PROPERTY LAW AND THE PUBLIC INTEREST: CASES AND MATERIALS

(2016–Pub.3096)

PROPERTY LAW AND THE PUBLIC INTEREST: CASES AND MATERIALS

Fourth Edition

DAVID L. CALLIES
Benjamin A. Kudo Professor of Law
University of Hawaii

DANIEL R. MANDELKER
Howard A. Stamper Professor of Law
Washington University

J. GORDON HYLTON
Professor of Law
University of Virginia

CAROLINA ACADEMIC PRESS
Durham, North Carolina

ISBN: 978-1-4224-9088-4 (Casebook)
ISBN: 978-1-4224-9089-1 (Looseleaf)

LCCN: 2016935463

Carolina Academic Press, LLC
700 Kent Street
Durham, NC 27701
Telephone (919) 489-7486
Fax (919) 493-5668
www.caplaw.com

Printed in the United States of America

(2016–Pub.3096)

Dedication

To

Laurie Callies
- D.L.C.

To all my children and grandchildren
- D.R.M.

Veronica, Elizabeth, Joseph, and Caroline
- J.G.H.

Preface

With the publication of this Fourth Edition, *Property Law and the Public Interest* remains committed to its central claims, that the concept of property is never static, that property law is both public and private, that property rules perform the socially critical function of mediating between competing claimants to the same resource or object, and that the law of property has always represented a balance between the claims of individual rights and the needs of the larger public.

However, the Fourth Edition does contain a number of alterations in the arrangements of the materials. For the first time, there is a separate chapter on estates in land and future interests. Concurrent estates and servitudes are now divided into distinct chapters while the materials on the police power and the power of eminent domain are now combined in a single chapter. In a similar way, many of the materials on the acquisition of property that previously appeared in a chapter on unintentional transfers are now incorporated into the opening chapter, which remains focused on the ways in which property and property rights are defined.

All of the chapters in this edition have been updated in light of developments since 2007, and the book continues to provide information in the notes on the historical context in which the featured cases have occurred. Whenever practical, a comparative perspective is provided. As has been the case since the appearance of the First Edition in 1998, Property Law and the Public Interest still consists of a collection of cases, edited to different degrees, and a series of notes written by the co-authors. It remains our belief that decisions regarding supplementary secondary sources are best left to the instructor. However, our notes do direct interested users to a wide variety of secondary sources.

As before, we are very much in debt to our editors at LexisNexis, to the library and administrative staffs at Washington University, the University of Hawaii, and the University of Virginia, and to research assistants at all of those institutions. Professor Callies thanks in particular Jacob Garmen, Derek Simons, and Ian Wesley-Smith, as well as his indefatigable faculty support specialist, Dana Lum, for her organizational skills in reassembling our manuscript. We are also anxious to receive feedback on this book from our users, both faculty and students. Such comments are always useful. They have helped shape future editions in the past, and they will certainly be taken into account during the preparation of the Fifth Edition.

David L. Callies
Daniel R. Mandelker
J. Gordon Hylton
October 2015

Table of Contents

Part I

Chapter 1

DEFINING PROPERTY AND ITS ACQUISITION

In his famous COMMENTARIES, William Blackstone observed that "There is nothing which so generally strikes the imagination, and engages the affections of mankind, as the right of property or that sole and despotic dominion which one man claims and exercises over the external things of the world, in total exclusion of the right of any other individual in the universe." 2 W. BLACKSTONE, COMMENTARIES ON THE LAWS OF ENGLAND 2 (1766). Since Blackstone's time, the Anglo-American legal tradition has honored this view, but the boundaries of the right of property have not always been easy to define. The legal system is routinely called upon to mediate among those who assert competing claims to the same resource, and in a democratic society, the resolution of such claims invariably requires the sovereign to take into account the interests of the general public as well as those of the individual claimants.

In the American system, the definition of "property" has constitutional implications. Both the Fifth and Fourteenth Amendments to the United States Constitution and corresponding provisions in all the state constitutions provide protection against improper governmental interference with the rights of private property owners. Once an interest is labeled "property," constitutional protections immediately attach.

The first part of this chapter addresses the question of how the American legal system historically allocated property rights in assets that had not yet been transferred to individual owners. By looking at cases involving natural resources — wild animals, water, oil and gas, land, and other persons — one can see the mixture of legal principles and policy arguments that have been invoked to justify the assignment of ownership rights. The second part continues the inquiry into what "entities" are properly labeled "property." The cases, drawn from the realm of what is usually called "intellectual property," involve property claims by those seeking exclusive control of intangible assets like public image, ideas, news, and computer time. These cases illustrate the difficulties courts have had in formulating precise rules and definitions that make it possible to distinguish between those entities that can be owned as "property" and those that cannot.

In keeping with the theme of this casebook that property law is more public than private, Chapter One demonstrates that nominally private disputes over the ownership of natural resources are in fact public disputes in which legislatures and courts are required to establish rules that serve the public interest, at least as it is understood at the time the dispute arises. Although legal treatises and hornbooks usually present property rules as though they were derived from neutral, objective principles or widely shared policy objectives, the historical record shows that this has rarely been the case.

[A.] PRIVATE OWNERSHIP OF NATURAL RESOURCES

The ability to own property is a right that most Americans take for granted. Similarly, most feel that there is little problem in defining what is property and what is not. Since most of one's property (or at least its components) is obtained from others (through gift, purchase, payment, inheritance, or find), most individuals spend little time pondering how property is acquired in the first instance. Cases like the ones that follow, however, force us to address the question of how individual private property rights are first established. The first case is one that has been used for almost a century to introduce students to the law of property.

[1.] Rights to Wild Animals

PIERSON v. POST

New York Supreme Court
3 Cai. R. 175 (1805)

Trespass on the case commenced in the justice's court by the present defendant. The declaration stated that Post, while hunting, chasing, and pursuing a fox with his dogs, and when in view of the animal, Pierson, knowing the fox was so hunted and pursued, did, in sight of Post, kill and carry it off. A verdict was rendered in favor of the plaintiff below; whereupon the defendant sued out a *certiorari*, assigning as error that the declaration and the matters therein stated were not sufficient to maintain the action.

By Court, TOMPKINS, J.

This cause comes before us on a return to a *certiorari* directed to one of the justices of Queen's county. The question submitted by the counsel in this cause for our determination is, whether Lodowick Post, by the pursuit with his hounds in the manner alleged in his declaration, acquired such a right to or property in the fox, as will sustain an action against Pierson for killing and taking him away. The cause was argued with much ability by the counsel on both sides, and presents for our decision a novel and nice question. It is admitted that a fox is an animal *ferae naturae*, and that property in such animals is acquired by occupancy only. These admissions narrow the discussion to the simple question of what acts amount to occupancy, applied to acquiring right to wild animals.

If we have recourse to the ancient writers upon general principles of law, the judgment below is obviously erroneous: Justinian's Institutes, lib. 2, tit. 1, s. 13, and Fleta, lib. 3, c. 2, p. 175, adopt the principle that pursuit alone vests no property or right in the huntsman; and that even pursuit, accompanied with wounding, is equally ineffectual for that purpose, unless the animal be actually taken. The same principle is recognized by Bracton, lib. 2, c. 1, p. 8. Puffendorf, lib. 4, c. 6, s. 2 and 10 defines occupancy of beasts *ferae naturae*, to be the actual corporal possession of them, and Bynkershock is cited as coinciding in this definition. It is indeed with hesitation that Puffendorf affirms that a wild beast mortally wounded, or greatly maimed, cannot be fairly intercepted by another, whilst the pursuit of the person inflicting the wound continues. The foregoing authorities are decisive to show that mere pursuit gave Post no legal right to the fox, but that he became the property of Pierson, who intercepted and killed him.

It, therefore, only remains to inquire whether there are any contrary principles or authorities to be found in other books, which ought to induce a different decision. Most of the cases which have occurred in England, relating to property in wild animals, have either been discussed and decided upon the principles of their positive statute regulations, or have arisen between the huntsman and the owner of the land upon which beasts *ferae naturae* have been apprehended; the former claiming them by title of occupancy, and the latter *ratione soli.* Little satisfactory aid can, therefore, be derived from the English reports.

Barbeyrac, in his notes on Puffendorf, does not accede to the definition of occupancy by the latter, but on the contrary affirms that actual bodily seizure is not, in all cases, necessary to constitute possession of wild animals. He does not, however, describe the acts which, according to his ideas, will amount to an appropriation of such animals to private use, so as to exclude the claims of all other persons, by title of occupancy, to the same animals; and he is far from averring that pursuit alone is sufficient for that purpose. To a certain extent, and so far as Barbeyrac appears to me to go, his objections to Puffendorf's definition of occupancy are reasonable and correct. That is to say, that actual bodily seizure is not indispensable to acquire right to or possession of wild beasts; but that, on the contrary, the mortal wounding of such beasts, by one not abandoning his pursuit, may, with the utmost propriety, be deemed possession of him; since thereby the pursuer manifests an unequivocal intention of appropriating the animal to his individual use, has deprived him of his natural liberty, and brought him within his certain control. So also encompassing and securing such animals with nets and toils, or otherwise intercepting them in such a manner as to deprive them of their natural liberty, and render escape impossible, may justly be deemed to give possession of them to those persons who, by their industry and labor, have used such means of apprehending them.

Barbeyrac seems to have adopted and had in view in his notes the more accurate opinion of Grotius with respect to occupancy. That celebrated author, lib. 2, c. 8, s. 3, p. 309, speaking of occupancy, proceeds thus: "*Requiritur autem corporalis quaedam; possessio ad donminium adipiscedum; atque ideo, vulnerasse non sufficit.*"[1] But in the following section he explains and qualifies this definition of occupancy: "*Sed possessio illa potest non solis manibus, sed instrumentis, ut decipulis, ratibus, laqueis dum duo adsint; primum ut ipsa instrumenta sint in nostra potestate, deinde ut fera, ita inclusa sit ut exire inde nequeat.*"[2] This qualification embraces the full extent of Barbeyrac's objection to Puffendorf's definition, and allows as great a latitude to acquiring property by occupancy, as can reasonably be inferred from the words or ideas expressed by Barbeyrac in his notes. The case now under consideration is one of mere pursuit, and presents no

---

[1] Editor's note: Roughly translated, "Some corporeal possession is required for obtaining dominion, and therefore wounding is not enough."

[2] Editor's note: Again, roughly, "But that possession can be not only with the hands, but with instruments, such as snares, nets, traps, so long as two elements are present: first, that the instruments themselves be in our power; second, that the wild things be so encompassed that they cannot get out."

circumstances or acts which can bring it within the definition of occupancy by Puffendorf or Grotius, or the ideas of Barbeyrac upon that subject.

The case cited from 11 Mod. 74-130, I think clearly distinguishable from the present; inasmuch as there the action was for maliciously hindering and disturbing the plaintiff in the exercise and enjoyment of a private franchise, and in the report of the same case, 3 Salk. 9, Holt, C.J., states that the ducks were in the plaintiff's decoy pond, and so in his possession, from which it is obvious the court laid much stress in their opinion upon the plaintiff's possession of the ducks, *ratione soli*.

We are the more readily inclined to confine possession or occupancy of beasts *ferae naturae* within the limits prescribed by the learned authors above cited, for the sake of certainty and preserving peace and order in society. If the first seeing, starting or pursuing such animals without having so wounded, circumvented or ensnared them so as to deprive them of their natural liberty and subject them to the control of their pursuer, should afford the basis of actions against others for intercepting and killing them, it would prove a fertile source of quarrels and litigation. However uncourteous or unkind the conduct of Pierson toward Post in this instance may have been, yet his act was productive of no injury or damage for which a legal remedy can be applied. We are of [the] opinion [that] the judgment below was erroneous and ought to be reversed.

LIVINGSTON, J.

My opinion differs from that of the court. Of six exceptions, taken to the proceedings below, all are abandoned except the third, which reduces the controversy to a single question. Whether a person who, with his own hounds, starts and hunts a fox on waste and uninhabited ground, and is on the point of seizing his prey, acquires such an interest in the animal, as to have a right of action against another, who in view of the huntsman and his dogs in full pursuit, and with knowledge of the chase, shall kill and carry him away?

This is a knotty point, and should have been submitted to the arbitration of sportsmen, without poring over Justinian, Fleta, Bracton, Puffendorf, Locke, Barbeyrac, or Blackstone, all of whom have been cited; they would have had no difficulty in coming to a prompt and correct conclusion. In a court thus constituted, the skin and carcass of poor reynard would have been properly disposed of, and a precedent set, interfering with no usage or custom which the experience of ages has sanctioned, and which must be so well known to every votary of Diana. But the parties have referred the question to our judgment, and we must dispose of it as well as we can, from the partial lights we possess, leaving to a higher tribunal, the correction of any mistake which we may be so unfortunate as to make. By the pleadings it is admitted that a fox is a "wild and noxious beast." Both parties have regarded him, as the law of nations does a pirate, "*hostem humani generis*," and although "*de mortuis nil nisi bonum*," be a maxim of our profession, the memory of the deceased has not been spared. His depredations on farmers and on barn yards have not been forgotten; and to put him to death wherever found, is allowed to be meritorious, and of public benefit. Hence it follows, that our decision should have in view the greatest possible encouragement to the destruction of an animal, so cunning and ruthless in his career. But who would keep a pack of hounds; or what gentleman, at the sound of the horn, and at peep of day, would mount his steed, and for hours together, "*sub jove frigido*," or a vertical sun, pursue the windings of this wily quadruped, if, just as night came on, and his stratagems and strength were nearly exhausted, a saucy intruder, who had not shared in the honours or labours of the chase, were permitted to come in at the death, and bear away in triumph the object of pursuit? Whatever Justinian may have thought of the matter, it must be recollected that his code was compiled many hundred years ago, and it would be very hard indeed, at the distance of so many centuries, not to have a right to establish a rule for ourselves. In his day, we read of no order of men who made it a business, in the language of the declaration in this cause, "with hounds and dogs to find, start, pursue, hunt, and chase," these animals, and that, too, without any other motive than the preservation of roman poultry; if this diversion had been then in fashion, the lawyers who composed his institutes would have taken care not to pass it by, without suitable encouragement. If anything, therefore, in the digests or pandects shall appear to militate against the defendant in error, who, on this occasion, was the fox hunter, we have only to say *tempora mutantur*; and if men themselves change with the times, why should not laws also undergo an alteration?

It may be expected, however, by the learned counsel, that more particular notice be taken of their authorities. I have examined them all, and feel great difficulty in determining, whether to acquire dominion over a thing, before in common, it be sufficient that we barely see it, or know where it is, or wish for it, or make a declaration of our will respecting it; or whether, in the case of wild beasts, setting a trap, or lying in wait, or starting, or pursuing, be enough; or if an actual wounding, or killing, or bodily tact and occupation be necessary. Writers on general law, who have favoured us with their speculations on these points, differ on them all; but, great as is the diversity of sentiment among them, some conclusion must be adopted on the question immediately before us. After mature deliberation, I embrace that of Barbeyrac, as the most rational, and least liable to objection. If at liberty, we might imitate the courtesy of a certain emperor, who, to avoid giving offense to the advocates of any of these different doctrines, adopted a middle course, and by ingenious distinctions, rendered it difficult to say (as often happens after a fierce and angry contest) to whom the palm of victory belonged. He ordained, that if a beast be followed with *large dogs and hounds*, he shall belong to the hunter, not to the chance occupant; and in like manner, if he be killed or wounded with a lance or sword; but if chased with *beagles only*, then he passed to the captor, not to the first pursuer. If slain with a dart, a sling, or a bow, he fell to the hunter, if still in chase, and not to him who might afterwards find and seize him.

Now, as we are without any municipal regulations of our own, and the pursuit here, for aught that appears on the case, being with dogs and hounds of *imperial stature*, we are at liberty to adopt one of the provisions just cited, which comports also with the learned conclusion of Barbeyrac, that property in animals *ferae naturae* may be acquired without bodily touch or manucaption, provided the pursuer be within reach, or have a *reasonable* prospect (which certainly existed here) of taking, what he has *thus* discovered an intention of converting to his own use.

When we reflect also that the interest of our husbandman, the most useful of men in any community, will be advanced by the destruction of a beast so pernicious and incorrigible, we cannot greatly err, in saying, that a pursuit like the present, through waste and unoccupied lands, and which must inevitably and speedily have terminated in corporal possession, or bodily *seisin*, confers such a right to the object of it, as to make any one a wrongdoer, who shall interfere and shoulder the spoil. The justice's judgment ought, therefore, in my opinion, to be affirmed.

NOTES AND QUESTIONS

1. *The Judges Who Decided* Pierson v. Post. The New York Supreme Court of 1805 was one of the most distinguished tribunals in American history. Justice Daniel Tompkins, the author of the majority opinion, was a well-known political figure who later served as Vice-President of the United States under President James Monroe. Members of the Court joining in Tompkins' opinion included Smith Thompson, a future United States Supreme Court Justice; James Kent, the Court's Chief Justice and whose COMMENTARIES ON AMERICAN LAW (1st ed. 1826) was one of the most influential legal treatises ever written in this country; and Ambrose Spencer, another prominent New York political figure of the post-Revolutionary War era. Justice Brockholst Livingston, the author of the dissent, was no less distinguished and was, in fact, appointed to the United States Supreme Court the following year (1806) by President Thomas Jefferson. Livingston was also a member of one of early New York's wealthiest families.

The two lawyers were equally prominent. Nathan Sanborn, Pierson's attorney, was prominent Long Island lawyer who was the current United States Attorney for New York and who would later serve two terms in the United States Senate and would eventually replace Kent as Chancellor. Post's lawyer, Cadwallader David Coldon was the previous U.S. Attorney for New York and in 1819 would be elected Mayor of New York City. The court was sitting in Albany at the time that it heard this case.

2. *Who Were Pierson and Post?* Jesse Pierson and Lodowick Post were both young men who were members of prominent families in Southampton, New York. Pierson was a member of a family that had been among the earliest settlers of the community in the 17th century and whose members had long been leaders in the community. The Posts, on the other hand, were a much less prominent family, although Nathan Post, the father of Lodowick, had arrived in Southampton in the 1770s, and had made a fortune in the West Indies trade after the Revolutionary War. Pierson, a school teacher, was apparently returning home from his job when he encountered the fox (which he supposedly killed with a broken fence rail). For additional details regarding the actual events of this case, see H. Hedges, *The Story of Bridgehampton, Long Island, 1660–1910*, *in* TRACING THE PAST: WRITINGS OF HENRY P. HEDGES 335, 350–51 (T. Twomey ed., 2000); H. HEDGES, A HISTORY OF THE TOWN OF EAST-HAMPTON, N.Y. (1897); W. HASLEY, SKETCHES FROM LOCAL HISTORY 131 (1935); J. ADAMS, MEMORIALS OF OLD BRIDGEHAMPTON 166ff. (1916); and the articles cited in Note 7, below.

Until recently, the principle source of information pertaining to the events in the case was Long Island resident and historian, Judge Henry Hedges who as a young man had known both the plaintiff and defendant. His account of the case first appeared in a local newspaper, the Sag-Harbor *Express*, on October 3, 1895. Note, however, that the court in this case relies upon the version of the facts set out in the complaint of Lodowick Post. (As the first paragraph of the opinion reveals, on appeal Pierson maintained that the allegations in Post's complaint were insufficient to support a cause of action.) The actual court records for *Pierson v. Post,* long believed lost, were located by Prof. Angela Fernandez in 2004 and 2005. *See* Note 7, below.

The case itself has an interesting genealogy. Given the relative insignificance of its subject matter (as opposed to its implications), the case might well have been forgotten. However, Chancellor Kent, one of the judges, considered it important enough to include a discussion of the case in his once widely read COMMENTARIES (mentioned above). Kent's treatise went through numerous editions, many of which were prepared by other editors following his death in 1847. The 12th edition (1873), was edited by future Supreme Court Justice Oliver Wendell Holmes, Jr., who knew of *Pierson v. Post* through Kent's work, and who discussed the case in his own legendary work, THE COMMON LAW (1881), which continues to be read long after Kent's treatise has become an historical relic. Finally, in 1915, Harvard Law Professor Edward H. "Bull" Warren, who knew the case from Holmes' work, decided to structure his new property casebook, SELECT CASES AND OTHER AUTHORITIES ON THE LAW OF PROPERTY, around the unifying concept of "possession." Warren's was arguably the first modern property law casebook in that it focused upon "property" as a jurisprudential concept rather than a collection of rules relating to real and personal property (usually taught as separate courses). For a course so conceived, *Pierson v. Post* was an obvious starting point, and for the past century most property law casebooks have begun with this case, or at least have included it with the introductory material.

3. *What Was Really Going on in This Case?* Although it would be a mistake to ignore the self-conscious humor of the judges in this case, *Pierson v. Post* provides a fascinating insight into the nature of the American legal system in the Early Republic. Since very little was at stake in terms of economic value, the lawsuit must have been pursued as a matter of principle (or pique). It is possible that Post violated some important community norm by interfering with the hunt of the fox. Both Pierson and Post were members of prominent families, and it seems highly unlikely that either was hunting the fox for the value of its carcass or its hide. Furthermore, although much of the terminology employed in the opinion sounds foreign or archaic to the modern ear, the "debate" between Tompkins and Livingston over the role and nature of precedent in allocating property rights among competing claimants is still a central question in American law.

4. *The Ownership of Wild Animals.* In some respects, the most important issue in *Pierson v. Post* is one left unaddressed by both the majority and the dissent: Why should either Pierson or Post be entitled to claim ownership of the dead fox, since neither owned the land upon which the fox was killed and neither had been explicitly authorized by the sovereign (the State of New York) to hunt foxes?

From the case report, it is impossible to say who, if anyone, owned the land upon which the fox at issue was killed. The location of the incident is described only as "on waste and uninhabited ground." "Waste" land, as understood at the time of this case, was any land that had never been brought under cultivation. Whether it was privately or publicly owned was immaterial. D. WALKER, THE OXFORD COMPANION TO LAW 1292 (1980). The historical record suggests that the land was part of a parcel of "community-owned" land set aside for the common use of local residents whose families had deep roots in the community. If the land in *Pierson v. Post* had been privately owned, and the owner had asserted a claim to the fox, would he have prevailed over both of the hunters? (Incidentally, the events in the case actually occurred in Suffolk County, New York, not Queens County, as the published opinion erroneously reports.)

There were few restrictions on the hunting of wild animals in the United States in the early 19th century, although under contemporary English law the right to hunt wild game was limited to a small number of wealthy landowners. In spite of the restrictive nature of English game laws, legal scholars disagreed on the question of who "owned" uncaptured wild animals. Some, like Blackstone, believed that the sovereign had exclusive rights to wild animals while others, like Edward Christian, believed that English law recognized that the owner of the land owned the game living on it. For Blackstone's position, see 2 W. BLACKSTONE, COMMENTARIES ON THE LAWS OF ENGLAND 414–19 (1766) and S. PURLEWENT, DIALOGUE BETWEEN A LAWYER AND A COUNTRY GENTLEMAN UPON THE SUBJECT OF THE GAME LAWS 46 (1771); for the contrary view, see E. CHRISTIAN, A TREATISE ON THE GAME LAWS (1817) and J. BELL, A COPIOUS AND PRACTICAL TREATISE ON THE GAME LAWS 5–7 (1839). Most American jurisdictions followed the Blackstonian model, concluding that in the absence of any prohibitions, the sovereign's implicit rule is that its citizens are free to hunt wild game.

5. *The Right to Hunt.* In fact, the right to hunt on undeveloped land was important enough to Americans of the Revolutionary generation that two states, Vermont and Pennsylvania, included it in their original state constitutions. Pa. Const. § 43 (1776), Vt. Const. § 39 (1777). There was also an effort to include such a provision in the United States Constitution. For an example of the argument that the United States Constitution ought to include a guarantee of the right to hunt on unenclosed lands, see *Address and Reasons of Dissent of the Minority of the Convention of the State of Pennsylvania to Their Constituents*, Dec. 12, 1787, *in* 2 B. SCHWARTZ, THE BILL OF RIGHTS: A DOCUMENTARY HISTORY 655 (1971).

Even without such a provision, many states recognized the right of private citizens to hunt on the undeveloped lands of others, even when the owner specifically objected. For such a case, see *M'Conico v. Singleton*, 4 S.C.L. (2 Mill.) 244 (1818). In Arkansas, this right was acknowledged as recently as 1953, *Shellnut v. Arkansas State Game & Fish Comm'n*, 258 S.W.2d 570 (Ark. 1953). For a discussion of the early American law of wild animals, see Lund, *Early American Wildlife Law*, 51 N.Y.U. L. REV. 703 (1976). In the 20th century, there has been a tendency to recognize a landowner's right to the wild game on his property. Comment *g* to § 450 of the RESTATEMENT (SECOND) OF PROPERTY (1977) states that a landowner may claim any game shot on his or her property by a trespasser or else recover damages for its conversion. (Conversion is the wrongful taking of property belonging to another.)

6. *Contemporary Views on the Ownership of Wild Animals.* Given the abundance of undeveloped land and wildlife in early American history, it was very easy to conceive of a right to hunt and the right to own what one killed and captured.

Today, prevailing attitudes are quite different. During most of the 20th century the hunting of game has been subject to strict regulation, even for those who own land; certain animals cannot be hunted at any time; and others can be hunted only in season and in certain locations. Many states have statutes authorizing the uncompensated seizure of animals killed out of season, even by landowners on their own land. See, for example, Wis. Stat. Ann. §§ 29.02 and 29.05(7), which provide that legal title to all wild animals in the state is vested in the state and authorizes the state's Department of Fish and Game to confiscate any wild animal caught or killed in violation of the state game laws. For a fascinating recent case concerning limits on the power of the United States government to dispose of wild animals in national forests, see *The Fund for Animals v. Thomas*, 932 F. Supp. 368 (D.D.C. 1996).

7. Nearly 200 years after the case was decided, the issues in *Pierson v. Post* continue to fascinate legal scholars and students of property law. For a recent examples, see Dharmapaia & Pitchford, *An Economic Analysis of "Riding to Hounds":* Pierson v. Post *Revisited*, 18 J.L. ECON. & ORG. 39 (2002); Berger, *It's Not About the Fox: The Untold History of* Pierson v. Post, 55 DUKE L.J. 1089 (2006); McDowell, *Legal Fictions in* Pierson v. Post, 105 MICH. L. REV. 735 (2007); Fernandez, *The Pushy Pedagogy of* Pierson v. Post *and the Fading Federalism of James Kent*, (May 2007), *available at* http://law.stanford.edu/wp-content/uploads/sites/default/files/event/266730/media/slspublic/Pierson_v_Post_1.pdf; Fernandez, *Capturing New Facts About the Fox: The Lost Record of* Pierson v. Post, *the Famous Fox Case*, 27 LAW & HIST. REV. 149 (2009); Fernandez, Pierson v. Post, *A Great Debate, James Kent, and the Project of Building a Learned Law for New York State*, 34 LAW & SOC. INQUIRY 301 (2009); Blackman, *Outfoxed* Pierson v. Post *and the Natural Law*, 51 AM. J. LEGAL HIST 417 (2011).

8. *Locke's Labor Theory of Value*. It is interesting that nowhere in the opinions of the justices in *Pierson v. Post* is there a citation to the works of John Locke, the 17th Century English philosopher whose theories of liberty and property have been widely associated with Revolutionary and Early National America. It is even more interesting, given that in a famous passage Locke wrote specifically concerning property rights arising out of the pursuit of wild animals (in his case, a hare, or rabbit). In regard to the origin of property generally, Locke wrote:

> Though the Earth, and all inferior Creatures be common to all Men, yet every Man has a *Property* in his own *Person*. This no Body has any Right to but himself. The *Labour* of his Body, and the *Work* of his Hands, we may say, are properly his. Whatsoever then he removes out of the State that Nature hath provided, and left it in, he hath mixed his *Labour* with, and joined to it something that is his own, and thereby makes it his *Property*. It being by him removed from the common state Nature placed it in, hath by this *Labour* something annexed to it, that excludes the common right of other Men.

SECOND TREATISE ON GOVERNMENT V § 27.

In regard to acquiring title to wild animals by pursuit, after noting that the killing of deer and the catching of fish make them the property of the "capturer," he further noted:

> And even amongst us the Hare that any one is Hunting, is thought his who pursues her during the Chase. For being a Beast that is still looked upon as common, and no Man's private Possession; whoever has imploy'd so much *Labour* about any of that kind, as to find and pursue her, has hereby removed her from the state of Nature, wherein she was common and has *begun a Property*.

Id. § 30.

The 18th century French jurist Jean Barbeyrac, whose views are described by the dissenter Livingston as "the most rational, and least liable to objection" is usually thought of as a disciple, of sorts, of Locke.

9. Pierson v. Post *and Legal Reasoning.* The clarity of the judicial reasoning in the case is one reason that law students are still asked to read *Pierson v. Post*, but its logical structure has also made it a well-known document in other fields as well. In the last several decades, the case has become an important benchmark in the field of artificial intelligence and law for computational models of argumentation. In 1993, language theorists Don Berman and Carole Hafner used the well-known case in an examination of the role of teleological reasoning in the law. Berman & Hafner, *Representing Teleological Structure in Case-Based Legal Reasoning: The Missing Link, in* PROCEEDINGS OF THE 4TH INTERNATIONAL CONFERENCE ON ARTIFICIAL INTELLIGENCE AND LAW 50–60 (1993). Since then, a number of artificial intelligence and legal scholars have made use of the case as a testing ground for models of legal argumentation. *See, e.g.*, Bench-Capon, *The Missing Link Revisited: The Role of Teleology in Representing Legal Argument*, 10 ARTIFICIAL INTELLIGENCE & L. 79 (2002); Gordon & Walton, Pierson vs. Post *Revisited, in* COMPUTATIONAL MODELS OF ARGUMENT: PROCEEDINGS OF COMMA 2006, 208–19 (Dunne & Bench, eds. 2006).

GHEN v. RICH

United States District Court, District of Massachusetts
8 F. 159 (1881)

NELSON, D.J.

This is a libel to recover the value of a fin-back whale. The libellant lives in Provincetown and the respondent in Wellfleet. The facts, as they appeared at the hearing, are as follows:

> In the early spring months the easterly part of Massachusetts bay is frequented by the species of whale known as the fin-back whale. Fishermen from Provincetown pursue them in open boats from the shore, and shoot them with bomb-lances fired from guns made expressly for the purpose. When killed they sink at once to the bottom, but in the course of from one to three days they rise and float on the surface. Some of them are picked up by vessels and towed into Provincetown. Some float ashore at high water and are left stranded on the beach as the tide recedes. Others float out to sea and are never recovered.

The person who happens to find them on the beach usually sends word to Provincetown, and the owner comes to the spot and removes the blubber. The finder usually receives a small salvage for his services. Try-works are established in Provincetown for trying out the oil. The business is of considerable extent, but, since it requires skill and experience, as well as some outlay of capital, and is attended with great exposure and hardship, few persons engage in it. The average yield of oil is about 20 barrels to a whale. It swims with great swiftness, and for that reason cannot be taken by the harpoon and line. Each boat's crew engaged in the business has its peculiar mark or device on its lances, and in this way it is known by whom a whale is killed.

The usage on Cape Cod, for many years, has been that the person who kills a whale in the manner and under the circumstances described, owns it, and this right has never been disputed until this case. The libellant has been engaged in this business for ten years past. On the morning of April 9, 1880, in Massachusetts bay, near the end of Cape Cod, he shot and instantly killed with a bomb-lance the whale in question. It sunk immediately, and on the morning of the 12th was found stranded on the beach in Brewster, within the ebb and flow of the tide, by one Ellis, 17 miles from the spot where it was killed.

Instead of sending word to Princeton,[3] as is customary, Ellis advertised the whale for sale at auction, and sold it to the respondent, who shipped off the blubber and tried out the oil. The libellant heard of the finding of the whale on the morning of the 15th, and immediately sent one of his boat's crew to the place and claimed it. Neither the respondent nor Ellis knew the whale had been killed by the libellant, but they knew or might have known, if they had wished, that it had been shot and killed with a bomb lance, by some person engaged in this species of business.

The libellant claims title to the whale under this usage. The respondent insists that this usage is invalid. It was decided by Judge Sprague, in *Taber v. Jenny*, 1 Sprague 315, that when a whale has been killed, and is anchored and left with marks of appropriation, it is the property of the captors; and if it is afterwards found, still anchored, by another ship, there is no usage or principle of law by which the property of the original captors is diverted, even though the whale may have dragged from its anchorage. The learned judge says: "When the whale had been killed and taken possession of by the boat of the Hillman, (the first taker,) it became the property of the owners of that ship, and all was done which was then practicable in order to secure it. They left it anchored, with unequivocal marks of appropriation."

In *Bartlett v. Budd*, 1 Low. 223, the facts were these: The first officer of the libellant's ship killed a whale in the Okhotsk sea, anchored it, attached a waif to the body, and then left it and went ashore at some distance for the night. The next

[3] Editor's Note: Although the reported opinion for this case uses the place name "Princeton," Judge Nelson almost certainly meant "Provincetown." There is a Princeton, Massachusetts, but it is located in the western part of the state and nowhere near the area where the recited events occurred.

morning the boats of the respondent's ship found the whale adrift, the anchor not holding, the cable coiled round the body, and no waif or irons attached to it. Judge Lowell held that, as the libellants had killed and taken actual possession of the whale, the ownership vested in them. In his opinion the learned judge says: "A whale, being ferae naturae, does not become property until a firm possession has been established by the taker. But when such possession has become firm and complete, the right of property is clear, and has all the characteristics of property."

He doubted whether a usage set up but not proved by the respondents, that a whale found adrift in the ocean is the property of the finder, unless the first taker should appear and claim it before it is cut in, would be valid, and remarked that "there would be great difficulty in upholding a custom that should take the property of A and give it to B, under so very short and uncertain a substitute for the statute of limitations, and one so open to fraud and deceit." Both the cases cited were decided without reference to usage, upon the ground that the property had been acquired by the first taker by actual possession and appropriation.

In *Swift v. Gifford*, 2 Low. 110, Judge Lowell decided that a custom among whalemen in the Arctic seas, that the iron holds the whale, was reasonable and valid. In that case a boat's crew from the respondent's ship pursued and struck a whale in the Arctic ocean, and the harpoon and the line attached to it remained in the whale, but did not remain fast to the boat. A boat's crew from the libellant's ship continued the pursuit and captured the whale, and the master of the respondent's ship claimed it on the spot. It was held by the learned judge that the whale belonged to the respondents. It was said by Judge Sprague, in *Bourne v. Ashley*, an unprinted case referred to by Judge Lowell in *Swift v. Gifford*, that the usage for the first iron, whether attached to the boat or not, to hold the whale was fully established; and he added that, although local usages of a particular port ought not to be allowed to set aside the general maritime law, this objection did not apply to a custom which embraced an entire business, and had been concurred in for a long time by everyone engaged in the trade.

In *Swift v. Gifford*, Judge Lowell also said: "The rule of law invoked in this case is one of very limited application. The whale fishery is the only branch of industry of any importance in which it is likely to be much used, and if a usage is found to prevail generally in that business, it will not be open to the objection that it is likely to disturb the general understanding of mankind by the interposition of an arbitrary exception."

I see no reason why the usage proved in this case is not as reasonable as that sustained in the cases cited. Its application must necessarily be extremely limited, and can affect but a few persons. It has been recognized and acquiesced in for many years. It requires in the first taker the only act of appropriation that is possible in the nature of the case. Unless it is sustained, this branch of industry must necessarily cease, for no person would engage in it if the fruits of his labor could be appropriated by any chance finder. It gives reasonable salvage for securing or reporting the property.

That the rule works well in practice is shown by the extent of the industry which has grown up under it, and the general acquiescence of a whole community interested to dispute it. It is by no means clear that without regard to usage the common law would not reach the same result. That seems to be the effect of the decisions in *Taber v. Jenny* and *Bartlett v. Budd*. If the fisherman does all that it is possible to do to make the animal his own, that would seem to be sufficient. Such a rule might well be applied in the interest of trade, there being no usage or custom to the contrary. HOLMES, COM. LAW, 217. But be that as it may, I hold the usage to be valid, and that the property in the whale was in the libellant. Decree for libellant for $71.05, without costs.

NOTES AND QUESTIONS

1. *Admiralty*. Admiralty is a body of private law that involves maritime matters, including legal issues that arise on internal navigable waterways. It has its own legal procedures and its own specialized vocabulary. For example, in admiralty, the first pleading by a plaintiff is called a "libel," while the plaintiff is the "libellant." Article III, § 2 of the United States Constitution gives the federal courts original jurisdiction over admiralty matters, and most admiralty cases are heard in federal court. In the American judicial system, there are no specialized admiralty courts or admiralty judges.

2. *The Role of Custom*. Is the ruling in this case consistent with the holding in *Pierson v. Post*? If it is, why does the trial judge devote so much attention to the issue of custom? Why are some customs relevant while others are not? Should the cases that United States District Judge Thomas Leverett Nelson cites be controlling? Given that the events in these cases occurred outside of United States territorial waters, are they even on point? Had the plaintiff Ghen really done all that he could reasonably do to locate and take possession of the whale? Should it matter that Judge Nelson was a resident of Worcester, Massachusetts, located well inland from Massachusetts Bay, and probably had no firsthand experience with the customs he discusses?

The proper role of customary practices in determining legal rules remains controversial. Some see past customs as evidence of an informal but just "legal" consensus that ought to be honored by formal legal institutions. On the other hand, others may view the same custom as a rule imposed by those who possessed economic or political power on those who did not, and thus not the product of either logic or justice. Cases that illustrate the dimensions of this ongoing debate include *Thornton v. Hay*, 462 P.2d 671 (Or. 1969), *Lucas v. South Carolina Coastal Council*, 505 U.S. 1003 (1992), *Public Access Shoreline Hawaii (PASH) v. Hawaii Planning Comm'n*, 903 P.2d 1246 (Haw. 1995). D. Callies & I. Wesley-Smith, *Beyond Blackstone: The Modern Emergence of Customary Law*, 4 BRIGHAM-KANNER PROP. RIGHTS CONF. J. 151 (2015).

3. *The American Whaling Industry in 1881*. By the time of *Ghen v. Rich*, the golden age of American whaling was a receding memory. In fact, the industry was on the verge of extinction. The increasing usage of petroleum and its by-products, particularly kerosene, had nearly destroyed the market for whale oil. Within a decade the American whaling industry would be effectively defunct. *See* D. YERGIN, THE PRIZE 1-51 (1991). Is this a factor that likely shaped Judge Nelson's opinion? Would it be proper to take such factors into account?

4. *Fast Fish and Loose Fish.* In Chapter 89 of his classic novel MOBY DICK (1851), Herman Melville provides an account of an English whaling case that allegedly occurred around the year 1800. According to Melville, the plaintiff's crew had succeeded in harpooning a whale in the Northern seas, but when the whale refused to die, the whalers had been forced to abandon their boat as well as the line connecting the harpoon to the boat. Shortly thereafter, the defendant, another whaler, arrived on the scene and killed the whale, still dragging the boat, lines, and harpoons, within the view of the plaintiff. The defendant refused to return the whale, the boat, the lines, or the harpoons, and upon his return to England, the plaintiff brought an action at law for whale-trover. (Trover was the common law form of action originally used for the recovery of damages against a person who had found another's goods and wrongfully converted them to his own use.)

In Melville's account, the judge hearing the case ordered that only the boat had to be returned to the plaintiff. In so ruling he applied "the fundamental principal of the unwritten law of whaling," that "a Fast-Fish belongs to the party fast to it" and "a Loose-Fish is fair game for anybody who can soonest catch it." The whale did not belong to the plaintiff because it was a "loose-fish" at the time of the defendant's arrival on the scene. Moreover, by escaping from the plaintiff's men with the harpoons and line in tow, the whale had acquired a property interest in those items which was transferred to the defendant when the whale was killed.

According to Melville's narrator, the "Fast Fish/Loose Fish" principle extends far beyond the law of whaling.

> What are the sinews and souls of Russian serfs and Republican slaves but Fast Fish, whereof possession is the whole of the law? What to the rapacious landlord is the widow's last mite but a Fast-Fish? What is the ruinous discount which Mordecai, the broker, gets from poor Woebegone, the bankrupt, on a loan to keep Woebegone's family from starvation; what is that ruinous discount but a Fast-Fish? What is the Archbishop of Savesoul's income of £100,000 seized from the scant bread and cheese of hundreds of thousands of broken-backed laborers (all sure of heaven without any of Savesoul's help)? What is that globular 100,000 but a Fast-Fish? What are the Duke of Dunder's hereditary towns and hamlets but Fast-Fish? What to that redoubted harpooner, John Bull, is poor Ireland, but a Fast-Fish? What to that apostolic lancer, Brother Jonathan, is Texas but a Fast-Fish? And concerning all these, is not Possession the whole of the law?
>
> But if the doctrine of Fast-Fish be pretty generally applicable, the kindred doctrine of Loose-Fish is still more widely so. That is internationally and universally applicable.
>
> What was American in 1492 but a Loose-Fish, in which Columbus struck the Spanish standard by way of waifing it for his royal master and mistress? What was Poland to the Czar? What Greece to the Turk? What India to England? What at last will Mexico be to the United States? All Loose-Fish.
>
> What are the Rights of Man and the Liberties of the World but Loose-Fish? What all men's minds and opinions but Loose-Fish? What is

> the principle of religious belief in them but a Loose-Fish? What to the ostentatious smuggling verbalists are the thoughts of thinkers but Loose-Fish? What is the great globe itself but a Loose-Fish? And what are you, reader, but a Loose-Fish and a Fast-Fish, too?

H. MELVILLE, MOBY DICK 1216–19 (Library of America ed., 1983).

5. *Difficulties in Capturing Whales.* Even a direct hit with a bomb lance of the sort used in *Ghen v. Rich* was no guarantee that the whale would be killed. In the spring of 2007, a 50-ton bowhead whale was killed by Eskimo hunters off the coast of Alaska. When the whale was "harvested," a 3.5 inch projectile was found lodged between its neck and shoulder blade. The projectile was one that had been fired by a bomb lance in the late 19th century which was likely manufactured in New Bedford, Massachusetts. The whale was an estimated 115 to 130 years old and was likely shot the first time somewhere around the year 1890. *See* N.Y. TIMES, June 17, 2007, at Sec. 4, col. 1.

[2.] Domestic Animals

SENTELL v. NEW ORLEANS & C.R. CO.

United States Supreme Court
166 U.S. 698 (1897)

In Error to the Court of Appeals for the Parish of Orleans in the State of Louisiana. This was an action originally instituted by [George W.] Sentell in the civil district court for the parish of Orleans, to recover the value of a Newfoundland bitch, known as 'Countess Lona,' alleged to have been negligently killed by the railroad company. The company answered, denying the allegation of negligence, and set up as a separate defense that plaintiff had not complied either with the requirements of the state law, or of the city ordinances, with respect to the keeping of dogs, and was therefore not entitled to recover. The law of the state was as follows:

> 'Section 1. . . . From and after the passage of this act dogs owned by citizens of this state are hereby declared to be personal property of such citizens, and shall be placed on the same guarantees of law as other personal property: provided, such dogs are given in by the owner thereof to the assessor.
>
> 'Sec. 2. . . . no dog shall be entitled to the protection of the law unless the same shall have been placed upon the assessment rolls.
>
> 'Sec. 3. . . . in civil actions for the killing of or for injuries done to dogs, the owner cannot recover beyond the amount of the value of such dog or dogs, as fixed by himself in the last assessment preceding the killing or injuries complained of. . . . Approved July 5, 1882.'

By the city ordinance, adopted July 1, 1890, No. 4613,'no dog shall be permitted to run or be at large upon any street, alley, highway, common or public square within the limits of the city of New Orleans: provided that this section shall not apply to any dog to which a tag, obtained from the treasurer, is attached.' By section

8 the treasurer was directed to furnish metal dog tags to all persons applying for the same at the rate of two dollars each, available only for the year in which they were issued.

Plaintiff denied the constitutionality of the state act; and the court charged the jury that the fact that the dog was not tagged, as required by the city ordinances, could not affect the right of the plaintiff to recover; that the above act of the legislature was unconstitutional, as destructive of the right of property; and that, a dog being property, a law which requires that property should not be protected, unless listed for taxation, was in conflict with the constitution of the United States, providing that no person shall be deprived of his life, liberty, or property without due process of law. The jury returned a verdict in favor of the plaintiff for $250, upon which judgment was entered.

The case was carried to the court of appeals, which reversed the judgment of the trial court, and entered judgment in favor of the defendant, holding that plaintiff should have shown a compliance with the law of the state and the ordinances of the city as a condition precedent to recover. Whereupon plaintiff sued out a writ of error from this court.

MR. JUSTICE BROWN, after stating the facts in the foregoing language, delivered the opinion of the court.

This case turns upon the constitutionality of a law of the state of Louisiana requiring dogs to be placed upon the assessment rolls, and limiting any recovery by the owner to the value fixed by himself for the purpose of taxation. The dog in question was a valuable Newfoundland bitch, registered in the American Kennel's stud book, and was kept by her owner for breeding purposes. It seems that, while following him in a walk upon the streets, she stopped on the track of the railroad company, and, being otherwise engaged for the moment, failed to notice the approach of an electric car which was coming towards her at great speed; and being, moreover, heavy with young, and not possessed of her usual agility, she was caught by the car and instantly killed. . . .

. . . [P]roperty in dogs is of an imperfect or qualified nature, and . . . they stand, as it were, between animals *ferae naturae*, in which, until killed or subdued, there is no property, and domestic animals, in which the right of property is perfect and complete. They are not considered as being upon the same plane with horses, cattle, sheep, and other domesticated animals, but rather in the category of cats, monkeys, parrots, singing birds, and similar animals, kept for pleasure, curiosity, or caprice. They have no intrinsic value, by which we understand a value common to all dogs as such, and independent of the particular breed or individual. Unlike other domestic animals, they are useful neither as beasts of burden, for draught (except to a limited extent), nor for food. They are peculiar in the fact that they differ among themselves more widely than any other class of animals, and can hardly be said to have a characteristic common to the entire race. While the higher breeds rank among the noblest representatives of the animal kingdom, and are justly esteemed for their intelligence, sagacity, fidelity, watchfulness, affection, and, above all, for their natural companionship with man, others are afflicted with such serious infirmities of temper as to be little better than a public nuisance. All are more or less subject to attacks of hydrophobic madness.

As it is practically impossible by statute to distinguish between the different breeds, or between the valuable and the worthless, such legislation as has been enacted upon the subject, though nominally including the whole canine race, is really directed against the latter class, and is based upon the theory that the owner of a really valuable dog will feel sufficient interest in him to comply with any reasonable regulation designed to distinguish him from the common herd. . . . [Justice Brown then cites a wide variety of cases from many different American jurisdictions that illustrate that the rights of dog owners to their dogs are frequently restricted by statutes and ordinances.] The only case to the contrary, to which our attention has been called is that of *Mayor v. Meigs*, 1 MacArthur 53 [Washington, D.C. 1873], in which a city ordinance of Washington requiring the owner of dogs to obtain a license for the keeping of the same was held to be illegal. The substance of the opinion seems to be that if the dog be a species of property, which was conceded, it is entitled to the protection of other property, and the owner should not be required to obtain a license for keeping the same.

Even if it were assumed that dogs are property in the fullest sense of the word, they would still be subject to the police power of the state, and might be destroyed or otherwise dealt with as in the judgment of the legislature is necessary for the protection of its citizens. That a state, in a *bona fide* exercise of its police power, may interfere with private property and even order its destruction is as well settled as any legislative power can be which has for its objects the welfare and comfort of the citizen. For instance, meats, fruits, and vegetables do not cease to become private property by their decay, but it is clearly within the power of the state to order their destruction in times of epidemic or whenever they are so exposed as to be deleterious to the public health. There is also property in rags and clothing, but that does not stand in the way of their destruction in case they become infected and dangerous to the public health. No property is more sacred than one's home, and yet a house may be pulled down or blown up by the public authorities if necessary to avert or stay a general conflagration, and that too without recourse against such authorities for the trespass. [Citations omitted.] Other instances of this are found in the power to kill diseased cattle, to destroy obscene books or pictures, or gambling instruments, and, in *Lawton v. Steele*, 152 U.S. 133 [1894], it was held to be within the power of a state to order the summary destruction of fishing nets the use of which was likely to result in the extinction of valuable fisheries within the waters of the state.

In Louisiana there is only a conditional property in dogs. If they are given in by the owner to the assessor, and placed upon the assessment rolls, they are entitled to the same legal guaranties as other personal property, though in actions for their death or injury the owner is limited in the amount of his recovery to the value fixed by himself in the last assessment. It is only under these restrictions that dogs are recognized as property. In addition to this, dogs are required by the municipal ordinance of New Orleans to be provided with a tag, obtained from the treasurer, for which the owner pays a license tax of two dollars. While these regulations are more than ordinarily stringent, and might be declared to be unconstitutional, if applied to domestic animals generally, there is nothing in them of which the owner of a dog has any legal right to complain. It is purely within the discretion of the legislature to say how far dogs shall be recognized as property . . . . The statute really puts a premium upon valuable dogs, by giving them a recognized position, and by permitting the owner to put his own estimate upon them.

There is nothing in this law that is not within the police power, or of which the plaintiff has a right to complain, and the judgment of the court of appeals is therefore affirmed.

NOTES AND QUESTIONS

1. *Jurisdiction of the Court.* One might ask why the United States Supreme Court is deciding a case concerning the liability of a railroad company to the owner of a dead dog. As the case indicates, the matter was originally tried in state court, but after an adverse decision by the Orleans Parish Court of Appeals, the dog owner appealed the case to the United States Supreme Court, as he was entitled to do. (Shades of *Pierson v. Post.*) The guarantee in Section 1 of the Fourteenth Amendment that no state shall "deprive any person of life, liberty, or property, without due process of law" has been one of the most litigated and most frequently interpreted clauses of the United States Constitution.

2. *Classification of Animals.* The Supreme Court here appears to agree that dogs can be placed in their own category of creatures, somewhere between domestic and wild animals. Does this mean that truly domestic animals, like horses, cattle, and sheep could not be subject to the requirements imposed on dogs by the statutes and ordinances imposed in this case? What does one make of the 1873 District of Columbia case acknowledged by the court that apparently reached a different decision regarding the legitimacy of a similar animal licensing ordinance? In 1857, in the case of *Wheatley v. Harris*, 36 Tenn. 468 (1857), the Tennessee Supreme Court ruled, "Upon the question whether the owner of a dog has such a property as will entitle him to maintain an action for killing or injuring the dog there can be no doubt." Can that sentiment be reconciled with the decision in *Sentell*?

3. *What About Theft?* Would the *Sentell* case be decided differently if the dog had been stolen rather than killed? In *Cummings v. Perham*, 1 Metcalf 555, 42 Mass. 555 (1840), the Massachusetts court opined, "Nor does the authority, given by statute, to kill a dog suffered to go without a collar, warrant a person to convert him to his own use. The object of the statute is, not to confer a benefit on an individual, but to rid society of a nuisance by killing the dog. This object would not be accomplished by a person's taking the dog to himself." Why the difference between killing and stealing?

4. *The Court that Decided* Sentell. The Supreme Court's opinion in Sentell was written by Henry Billings Brown (1836–1913), a New England native who studied at both Yale and Harvard before emigrating to Michigan where he rose to the highest ranks of the legal profession. He was appointed to the United States Supreme Court in 1890 by President Benjamin Harrison. Less than a year before his *Sentell* decision, Brown authored the Supreme Court's infamous opinion in *Plessy v. Ferguson*, 163 U.S. 537 (1896). In that case, Brown also upheld the power of the state of Louisiana to classify its citizens on the basis of race and to require them to take separate accommodations on public conveyances. In *Plessy*, Brown's colleague John Marshall Harlan, a former slave-holder from Kentucky famously dissented, and his Yale College classmate, David Josiah Brewer, abstained. In *Sentell*, the decision was unanimous.

[3.] Rights to Persons

Although it is one of the abhorrent facts of American history, African-American slavery existed as a form of American property from the 17th century until the ratification of the Thirteenth Amendment in 1865. The precise nature of slave property, particularly in states where slavery was not permitted, was a very complicated question that went to the heart of what it meant to designate something "property."

COMMONWEALTH v. AVES

Massachusetts Supreme Judicial Court
35 Mass. (18 Pick.) 193 (1836)

[On May 1, 1836, Mary Slater, a resident of New Orleans, Louisiana, entered the state of Massachusetts accompanied by an 8 year old slave girl named Med. Med had been purchased in Louisiana, along with her mother, three years earlier by Mary's husband Samuel Slater. Mary Slater and Med remained in Massachusetts throughout that summer. On August 17, 1836, Levin H. Harris, a Boston abolitionist, obtained a writ of habeas corpus against Thomas Aves, also of Boston, into whose custody Med had been temporarily intrusted. Aves was summoned before the Supreme Judicial Court of Massachusetts to explain why he was not unlawfully restraining Med of her liberty. Harris did not contest the fact that under the laws of Louisiana, Med was the property of Samuel Slater and that Mary Slater and Thomas Aves were his lawful agents.]

Shaw, C.J. delivered the opinion of the Court.

The precise question presented by the claim of the respondent is, whether a citizen of any one of the United States, where Negro slavery is established by law, coming into this State, for any temporary purpose of business or pleasure, staying some time, but not acquiring a domicil here, who brings a slave with him as a personal attendant, may restrain such slave of his liberty during his continuance here, and convey him out of this State on his return, against his consent.

It is now to be considered as an established rule, that by the constitution and law of this Commonwealth, before the adoption of the constitution of the United States, in 1789, slavery was abolished, as being contrary to the principles of justice, and of nature, and repugnant to the provisions of the declaration of rights, which is a component part of the constitution of the State. Such being the general rule of law, it becomes necessary to inquire how far it is modified or controlled in its operation; either: 1. By the law of other nations and states, as admitted by the comity of nations to have a limited operation within a particular state; or 2. By the constitution of the United States.

Although slavery and the slave trade are deemed contrary to natural right, yet it is settled by the judicial decision of this country and of England that it is not contrary to the law of nations. *Sommersett's* case [an 18th century English case holding that a West Indian slave owned by a British subject cannot be held as a slave in England] decides that slavery, being odious and against natural right, cannot exist, except by force of positive law. But it clearly admits, that it may exist by force of positive law.

This view of the law applicable to slavery, marks strongly the distinction between the relation of master and slave, as established by the local law of particular states, and in virtue of that sovereign power and independent authority which each independent state concedes to every other, and those natural and social relations, which are everywhere and by all people recognized, and which, though they may be modified and regulated by municipal law, are not founded upon it, such as the relation of parent and child, and husband and wife. Such also is the principle upon which the general right of property is founded, being in some form universally recognized as a natural right, independently of municipal law.

This affords an answer to the argument drawn from the maxim, that the right of personal property follows the person, and therefore, where by the law of a place a person there domiciled acquires personal property, by the comity of nations the same must be deemed his property everywhere. It is obvious, that if this were true, in the extent in which the argument employs it, if slavery exists anywhere, and if by the laws of any place a property can be acquired in slaves, the law of slavery must extend to every place where such slaves may be carried. The maxim, therefore, and the argument can apply only to those commodities which are everywhere, and by all nations, treated and deemed subjects of property. But it is not speaking with strict accuracy to say, that a property can be acquired in human beings, by local laws. Each state may, for its own convenience, declare that slaves shall be personal property, and that the relations and laws of personal chattels shall be deemed to apply to them. But it would be a perversion of terms to say, that such local laws do in fact make them personal property generally; they can only determine, that the same rules of law shall apply to them as applicable to property, and this effect will follow only so far as such law *proprio vigore* can operate. [Shaw then concludes that the Constitution and laws of the United States "are confined to cases of slaves escaping from other States and coming within the limits of this State without the consent and against the will of their masters." This, clearly, was not Med's situation since her owners had voluntarily brought her into Massachusetts.]

It is upon these grounds we are of opinion, that an owner of a slave in another State where slavery is warranted by law, voluntarily bringing such slave into this State, has no authority to detain him against his will, or to carry him out of the State against his consent, for the purpose of being held in slavery. We are of opinion that his [Aves'] custody is not to be deemed by the Court a proper and lawful custody. Under a suggestion made in the outset of this inquiry, that a probate guardian would probably be appointed, we shall for the present order the child into temporary custody, to give time for an application to be made to the judge of probate.

NOTES AND QUESTIONS

1. *Natural Law and Positive Law.* Chief Justice Lemuel Shaw describes the right to own property as a natural right, but characterizes slavery as contrary to natural law. How persuasive is his argument that Louisiana laws and customs that permit the ownership of African-American slaves do not convert slaves into property? If Shaw is wrong, what does it say about the nature of property if an item can cease to be property by the simple fact of its owner crossing state lines? Would it make a difference if this case were about captive wild animals, or firearms, or, perhaps a little anachronistically, automobile radar detectors, rather than slavery? Would the result be any different if ownership of these items was prohibited by Massachusetts law?

2. *Slavery and the Constitution.* Somewhat ironically, Aves' lawyer in the above case was Benjamin Robbins Curtis, who two decades later would be one of only two United States Supreme Court justices to dissent from the majority holding in *Dred Scott v. Sandford*, 60 U.S. 393 (1857). This infamous decision held, among other things, that the slave Dred Scott's long residence with his owner in free territory did not automatically emancipate him. Keep in mind that Med had been brought into Massachusetts by her owner and was not an escaped slave and therefore was not subject to the provisions of the Fugitive Slave Act of 1793 which required the return of escaped slaves to their masters. Fifteen years later, in *Thomas Sims' Case*, 61 Mass. 285 (1851), Chief Justice Shaw, to the dismay of many Massachusetts abolitionists, ruled that under the laws of the United States, Sims, an escaped slave, had to be returned to his master in Georgia. In other words, the Fugitive Slave Act (revised and strengthened in 1850) provided the positive law that was missing in *Commonwealth v. Aves*.

Chief Justice Taney's opinion for the Court in *Dred Scott* also asserted that "the right of property in a slave is distinctly and expressly affirmed in the Constitution" and that the Due Process and Just Compensation Clauses of the Fifth Amendment prevented Congress from outlawing slavery in the congressionally controlled territories on the grounds that doing so would deprive slave owners of their property. 60 U.S. 449–52.

3. *Ownership of the Human Body.* While slavery ended with the ratification of the Thirteenth Amendment in 1865, the issue of the ownership of the human body remains with us. Certain parts of the body are treated as though they were the property of the owner, but other parts are not. Under current law, a living individual can sell some parts of his or her body, particularly if they can be replenished and do not harm the health of the vendor — hair and blood are the two most obvious examples — but the individual is barred by law from selling organs, including those like kidneys, eyes, and the spleen, the removal of which are ordinarily not fatal. National Organ Transplant Act of 1984, 98 Stat. 2339 (1984), now 42 U.S.C. § 274e. In *Moore v. Regents of the Univ. of Cal.*, 793 P.2d 479 (Cal. 1990), the plaintiff argued that his physician's use of cells taken from his cancerous spleen (which the doctor had removed) for potentially profitable medical research was a conversion of his property. Although the California Supreme Court ruled on Moore's behalf on other grounds, it refused to characterize the use of the cells as the conversion of his property. So far, American courts have been similarly reluctant to apply ordinary

rules of property to frozen human sperm, ova, and pre-embryos. *See, e.g., Hecht v. Superior Court*, 16 Cal. App. 4th 836 (1993); *Kass v. Kass*, 235 A.D.2d 150 (N.Y. App. Div. 1997). What explains this hesitancy?

Although the topic strikes many as too gruesome to be a matter of public debate, the common law principle that no property rights exist in the body after death has been seriously challenged by developments in transplant technology and genetic research and by the growth of a market for body parts. The traditional rule was that the next of kin had no property rights in the body of the deceased except for a limited right to possess the body for burial purposes. *See generally* P. JACKSON, THE LAW OF CADAVERS AND OF BURIAL AND BURIAL PLACES (2d ed. 1950). However, it is now undeniable that if the corpse was treated as part of the decedent's estate, some corpses would have value, either for the still functioning body parts or, in some cases, for the macabre fascination they might hold for the public. (One thinks of the furor surrounding the requested auction of the personal belongings of Jeffrey Dahmer by the judgment creditors of the deceased serial killer.) For an unsuccessful effort to have Florida's Corneal Removal Statute declared unconstitutional as a taking of property without just compensation in violation of the Fifth and Fourteenth Amendments, see *Florida v. Powell*, 497 So. 2d 1188 (Fla. 1986). The Florida statute provided for the removal of corneal tissue during statutorily required autopsies when such tissue was needed for transplantation. The statute prohibited the removal of the tissue if the next-of-kin objected but did not require notification of the procedure.

Although there continues to be a general reluctance to recognize a "saleable" property interest in the body after death, "gifts" of body parts are widely encouraged. Every state has adopted the Uniform Anatomical Gift Act (1968, 1987) in some form as a way of increasing the number of cadaver organs available for transplant. Aside from the obvious public health interest in ensuring that dead bodies are disposed of in a timely fashion, are there valid public policy reasons for refusing to include the decedent's body as part of his or her estate?

[4.] Rights to Land — Priority of Possession

The owner of land is said to have "title" to the parcel. While someone without title may possess land and enjoy certain rights to it, possessory rights are inferior to those of the holder of title. Title to land in the United States ordinarily originated with an express grant from the sovereign (originally the British government and later the United States or one of the states). Title is normally represented by a written document known as a patent or a deed.

While title to land was granted in a variety of ways, the most common method of transferring the public domain to private hands after independence from Britain was sale of relatively small parcels at public auction. Although the bidding was open to all, payment in cash requirements often favored land speculators over actual settlers. However, from 1830 onward, government land sales actually favored those who were already possessing (or "squatting" on) the public domain. Through a process known as preemption, squatters were given the first opportunity to purchase "their" land at a set (and usually quite low) price. After 1862, the Homestead Act also made it possible to obtain undeveloped land from the

United States government without paying for it at all, although the Act required prior registration and a period of residency (usually five years) before a formal deed was issued by the government.

If the purpose of the United States land policy was to get public land into private hands as quickly as possible, it was a rousing success. Between 1854 and 1862, nearly 300 million acres were transferred to private owners; between 1862 and 1904, the total was in excess of 758 million. By 1940, the total acreage granted by the United States government to private owners exceeded one billion acres. (At the same time, title to more than 1.4 billion acres remained in the United States.) For a list of federal land legislation between 1785 and 1965 and statistics pertaining to land transfers, see R. Morris, Encyclopedia of American History 461–66 (1965).

Issues of land ownership were particularly important in California which became part of the United States in 1848 as a consequence of the Mexican-American War. As part of the Treaty of Guadalupe Hildago that ended the war, the United States promised to honor all land titles previously granted by the Spanish or Mexican governments in lands ceded to the United States (which included California). Treaty of Guadalupe Hildago, Art. VIII, 9 Stat. 929. Mexican grants encompassed over 10,000,000 acres of land, and several decades passed before many of these titles were confirmed. Land that had not been transferred to private ownership came under the control of the United States government. On California land titles generally, see W. Robinson, Land in California (1948).

As the following case shows, disputes over legal entitlement to land frequently arose, and in many cases, it was not possible to identify the true owner.

PLUME v. SEWARD & THOMPSON

California Supreme Court
4 Cal. 94 (1854)

Mr. Ch. J. Murray delivered the opinion of the Court.

This was an action of ejectment to recover a lot in the city of Marysville.[4] On the trial of the cause, the plaintiff proved that Covillaud and others, from whom he claimed, were in the year 1849, in possession of a tract of land, lying between the Yuba river and a slough, which was enclosed by a ditch on each side, running [from] the river to the slough; and had within said enclosure a trading post, a corral and a wheat field. The lot in dispute was not a portion of the wheat field or corral, but was included in the premises thus designated or enclosed by them; their right of possession remaining unquestioned and undisturbed. The land was afterwards laid out into lots and streets, upon the official map of the city of Marysville, many of which were sold by said Covillaud and others.

There is no pretense of an abandonment of the premises thus enclosed; but evidence that Covillaud continued to assert title and exercise acts of ownership over them. At the last term of this Court we decided, possession was prima facie evidence

[4] Editor's note: By the time of this case, California (and many other states) had abandoned the legal fiction that an action of ejectment could be brought only by a tenant.

of title, and sufficient to maintain ejectment. What acts of ownership were necessary to constitute possession was not involved in that decision.

From a careful examination of the authorities, I am satisfied, there must be an actual *bona fide* occupation, a *possessio pedis*, a subjection to the will and control, as contradistinguished from the mere assertion of title, and the exercise of casual acts of ownership, such as recording deeds, paying taxes, & etc.

This being the case, it becomes necessary to inquire if a party, who enters on land with no higher claim of title than that which the law presumes from his possession, is entitled to claim more than the quantity thus actually occupied by him.

This question has been frequently decided in most of the Western States, where entries have been made upon public lands by persons unable to reduce the whole of the lands to actual occupation by fencing and cultivation. These entries have for the most part been made by settlers claiming 160 acres under pre-emption laws, or some local custom on the subject.

In many cases the occupation of a portion of the land and the blazing of trees, so as to distinctly mark the extent and boundaries of the claim, have been held to operate as notice, and carry the possession to the whole tract; so the [falling] of timber around a tract of land, and the building of a brush fence, have been held as sufficient acts of the party in occupation of a part to draw after the possession of the land so enclosed.

The character of the improvement must, in a great measure, depend upon the locality. It is not necessary the occupant should cultivate the property thus claimed; it is sufficient if it be subject to his use in the manner pointed out. Neither is any particular kind of enclosure required where a party is in possession of land marked by distinct monuments of boundary, whether the same be a natural or artificial inclosure. Claiming title to the whole tract, the possession of the part so occupied will draw after it the possession of the whole.

It is said that this doctrine would give to Covillaud and others all the land claimed by them running from Yuba river to the mountains. We know nothing of their claim; but if they should establish their possession in the manner already indicated, we can see no reason for a different rule. Laying off the premises into town lots, selling the same, and exercising other acts of ownership over them, does not operate as an abandonment, but taken in connection with previous acts of ownership, would rather seem to strengthen the plaintiff's possession.

From this it follows that the Court below erred in ordering the plaintiff to be nonsuited. The evidence of the character of the possession, and the nature of the inclosure were before the jury, and they ought to have been allowed to pass on the sufficiency of them. Judgment reversed with costs and new trial ordered.

NOTES AND QUESTIONS

1. *What Happened in the Trial Court?* To understand the "property" question involved in this case, one must first understand what happened at trial. The plaintiff (Plume), claiming the right to the land from a sale by Covillaud, brought an action of ejectment against the defendants (who by necessity must have been in present possession of the lot). After hearing the plaintiff's evidence, the trial judge, presumably at the request of the defendants, dismissed the plaintiff's claim, thus leaving the defendants in possession of the lot. On what grounds could the trial judge have so ruled?

2. *The Historical Background to* Plume v. Seward & Thompson. The village of Marysville, California was located within the boundaries of an 11 legua (approximately 76 square miles) land grant given in 1842 to Swiss-born John Sutter by California's Mexican governor, Juan Bautista Alvarado. (At this time, Sutter was a naturalized Mexican citizen.) The grant also included the site of modern day Sacramento, as well as Sutter's Mill where gold would be discovered in January 1848. The settlement that included the city lot in dispute in the above case was first called Nye's Ranch, then Yubaville, and finally Marysville. (The town was named for Mary Murphy Covillaud, a survivor of the ill-fated Donner Party and the new wife of town founder Charles Covillaud.)

Later in 1842, Sutter granted Theodor Cordura, a Mexican resident of California, a 19-year lease to farm the portion of the grant which lay north of the Yuba and east of the Feather rivers. Two years later Cordura obtained from the Mexican government a large land grant lying north of Sutter's grant. In October 1848, eight months after the Treaty of Guadalupe Hildago transferred California from Mexico to the United States, Cordura sold half of his interest in the lease to the above-mentioned Covillaud, a French trapper and trader who had worked as Cordura's overseer and who had recently struck it rich in the gold fields. Shortly thereafter, Cordura sold the remainder of his interest to Covillaud's brothers-in-law Michael C. Nye and William Foster. On September 1849, Nye and Foster sold their interest to Covillaud, and four days later, Covillaud sold the majority of his interest to two Chileans, Jose Manuel Ramirez and John Sampson, and part to another Frenchman, Theodore Sicard.

Although technically Covillaud and his partners owned only the remaining years of a lease scheduled to expire in 1861, they treated the land as though they owned it absolutely. In December 1849, the Covillaud partnership had the town surveyed and began selling lots (including the one involved in this case). In spite of the "title" problem, lots sold at a furious pace as the Gold Rush brought new residents to Marysville every day. To remove the one problem — the developers holding only a lease to the property — Covillaud and his partners purchased title to the land from John Sutter in January 1850. By 1853, the population of Marysville had exceeded 10,000 residents. The story of the founding of Marysville is told in Thompson & West, *History of Yuba County California* (1879), *rprt. in* A MEMORIAL AND BIOGRAPHICAL HISTORY OF NORTHERN CALIFORNIA (1891). *See* P. KENS, JUSTICE STEPHEN FIELD: SHAPING LIBERTY FROM THE GOLD RUSH TO THE GILDED AGE 25–27 (1998); *see also Marysville's Golden History*, http://www.syix.com/yubacity/msvlhistory.html. For a critical appraisal of the situation in *Plume v. Seward* and *Thompson*, in the context of the problems faced by Mexican landowners after the annexation of California, see Chanbonpin, *How the Border Crossed Us: Filling the Gap Between* Plume v. Seward *and the Dispossession of Mexican Landowners in California After 1848*, 52 CLEV. ST. L. REV. 297 (2005).

3. *Who Actually Owned the Lot?* Based on the evidence in the historical record (though not in the opinion), it appears that Plume probably was the owner of the lot. The land was originally given to Sutter by the Mexican government (the sovereign in 1842). It was then leased to Cordura and the lease was transferred through a series of transactions to Covillaud and his partners. Even though Covillaud and his partners may have only possessed a leasehold interest in the lot at the time it was sold to Plume, that lease was scheduled to run until 1861, which was still years in the future when Plume filed his action to eject Seward & Thompson. Subsequent to the sale of many of the lots in Marysville, Covillaud and his partners acquired Sutter's reversionary interest in the tract, giving them actual title. (Because of a real property doctrine known as "estoppel by deed," the Covillaud group could not recover the land from the purchasers when the lease expired, if they had represented to the buyers that they had title to the lots in question.)

4. *Why Did Plume Proceed on a Theory of Possession Rather than Ownership?* If Covillaud was the owner of the lot prior to its sale to Plume, why did Plume base his argument for ejectment on Covillaud's possession, rather than his title to the property? Mostly likely, it was the product of uncertainty concerning the validity of Sutter's 1842 land grant. (Remember, the validity of Plume's title traces back to the legitimacy of Sutter's grant.) By the early 1850s, the large, geographically amorphous nature of Sutter's grant combined with the presence of a number of obligations stated in the grant which Sutter may not have met led a number of Californians to challenge the legitimacy of the grant before the Federal Land Claims Commission. Although Sutter's grant was eventually upheld by the Commission in 1857, and effectively confirmed by the United States Supreme Court the next year in *United States v. Fossat*, 61 U.S. 413 (1858), Plume and his lawyer may have decided in the early 1850s that it was too risky to stake their claim for ejectment on a title that might be declared invalid at any time. *See* A. HURTADO, JOHN SUTTER: A LIFE ON THE NORTH AMERICAN FRONTIER (2006).

5. *Ownership vs. Possession.* In the 19th century (and, presumably, today) most states favor the claims of a prior possessor without legal title over a subsequent occupier of the land, so long as it could be shown that the land had not been abandoned and that the subsequent occupier did not possess legal title. *See, e.g., Tapscott v. Lessee of Cobbs*, 52 Va. (11 Gratt.) 172 (1854). The same principle applies when the right to personal, rather than real, property is in dispute. Property law hornbooks have long stated that possession of a chattel, even without claim of title, gives the possessor a superior right to the chattel against everyone but the true owner. In *Anderson v. Gouldberg*, 53 N.W. 636 (Minn. 1892), a trespasser who had cut down trees to which he had no claim of right was found to have a valid cause of action against the operator of a saw mill who refused to return them to him. The court, in that case, reasoned that without a rule favoring the prior possessor, there would be "an endless series of unlawful seizures and reprisals in every case where property had once passed out of the possession of the rightful owner."

Professor Richard Helmholz of the University of Chicago, however, has argued that, contrary to the hornbook assertion, American courts have not ordinarily been willing to apply this principle in cases involving two wrongful possessors. In his view, concerns for the security of property rights have competed with notions of fairness and the latter have frequently prevailed. *See* Helmholz, *Wrongful Posses-*

sion of Chattels: Hornbook Law and Case Law, 80 Nw. U. L. Rev. 1221 (1986).

6. *What Constitutes Possession of Land?* In *Brumagin v. Bradshaw*, 39 Cal. 24, 50 (1870), another case involving events arising out of the California Gold Rush, the California Supreme Court stated:

> The general principle pervading all this class of cases, where the inclosure consists wholly or partially of natural barriers, is, that the acts of dominion and ownership which establish a *possessio pedis* must correspond, in a reasonable degree, with the size of the tract, its condition and appropriate use, and must be such as usually accompany the ownership of land similarly situated.

In *Brumagin*, the claim of possession was based upon the construction of a wall and a ditch in 1850 that sealed off access to a peninsula near San Francisco. The "possessor" then used the 1000-acre peninsula for the pasturage of several hundred horses. Twenty years later, the peninsula (known as Potrero) had become part of the City of San Francisco and was divided into lots, blocks, and streets. In a dispute between a present occupant and the administrator of the estate of one of the individuals who had used the peninsula for pasturage, the court was called upon to decide if the enclosure of one side and the use of 1000-acres for grazing were acts sufficient to constitute possession.

7. *Rights to Publically Owned Land.* Despite of the provisions of the treaty of Guadalupe Hildago which recognized the validity of Spanish and Mexican land grants, much of California remained part of the public domain at the time of the United States takeover. Even if the American government had wanted to transfer public land to private hands quickly, the reality of the Gold Rush made that impossible. Settlement on public lands, and the exploration for gold on public lands, far exceeded the capacity of the United States government to transfer public land into private hands in an orderly fashion. Consequently, much of the public domain was occupied, and disputes frequently arose among settlers and miners who claimed the right to specific parcels.

Shortly after California became a state in 1850, its legislature adopted a "Possessory Act" which provided that persons in possession of public lands for cultivation or grazing purposes were to be treated as though they held actual title. Act of Apr. 11, 1850, ch. 83, 1849–50 Cal. Stat. 203. A similar approach was adopted for miners as well.

George Plume's lawyer in the above case was Stephen J. Field. Field was himself a resident of Marysville, having settled in the community in January 1850, when it consisted of nothing more than an old adobe building and numerous tents. (Field had also represented Covillaud in the purchase of the land from Sutter in 1850 shortly after he arrived in Marysville.) Field, a native of Massachusetts and a member of a distinguished family, was elected to the California Supreme Court in 1857 and appointed to the United States Supreme Court in 1863, a position that held until 1897. In 1860, Field, by then Chief Justice of the California Supreme Court, summarized the California approach to questions of land ownership in the following way:

> The larger portion of the mining lands within the State [of California] belong to the United States, and yet that fact has never been considered as a sufficient answer to the prosecution of actions for the recovery of portions of such lands. Actions for the possession of mining claims, water privileges and the like, situated upon the public lands, are matters of daily occurrence, and if the proof of the paramount title of the Government would operate to defeat them, confusion and ruin would be the result. In determining controversies between parties thus situated, this Court proceeds upon the presumption of a grant from the Government to the first appropriator of mines, water privileges and the like. This presumption, which would have no place for consideration as against the assertion of the rights of the superior proprietor, is held absolute in all those controversies. And with the public lands which are not mineral lands, the title, as between citizens of the State, where neither connects himself with the Government, is considered as vested in the first possessor, and to proceed from him.

Coryell v. Cain, 16 Cal. 567, 572–73 (1860).

From all indications, the United States government did not object to California's approach to possessory rights in public lands.

8. *Possession as the Root of Title.* Modern Jurisprudential literature is replete with studies of the relationship of "title," or ownership to possession. The modern literature begins with Martin, *Possession as a Root of Title*, 61 U. PENN. L. REV. 647 (1913), and includes, among many others, Epstein, *Possession as the Root of Title*, 13 GA. L. REV. 1221 (1979), and Rose, *Possession as the Root of Property*, 52 U. CHI. L. REV. 73 (1985).

9. *Special Rules Affecting the Transfer of Land.* Because of the unique nature of land as property, special rules govern its transfer. Ordinarily, land can be transferred only by a written deed, and the deed must be recorded in the local land registry for the owner to secure full protection of his or her property. Procedures that would be perfectly acceptable to transfer valuable jewels or large amounts of stock may prove ineffective to transfer a small, relatively valueless parcel of land. Such rules are the subject of Chapter 9.

10. *The Critical Role of the Transfer from the Sovereign to the First Private Owner.* Arguments that productive use of land should be a precondition of ownership have been advanced throughout American history, but the fact is that the American legal system has ultimately recognized only those claims traceable back to a sovereign grant. (Even those who establish title by adverse possession, discussed below, must demonstrate that they have adversely possessed against the claimant who can trace title back to the sovereign before they can be said to have superior title to all competing claimants.)

Nowhere was this point made more dramatically than in *Johnson & Graham's Lessee v. M'Intosh*, 21 U.S. (8 Wheat.) 543 (1823). In that case, Chief Justice John Marshall was called upon to decide which of two parties had the superior claim to a large tract of land in the State of Illinois. Joshua Johnson and Thomas Graham, who were represented by none other than Senator Daniel Webster, claimed title through the will of their ancestor Thomas Johnson, who had been a member of a group of individuals who had purchased a large tract of land from the Piankeshaw and Illinois Indians in 1775. (The "lessee" in the title of the case was entirely fictitious, a fact that was known to all parties. The case was initiated as an action for ejectment which, technically, could only be brought by a tenant.) M'Intosh, by contrast, had purchased the land in question in 1818 from the United States government which had entered into a treaty with the Piankeshaws and the Illinois after the 1775 transfer.

Although Chief Justice Marshall acknowledged that the tribes involved in the earlier sale were in lawful possession of the land they purported to transfer, he held for a unanimous court that M'Intosh had the superior claim to the property. After analyzing at length the effect of European conquest upon the rights of Native American tribes, Marshall concluded that "the Indian inhabitants are to be considered merely as occupants, to be protected, indeed, while in peace, in the possession of their lands, but to be deemed incapable of transferring the absolute title to others. However this restriction may be opposed to natural right, and to the usages of civilized nations, yet, if it be indispensable to that system under which the country has been settled, and be adapted to the actual condition of the two people, it may, perhaps, be supported by reason, and certainly cannot be rejected by Courts of justice."

Consequently, the Indian tribes had no right to convey an interest to Thomas Johnson and his cohorts in 1775. Through a treaty with the same tribes, the United States had subsequently extinguished the Indians' occupancy rights to the property and had then conveyed valid legal title to M'Intosh. For a study of how the unowned lands of North America were initially transformed into commodities that could be owned, see K. MacMillan, Sovereignty and Possession in the English New World: The Legal Foundations of Empire, 1576–1640 (2006).

11. *Aboriginal Property Rights.* The legal inability of Native Americans to transfer their legal interests in land to private parties, acknowledged in *Johnson v. M'Intosh,* was also extended to situations involving transfers to state governments after the passage of the Indian Non-Intercourse Act of 1790. Under this act, Congress, acting pursuant to Art. I, § 8 of the Constitution, which gives the United States government authority "to regulate Commerce . . . with the Indian Tribes," prohibited the sale of Indian Lands unless the sale was "duly executed at some public treaty, held under the authority of the United States." Act of July 22, 1790, ch. 33, 1 Stat. 137, 138. In the 20th century, Native American tribes have successfully recovered damages from states that unlawfully obtained land from them after 1790. *See, e.g., Oneida Indian Nation v. County of Oneida,* 414 U.S. 661 (1974). In a widely noted decision handed down in 1992, the High Court of Australia reversed that country's traditional rejection of aboriginal rights to land occupied at the time of European settlement. *Mabo v. State of Queensland,* 107 A.L.R. 1 (1992).

12. *Land That Cannot Be Owned.* While the private ownership of land has long been one of the bedrocks of American democracy, at least one type of "land" — the bottoms of navigable waterways — cannot be owned even with the sovereign's permission. The public trust doctrine obligates the sovereign to retain control of these assets for the benefit of the public as a whole. Should a public trust asset be transferred into private hands to the extent that the sovereign relinquishes control of the asset, it can be reclaimed by the sovereign without compensation. This happened in the late 19th century when the Illinois legislature ceded control of the Chicago harbor to the Illinois Central Railroad only to reclaim it several years later. Illinois' right to do this was confirmed by the United States Supreme Court in *Illinois Central Railroad Co. v. Illinois*, 146 U.S. 387 (1892), in an opinion written by the above-mentioned Justice Stephen Field. In most American states, the same approach is taken toward tidal lands as well. The *Illinois Central* case and the public trust doctrine are examined in detail later in this book.

[5.] Adverse Possession

MARENGO CAVE CO. v. ROSS

Indiana Supreme Court
10 N.E.2d 917 (1937)

ROLL, JUDGE.

Appellee and appellant were the owners of adjoining land in Crawford County, Ind. On appellant's land was located the opening to a subterranean cavity known as "Marengo Cave." This cave extended under a considerable portion of appellant's land, and the southeastern portion thereof extended under lands owned by appellee. This action arose out of a dispute as to the ownership of that part of the cave that extended under appellee's land. Appellant was claiming title to all the cave and [c]avities, including that portion underlying appellee's land. Appellee instituted this action to quiet his title as by a general denial and filed a cross-complaint wherein he sought to quiet its title to all the cave, including that portion underlying appellee's land. There was a trial by jury which returned a verdict for the appellee. Appellant filed its motion for a new trial which was overruled by the court, and this the only error assigned on appeal. Appellant assigns as grounds for a new trial that the verdict of the jury is not sustained by sufficient evidence, and is contrary to law. These are the only grounds urged for a reversal of this cause.

The facts as shown by the record are substantially as follows: In 1883 one Stewart owned the real estate now owned by appellant, and in September of that year some young people who were upon that land discovered what afterwards proved to be the entrance to the cavern since known as Marengo Cave, this entrance being approximately 700 feet from the boundary line between the lands now owned by appellant and appellee, and the only entrance to said cave. Within a week after discovery of the cave, it was explored, and the fact of its existence received wide publicity through newspaper articles, and otherwise. Shortly thereafter the then owner of the real estate upon which the entrance was located took complete possession of the entire cave as now occupied by appellant and used for exhibition purposes, and began to charge an admission fee to those who desired to enter and view the cave, and to exclude therefrom those who were unwilling to pay for admission. This practice continued from 1883, except in some few instances when persons were permitted by the persons claiming to own said cave to enter same without payment of the usual required fee, and during the following years the successive owners of the land upon which the entrance to the cave was located, advertised the existence of said cave through newspapers, magazines, posters, and otherwise, in order to attract visitors thereto; also made improvements within the cave, including the building of concrete walks, and concrete steps where there was a difference in elevation of said cavern, widened and heightened portions of passageways; had available and furnished guides, all in order to make the cave more easily accessible to visitors desiring to view the same; and continuously, during all this time, without asking or obtaining consent from any one, but claiming a right so to do, held and possessed said subterranean passages constituting said cave, excluding therefrom the "whole world," except such persons as entered after paying admission for the privilege of so doing, or by permission.

Appellee has lived in the vicinity of said cave since 1903, and purchased the real estate which he now owns in 1908. He first visited the cave in 1895, paying an admission fee for the privilege, and has visited said cave several times since. He has never, at any time, occupied or been in possession of any of the subterranean passages or cavities of which the cave consists, and the possession and use of the cave by those who have done so has never interfered with his use and enjoyment of the lands owned by him. For a period of approximately 25 years prior to the time appellee purchased his land, and for a period of 21 years afterwards, exclusive possession of the cave has been held by appellant, its immediate and remote grantors.

The cave, as such, has never been listed for taxation separately from the real estate wherein it is located, and the owners of the respective tracts of land have paid the taxes assessed against said tracts.

A part of said cave at the time of its discovery and exploration extended beneath real estate now owned by appellee, but this fact was not ascertained until the year 1932, when the boundary line between the respective tracts through the cave was established by means of a survey made by a civil engineer pursuant to an order of court entered in this cause. Previous to this survey neither of the parties to this appeal, nor any of their predecessors in title, knew that any part of the cave was in fact beneath the surface of a portion of the land now owned by appellee. Possession of the cave was taken and held by appellant's remote and immediate grantors, improvements made, and control exercised, with the belief on the part of such grantors that the entire cave as it was explored and held was under the surface of lands owned by them. There is no evidence of and dispute as to ownership of the cave, or any portion thereof, prior to the time when in 1929 appellee requested a survey, which was approximately 46 years after discovery of the cave and the exercise of complete dominion thereover by appellant and its predecessors in title.

It is appellant's contention that it has a fee-simple title to all of the cave; that it owns that part underlying appellee's land by adverse possession. Section 2-602, Burns' Ann.St.1933, section 61, Baldwin's Ind.St.1934, provides as follows: "The following actions shall be commenced within the periods herein prescribed after the cause of action has accrued, and not afterward: . . . Sixth. Upon contracts in writing other than those for the payment of money, on judgments of courts of record, and for the recovery of the possession of real estate, within twenty (20) years."

It will be noted that appellee nor his predecessors in title had never effected a severance of the cave from the surface estate. Therefore the title of the appellee extends from the surface to the center but actual possession is confined to the surface. Appellee and his immediate and remote grantors have been in possession of the land and estate here in question at all times, unless it can be said that the possession of the cave by appellant as shown by the evidence above set out has met all the requirements of the law relating to the acquisition of land by adverse possession. A record title may be defeated by adverse possession. All the authorities agree that, before the owner of the legal title can be deprived of his land by another's possession, through the operation of the statute of limitation, the possession must have been actual, visible, notorious, exclusive, under claim of ownership and hostile to the owner of the legal title and to the world at large (except only the government), and continuous for the full period prescribed by the statute. The rule is not always stated in exactly the same words in the many cases dealing with the subject of adverse possession, yet the rule is so thoroughly settled that there is no doubt as to what elements are essential to establish a title by adverse possession.

(1) The possession must be actual. It must be conceded that appellant in the operation of the "Marengo Cave" used not only the cavern under its own land but also that part of the cavern that underlaid appellee's land, and assumed dominion over all of it. Yet it must also be conceded that during all of the time appellee was in constructive possession, as the only constructive possession known to the law is that which inheres in the legal title and with which the owner of that title is always endowed. Whether the possession was actual under the peculiar facts in this case we need not decide.

(2) The possession must be visible. The owner of land who, having notice of the fact that it is occupied by another who is claiming dominion over it, nevertheless stands by during the entire statutory period and makes no effort to eject the claimant or otherwise protect his title, ought not to be permitted, for reasons of public policy, thereafter to maintain an action for the recovery of his land. But, the authorities assert, in order that the possession of the occupying claimant may constitute notice in law, it must be visible and open to the common observer so that the owner or his agent on visiting the premises might readily see that the owner's rights are being invaded. What constitutes open and visible possession has been stated in general terms, thus; it is necessary and sufficient if its nature and character is such as is calculated to apprise the world that the land is occupied and who the occupant is[,] and such an appropriation of the land by claimant as to apprise, or convey visible notice to the community or neighborhood in which it is situated that it is in his exclusive use and enjoyment.

(3) The possession must be open and notorious. The mere possession of the land is not enough. It is knowledge, either actual or imputed, of the possession of his lands by another, claiming to own them bona fide and openly, that affects the legal owner thereof. Where there has been no actual notice, it is necessary to show that the possession of the disseisor was so open, notorious, and visible as to warrant the inference that the owner must or should have known of it.

And again, the possession must be notorious. It must be so conspicuous that it is generally known and talked of by the public. "It must be manifest to the community."

(4) The possession must be exclusive. It is evident that two or more persons cannot hold one tract of land adversely to each other at the same time.

The facts as set out above show that appellee and his predecessors in title have been in actual and continuous possession of his real estate since the cave was discovered in 1883. At no time were they aware that any one was trespassing upon their land. No one was claiming to be in possession of appellee's land. It is true that appellant was asserting possession of the "Marengo Cave." There would seem to be quite a difference in making claim to the "Marengo Cave," and making claim to a portion of appellee's land, even though a portion of the cave extended under appellee's land, when this latter fact was unknown to any one. The evidence on both sides of this case is to the effect that the "Marengo Cave" was thought to be altogether under the land owned by appellant, and this erroneous supposition was not revealed until a survey was made at the request of appellee and ordered by the court in this case. It seems to us that the following excerpt from *Lewey v. H.C. Frick Coke Co.* (Pa. 1895) 31 A. 261, 263, is peculiarly applicable to the situation here presented, inasmuch as we are dealing with an underground cavity. It was stated in the above case:

> The title of the plaintiff extends from the surface to the center, but actual possession is confined to the surface. Upon the surface he must be held to know all that the most careful observation by himself and his employees could reveal, unless his ignorance is induced by the fraudulent conduct of the wrongdoer. But in the coal veins, deep down in the earth, he cannot see. Neither in person nor by his servants nor employees can he explore their recesses in search for an intruder. If an adjoining owner goes beyond his own boundaries in the course of his mining operations, the owner on whom he enters has no means of knowledge within his reach. Nothing short of an accurate survey of the interior of his neighbor's mines would enable him to ascertain the fact. This would require the services of a competent mining engineer and his assistants, inside the mines of another, which he would have no right to insist upon. To require an owner, under such circumstances, to take notice of a trespass upon his underlying coal at the time it takes place, is to require an impossibility; and to hold that the statute begins to run at the date of the trespass is in most cases to take away the remedy of the injured party before he can know that an injury has been done him. A result so absurd and so unjust ought not to be possible.
>
> The reason for the distinction exists in the nature of things. The owner of land may be present by himself or his servants on the surface of his possessions, no matter how extensive they may be. He is for this reason held to be constructively present wherever his title extends. He cannot be present in the interior of the earth. No amount of vigilance will enable him to detect the approach of a trespasser who may be working his way through the coal seams underlying adjoining lands. His senses cannot inform him of the encroachment by such trespasser upon the coal that is hidden in the rocks under his feet. He cannot reasonably be held to be constructively

> present where his presence is, in the nature of things, impossible. He must learn of such a trespass by other means than such as are within his own control, and, until these come within his reach, he is necessarily ignorant of his loss. He cannot reasonably be required to act until knowledge that action is needed is possible to him.

We are not persuaded that this case falls within the rule of mistaken boundary as announced in *Rennert v. Shirk*, wherein this court said: "Appellant insists, however, that, if one takes and holds possession of real estate under a mistake as to where the true boundary line is, such possession cannot ripen into a title. In this state, when an owner of land, by mistake as to the boundary line of his land, takes actual, visible, and exclusive possession of another's land, and holds it as his own continuously for the statutory period of 20 years, he thereby acquires the title as against the real owner. The possession is regarded as adverse, without reference to the fact that it is based on mistake; it being prima facie sufficient that actual, visible, and exclusive possession is taken under a claim of right."

The reason for the above rule is obvious. Under such circumstances appellant was in possession of the necessary means of ascertaining the true boundary line, and to hold that a mere misapprehension on the part of appellant as to the true boundary line would nullify the well-established law on adverse possession. The facts in the present case are far different. Here the possession of appellant was not visible. No one could see below the earth's surface and determine that appellant was trespassing upon appellee's lands. This fact could not be determined by going into the cave. Only by a survey could this fact be made known. The same undisputed facts clearly show that appellant's possession was not notorious. Not even appellant itself nor any of its remote grantors knew that any part of the "Marengo Cave" extended beyond its own boundaries, and they at no time even down to the time appellee instituted this action made any claim to appellee's lands. Appellee and his predecessors in title at all times have been in possession of the land which he is now claiming. No severance by deed or written instrument was ever made to the cave, from the surface. In the absence of a separate estate could appellant be in the exclusive possession of the cave that underlies appellee's land?

"If there is no severance, an entry upon the surface will extend downward, and draw to it a title to the underlying minerals; so that he who disseizes another, and acquires title by the statute of limitations, will succeed to the estate of him upon whose possession he has entered." *Delaware & Hudson Canal Co. v. Hughes* (Pa. 1897) 38 A. 568, 570.

Even though it could be said that appellant's possession has been actual, exclusive, and continuous all these years, we would still be of the opinion that appellee has not lost his land. It has been the uniform rule in equity that the statute of limitation does not begin to run until the injured party discovers, or with reasonable diligence might have discovered, the facts constituting the injury and cause of action. Until then the owner cannot know that his possession has been invaded. Until he has knowledge, or ought to have such knowledge, he is not called upon to act, for he does not know that action in the premises is necessary and the law does not require absurd or impossible things of any one.

So in the case at bar, appellant pretended to use the "Marengo Cave" as his property and all the time he was committing a trespass upon appellee's land. After 20 years of secret user, he now urges the statute of limitation, section 2-602, Burns' St.1933, section 61, Baldwin's Ind.St.1934, as a bar to appellee's action. Appellee did not know of the trespass of appellant, and had no reasonable means of discovering the fact. It is true that appellant took no active measures to prevent the discovery, except to deny appellee the right to enter the cave for the purpose of making a survey, and disclaiming any use of appellee's lands, but nature furnished the concealment, or where the wrong conceals itself. It amounts to the taking of another's property without his knowledge of the fact that it is really being taken from him. In most cases the ignorance is produced by artifice. But in this case nature has supplied the situation which gives the trespasser the opportunity to occupy the recesses on appellee's land and caused the ignorance of appellee which he now seeks to avail himself. We cannot assent to the doctrine that would enable one to trespass upon another's property through a subterranean passage and under such circumstances that the owner does not know, or by the exercise of reasonable care could not know, of such secret occupancy, for 20 years or more and by so doing obtained a fee-simple title as against the holder of the legal title. The fact that appellee had knowledge that appellant was claiming to be the owner of the "Marengo Cave," and advertised it to the general public, was no knowledge to him that it was in possession of appellee's land or any part of it. We are of the opinion that appellant's possession for 20 years or more of that part of "Marengo Cave" underlying appellee's land was not open, notorious, or exclusive, as required by the law applicable to obtaining title to land by adverse possession.

We cannot say that the evidence is not sufficient to support the verdict or that the verdict is contrary to law. Judgment affirmed.

NOTES AND QUESTIONS

1. *The Elements of Adverse Possession.* Although there are many variations of the formula, most versions emphasize that the possession must be actual, exclusive, open and notorious, adverse or hostile, under a claim of right, and continuous for the statutory period. What constitutes "actual" possession seems to vary slightly from jurisdiction to jurisdiction, but it clearly requires more than mere presence. The location, character, and nature of the land will usually help determine what type of use amounts to "actual possession." Other elements of adverse possession are discussed in the notes following the next case.

2. *What Happened Next in Marengo Cave?* As it turned out, Marengo Cave consisted of almost five miles of passages, approximately 700 feet of which lay underneath the land of John E. "Ed" Ross. When the owners of the largest part of the cave were unable to acquire either Ross' interest in the cave or his permission to include his portion in cave tours, a fence was constructed along the subterranean property line that allowed visitors to the cave to look into Ross portion of the cave but prevented them from entering it. The fence remained in place until Ross died in 1972, and in 1978, the Ross portion was opened to cave visitors. The cave, which features a stunning landscape of stalactites and stalagmites, was designated a National Landmark in 1984, and today it remains one of the primary tourist attractions in southern Indiana. For an outline of the cave's history, see *Show Cave*

of the United States of America: Marengo Cave National Landmark, www.showcaves.com/english/usa/showcaves/Marengo.html. The cave's own website is www.marengocave.com.

3. Note that the court in *Marengo Cave* accepts as a given that absent an adverse possession Ross owns the part of the cave beneath his land, even though he has no access to it. This decision was handed down eight years after the decision of the Kentucky Court of Appeals in *Edwards v. Sims*, 24 S.W.2d 619 (Ky. Ct. App. 1929), discussed in the notes following the *Geller* decision in Chapter 2. Does the result in this case suggest that there ought to a special rule pertaining to the ownership of caves, or at least an exception to the rules for adverse possession? Why should Ross have the right to exclude the world from a place that he cannot reach, let alone use productively? Would a rule that gave ownership rights to the owners of the cave entrances be a better rule? What if there were multiple entrances located on parcels with different owners? Alternatively, should the open and notorious requirement of adverse possession be relaxed for caves?

4. What should happen if an adverse possessor meets the requirements of adverse possession on a parcel of land in which the mineral rights (as in *Penn Coal*) or the "cave rights" (which, from the Court's opinion, seems possible in Indiana) had been transferred to a third party prior to the start of the adverse possession? The standard answer is that possession of the surface alone who not divest the owners of the subsurface estate of their ownership interests. Does this make sense? What would happen if the adverse possessor started mining for minerals or using the cave? Should adverse possession of the surface include adverse possession of the underlying mineral rights if the rights have not been transferred? In *Failoni v. Chicago & North Western Ry. Co.*, 195 N.E.2d 619 (Ill. 1964), the Illinois Supreme Court ruled that the adverse possessor of the surface had not adversely possessed the subsurface mineral rights even though they had not been severed from the original parcel. Is such a holding consistent with the general theory of adverse possession? What is the general theory of adverse possession? For one attempt to answer the last question, see Sprankling, *An Environmental Critique of Adverse Possession*, 79 CORNELL L. REV. 816 (1994). What if the doctrine depended on ownership rather than use? *See* Brown & Williams, *Rethinking Advanced Possession: An Essay on Ownership and Possession*, 60 SYRACUSE L. REV. 583 (2010).

5. *Origins of the Doctrine of Adverse Possession.* Adverse possession as an Anglo-American legal principle dates to the Statute of Westminister which was enacted by the English parliament in 1275. State of Westminister I, 3 Edw. I, c. 39 (1275). For the first time, plaintiffs were barred from bringing long-standing claims for the recovery of land. The 1639 Statute of Limitations, enacted at the outset of English colonization of North America, required such actions to be filed no later than 20 years after the cause arose. 21 Ja. I, ch. 16 (1623). Because of the uncertain nature of many early American land titles, particularly in regard to boundaries, the doctrine played an important role in the early American land system. Although the "legality" of the doctrine was not at issue, the United States Supreme Court affirmed the utility of the principle in 1839. *Clark v. Smith*, 13 U.S. 195 (1839).

CAMPBELL v. HIPAWAI CORP.

Hawaii Appellate Court
639 P.2d 1119 (1982)

Per Curiam.

This is a dispute between two landowners over the location of the common boundary between their properties. The property in question is located in Manoa Valley, Oahu, and is designated by the exhibits in evidence as parcel 15, TMK 2-29-23-15. It consists of 2,016 square feet and is bordered on the west by parcel 14, owned by defendant-appellant, and on the east by parcel 4, owned by plaintiff-appellee. Appellee claimed paper title to the property by virtue of Royal Patent No. 1273, issued in 1853 to Kaaukai by King Kamehameha III. Appellant claimed title to the same parcel by mesne conveyances and by adverse possession, established by its predecessors in interest. After a trial by jury, the court below entered a judgment quieting title in appellee. Appellant appeals contending that the jury was erroneously instructed on the period of limitations applicable to its claim of adverse possession. We agree and accordingly, reverse.

In the trial below, there was evidence adduced from which the jury may have found that appellant had acquired title to parcel 15 by adverse possession.

James Woolsey, one of appellant's predecessors in interest, stated that as far back as 1918, parcel 15 was being cultivated as part of parcel 14 by Rose Hao and her husband Makahi. In 1942, Woolsey's mother, Annie Harris, conveyed parcels 14 and 15 to Hattie Smith (the adopted daughter of Rose and Makahi) by an unrecorded agreement of sale. Woolsey stated that up until Hattie's death in 1957, Hattie and her husband, John Smith, continued to farm and cultivate parcel 15. In 1949, Woolsey succeeded to his mother's estate. In 1957, Woolsey and Smith conveyed their respective interests in the property to Leon Chun.

John Smith testified that he married Hattie in 1913 and had resided on the property in question between the years 1910 through 1913 and 1929 through 1959. Smith stated that as far as he could remember, parcel 15 had always been cultivated as part of parcel 14. Smith also stated that when appellee's predecessor in interest, Alice Campbell, first began to reside on parcel 4 in 1936, she never questioned their use and cultivation of parcel 15.

Leon Chun, appellant's grantor, testified that he acquired parcel 14 and 15 by deed on October 23, 1957. Chun stated that in 1958, he moved a second house onto the property and placed it immediately adjacent to the boundary between parcel 14 and 15. Chun then visited Alice Campbell to discuss the multiple tax claimant problem which existed with respect to parcel 15 but apparently nothing was resolved. Shortly thereafter, Chun discovered that a chain link fence had been erected between parcel 14 and 15. He immediately tore it down. In 1967, appellee inherited parcel 4 and began to reside there. Chun stated he approached her to discuss the multiple tax claimant problem which still existed. Appellee referred Chun to her lawyers but again, nothing was resolved. On January 1, 1968, Chun conveyed the property to appellant. Sometime in 1977, Chun discovered that appellee was clearing parcel 15 of underbrush and that the chain link fence had been

* - a conveyance occupying an intermediate position in a chain of title between the first grantee and the present holder.

restored. He again tore the fence down. Appellee filed her complaint on August 23, 1977.

Appellant contends that the trial court erred in instructing the jury that the applicable period of limitations governing its claim of adverse possession is twenty years. We agree.

Plaintiff's Instruction No. 2, given over appellant's objections, is as follows:

> If the jury finds from the evidence that the plaintiff obtained legal title to the whole of the lands described in the complaint and her right to possession thereof, then the burden is on the defendant to show title by adverse possession to said property for a period of not less than 20 years before the commencement of the suit by clear and positive evidence.

Plaintiff's Instruction No. 11 states that:

> Adverse possession requires five elements. It must be [(1)] hostile or adverse; (2) actual; (3) visible, notorious and exclusive; (4) continuous; and (5) under claim of ownership. The party who claims adverse possession has the burden of proving that the foregoing elements have existed for the statutory period of not less than 20 years. In addition, he must prove, by clear and positive evidence the location of the boundaries he claims. Such boundaries must be established at the inception, during the continuance, and at the completion of the period of adverse possession.
>
> If the jury finds that the defendant or any of its predecessors in interest did comply with and satisfy the five elements required in adverse possession as stated above, over a continuous period of 20 years, then you must find for the defendant.

The above instructions were based on the period of limitations governing claim of adverse possession set forth under the provisions of HRS §§ 657-31[5] and 669-1.[6] These statutes amended pre-existing law by increasing the period of limitations from ten years to twenty. See, Steadman, *The Statutory Elements of Hawaii's Adverse Possession Law*, 14 HBJ, No. 2, Summer 1978. The amendments became effective on May 4, 1973, by Act 26, S.B. 660. However, Section 6 of the Act states:

> This Act shall take effect upon its approval and shall govern any case or controversy which shall arise after the effective date of this Act; provided,

---

[5] [1] HRS § 657-31 states that:

> No person shall commence an action to recover possession of any lands, or make any entry thereon, unless within twenty years after the right to bring the action first accrued.

[6] [2] HRS § 669-1 states that:

> (a) Action may be brought by any person against another person who claims, or who may claim adversely to the plaintiff, an estate or interest in real property, for the purpose of determining the adverse claim.
>
> (b) Action for the purpose of establishing title to real property may be brought by any person who has been in adverse possession of the real property for not less than twenty years.
>
> (c) Action under subsection (a) or (b) shall be brought in the circuit court of the circuit in which the property is situated.

however, that this Act does not affect rights and duties that matured, penalties that were incurred, and proceedings that were begun, before its effective date.

This savings clause was prompted by the legislature's concern over protecting vested rights. The bill was specifically amended to insure that "this Act will be prospective in nature and will not affect those rights and duties existing under present law." H. Stand. Comm. Rep. No. 878 on S.B. 660, 1973 H. Jour. 1163–1164.

At oral argument, appellee argued that even if the instructions were erroneous, there was no evidence to support the claim of a matured 10-year period of adverse possession prior to the amendment of the statute. We cannot agree. The testimony of Woolsey, Smith and Chun, summarized above, was sufficient to create a jury question on the issue. Thus, an instruction based on the 10-year period of limitations should have been given. It should have included appropriate language to the effect that once title by adverse possession had vested, continued possession was not required. Had the jury been properly instructed, they may have found that appellant had established title by adverse possession.

The function served by jury instructions is to inform the jury of the law applicable to the current case. *Tittle v. Hurlbutt*, 497 P.2d 1354 (Haw. 1972). It is reversible error for the trial judge to fail to instruct the jury on the proper rule of law to be applied in a particular case. *City & County of Honolulu v. Bonded Inv. Co., Ltd.*, 507 P.2d 1084 (Haw. 1973).

Appellant's other specifications of error are without merit. We hold that the trial court erred in failing to instruct the jury that a ten-year period of limitations was applicable to appellant's claim where it was warranted by the evidence. Reversed and remanded.

NOTES AND QUESTIONS

1. *Adverse Possession Through Mistaken Boundary.* In *Marengo*, the court suggests that the possessor of the land under a "mistaken boundary" may acquire land by adverse possession because the landowner is "in possession of the necessary means of ascertaining the true boundary line." But why would the "true owner" take advantage of such means? Doesn't such a mistake alter the meaning of intent? If not, doesn't such a rule appear to require a landowner to recheck boundaries every few years to avoid loss of land through adverse possession? Is this the purpose of common law and statutory adverse possession?

2. *The Amount of Land.* How much of the "possession" in *Campbell* does the court intimate is adverse? What about the "cultivation," if it could be shown to be continuous between 1918 and 1942? What about the "residence" of Chun's transferor's mother between 1929 and 1959? Some states draw a distinction between adverse possessors who hold under color of title (usually a defective deed or an invalid will) and those who simply take possession. The latter are entitled only to the land that they actually possess whereas the former are often deemed to be in constructive possession of all lands described in the invalid document, whether or not they are actually possessing it.

3. *"Tacking" and the Statutory Period.* In *Campbell*, the adversely-possessed land changed hands several times. If none of the adverse possessors held the land for the statutory period, should it be sufficient to meet the statutory period if their collective adverse possession exceeds 20 years? The traditional rule is that consecutive, continuous periods of adverse possession can be "tacked" together if there is "privity" between the successors in the adverse possession. In this context, privity means either that the previous adverse possessor transferred his or her "interest" to the successor with a deed or similar document or else that the successor was the heir or devisee of the previous possessor. Consequently, an adverse possessor who ousts the prior adverse occupant will not gain the benefit of his predecessor's possession. *Glenn v. Shuey*, 595 A.2d 606 (Pa. Super. Ct. 1991). *See generally* J. SPRANKLING, UNDERSTANDING PROPERTY LAW 462 (2d ed. 2007).

4. *Interruption of Adverse Possession.* What action is sufficient by way of interruption of an adverse possession by the second owner? Campbell put up a fence. What if she had merely sent a letter to Chun? Commenced a lawsuit? At least two of the "adverse" claimants built a dwelling. Is this sufficient to commence adverse possession? How much of the land was claimed by another by record title?

5. *What About the Payment of Taxes?* Should it make a difference in the proceedings if one or the other party has a deed? This normally satisfies the "color of title" requirement which is an additional requirement in some states. (*See* Note 2, above.) What about the payment of taxes? In some states, most of which are located in the American West, payment of taxes during the statutory period is an additional requirement for a successful adverse possession. *See* POWELL ON REAL PROPERTY § 91.09(2) (Michael Alan Wolf ed. 2007). Most of these statutes were designed to protect the interests of owners of large tracts of undeveloped land from the unauthorized possession of parts of their land by squatters.

6. *Use and Occupancy.* What kinds of use and occupancy constitute sufficient possession for title to pass by adverse possession? According to one court, the established rule is: "It is sufficient if the acts of ownership are of such a character as to openly and publicly indicate an assumed control or use such as are consistent with the character of the premises in question." *Murray v. Hudson*, 32 N.W. 889, 891 (Mich. 1887). Does occasionally cutting hay, planting trees, and renting to a hunting club during hunting season suffice? *See Whitaker v. Erie Shooting Club*, 60 N.W. 983 (Mich. 1894). What about building a succession of hunting cabins, coupled with paying taxes? *See Monroe v. Rawlings*, 49 N.W.2d 55 (Mich. 1951). What about renting to a farmer coupled with regular recreational use? *Okuna v. Nakahuna*, 594 P.2d 128 (Haw. 1979).

7. *No Adverse Possession Against Government.* It is generally agreed that one cannot acquire title by adverse possession from a government owner. *See, e.g., United Congregational & Evangelical Churches of Moku'aikaua & Helani v. Heirs of Kamamalu*, 582 P.2d 208 (Haw. 1978). What policies support such an exemption? Some states will permit adverse possession of government-owned lands if they are held for income rather than a direct public purpose. *See Jarvis v. Gillespie*, 587 A.2d 981 (Vt. 1991).

8. *Amended Statute's Effect on Existing Rights Regarding Time Period.* What happens when a statute changes the existing statutory period for adverse posses-

sion by shortening it? As you see from the *Campbell* case, the intent of the legislature was not to affect existing rights. Which claimant does the language protect? All adverse possessors who, upon possession, have held land openly, notoriously, continuously, etc., for at least 10 years? What if the period is lengthened by 10 years, from 10 years to 20 years? Surely, titles which have "passed" by adverse possession during the time the 10 year period is in effect should be deemed settled. Is it clear that an adverse possessor holding land for nine years must wait an additional 11 years, or should the right to the 10 year period be regarded as "vested"?

9. *Amended Statute's Effect on Existing Rights Regarding Amount of Land.* What if the legislature decides by statute to affect the *amount* of land that can change ownership by adverse possession? Hawaii, for example, reduced to four acres the land area that can be so transferred. Should the same analysis apply with the same result as in the preceding note?

10. *Length of the Statutory Period.* At the outset of the 21st century, statutory periods in the United States ranged from five years to 40 years. The most common statutory period was 10 years (16 states) with 20 years ranking second (12 states). The three states with the shortest periods (all five years) are California, Idaho, and Montana. The three states with the longest periods are Louisiana (30 years), New Jersey (30 years), and Iowa (40 years). Some states have shorter periods for adverse possessors who have paid taxes on the land or who claim the land under color of title. Louisiana has the widest gap with a 10 year period for "good faith" adverse possessors and a 30 year period for those who occupy in bad faith. La. Civ. Code arts. 2486, 3473, 3475.

11. *Exceptions to the Time Period.* Many adverse possession statutes have a section on disabilities whereby minors, those in prison, and those adjudged insane or otherwise incompetent to manage their affairs are given a period of years or an unlimited period of time to eject those who are adversely possessing land to which they claim title by record. Haw. Rev. Stat. § 657-34 thus provides:

> If, when right of entry or of action first accrues as aforesaid, the person entitled to the entry or action is within the age of eighteen years, or insane, or imprisoned, such person, or anyone claiming from, by, or under the person, may make the entry or bring the action at any time within five years after the disability is removed, notwithstanding the twenty years before limited in that behalf, have expired.

12. *How Adverse Possessors Establish Title.* Once an adverse possessor meets the requirements of the jurisdiction in which the land is located, he or she becomes the owner of the property. However, the local land records will still show the owner as the previous title-holder, and the adverse possessor is likely to have difficulty selling his new parcel. To allow the adverse possessor to become the new owner of record, all states allow the new owner to file an "action to quiet title" which will result in the issuance of a new deed.

[6.] Rights to Water

Contemporary issues of ownership have increasingly involved property claims to items that are intangible — ideas, genetic codes, computer programs, airspace, and sunlight, to name a few. The challenges facing those who must decide the apportionment of rights in these areas are reminiscent of those involving claims of ownership of water in an earlier era. Although water is "tangible," it also has a furtive character not unlike that of more ephemeral objects. Water, moreover, was not only a necessity; it also provided much of the energy for industrial development in the early United States. The individual who controlled water exercised considerable power, especially in those regions in which water was not abundant.

EVANS v. MERRIWEATHER
Illinois Supreme Court
4 Ill. 491 (1842)

JUSTICE LOCKWOOD delivered the opinion of the court.

This was an action on the case, brought in the Greene Circuit Court, by Merriweather against Evans, for obstructing and diverting a water course. The plaintiff obtained a verdict, and judgment was rendered thereon.

After the cause was brought into this court, the parties agreed upon the following statement of facts: Smith and Baker, in 1834, bought of T. Carlin six acres of land, through which a branch ran, and erected a steam mill thereon. They depended upon a well and the branch for water in running their engine. About one or two years afterwards, John Evans bought of T. Carlin six acres of land, on the same branch, above and immediately adjoining the lot owned by Smith & Baker, and erected thereon a steam mill, depending upon a well and the branch for water in running his engine. Smith & Baker, after the erection of Evans' mill, in 1836 or 1837, sold the mill and appurtenances to Merriweather, for about $8,000. Evans' mill was supposed to be worth $12,000.

Ordinarily there was an abundance of water for both mills; but in the fall of 1837, there being a drought, the branch failed, so far that it did not afford water sufficient to run the upper mill continually. Evans directed his hands not to stop, or divert the water, in the branch; but one of them employed about the mill did make a dam across the branch, just below Evans' mill, and thereby diverted all the water in the branch into Evans' well. After the diversion of the water in to Evans' well, as aforesaid, the branch went dry below, and Merriweather's mill could not and did not run, in consequence of it more than one day in a week, and was then supplied with water from his well. Merriweather then brought this suit, in three or four weeks after the putting of the dam across the branch for the diversion of the water, and obtained a verdict for $150.

This suit, it is admitted, is the first between the parties litigating the right as to the use of the water. It is further agreed, that the branch afforded usually sufficient water for the supply of both mills, without materially affecting the size of the current, though the branch was not depended upon exclusively for that purpose. Furthermore, that at the time of the grievances complained of by the plaintiff below, the defendant had water hauled in part for the supply of his boilers. That the dam was made below the defendant's well, across the branch, which diverted as well the water hauled and poured out into the branch above the well, as the water of the branch, into the defendant's well.

Upon this state of facts, the question is presented, as to what extent riparian proprietors, upon a stream not navigable, can use the water of such stream? The branch mentioned in the agreed statement of facts, is a small natural stream of water, not furnishing, at all season of the year, a supply of water sufficient for both mills. There are no facts in the case showing that the water is wanted for any other than milling purposes, and for those purposes to be converted into steam, and thus entirely consumed.

In an early case decided in England, it is laid down that "A water course begins '*ex jure naturae*,' and having taken a certain course naturally, can not be diverted." The language of all the authorities is that water flows in its natural course, and should be permitted thus to flow, so that all through whose land it naturally flows, may enjoy the privilege of using it. The property in the water, therefore, by virtue of the riparian ownership, is in its nature usufructuary, and consists, in general, not so much of the fluid itself, as of the advantage of its impetus. A riparian proprietor, therefore, though he has an undoubted right to use the water for hydraulic or manufacturing purposes, must so use it as to do no injury to any other riparian proprietor.

Some decisions, in laying down the rights of riparian proprietors of water courses, have gone so far as to restrict their right in the use of water flowing over their land, so that there shall be no diminution in the quantity of the water, and no obstruction to its course. The decisions last referred to cannot, however, be consider as furnishing the true doctrine on this subject. Mr. Justice Storey [sic]; in delivering the opinion of the court, in the case of *Tyler v. Wilkinson*, 4 Mason, 400, says, "I do not mean to be understood as holding the doctrine that there can be no diminution whatever, and no obstruction or impediment whatever, by a riparian proprietor in the use of water as it flows; for that would be to deny any valuable use of it. There may be, and there must be, of that which is common to all, a reasonable use. The true test of the principle and extent of the use is, whether it is to the injury of the other proprietors or not. There may be diminution in quantity, or a retardation or acceleration of the natural current, indispensable for the general and valuable use of the water, perfectly consistent with the use of the common right. The diminution, retardation, or acceleration, not positively and sensibly injurious, by diminishing the value of the common right, is an implied element in the right of using the stream at all."

Where all have a right to participate in a common benefit, and none can have an exclusive enjoyment, no rule, [from] the very nature of the case, can be laid down, as to how much each may use without infringing upon the rights of others. In such cases, the question must be left to the judgment of the jury, whether the party complained of has used, under all the circumstances, more than his just proportion.

It appears, from the facts agreed on, that Evans obstructed the water by a dam, and diverted the whole into his well. This diversion, according to all the cases, both English and American, was clearly illegal. For this diversion, an action will lie. For these reasons I am of opinion that the judgment ought to be affirmed, with costs.

NOTES AND QUESTIONS

1. *The Special Character of Water*. In *Evans v. Merriweather*, Justice Samuel Lockwood asserts, "The property in the water, therefore, by virtue of the riparian ownership, is in its nature usufructuary (i.e., the right to use what one does not own), and consists, in general, not so much of the fluid itself, as of the advantage of its impetus." Why should this be? Why should property rights in a commodity be limited to a right to use? If Pierson or Post could own the fox by capturing it, why shouldn't Evans be able to capture the water as it runs across his land?

That running waters were common to all men was an ancient principle, recognized by Roman law. According to Title I, § 1 of the Institutes of Justinian: "By natural law all these things are common, viz: air, running water, the sea and as a consequence the shores of the sea." THE INSTITUTES OF JUSTINIAN 158 (Sandars ed., 1876). Blackstone described the special status of these resources in the following manner: "There are some few things which, notwithstanding the general introduction and continuance of property, must still unavoidably remain in common . . . . Such (among others) are the elements of light, air, and water . . . . A man can have no absolute permanent property in these, as he may in the earth and land, since these are of a vague and fugitive nature." 2 W. BLACKSTONE, COMMENTARIES ON THE LAWS OF ENGLAND 14, 18 (1766).

Nevertheless, it is widely acknowledged that a riparian owner who lawfully removes water from a flowing stream is the owner of the water. As a New York court noted at the end of the 19th century, "Water, when reduced to possession, is property, and it may be bought and sold and have a market value, but it must be in actual possession, subject to control and management." *City of Syracuse v. Stacey*, 62 N.E. 354, 355 (N.Y. 1901). In other words, if A lawfully withdraws water from a stream and places it in barrels, and B then steals the barrels, B is guilty of the theft of the water as well as of the barrels. If this is the case, why doesn't Evans own the water he diverted from the stream?

2. *Navigability*. Justice Lockwood also emphasized that the stream in question was not navigable. Why should this matter? Under English and American law, navigable waterways, along with certain other unique assets, were deemed to be held in trust by the sovereign and therefore could not be owned by private individuals. (This concept is known generally as the Public Trust doctrine.) Should the non-navigability of the stream give Merriweather a stronger claim to ownership of the water?

3. *Surface Water vs. Underground Water*. In *Acton v. Blundell*, 12 Mees. and W. 324, 152 Eng. Rep. 1223 (Exch. 1843), an English court was called upon to resolve a dispute over rights to underground water. Acton was the owner of a cotton mill. In 1821, a predecessor owner had sunk a well for "raising water for the working of the mill." In 1837 and 1840, Blundell sank coal pits within three quarters of a mile of Acton's well. The effect of the coal pits was to drain water away from Acton's well, making it "altogether insufficient for the purposes of the mill."

After noting that "no case has been cited on either side bearing directly on the subject in dispute," the English court held that the rules that applied to rivers and flowing streams did not apply to underground water. In a decision rendered the year after *Evans v. Merriweather*, the court asserted: "[I]t rather falls within that principle, which gives to the owner of the soil all that lies beneath his surface; that the land immediately below is his property, whether it is solid rock, or porous ground, or venous earth, or part soil, part water; that the person who owns the surface may dig therein, and apply all that is there found to his own purposes at his free will and pleasure; and that if, in the exercise of such right, he intercepts or drains off the water collected from underground springs in his neighbour's well, this inconvenience to his neighbour falls within the description of *damnum absque injuria*, which cannot become the ground of an action." This became known as the "absolute ownership" rule, and "captured" water could be sold to others. For a case citing *Pierson v. Post* for the principle that ownership rights attach to the first person to drill a well and capture the water, see *City of San Marcos v. Texas Comm'n on Envtl. Quality*, 128 S.W.3d 264, 270 (Tex. App. 2004).

Does it make sense to distinguish between the rights to surface and underground water in this manner? While American courts initially followed the rule in *Acton v. Blundell*, the courts in most jurisdictions later modified it in important ways. Ground water (i.e., water moving diffusely through the ground) was distinguished from water flowing in discrete underground streams, and the rules that applied to surface water were applied to the latter. More significantly, American courts began to further require that water extracted from underneath the surface be used for reasonable (i.e., non-wasteful) purposes and that it not be transported away from the land from which it was extracted. In arid parts of the American west, this latter restriction was particularly significant since it limited the ability of densely populated areas to transport water from distant aquifers. *See, e.g.*, *Bristor v. Cheatham*, 255 P.2d 173 (Ariz. 1953). With such qualifications, can it still be said that the owner of the surface "owns" the water he extracts from underneath his soil?

Surface waters that do not flow in a fixed watercourse — that is, flood waters — are sometimes governed by different rules. At one time, most American jurisdictions followed the common enemy rule, which, as its name suggests, implied that landowners can legally do whatever they can to steer such waters away from their land. The "civil law rule" recognized a servitude over the lands where the diffuse surface water would naturally flow, but restricted the right of landowners to redirect the water in a direction that it would not have otherwise taken. The model rule is one of reasonable use, involving a balancing test similar to that of the law of nuisance and rules that apply to other forms of water transit. This topic is addressed in more detail in Chapter 2.

4. *The Rights of Prior Users.* In *Acton v. Blundell*, the English court was careful to emphasize that Acton and his predecessors had been using their well for less than 20 years at the time the injury occurred. The court noted, "We intimate no opinion whatever as to what might be the rule of law, if there had been an uninterrupted user of the right for more than the last twenty years." English law recognized property rights in those who had made use of water for more than 20 years even if they could not establish any independent right to it. Under what theory of property rights could this be relevant?

In the 19th century, many states in the arid American west rejected the "reasonable use" riparian system for surface water and instead embraced a system known as "prior appropriation." Although not based on a theory of prescription by long use, the prior appropriation system assigned first users a legal right to the amount of water they were already using, so long as it was put to a beneficial use. *See, e.g.*, *Coffin v. Left Handed Ditch Co.*, 6 Colo. 443 (1882). Do you see why this approach might be more desirable in regions where water is in short supply? The limitations that the law imposes on those who are entitled to use various types of water are explored in Chapter 2.

[7.] Rights to Oil and Gas

Until the 20th century, it was a widely accepted maxim of English and American property law that the owner of land owned everything from the heavens above his land to the center of the earth below it. (Or as it was frequently rendered in Latin: *cujus est solum, ejus est usque ad coelum et ad inferos*.) When applied to minerals, this meant that the owner of a tract of land owned whatever lay below the surface. (As the notes following the case suggest, this was not the case in most countries of the world.) However, from the 1850s onward, the fugacious nature of oil and gas posed special problems. Unlike minerals such as coal or valuable metals that remained in place until removed, oil and gas molecules were constantly in motion. This feature, combined with their great economic value to whomever could draw them from beneath the earth's surface, challenged the limits of the *ad coelum* principle.

BARNARD v. MONONGAHELA NATURAL GAS CO.

Pennsylvania Supreme Court
65 A. 801 (1907)

Bill in equity for an injunction and an accounting.

MCILVAINE, P.J.

The court finds the facts in this case to be as follows:

1. Daniel Barnard and Elizabeth Barnard, the plaintiffs in this case, are the owners in fee of a tract of land in Deemston borough, in this county [Washington], containing sixty-six acres, more or less.

2. James B. Barnard owns in fee a tract of land adjoining the plaintiffs' land and containing 156 acres.

3. The Monongahela Natural Gas Company, a corporation in the business of producing and marketing natural gas, holds a lease on each of these farms "for the purpose and with the exclusive right of drilling and operating thereon for petroleum and gas," which said leases were in full force and effect when the bill herein was filed and are yet in force and effect. By the terms of these leases the Monongahela Natural Gas Company is to pay to the respective lessors a fixed sum per year for the gas from each well drilled on their or his farm "so long as it shall be sold therefrom."

4. The farm of James B. Barnard joins the farm of the plaintiffs, Daniel and Elizabeth Barnard.

5. That the Monongahela Natural Gas Company, the defendant, lately drilled a well on the James B. Barnard farm. This well was drilled on the location chosen after the plaintiffs had protested against it being located so near their [boundary] lines.

6. That since this well was drilled on the James B. Barnard farm the defendant company has drilled a well on the plaintiffs' farm 1,350 feet away from the James B. Barnard well. This well when completed failed to produce any gas.

7. A gas well in time will drain ten acres, more or less, of land and if the gas producing sand is equally porous the gas will be drawn along all the radii of a circle of which the well is the center.

8. The Monongahela Natural Gas Company, the defendant, when it located its well on the corner of the James B. Barnard farm did not do so with intent to fraudulently deprive the plaintiffs of their rights.

Conclusions of Law

1. That the drilling of the well on the farm of James B. Barnard by the defendant company and taking the gas therefrom in no way invades the plaintiffs' property rights.

2. That the defendant company, under all the facts of this case is not guilty of either actual or legal fraud in that it drilled the James B. Barnard well where it did and drained gas from the plaintiffs' farm.

Comments

The facts in this case are not complicated and are substantially undisputed. But the plaintiffs' contention raises a question of law that is both novel and interesting, and if sustained by the highest court of our state would revolutionize the manner of developing oil and gas leaseholds. "What the law ought to be" and "what the law is" are different questions. The Supreme Court, ignoring the principle of stare decisis, on account of changed conditions or for any reason justifying it, may declare "what ought to be the law" to be henceforth "the law," but the lower courts have no such authority; our duty is to follow the lead of the decisions, not to qualify, explain, modify, overrule or reverse them.

What then are the questions of law involved in this case, and under existing decisions how must they be answered?

The first question stated broadly is this: "Can a landowner in gas territory, drill a well on his farm close to the line of his adjoining landowner and draw from the land of the latter three-fourths of the gas that his well may produce without so invading the property rights of the adjoining landowner as to be legally accountable therefor." There is no doubt that the oil and gas confined in the oil and gas-bearing sands of a farm belong to the one who holds title to the farm, but it is also recognized both as a question of fact and law that oil and gas are fugitive in their nature and will by reason of inherent pressure seek any opening from the earth's surface that may reach the sand where they are confined.

"The right of every landowner to drill a well on his own land at whatever spot he may see fit" certainly must be conceded. If then the landowner drills on his own land at such a spot as best subserves his purposes what is the standing of the adjoining landowner whose oil or gas may be drained by this well? He certainly ought not to be allowed to stop his neighbor from developing his own farm. There is no certain way of ascertaining how much of the oil and gas that comes out of the well was when in situ under this farm and how much under that. What then has been held to be the law? — it is this, as we understand it, every landowner or his lessee may locate his wells wherever he pleases regardless of the interests of others. He may distribute them over the whole farm or locate them only on one part of it. He may crowd the adjoining farms so as to enable him to draw the oil and gas from them. What then can the neighbor do? Nothing, only go and do likewise. He must protect his own oil and gas. He knows it is wild and will run away if it finds an opening and it is his business to keep it at home. This may not be the best rule, but neither the legislature nor our highest court has given us any better. No doubt many thousands of dollars have been expended "in protecting lines" in oil and gas territory that would not have been expended if some rule had existed by which it could have been avoided. Injunction certainly is not the remedy. If so, just how far must the landowner be from the line of his neighbor to avoid the blow of "this strong arm of the law"?

This brings us to the second question in the case, and that is this, "Will a lessee who has a lease on each of two adjoining farms be enjoined at the instance of one of the landowners from drilling a well on the farm of the other at such a point as will drain most of the gas that it produces from the land of the first?" [The Court then concludes that there was no fraud on the part of the defendant as would entitle the plaintiffs to either an injunction or an accounting for damages.]

Per Curiam, January 7, 1907: Decree affirmed on the opinion of the court below.

NOTES AND QUESTIONS

1. *The Power of Courts to Make Law.* In *Barnard*, the trial court, whose opinion is accepted without modification by the Pennsylvania Supreme Court, asserts that it lacks the power to change the rules pertaining to ownership of oil, even if they are unfair. On the other hand, it acknowledges that "the Supreme Court [of Pennsylvania], ignoring the principle of stare decisis, on account of changed conditions or for any reason justifying it, may declare 'what ought to be the law' to be henceforth 'the law.' " What justifies such a distinction?

2. *Ownership of Oil and Other Minerals.* In the first recorded case involving the question of the ownership of oil and gas, *Hail v. Reed*, 54 Ky. (15 B. Mon.) 479 (1854), the Kentucky Supreme Court considered but rejected the *ad coelum* approach to the question of the ownership of oil. In a decision rendered five years before the historic drilling of the first commercial oil well at Titusville, Pennsylvania, the court was called upon to rule on the plaintiff's claim for damages for oil taken from a well on his property. Rejecting the idea that the oil in the well was automatically the plaintiff's property merely because it was taken from below the surface of his land, the court characterized oil as "a peculiar liquid not necessary nor indeed suitable for the common use of man." Reasoning that oil was more like water than hard minerals, it concluded that the oil was in fact the plaintiff's property, but only because he had captured it in his well.

3. *Defining the Rights of Surface Owners.* In *Barnard*, the trial court's opinion included the comment that "There is no doubt that the oil and gas confined in the oil and gas-bearing sands of a farm belong to the one who holds title to the farm." Is such a statement consistent with the holding in this case which permits the owner of one tract of land to pump out the oil previously lying beneath the surface of an adjacent tract? If the mineral at issue were coal rather than gas, would the owner of one tract be permitted to dig a horizontal underground shaft to remove coal resting underneath the surface of an adjacent landowner? What explains the difference?

4. *The Utility of the Capture Theory.* The early American law of oil and gas was rooted in the "capture theory" developed in wild animal cases like *Pierson v. Post* and underground water cases like *Acton v. Blundell* and its American counterparts. Recognizing the fugitive nature of oil and gas, courts found it useful to draw an analogy between these minerals and wild animals on the one hand and with water on the other. For example, in *Funk v. Haldeman*, 53 Pa. 229 (1867), one of the earliest oil and gas cases, the Pennsylvania Supreme Court described oil as "a moveable, wandering, fugitive thing in the bowels of the earth, and must, of necessity, continue common like water, so that one can only have a usufructuary property therein."

In *Hammonds v. Central Ky. Natural Gas Co.*, 75 S.W.2d 204 (Ky. 1934), a landowner withdrew natural gas from underneath his land, only to later pump it back under the ground to store it for future use. A neighboring landowner, drilling on his own land, subsequently tapped into the underground pool of gas and withdrew it for his own use and sale. In upholding the second landowner's right to the gas, the Kentucky Supreme Court reasoned that gas pumped back into the ground was analogous to a wild animal returned to the wild. (The general rule of *ferae naturae* is that, while a captured wild animal may be owned, all ownership rights are extinguished if and when the animal returns to the wild.) Do such analogies make sense?

5. *Law and Technological Innovation.* Until well into the 20th century, geologists lacked the technological capacity to measure the size and dimensions of underground pools of oil and gas. They also failed to appreciate the connections between subsurface waters and the hydrological cycle. How significant were such factors in the formulation of rules like those relied upon in *Barnard* and *Acton v. Blundell*?

With a fuller understanding of reservoir mechanics in the 20th century, the limitations of the analogies to water and wild animals became apparent. In 1926, John Ise, a nationally recognized expert on energy policy, wrote: "The law pertaining to oil deposits has been an absurd, almost idiotic, conception anyhow. It is difficult to understand how it could have been tolerated by an intelligent people." J. Ise, The United States Oil Policy 217 (1926). Modifications of the capture rule in oil and gas producing states include the doctrine of correlative rights which posits that each owner has a right to a fair and equitable share of the oil and gas under his land as well as the right to protection from negligent damage to the producing formation, and various oil and gas conservation statutes which regulate production to prevent wasteful drilling techniques and encourage rational development of the resources. For example, see *Elliff v. Texon Drilling Co.*, 210 S.W.2d 558 (Tex. 1948). Even with such changes, states still differ on the question of whether the owner of the surface owns the oil and gas underneath his property until it migrates (the "ownership in place" theory) or merely has the right to search for and reduce them to possession (the "non-ownership" theory). *See* R. HEMINGWAY, THE LAW OF OIL AND GAS 27–34 (3d ed. 1991).

6. *The Rule in Other Countries.* Although it seems natural to most Americans that the owner of the surface would have a claim to valuable commodities below the surface, this is, in fact, *not* the rule in most countries of the world. In virtually all other countries, whether capitalist or socialist, the sovereign (and through the sovereign, the public) retains ownership rights of subsurface minerals and other valuable commodities below the surface. For example, Article 13 of the Constitution of Ukraine states: "The land, its mineral wealth, atmosphere, water and other natural resources within the territory of Ukraine, the natural resources of its continental shelf, and the exclusive (maritime) economic zone, are objects of the right of property of the Ukrainian people. Ownership rights on behalf of the Ukrainian people are exercised by bodies of state power and bodies of local self-government within the limits determined by this Constitution." The traditional rule in the United Kingdom resembled that of the United States except that the crown held a prerogative right to any silver or gold under the surface. In Australia, control over subsurface minerals (other than silver and gold) initially passed with ownership of the surface, but since the late 19th century, in new transactions it has regularly been reserved for the Crown (i.e., the sovereign). FORBES & LANG, AUSTRALIAN MINING AND PETROLEUM LAWS 14-31 (1987) (describing the laws of both the United Kingdom and Australia).

7. *Ownership of Matter that Falls from the Heavens.* The ownership of meteorites that imbed themselves in land on the surface of the earth has been as issue that has been litgated for more than a century. In *Goddard v. Winchell*, 52 N.W. 1124 (Iowa, 1892), John Goddard was the owner of a tract of prairie land in Winnebago County Iowa, that was leased to a man named John Erickson. On May 2, 1890, during the term of the lease, a 66-pound aerolite (meteorite) crased into Goddard's tract and imbedded itself into the soil. The large rock was removed from the property by Peter Hoagland, an acquaintance of the tenant who had watched it fall from the sky. Hoagland then sold the object to a man named H. V. Winchell for $105. Goddard sued Winchell for the value of the rock. The trail court ruled on Goddard's behalf on grounds that the extraterrestrial object had become part of the soil when it hit the earth. The ruling was upheld by the Iowa Supreme Court. Although the latter court qualified its ruling with the observation, "Our conclusions are announced with some doubts as to their correctness," most American courts have reach a similar conclusion.

8. *Hydraulic Fracturing: A Different Analysis?* A number of jurisdictions have dealt with fracking, some by means of a comprehensive statute (Illinois) and some

through interpretation of existing oil and gas statutes by the courts (e.g. New York, Pennsylvania and Colorado). So far, most litigation is over which level of government — state or local — may regulate fracking. The federal government is not much nvolved thanks to a specific provision in the Safe Drinking Water Act (the logical place for such regulation) that exempts fracking. The regulation of fracking outside the United States has also become an issue in Europe and Asia, with most foreign jurisdictions banning fracking altogether. *See* Hannah Wiseman, *Governing Fracking from the Ground Up*, Tex. L. Rev. 29 (2015); Bruce M. Kramer, A Short History of Federal Statutory and Regulatory Concerns Relating to Hydraulic Fracturing (2011); David L. Callies & Chynna Stone, *Regulation of Hydraulic Fracturing*, 1 J. Int'l & Comp. L. 1 (2014). For a thorough examination of the issues surrounding fracking, see Erica Levine Powers & Beth E. Kinne (eds.), Beyond the Fracking Wars: A Guide for Lawyers, Public Officials, Planners and Citizens (ABA Press 2013). For a timely suggestion for a different theoretical construct, see Bret Wells, *The Dominant Mineral Estate in the Horizontal Well Context*, 53 Hous. L. Rev. 193 (2015).

[B.] OWNERSHIP OF PERSONAL PROPERTY

[1.] Transfer by Gift

HOCKS v. JEREMIAH
Oregon Court of Appeals
759 P.2d 312 (1988)

Rossman, Judge.

Plaintiff, personally and as personal representative of the estate of Robert Hocks (Hocks), appeals from a judgment after trial to the court dismissing her action against Hocks' sister, defendant Jeremiah, for replevin and conversion of personal property. Defendant asserted that Hocks gave the property to her before his death, and the trial court agreed. . . .

We recite the facts in the light most favorable to defendant. On December 29, 1980, Hocks arranged to meet defendant at a restaurant in Portland. He handed her two envelopes, each containing two $5,000 bearer bonds. He said "Here, I have something I want to give you. . . . This is just the beginning. I plan to give you a lot more." He told her that he was giving her the bonds because he loved her, because he was grateful for what she had done for their mother in her last years and to satisfy a promise he had made to their mother.

Hocks suggested to defendant that she place the bonds in a safety deposit box. He told her that everything in the box would be hers. They then went to a nearby bank and jointly rented a safety deposit box. Each signed the signature card, and each retained a key to the box. Defendant testified that she offered to pay the rent on the box, but that her brother refused, saying, "Your money isn't any good." Hocks explained to defendant that the bonds were like cash and that the interest on them could be collected by clipping and redeeming the coupons. Defendant told

Hocks that she and her husband did not need the money and that she preferred that he collect the interest on the bonds. He told her that that was fine but that, if she ever needed money, she should go to the box and clip the coupons, letting him know so that he did not waste a trip to the bank. Defendant and Hocks never talked about the interest coupons again.

In 1981, shortly after they opened the box, Hocks told defendant that he was giving her an "investment" diamond and that he had put it in the safety deposit box. Over the years, Hocks mentioned to defendant when they met or spoke that he had added more bonds to the box. By the time of his death in March, 1985, he had added 22 bonds to the box. From December 12, 1980, until two days after Hocks' death, defendant never opened the box. She testified that, although she did not believe that she needed Hocks' authorization to open and remove the bonds or coupons, she would not have done so without it. Hocks visited the box regularly to clip the coupons and to add more bonds and the diamond.

Defendant testified that, one day in the summer of 1984, over coffee at the restaurant, she asked her brother to leave a note in the safety deposit box indicating her interest, because, in the event of his death, it would save her "a lot of hassle." She was concerned at the time that there would be problems with her sister-in-law, plaintiff here. She thought that a note from Hocks would "put the icing on the cake." Hocks placed two handwritten notes in the box. The first, dated August 17, 1979, stated: "To whom it may concern: In the event of my death, I do hereby give and bequeath this diamond to my sister Joan, with all my love[.]" The second note, dated August 23, 1984, stated: "To whom it may concern: Upon my death, the contents of this safety deposit box # 7069 will belong to and are to be removed only by my sister Joan Jeremiah."

Defendant acknowledged in her testimony that the notes indicate an intention on the part of Hocks that the gift of the diamond and bonds take effect on his death. She testified, however, that, although he had the power to do so, Hocks would not have considered removing the contents of the box for his own use. "[M]y brother was not that way. I mean, I suppose some people are that way. When my brother gave a gift, it was a gift. It was mine." Yet, when asked why, if Hocks had made an outright gift and in view of potential problems with plaintiff, she did not remove the bonds and diamond and place them in her own safety deposit box, she answered, "Bob was still living, Bob was still living."

Burrows, Hocks' long-time friend and former attorney, testified that Hocks had told him about his plan to leave the bonds and diamond to his sister on his death, but not as a part of his testamentary disposition. Two days after Hocks' death, defendant entered the safety deposit box in Burrows' presence and removed the bonds and the diamond. . . . Defendant has retained the bonds and diamond and has collected the interest on the bonds and has cashed one of them when it became due.

An action for replevin requires proof that the defendant holds property that rightfully belongs to the plaintiff. . . . The rules for the establishment of an *inter vivos* gift are strict. Every element must be shown by clear and convincing evidence. *Estate of McConnell v. McConnell*, 71 Or. App. 795, 694 P.2d 982 (1985). "Clear and convincing" means that the evidence is free from confusion, fully intelligible and distinct and that the truth of the facts asserted is highly probable. *Riley Hill General Contractor v. Tandy Corp.*, 303 Or. 390, 407, 737 P.2d 595 (1987).

Proof of a gift requires a showing that the donor . . . [deliver] . . . the property to the donee by the transfer of possession and absolute dominion over the property, accompanied by a manifested intention to make a present gift. *Johnson v. Steen*, [281 Or. 361, 369, 575 P.2d 141, 146 (1978)]. A gift to take effect in the future is ineffective. If no present interest is created at the time of delivery, there is only a gratuitous promise to make a gift in the future. If no interest is created until after the donor's death, the transaction is testamentary and ineffective, unless it is executed with the formalities required for a will. *Allen v. Hendrick*, 104 Or. 202, 218, 206 P. 733 (1922).

We affirm the trial court's determination that Hocks gave defendant the first four bonds. He hand delivered them to her. He told her then that they and the interest income from them were hers. She accepted the bonds but said that she would like him to have the interest from them. The facts that Hocks later had possession of the bonds, collected the interest on them and indicated that he wanted the four bonds, along with the others, to pass to defendant on his death does not negate the evidence of a completed gift. *In re Norman's Estate*, 161 Or. 450, 88 P.2d 977 (1939); *Gilbert v. Brown*, 71 Or. App. 809, 817, 693 P.2d 1330 (1985). That evidence is sufficient to support the trial court's finding of a gift as to the first four bonds.

As to the remainder of the property, however, the evidence was insufficient to enable the trial court to find that Hocks had made a gift. Assuming, without deciding, that the evidence was sufficient to support a finding that Hocks *intended* to make a present gift of the property, it is insufficient to support a finding that he transferred possession and absolute dominion over those items. *See Beach v. Holland*, 172 Or. 396, 405, 142 P.2d 990 (1943).

Even if, in some circumstances, the joint lease of a safety deposit box is sufficient to constitute delivery by the transfer of possession and control . . . it is not sufficient in this case. Hocks had access to the contents of the box and could have removed the bonds or disposed of them at any time. He, exclusively, paid for and used the box, visiting it frequently. He continued to collect the interest, thereby retaining that element of ownership. In 1983, he listed the bonds that were in the box at that time among his assets available as collateral for a loan. Defendant testified that she never sought access to the box until after her brother's death and that she would not have removed items from the box while he was alive, indicating her understanding that her interest would not become possessory until his death. She was not even aware of the exact contents of the box until she opened it after Hocks' death. The two notes that Hocks placed in the box show his belief that he owned the contents.

In short, other than with regard to the first four bonds, although there is much evidence that Hocks retained and believed that he retained ownership and control of the contents of the box, there is no evidence the trier of fact could find clear and convincing that Hocks parted with control and possession of the property. We conclude, therefore, that the evidence was insufficient to enable the trial court to find that Hocks made an *inter vivos* gift of the remaining contents. Reversed and remanded for proceedings not inconsistent with this opinion.

NOTES AND QUESTIONS

1. *The Delivery Requirement.* Although a valid delivery (and acceptance) are normally required for a valid gift (along with donative intent), there are several mechanisms that can substitute for actual or constructive delivery. (Constructive delivery occurs when the donor gives the done exclusive control over the gifted property even though the property itself is not delivered. The classic example of constructive delivery is the delivery of the car keys to the donor.) Direct delivery can also be avoided by transferring the gift, irrevocably, to a third party escrow (or agent). Although the agent may be instructed to deliver the property to the done at some future time, the gift is valid, so long as the donor has no right to reclaim the property or cancel the gift. The fact that delivery may be delayed until after the donor's death is not problematic, although there might be federal gift tax consequences (as in presently oweable taxes) if the girt is sufficiently large. *See* BARLOW BURKE, PERSONAL PROPERTY 235 (1983).

In some jurisdictions, an express declaration that a gift has been made will lead to a finding of a valid gift, even if no transfer took place. *See Hengst v. Hengst*, 420 A.2d 370 (Pa. 1980) (husband stated that United States savings bonds issued to him by his employer were jointly owned with wife in a non-community property state); Jones, *Corroborating Evidence as a Substitute for Delivery in Gifts of Chattels*, 12 SUFF. U. L. REV. 16 (1978). Property held in trust by the creator of the trust for the benefit of a third party also belongs to the beneficiary of the trust, even if the trust is a self-declared oral trust. Restatement (Second) Trusts, § 24, comment b, illustration 1. Some commentators have called for the elimination of the delivery requirement altogether when there is clear evidence of present donative intent. McGowan, *Special Delivery: Does the Postman Have to Ring At All — The Current State of the Delivery Requirement for Valid Gifts*, 31 REAL PROP. PROB. & TR. L.J. 357, 360 (1996). However, such a change does not appear to be on the horizon.

2. *Gifts Causa Mortis.* Such gifts are an old-fashion mechanism for transferring property immediately before death without having to comply with the requirements of the jurisdiction's Wills Act. The *donation causa mortis* option applies only to personal property and requires donative intent, delivery, and acceptance. However, such transfers have many features in common with wills. First of all, the gift is automatically revoked if the donor survives the impending peril which he or she anticipates will result in his or her death. Even if the donor does die, he or she has the right to revoke the gift while still alive, and should the donee die before the donor, the property goes to the heirs or successors of the donor, not those of the done. Although the formal rule is that there must be actual or constructive delivery (and not merely symbolic delivery) for a valid gift *causa mortis*, court do often seem willing to relax the standards for constructive delivery. *See, e.g., Edinburg v. Edinburg*, 492 N.E.2d 1164 (Mass. App. Ct. 1986) (donor placed donee's name on container holding valuable drawings, kept container in her vault for security, and signed documents confirming she had made the gift; held: valid delivery of drawings). Acceptance of the gift is also still a requirement. A dying person cannot force their cat or other pet on to an unwilling donee, even if the animal is handed to the intended new owner.

3. *Bailments*. A bailment occurs when the owner or possessor of personal property delivers that property to another for a specific purpose, with a contract, express or implied, that the purpose will be faithfully executed, and that the property will be returned or duly accounted for when the special purpose is accomplished, or kept until the bailor reclaims it. The bailee takes possession of, but not title to, the property. Bailments arise, for example, when people loan property to friends, take their clothes to a dry cleaner, leave a car in a parking garage, check luggage with an airline, or exchange an item of personal property for money at a pawn shop.

The bailee is under a duty to take reasonable care of the property entrusted to his or her, or its, care. If the property is damaged, there is a presumption of negligence on the part of the bailee. The presumption is rebuttable, but unlike the case in a normal negligence action, the defendant has the burden of demonstrating that he or she was not at fault. If the bailee refuses to return the property, then the bailor has an action for conversion. Contracts can also be used to raise or lower the duties that are normally implied from the creation of a bailment.

4. *Bailment Remedies*. A bailor whose chattel is improperly withheld by the bailee may sue (a) for conversion or replevin, to recover the item; (b) for damages for making any necessary repairs; and (c) for loss of use, which is usually the rental value of the item during the time it was improperly withheld. *See generally Alaska Const. Equipment, Inc. v. Star Trucking, Inc.*, 128 P.3d 164 (Alaska 2006). In *Jeter v. Mayo Clinic Arizona*, 121 P.3d 1256 (Ariz. Ct. App. 2005), the court applied bailment law to three-day old, cryo-preserved human eggs, which the court referred to as pre-embryos. The Jeters had 10 pre-embryos cryo-preserved by the Mayo Clinic, but when the Jeters asked to have the pre-embryos transferred to another facility where the Jeters were to have the pre-embryos implanted, the Mayo Clinic transferred only five pre-embryos and could not account for the other five. Mrs. Jeter conceived and bore a daughter at the other facility, and then the Jeters sued the Mayo Clinic for losing the other five pre-embryos. The Jeters were concerned that the pre-embryos had been destroyed or provided to someone else for implantation. Among other claims, the Jeters asserted a bailment cause of action. The court found that the Clinic had expressly promised to store the Jeters' pre-embryos, and that the Jeters were entitled to proceed with their claim that Mayo breached the bailment contract.

[2.] The Law of Finds

BENJAMIN v. LINDNER AVIATION, INC.

Iowa Supreme Court
534 N.W.2d 400 (1995)

Ternus, Justice.

Appellant, Heath Benjamin, found over $18,000 in currency inside the wing of an airplane. At the time of this discovery, appellee, State Central Bank, owned the plane and it was being serviced by appellee, Lindner Aviation, Inc. All three parties claimed the money as against the true owner. After a bench trial, the district court held that the currency was mislaid property and belonged to the owner of the plane. The court awarded a finder's fee to Benjamin. Benjamin appealed and Lindner Aviation and State Central Bank cross-appealed. We reverse on the bank's cross-appeal and otherwise affirm the judgment of the district court.

I. *Background Facts and Proceedings.*

In April of 1992, State Central Bank became the owner of an airplane when the bank repossessed it from its prior owner who had defaulted on a loan. In August of that year, the bank took the plane to Lindner Aviation for a routine annual inspection. Benjamin worked for Lindner Aviation and did the inspection. As part of the inspection, Benjamin removed panels from the underside of the wings. . . . Benjamin testified that the [left wing] panel probably had not been removed for several years. Inside the left wing Benjamin discovered two packets approximately four inches high and wrapped in aluminum foil. He removed the packets from the wing and took off the foil wrapping. Inside the foil was paper currency, tied in string and wrapped in handkerchiefs. The currency was predominately twenty-dollar bills with mint dates before the 1960s, primarily in the 1950s. The money smelled musty.

Benjamin took one packet to his jeep and then reported what he had found to his supervisor, offering to divide the money with him. However, the supervisor reported the discovery to the owner of Lindner Aviation, William Engle. Engle insisted that they contact the authorities and he called the Department of Criminal Investigation. The money was eventually turned over to the Keokuk police department. Two days later, Benjamin filed an affidavit with the county auditor claiming that he was the finder of the currency under the provisions of Iowa Code chapter 644 (1991). Lindner Aviation and the bank also filed claims to the money. The notices required by chapter 644 were published and posted. *See* Iowa Code § 644.8 (1991). No one came forward within twelve months claiming to be the true owner of the money. *See id.* § 644.11 (if true owner does not claim property within twelve months, the right to the property vests in the finder).

Benjamin filed this declaratory judgment action against Lindner Aviation and the bank to establish his right to the property. The parties tried the case to the court. The district court held that chapter 644 applies only to "lost" property and the money here was mislaid property. The court awarded the money to the bank, holding that it was entitled to possession of the money to the exclusion of all but the true owner. The court also held that Benjamin was a "finder" within the meaning of chapter 644 and awarded him a ten percent finder's fee. *See id.* § 644.13 (a finder of lost property is entitled to ten percent of the value of the lost property as a reward).

Benjamin appealed. He claims that chapter 644 governs the disposition of all found property and any common law distinctions between various types of found property are no longer valid. He asserts alternatively that even under the common law classes of found property, he is entitled to the money he discovered. He claims that the trial court should have found that the property was treasure trove or was lost or abandoned rather than mislaid, thereby entitling the finder to the property. The bank and Lindner Aviation cross-appealed. Lindner Aviation claims that if the money is mislaid property, it is entitled to the money as the owner of the premises on which the money was found, the hangar where the plane was parked. It argues in the alternative that it is the finder, not Benjamin, because Benjamin discovered the money during his work for Lindner Aviation. The bank asserts in its cross-appeal that it owns the premises where the money was found — the airplane — and that no one is entitled to a finder's fee because chapter 644 does not apply to mislaid property.

II. *Standard of Review.*

Whether the money found by Benjamin was treasure trove or was mislaid, abandoned or lost property is a fact question. . . . Therefore, the trial court's finding that the money was mislaid is binding on us if supported by substantial evidence. . . .

III. *Does Chapter 644 Supersede the Common Law Classifications of Found Property?*

Benjamin argues that chapter 644 governs the rights of finders of property and abrogates the common law distinctions between types of found property. As he points out, lost property statutes are intended "to encourage and facilitate the return of property to the true owner, and then to reward a finder for his honesty if the property remains unclaimed." . . . . These goals, Benjamin argues, can best be achieved by applying such statutes to all types of found property. Although a few courts have adopted an expansive view of lost property statutes . . . Iowa law is to the contrary. In . . . *Zornes v. Bowen*, 223 Iowa 1141, 1145, 274 N.W. 877, 879 (1937) . . . [we held] that chapter 644 does not abrogate the common law classifications of found property. We note this position is consistent with that taken by most jurisdictions. . . . [C]hapter 644 applies only if the property discovered can be categorized as "lost" property as that term is defined under the common law. Thus, the trial court correctly looked to the common law classifications of found property to decide who had the right to the money discovered here.

IV. *Classification of Found Property.*

Under the common law, there are four categories of found property: (1) abandoned property, (2) lost property, (3) mislaid property, and (4) treasure trove. . . . The rights of a finder of property depend on how the found property is classified. . . .

A. *Abandoned property.*

Property is abandoned when the owner no longer wants to possess it. . . . Abandonment is shown by proof that the owner intends to abandon the property and has voluntarily relinquished all right, title and interest in the property. . . . Abandoned property belongs to the finder of the property against all others, including the former owner. . . .

B. *Lost property.*

"Property is lost when the owner unintentionally and involuntarily parts with its possession and does not know where it is." . . . Stolen property found by someone who did not participate in the theft is lost property. . . . Under chapter 644, lost property becomes the property of the finder once the statutory procedures are followed and the owner makes no claim within twelve months. Iowa Code § 644.11 (1991).

C. *Mislaid property.*

Mislaid property is voluntarily put in a certain place by the owner who then overlooks or forgets where the property is. . . . It differs from lost property in that the owner voluntarily and intentionally places mislaid property in the location where it is eventually found by another. . . . In contrast, property is not considered lost unless the owner parts with it involuntarily. . . . The finder of mislaid property acquires no rights to the property. . . . The right of possession of mislaid property belongs to the owner of the premises upon which the property is found, as against all persons other than the true owner. . . .

D. *Treasure trove.*

Treasure trove consists of coins or currency concealed by the owner. *Id.* It includes an element of antiquity. . . . To be classified as treasure trove, the property must have been hidden or concealed for such a length of time that the owner is probably dead or undiscoverable. . . . Treasure trove belongs to the finder as against all but the true owner. . . .

V. *Is There Substantial Evidence to Support the Trial Court's Finding That the Money Found by Benjamin Was Mislaid?*

We think there was substantial evidence to find that the currency discovered by Benjamin was mislaid property. . . . [The] location where the money was found [is] a factor in determining whether the money was lost property. . . . The place where Benjamin found the money and the manner in which it was hidden are . . . important . . . . The bills were carefully tied and wrapped and then concealed in a location that was accessible only by removing screws and a panel. These circumstances support an inference that the money was placed there intentionally. This inference supports the conclusion that the money was mislaid. . . .

The same facts that support the trial court's conclusion that the money was mislaid prevent us from ruling as a matter of law that the property was lost. Property is not considered lost unless considering the place where and the conditions under which the property is found, there is an inference that the property was left there unintentionally. . . . Contrary to Benjamin's position the circumstances here do not support a conclusion that the money was placed in the wing of the airplane unintentionally. Additionally, as the trial court concluded, there was no evidence suggesting that the money was placed in the wing by someone other than the owner of the money and that its location was unknown to the owner.

For these reasons, we reject Benjamin's argument that the trial court was obligated to find that the currency Benjamin discovered was lost property.

We also reject Benjamin's assertion that as a matter of law this money was abandoned property. Both logic and common sense suggest that it is unlikely someone would voluntarily part with over $18,000 with the intention of terminating his ownership. The location where this money was found is much more consistent with the conclusion that the owner of the property was placing the money there for safekeeping. *See* [*Ritz v. Selma United Methodist Church*, 467 N.W.2d 266, 269 (Iowa 1991)] (property not abandoned where money was buried in jars and tin cans, indicating a desire by the owner to preserve it); [*Jackson v. Steinberg*, 200 P.2d 376, 378 (Or. 1948)] (because currency was concealed intentionally and deliberately, the bills could not be regarded as abandoned property); 1 Am. Jur. 2d *Abandoned Property* § 13, at 17 (where property is concealed in such a way that the concealment appears intentional and deliberate, there can be no abandonment). We will not presume that an owner has abandoned his property when his conduct is consistent with a continued claim to the property. . . . Therefore, we cannot rule that the district court erred in failing to find that the currency discovered by Benjamin was abandoned property.

Finally, we also conclude that the trial court was not obligated to decide that this money was treasure trove. Based on the dates of the currency, the money was no older than thirty-five years. The mint dates, the musty odor and the rusty condition of a few of the panel screws indicate that the money may have been hidden for some time. However, there was no evidence of the age of the airplane or the date of its last inspection. These facts may have shown that the money was concealed for a much shorter period of time. Moreover, it is also significant that the airplane had a well-documented ownership history. The record reveals that there were only two owners of the plane prior to the bank. One was the person from whom the bank repossessed the plane; the other was the original purchaser of the plane when it was manufactured. Nevertheless, there is no indication that Benjamin or any other party attempted to locate and notify the prior owners of the plane, which could very possibly have led to the identification of the true owner of the money. Under these circumstances, we cannot say as a matter of law that the money meets the antiquity requirement or that it is probable that the owner of the money is not discoverable.

We think the district court had substantial evidence to support its finding that the money found by Benjamin was mislaid. The circumstances of its concealment and the location where it was found support inferences that the owner intentionally placed the money there and intended to retain ownership. We are bound by this factual finding.

VI. *Is the Airplane Or the Hangar the "Premises" Where the Money Was Discovered?*

Because the money discovered by Benjamin was properly found to be mislaid property, it belongs to the owner of the premises where it was found. Mislaid property is entrusted to the owner of the premises where it is found rather than the finder of the property because it is assumed that the true owner may eventually recall where he has placed his property and return there to reclaim it. . . . We think that the premises where the money was found is the airplane, not Lindner Aviation's hangar where the airplane happened to be parked when the money was discovered. The policy behind giving ownership of mislaid property to the owner of the premises where the property was mislaid supports this conclusion. If the true owner of the money attempts to locate it, he would initially look for the plane; it is unlikely he would begin his search by contacting businesses where the airplane might have been inspected. Therefore, we affirm the trial court's judgment that the bank, as the owner of the plane, has the right to possession of the property as against all but the true owner.

VII. *Is Benjamin Entitled to a Finder's Fee?*

Benjamin claims that if he is not entitled to the money, he should be paid a ten percent finder's fee under section 644.13. The problem with this claim is that only the finder of "*lost* goods, money, bank notes, and other things" is rewarded with a finder's fee under chapter 644. Iowa Code § 644.13 (1991). Because the property found by Benjamin was mislaid property, not lost property, section 644.13 does not apply here. The trial court erred in awarding Benjamin a finder's fee.

VIII. *Summary.*

We conclude that the district court's finding that the money discovered by Benjamin was mislaid property is supported by substantial evidence. Therefore, we affirm the district court's judgment that the bank has the right to the money as against all but the true owner. This decision makes it unnecessary to decide whether Benjamin or Lindner Aviation was the finder of the property. We reverse the court's decision awarding a finder's fee to Benjamin. . . .

SNELL, JUSTICE (dissenting). [HARRIS and ANDREASEN, JJ., join this dissent.]

[The] facts satisfy the requirement that the property was voluntarily put in a certain place by the owner. But the second [part of the] test for [concluding] . . . that property is mislaid is that the owner "overlooks or forgets where the property is." . . . I do not believe that the facts, logic, or common sense lead to a finding that this requirement is met. It is not likely or reasonable to suppose that a person would secrete $18,000 in an airplane wing and then forget where it was. . . . After finding the money, Benjamin proceeded to give written notice of finding the property as prescribed in Iowa Code chapter 644 (1993) . . . .

The purpose of this type of legal notice is to give people the opportunity to assert a claim if they have one. . . . If no claim is made, the law presumes there is none or for whatever reason it is not asserted. Thus, a failure to make a claim after legal notice is given is a bar to a claim made thereafter. . . . Benjamin followed the law in giving legal notice of finding property. None of the parties dispute this. The suggestion that Benjamin should have initiated a further search for the true owner is not a requirement of the law, is therefore irrelevant, and in no way diminishes Benjamin's rights as finder. The scenario unfolded in this case convinces me that the money found in the airplane wing was abandoned. . . . The money had been there for years, possibly thirty. No owner had claimed it in that time. No claim was made by the owner after legally prescribed notice was given that it had been found. Thereafter, logic and the law support a finding that the owner has voluntarily relinquished all right, title, and interest in the property. Whether the money was abandoned due to its connection to illegal drug trafficking or is otherwise contraband property is a matter for speculation. In any event, abandonment by the true owner has legally occurred and been established. I would hold that Benjamin is legally entitled to the entire amount of money that he found in the airplane wing as the owner of abandoned property.

NOTES AND QUESTIONS

The Common Law of Finds. Many commentators have debated whether the four traditional common law categories of finders discussed in the above case do more to achieve or impede justice. *See, e.g.*, R.H. Helmholz, *Wrongful Possession of Chattels: Hornbook Law and Case Law*, 80 Nw. U. L. Rev. 1221, 1230 (1986) ("the law of finders contains contradictory decisions and artificial distinctions"); Edward R. Cohen, *The Finders Cases Revisited*, 48 Tex. L. Rev. 1001 (1970) (these cases present the task of attempting "to reconcile the irreconcilable," quoting *Hibbert v. McKiernan*, 2 K.B. 142, 149 (1948)). For an argument that the both the majority and the dissent in the above case got almost everything wrong, see Jennifer S. Moorman, *Finders Weepers, Losers Weepers?:* Benjamin v. Lindner Aviation, Inc., 82 Iowa L. Rev. 717, 733 (1997) (court should have adopted all-inclusive definition of "lost goods"; bright-line rule would avoid arbitrary decisions such as *Benjamin*; common law classifications are artificial, tenuous, and arbitrary, and difficult to apply).

[3.] Abandonment

COLUMBUS-AMERICA DISCOVERY GROUP v. ATLANTIC MUTUAL INSURANCE CO.

United States Court of Appeals, Fourth Circuit
974 F.2d 450 (1992)

Donald Russell, Circuit Judge.

"When Erasmus mused that '[a] common shipwreck is a source of consolation to all,' Adagia, IV.iii.9 (1508), he quite likely did not foresee inconcinnate free-for-alls among self-styled salvors." *Martha's Vineyard Scuba HQ, Inc. v. The Unidentified, Wrecked and Abandoned Steam Vessel*, 833 F.2d 1059, 1061 (1st Cir. 1987). Without doubt the Dutch scholar also could not imagine legal brawls involving self-styled "finders" from Ohio, British and American insurance underwriters, an heir to the Miller Brewing fortune, a Texas oil millionaire, an Ivy League university, and an Order of Catholic monks. Yet that is what this case involves, with the prize being up to one billion dollars in gold.

This gold was deposited on the ocean floor, 8,000 feet below the surface and 160 miles off the South Carolina coast, when the S.S. CENTRAL AMERICA sank in a hurricane on September 12, 1857. The precise whereabouts of the wreck remained unknown until 1988, when it was located by the Columbus-America Discovery Group ("Columbus-America"). This enterprise has since been recovering the gold, and last year it moved in federal district court to have itself declared the owner of the treasure. Into court to oppose this maneuvre came British and American insurers who had originally underwritten the gold for its ocean voyage and then had to pay off over a million dollars in claims upon the disaster. Also attempting to get into the stew were three would-be intervenors who claimed that Columbus-America had used their computerized "treasure map" to locate the gold. The district court allowed the intervention, but it did not give the intervenors any time for discovery.

After a ten-day trial, the lower Court awarded Columbus-America the golden treasure in its entirety, 742 F. Supp. 1327 [(E.D. Va. 1990)]. It found that the underwriters had previously abandoned their ownership interests in the gold by deliberately destroying certain documentation. As for the intervenors, the Court held that there was no evidence showing that Columbus-America used their information in any way in locating the wreck.

I

On August 14, 1990, the Court found for Columbus-America on all the issues, dismissing the claims of the underwriters, Columbia, John, and Grimm. *Columbus-America Discovery Group v. The Unidentified, Wrecked and Abandoned Sailing Vessel*, 742 F. Supp. 1327 (E.D. Va. 1990). On the finder/salvor issue, the district court held that the underwriters had abandoned the gold, and thus Columbus-America was its finder and sole owner. The Court based this finding of abandonment primarily on the supposed fact that the underwriters had intentionally destroyed any documentation they had once had concerning the case. *Id.* at 1344–48. As for the intervenors, the Court found that they failed to prove that the information furnished Thompson[, the Columbus-American president,] could have assisted in locating the ship, that Columbus-America used this information in any way, or "even if the information was of value and was used, that any such use would entitle them to share in any recovery." *Id.* at 1341.

The underwriters and the intervenors now appeal.

II

A

Historically, courts have applied the maritime law of salvage when ships or their cargo have been recovered from the bottom of the sea by those other than their owners. Under this law, the original owners still retain their ownership interests in such property, although the salvors are entitled to a very liberal salvage award. Such awards often exceed the value of the services rendered, and if no owner should come forward to claim the property, the salvor is normally awarded its total value.

A related legal doctrine is the common law of finds, which expresses "the ancient and honorable principle of 'finders, keepers.' " Traditionally, the law of finds was applied only to maritime property which had never been owned by anybody, such as ambergris, whales, and fish. A relatively recent trend in the law, though, has seen the law of finds applied to long lost and abandoned shipwrecks.

Courts in admiralty favor applying salvage law rather than the law of finds. As has been succinctly stated by Judge Abraham D. Sofaer:

> The law of finds is disfavored in admiralty because of its aims, its assumptions, and its rules. The primary concern of the law of finds is title. The law of finds defines the circumstances under which a party may be said to have acquired title to ownerless property. Its application necessarily assumes that the property involved either was never owned or was abandoned. To justify an award of title (albeit of one that is defeasible), the law of finds requires a finder to demonstrate not only the intent to acquire the property involved, but also possession of that property, that is, a high degree of control over it. These rules encourage certain types of conduct and discourage others. A would-be finder should be expected to act acquisitively, to express a will to own by acts designed to establish the high degree of control required for a finding of possession. The would-be finder's longing to acquire is exacerbated by the prospect of being found to have failed to establish title. If either intent or possession is found lacking, the would-be finder receives nothing; neither effort alone nor acquisition unaccompanied by the required intent is rewarded. Furthermore, success as a finder is measured solely in terms of obtaining possession of specific property; possession of specific property can seldom be shared, and mere contribution by one party to another's successful efforts to obtain possession earns no compensation. Would-be finders are encouraged by these rules to act secretly, and to hide their recoveries, in order to avoid claims of prior owners or other would-be finders that could entirely deprive them of the property.

Hener v. United States, 525 F. Supp. 350, 356 (S.D.N.Y. 1981).

In sharp contrast to "the harsh, primitive, and inflexible nature of the law of finds" is the law of salvage.

> Admiralty favors the law of salvage over the law of finds because salvage law's aims, assumptions, and rules are more consonant with the needs of marine activity and because salvage law encourages less competitive and secretive forms of conduct than finds law. The primary concern of salvage law is the preservation of property on oceans and waterways. Salvage law specifies the circumstances under which a party may be said to have acquired, not title, but the right to take possession of property (e.g., vessels, equipment, and cargo) for the purpose of saving it from destruction, damage, or loss, and to retain it until proper compensation has been paid.
>
> Salvage Law assumes that the property being salved is owned by another, and thus that it has not been abandoned. Admiralty courts have adhered to the traditional and realistic premise that property previously owned but lost at sea has been taken involuntarily out of the owner's possession and control by the forces of nature at work in oceans and

> waterways; in fact, property may not be "salvaged" under admiralty law unless it is in some form of peril.
>
> Salvage law requires that to be a salvor a party must have the intention and the capacity to save the property involved, but the party need not have the intention to acquire it. Furthermore, although the law of salvage, like the law of finds, requires a salvor to establish possession over property before obtaining the right to exclude others, "possession" means something less in salvage law than in finds law. In the salvage context, only the right to compensation for service, not the right to title, usually results; "possession" is therefore more readily found than under the law of finds . . . . Moreover, unlike the would-be finder, who is either a keeper or a loser, the salvor receives a payment, depending on the value of the service rendered, that may go beyond quantum meruit. Admiralty's equitable power to make an award for salvage — recognized since ancient times in maritime civilizations — is a corollary to the assumption of nonabandonment and has been applied irrespective of the owner's express refusal to accept such service.
>
> These salvage rules markedly diminish the incentive for salvors to act secretly, to hide their recoveries, or to ward off competition from other would-be salvors. In short, although salvage law cannot alter human nature, its application enables courts to encourage open, lawful, and cooperative conduct, all in the cause of preserving property (and life).

Id. at 357–58; *see also* 3A BENEDICT ON ADMIRALTY § 158, at 11-15 to 11-16.

Today, finds law is applied to previously owned sunken property only when that property has been abandoned by its previous owners. Abandonment in this sense means much more than merely leaving the property, for it has long been the law that "[w]hen articles are lost at sea the title of the owner in them remains." *THE AKABA*, 54 F. 197, 200 (4th Cir. 1893). Once an article has been lost at sea, "lapse of time and nonuser are not sufficient, in and of themselves, to constitute an abandonment." In addition, there is no abandonment when one discovers sunken property and then, even after extensive efforts, is unable to locate its owner.

While abandonment has been simply described as "the act of deserting property without hope of recovery or intention of returning to it," in the lost property at sea context, there is also a strong actus element required to prove the necessary intent. "Abandonment is said to be a voluntary act which must be proved by a clear and unmistakable affirmative act to indicate a purpose to repudiate ownership." The proof that need be shown must be "strong . . . , such as the owner's express declaration abandoning title."

There are only a handful of cases which have applied the law of finds, all of which fit into two categories. First, there are cases where owners have expressly and publicly abandoned their property. In the second type of case, items are recovered from ancient shipwrecks and no owner appears in court to claim them. Such circumstances may give rise to an inference of abandonment, but should an owner appear in court and there be no evidence of an express abandonment, the law of salvage must be applied. We agree with the author of ADMIRALTY AND MARITIME LAW that:

> In the treasure salvage cases, often involving wrecks hundreds of years old, the inference of abandonment may arise from lapse of time and nonuse of the property, or there may even be an express disclaimer of ownership. This calls for the application of the law of finds. By contrast, parties who intend to assert a claim of ownership may be identified. In such a case the law of salvage is applied.

The case below appears to be the only reported decision involving salvaged treasure from ancient shipwrecks wherein a court has applied the law of finds despite the fact that the previous owner appeared in court. In all other finds law cases, no prior owner has appeared. One example is the Treasure Salvors set of cases, all of which involved the salvage of Spanish treasure ships sunk off the Florida Keys in 1622. Widely quoted is the Fifth Circuit's phrase that "[d]isposition of a wrecked vessel whose very location has been lost for centuries as though its owner were still in existence stretches a fiction to absurd lengths." *Treasure Salvors, Inc. v. The Unidentified Wrecked and Abandoned Sailing Vessel*, 569 F.2d 330, 337 (5th Cir. 1978). Yet the Court there also took the trouble to note that it had been stipulated by all parties involved that the original owners had abandoned the wrecks.

In maintaining the position that previous owners can abandon sunken vessels even without any affirmative acts, Columbus-America relies especially on two state supreme court cases decided before the Civil War, *Eads v. Brazelton*, 22 Ark. 499 (1861) and *Wyman v. Hurlburt*, 12 Ohio 81 (1843). *Eads* involved the steamboat AMERICA which partially sank in the Mississippi River in 1827. The boat contained much valuable property, and in the two weeks after its sinking the owners conducted salvage operations in which they rescued all of the fur and government-owned specie on board, as well as one-half of the six hundred pigs of lead and a portion of the shot. Also, all of the machinery of the ship, including the boilers, was successfully removed. After this salvage, the owners physically abandoned the wreck and two years later an island began forming about it, on which trees would eventually grow to a height of thirty or forty feet.

The actual case concerned which of two would-be finders/salvors owned the remaining pigs of lead. As for the original owners, the Court declared that the cargo had been abandoned and then, in dicta, noted that "in extreme cases property wholly derelict and abandoned has been held to belong to the finder against the former owner." *Id.* at 509. Such was not the case here, though, for the former owners made no attempt to claim an ownership interest in the lead.[7] Because the boat and its contents were partially salvaged shortly after the wreck, the remaining cargo was easily salvageable for at least two years thereafter, and, most importantly, the original owners made no claim to the property once the remaining lead was salvaged, we find *Eads* inapposite.

---

[7] [4] In fact, the only person originally connected with THE AMERICA who was mentioned by the Court, its Captain, Swan, far from claiming any ownership interest in the boat, actually supplied information to one of the salvors as to the location of the wreck.

The facts of *Wyman* are more on point, although we doubt its precedential value. There, a schooner, THE G.S. WILLIS, sank in Lake Erie during the fall of 1835. The next year it was raised by another party and $865 in specie was discovered in the cabin. Truman Wyman, the original owner of this money, then filed an action of trover in Ohio state court against the finders/salvors. The case was tried before a jury in the Supreme Court of Ashtabula County, and they returned a special verdict which included the finding that "at the time the said schooner was seized by the defendants, the same was abandoned by the plaintiff, and that said schooner was, on the day and year aforesaid, derelict property, and when found in the bottom of the Lake was worth nothing." 12 Ohio at 85.

A majority of the Ohio Supreme Court held for the finders/salvors, awarding them the entire amount. The Court based this decision on the jury's finding of abandonment, which the majority supposed was intended "to be understood that all hope, expectation, and intention to recover the property were utterly and entirely relinquished." *Id.* at 86–87. A seventy-two word dissenting opinion was filed, though, by Chief Justice Ebenezer Lane. Lane was "not entirely certain that [his brethren] adopt[ed] the true sense of the word 'abandoned,' [as it was employed] in the special verdict." Instead, the Chief Justice was "incline[d] to think the jury meant nothing more than a want of the plaintiff's pursuing active measures to reclaim his property, and not a positive relinquishment of his right. If this be the true meaning, it would change the judgment." *Id.* at 88.

Because of the meager information supplied by the court, it is impossible to know which of Wyman's acts, or omissions, the jury relied on in finding an abandonment. Also, like Chief Justice Lane, we find it difficult to know exactly what the jury meant when it found the ship to have been "abandoned." What is clear, though, is that the Chief Justice was entirely correct when he stated that an abandonment of sunken cargo so as to lose possession must be shown not by the mere cessation of attempts to recover, but by the owner's positive relinquishment of his rights in the property. We find that this is the only principle of note to be gleaned from *Wyman*.

In conclusion, when sunken ships or their cargo are rescued from the bottom of the ocean by those other than the owners, courts favor applying the law of salvage over the law of finds. Finds law should be applied, however, in situations where the previous owners are found to have abandoned their property. Such abandonment must be proved by clear and convincing evidence, though, such as an owner's express declaration abandoning title. Should the property encompass an ancient and longlost shipwreck, a court may infer an abandonment. Such an inference would be improper, though, should a previous owner appear and assert his ownership interest; in such a case the normal presumptions would apply and an abandonment would have to be proved by strong and convincing evidence.

B

Before addressing whether the district court correctly found that the insured shipments of gold were abandoned by the underwriters, several points should be noted. First, the CENTRAL AMERICA herself was self-insured, and successors in interest to the U.S. Mail and Steamship Company have made no attempt to claim an ownership interest in the wreck. Also, there appears to have been a fairly significant amount of passenger gold aboard, but this case, almost surprisingly, has failed to see descendants of any of the passengers attempt to gain a share of the treasure. Thus, an abandonment may be found, and Columbus-America may be declared the finder and sole owner, as to any recovered parts of the ship, all passenger possessions, and any cargo besides the insured shipments.[8]

As for the insured gold, to "prima facially" prove their ownership interests at trial, the underwriters produced several original documents: entries from the Atlantic Mutual's Vessel Disasters Book concerning the disaster (one of which contained the scribbled notation, "e[stimated] l[oss] $150,000"); records of Board resolutions to pay claims; minutes from an underwriters' board meeting discussing the CENTRAL AMERICA; a study prepared by the New York Board of Underwriters regarding the disaster; and the salvage contract between the underwriters and Brutus de Villeroi. The insurers also produced a great many period newspaper articles. These discussed the amount of treasure on board; the insurers of this treasure and the amounts they insured; the willingness of the insurers to pay off claims; the general satisfaction the insureds received from having their claims promptly settled; and the salvage negotiations between the underwriters and the Boston Submarine Armor Company.

On appeal, Columbus-America exerts much effort in asserting that there exists insufficient evidence to prove that the underwriters who are now parties in this litigation actually insured and paid off claims upon the gold. The lower court, though, found "prima facially" that the underwriters did insure the treasure and that they received ownership interests in the gold once the claims were paid. Because of the extent of the catastrophe involved, and its feared repercussions in the American economy, newspapers around the country devoted much space and attention not only to the human aspects of the tragedy, but also the financial. Articles abounded on the quantity of gold aboard, its owners, and its insurers. Some of these articles do contradict others as to the exact amount certain underwriters insured. Still, we find that the district court did not err when it held that the underwriters who are now parties, or their predecessors in interests, paid off claims upon and became the owners of the commercial shipment of gold in 1857.

Despite finding that the underwriters owned the gold in 1857, the district court applied the law of finds and awarded Columbus-America the entire treasure. This was because at some point the insurers had abandoned their interests in the gold. On appeal, Columbus-America asserts that the lower court found an abandonment because of "20 distinct factors." It is clear, though, that the Court ruled as it did because of only two: the underwriters did nothing to recover the gold after 1858, and they supposedly destroyed all documentation they had regarding payment of claims for the gold.

During trial, the underwriters did not produce any of the original insurance contracts with the insureds, statements from shippers that goods were aboard, bills

---

[8] [6] Should Columbus-America be able to prove, for example from a location on the ocean floor inconsistent with the bulk of the treasure, that certain gold was, more likely than not, passenger gold, rather than part of the insured shipment, this gold should be awarded to Columbus-America in its entirety. Also, should more than $1,219,189 (1857 valuation) of gold be rescued, Columbus-America should be found the owner of any surplus.

of lading, or canceled checks or receipts from paying off the claims. While such documents would have existed in 1857, none could be located in 1990. Thus, because an insurance executive testified that the usual practice today is for insurance companies to destroy worthless documents after five years, the district court found that the above documentation concerning the CENTRAL AMERICA must have been intentionally destroyed in the ordinary course of business. Such destruction, coupled with 130 years of nonuse, equalled [sic], according to the Court, an abandonment.

Contrary to the district court, we cannot find any evidence that the underwriters intentionally or deliberately destroyed any of their documents about the CENTRAL AMERICA. Instead, the only evidence we have is that after 134 years, such documents that may have once existed can no longer be located. With such a passing of time, it seems as, if not more, likely that the documents were lost or unintentionally destroyed, rather than being intentionally destroyed.

It is undoubtedly true that in our case some of the insurance documents from 134 years ago are missing. Yet, the underwriters did present several other original documents from their files concerning this case, and in at least one instance all the documents in an insurer's file on the CENTRAL AMERICA were stolen by a would-be salvor. Also, almost all of the evidence in the record actually seems to indicate a specific predisposition on the underwriters' part not to abandon the treasure.

[The court summarizes various contacts with salvors shortly after the sinking and again in the 1970s and 1980s].

In conclusion, when a previous owner claims long lost property that was involuntarily taken from his control, the law is hesitant to find an abandonment and such must be proved by clear and convincing evidence. Here, we are unable to find the requisite evidence that could lead a court to conclude that the underwriters affirmatively abandoned their interest in the gold. Thus, we hold that the lower court clearly erred when it found an abandonment and applied the law of finds. Accordingly, the case is remanded to the district court for further proceedings.

On remand, the district court is to apply the law of salvage, and in so doing it must determine what percentage of the gold each underwriter insured. Equally, if not more, important, the Court must also determine the proper salvage award for Columbus-America. Although this is a decision that must be left to the lower court, we are hazarding but little to say that Columbus-America should, and will, receive by far the largest share of the treasure. Reversed and Remanded.

WIDENER, CIRCUIT JUDGE, dissenting.

I respectfully dissent. In *Anderson v. Bessemer City*, [470 U.S. 564 (1985),] of course, the Court emphasized that the findings of fact of a district court, especially when the judge has heard the witnesses ore tenus in open court, shall not be set aside unless clearly erroneous, with due regard being given to the opportunity of the trial court to judge the credibility of the witnesses.

In my view, throughout its opinion, the majority has disregarded the rules set forth by the Supreme Court in *Bessemer City*. The majority, in contravention of the mandate that "[w]here there are two permissible views of evidence, the factfinder's choice between them cannot be clearly erroneous," reverses the district court's factual finding as clearly erroneous simply because, in my opinion, "it would have decided the case differently." *Bessemer City*.

The district court found as a fact that the property taken from the CENTRAL AMERICA had been abandoned by its owners. I would hold that the district court was not clearly erroneous in making that determination. The circumstances of the insurance companies' failure to retain any indicia of ownership, such as bills of lading or commercial invoices, or to make any attempt to recover the property since 1858, coupled with the passage of more than 100 years, is ample evidence (not to mention details) to support the district court's finding that any claim the insurance companies may have had in the cargo of the CENTRAL AMERICA has been abandoned.

I disagree with the majority's decision to apply the law of salvage to the facts of this case. It appears to base its decision on the erroneous belief that courts favor applying salvage law rather than the law of finds. In fact, in the context of long lost wrecks, such as the instant case, courts, almost without exception, apply the law of finds.

NOTES AND QUESTIONS

1. *The Law of Finds*. If the law of salvage does not apply in this case, the law of finds apparently would (as the dissent would have it, and as the District Court found in 1990). What acts of the "owners" constitute abandonment? Are those acts sufficient? What acts would more clearly demonstrate an intent by the "owners" to abandon the insured property?

2. *The Rights of the Insured*. What rules of abandonment applies to the situation where the missing or inaccessible property was insured in a way that passed title to the insurer? What steps should *those* owners, the underwriters in this case, have taken to avoid charges that they had "abandoned" their interests?

3. *Allegations of Intervenors*. The three intervenors claim that Columbus-America misused and misappropriated their data in order to find the CENTRAL AMERICA. (It was found where the intervenors had "imaged" a "target" in 1984). A research vessel named ROBERT D. CONRAD was used to conduct a sonar survey of an area of the ocean floor thought to be the final resting place of the CENTRAL AMERICA. The information gathered is referred to as CONRAD data. If the court ruled that Columbus-America had indeed "misappropriated" the CONRAD data, how would that have altered the comparative rights of Columbus-America and CONRAD under the law of finds?

4. *What Should Be the Salvage Award?* To how much of the gold should the salvor, Columbus-America, be entitled? What factors should be taken into account? In the subsequent litigation, the trial court awarded the finders 90% (!) of the recovery. Is this the proper percentage? *See Columbus-America Discovery Group v. Atlantic Mutual Ins. Co.*, 56 F.3d 556 (4th Cir. 1005).

5. *Abandonment by the Sovereign.* On July 9, 1776, a band of patriots, hearing news of the Declaration of Independence, toppled the equestrian statue of King George III, which was located in Bowling Green Park in lower Manhattan, New York. The statue, of gilded lead, was then hacked apart and the pieces ferried over Long Island Sound and loaded onto wagons at Norwalk, Connecticut, to be hauled some 50 miles northward to Oliver Wolcott's bullet-molding foundry in Litchfield, there to be cast into bullets. On the journey to Litchfield, the wagoners halted at Wilton, Connecticut, and while the patriots were imbibing, loyalists managed to steal back pieces of the statue. The wagon load of the pieces lifted by the Tories was scattered about in the area of the Davis swamp in Wilton. Nearly 200 years later, Louis Miller, a treasure hunter with a metal detector who was looking for pieces of the statue, located a portion of it in the Davis swamp (which was still a swamp). The fragment was embedded 10 inches below the soil. The land was privately owned, and Miller lacked permission to be on the property. Who should have the superior claim to the fragment? Miller the finder? The owner of the swamp? The British government? The United States government? For a decision favoring the landowner over the finder, see *Favorite v. Miller*, 407 A.2d 974 (Conn. 1978).

6. *The Ownership of Baseballs.* In recent years, much ink has been spilled in law reviews over the issue of the ownership of baseballs hit into the stands at professional baseball games. Among the fans scrambling after the balls, *Pierson v. Post*-like rules of possession clearly apply, but why do fans get to keep the balls in the first place? (No such right exists at professional football or basketball games, although it does in professional hockey.) Most analysts assume that the balls are abandoned by the teams that own them, *see* Finkelman, *Fugitive Baseballs and Abandoned Property: Who Owns the Home Run Ball?*, 23 CARDOZO L. REV. 1609 (2002); Semeraro, *An Essay on Property Rights in Milestone Home Run Baseballs*, 56 SMU L. REV. 2281 (2004); Adomeit, *The Barry Bonds Baseball Case — An Empirical Approach — Is Fleeting Possession Five Tenths of the Ball?*, 48 ST. LOUIS U. L.J. 475 (2004), but are the balls really abandoned? Aren't they more like gifts to the lucky fan who catches (or captures) the ball? Given that everyone knows that fans get to keep baseballs hit into the stands and that fans expect this to be one of the benefits of going to a game, isn't the fan's right actually contractual? Part of what one pays for when he or she purchases a ticket to a game is the right to keep balls batted or thrown into the stand. This practice, while dating only from the 1920s, has become so institutionalized that one could argue that it is an implicit component of the contract for the sale of a ticket to a baseball game. Presumably, the home teams which own the balls while they are in play could demand that they be returned (as is the case in college and amateur baseball), but a rule change of this nature would have to be stated explicitly at the time that admission tickets were sold.

[4.] Adverse Possession of Personal Property

SONGBYRD, INC. v. ESTATE OF ALBERT B. GROSSMAN

United States District Court, Northern District of New York
23 F. Supp. 2d 219 (1998)

David R. Homer, United States Magistrate Judge.

Plaintiff Songbyrd, Inc. ("Songbyrd") brought this action seeking monetary damages and a declaration of rights in certain recorded music tracks. Presently pending is a motion by defendant Estate of Albert B. Grossman, doing business as Bearsville Records, Inc. ("Bearsville") for summary judgment pursuant to Fed. R. Civ. P. 56 on the ground that the action is barred by the applicable statute of limitations. Songbyrd opposes the motion. For the reasons which follow, the motion is granted.

I. Facts

The undisputed facts of this matter, including its musical background and context, are detailed in an earlier opinion from the Fifth Circuit Court of Appeals. *See Songbyrd, Inc. v. Bearsville Records, Inc.*, 104 F.3d 773, 774–75 (5th Cir. 1997). This case concerns the possession, ownership, and usage of several master recordings of musical performances made in the early 1970s by New Orleans musician Henry Roeland Byrd, who was professionally known as "Professor Longhair" ("Byrd"). (Songbyrd incorporated in 1993 and conducts business as a successor in interest to Byrd.) The tapes were produced in a Baton Rouge, Louisiana recording studio and soon thereafter came into the possession of a predecessor in interest to Bearsville located in Woodstock, New York. Over time several requests have been made by representatives of Byrd to secure return of the tapes. It is unclear what if any response those requests received, but the tapes have remained in the physical custody of Bearsville continuously since the 1970s.

In August 1986, Bearsville licensed certain of the master recordings to Rounder Records Corporation, which in 1987 released an album of Byrd's music produced from the recordings. In 1991, another recording based on the disputed master recordings was released by Rhino Records. That release was made possible by a licensing agreement between Bearsville and the production company.

II. Procedural Background

Originally filed in Louisiana state court in 1995, this action was removed by Bearsville to the United States District Court for the Eastern District of Louisiana. Bearsville then moved pursuant to Fed. R. Civ. P. 12(b) to dismiss the claim on the ground that the court lacked personal jurisdiction and the claim was barred by Louisiana's period of prescription. The district court held that the action was barred by the applicable prescriptive period and granted the motion without addressing the jurisdictional question. *Songbyrd, Inc. v. Bearsville Records, Inc.*, 1996 U.S. Dist. LEXIS 8728, Civ. A. No. 95-3706 (E.D. La. June 18, 1996). Songbyrd appealed and the Fifth Circuit Court of Appeals reversed, holding that the claim was not prescribed under Louisiana law. 104 F.3d 773, 779 (5th Cir. 1997). On remand, the district court considered the question of personal jurisdiction, concluded that jurisdiction was lacking, and transferred the action to this district. [Both parties agreed that New York law was controlling in this case.]

III. Summary Judgment Standard

[Omitted.]

IV. Discussion

This action is governed by the three year statute of limitations for recovery of chattel provided in N.Y. Civ. Prac. L. & R. § 214(3) (McKinney 1990). *Johnson v. Smithsonian Inst.*, 9 F. Supp. 2d 347, 354 (S.D.N.Y. 1998) (New York statute of limitations for conversion and replevin is three years). The issue presented here is when the claim accrued for statute of limitations purposes.

The statute of limitations for conversion begins to run at the time of the conversion. *Sporn v. MCA Records, Inc.*, 448 N.E.2d 1324 (N.Y. 1983). In *Sporn*, New York's Court of Appeals was presented with a case very similar to the case at bar. There, the plaintiff, the successor in interest to the purported owner of rights in certain master recordings, sued the defendant record company for commercially exploiting the master recordings contrary to the plaintiff's interests. The record company defended on the ground that the three year limitations period had begun to run at the time it began using the master recordings contrary to the plaintiff's purported interest and had expired prior to the commencement of the action. Holding that the statute of limitations for conversion begins to run at the time of the conversion, the Court of Appeals affirmed the grant of summary judgment in favor of the record company.

Songbyrd contends that *Solomon R. Guggenheim Found. v. Lubell*, 569 N.E.2d 426 (N.Y. 1991) ("*Guggenheim*"), not *Sporn*, governs this action. In *Guggenheim*, the New York Court of Appeals held that "a cause of action for replevin against a good-faith purchaser of a stolen chattel accrues when the true owner makes demand for return of the chattel and the person in possession of the chattel refuses to return it." Songbyrd argues that under *Guggenheim* the statute of limitations does not begin to run until after a demand for return has been refused, that such a demand has been made but not refused here and as a result the limitations period has not yet begun to run. *Guggenheim*, however, addresses the different circumstance of possession of a chattel by a bona fide purchaser for value and does not, therefore, provide the controlling rule of law here.

Guggenheim, in fact, recognized that a different rule applies when the stolen chattel remains in the possession of the thief. Citing *Sporn*, the court stated that in such a circumstance the statute of limitations begins to run from the time of the theft. Here, the chattel at issue has remained in the possession of Bearsville, the party alleged to have committed the wrongful taking. There is no evidence that Bearsville was ever a bona fide purchaser for value. Thus, the statute of limitations here began to run at the time Bearsville converted the master recordings. *See*

Vigilant Ins. Co. of Am. v. Housing Auth. of the City of El Paso, Tex., 660 N.E.2d 1121 (N.Y. 1995) (in a case not involving a bona fide purchaser, a conversion claim accrues at the time of the conversion). Thus, *Guggenheim* is limited to circumstances involving a bona fide purchaser's possession of the chattel.

Having concluded that Songbyrd's conversion claim accrued at the time of the conversion, the question becomes when the master recordings were allegedly converted. "The tort of conversion is established when one who owns and has a right to possession of personal property proves that the property is in the unauthorized possession of another who has acted to exclude the rights of the owner." *Key Bank of N.Y. v. Grossi*, 227 A.D.2d 841 (N.Y. App. Div. 1996). A party acts to the exclusion of the rights of another by exercising dominion and control over the property that is inconsistent with the interests of the true owner. *Shaw v. Rolex Watch, U.S.A., Inc.*, 673 F. Supp. 674, 682 (S.D.N.Y. 1987). Accepting this definition of conversion, the decisive issue is when Bearsville began unauthorized possession of the master recordings.

Bearsville undeniably had lawful and authorized possession of the master tapes when they were first transferred to its predecessor in 1972. In August 1986, the master recordings were licensed by Bearsville to Rounder Records. The result of this agreement was the 1987 release of an album of Byrd's music taken from the master recordings. This licensing agreement clearly demonstrated Bearsville's intent to exercise control over the Byrd recordings to the exclusion of Songbyrd. *See Jaywyn Video Prod., Ltd. v. Servicing All Media, Inc.*, 179 A.D.2d 397 (N.Y. App. Div. 1992) (licensing of property rights demonstrates exercise of dominion and control). Any claim for conversion, therefore, accrued no later than August 1986 and was time barred at the time this action was filed in 1995. That Songbyrd may not have known of the conversion at the time it occurred is of no moment. *Two Clinton Square Corp. v. Friedler*, 91 A.D.2d 1193 (N.Y. App. 1983); *Memorial Hosp. v. McGreevy*, 152 Misc. 2d 127 (N.Y. Sup. Ct. 1991) (claim accrues at time of conversion "even though the plaintiff may have been unaware of the occurrence").

Where, as here, "the conduct of the defendant certainly constituted a denial of both the plaintiff's right to the master recording and a total usurping of plaintiff's right to possess the master recording," the claim is properly stated as one for conversion. That claim is clearly untimely. The time bar arose in August 1989, three years following the licensing agreement with Rounder Records.[9] Conversion is not a continuing wrong for which every new act that might constitute conversion restarts a new limitations period. *Tinker v. Abrams*, 640 F. Supp. 229, 232 (S.D.N.Y. 1986) (citing *Sporn*). Here, Songbyrd simply failed to commence this action within the applicable statute of limitations. Bearsville's motion [for summary judgment] must, therefore, be granted.

---

[9] [6] In the alternative the conversion occurred no later than August 1991 when Bearsville licensed the master recordings to Rhino Records. That agreement resulted in the 1991 Rhino Records release of an album containing seven tracks produced from the master recordings. The exact date of the Rhino Records licensing deal is not clear in the record but necessarily occurred in or before 1991. Thus, with 1991 as the date of conversion, Songbyrd's claim was time barred prior to the commencement of this action in 1995.

NOTES AND QUESTIONS

1. *Who Were Grossman and Professor Longhair?* Albert Grossman (1926–1986) was a major figure in American popular music in the middle of the 20th century. He organized the first Newport Folk Festival in 1959, and during the 1960s, he served as the manager or mentor for Bob Dylan, Peter, Paul and Mary, Gordon Lightfoot, Janis Joplin, the Band, and other folk and rock stars of the era. Bearsville Records is a recording studio and record company located in the small town of Bearsville, New York (which is near Woodstock), that was founded by Grossman.

The following description of the career of Professor Longhair appears in the Fifth Circuit's 1997 opinion in *Songbyrd, Inc. v. Bearsville Records, Inc.*

> The late Henry Roeland Byrd, also known as "Professor Longhair," was an influential New Orleans rhythm-and-blues pianist and composer, and is widely regarded as one of the primary inspirations for the renaissance of New Orleans popular music over the last thirty years. His numerous hits included original compositions such as "Tipitina" and "Go to the Mardi Gras," as well as his famous renditions of Earl King's "Big Chief." After achieving modest commercial success as a local performer and recording artist in the 1940's and 1950's, Byrd fell on hard times during the 1960's. His fortunes began to change for the better in 1970, however, when New Orleans music aficionado Arthur "Quint" Davis, along with others, founded the New Orleans Jazz and Heritage Festival ("JazzFest"). Needing talented performers for JazzFest, Davis located Byrd in 1971 working in an obscure record store in New Orleans and transformed him into a perennial star attraction of the JazzFest and other venues from that time until his death in 1980.

1997 U.S. App. LEXIS 12684, 2 (5th Cir. Feb. 4, 1997).

2. *Period of Prescription.* The "period of prescription" in civil law jurisdictions like Louisiana (mentioned in the above opinion) is generally synonymous with the common law concept of a statute of limitations. *See FDIC v. Barton*, 96 F.3d 128, 131 n.2 (5th Cir. 1996).

3. Grossman acquired the tapes from Byrd in the early 1970s. Why does the statute of limitations not start to run until 1986? Are the policy justifications for a principle of adverse possession of personal property the same as those for the same principle applied to land? Why is the statutory period for personal property so much shorter than the corresponding period for real property? (In New York, the statutory period for land is 10 years. N.Y. Real Prop. Acts §§ 501–552.)

4. *O'Keefe v. Snyder.* Perhaps the best known adverse possession of personal property case is *O'Keefe v. Snyder*, 416 A.2d 862 (N.J. 1980). In that case, the famous American painter Georgia O'Keefe sued New York gallery owner Barry Snyder for the recovery of three of her paintings which had apparently been stolen 30 years earlier. Snyder had purchased the paintings for $35,000 from a man named Ulrich A. Frank who had inherited the paintings from his father. Snyder maintained that O'Keefe's right to recover the paintings was barred by New Jersey's six year statute of limitations which, he insisted, had begun to run when the paintings were stolen. O'Keefe insisted that the statute of limitations did not begin to run until she learned where the stolen paintings were located.

The court agreed with O'Keefe, holding that the statute does not begin to run until the owner knows, or should know, where the stolen objects are located. (The owner must use "due diligence" to discover the whereabouts of the purloined works.) The New Jersey approach is known as the "discovery" rule.

5. *The New York Rule.* As the *Songbyrd* decision indicates, New York courts have adopted a somewhat different approach, favoring a "demand-and-refusal" rule which delays the running of the statute of limitations until the owner demands the return of the property from "a good faith purchaser of a stolen chattel." This was the holding in the *Guggenheim v. Lubell* decision discussed in *Songbyrd.* Was the court in the latter case correct in holding that the "demand and refusal" rule did not apply to its particular facts? As a general matter, which rule is more favorable to original owners: the "discovery" rule, or the "demand and refusal" rule?

6. *Ranking the Rights of Thieves, Innocent Purchasers for Value, Finders, Owners of the Premises, and the True Owner.* Neither the unlawful possessor of property nor the innocent third-party purchaser acquire any interest against the true owner, although such parties do, at least in theory, obtain a property interest against subsequent wrongful possessors. Adverse possession statutes, however, have the potential to create property rights for those whose claims were initially illegitimate. As the above material illustrates, property that is lost but not abandoned still belongs to the unlucky owner. In suits between the non-owner finder and the owner of the land on which the lost object is found, American courts usually favor the landowner rather than the finder.

[C.] PROPERTY IN INTANGIBLES

[1.] The Right to Publicity

TENNESSEE EX REL. THE ELVIS PRESLEY INTERNATIONAL MEMORIAL FOUNDATION v. CROWELL

Tennessee Court of Appeals
733 S.W.2d 89 (1987)

William C. Koch, Jr., J.

This appeal involves a dispute between two not-for-profit corporations concerning their respective rights to use Elvis Presley's name as part of their corporate names. The case began when one corporation filed an unfair competition action in the Chancery Court for Davidson County to dissolve the other corporation and to prevent it from using Elvis Presley's name. Elvis Presley's estate intervened on behalf of the defendant corporation. It asserted that it had given the defendant corporation permission to use Elvis Presley's name and that it had not given similar permission to the plaintiff corporation.

The trial court determined that Elvis Presley's right to control his name and image descended to his estate at his death and that the Presley estate had the right to control the commercial exploitation of Elvis Presley's name and image. Thus, the trial court granted the defendant corporation's motion for summary judgment and dismissed the complaint.

The plaintiff corporation has appealed. Its primary assertion is that there is no descendible right of publicity in Tennessee and that Elvis Presley's name and image entered into the public domain when he died. It also asserts that the trial court should not have granted a summary judgment because there are disputed factual issues and that the trial court should not have permitted the corporation representing Elvis Presley's estate to intervene. We concur with the trial court's determination that Elvis Presley's right of publicity is descendible under Tennessee law. However, for the reasons stated herein, we vacate the summary judgment and remand the case for further proceedings.

Elvis Presley's career is without parallel in the entertainment industry. From his first hit record in 1954 until his death in 1977, he scaled the heights of fame and success that only a few have attained. His twenty-three year career as a recording star, concert entertainer and motion picture idol brought him international recognition and a devoted following in all parts of the nation and the world.

Elvis Presley was aware of this recognition and sought to capitalize on it during his lifetime. He and his business advisors entered into agreements granting exclusive commercial licenses throughout the world to use his name and likeness in connection with the marketing and sale of numerous consumer items. As early as 1956, Elvis Presley's name and likeness could be found on bubble gum cards, clothing, jewelry and numerous other items. The sale of Elvis Presley memorabilia has been described as the greatest barrage of merchandise ever aimed at the teenage set. It earned millions of dollars for Elvis Presley, his licensees and business associates.

Elvis Presley's death on August 16, 1977 did not decrease his popularity. If anything it preserved it. Now Elvis Presley is an entertainment legend, somewhat larger than life, whose memory is carefully preserved by his fans, the media and his estate.

The demand for Elvis Presley merchandise was likewise not diminished by his death. The older memorabilia are now collector's items. New consumer items have been authorized and are now being sold. Elvis Presley Enterprises, Inc., a corporation formed by the Presley estate, has licensed seventy-six products bearing his name and likeness and still controls numerous trademark registrations and copyrights. Graceland, Elvis Presley's home in Memphis, is now a museum that attracts approximately 500,000 paying visitors a year. Elvis Presley Enterprises, Inc. also sells the right to use portions of Elvis Presley's filmed or televised performances. These marketing activities presently bring in approximately fifty million dollars each year and provide the Presley estate with approximately $4.6 million in annual revenue. The commercial exploitation of Elvis Presley's name and likeness continues to be a profitable enterprise. It is against this backdrop that this dispute between these two corporations arose.

A group of Elvis Presley fans approached Shelby County officials sometime in 1979 concerning the formation of a group to support a new trauma center that was part of the Memphis and Shelby County hospital system. This group, calling themselves the Elvis Presley International Memorial Foundation, sought a charter as a Tennessee not-for-profit corporation in October, 1980. The Secretary of State denied their application on November 12, 1980, stating that "the name Elvis Presley cannot be used in the charter."

Lawyers representing the group of fans and the Presley estate met to discuss the group's use of Elvis Presley's name following the Secretary of State's rejection of the charter application. In December, 1980, the Presley estate and its trademark counsel formally declined to give the group the unrestricted right to use Elvis Presley's name and likeness. However, the Presley estate offered the group a royalty-free license to use Elvis Presley's name and likeness if the group agreed to abide by eight conditions limiting the group's activities. The group declined the offer of a royalty-free license.

The Presley estate incorporated Elvis Presley Enterprises, Inc. on February 24, 1981. Two days later on February 26, 1981, the Secretary of State, reversing its original decision, granted the fan group's renewed application and issued a corporate charter to the Elvis Presley International Memorial Foundation (International Foundation). The International Foundation raises funds by charging membership fees and dues and by sponsoring an annual banquet in Memphis. It uses its funds to support the trauma center of the new City of Memphis Hospital which was named after Elvis Presley and to provide an annual award of merit.

The Presley estate and Elvis Presley Enterprises, Inc. incorporated the Elvis Presley Memorial Foundation, Inc. (Foundation) as a Tennessee not-for-profit corporation on May 14, 1985. The Foundation is soliciting funds from the public to construct a fountain in the shopping center across the street from Elvis Presley's home.

The International Foundation's heretofore amicable relationship with the Presley estate and Elvis Presley Enterprises, Inc. deteriorated after the formation of the Foundation. On July 17, 1985, the International Foundation filed this action seeking to dissolve the Foundation and to enjoin it using a deceptively similar name.

II

[In this portion of the opinion, the court ruled that the trial court did not err in allowing Elvis Presley Enterprises, Inc. to intervene as a defendant in this action.]

III

Elvis Presley's Right of Publicity

We are dealing in this case with an individual's right to capitalize upon the commercial exploitation of his name and likeness and to prevent others from doing so without his consent. This right, now commonly referred to as the right of publicity, is still evolving and is only now beginning to step out of the shadow of its more well known cousin, the right of privacy.

The confusion between the right of privacy and the right of publicity has caused one court to characterize the state of the law as a "haystack in a hurricane." *Ettore v. Philco Television Broadcasting Corp.*, 229 F.2d 481, 485 (3d Cir. 1956). This confusion will not retard our recognition of the right of publicity because Tennessee's common law tradition, far from being static, continues to grow and to accommodate the emerging needs of modern society. [Citations omitted.]

A

The right of privacy owes its origin to Samuel Warren's and Louis Brandeis' now famous 1890 law review article. Warren & Brandeis, *The Right to Privacy*, 4 HARV. L. REV. 193 (1890). The authors were concerned with the media's intrusion into the affairs of private citizens and wrote this article to vindicate each individual's "right to be left alone." The privacy interest they sought to protect was far different from a celebrity's interest in controlling and exploiting the economic value of his name and likeness.

Writing in 1890, Warren and Brandeis could not have foreseen today's commercial exploitation of celebrities. They did not anticipate the changes that would be brought about by the growth of the advertising, motion picture, television and radio industries. American culture outgrew their concept of the right of privacy and soon began to push the common law to recognize and protect new and different rights and interests.

It would be difficult for any court today, especially one sitting in Music City U.S.A. practically in the shadow of the Grand Ole Opry, to be unaware of the manner in which celebrities exploit the public's recognition of their name and image. The stores selling Elvis Presley tee shirts, Hank Williams, Jr. bandannas or Barbara Mandrell satin jackets are not selling clothing as much as they are selling the celebrities themselves. We are asked to buy the shortening that makes Loretta Lynn's pie crusts flakier or to buy the same insurance that Tennessee Ernie Ford has or to eat the sausage that Jimmy Dean makes.

There are few every day activities that have not been touched by celebrity merchandising. This, of course, should come as no surprise. Celebrity endorsements are extremely valuable in the promotion of goods and services. They increase audience appeal and thus make the commodity or service more sellable. These endorsements are of great economic value to celebrities and are now economic reality.

The first decision to recognize the right of publicity as a right independent from the right of privacy was *Haelan Laboratories, Inc. v. Topps Chewing Gum, Inc.*, 202 F.2d 866 (2d Cir.), *cert. denied*, 346 U.S. 816 (1953). The United States Court of Appeals for the Second Circuit stated:

> This right might be called a "right of publicity." For it is common knowledge that many prominent persons (especially actors and ballplayers), far from having their feelings bruised through public exposure of their likenesses, would feel sorely deprived if they no longer received money for authorizing advertisements, popularizing their countenances, displayed in newspapers, magazines, busses, trains and subways. This right

> of publicity would usually yield them no money unless it could be made the subject of an exclusive grant which barred any other advertiser from using their pictures.

Id. at 868.

The concept of an independent right of publicity did not achieve immediate recognition. Dean Prosser, in his authoritative discussions of the right of privacy, continued to include the right of publicity as one of the four distinct interests protected by the right of privacy. W. Prosser, Handbook of the Law of Torts § 97, at 637 & 639 (2d ed. 1955). In his later writings, Prosser characterized the right of publicity as an exclusive right in the individual plaintiff to a species of trade name, his own, and a kind of trade mark in his likeness. It seems quite pointless to dispute over whether such a right is to be classified as "property;" it is at least clearly proprietary in nature. W. Prosser, Handbook of the Law of Torts § 117, at 807 (4th ed. 1971). *See also* W. Keeton, Prosser and Keeton on the Law of Torts § 117, at 854 (5th ed. 1984).

The Restatement (Second) of Torts adopted Prosser's analytic conception of the scope of the right of privacy. Restatement (Second) of Torts § 652A (1976) embodies his four right of privacy categories. However, the American Law Institute recognized that the nexus between the right of publicity and the other three categories is tenuous. Restatement (Second) of Torts § 652A(2) comm. b (1976). Based upon this difference, the Restatement (Second) of Torts § 652I (1976) recognizes that the right of publicity may be descendible even if the other categories are not.

The legal experts have consistently called for the recognition of the right of publicity as a separate and independent right. In 1977, the United States Supreme Court recognized that the right of publicity was distinct from the right of privacy. *Zacchini v. Scripps-Howard Broadcasting Co.*, 433 U.S. 562, 571–74 (1977). Now, courts in other jurisdictions uniformly hold that the right of publicity should be considered as a free standing right independent from the right of privacy. *Baltimore Orioles, Inc. v. Major League Baseball Players Association*, 805 F.2d 663, 677–78 n.26 (7th Cir. 1986), *petition for cert. filed*, 55 U.S.L.W. 3644 (U.S. Jan. 27, 1987); *Carson v. Here's Johnny Portable Toilets, Inc.*, 698 F.2d 831, 834 (6th Cir. 1983); *Martin Luther King, Jr. Center for Social Change, Inc. v. American Heritage Products, Inc.*, 694 F.2d 674, 674–75 (11th Cir. 1983); *Estate of Elvis Presley v. Russen*, 513 F. Supp. 1339, 1353 (D.N.J. 1981); *Martin Luther King, Jr. Center for Social Change, Inc. v. American Heritage Products, Inc.*, 296 S.E.2d 697, 703 (Ga. 1982); and *House v. Sports Films & Talents, Inc.*, 351 N.W.2d 684, 685 (Minn. App. 1984).

B

The status of Elvis Presley's right of publicity since his death has been the subject of four proceedings in the Federal courts. The conflicting decisions in these cases mirror the difficulty other courts have experienced in dealing with the right of publicity. The first case originated in Tennessee and involved the sale of pewter statuettes of Elvis Presley without the exclusive licensee's permission. The United States District Court recognized Elvis Presley's independent right of publicity and held that it had descended to the Presley estate under Tennessee law. *Memphis Development Foundation v. Factors, Etc. Inc.*, 441 F. Supp. 1323, 1330 (W.D. Tenn. 1977). The United States Court of Appeals for the Sixth Circuit reversed. Apparently without considering Tennessee law, the court held that Tennessee courts would find that the right of publicity would not survive a celebrity's death. *Memphis Development Foundation v. Factors, Etc., Inc.*, 616 F.2d 956, 958 (6th Cir.), *cert. denied*, 449 U.S. 953 (1980).

The second and third cases originated in New York and were originally decided under New York law. On two successive days, Judge Charles H. Tenney recognized Elvis Presley's right of publicity and held that it descended at death like any other intangible property right. *Factors Etc. Inc. v. Creative Card Co.*, 444 F. Supp. 279, 284 (S.D.N.Y. 1977) and *Factors Etc., Inc. v. Pro Arts, Inc.*, 444 F. Supp. 288, 290 (S.D.N.Y. 1977). Pro Arts, Inc. appealed, and the United States Court of Appeals for the Second Circuit, applying New York law, agreed that Elvis Presley's right of publicity survived his death and remanded the case. *Factors Etc., Inc. v. Pro Arts, Inc.*, 579 F.2d 215, 221 (2d Cir. 1978), *cert. denied*, 440 U.S. 908 (1979).

The dispute between Factors, Etc., Inc. and Pro Arts, Inc. did not end. On remand, Judge Tenney permanently enjoined Pro Arts from making any commercial use of Elvis Presley's name and likeness. Pro Arts, Inc. again appealed to the United States Court of Appeals for the Second Circuit. This time Pro Arts insisted that the controversy was governed by Tennessee law and that the United States Court of Appeals for the Sixth Circuit's opinion in *Memphis Development Foundation v. Factors, Etc., Inc.* should control.

The United States Court of Appeals for the Second Circuit agreed that Tennessee law controlled the case. While it expressly disagreed with the Sixth Circuit's holding in *Memphis Development Foundation v. Factors, Etc., Inc.* it concluded that it was required to accept the Sixth Circuit's decision as controlling authority. *Factors Etc., Inc. v. Pro Arts, Inc.*, 652 F.2d 278, 282–83 (2d Cir. 1981), *cert. denied*, 456 U.S. 927 (1982).

The fourth case originated in New Jersey and involved an Elvis Presley impersonator. Applying New Jersey law, the United States District Court recognized Elvis Presley's right of publicity and held that it would be descendible under New Jersey law. *Estate of Elvis Presley v. Russen*, 513 F. Supp. 1339, 1354–55 (D.N.J. 1981).

The courts in each of these cases recognized the existence of Elvis Presley's right of publicity. All the courts, except one, also recognized that this right was descendible upon Elvis Presley's death. The reasoning employed by the United States Court of Appeals for the Sixth Circuit to deny the descendibility of Elvis Presley's right of publicity has not been widely followed. The United States Court of Appeals for the Second Circuit specifically disagreed with it. *Factors Etc., Inc. v. Pro Arts, Inc.*, 652 F.2d 278, 282 (2d Cir. 1981). It has also been consistently criticized in the legal literature. [Citations omitted.]

C

The appellate courts of this State have had little experience with the right of publicity. The Tennessee Supreme Court has never recognized it as part of our common law or has never undertaken to define its scope. However, the recognition of individual property rights is deeply embedded in our jurisprudence. These rights are recognized in Article I, Section 8 of the Tennessee Constitution and have been called "absolute" by the Tennessee Supreme Court. *Stratton Claimants v. Morris Claimants*, 15 S.W. 87, 90 (Tenn. 1891). This Court has noted that the right of property "has taken deep root in this country and there is now no substantial dissent from it." *Davis v. Mitchell*, 178 S.W.2d 889, 910 (Tenn. App. 1943).

The concept of the right of property is multi-faceted. It has been described as a bundle of rights or legally protected interests. These rights or interests include: (1) the right of possession, enjoyment and use; (2) the unrestricted right of disposition; and (3) the power of testimonial disposition. *Weiss v. Broadway National Bank*, 322 S.W.2d 427, 431 (Tenn. 1959); *Sanford-Day Iron Works v. Enterprise Foundry & Machine Co.*, 198 S.W. 258, 259 (Tenn. 1917); and *Third National Bank v. Divine Grocery Co.*, 37 S.W. 390, 392 (Tenn. 1896).

In its broadest sense, property includes all rights that have value. It embodies all the interests a person has in land and chattels that are capable of being possessed and controlled to the exclusion of others. *Watkins v. Wyatt*, 68 Tenn. (9 Baxt.) 250, 255 (1877) and *Townsend v. Townsend*, 7 Tenn. (1 Peck) 1, 17 (1821). Chattels include intangible personal property such as choses in action or other enforceable rights of possession. *Childress v. Childress*, 569 S.W.2d 816, 818 (Tenn. 1978); *North v. Puckett*, 46 S.W.2d 73, 74 (Tenn. 1932); and *Sharp v. Cincinnati, N.O. & T.P.R. Co.*, 179 S.W. 375, 376 (Tenn. 1915).

Our courts have recognized that a person's "business," a corporate name, a trade name and the good will of a business are species of intangible personal property. *M.M. Newcomer Co. v. Newcomer's New Store*, 217 S.W. 822, 825 (Tenn. 1919) [trade name]; *Sanford-Day Iron Works v. Enterprise Foundry & Machine Co.*, 198 S.W. 258, 259 (Tenn. 1917) ["one's business"]; *Bradford & Carson v. Montgomery Furniture Co.*, 92 S.W. 1104, 1106 (Tenn. 1905) [good will]; and *Robinson v. Robinson's, Inc.*, 9 Tenn. App. 103 (1928) [corporate name].

Tennessee's common law thus embodies an expansive view of property. Unquestionably, a celebrity's right of publicity has value. It can be possessed and used. It can be assigned, and it can be the subject of a contract. Thus, there is ample basis for this Court to conclude that it is a species of intangible personal property.

D

Today there is little dispute that a celebrity's right of publicity has economic value. Courts now agree that while a celebrity is alive, the right of publicity takes on many of the attributes of personal property. It can be possessed and controlled to the exclusion of others. Its economic benefits can be realized and enjoyed. It can also be the subject of a contract and can be assigned to others.

What remains to be decided by the courts in Tennessee is whether a celebrity's right of publicity is descendible at death under Tennessee law. Only the law of this State controls this question. *Hartman v. Duke*, 22 S.W.2d 221–22 (Tenn. 1929) and *Jones v. Marable*, 25 Tenn. (6 Humph.) 116, 118 (1845). The only reported opinion holding that Tennessee law does not recognize a postmortem right of publicity is *Memphis Development Foundation v. Factors, Etc., Inc.*, 616 F.2d 956 (6th Cir.), *cert. denied*, 449 U.S. 953 (1980). We have carefully reviewed this opinion and have determined that it is based upon an incorrect construction of Tennessee law and is inconsistent with the better reasoned decisions in this field.

The United States Court of Appeals for the Sixth Circuit appears to believe that there is something inherently wrong with recognizing that the right of publicity is descendible. *Memphis Development Foundation v. Factors, Etc., Inc.*, 616 F.2d 956, 959–60 (6th Cir. 1980). We do not share this subjective policy bias. Like the Supreme Court of Georgia, we recognize that the "trend since the early common law has been to recognize survivability, notwithstanding the legal problems which may thereby arise." *Martin Luther King Center for Social Change Inc. v. American Heritage Products, Inc.*, 296 S.E.2d 697, 705 (Ga. 1982).

We have also concluded that recognizing that the right of publicity is descendible promotes several important policies that are deeply ingrained in Tennessee's jurisprudence. First, it is consistent with our recognition that an individual's right of testamentary distribution is an essential right. If a celebrity's right of publicity is treated as an intangible property right in life, it is no less a property right at death. *See Price v. Hal Roach Studios, Inc.*, 400 F. Supp. 836, 844 (S.D.N.Y. 1975).

Second, it recognizes one of the basic principles of Anglo-American jurisprudence that "one may not reap where another has sown nor gather where another has strewn." *M.M. Newcomer Co. v. Newcomer's New Store*, 217 S.W. 822, 825 (Tenn. 1919). *See also Zacchini v. Scripps-Howard Broadcasting Co.*, 433 U.S. 562, 580 n.2 (1977) (Powell, J., dissenting); *Bi-Rite Enterprises, Inc. v. Bruce Miner Co.*, 757 F.2d 440, 444 (1st Cir. 1985); *Carson v. Here's Johnny Portable Toilets, Inc.*, 698 F.2d 831, 838 (6th Cir. 1983); and *Hirsch v. S. C. Johnson & Son, Inc.*, 280 N.W.2d 129, 134 (Wis. 1979). This unjust enrichment principle argues against granting a windfall to an advertiser who has no colorable claim to a celebrity's interest in the right of publicity. *Factors Etc., Inc. v. Pro Arts, Inc.*, 579 F.2d 215, 221 (2d Cir. 1978), *cert. denied*, 440 U.S. 908 (1979) and *Martin Luther King, Jr. Center for Social Change, Inc. v. American Heritage Products, Inc.*, 296 S.E.2d 697, 705 (Ga. 1982).

Third, recognizing that the right of publicity is descendible is consistent with a celebrity's expectation that he is creating a valuable capital asset that will benefit his heirs and assigns after his death. It is now common for celebrities to include their interest in the exploitation of their right of publicity in their estate. While a celebrity's expectation that his heirs will benefit from his right of publicity might not, by itself, provide a basis to recognize that the right of publicity is descendible, it does recognize the effort and financial commitment celebrities make in their careers. This investment deserves no less recognition and protection than investments celebrities might make in the stock market or in other tangible assets.

Fourth, concluding that the right of publicity is descendible recognizes the value of the contract rights of persons who have acquired the right to use a celebrity's name and likeness, The value of this interest stems from its duration and its exclusivity, If a celebrity's name and likeness were to enter the public domain at death, the value of any existing contract made while the celebrity was alive would be greatly diminished.

Fifth, recognizing that the right of publicity can be descendible will further the public's interest in being free from deception with regard to the sponsorship, approval or certification of goods and services, Falsely claiming that a living celebrity endorses a product or service violates Tenn. Code Ann. § 47-18-104(b)(2), (3) and (5), It should likewise be discouraged after a celebrity has died. Finally, recognizing that the right of publicity can be descendible is consistent with the policy against unfair competition through the use of deceptively similar corporate names.

The legal literature has consistently argued that the right of publicity should be descendible, A majority of the courts considering this question agree, *Acme Circus Operating Co. v. Kuperstock*, 711 F.2d 1538, 1543–44 (11th Cir. 1983); *Martin Luther King, Jr. Center for Social Change Inc. v. American Heritage Products, Inc.*, 694 F.2d 674 (11th Cir. 1983); *Factors, Etc., Inc. v. Pro Arts, Inc.*, 579 F.2d 215, 222 (2d Cir. 1978), *cert. denied*, 440 U.S. 908 (1979); *Price v. Hal Roach Studios, Inc.*, 400 F. Supp. 836, 844 (S.D.N.Y. 1975); *Lugosi v. Universal Pictures*, 603 P.2d 425, 431 (Cal. 1979); and *Martin Luther King, Jr. Center for Social Change, Inc. v. American Heritage Products, Inc.*, 296 S.E.2d 697, 705 (Ga. 1982). We find this authority convincing and consistent with Tennessee's common law and, therefore, conclude that Elvis Presley's right of publicity survived his death and remains enforceable by his estate and those holding licenses from the estate.

E

While Tennessee's courts are capable of defining the parameters of the right of publicity on a case by case basis, the General Assembly also has the prerogative to define the scope of this right. The General Assembly undertook to do so in 1984 when it enacted Tenn. Code Ann. § 47-25-1101 *et seq.* which is known as "The Personal Rights Protection Act of 1984." Tenn. Code Ann. § 47-25-1103(a) recognizes that an individual has "a property right in the use of his name, photograph or likeness in any medium in any manner." Tenn. Code Ann. § 47-25-1103(b) provides that this right is descendible. Tenn. Code Ann. § 47-25-1104(a) & (b)(1) provide that the right is exclusive in the individual or his heirs and assigns until it is terminated. Tenn. Code Ann. § 47-25-1104(b)(2) provides that the right is terminated if it is not used after the individual's death.

Our decision concerning the descendibility of Elvis Presley's right of publicity is not based upon Tenn. Code Ann. § 47-25-1101*et seq.* but rather upon our recognition of the existence of the common law right of publicity. We note, however, that nothing in Tenn. Code Ann. § 47-25-1101*et seq.* should be construed to limit vested rights of publicity that were in existence prior to the effective date of the act. To do so would be contrary to Article I, Section 20 of the Tennessee Constitution. A statute cannot be applied retroactively to impair the value of a contract right in existence when the statute was enacted. *Massey v. Sullivan County*, 464 S.W.2d 548, 549 (Tenn. 1971) and *Collier v. Memphis Light, Gas & Water Division*, 657 S.W.2d 771, 775 (Tenn. App. 1983).

IV–V

[Although finding that Elvis Presley's estate retained the exclusive right to control the commercial exploitation of his name and likeness, the court ruled that the trial court had erred in granting the Foundation's motion for a summary judgment, since it could not be shown *as a matter of law* that the International Foundation's argument that the Foundation had waived its rights was without merit. The summary judgment granted in favor of Elvis Presley Enterprises, Inc. was vacated, and the case was remanded for further proceedings consistent with this opinion.]

NOTES AND QUESTIONS

1. Elvis Presley Enterprises' CEO and President Jack Soden was instrumental in securing passage of Tennessee's "Personal Rights Protection Act of 1984" (Tenn. Code Ann. § 47-25-1101 *et seq.*) which guaranteed that the Presley estate would be able to commercially exploit the King of Rock and Roll's name and image. Soden later explained that he believed that the alternative rule — that a person's exclusive publicity rights died with them — was morally wrong. As Soden put it, "If Elvis Presley had spent 30 years building a tire factory instead of a vast value to his image and likeness, would the law have held on the day he died that everybody in town could kick open the doors and go take all the tires because Elvis didn't need the tires anymore?" *National Public Radio Weekly Edition* (National Public Radio, Aug. 16, 1997, transcript # 97081608-213). Is Soden, who never met Elvis, correct in his assertion that Elvis' image and automobile tires belong in the same category of property interests?

Events of the past four decades have proven the image of Elvis Presley to be an even more valuable commodity today than it was at the time of the singer's death in 1977. Elvis Presley Enterprises ("EPE") eventually licensed more than 100 companies to produce Elvis-related items, and its lawyers aggressively pursued those who attempted to use the Presley likeness without permission. To control the quality of licensed merchandise, EPE requires the holders of its licenses to comply with strict guidelines spelled out in an official style book. For example, the guidelines restrict the way in which Elvis' hair can be depicted and licensees are forbidden to refer to Elvis as simply "The King," even though he is widely known by that name. (The latter rule stems from Elvis' view that this nickname was sacrilegious.) According to National Public Radio, in 1997, Elvis Presley Enterprises, then run by Soden and Elvis' ex-wife Priscilla, grossed in the neighborhood of $250,000,000 annually. By the end of the 1990's, more than 700,000 people visited Graceland each year, making it America's second most visited house following the White House. *National Public Radio Weekly Edition*, Aug. 16, 1997.

Although interest in Elvis has waned somewhat, in the second decade of the 21st Century more than 600,000 visitors come to Graceland each year, making it now one of the five most visited homes in the United States. As of 2015, Jack Soden was still running EPE, although Priscilla Presley stepped down as Chairman of the Board in 2005.

2. *Who Decides What Is Property?* Identifying interests that are classified as "property" is usually a matter of state law. Consequently, the Tennessee legislature and the Tennessee Supreme Court have the authority to say what is and is not recognized as property within the boundaries of the Volunteer State. Federal courts are expected to follow state courts on this issue. However, there are times when federal courts are required to rule on the nature of property interests in an area in which state law is silent. In such a situation, the federal court is supposed to rule as it believes a state court would, given similar facts. This happened in *Memphis Dev. Found. v. Factors, Etc., Inc.*, 441 F. Supp. 1323, 1330 (W.D. Tenn. 1977), and 616 F.2d 956, 958 (6th Cir. 1980), where the Sixth Circuit Court of Appeals concluded that under Tennessee law, the right of publicity did not survive the death of the individual. The Tennessee Court of Appeals rejected the reasoning of the Sixth Circuit's opinion when it reached an opposite conclusion and further characterized the federal court decision as having been made "apparently without considering Tennessee law."

3. *Tort or Property?* As the above opinion notes, for many years, courts and legal scholars debated whether or not the right to publicity represented a separate property right or merely the right to be free from tortious interference (i.e., the invasion of privacy). To use the language of the old common law, is someone who uses the image of a celebrity without permission committing an act of trespass on the case (an "injury resulting . . . from the wrongful act of another, unaccompanied by direct or immediate force") or one of trover (the "wrongful appropriation of goods, chattels, or personal property [of another] which is specific enough to be identified")? (Definitions from Black's Law Dictionary 1675, 1679 (4th ed. 1968).) In the past, courts have found it easier to address questions of this sort as "tort" rather than "property" cases. (See the discussion of *International News Serv. v. Associated Press*, below.) Why should that be?

At the beginning of the 20th century, courts were resistant to the idea of a property interest in a name. In *Atkinson v. John E. Doherty & Co.*, 80 N.W. 285 (Mich. 1899), a Michigan cigar company placed the name and likeness of Col. John Atkinson, a recently deceased lawyer and politician, on the labels of its line of cigars which it named "the Col. John Atkinson cigar." The company sought neither the permission of Atkinson during his lifetime nor of his widow after his death. The court concluded that Atkinson would have had no cause of action against the cigar manufacturer were he still alive unless the action was libelous, and the court found nothing libelous about naming a cigar in honor of a well-known figure. However, as the Tennessee court noted in the *Elvis Presley* case, that idea broke down over the course of the century, and the modern trend is clearly toward the recognition of a property right in publicity.

4. *Origins of the Right of Publicity.* The court above identifies *Haelan Laboratories, Inc. v. Topps Chewing Gum, Inc.*, 202 F.2d 866 (2d Cir. 1953), as the first American case recognizing an independent right of property in publicity. Haelan produced cards containing photographs of major league baseball players which were inserted into packages of bubble gum. The players pictured on the cards had signed exclusive contracts with Haelan. However, several of the players signed later agreed to permit Topps to produce baseball cards bearing their image to be packaged with bubble gum. When Haelan sought to enjoin Topps from selling the

cards, Topps argued that the players in question had no property interest in their own photographs and that all that the exclusive contracts meant was that the players had bargained away their right to sue the card manufacturers for invasion of privacy.

In rejecting this argument, the *Haelan* court issued the statement quoted previously in *Tennessee ex rel. The Elvis Presley International Memorial Foundation v. Crowell*. In so ruling, the court rejected an earlier decision of the Fifth Circuit Court of Appeals which had held that professional baseball players had no property interest in their names or their fame. *Hanna Mfg. Co. v. Hillerich & Bradsby Co.*, 78 F.2d 763 (5th Cir. 1935) (involving contracts giving manufacturers exclusive right to use player names on baseball bats). In that case, the court asserted, "Fame is not merchandise. It would help neither sportsmanship nor business to uphold the sale of a famous name to the highest bidder as property." 78 F.2d at 766. For more on this case, see Hylton, *Baseball Cards and the Birth of the Right of Publicity: The Curious Case of* Haelan Laboratories v. Topps Chewing Gum, 12 MARQ. SPORTS L. REV. 273 (2001).

5. *How Broad Are the Rights Protected?* Many courts have extended the protection provided by the Right of Publicity well beyond the protection of names and images. Well-known cases have protected the distinctive voices of singers Bette Midler and Tom Waits (*Midler v. Ford Motor Co.*, 849 F.2d 460 (9th Cir. 1996); *Waits v. Frito-Lay, Inc.*, 978 F.2d 1093 (9th Cir. 1992)); talk show host Johnny Carson's "Here's Johnny" slogan (*Carson v. Here's Johnny Portable Toilets*, 698 F.2d 831 (6th Cir. 1983)); Vanna White's identity as a "blonde letter-turner" in Wheel of Fortune-like games (*White v. Samsung Electronics America*, 971 F.2d 1395 (9th Cir. 1992)); and the name of basketball-great Kareem Abdul-Jabbar as the answer to a trivia question (*Abdul-Jabbar v. General Motors*, 75 F.3d 1391 (9th Cir. 1996)).

Whether or not the right of publicity gives well-known athletes the power to control the use of their names and "statistics" against unauthorized usage by the producers and players of simulated and fantasy sports games is still a matter of controversy in many jurisdictions. Initially, the answer seemed to be yes. *See, e.g., Palmer v. Schonhorn Enters.*, 232 A.2d 458 (N.J. Super. 1967); *Uhlaender v. Henricksen*, 316 F. Supp. 1277 (D. Minn. 1970). More recently, however, there has been a movement in the general direction of protecting the right of unlicensed use of such information on First Amendment grounds. See *C.B.C. Distribution and Marketing, Inc. v. Major League Baseball Advanced Media*, 443 F. Supp. 2d 1077 (W.D. Mo. 2006); 505 F.3d 818 (8th Cir. 2007), and the discussion of the relationship of the First Amendment to the Right of Publicity at Note 9, below. Because of the state-by-state variations in the protection of publicity rights, the same facts can produce different results in different states. *See Keller v. Electronic Arts, Inc.*, 724 F.3d 1268 (9th Cir. 2013) (claim involving popular Madden video game dismissed under Indiana law, but upheld as valid under California law).

6. *Does the Right of Publicity Survive the Death of the Individual?* In a footnote in *Tennessee ex rel. The Elvis Presley International Memorial Foundation v. Crowell* not reproduced above, the Tennessee Court of Appeals noted: "There is some dispute concerning whether the right of publicity must be exercised while a celebrity is alive in order to render it descendible. We need not decide this question

in this case. There is no dispute in this record that Elvis Presley commercially exploited his right of publicity while he was alive." In *Hicks v. Casablanca Records*, 464 F. Supp. 426 (S.D.N.Y. 1978), the United States District Court for the Southern District of New York suggested that there should be such a requirement.

While such a requirement obviously posed no problem for the estate of Elvis Presley, it did for the heirs of the Rev. Martin Luther King when they sought to block the sale of an unauthorized King memento consisting of a plastic bust of the civil rights leader seated on a coffin. Although King was one of the best known Americans of his time, he had never attempted to exploit his fame for personal financial gain. In *Martin Luther King, Jr. Ctr. for Social Change, Inc. v. American Heritage Prods., Inc.*, 296 S.E.2d 697, 705 (Ga. 1982), the Georgia Supreme Court refused to recognize such a requirement, asserting that the right of King's family to "preserve and extend his status and memory" should not turn on King's failure to "commercialize himself during his lifetime."

States that recognize the survivability of the Right of Publicity differ as to when the right should finally expire. In Virginia, the right expires 20 years after the individual's death. In Florida, the period is 40 years; in Kentucky, Nevada, and Texas, 50 years; in California, 70 years; in Washington, 75 years; and in Indiana and Oklahoma, 100 years. In Tennessee, the right is potentially infinite, but it expires if the successors go 10 years without exercising the right. In a few states, like New York and Wisconsin, the right dies with the individual. In slightly more than 20 states, there does not appear to be any recognized right of publicity, but it is not at all clear what this means in an age of a truly national marketplace and the Internet.

7. *Is the Right of Publicity Retroactive?* What about celebrities who died before the states in which they lived and operated recognized the right of publicity? Do their heirs or assigns currently possess the deceased's publicity rights? Many states have said no. In *Shaw Family Archives, Ltd. v. CMG Worldwide, Inc.*, 486 F. Supp. 2d 309 (S.D.N.Y. 2007), a New York federal court ruled that the successors to Marilyn Monroe, who died in 1963, had acquired no publicity rights because none of the possible forum states (New York or California, where she resided, or Indiana, where the dispute over control of her name and likeness arose) recognized a descendible right of publicity at the time of her death. The court's ruling in regard to Indiana law was confirmed by an Indiana federal court in 2011 in a case involving the alleged publicity rights of gangster John Dillinger who was gunned down by FBI agents in 1943, 51 years before the passage of Indiana's 1994 Right of Publicity Statute (its first such act). *Dillinger, LLC v. Elec. Arts, Inc.*, 795 F. Supp. 2d 829 (S.D. Ind. 2011).

8. *Is the Right of Publicity a Good Idea?* Not everyone is enamored with the recent developments regarding the right of publicity, and the aggressive approach of the Elvis Presley Foundation in protecting its property rights has been criticized by other keepers of the Elvis flame. For the past 20 years, Yale Ph.D. Vernon Chadwick, a former professor of English at the University of Mississippi and the founder of the annual International Conference on Elvis Presley, has questioned the propriety of treating the image of Elvis as a privately owned commodity. According to Chadwick, "Elvis as property, as trademark, copyright, intellectual publicity property, seems to me actually contrary to the spirit of Elvis. Elvis belongs to the

people, which means that the image of Elvis will evolve with the people's fancy, with the people's imagination." *National Public Radio Weekly Edition*, August 16, 1997.

Nor is this sentiment limited to disgruntled Elvis fans. In *White v. Samsung Electronics America*, 971 F.2d 1395 (9th Cir. 1992), mentioned above, the Ninth Circuit Court of Appeals ruled that the game show *Wheel-of-Fortune*'s famous hostess and letter-turner Vanna White could bring an action against Samsung Electronics for violating her common law right of publicity. At issue was a television advertisement sponsored by Samsung that featured a futuristic robot dressed to resemble White standing next to a *Wheel-of-Fortune* style game board. The court ruled that the right of publicity could apply in this situation even though Samsung had not used White's "name, likeness, voice, or signature."

In a dissenting opinion filed to a denial of a request for a hearing *en banc* in the *White* case, Judge Alex Kozinski warned: "Something very dangerous is going on here. Private property, including intellectual property, is essential to our way of life. . . . But reducing too much to private property can be bad medicine. . . . Overprotecting intellectual property is as harmful as under-protecting it. Creativity is impossible without a rich public domain. Nothing today, like nothing since we tamed fire, is genuinely new: Culture, like science and technology, grows by accretion, each new creator building on the works of those who came before. Over-protection stifles the very creative forces it's supposed to nurture." 989 F.2d at 1513. What theory of property, if any, undergirds the comments of Dr. Chadwick and Judge Kozinski? How does it differ from that embraced by Judge Koch in *Tennessee, ex rel. The Elvis Presley International Memorial Foundation v. Crowell*? For what it is worth, British law still rejects the property-based right of publicity, although it does recognize a right of privacy. J. THOMAS MCCARTHY, THE RIGHTS OF PRIVACY AND PUBLICITY § 6.21 (2007).

9. *The First Amendment and the Right of Publicity.* The guarantees of freedom of speech and of the press contained in the First Amendment to the United States Constitution limit the right of publicity, particularly as applied to the news media. A prominent individual or celebrity cannot claim that her right of publicity has been violated when her picture appears on the front page of the *New York Times* or the cover of *People Magazine* or *Sports Illustrated*, even if the choice of covers was at least in part motivated by a desire to sell more newspapers or magazines. However, there are limits to what media outlets can do without running afoul of the right of publicity.

In *Zacchini v. Scripps-Howard Broadcasting Co.*, 433 U.S. 562 (1977), the United States Supreme Court ruled that the First Amendment did not protect an Ohio television station that broadcast as part of its newscast the entire 15-second act of Hugo Zaccini, the "human cannonball." Zaccini's entire act involved his being fired out of a cannon into a net 200 feet away. While performing at the Geauga County Fair in Burton, Ohio, Zaccini's act was filmed by a free-lance television reporter and later shown on the defendant's 11:00 p.m. newscast. Although the story was highly flattering to Zaccini, he nevertheless sued on right of publicity grounds. In a 5-4 decision, the Court found that the television station had exceeded the boundaries of the protections supplied by the First Amendment.

More recently, courts have begun to hold that the free speech provisions of the First Amendment also immunize artists from right of publicity liability, at least if their works are sufficiently "transformative," that is, that they are not just photograph-like reproductions of the subject's image. In *ETW Corp. v. Jireh Pub., Inc.*, 332 F.3d 915 (6th Cir. 2003), the court found that Ohio artist Rick Rush's painting of Tiger Woods at the 1997 Masters Tournament was sufficiently transformative to be protected by the First Amendment. In *Cardtoons, L.C. v. Major League Baseball Players Ass'n*, 335 F.3d 1161 (10th Cir. 2003), another court found that a set of "parody" baseball cards also fell within the ambit of the First Amendment, and therefore the players who were clearly the subject of the cards were barred from bringing a right of publicity claim. In the above-mentioned *C.B.C. Distribution and Marketing, Inc. v. Major League Baseball Advanced Media*, the Sixth Circuit Court of Appeals found that the First Amendment prevented states from allowing Major League baseball players to control the dissemination of statistical information pertaining to their playing careers.

[2.] Property in Ideas

DOWNEY v. GENERAL FOODS

New York Court of Appeals
286 N.E.2d 257 (1972)

CHIEF JUDGE FULD.

The plaintiff, an airline pilot, brought this action against the defendant General Foods Corporation to recover damages for the alleged misappropriation of an idea. [Although the complaint's demand was for $34,600,000, that amount was changed, by stipulation, to $2,800,000, representing $200,000 of damages for each of the complaint's 14 causes of action.] It is his claim that he suggested that the defendant's own gelatin product, "Jell-O," be named "Wiggley" or a variation of that word, including "Mr. Wiggle," and that the product be directed towards the children's market; that, although the defendant disclaimed interest in the suggestion, it later offered its product for sale under the name "Mr. Wiggle." The defendant urges — by way of affirmative defense — that the plaintiff's "alleged 'product concept and name' was independently created and developed" by it. The plaintiff moved for partial summary judgment "on the question of liability" on 5 of its 14 causes of action and the defendant cross-moved for summary judgment dismissing the complaint. The court at Special Term denied both motions, and the Appellate Division affirmed, granting leave to appeal to this court on a certified question.

The plaintiff relies chiefly on correspondence between himself and the defendant, or, more precisely, on letters over the signature of a Miss Dunham, vice-president in charge of one of its departments. On February 15, 1965, the plaintiff wrote to the defendant, stating that he had an "excellent idea to increase the sale of your product Jell-O . . . making it available for children." Several days later, the defendant sent the plaintiff an "Idea Submittal Form" (ISF) which included a form letter and a space for explaining the idea.[10] In that form, the plaintiff suggested, in essence, that the product "be packaged & distributed to children under the name 'wig-l-e' (meaning wiggly or wiggley) or 'wiggle-e' or 'wiggle-eee' or 'wigley.' " He explained that, although his children did not "get especially excited about the Name Jell-O, or wish to eat it," when referred to by that name, "the kids really took to it fast" when his wife "called it 'wiggle-y,' " noting that they then "[associated] the name to the 'wiggle-ing' dessert." Although this is the only recorded proof of his idea, the plaintiff maintains that he sent Miss Dunham two handwritten letters in which he set forth other variations of "Wiggiley," including "Mr. Wiggley, Wiggle, Wiggle-e."

A letter, dated March 8, 1965, over the signature of Miss Dunham, acknowledged the submission of the ISF and informed the plaintiff that it had no interest in promoting his suggestion. However, in July, the defendant introduced into the market a Jell-O product which it called "Mr. Wiggle." The plaintiff instituted the present action some months later. In addition to general denials, the answer contains several affirmative defenses, one of which, as indicated above, recites that the defendant independently created the product's concept and name before the plaintiff's submission to it.

In support of its position, the defendant pointed to depositions taken by the plaintiff from its employees and from employees of Young & Rubicam, the firm which did its advertising. From these it appears that the defendant first began work on a children's gelatin product in May, 1965 — three months after the plaintiff had submitted his suggestion — in response to a threat by Pillsbury Company to enter the children's market with a product named "Jiggly." Those employees of the defendant in charge of the project enlisted the aid of Young & Rubicam which, solely on its own initiative, "came up with the name 'Mr. Wiggle.' " In point of fact, Miss Dunham swore in her deposition that she had had no knowledge whatever of the plaintiff's idea until late in 1966, shortly before commencement of his suit; that ideas submitted by the general public were kept in a file by an assistant of hers "under lock and key;" and that no one from any other of the defendant's departments ever asked to research those files. The assistant, who had alone handled the correspondence with the plaintiff over Miss Dunham's signature — reproduced by means of a signature duplicating machine — deposed that she had no contact whatsoever with Young & Rubicam and had never discussed the name "Wiggle" or "Mr. Wiggle" with any one from that firm.

In addition to the depositions of its employees and the employees of its advertising agency, the defendant submitted documentary proof of its prior use of some form of the word "wiggle" in connection with its endeavor to sell Jell-O to children. Thus, it submitted (1) a copy of a report which Young & Rubicam furnished it in June of 1959 proposing "an advertising program directed at children as a means of securing additional sales volume"; (2) a copy of a single dimensional

---

[10] Editor's note: The form letter which Downey signed and returned to General Foods stated: "I submit this suggestion with the understanding, which is conclusively evidenced by my use and transmittal to you of this form, that this suggestion is not submitted to you in confidence, that no confidential relationship has been or will be established between us and that the use, if any, to be made of this suggestion by you and the compensation to be paid therefor, if any, if you use it, are matters resting solely in your discretion."

reproduction of a television commercial, prepared in 1959 and used thereafter by the defendant in national and local television broadcasts, which contained the phrase, "all that wiggles is not Jell-O"; and (3) a copy of a newspaper advertisement that appeared in 1960, depicting an Indian "squaw" puppet and her "papoose" preparing Jell-O — the "top favorite in every American tepee" — and suggesting to mothers that they "[make] a wigglewam of Jell-O for your tribe tonight!"

The critical issue in this case turns on whether the idea suggested by the plaintiff was original or novel. An idea may be a property right. But, when one submits an idea to another, no promise to pay for its use may be implied, and no asserted agreement enforced, if the elements of novelty and originality are absent, since the property right in an idea is based upon these two elements. (*See Soule v. Bon Ami Co.*, 201 App. Div. 794, 796, *aff'd*, 235 N.Y. 609; *Bram v. Dannon Milk Prods.*, 33 A.D.2d 1010; *Santilli v. Philip Morris & Co.*, 283 F.2d 6, 7; *Lueddecke v. Chevrolet Motor Co.*, 70 F.2d 345; *Puente v. President & Fellows of Harvard Coll.*, 149 F. Supp. 33, 34, *aff'd*, 248 F.2d 799 *cert. denied* 356 U.S. 947.) The *Bram* case is illustrative; in reversing Special Term and granting summary judgment dismissing the complaint, the Appellate Division made it clear that, despite the asserted existence of an agreement, the plaintiff could not recover for his idea if it was not original and had been used before (33 A.D.2d, at p. 1010): "The idea submitted by the plaintiff to the defendants, the concept of depicting an infant in a highchair eating and enjoying yogurt, was lacking in novelty and had been utilized by the defendants . . . prior to its submission. Lack of novelty in an idea is fatal to any cause of action for its unlawful use. In the circumstances a question of fact as to whether there existed an oral agreement between the parties would not preclude summary judgment."

In the case before us, the record indisputably establishes, first, that the idea submitted — use of a word ("wiggley" or "wiggle") descriptive of the most obvious characteristic of Jell-O, with the prefix "Mr." added — was lacking in novelty and originality and, second, that the defendant had envisaged the idea, indeed had utilized it, years before the plaintiff submitted it. As already noted, it had made use of the word "wiggles" in a 1959 television commercial and the word "wigglewam" in a 1960 newspaper advertisement. It was but natural, then, for the defendant to employ some variation of it to combat Pillsbury's entry into the children's market with its "Jiggly." Having relied on its own previous experience, the defendant was free to make use of "Mr. Wiggle" without being obligated to compensate the plaintiff.

It is only necessary to add that, in light of the complete pretrial disclosure in this case of every one who had any possible connection with the creation of the name, the circumstance, adverted to by the courts below, that the facts surrounding the defendant's development of the name were within the knowledge of the defendant and its advertising agency does not preclude a grant of summary judgment. In the present case, it was shown beyond peradventure that there was no connection between Miss Dunham's department and the defendant's other employees or the employees of the advertising outfit who took part in the creation of "Mr. Wiggle." In exhaustive discovery proceedings — which included examinations of all parties concerned either with that name or the defendant's idea files — the plaintiff was furnished with every conceivable item of information in the defendant's possession bearing on the privacy and confidentiality of such files and on the absence of access to them by those outside of Miss Dunham's department. The hope, expressed by the plaintiff that he may be able to prove that the witnesses who gave testimony in examinations before trial lied, is clearly insufficient to create an issue of fact requiring a trial or defeat the defendant's motion for summary judgment.

The order appealed from should be reversed, without costs, the question certified answered in the negative and the defendant's motion for summary judgment dismissing the complaint granted.

NOTES AND QUESTIONS

1. It has long been a maxim of American intellectual property law that there can be no property right in an idea, no matter how novel. The law of both copyright and patent go to some length to insure that it is the concrete expression of an idea that is protected and not the idea itself. To borrow Herman Melville's metaphor, ideas are loose fish that cannot be owned, at least not until they are captured and secured to something more tangible than just the mind of their creator. Even when the idea reflects a genuinely remarkable insight, those who formulate it possess no special claim to it, any more than the first hunter who spies the fox. As Chief Justice Burger observed in a patent case: "Einstein could not patent his celebrated law that $E = mc^2$; nor could Newton have patented the law of gravity." *Diamond v. Chakrabarty*, 447 U.S. 303, 309 (1980).

2. *Idea Submission Rights*. Nevertheless, the court in *Downey* says, "An idea may be a property right." What does it mean by this statement? The opinion suggests that the key question is whether or not the idea was "original or novel," but this raises the question of how one determines originality or novelty. Moreover, even if the idea is novel, why should it be protected as property, particularly if the idea's originator has no capacity to act upon it? Should the first person to have come up with the idea of a mechanical dollar bill changer have had a property interest in his idea if he had no idea how to build such an invention?

To prevent the unjust enrichment of those who unfairly use the ideas of others without "commodifying" ordinary ideas, many states have adopted an exception to the "no property rights in an idea" principle known as "idea submission" rights. Under this theory, if a novel idea is submitted in confidence from one party to another with the intention of being compensated if the idea is used, then the second party is liable to the first if it in fact uses the idea. This is apparently what Downey believed to have occurred in the previous case. To prevail under such a claim, the plaintiff would have to establish (1) that the idea was novel; (2) that it was conveyed to the defendant in confidence; and (3) that the defendant made use of the idea after learning of it from the plaintiff. The existing case law suggests that it is difficult to prevail in such a case. *See Murray v. National Broadcasting Co.*, 844 F.2d 988 (2d Cir. 1988) (suggestion of a television comedy about a middle-class black family not sufficiently novel in a suit claiming the idea behind "The Cosby Show"); *Ahlert v. Hasbro*, 325 F. Supp. 2d 509 (D.N.J. 2004) (no proof that defendant did not develop its own high-powered toy water gun independent of plaintiff's confidential presentation of his design for a toy known as the "Water Rat").

3. *Trade Secrets.* Another form of idea protection is provided by the law of trade secrets. A trade secret is "any formula, pattern, device or compilation of information which is used in one's business, and which gives him an opportunity to obtain an advantage over competitors who do not know or use it." RESTATEMENT OF TORTS § 757, cmt. b (1939). (The most famous trade secret is probably the formula for Coca-Cola which has never been divulged.) Courts will enjoin the inappropriate disclosure of trade secrets and will prevent competitors from benefiting from inappropriately disclosed trade secrets. Whether a trade secret is technically a form of "property" has been much debated — United States Supreme Court Justice Oliver Wendell Holmes, Jr. (who figures prominently in the next case) once observed that the label "property" as applied to trade secrets was only an "unanalyzed expression" and that the real offense was not the taking of property but the breach of a "special confidence." *E.I. Du Pont v. Masland*, 244 U.S. 100, 102 (1917). However, more recently the Supreme Court has acknowledged that trade secrets are a form of private property. *Ruckelshaus v. Monsanto Co.*, 467 U.S. 986, 1001–04 (1984).

4. Property interests in ideas may also be created by contract, as where A promises to share his new idea with B if B pays him $5,000. If A fulfills his promise and B refuses to pay, A clearly has a cause of action. Does such a right suggest that the originator of the idea had an *a priori* property right in the idea itself independent of the contract?

5. *Intellectual Property.* Once an idea takes specific form, it may be recognized as legally protected property, at least as long as the developer of the idea has complied with specific statutory guidelines. (In the *Diamond* case cited above, for example, the United States Supreme Court held that a new strain of bacterium was a proper subject for a patent and thus a protected form of property.) Drawing the line between what is merely an idea, and thus not protected property, and a concrete embodiment of that idea, which can be asserted as a form of property, is the central task of the law of intellectual property.

[3.] Copyright and Patent

HOLMES v. HURST

United States Supreme Court
174 U.S. 82 (1899)

This was a bill in equity by the executor of the will of the late Dr. Oliver Wendell Holmes, praying for an injunction against the infringement of the copyright of a book originally published by plaintiff's testator under the title of "The Autocrat of the Breakfast Table."

The case was tried upon an agreed statement of facts, the material portions of which are as follows: Dr. Holmes, the testator, was the author of "The Autocrat of the Breakfast Table," which, during the years 1857 and 1858, was published by Phillips, Sampson & Company of Boston, in twelve successive numbers of the Atlantic Monthly, a periodical magazine published by them, and having a large circulation. Each of these twelve numbers was a bound volume of 128 pages, consisting of a part of "The Autocrat of the Breakfast Table," and of other literary compositions. These twelve parts were published under an agreement between Dr.

Holmes and the firm of Phillips, Sampson & Company, whereby the author granted them the privilege of publishing the same, the firm stipulating that they should have no other right in or to said book. No copyright was secured, either by the author or by the firm or by any other person, in any of the twelve numbers so published in the Atlantic Monthly; but on November 2, 1858, after the publication of the last of the twelve numbers, Dr. Holmes deposited a printed copy of the title of the book in the clerk's office of the District Court of the District of Massachusetts, wherein the author resided, which copy the clerk recorded. The book was published by Phillips, Sampson & Company in a separate volume on November 22, 1858, and upon the same day a copy of the same was delivered to the clerk of the District Court. The usual notice, namely, "Entered according to act of Congress, 1858, by Oliver Wendell Holmes, in the Clerk's Office of the District Court of the District of Massachusetts," was printed in every copy of every edition of the work subsequently published, with a slight variation of the edition published in June, 1874.

On July 12, 1886, Dr. Holmes recorded the title a second time; sent a printed copy of the title to the Librarian of Congress, who recorded the same in a book kept for that purpose, and also caused a copy of this record to be published in the Boston Weekly Advertiser; and in the several copies of every edition subsequently published was the following notice: "Copyright, 1886, by Oliver Wendell Holmes."

Since November 1, 1894, defendant has sold and disposed of a limited number of copies of the book entitled "The Autocrat of the Breakfast Table," all of which were copied by the defendant from the twelve numbers of the Atlantic Monthly exactly as they were originally published, and upon each copy so sold or disposed of a notice appeared that the same was taken from the said twelve numbers of the Atlantic Monthly.

The case was heard upon the pleadings and this agreed statement of facts, by the Circuit Court for the Eastern District of New York, and the bill dismissed. From this decree an appeal was taken to the Circuit Court of Appeals for the Second Circuit, by which the decree of the Circuit Court was affirmed. Whereupon plaintiff took an appeal to this court.

MR. JUSTICE BROWN, after stating the case, delivered the opinion of the court.

This case raises the question whether the serial publication of a book in a monthly magazine, prior to any steps taken toward securing a copyright, is such a publication of the same within the meaning of the act of February 3, 1831, c. 16, 4 Stat. 436, as to vitiate a copyright of the whole book, obtained subsequently but prior to the publication of the book as an entirety.

The right of an author, irrespective of statute, to his own productions and to a control of their publication, seems to have been recognized by the common law, but to have been so ill defined that from an early period legislation was adopted to regulate and limit such right. The earliest recognition of this common law right is to be found in the charter of the Stationers' Company, and certain decrees of the Star Chamber promulgated in 1556, 1585, 1623 and 1637, providing for licensing and regulating the manner of printing, and the number of presses throughout the Kingdom, and prohibiting the publication of unlicensed books. Indeed, the Star

Chamber seems to have exercised the power of search, confiscation and imprisonment without interruption from Parliament, up to its abolition in 1641. From this time the law seems to have been in an unsettled state — although Parliament made some efforts to restrain the licentiousness of the press — until the eighth year of Queen Anne, when the first copyright act was passed, giving authors a monopoly in the publication of their works for a period of from fourteen to twenty-eight years. Notwithstanding this act, however, the chancery courts continued to hold that, by the common law and independently of legislation, there was a property of unlimited duration in printed books. This principle was affirmed so late as 1769 by the Court of King's Bench in the very carefully considered case of *Millar v. Taylor*, 4 Burrows, 2303, in which the right of the author of "Thompson's Seasons," to a monopoly of this work, was asserted and sustained. But a few years thereafter the House of Lords, upon an equal division of the judges, declared that the common law right had been taken away by the statute of Anne, and that authors were limited in their monopoly by that act. *Donaldsons v. Becket*, 4 Burrows, 2408. This remains the law of England to the present day.

An act similar in its provisions to the statute of Anne was enacted by Congress in 1790, and the construction put upon the latter in *Donaldsons v. Becket*, was followed by this court in *Wheaton v. Peters*, 8 Pet. 591. While the propriety of these decisions has been the subject of a good deal of controversy among legal writers, it seems now to be considered the settled law of this country and England that the right of an author to a monopoly of his publications is measured and determined by the copyright act — in other words, that while a right did exist by common law, it has been superseded by statute.

The right thus secured by the copyright act is not a right to the use of certain words, because they are the common property of the human race, and are as little susceptible of private appropriation as air or sunlight; nor is it the right to ideas alone, since in the absence of means of communicating them they are of value to none but the author. But the right is to that arrangement of words which the author has selected to express his ideas. Or, as Lord Mansfield describes it, "an incorporeal right to print a set of intellectual ideas, or modes of thinking, communicated in a set of words or sentences, and modes of expression. It is equally detached from the manuscript, or any other physical existence whatsoever." 4 Burrows, 2396. The nature of this property is perhaps best defined by Mr. Justice Erle in *Jefferys v. Boosey*, 4 H.L.C. 815, 867: "The subject of property is the order of words in the author's composition; not the words themselves, they being analogous to the elements of matter, which are not appropriated unless combined, nor the ideas expressed by those words, they existing in the mind alone, which is not capable of appropriation."

The right of an author to control the publication of his works, at the time the title to the "Autocrat" was deposited, was governed by the act of February 3, 1831, c. 16, 4 Stat. 436, wherein it is enacted:

> SEC. 1. That from and after the passing of this act, any person or persons, being a citizen or citizens of the United States, or resident therein, who shall be the author or authors of a book or books, map, chart or musical composition, which may be now made or composed, and not printed and

> published, or shall hereafter be made or composed, . . . shall have the sole right and liberty of printing, reprinting, publishing and vending such book or books, . . . in whole or in part, for the term of twenty-eight years from the time of recording the title thereof, in the manner hereinafter directed.
>
> SEC. 4. That no person shall be entitled to the benefit of this act, unless he shall, before publication, deposit a printed copy of the title of such book or books . . . in the clerk's office of the District Court of the District wherein the author or proprietor shall reside, etc. And the author and proprietor of any such book . . . shall, within three months from the publication of said book, . . . deliver or cause to be delivered a copy of the same to the clerk of said District.

The substance of these enactments is that, by section one, the author is only entitled to a copyright of books not printed and published; and by section four, that, as a preliminary to the recording of a copyright, he [must], before publication, deposit a printed copy of the title of such book, etc.

The argument of the plaintiff in this connection is, that the publication of the different chapters of the book in the Atlantic Monthly was not a publication of the copyright book which was the subject of the statutory privilege; that if Dr. Holmes had copyrighted and published the twelve parts, one after the other, as they were published in the magazine, or separately, there would still have remained to him an inchoate right, having relation to the book as a whole; that his copyright did not cover and include the publication of the twelve parts printed as they were printed in the Atlantic Monthly, and that while the defendant had a right to make copies of those parts and to sell them separately or collectively, he had no right to combine them into a single volume, since that is the real subject of the copyright.

Counsel further insisted that, if the author had deposited the twelve parts of the book, one after the other, as they were composed, he would not have acquired the statutory privilege to which he seeks to give effect; that to secure such copyright it was essential to do three things: (1) deposit the title "The Autocrat of the Breakfast Table;" (2) deposit a copy of the book "The Autocrat of the Breakfast Table;" and (3) comply with the provisions concerning notice; that he could acquire the privilege of copyright only by depositing a copy of the very book for which he was seeking protection; that if the taking of a copyright for each chapter created a privilege which was less than the privilege which would have been acquired by withholding the manuscript until the book was completed, and then taking the copyright, this copyright is valid. His position briefly if that no one of the twelve copyrights, if each chapter were copyrighted, nor all of them combined, could be held to be a copyright, in the sense of the statute, of the book, which is the subject of the copyright in question; and that neither separately nor collectively could they constitute the particular privilege, which is the subject of the copyright of "The Autocrat of the Breakfast Table," as a whole.

That there was a publication of the contents of the book in question, and of the entire contents, is beyond dispute. It follows from this that defendant might have republished in another magazine these same numbers as they originally appeared in the Atlantic Monthly. He might also, before the copyright was obtained, have published them together, paged them continuously, and bound them in a volume.

Indeed, the learned counsel for the plaintiff admits that the defendant had the right to make copies of these several parts, and to sell them separately or collectively; but insists that he had no right to combine them in a single volume. The distinction between publishing these parts collectively and publishing them in a single volume appears to be somewhat shadowy; but assuming that he had no such right, it must be because the copyright protected the author, not against the republishing of his intellectual productions or "the order of his words," but against the assembling of such productions in a single volume. The argument leads to the conclusion that the whole is greater than the sum of all the parts — a principle inadmissible in logic as well as in mathematics. If the several parts had been once dedicated to the public, and the monopoly of the author thus abandoned, we do not see how it could be reclaimed by collecting such parts together in the form of a book, unless we are to assume that the copyright act covers the process of aggregation as well as that of intellectual production. The contrary is the fact.

If the patent law furnishes any analogy in this particular — and we see no reason why it may not — then there is nothing better settled than that a mere aggregation of familiar elements, producing no new result, is not a patentable combination. But if there were anything more than mechanical skill involved in the collocation of the several parts of this work, it would be the exercise of inventive genius and the subject of a patent rather than a copyright. If an author permit[s] his intellectual production to be published either serially or collectively, his right to a copyright is lost as effectually as the right of an inventor to a patent upon an invention which he deliberately abandons to the public — and this, too, irrespective of his actual intention not to make such abandonment. It is the intellectual production of the author which the copyright protects and not the particular form which such production ultimately takes, and the word "book" as used in the statute is not to be understood in its technical sense of a bound volume, but any species of publication which the author selects to embody his literary product. We are quite unable to appreciate the distinction between the publication of a book and the publication of the contents of such book, whether such contents be published piecemeal or en bloc.

If, as contended by the plaintiff, the publication of a book be a wholly different affair from the publication of the several chapters serially, then such publication of the parts might be permitted to go on indefinitely before a copyright for the book is applied for, and such copyright used to enjoin a sale of books which was perfectly lawful when the books were published. There is no fixed time within which an author must apply for a copyright, so that it be "before publication;" and if the publication of the parts serially be not a publication of the book, a copyright might be obtained after the several parts, whether published separately or collectively, had been in general circulation for years. Surely, this cannot be within the spirit of the act.

We have not overlooked the inconvenience which our conclusions will cause, if, in order to protect their articles from piracy, authors are compelled to copyright each chapter or installment as it may appear in a periodical; nor the danger and annoyance it may occasion to the Librarian of Congress, with whom copyrighted articles are deposited, if he is compelled to receive such articles as they are published in newspapers and magazines; but these are evils which can be easily remedied by an amendment of the law.

The infringement in this case consisted [of] selling copies of the several parts of "The Autocrat of the Breakfast Table" as they were published in the Atlantic Monthly, and each copy so sold was continuously paged so as to form a single volume. Upon its title page appeared a notice that it was taken from the Atlantic Monthly. There can be no doubt that the defendant had the right to publish the numbers separately as they originally appeared in the Atlantic Monthly, (since those numbers were never copyrighted,) even if they were paged continuously. When reduced to its last analysis, then, the infringement consists in binding them together in a single volume. For the reasons above stated, this act is not the legitimate subject of a copyright.

The decree of the court below must therefore be affirmed.

NOTES AND QUESTIONS

1. *Justice Holmes' Role in* Holmes v. Hurst. The appellant in this case, the executor of the estate of Oliver Wendell Holmes, Sr., was Oliver Wendell Holmes, Jr., who was at the time the Chief Justice of the Supreme Judicial Court of Massachusetts. Five years later, the younger Holmes was appointed to the United States Supreme Court. Holmes is apparently the only justice in the Supreme Court's history to have appeared before it as a party to a case. (Several, including both Justices Marshall, appeared before it as lawyers.) Holmes' later views on the right of property in ideas are discussed below.

2. *Congressionally Defined Intellectual Property.* Congressional authority to legislate in the area of intellectual property stems from Article 1, Section 8 of the United States Constitution which provides Congress the power "to promote the Progress of Science and useful arts by securing for limited time to authors and inventors the exclusive right to their respective writings and discoveries." To this end, the first United States Congress enacted copyright and patents acts in 1790. To distinguish between the two acts and their successor statutes, the United States Supreme Court drew a line between expression and ideas in *Baker v. Selden*, 101 U.S. 99 (1879). In a case involving an effort on the part of the developer of a bookkeeping system published in a copyrighted book to prevent a competitor from making use of account books "arranged on substantially the same system," the Court denied the plaintiff's claim that his copyright had been infringed. According to the Court: "The description of the art in a book, though entitled to the benefit of copyright, lays no foundation for an exclusive claim to the art itself. The object of the one is explanation; the object of the other is use. The former may be secured by copyright. The latter can only be secured, if it can be secured at all, by letters-patent." 101 U.S. at 105. The distinction made by the Court in this case has come to be known as the "idea-expression dichotomy."

3. *Copyrights.* Consistent with this distinction, copyrights are awarded for the unique manner of expression of an idea but not for the idea itself. The expression may be by writings, recordings, paintings, sculpture, motion pictures, photographs, computer programs, or even industrial designs. The protection provided to authors extends not just to actual copies but to derivative works as well. Drawing the line between works that are legally derived from other works, as opposed to merely inspired, is often a difficult process. For an example of a case involving derivative

works and computer software (in this case, the legendary computer game, Duke Nukem), see *Micro Star v. Formgen Inc.*, 154 F.3d 1107 (9th Cir. 1998).

Today, most copyright issues are resolved under the congressional Copyright Act of 1976. 17 U.S.C. §§ 101–810, 1101–1110 (1994). The current copyright term is defined as the remaining life of the author plus 70 years. In 1998, Congress extended by 20 years the terms of all copyrights originally acquired before January 1, 1977 (the effective date of the 1976 Act). In *Eldred v. Ashcroft*, 537 U.S. 186 (2003), the United States Supreme Court upheld the right of Congress to adopt such a term extension (which among other effects, extended the lives of the Disney character copyrights). However, the "limited term" language of Article I, Section 8 presumably rules out the possibility of a Congressionally-created perpetual copyright.

Although producers of copyrighted material were once required to register their copyrights with the United States Copyright Office, they are no longer required to do so. (There are nevertheless very real advantages to registration.) The application of the current act is discussed in *National Basketball Ass'n v. Motorola*, below.

4. *Fair Use.* Even though an individual may "own" a valid copyright, not all uses by others can be prohibited. The right of "fair use" entitles a third party to use a copyrighted work without the copyright holder's consent so long as the use is "reasonable." The right of fair use was first recognized by an American court in 1841 in *Folsom v. Marsh*, 9 F. Cas. 342 (C.C.D. Mass. 1841), and was incorporated in the Copyright Act of 1976. 17 U.S. Code § 107. What constitutes a "fair use" has been the source of endless litigation. While it is generally acknowledged that copyrighted material can fairly be used without permission for criticism, comment, news reporting, teaching, scholarship, and research, the boundary lines between fair and unfair uses is anything but clear. For a recent, highly publicized case involving a finding that the sharing of digital copies of copyrighted music through an Internet service was not a fair use, see *A & M Records, Inc. v. Napster, Inc.*, 239 F.3d 1004 (9th Cir. 2001). Why should a copyright be subject to a fair use limitation when other forms of property are not? Why shouldn't other users be required to obtain the copyright holder's permission in all cases?

5. *Patents.* To be patented, an invention must have social utility, must be novel, and must show "invention." Patents are granted for processes, machines, and substances, but not merely for ideas. For example, in the classic case of *O'Reilly v. Morse*, 56 U.S. 62 (1853), Samuel Morse was permitted a patent for his inventions that made possible the development of the telegraph, but his request that he be granted a patent for the general use of electromagnetism was denied. The Patent Act of 1952, modified by numerous amendments, provides the foundation for modern patent law. 35 U.S.C. §§ 1–376 (1994). Both patents and copyrights grant their holders a monopoly over the protected property for a specific period of time. Although under some circumstances, the patent and copyright may be renewed, once the period of time expires, the product or literary effort passes into the public domain and may be used by anyone.

6. *Other Forms of Intellectual Property.* Intellectual property also includes trademarks, trade dress, and trade secrets (discussed above). Unlike the case with patents and copyrights, which are granted to encourage particular types of creative activities, trademark and trade dress statutes (the most important of which is the

Lanham Act, 15 U.S.C. §§ 1051–1127) are designed to protect consumers against sellers pretending to be something they are not. Trade secret laws are laws that prohibit the misappropriation of confidential information. For a case illustrating the complexity of modern trademark law, see *Two Pesos, Inc. v. Taco Cabana, Inc.*, 505 U.S. 763 (1992), in which the Supreme Court upheld a lower court finding that the specific decor of a chain of Mexican restaurants was protected by the Trademark Act of 1946 (the Lanham Act).

Some states provide property status to aspects of intellectual property not protected by federal law. In *Golding v. R.K.O. Pictures, Inc.*, 221 P.2d 95 (Cal. 1950), the California Supreme Court, while denying that there could be property in an idea not reduced to concrete form, found that an author had a property interest in the "basic dramatic core" of a literary work apart from any copyright protection the right might enjoy. Is this in fact a recognition of a property right in an idea? Three years later, the same court concluded that a revision of § 980 of the California Code of Civil Procedure, which pertained to the protection of literary works, had eliminated this protection. *Weitzenkorn v. Lesser*, 256 P.2d 947 (Cal. 1953). At least one New York court has acknowledged that under certain circumstances there could be a protected property interest in the spoken word. *Hemingway v. Random House, Inc.*, 244 N.E.2d 250 (N.Y. Ct. App. 1968).

7. *Why Is There No Property Right in an Idea?* Although it appears that Hurst has done nothing wrong under the existing copyright act, should the Supreme Court have recognized a common law property right in the work at issue in the above case? What harm would be done if Holmes were permitted to prevail in this case? Is there any question that the senior Holmes was the author of the literary work at issue? Why shouldn't his estate continue to reap the benefits of his efforts? Is an author's right to his written work really like a patent as Justice Brown suggests? Is there a chance that someone else might independently write "The Autocrat at the Breakfast Table"?

8. *The Concept of the Author's Moral Rights.* Most European legal systems recognize an author's or artist's "moral right" to his or her work separate and apart from any copyright claim that he might possess. This right guarantees that the producer of the work of art will receive credit for the work and will be protected against false attribution even if he or she gives up all rights to the work. It further guarantees that the work will not be distorted or destroyed after it leaves the creator's control. The moral right lasts at least for the life of the author and in most instances for a number of years after his or her death. In France, the moral right is perpetual. In the United States, the owner of a work of art of great value is free to destroy it if he chooses to do so. Does it make sense to define the right of private property in such a way that it gives the owner the power to destroy objects of great cultural significance?

[4.] News and Its Presentation

A NOTE ON *INTERNATIONAL NEWS SERVICE v. ASSOCIATED PRESS*

International News Service v. Associated Press, 248 U.S. 215 (1918), is one of the most thoroughly studied property cases in American history. In 1916, the International News Service (or INS), one of two major American newswire services — the other was the Associated Press (or AP) — was barred from sending cables back to the United States from England and other western European countries because of its failure to comply with guidelines imposed by British government censors. To compensate, INS began to obtain information covertly from the AP. In addition to secretly buying news from an employee of an AP newspaper in Cleveland, INS had taken news from public bulletin boards outside the AP office in New York and from early editions of East Coast newspapers who subscribed to the AP service. This news was then transmitted to INS' western clients without any indication as to its source. AP filed suit in federal court requesting a restraining order on the grounds that INS was "pirating" its property.[11] Both parties agreed that news was not protected by the copyright laws of the United States. (This story is told, albeit from the perspective of a long-time employee of the Associated Press, in O. GRAMLING, AP: THE STORY OF THE NEWS (1940).)

In his opinion for the Court, Justice Mahlon Pitney observed near the outset, "We need spend no time, however, upon the general question of property in news matter at common law, or the application of the copyright act, since it seems to us the case must turn upon the question of unfair competition in business." In concluding that INS' actions did constitute unfair competition, Pitney maintained that while AP *may* not have had a property right in its news against the public generally once it was published, it continued to have at least a "quasi property" right against a competitor such as INS. According to Pitney:

> The right of the purchaser of a single newspaper to spread knowledge of its contents gratuitously, for any legitimate purpose not unreasonably interfering with complainant's right to make merchandise of it, may be admitted; but to transmit that news for commercial use, in competition with complainant — which is what defendant has done and seeks to justify — is a very different matter.

Consequently, Pitney concluded, the actions of INS constituted unfair competition in business and the order of the lower court enjoining INS from taking the words or substance of AP's news was affirmed.

Justice Oliver Wendell Holmes, Jr., the official plaintiff in *Holmes v. Hurst*, concurred in the result. However, he disagreed with Pitney's "quasi property"

[11] In its bill of complaint, the Associated Press also accused the defendant of bribing and otherwise inducing the employees of Associated Press-member newspapers to reveal news to it prior to publication. However, the only issue argued before the Supreme Court pertained to the news taken from the bulletin boards and already published newspapers.

analysis and found instead that the unfair trade violation came in the failure of INS to reveal the source of its news. Holmes concluded his concurring opinion with the observation: "I think that within the limits recognized by the decision of the Court the defendant should be enjoined from publishing news obtained from the Associated Press for ______ [blank to be filled in] hours after publication by the plaintiff unless it gives express credit to the Associated Press; the number of hours and the form of acknowledgment to be settled by the District Court." In other words, had INS simply credited AP as the source of its information, Holmes would have found nothing illegal about its conduct.

Only Justice Louis Brandeis dissented. He argued that competition was "not unfair in a legal sense merely because the profits gained are unearned" and that in many situations the law actually encouraged others to seek profits "due largely to the labor and expense of the first adventurer." Moreover, he found nothing objectionable about the way in which INS obtained news gathered by the Associated Press. More importantly, Brandeis was uncomfortable with the idea that the Supreme Court should recognize a new private right in news, even one as qualified as Justice Pitney's "quasi property right." As Brandeis put it, "Courts are ill-equipped to make the investigations which should precede a determination of the limitations which should be set upon any property right in news or of the circumstances under which news gathered by a private agency should be deemed affected with a public interest. . . . Considerations such as these should lead us to decline to establish a new rule of law in the effort to redress a newly-disclosed wrong, although the propriety of some remedy appears to be clear."

The Court's decision actually did little to clarify the situation with news. The appearance of radio, and later television, only intensified the conflict at issue in *INS v. AP*. In their infancy, radio stations often satisfied their listeners' interest in the news by reading the day's newspapers over the air, sometimes identifying the source of the information and other times, not. In 1935, the Associated Press obtained an injunction against Bellingham, Washington, radio station KVOS for engaging in just such a practice. *Associated Press v. KVOS, Inc.*, 80 F.2d 575 (9th Cir. 1935), *rev'd on other grounds*, *KVOS, Inc. v. Associated Press*, 299 U.S. 269 (1936). As the following case demonstrates, eight decades after the decision in *INS v. AP*, key questions pertaining to the ownership of newsworthy information remained unresolved (and to some extent still are.)

NATIONAL BASKETBALL ASS'N v. MOTOROLA

United States Circuit Court of Appeals, Second Circuit
105 F.3d 841 (1997)

WINTER, CIRCUIT JUDGE.

Motorola, Inc. and Sports Team Analysis and Tracking Systems ("STATS") appeal from a permanent injunction entered by Judge Preska [of the United States District Court for the Southern District of New York]. The injunction concerns a handheld pager sold by Motorola and marketed under the name "SportsTrax," which displays updated information of professional basketball games in progress. The injunction prohibits appellants, absent authorization from the National Basketball Association and NBA Properties, Inc. (collectively the "NBA"), from transmitting scores or other data about NBA games in progress via the pagers, STATS's site on America On-Line's computer dial-up service, or "any equivalent means."

The crux of the dispute concerns the extent to which a state law "hot-news" misappropriation claim based on *International News Service v. Associated Press*, 248 U.S. 215 (1918) ("*INS*"), survives preemption by the federal Copyright Act and whether the NBA's claim fits within the surviving *INS*-type claims. We hold that a narrow "hot-news" exception does survive preemption. However, we also hold that appellants' transmission of "real-time" NBA game scores and information tabulated from television and radio broadcasts of games in progress does not constitute a misappropriation of "hot news" that is the property of the NBA.

The facts are largely undisputed. Motorola manufactures and markets the SportsTrax paging device while STATS supplies the game information that is transmitted to the pagers. The product became available to the public in January 1996, at a retail price of about $200. SportsTrax's pager has an inch-and-a-half by inch-and-a-half screen and operates in four basic modes: "current," "statistics," "final scores" and "demonstration." It is the "current" mode that gives rise to the present dispute. In that mode, SportsTrax displays the following information on NBA games in progress: (i) the teams playing; (ii) score changes; (iii) the team in possession of the ball; (iv) whether the team is in the free-throw bonus; (v) the quarter of the game; and (vi) time remaining in the quarter. The information is updated every two to three minutes, with more frequent updates near the end of the first half and the end of the game. There is a lag of approximately two or three minutes between events in the game itself and when the information appears on the pager screen.

SportsTrax's operation relies on a "data feed" supplied by STATS reporters who watch the games on television or listen to them on the radio. The reporters key into a personal computer changes in the score and other information such as successful and missed shots, fouls, and clock updates. The information is relayed by modem to STATS's host computer, which compiles, analyzes, and formats the data for retransmission. The information is then sent to a common carrier, which then sends it via satellite to various local FM radio networks that in turn emit the signal received by the individual SportsTrax pagers.

The issues before us are ones that have arisen in various forms over the course of this century as technology has steadily increased the speed and quantity of information transmission. Today, individuals at home, at work, or elsewhere, can use a computer, pager, or other device to obtain highly selective kinds of information virtually at will. *International News Service v. Associated Press*, 248 U.S. 215 (1918) ("*INS*") was one of the first cases to address the issues raised by these technological advances, although the technology involved in that case was primitive by contemporary standards. *INS* involved two wire services, the Associated Press ("AP") and International News Service ("INS"), that transmitted news stories by wire to member newspapers. *Id.* INS would lift factual stories from AP bulletins and send them by wire to INS papers. *Id.* at 231. INS would also take factual stories from east coast AP papers and wire them to INS papers on the west coast that had yet to publish because of time differentials. *Id.* at 238. The Supreme Court held that INS's conduct was a common-law misappropriation of AP's property. *Id.* at 242.

With the advance of technology, radio stations began "live" broadcasts of events such as baseball games and operas, and various entrepreneurs began to use the transmissions of others in one way or another for their own profit. In response, New York courts created a body of misappropriation law, loosely based on *INS*, that sought to apply ethical standards to the use by one party of another's transmissions of events.

Federal copyright law played little active role in this area until 1976. Before then, it appears to have been the general understanding — there being no case law of consequence — that live events such as baseball games were not copyrightable. Moreover, doubt existed even as to whether a recorded broadcast or videotape of such an event was copyrightable. In 1976, however, Congress passed legislation expressly affording copyright protection to simultaneously-recorded broadcasts of live performances such as sports events. *See* 17 U.S.C. § 101. Such protection was not extended to the underlying events.

The 1976 amendments also contained provisions preempting state law claims that enforced rights "equivalent" to exclusive copyright protections when the work to which the state claim was being applied fell within the area of copyright protection. *See* 17 U.S.C. § 301. Based on legislative history of the 1976 amendments, it is generally agreed that a "hot-news" *INS*-like claim survives preemption. H.R. No. 94-1476 at 132 (1976), *reprinted in* 1976 U.S.C.C.A.N. 5659, 5748. However, much of New York misappropriation law after *INS* goes well beyond "hot-news" claims and is preempted.

We hold that the surviving "hot-news" *INS*-like claim is limited to cases where: (i) a plaintiff generates or gathers information at a cost; (ii) the information is time-sensitive; (iii) a defendant's use of the information constitutes free-riding on the plaintiff's efforts; (iv) the defendant is in direct competition with a product or service offered by the plaintiffs; and (v) the ability of other parties to free-ride on the efforts of the plaintiff or others would so reduce the incentive to produce the product or service that its existence or quality would be substantially threatened. We conclude that SportsTrax does not meet that test.

Sports events are not "authored" in any common sense of the word. There is, of course, at least at the professional level, considerable preparation for a game. However, the preparation is as much an expression of hope or faith as a determination of what will actually happen. Unlike movies, plays, television programs, or operas, athletic events are competitive and have no underlying script. Preparation may even cause mistakes to succeed, like the broken play in football that gains yardage because the opposition could not expect it. Athletic events may also result in wholly unanticipated occurrences, the most notable recent event being in a championship baseball game in which interference with a fly ball caused an umpire to signal erroneously a home run.

What "authorship" there is in a sports event, moreover, must be open to copying by competitors if fans are to be attracted. If the inventor of the T-formation in football had been able to copyright it, the sport might have come to an end instead of prospering. Even where athletic preparation most resembles authorship — figure skating, gymnastics, and, some would uncharitably say, professional wrestling — a performer who conceives and executes a particularly graceful and difficult — or, in the case of wrestling, seemingly painful — acrobatic feat cannot copyright it without impairing the underlying competition in the future. A claim of being the only athlete to perform a feat doesn't mean much if no one else is allowed to try.

Concededly, case law is scarce on the issue of whether organized events themselves are copyrightable, but what there is indicates that they are not. *See Production Contractors, Inc. v. WGN Continental Broadcasting Co.*, 622 F. Supp. 1500 (N.D. Ill. 1985) (Christmas parade is not a work of authorship entitled to copyright protection).

[The court then concluded that New York misappropriation law, which was considerably broader than that embraced by the United States Supreme Court in *INS*, had been preempted by the Copyright Act of 1976 and that it was therefore an error for the district court to rely on this standard in finding for the plaintiffs.] Our conclusion, therefore, is that only a narrow "hot-news" misappropriation claim survives preemption for actions concerning material within the realm of copyright.

INS is not about ethics; it is about the protection of property rights in time-sensitive information so that the information will be made available to the public by profit-seeking entrepreneurs. If services like AP were not assured of property rights in the news they pay to collect, they would cease to collect it. The ability of their competitors to appropriate their product at only nominal cost and thereby to disseminate a competing product at a lower price would destroy the incentive to collect news in the first place. The newspaper-reading public would suffer because no one would have an incentive to collect "hot news."

We therefore find the extra elements — those in addition to the elements of copyright infringement — that allow a "hot news" claim to survive preemption are: (i) the time-sensitive value of factual information, (ii) the free-riding by a defendant, and (iii) the threat to the very existence of the product or service provided by the plaintiff.

We conclude that Motorola and STATS have not engaged in unlawful misappropriation under the "hot-news" test set out above. To be sure, some of the elements of a "hot-news" *INS* claim are met. The information transmitted to SportsTrax is not precisely contemporaneous, but it is nevertheless time-sensitive. Also, the NBA does provide, or will shortly do so, information like that available through SportsTrax. It now offers a service called "Gamestats" that provides official play-by-play game sheets and half-time and final box scores within each arena. It also provides such information to the media in each arena. In the future, the NBA plans to enhance Gamestats so that it will be networked between the various arenas and will support a pager product analogous to SportsTrax. SportsTrax will of course directly compete with an enhanced Gamestats.

However, there are critical elements missing in the NBA's attempt to assert a "hot-news" *INS*-type claim. As framed by the NBA, their claim compresses and confuses three different informational products. The first product is generating the information by playing the games; the second product is transmitting live, full descriptions of those games; and the third product is collecting and retransmitting strictly factual information about the games. The first and second products are the NBA's primary business: producing basketball games for live attendance and licensing copyrighted broadcasts of those games. The collection and retransmission of strictly factual material about the games is a different product: e.g., box-scores in newspapers, summaries of statistics on television sports news, and real-time facts to be transmitted to pagers. In our view, the NBA has failed to show any competitive effect whatsoever from SportsTrax on the first and second products and a lack of any free-riding by SportsTrax on the third.

With regard to the NBA's primary products — producing basketball games with live attendance and licensing copyrighted broadcasts of those games — there is no evidence that anyone regards SportsTrax as a substitute for attending NBA games or watching them on television. In fact, Motorola markets SportsTrax as being designed "for those times when you cannot be at the arena, watch the game on TV, or listen to the radio . . . ."

The NBA argues that the pager market is also relevant to a "hot-news" *INS*-type claim and that SportsTrax's future competition with Gamestats satisfies any missing element. We agree that there is a separate market for the real-time transmission of factual information to pagers or similar devices. However, we disagree that SportsTrax is in any sense free-riding off Gamestats.

An indispensable element of an *INS* "hot-news" claim is free-riding by a defendant on a plaintiff's product, enabling the defendant to produce a directly competitive product for less money because it has lower costs. SportsTrax is not such a product. The use of pagers to transmit real-time information about NBA games requires: (i) the collecting of facts about the games; (ii) the transmission of these facts on a network; (iii) the assembling of them by the particular service; and (iv) the transmission of them to pagers or an on-line computer site. Appellants are in no way free-riding on Gamestats. Motorola and STATS expend their own resources to collect purely factual information generated in NBA games to transmit to SportsTrax pagers. They have their own network and assemble and transmit data themselves.

To be sure, if appellants in the future were to collect facts from an enhanced Gamestats pager to retransmit them to SportsTrax pagers, that would constitute free-riding and might well cause Gamestats to be unprofitable because it had to bear costs to collect facts that SportsTrax did not. However, that is not the case in the instant matter. SportsTrax and Gamestats are each bearing their own costs of collecting factual information on NBA games, and, if one produces a product that is cheaper or otherwise superior to the other, that producer will prevail in the marketplace. This is obviously not the situation against which *INS* was intended to prevent: the potential lack of any such product or service because of the anticipation of free-riding. For the foregoing reasons, the NBA has not shown any damage to any of its products based on free-riding by Motorola and STATS, and the NBA's misappropriation claim based on New York law is preempted.

NOTES AND QUESTIONS

1. *Similarities Between* NBA v. Motorola *and* INS v. AP. When Judge Winter describes the case as holding that "INS's conduct was a common-law misappropriation of AP's property," he may be over simplifying Justice Pitney's holding. Some have read the majority opinion in that case as avoiding the issue of whether the AP's interest in its news can properly be labeled "property." Others have credited Justice Pitney with a sophisticated understanding of the term "property" and suggest that his opinion represents a belief that property can only be defined in terms of the rights that one party can exercise against another. Does it really matter whether or not we describe the relationship of AP and its news (or the NBA and the content of its games) as property?

2. *Federal Preemption of State Law.* The concept of preemption, to which much of the Second Circuit's opinion is devoted (although omitted above), is rooted in the Supremacy Clause of the United States Constitution (Art. VI, cl. 2) which negates state laws that conflict with properly enacted federal legislation. But for the Copyright Act of 1976, the NBA would have prevailed in this case, at least in the state of New York. But it is important to realize that New York has consciously chosen to provide additional protection to parties like the NBA in this case through its law of misappropriation.

3. *The Property Value of Sports Scores in Ongoing Games.* Although the existence of the Internet and cell phones have accustomed modern Americans to expectations of real time information, the rights of leagues and team owners to control the publicity surrounding sporting events has been a recurring issue in the history of American sport. In 1876, the first year of operation of the National Baseball League, the league's Hartford Blues adopted a rule barring newspaper reporters from transmitting inning by inning scores back to their newsrooms where they were regularly posted on public bulletin boards. This decision prompted the *Chicago Tribune* to observe, "One of the stupidest ideas that ever entered into the head of base-ball managers is the new arrangement on the Hartford grounds, by which they refuse to permit the transmission of any report of the game by innings. As the 'Courant' [Hartford's leading newspaper] well says, those who have been visitors to the bulletins are those who have an interest in the game, which is kept alive by their opportunity of watching the board, and the increased interest they have had has made them visitors to the games when a game of special interest has been played, or when they could get away from their business to attend. Not to continue the score by innings is to remove a very excellent and cheap feature of advertising, and, in a money way, to cause a loss to the ball manager." CHI. TRIB., June 8, 1876.

Reported courts cases involving similar issues (and similarly primitive technology) include *Detroit Baseball Club v. Deppart*, 27 N.W. 856 (Mich. 1886), where the court refused to enjoin a neighboring property owner from selling seats on the roof of his barn overlooking baseball field to view the home games of the Detroit Wolverines of the National League; *Pittsburgh Athletic Co. v. KQV Broadcasting Co.*, 24 F. Supp. 490 (W.D. Pa. 1938), where a radio station was enjoined from using individuals positioned outside of Forbes Field with a view of the field to broadcast play-by-play accounts of Pittsburgh Pirate games; and *National*

Exhibition Co. v. Fass, 143 N.Y.S.2d 767 (Sup. Ct. 1955), where a teletype operator was enjoined from sending play-by-play information from New York Giants baseball broadcasts to competing radio stations for immediate rebroadcast. In an apparent replay of the *Deppart* case more than a century later, the Chicago Cubs baseball team filed suit in December 2002 against the owners of nine buildings adjacent to Wrigley Field (the Cubs' home ballpark), claiming that the building owners had unlawfully allowed individuals, for a fee, to watch Cub games from the rooftops of the buildings. N.Y. TIMES, Dec. 17, 2002, at C20. This case, and others like it, were eventually settled with the roof top owners agreeing to pay the Cubs part of their profits.

[5.] Property Rights in Cyberspace

It is often said that a lawyer's time is his stock in trade. However, the question of whether time itself can be treated as an item of property is an extremely complex one, as the following case illustrates.

LUND v. COMMONWEALTH

Virginia Supreme Court
232 S.E.2d 745 (1977)

I'ANSON, C.J., delivered the opinion of the court.

Defendant, Charles Walter Lund, was charged in an indictment with the theft of keys, computer cards, computer print-outs and using "without authority computer operation time and services of Computer Center Personnel at Virginia Polytechnic Institute and State University [V.P.I. or University] with intent to defraud, such property and services having a value of one hundred dollars or more." Code §§ 18.1-100 and 18.1-118 were referred to in the indictment as the applicable statutes. Defendant pleaded not guilty and waived trial by jury. He was found guilty of grand larceny and sentenced to two years in the State penitentiary. The sentence was suspended, and defendant was placed on probation for five years.

Defendant was a graduate student in statistics and a candidate for a Ph.D. degree at V.P.I. The preparation of his dissertation on the subject assigned to him by his faculty advisor required the use of computer operation time and services of the computer center personnel at the University. His faculty advisor neglected to arrange for defendant's use of the computer, but defendant used it without obtaining the proper authorization.

The computer used by the defendant was leased on an annual basis by V.P.I. from the IBM Corporation. The rental was paid by V.P.I. which allocates the cost of the computer center to various departments within the University by charging it to the budget of that department. This is a bookkeeping entry, and no money actually changes hands. The departments are allocated "computer credits [in dollars] back for their use [on] a proportional basis of their [budgetary] allotments." Each department manager receives a monthly statement showing the allotments used and the running balance in each account of his department.

An account is established when a duly authorized administrator or "department head" fills out a form allocating funds to a department of the University and an individual. When such form is received, the computer center assigns an account number to this allocation and provides a key to a locked post office box which is also numbered to the authorized individual and department. The account number and the post office box number are the access code which must be provided with each request before the computer will process a "deck of cards" prepared by the user and delivered to computer center personnel. The computer print-outs are usually returned to the locked post office box. When the product is too large for the box, a "check" is placed in the box, and it is used to receive the print-outs at the "computer center main window."

Defendant came under surveillance on October 12, 1974, because of complaints from various departments that unauthorized charges were being made to one or more of their accounts. When confronted by the University's investigator, defendant initially denied that he had used the computer service, but later admitted that he had. He gave to the investigator seven keys for boxes assigned to other persons. One of these keys was secreted in his sock. He told the investigating officer he had been given the keys by another student. A large number of computer cards and print-outs were taken from defendant's apartment.

The director of the computer center testified that the unauthorized sum spent out of the accounts associated with the seven post office box keys, amounted to $5,065. He estimated that on the basis of the computer cards and print-outs obtained from the defendant, as much as $26,384.16 in unauthorized computer time had been used by the defendant. He said, however, that the value of the cards and print-outs obtained from the defendant was "whatever scrap paper is worth."

Defendant testified that he used the computer without specific authority. He stated that he knew he was a large computer user, but, because he was doing work on his doctoral dissertation, he did not consider this use excessive or that "he was doing anything wrong."

Four faculty members testified in defendant's behalf. They all agreed that computer time "probably would have been" or "would have been" assigned to defendant if properly requested. Dr. Hinkleman, who replaced defendant's first advisor, testified that the computer time was essential for the defendant to carry out his assignment. He assumed that a sufficient number of computer hours had been arranged by Lund's prior faculty advisor.

The head of the statistics department, at the time of the trial, agreed with the testimony of the faculty members that Lund would have been assigned computer time if properly requested. He also testified that the committee which recommended the awarding of degrees was aware of the charges pending against defendant when he was awarded his doctorate by the University.

The defendant contends that his conviction of grand larceny of the keys, computer cards, and computer print-outs cannot be upheld under the provisions of Code § 18.1-100 because (1) there was no evidence that the articles were stolen, or that they had a value of $100 or more, and (2) computer time and services are not the subject of larceny under the provisions of Code §§ 18.1-100 or 18.1-118.

Code § 18.1-100 (now § 18.2-95) provides as follows: "Any person who: (1)

Commits larceny from the person of another of money or other thing of value of five dollars or more, or (2) Commits simple larceny not from the person of another of goods and chattels of the value of one hundred dollars or more, shall be deemed guilty of grand larceny . . . ."

Section 18.1-118 (now § 18.2-178) provides as follows: "If any person obtain, by any false pretense or token, from any person, with intent to defraud, money or other property which may be the subject of larceny, he shall be deemed guilty of larceny thereof; . . . ."

The Commonwealth concedes that the defendant could not be convicted of grand larceny of the keys and computer cards because there was no evidence that those articles were stolen and that they had a market value of $100 or more. The Commonwealth argues, however, that the evidence shows the defendant violated the provisions of § 18.1-118 when he obtained by false pretense or token, with intent to defraud, the computer print-outs which had a value of over $5,000.

Under the provisions of Code § 18.1-118, for one to be guilty of the crime of larceny by false pretense, he must make a false representation of an existing fact with knowledge of its falsity and, on that basis, obtain from another person money or other property which may be the subject of larceny, with the intent to defraud.

At common law, larceny is the taking and carrying away of the goods and chattels of another with intent to deprive the owner of the possession thereof permanently. Code § 18.1-100 defines grand larceny as a taking from the person of another money or other thing of value of five dollars or more, or the taking not from the person of another goods and chattels of the value of $100 or more. The phrase "goods and chattels" cannot be interpreted to include computer time and services in light of the often repeated mandate that criminal statutes must be strictly construed.

At common law, labor or services could not be the subject of the crime of false pretense because neither time nor services may be taken and carried away. It has been generally held that, in the absence of a clearly expressed legislative intent, labor or services could not be the subject of the statutory crime of false pretense. Some jurisdictions have amended their criminal codes specifically to make it a crime to obtain labor or services by means of false pretense. E.g., New York Penal Code § 165.15; New Jersey Penal Code ch. 2A:111; and California Criminal Code § 322. We have no such provision in our statutes.

Furthermore, the unauthorized use of the computer is not the subject of larceny. Nowhere in Code § 18.1-100 or § 18.1-118 do we find the word "use." The language of the statutes connotes more than just the unauthorized use of the property of another. It refers to a taking and carrying away of a certain concrete article of personal property. We hold that labor and services and the unauthorized use of the University's computer cannot be construed to be subjects of larceny under the provisions of Code §§ 18.1-100 and 18.1-118. For the reasons stated, the judgment of the trial court is reversed, and the indictment is quashed.

Labor and time cannot be subject of larceny because they cannot be taken and carried away.

NOTES AND QUESTIONS

1. *Computer Time as a Commodity.* The Virginia statute defines grand larceny as the theft of "goods and chattels of the value of one hundred dollars or more." Why wasn't more than $20,000 worth of computer time a "good" or "chattel"? Given the date of this case (1977), is it possible that the justices of the Virginia Supreme Court were simply too unfamiliar with computers to grasp the nature of the commodity at issue in this case?

In *People v. Ashworth*, 220 A.D. 498 (N.Y. App. Div. 1927), a New York court held that the unauthorized use of machinery and spinning facilities of another to process wool did not constitute larceny under New York's false pretense statute (which was similar to the Virginia statute quoted in *Lund*). Is the unauthorized use of a computer any different than the unauthorized use of a loom or a piano? Or is it possible to think of computer time as a commodity separate and apart from the time spent using the computer? Is taking "time" out of a computer like taking oil out of a well? Does the fact that the new oil rushes into the well to replace what is removed make the unauthorized removal of the oil any less larcenous?

2. *Resolving the Problem.* Most jurisdictions have solved the problem posed by the *Lund* case by simply enacting a new statute defining the unauthorized use of a computer as a crime with penalties comparable to larceny. At its next session following the announcement of the *Lund* decision, the Virginia legislature amended the state's larceny statute with the following provision:

> Va. Code. Ann. § 18.2-98.1. Computer time, services, subject of larceny. — Computer time or services or data processing services or information or data stored in connection therewith is hereby defined to be property which may be the subject of larceny under §§ 18.2-95 or 18.2-96, or embezzlement under § 18.2-111, or false pretenses under § 18.2-178.

1978 Va. Acts ch. 1120.

Does this decision to reverse the *Lund* holding by legislation reflect the Virginia legislature's view that the state supreme court incorrectly interpreted the existing law, or did the legislature intend to recognize a new form of property with this statute?

3. *Trespass in Cyberspace.* With the growth of access to the Internet and its increasing commercialization in the 1980s and 1990s, many questions arose in regard to the meaning of property and property rights in an electronic medium. Although the legal issues in cyberspace seemed to many to be similar to those in the physical world, the way in which information is disseminated on-line has made the application of traditional legal principles especially troublesome. (As the court noted in *ImOn, Inc. v. ImaginOn, Inc.*, 90 F. Supp. 2d 345, 350, (S.D.N.Y. 2000), the Internet is "one of the most fluid, rapidly developing, and virtually daily changing areas of commerce that the law has had to focus upon and endeavor to apply established principles to.")

Disputes involving the non-permissive access to computers are a regular feature of modern Internet litigation. Today, it is usually another computer that is "improperly" gaining access to a host computer. Such cases are normally deemed to be about trespass (unlawful presence on or use of the property of another) rather than conversion (the unlawful taking of another's property). Although it would appear that most cases of this nature would be treated as trespasses to chattels (the other computer), in many ways the more apt comparison is trespass on land. The latter approach is particularly important because it allows for the remedy of injunctive relief. In *eBay, Inc. v. Bidder's Edge, Inc.*, 100 F. Supp. 2d 1058 (N.D. Cal. 2000), defendant's computer bots were programmed to crawl eBay's auction website for the purpose of using e-Bay's data, with data from other auction websites, to yield a larger aggregate auction website. In its analysis the court rejected conversion (i.e., unlawful taking of property) analogies, and applied trespass to chattels principles instead. For a comprehensive effort to sort out the subject matter of property rights in cyberspace, see Hylton, *Property Rules, Liability Rules, and Immunity: An Application to Cyberspace*, 87 B.U. L. REV. 1 (2007).

4. *Parceling Out the Internet Domain.* An early example of the difficulty of applying traditional property concepts to the Internet was the controversy in the early and mid-1990's concerning the ownership of Internet domain names. In May of 1993, an anticipated increase in private sector demand for domain addresses led the National Science Foundation to "privatize" the name acquisition process by authorizing Network Solutions, Inc., a Herndon, Virginia-based private company to administer the process. Initially, domain names were assigned by Network Solutions on a first come, first serve basis. Applicants paid an initial fee of $100 and were assessed an annual fee of $50 to maintain their rights to the name. Once a name was acquired, it could be used or sold at the discretion of the name-holder.

Certain individuals, anticipating that the Internet would grow in importance, early on acquired domain names that were unrelated to their business but which included either the trade name of another business or a trademark registered to it. Called "prospectors" or "cyber-squatters," these individuals registered domain names in hopes of selling them for a substantial profit. One of the leaders of the cyber-squatters, Dennis Toeppen, registered more than 240 well-known names including www.aircanada.com, www.anaheimstadium.com, www.australia.com, www.camdenyards.com, www.deltaairlines.com, www.eddiebauer.com, www.lufthansa.com, www.nieman-marcus.com, www.ussteel.com, and www.yankeestadium.com, without having any connection to any of the companies identified by the domain name. Toeppen typically charged between $5,000 and $13,000 to relinquish the names he registered. *See The Internet's Gatekeeper May Cash In on Its Role*, N.Y. TIMES, Sept. 12, 1996, at A1; *What Are Your Rights to an Internet Domain Name?*, N.Y. TIMES, Sept. 12, 1996, at A1; THE METROPOLITAN CORPORATE COUNSEL, Mar. 1997. While many companies hoping to establish an Internet site simply purchased the domain address from its holder, others filed suit against the registrant of the address, alleging trademark infringement. See, for example, *MTV Networks v. Curry*, 867 F. Supp. 202 (S.D.N.Y. 1994), which involved Curry's acquisition of the address "www.mtv.com."

In July 1995, Network Solutions announced that it would suspend use of a domain name if the first individual to register refused to relinquish it to the company that owns the trademark. WALL ST. J., July 27, 1995, B14. Congress has also addressed the process of divesting a cyber-squatter of his rights to a registered address in the Federal Trademark Dilution Act of 1995, which relieves trademark holders of any obligation to show either competition between themselves and the parties holding rights to the domain address or the likelihood of confusion if both parties were to use the mark. Section 43(c) of the Lanham Act had previously required such a showing. After the passage of the act, Dennis Toeppen was ordered to give up domain names by federal courts in California and his home state of Illinois. In 1999, Congress went even further with the Anticybersquatting Consumer Protection Act which was signed into law by President Clinton on November 29, 1999. The Act was designed to "protect" the public from the "bad faith, abusive registration of Internet domain names." The Act directed the Secretary of Commerce to recommend to Congress appropriate "guidelines and procedures for resolving disputes involving the registration or use by a person of a domain name that includes the personal name of another person, in whole or in part, or a name confusingly similar thereto." 15 U.S.C. §§ 1051, 1114, 1116.

How should the United States government have disposed of these valuable pieces of property? Should there have been a lesson to be learned from the experience with the transfer of the public lands into private hands, discussed above in the notes following *Plume v. Seward & Thompson*?

5. *Contrasting Views on the Ownership of Intangibles.* Are the problems presented by cases like *Presley v. Crowell, INS v. AP, NBA v. Motorola*, and *Lund v. Virginia* the result of the view of the American legal system that there can be such a thing as "property" in an intangible entity? Western European legal systems based on Roman law limit the term "ownership" to tangible things. English and American law, in contrast, recognize a wide variety of intangible interests as property. Whereas debts, mortgages, franchises, shares in companies, patents, and copyrights are viewed merely as causes of action in continental law, the Anglo-American legal system has no problem characterizing these interests as property even though such a characterization automatically invokes all the legal and constitutional protections associated with that legal category. Are publicity rights, news, and computer time any different than these other intangible items of property? Would we be better off if we restricted the term "property" to tangible objects?

6. *What Is Property?* In 1937, economist Walter Hamilton defined "property" as "a euphonious collection of letters which serves as a general term for the miscellany of equities that persons hold in the commonwealth." 11 ENCYCLOPEDIA OF THE SOCIAL SCIENCES 528 (1937 ed.). One could argue that Hamilton was simply restating the American statesman Henry Clay's observation of a century earlier: "That is property which the law declares to be property." 8 THE WORKS OF HENRY CLAY 152 (Colton ed., 1904). In light of the cases in this chapter, is it possible to improve on this definition? For an early 20th century effort to do so, see Mossof, *What Is Property? Putting the Pieces Back Together*, 45 ARIZ. L. REV. 371 (2003). For a survey of the history of property theories generally, see L. UNDERKUFFLER, THE IDEA OF PROPERTY: ITS MEANING AND POWER (2002) and L.ALEXANDER & E. PENALVER, AN INTRODUCTION TO PROPERTY THEORY (2012).

Chapter 2

PROPERTY RIGHTS AND THEIR LIMITATIONS

Property rights are not unqualified. They are affected by both public and private limitations. This chapter serves as an introduction to those limitations which we explore in greater depth in the chapters that follow.

[A.] THE RIGHT TO EXCLUDE

[1.] The Right Defined

The following United States Supreme Court case contains one of the most thorough expositions of the concept of the right to exclude.

KAISER AETNA v. UNITED STATES

United States Supreme Court
444 U.S. 164 (1979)

MR. JUSTICE REHNQUIST delivered the opinion of the Court.

The Hawaii Kai Marina was developed by the dredging and filling of Kuapa Pond, which was a shallow lagoon separated from Maunalua Bay and the Pacific Ocean by a barrier beach. Although under Hawaii law Kuapa Pond was private property, the Court of Appeals for the Ninth Circuit held that when petitioners converted the pond into a marina and thereby connected it to the bay, it became subject to the "navigational servitude" of the Federal Government. Thus, the public acquired a right of access to what was once petitioners' private pond. We granted certiorari because of the importance of the issue and a conflict concerning the scope and nature of the servitude.

I

Kuapa Pond was apparently created in the late Pleistocene Period, near the end of the ice age, when the rising sea level caused the shoreline to retreat, and partial erosion of the headlands adjacent to the bay formed sediment that accreted to form a barrier beach at the mouth of the pond, creating a lagoon. It covered 523 acres on the island of Oahu, Hawaii, and extended approximately two miles inland from Maunalua Bay and the Pacific Ocean. The pond was contiguous to the bay, which is a navigable waterway of the United States, but was separated from it by the barrier beach.

Early Hawaiians used the lagoon as a fishpond and reinforced the natural sandbar with stone walls. Prior to the annexation of Hawaii, there were two openings from the pond to Maunalua Bay. The fishpond's managers placed removable sluice gates in the stone walls across these openings. Water from the bay and ocean entered the pond through the gates during high tide, and during low tide the current flow reversed toward the ocean. The Hawaiians used the tidal action to raise and catch fish such as mullet.

Kuapa Pond, and other Hawaiian fishponds, have always been considered to be private property by landowners and by the Hawaiian government. Such ponds were once an integral part of the Hawaiian feudal system. And in 1848 they were allotted as parts of large land units, known as "ahupuaas," by King Kamehameha III during the Great Mahele or royal land division. Titles to the fishponds were recognized to the same extent and in the same manner as rights in more orthodox fast land. Kuapa Pond was part of an ahupuaa that eventually vested in Bernice Pauahi Bishop and on her death formed a part of the trust corpus of petitioner Bishop Estate, the present owner.

In 1961, Bishop Estate leased a 6,000 acre area, which included Kuapa Pond, to petitioner Kaiser Aetna for subdivision development. The development is now known as "Hawaii Kai." Kaiser Aetna dredged and filled parts of Kuapa Pond, erected retaining walls and built bridges within the development to create the Hawaii Kai Marina. Kaiser Aetna increased the average depth of the channel from two to six feet. It also created accommodations for pleasure boats and eliminated the sluice gates.

When petitioners notified the Army Corps of Engineers of their plans in 1961, the Corps advised them they were not required to obtain permits for the development of and operations in Kuapa Pond. Kaiser Aetna subsequently informed the Corps that it planned to dredge an 8 foot deep channel connecting Kuapa Pond to Maunalua Bay and the Pacific Ocean, and to increase the clearance of a bridge of the Kalanianaole Highway which had been constructed during the early 1900s along the barrier beach separating Kuapa Pond from the bay and ocean to a maximum of 13.5 feet over the mean sea level. These improvements were made in order to allow boats from the marina to enter into and return from the bay, as well as to provide better waters. The Corps acquiesced in the proposals, its chief of construction commenting only that the "deepening of the channel may cause erosion of the beach."

At the time of trial, a marina style community of approximately 22,000 persons surrounded Kuapa Pond. It included approximately 1,500 marina waterfront lot lessees. The waterfront lot lessees, along with at least 86 nonmarina lot lessees from Hawaii Kai and 56 boat owners who are not residents of Hawaii Kai, pay fees for maintenance of the pond and for patrol boats that remove floating debris, enforce boating regulations, and maintain the privacy and security of the pond. Kaiser Aetna controls access to and use of the marina. It has generally not permitted commercial use, except for a small vessel, the Marina Queen, which could carry 25 passengers and was used for about five years to promote sales of marina lots and for a brief period by marina shopping center merchants to attract people to their shopping facilities.

In 1972, a dispute arose between petitioners and the Corps concerning whether

(1) petitioners were required to obtain authorization from the Corps, in accordance with § 10 of the Rivers and Harbors Appropriation Act of 1899, 33 U.S.C. § 403, for future construction, excavation, or filling in the marina, and (2) petitioners were precluded from denying the public access to the pond because, as a result of the improvements, it had become a navigable water of the United States. The dispute foreseeably ripened into a lawsuit by the United States Government against petitioners in the United States District Court for the District of Hawaii. In examining the scope of Congress' regulatory authority under the Commerce Clause, the District Court held that the pond was "navigable water of the United States" and thus subject to regulation by the Corps under § 10 of the Rivers and Harbors Appropriation Act. It further held, however, that the Government lacked the authority to open the now dredged pond to the public without payment of compensation to the owner. *Id.*, at 54. In reaching this holding, the District Court reasoned that although the pond was navigable for the purpose of delimiting Congress' regulatory power, it was not navigable for the purpose of defining the scope of the federal "navigational servitude" imposed by the Commerce Clause. *Ibid.* Thus, the District Court denied the Corps' request for an injunction to require petitioners to allow public access and to notify the public of the fact of the pond's accessibility.

II

The Government contends that petitioners may not exclude members of the public from the Hawaii Kai Marina because "[t]he public enjoys a federally protected right of navigation over the navigable waters of the United States." It claims the issue in dispute is whether Kuapa Pond is presently a "navigable water of the United States." When petitioners dredged and improved Kuapa Pond, the Government continues, the pond although it may once have qualified as fast land became navigable water of the United States. The public thereby acquired a right to use Kuapa Pond as a continuous highway for navigation, and the Corps of Engineers may consequently obtain an injunction to prevent petitioners from attempting to reserve the waterway to themselves.

It is true that Kuapa Pond may fit within definitions of "navigability" articulated in past decisions of this Court. But it must be recognized that the concept of navigability in these decisions was used for purposes other than to delimit the boundaries of the navigational servitude: for example, to define the scope of Congress' regulatory authority under the Interstate Commerce Clause, *see, e.g., United States v. Appalachian Power Co.*, 311 U.S. 377 (1940); *South Carolina v. Georgia*, 93 U.S. 4 (1876); *The Montello*, 20 Wall. 430 (1874); *The Daniel Ball*, 10 Wall. 557 (1871), to determine the extent of the authority of the Corps of Engineers under the Rivers and Harbors Appropriation Act of 1899, and to establish the limits of the jurisdiction of federal courts conferred by Art. III, § 2, of the United States Constitution over admiralty and maritime cases. Although the Government is clearly correct in maintaining that the now dredged Kuapa Pond falls within the definition of "navigable waters" as this Court has used that term in delimiting the boundaries of Congress' regulatory authority under the Commerce Clause, *see, e.g., The Daniel Ball, supra*, 10 Wall., at 563; *The Montello, supra*, 20 Wall., at 441 442; *United States v. Appalachian Power Co., supra*, 311 U.S. at 407–408, this Court has never held that the navigational servitude creates a blanket exception to the Takings Clause whenever Congress exercises its Commerce Clause authority to promote navigation. Thus, while Kuapa Pond may be subject to regulation by the Corps of Engineers, acting under the authority delegated it by Congress in the Rivers and Harbors Appropriation Act, it does not follow that the pond is also subject to a public right of access.

A

Reference to the navigability of a waterway adds little if anything to the breadth of Congress' regulatory power over interstate commerce. It has long been settled that Congress has extensive authority over this Nation's waters under the Commerce Clause. Early in our history this Court held that the power to regulate commerce necessarily includes power over navigation. *Gibbons v. Ogden*, 9 Wheat. 1, 189 (1824). As stated in *Gilman v. Philadelphia*, 3 Wall. 713, 724–725 (1866):

> Commerce includes navigation. The power to regulate commerce comprehends the control for that purpose, and to the extent necessary, of all the navigable waters of the United States which are accessible from a State other than those in which they lie. For this purpose they are the public property of the nation, and subject to all the requisite legislation by Congress.

The pervasive nature of Congress' regulatory authority over national waters was more fully described in *United States v. Appalachian Power Co., supra*, 311 U.S. at 426–427:

> [I]t cannot properly be said that the constitutional power of the United States over its waters is limited to control for navigation. In truth the authority of the United States is the regulation of commerce on its waters. Navigability . . . is but a part of this whole. Flood protection, watershed development, recovery of the cost of improvements through utilization of power are likewise parts of commerce control. [The] authority is as broad as the needs of commerce. The point is that navigable waters are subject to national planning and control in the broad regulation of commerce granted the Federal Government.

Appalachian Power Co. indicates that congressional authority over the waters of this Nation does not depend on a stream's "navigability." And, as demonstrated by this Court's decisions in *NLRB v. Jones & Laughlin Steel Corp.*, 301 U.S. 1 (1937), *United States v. Darby*, 312 U.S. 100 (1941), and *Wickard v. Filburn*, 317 U.S. 111 (1942), a wide spectrum of economic activities "affect" interstate commerce and thus are susceptible of congressional regulation under the Commerce Clause irrespective of whether navigation, or, indeed, water, is involved. The cases that discuss  Congress' paramount authority to regulate waters used in interstate commerce are consequently best understood when viewed in terms of more traditional Commerce Clause analysis than by reference to whether the stream in fact is capable of supporting navigation or may be characterized as "navigable water of the United States." With respect to the Hawaii Kai Marina, for example, there is no doubt that Congress may prescribe the rules of the road, define the conditions under which running lights shall be displayed, require the removal of obstructions to navigation, and exercise its authority for such other reason as may seem to it in the interest of furthering navigation or commerce.

B

In light of its expansive authority under the Commerce Clause, there is no question but that Congress could assure the public a free right of access to the Hawaii Kai Marina if it so chose. Whether a statute or regulation that went so far amounted to a "taking," however, is an entirely separate question. *Pennsylvania Coal Co. v. Mahon*, 260 U.S. 393, 415 (1922). As was recently pointed out in Penn Central Transportation Co. v. New York City, 438 U.S. 104, 98 S. Ct. 2646, 57 L. Ed. 2d 631 (1978), this Court has generally "been unable to develop any 'set formula' for determining when 'justice and fairness' require that economic injuries caused by public action be compensated by the government, rather than remain disproportionately concentrated on a few persons." *Id.*, at 124, 98 S. Ct., at 2659. Rather, it has examined the "taking" question by engaging in essentially ad hoc, factual inquiries that have identified several factors-such as the economic impact of the regulation, its interference with reasonable investment backed expectations, and the character of the governmental action-that have particular significance. Ibid. . . .

C

The navigational servitude is an expression of the notion that the determination whether a taking has occurred must take into consideration the important public interest in the flow of interstate waters that in their natural condition are in fact capable of supporting public navigation.

For over a century, a long line of cases decided by this Court involving Government condemnation of "fast lands" delineated the elements of compensable damages that the Government was required to pay because the lands were riparian to navigable streams. The Court was often deeply divided, and the results frequently turned on what could fairly be described as quite narrow distinctions. But this is not a case in which the Government recognizes any obligation whatever to condemn "fast lands" and pay just compensation under the Eminent Domain Clause of the Fifth Amendment to the United States Constitution. It is instead a case in which the owner of what was once a private pond, separated from concededly navigable water by a barrier beach and used for aquatic agriculture, has invested substantial amounts of money in making improvements. The Government contends that as a result of one of these improvements, the pond's connection to the navigable water in a manner approved by the Corps of Engineers, the owner has somehow lost one of the most essential sticks in the bundle of rights that are commonly characterized as property — the right to exclude others.

There is no denying that the strict logic of the more recent cases limiting the Government's liability to pay damages for riparian access, if carried to its ultimate conclusion, might completely swallow up any private claim for "just compensation" under the Fifth Amendment even in a situation as different from the riparian condemnation cases as this one. But, as Mr. Justice Holmes observed in a very different context, the life of the law has not been logic, it has been experience. The navigational servitude, which exists by virtue of the Commerce Clause in navigable streams, gives rise to an authority in the Government to assure that such streams retain their capacity to serve as continuous highways for the purpose of navigation in interstate commerce. Thus, when the Government acquires fast lands to improve navigation, it is not required under the Eminent Domain Clause to compensate landowners for certain elements of damage attributable to riparian location, such as the land's value as a hydroelectric site, *Twin City Power Co.*, [350 U.S. 222 (1956)], or a port site, *United States v. Rands*, [389 U.S. 121 (1967)]. But none of these cases ever doubted that when the Government wished to acquire fast lands, it was required by the Eminent Domain Clause of the Fifth Amendment to condemn and pay fair value for that interest.

We think, however, that when the Government makes the naked assertion it does here, that assertion collides with not merely an "economic advantage" but an "economic advantage" that has the law back of it to such an extent that courts may "compel others to forbear from interfering with [it] or to compensate for [its] invasion." *United States v. Willow River Co.*, 324 U.S. 499 (1945).

Here, the Government's attempt to create a public right of access to the improved pond goes so far beyond ordinary regulation or improvement for navigation as to amount to a taking under the logic of *Pennsylvania Coal Co. v. Mahon*, 260 U.S. 393 (1922). More than one factor contributes to this result. It is clear that prior to its improvement, Kuapa Pond was incapable of being used as a continuous highway for the purpose of navigation in interstate commerce. Its maximum depth at high tide was a mere two feet, it was separated from the adjacent bay and ocean by a natural barrier beach, and its principal commercial value was limited to fishing. It consequently is not the sort of "great navigable stream" that this Court has previously recognized as being "[incapable] of private ownership." *See, e.g.*, *United States v. Chandler Dunbar Co.*, 229 U.S. at 69; *United States v. Twin City Power Co.*, *supra*, at 228. And, as previously noted, Kuapa Pond has always been considered to be private property under Hawaiian law. Thus, the interest of petitioners in the now dredged marina is strikingly similar to that of owners of fast land adjacent to navigable water.

We have not the slightest doubt that the Government could have refused to allow such dredging on the ground that it would have impaired navigation in the bay, or could have conditioned its approval of the dredging on petitioners' agreement to comply with various measures that it deemed appropriate for the promotion of navigation. But what petitioners now have is a body of water that was private property under Hawaiian law, linked to navigable water by a channel dredged by them with the consent of the Government. While the consent of individual officials representing the United States cannot "estop" the United States, it can lead to the fruition of a number of expectancies embodied in the concept of "property" expectancies that, if sufficiently important, the Government must condemn and pay for before it takes over the management of the landowner's property. In this case, we hold that the "right to exclude," so universally held to be a fundamental element of the property right, falls within this category of interests that the Government cannot take without compensation.

This is not a case in which the Government is exercising its regulatory power in a manner that will cause an insubstantial devaluation of petitioners' private property; rather, the imposition of the navigational servitude in this context will result in an actual physical invasion of the privately owned marina. Compare *Andrus v. Allard*, 444 U.S. 51 at 65, 66, with the traditional taking of fee interests in *United States ex rel. TVA v. Powelson*, 319 U.S. 266 (1943), and in *United States v. Miller*, 317 U.S. 369 (1943). And even if the Government physically invades only an easement in property, it must nonetheless pay just compensation. *See United States v. Causby*, 328 U.S. 256, 265 (1946); *Portsmouth Co. v. United States*, 260 U.S. 327 (1922). Thus, if the Government wishes to make what was formerly Kuapa Pond into a public aquatic park after petitioners have proceeded as far as they have here, it may not, without invoking its eminent domain power and paying just compensation, require them to allow free access to the dredged pond while petitioners' agreement with their customers calls for an annual $72 regular fee.

Accordingly the judgment of the Court of Appeals is reversed.

[The dissenting opinion of Justice Blackmun, which was joined by Justices Brennan and Marshall, is omitted.]

NOTES AND QUESTIONS

1. *The Navigation Servitude.* The limitations imposed on private property rights by the United States' navigation servitude are critical to the resolution of this case. Property owners who acquire land adjacent to navigable waterways take ownership subject to the sovereign's pre-existing right. For example, in *United States v. Willow River Co.*, 324 U.S. 499 (1945), cited in *Kaiser Aetna*, the owners of a Wisconsin hydroelectric power plant where found to be without remedy against the U.S. government, even though the plant had been rendered virtually inoperable by a government-built dam on the upper Mississippi River.

Is Justice (later Chief Justice) Rehnquist's argument that the navigation servitude does not extend to Kuapa Pond under these circumstances convincing? In his dissenting opinion Justice Blackmun wrote:

> My disagreement with the Court lies in four areas. First, I believe the Court errs by implicitly rejecting the old and long-established "ebb and flow" test of navigability as a source for the navigational servitude the Government claims. Second, I cannot accept the notion, which I believe to be without foundation in precedent, that the federal "navigational servitude" does not extend to all "navigable waters of the United States." Third, I reach a different balance of interests on the question whether the exercise of the servitude in favor of public access requires compensation to private interests where private efforts are responsible for creating "navigability in fact." And finally, I differ on the bearing that state property law has on the questions before us today.

444 U.S. at 181.

2. *The Extent of the Invasion.* The right to exclude exists independent of the extent of the invasion. That no harm was done to the property is not a defense in an action for trespass. In *Loretto v. Teleprompter Manhattan CATV Corp.*, 458 U.S. 419 (1982), the United States Supreme Court ruled that a government requirement that building owners permit the installation of a small cable T.V. box and wires amounted to an infringement of the owner's right to exclude. Because this was a government-mandated "trespass" that resulted in a permanent, non-permissive presence on the property, the Court ruled that the State of New York had "taken" a portion of the plaintiff's property and was required by the Fifth and Fourteenth Amendments to compensate the building owner. Although the extent of the occupation was small, the court insisted that that factor was relevant to the amount of damages but not to the issue of governmental liability. (Evidence in the case suggested that the presence of the cable box had no adverse effect on the value of the building owner's property and in fact may have made it more valuable. On remand, Ms. Loretto was awarded damages of only $1 for that very reason. *Loretto v. Teleprompter Manhattan CATV Corp.*, 446 N.E. 2d 428 (N.Y. 1983). While, the Supreme Court did emphasize that this ruling applied to permanent physical presences and not to temporary governmental invasions of private property which did not constitute compensable takings. *See Nollan v. California Coastal Comm'n*, 483 U.S. 825 (1987), in which the Court held even crossing private land was an impermissible intrusion (discussed in Chapter 3).

3. *Who Possesses the Right to Exclude?* The right to exclude extends not just to those who own title to the property but also to those who are in lawful possession of it. The 1936 edition of the American Law Institute's RESTATEMENT OF THE LAW OF PROPERTY § 7 describes the holders of possessory interests in land as those who "exercise such control as to exclude other members of society in general from any present occupation of the land." Tenants, for example, have the right to exclude during the term of their lease. The right to exclude is not limited to real property but extends to personal property as well. For a controversial application of this principle to presidential papers of the 37th President of the United States by the District of Columbia Court of Appeals, see *Nixon v. United States*, 978 F.2d 1269 (D.C. Cir. 1992).

4. *The Bundle of Sticks.* In discussions of property rights, the metaphor of the "bundle of sticks" is often use to convey the idea that property rights are a collection of separate rights bound together but ultimately severable. The first use judicial use of this metaphor was apparently by United States District Court for the Southern District of Ohio in a 1960 tax case, *Rundle v. Welch*, 184 F. Supp. 777, 780 (S.D. Ohio 1960). The United States Supreme Court first used this phrase in 1977 in the case of *Frank Lyon Co. v. United States*, 435 U.S. 561 (1977), and has used the concept to define the right to exclude on numerous occasions over the past 30 years, though not always consistently. In *Loretto v. Teleprompter Manhattan CATV Corp.*, cited in the previous note, the Court described physical invasion as "chopping through the bundle taking a slice of every strand." *Id.* at 435. However, in *Hodel v. Irving*, 481 U.S. 704 (1987), a case involving inheritance rights, the Court described the right to exclude as one of the most essential sticks in the bundle. *Id.* at 716. For additional commentary on the importance of the concept of the right to exclude in the definition of rights in land, see Michelman, *Property, Utility and Fairness: Comments on the Foundations of "Just Compensation" Law*, 80 HARV. L. REV. 1165, 1186 (1967); L. TRIBE, AMERICAN CONSTITUTIONAL LAW 604–05 n.33 (2d ed. 1988), and

Callies & Breemer, *Selected Legal and Policy Trends in Takings Law: Background Principles Custom, and Public Trust "Exceptions" and the (Mis)Use of Investment-Backed Expectations*, 36 VAL. U. L. REV. 339 (2002).

5. *Limitations on the Right to Exclude.* In spite of the critical importance of the right to exclude, courts have recognized various exceptions to the right to exclude. As the following cases in this section illustrate, limitations on the right to exclude can raise serious constitutional questions (as they did in *Kaiser Aetna*).

[2.] Custom and Public Access

The 18th century official Vinerian lecturer William Blackstone set out a number of requirements for custom to be valid in his famous *Commentaries* at least in part for fear that custom would swallow up too much of the common law, of which he was a staunch defender. 1 William Blackstone, Commentaries, 76–78. Many of these requirements are noted in the *Thornton* case, which introduces customary law at this point. Do the judges follow Blackstonian custom or not? Does it matter? The doctrines of custom and public trust have long been regarded as in derogation private property rights. Callies, *Custom and Public Trust: Background Principles of State Property Law?*, 30 ENVTL. L. REP. 10003 (2000); D. Bederman, *The Curious Resurrection of Custom: Beach Access and Judicial Takings*, 96 COLUM. L. REV. 1375 (1996). They are of particular relevance today also because several courts and commentators have held them to be "background principles of a state's law of property," so that police power regulations which codify them may deprive a landowner of "all economically beneficial use" without the usual compensation requirements of the 5th Amendment when government takes property. *Lucas v. South Carolina Coastal Council*, 424 S.E.2d 484 (S.C. 1992). *See, e.g., Stevens v. City of Cannon Beach*, 854 P.2d 449 (Or. 1993); and *Esplanade Properties, LLC v. City of Seattle*, 307 F.3d 978 (9th Cir. 2002).

STATE OF OREGON EX REL. THORNTON v. HAY

Oregon Supreme Court
462 P.2d 671 (1969)

GOODWIN, JUSTICE.

William and Georgianna Hay, the owners of a tourist facility at Cannon Beach, appeal from a decree which enjoins them from constructing fences or other improvements in the dry sand area between the sixteen foot elevation contour line and the ordinary high tide line of the Pacific Ocean. The issue is whether the state has the power to prevent the defendant landowners from enclosing the dry sand area contained within the legal description of their ocean front property.

The state asserts two theories: (1) the landowners' record title to the disputed area is encumbered by a superior right in the public to go upon and enjoy the land for recreational purposes; and (2) if the disputed area is not encumbered by the asserted public easement, then the state has power to prevent construction under zoning regulations made pursuant to ORS 390.640.[1]

From the trial record, applicable statutes, and court decisions, certain terms and definitions have been extracted and will appear in this opinion. A short glossary follows:

ORS 390.720 refers to the "ordinary" high tide line, while other sources refer to the "mean" high-tide line. For the purposes of this case the two lines will be considered to be the same. The mean high-tide line in Oregon is fixed by the 1947 Supplement to the 1929 United States Coast and Geodetic Survey data.

The land area in dispute will be called the dry sand area. This will be assumed to be the land lying between the line of mean high tide and the visible line of vegetation. The vegetation line is the seaward edge of vegetation where the upland supports vegetation. It falls generally in the vicinity of the sixteen foot elevation contour line, but is not at all points necessarily identical with that line. Differences between the vegetation line and the sixteen foot line are irrelevant for the purposes of this case.

The sixteen foot line, which is an engineering line and not a line visible on the ground, is mentioned in ORS 390.640, and in the trial court's decree. The extreme high tide-line and the high-water mark are mentioned in the record, but will be treated as identical with the vegetation line. While technical differences between extreme high tide and the high-water mark, and between both lines and the sixteen foot line, might have legal significance in some other litigation, such differences, if any, have none in this case. We cite these variations in terminology only to point out that the cases and statutes relevant to the issues in this case, like the witnesses, have not always used the same words to describe similar topographical features.

Below, or seaward of, the mean high tide line, is the state owned foreshore, or wet sand area, in which the landowners in this case concede the public's paramount right, and concerning which there is no justiciable controversy.

The only issue in this case, as noted, is the power of the state to limit the record owner's use and enjoyment of the dry sand area, by whatever boundaries the area may be described.

The trial court found that the public had acquired, over the years, an easement for recreational purposes to go upon and enjoy the dry sand area, and that this easement was appurtenant to the wet sand portion of the beach which is admittedly owned by the state and designated as a "state recreation area."

Because we hold that the trial court correctly found in favor of the state on the rights of the public in the dry sand area, it follows that the state has an equitable right to protect the public in the enjoyment of those rights by causing the removal

---

1 [1] ORS 390.720 provides:

> Ownership of the shore of the Pacific Ocean between ordinary high tide and extreme low tide, and from the Oregon and Washington state line on the north to the Oregon and California state line on the south, excepting such portions as may have been disposed of by the state prior to July 5, 1947, is vested in the State of Oregon, and is declared to be a state recreation area. No portion of such ocean shore shall be alienated by any of the agencies of the state except as provided by law.

of fences and other obstacles. In order to explain our reasons for affirming the trial court's decree, it is necessary to set out in some detail the historical facts which lead to our conclusion.

The dry sand area in Oregon has been enjoyed by the general public as a recreational adjunct of the wet sand or foreshore area since the beginning of the state's political history. The first European settlers on these shores found the aboriginal inhabitants using the foreshore for clam digging and the dry sand area for their cooking fires. The newcomers continued these customs after statehood. Thus, from the time of the earliest settlement to the present day, the general public has assumed that the dry sand area was a part of the public beach, and the public has used the dry sand area for picnics, gathering wood, building warming fires, and generally as a headquarters from which to supervise children or to range out over the foreshore as the tides advance and recede. In the Cannon Beach vicinity, state and local officers have policed the dry sand, and municipal sanitary crews have attempted to keep the area reasonably free from manmade litter.

Perhaps one explanation for the evolution of the custom of the public to use the dry sand area for recreational purposes is that the area could not be used conveniently by its owners for any other purpose. The dry sand area is unstable in its seaward boundaries, unsafe during winter storms, and for the most part unfit for the construction of permanent structures. While the vegetation line remains relatively fixed, the western edge of the dry sand area is subject to dramatic moves eastward or westward in response to erosion and accretion. For example, evidence in the trial below indicated that between April 1966 and August 1967 the seaward edge of the dry sand area involved in this litigation moved westward 180 feet. At other points along the shore, the evidence showed, the seaward edge of the dry sand area could move an equal distance to the east in a similar period of time.

Until very recently, no question concerning the right of the public to enjoy the dry sand area appears to have been brought before the courts of this state. The public's assumption that the dry sand as well as the foreshore was "public property" had been reinforced by early judicial decisions. See *Shively v. Bowlby*, 152 U.S. 1 (1894), which affirmed *Bowlby v. Shively*, 30 P. 154 (Or. 1892). These cases held that landowners claiming under federal patents owned seaward only to the "high water" line, a line that was then assumed to be the vegetation line.

Recently, however, the scarcity of oceanfront building sites has attracted substantial private investments in resort facilities. Resort owners like these defendants now desire to reserve for their paying guests the recreational advantages that accrue to the dry sand portions of their deeded property. Consequently, in 1967, public debate and political activity resulted in legislative attempts to resolve conflicts between public and private interests in the dry sand area:

ORS 390.610

(1) The Legislative Assembly hereby declares it is the public policy of the State of Oregon to forever preserve and maintain the sovereignty of the state heretofore existing over the seashore and ocean beaches of the state from the Columbia River on the North to the Oregon California line on the South so that the public may have the free and uninterrupted use thereof.

> (2) The Legislative Assembly recognizes that over the years the public has made frequent and uninterrupted use of lands abutting, adjacent and contiguous to the public highways and state recreation areas and recognizes, further, that where such use has been sufficient to create easements in the public through dedication, prescription, grant or otherwise, that it is in the public interest to protect and preserve such public easements as a permanent part of Oregon's recreational resources.
>
> (3) Accordingly, the Legislative Assembly hereby declares that all public rights and easements in those lands described in subsection (2) of this section are confirmed and declared vested exclusively in the State of Oregon and shall be held and administered in the same manner as those lands described in ORS 390.720.

The state concedes that such legislation cannot divest a person of his rights in land, *Hughes v. Washington*, 389 U.S. 290 (1967), and that the defendants' record title, which includes the dry sand area, extends seaward to the ordinary or mean high tide line. The landowners likewise concede that since 1899 the public's rights in the foreshore have been confirmed by law as well as by custom and usage. Oregon Laws 1899, p. 3, provided:

> That the shore of the Pacific ocean, between ordinary high and extreme low tides, and from the Columbia river on the north to the south boundary line of Clatsop county on the south, is hereby declared a public highway, and shall forever remain open as such to the public.

The disputed area is *sui generis*. While the foreshore is "owned" by the state, and the upland is "owned" by the patentee or record title holder, neither can be said to "own" the full bundle of rights normally connoted by the term "estate in fee simple." 1 POWELL, REAL PROPERTY 163, at 661 (1949).

In addition to the *sui generis* nature of the land itself, a multitude of complex and sometimes overlapping precedents in the law confronted the trial court. Several early Oregon decisions generally support the trial court's decision, i.e., that the public can acquire easements in private land by long continued user that is inconsistent with the owner's exclusive possession and enjoyment of his land. A citation of the cases could end the discussion at this point. But because the early cases do not agree on the legal theories by which the results are reached, and because this is an important case affecting valuable rights in land, it is appropriate to review some of the law applicable to this case.

One group of precedents relied upon in part by the state and by the trial court can be called the "implied dedication" cases. The doctrine of implied dedication is well known to the law in this state and elsewhere. Dedication, however, whether express or implied, rests upon an intent to dedicate. In the case at bar, it is unlikely that the landowners thought they had anything to dedicate, until 1967, when the notoriety of legislative debates about the public's rights in the dry sand area sent a number of ocean front landowners to the offices of their legal advisers.

A second group of cases relied upon by the state, but rejected by the trial court, deals with the possibility of a landowner's losing the exclusive possession and enjoyment of his land through the development of prescriptive easements in the public. In Oregon, as in most common law jurisdictions, an easement can be created in favor of one person in the land of another by uninterrupted use and enjoyment of the land in a particular manner for the statutory period, so long as the user is open, adverse, under claim of right, but without authority of law or consent of the owner.

The public use of the disputed land in the case at bar is admitted to be continuous for more than sixty years. There is no suggestion in the record that anyone's permission was sought or given; rather, the public used the land under a claim of right. Therefore, if the public can acquire an easement by prescription, the requirements for such an acquisition have been met in connection with the specific tract of land involved in this case.

The owners argue, however, that the general public, not being subject to actions in trespass and ejectment, cannot acquire rights by prescription, because the statute of limitations is irrelevant when an action does not lie.

While it may not be feasible for a landowner to sue the general public, it is nonetheless possible by means of signs and fences to prevent or minimize public invasions of private land for recreational purposes. In Oregon, moreover, the courts and the Legislative Assembly have both recognized that the public can acquire prescriptive easements in private land, at least for roads and highways. See ORS 368.405, which provides for the manner in which counties may establish roads. The statute enumerates the formal governmental actions that can be employed, and then concludes: "This section does not preclude acquiring public ways by adverse user."

Another statute codifies a policy favoring the acquisition by prescription of public recreational easements in beach lands. See ORS 390.610. While such a statute cannot create public rights at the expense of a private landowner the statute can, and does, express legislative approval of the common law doctrine of prescription where the facts justify its application. Consequently, we conclude that the law in Oregon, regardless of the generalizations that may apply elsewhere, does not preclude the creation of prescriptive easements in beach land for public recreational use.

Because many elements of prescription are present in this case, the state has relied upon the doctrine in support of the decree below. We believe, however, that there is a better legal basis for affirming the decree. The most cogent basis for the decision in this case is the English doctrine of custom. Strictly construed, prescription applies only to the specific tract of land before the court, and doubtful prescription cases could fill the courts for years with tract by tract litigation. An established custom, on the other hand, can be proven with reference to a larger region. Ocean front lands from the northern to the southern border of the state ought to be treated uniformly.

The other reason which commends the doctrine of custom over that of prescription as the principal basis for the decision in this case is the unique nature of the lands in question. This case deals solely with the dry sand area along the Pacific shore, and this land has been used by the public as public recreational land according to an unbroken custom running back in time as long as the land has been inhabited.

A custom is defined in 1 BOUVIER'S LAW DICTIONARY, Rawle's Third Revision, p. 742 as "such a usage as by common consent and uniform practice has become the law of the place, or of the subject matter to which it relates." In 1 BLACKSTONE, COMMENTARIES, Sir William Blackstone set out the requisites of a particular custom. Paraphrasing Blackstone, the first requirement of a custom, to be recognized as law, is that it must be ancient. It must have been used so long "that the memory of man runneth not to the contrary." Professor Cooley footnotes his edition of Blackstone with the comment that "long and general" usage is sufficient. In any event, the record in the case at bar satisfies the requirement of antiquity. So long as there has been an institutionalized system of land tenure in Oregon, the public has freely exercised the right to use the dry sand area up and down the Oregon coast for the recreational purposes noted earlier in this opinion.

The second requirement is that the right be exercised without interruption. A customary right need not be exercised continuously, but it must be exercised without an interruption caused by anyone possessing a paramount right. In the case at bar, there was evidence that the public's use and enjoyment of the dry sand area had never been interrupted by private landowners. Blackstone's third requirement, that the customary use be peaceable and free from dispute, is satisfied by the evidence which related to the second requirement.

The fourth requirement, that of reasonableness, is satisfied by the evidence that the public has always made use of the land in a manner appropriate to the land and to the usages of the community. There is evidence in the record that when inappropriate uses have been detected, municipal police officers have intervened to preserve order. The fifth requirement, certainty, is satisfied by the visible boundaries of the dry sand area and by the character of the land, which limits the use thereof to recreational uses connected with the foreshore.

The sixth requirement is that a custom must be obligatory; that is, in the case at bar, not left to the option of each landowner whether or not he will recognize the public's right to go upon the dry sand area for recreational purposes. The record shows that the dry sand area in question has been used, as of right, uniformly with similarly situated lands elsewhere, and that the public's use has never been questioned by an upland owner so long as the public remained on the dry sand and refrained from trespassing upon the lands above the vegetation line. Finally, a custom must not be repugnant, or inconsistent, with other customs or with other law. The custom under consideration violates no law, and is not repugnant.

Two arguments have been arrayed against the doctrine of custom as a basis for decision in Oregon. The first argument is that custom is unprecedented in this state, and has only scant adherence elsewhere in the United States. The second argument is that because of the relative brevity of our political history it is inappropriate to rely upon an English doctrine that requires greater antiquity than a newly settled land can muster. Neither of these arguments is persuasive.

The custom of the people of Oregon to use the dry sand area of the beaches for public recreational purposes meets every one of Blackstone's requisites. While it is not necessary to rely upon precedent from other states, we are not the first state to recognize custom as a source of law. See *Perley et ux'r v. Langley*, 7 N.H. 233 (1834). On the score of the brevity of our political history, it is true that the Anglo American legal system on this continent is relatively new. Its newness has made it possible for government to provide for many of our institutions by written law rather than by customary law. This truism does not, however, militate against the validity of a custom when the custom does in fact exist. If antiquity were the sole test of validity of a custom, Oregonians could satisfy that requirement by recalling that the European settlers were not the first people to use the dry sand area as public land.

Finally, in support of custom, the record shows that the custom of the inhabitants of Oregon and of visitors in the state to use the dry sand as a public recreation area is so notorious that notice of the custom on the part of persons buying land along the shore must be presumed. In the case at bar, the landowners conceded their actual knowledge of the public's long standing use of the dry sand area, and argued that the elements of consent present in the relationship between the landowners and the public precluded the application of the law of prescription. As noted, we are not resting this decision on prescription, and we leave open the effect upon prescription of the type of consent that may have been present in this case. Such elements of consent are, however, wholly consistent with the recognition of public rights derived from custom.

Because so much of our law is the product of legislation, we sometimes lose sight of the importance of custom as a source of law in our society. It seems particularly appropriate in the case at bar to look to an ancient and accepted custom in this state as the source of a rule of law. The rule in this case, based upon custom, is salutary in confirming a public right, and at the same time it takes from no man anything which he has had a legitimate reason to regard as exclusively his.

For the foregoing reasons, the decree of the trial court is affirmed.

NOTES AND QUESTIONS

1. *The Role of Custom.* The Oregon Supreme Court ultimately grounds its decision in the law of custom, citing BLACKSTONE'S COMMENTARIES, a fertile source for the English common law that formed the basis for private law in most states. Most American states have a reception clause in their state constitutions that declares the common law of England as of a particular date to be the law of the state except as modified or amended by statute. However, whether "custom" was part of the common law is a complicated question. Also, which branch of government should decide what is customary and what is not? Is the declaration of custom a proper judicial function? Is custom a legitimate place for the court to look for the law? If it is, should the courts be free to disregard the usual limitations on construing law? For the view of one of the casebook editors, see Callies, *Custom & Public Trust: Background Principles of State Property Law?*, 30 ENVTL. L. REP. 10003 (2000). For a different view that rejects the custom analysis of the principal case, see *Severance v. Patterson*, 370 S.W.3d 705 (Tex. 2012).

2. *Adverse Use.* Although the court chose to rest its decision on the law of custom rather than prescriptive right, open, adverse, non-permissive use of private

land often results in the user's acquisition of an easement. (Prescriptive rights are examined in Chapter 7.) In Oregon, the prescriptive period is 10 years. Or. Rev. Stat. § 12.050. *See Feldman et ux. v. Knapp et ux.*, 250 P.2d 92 (Or. 1952); *Coventon v. Seufert*, 32 P. 508 (Or. 1893). Should beachgoers have the right to continue to pass between two private dwellings to a public beach — which they can demonstrate they have done for over 20 years — if the owners decide to "gate" the path (assuming there is no evidence of permissive use)? Should such a prescriptive right extend to more diffuse and less "channeled" non-permissive uses, say to grazing cattle on unfenced land? In *Sanchez v. Taylor*, 377 F.2d 733 (10th Cir. 1967), the court refused to recognize such a right for the appellants even though they and their predecessors had, with the owner's permission, grazed cattle on the tract in question for 108 years.

3. *Customary Rights in Hawaii.* In *Public Access Shoreline Hawaii v. Hawaii Planning Comm'n*, 903 P.2d 1246 (Haw. 1995) ("*PASH*"), the Hawaii Supreme Court redefined custom so as to permit "Native Hawaiians" (about one-sixth of Hawaii's population) to go upon any land in the state, public or private, developed or undeveloped, to exercise "all rights customarily and traditionally exercised for subsistence, cultural and religious purposes." (The state is required by Article XII, § 7 of the Hawaii State Constitution to "protect" such rights.) Many of these customs have not been practiced for as long as 100 years, and it is clear that some "customs" — like hunting and native worship — would today amount to trespass.

Is the Hawaii Supreme Court "redefining" custom beyond the rationale and parameters set out in *Hay*, and by implication Blackstone? The *PASH* court also opined that "Hawaiian history leads us to the conclusion that the western concept of exclusivity is not universally applicable in Hawaii. The issuance of Hawaiian land patent confirmed a limited property interest as compared with typical land patents governed by western concepts of property." Based upon *Kaiser Aetna*, how would the U.S. Supreme Court respond to such language? *See* Sullivan, *Customary Revolutions: The Law of Custom and the Conflict of Traditions in Hawaii*, 20 U. Haw. L. Rev. 99 (1999). The Hawaii legislature now requires all land developers to dedicate access ways to the beach in all coastal land development projects. Hawaii Rev. Stat. § 46-6.5. Is such a statute a good idea? Is it fair? Is it constitutional? Consider the latter question after reading the materials on exactions, dedications, and other land development conditions in Chapter 3.

4. *Is There a Constitutional Problem in* Thornton v. Hay? If Or. Rev. Stat. § o390.640 (the statute at issue in the above case) were applied as a zoning regulation to lands upon which the public had not acquired an easement for recreational use, it would almost certainly constitute a taking of property and the state would be constitutionally obligated to pay just compensation. *See Opinion of the Justices*, 649 A.2d 604 (N.H. 1999), in Chapter 3.Is the state in this case really just trying to avoid compensating the owners of beachfront property?

5. *Subsequent Developments.* Twenty years later, the Oregon Supreme Court narrowed the effect of *Thornton v. Hay* somewhat by ruling that the customary easement recognized in the earlier case did not apply to the entire Oregon coastline but just to those tracts of land that historically had been used by the public for recreational purposes. *McDonald v. Halvorson*, 780 P.2d 714 (Or. 1989). However, the legitimacy of the custom rationale was reaffirmed by the same court four years later in *Stevens v. Cannon Beach*, 510 U.S. 1207 (1994). For a scathing criticism of the rationale in *Thornton* and *Stevens*, see Justice Antonin Scalia's dissenting opinion accompanying the United States Supreme Court's denial of certiorari in the *Stevens* case. 510 U.S. 1207 (1994).

6. *The Right to Exclude Outside the United States*. The right to exclude has occasionally arisen as a legal issue outside the United States. It achieved international status in 1999 when the European Court of Human Rights decided *Chassagnou and Others v. France*, Applic. Nos. 25088/94, 28331/65, and 28443/95. There, three farmers who objected to a French law that permitted the transfer of hunting rights on their farms to a local hunters' association successfully challenged the applicable statute as a violation of the European Convention for the Protection of Human Rights and Fundamental Freedoms. For further explanation and analysis, see Callies, *Case Note*, 2 Business Law International 107 (2000). *See also* T. Allen, Property in the Human Rights Act 1998 (2005); Allen, *Property as a Fundamental Right in India, Europe and South Africa*, 15 Asia Pacific L. Rev. 193 (2007).

[3.] Access by the Public and First Amendment Rights

STATE v. SHACK

New Jersey Supreme Court
277 A.2d 369 (1971)

Weintraub, C.J.

Defendants entered upon private property to aid migrant farmworkers employed and housed there. Having refused to depart upon the demand of the owner, defendants were [convicted of] . . . violating N.J.S.A. 2A:170-31 which provides that '(a)ny person who trespasses on any lands * * * after being forbidden so to trespass by the owner * * * is a disorderly person and shall be punished by a fine of not more than $50.' . . .

Before us, no one seeks to sustain these convictions. The complaints were prosecuted in the Municipal Court and in the County Court by counsel engaged by the complaining landowner, Tedesco. However Tedesco did not respond to this appeal, and the county prosecutor, while defending abstractly the constitutionality of the trespass statute, expressly disclaimed any position as to whether the statute reached the activity of these defendants.

Complainant, Tedesco, a farmer, employs migrant workers for his seasonal needs. As part of their compensation, these workers are housed at a camp on his property.

Defendant Tejeras is a field worker for the Farm Workers Division of the Southwest Citizens Organization for Poverty Elimination, known by the acronym SCOPE, a nonprofit corporation funded by the Office of Economic Opportunity pursuant to an act of Congress, 42 U.S.C.A. §§ 2861–2864. The role of SCOPE includes providing for the 'health services of the migrant farm worker.'

Defendant Shack is a staff attorney with the Farm Workers Division of Camden Regional Legal Services, Inc., known as 'CRLS,' also a nonprofit corporation funded by the Office of Economic Opportunity pursuant to an act of Congress, 42 U.S.C.A. § 2809(a)(3). The mission of CRLS includes legal advice and representation for these workers.

Differences had developed between Tedesco and these defendants prior to the events which led to the trespass charges now before us. Hence when defendant Tejeras wanted to go upon Tedesco's farm to find a migrant worker who needed medical aid for the removal of 28 sutures, he called upon defendant Shack for his help with respect to the legalities involved. Shack, too, had a mission to perform on Tedesco's farm; he wanted to discuss a legal problem with another migrant worker there employed and housed. Defendants arranged to go to the farm together. Shack carried literature to inform the migrant farmworkers of the assistance available to them under federal statutes, but no mention seems to have been made of that literature when Shack was later confronted by Tedesco.

Defendants entered upon Tedesco's property and as they neared the camp site where the farmworkers were housed, they were confronted by Tedesco who inquired of their purpose. Tejeras and Shack stated their missions. In response, Tedesco offered to find the injured worker, and as to the worker who needed legal advice, Tedesco also offered to locate the man but insisted that the consultation would have to take place in Tedesco's office and in his presence. Defendants declined, saying they had the right to see the men in the privacy of their living quarters and without Tedesco's supervision. Tedesco thereupon summoned a State Trooper who, however, refused to remove defendants except upon Tedesco's written complaint. Tedesco then executed the formal complaints charging violations of the trespass statute.

The constitutionality of the trespass statute, as applied here, is challenged on several scores. . . .

These constitutional claims are not established by any definitive holding. We think it unnecessary to explore their validity. The reason is that we are satisfied that under our State law the ownership of real property does not include the right a bar access to governmental services available to migrant workers and hence there was no trespass within the meaning of the penal statute. The policy considerations which underlie that conclusion may be much the same as those which would be weighed with respect to one or more of the constitutional challenges, but a decision in nonconstitutional terms is more satisfactory, because the interests of migrant workers are more expansively served in that way than they would be if they had no more freedom than these constitutional concepts could be found to mandate if indeed they apply at all.

Property rights serve human values. They are recognized to that end, and are limited by it. Title to real property cannot include dominion over the destiny of persons the owner permits to come upon the premises. Their well-being must remain the paramount concern of a system of law. Indeed the needs of the occupants may be so imperative and their strength so weak, that the law will deny the occupants the power to contract away what is deemed essential to their health, welfare, or dignity.

Here we are concerned with a highly disadvantaged segment of our society. We are told that every year farmworkers and their families numbering more than one million leave their home areas to fill the seasonal demand for farm labor in the United States. . . . The migrant farmworkers come to New Jersey in substantial numbers. . . .

The migrant farmworkers are a community within but apart from the local scene. They are rootless and isolated. Although the need for their labors is evident, they are unorganized and without economic or political power. It is their plight alone that summoned government to their aid. In response, Congress provided under Title III-B of the Economic Opportunity Act of 1964 (42 U.S.C.A. § 2701 et seq.) for 'assistance for migrant and other seasonally employed farmworkers and their families.' . . .

These ends would not be gained if the intended beneficiaries could be insulated from efforts to reach them. It is in this framework that we must decide whether the camp operator's rights in his lands may stand between the migrant workers and those who would aid them. The key to that aid is communication. Since the migrant workers are outside the mainstream of the communities in which they are housed and are unaware of their rights and opportunities and of the services available to them, they can be reached only by positive efforts tailored to that end. . . .

A man's right in his real property of course is not absolute. It was a maxim of the common law that one should so use his property as not to injure the rights of others. . . . Although hardly a precise solvent of actual controversies, the maxim does express the inevitable proposition that rights are relative and there must be an accommodation when they meet. Hence it has long been true that necessity, private or public, may justify entry upon the lands of another. . . .

The process involves not only the accommodation between the right of the owner and the interests of the general public in his use of this property, but involves also an accommodation between the right of the owner and the right of individuals who are parties with him in consensual transactions relating to the use of the property. . . .

. . . The quest is for a fair adjustment of the competing needs of the parties, in the light of the realities of the relationship between the migrant worker and the operator of the housing facility.

Thus approaching the case, we find it unthinkable that the farmer-employer can assert a right to isolate the migrant worker in any respect significant for the worker's well-being. The farmer, of course, is entitled to pursue his farming activities without interference, and this defendants readily concede. But we see no legitimate need for a right in the farmer to deny the worker the opportunity for aid available from federal, State, or local services, or from recognized charitable groups seeking to assist him. Hence representatives of these agencies and organizations may enter upon the premises to seek out the worker at his living quarters. So, too, the migrant worker must be allowed to receive visitors there of his own choice, so long as there is no behavior hurtful to others, and members of the press may not be denied reasonable access to workers who do not object to seeing them.

It is not our purpose to open the employer's premises to the general public if in fact the employer himself has not done so. We do not say, for example, that solicitors or peddlers of all kinds may enter on their own; we may assume for the present that the employer may regulate their entry or bar them, at least if the employer's purpose is not to gain a commercial advantage for himself or if the regulation does not deprive the migrant worker of practical access to things he needs.

And we are mindful of the employer's interest in his own and in his employees' security. Hence he may reasonably require a visitor to identify himself, and also to state his general purpose if the migrant worker has not already informed him that the visitor is expected. But the employer may not deny the worker his privacy or interfere with his opportunity to live with dignity and to enjoy associations customary among our citizens. These rights are too fundamental to be denied on the basis of an interest in real property and too fragile to be left to the unequal bargaining strength of the parties. . . .

It follows that defendants here invaded no possessory right of the farmer-employer. Their conduct was therefore beyond the reach of the trespass statute. The judgments are accordingly reversed and the matters remanded to the County Court with directions to enter judgments of acquittal.

NOTES AND QUESTIONS

1. *Relevant "Sticks" in the Bundle of Rights.* What "sticks" in the bundle of rights did Tedesco claim were being affected?

2. *Procedure.* This is a criminal case which Tedesco, through his own counsel, prosecuted in the lower courts. Why should a private party be able to bring a criminal case? Why is this a case about property rights? Since no one appeared in the New Jersey Supreme Court to sustain the convictions — and the county prosecutor, who was the only person who appeared in that court, "expressly disclaimed" any position about whether the statute reached this particular case — why didn't the New Jersey Supreme Court summarily overturn the convictions without a lengthy opinion?

3. *Basis of Decision.* Is this a constitutional, statutory or common law case?

4. *Whose Rights?* Whose rights did the court define? Were Tedesco's rights diminished? Were the farmworker's rights enhanced? Were the defendants' rights enhanced?

5. *"Public" Interest?* Does the court's decision implement the *public* interest, or only the individual interests of the farmworkers, and also perhaps those of the defendants? What about the interests of the farmer? Can it be said that each of those parties not only represents their own, individual interests, but also stands as a *proxy* for broader public interests? If so, what public interests does each represent? How does the court determine that in this particular situation, the interests represented by the farmworkers and defendants prevail over the interests represented by the farmer?

6. *Scope of Decision.* Consider the various people involved: the landowner, the farmworkers and the intruders (the defendants). Are all employers covered, or is the decision limited to farmers? Are all farmworkers covered, or only farmworkers

who live on the farm? Are all employees covered, or only farmworkers? Are intruders covered, or only those seeking to implement federally-funded program *State v. Fields*, 2015 N.J. Super. Unpub. LEXIS 257, at *7 (Feb. 12, 2015), held th "the primary focus of the Court in *Shack* is the protection of a disadvantaged clas

PRUNEYARD SHOPPING CENTER v. ROBINS

United States Supreme Court
447 U.S. 74 (1980)

MR. JUSTICE REHNQUIST delivered the opinion of the Court.

We postponed jurisdiction of this appeal from the Supreme Court of California to decide the important federal constitutional questions it presented. Those are whether state constitutional provisions, which permit individuals to exercise free speech and petition rights on the property of a privately owned shopping center to which the public is invited, violate the shopping center owner's property rights under the Fifth and Fourteenth Amendments or his free speech rights under the First and Fourteenth Amendments.

I

Appellant PruneYard is a privately owned shopping center in the City of Campbell, Cal. It covers approximately 21 acres 5 devoted to parking and 16 occupied by walkways, plazas, sidewalks, and buildings that contain more than 65 specialty shops, 10 restaurants, and a movie theater. The PruneYard is open to the public for the purpose of encouraging the patronizing of its commercial establishments. It has a policy not to permit any visitor or tenant to engage in any publicly expressive activity, including the circulation of petitions, that is not directly related to its commercial purposes. This policy has been strictly enforced in a nondiscriminatory fashion. The PruneYard is owned by appellant Fred Sahadi.

Appellees are high school students who sought to solicit support for their opposition to a United Nations resolution against "Zionism." On a Saturday afternoon they set up a card table in a corner of PruneYard's central courtyard. They distributed pamphlets and asked passersby to sign petitions, which were to be sent to the President and Members of Congress. Their activity was peaceful and orderly and so far as the record indicates was not objected to by PruneYard's patrons.

Soon after appellees had begun soliciting signatures, a security guard informed them that they would have to leave because their activity violated PruneYard regulations. The guard suggested that they move to the public sidewalk at the PruneYard's perimeter. Appellees immediately left the premises and later filed this lawsuit in the California Superior Court of Santa Clara County. They sought to enjoin appellants from denying them access to the PruneYard for the purpose of circulating their petitions.

The Superior Court held that appellees were not entitled under either the Federal or California Constitution to exercise their asserted rights on the shopping center property. It concluded that there were "adequate, effective channels of communication for [appellees] other than soliciting on the private property of the [PruneYard]." The California Court of Appeal affirmed.

The California Supreme Court reversed, holding that the California Constitution protects "speech and petitioning, reasonably exercised, in shopping centers even when the centers are privately owned." It concluded that appellees were entitled to conduct their activity on PruneYard property. In rejecting appellants' contention that such a result infringed property rights protected by the Federal Constitution, the California Supreme Court observed:"

> It bears repeated emphasis that we do not have under consideration the property or privacy rights of an individual homeowner or the proprietor of a modest retail establishment. As a result of advertising and the lure of a congenial environment, 25,000 persons are induced to congregate daily to take advantage of the numerous amenities offered by the [shopping center]. A handful of additional orderly persons soliciting signatures and distributing handbills in connection therewith, under reasonable regulations adopted by defendant to assure that these activities do not interfere with normal business operations, would not markedly dilute defendant's property rights.

Before this Court, appellants contend that their constitutionally established rights under the Fourteenth Amendment to exclude appellees from adverse use of appellants' private property cannot be denied by invocation of a state constitutional provision or by judicial reconstruction of a State's laws of private property. We postponed consideration of the question of jurisdiction until the hearing of the case on the merits. We now affirm.

[The portions of this opinion dealing with the Supreme Court's jurisdiction to hear this appeal (part II) and the application of the First Amendment to the facts of this case (parts III and V) are omitted.]

IV

Appellants next contend that a right to exclude others underlies the Fifth Amendment guarantee against the taking of property without just compensation and the Fourteenth Amendment guarantee against the deprivation of property without due process of law.

It is true that one of the essential sticks in the bundle of property rights is the right to exclude others. *Kaiser Aetna v. United States*, 444 U.S. 164 (1979). And here there has literally been a "taking" of that right to the extent that the California Supreme Court has interpreted the State Constitution to entitle its citizens to exercise free expression and petition rights on shopping center property.[2] But it is

---

[2] [6] The term "property" as used in the Taking Clause includes the entire "group of rights inhering in the citizen's [ownership]." *United States v. General Motors Corp.*, 323 U.S. 373 (1945). It is not used in the "vulgar and untechnical sense of the physical thing with respect to which the citizen exercises rights recognized by law. [Instead, it] denote[s] the group of rights inhering in the citizen's relation to the physical thing, as the right to possess, use and dispose of it. The constitutional provision is addressed

well established that "not every destruction or injury to property by governmental action has been held to be a 'taking' in the constitutional sense." *Armstrong v. United States*. 364 U.S. 40 (1960). Rather, the determination whether a state law unlawfully infringes a landowner's property in violation of the Taking Clause requires an examination of whether the restriction on private property "forc[es] some people alone to bear public burdens which, in all fairness and justice, should be borne by the public as a whole." *Id.*[3] This examination entails inquiry into such factors as the character of the governmental action, its economic impact, and its interference with reasonable investment backed expectations. *Kaiser Aetna, supra.* When "regulation goes too far it will be recognized as a taking." *Pennsylvania Coal Co. v. Mahon*, 260 U.S. 393 (1922).

Here the requirement that appellants permit appellees to exercise state protected rights of free expression and petition on shopping center property clearly does not amount to an unconstitutional infringement of appellants' property rights under the Taking Clause. There is nothing to suggest that preventing appellants from prohibiting this sort of activity will unreasonably impair the value or use of their property as a shopping center. The PruneYard is a large commercial complex that covers several city blocks, contains numerous separate business establishments, and is open to the public at large. The decision of the California Supreme Court makes it clear that the PruneYard may restrict expressive activity by adopting time, place, and manner regulations that will minimize any interference with its commercial functions. Appellees were orderly, and they limited their activity to the common areas of the shopping center. In these circumstances, the fact that they may have "physically invaded" appellants' property cannot be viewed as determinative.

This case is quite different from *Kaiser Aetna v. United States, supra. Kaiser Aetna* was a case in which the owners of a private pond had invested substantial amounts of money in dredging the pond, developing it into an exclusive marina, and building a surrounding marina community. The marina was open only to fee paying members, and the fees were paid in part to "maintain the privacy and security of the pond." *Id.* The Federal Government sought to compel free public use of the private marina on the ground that the marina became subject to the federal navigational servitude because the owners had dredged a channel connecting it to "navigable water."

The Government's attempt to create a public right of access to the improved pond interfered with Kaiser Aetna's "reasonable investment backed expectations." We held that it went "so far beyond ordinary regulation or improvement for navigation as to amount to a taking." *Id.* Nor as a general proposition is the United States, as opposed to the several States, possessed of residual authority that enables it to define "property" in the first instance. A State is, of course, bound by

to every sort of interest the citizen may possess." *Id.*

[3] [7] Thus, as this Court stated in *Monongahela Navigation Co. v. United States*, 148 U.S. 312 (1893), the Fifth Amendment "prevents the public from loading upon one individual more than his just share of the burdens of government, and says that when he surrenders to the public something more and different from that which is exacted from other members of the public, a full and just equivalent shall be returned to him."

the Just Compensation Clause of the Fifth Amendment, but here appellants have failed to demonstrate that the "right to exclude others" is so essential to the use or economic value of their property that the state authorized limitation of it amounted to a "taking."

There is also little merit to appellants' argument that they have been denied their property without due process of law. In *Nebbia v. New York*, this Court stated:

> [N]either property rights nor contract rights are absolute . . . . Equally fundamental with the private right is that of the public to regulate it in the common interest . . . . [T]he guaranty of due process, as has often been held, demands only that the law shall not be unreasonable, arbitrary or capricious, and that the means selected shall have a real and substantial relation to the objective sought to be attained.

Appellants have failed to provide sufficient justification for concluding that this test is not satisfied by the State's asserted interest in promoting more expansive rights of free speech and petition than conferred by the Federal Constitution.

Affirmed.

MR. JUSTICE BLACKMUN joins the opinion of the Court except that sentence thereof, which reads: "Nor as a general proposition is the United States, as opposed to the several States, possessed of residual authority that enables it to define 'property' in the first instance."

MR. JUSTICE MARSHALL, concurring.

I join the opinion of the Court, but write separately to make a few additional points.

I do not understand the Court to suggest that rights of property are to be defined solely by state law, or that there is no federal constitutional barrier to the abrogation of common law rights by Congress or a state government. The constitutional terms "life, liberty, and property" do not derive their meaning solely from the provisions of positive law. They have a normative dimension as well, establishing a sphere of private autonomy which government is bound to respect. Quite serious constitutional questions might be raised if a legislature attempted to abolish certain categories of common law rights in some general way. Indeed, our cases demonstrate that there are limits on governmental authority to abolish "core" common law rights, including rights against trespass, at least without a compelling showing of necessity or a provision for a reasonable alternative remedy.

That "core" has not been approached in this case. The California Supreme Court's decision is limited to shopping centers, which are already open to the general public. The owners are permitted to impose reasonable restrictions on expressive activity. There has been no showing of interference with appellants' normal business operations. The California court has not permitted an invasion of any personal sanctuary. *Cf. Stanley v. Georgia*, 394 U.S. 557 (1969). No rights of privacy are implicated. In these circumstances there is no basis for strictly scrutinizing the intrusion authorized by the California Supreme Court.

MR. JUSTICE POWELL, with whom MR. JUSTICE WHITE joins, concurring in part and in the judgment.

Although I join the judgment, I do not agree with all of the reasoning in Part V of the Court's opinion. I join Parts I–IV on the understanding that our decision is limited to the type of shopping center involved in this case. Significantly different questions would be presented if a State authorized strangers to picket or distribute leaflets in privately owned, freestanding stores and commercial premises. Nor does our decision today apply to all "shopping centers." This generic term may include retail establishments that vary widely in size, location, and other relevant characteristics. Even large establishments may be able to show that the number or type of persons wishing to speak on their premises would create a substantial annoyance to customers that could be eliminated only by elaborate, expensive, and possibly unenforceable time, place, and manner restrictions. As the Court observes, state power to regulate private property is limited to the adoption of reasonable restrictions that "do not amount to a taking without just compensation or contravene any other federal constitutional provision."

Restrictions on property use, like other state laws, are invalid if they infringe the freedom of expression and belief protected by the First and Fourteenth Amendments. In Part V of today's opinion, the Court rejects appellants' contention that "a private property owner has a First Amendment right not to be forced by the State to use his property as a forum for the speech of others." *Ante.* I agree that the owner of this shopping center has failed to establish a cognizable First Amendment claim in this case. But some of the language in the Court's opinion is unnecessarily and perhaps confusingly broad. In my view, state action that transforms privately owned property into a forum for the expression of the public's views could raise serious First Amendment questions.

Because appellants have not shown that the limited right of access held to be afforded by the California Constitution burdened their First and Fourteenth Amendment rights in the circumstances presented, I join the judgment of the Court. I do not interpret our decision today as a blanket approval for state efforts to transform privately owned commercial property into public forums. Any such state action would raise substantial federal constitutional questions not present in this case.

NOTES AND QUESTIONS

1. *Commercial Establishments and the Right to Exclude.* Although it was well-established that the operators of common carriers and innkeepers were required to accept any customer who sought their services, the traditional American common law rule was that individuals who operated an establishment open to the public were free to select their customers in a discriminatory fashion, if they chose to do so. *See McCrea v. Marsh*, 78 Mass. 211 (1858) (allowing operators of places of public entertainment to exclude customers on the basis of race). The freedom to discriminate on the basis of race, gender, national origin, religion, and disability have been severely limited by state and federal civil rights statutes, but the general right to exclude appears to remain intact, so long as it is not exercised in a way that affects those protected by the civil rights statutes.

There is some evidence, however, that this "right" is slowly eroding. The New Jersey Supreme Court, for example, has held that property owners who open their premises to the public have no right to exclude individuals "unreasonably," a holding that appears to be at odds with the traditional common law principle. *Uston v. Resorts Int'l Hotel, Inc.*, 445 A.2d 370 (N.J. 1982). New Jersey courts have also recognized a state constitutional right to distribute leaflets in a shopping mall similar to that recognized by the California Supreme Court in *Pruneyard. New Jersey Coalition Against War in the Middle East v. J.M.B. Realty Corp.*, 650 A.2d 757 (N.J. 1994). For a review of the cases, see *Mazdabrook Commons Homeowners' Ass'n v. Khan*, 46 A.3d 507 (N.J. 2012).

2. *The Right to Exclude and the First Amendment.* Ordinarily, the free speech protections provided by the First and Fourteenth Amendments to the United States Constitution apply only against the actions of government entities. Private property owners are thus generally free to deny access to individuals who wish to use their property for speech purposes. However, in 1946, the United States Supreme Court ruled that the operators of a "company town" — a community where streets, homes, businesses, schools, and other "public areas" were all owned by the employer of the residents — could not deny individuals the free speech rights that they would have in an ordinary community. *Marsh v. Alabama*, 326 U.S. 501 (1946).

In 1968, the Supreme Court appeared to expand upon *Marsh v. Alabama* when it held that a private shopping center that was open to the public was the equivalent of a business district in a community and that, therefore, individuals had the right to "picket" a particular store that refused to hire non-union labor. *Amalgamated Food Employees Union Local 590 v. Logan Valley Plaza, Inc.*, 391 U.S. 308 (1968). The broad implications of *Logan Valley* were cut back rather quickly, however, when a Supreme Court, including four recent appointees of President Richard Nixon, found that contrary to the holding in *Logan Valley*, a shopping center was not a public square and therefore its owners were not required to recognize the First Amendment rights of individual visitors. In *Lloyd Corp., Ltd. v. Tanner*, 407 U.S. 551 (1972), the Court held that a shopping center was not required to allow leafleting on its premises.

As the *PruneYard* case indicates, some states have applied free speech protections to shopping centers and other privately controlled spaces. While it appears that only California and New Jersey recognize a general right of access for speech purposes, other states permit access for more limited goals, primarily related to the electoral or public referendum processes. For discussion, see *Developments in the Law, VI. Public Space, Private Deed: The State Action Doctrine and Freedom of Speech on Private Property*, 123 HARV. L. REV. 1303, 1308 (2010), noting that a majority of states have rejected California's interpretation. The article notes that "[o]ne approach is the Supreme Court's refusal to extend speech rights into private shopping malls by setting government ownership as the standard for state action. California's alternate approach to state action makes a location's openness to the public sufficient to sustain a state constitutional challenge." *Id.* at 1313–14. For a restatement of the California view in more conventional terms, see *Golden Gateway Ctr. v. Golden Gateway Tenants Ass'n*, 29 P.3d 797, 810 (Cal. 2001).

The general right to exclude can also be limited by a variety of factors, such as the acquisition of easements by prescription. *See* Chapter 7. *See also Desnick v. ABC, Inc.*, 44 F.3d 1345 (7th Cir. 1995) (investigative journalists have a right to enter property during the course of an investigation, even if they do so under false pretenses).

3. In much of the United States there was, in its early history, an implicit right to "trespass" on undeveloped land, at least if the owner sent no message to the contrary. The practice of posting "No Trespassing" or "Posted" signs on undeveloped property developed as a way to limit the exercise of this "right." As discussed earlier, this right of access was often coupled with a right to hunt. (*See* Chapter 1, Section A-1, Note 4.) The principle of the open range — that cattle and hogs were free to roam and forage on private property unless the property owner chose to "fence out" the livestock — was a related principle. Although the "open range" has disappeared in most places, it appears to be still the law in Wyoming, at least in regard to cattle. *See* Wyo. Stat. § 11-26-101 (prohibiting swine, goats, and domestic elk from running at large in the state, but not extending the prohibition to cattle and horses).

Several Scandinavian countries still recognize "allemansratt," or "allmansret" (literally, "everyman's right") which is a right to travel on foot through privately owned lands that are untilled or undeveloped. It is sometimes described as a right "to walk freely in nature." Those exercising the right are obligated to respect the land on which they are traveling and while there is a right to camp, it is normally limited to one night. In Great Britain, the ramblers, an informal association of long-distance hikers and nature lovers, have lobbied with some success for governmental recognition of a "right to roam." In 2000, the British Parliament adopted the Countryside and Rights of Way Act which created a right of way for foot travel through nearly four million acres of open, undeveloped land in England and Wales, an area amounting to almost 10% of the land in those parts of the United Kingdom. A similar act was adopted in Scotland. *See Right to Roam Laws Let British Walk Over Class Lines*, N.Y. Times, Sept. 20, 2004, Sec. A, at 4; Sprankling, Coletta & Mirow, Global Issues in Property Law 88–94 (2006).

4. *State Definition of Property Rights*. Some commentators have characterized the *Pruneyard* case as primarily about the states' ability to define their own property rights free from federal interference. Is this a fair reading of *PruneYard*? Would Justice Marshall concur? In the Hawaii Supreme Court's *PASH* opinion, 903 P.2d 1246 (Haw. 1995), discussed above, the court suggested that the complaining landowner placed undue reliance on the western understandings of property law that are not universally applicable in Hawaii. Is that language consistent with the holding here?

[4.] Control of Airspace

GELLER v. BROWNSTONE CONDOMINIUM ASS'N
Illinois Court of Appeals
402 N.E.2d 807 (1980

McNamara, Justice.

Plaintiff, Donald Geller, appeals from an order of the circuit court of Cook County dismissing his amended complaint in which he had sought injunctive relief and damages from defendants.

Plaintiff is the owner of real estate located at 1448 North State Parkway in Chicago on which he is constructing a three story residence. Defendant Brownstone Condominium Association is the owner of a high rise condominium immediately south of plaintiff's property; defendant American Invesco Co. is manager of the condominium. The amended complaint recited in two counts that during construction of his residence workmen would be on plaintiff's property, and that after construction plaintiff and his family would reside there. Paragraphs 4 and 5 of count I charged as follows:

> 4. In performing any maintenance or other work on the North wall of its building, Defendants have, and if not prohibited will continue to encroach and trespass upon Plaintiff's property to perform work on its own property, either by erecting and operating a movable scaffolding or any other structure on its own property and extending over Plaintiff's property to the irreparable injury and great damage to the Plaintiff, for which Plaintiff has no adequate remedy at law.
>
> 5. The aforesaid structure and extensions have and will continue to interfere with Plaintiff's use of light and air and constitute a continuing and illegal trespass of Plaintiff's air rights.

Paragraphs 5 and 6 of Count II charged as follows:

> 5. Either defect of the scaffolding or negligence in construction, use or maintenance thereof would cause the scaffolding which Defendants erect over Plaintiff's property, or any object on the scaffolding, to fall on Plaintiff's building and work site causing serious injury or death to workmen or others on the property.
>
> 6. Maintenance of extensions by Defendants over Plaintiff's property constitutes encroachment by Defendants upon Plaintiff's property, light and air and exposes Plaintiff, his family, and others, to great hazard upon the malfunction or negligent use of said scaffolding for any reason or from objects falling from said scaffolding.

The complaint asked that defendants be permanently enjoined from installing or operating any scaffolding upon the north wall of their building. Plaintiff also asked that he be awarded damages for the unlawful trespass and taking of property and air rights.

Defendants filed a motion to dismiss the amended complaint. They argued that the complaint failed to state a cause of action, and that the court was without authority to enjoin future negligence. After considering the pleadings, memoranda, and arguments of counsel, the trial court dismissed the action.

A motion to dismiss a complaint admits only facts well pleaded, not conclusions of law. Here, the well pleaded facts and the threatened harm which plaintiff sought to enjoin were set forth in the paragraphs above. Pointing out that defendant's condominium was erected with its north wall on defendants' property line, plaintiff sought to prevent defendants from using temporary scaffolding on that wall. Plaintiff maintains that scaffolding on that wall extends into his air space and constitutes a continuing trespass. Plaintiff also urges that sometime in the future, defendants' workmen may be negligent while on the scaffolding, thus causing objects to fall on plaintiff's family or property. We do not believe that the well pleaded facts are legally sufficient to state a cause of action, and we believe the trial court properly dismissed the amended complaint.

In *United States v. Causby*, 328 U.S. 256 (1946), the Supreme Court held that a landowner owns at least as much of the space above the ground as he can occupy or use in connection with the land. In that case, the court ruled that planes in a flight pattern regularly flying over plaintiff's farm at a height of 83 feet above the ground came so close as to affect plaintiff's actual use of the land and thus constituted an intrusion. In *Hinman v. Pacific Air Transport*, 84 F.2d 755 (9th Cir. 1936), the plaintiff landowner sought to enjoin the defendant airline from operating its planes across plaintiff's land at a height of approximately 150 feet. In affirming the dismissal of the complaint, the court stated at p. 758:

> We own so much of the space above the ground as we can occupy or make use of, in connection with the enjoyment of our land. This right is not fixed. It varies with our varying needs and is coextensive with them. The owner of land owns as much of the space above him as he uses, but only so long as he uses it.
>
> Any use of such air or space by others which is injurious to his land, or which constitutes an actual interference with his possession or his beneficial use thereof, would be a trespass for which he would have remedy. But any claim of the landowner beyond this cannot find a precedent in law, nor support in reason.

The fundamental principle to be gleaned from *Causby* and *Hinman* is that a property owner owns only as much air space above his property as he can practicably use. And to constitute an actionable trespass, an intrusion has to be such as to subtract from the owner's use of the property. In the present case, plaintiff's complaint does not even allege use of the air space above the residence under construction. Defendants' use of temporary scaffolding in the air and space above that residence cannot be deemed actionable. The trial court correctly dismissed the matter.

Cases cited by plaintiff are distinguishable from the present case. In each case cited, there was an actual intrusion on the landowner's property interfering with the owner's use. In *Checkley v. Illinois Central R.R. Co.*, 100 N.E. 942 (Ill. 1913), the landlord's agent went on the tenant's property to burn grass and weeds, and the ensuing fire went out of control and damaged a building on the property. In *Miller v. Simon*, 241 N.E.2d 697 (Ill. App. 1968), the property owner had trees and topsoil taken from his land. In *Scioscia v. Iovieno*, 63 N.E.2d 898 (Mass. 1945), on which plaintiff places heavy reliance, defendants ran clothes reels with laundry onto plaintiff's property and actually interfered with plaintiff's use of the premises. In *Maton Bros. Inc. v. Central Illinois Public Service Co.*, 191 N.E. 321 (Ill. 1933), gas pipes maintained by defendant leaked onto plaintiff's property and destroyed plants. And in *Gerrard v. Procheddu*, 243 Ill. App. 562 (1927), defendant caused a fire on plaintiff's property by discharging fireworks. In the present case, the complaint alleged no such intrusion.

Running through the complaint is the suggestion that plaintiff is attempting to enjoin future acts of negligence by defendants' employees. Plaintiff insists that his complaint addresses itself to a present trespass rather than future negligence. In any event, the elements of a negligence action are absent, and the complaint is insufficient to state a cause of action in negligence.

For the reasons stated, the judgment of the circuit court of Cook County dismissing plaintiff's amended complaint is affirmed. Judgment affirmed.

NOTES AND QUESTIONS

1. *What Constitutes an Intrusion?* Is there no intrusion in the principal case, or no actionable intrusion? Does this distinction matter? What if the intrusion consisted of flagpoles extending over the property and into plaintiff's airspace? What about very tall trees whose upper branches extend over the property line? How about balconies? What if the plaintiff makes plans to construct his own high-rise? Is the key to an actionable trespass that the intrusion be into that portion of plaintiff's airspace that he is currently using, or would it suffice if the intrusion were into a portion of the airspace that *could* be used? Would a permanent intrusion be different than a temporary one? Why? *See Standard Realty Associates, Inc. v. Chelsea Gardens Corp.*, 964 N.Y.S.2d 94 (App. Div. 2013) (intrusion of advertising sign into plaintiff's airspace actionable as trespass).

2. *The Upper Limits to Ownership.* In 1926, the United States Congress declared the navigable airspace above the country to be in the public domain. Air Commerce Act of 1926, ch. 344 § 10, 44 Stat. 574. At least one court found that this declaration to preempt the ancient doctrine that he who owns the land owns the airspace above it. *Allegheny Airlines, Inc. v. Village of Cedarhurst*, 132 F. Supp. 871 (E.D.N.Y. 1955). However, in *Southwest Weather Research, Inc. v. Rounsaville*, 320 S.W.2d 211 (Tex. Civ. App. 1958), the court upheld an injunction against the appellant seeding clouds (to induce rain) over Rounsaville's land. (However, in *Rounsaville*, the court seemed more concerned about the "intrusion" of the rain caused by the cloud seeding than it did about the overflights themselves.) Should the 1926 Commerce Act have a bearing on the resolution of a case like *Geller*?

3. *An Easement Is a Real Property Interest.* What about the prescriptive easement that formed the basis for the U.S. Supreme Court's decision in *United States v. Causby*, discussed in *Geller*? As you will see in Chapter 8, an easement is

a real property interest in the land of another. In *Causby*, the Court held the taking of an easement by the federal government, whether or not intentional, amounts to a taking of property requiring compensation under the Fifth Amendment. Courts also recognize the taking of easements "by necessity" by private persons under certain circumstances. Do the facts in the principal case give rise to such circumstances? If so, what compensation, if any, should be due the plaintiff? Is this a better way to resolve the issue than declaring that this is not an intrusion because the plaintiff cannot, or is not, using the space? For a ruling that frequent overflights within 500 feet of the surface by United States Air Force planes might constitute a taking, see *Brown v. United States*, 73 F.3d 1100 (Fed. Cir. 1996).

4. *Easements in Air Space?* The issue looks trivial given the facts of the principal case; however, if the space being invaded were over, say, a railroad terminal in New York City, how would you expect a court to react to the argument that the railroad is not using the space over the terminal, and therefore any intrusion is not actionable? *See Penn Central Transp. Co. v. City of New York*, 438 U.S. 104 (1978), discussed in Chapter 3.

5. *Airspace and International Law.* It is universally accepted that a sovereign nation has the right to control its own airspace, but how far upward does that zone of control extend? Airspace is usually defined as "navigable airspace," but how does one draw the line between airspace and outer space? The most widely accepted position today is that the boundary between navigable airspace and outer space should be the lowest altitude (perigee) at which artificial satellites can remain in orbit without being destroyed by friction with the air. (At the present time, this is approximately 90 kilometers or 56 miles.) *See* Beckman, *Citizens Without a Forum: The Lack of an Appropriate and Consistent Remedy for United States Citizens Injured or Killed as the Result of Activity Above the Territorial Air Space*, 22 B.C. INT'L & COMP. L. REV. 249 (1999).

6. *Subsurface Trespasses.* Under the traditional American theory of ownership, ownership of land includes ownership of everything below the surface down to the center of the earth. Taken literally, this would mean that every parcel was essentially cone-shaped. While the right to control the area above the surface has been subjected to a "reasonableness" limitation, American courts still protect the surface owner's unrestricted right to control access to the subsurface. (The issue arises in regard to mining, the instillation of pipelines, exploration of caves, and other underground activities.) The leading case on this topic is still *Edwards v. Sims*, 24 S.W.2d 619 (Ky. Ct. App. 1929), which involved a dispute over the ownership of the Great Onyx Cave in Kentucky. The court barred the owner of the entrance of the cave from trespassing on the portion of the cave that ran underneath the plaintiff's land, even though the plaintiff had no access to his portion of the cave. (For more on this issue, see the discussion of *Marengo Cave Co. v. Ross*, 10 N.E.2d 917 (Ind. 1937), in Chapter 4.)

[B.] THE RIGHT TO USE

[1.] Nuisance

A nuisance is an unreasonable interference with another's use or enjoyment of land. Of course, "unreasonable" is a subjective term. The RESTATEMENT (SECOND) OF TORTS §§ 827 and 828, contains a frequently used formula for determining whether a nuisance exists. The formula weighs the gravity of the harm to the plaintiff against the utility of the defendant's use. Regarding the plaintiff's harm, the RESTATEMENT directs one to look at (1) the character of the harm; (2) the social value of the use invaded; and (3) the suitability of that use to the character of the area. The overriding question is whether it is reasonable for the defendant to be doing what he or she is doing where he or she is doing it.

Nuisances can be public and/or private, and they can be *per se* or *per accidens.* A private nuisance involves an invasion of the interest in the enjoyment of land (as in *Bove v. Donner-Hanna*, below), while a public nuisance involves an interference with the rights of the public. Frequently, a particular episode of unreasonable conduct will give rise simultaneously to both a public and a private nuisance. A nuisance *per se*, or at law, is conduct that is a nuisance itself (like the operation of an illegal house of prostitution or a dog-fighting business) while a nuisance *per accidens* is otherwise lawful conduct that is wrongful because of the particular circumstances of the case where it is located. Halfway houses and soup kitchens might be nuisances in residential areas, but they are not nuisances *per se* because there are settings where they are perfectly reasonable. What constitutes a nuisance has assumed critical importance in so-called "total" regulatory takings since, as the U.S. Supreme Court made clear in *Lucas*, a nuisance constitutes an exception to the categorical rule that a regulation depriving an owner of all economic beneficial use is the equivalent of an eminent domain taking requiring compensation. *See* Chapter 3.

BOVE v. DONNER-HANNA COKE CORP.

New York Supreme Court
258 N.Y.S. 229 (1932)

EDGCOMB, J.

In 1910 plaintiff purchased two vacant lots at the corner of Abby and Baraga streets in the city of Buffalo, and two years later built a house thereon. The front of the building was converted into a grocery store, and plaintiff occupied the rear as a dwelling. She rented the two apartments on the second floor.

Defendant operates a large coke oven on the opposite side of Abby street. The plant runs twenty-four hours in the day, and three hundred sixty-five days in the year. Of necessity, the operation has to be continuous, because the ovens would be ruined if they were allowed to cool off. The coke is heated to a temperature of around 2,000 degrees F., and is taken out of the ovens and run under a "quencher," where five or six hundred gallons of water are poured onto it at one time. This is a necessary operation in the manufacture of coke. The result is a tremendous cloud of steam, which rises in a shaft and escapes into the air, carrying with it minute portions of coke and more or less gas. This steam and the accompanying particles of dirt, as well as the dust which comes from a huge coal pile, necessarily kept on the premises, and the gases and odors which emanate from the plant, are carried by the wind in various directions, and frequently find their way onto the plaintiff's premises and into her house and store. According to the plaintiff, this results in an unusual amount of dirt and soot accumulating in her house, and prevents her opening the windows on the street side. She also claims that she suffers severe headaches by breathing the impure air occasioned by this dust and these offensive odors, and that her health and that of her family has been impaired, all to her very great discomfort and annoyance. She also asserts that this condition has lessened the rental value of her property, and has made it impossible at times to rent her apartments.

Claiming that such use of its plant by the defendant deprives her of the full enjoyment of her home, invades her property rights, and constitutes a private nuisance, plaintiff brings this action in equity to enjoin the defendant from the further maintenance of said nuisance, and to recover the damages which she asserts she has already sustained.

As a general rule, an owner is at liberty to use his property as he sees fit, without objection or interference from his neighbor, provided such use does not violate an ordinance or statute. There is, however, a limitation to this rule; one made necessary by the intricate, complex, and changing life of today. The old and familiar maxim that one must so use his property as not to injure that of another (*sic utere tuo ut alienum non laedas*) is deeply imbedded in our law. An owner will not be permitted to make an unreasonable use of his premises to the material annoyance of his neighbor, if the latter's enjoyment of life or property is materially lessened thereby.

Such a rule is imperative, or life today in our congested centers would be intolerable and unbearable. If a citizen was given no protection against unjust harassment arising from the use to which the property of his neighbor was put, the comfort and value of his home could easily be destroyed by any one who chose to erect an annoyance nearby, and no one would be safe, unless he was rich enough to buy sufficient land about his home to render such disturbance impossible. When conflicting rights arise, a general rule must be worked out which, so far as possible, will preserve to each party that to which he has a just claim.

While the law will not permit a person to be driven from his home, or to be compelled to live in it in positive distress or discomfort because of the use to which other property nearby has been put, it is not every annoyance connected with business which will be enjoined. Many a loss arises from acts or conditions which do not create a ground for legal redress. *Damnum absque injuria* is a familiar maxim. Factories, stores, and mercantile establishments are essential to the prosperity of the nation. They necessarily invade our cities, and interfere more or less with the peace and tranquility of the neighborhood in which they are located.

One who chooses to live in the large centers of population cannot expect the quiet of the country. Congested centers are seldom free from smoke, odors, and other pollution from houses, shops, and factories, and one who moves into such a region cannot hope to find the pure air of the village or outlying district. A person who prefers the advantages of community life must expect to experience some of the resulting inconveniences. Residents of industrial centers must endure without redress a certain amount of annoyance and discomfiture which is incident to life in such a locality. Such inconvenience is of minor importance compared with the general good of the community.

Whether the particular use to which one puts his property constitutes a nuisance or not is generally a question of fact, and depends upon whether such use is reasonable under all the surrounding circumstances. What would distress and annoy one person would have little or no effect upon another; what would be deemed a disturbance and a torment in one locality would be unnoticed in some other place; a condition which would cause little or no vexation in a business, manufacturing, or industrial district might be extremely tantalizing to those living in a restricted and beautiful residential zone; what would be unreasonable under one set of circumstances would be deemed fair and just under another. Each case is unique. No hard and fast rule can be laid down which will apply in all instances.

The inconvenience, if such it be, must not be fanciful, slight, or theoretical, but certain and substantial, and must interfere with the physical comfort of the ordinarily reasonable person.

Applying these general rules to the facts before us, it is apparent that defendant's plant is not a nuisance *per se*, and that the court was amply justified in holding that it had not become one by reason of the manner in which it had been conducted. Any annoyance to plaintiff is due to the nature of the business which the defendant conducts, and not to any defect in the mill, machinery, or apparatus. The plant is modern and up-to-date in every particular. It was built under a contract with the federal government, the details of which are not important here. The plans were drawn by the Kopperas Construction Company, one of the largest and best-known manufacturers of coke plants in the world, and the work was done under the supervision of the War Department. No reasonable change or improvement in the property can be made which will eliminate any of the things complained of. If coke is made, coal must be used. Gas always follows the burning of coal, and steam is occasioned by throwing cold water on red hot coals.

The cases are legion in this and other states where a defendant has been held guilty of maintaining a nuisance because of the annoyance which he has caused his neighbor by reason of noise, smoke, dust, noxious gases, and disagreeable smells which have emanated from his property. But smoke and noisome odors do not always constitute a nuisance. I find none of these cases controlling here; they all differ in some particular from the facts in the case at bar.

It is true that the appellant was a resident of this locality for several years before the defendant came on the scene of action, and that, when the plaintiff built her house, the land on which these coke ovens now stand was a hickory grove. But in a growing community changes are inevitable. This region was never fitted for a residential district; for years it has been peculiarly adapted for factory sites. This was apparent when plaintiff bought her lots and when she built her house. The land is low and lies adjacent to the Buffalo river, a navigable stream connecting with Lake Erie. Seven different railroads run through this area. Freight tracks and yards can be seen in every direction. Railroads naturally follow the low levels in passing through a city. Cheap transportation is an attraction which always draws factories and industrial plants to a locality. It is common knowledge that a combination of rail and water terminal facilities will stamp a section as a site suitable for industries of the heavier type, rather than for residential purposes. In 1910 there were at least eight industrial plants, with a total assessed valuation of over a million dollars, within a radius of a mile from plaintiff's house.

With all the dirt, smoke, and gas which necessarily comes from factory chimneys, trains, and boats, and with full knowledge that this region was especially adapted for industrial rather than residential purposes, and that factories would increase in the future, plaintiff selected this locality as the site of her future home. She voluntarily moved into this district, fully aware of the fact that the atmosphere would constantly be contaminated by dirt, gas, and foul odors, and that she could not hope to find in this locality the pure air of a strictly residential zone. She evidently saw certain advantages in living in this congested center. This is not the case of an industry, with its attendant noise and dirt, invading a quiet residential district. It is just the opposite. Here a residence is built in an area naturally adapted for industrial purposes and already dedicated to that use. Plaintiff can hardly be heard to complain at this late date that her peace and comfort have been disturbed by a situation which existed, to some extent at least, at the very time she bought her property, and which condition she must have known would grow worse rather than better as the years went by.

Today there are twenty industrial plants within a radius of less than a mile and three-quarters from appellant's house, with more than sixty-five smokestacks rising in the air, and belching forth clouds of smoke. Every day there are one hundred and forty-eight passenger trains, and two hundred and twenty-five freight trains, to say nothing of switch engines, passing over these various railroad tracks near to the plaintiff's property. Over ten thousand boats, a large portion of which burn soft coal, pass up and down the Buffalo river every season. Across the street, and within three hundred feet from plaintiff's house, is a large tank of the Iroquois Gas Company which is used for the storage of gas.

The utter abandonment of this locality for residential purposes, and its universal use as an industrial center, becomes manifest when one considers that in 1929 the assessed valuation of the twenty industrial plants above referred to aggregated over $20,000,000, and that the city in 1925 passed a zoning ordinance putting this area in the third industrial district, a zone in which stockyards, glue factories, coke ovens, steel furnaces, rolling mills, and other similar enterprises were permitted to be located.

One has only to mention these facts to visualize the condition of the atmosphere in this locality. It is quite easy to imagine that many of the things of which the plaintiff complains are due to causes over which the defendant has no control. At any rate, if appellant is immune from the annoyance occasioned by the smoke and odor which must necessarily come from these various sources, it would hardly seem that she could consistently claim that her health has been impaired, and that the use and enjoyment of her home have been seriously interfered with solely because of the dirt, gas, and stench which have reached her from defendant's plant.

It is very true that the law is no respecter of persons, and that the most humble citizen in the land is entitled to identically the same protection accorded to the master of the most gorgeous palace. However, the fact that the plaintiff has voluntarily chosen to live in the smoke and turmoil of this industrial zone is some evidence, at least that any annoyance which she has suffered from the dirt, gas, and odor which have emanated from defendant's plant is more imaginary and theoretical than it is real and substantial.

I think that the trial court was amply justified in refusing to interfere with the operation of the defendant's coke ovens. No consideration of public policy or private rights demands any such sacrifice of this industry.

Plaintiff is not entitled to the relief which she seeks for another reason.

Subdivision 25 of section 20 of the General City Law, added by Laws 1917, c. 483, gives to the cities of this state authority to regulate the location of industries, and to district the city for that purpose. Pursuant to such authority the common council of the city of Buffalo adopted an ordinance setting aside the particular area in which defendant's plant is situated as a zone in which coke ovens might lawfully be located.

After years of study and agitation it has been found that development in conformity with some well-considered and comprehensive plan is necessary to the welfare of any growing municipality. The larger the community the greater becomes the need of such plan. Haphazard city building is ruinous to any city. Certain areas must be given over to industry, without which the country cannot long exist. Other sections must be kept free from the intrusion of trade and the distraction of business, and be set aside for homes, where one may live in a wholesome environment. Property owners, as well as the public, have come to recognize the absolute necessity of reasonable regulations of this character in the interest of public health, safety, and general welfare, as well as for the conservation of property values. Such is the purpose of our zoning laws.

After due consideration the common council of Buffalo decreed that an enterprise similar to that carried on by the defendant might properly be located at the site of this particular coke oven. It is not for the court to step in and override such decision, and condemn as a nuisance a business which is being conducted in an approved and expert manner, at the very spot where the council said that it might be located. A court of equity will not ordinarily assume to set itself above officials to whom the law commits a decision, and reverse their discretion and judgment, unless bad faith is involved. No such charge is made here.

Other defenses have been urged by the defendant, which it is unnecessary to discuss, in view of the conclusion which has already been reached. I see no good reason why the decision of the Special Term should be disturbed. I think that the judgment appealed from should be affirmed.

NOTES AND QUESTIONS

1. *What Is a Nuisance?* Cement plants and piggeries make for relatively easy nuisance cases if they are located in the wrong place. But what about funeral parlors, halfway houses, homes for abused women, homes for AIDS patients, and abortion clinics? How important should the social value factor be in making the

nuisance determination? A soup kitchen conducted by a church in a residential area was held to be a nuisance in *Armory Park Neighborhood Ass'n v. Episcopal Community Servs. in Arizona*, 712 P.2d 914 (Ariz. 1985). In *Smith v. Gill*, 310 So. 2d 214, 218 (Ala. 1975), a halfway house for a "mental patients" was found to be a nuisance in a residential area.

2. *Industrial vs. Residential.* In *Bove*, how does the court decide that the area is more suitable for industry than residential use? Examine the court's description of what the area was like when the plaintiff acquired her land compared to what it was like at the time the case was tried. Wasn't she there first? Is it fair to force her to have foreseen the way the area would develop?

Agricultural uses frequently clash with residential uses as well. Based on *Bove*, what would a court do with the following facts? In 1949, a pig farmer set up his piggery in a rural community. His business proved successful and the number of pigs increased; he satisfactorily operated the piggery (as in *Bove* there is no negligence on his part), but it did smell. By 1960, development had grown out toward the pig farmer and a small subdivision was built on the land near him. His new neighbors, bothered by the smell, wanted his operation shut down. Should they be able to secure a legal determination that the farm is a nuisance?

In *Pendoley v. Ferreira*, 187 N.E.2d 142 (Mass. 1963), on similar facts, the court held the farmer was conducting a nuisance and ordered him to liquidate his business. Is such a holding fair? The farm preservation movement has led to the adoption of "right to farm" statutes in some states that immunize certain farm operations from being declared nuisances. These statutes are discussed in Note 6 below.

3. *The Changing Definition of Nuisance.* How does nuisance law deal with changing times? What may be a nuisance in one era is not necessarily one in another. Funeral parlors in residential areas, for example, were not viewed as nuisances in the 19th century, but have been so-classified in the modern era. *Compare Wescott v. Middleton*, 11 A. 490 (N.J. 1887) (held not a nuisance per se), *with Powell v. Taylor*, 263 S.W.2d 906 (Ark. 1954) (enjoined as a nuisance). What will be deemed a nuisance will be particularly hard to predict in times of changing attitudes.

4. *Remedies for Nuisances.* Public nuisances were subject to abatement without compensation by the state. In a private nuisance case, traditionally a successful plaintiff was entitled to both money damages and injunctive relief. The latter followed automatically from the finding of nuisance and was particularly useful because it could restore the previous status quo.

When *Bove* was decided, New York case law provided an absolute right to an injunction once a nuisance was found. Thus, had the court found the coke plant to be a nuisance, it would have had to enjoin its operation. Imagine the implications of a court doing so in 1932 during the depths of the Great Depression. Could it be that the mandatory injunction rule colored the court's view of Bove's claim? In *Boomer v. Atlantic Cement Co.*, 257 N.E.2d 870 (N.Y. 1970), the same court a generation later affirmed a finding that a cement plant was a nuisance but refused to follow its longstanding injunction rule and awarded permanent damages to the neighbors.

The plant was a major employer and taxpayer in the town, and on balance the rights of the plant's neighbors to be free from a nuisance simply were overwhelmed. Had the *Boomer* rule been in effect at the time of *Bove*, would it have been proper to award Ms. Bove damages?

In *Spur Indus. v. Del Webb Corp.*, 494 P.2d 700 (Ariz. 1972), the court found that defendant's commercial cattle feedlot had become a nuisance because the land around it had been developed as a residential community. Although the public interest required closing the feedlot, the court found that the plaintiff, a major developer, had caused the problem and ordered it to pay the defendant's costs incurred in shutting down the operation and relocating. Is this a better solution? Although the *Spur* case has been much discussed over the past 35 years, no other court has adopted its approach. *See* Lewin, *Compensated Injunctions and the Evolution of Nuisance Law*, 71 IOWA L. REV. 775 (1986). Is this an appropriate approach?

5. *Defenses to Nuisance Actions*. The most obvious defense, of course, is that the complained of conduct is not unreasonable. Even when the conduct is deemed unreasonable, the defendant may have a number of defenses to liability. First, the plaintiff must bring his action in a timely fashion. If there is a statute of limitations, it must be complied with, and even if there is not, a long period of acquiescence may prevent the plaintiff from prevailing. If the offending activity has been preceding for the necessary time, it is possible that the defendant has acquired a prescriptive easement (as discussed in *Thornton v. Hay*, above) for the allegedly unreasonable actions. In addition, many jurisdictions once recognized a "coming to the nuisance" defense that protected first-in-time use. This defense has largely fallen out of favor — think of how it would apply to the cases already discussed — but it is still taken into account as a factor in the determination of reasonableness. *See* SPRANKLING, UNDERSTANDING PROPERTY LAW § 29.05[B] (3d ed. 2012).

6. *Right to Farm Statutes*. To protect farms from suburban sprawl, a majority of states have adopted statutes that insulate farms from nuisance liability. As such, they work to revive the "coming to a nuisance" defense. There is some variation from state to state, but the Texas statute is representative. It protects any farming operation that has been in business for more than one year so long as its activities are "substantially unchanged since the established date of operation." If a plaintiff sues a protected farmer, the farmer not only prevails but is entitled to collect legal fees, court costs, travel expenses, and any other related costs from the plaintiff. Tex. Agric. Code Ann. § 251.004. The constitutional legitimacy of these statutes has generally been upheld, although in Iowa (of all places) a right to farm statute was struck down as a regulatory taking of property prohibited by the Fifth and Fourteenth Amendments of the United States Constitution. *Bormann v. Board of Supervisors*, 584 N.W.2d 309 (Iowa 1998). Not all courts have followed *Bormann*.

7. *Importance of Zoning Classification*. Note how the *Bove* court used the fact that the area in Buffalo where the parties were located was zoned industrial. Should the zoning classification be conclusive evidence of suitability of use in the area? Ordinarily it is an important factor in determining reasonableness, but it is normally not absolutely conclusive.

[2.] Lateral Support

VIKELL INVESTORS PACIFIC, INC. v. HAMPDEN, LTD.

Colorado Court of Appeals
946 P.2d 589 (1997)

Opinion by Judge Davidson.

Plaintiff, Vikell Investors Pacific, Inc., (Vikell) appeals from a judgment entered on a jury verdict finding defendant Kip Hampden, Ltd., (Kip Hampden) not liable for the subsidence of real property owned by Vikell. Vikell also appeals from a directed verdict by the trial court dismissing its claim against defendants George Morris and his company, Lincoln DeVore, Inc., (collectively Morris) for breach of fiduciary duty. We affirm.

This controversy centers around the subsidence of a hill in Colorado Springs. Vikell owned real property at the top of the hill, located on which was a large apartment complex called Woodstone Apartments (Woodstone). Kip Hampden owned adjoining property, occupied by a car dealership, at the bottom of the hill, directly below Woodstone.

In 1987, Kip Hampden decided to improve its property by grading the base of the hill and expanding a parking lot used by the car dealership. Kip Hampden hired Morris, an engineering consultant, to determine whether the excavation could be done safely and, if so, to plan the project. After Morris tested the slope stability, which test revealed water seepage in the hillside, he issued a report to Kip Hampden indicating that the hillside was subject to movement and landslides. Nevertheless, the report included a detailed plan for grading the base of the hill and expanding the parking lot.

Pursuant to Morris' plan, Kip Hampden began the excavation and had thousands of cubic yards of soil removed from the base of the hill below Woodstone.

In 1989, when Vikell acquired the Woodstone property, it hired several consultants and contractors to refurbish and repair the apartment complex, which had fallen into disrepair after its prior owner declared bankruptcy.

Vikell hired a soils engineer to examine several of the Woodstone buildings, which were experiencing foundation cracking and other problems. That engineer advised that the buildings were moving, causing the foundation cracking, and he identified three possible reasons: expansive soils, slope instability, and foundation settlement caused by consolidation of non-compact fill used in the original building construction. He recommended that Vikell pay special attention to controlling water in the hillside, which he indicated could be aggravating the building movement.

A structural engineer hired by the bankruptcy court in 1988 to help bring Woodstone up to a reasonable standard of maintenance also advised Vikell representatives that controlling water in and around the hillside was critical to the repair project because water could be aggravating any downhill building movement.

Pursuant to the engineers' recommendations, Vikell attempted to correct surface drainage problems and utility leaks in order to reduce the amount of water in the hillside and stop the building movement. After several repairs, all of the buildings stabilized with the exception of Woodstone buildings 410 and 420, which continued to move and crack.

In 1991, Vikell hired Morris as its new soils engineer to study and solve the remaining problems with building movement. Morris did not inform Vikell that Kip Hampden had excavated the base of the hill in 1987 or that he had worked for Kip Hampden on the project.

Morris first theorized that the movement of buildings 410 and 420 was due to simple building settlement, and he recommended pressure grouting beneath the buildings to provide them with additional support. When the buildings continued to move, Morris shifted his focus to water problems. He dug up various parts of Vikell's property to check for groundwater but, despite his earlier report to Kip Hampden that there was water seepage in the hillside, he found little, if any, water. Morris next recommended a second pressure grouting. After the second grouting, however, the building movement accelerated.

In 1994, Morris suggested that, although "unthinkable," the entire hillside might be subsiding toward Kip Hampden's property, causing buildings 410 and 420 to slide down the hillside. He performed a slope failure analysis and confirmed that the stability of the hillside had decreased. Morris' report also revealed that Kip Hampden had cut away the base of the slope in 1987. However, his report did not indicate that he had worked on the project.

Shortly thereafter, Vikell hired a new soils expert who investigated the nature and cause of the building movement and determined that Kip Hampden's removal of soil from the base of the hill contributed to the ongoing slope subsidence.

In 1995, major slope failures occurred and Vikell was forced to abandon and demolish buildings 410 and 420. Kip Hampden denied any responsibility for the slope failures. In a meeting between representatives of Vikell and Kip Hampden, Morris revealed for the first time that he was the soils engineer who had assisted Kip Hampden with its downhill excavation.

As a result of the damage caused by the slope subsidence, Vikell sued Kip Hampden for strict liability and for vicarious liability arising from Morris' allegedly negligent work in planning the 1987 excavation. Vikell also sued Morris directly for negligence and breach of fiduciary duty. The trial court directed a verdict in favor of Morris on the claim for breach of fiduciary duty. The remaining issues were submitted to a jury, which found that Kip Hampden was neither strictly liable nor vicariously liable, that Morris was not negligent, and that Vikell was negligent. This appeal followed.

I.

Vikell first contends that the trial court erred in instructing the jury on the appropriate standard of strict liability in lateral support cases. Specifically, it maintains that it was error to instruct the jury that additional subsurface water and groundwater are artificial additions or improvements that a plaintiff must prove did

not materially contribute to slope subsidence. We disagree.

As a general matter, one who withdraws naturally necessary lateral support of land in another's possession is strictly liable for a subsidence of the land, as well as for harm to artificial additions resulting from the subsidence. Restatement (Second) of Torts § 817 (1979). For strict liability to apply, however, a jury first must find that the weight of the buildings, artificial additions, and fill on the plaintiff's land did not materially increase the lateral pressure and thus that such added weight was not a proximate cause of the damage to the property. In fact, there is a legal presumption that the weight of the buildings, artificial additions, and fill did contribute to the subsidence, and the burden is on the plaintiff to overcome this presumption. *Gladin v. Von Engeln*, 575 P.2d 418 (Colo. 1978).

Here, the trial court instructed the jury that:

> Kip Hampden, Ltd. alleges that the artificial additions and fill have created additional sub-surface water and groundwater on Plaintiff's property . . . [and] the burden is upon the Plaintiff to overcome this presumption . . . and to prove . . . that the additional sub-surface water and groundwater has not materially contributed to the existing subsidences . . . .

The parties agree that Vikell's land, improved by Woodstone, was not in its natural state. They also agree that the weight of the Woodstone buildings did not significantly increase lateral pressure on the land and thus was not a proximate cause of the hill's subsidence. Furthermore, the parties do not dispute that additional sub-surface water and groundwater in the hill contributed to the hill's subsidence.

At issue, then, is whether collateral consequences of artificial additions to land — specifically, the additional water in the hill caused by the presence of the Woods tone complex — are incorporated in the legal presumption against strict liability.

Vikell contends that, according to *Gladin*, in order to overcome the legal presumption against strict liability, it must prove only that the weight of its buildings did not increase lateral pressure on the land and thus materially contribute to the hill's subsidence. Accordingly, Vikell contends that the trial court's instruction improperly included additional water in the legal presumption. In contrast, Kip Hampden contends that the instruction was proper because the legal presumption prescribed in *Gladin* is broad, extending beyond increased lateral pressure from the weight of buildings or improvements to include any changes to the land occurring as collateral consequences of artificial additions to the land. We agree with Kip Hampden.

In *Gladin*, the supreme court determined that the applicability of strict liability in a lateral support case hinges on whether an artificial condition created on the plaintiff's land contributed to the injury, or whether the subsidence would have occurred even if the land had remained in its natural state. That opinion makes it clear that increased lateral pressure from the weight of buildings or improvements is an artificial condition created on the land. However, neither *Gladin* nor any subsequent Colorado appellate court opinion has addressed the issue whether changes to the land occurring as collateral consequences of buildings or improvements also qualify as artificial conditions created on the land.

By common law tradition, a landowner is absolutely entitled to the lateral support of his or her soil in its natural state by the soil of adjoining lands.

When land is no longer in its natural state, but has been filled or altered, the entitlement to lateral support from adjoining land is not forfeited, but the landowner is entitled only to the lateral support from adjoining property that the land would have needed in its natural state, before it was filled or altered. *See* Restatement (Second) of Torts § 817 comments b & d (1979).

The measure of this entitlement, and of the duty of the adjoining landowner to provide lateral support, is the natural dependence of the land, and the entitlement and duty are not enlarged by alterations of the natural condition. *See* Restatement (Second) of Torts § 817 comment c (1979).

Similarly, land that is entitled to maintenance of lateral support from adjoining land likewise is expected to provide its own lateral support. Strict liability does not apply in circumstances in which a subsidence of land is caused by the removal of additional lateral support required because alterations in the supported land have impaired its cohesiveness and stability. (The court cited cases where digging or mining superimposed unnatural with or diminished land's supporting power. — Eds.) *See* Restatement (Second) of Torts § 817 comment e (1979).

Underlying this limitation on strict liability is the fundamental notion that a landowner cannot, by placing improvements on its land, increase its neighbor's duty to support the land laterally. Otherwise, the party with the duty to maintain the lateral support would be responsible for improving the support to hold more than the natural land would have held.

In light of these principles, which emphasize a comparison of the support required by land in its natural state with the support required by the same land in its improved state, we conclude that, for purposes of strict liability in lateral support cases, any alteration by a plaintiff of its land, whether a purposeful improvement added to the land or an unforeseen collateral consequence of such an improvement, is an artificial condition on the land.

Here, because the jury found that the additional water in the hill was not a natural occurrence but was caused by Woodstone's construction, such water was necessarily an artificial condition on Vikell's land. Consequently, because according to *Gladin* the applicability of strict liability in a lateral support case hinges on whether an artificial condition created on the plaintiff's land contributed to the injury, we further conclude that the trial court's instruction properly included additional water in the legal presumption against strict liability.

Vikell, however, contends that, by including any additional water in the land associated with construction thereon as being an artificial addition or improvement that a plaintiff must prove did not contribute to slope subsidence, we are effectively eliminating strict liability as a claim for relief in all lateral support cases. We disagree. Nothing precludes a plaintiff from overcoming the presumption against strict liability by proving that additional water — or any other collateral consequence of artificial additions to land — did not materially contribute to subsidence of its land.

Moreover, contrary to Vikell's contention that *Gladin* contradicts established tort principles, we note simply that actions for strict liability in lateral support cases involve an impure form of that theory. *See generally* W. Keeton, *Prosser & Keeton on Torts* §§ 75, 79, 81 (5th ed. 1984). Although in a strict liability lateral support case there is a burden placed on a plaintiff to overcome the legal presumption that artificial conditions contributed to the subsidence of its land, nevertheless, once the plaintiff overcomes that presumption, it need prove merely that the withdrawal of such support was a cause of its damages. . . .

The judgment is affirmed.

Chief Judge Sternberg and Judge Plank concur.

NOTES AND QUESTIONS

1. *Lateral vs. Subjacent Support.* Landowners are entitled to both lateral and subjacent support. The former is the right to have land supported in its natural condition by adjoining parcels of land; the latter, is the right to have land supported in its natural condition by the earth below. Liability for both is normal strict liability, so long as the land is in its natural state. However, if the land contains buildings or other structures and the defendants' excavation would not have caused subsidence were the land still in its natural state, then the standard of liability is one of reasonableness or negligence. Moreover, collateral damage caused by material additions may also eliminate strict liability. The defendant's actions in doing excavation caused the subsidence in the principal case, but strict liability can attach for a failure to maintain support when there is a duty to act. *Noone v. Price*, 298 S.E.2d 218 (W. Va. 1982).

As a practical matter, when the issue is subjacent support, liability will almost always be strict, since it is likely that the surface would have collapsed when undermined from below whether or not there were structures on it. Subjacent support cases usually occur in the context of underground mining when the mineral rights are owned by someone other than the surface owner. Legislation may require measures to prevent subsidence from mining. This legislation can raise takings problems. *See* Chapter 3.

2. *A Fair Rule?* In today's urban settings, the right to support is a narrow entitlement. Even if a material addition such as a major building does not cause subsidence, a plaintiff might not be able to claim strict liability if there is "collateral damage," and negligence may be difficult to prove. The right to support also favors the uphill owner. Why should this be so? Development on hillsides is disfavored today, and communities often adopt land use regulations that prohibit or severely limit hillside development. *See* R. Olshansky, *Planning for Hillside Development*, American Planning Association, Planning Advisory Service Rep. No. 466 (1996).

The origins of the right to support are unclear. For a holding that the right has its origins in nuisance law, see *Dalton v Henry Angus & Co*, (1881) 6 App. Cas. 740, 746.

3. *A Special Problem.* A complicated situation arises when careful excavation by the defendant results in the disturbance of underground "quicksand" (a mixture of soil and water with more attributes of the latter than the former). If plaintiff's land "subsides," should the plaintiff prevail on subsidence grounds, or should the court examine the law of the jurisdiction on subsurface water rights? Traditionally, a landowner was not liable for the consequences of withdrawing underground water, but was liable for excavations that resulted in subsidence. *See Prete v. Cray*, 141 A. 609 (R.I. 1928) (city not liable when construction of sewer system caused plaintiff's land to collapse); *Finley v. Teeter Stone, Inc.*, 248 A.2d 106 (Md. 1968) (no liability when operation of a quarry involved continued pumping of accumulated water from quarry pits cause sinkholes on neighboring property). The reasonable and unreasonable use of water is discussed below in Subsection 3b. Is the issue here one of lateral or subjacent support?

[3.] Reasonable Use of Natural Resources

[a.] Water

YONADI v. HOMESTEAD COUNTRY HOMES

New Jersey Superior Court
114 A.2d 564 (1955)

The opinion of the court was delivered by Clapp, S.J.A.D.

This appeal has to do with the law of casual surface waters. The principal question presented (to state the case very generally) is whether a person improving a tract of land and constructing and maintaining drains therein is to be charged with liability for a resultant increase in the flow of surface water which runs off the tract upon plaintiffs' lands.

Plaintiffs own a golf course and restaurant located on the south side of Allaire Road, Spring Lake Heights. The tract mentioned, consisting of 40 acres, lying across the road on the north side, had been farming land until 1950, but since then the private corporate defendants, or one of them, have erected on it 169 houses. Generally speaking, the natural drainage of this land is southerly, passing from this tract through ditches and a swale once existing on the property now constituting the golf course, and so eventually to the Atlantic Ocean. There was testimony that the run-off from improved residential areas, such as the development here with its catch basins and sub-surface drains, is about 3 1/2 times that coming from the more absorbent soil of the farm land formerly here. In times of heavy rain, excess water has produced flood conditions on plaintiffs' property.

The court sitting without a jury gave judgment for the plaintiff against the borough and the two private corporations, awarding damages of $2,500 against all three defendants, and (a) restraining them from "using or permitting the artificial collection of waters, and from collecting and diverting it thereby on the lands of the plaintiffs, to the harm of the plaintiffs," and (b) ordering defendants "to accomplish this work" within 90 days.

The trial court seems to have been of the view that the casting of surface waters, in unusual or substantial quantities, through artificial means, on the land of another, was, without more, unlawful and actionable. This, we think, is error.

The general rule is that neither the diversion nor the altered transmission, repulsion or retention of surface water gives rise to an actionable injury. Generally, therefore, he who improves or alters land is not subjected to liability because of the consequences of his acts upon the flow of surface water. *Bowlsby v. Speer*, 31 N.J.L. 351 (Sup. Ct. 1865). [Other citations omitted.]

Under this rule it matters not that the flow of water upon plaintiffs' property is much increased or accelerated or its force aggravated. In pursuance of this rule, it has been held that the mere filling in of a tract of land "to such an extent as to work a change in the topography of the land, and to cause the surface water to run in a southerly, instead of, as formerly, in an easterly course," is not actionable.

There are or may be a number of exceptions to this rule. [Summary of exceptions omitted.] But we need consider only one of them.

This exception arises where a defendant improving or altering land interferes with the flow of surface water, not by making a change in the grade or surface of the land, but by means of drains, ditches or other artificial contrivances for the very purpose of transmitting the water. Under this exception, a defendant renders himself absolutely liable if by means of such an artificial device he causes surface water to be carried in a body large enough to do substantial injury (usually drainage from a large tract) and thereby casts it on plaintiff's lands away from where it otherwise would have flowed. *Inhabitants of Township of West Orange v. Field*, 37 N.J. Eq. 600 (E. & A. 1883).

But this exception does not apply where the surface water is brought to the locality substantially where it otherwise would have flowed. In such a case we are thrown back upon the general rule. Thus, if through a drain or other artificial means, a defendant effects a concentration in the flow of surface water but brings it to the locality substantially where it otherwise would have flowed, the damage is not actionable. *See Jessup v. Bamford Bros. Silk Mfg. Co.*, 66 N.J.L. 641, 645 (E. & A. 1901).

While the New Jersey cases do not deal with the matter explicitly, we conclude that where surface water is concentrated through a drain or other artificial means and is conducted to some place substantially where it otherwise would have flowed, the defendant will not be liable even though by reason of improvements he has made in the land, the water is brought there in larger quantities and with greater force than would have occurred prior to the improvements. The policies underlying the general rule come to bear here. What reasonably could the upland proprietor or occupant do in the present case with this excess water? Rather than require him to dispose of it — and so perhaps require him to secure the cooperation of a number of lowland properties through which the water must eventually be brought — the burden is cast on each lowland proprietor to protect his own land.

There are three rules in this country as to surface water. First, there is the Massachusetts and New Jersey rule — the general rule above stated — adopted in some 22 jurisdictions. It is known as the common enemy rule, after a phrase employed by Beasley, C.J., in *Town of Union v. Durkes*, 38 N.J.L. 21, 22 (Sup. Ct. 1875), which, though apparently inaccurate in its allusion, nevertheless is a not inappropriate appellation of the fundamental concept of the rule. This rule obviously favors the improver of property, at the expense of neighbors who are affected by his disposition of the surface water.

Second, there is the civil law rule prevailing in some measure in 18 states, including Illinois and Pennsylvania. Under it the proprietor of the higher land has a natural servitude in the lower land to accommodate the natural flow (and no more than the natural flow) of surface water from his land. This servitude, the proprietor of the lowland cannot obstruct.

There is a third rule in force only in two jurisdictions, nevertheless representative also of a recent tendency in the law of other jurisdictions. Under it a person altering his land is placed under a duty in connection with surface water not to act unreasonably under the circumstances. Prosser, Torts 587 (1941); 6A American Law of Property 190 (1954); 12 A.L.R. 2d 1340; *Brownsey v. General Printing Ink Corp.*, 118 N.J.L. 505 (Sup. Ct. 1937). The Restatement of Torts, § 833, has adopted this view.

It will be found that the law of surface waters in this country, including this State, was first laid down about a century ago in the light of the law of private nuisances as it then stood. And it may therefore be said by some students of the matter — having regard to the tendency then to look upon an interference with the use or enjoyment of land, as an absolute, either black or white, imposing either absolute liability or absolute non-liability — that the law as to surface waters is out of keeping with the notions of today as to private nuisances.

But the question is not as easily disposed of as that. The strong public policies favoring the development of land, which underlie the common enemy doctrine, not to speak of the practicalities of the doctrine, have made themselves felt under the rule of reasonable user also. So under the latter rule the erection of buildings in an urban locality is regarded as of such high utility that in the absence of exceptional circumstances, the resultant invasion of another's enjoyment of land, through surface waters, is not actionable. Restatement of Torts § 833b. Thus, under the doctrine of reasonable user there are rules, limited it is true, but nevertheless representative of a crystallization of judicial opinion, as to what under certain circumstances is reasonable or unreasonable as a matter of law. Restatement of Torts § 826d. In our view the common enemy doctrine and the exception to it above stated are crystallizations of this very sort.

The problem before us then is simply to apply the above stated rule and exception to the circumstances here. Of the 40 acres, 28 and another two acres still drain to the locality substantially where they would otherwise drain, had there been no development. In these 30 acres, as above indicated, not only has there been an increase in the flow of the surface water as a result of the development, but catch-basins and drains have been constructed and the land seems in places to have been elevated; however, in our view, the plaintiffs cannot complain of any of these acts. Furthermore the mere fact that at one point a level 15-inch pipe was tied into a 12-inch pipe running under Allaire Road (it has been said that these two pipes have recently been disconnected) creates at most a concentration of the water which, as above indicated, is not actionable.

Hence, with respect to 30 acres the defendants are all exonerated under the general rule. Illustrative of the virtue of the simple rules of thumb which have been adopted in this State — in contrast to the rule of reason which ordinarily calls for a determination by the trier of fact in each case as to what is reasonable under the circumstances, Restatement of Torts §§ 826d, 833b — and illustrative too of the virtue of stare decisis, is the plan here of the engineer for the development. His original scheme proceeded upon the premise that the bringing of the surface water to substantially the place where it would naturally flow relieved the developer of liability.

The defendant borough claims it has accepted only streets and drains lying within the 28 acres. If this is so (the matter is not entirely clear on the record before us), there is no cause of action as against it. This question we therefore leave to the trial court to be disposed of on the remand.

The next question in the case is whether there is any liability with respect to the ten acres remaining from the 40, after deducting the 30 acres mentioned. There is testimony that the surface water here was drained away from the place where it would otherwise flow; and so in connection with these ten acres we are concerned with the exception stated above. However, there is also testimony that even as to this land, the water was brought to the Helbig ditch, "the ultimate point of disposal, regardless of whether pipes were put in or not." The proofs being unclear on the point, the case will have to be remanded to determine in what respects, if any, there is, as to this ten acres, liability under the principles above stated. If such liability is established, plaintiffs are entitled to injunctive relief and to such damages as are allocable to the ten acres.

If the drainage water from these ten acres has been carried away from the place where it otherwise would flow, defendants may relieve themselves of liability as to the same in the future, provided they re-channel this water back substantially to that place — that is, to the place where under the engineer's original design of the development, it was intended to go. This follows from what has already been said.

Reversed and remanded.

NOTES AND QUESTIONS

1. *Adopting the Modern Standard.* One year after the above opinion was handed down, the Supreme Court of New Jersey officially adopted the "reasonable use" standard for cases involving diffuse surface water. *See Armstrong v. Francis Corp.*, 120 A.2d 4 (N.J. 1956). The overwhelming majority of the states now follow the reasonable use rule. Powell on Real Property § 65.12[2]. The remainder of the states generally have taken the approach of imposing a reasonableness overlay on top of existing civil law or common enemy rules. *See Kurpiel v. Hicks*, 731 S.E.2d 921 (Va. 2012) (common enemy rule; must be reasonable good faith use of land so as not to inflict injury beyond what is necessary). For a relatively recent defense of the common enemy rule, see *Argyelan v. Haviland*, 435 N.E.2d 973 (Ind. 1982). Most civil law jurisdictions permit the upper owner to accelerate water flow or modify the drainage pattern if the changes are not substantial and do not unreasonably or

negligently cause harm to the lower owner. POWELL, *supra*.

2. At this point, you are encouraged to review *Evans v. Merriweather* and the accompanying notes in Chapter 1. How do the issues in *Evans v. Merriweather* compare with those in the *Yonadi* case? How does the right to utilize a resource compare with the right to be free from harm caused by a neighbor's misuse of a resource?

[b.] Vegetation

WHITESELL v. HOULTON

Hawaii Intermediate Court of Appeals
632 P.2d 1077 (1981)

BURNS, JUDGE.

In this case, the district court held an owner of a banyan[4] tree liable for damages it caused to a neighbor's property and for the cost incurred by the neighbor in cutting it back. The primary issues are whether a tree owner has a duty to prevent his tree from damaging his neighbor's property and whether he is liable for the damage caused. We answer yes to both questions and we affirm.

Plaintiffs Appellees Whitesells and Defendant Appellant Houlton own and occupy adjoining residential properties. Houlton's property contains a banyan tree 80 to 90 feet high with foliage extending 100 to 110 feet. Said banyan overhangs the Whitesells' property and the two lane street fronting both properties.

In April 1975, the Whitesells asked Houlton to cut the intruding branches, but he refused to do so.

In June 1975, the Whitesells rented equipment and cut some of the banyan's intruding branches.

In July 1975, the Whitesells repaired their garage roof because of damage previously caused by the branches of Houlton's tree.

In January 1976, the Whitesells drove their Volkswagen van on the street fronting the properties, and it was damaged by the branches of Houlton's tree.

In February 1976, the Whitesells advised Houlton by letter that a recent storm had broken a number of large branches near the top of the banyan tree, which branches were dangling directly over the Whitesells' driveway and carport and very likely to fall and cause damage.

Houlton failed to respond to the letter in any manner; thus, in May 1976, the Whitesells hired a professional tree trimmer who cut the banyan's branches back to Houlton's property line.

---

[4] [1] A "banyan" tree is a large evergreen tree of the fig family (moraceae). Generally, its branches send out aerial roots which grow down to the soil to form secondary trunks. In this case, we do not know if the tree is an Indian banyan, ficus benghalensis, or a Malayan or Chinese banyan, ficus retusa. However, the record indicates that its "trunk" is approximately 12 feet in diameter.

The lower court gave the Whitesells judgment for, inter alia, the cost of renting the equipment in June 1975, the cost of repairing the garage roof in July 1975, one half the cost of the tree trimmer hired in May 1976, and the cost of repairing the van.

On appeal, Houlton first contends that the damage to the van was caused by the Whitesells' contributory negligence.

Although the evidence raised the possibility of contributory negligence and the lower court made no express finding on this issue, the result clearly indicates that it did not find any. We perceive no error in the failure to find contributory negligence.

Houlton next contends that he had no duty to cut the branches extending into the Whitesells' property and, therefore, he is not liable for any resulting damage or the cost of cutting the branches.

This being an issue of first impression in Hawaii, we can choose between the Massachusetts, Washington, D.C. view which says Houlton had no duty, or the California, Washington, New Jersey view which says Houlton had a duty whether or not damage has occurred to his neighbor's property, or the Virginia view which says Houlton had a duty to prevent his tree from causing sensible damage to his neighbor's property.

In *Sterling v. Weinstein*, 75 A.2d 144 (D.C. 1950), Judge Hood did an in depth review of the various views and chose the Massachusetts rule which says that if the branches and roots from your neighbor's tree offend you or your property, you must cut them back yourself; you may not require him to do so or to pay for the damages.

We agree with Judge Hood that the Massachusetts rule is "simple and certain." However, we question whether it is realistic and fair. Because the owner of the tree's trunk is the owner of the tree, we think he bears some responsibility for the rest of the tree. It has long been the rule in Hawaii that if the owner knows or should know that his tree constitutes a danger, he is liable if it causes personal injury or property damage on or off of his property. Such being the case, we think he is duty bound to take action to remove the danger before damage or further damage occurs.

Consequently, we prefer a modified Virginia rule. We hold that non-noxious plants ordinarily are not nuisances; that overhanging branches which merely cast shade or drop leaves, flowers, or fruit are not nuisances; that roots which interfere only with other plant life are not nuisances; that overhanging branches or protruding roots constitute a nuisance only when they actually cause, or there is imminent danger of them causing, sensible harm to property other than plant life, in ways other than by casting shade or dropping leaves, flowers, or fruit; that when overhanging branches or protruding roots actually cause, or there is imminent danger of them causing, sensible harm to property other than plant life, in ways other than by casting shade or dropping leaves, flowers, or fruit, the damaged or imminently endangered neighbor may require the owner of the tree to pay for the damages and to cut back the endangering branches or roots and, if such is not done within a reasonable time, the damaged or imminently endangered neighbor may cause the cutback to be done at the tree owner's expense.

However, we also hold that a landowner may always, at his own expense, cut away only to his property line above or below the surface of the ground any part of the adjoining owner's trees or other plant life.

We find all of Mr. Houlton's other points of error to be without merit.

Affirmed.

NOTES AND QUESTIONS

1. *Fusion of Property and Tort Law.* Here as elsewhere in this section, property rights are defined in light of tort principles. Is the court's conclusion that a neighboring property owner may "always" cut away such plant life based on trespass, or on the property right to exclude? Should the same principles apply to roots as branches? (Generally they do.) Can trespassing branches or roots that do no damage to the neighboring property be the basis of a prescriptive easement? (Prescriptive easements are discussed in greater detail in Chapter 7.) *See also Herring v. Lisbon Partners Credit Fund, Ltd. P'ship*, 823 N.W.2d 493 (N.D. 2012) (adopts Hawaii rule). For a review of the rules, and rejection of an "urban-tree" rule that would impose a duty to act reasonably in exercising the self-help remedy, see *Alvarez v. Katz*, 124 A.3d 839 (Vt. 2015). The duty to cut trees and vegetation changes when solar access is involved. See the next reproduced case.

2. *Liability for Damage Caused During Self-Help.* While states differ as to when damages may be awarded — some states limit damages to situations where the intruding trees are classified as "noxious or poisonous" and others require damage to something other than vegetation — all states agree that owners of adjacent land have the right of self-help to cut away offending roots and branches. What if the landowner, into or out of whose land an offending root or branch grows, cuts it so carelessly that the plant dies? Or so that, without the "trespassory" root(s), the neighbor's tree simply falls or blows down onto the owner's garage? What if the self-help damages the neighbor's garage? For the efforts of one state to deal with these issues, see *Abbinett v. Fox*, 703 P.2d 177 (N.M. Ct. App. 1985), and *Garcia v. Sanchez*, 772 P.2d 1311 (N.M. Ct. App. 1989).

3. *Temporary Invasion.* Some plants and trees, such as palm trees, sway excessively, especially in strong winds. What if such a palm tree drops large coconuts from a height of 25 feet, for example, onto a neighbor's car during a high wind? Can a neighbor whack off such swaying branches as they cross the property line? How about "harvesting" fruit like avocados, guavas, or grapefruit during such cross-boundary "swaying"?

4. *Split Down the Middle.* In *Willis v. Maloof*, 361 S.E.2d 512 (Ga. App. 1987), Maloof was injured by the falling of a tree that straddled the property line between lots owned by Willis and Maloof. The court refused to allow Maloof to recover against Willis on the theory that each man owned the portion of the tree that rested on his side of the property line and that each possessed an "easement of support" for the other. Both parties were responsible for maintaining the tree and since neither had done so, neither could be liable to the other. In so ruling, the court drew an analogy to party walls, the situation that exists when adjoining properties share a common wall.

[c.] Sunlight

PRAH v. MARETTI
Wisconsin Supreme Court
321 N.W.2d 182 (1982)

ABRAHAMSON, JUSTICE.

According to the complaint, the plaintiff is the owner of a residence which was constructed during the years 1978–1979. The complaint alleges that the residence has a solar system which includes collectors on the roof to supply energy for heat and hot water and that after the plaintiff built his solar heated house, the defendant purchased the lot adjacent to and immediately to the south of the plaintiff's lot and commenced planning construction of a home. The complaint further states that when the plaintiff learned of defendant's plans to build the house he advised the defendant that if the house were built at the proposed location, defendant's house would substantially and adversely affect the integrity of plaintiff's solar system and could cause plaintiff other damage. Nevertheless, the defendant began construction. The complaint further alleges that the plaintiff is entitled to "unrestricted use of the sun and its solar power" and demands judgment for injunctive relief and damages.

Plaintiff's home was the first residence built in the subdivision, and although plaintiff did not build his house in the center of the lot it was built in accordance with applicable restrictions. Plaintiff advised defendant that if the defendant's home were built at the proposed site it would cause a shadowing effect on the solar collectors which would reduce the efficiency of the system and possibly damage the system. To avoid these adverse effects, plaintiff requested defendant to locate his home an additional several feet away from the plaintiff's lot line, the exact number being disputed. Plaintiff and defendant failed to reach an agreement on the location of defendant's home before defendant started construction. The Architectural Control Committee and the Planning Commission of the City of Muskego approved the defendant's plans for his home, including its location on the lot. After such approval, the defendant apparently changed the grade of the property without prior notice to the Architectural Control Committee. The problem with defendant's proposed construction, as far as the plaintiff's interests are concerned, arises from a combination of the grade and the distance of defendant's home from the defendant's lot line.

The plaintiff presents three legal theories to support his claim that the defendant's continued construction of a home justifies granting him relief: (1) the construction constitutes a common law private nuisance; (2) the construction is prohibited by sec. 844.01, Stats. 1979–80;[5] and (3) the construction interferes with

---

[5] [3] Sec. 844.01, Stats. 1979–80, provides:

> (1) Any person owning or claiming an interest in real property may bring an action claiming physical injury to, or interference with, the property or his interest therein; the action may be to redress past injury, to restrain further injury, to abate the source of injury, or for other appropriate relief.
>
> (2) Physical injury includes unprivileged intrusions and encroachments; the injury may be

the solar easement plaintiff acquired under the doctrine of prior appropriation.[6]

We consider first whether the complaint states a claim for relief based on common law private nuisance. This state has long recognized that an owner of land does not have an absolute or unlimited right to use the land in a way which injures the rights of others. The rights of neighboring landowners are relative; the uses by one must not unreasonably impair the uses or enjoyment of the other. When one landowner's use of his or her property unreasonably interferes with another's enjoyment of his or her property, that use is said to be a private nuisance.

The private nuisance doctrine has traditionally been employed in this state to balance the rights of landowners, and this court has recently adopted the analysis of private nuisance set forth in the Restatement (Second) of Torts. The Restatement defines private nuisance as "a nontrespassory invasion of another's interest in the private use and enjoyment of land." Restatement (Second) of Torts sec. 821D (1977). The phrase "interest in the private use and enjoyment of land" as used in sec. 821D is broadly defined to include any disturbance of the enjoyment of property. The comment in the Restatement describes the landowner's interest protected by private nuisance law as follows:

> The phrase "interest in the use and enjoyment of land" is used in this Restatement in a broad sense. It comprehends not only the interests that a person may have in the actual present use of land for residential, agricultural, commercial, industrial and other purposes, but also his interests in having the present use value of the land unimpaired by changes in its physical condition. Thus the destruction of trees on vacant land is as much an invasion of the owner's interest in its use and enjoyment as is the destruction of crops or flowers that he is growing on the land for his present use. "Interest in use and enjoyment" also comprehends the pleasure, comfort and enjoyment that a person normally derives from the occupancy of land. Freedom from discomfort and annoyance while using land is often as important to a person as freedom from physical interruption with his use or freedom from detrimental change in the physical condition of the land itself.

Restatement (Second) of Torts, Sec. 821D, Comment *b*, p. 101 (1977).

Although the defendant's obstruction of the plaintiff's access to sunlight appears to fall within the Restatement's broad concept of a private nuisance as a nontrespassory invasion of another's interest in the private use and enjoyment of land, the

---

surface, subsurface or suprasurface; the injury may arise from activities on the plaintiff's property, or from activities outside the plaintiff's property which affect plaintiff's property.

(3) Interference with an interest is any activity other than physical injury which lessens the possibility of use or enjoyment of the interest.

(4) The lessening of a security interest without physical injury is not actionable unless such lessening constitutes waste.

We can find no reported cases in which sec. 844.01 has been interpreted and applied, and the parties do not cite any.

[6] [4] Under the doctrine of prior appropriation the first user to appropriate the resource has the right of continued use to the exclusion of others.

defendant asserts that he has a right to develop his property in compliance with statutes, ordinances and private covenants without regard to the effect of such development upon the plaintiff's access to sunlight. In essence, the defendant is asking this court to hold that the private nuisance doctrine is not applicable in the instant case and that his right to develop his land is a right which is *per se* superior to his neighbor's interest in access to sunlight. This position is expressed in the maxim "*cujus est solum, ejus est usque ad coelum et ad infernos*," that is, the owner of land owns up to the sky and down to the center of the earth. The rights of the surface owner are, however, not unlimited.

The defendant is not completely correct in asserting that the common law did not protect a landowner's access to sunlight across adjoining property. At English common law a landowner could acquire a right to receive sunlight across adjoining land by both express agreement and under the judge made doctrine of "ancient lights." Under the doctrine of ancient lights if the landowner had received sunlight across adjoining property for a specified period of time, the landowner was entitled to continue to receive unobstructed access to sunlight across the adjoining property. Under the doctrine the landowner acquired a negative prescriptive easement and could prevent the adjoining landowner from obstructing access to light.

Although American courts have not been as receptive to protecting a landowner's access to sunlight as the English courts, American courts have afforded some protection to a landowner's interest in access to sunlight. American courts honor express easements to sunlight. American courts initially enforced the English common law doctrine of ancient lights, but later every state which considered the doctrine repudiated it as inconsistent with the needs of a developing country. Indeed, for just that reason this court concluded that an easement to light and air over adjacent property could not be created or acquired by prescription and has been unwilling to recognize such an easement by implication.

Many jurisdictions in this country have protected a landowner from malicious obstruction of access to light (the spite fence cases) under the common law private nuisance doctrine. If an activity is motivated by malice it lacks utility and the harm it causes others outweighs any social values. This court was reluctant to protect a landowner's interest in sunlight even against a spite fence, only to be overruled by the legislature. Shortly after this court upheld a landowner's right to erect a useless and unsightly sixteen foot spite fence four feet from his neighbor's windows, the legislature enacted a law specifically defining a spite fence as an actionable private nuisance. Thus a landowner's interest in sunlight has been protected in this country by common law private nuisance law at least in the narrow context of the modern American rule invalidating spite fences.

This court's reluctance in the nineteenth and early part of the twentieth century to provide broader protection for a landowner's access to sunlight was premised on three policy considerations. First, the right of landowners to use their property as they wished, as long as they did not cause physical damage to a neighbor, was jealously guarded.

Second, sunlight was valued only for aesthetic enjoyment or as illumination. Since artificial light could be used for illumination, loss of sunlight was at most a personal annoyance which was given little, if any, weight by society.

Third, society had a significant interest in not restricting or impeding land development. This court repeatedly emphasized that in the growth period of the nineteenth and early twentieth centuries change is to be expected and is essential to property and that recognition of a right to sunlight would hinder property development. The court expressed this concept as follows:

> As the city grows, large grounds appurtenant to residences must be cut up to supply more residences. The cistern, the outhouse, the cesspool, and the private drain must disappear in deference to the public waterworks and sewer; the terrace and the garden, to the need for more complete occupancy. Strict limitation [on the recognition of easements of light and air over adjacent premises is] in accord with the popular conception upon which real estate has been and is daily being conveyed in Wisconsin and to be essential to easy and rapid development at least of our municipalities.

Considering these three policies, this court concluded that in the absence of an express agreement granting access to sunlight, a landowner's obstruction of another's access to sunlight was not actionable. These three policies are no longer fully accepted or applicable. They reflect factual circumstances and social priorities that are now obsolete.

First, society has increasingly regulated the use of land by the landowner for the general welfare. *Euclid v. Ambler Realty Co.*, 272 U.S. 365 (1926); *Just v. Marinette*, 201 N.W.2d 761 (Wis. 1972).

Second, access to sunlight has taken on a new significance in recent years. In this case the plaintiff seeks to protect access to sunlight, not for aesthetic reasons or as a source of illumination but as a source of energy. Access to sunlight as an energy source is of significance both to the landowner who invests in solar collectors and to a society which has an interest in developing alternative sources of energy.[7]

The federal government has also recognized the importance of solar energy and currently encourages its utilization by means of tax benefits, direct subsidies and government loans for solar projects.

Third, the policy of favoring unhindered private development in an expanding economy is no longer in harmony with the realities of our society. *State v. Deetz*, 224 N.W.2d 407 (Wis. 1974). The need for easy and rapid development is not as great today as it once was, while our perception of the value of sunlight as a source of energy has increased significantly.

Courts should not implement obsolete policies that have lost their vigor over the course of the years. The law of private nuisance is better suited to resolve landowners' disputes about property development in the 1980s than is a rigid rule which does not recognize a landowner's interest in access to sunlight.

Yet the defendant would have us ignore the flexible private nuisance law as a means of resolving the dispute between the landowners in this case and would have us adopt an approach, already abandoned in *Deetz*, of favoring the unrestricted

---

[7] [11] State and federal governments are encouraging the use of the sun as a significant source of energy. In this state the legislature has granted tax benefits to encourage the utilization of solar energy.

development of land and of applying a rigid and inflexible rule protecting his right to build on his land and disregarding any interest of the plaintiff in the use and enjoyment of his land. This we refuse to do.[8]

Private nuisance law, the law traditionally used to adjudicate conflicts between private landowners, has the flexibility to protect both a landowner's right of access to sunlight and another landowner's right to develop land. Private nuisance law is better suited to regulate access to sunlight in modern society and is more in harmony with legislative policy and the prior decisions of this court than is an inflexible doctrine of non-recognition of any interest in access to sunlight across adjoining land.

We therefore hold that private nuisance law, that is, the reasonable use doctrine as set forth in the Restatement, is applicable to the instant case. Recognition of a nuisance claim for unreasonable obstruction of access to sunlight will not prevent land development or unduly hinder the use of adjoining land. It will promote the reasonable use and enjoyment of land in a manner suitable to the 1980s. That obstruction of access to light might be found to constitute a nuisance in certain circumstances does not mean that it will be or must be found to constitute a nuisance under all circumstances. The result in each case depends on whether the conduct complained of is unreasonable.

Accordingly we hold that the plaintiff in this case has stated a claim under which relief can be granted. Nonetheless we do not determine whether the plaintiff in this case is entitled to relief. In order to be entitled to relief the plaintiff must prove the elements required to establish actionable nuisance, and the conduct of the defendant herein must be judged by the reasonable use doctrine.

Our examination of the record leads us to conclude that the record does not furnish an adequate basis for the circuit court to apply the proper legal principles on summary judgment. The application of the reasonable use standard in nuisance cases normally requires a full exposition of all underlying facts and circumstances.

---

[8] [13] Defendant's position that a landowner's interest in access to sunlight across adjoining land is not "legally enforceable" and is therefore excluded per se from private nuisance law was adopted in *Fontainebleau Hotel Corp. v. Forty-five Twenty-five, Inc.*, 114 So. 2d 357 (Fla. App. 1959), *cert. denied*, 117 So. 2d 842 (Fla. 1960). The Florida district court of appeals permitted construction of a building which cast a shadow on a neighboring hotel's swimming pool. The court asserted that nuisance law protects only those interests "which [are] recognized and protected by law," and that there is no legally recognized or protected right to access to sunlight. A property owner does not, said the Florida court, in the absence of a contract or statute, acquire a presumptive or implied right to the free flow of light and air across adjoining land. The Florida court then concluded that a lawful structure which causes injury to another by cutting off light and air whether or not erected partly for spite does not give rise to a cause of action for damages or for an injunction. *See also People ex rel. Hoogasian v. Sears, Roebuck & Co.*, 287 N.E.2d 677 (Ill. 1972).

We do not find the reasoning of *Fontainebleau* persuasive. The court leaped from rejecting an easement by prescription (the doctrine of ancient lights) and an easement by implication to the conclusion that there is no right to protection from obstruction of access to sunlight. The court's statement that a landowner has no right to light should be the conclusion, not its initial premise. The court did not explain why an owner's interest in unobstructed light should not be protected or in what manner an owner's interest in unobstructed sunlight differs from an owner's interest in being free from obtrusive noises or smells or differs from an owner's interest in unobstructed use of water. The recognition of a *per se* exception to private nuisance law may invite unreasonable behavior

Too little is known in this case of such matters as the extent of the harm to the plaintiff, the suitability of solar heat in that neighborhood, the availability of remedies to the plaintiff, and the costs to the defendant of avoiding the harm. Summary judgment is not an appropriate procedural vehicle in this case when the circuit court must weigh evidence which has not been presented at trial.

Because the plaintiff has stated a claim of common law private nuisance upon which relief can be granted, the judgment of the circuit court must be reversed. We need not, and do not, reach the question of whether the complaint states a claim under sec. 844.01, Stats. 1979–80, or under the doctrine of prior appropriation.

CALLOW, JUSTICE (dissenting).

The majority has adopted the Restatement's reasonable use doctrine to grant an owner of a solar heated home a cause of action against his neighbor who, in acting entirely within the applicable ordinances and statutes, seeks to design and build his home in such a location that it may, at various times during the day, shade the plaintiff's solar collector, thereby impeding the efficiency of his heating system[9] during several months of the year. Because I believe the facts of this case clearly reveal that a cause of action for private nuisance will not lie, I dissent.

It is a fundamental principle of law that a "landowner owns at least as much of the space above the ground as he can occupy or use in connection with the land." As stated in the frequently cited and followed case of *Fontainebleau Hotel Corp. v. Forty-Five Twenty-Five, Inc.*, 114 So. 2d 357 (Fla. Dist. Ct. App. 1959), *cert. denied*, 117 So. 2d 842 (Fla. 1960):

> There being, then, no legal right to the free flow of light and air from the adjoining land, it is universally held that where a structure serves a useful and beneficial purpose, it does not give rise to a cause of action, either for damages or for an injunction under the maxim *sic utere tuo ut alienum non laedas*, even though it causes injury to another by cutting off the light and air and interfering with the view that would otherwise be available over adjoining land in its natural state, regardless of the fact that the structure may have been erected partly for spite.

Id. at 359. *See Venuto v. Owens Corning Fiberglas Corp.*, 99 Cal. Rptr. 350, 357 (Cal. App. 1971). I firmly believe that a landowner's right to use his property within the limits of ordinances, statutes, and restrictions of record where such use is necessary to serve his legitimate needs is a fundamental precept of a free society which this court should strive to uphold.

As one commentator has suggested:

> It is fashionable to dismiss such values as deriving from a bygone era in which people valued development as a "goal in itself," but current market prices for real estate, and more particularly the premiums paid for land

---

[9] [1] Plaintiff testified that he has a backup electrical system as required by law in this state. Thus, if the solar system fails or loses efficiency, he may resort to the electrical system

whose zoning permits intensive use, suggest that people still place very high values on such rights."

Williams, *Solar Access and Property Rights: A Maverick Analysis*, 11 CONN. L. REV. 430, 443 (1979).

I know of no cases repudiating policies favoring the right of a landowner to use his property as he lawfully desires or which declare such policies are "no longer fully accepted or applicable" in this context. The right of a property owner to lawful enjoyment of his property should be vigorously protected, particularly in those cases where the adjacent property owner could have insulated himself from the alleged problem by acquiring the land as a defense to the potential problem or by provident use of his own property.

The majority concludes that sunlight has not heretofore been accorded the status of a source of energy, and consequently it has taken on a new significance in recent years. Solar energy for home heating is at this time sparingly used and of questionable economic value because solar collectors are not mass produced, and consequently, they are very costly. Their limited efficiency may explain the lack of production.

Regarding the third policy the majority apparently believes is obsolete (that society has a significant interest in not restricting land development), it cites *State v. Deetz*. I concede the law may be tending to recognize the value of aesthetics over increased volume development and that an individual may not use his land in such a way as to harm the public. The instant case, however, deals with a private benefit.

I conclude that plaintiff's solar heating system is an unusually sensitive use. In other words, the defendant's proposed construction of his home, under ordinary circumstances, would not interfere with the use and enjoyment of the usual person's property. *See* W. PROSSER, LAW OF TORTS, sec. 87 at 578–79 (4th ed. 1971). "The plaintiff cannot, by devoting his own land to an unusually sensitive use, such as a drive in motion picture theater easily affected by light, make a nuisance out of conduct of the adjoining defendant which would otherwise be harmless." *Id.* at 579.

NOTES AND QUESTIONS

1. *What Happened Next?* The case of *Prah v. Maretti* never went to trial on the issue of whether Maretti's building constituted a nuisance under these circumstances. After the above ruling of the Wisconsin Supreme Court, Glenn Prah, a pilot for American Airlines, and Richard Maretti, a salesman, decided to discontinue their lawsuit, at least in part because both were uncomfortable with the national attention that their case had attracted. For example, see *A Shadow Has Been Cast Over the Sunny Days of Glenn Prah*, UNITED PRESS INTERNATIONAL, Nov. 14, 1980 (reporting trial court results), and *Landmark Decision on Sun Access*, N.Y. TIMES July 10, 1982 at Sec. 1, p. 46. The two lived next door to each other for many years, although as Prah told an interviewer in the early 1990s, they "were neighbors, but not friends."

2. *The Role of Legal History.* Justice (now Chief Justice) Shirley Abrahamson, the author of the majority opinion in *Prah v. Maretti*, held an S.J.D. degree in legal history and was a student of the famous American legal historian, J. Willard Hurst of the University of Wisconsin. Does her use of historical explanations strengthen her opinion? What is the difference between history and precedent?

3. *Doctrine of Ancient Lights.* The doctrine of ancient lights, discussed in the above opinion, was virtually never applied in the United States and was formally abandoned at an early date in most jurisdictions. See, for example, *Parker & Edgerton v. Foote*, 19 Wend. 309 (N.Y. 1838) (British doctrine of ancient lights "is an anomaly in the law"). However, in the United Kingdom, it remains the law, although it was modified to facilitate the rebuilding of post-World War II Britain. *See* Rights of Light Act, 7 & 8 Eliz. 2, c. 56 (1959). Early American courts rejected "ancient lights" because it would have, as the court in *Parker & Edgerton v. Foote* noted, "the most mischievous consequences" for "the growing cities and villages of this country." One hundred and seventy years later, the United States is a country of more than 300 million people. Would the consequences of a doctrine like "ancient lights" still be mischievous?

4. *Solar Access Laws and Statutes.* Legislation can overcome the limitations of the common law in protecting solar access. Over half the states protect access to solar energy by authorizing the voluntary creation of solar easements. *See, e.g.*, N.H. Rev. Stat. Ann. § 477:49. New Mexico is one of two states that recognizes the natural resource of solar energy as a property right to an "unobstructed line of sight" between the solar collector and the sun. Disputes over the use of solar energy are resolved by the beneficial use and prior appropriation doctrines. N.M. Stat. Ann. §§ 43-3-1 to 5. For discussion of the statute see Stromberg, *Has the Sun Set on Solar Rights? Examining the Practicality of the Solar Rights Acts*, 50 NAT. RESOURCES J. 211 (2010). For a web site that collects solar access laws see Solar Access Laws, DSIRE Solar, http://ncsolarcen-prod.s3.amazonaws.com/wp-content/uploads/2015/09/Solar-Policy-Guide.pdf. Some states require compensation to the landowner who is burdened by a solar easement.

States may authorize local regulation of solar access, and states like Wisconsin have a permit system that authorizes permits if the solar system does not impermissibly interfere with the use of land, and its benefits outweigh its burdens. Local ordinances can deal with issues such as solar setback, performance standards, vegetation removal, and permitting. Weismantle, *Building A Better Solar Energy Framework*, 26 ST. THOMAS L. REV. 221 (2014). *See also* Bronin, *Solar Rights*, 89 B.U. L. REV. 1217 (2009). Professor Bronin "advocates an approach that recognizes sunlight's natural qualities, assigns the initial entitlement to the property owner whose use of sunlight will most benefit society, and works within existing legal forms." *Modern Lights*, 80 U. COLO. L. REV. 881, 920 (2009).

5. *Spite Fences.* What about a fence designed solely for the purpose of preventing sunlight from reaching a neighbor's property, or a "spite building" constructed in such a fashion as to block sunlight from a neighboring hotel's swimming pool? *See Fontainbleau Hotel Corp. v. Forty-Five Twenty-Five, Inc.*, 114 So. 2d 357 (Fla. Dist. Ct. App. 1959). Although the court recognized that there could be a nuisance action in these situations, it found that the facts did not warrant such a holding in that case, since the addition served "a useful and beneficial purpose." While it does not appear from the report of the case, the Fountainbleau Hotel's

expansion on the side facing the Eden Roc Hotel resembled a multi-story factory wall, with its white face unrelieved by architectural features of any sort. There is also evidence that bad blood between the owners of the two hotels prompted the Fountainbleau's expansion to take the form that it did. Does nuisance provide an adequate framework for the resolution of disputes like this one? Should the motive of the Fountainbleu's owner matter if the expansion serves it official purpose of expanding the capacity of the hotel?

6. *Protection of Solar Rights.* Technically, all the Wisconsin Supreme Court says in the above opinion is that the construction of a house in such a way that it blocked solar collectors "might" be a nuisance. How would the jury likely have ruled if the case had gone to trial? Would the result in 1982 be different than it might be today? For a refusal to apply the reasoning of *Prah v. Maretti* to a case involving an effort to protect a "solar house" built to take advantage of its orientation on its lot, see *Sher v. Leiderman*, 181 Cal. App. 3d 867 (1986). In *Sher*, the court adopted the logic of the dissenting Justice Callows in *Prah v. Maretti. See also Van Baalen v. Jones*, 2014 Ariz. App. Unpub. LEXIS 987 (July 31, 2014) (obstruction of a landowner's view does not constitute a private nuisance absent a statute or an easement to the contrary).

For an international perspective on these issues, see Zaidi, *Solar Energy Policy in Canada: An Overview of Recent Legislative and Community-Based Trends Toward A Coherent Renewable Energy Sustainability Framework*, 17 Mo. Envtl. L. & Pol'y Rev. 108 (2009).

Chapter 3

GOVERNMENTAL POWER AND THE RIGHTS OF PROPERTY OWNERS

Government affects the private rights, including use, of land in two basic ways: taking it by compulsory purchase, or eminent domain, and regulating it under its police power. This chapter introduces and analyzes the historical roots of, and current practices under, these two governmental powers. For a fascinating reorientation of the jurisprudence flowing from the exercise of these powers, see Donald J. Kochan, *Keepings*, 23 N.Y.U. Envtl. L.J. 255 (2015).

[A.] THE POWER OF EMINENT DOMAIN

The authority of government to take land is centuries old. Until the 19th century, however, the use of eminent domain powers by public agencies was limited by the restricted role of government in public affairs and the simpler needs of a less complicated economy. In the 20th century, as government intervention in public affairs widened to include programs like urban redevelopment and the national interstate highway network, the use of eminent domain by government increased dramatically. In addition to regulating the use of land, governmental agencies now acquire interests in land for a variety of purposes.

This section examines legal issues arising in the use of eminent domain. It first considers the public use doctrine that controls the purposes for which government can exercise the power, especially the often controversial use of eminent domain in urban renewal and redevelopment programs. Next, it looks at situations where compensation is payable because of governmental activities that result in an involuntary acquisition of land by indirect means. It concludes with an examination of highway access and special benefit issues that can arise in the use of eminent domain for highway programs.

[1.] The Public Use Doctrine

The public use doctrine, which is based on the Fifth Amendment to the federal Constitution and comparable state constitutional provisions, developed differently in the states and in the federal courts. For a concise history of the doctrine before 1950, see the classic Comment, *The Public Use Limitation on Eminent Domain: An Advance Requiem*, 58 Yale L.J. 599 (1949). The Fifth Amendment states that property can be taken only for "public use" with just compensation. State constitutions either have similar provisions, or courts find a similar implied limitation on the eminent domain power. Concerned about the possible use of eminent domain for private purposes, state courts at first held that government agencies could condemn interests in land only if the land was subsequently used by the public. (Turnpikes and canals were classic examples.) At the same time, there were widely accepted examples where the eminent domain power was used for purposes that did not involve direct public use. The mills acts of the early 19th century, for example, allowed private owners to maintain mills if they compensated upstream landowners for flooding caused by the mill operation.

Courts eventually began to define the public use test more broadly, finding it to be satisfied if the use "benefited" the public. This shift in emphasis opened the way for a more aggressive use of the eminent domain power, especially since the public benefit that would justify the use was open to judicial interpretation and extension. The "benefit to the public" test also opened the way for programs that required social engineering and that transferred wealth from one private entity to another. An example is an urban redevelopment project, where a city condemns land from one private owner and conveys it to another private owner at a below-market cost or no cost at all for redevelopment.

The public use doctrine in the Supreme Court. Although there is an extensive state jurisprudence on the public use doctrine, the decisions of the United States Supreme Court have long dominated the law of public use. The Court embraced an expansive view of the public use doctrine early in the 20th century. In 1916, Justice Holmes wrote for the Court in *Mount Vernon-Woodberry Cotton Duck Co. v. Alabama Interstate Power Co.*, 240 U.S. 30, 32 (1916), and expressly repudiated the use by the public test. Three decades later, in *Tennessee Valley Authority v. Welch*, 327 U.S. 546 (1946), the Court announced that it would pay considerable deference to and would be reluctant to question a legislative declaration of public use.

A critical test for the use of eminent domain came several years later, when the Supreme Court was asked to consider its use in the new urban renewal program that had been given federal subsidies Congress in the Housing Act of 1949. The test case arose in the District of Columbia, where eminent domain was proposed to clear and redevelop the southwest Washington slums which had once been pictured on the cover of *Life* magazine at the doorstep of the nation's capital.

BERMAN v. PARKER

United States Supreme Court
348 U.S. 26 (1954)

MR. JUSTICE DOUGLAS delivered the opinion of the Court.

This is an appeal from the judgment of a three-judge District Court which dismissed a complaint seeking to enjoin the condemnation of appellants' property under the District of Columbia Redevelopment Act of 1945. The challenge was to the constitutionality of the Act, particularly as applied to the taking of appellants' property. The District Court sustained the constitutionality of the *Act*.

By § 2 of the Act, Congress made a "legislative determination" that "owing to technological and sociological changes, obsolete lay-out, and other factors, conditions existing in the District of Columbia with respect to substandard housing and blighted areas, including the use of buildings in alleys as dwellings for human habitation, are injurious to the public health, safety, morals, and welfare; and it is hereby declared to be the policy of the United States to protect and promote the welfare of the inhabitants of the seat of the Government by eliminating all such injurious conditions by employing all means necessary and appropriate for the purpose."[1]

Section 2 goes on to declare that acquisition of property is necessary to eliminate these housing conditions.

Congress further finds in § 2 that these ends cannot be attained "by the ordinary operations of private enterprise alone without public participation"; that "the sound replanning and redevelopment of an obsolescent or obsolescing portion" of the District "cannot be accomplished unless it be done in the light of comprehensive and coordinated planning of the whole of the territory of the District of Columbia and its environs"; and that "the acquisition and the assembly of real property and the leasing or sale thereof for redevelopment pursuant to a project area redevelopment plan . . . is hereby declared to be a public use."

Section 4 creates the District of Columbia Redevelopment Land Agency (hereinafter called the Agency), composed of five members, which is granted power by § 5 (a) to acquire and assemble, by eminent domain and otherwise, real property for "the redevelopment of blighted territory in the District of Columbia and the prevention, reduction, or elimination of blighting factors or causes of blight."

Section 6 (a) of the Act directs the National Capital Planning Commission (hereinafter called the Planning Commission) to make and develop "a comprehensive or general plan" of the District, including "a land-use plan" which designates land for use for "housing, business, industry, recreation, education, public buildings, public reservations, and other general categories of public and private uses of the land." Section 6 (b) authorizes the Planning Commission to adopt redevelopment plans for specific project areas. These plans are subject to the approval of the District Commissioners after a public hearing; and they prescribe the various public and private land uses for the respective areas, the "standards of population density and building intensity," and "the amount or character or class of any low-rent housing." § 6 (b).

Once the Planning Commission adopts a plan and that plan is approved by the Commissioners, the Planning Commission certifies it to the Agency. § 6 (d). At that point, the Agency is authorized to acquire and assemble the real property in the area. *Id.*

After the real estate has been assembled, the Agency is authorized to transfer to public agencies the land to be devoted to such public purposes as streets, utilities, recreational facilities, and schools, § 7 (a), and to lease or sell the remainder as an entirety or in parts to a redevelopment company, individual, or partnership. § 7 (b),

---

[1] [*]The Act does not define either "slums" or "blighted areas." Section 3 (r), however, states:

"'Substandard housing conditions' means the conditions obtaining in connection with the existence of any dwelling, or dwellings, or housing accommodations for human beings, which because of lack of sanitary facilities, ventilation, or light, or because of dilapidation, overcrowding, faulty interior arrangement, or any combination of these factors, is in the opinion of the Commissioners detrimental to the safety, health, morals, or welfare of the inhabitants of the District of Columbia."

(f). The leases or sales must provide that the lessees or purchasers will carry out the redevelopment plan and that "no use shall be made of any land or real property included in the lease or sale nor any building or structure erected thereon" which does not conform to the plan, §§ 7 (d), 11. Preference is to be given to private enterprise over public agencies in executing the redevelopment plan. § 7 (g).

The first project undertaken under the Act relates to Project Area B in Southwest Washington, D. C. In 1950 the Planning Commission prepared and published a comprehensive plan for the District. Surveys revealed that in Area B, 64.3% of the dwellings were beyond repair, 18.4% needed major repairs, only 17.3% were satisfactory; 57.8% of the dwellings had outside toilets, 60.3% had no baths, 29.3% lacked electricity, 82.2% had no wash basins or laundry tubs, 83.8% lacked central heating. In the judgment of the District's Director of Health it was necessary to redevelop Area B in the interests of public health. The population of Area B amounted to 5,012 persons, of whom 97.5% were Negroes.

The plan for Area B specifies the boundaries and allocates the use of the land for various purposes. It makes detailed provisions for types of dwelling units and provides that at least one-third of them are to be low-rent housing with a maximum rental of $17 per room per month.

After a public hearing, the Commissioners approved the plan and the Planning Commission certified it to the Agency for execution. The Agency undertook the preliminary steps for redevelopment of the area when this suit was brought.

Appellants own property in Area B at 712 Fourth Street, S. W. It is not used as a dwelling or place of habitation. A department store is located on it. Appellants object to the appropriation of this property for the purposes of the project. They claim that their property may not be taken constitutionally for this project. It is commercial, not residential property; it is not slum housing; it will be put into the project under the management of a private, not a public, agency and redeveloped for private, not public, use. That is the argument; and the contention is that appellants' private property is being taken contrary to two mandates of the *Fifth Amendment* — (1) "No person shall . . . be deprived of . . . property, without due process of law"; (2) "nor shall private property be taken for public use, without just compensation." To take for the purpose of ridding the area of slums is one thing; it is quite another, the argument goes, to take a man's property merely to develop a better balanced, more attractive community. The District Court, while agreeing in general with that argument, saved the Act by construing it to mean that the Agency could condemn property only for the reasonable necessities of slum clearance and prevention, its concept of "slum" being the existence of conditions "injurious to the public health, safety, morals and welfare."

The power of Congress over the District of Columbia includes all the legislative powers which a state may exercise over its affairs. We deal, in other words, with what traditionally has been known as the police power. An attempt to define its reach or trace its outer limits is fruitless, for each case must turn on its own facts. The definition is essentially the product of legislative determinations addressed to the purposes of government, purposes neither abstractly nor historically capable of complete definition. Subject to specific constitutional limitations, when the legislature has spoken, the public interest has been declared in terms well-nigh conclusive.

In such cases the legislature, not the judiciary, is the main guardian of the public needs to be served by social legislation, whether it be Congress legislating concerning the District of Columbia or the States legislating concerning local affairs. This principle admits of no exception merely because the power of eminent domain is involved. The role of the judiciary in determining whether that power is being exercised for a public purpose is an extremely narrow one.

Public safety, public health, morality, peace and quiet, law and order — these are some of the more conspicuous examples of the traditional application of the police power to municipal affairs. Yet they merely illustrate the scope of the power and do not delimit it. See Miserable and disreputable housing conditions may do more than spread disease and crime and immorality. They may also suffocate the spirit by reducing the people who live there to the status of cattle. They may indeed make living an almost insufferable burden. They may also be an ugly sore, a blight on the community which robs it of charm, which makes it a place from which men turn. The misery of housing may despoil a community as an open sewer may ruin a river.

We do not sit to determine whether a particular housing project is or is not desirable. The concept of the public welfare is broad and inclusive. The values it represents are spiritual as well as physical, aesthetic as well as monetary. It is within the power of the legislature to determine that the community should be beautiful as well as healthy, spacious as well as clean, well-balanced as well as carefully patrolled. In the present case, the Congress and its authorized agencies have made determinations that take into account a wide variety of values. It is not for us to reappraise them. If those who govern the District of Columbia decide that the Nation's Capital should be beautiful as well as sanitary, there is nothing in the *Fifth Amendment* that stands in the way.

Once the object is within the authority of Congress, the right to realize it through the exercise of eminent domain is clear. For the power of eminent domain is merely the means to the end. Once the object is within the authority of Congress, the means by which it will be attained is also for Congress to determine. Here one of the means chosen is the use of private enterprise for redevelopment of the area. Appellants argue that this makes the project a taking from one businessman for the benefit of another businessman. But the means of executing the project are for Congress and Congress alone to determine, once the public purpose has been established. The public end may be as well or better served through an agency of private enterprise than through a department of government — or so the Congress might conclude. We cannot say that public ownership is the sole method of promoting the public purposes of community redevelopment projects. What we have said also disposes of any contention concerning the fact that certain property owners in the area may be permitted to repurchase their properties for redevelopment in harmony with the over-all plan. That, too, is a legitimate means which Congress and its agencies may adopt, if they choose.

In the present case, Congress and its authorized agencies attack the problem of the blighted parts of the community on an area rather than on a structure-by-structure basis. That, too, is opposed by appellants. They maintain that since their building does not imperil health or safety nor contribute to the making of a slum or a blighted area, it cannot be swept into a redevelopment plan by the mere dictum of the Planning Commission or the Commissioners. The particular uses to be made of the land in the project were determined with regard to the needs of the particular community. The experts concluded that if the community were to be healthy, if it were not to revert again to a blighted or slum area, as though possessed of a congenital disease, the area must be planned as a whole. It was not enough, they believed, to remove existing buildings that were insanitary or unsightly. It was important to redesign the whole area so as to eliminate the conditions that cause slums — the overcrowding of dwellings, the lack of parks, the lack of adequate streets and alleys, the absence of recreational areas, the lack of light and air, the presence of outmoded street patterns. It was believed that the piecemeal approach, the removal of individual structures that were offensive, would be only a palliative. The entire area needed redesigning so that a balanced, integrated plan could be developed for the region, including not only new homes but also schools, churches, parks, streets, and shopping centers. In this way it was hoped that the cycle of decay of the area could be controlled and the birth of future slums prevented. Such diversification in future use is plainly relevant to the maintenance of the desired housing standards and therefore within congressional power.

The District Court below suggested that, if such a broad scope were intended for the statute, the standards contained in the Act would not be sufficiently definite to sustain the delegation of authority. We do not agree. We think the standards prescribed were adequate for executing the plan to eliminate not only slums as narrowly defined by the District Court but also the blighted areas that tend to produce slums. Property may of course be taken for this redevelopment which, standing by itself, is innocuous and unoffending. But we have said enough to indicate that it is the need of the area as a whole which Congress and its agencies are evaluating. If owner after owner were permitted to resist these redevelopment programs on the ground that his particular property was not being used against the public interest, integrated plans for redevelopment would suffer greatly. The argument pressed on us is, indeed, a plea to substitute the landowner's standard of the public need for the standard prescribed by Congress. But as we have already stated, community redevelopment programs need not, by force of the Constitution, be on a piecemeal basis — lot by lot, building by building. It is not for the courts to oversee the choice of the boundary line nor to sit in review on the size of a particular project area. Once the question of the public purpose has been decided, the amount and character of land to be taken for the project and the need for a particular tract to complete the integrated plan rests in the discretion of the legislative branch. The District Court indicated grave doubts concerning the Agency's right to take full title to the land as distinguished from the objectionable buildings located on it. We do not share those doubts. If the Agency considers it necessary in carrying out the redevelopment project to take full title to the real property involved, it may do so. It is not for the courts to determine whether it is necessary for successful consummation of the project that unsafe, unsightly, or insanitary buildings alone be taken or whether title to the land be included, any more than it is the function of the courts to sort and choose among the various parcels selected for condemnation.

The rights of these property owners are satisfied when they receive that just compensation which the *Fifth Amendment* exacts as the price of the taking.

The judgment of the District Court, as modified by this opinion, is *Affirmed.*

NOTES AND QUESTIONS

1. *Understanding* Berman v. Parker. *Berman v. Parker* critically tested a key element of the new urban renewal program, which required a conveyance of land in the redevelopment area to a private entity for redevelopment once the area was cleared. This raised the problem under the public use clause that property would be conveyed from private entity to another, which Justice Douglas managed to avoid. Do you see how he did this by deferring to congressional selection of ends and means? (Congress enacted laws for the District at that time.) The District of Columbia statute was based on model legislation drafted in the national housing agency for adoption in the states, which based the project on a finding of blight. Justice Douglas did not address this issue either, so the case does not tell us much about when the use of eminent domain to clear blight satisfies the public use requirement. The opinion's heavy reliance on legislative deference left much to state legislatures and local governments. Problems arose later at the state level because the model legislation defined blight as economic as well as social blight, opening the door for projects that had an economic rather than a slum clearance purpose.

The history and background of the southwest Washington project is detailed in Lavine, *Urban Renewal and the Story of Berman v. Parker*, 42 URB. LAW. 423 (2010). Southwest Washington was a poor but diverse and thriving community that was largely replaced by upscale residential housing. Physical conditions were substandard. Forty-three percent of the dwellings in the area had only outhouses, and 70% has no central heating. Redevelopment was intended to attract higher-income residents, displacing the area's lower income population, who were not adequately relocated. Lately the area has become more diverse, racially and economically. Should proof of an acceptable public use require proof that relocation plans will be adequate?

2. *The* Midkiff *Case*. The Court returned to the public use question in eminent domain 30 years later in *Hawaii Housing Authority v. Midkiff*, 467 U.S. 229 (1984), where it substantially broadened the definition of public use in a case upholding Hawaii's Land Reform Act. A considerable majority of land in Hawaii is held under leasehold. Under the Act, a state agency could condemn a leasehold interest and then convey fee title to the lessee. Justice O'Connor reviewed *Berman v. Parker*, noted the narrow role of the courts in deciding what is a public use, and spoke approvingly of the Hawaii law:

> But where the exercise of the eminent domain power is rationally related to a conceivable public purpose, the Court has never held a compensated taking to be proscribed by the Public Use Clause. [citations omitted] . . . The people of Hawaii have attempted, much as the settlers of the original 13 Colonies did, to reduce the perceived social and economic evils of a land oligopoly traceable to their monarchs. The land oligopoly has, according to the Hawaii Legislature, created artificial deterrents to the normal functioning of the State's residential land market and forced thousands of individual homeowners to lease, rather than buy, the land underneath their homes. Regulating oligopoly and the evils associated with it is a classic exercise of a State's police powers.

Id. at 241–242.

3. *The Public Use Doctrine After* Berman *and* Midkiff. The Supreme Court's public use cases opened the door for an expansive use of the eminent domain power in redevelopment projects. As the nation's slums were gradually cleared, many of these projects called for economic development in areas that were not physically blighted. In *Levin v. Township Comm.*, 274 A.2d 1 (N.J. 1971), for example, the court had no trouble accepting the legitimacy of the condemnation of vacant land for development as a shopping mall. In what became known as an infamous decision, *Poletown Neighborhood Council v. City of Detroit*, 304 N.W.2d 455 (Mich. 1981), the court held the benefit to the city from the condemnation of a still vibrant ethnic neighborhood for purposes of allowing General Motors to build a new factory was "clear and significant" and that the "private interest [of General Motors] is merely incidental." In *State ex rel. United States Steel v. Koehr*, 811 S.W.2d 385 (Mo. 1991), the City of St. Louis Board of Aldermen approved an urban renewal plan and declared a particular area blighted. The city land clearance authority decided a privately owned parking lot next to a hotel that was to be renovated under the plan was essential to provide parking for the hotel and to provide for its possible expansion. The city sued to acquire the parking lot in eminent domain after negotiations to buy it failed. Relying on *Berman v. Parker*, the court held that "the fact that [the property] is not blighted is irrelevant to the question of public use."

Although their decisions received relatively little attention, there were some state courts in the final third of the 20th century that adopted a more aggressive position in reviewing condemnations for redevelopment. For example, in *Port Authority of St. Paul v. Groppoli*, 202 N.W.2d 371 (Minn. 1972), the Minnesota Supreme Court refused to permit the condemnation of a beer distributor's warehouse, which was to be transferred "as is" to another distributor. In *City of Center Line v. Chmelko*, 416 N.W.2d 401 (Mich. Ct. App. 1987). The court invalidated the city's exercise of eminent domain to condemn allegedly blighted commercial buildings adjacent to a car dealership so it could expand and not leave its location, as it had threatened. *See also Mayor & Aldermen of the City of Vicksburg v. Thomas*, 645 So. 2d 940 (Miss. 1994) (court found no primary and public purpose in acquisition of land for casino development).

After 2000, a number of courts became even more outspoken in their opposition to the use of eminent domain for purposes of economic development. In *Southwestern Illinois Dev. Auth. v. National City Envtl., L.L.C.*, 768 N.E.2d 1 (Ill. 2002), the court invalidated a condemnation of an automobile recycling facility which was to be converted into a parking lot for a race track that wanted to expand. The authority claimed the condemnation would foster economic development, promote public safety, and prevent or eliminate blight. However, the court noted the authority did not conduct a study or formulate an economic plan and advertised it would condemn land for the private use of developers. In a Michigan case, *County of Wayne v. Hathcock*, 684 N.W.2d 765 (Mich. 2004), the state supreme court explicitly overruled its *Poletown* decision, and declared that a private business park was not a public use under the Michigan Constitution. Similar results were reached in *Manufactured Housing Communities of Washington v. Washington*, 13 P.3d 183 (Wash. 2000); *99 Cents Only Stores v. Lancaster Redevelopment Agency*, 237 F. Supp. 2d 1123 (C.D. Cal. 2001); *Pequonnock Yacht Club, Inc. v. City of Bridgeport*, 790 A.2d 1178 (Conn. 2002); *Township of West Orange v. 769 Assocs., L.L.C.*, 800 A.2d 86 (N.J. 2002);

Georgia Dept. of Transportation v. Jasper County, 586 S.E.2d 853 (S.C. 2003).

Such was the state of the law on public use when the Supreme Court again considered the public use question:

KELO v. CITY OF NEW LONDON

United States Supreme Court
545 U.S. 469 (2005)

JUSTICE STEVENS delivered the opinion of the Court.

In 2000, the city of New London approved a development plan that, in the words of the Supreme Court of Connecticut, was "projected to create in excess of 1,000 jobs, to increase tax and other revenues, and to revitalize an economically distressed city, including its downtown and waterfront areas." 843 A.2d 500, 507 (Conn. 2004). In assembling the land needed for this project, the city's development agent has purchased property from willing sellers and proposes to use the power of eminent domain to acquire the remainder of the property from unwilling owners in exchange for just compensation. The question presented is whether the city's proposed disposition of this property qualifies as a "public use" within the meaning of the Takings Clause of the Fifth Amendment to the Constitution.

I

The city of New London (hereinafter City) sits at the junction of the Thames River and the Long Island Sound in southeastern Connecticut. Decades of economic decline led a state agency in 1990 to designate the City a "distressed municipality." In 1996, the Federal Government closed the Naval Undersea Warfare Center, which had been located in the Fort Trumbull area of the City and had employed over 1,500 people. In 1998, the City's unemployment rate was nearly double that of the State, and its population of just under 24,000 residents was at its lowest since 1920.

These conditions prompted state and local officials to target New London, and particularly its Fort Trumbull area, for economic revitalization. To this end, respondent New London Development Corporation (NLDC), a private nonprofit entity established some years earlier to assist the City in planning economic development, was reactivated. In January 1998, the State authorized a $5.35 million bond issue to support the NLDC's planning activities and a $10 million bond issue toward the creation of a Fort Trumbull State Park. In February, the pharmaceutical company Pfizer Inc. announced that it would build a $300 million research facility on a site immediately adjacent to Fort Trumbull; local planners hoped that Pfizer would draw new business to the area, thereby serving as a catalyst to the area's rejuvenation. After receiving initial approval from the city council, the NLDC continued its planning activities and held a series of neighborhood meetings to educate the public about the process. In May, the city council authorized the NLDC to formally submit its plans to the relevant state agencies for review. Upon obtaining state-level approval, the NLDC finalized an integrated development plan focused on 90 acres of the Fort Trumbull area.

The Fort Trumbull area is situated on a peninsula that juts into the Thames River. The area comprises approximately 115 privately owned properties, as well as the 32 acres of land formerly occupied by the naval facility (Trumbull State Park now occupies 18 of those 32 acres). The development plan encompasses seven parcels. Parcel 1 is designated for a waterfront conference hotel at the center of a "small urban village" that will include restaurants and shopping. This parcel will also have marinas for both recreational and commercial uses. A pedestrian "riverwalk" will originate here and continue down the coast, connecting the waterfront areas of the development. Parcel 2 will be the site of approximately 80 new residences organized into an urban neighborhood and linked by public walkway to the remainder of the development, including the state park. This parcel also includes space reserved for a new U.S. Coast Guard Museum. Parcel 3, which is located immediately north of the Pfizer facility, will contain at least 90,000 square feet of research and development office space. Parcel 4A is a 2.4-acre site that will be used either to support the adjacent state park, by providing parking or retail services for visitors, or to support the nearby marina. Parcel 4B will include a renovated marina, as well as the final stretch of the riverwalk. Parcels 5, 6, and 7 will provide land for office and retail space, parking, and water-dependent commercial uses.

The NLDC intended the development plan to capitalize on the arrival of the Pfizer facility and the new commerce it was expected to attract. In addition to creating jobs, generating tax revenue, and helping to "build momentum for the revitalization of downtown New London," the plan was also designed to make the City more attractive and to create leisure and recreational opportunities on the waterfront and in the park.

The city council approved the plan in January 2000, and designated the NLDC as its development agent in charge of implementation. The city council also authorized the NLDC to purchase property or to acquire property by exercising eminent domain in the City's name. The NLDC successfully negotiated the purchase of most of the real estate in the 90-acre area, but its negotiations with petitioners failed. As a consequence, in November 2000, the NLDC initiated the condemnation proceedings that gave rise to this case.

II

Petitioner Susette Kelo has lived in the Fort Trumbull area since 1997. She has made extensive improvements to her house, which she prizes for its water view. Petitioner Wilhelmina Dery was born in her Fort Trumbull house in 1918 and has lived there her entire life. Her husband Charles (also a petitioner) has lived in the house since they married some 60 years ago. In all, the nine petitioners own 15 properties in Fort Trumbull — 4 in parcel 3 of the development plan and 11 in parcel 4A. Ten of the parcels are occupied by the owner or a family member; the other five are held as investment properties. There is no allegation that any of these properties is blighted or otherwise in poor condition; rather, they were condemned only because they happen to be located in the development area.

[In December 2000, the petitioners filed suit in Connecticut state court, claiming that the taking of their properties violated the "public use" restriction in the Fifth

Amendment. Although Ms. Kelo and her associates prevailed in the trial court, the Connecticut Supreme Court reversed the decision, holding that the taking was constitutionally valid. Three justices dissented, and Kelo successfully petitioned the United States Supreme Court for a writ of certiorari.]

III

Two polar propositions are perfectly clear. On the one hand, it has long been accepted that the sovereign may not take the property of *A* for the sole purpose of transferring it to another private party *B*, even though *A* is paid just compensation. On the other hand, it is equally clear that a State may transfer property from one private party to another if future "use by the public" is the purpose of the taking; the condemnation of land for a railroad with common-carrier duties is a familiar example. Neither of these propositions, however, determines the disposition of this case.

As for the first proposition, the City would no doubt be forbidden from taking petitioners' land for the purpose of conferring a private benefit on a particular private party. *See Midkiff*, 467 U.S., at 245 ("A purely private taking could not withstand the scrutiny of the public use requirement; it would serve no legitimate purpose of government and would thus be void"); *Missouri Pacific R. Co. v. Nebraska*, 164 U.S. 403 (1896). Nor would the City be allowed to take property under the mere pretext of a public purpose, when its actual purpose was to bestow a private benefit. The takings before us, however, would be executed pursuant to a "carefully considered" development plan. 843 A.2d, at 536. The trial judge and all the members of the Supreme Court of Connecticut agreed that there was no evidence of an illegitimate purpose in this case. Therefore, the City's development plan was not adopted "to benefit a particular class of identifiable individuals."

On the other hand, this is not a case in which the City is planning to open the condemned land — at least not in its entirety — to use by the general public, [but] this "Court long ago rejected any literal requirement that condemned property be put into use for the general public." 467 U.S. at 244. Indeed, while many state courts in the mid-19th century endorsed "use by the public" as the proper definition of public use, that narrow view steadily eroded over time. Accordingly, when this Court began applying the Fifth Amendment to the States at the close of the 19th century, it embraced the broader and more natural interpretation of public use as "public purpose." *See, e.g., Fallbrook Irrigation Dist. v. Bradley*, 164 U.S. 112 (1896). Thus, in a case upholding a mining company's use of an aerial bucket line to transport ore over property it did not own, Justice Holmes' opinion for the Court stressed "the inadequacy of use by the general public as a universal test." *Strickley v. Highland Boy Gold Mining Co.*, 200 U.S. 527 (1906). We have repeatedly and consistently rejected that narrow test ever since.

The disposition of this case therefore turns on the question whether the City's development plan serves a "public purpose." Without exception, our cases have defined that concept broadly, reflecting our longstanding policy of deference to legislative judgments in this field.

. . . .

[The Court discussed and summarized *Berman v. Parker*.]

In *Hawaii Housing Authority v. Midkiff*, 467 U.S. 229 (1984), the Court considered a Hawaii statute whereby fee title was taken from lessors and transferred to lessees (for just compensation) in order to reduce the concentration of land ownership. We unanimously upheld the statute and rejected the Ninth Circuit's view that it was "a naked attempt on the part of the state of Hawaii to take the property of A and transfer it to B solely for B's private use and benefit." *Id.*, at 235. Reaffirming *Berman*'s deferential approach to legislative judgments in this field, we concluded that the State's purpose of eliminating the "social and economic evils of a land oligopoly" qualified as a valid public use. 467 U.S., at 241–242. Our opinion also rejected the contention that the mere fact that the State immediately transferred the properties to private individuals upon condemnation somehow diminished the public character of the taking. "[I]t is only the taking's purpose, and not its mechanics," we explained, that matters in determining public use. *Id.*, at 244.

[The Court's discussion of the similar result in *Ruckelshaus v. Monsanto Co.*, 467 U.S. 986 (1984), is omitted.]

Viewed as a whole, our jurisprudence has recognized that the needs of society have varied between different parts of the Nation, just as they have evolved over time in response to changed circumstances. Our earliest cases in particular embodied a strong theme of federalism, emphasizing the "great respect" that we owe to state legislatures and state courts in discerning local public needs. For more than a century, our public use jurisprudence has wisely eschewed rigid formulas and intrusive scrutiny in favor of affording legislatures broad latitude in determining what public needs justify the use of the takings power.

IV

Those who govern the City were not confronted with the need to remove blight in the Fort Trumbull area, but their determination that the area was sufficiently distressed to justify a program of economic rejuvenation is entitled to our deference. The City has carefully formulated an economic development plan that it believes will provide appreciable benefits to the community, including — but by no means limited to — new jobs and increased tax revenue. As with other exercises in urban planning and development, the City is endeavoring to coordinate a variety of commercial, residential, and recreational uses of land, with the hope that they will form a whole greater than the sum of its parts. To effectuate this plan, the City has invoked a state statute that specifically authorizes the use of eminent domain to promote economic development. Given the comprehensive character of the plan, the thorough deliberation that preceded its adoption, and the limited scope of our review, it is appropriate for us, as it was in *Berman*, to resolve the challenges of the individual owners, not on a piecemeal basis, but rather in light of the entire plan. Because that plan unquestionably serves a public purpose, the takings challenged here satisfy the public use requirement of the Fifth Amendment.

To avoid this result, petitioners urge us to adopt a new bright-line rule that economic development does not qualify as a public use. Putting aside the unpersuasive suggestion that the City's plan will provide only purely economic benefits, neither precedent nor logic supports petitioners' proposal. Promoting economic development is a traditional and long accepted function of government. There is, moreover, no principled way of distinguishing economic development from the other public purposes that we have recognized. In our cases upholding takings that facilitated agriculture and mining, for example, we emphasized the importance of those industries to the welfare of the States in question, *see, e.g., Strickley*, 200 U.S. 527; in *Berman*, we endorsed the purpose of transforming a blighted area into a "well-balanced" community through redevelopment, 348 U.S., at 33; in *Midkiff*, we upheld the interest in breaking up a land oligopoly that "created artificial deterrents to the normal functioning of the State's residential land market," 467 U.S., at 242, and in *Monsanto*, we accepted Congress' purpose of eliminating a "significant barrier to entry in the pesticide market," 467 U.S., at 1014–1015. It would be incongruous to hold that the City's interest in the economic benefits to be derived from the development of the Fort Trumbull area has less of a public character than any of those other interests. Clearly, there is no basis for exempting economic development from our traditionally broad understanding of public purpose.

Petitioners contend that using eminent domain for economic development impermissibly blurs the boundary between public and private takings. Again, our cases foreclose this objection. Quite simply, the government's pursuit of a public purpose will often benefit individual private parties. The owner of the department store in *Berman* objected to "taking from one businessman for the benefit of another businessman," 348 U.S., at 33, referring to the fact that under the redevelopment plan land would be leased or sold to private developers for redevelopment. Our rejection of that contention has particular relevance to the instant case: "The public end may be as well or better served through an agency of private enterprise than through a department of government — or so the Congress might conclude. We cannot say that public ownership is the sole method of promoting the public purposes of community redevelopment projects." *Id.*, at 34.

It is further argued that without a bright-line rule nothing would stop a city from transferring citizen *A*'s property to citizen *B* for the sole reason that citizen *B* will put the property to a more productive use and thus pay more taxes. Such a one-to-one transfer of property, executed outside the confines of an integrated development plan, is not presented in this case. While such an unusual exercise of government power would certainly raise a suspicion that a private purpose was afoot, the hypothetical cases posited by petitioners can be confronted if and when they arise. They do not warrant the crafting of an artificial restriction on the concept of public use.

Alternatively, petitioners maintain that for takings of this kind we should require a "reasonable certainty" that the expected public benefits will actually accrue. Such a rule, however, would represent an even greater departure from our precedent. "When the legislature's purpose is legitimate and its means are not irrational, our cases make clear that empirical debates over the wisdom of takings — no less than debates over the wisdom of other kinds of socioeconomic legislation — are not to be carried out in the federal courts." *Midkiff*, 467 U.S., at 242. The disadvantages of a heightened form of review are especially pronounced in this type of case. Orderly implementation of a comprehensive redevelopment plan obviously requires that the legal rights of all interested parties be established before new construction can be commenced. A constitutional rule that required postponement of the judicial approval of every condemnation until the likelihood of success of the plan had been assured would unquestionably impose a significant impediment to the successful consummation of many such plans.

Just as we decline to second-guess the City's considered judgments about the efficacy of its development plan, we also decline to second-guess the City's determinations as to what lands it needs to acquire in order to effectuate the project. "It is not for the courts to oversee the choice of the boundary line nor to sit in review on the size of a particular project area. Once the question of the public purpose has been decided, the amount and character of land to be taken for the project and the need for a particular tract to complete the integrated plan rests in the discretion of the legislative branch." *Berman*, 348 U.S., at 35–36.

In affirming the City's authority to take petitioners' properties, we do not minimize the hardship that condemnations may entail, notwithstanding the payment of just compensation. We emphasize that nothing in our opinion precludes any State from placing further restrictions on its exercise of the takings power. Indeed, many States already impose "public use" requirements that are stricter than the federal baseline. Some of these requirements have been established as a matter of state constitutional law, while others are expressed in state eminent domain statutes that carefully limit the grounds upon which takings may be exercised. As the submissions of the parties and their *amici* make clear, the necessity and wisdom of using eminent domain to promote economic development are certainly matters of legitimate public debate. This Court's authority, however, extends only to determining whether the City's proposed condemnations are for a "public use" within the meaning of the Fifth Amendment to the Federal Constitution. Because over a century of our case law interpreting that provision dictates an affirmative answer to that question, we may not grant petitioners the relief that they seek.

The judgment of the Supreme Court of Connecticut is affirmed.

JUSTICE KENNEDY, concurring.

I join the opinion for the Court and add these further observations. This Court has declared that a taking should be upheld as consistent with the Public Use Clause, as long as it is "rationally related to a conceivable public purpose." The determination that a rational-basis standard of review is appropriate does not, however, alter the fact that transfers intended to confer benefits on particular, favored private entities, and with only incidental or pretextual public benefits, are forbidden by the Public Use Clause.

A court applying rational-basis review under the Public Use Clause should strike down a taking that, by a clear showing, is intended to favor a particular private party, with only incidental or pretextual public benefits, just as a court applying rational-basis review under the Equal Protection Clause must strike down a government classification that is clearly intended to injure a particular class of private parties, with only incidental or pretextual public justifications.

A court confronted with a plausible accusation of impermissible favoritism to private parties should treat the objection as a serious one and review the record to see if it has merit, though with the presumption that the government's actions were reasonable and intended to serve a public purpose. My agreement with the Court that a presumption of invalidity is not warranted for economic development takings in general, or for the particular takings at issue in this case, does not foreclose the possibility that a more stringent standard of review than that announced in *Berman* and *Midkiff* might be appropriate for a more narrowly drawn category of takings.

JUSTICE O'CONNOR, with whom THE CHIEF JUSTICE, JUSTICE SCALIA, and JUSTICE THOMAS join, dissenting. [Only a part of Justice O'Connor's opinion is reproduced here.]

Over two centuries ago, just after the Bill of Rights was ratified, Justice Chase wrote:

> An ACT of the Legislature (for I cannot call it a law) contrary to the great first principles of the social compact, cannot be considered a rightful exercise of legislative authority . . . . A few instances will suffice to explain what I mean . . . . [A] law that takes property from A. and gives it to B: It is against all reason and justice, for a people to entrust a Legislature with SUCH powers; and, therefore, it cannot be presumed that they have done it.

Calder v. Bull, 3 U.S. 386 (1798) . . . .

[Justice O'Connor reviewed *Berman* and *Midkiff I*, noted that they did not qualify the "bedrock principle" that land may not be taken for a private use, and backed away from her *MidKiff* opinion by noting that both that decision and *Berman* contained "errant language." Her opinion includes the much-quoted phrase that "[n]othing [in the Court's decision] is to prevent the State from replacing any Motel 6 with a Ritz-Carlton, any home with a shopping mall, or any farm with a factory."]

Today the Court abandons this long-held, basic limitation on government power. Under the banner of economic development, all private property is now vulnerable to being taken and transferred to another private owner, so long as it might be upgraded — *i.e.*, given to an owner who will use it in a way that the legislature deems more beneficial to the public — in the process. To reason, as the Court does, that the incidental public benefits resulting from the subsequent ordinary use of private property render economic development takings "for public use" is to wash out any distinction between private and public use of property — and thereby effectively to delete the words "for public use" from the Takings Clause of the Fifth Amendment. Accordingly I respectfully dissent.

. . . .

It was possible after *Berman* and *Midkiff* to imagine unconstitutional transfers from A to B. Those decisions endorsed government intervention when private property use had veered to such an extreme that the public was suffering as a consequence. Today nearly all real property is susceptible to condemnation on the Court's theory . . . . Any property may now be taken for the benefit of another private party, but the fallout from this decision will not be random. The beneficiaries are likely to be those citizens with disproportionate influence and power in the political process, including large corporations and development firms. As for the victims, the government now has license to transfer property from those with fewer resources to those with more. The Founders cannot have intended this perverse result. "That alone is a *just* government," wrote James Madison, "which *impartially* secures to every man, whatever is his *own*." For the National Gazette, Property, (Mar. 29, 1792), *reprinted in* 14 PAPERS OF JAMES MADISON 266 (R. Rutland et al. eds. 1983).

I would hold that the takings in both Parcel 3 and Parcel 4A are unconstitutional, reverse the judgment of the Supreme Court of Connecticut, and remand for further proceedings.

JUSTICE THOMAS, dissenting.

[Omitted.]

NOTES AND QUESTIONS

1. *What* Kelo *Means*. The majority in *Kelo* seem to be saying that its opinion is entirely consistent with its earlier decisions, but Justice O'Connor insisted that the majority had greatly weakened the "public use" test. To what extent (if any) has the Court changed the rules in *Kelo* from what they were in *Berman* and *Midkiff*? Is the Court basically saying that the redistribution of wealth is a public use, or is it saying that the redistribution of wealth is a constitutionally acceptable means of accomplishing a public purpose, so long as compensation is required, or is it saying that it will defer to virtually all legislative determinations of what constitutes a public use? If the City of New London has the power to purchase private lots from homeowners who wish to sell, why shouldn't it be able to use the power of eminent domain for those who won't sell? Perhaps it is all about Federalism, as David Callies suggested in *Kelo v. New London: Of Planning, Federalism, and a Switch in Time*, 28 HAWAII L. REV. 327 (2006).

Justice Stevens emphasized the planning that had been done for the New London project as a reason finding a public use. This emphasis is of interest considering that federal agency decision makers rejected a reliance on planning as a basis for claiming a public use in favor of a defense resting on the removal of slums and blight. *See* Mandelker, Kelo*'s Lessons for Urban Redevelopment: History Forgotten* (2009), http://law.wustl.edu/landuselaw/Articles/Mandelker%20article%20-%20EIC%20edit%20final%20%28clean%29.pdf. Nicole Garnett has discussed the role of planning in public use litigation, and has suggested that takings for economic development that occur outside a comprehensive plan may be constitutionally suspect. *Planning as Public Use?*, 34 ECOLOGY L.Q. 443, 455 (2007).

2. *The Public Reaction to* Kelo. Public reaction to the *Kelo* decision was swift and furious. As one commentator noted, once the case was decided, "All Hell broke loose." Cole, *Why Kelo Is Not Good News for Local Planners and Developers*, 22 GA. ST. U.L. REV. 803, 803 (2006) In fact, the case spawned the most intense public reaction ever to a Supreme Court decision not involving race or abortion. Critics

quickly emerged from both the right and the left. Conservatives saw the decision as an attack on the foundation of private property while progressives saw it as further evidence that local governmental agencies were in the hip pockets of large corporations and real estate developers. As two commentators noted, "Everyone hates *Kelo*." Bell & Parchomovsky, *The Uselessness of Public Use*, 106 COLUM. L. REV. 1412, 1413 (2006).

Does the extremely hostile popular reaction to the *Kelo* decision mean that the majority was wrong? Does it vindicate the views of either O'Connor or Thomas?

3. *Judicial Decisions Post-*Kelo. Some courts accepted its invitation to take a more rigorous position under state public use clauses. In an influential case, for example, the Supreme Court of Ohio applied the Ohio Constitution to hold that "an economic or financial benefit alone is insufficient to satisfy the public-use requirement" of the Ohio Constitution. *City of Norwood v. Horney*, 853 N.E.2d 1115 (Ohio 2006). The opinion concluded that modern public-private partnership economic development strategy carries with it the "danger . . . that the state's decision to take may be influenced by the financial gains that would flow to it or to the private entity because of the taking." Thus, "both common sense and the law command independent judicial review of the taking." The court also held that local governments in Ohio could not base takings solely on the fact that property is in a "deteriorating area," characterized by the municipal code of the City of Norwood as an area with incompatible land uses, nonconforming uses, faulty street arrangement, diversity of ownership and the like, because the term "describes almost any city" and thus was too vague to give appropriate notice to landowners of the possibility that their land could be subject to eminent domain proceedings. *See also Franco v. National Capital Revitalization Corp.*, 930 A.2d 160 (D.C. 2007) (opinion contains extensive survey of state eminent domain opinions since *Kelo*); *Gallenthin Realty Dev. Inc. v. Borough of Paulsboro*, 924 A.2d 447 (N.J. 2007) (land may not be condemned for redevelopment because it is not fully productive)

Two New York high court cases, however, confirmed judicial deference to the use of eminent domain for economic redevelopment. One involved the Atlantic Yards project, a 22-acre site near downtown Brooklyn that is to be developed with a sports stadium and mixed uses. Lavine & Oder, *Urban Redevelopment Policy, Judicial Deference to Unaccountable Agencies, and Reality in Brooklyn's Atlantic Yards Project*, 42 URB. LAW. 287 (2010), criticize the project for lack of public accountability, procedural transparency and thorough governmental oversight, but federal and state courts approved the use of eminent domain while rejecting pretext arguments. *Goldstein v. Pataki*, 516 F.3d 50 (2d Cir. 2008); *Matter of Goldstein v. New York State Urban Dev. Corp.*, 921 N.E.2d 164 (N.Y. 2009). In *Matter of Kaur v. New York State Urban Dev. Corp.*, 933 N.E.2d 721 (N.Y. 2010), the court reversed an angry intermediate appellate court decision and upheld an expansion project by Columbia University in upper Manhattan. The appellate court had found that the finding of public use was unsupported, that the blight finding was false, and that there was no benefit to the public. *See* Hirokawa & Salkin, *Can Urban University Expansion and Sustainable Development Co-Exist?: A Case Study in Progress on Columbia University*, 37 FORDHAM URB. L.J. 637 (2010).

4. *Statutory and Constitutional Change.* Virtually every state commenced some sort of legal change — most commonly in the form of legislation or constitutional amendment — to "roll back" the broad definition of public use which the majority articulated in *Berman, Midkiff,* and *Kelo.* More than half the states (including post-Katrina Louisiana) have adopted constitutional amendments or legislation by popular initiative or have passed legislation modifying their redevelopment statutes to limit condemnation. This legislation or constitutional amendment either 1) prohibits the use of eminent domain for redevelopment or limits it to tightly-defined blighted areas, 2) imposes more rigorous procedural protections, or 3) requires fair compensation when a principal residence is taken. Although the intensity of the outrage has subsided, the campaign to restrict, or elimination, the use of eminent domain for economic redevelopment continues. For a recent review of this response, see D. Callies, 50 STATE REPORT CARD; TRACKING EMINENT DOMAIN SINCE *KELO* (2007), www.castlecoalition.org. What are the consequences of such enactments for the substantial percentage of Americans who live in older suburbs in need of renewal and redevelopment? *See* R. Puentes & D. Warren, ONE-FIFTH OF AMERICA: A COMPREHENSIVE GUIDE TO AMERICA'S FIRST SUBURBS (2006).

Eagle & Perotti, *Coping with Kelo: A Potpourri of Legislative and Judicial Responses,* 42 REAL PROP. PROB. & TR. J. 799 (2008), group legislation and constitutional amendments on public use into the following categories: 1) inclusionary definitions of public use, such as the "possession, occupation, and enjoyment" of property by the public or public entities, which would seem to prohibit public-private partnerships; 2) exclusionary definitions of public use, such as exercise of eminent domain for "the purpose of achieving the public benefits of an increase in the tax base, an increase in tax revenue, more employment, or general economic stability"; 3) hybrid provisions that specify public uses but also state that economic redevelopment is not a public use; and 4) exemptions from exclusionary definitions that allow takings of blighted properties and for traditional uses that are publicly owned or operated.

City of Omaha v. Tract No. 1, 778 N.W.2d 122 (Neb. Ct. App. 2010), considered a statute with language similar to that quoted in category 2. The city acquired a strip of land through eminent domain to install a deceleration lane to handle increased traffic that would access a new retail development. The court rejected an argument that the property had been taken primarily for the economic purpose of serving the retailer. It held that the primary users of the deceleration lane would be the public, that it would not generate taxes, that the purpose of acquiring the deceleration lane was not related to job creation, and that the city's use of the eminent domain power was not affected by general economic conditions. Is there a contrary argument? *See also* Somin, *The Limits of Backlash: Assessing the Political Response to Kelo,* 93 MINN. L. REV. 2100 (2009).

5. *Commentary.* There is extensive commentary on the *Kelo* decision and its aftermath. For representative commentary, see J. RYSKAMP, THE EMINENT DOMAIN REVOLT (2007); EMINENT DOMAIN USE AND ABUSE: *KELO* IN CONTEXT (D. Merriam & M. Massaron, eds. 2006); Bell & Parchomovsky, *Essay: The Uselessness of Public Use,* 106 COLUM. L. REV. 1412 (2006); Hafetz, *Ferreting Out Favoritism: Bringing PreText Claims After Kelo,* 77 FORDHAM L. REV. 3095 (2009); Mihaly, *Living in the Past: The Kelo Court and Public-Private Economic Redevelopment,* 34 ECOLOGY

L.Q. 1 (2007); Sax, Kelo*: A Case Rightly Decided*, 28 HAWAII L. REV. 365 (2006); Zeiner, *Eminent Domain Wolves in Sheep's Clothing: Private Benefit Masquerading as Classic Public Use*, 28 VA. ENVTL. L.J. 1 (2010).

[2.] Consequential Damages

In the discussion of public use, it was assumed the government agency took full title to land. But government can also condemn or impair interests in land that are less than full title. The following is an early case that explains the consequential damage concept, and why consequential damages can require compensation.

PUMPELLY v. GREEN BAY COMPANY

United States Supreme Court
80 U.S. 166 (1872)

JUSTICE MILLER delivered the opinion of the Court.

The Constitution of Wisconsin ordains that "The property of no person shall be taken for public use without just compensation therefor." With this provision in force as fundamental law, one Pumpelly, in September, 1867, brought trespass on the case against the Green Bay and Mississippi Canal Company for overflowing 640 acres of his land, by means of a dam erected across Fox River, the northern outlet of Lake Winnebago, by which, as the declaration averred, the waters of the lake were raised so high as to forcibly and with violence overflow all his said land, from the time of the completion of the dam in 1861 to the commencement of this suit; the water coming with such a violence, the declaration averred, as to tear up his trees and grass by the roots, and wash them, with his hay by tons, away, to choke up his drains and fill up his ditches, to saturate some of his lands with water, and to dirty and injure other parts by bringing and leaving on them deposits of sand, and otherwise greatly injuring him.

The plea averred that Reed and an associate commenced the building of this dam; that by certain legislation of Wisconsin (now become a State) it was afterwards adopted as part of the system of improving the navigation of the Fox River, and became the property of the defendants.

The plea then set out the legislation in regard to the improvement, the incorporation of the Fox and Wisconsin Improvement Company, the organization, incorporation, and title of the canal company (the defendant), as set forth before, and further alleged that the dam was built and maintained under the authority of the laws of the United States and of the State of Wisconsin, and the board of public works; that as constructed and maintained, it was and is an essential portion of the works for the improvement of the navigability of the Fox and Wisconsin Rivers, and to the proper development as common navigable highways . . . .

The legislature of Wisconsin, after it became a State, projected a system of improving the navigation of the Fox and Wisconsin Rivers, which adopted the dam of Reid and Doty, then in process of construction, as part of that system; and that, under that act, a board of public works was established, which made such arrangements with Reid and Doty that they continued and completed the dam; and that, by subsequent legislation, changing the organization under which the work was carried on, the defendants finally became the owners of the dam, with such powers concerning the improvement of the navigation of the river as the legislature could confer in that regard. But it does not appear that any statute made provision for compensation to the plaintiff, or those similarly injured, for damages to their lands. So that the plea, as thus considered, presents substantially the defense that the State of Wisconsin, having, in the progress of its system of improving the navigation of the Fox River, authorized the erection of the dam as it now stands, without any provision for compensating the plaintiff for the injury which it does him, the defendant asserts the right, under legislative authority, to build and continue the dam without legal responsibility for those injuries.

And counsel for the defendant, with becoming candor, argue that the damages of which the plaintiff complains are such as the State had a right to inflict in improving the navigation of the Fox River, without making any compensation for them.

This requires a construction of the Constitution of Wisconsin; for though the Constitution of the United States provides that private property shall not be taken for public use without just compensation, it is well settled that this is a limitation on the power of the Federal government, and not on the States. The Constitution of Wisconsin, however, has a provision almost identical in language, viz.: that "the property of no person shall be taken for public use without just compensation therefor." Indeed this limitation on the exercise of the right of eminent domain is so essentially a part of American constitutional law that it is believed that no State is now without it, and the only question that we are to consider is whether the injury to plaintiff's property, as set forth in his declaration, is within its protection.

The declaration states that, by reason of the dam, the water of the lake was so raised as to cause it to overflow all his land, and that the overflow remained continuously from the completion of the dam, in the year 1861, to the commencement of the suit in the year 1867, and the nature of the injuries set out in the declaration are such as show that it worked an almost complete destruction of the value of the land.

The argument of the defendant is that there is no *taking* of the land within the meaning of the constitutional provision, and that the damage is a consequential result of such use of a navigable stream as the government had a right to for the improvement of its navigation.

It would be a very curious and unsatisfactory result, if in construing a provision of constitutional law, always understood to have been adopted for protection and security to the rights of the individual as against the government, and which has received the commendation of jurists, statesmen, and commentators as placing the just principles of the common law on that subject beyond the power of ordinary legislation to change or control them, it shall be held that if the government refrains from the absolute conversion of real property to the uses of the public it can destroy its value entirely, can inflict irreparable and permanent injury to any extent, can, in effect, subject it to total destruction without making any compensation, because, in the narrowest sense of that word, it is not *taken* for the public use. Such a construction would pervert the constitutional provisions into a restriction upon the rights of the citizen, as those rights stood at the common law, instead of the government, and make it an authority for invasion of private right under the pretext of the public good, which had no warrant in the laws or practices of our ancestors.

In the case of *Gardner v. Newburgh,* 2 Johnson's Chancery, 162. [New York 1816] Chancellor Kent granted an injunction to prevent the trustees of Newburg from diverting the water of a certain stream flowing over plaintiff's land from its usual course, because the act of the legislature which authorized it had made no provision for compensating the plaintiff for the injury thus done to his land. And he did this though there was no provision in the Constitution of New York such as we have mentioned, and though he recognized that the water was taken for a public use. After citing several continental jurists on this right of eminent domain, he says that while they admit that private property may be taken for public uses when public necessity or utility requires, they all lay it down as a clear principle of natural equity that the individual whose property is thus sacrificed must be indemnified. And he adds that the principles and practice of the English government are equally explicit on this point. It will be seen in this case that it was the diversion of the water from the plaintiff's land, which was considered as taking private property for public use, but which, under the argument of the defendant's counsel, would, like overflowing the land, be called only a consequential injury . . . . [Other cases discussed have been omitted.]

We are not unaware of the numerous cases in the State courts in which the doctrine has been successfully invoked that for a consequential injury to the property of the individual arising from the prosecution of improvements of roads, streets, rivers, and other highways, for the public good, there is no redress; and we do not deny that the principle is a sound one, in its proper application, to many injuries to property so originating. And when, in the exercise of our duties here, we shall be called upon to construe other State constitutions, we shall not be unmindful of the weight due to the decisions of the courts of those States.

But we are of opinion that the decisions referred to have gone to the uttermost limit of sound judicial construction in favor of this principle, and, in some cases, beyond it, and that it remains true that where real estate is actually invaded by superinduced additions of water, earth, sand, or other material, or by having any artificial structure placed on it, so as to effectually destroy or impair its usefulness, it is a taking, within the meaning of the Constitution, and that this proposition is not in conflict with the weight of judicial authority in this country, and certainly not with sound principle. Beyond this we do not go, and this case calls us to go no further.

We do not think it necessary to consume time in proving that when the United States sells land by treaty or otherwise, and parts with the fee by patent without reservations, it retains no right to take that land for public use without just compensation, nor does it confer such a right on the State within which it lies; and that the absolute ownership and right of private property in such land is not varied by the fact that it borders on a navigable stream.

The demurrer to this plea [by the defendant] should also have been sustained.

NOTES AND QUESTIONS

1. *Liability for Consequential Damage.* The recognition that the Fifth Amendment and its counterparts in state constitutions applied when property was directly damaged by certain types of government actions was one of the most important developments in the constitutional law of property in the 19th century. See the discussion of this topic in J. ELY, THE GUARDIAN OF EVERY OTHER RIGHT (1998), M. HORWITZ, THE TRANSFORMATION OF AMERICAN LAW (1977), and Mossoff, *What Is Property? Putting the Pieces Back Together*, 45 ARIZ. L. REV. 371, 432–36 (2003).

In 1870, a new section was added to the Illinois Constitution that provided for compensation for private property that was "taken or damaged" by the state for a public use. Even before the adoption of the new provision, the Illinois Supreme Court had ruled that a municipality was liable for damages incurred by private property owners as a result of changes in the grade of a city street. *Nevins v. City of Peoria*, 41 Ill. 502 (1866). Two years later, West Virginia added a similar provision to its state constitution, and the consequential damages principle was accepted in most jurisdictions whether or not the state constitution made specific references to "damaged" property. Note that the Wisconsin Constitution in *Pumpelly* lacked such language. In *Pumpelly*, the United States Supreme Court was called upon to interpret the Wisconsin state constitution, not the United States Constitution. The decision was handed down in 1871, only three years after the ratification of the Fourteenth Amendment and before it was clear that this amendment imposed limitations on the police power of the states.

2. *The Limits of Recovery.* In *Pumpelly*, the Court referred to state cases where courts held that "for consequential injury . . . there is no redress." How is the line to be drawn? Did the taking of a "property" interest in *Pumpelly* lead the Court to award compensation? See *Eaton v. Boston*, C. & M.R.R., 51 N.H. 504 (1872), where the court held that an interference with the use of land was compensable as a taking of property. Consider the following:

Felts v. Harris County, 915 S.W.2d 482 (Tex. 1996). Landowners sought damages in inverse condemnation for roadway traffic noise caused by a four-lane "major thoroughfare" adjacent to plaintiff's property. Recovery was denied because roadway noise had a "similar impact on the community as a whole," and thus any damages suffered by the plaintiffs were community damages "not connected with the landowner's use and enjoyment." Under exceptional circumstances, however, the court indicated that traffic noise may be so significant that it severely impairs the ownership interest in property. *Accord*, *Texas Dep't of Transp. v. City of Sunset Valley*, 146 S.W.3d 637 (Tex. 2004) (no recovery for damage claimed from lights from highway).

Varjabedian v. City of Madera, 572 P.2d 43 (Cal. 1977). The court allowed recovery of compensation to plaintiffs, who owned a vineyard, for septic smells coming from the city's landfill. The court held that physical invasion was not necessary for recovery, and applied the holding in *Richards v. Washington Terminal Co.*, 233 U.S. 546 (1914), that recovery is allowable when damages are a direct, peculiar, and substantial burden on plaintiff's property. Compare *Oliver v. AT & T Wireless Servs.*, 76 Cal. App. 4th 521 (1999), rejecting a compensation claim based on aesthetic injuries allegedly caused by a cellular telephone transmission tower and distinguishing *Madera.*

Estate of Kirkpatrick v. City of Olathe, 215 P.3d 561 (Kan. 2009). The court awarded compensation for the flooding of a house caused by grading for a highway roundabout. It held that damage is compensable if it is "substantial and . . . the planned or inevitable result of government action undertaken for public benefit," but that "[d]amage that is tangential or consequential to a government action is more appropriately addressed in the realm of tort law."

Recall *United States v. Causby*, a U.S. Supreme Court cases discussed in the *Geller* case in Chapter 2, where the Court upheld compensation awarded for airplane overflights that caused damage to the plaintiff's property. Is that case different because it was an invasion of a property right? The highway access cases that follow present another example where compensation may be awarded for the taking of a property right. For discussion of these issues see Ball, *The Curious Intersection of Nuisance and Takings Law*, 86 B.U.L. Rev. 819 (2006); Mandelker, *Inverse Condemnation: The Constitutional Limits of Public Responsibility*, 1966 Wis. L. Rev. 3.

[3.] Limitations on Highway Access

In the discussion of public use, it was assumed the government agency took full title to land. But government can also condemn or impair interests in land that are less than full title. Highway and street access is a case in point. Individuals need access to be able to enter and leave their properties. Businesses need access so they will be readily accessible to patrons. Without access, a business may fail.

In the early days of the construction of the national, limited-access, interstate highway system through the 1970s, denial of access problems often arose when the construction of a new limited-access highway diverted traffic away from an older and established road where access was unlimited. Businesses on the old road then lost most of their clientele and were forced to close. A property owner might then sue, claiming she had been deprived of her property right to highway access. Now that the interstate system is completed, denial of access problems are more likely to arise when highways are reconstructed or improved, as the following case demonstrates.

STATE OF INDIANA v. DUNN

Indiana Court of Appeals
888 N.E.2d 858 (2008)

Vaidik, Judge

Case Summary

The State's construction of a median strip that makes the route of travel to a business property more circuitous is not a compensable taking. We therefore reverse the trial court's partial summary judgment in favor of business owner John

M. Dunn against the State and the subsequent damages awarded to Dunn by a jury.

Facts and Procedural History

Dunn entered the hotel business in 1978. Since that time, he has developed, owned, and operated more than twenty hotel properties. One of these properties is located at 100 South Green River Road in Evansville, Indiana ("Subject Property").

In the late 1980s, the State decided to construct the Lloyd Expressway near the Subject Property. When the Lloyd Expressway was initially constructed, all entrances connecting the Subject Property to Green River Road were eliminated. However, the State then initiated condemnation proceedings to acquire a nearby strip of land belonging to Dunn in order to build a service road connecting the western boundary of the Subject Property to Green River Road. at 130. The State successfully acquired the land and constructed the service road, and Dunn received compensation for the taking.

Thereafter, the Subject Property had access, via the service road, to and from the northbound and southbound lanes of Green River Road. This changed in July 2004, when the State, acting through the Indiana Department of Transportation, installed a concrete median in the center of Green River Road, *id.* at 116, 118, near that road's interchange with State Road 66. This median prevents southbound traffic from Green River Road from making left turns into the service road entrance to the Subject Property. The elimination of left-hand turns onto the service road "was designed as a safety measure," as a southbound driver making such a turn would have to cross five lanes of oncoming northbound traffic. The service road remains accessible to the public, although southbound drivers on Green River Road must follow a circuitous route to reach the service road and, hence, the Subject Property. The State undertook this project pursuant to its authority under Indiana Code § 8-23-8-1 to build and improve limited access facilities.[2]

After the State released its plan for the construction of the median but before its actual construction, Dunn, anticipating a loss in clientele because of the reduced convenience of the hotel's entrance, began remodeling the hotel in November 2003 to increase its customer base. While the hotel had apparently operated successfully from approximately 1978 until 2004, Dunn characterizes the hotel's occupancy rates between November 2003 until the end of 2004 as "disappointing."

Dunn filed an inverse condemnation action against the State, alleging that the erection of the median "has completely eliminated all access to the Hotel and Subject Property from the southbound lane of Green River Road," as it "prevents all left-hand turns from the southbound lanes of Green River Road into the Hotel's vehicular entrance." Therefore, according to Dunn, the median "substantially and materially limited and impaired vehicular access to the Subject Property and

---

[2] [3] A "limited access facility" is a "highway or street designed for through traffic, over, from, or to which owners or occupiers of abutting land or other persons have either no right or easement of direct access, light, air, or view because their property abuts upon the limited access facility or for any other reason. The highways or streets may be parkways from which trucks, busses, and other commercial vehicles are excluded or freeways open to use by all customary forms of highway and street traffic." Ind. Code § 8-23-1-28.

vehicular egress from the Subject Property," and this constitutes "a taking of [his] property without just compensation." He sought monetary compensation for the taking. The State answered and acknowledged that the median "prohibit[ed] left hand turns to and from Green River Road and the public service road." However, the State contended that Dunn is not entitled to compensation as a matter of law because the erection of medians resulting in circuitous travel to a business is conducted according to the State's police powers and does not effect a compensable taking. Both parties subsequently filed motions for summary judgment, and the trial court granted Dunn's motion for partial summary judgment, concluding that "a taking of Plaintiffs property rights by the Defendant, State of Indiana, has occurred." The suit thereafter proceeded to jury trial on the issue of damages. The jury returned a verdict in favor of Dunn in the amount of $3,650,000, and the trial court entered judgment accordingly. Upon Dunn's later motion, the trial court awarded him an additional $1,049,600 in prejudgment interest, $109 in costs, and $25,000 in attorneys' fees. The State now appeals.

Discussion and Decision

Article I, § 21 of the Indiana Constitution provides that "[n]o person's property shall be taken by law, without just compensation; nor, except in case of the State, without such compensation first assessed and tendered." Indiana Code § 32-24-1-16 further provides that "[a] person having an interest in property that has been or may be required for a public use without the procedures of [the eminent domain] article or any prior law followed is entitled to have the person's damages assessed" under Indiana's statutory eminent domain procedure, found at Indiana Code chapter 32-24-1. Cases brought pursuant to Indiana Code § 32-24-1-16 are known as inverse condemnation actions. As we have observed in the past, condemnation proceedings are comprised of two stages: (1) an initial or summary phase, and (2) the phase during which the fact finder determines damages. *City of Hammond v. Marina Entm't Complex, Inc.*, 733 N.E.2d 958, 966 (Ind. App. 2000). "During the initial or summary phase of the proceedings, the action consists solely of legal issues which are decided by the trial court." *Id.* "During the second stage of the condemnation proceedings the fact finder must determine the amount of damages sustained by the landowner." *Id.*

The State raises four issues on appeal, pertaining to both the initial phase and the damages phase of the adjudication of Dunn's inverse condemnation complaint. We find one issue dispositive: whether the trial court erred as a matter of law in granting partial summary judgment in favor of Dunn and against the State when the State built a median that forces traffic moving in certain directions to travel a more circuitous route to and from Dunn's business property. We therefore will not reach the remaining issues. . . .

[The court applied the standard of review of a summary judgment ruling, which is whether "the evidence shows there is no genuine issue of material fact and the moving party is entitled to a judgment as a matter of law." It added that "[w]hether a taking has occurred is a question of law, and we review questions of law *de novo*."]

The State contends that Dunn was not entitled to summary judgment as a matter of law because the construction of a median, resulting in a circuitous route of ingress and egress for a property, does not constitute a compensable taking under Indiana eminent domain law. Dunn counters that he is entitled to compensation under Indiana Code § 8-23-8-1, and that Indiana case law "holds that a determination of a 'taking' relative to a business owner's loss of access requires a fact-sensitive inquiry to consider whether the State action interferes with the distinct investment-backed expectations of the owner and whether the State action interfered with the present use of the property so as to substantially diminish the value of the property."

In order to determine whether a taking of property has occurred, we look at whether the plaintiff landowner has shown that he or she "has an interest in land which has been taken for a public use without having been appropriated under eminent domain laws." *Jenkins v. Bd. of County Comm'rs of Madison County*, 698 N.E.2d 1268, 1270 (Ind. App. 1998). The threshold question in determining whether a taking has occurred is whether the plaintiff landowner has a property interest in the property that has been acquired by the State. *See* Ind. Code § 32-24-1-16 (allowing inverse condemnation suits where a "person ha[s] an interest in property").

" 'Property' in its legal sense means a valuable right or interest in something rather than the thing itself, and is the right to possess, use and dispose of that something in such a manner as is not inconsistent with law." *State v. Ensley*, 164 N.E.2d 342, 348–49 (Ind. 1960). It is well settled that "the right of ingress and egress is a property right which cannot be taken without compensation." *Jenkins*, 698 N.E.2d at 1270. However, "[a] property owner is not entitled to unlimited access to abutting property at all points along the highway," *Jenkins*, 698 N.E.2d at 1271, and our Supreme Court has made clear that a taking does not "occur where ingress and egress is made more circuitous and difficult," *Town Council of New Harmony v. Parker*, 726 N.E.2d 1217, 1222 (Ind. 2000). This is because "[t]he general rule is that there is no property right of an abutting property owner in the free flow of traffic past his property" and economic damage to a business due to a State action resulting in such a route "is not compensable because [the landowners] have no property right in the free flow of traffic past their place of business." *Ensley*, 164 N.E.2d at 350.

Our Supreme Court has decided a case directly on point with the one before us today. In the case of *State v. Ensley*, the Court addressed whether an interference with a property owner's right of ingress and egress resulting from the construction of a divider strip, or median, was compensable. In that case, just as in this one, the construction of a median compelled traffic to and from a business to travel a more circuitous route. *Ensley* involved, in part, the construction of a divider strip on a busy road in Indianapolis. The divider strip blocked northbound traffic from turning directly into a business property: "Northbound traffic, instead of turning directly into the . . . entrance, [had to] continue to [an] intersection . . . where it then [could] make a left turn and drive west approximately one-half block and enter [the business]" from another entrance. *Id.* at 346. The State contended that the construction of the divider strip was an exercise of the State's police power and was, as such, not a compensable taking. *See State v. Tolliver*, 205 N.E.2d 672, 675 (Ind. 1965) (noting that where the State exercises its police power, no compensation is given). The business owners countered that a provision of Indiana's eminent domain statute, Burns Ind. Stat. Ann. § 3-1706 P 4 (Bobbs-Merrill 1946 Replacement),[3] expressly provided for compensation under the facts. The statute provided for damages as follows: "Such other damages, if any, as will result to any persons or corporation from the construction of the improvements in the manner proposed by the plaintiff." Burns Ind. Stat. Ann. § 3-1706 P 4 (Bobbs-Merrill 1946 Replacement).

In addressing the parties' competing claims, *Ensley* articulated the rule that in order to be compensated for a loss of right of access to a property, the landowner's rights must be substantially or materially affected:

> In order to recover for the alleged impairment of their right of access [landowners] must suffer a particular private injury, and not merely an inconvenience or annoyance, even though it may be greater in degree than such as is suffered by the public generally. . . . Nor is an abutting property owner entitled to damages merely for "a partial limitation and obstruction" of the right of access. Such right must be *substantially or materially interfered with or taken away.*

Ensley, 164 N.E.2d at 347, 351. With this general rule in mind, the landowners contended that the damages suffered as a result of the construction of the divider strip were substantial and material and that they were therefore entitled to compensation. They presented evidence that the damages resulting solely from the divider strip were $157,650.[4] *Id.* at 345. However, the *Ensley* Court pointed out that landowners have no property right in the free flow of traffic past their land and therefore concluded that the landowners were not entitled to compensation for losses resulting from the construction of the divider strip:

> Since [the business owners] have no property right in the free flow of traffic past their premises, the construction of the divider strip does not deprive them of any property right, and hence, any damage sustained thereby, by loss of business or depreciation in the value of their property, would not, for this further person, be compensable under the Indiana eminent domain statute. *Id.* at 350.

Thus, large financial loss is not the key to determining whether a taking has occurred. Instead, to have suffered a compensable injury under Indiana eminent domain law, the landowner *must* have been, first and foremost, deprived of a property right. *Ensley* makes clear that because there is "no property right in the free flow of traffic past [a landowner's] premises," the construction of a divider strip or median that acts to create a more circuitous route to and from a parcel of land "does not deprive [the landowner] of any property right" and any "loss of business or depreciation in the value of the [ ] property" is simply non-compensable. *Id.*

Ensley's legacy is a clarification of the very different treatments that two types of loss of access claims will receive under Indiana law. On the one hand, cases which allege damages resulting from an alteration of traffic flow ("traffic flow cases") present no cognizable claim for compensation under Indiana eminent domain law

---

[3] [7] The present version of this statute, found at Indiana Code § 32-24-1-9(c)(4), is almost identical to the statute discussed in *Ensley*.

[4] [8] We bear in mind that these were the calculated damages in 1960 or earlier.

because landowners do not have a property right in the free flow of traffic past their land. On the other hand, cases which allege interference with a landowner's rights of ingress and egress ("ingress/egress cases") may present a compensable taking where the interference is substantial or material. Since *Ensley*, our Supreme Court has addressed a number of cases involving landowners' loss of access claims. However, our Supreme Court has never retreated from its *Ensley* analysis. Instead, subsequent cases from that Court have split into two lines, adhering to the different treatments of these two types of claims. [The court then discussed later Indiana cases]

. . . .

We return now to the question before us: did Dunn suffer a compensable taking when the State constructed a median on Green River Road that compelled customers entering and exiting Dunn's hotel property, heading in certain directions, to travel a more circuitous route? To answer this question, we must determine whether to treat Dunn's suit as a traffic flow claim or an ingress/egress claim. Dunn would have us treat it as an ingress/egress claim, arguing that Indiana eminent domain law provides for a fact-sensitive inquiry into his damages to determine whether a taking has occurred. He interprets the applicable case law to emphasize the issue of whether the impact upon a property is substantial and material in answering the question of whether a compensable taking has occurred. This is, however, a contention that we examined and rejected in *Cheris*, concluding that the degree of interference in traffic flow cases is simply irrelevant to the question of whether a compensable taking has occurred. [*State v. Cheris*, 287 N.E.2d 777, 780 (Ind. App. 1972).] In reaching this conclusion, *Cheris* applied *Ensley*, the case that still controls today.

Ensley instructs us that the construction of a divider strip, or median, that causes traffic to and from a property to travel a more circuitous route does not constitute a compensable taking under Indiana eminent domain law because the landowner does not, as a matter of law, have a property right in the flow of traffic past his or her land. *Ensley*, 164 N.E.2d at 350. In a nutshell, Dunn's argument is that because of the median, access to his hotel property became less convenient for potential guests, which led to lower occupancy rates and economic losses. Despite Dunn's efforts to distinguish his claim from that made in *Ensley*, we agree with the State that "Dunn's claim [is] one essentially showing nothing more than a non-actionable and non-compensable loss of convenient access to the hotel property." As a matter of Indiana law, this does not constitute a compensable taking. Therefore, Dunn was not entitled to summary judgment as a matter of law.

Dunn criticizes *Ensley* as "shoddy work," which is wholly unhelpful, and we decline his request that we not apply it to this case. As explained in this opinion, *Ensley* is directly on point with the issue before us today, and its progeny have done nothing to weaken its effect. We observe that Indiana is in the firm majority of jurisdictions that have addressed whether the construction of medians in roadways constitutes a compensable taking and have concluded that it does not. . . . [Citing cases.]

In conclusion, landowners have no property right to the free flow of traffic past their properties. Thus, the construction of a median in a roadway that causes traffic traveling to and from an abutting property to travel a circuitous route does not constitute a compensable taking under Indiana eminent domain law. Therefore, Dunn was not entitled to judgment as a matter of law on the issue of whether he suffered a compensable taking, and the trial court erred in granting Dunn's motion for partial summary judgment. Reversed.

Darden, J., concurs.

Barnes, J., concurs in result with separate opinion.

[Omitted.]

NOTES AND QUESTIONS

1. *The Setting of the Case.* In the public use condemnation cases, the government agency acquires full title to the land, and the question is whether the governmental purpose justifies the taking. In the access cases, like *Dunn*, there is no question about the legitimacy of the governmental purpose. The question is whether there was a taking of the landowner's property interest in access. Dunn argued that the compensation paid for the earlier taking for a service road was not enough.

In cases like this, the property owner will bring an action known as inverse condemnation. The claim is that there has been effective taking of property even though there is no formal exercise of the power of eminent domain. In other words, the property owner brings an action in which he states that he has not been compensated by the government, that he/she is entitled to compensation, and that the court should award it. This is the way in which *Dunn* came to court.

Notice also the way in which the court characterizes the issues. Compensation is not payable in the "traffic flow" cases, but it is payable in the "ingress/egress" cases. Do the cases discussed by the court give you a bright-line rule for distinguishing these two types of cases? The court also refers to the traffic flow cases as an exercise of the police power. For example, in *Cohen v. City of Hartford*, 710 A.2d 746 (Conn. 1998), the city restored a street to its historic state and prohibited traffic during the midday hours. The court held there was no denial of access. Why isn't an elimination of access an exercise of the police power?

2. *Drawing the Lines.* There are some well-established rules in access denial cases, but applying them is the problem. All courts recognize that the right of access is a property right. Defining that right is another matter. Some courts hold that access must be reasonable, convenient, and suitable to an abutting highway. *Hendrickson v. State*, 127 N.W.2d 165 (Minn. 1964). Yet, as the *Dunn* case points out, there is no guarantee of a flow of traffic, and mere diversion and circuity of travel is not enough for a denial. *See Department of Transp. v. Fisher*, 958 So. 2d 586 (Fla. Dist. Ct. App. 2007) (placing a car wash that previously had access to a main highway on a service road not compensable); *Hardin v. South Carolina Dept. of Transp.*, 641 S.E. 2d 437 (S.C. 2007) (closing of "break" in median that allowed

access to property owner's business held not compensable; enough if property still has access to public road system).

Compare the facts of the *Dunn* case with *Palm Beach County v. Tessler*, 538 So. 2d 846 (Fla. 1989). The property owners had a beauty salon on Palmetto Park Road in Boca Raton, but the county planned to build a retaining wall in front of the property that would block all access to and visibility of the property from the adjacent road. Customers could only access the property by winding 600 yards through a residential neighborhood. The court held that compensation was payable even though access to the business was not totally cut off. Quoting from the district court, the court stated:

> They have shown that the retaining wall will require their customers to take a tedious and circuitous route to reach their business premises which is patently unsuitable and sharply reduces the quality of access to their property. The wall will also block visibility of the commercial storefront from Palmetto Park Road.

Id. at 850.

The court also held that damages had to be special and not common to the general public. *Id.* at 849. Would the Indiana court reach the same result?

3. *Other Examples*. The law of highway access is clearly fact-sensitive, and courts are divided on when compensation for a denial of access is required. Consider the following sampling of cases and whether they conflict with the principal case or any of the cases discussed in these Notes:

Department of Transp. v. Harkey, 301 S.E.2d 64 (N.C. 1983). A property had access to three streets. Access to one street was eliminated by construction of a controlled access highway along that street, while access to the highway from the other two streets was blocked. The court found a taking even though circuitous access through surrounding streets was available. *See also State ex rel. Thieken v. Proctor*, 904 N.E.2d 619 (Ohio Ct. App. 2008) (compensation payable when state closed access to one of two streets by filling station and replaced second access with narrow roadway, forcing tanker trucks to back in or out).

State v. DuPree, 961 P.2d 232 (Or. Ct. App. 1998). The state revoked one access point for a property on which a restaurant was located when a state highway was declared an Access Oregon Highway. The landowner claimed he was entitled to compensation for the denial of access because a restaurant requires two access points to a highway, but the court disagreed. Compensation is not payable for any inconvenience, reduction in business or reduction in the value of the property caused by the denial of the access point.

City of Wichita v. McDonald's Corp., 971 P.2d 1189 (Kan. 1999). A highway project impaired access to a Wal-Mart store (which was also a party to the case). Before the project, the store had four exits and entrances. All four remained after the project, but the work eliminated access to one street and converted two service roads from two-way to one-way traffic. As a result, the route to the store became more circuitous. Compensation was not owed. Wal-Mart had the same access it had before, and the changes that "heavily" affected it were "changes in the direction and flow of traffic."

Union Elevator & Warehouse Co., Inc. v. State, 980 P.2d 779 (Wash. Ct. App. 1999). A cul-de-sac at an intersection in a highway improvement project eliminated direct access to a grain elevator, which did not abut the road closure. Customers who wished to use the grain elevator then had to travel a longer, more difficult and unsafe route, and the business closed. Though noting that nonabutters are usually denied compensation for access, the court held it was possible that "access has been so substantially impeded that Union has suffered damages different from the general public and is, therefore, entitled to compensation."

[4.] Off-Set of Special Benefits

So far we have been reading cases where a landowner has asked for compensation for a taking for highway purposes. In some cases, however, a highway or other public improvement may confer benefits on a property owner that increase the value of her property. The question in this kind of case is whether the public agency should be able to recoup, or at least off-set, the benefits that are conferred.

ACIERNO v. STATE OF DELAWARE

Delaware Supreme Court
643 A.2d 1328 (1994)

WALSH, J.

This is an appeal from a condemnation award in the Superior Court. The condemning authority, the Delaware Department of Transportation ("State"), sought to acquire 59.0149 acres of land in New Castle County for the realignment of Delaware Route 7 ("Route 7") and the construction of a regional interchange. The property owner, Frank E. Acierno ("Acierno"), contends that the amount awarded by the condemnation commissioners, $266,000, is grossly inadequate. [W]e affirm the condemnation award and judgment of the Superior Court.

Since 1972, Acierno and Albert Marta ("Marta") have owned, as tenants in common, 401.3 acres of unimproved land ("Acierno/Marta property") located about one-half mile southeast of the intersection of Interstate 95 and Route 7 in an area known as the Christiana Metroform. The property abuts the Christiana Mall, a regional shopping mall, to the north, and Route 7 to the east. When originally purchased, the property had a zoning classification of R-2, i.e., for agricultural and general purposes. This classification is considered a "holding category" for land for which the highest use or zoning classification has yet to be established. The Christiana Metroform is a strong commercial and residential district and, as such, is one of the fastest growing areas in New Castle County.

The increased traffic flow associated with commercial activity caused Route 7 eventually to become heavily congested and incapable of handling further development. As a result, the New Castle County Department of Planning began to design the eventual realignment of Route 7 from Interstate 95 to U.S. Route 13, with a major interchange at the Christiana Mall to alleviate the traffic flow problems in the area ("Highway Project"). The realigned Route 7 was designed as a four-lane highway and was to be constructed on the western part of the Acierno/Marta property.

In connection with the new construction project, Acierno and Marta submitted an application to reclassify the zoning of their land into separate parcels. On November 23, 1982, Acierno and Marta, in connection with the potential rezoning of their property, executed and recorded a Declaration of Restrictions ("Declaration"). The Declaration imposed several covenants on the property restricting its use in relation to the rezoning and Highway Project. The Declaration also provided that Acierno and Marta would donate to the State any land necessary for the realignment of Route 7, exclusive of any land necessary for the proposed interchange.[5] The New Castle County Council approved the Marta/Acierno rezoning. As approved, the ordinance divided the property into five separate parcels with the following zoning designations:

> Parcel #1, containing about 78 acres, was rezoned to O-2 classification (General & Research Offices).
>
> Parcel #2, containing about 48 acres, was rezoned to R-4 classification (Multi-Family Residential).
>
> Parcel #3, containing about 159 acres, was rezoned to C-3 classification (general commercial/business).
>
> Parcel #4, containing about 39 acres, was rezoned to R-3-G classification (group housing other than apartments or multi family structures (townhouses)).
>
> Parcel #5, the remainder, containing about 78 acres, remained as R-2 zoning classification.

Following the recording of the restrictions, the State began extended negotiations with Marta and Acierno for their donation of the property necessary for the State to construct the regional interchange. The parties could not reach an agreement, however, because Acierno objected to the design and configuration of the interchange. On September 20, 1988, Acierno and Marta granted the State a right of entry onto their land to commence construction but the parties could not reach agreement on the donation. As a result, the State instituted the present condemnation proceeding in the Superior Court.

The parties stipulated that the land acquired by the State for purposes of the highway and interchange amounts to 59.0149 acres, consisting of 18.0453 acres for the highway, 35.3652 acres for the interchange, 5.5258 acres for wetland mitigation, and .0785 acres for a permanent drainage easement. The parties used September 20, 1988, as the date of the taking since that is the date Acierno and Marta granted the State a right of entry onto the land.

. . . .

[5] Editor's note: It is not unusual for a landowner to agree to a land dedication of this kind in exchange for a rezoning of his property.

[Marta entered into a settlement agreement with the State and was dismissed from the condemnation action. The Superior Court, in a pretrial ruling, ruled that Acierno's donation was limited to the 18.0453 acres necessary to accommodate the realignment of Route 7, but that Acierno was entitled to be compensated for the remaining 41 acres.]

At trial, the State presented evidence that the Acierno property increased in value as a result of the taking. Robert H. McKennon ("McKennon") originally appraised the property on behalf of the State. McKennon valued the property as of October 24, 1988, but viewed its "before" value according to its pre-1982 zoning. McKennon disregarded the subsequent rezoning of Acierno's property because he perceived that the new classifications were enhancements contingent on completion of the highway construction. McKennon opined that the Acierno property's highest and best use after the taking was to be fully developed consistent with the rezoning and Highway Project. McKennon estimated the value before the taking to be $26,088,000 and the value after the taking to be $32,288,000, resulting in a condemnation award of zero.

After Marta was dismissed from the suit and the Superior Court had made its finding that Acierno donated 18 acres of his land, the State asked McKennon to submit a supplemental appraisal considering these factors and a separate appraisal of three parcels of land within the original tract. McKennon's estimate that just compensation was zero was unaffected by the donation. The three residual parcels were valued by McKennon at $530,930, with Acierno's undivided one-half interest being $266,000.

Gary V. Parker ("Parker") tendered a separate appraisal on behalf of the State. His appraisal report concluded that the highest and best use of the land before the taking was to leave the land vacant until significant improvements were performed on Route 7. Parker believed that the rezoning was contingent upon the Route 7 improvement because full development of the property would not be otherwise attainable. The appraisal report indicated that the highest and best use after the taking was development of the property as rezoned. Considering these factors, Parker estimated that the before taking value of the property was $9,000,000. The property after the taking, considering the rezoned parcels affected by the improvements of the Highway Project, was valued at $31,000,000, resulting in just compensation of zero.

Parker also submitted another appraisal report valuing the three residual parcels. The State had requested an estimate of the fair market value of the parcels independent of any set off benefits. Parker estimated their collective value at $395,100, with Acierno's one-half undivided interest equaling $197,550.

Raymond Harbeson ("Harbeson"), Chief Engineer and acting Director of Preconstruction for the Department of Transportation, testified for the State that the plans for the Highway Project were finalized in 1988 with contract bid advertisements in January 1990. Harbeson indicated that, at the time of trial, the interchange adjacent to the Acierno land was not fully constructed in accordance with its original planned design. The Highway Project contemplated building a four-lane bridge across Route 7, with a ramp at its intersection with the interchange. Due to public opposition to extensive construction in an area without active commercial development, the bridge was constructed as a two-lane highway and the ramp was not built according to the final design. Harbeson testified that it was common for the State to construct such projects in phases and not to over-build in the first phase. He testified that the State was committed to constructing the additional improvements to the Highway Project in the future after Acierno began development of his property. He conceded that as currently built, the interchange cannot accommodate the full development of the Acierno property.

Arnold S. Tesh ("Tesh") also appraised the property and testified for Acierno. Tesh's appraisal estimated the value of the land before the taking at $51,450,000 and the value after the take at $20,950,000. Just compensation was estimated by Tesh at $30,500,000, with Acierno's one-half interest valued at $15,250,000.

The commissioners awarded Acierno $266,000 as just compensation for his taken property. Acierno timely moved for a new trial and judgment notwithstanding the verdict following the commissioners' award. The trial court denied Acierno's post-trial motions and this appeal followed.

II

Acierno first claims that the State failed to introduce sufficient evidence to establish that the highway and interchange construction constituted a "special benefit" to his property beyond the general benefit shared by the community at large. At the close of the State's evidence, Acierno moved for a directed verdict on the special benefits issue. The trial court denied Acierno's motion but Acierno renewed his motion at the time the commissioners were instructed. Acierno's objection was properly before the trial court in his motion for directed verdict and his post-trial motions. Accordingly, we review the claim.

In a partial taking case such as this, just compensation is calculated by computing the difference in value of the whole property before the taking and the value of the remainder after the taking. Any benefits or advantages inuring to the landowners which result from the taking will be set off against whatever damages are caused by the severance. In Delaware, both the value of the taken property and any damages to the remaining land may be reduced by the benefits to the landowner. This set off rule is inherent in the constitutional requirement of just compensation. However, such a reduction is permissible only with respect to special benefits accruing to the remaining land. General benefits, i.e., benefits accruing to the entire community by reason of the improprieties contemplated by the taking, may not be set off.

This Court has had no occasion to define special benefits with precision and, as will be seen, the distinction between special and general benefits is nebulous at best. As a leading commentator has stated:

> Upon this subject there is a great diversity of opinion and more rules, different and inconsistent with each other, have been laid down than upon any other point in the law of eminent domain.

3 JULIUS L. SACKMAN, NICHOLS' THE LAW OF EMINENT DOMAIN § 8A.03 at 8A-26 n.1

(rev. 3d ed. 1991). A close analysis of the special benefits doctrine is required to evaluate Acierno's claim in this case.

Whether characterized as general or special, conditions which result from the partial taking of a condemnee's land may serve to increase the value of the remaining property. For such benefits to be considered in a partial taking, they may not be so remote, uncertain, or speculative that they are incapable of being estimated in monetary value. Prospective benefits, which merely pose the future possibility of enhancement of the present value of the property affected, may not be considered in a condemnation proceeding. There must be a sufficient certainty that the benefits will be realized.

Special benefits directly and proximately affect the property remaining after the partial taking while general benefits are incidental and shared by the general public within the area of the taking. General benefits arise from the fulfillment of the public project which justified the taking while special benefits arise from the peculiar or unique relation of the property in question to the public improvement. Special benefits, unlike general benefits, add to the convenience, accessibility, and use of the property resulting from physical changes to the owner's remaining land or its proximity to the public project. Special benefits are further differentiated from general benefits where the differences are in nature or kind not enjoyed by the public at large. A benefit may be special with respect to the taken property even if the benefit is shared by other property in the area. While the burden is usually upon the condemnee to prove the value of his damages, the burden is properly upon the State to demonstrate that the condemnee has specially benefitted from the taking.

Whether a given benefit is special or general is determined largely by the facts and circumstances of each case. Despite the sometimes shadowy distinction between general and special benefits, a few general trends are discernable when the condemnor has taken land for highway construction. As a general rule, increased traffic flow resulting from the construction of a new highway or public access, by itself, is generally insufficient to qualify as a special benefit. Some courts have created a presumption that any property which is adjacent to a newly constructed highway receives special benefits from the construction. *See, e.g., State ex rel. State Highway Comm'n v. Gatson*, Mo. App., 617 S.W.2d 80 (1981). Special benefits are generally found when the highway construction changes the available use of the land to a higher and better use. *State ex rel. State Highway Comm'n v. Koziatek*, 639 S.W.2d 86, 88 ([Mo. App.] 1982). A benefit may be special to a particular property in a highway improvement case although the benefit is shared with other property in the vicinity, especially if the project either provides a separate access to the property or enables it to become available for a new or more productive use. When a public project enhances the commercial or residential value of property in the vicinity of the highway improvement, it generally constitutes a special benefit. The physical proximity of the public improvement to the remaining land is a strong factor in demonstrating a special benefit. Thus, land immediately abutting or fronting upon a highway may be considered specially benefitted from the public improvement, even if other property abutting the highway is not taken.

Acierno argues that the State failed to introduce evidence establishing that Acierno specially benefitted from the highway alignment and interchange construction. He contends that the State failed to build the interchange as originally planned and is not legally bound to make the necessary improvements to accommodate the full development of his property. Thus, he concludes, any benefits accruing to the Acierno property are too remote or speculative to constitute special benefits and the trial court should have directed a verdict on this issue at the close of the State's evidence.

We do not share Acierno's view of the record. To the contrary, the State did introduce evidence indicating that the Acierno land specially benefitted from the highway realignment. The State presented testimony indicating that the Highway Project enabled Acierno to develop his property to a greater extent than before the taking. McKennon's appraisal report, admitted into evidence, specifically stated that Acierno's land was specially benefitted. Harbeson testified during cross-examination that the interchange was built simply to serve the Acierno property and other properties along Route 7. He further testified that the State was committed to completing the Highway Project in the future when Acierno began development of his property. Moreover, Parker testified on cross-examination that the highway improvements benefitted all real estate in the area generally while benefitting the Acierno property specially. It is also significant that the Declaration executed by Acierno recited that the Highway Project would serve the Acierno/Marta construction project in addition to relieving the traffic problem in the area.

The fact that owners of property abutting Route 7 and the Christiana Mall will also benefit from the highway improvements without a similar loss of land does preclude a showing that Acierno himself has received special benefits. The highway improvement provided Acierno a means of egress and ingress onto the interchange as well as direct exposure and frontage along a major state roadway. The close proximity of Acierno's land to the interchange increased its development potential and fair market value. The evidence demonstrates that the Acierno property benefitted from the Highway Project beyond the enjoyment flowing to the surrounding community and created a factual issue for the commissioners' consideration in fixing the value of the taking.

The State's claim of special benefits is conditioned upon Harbeson's representation at trial that the State is committed to the future improvements necessary for the full development of the Acierno property. Indeed the State argued at trial, and repeats the contention here, that the benefits were neither speculative nor remote. We view the State as legally bound by its representations which had the effect of reducing its exposure to a larger condemnation award.

NOTES AND QUESTIONS

1. *The Special Benefit Problem.* A government agency can claim a special benefit offset only when it takes part of a landowner's land. When there is a total taking, no land is left to the landowner upon which a special benefits claim can be made. When none of the land of a landowner is taken, there is obviously no compensation payable and nothing to offset. The inability to obtain special benefit offsets when no land is taken also creates a fairness problem. Government agencies can claim special benefits offsets against land they have partially taken, but are powerless to claim special benefit offsets when no land is condemned, even though a landowner may be equally benefited.

Notice that in the *Acierno* case, there might also have been damage to the remainder of the property from the construction of the highway improvements. This kind of damage is called severance damage, and requires the payment of compensation. Compensation for severance damage is in addition to the compensation paid for the part taken. If there is a general rule, it is that almost all jurisdictions allow the deduction of special benefits from severance damages to the remainder. A majority of states do not allow the value of special benefits to be deducted from the value of the part taken, although the federal rule is in the minority on this point. *Bauman v. Ross*, 167 U.S. 548 (1897). The federal rule means that a landowner may receive no compensation at all if special benefits are greater than the value of the land physically taken by the government.

2. *Offset of General Damages*. A minority of courts allow the offset of both general and special benefits. California is in this group. *Los Angeles County Metropolitan Transp. Auth. v. Continental Dev. Corp.*, 941 P.2d 809 (Cal. 1997). The Authority sued to acquire a narrow easement for an elevated light rail line known as the Green Line along one side of land owned by Continental. A station was located within a 10-minute walk from Continental's property. There was an office building on the property, and there was evidence that proximity to the station increased the property's value by 4.1 million dollars. However, 565 parcels were located within 1,700 feet of the station, but only seven were condemned for construction of the Green Line.

The court noted that a decision either to offset or not offset general benefits created difficulties:

> If Continental is subjected to setoff of general benefits resulting from proximity to the Douglas Street station, one might say it pays more than its proper share of the cost of this transit project because it loses an expectation of gain that other property owners, from whom no land is taken, are allowed to keep. If, on the other hand, Continental is permitted both to recover severance damages and to retain the general enhancement in the value of its property, one could with equal validity say it thereby pays less than its proper share of the project cost vis-a-vis those property owners from whom no property is taken, and who cannot recover damages for the diminution in the value of their property resulting from the operation of the transit line, when those effects are not sufficiently deleterious to support an action in inverse condemnation or nuisance. The law has no mechanism by which to ensure an absolutely fair distribution of costs and benefits across the entire community. We must instead search for the rule of greatest relative fairness, or least unfairness.

Id. at 823. The court then held that "in determining a landowner's entitlement to severance damages, the fact finder henceforth shall consider competent evidence relevant to any conditions caused by the project that affect the remainder property's fair market value, insofar as such evidence is neither conjectural nor speculative." *Id.* Is this a fair solution? *See* Comment, *Assessing the Benefits of*

California's New Valuation Rule for Partial Condemnations, 88 CAL. L. REV. 565 (2000).

Joining California in the minority rule, Michigan, New Mexico, New York, South Carolina, and West Virginia courts have held that all benefits can be used to offset just compensation owed. Notably, North Carolina, and also Alabama, allow an offset of general benefits in highway and related takings, but not other in types of acquisitions. *See North Carolina Dep't of Transp. v. Rowe*, 549 S.E.2d 203 (N.C. 2001) (upholding statute allowing offset of general benefits because a general benefit "is no less real simply because it is shared by a condemnee's neighbor.") Iowa and Mississippi do not allow the offset of benefits at all. Other states, such as Colorado and Hawaii, have different rules for highway cases as opposed to other types of cases. For a detailed look at varying state law and cases on benefits, see Sperber, *How Does Your State Stack Up? A National Survey of Selected Compensation Laws and Rules*, in Eminent Domain and Land Valuation Litigation, at 647–648 (ALI-ABA Continuing Legal Education 2005).

3. *The Special Benefits Rule Applied.* The construction of a highway interchange or public transit station or highway improvement is likely to increase the value of property because of its greater access to the public transportation system and, in the case of a highway, because of increased traffic flow. It is difficult in these situations to determine whether property taken for the improvement has received a special benefit because other properties in the area that have not been taken may enjoy the same benefit, as in the *Continental* case. Consider the following cases that decided whether highway improvements conferred a special benefit on the property taken:

State ex rel. State Highway Comm'n v. Koziatek, cited in the principal case. A condemnation to relocate and improve a roadway intersection took approximately three acres of a 93 acre tract of land owned by the defendant. The relocation severed .38 of an acre of defendant's property and left it adjoined to an executive park. Testimony from state highway experts assumed a commercial rezoning for the severed parcel, which would be the only part of the executive park visible from highway thoroughfares. The court found a special benefit and said "[a] prime example of a special benefit, which the Highway Commission argues occurred here, is when highway construction changes available use of land to a higher and better use."

Territory of Hawaii v. Mendonca, 375 P.2d 6 (Haw. 1962). A condemnation for a limited access highway cut the Mendonca land in two. There was no direct access to the limited access highway except through Valley View Drive, a street running between the Mendonca land and another subdivision. The benefit was general because it was shared with the other subdivision.

Hero Int'l Corp. v. Massachusetts, 618 N.E.2d 1386 (Mass. Ct. App. 1993). The Commonwealth of Massachusetts took 11.08 acres from the plaintiff's 112.95 acre lot to widen two highways and to construct a limited access highway leading to the municipal airport. The taking included three small parcels along the highways and a 10.18 acre swath running through 98.70 acres of industrial land. The court found the taking had specially benefited the remaining industrial property. The taking provided greater access by increasing the frontage of the remaining industrial land

and also caused the remainder to become a "corner location," which has greater utility because it can be developed either "front or back." The court added that the location of a parcel on, or with access to, a limited access highway strongly suggests special benefit.

Taub v. City of Deer Park, 882 S.W.2d 824 (Tex. 1994). The city, in part, condemned 14.56 acres from Taub's land to construct drainage ditch structures which would run along the southeastern side of the tract, extend across the tract to the western edge, and then continue along the northwestern section of the tract. The court held the benefit was general because it benefited the entire eastern half of the city as well as Taub's land. Compare *Board of Comm'rs of Great Neck Park Dist. v. Kings Point Heights, LLC*, 74 A.D.3d 804 (N.Y. App. Div. 2010) (value of remaining parcel enhanced by existence of park on condemned portion of property).

4. *The Set-Off Problem in American History*. In the 19th century, liberal use of the set-off principle, i.e., allowing those responsible for paying eminent domain damages (often private internal improvement companies) to reduce payments by the amount of benefit added to the landowner's remaining property, greatly reduced the cost of constructing the nation's transportation network. Although the set-off principle was initially accepted in most states by the final third of the century, a wide-spread reaction against set-off had set in. A refusal to reduce eminent domain awards by the amount of general benefit was a common response. For a more detailed account, see the relevant portions of HORWITZ, TRANSFORMATION OF AMERICAN LAW and ELY, GUARDIAN OF EVERY OTHER RIGHT, discussed above in the Notes following *Pumpelly*.

[5.] Judicial Fiat

In *Stop the Beach Renourishment Inc. v. Florida Dept. of Environmental Protection*, 560 U.S. 702 (2010), the U.S. Supreme Court dealt with the property rights of littoral landowners. (*See* Note 5, page 237, *infra*.) One of the critical issues in the Petition for Certiorari in that case was whether there was — or could be — a "judicial" taking. The Court could not form a majority on the question — four justices said there could be, but not in the instant case given the heavy reliance on state statutory law — but it remains an intriguing question, which, if the Court had meant to address it, would have more appropriately been taken up in the case below.

ROBINSON v. ARIYOSHI

United States Court of Appeals, Ninth Circuit
753 F.2d 1468 (1985)

GOODWIN, CIRCUIT JUDGE.

The district court, in an action brought under 42 U.S.C. § 1983 challenging an alleged threat to divest plaintiffs' irrigation water rights, enjoined the named state officials from taking any action to enforce a recent decree of the state courts that appeared to be adverse to the property rights of the plaintiffs. The state officials appeal, raising a number of procedural and substantive issues. We will first set out the factual context in which this dispute has kept territorial, state, and federal courts intermittently busy for more than sixty years.

Background

In 1889 the predecessors in title of the plaintiffs, Gay and Robinson, owned substantial land grants within the ahupuaa of Hanapepe, a local designation of land extending from the top of the central mountain mass of the Island of Kauai to the sea and roughly encompassing the drainage of the Hanapepe River. At the mauka, or upper part of the ahupuaa, the annual rainfall ranges from four to five hundred inches. At lower elevations rainfall averages as little as twenty-three inches and in many parts of the ahupuaa most types of agriculture are not possible without irrigation.

In the early days of the development of sugar cane fields on Kauai, the owners and lessees of the privately-owned lands built dams, flumes and ditches in order to distribute the abundant rainfall from the wettest portions of their lands to fertile but dry neighboring land areas. As the years went by and more lands were brought into production, the irrigation works became fairly elaborate. By 1922 Gay and Robinson had been to court at least once and had their title confirmed by the territorial courts to a substantial portion of the lands. The lands known as the Ili of Koula were drained by the Koula branch of the Hanapepe River, and from this drainage substantial volumes of irrigation water were diverted into a dry area that was outside the Hanapepe ahupuaa. Similar diversions of water to dry land were being made contemporaneously by Gay and Robinson from their nearby lands in the Ili of Manuahi, the other principal branch feeding the Hanapepe River. This state of affairs had evolved gradually over the years, beginning before 1891, and has been in effect more or less continually until the present time.

In the 1920s the territorial government's increasing interest in water for the development of dry lands at lower elevations, some of which were owned or controlled by the Territory of Hawaii, produced litigation which in 1931 resulted in a decree of the Territorial Court. The Territorial Court held that Gay and Robinson were the owners of "normal surplus" water flowing from their Ilis of Koula and Manuahi into the Hanapepe River, and confirmed their right to divert that water for use outside the Hanapepe drainage.

In 1941 the Olokele Sugar Company succeeded to certain lands that were being supplied with irrigation water from the Gay and Robinson engineering efforts, and in 1949 the Gay and Robinson successors opened a new tunnel to supply water to their own and Olokele lands known locally as the Makaweli district.

The Hawaiian Statehood Act, Pub. L. No. 86-3, 73 Stat. 4, reprinted in 1959 U.S. Code Cong. & Ad. News 5, inter alia, confirmed existing statutory law of the territory and approved the new state's constitution. Gay and Robinson claim that the state constitution includes protection of their court-decreed and vested right to divert and use water from their mauka lands drained by the Koula and Manuahi branches of the Hanapepe.[6] The state officials, however, argue as if the matter were

[6] [1] Hawaii Const. art. XVIII, § 9, reprinted in 1 Hawaii Rev. Stat. (1968, Supp. 1983) provides:

open for a fresh decision, that the private use outside the ahupuaa of a large volume of Hanapepe water by Gay and Robinson and their associates is both undesirable and contrary to state law.

In 1959 the McBryde Sugar Company commenced in the new state court an action against a number of defendants, among whom Gay and Robinson were named. McBryde sued the state, Olokele, Gay and Robinson, and others referred to as the "small owners" to obtain a declaration of the rights of various parties along the Hanapepe upstream and downstream to various water rights, appurtenant, prescriptive, "ancient," or otherwise derived. The Hawaii state trial court in 1968 declared in a 65-page decision the rights of the parties including "other" small holders whose "ancient" and "appurtenant" rights were acknowledged by the principal parties in the controversy. Both the state and the larger owners appealed to the Supreme Court of Hawaii, challenging various portions of the trial court's decree. No party questioned existing Hawaii water law as announced in a number of earlier territorial cases.

The Supreme Court of Hawaii in 1973 sua sponte overruled all territorial cases to the contrary and adopted the English common law doctrine of riparian rights. *McBryde Sugar Co. v. Robinson, et al.*, 504 P.2d 1330, 1344 (Haw. 1973). In this decision, which we will refer to as *McBryde I*, the court also held sua sponte that there was no such legal category as "normal daily surplus water" and declared that the state, as sovereign, owned and had the exclusive right to control the flow of the Hanapepe River. *McBryde I* further announced that because the flow of the Hanapepe was the sovereign property of the State of Hawaii, McBryde's claim of a prescriptive right to divert water could not be sustained against the state.

The parties adversely affected by the holding in *McBryde I* petitioned for rehearing and the state supreme court allowed a rehearing on the limited issue of the proper construction of Hawaii Rev. Stat. § 7-1 (a century-old territorial statute dealing largely with drinking water and rights of way on roads over private lands) and the meaning of the word "appurtenant." The parties attempted to enlarge the scope of the rehearing to include state and federal constitutional claims but their attempt was summarily rejected. In 1974 this litigation began in the United States District Court for the District of Hawaii. The decision in the district court permanently enjoined the named state officials from enforcing against these plaintiffs any "new law" announced in *McBryde I* and *II*.

The leisurely pace of this litigation has produced three oral arguments in this court, two of which were followed by referral of certified questions to the Supreme Court of Hawaii. Following the publication of the state court's answers to the certified questions, the parties briefed the remaining issues that had been narrowed by the earlier proceedings and reargued the case. A number of complex questions remain, but to expedite the matter we will discuss only those essential to a resolution of the main question: Can the state, by a judicial decision which creates a major change in property law, divest property interests?

Except as otherwise provided by amendments to this constitution, all existing . . . judgments, . . . orders, decrees, . . . titles and rights shall continue unaffected notwithstanding the taking effect of the amendments.

The state conceded at oral argument that the Fourteenth Amendment would require it to pay just compensation if it attempted to take vested property rights. The substantive question, therefore, is whether the state can declare, by court decision, that the water rights in this case have not vested. The short answer is no.

The district court's opinion in *Robinson I* makes clear that considerable property interests were at stake. In summary form, the interests affected by *McBryde I* and *II* include:

(1) The water rights which as private property had been bought, sold and leased freely, and which had been the subject of state and local taxation as well as condemnation for ditch rights-of-way;

(2) The expenditures by G & R and Olokele of almost one million dollars in building an extensive water transportation system for irrigation of their sugar lands, lands now potentially destined to become pasture; and

(3) The interests of McBryde Sugar Company, which stands, if its rights are vested, in the same position as Gay and Robinson.

On April 28, 1930, the Supreme Court of the Territory of Hawaii, in litigation between substantially the same parties that are here today, except for the McBryde Sugar Company, held that the common law doctrine of riparian rights was not in force in Hawaii with reference to surplus waters of the normal flow of a stream. The same court further held that the owner (konohiki) of the land (ili) could use the water collected on his ili as he saw fit, subject to the rights of downstream owners to drinking water and other domestic uses that the parties in all this litigation have agreed have not been in controversy. *Territory I*, 31 Hawaii at 387–88, 395. When that case reached this court, we affirmed in an opinion which stated that the definition of property rights and water rights in light of the feudal history of land tenure in the islands was best left to the local courts. *Territory of Hawaii v. Gay*, 52 F.2d 356, 359 (9th Cir. 1931) ("*Territory II*"). The water law, at least between the territorial government and the Gay and Robinson interests, thereafter remained settled until statehood.

Relying upon the decrees in *Territory I* and *II*, Gay and Robinson proceeded with further development of their plantations. By the time this litigation reached the district court, in *Robinson I*, improvements costing many millions of dollars had been constructed on the affected lands. By any reasonable interpretation of the word "vested," Gay and Robinson's rights to the continued use of their water and related engineering works had become vested.

The *Robinson I* court found that McBryde Sugar Company also relied upon the law set forth in *Territory II*, and developed water rights that became vested. (Territorial cases are collected in *Territory I*, 31 Hawaii at 384.) The extent of McBryde's rights, however, the district court left for further litigation in the state courts.

The parties concede that the State of Hawaii has the sovereign power to change its laws from time to time as its legislature may see fit, and may, by changing its laws, radically change the definitions of property rights and the manner in which property rights can be controlled or transferred.

The state may also change its laws by judicial decision as well as by legislative action. Insofar as judicial changes in the law operate prospectively to affect property rights vesting after the law is changed, no specific federal question is presented by the state's choice of implement in changing state law.

We assume, therefore, for the purposes of this case, that the Supreme Court of Hawaii was acting well within its judicial power under the state constitution when it overruled earlier cases and declared for the first time, after more than a century of a different law, that the common law doctrine of riparian ownership was the law of Hawaii. This declaration of a change in the water law of Hawaii may be effective with respect to real property rights created in Hawaii after the *McBryde I* decision became final. New law, however, cannot divest rights that were vested before the court announced the new law.

There is no constitutional barrier to the state's exercise of its power of eminent domain to condemn and take vested property rights for public purposes. The state has the power to take over the water works constructed by Gay and Robinson and their associates upon exercising the powers of eminent domain in a manner compatible with the Fourteenth Amendment.

In light of the above authorities, the plaintiffs in this case, having acquired through judicial process a de jure vested right to divert water from their lands within the Hanapepe watershed to their own or related lands outside the watershed, cannot now be divested of this right without just compensation.

It has been clear since *Territory I* that the downstream rights of small owners to domestic water and "ancient" rights to water for taro cultivation on lands that were wet lands before the litigation commenced have never been contested by Gay and Robinson. These rights were specifically left open by the trial court in the first territorial litigation arising out of the earliest diversions of water. The rights of the small holders that were declared in *McBryde I* and *II* were not disturbed in the district court in the case at bar but were left to be sorted out by the state courts consistent with the recognition of any rights that vested before 1973.

As noted, the district court entered a decree granting injunctive relief against named state officials. Because the state officers in these proceedings have taken no steps to interfere with plaintiffs' property, and have denied that they are presently planning to take such steps, the injunction may have been premature. (The officers still argue, however, that the state is free under *McBryde I* and *II*, to take any action it may see fit in the future to control the flow of the river.) A declaration of the rights of the parties would appear to be sufficient to assure the owners of the rights confirmed in *Territory II*. The state must bring condemnation proceedings before it can interfere with vested water rights and the enjoyment of the improvements made in reliance thereon.

The judgment of the district court is affirmed in all respects insofar as it declares the rights of the parties. The injunctions against the named defendants are vacated without prejudice to the continuing jurisdiction of the district court to enjoin future state officeholders from conduct, if any, in violation of the rights of the plaintiffs should such a case arise. The plaintiffs are entitled to costs and such attorneys' fees as the district court may determine to be reasonable pursuant to 42 U.S.C. § 1988.

Affirmed in part, vacated in part, and remanded for the entry of a modified judgment.

NOTES AND QUESTIONS

1. *Can the Changing of Water Rights Rules Be a Taking?* The United States Supreme Court subsequently vacated the Ninth Circuit Court decision on ripeness grounds, *Robinson v. Ariyoshi*, 477 U.S. 902 (1986), a decision which prompted blunt judicial criticism by the federal district court. *See Robinson v. Ariyoshi*, 703 F. Supp. 1412 (D. Haw. 1989), *rev'd and vacated*, 933 F.2d 781 (9th Cir. 1991). Notwithstanding the vacation of the judgment, the 1985 circuit court decision raises important questions concerning judicial power to take property, such as how far does the compensation requirement extend and when do rights vest? For a discussion of judicial takings generally, see Thompson, *Judicial Takings*, 76 VA. L. REV. 1449 (1990). More recently, the Supreme Court of Texas has cited to *Stop the Beach Renourishment* in noting that judicial decrees that create limitations on private property raise serious Constitutional concerns. *See Severance v. Patterson*, 370 S.W.3d 705, n.5 (Tex. 2012).

2. In *Pele Defense Fund v. Paty*, 837 P.2d 1247 (Haw. 1992), and *PASH v. Hawaii Planning Comm'n*, 903 P.2d 1246 (Haw. 1995), the Hawaii Supreme Court held that Native Hawaiians may enter any lands in the state, public or private, to engage in largely undefined "customary," cultural, religious and sustenance activities, specifically holding that worshiper of Pele (a Volcano goddess) could enter private land to conduct ceremonies. It makes no difference, said the court, whether such land is developed or undeveloped. The case has been used to rebut charges of trespass, and to claim that a local government decision, which permits a series of wooded-platformed tents placed on a long hiking "trail" among thousands of acres of private ranch land, should be reviewed to see if the tents interfere with customary native Hawaiian hunting practices. Do the private landowners in these cases have vested right to be free from the exercise of such rights under the reasoning in the *Robinson* decision? If so, what remedies are available to the landowner?

3. *Historical Background.* The United States Supreme Court first dealt with the issue of judicial takings in the case of *Muhlker v. New York and Harlem Railroad Company*, 197 U.S. 544 (1905). New York state courts had initially ruled that urban landowners had easements of light, air, and access to public streets and that loss of these easements because of the construction of elevated railroads in New York City required compensation. In a later decision, the New York Court of Appeals reversed itself and ruled that property owners had no such interests and thus were not entitled to compensation. In reviewing the constitutionality of the rule change, the Supreme Court had great difficulty in answering the questions posed by the *Muhlker* case. Although five of the justices believed that compensation was required, they could not agree on a common rationale for so ruling. Writing for the dissenters, Justice Holmes insisted that property owners had no constitutional right to have general legal propositions remain unchanged. For a discussion of this case, see ELY, THE CHIEF JUSTICESHIP OF MELVILLE W. FULLER, 1888–1910, at 109–10 (1995). For extended commentary on judicial takings, see Barros, *The Complexities of Judicial Takings*, 45 U. RICH. L. REV. 903 (2011).

[6.] The Public Trust Doctrine

As traditionally defined, the public trust doctrine "'provides that submerged and submersible lands are preserved for public use in navigation, fishing and recreation and the state, as trustee for the people, bears responsibility of preserving and protecting the right of the public use of the waters for those purposes.' *Oregon Shores Conservation Coalition v. Oregon Fish & Wildlife Comm'n*, 662 P.2d 356, 364 [(Or. Ct. App. 1983)]." BLACK'S LAW DICTIONARY 1232 (6th ed. 1990). "Submerged and submersible" lands include tide lands and, by implication, coastlines, harbors, and navigable bodies of water. Grounded in Roman law, the public trust doctrine includes both public use (*use publicum*) and private use (use *privatem*) of public trust land and water. *See* COASTAL STATES ORGANIZATION, INC., PUTTING THE PUBLIC TRUST DOCTRINE TO WORK 1–2 (2d ed. 1994). However, because the sovereign is obligated to protect these assets, the doctrine imposes a limit on the sovereign's ability to transfer them to private owners. Not so clear is whether public access to such public trust assets is part of the public trust doctrine. The seminal public trust case in American law is *Illinois Central Railroad Co. v. Illinois*, 146 U.S. 387 (1892).

ILLINOIS CENTRAL RAILROAD COMPANY v. ILLINOIS

United States Supreme Court
146 U.S. 387 (1892)

MR. JUSTICE FIELD delivered the opinion of the court.

The object of the suit is to obtain a judicial determination of the title of certain lands on the east or lake front of the city of Chicago, situated between the Chicago River and Sixteenth Street, which have been reclaimed from the waters of the lake, and are occupied by the tracks, depots, warehouses, piers and other structures used by the railroad company in its business; and also of the title claimed by the company to the submerged lands, constituting the bed of the lake, lying east of its tracks, within the corporate limits of the city, for the distance of a mile, and between the south line of the south pier near Chicago River extended eastwardly, and a line extended, in the same direction, from the south line of lot 21 near the company's round-house and machine shops. The determination of the title of the company will involve a consideration of its right to construct, for its own business, as well as for public convenience, wharves, piers and docks in the harbor.

The State prays a decree establishing and confirming its title to the bed of Lake Michigan and exclusive right to develop and improve the harbor of Chicago by the *construction* of docks, wharves, piers and other improvements, against the claim of the railroad company, that it has an absolute title to such submerged lands by the act of 1869, and the right, subject only to the paramount authority of the United States in the regulation of commerce, to fill all the bed of the lake within the limits above stated, for the purpose of its business; and the right, by the construction and promotion generally of commerce and navigation. And the State, insisting that the company has, without right, erected and proposes to continue to erect wharves and piers upon its domain, asks that such alleged unlawful structures may be ordered to be removed, and the company be enjoined from erecting further structures of any kind.

The lands granted were made subject to the disposition of the legislature of the State; and it was declared that the railroad and its branches should be and remain a public highway for the use of the government of the United States, free from toll or other charge upon the transportation of their property or troops.

We proceed to consider the claim of the railroad company to the ownership of submerged lands in the harbor, and the right to construct such wharves, piers, docks and other works therein as it may deem proper for its interest and business.

The question, therefore, to be considered is whether the legislature was competent to thus deprive the State of its ownership of the submerged lands in the harbor of Chicago, and of the consequent control of its waters; or, in other words, whether the railroad corporation can hold the lands and control the waters by the grant, against any future exercise over them by the State.

That the State holds the title to the lands under the navigable waters of Lake Michigan, within its limits, in the same manner that the State holds title to soils under tide water, by the common law, we have already shown, and that title necessarily carries with it control over the waters above them whenever the lands are subjected to use. But it is a title different in character from the title which the United States hold in the public lands which are open to preemption and sale. It is a title held in trust for the people of the State that they may enjoy the navigation of the waters, carry on commerce over them, and have liberty of fishing therein freed from the obstruction or interference of private parties. The interest of the people in the navigation of the waters and in commerce over them may be improved in many instances by the erection of wharves, docks and piers therein, for which purpose the State may grant parcels of the submerged lands; and, so long as their disposition is made for such purpose, no valid objections can be made to the grants. It is grants of parcels of lands under navigable waters, that may afford foundation for wharves, piers, docks and other structures in aid of commerce, and grants of parcels which, being occupied, do not substantially impair the public interest in the lands and waters remaining, that are chiefly considered and sustained in the adjudged cases as a valid exercise of legislative power consistently with the trust to the public upon which such lands are held by the state. But that is a very different doctrine from the one which would sanction the abdication of the general control of the State over lands under the navigable waters of an entire harbor or bay, or of a sea or lake. Such abdication is not consistent with the exercise of that trust which requires the government of the State to preserve such waters for the use of the public. The trust devolving upon the State for the public, and which can only be discharged by the management and control of property in which the public has an interest, cannot be relinquished by a transfer of the property. The control of the State for the purposes of the trust can never be lost, except as to such parcels as are used in promoting the interests of the public therein, or can be disposed of without any substantial impairment of the public interest in the lands and waters remaining. It is only by observing the distinction between a grant of such parcels for the improvement of the public interest, or which when occupied do not substantially impair the public interest in the lands and waters remaining, and a grant of the whole property in which the public is interested, that the language of the adjudged cases can be reconciled. General language sometimes found in opinions of the court, expressive of absolute ownership and control by the State of lands under navigable waters, irrespective of any trust as to their use and disposition, must be read and construed with reference to the special facts of the particular cases. A grant of all the lands under the navigable waters of a State has never been adjudged to be within legislative power; and any attempted grant of the kind would be held, if not absolutely void on its face, as subject to revocation. The State can no more abdicate its trust over property in which the whole people are interested, like navigable waters and soils under them, so as to leave them entirely under the use and control of private parties, except in the instance of parcels mentioned for the improvement of the navigation and use of the waters, or when parcels can be disposed of without impairment of the public interest in what remains, that it can abdicate its police powers in the administration of government and the preservation of the peace. In the administration of government the use of such powers may be for a limited period be delegated to a municipality or other body, but there always remains with the State the right to revoke those powers and exercise them in a more direct manner, and one more conformable to its wishes. So with trusts connected with public property, or property of a special character, like lands under navigable water, they cannot be placed entirely beyond the direction and control of the State.

Any grant of the kind is necessarily revocable, and the exercise of the trust by which the property was held by the state can be resumed at any time. Undoubtedly there may be expenses incurred in improvements made under such a grant which the State ought to pay; but, be that as it may, the power to resume the trust whenever the State judges best is, we think, incontrovertible. The position advanced by the railroad company in support of its claim to the ownership of the submerged lands and the right to the erection of wharves, piers and docks at its pleasure, or for its business in the harbor of Chicago, would place every harbor in the country at the mercy of a majority of the legislature of the State in which the harbor is situated.

We cannot, it is true, cite any authority where a grant of this kind has been held invalid, for we believe that no instance exists where the harbor of a great city and its commerce have been allowed to pass into the control of any private corporation. But the decisions are numerous which declare that such property is held by the State, by virtue of its sovereignty, in trust for the public. The ownership of the navigable waters of the harbor and of the lands under them is a subject of public concern to the whole people of the State. The trust with which they are held, therefore, is governmental and cannot be alienated, except in those instances mentioned of parcels used in the improvement of the interest thus held, or when parcels can be disposed of without detriment to the public interest in the lands and waters remaining.

This follows necessarily from the public character of the property, being held by the whole people for purposes in which the whole people are interested.

We hold, therefore, that any attempted cession of the ownership and control of the State in and over the submerged lands in Lake Michigan, by the Act of April 16, 1869, was inoperative to affect, modify or in any respect to control the sovereignty and dominion of the State over the lands, or its ownership thereof, and that any such attempted operation of the act was annulled by the repealing act of April 15, 1873, which to that extent was valid and effective. There can be no irrepealable contract in a conveyance of property by a grantor in disregard of a public trust, under which he was bound to hold and manage it.

MR. JUSTICE SHIRAS, with whom concurred MR. JUSTICE GRAY and MR. JUSTICE BROWN, dissenting.

[Omitted.]

NOTES AND QUESTIONS

1. Justice Field's *Illinois Central* opinion acknowledged that not every transfer of an interest in public trust to a private party is invalid — "parcels used in the improvement of the interest thus held, or when parcels can be disposed of without detriment to the public interest in the lands and waters remaining" is how he described the acceptable transfers. How does one decide which transfers are valid and which are not? This is not an academic question. One comprehensive source reports that fully one-third of public trust property is in private, rather than public, hands. COSTAL STATE ORGANIZATION, INC., PUTTING THE PUBLIC TRUST DOCTRINE TO WORK 230 (2d ed. 1997).

2. *The Continuing Role of the* Illinois Central *Case*. A number of courts have relied on *Illinois Central* as the basis for the public trust doctrine. *See, e.g., Arizona Ctr. For Law in the Pub. Interest v. Hassell*, 837 P.2d. 158, 168 (Ariz. Ct. App. 1991). For an argument that *Illinois Central* is no longer the authoritative source for the doctrine, see Pearson, *Illinois Central and the Public Trust Doctrine in State Law*, 15 VA. ENVTL. L.J. 713 (1996). *See also* J. Kearney & T. Merrill, *The Origins of the American Public Trust Doctrine: What Really Happened in* Illinois Central, 71 U. CHI. L. REV. 799 (2004).

3. The Ninth Circuit has held that the public trust doctrine is a "background principles of a state's law of property." *Esplanade Properties v. City of Seattle*, 307 F.3d 978 (9th Cir. 2002). Does such a determination immunize the state from all takings challenges involving public trust property?

MATTHEWS v. BAY HEAD IMPROVEMENT ASSOCIATION

New Jersey Supreme Court
471 A.2d 355 (1984)

The opinion of the Court was delivered by SCHREIBER, J.

The public trust doctrine acknowledges that the ownership, dominion and sovereignty over land flowed by tidal waters, which extend to the mean high water mark, is vested in the State in trust for the people. The public's right to use the tidal lands and water encompasses navigation, fishing and recreational uses, including bathing, swimming, and other shore activities. *Borough of Neptune City v. Borough of Avon-by-the-Sea*, 61 N.J. 296, 309 (1972). In *Avon* we held that the public trust applied to the municipality-owned dry sand beach immediately landward of the high water mark. The major issue in this case is whether, ancillary to the public's right to enjoy the tidal lands, the public has a right to gain access through and to use the dry sand area not owned by a municipality but by a quasi-public body.

The Borough of Point Pleasant instituted this suit against the Borough of Bay Head and the Bay Head Improvement Association (Association), generally asserting that the defendants prevented Point Pleasant inhabitants from gaining access to the Atlantic Ocean and the beachfront in Bay Head. The proceeding was dismissed as to the Borough of Bay Head because it did not own or control the beach. Subsequently, Virginia Matthews, a resident of Point Pleasant who desired to swim and bathe at the Bay Head beach, joined as a party plaintiff, and Stanley Van Ness, as Public Advocate, joined as plaintiff-intervenor. The trial court entered a final judgment in favor of the defendants. Upon plaintiff's appeal, the Appellate Division affirmed.

Facts

The Borough of Bay Head (Bay Head) borders the Atlantic Ocean. Adjacent to it on the north is the Borough of Point Pleasant Beach, on the south the Borough of Mantoloking, and on the west Barnegat Bay. Bay Head consists of a fairly narrow strip of land, 6,667 feet long (about 1 1/4 miles). A beach runs along its entire length adjacent to the Atlantic Ocean. There are 76 separate parcels of land that border the beach. All except six are owned by private individuals. Title to those six is vested in the Association.

The Association was founded in 1910 and incorporated as a nonprofit corporation in 1932. Its certificate of incorporation states that its purposes are

> the improving and beautifying of the Borough of Bay Head, New Jersey, cleaning, policing and otherwise making attractive and safe the bathing beaches in said borough, and the doing of any kind of act which may be found necessary or desirable for the greater convenience, comfort and enjoyment of the residents.

Its constitution delineates the Association's object to promote the best interests of the Borough and "in so doing to own property, operate bathing beaches, hire lifeguards, beach cleaners and policeman."

Nine streets in the Borough, which are perpendicular to the beach, end at the dry sand. The Association owns the land commencing at the end of seven of these streets for the width of each street and extending through the upper dry sand to the mean high water line, the beginning of the wet sand area or foreshore. In addition, the Association owns the fee in six shore front properties, three of which are contiguous and have a frontage aggregating 310 feet. Many owners of beachfront property executed and delivered to the Association leases of the upper dry sand area. These leases are revocable by either party to the lease on thirty days' notice. Some owners have not executed such leases and have not permitted the Association to use their beaches. Some also have acquired riparian grants from the State extending approximately 1,000 feet east of the high water line.

The Association controls and supervises its beach property between the third week in June and Labor Day. It engages about 40 employees, who serve as lifeguards, beach police and beach cleaners. Lifeguards, stationed at five operating beaches, indicate by use of flags whether the ocean condition is dangerous (red), requires caution (yellow), or is satisfactory (green). In addition to observing and, if need be, assisting those in the water, when called upon lifeguards render first aid. Beach cleaners are engaged to rake and keep the beach clean of debris. Beach police are stationed at the entrances to the beaches where the public streets lead into the beach to ensure that only Association members or their guests enter. Some beach police patrol the beaches to enforce its membership rules.

Membership is generally limited to residents of Bay Head. Class A members are property owners. Class B are non-owners. Large families (six or more) pay $90 per year and small families pay $60 per year. Upon application residents are routinely accepted. Membership is evidenced by badges that signify permission to use the beaches. Members, which include local hotels, motels and inns, can also acquire badges for guests. The charge for each guest badge is $12. Members of the Bay Head Fire Company, Bay Head Borough employees, and teachers in the municipality's school system have been issued beach passes irrespective of residency.

Except for fishermen, who are permitted to walk through the upper dry sand area to the foreshore, only the membership may use the beach between 10:00 a.m. and 5:30 p.m. during the summer session. The public is permitted to use the Association's beach from 5:30 p.m. to 10:00 a.m. during the summer and, with no hourly restrictions, between Labor Day and mid-June.

No attempt has ever been made to stop anyone from occupying the terrain east of the high water mark. During certain parts of the day, when the tide is low, the foreshore could consist of about 50 feet of sand not being flowed by the water. The public could gain access to the foreshore by coming from the Borough of Point Pleasant Beach on the north or from the Borough of Mantoloking on the south.

Association membership totals between 4,800 to 5,000. The Association President testified during depositions that its restrictive policy, in existence since 1932, was due to limited parking facilities and to the overcrowding of the beaches. The Association's avowed purpose was to provide the beach for the residents of Bay Head.

There is also a public boardwalk, about one-third of a mile long, parallel to the ocean on the westerly side of the dry sand area. The boardwalk is owned and maintained by the municipality.

The Public Trust

In *Borough of Neptune City v. Borough of Avon-by-the-Sea*, 61 N.J. 296, 303 (1972), Justice Hall alluded to the ancient principle "that land covered by tidal waters belonged to the sovereign, but for the common use of all the people." The genesis of this principle is found in Roman jurisprudence, which held that "[b]y the law of nature" "the air, running water, the sea and consequently the shores of the sea" were "common to mankind." Justinian, Institutes 2.1.1. (T. Sanders trans. 1st Am. ed. 1876). No one was forbidden access to the sea, and everyone could use the seashore "to dry his nets there, and haul them from the sea." *Id.*, 2.1.5. The seashore was not private property, but "subject to the same law as the sea itself, and the sand or ground beneath it." *Id.* This underlying concept was applied in New Jersey in *Arnold v. Mundy*, 6 N.J.L. 1 (Sup. Ct. 1821).

In Avon, Justice Hall reaffirmed the public's right to use the waterfront as announced in *Arnold v. Mundy*. He observed that the public has a right to use the land below the mean average high water mark where the tide ebbs and flows. These uses have historically included navigation and fishing. In *Avon* the public's rights were extended "to recreational uses, including bathing, swimming and other shore activities." 61 N.J. at 309. *Compare Blundell v. Catterall*, 5 B. & Ald. 268, 106 Eng. Rep. 1190 (K.B.1821) (holding no right to swim in common property) *with Martin v. Waddell's Lessee*, 41 U.S. (16 Pet.) 367, 10 L. Ed. 997 (1842) (indicating right to bathe in navigable waters). It has been said that "[h]ealth, recreation and sports are encompassed in and intimately related to the general welfare of a well-balanced state." *N.J. Sports & Exposition Authority v. McCrane*, 119 N.J. Super. 457, 488 (Law Div. 1971), *aff'd*, 61 N.J. 1, *appeal dismissed sub nom., Borough of East Rutherford v. N.J. Sports & Exposition Authority*, 409 U.S. 943 (1972). Extension of the public trust doctrine to include bathing, swimming and other shore activities is consonant with and furthers the general welfare. The public's right to enjoy these privileges must be respected.

In order to exercise these rights guaranteed by the public trust doctrine, the public must have access to municipally-owned dry sand areas as well as the foreshore. The extension of the public trust doctrine to include municipally-owned dry sand areas was necessitated by our conclusion that enjoyment of rights in the foreshore is inseperable from use of dry sand beaches. *See Lusardi v. Curtis Point Property Owner's Ass'n*, 86 N.J. 217, 228 (1981). In *Avon* we struck down a municipal ordinance that required nonresidents to pay a higher fee than residents for the use of the beach. We held that where a municipal beach is dedicated to public use, the public trust doctrine "dictates that the beach and the ocean waters must be open to all on equal terms and without preference and that any contrary state or municipal action is impermissible." 61 N.J. at 309.

Public Rights in Privately-Owned Dry Sand Beaches

In *Avon* our finding of public rights in dry sand areas was specifically and appropriately limited to those beaches owned by a municipality. We now address the extent of the public's interest in privately-owned dry sand beaches.

Beaches are a unique resource and are irreplaceable. The public demand for beaches has increased with the growth of population and improvement of transportation facilities. Exercise of the public's right to swim and bathe below the mean high water mark may depend upon a right to pass across the upland beach. Without some means of access the public right to use the foreshore would be meaningless. To say that the public trust doctrine entitles the public to swim in the ocean and to use the foreshore in connection therewith without assuring the public of a feasible access route would seriously impinge on, if not effectively eliminate, the rights of the public trust doctrine. This does not mean the public has an unrestricted right to cross at will over any and all property bordering on the common property. The public interest is satisfied so long as there is reasonable access to the sea.

We see no reason why rights under the public trust doctrine to use of the upland dry sand area should be limited to municipally-owned property. It is true that the private owner's interest in the upland dry sand area is not identical to that of a municipality. Nonetheless, where use of dry sand is essential or reasonably necessary for enjoyment of the ocean, the doctrine warrants the public's use of the upland dry sand area subject to an accommodation of the interests of the owner.

We perceive no need to attempt to apply notions of prescription, dedication, or custom as an alternative to application of the public trust doctrine. Archaic judicial responses are not an answer to a modern social problem. Rather, we perceive the public trust doctrine not to be "fixed or static," but one to be "molded and extended to meet changing conditions and needs of the public it was created to benefit." *Avon*, 61 N.J. at 309.

Precisely what privately-owned upland sand area will be available and required to satisfy the public's rights under the public trust doctrine will depend on the circumstances. Location of the dry sand area in relation to the foreshore, extent and availability of publicly-owned upland sand area, nature and extent of the public demand, and usage of the upland sand land by the owner are all factors to be weighed and considered in fixing the contours of the usage of the upper sand.

Today, recognizing the increasing demand for our State's beaches and the dynamic nature of the public trust doctrine, we find that the public must be given both access to and use of privately-owned dry sand areas as reasonably necessary. While the public's rights in private beaches are not co-extensive with the rights enjoyed in municipal beaches, private landowners may not in all instances prevent the public from exercising its rights under the public trust doctrine. The public must be afforded reasonable access to the foreshore as well as a suitable area for recreation on the dry sand.

NOTES AND QUESTIONS

1. *Defining the Boundaries of Publicly Owned Areas.* In New Jersey, the dry sand area is generally defined as the land that lies landward of the high water mark to the vegetation line, or, where there is no vegetation to a seawall, road, parking lot or boardwalk. NEW JERSEY BEACH ACCESS STUDY COMMISSION, PUBLIC ACCESS TO THE OCEANFRONT BEACHES: A REPORT TO THE GOVERNOR AND LEGISLATURE OF NEW JERSEY 2 (1977). The high water mark is the "line formed by the intersection of the tidal plane of mean high tide with the shore." *O'Neill v. State Hwy. Dep't*, 235 A.2d 1, 9 (N.J. 1967). The mean or ordinary high tide is a mean of all high tides over a period of 18.6 years. *Id.* at 324; *see also Borax Consolidated, Ltd v. City of Los Angeles*, 296 U.S. 10, 26–27 (1935). For one view on the implications of the New Jersey cases, see Marc Poirier, *Modified Private Property: New Jersey's Public Trust Doctrine, Private Development and Exclusion, and Shared Public Uses of Natural Resources*, 15 SOUTHEASTERN ENVTL. L.J. 71 (2006).

2. *The Remedy in* Matthews v. Bay Head. In the final portion of its opinion, not reproduced above, the New Jersey Supreme Court addressed the issue of the proper remedy for those who had been denied access to public trust lands. The Court instructed the Bay Head Improvement Association to open its membership to

the public at large and to make available a "reasonable quantity" of daily and seasonal badges for nonresidents. The Association was permitted to charge fees and enforce its regulations so long as both were done in a non-discriminatory manner.

What if there had been no Association, only a group of private owners of beachfront land who individually denied the public access to the wet sand areas? Under the logic of the *Matthews* decision, would the New Jersey Supreme Court have been warranted in requiring private landowners to give the public a reasonable right-of-way across their property? Could this be done constitutionally without the payment of compensation? Can there be such a thing as a reserved public trust easement?

3. *Other States*. While few states have gone as far as New Jersey in recognizing public trust easements, the Connecticut Court of Appeals found that the state's public trust doctrine dictated that beach front property was part of the public trust, and, consequently, the Town of Greenwich could not limit access to a town-owned beach-front park to local residents. *Leydon v. Town of Greenwich*, 750 A.2d 1122 (Conn. App. Ct. 2000). As illustrated above, Oregon has reached a similar result through the application of the doctrine of custom. However, other states have rejected the idea that the public implicitly reserved a right of access through lands above the high water mark even when codified in a state statute. For an example of this view, which still appears to be the majority rule, see *Opinion of the Justices*, 313 N.E.2d 561 (Mass. 1974) (same).

Other extensions have involved incorporating additional assets into the public trust. In *National Audubon Society v. Superior Court of Alpine County*, 658 P.2d 709 (Cal. 1983), the court accepted the application of the concept to Mono Lake, a large inland body of water that was not legally navigable since it was fed by non-navigable streams. The Mono Lake case represents a clear trend to extend the doctrine to water resources generally. Lazarus, *Changing Conceptions of Property and Sovereignty in Natural Resources: Questioning the Public Trust Doctrine*, 71 Iowa L. Rev. 631 (1986), notes that courts have also extended the public trust doctrine beyond aquatic resources to "embrace the dry sand area of a beach, rural parklands, a historic battlefield, wildlife, archaeological remains, and even a downtown area." *Id.* at 649. *See also Save Ourselves, Inc. v. Louisiana Envtl. Control Comm'n*, 452 So. 2d 1152, 1154 n.102, 1157 (La. 1984) (doctrine applies to all natural resources). Of course, not all public land is held in public trust. For the view that judicial expansion of traditional public trust doctrine is both dangerous and counterproductive, see G. Smith and M. Sweeney, *The Public Trust Doctrine and Natural Law: Emanations Within a Penumbra*, 33 B.C. Envtl. Aff. L. Rev. 307 (2006). For a broader contextual discussion, see Barton H. Thompson, *The Public Trust Doctrine: A Conservative Reconstruction & Defense*, 15 Southeastern Envtl. L.J. 47 (2006).

OPINION OF THE JUSTICES (PUBLIC USE OF COASTAL BEACHES)

New Hampshire Supreme Court
649 A.2d 604 (1994)

To the Honorable House:

The undersigned justices of the supreme court submit the following reply to your questions of May 5, 1994. Following our receipt of your resolution, we invited interested parties to file memoranda with the court on or before September 1, 1994.

SB 636 (the bill), as amended, proposes to amend RSA chapter 483-B (1992) by inserting after section 9 a new section, 483-B:9-a, titled, "Public Use of Coastal Beaches." The legislature's purpose is set out in the bill as follows:

> It is the purpose of the general court [the legislature] in this section to recognize and confirm the historical practice and common law right of the public to enjoy the existing public easement in the greatest portion of New Hampshire coastal beach land subject to those littoral rights recognized as common law. This easement presently existing over the greater portion of that beachfront property extending from where the "public trust" ends across the commonly used portion of sand and rocks to the intersection of the beach and the high ground, often but not always delineated by a seawall, or the line of vegetation, or the seaward face of the foredunes, this being that beach where violent sea action occurs at irregular frequent intervals making its use for the usual private constructions uneconomical and physically impractical.

The bill defines "coastal beaches" as "that portion of the beach extending from where the public trust shoreline ends, across the commonly used portion of sand and rocks to the intersection of the beach and high ground, often but not always delineated by a seawall, or the line of vegetation, or the seaward face of the foredunes."

The bill states that "New Hampshire holds in 'public trust' rights in all shorelands subject to the ebb and flow of the tide and subject to those littoral rights recognized at common law" and that the " 'public trust' shoreland establishes the extreme seaward boundary extension of all private property rights in New Hampshire except for those 'jus privatum' rights validly conveyed by legislative act without impairment on New Hampshire's 'jus publicum' interests."

The bill then provides that for an historical period extending back well over 20 years the public has made recognized, prevalent and uninterrupted use of the vast majority of New Hampshire's coastal beaches above the " 'public trust shoreland. The legislature recognizes that some public use of the beach area above the public trust lands is necessary to the full enjoyment of the land. The general court recognizes and confirms a public easement flowing from and demonstrated by this historical practice in the coastal beaches contiguous to the public trust shoreland where the public has traditionally had access and which easement has been created by virtue of such uninterrupted public use.

Further, the bill states that "[a]ny person may use the coastal beaches of New Hampshire where such a public easement exists for recreational purposes subject to the provisions of municipal ordinances," but "[t]he provisions of [the bill] shall in no way be construed as affecting the title of property owners of land contiguous to the land subject to a public easement." Finally, the new section provides that "[i]n a suit brought or defended under this section, or whose determination is affected by this section, a showing that the area in dispute is within the area defined as 'coastal beach' shall be prima facie evidence that a public easement exists."

Your first question asks "[w]hether New Hampshire law identifies a particular coastal feature or tidal event as outlining the maximum shoreward extension of the public trust area boundary . . . beyond which the probable existence of private property rights may, without a public easement arising from historical practice, restrict any public access under the provisions of Part I, Article 12 of the New Hampshire Constitution and the 5th amendment of the United States Constitution." We answer in the affirmative.

Part I, article 12 of the New Hampshire Constitution provides that "no part of a man's property shall be taken from him, or applied to public uses, without his own consent, or that of the representative body of the people." This clause requires just compensation in the event of a taking. *Piscataqua Bridge v. N.H. Bridge*, 7 N.H. 35, 66–70 (1834). "The same principle was embodied in the Fifth Amendment to the Constitution of the United States at the insistence of a majority of the States, including New Hampshire, in ratifying the Constitution." *Burrows v. City of Keene*, A.2d 15, 18 (N.H. 1981). The fifth amendment of the Federal Constitution provides that "no person shall . . . be deprived of life, liberty, or property, without due process of law; nor shall private property be taken for public use, without just compensation."

The public trust has its origins in the concept of the jus publicum, an English common law doctrine under which the tidelands and navigable waters were held by the king in trust for the general public. *See* Sax, *The Public Trust Doctrine in Natural Resource Law: Effective Judicial Intervention*, 68 Mich. L. Rev. 471, 475–76 (1970). The English common law was based, in turn, upon the ancient Roman concept of "natural law" that held that certain things, including the shores, by their nature are common to all. *See* Comment, *The Public Trust Doctrine in Maine's Submerged Lands: Public Rights, State Obligation and the Role of the Courts*, 37 Me. L. Rev. 105, 107–08 (1985). At common law, the king had "both the title and the dominion of the sea, and of rivers and arms of the sea, where the tide ebbs and follows, and all of the lands below high-water mark, within the jurisdiction of the crown of England." *Shively v. Bowlby*, 152 U.S. 1, 11 (1894). The king held the title to intertidal lands, or just privatum, absolutely, and in his role as sovereign he held the public rights, or jus publicum, in trust for the benefit of the public. *Id.* at 13. The jus publicum included uses "for highways of navigation and commerce, domestic and foreign, and for the purpose of fishing by all the King's subjects." *Id.*

Following the American Revolution, "the people of each state became themselves sovereign; and in that character hold the absolute right to all their navigable waters and the soils under them for their own common use, subject only to the rights since surrendered by the Constitution to the general government." *Martin v. Waddell*, 41

U.S. 367 (1842). Upon entering the Union, the original thirteen states and all new States acquired title to lands under waters subject to the ebb and flow of the tide. *Phillips Petroleum Co. v. Mississippi*, 484 U.S. 469, 476 (1988). As sovereigns, the States hold the intertidal lands in trust for the public and "have the authority to define the limits of the lands held in public trust and to recognize private rights in such lands as they see fit." *Id.* at 475.

In 1889, this court rejected a Massachusetts law that adopted the low water mark as the boundary between public and private ownership. *Concord Mfg. Co. v. Robertson*, 25 A. 721, 730–31 (N.H. 1889). The Massachusetts rule, embodied in a 1647 ordinance, extended private titles "to encompass land as far as mean low water line or 100 rods from the mean high water line, whichever was the lesser measure." *In re Opinion of the Justices*, 313 N.E.2d 561, 565 (Mass. 1974). The purpose of the ordinance was "to encourage littoral owners to build wharves." *Id.*

The *Robertson* court rejected the need to vest New Hampshire private property owners with fee title to the tidelands below high water mark:

> While the [Massachusetts] ordinance maintains the public title of large ponds, it converts into private property, and gives away, a great amount of tide-land. In this state, the transfer of the fee to the abutters has not been necessary to encourage improvements below high-water mark. Their common-law right of reasonable use has been sufficient for all the purposes for which the [Massachusetts] ordinance changed the common-law title. Private ownership of so much of the tide-land (not exceeding 100 rods inwidth) as is bare twice a day, and public ownership where vessels can cometo a wharf at low tide, is not an adequate or useful adjustment of rights forcommercial purposes. Where tide-land ought to be improved and occupiedby the abutter, above and below low-water mark, he has a common-lawright to improve and occupy it.

25 A. at 730. The court noted that "no serious inconvenience has arisen from the adoption of the water's edge as the boundary of public and private ownership." *Id.* at 727. "The experience of more than 250 years has shown no practical difficulty in the question of the abutters' reasonable private use, and no defect in the law calling for such amendments as have been made in Massachusetts in relation to tidewaters." *Id.* Regarding ownership of the shore, the court concluded that "[t)he introduction of any line other than high-water mark as the marine boundary would overturn common-law rights that had been established here, by a usage and traditional understanding of two hundred years' duration." *Id.* at 730–31.

Robertson still represents the law in New Hampshire. While it is settled, therefore, that the public trust in tidewaters in this State extends landward to the high water mark, the following common law questions are not settled: what is the high water mark; where is it located; and how is it located. We do not purport to determine in this opinion answers to such questions

Your second question asks "[w]hether the effect of [the bill], which recognizes that the public trust extends to those lands 'subject to ebb and flow of the tide' infringes upon existing private property rights as protected by Part I, Article 12 of the New Hampshire Constitution and the 5th amendment of the United States

Constitution." We answer in the negative.

As already set out in our answer to your first question, New Hampshire has long recognized that lands subject to the ebb and flow of the tide are held in public trust. "Land covered by public water is capable of many uses." *Concord Mfg. Co. v. Robertson*, 25 A. at 721. "Rights of navigation and fishery are not the whole estate" but rather the public trust lands are held "for the use and benefit of all the [public], for all useful purposes." *Id.* at 721; *see St. Regis Paper Co. v. Board*, 26 A.2d 832, 837–38 (N.H. 1942) (public trust encompasses "all useful and lawful purposes"); *State v. Sunapee Dam Co.*, 50 A. 108, 110 (N.H. 1900) ("in this state the law of public waters is what justice and reason require"). These uses include recreational uses. *See Hartford v. Gilmantown*, 146 A.2d 851, 853 (N.H. 1958) (public waters may be used to boat, bathe, fish, fowl, skate, and cut ice).

In addition, we have uniformly held that owners of property adjacent to lands held in public trust have common law rights which are "more extensive than those of the public generally." *Sundell v. Town of New London*, 409 A.2d 1315, 1317 (N.H. 1979).

These rights, recognized at common law, constituted property which could not be taken without compensation. These private rights of littoral owners include but are not necessarily limited to the right to use and occupy the waters adjacent to their shore for a variety of recreational purposes, the right to erect boat houses and to wharf out into the water. We have also held that these private littoral rights are incidental property rights which are severable from the shore property itself and may be conveyed separate from the littoral property.

Because these littoral rights are an incident of ownership of shore property, their value is reflected in the fact that shorefront property commonly is substantially more valuable than property otherwise situated. *Id.* at 1318. "The right of littoral owners on public waters are," however, always subject to the paramount right of the State to control them reasonably in the interests of navigation, fishing and other public purposes. In other words, the rights of these owners are burdened with a servitude in favor of the State which comes into operation when the State properly exercises its power to control, regulate, and utilize such waters. *Sibson v. State*, 259 A.2d 397, 400 (N.H. 1969). Private shorefront owners are entitled to exercise their property rights in the tidelands so long as they do not unreasonably interfere with the rights of the public. *See Concord Mfg. Co. v. Robertson*, 25 A. at 727.

Therefore, to the extent that the term "lands subject to ebb and flow of the tide" applies to tidelands below the high water mark, the bill simply codifies the common law and does not infringe upon private property rights. Where private title to tidelands is already burdened by preexisting public rights, a regulation designed to protect those same rights will not constitute a taking of property without just compensation.

Your third question asks "[w]hether the provisions of [the bill], which recognize a public easement in the 'dry sand area' of historically accessible coastal beaches is a taking of private property for a public purpose without just compensation in violation of Part I, Article 12 of the New Hampshire Constitution and the 5th amendment of the United States Constitution." Except for those areas where there is an established and acknowledged public easement and subject to the assumptions contained in the discussion below, we answer in the affirmative.

The bill apparently recognizes two property interests in two distinct areas of shoreland. First, the bill establishes that "New Hampshire holds in 'public trust' rights in all shorelands subject to the ebb and flow of the tide." Second, the bill establishes a public easement in land "extending from where the public trust ends across the commonly used portion of sand and rocks to the intersection of the beach and the high ground, often but not always delineated by a sea wall, or the line of vegetation, or the seaward face of the foredunes." This high ground is generally known as the "dry sand" area. The bill states that "for an historical period extending back well over 20 years the public has made recognized, prevalent and uninterrupted use of the vast majority of New Hampshire's coastal beaches above the 'public trust' shoreland." The general court recognizes and confirms a public easement flowing from and demonstrated by this historical practice in the coastal beaches contiguous to the public trust shoreland where the public has traditionally had access and which easement has been created by virtue of such uninterrupted public use.

As noted in our answer to your first question, this court has not defined the term "high water mark." Because, however, the bill states that the dry sand area is not within the public trust we will, for purposes of this opinion, base our analysis on that assumption. We construe the bill, therefore, as recognizing public trust rights below the dry sand area and a prescriptive easement in the dry sand. See *Waterville Estates Assoc. v. Town of Campton*, 446 A.2d 1167, 1168 (N.H. 1982) ("easement is a non-possessory interest in realty which can only be created by prescription, written conveyance or implication").

"To establish a prescriptive easement, the plaintiff must prove by a balance of probabilities twenty years' adverse, continuous, uninterrupted use of the land [claimed] in such a manner as to give notice to the record owner that an adverse claim was being made to it." *Mastin v. Prescott*, 444 A.2d 556, 558 (N.H. 1982). Although the general public is capable of acquiring an easement by prescription, *Elmer v. Rodgers*, 214 A.2d 750, 752 (N.H. 1965), [e]vidence of continuous and uninterrupted public use of the premises for the statutory period . . . is insufficient alone to establish prescriptive title as a matter of law. The nature of the use must be such as to show the owner knew or ought to have known that the right was being exercised, not in reliance upon his toleration or permission, but without regard to his consent. *Vigeant v. Donel Realty Trust*, 540 A.2d 1243, 1244 (N.H. 1988).

While the fact that the owner was also using the premises for the same purposes would not prevent a finding of adverse use by the general public, *Elmer v. Rodgers*, 214 A.2d at 752, "[a] permissive use no matter how long or how often exercised cannot ripen into an easement by prescription." *Ucietowski v. Nowak*, 152 A.2d 614, 618 (1959). The general public may, therefore, acquire coastal beach land by prescription in New Hampshire.

Problems militate, however, against the use of the prescriptive doctrine. "First, there is the obvious problem of establishing factual evidence of the specialized type of adverse use for the requisite period of time . . . needed to create an easement by prescription." 3 R. Powell, Powell on Real Property § 34.11[6], at 34-171 (1994).

"Secondly, prescriptive easements, by their nature, can be utilized only on a tract-by-tract basis, and thus cannot be applied to all beaches within a state." *Id.* In a suit to quiet title, adequate evidence may well exist to prove that on a given piece of property, the area landward of the public trust across the dry sand is subject to a public easement. Such a determination is, however, a judicial one.

It is the constitutional mandate that questions of law belong to the judiciary for final determination, as a necessary deduction of the required separation of the legislative, executive and judicial powers of government. (Const., Part I, Art. 37). It follows that legislation cannot bar or restrict this power of the judiciary, and the courts have inherent power, through appropriate process, to act upon and decide such questions, if they are not of a strictly political nature. *Cloutier v. State Milk Control Board*, 28 A.2d 554, 556 (N.H. 1942).

Although the bill does not completely deprive private property owners of use of their property, "[t]he interference ,with private property here involves a wholesale denial of an owner's right to exclude the public." *Bell v. Town of Wells*, 557 A.2d 168, 178 (Me. 1989). "If a possessory interest in real property has any meaning at all it must include the general right to exclude others." *Id.*

"Property," in the constitutional sense, is not the physical thing itself but is rather the group of rights which the owner of the thing has with respect to it. The term refers to a person's right to possess, use, enjoy and dispose of a thing and is not limited to the thing itself. The property owner's right of indefinite user (or of using indefinitely) . . . necessarily includes the right . . . to exclude others from using the property, whether it be land or anything else. From the very nature of these rights of user and of exclusion, it is evident that they cannot be materially abridged without, ipso facto, taking the owner's property. The principle must be the same whether the owner is wholly deprived of the use of his land, or only partially deprived of it. *Burrows v. City of Keene*, 432 A.2d at 19; *see Claridge v. New Hampshire Wetlands Bd.*, 485 A.2d 287, 291 (N.H. 1984).

When the government unilaterally authorizes a permanent, public easement across private lands, this constitutes a taking requiring just compensation. *See Nollan v. California Coastal Comm'n*, 483 U.S. 825, 831 (1987). In *Nollan* the United States Supreme Court stated:

> [A]s to property reserved by its owner for private use, the right to exclude [others is] one of the most essential sticks in the bundle of rights that are commonly characterized as property. [O]ur cases uniformly have found a taking to the extent of the occupation, without regard to whether the action achieves an important public benefit or has only minimal economic impact on the owner. We think a permanent physical occupation has occurred, for purposes of that rule, where individuals are given a permanent and continuous right to pass to and fro, so that the real property may continuously be traversed, even though no particular individual is permitted to station himself permanently upon the premises.

Id. at 831–32; *see Loretto v. Teleprompter Manhattan CATV Corp.*, 458 U.S. 419, 426–27 & n. 5 (1982).

Because the bill provides no compensation for the landowners whose property may be burdened by the general recreational easement established for public use, it violates the prohibition contained in our State and Federal Constitutions against the taking of private property for public use without just compensation. Although the State has the power to permit a comprehensive beach access and use program by using its eminent domain power and compensating private property owners, it may not take property rights without compensation through legislative decree. *See Eaton v. B.C. & M.R.R.*, 51 N.H. 504, 510–11 (1872). "[A] strong public desire to improve the public condition is not enough to warrant achieving the desire by a shorter cut than the constitutional way of paying for the change." *Appeal of Public Serv. Co. of N.H.*, 454 A.2d 435, 440 (N.H. 1982); *see Eaton*, 51 N.H. at 518 ("if the work is one of great public benefit, the public can afford to pay for it").

Based on our response to your third question, we deem it unnecessary to answer your fourth question.

We emphasize that this opinion does not amount to a judicial decision. An opinion of the justices on proposed legislation is not binding upon the court in the event the proposed legislation should become law and a case should arise requiring its construction. *Opinion of the Justices*, 25 N.H. 537, 538 (1852).

NOTES AND QUESTIONS

1. The approach of the New Hampshire Supreme Court to the issue of public rights above the high water mark is more representative of how states view the relationship between the public trust and private ownership rights than the New Jersey Supreme Court's opinion in *Matthews v. Bay Head Imp. Ass'n*, 471 A.2d 355 (N.J. 1984).

2. *Advisory Opinions.* The above opinion, called an advisory opinion, was issued by the New Hampshire court in response to questions posed by the New Hampshire legislature concerning the constitutionality of a proposed piece of legislation rather than by an actual case or controversy before the court. It has long been an established principle of American constitutional law that the United States Supreme Court does not issue advisory opinions — *see* Letter from the Justices to George Washington (Aug. 8, 1793) (declining to express an opinion on a number of legal questions arising out of the ongoing hostilities between Britain and France and the application of American neutrality laws), *reprinted in* P. BATOR, ET AL., HART & WECHSLER'S THE FEDERAL COURTS AND THE FEDERAL SYSTEM, 65–66 (2d ed. 1973). However, a number of states, including New Hampshire, do issue such opinions.

3. *The Public Trust Doctrine and Environmental Protection.* The public trust doctrine is not just about the sovereign reclaiming property from private landowners. It also operates as an important limitation on the ability of the sovereign to misuse or mismanage natural resources. In fact, the transformation of the public trust doctrine into a major doctrine for the protection of environmental resources is one of the most dramatic changes in property law in the last several decades.

Professor Dan Tarlock has explained the origins and original scope of the public trust doctrine, and how courts extended it beyond its original meaning to make it a basis for environmental protection:

> Early in the environmental movement, Professor Joseph Sax saw the majoritarian problem of recognizing a constitutional right to a decent environment and tried to avoid it by using the public trust doctrine to create nonconstitutional rights. The public trust is a curious doctrine that expresses three ideas, one grounded in Roman law and the other two resulting from Anglo-American common law. The first is that public waters, generally defined as navigable waters, are subject to a public servitude for navigation, commerce, and, later, fisheries. The second idea is that the public owns the beds of submerged waters. The third idea is that the sovereign must use these submerged lands only for trust purposes. Environmental lawyers used the third aspect of the public trust doctrine to make the following arguments: (1) Legislative and administrative decisions that authorized nonenvironmentally sensitive uses of any public resource were subject to heightened judicial scrutiny; and (2) courts should recognize pre-existing but long-ignored public rights in common property resources.

Tarlock, *Earth and Other Ethics: The Institutional Issues*, 56 TENN. L. REV. 43, 56 (1988). Tarlock refers to Sax, *The Public Trust Doctrine in Natural Resource Law: Effective Judicial Intervention*, 68 MICH. L. REV. 471 (1970), in which the author called for an expansion of the doctrine beyond its traditional limits. After outlining the traditional scope of the doctrine, Sax argued: "If any of the analysis in this Article makes sense, it is clear that the judicial techniques developed in public trust cases need not be limited either to these few conventional interests or to questions of disposition of public properties. Public trust problems are found whenever governmental regulation comes into question, and they occur in a wide range of situations in which diffuse public interests need protection against tightly organized groups with clear and organized goals." *Id.* at 556.

4. *Rights of Littoral Owners.* While the public as a whole has rights to land held in public trust, some states afford the owners of private land adjacent to public trust land (particularly coastal land) greater rights to use the public trust land than those of the general public. *Sundell v. Town of New London*, 409 A.2d 1315 (N.H. 1979). These rights include the right to use and occupy the waters adjacent to the shore for a variety of recreational purposes and the right to erect boathouses and wharfs. *Id.* at 1318. These rights can be severed from shore property and separately alienated, and they cannot be abrogated by the state except for a public purpose and with the payment of just compensation. The state can, of course, control them in the interests of navigation, fishing, and other public purposes.

5. *Accretion and Reliction.* In *Stop the Beach Renourishment, Inc. v. Florida Dept. of Environmental Protection*, 560 U.S. 702 (2010), the Supreme Court attempted to resolve some of the issues arising in the events of reliction or accretion, concepts related to private property rights to land which adjoins public lands, essentially concluding that beachfront littoral landowners had no property right under state law to additions to their lands from accretions or relictions nor to have their lands touch the water, hence were not subjected to unconstitutional takings by the beach restoration project.

In an opinion by Justice Scalia announcing the judgment of the Court, joined with respect to Parts I, IV, and V by Chief Justice Roberts and Justices Kennedy, Thomas, Ginsburg, Breyer, Alito and Sotomayor, the Court held that Florida beachfront landowners had no established property right under Florida law — to additions to their lands resulting from accretions (the slow, gradual and imperceptible deposit of additional sand, sediment or other deposits) and relictions (the exposure of land resulting from receding of water), nor to have their lands touch the water — superior to the State's right to fill in its submerged land.

The 1961 Florida Beach and Shore Preservation Act, Fla. Stat. §§ 161.011–162.45, established procedures for beach restoration and nourishment projects. In 2003, the city of Destin and Walton county obtained permits to restore 6.9 miles of beach within their jurisdictions that had been eroded by several hurricanes. The project would add about 75 feet of dry sand seaward of an "erosion control line" (ECL) — which in this case was established to coincide with the mean high-water line. However, once the ECL was established, the littoral landowners' lands no longer would benefit from the accretions or relictions seaward of the ECL, and their lands would no longer touch the water. Littoral landowners administratively challenged the project and appealed the adverse administrative determination to the state courts. Although the state court's decision focused on the state constitution, and the federal constitutional question was not raised until a petition for rehearing which was denied, the United States Supreme Court nevertheless held that the federal constitutional question was properly presented.

The United States Supreme Court held that two principles of Florida property law intersected in the case: First, the state as owner of the submerged land adjacent to beachfront (or "littoral") land has the right to fill its land so long as it does not interfere with the rights of the public or those of the littoral landowners; second, if an avulsion (a sudden or perceptible addition of land by the action of water) exposes land seaward of the littoral lands which had previously been submerged, that newly-exposed land belongs to the state even if the state interrupts the littoral owner's contact with the water. The issue, therefore, became whether there was an exception to the second principle when the state itself was the cause of the avulsion. The Court cited two Florida state cases suggesting that no such exception existed: *Martin v. Busch*, 112 So. 274 (Fla. 1927), held that when the state drained water from a lakebed belonging to the state, the land below the high-water line thereby exposed continued to belong to the state. *Bryant v. Peppe*, 238 So. 2d 836, 838–39 (Fla. 1970), analogized the situation in *Martin* to an avulsion, and also confirmed that the doctrines of accretion and reliction did not apply to the (formerly) littoral lands. The United States Supreme Court noted that this was not surprising, since there could be no accretions or relictions with respect to land that no longer abutted the water.

Accordingly, the Court held that since the Florida law prior to the events in this case allowed the state to fill in its own seabed, with the resulting sudden exposure of previously submerged land treated like an avulsion whereby the newly-exposed land belonged to the state, therefore the littoral landowners here had no protectable property right to accretions or relictions under Florida law in the circumstances. With respect to the littoral landowners' claim that they had a property right to maintain contact with the water, the Court emphasized — and the parties agreed —

that the ECL line here was established to coincide with the existing mean high-water line. Indeed, the state conceded that if the ECL had been established landward of the mean high-water line, "the State would have taken property." However, the Court quoted *Board of Trustees of the Internal Imp. Trust Fund v. Sand Key Associates, Ltd.*, 512 So. 2d 934, 936 (Fla. 1987), which stated that a littoral landowner had "no independent right of contact with the water," but only a "right of access to water." Thus, the littoral landowners continued to have what the previously had.

In Parts II and III of Justice Scalia's opinion, joined by Chief Justice Roberts and Justices Thomas and Alito, he declared that unconstitutional takings of private property in violation of the Just Compensation Clause may arise in the "judicial takings" setting, in which a court declares that what was once an established right to private property no longer exists. In a separate opinion by Justice Kennedy, joined by Justice Sotomayor, as well as in a separate opinion by Justice Breyer, joined by Justice Ginsberg, those Justices refused to go along with Parts II and III of Justice Scalia's opinion because they concluded that the issue of judicial takings was not posed, and hence should not be addressed, in this case.

Justice Stevens did not participate in the case.

[B.] PHYSICAL INVASIONS AND THE TAKING OF PERSONAL PROPERTY

While they are usually treated entirely separately, eminent domain — the compulsory purchase of interests in land as described in Part A of this chapter — and taking by regulation, which follows in the rest of this chapter, the distinction is, as with much of law, blurred at the edges. Thus, for example, what about government regulations which work as a physical invasion of property, or act primarily on what is clearly an interest in property which traditionally has nothing to do with real property? The following cases deal with these issues, both decided by the US Supreme Court and both resulting in compensation for the taking of property as a result of a governmental regulation.

HORNE v. DEPARTMENT OF AGRICULTURE

United States Supreme Court
135 S. Ct. 2419 (2015)

Chief Justice Roberts delivered the opinion of the Court.

Under the United States Department of Agriculture's California Raisin Marketing Order, a percentage of a grower's crop must be physically set aside in certain years for the account of the government, free of charge. The Government then sells, allocates, or otherwise disposes of the raisins in ways it determines are best suited to maintaining an orderly market. The question in whether the Takings Clause of the Fifth Amendment bars the Government from imposing such a demand on the growers without just compensation.

II.

The petition for certiorari poses three questions, which we answer in turn.

A

The first question presented asks "Whether the government's 'categorical duty' under the Fifth Amendment to pay just compensation when it 'physically takes possession of an interest in property,' *Arkansas Game & Fish Comm'n v. United States*, ___U.S.___, 133 S. Ct. 511, 518, 184 L. Ed. 2d 417 (2012), applies only to real property and not to personal property. The answer is no.

1

There is no dispute that the "classic taking [is on] in which the government directly appropriates private property for its own use." *Tahoe-Sierra Preservation Council, Inc., v. Tahoe Regional Planning Agency*, 535 U.S. 302, 324, 122 S. Ct. 1465, 152 L. Ed. 2d 517 (2002) (brackets and internal quotation marks omitted). Nor is there any dispute that, in the case of real property, such an appropriation is a *per se* taking that requires just compensation. See *Loretto v. Teleprompter Manhattan CATV Corp.*, 458 U.S. 419, 426–435, 102 S. Ct. 3164, 73 L. Ed. 2d 868 (1982).

Nothing in the text or history of the Takings Clause, or our precedents, suggests that the rule is any different when it comes to appropriation of personal property. The Government has a categorical duty to pay just compensation when it takes your car, just as when it takes your home.

The Takings Clause provides: "[N]or shall private property be taken for public use, without just compensation." U.S. Const., Amdt. 5. It protects "private property" without any distinction between different types. The principle reflected in the Clause goes back at least 800 years to Magna Carta, which specifically protected agricultural crops from uncompensated takings. Clause 28 of that charter forbade any "constable or other bailiff" from taking "corn or other provisions from any one without immediately tendering money therefor, unless he can have postponement thereof by permission of the seller." Cl. 28 (1215) in W. McKechnie, Magna Carta, A Commentary on the Great Charter of King John 329 (2d ed. 1914).

The colonists brought the principles of Magna Carta with them to the New World, including that charter's protection against uncompensated takings of personal property. In 1641, for example, Massachusetts adopted its Body of Liberties, prohibiting "mans Cattel or goods of what kinde soever" from "being pressed or taken for any publique use or service, unlesse it be by warrant grounded upon some act of the generall Court, not without such reasonable prices and hire as the ordinarie rates of the Countrie do afford." Massachusetts Body of Liberties ¶ 8, in R. Perry, Sources of Our Liberties 149 (1978). Virginia allowed the seizure of surplus "livestock or beef, pork, or bacon" for the military, but only upon "paying or tendering to the owner the price so estimated by the appraisers." 1777 Va. Acts ch. XII. And South Carolina authorized the seizure of "necessaries" for public use, but provided that "said articles so seized shall be paid for agreeable to the prices such and the like articles sold for on the ninth day of October last." 1779 S.C. Acts § 4.

Given that background, it is not surprising that early Americans bridled at appropriations of their personal property during the Revolutionary War, at the hands of both sides. John Jay, for example, complained to the New York Legislature about military impressment by the Continental Army of "Horses, Teems, and Carriages," and voiced his fear that such action by the "little Officers" of the Quartermasters Department might extend to "Blankets, Shoes, and many other articles." A Hint to the Legislature of the State of New York (1778), in John Jay, The Making of a Revolutionary 461–463 (R. Morris ed. 1975)(emphasis deleted). The legislature took the "hint," passing a law that, among other things, provided for compensation for the impressment of horses and carriages. 1778 N.Y. Laws ch. 29. According to the author of the first treatise on the Constitution, St. George Tucker, the Takings Clause was "probably" adopted in response to "the arbitrary and oppressive mode of obtaining supplies for the army, and other public uses, by impressment, as was too frequently practised during the revolutionary war, without any compensation whatever." 1 Blackstone's Commentaries, Editor's App. 305–306 (1803).

Nothing in this history suggests that personal property was any less protected against U.S. 356, 358, 26 L. Ed. 786 (1882), a case concerning the alleged appropriation of a patent by the Government:

> "[A patent] confers upon the patentee as exclusive property in the patented invention which cannot be appropriated or used by the government itself, without just compensation, any more than it can appropriate or use without compensation land which has been patented to a private purchaser."

Prior to this Court's decision in *Pennsylvania Coal Co. v. Mahon*, 260 U.S. 393, 43 S. Ct. 158, 67 L. Ed. 322 (1922), the Takings Clause was understood to provide protection only against a direct appropriation of property — personal or real. *Pennsylvania Coal* expanded the protection of the Takings Clause, holding that compensation was also required for a "regulatory taking" — a restriction on the use of property that went "too far." *Id.*, at 415. And in *Penn Central Transp. Co. v. New York City*, 438 U.S. 104, 124, 98 S. Ct. 2646, 57 L. Ed. 2d 631 (1978), the Court clarified that the test for how far was "too far" required an "ad hoc" factual inquiry. That inquiry required considering factors such as the economic impact of the regulation, its interference with reasonable investment-backed expectations, and the character of the government action.

Four years after *Penn Central*, however, the Court reaffirmed the rule that a physical *appropriation* of property gave rise to a *per se* taking, without regard to other factors. In *Loretto*, the Court held that requiring an owner of an apartment building to allow installation of a cable box on her rooftop was a physical taking of real property, for which compensation was required. That was true without regard to the claimed public benefit or the economic impact on the owner. The Court explained that such protection was justified not only by history, but also because "[s]uch an appropriation is perhaps the most serious form of invasion of an owner's property interests," depriving the owner of the "rights to possess, use and dispose of" the property. 458 U.S., at 435, 102 S. Ct. 3164 (internal quotation marks omitted). That reasoning — both with respect to history and logic — is equally applicable to a physical appropriation of personal property.

The Ninth Circuit based its distinction between real and personal property on this Court's discussion in *Lucas v. South Carolina Coastal Council*, 505 U.S. 1003, 112 S. Ct. 2886, 120 L. Ed. 2d 798 (1992), a case involving extensive limitations on the use of shorefront property. 750 F. 3d at 1139–1141. *Lucas* recognized that while an owner of personal property "ought to be aware of the possibility that new regulation might even render his property economically worthless," such an "implied limitation" was not reasonable in the case of land. 505 U.S., at 1027–1028, 112 S. Ct. 2886.

Lucas, however, was about regulatory takings, not direct appropriations. Whatever *Lucas* had to say about reasonable expectations with regard to regulations, people still do not expect their property, real or personal, to be actually occupied or taken away. Our cases have stressed the "longstanding distinction" between governmental acquisitions or property and regulations. *Tahoe-Sierra Preservation Council*, 535 U.S., at 323, 122 S. Ct. 1465. The different treatment of real and personal property in a regulatory case suggested by *Lucas* did not alter the established rule of treating direct appropriations of real and personal property alike. See 535 U.S., at 323. (It is "inappropriate to treat cases involving physical takings as controlling precedents for the evaluation of a claim that there has been a 'regulatory taking,' and vice versa" (footnote omitted)).

2

The reserve requirement imposed by the Raisin Committee is a clear physical taking. Actual raisins are transferred from the growers to the Government. Title to the raisins passes to the Raisin Committee. App. To Pet. for Cert. 179a; Tr. of Oral Arg. 31. The Committee's raisings must be physically segregated from free-tonnage raisins. 7 CFR § 989.66(b)(2). Reserve raisins are sometimes left on the premises of handlers, but they are held "for the account" of the Government. § 989.66(a). The Committee disposes of what becomes its raisins as it wishes, to promote the purposes of the raisin marketing order.

Raisin growers subject to the reserve requirement thus lose the entire "bundle" or property rights in the appropriated raisins — "the rights to possess, use and dispose" of them. *Loretto*, 458 U.S., at 435, 102 S. Ct. 3164 (internal quotation marks omitted) — with the exception of the speculative hope that some residual proceeds may be left when the Government is done with the raisins and has deducted the expenses of implementing all aspects of the marketing order. The Government's "actual taking of possession and control" of the reserve raisins gives rise to a taking as clearly "as if the Government held full title and ownership," *id.*, at 431, 102 S. Ct. 3164 (internal quotation marks omitted), as it essentially does. The Government's formal demand that the Hornes turn over a percentage of their raisin crop without charge, for the Government's control and use, is "of such a unique character that it is a taking without regard to other factors that a court might ordinarily examine." *Id.*, at 432, 102 S. Ct. 3164.

The Government thinks it "strange" and the dissent "baffling" that the Hornes object to the reserve requirement, when they nonetheless concede that "the government may prohibit the sale of raisins without effecting a per se taking." Brief for Respondent 35; *post*, at ______ (SOTOMAYOR, J., dissenting). But that distinction flows naturally from the settled difference in our takings jurisprudence between appropriation and regulation. A physical taking of raisins and a regulatory limit on production may have the same economic impact on a grower. The Constitution, however, is concerned with means as well as ends. The Government has broad powers, but the means it uses to achieve its ends must be "consist[end] with the letter and spirit of the constitution." *McCulloch v. Maryland*, 4 Wheat. 316, 421, 4 L. Ed. 579 (1819). As Justice Holmes noted, "a strong public desire to improve the public condition is not enough to warrant achieving the desire by a shorter cut than the constitutional way." *Pennsylvania Coal*, 260 U.S., at 416, 43 S. Ct. 158.

B.

The second question presented asks "Whether the government may avoid the categorical duty to pay just compensation for a physical taking of property by reserving to the property owner a contingent interest in a portion of the value of the property, set at the government's discretion." The answer is no.

The Government and dissent argue that raisins are fungible goods whose only value is in the revenue from their sale. According to the Government, the raisin marketing order leaves that interest with the raisin growers: After selling reserve raisins and deducting expenses and subsidies for exporters, the Raisin Committee returns any net proceeds to the growers. 7 CFR §§ 989.67(d), 989.82, 989.53(a), 989.66(h). The Government contends that because growers are entitled to these net proceeds, they retain the most important property interest in the reserve raisins, so there is no taking in the first place. The dissent agrees, arguing that this possible future revenue means there has been no taking under *Loretto*. See *post*, at ______.

But when there has been a physical appropriation, "we do not ask . . . whether it deprives the owner of all economically valuable use" of the item taken. *Tahoe-Sierra Preservation Council*, 535 U.S., at 323, 122 S. Ct. 1465; see *id*., at 322, 122 S. Ct. 1465 ("When the government physically takes possession of an interest in property for some public purpose, it has a categorical duty to compensate the former owner, regardless of whether the interest that is taken constitutes an entire parcel or merely a part thereof." (citation omitted)). For example, in *Loretto*, we held that the installation of a cable box on a small corner of Loretto's rooftop was a *per se* taking, even though she could of course still sell and economically benefit from the property. 458 U.S., at 430, 436, 102 S. Ct. 3164. The fact that the growers retain a contingent interest of indeterminate value does not mean there has been no physical taking, particularly since the value of the interest depends on the discretion of the taker, and may be worthless, as it was for one of the two years at issue here.

The dissent points to *Andrus v. Allard*, 444 U.S. 51, 100 S. Ct. 318, 62 L. Ed. 2d 210 (1979), noting that the Court found no taking in that case, even though the owner's artifacts could not be sold at all. *Post*, at ______. The dissent suggests that the Hornes should be happy, because they might at least get *something* from what had been their raisins. But *Allard* is a very different case. As the dissent recognizes, the owners in that case retained the rights to possess, donate, and devise their property. In finding no taking, the Court emphasized that the Government did not "compel the surrender of the artifacts, and there [was] no physical invasion or restraint upon them." 444 U.S., at 65–66. Here of course the raisin program requires physical surrender of the raisins and transfer of title, and the growers lose any right to control their disposition.

The Government and dissent again confuse our inquiry concerning *per se* takings with our analysis for regulatory takings. A regulatory restriction on use that does not entirely deprive an owner of property rights may not be a taking under *Penn Central*. That is why, in *PruneYard Shopping Center v. Robins*, 447 U.S. 74, 100 S. Ct. 2035, 64 L. Ed. 2d 741 (1980), we held that a law limiting a property owner's right to exclude certain speakers from an already publicly accessible shopping center did not take the owner's property. The owner retained the value of the use of the property as a shopping center largely unimpaired, so the regulation did not go "too far." *Id.*, at 83 (quoting *Pennsylvania Coal Co.*, 260 U.S., at 415). But once there is a taking, as in the case of a physical appropriation, any payment from the Government in connection with that action goes, at most, to the question of just compensation. See *Suitum v. Tahoe Regional Planning Agency*, 520 U.S. 725, 747–748, 117 S. Ct. 1659, 137 L. Ed. 2d 980 (1997) (SCALIA, J., concurring in part and concurring in judgment). That is not an issue here: The Hornes did not receive any net proceeds from Raisin Committee sales for the years at issue, because they had not set aside any reserve raisins in those years (and, in any event, there were no net proceeds in one of them).

C

The third question presented asks "Whether a governmental mandate to relinquish specific, identifiable property as a 'condition' on permission to engage in commerce effects a per se taking." The answer, at least in this case, is yes.

The Government contends that the reserve requirement is not a taking because raisin growers voluntarily choose to participate in the raisin market. According to the Government, if raisin growers don't like it, they can "plant different crops," or "sell their raisin-variety grapes as table grapes of for use in juice or wine." Brief for Respondent 32 (brackets and internal quotation marks omitted).

"Let them sell wine" is probably not much more comforting to the raisin growers than similar retorts have been to others throughout history. In any event, the Government is wrong as a matter of law. In *Loretto*, we rejected the argument that the New York law was not a taking because a landlord could avoid the requirement by ceasing to be a landlord. We held instead that "a landlord's ability to rent his property may not be conditioned on his forfeiting the right to compensation for a physical occupation." 458 U.S., at 439, n. 17. As the Court explained, the contrary argument "proves too much":

> "For example, it would allow the government to require a landlord to devote a substantial portion of his building to vending and washing machine, with all profits to be retained by the owners of these services and with no compensation for the deprivation of space. It would even allow the government to requisition a certain number of apartments as permanent government offices." *Ibid.*

As the Court concluded, property rights "cannot be so easily manipulated." *Ibid.*

The Government and dissent rely heavily on *Ruckelshaus v. Monsanto Co.*, 467 U.S. 986, 104 S. Ct. 2862, 81 L. Ed. 2d 815 (1984). There we held that the Environmental Protection Agency could require companies manufacturing pesticides, fungicides, and rodenticides to disclose health, safety, and environmental information about their products as a condition to receiving a permit to sell those products. While such information included trade secrets in which pesticide manufacturers had a property interest, those manufacturers were not subjected to a taking because they received a "valuable Government benefit" in exchange — a license to sell dangerous chemicals. *Id.*, at 1007; see *Nollan*, 483 U.S., at 834, n. 2, 107 S. Ct. 3141 (discussing *Monsanto*).

The taking here cannot reasonably be characterized as part of a similar voluntary exchange. In one of the years at issue here, the Government insisted that the Hornes turn over 47 percent of their raisin crop, in exchange for the "benefit" of being allowed to sell the remaining 53 percent. The next year, the toll was 30 percent. We have already rejected the idea that *Monsanto* may be extended by regarding basic and familiar uses of property as a "Government benefit" on the same order as a permit to sell hazardous chemicals. See *Nollan*, 483 U.S., at 834, n. 2, 107 3141 (distinguishing *Monsanto* on the ground that "the right to build on one's own property — even though its exercise can be subjected to legitimate permitting requirements — cannot remotely be described as a 'governmental benefit' "). Selling produce in interstate commerce, although certainly subject to reasonable government regulation, is similarly not a special governmental benefit that the Government may hold hostage, to be ransomed by the waiver of constitutional protection. Raisins are not dangerous pesticides; they are a healthy snack. A case about conditioning the sale of hazardous substances on disclosure of health, safety, and environmental information related to those hazards are hardly on point.

Leonard & Leonard v. Earle, 279 U.S. 392, 49 S. Ct. 372, 73 L. Ed. 754 (1929), is also readily distinguishable. In that case, the Court upheld a Maryland requirement that oyster packers remit ten percent of the marketable detached oyster shells or their monetary equivalent to the State for the privilege of harvesting the oysters. But the packers did "not deny the power of the State to declare their business as a privilege," and the power of the State to impose a "privilege tax" was "not questioned by counsel." *Id.*, at 396. The oysters, unlike raisins, were "feræ naturæ" that belonged to the State under state law, and "[n]o individual ha[d] any property rights in them other than such as the state may permit him to acquire." *Leonard v. Earle*, 155 Md. 252, 258, 141 A. 714, 716 (1928). The oyster packers did not simply seek to sell their property; they sought to appropriate the State's. Indeed, the Maryland Court of Appeals saw the issue as a question of "a reasonable and fair compensation" *from* the packers *to* "the state, as owner of the oysters." *Id.*, at 259, 141 A., at 717 (internal quotation marks omitted).

Raisins are not like oysters: they are private property — the fruit of the growers' labor — not "public things subject to the absolute control of the state," *id.*, at 258, 141 A., at 716. Any physical taking of them for public use must be accompanied by just compensation.

III

The Government correctly points out that a taking does not violate the Fifth Amendment unless there is no just compensation, and argues that the Hornes are free to seek compensation for any taking by bringing a damages action under the Tucker Act in the Court of Federal Claims. See 28 U.S.C. § 1491(a)(1); *Monsanto*, 467 U.S., at 1020, 104 S. Ct. 2862. But we held in *Horne I* that the Hornes may, in their capacity as handlers, raise a takings-based defense to the fine levied against them. We specifically rejected the contention that the Hornes were required to pay the fine and then seek compensation under the Tucker Act. See 569 U.S., at ___, 133, at 2063 ("We . . . conclude that the [Agricultural Marketing Agreement Act] withdraws Tucker Act jurisdiction over [the Hornes'] takings claim. [The Hornes](as handlers) have no alternative remedy, and their takings claim was not 'premature' when presented to the Ninth Circuit.").

As noted, the Hornes are both growers and handlers. Their situation is unusual in that, as handlers, they have the full economic interest in the raisins the government alleges should have been set aside for its account. They own the raisins they handle for other growers, having paid those growers for all their raisins (not just the free-tonnage amount, as is true with respect to most handlers). See *supra*, at ___; Tr. of Oral Arg. 3–4. The penalty assessed against them as handlers included the dollar equivalent of the raisins they refused to set aside — their raisins. 750 F. 3d, at 1135, n. 6; Brief for Petitioners 15. They may challenge the imposition of that fine, and do not have to pay it first and then resort to the Court of Federal Claims.

Finally, the Government briefly argues that if we conclude that the reserve requirement effects a taking, we should remand for the Court of Appeals to calculate "what compensation would have been due if petitioners had complied with the reserve requirement." Brief for Respondent 55. The Government contends that the calculation must consider what the value of the reserve raisins would have been without the price support program, as well as "other benefits . . . from the regulatory program, such as higher consumer demand for raisins spurred by enforcement of quality standards and promotional activities." *Id.*, at 55–56. Indeed, according to the Government, the Hornes would "likely" have a net gain under this theory. *Id.*, at 56.

The best defense may be a good offense, but the Government cites no support for its hypothetical-based approach, or its notion that general regulatory activity such as enforcement of quality standards can constitute just compensation for a specific physical taking. Instead, our cases have set forth a clear and administrable rule for just compensation: "The Court has repeatedly held that just compensation normally is to be measured by 'the market value of the property at the time of the taking.' " *United States v. 50 Acres of Land*, 469 U.S. 24, 29, 105 S. Ct. 451, 83 L. Ed. 2d 376 (1984) (quoting *Olsen v. United States*, 292 U.S. 246, 255, 54 S. Ct. 704, 78 L. Ed. 1236 (1934)).

Justice Breyer is concerned that applying this rule in this case will affect provisions concerning whether a condemning authority may deduct special benefits — such as new access to a waterway or highway, or filling in of swampland — from the amount of compensation it seeks to pay a landowner suffering a partial taking. *Post*, at ______ (opinion concurring in part and dissenting in part); see *Bauman v.*

Ross, 167 U.S. 548, 17 S. Ct. 966, 42 L. Ed. 270, (1897) (laying out the streets and subdivisions in the District of Columbia). He need not be. Cases of that sort can raise complicated questions involving the exercise of the eminent domain power, but they do not create a generally applicable exception to the usual compensation rule, based on asserted regulatory benefits of the sort at issue here. Nothing in the cases Justice Breyer labels "*Bauman* and its progeny," *post*, at ______, suggests otherwise, which may be why the Solicitor General does not cite them.

In any event, this litigation presents no occasion to consider the broader issues discussed by Justice Breyer. The Government has already calculated the amount of just compensation in this case, when it fined the Hornes the fair market value of the raisins: $483,843.53. 750 F.3d, at 1135, n.6. The Government cannot now disavow that valuation, see Reply Brief 21–23, and does not suggest that the marketing order affords the Hornes compensation in that amount. There is accordingly no need for a remand; the Hornes should simply be relieved of the obligation to pay the fine and associated civil penalty they were assessed when they resisted the Government's effort to take their raisins. This case, in litigation for more than a decade, has gone on long enough.

The judgment of the United States Court of Appeals for the Ninth Circuit is reversed.

It is so ordered.

LORETTO v. TELEPROMPTER MANHATTAN CATV CORP.

United States Supreme Court
458 U.S. 419 (1982)

Justice Marshall delivered the opinion of the Court.

This case presents the question whether a minor but permanent physical occupation of an owner's property authorized by government constitutes a "taking" or property for which just compensation is due under the Fifth and Fourteenth Amendments of the Constitution. New York law provides that a landlord must permit a cable television company to install its cable facilities upon his property. In this case, the cable installation occupied portions of appellant's roof and the side of her building. The New York Court of Appeals ruled that this appropriation does not amount to a taking. 53 N.Y.2d 124, 440 N.Y.S.2d 843, 423 N.E.2d 320 (1981). Because we conclude that such a physical occupation of property is a taking, we reverse.

Appellant Jean Loretto purchased a five-story apartment building located at 303 West 105th Street, New York City, in 1971. The previous owner had granted appellees Teleprompter Corp. and Teleprompter Manhattan CATV (collectively Teleprompter) permission to install a cable on the building and the exclusive privilege of furnishing cable television (CATV) services to the tenants. The New York Court of Appeals described the installations as follows:

"On June 1, 1970, TelePrompter installed a cable slightly less than one-half inch in diameter and of approximately 30 feet in length along the length of the building about 18 inches above the roof top, and directional of the roof. By June 8, 1970 the cable had been extended another 4 to 6 feet and cable had been run from the directional taps to the adjoining building at 305 West 105th Street."

Teleprompter also installed two large silver boxes along the roof cables. The cables are attached by screws or nails penetrating the masonry at approximately two-foot intervals, and other equipment is installed by bolts.

Initially, Teleprompter's roof cables did not service appellant's building. They were part of what could be described as a cable "highway" circumnavigating the city block, with service cables periodically dropped over the front or back of a building in which a tenant desired service. Crucial to such a network is the use of so-called "crossovers" — cable lines extending from one building to another in order to reach a new group of tenants. Two years after appellant purchased the building, Teleprompter connected a "noncrossover" line — i.e., one that provided CATV service to appellant's own tenants — by dropping a line to the first floor down the front of the appellant's building.

Prior to 1973, Teleprompter routinely obtained authorization for its installations from property owners along the cable's route, compensating the owners at the standard rate of 5% of the gross revenues that Teleprompter realized from the particular property. To facilitate tenant access to CATV, New York enacted § 828 of the Executive Law, which provides that a landlord may not "interfere with the installation of cable television facilities upon his property or premises," and may not demand payment from any tenant for permitting CATV, or demand payment from any CATV company "in excess of any amount which the [State Commission on Cable Television] shall, by regulation, determine to be reasonable." The landlord may, however, require the CATV company or the tenant to bear the cost of installation and to indemnify for any damage caused by the installation. Pursuant to § 828(1)(b), the State Commission has ruled that a one-time $1 payment is the normal fee to which a landlord is entitled. The Commission ruled that this nominal fee, which the Commission concluded was equivalent to what the landlord would receive if the property were condemned pursuant to New York's Transportation Corporations Law, satisfied constitutional requirements "in the absence of a special showing of greater damages attributable to the taking."

Appellant did not discover the existence of the cable until after she had purchased the building. She brought a class action against Teleprompter in 1976 on behalf of all owners of real property in the State on which Teleprompter has placed CATV components, alleging that Teleprompter's installation was a trespass and, insofar as it relied on § 828, a taking without just compensation. She requested damages and injunctive relief. * * *

The Court of Appeals determined that § 828 serves the legitimate public purpose of "rapid development of and maximum penetration by a means of communication which has important educational and community aspects," 423 N.E.2d, at 329, and thus is within the State's police power. We have no reason to question that determination, however, whether an otherwise valid regulation so frustrates property rights that compensation must be paid.

In *Penn Central Transportation Co. v. New York City*, 438 U.S. 104 (1978), the Court surveyed some of the general principles governing the Takings Clause. The

Court noted that no "set formula" existed to determine, in all cases, whether compensation is constitutionally due for a government restriction of property. Ordinarily, the Court must engage in "essentially ad hoc, factual inquiries." *Id.*, at 124. But the inquiry is not standardless. The economic impact of the regulation, especially the degree of interference with investment-backed expectations, is of particular significance. "So, too, is the character of the governmental action. A 'taking' may more readily be found when the interference with property can be characterized as a physical invasion by government, than when interference arises from some public program adjusting the benefits and burdens of economic life to promote the common good."

As *Penn Central* affirms, the Court has often upheld substantial regulation of an owner's use of his own property where deemed necessary to promote the public interest. At the same time, we have long considered a physical intrusion by government to be a property restriction of an unusually serious character for purposes of the Taking Clause. Our cases further establish that when the physical intrusion reaches the extreme form of a permanent physical occupation, a taking has occurred. In such a case, "the character of the government action" not only is an important factor in resolving whether the action works a taking but is determinative.

When faced with a constitutional challenge to a physical occupation of real property, this Court has invariably found a taking. As early as 1871, in *Pumpelly v. Green Bay Company*, 13 Wall. (80 U.S.) 166, 20 L. Ed. 557 (1871), this Court held that the defendant's construction, pursuant to state authority, of a dam which permanently flooded plaintiff's property constituted a taking. A unanimous Court stated, without qualification, that "where real estate is actually invaded by superinduced additions of water, earth, sand, or other material, or by having any artificial placed on it, so as to effectually destroy or impair its usefulness, it is a taking, within the meaning of the Constitution."

Since these early cases, this Court has consistently distinguished between flooding cases involving a permanent physical occupation and cases involving a more temporary invasion, or government action outside the owner's property that causes consequential damages within. A taking has always been found only in the former situation.

In *St. Louis v. Western Union Telegraph Co.*, 148 U.S. 92 (1893), the Court applied the principles enunciated in *Pumpelly* to a situation closely analogous to the one presented today. In that case, the Court held that the city of St. Louis could exact reasonable compensation for a telegraph company's placement of telegraph poles on the city's public streets. The Court reasoned:

> The use which the [company] makes of the streets is an exclusive and permanent one, and not one temporary, shifting and in common with the general public. The ordinary traveler, whether on foot or in a vehicle, passes to and fro along the streets, and his use and occupation thereof are temporary and shifting. The space he occupies one moment he abandons the next to be occupied by any other traveler . . . . *But the use made by the telegraph company is, in respect to so much of the space as it occupies with its poles, permanent and exclusive.* It as effectually and permanently

dispossesses the general public as if it had destroyed that amount of ground.

. . . .

More recent cases confirm the distinction between a permanent physical occupation, a physical invasion short of an occupation, and a regulation that merely restricts the use of property. In *United States v. Causby*, 328 U.S. 256 (1946), the Court ruled that frequent flights immediately above a landowner's property constituted a taking.

The Court concluded that the damages to the respondents "were not merely consequential. They were the product of a direct invasion of respondents' domain." *Id.*, at 265–266. See also *Griggs v. Allegheny County*, 369 U.S. 84 (1962).

Although this Court's most recent cases have not addressed the precise issue before us, they have emphasized that physical invasion cases are special and have not repudiated the rule that any permanent physical occupation is a taking. The cases state or imply that a physical invasion is subject to a balancing process, but they do not suggest that a permanent physical occupation would ever be exempt from the Takings Clause.

Penn Central Transportation Co. v. New York City, as noted above, contains one of the most complete discussions of the Takings Clause. The Court explained that resolving whether public action works a taking is ordinarily an ad hoc inquiry in which several factors are particularly significant — the economic impact of the regulation, the extent to which it interferes with investment-backed expectations, and the character of the government action. The opinion does not repudiate the rule that a permanent physical occupation is a government action of such a unique character that it is a taking without regard to other factors that a court might ordinarily assume.

In *Kaiser Aetna v. United States*, 444 U.S. 164 (1979), the Court held that the government's imposition of a navigational servitude requiring public access to a pong was a taking where the land owner had reasonably relied on government consent in connecting the pond to navigable water. The Court emphasized that the servitude took the land owner's right to exclude, "one of the most essential sticks in the bundle of rights that are commonly characterized as property."

Although the easement of passage, not being a permanent occupation of land, was not considered a taking per se, *Kaiser Aetna* reemphasizes that a physical invasion is a government intrusion of an unusually serious character.

In short, when the "character of the governmental action," *Penn Central*, 438 U.S. at 124, is a permanent physical occupation of property, our cases uniformly have found a taking to the extent of the occupation, without regard to whether the action achieves an important public benefit or has only minimal economic impact on the owner.

The historical rule that a permanent physical occupation of another's property is a taking has more than tradition to commend it. Such an appropriation is perhaps the most serious form of invasion of an owner's property interests. To borrow a metaphor, cf. *Andrus v. Allard*, 444 U.S., at 65–66, 100, at 326–327, the government does not simply take a single "strand" from the "bundle" of property rights: it chops through the bundle, taking a slice of every strand.

Property rights in a physical thing have been described as the rights "to possess, use and dispose of it." *United States v. General Motors Corp.*, 323 U.S. 373, 378 (1945). To the extent that the government permanently occupies physical property, it effectively destroys each of these rights. First, the owner has no right to possess the occupied space himself, and also has no power to exclude the occupier from possession and use of the space. The power to exclude has traditionally been considered one of the most treasured strands in an owner's bundle of property rights. See *Kaiser Aetna*, 444 U.S., at 179–180; see also Restatement of Property § 7 (1936). Second, the permanent physical occupation of property forever denies the owner any power to control the use of the property; he not only cannot exclude others, but can make no non-possessory use of the property. Although deprivation of the right to use and obtain a profit from property is not, in every case, independently sufficient to establish a taking, see *Andrus v. Allard*, 444 U.S., at 66, it is clearly relevant. Finally, even though the owner may retain the bare legal right to dispose of the occupied space by a transfer of sale, the permanent occupation of that space by a stranger will ordinarily empty the right of any value, since the purchaser will also be unable to make any use of the property.

Moreover, an owner suffers a special kind of injury when a stranger directly invades and occupies the owner's property. As section II-A, *supra*, indicates, property law has long protected an owner's expectation that he will be relatively undisturbed at least in the possession of his property. To require, as well, that the owner permit another to exercise complete dominion literally adds insult to injury. See Michelman, Property, Utility, and Fairness: Comments on the Ethical Foundation of "Just Compensation" Law, 80 Harv. L. Rev. 1165, 1228, and n. 110 (1967). Furthermore, such an occupation is qualitatively more severe than a regulation of the *use* of property, even if a regulation that imposes affirmative duties on the owner, since the owner may have no control over the timing, extent, or nature of the invasion.

Finally, whether a permanent physical occupation has occurred presents relatively few problems of proof. The placement of a fixed structure on land or real property is an obvious fact that will rarely be subject to dispute. Once the fact of occupation is shown, of course, a court should consider the *extent* of the occupation as one relevant factor in determining the compensation due. For that reason, moreover, there is less need to consider the extent of the occupation in determining whether there is a taking in the first instance.

Teleprompter's cable installation on appellant's building constitutes a taking under the traditional test. The installation involved a direct physical attachment of plates, boxes, wires, bolts and screws to the building, completely occupying space immediately above and upon the roof and along the building's exterior wall.

In light of our analysis, we find no constitutional difference between a crossover and a noncrossover installation. The portions of the installation necessary for both crossovers and noncrossovers permanently appropriate appellant's property. Accordingly, each type of installation is a taking.

Appellees raise a series of objections to application of the traditional rule here. Teleprompter notes that the law applies only to buildings used as rental property, and draws the conclusion that the law is simply a permissible regulation of the use of real property. We fail to see, however, why a physical occupation of one type of property but not another type is any less a physical occupation. Insofar as Teleprompter means to suggest that this is not a permanent physical invasion, we must differ. So long as the property remains residential and a CATV company wishes to retain the installation, the landlord must permit it.[7]

Teleprompter also asserts the related argument that the State has effectively granted a tenant the property right to have a CATV installation placed on the roof of his building, as an appurtenance to the tenant's leasehold. The short answer is that § 828(1)(a) does not purport to give the *tenant* any enforceable property rights with respect to CATV installation, and the lower courts did not rest their decisions on this ground. Of course, Teleprompter, not appellant's tenants, actually owns the installation. Moreover, the government does not have unlimited power to redefine property rights. See *Webb's Fabulous Pharmacies, Inc. v. Beckwith*, 449 U.S. 155, 164, (1980) ("a State, by *ipse dixit*, may not transform private property into public property without compensation").

Finally, we do not agree with appellees that application of the physical occupation rule will have dire consequences for the government's power to adjust landlord-tenant relationships. This Court has consistently affirmed that States have broad power to regulate housing conditions in general and the landlord-tenant relationship in particular without paying compensation for all economic injuries that such regulation entails. In none of these cases, however, did the government authorize the permanent occupation of the landlord's property by a third party. Consequently, our holding today in no way alters the analysis governing the State's power to require landlords to comply with building codes and provide utility connections, mailboxes, smoke detectors, fire extinguishers, and the like in the common area of a building. So long as these regulations do not require the landlord to suffer the physical occupation of a portion of his building by a third party, they will be analyzed to non-possessory governmental activity. See *Penn Central*.[8]

Our holding today is very narrow. We affirm the traditional rule that a permanent

---

[7] [17] It is true that the landlord could avoid the requirements of § 828 by ceasing to rent the building to tenants. But a landlord's ability to rent his property may not be conditioned on his forfeiting the right to compensation for a physical occupation. Teleprompter's broad "use-dependency" argument proves too much. For example, it would allow the government to require a landlord to devote a substantial portion of his building to vending and washing machines, with all profits to be retained by the owners of these services and with no compensation for the deprivation of space. It would even allow the government to requisition a certain number of apartments as permanent government offices. The right of a property owner to exclude a stranger's physical occupation of his land cannot be so easily manipulated.

[8] [19] If § 828 required landlords to provide cable installation if a tenant so desires, the statute might present a different question from the question before us, since the landlord would own the installation. Ownership would give the landlord rights to the placement, manner, use, and possibly the disposition of the installation. The fact of ownership is, contrary to the dissent, not simply "incidental,"; it would give a landlord (rather than a CATV company) full authority over the installation except only as government specifically limited that authority. The *landlord* would decide how to comply with applicable government regulations concerning CATV and therefore could minimize the physical, aesthetic, and other effects of the installation. Moreover, if the landlord wished to repair, demolish, or construct in the area of the

physical occupation of property is a taking. In such a case, the property owner entertains an historically-rooted expectation of compensation, and the character of the invasion is qualitatively more intrusive than perhaps any other category of property regulation. We do not, however, question the equally substantial authority upholding a State's broad power to impose appropriate restrictions upon an owner's *use* of his property.

Furthermore, our conclusion that § 828 works a taking of a portion of appellant's property does not presuppose that the fee which many landlords have obtained from Teleprompter prior to the law's enactment is a proper measure of the value of the property taken. The issue of the amount of compensation that is due, on which we express no opinion, is a matter for the state courts to consider on remand.

The judgment of the New York Court of Appeals is reversed and the case is remanded for further proceedings not inconsistent with this opinion.

It is so ordered.

JUSTICE BLACKMUN, with whom JUSTICE BRENNAN and JUSTICE WHITE join, dissenting.

If the Court's decisions construing the Takings Clause state anything clearly, it is that "[t]here is no set formula to determine where regulation ends and takings begins." *Goldblatt v. Town of Hempstead*, 369 U.S. 590, 594 (1962).

In a curiously anachronistic decision, the Court today acknowledges its historical disavowal of set formulae in almost the same breath as it constructs a rigid per se takings rule: "a permanent physical occupation authorized by the government is a taking without regard to the public interests that it may serve." To sustain its rule against our recent precedents, the Court erects a strained and untenable distinction between "temporary physical invasions," whose constitutionality concededly "is subject to a balancing process," and "permanent physical occupations," which are "taking[s] without regard to other factors that a court might ordinarily examine."

In my view, the Court's approach "reduces the constitutional issue to a formalistic quibble" over whether property has been "permanently occupied" or "temporarily invaded." Sax, Takings and the Police Power, 74 Yale L.J. 36, 37 (1964). The Court's application of its formula to the facts of this case vividly illustrates that its approach is potentially dangerous as well as misguided. Despite its concession that "States have broad power to regulate . . . the landlord-tenant relationship . . . without paying compensation for all economic injuries that such regulation entails," the Court uses its rule to undercut a carefully considered legislative judgment concerning landlord-tenant relationships. I therefore respectfully dissent.

---

building where the installation is located, he need not incur the burden of obtaining the CATV company's cooperation in moving the cable.

In this case, by contrast, appellant suffered injury that might have been obviated if she had owned the cable and could exercise control over its installation. The drilling and stapling that accompanied installation apparently caused physical damage to appellant's building. Appellant, who resides in her building, further testified that the cable installation is "ugly." Although § 828 provides that a landlord may require "reasonable" conditions that are "necessary" to protect the appearance of the premises and may seek indemnity for damage, these provisions are somewhat limited. Even if the provisions are effective, the inconvenience to the landlord of initiating the repairs remain a cognizable burden.

NOTES: THE REACH OF THE "PER SE" PHYSICAL TAKINGS RULE

1. Physical invasions sufficient to support an action for inverse condemnation have been found in a variety of circumstances, some permanent, like *Loretto*, and some temporary. *See, e.g.*, *Kaiser Aetna v. United States*, 444 U.S. 164 (1979), cited in *Loretto* as an example of a temporary invasion, finding a taking where the owners of a private lagoon made it accessible to navigable waters and were then forced to allow the public to use the lagoon. In the pre-*Loretto* case of *United States v. Causby*, 328 U.S. 256 (1946), frequent overflights of land adjoining a municipal airport leased to the federal government had rendered plaintiff's land unusable as a chicken farm. The Court noted:

> If, by reason of the frequency and altitude of the flights, respondents could not use this land for any purpose, their lose would be complete. It would be as complete as if the United States had entered upon the surface of the land and taken exclusive possession of it. * * * We would not doubt that, if the United States erected an elevated railway over respondents' land at the precise altitude where its planes now fly, there would be a partial taking, even though none of the supports of the structure rested on the land. The reason is that there would be an intrusion so immediate and direct as to subtract from the owner's full enjoyment of the property and to limit his exploitation of it.

Id. at 261, 264–65.

In *McCarran International Airport v. Sisolak*, 137 P.3d 1110 (Nev. 2006), the Nevada supreme court found that an ordinance imposing a height restriction was a permanent avigation easement constituting a taking under *Loretto*. *See also Judlo, Inc. v. Vons Cos.*, 211 Cal. App. 3d 1020 (1989) (holding that an injunction issued pursuant to a state constitutional clause protecting freedom of speech, which required a store owner to permit a newspaper publisher to place a news rack in front of the store, was a permanent physical occupation amounting to a taking).

2. How does the Court deal with the fact that the Hornes are entitled to some of the value of the raisins sold by the government? Does this mitigate the taking or affect just compensation?

3. Under the Court's analysis in *Horne* and *Loretto*, would the outcome in *Horne* be different if the government confiscated, say, a bushel of raisins? Ten raisins? One raisin? If the government regularly returned to the Hornes the equivalent, or more, at the value of the raisins confiscated?

4. Note the Court in *Horne* opines that under this and other former rulings, "basic and familiar uses of property" are not privileges conferred by government, but property rights. Such as? How far can government regulate these rights? *See* Part B *infra*.

5. The Hawai'i Supreme Court has declared that native Hawaiians, who make up 20% of the state's population, may enter any "undeveloped" private property to undertake traditional and customary subsistence, cultural, and religious activities. *Pele Defense Fund v. Paty*, 837 P.2d 1247 (Haw. 1992). The court then held in *Public*

Access Shoreline Hawai'i v. Hawai'i County Planning Commission, 903 P.2d 1246 (Haw. 1995) that such "traditional and customary" rights-here access over a hotel development site — may be exercised on developed land as well, and that "[W]estern concepts" of property rights "may not be applicable in Hawai'i."[9] Is this type of physical invasion that the U.S. Supreme Court — and the Fifth Amendment — prohibit without compensation? Who defines property?

6. John Costonis suggests that "physical invasions be characterized as either location-contingent or use-dependent." Constonis, *Presumptive and Per Se Takings: A Decisional Model for the Taking Issue*, 58 N.Y.U. L. Rev 465, 492 (1983). Location-contingent invasions are those that burden land because of its location, while use-dependent invasions are imposed because of the way the land is used. The former are takings; the latter are not. Which was *Loretto*? *Nollan*? Recall that *Nollan* involved the imposition of a lateral access easement on the beachfront side of a lot to be developed for residential purposes. According to Justice Scalia the easement was location-contingent; according to Justice Brennan, it was use-dependent. What explains their different conclusions?

[C.] LAND DEVELOPMENT AND THE POLICE POWER

There is no more basic governmental power than that of "police," the power of government to regulate on behalf of the health, welfare, and safety of the community. As Justice Lemuel Shaw of the Massachusetts Supreme Judicial Court noted in 1851:

> [I]t is a well-settled principle, growing out of the nature of well-ordered civil society, that every holder of property, however absolute and unqualified may be his title, holds under the implied liability that his use of it may be so regulated that it shall not be injurious to the equal enjoyment of others having an equal right to the enjoyment of their property, nor injurious to the right of the community.

Commonwealth v. Alger, 61 Mass. 84–85 (1851).

A little more than a half century later, during the Progressive Era, former President Theodore Roosevelt made the same point when he proclaimed, "[E]very man holds his property subject to the general right of the community to regulate its use to whatever degree the public welfare may require it." Roosevelt, *The New Nationalism*, Aug. 31, 1910, *in* Social Justice and Popular Rule (1926).

While the wide range and scope of the police power was always conceded, its boundaries were sometimes hard to define, particularly when the police power collided with constitutionally protected property rights. At least since the 1868 ratification of the Fourteenth Amendment, which forbids states from depriving citizens of property without due process of law, one of the primary functions of the

[9] In *State v. Hanapi*, 970 P.2d 485 (Haw. 1998), the Hawai'i Supreme Court clarified its PASH decision by holding that a residential lot with a house on it was always "developed" and so not subject to native Hawaiian traditional and customary rights. In *Hanapi*, the lot was several acres with only one house, raising a presumption that the Court will permit such exercise only on land which is substantially open space.

United States Supreme Court has been to define the acceptable boundaries of the police power when it is used to regulate the use of property.

During the nation's first century, an abundance of land combined with a largely agrarian economy and a strong belief in property rights restricted most land use disputes to the realm of private nuisance law. Legislative land use controls adopted pursuant to the police power appeared comparatively late in American history, although their roots date back to the colonial period. The bulk of these controls accompanied the rapid urbanization that occurred after the Civil War. Restrictions initially took the form of prohibitions of specific uses, like operating a slaughter house or a livery stable. In the 20th century, however, efforts to regulate the use of land became more systematic, culminating with the system we know as zoning.

Regulations under the police power for the benefit of the general health, safety, and welfare of the public invariably clash with the interests of private property owners who find themselves subject to regulations and restrictions that they may not support. Throughout the 20th century and into the 21st, the United States Supreme Court has been called upon repeatedly to define the boundary between acceptable and unacceptable regulation. This chapter traces that story through an examination of several of the most important Supreme Court cases dealing with issues of constitutionality and the police power.

For more on the early history of land use control in the United States, see WOLF, THE ZONING OF AMERICA (2008); Hart, *Colonial Land Use Law and Its Significance for Modern Takings Doctrine*, 109 HARV. L. REV. 1252 (1996); Hylton, *Prelude to* Euclid*: The United States Supreme Court and the Constitutionality of Land Use Regulation, 1900–1920*, 3 WASH. U. J.L. & POL'Y 1 (2000); F. BOSSELMAN, D. CALLIES & J. BANTA, THE TAKING ISSUE: AN ANALYSIS OF THE CONSTITUTIONAL LIMITS OF LAND USE CONTROL Chs. 5 & 6 (1973); R. BABCOCK, THE ZONING GAME Ch. 1 (1967).

[1.] Foundation: Police Power and Land Use

The notion that the exercise of regulatory power by a governmental agency can constitute a "taking" of property is a relatively new phenomenon in the law of zoning and land use. Before the 20th century, courts universally found that a taking occurred only when property was actually physically taken for the use of the state. The case that follows is generally viewed as the origin of the regulatory taking doctrine — the principle that a police power regulation can, if excessive, amount to a Fifth Amendment taking.

PENNSYLVANIA COAL CO. v. MAHON

United States Supreme Court
260 U.S. 393 (1922)

MR. JUSTICE HOLMES delivered the opinion of the Court.

This is a bill in equity brought by the defendants in error to prevent the Pennsylvania Coal Company from mining under their property in such way as to remove the supports and cause a subsidence of the surface and of their house. The bill sets out a deed executed by the Coal Company in 1878, under which the plaintiffs claim. The deed conveys the surface but in express terms reserves the right to remove all the coal under the same and the grantee takes the premises with the risk and waives all claim for damages that may arise from mining out the coal. But the plaintiffs say that whatever may have been the Coal Company's rights, they were taken away by an Act of Pennsylvania, approved May 27, 1921 (P.L. 1198), commonly known there as the Kohler Act. The Court of Common Pleas found that if not restrained the defendant would cause the damage to prevent which the bill was brought but denied an injunction, holding that the statute if applied to this case would be unconstitutional. On appeal the Supreme Court of the State agreed that the defendant had contract and property rights protected by the Constitution of the United States, but held that the statute was a legitimate exercise of the police power and directed a decree for the plaintiffs. A writ of error was granted bringing the case to this Court.

The statute forbids the mining of anthracite coal in such way as to cause the subsidence of, among other things, any structure used as a human habitation, with certain exceptions, including among them land where the surface is owned by the owner of the underlying coal and is distant more than one hundred and fifty feet from any improved property belonging to any other person. As applied to this case the statute is admitted to destroy previously existing rights of property and contract. The question is whether the police power can be stretched so far.

Government hardly could go on if to some extent values incident to property could not be diminished without paying for every such change in the general law. As long recognized some values are enjoyed under an implied limitation and must yield to the police power. But obviously the implied limitation must have its limits or the contract and due process clauses are gone. One fact for consideration in determining such limits is the extent of the diminution. When it reaches a certain magnitude, in most if not in all cases there must be an exercise of eminent domain and compensation to sustain the act. So the question depends upon the particular facts. The greatest weight is given to the judgment of the legislature but it always is open to interested parties to contend that the legislature has gone beyond its constitutional power.

This is the case of a single private house. No doubt there is a public interest even in this, as there is in every purchase and sale and in all that happens within the commonwealth. Some existing rights may be modified even in such a case. *Rideout v. Knox*, 19 N.E. 390 (Mass.). But usually in ordinary private affairs the public interest does not warrant much of this kind of interference. A source of damage to such a house is not a public nuisance even if similar damage is inflicted on others in different places. The damage is not common or public. *Wesson v. Washburn Iron Co.*, 13 Allen (Mass.) 96, 103. The extent of the public interest is shown by the statute to be limited, since the statute ordinarily does not apply to land when the surface is owned by the owner of the coal. Furthermore, it is not justified as a protection of personal safety. That could be provided for by notice. Indeed the very foundation of this bill is that the defendant gave timely notice of its intent to mine under the house. On the other hand the extent of the taking is great. It purports to abolish what is recognized in Pennsylvania as an estate in land, a very valuable estate, and what is declared by the Court below to be a contract hitherto binding the plaintiffs.

It is our opinion that the act cannot be sustained as an exercise of the police power, so far as it affects the mining of coal under streets or cities in places where the right to mine such coal has been reserved. What makes the right to mine coal valuable is that it can be exercised with profit. To make it commercially impracticable to mine certain coal has very nearly the same effect for constitutional purposes as appropriating or destroying it. Thus we think that we are warranted in assuming that the statute does.

It is true that in *Plymouth Coal Co. v. Pennsylvania*, 232 U.S. 531, it was held competent for the legislature to require a pillar of coal to be left along the line of adjoining property, that with the pillar on the other side of the line would be a barrier sufficient for the safety of the employees of either mine in case the other should be abandoned and allowed to fill with water. But that was a requirement for the safety of employees invited into the mine, and secured an average reciprocity of advantage that has been recognized as a justification of various laws.

The rights of the public in a street purchased or laid out by eminent domain are those that it has paid for. If in any case its representatives have been so short sighted as to acquire only surface rights without the right of support we see no more authority for supplying the latter without compensation than there was for taking the right of way in the first place and refusing to pay for it because the public wanted it very much. The protection of private property in the Fifth Amendment presupposes that it is wanted for public use, but provides that it shall not be taken for such use without compensation. A similar assumption is made in the decisions upon the Fourteenth Amendment. When this seemingly absolute protection is found to be qualified by the police power, the natural tendency of human nature is to extend the qualification more and more until at last private property disappears. But that cannot be accomplished in this way under the Constitution of the United States.

The general rule at least is that while property may be regulated to a certain extent, if regulation goes too far it will be recognized as a taking.

We are in danger of forgetting that a strong public desire to improve the public condition is not enough to warrant achieving the desire by a shorter cut than the constitutional way of paying for the change. As we already have said this is a question of degree, and therefore cannot be disposed of by general propositions. But we regard this as going beyond any of the cases decided by this Court.

We assume, of course, that the statute was passed upon the conviction that an exigency existed that would warrant it, and we assume that an exigency exists that would warrant the exercise of eminent domain. But the question at bottom is upon whom the loss of the changes desired should fall. So far as private persons or communities have seen fit to take the risk of acquiring only surface rights, we cannot see that the fact that their risk has become a danger warrants the giving to them greater rights than they bought.

Decree reversed.

MR. JUSTICE BRANDEIS, dissenting.

Every restriction upon the use of property imposed in the exercise of the police power deprives the owner of some right theretofore enjoyed, and is, in that sense, an abridgment by the State of rights in property without making compensation. But restriction imposed to protect the public health, safety or morals from dangers threatened is not a taking. The restriction here in question is merely the prohibition of a noxious use. The property so restricted remains in the possession of its owner. The State does not appropriate it or make any use of it. The State merely prevents the owner from making a use which interferes with paramount rights of the public. Whenever the use prohibited ceases to be noxious, — as it may because of further change in local or social conditions, — the restriction will have to be removed and the owner will again be free to enjoy his property as heretofore.

The restriction upon the use of this property can not, of course, be lawfully imposed, unless its purpose is to protect the public. But the purpose of a restriction does not cease to be public, because incidentally some private persons may thereby receive gratuitously valuable special benefits. Thus, owners of low buildings may obtain, through statutory restrictions upon the height of neighboring structures, benefits equivalent to an easement of light and air. *Welch v. Swasey*, 214 U.S. 91. Compare *Lindsley v. Natural Carbonic Gas Co.*, 220 U.S. 61; *Walls v. Midland Carbon Co.*, 254 U.S. 300. Furthermore, a restriction, though imposed for a public purpose, will not be lawful, unless the restriction is an appropriate means to the public end. But to keep coal in place is surely an appropriate means of preventing subsidence of the surface; and ordinarily it is the only available means. Restriction upon use does not become inappropriate as a means, merely because it deprives the owner of the only use to which the property can then be profitably put. The liquor and the oleomargarine cases settled that. *Mugler v. Kansas*, 123 U.S. 623, 668, 669; *Powell v. Pennsylvania*, 127 U.S. 678, 682. See also *Hadacheck v. Los Angeles*, 239 U.S. 394; *Pierce Oil Corporation v. City of Hope*, 248 U.S. 498. Nor is a restriction imposed through exercise of the police power inappropriate as a means, merely because the same end might be effected through exercise of the power of eminent domain, or otherwise at public expense. Every restriction upon the height of buildings might be secured through acquiring by eminent domain the right of each owner to build above the limiting height; but it is settled that the State need not resort to that power. Compare *Laurel Hill Cemetery v. San Francisco*, 216 U.S. 358; *Missouri Pacific Ry. Co. v. Omaha*, 235 U.S. 121. If by mining anthracite coal the owner would necessarily unloose poisonous gasses, I suppose no one would doubt the power of the State to prevent the mining, without buying his coal fields. And why may not the State, likewise, without paying compensation, prohibit one from digging so deep or excavating so near the surface, as to expose the community to like dangers? In the latter case, as in the former, carrying on the business would be a public nuisance.

It is said that one fact for consideration in determining whether the limits of the police power have been exceeded is the extent of the resulting diminution in value; and that here the restriction destroys existing rights of property and contract. But values are relative. If we are to consider the value of the coal kept in place by the restriction, we should compare it with the value of all other parts of the land. That is, with the value not of the coal alone, but with the value of the whole property. The rights of an owner as against the public are not increased by dividing the interests in his property into surface and subsoil. The sum of the rights in the parts can not be greater than the rights in the whole. The estate of an owner in land is grandiloquently described as extending ab orco usque ad coelum. But I suppose no one would contend that by selling his interest above one hundred feet from the surface he could prevent the State from limiting, by the police power, the height of structures in a city. And why should a sale of underground rights bar the State's power? For aught that appears the value of the coal kept in place by the restriction may be negligible as compared with the value of the whole property, or even as compared with that part of it which is represented by the coal remaining in place and which may be extracted despite the statute.

NOTES AND QUESTIONS

1. For decades it was the position of some courts and commentators that the "takings" language of Justice Holmes in *Pennsylvania Coal* was merely symbolic, at least in the sense that the remedy for a regulatory taking was not the mandated just compensation of the Fifth Amendment, but invalidation of the ordinance. In 1987, the Court rejected that view. *See First English Evangelical Lutheran Church v. County of Los Angeles*, 482 U.S. 304 (1987).

2. There is much debate over the historical underpinnings of *Pennsylvania Coal*. *See, e.g.*, James W. Ely, Jr., *The Fuller Court and Takings Jurisprudence*, 1961 J. SUP. CT. HISTORY, VOL. II 120 (1996); Robert Brauneis, *The Foundation of Our "Regulatory Takings" Jurisprudence: The Myth and Meaning of Justice Holmes's Opinion in Pennsylvania Coal Co. v. Mahon*, 106 YALE L.J. 613 (1996).

3. "*England's Impression of the American Regulatory Taking*. The notion that a regulation could constitute a 'taking' was so odd to the English law lords that they assumed that the sole dissenting opinion by Justice Brandeis in *Pennsylvania Coal* represented the opinion of the country, on the grounds that no right-thinking person could hold otherwise [. . . .]"

4. In his *Mahon* dissent, Brandeis argued that a "restriction imposed to protect the public health, safety or morals from dangers threatened is not a taking" and that the diminution in value should be measured against the value of the whole property and not just the value of the coal retained by the company. *Belfast Corp. v. O.D. Cars, Ltd.*, House of Lords [1960] 1 All. E.R. 65. *See also* ALTERMAN (ED.), TAKINGS INTERNATIONAL, A COMPARATIVE PERSPECTIVE ON LAND USE REGULATIONS AND COMPENSATION RIGHTS (2010); Mandelker, et al., *Symposium on Regulatory Takings in Land-Use Law: A Comparative Perspective on Compensation Rights*, 5 WASH. U. GLOBAL STUD. L. REV. 469 (2006); Kotaka & Callies (eds.) TAKING LAND: COMPULSORY PURCHASE AND REGULATION IN ASIAN-PACIFIC COUNTRIES (2002).

5. For a recent overview of takings law generally, see J. MARTINEZ, GOVERNMENT TAKINGS (2006). For a recent article on contemporary trends in taking law, see David Callies, *Through a Glass Clearly: Predicting the Future in Land Use Takings Law*, 34 Washburn L.J. 43 (2015).

VILLAGE OF EUCLID, OHIO v. AMBLER REALTY CO

United States Supreme Court

272 U.S. 365 (1926)

MR. JUSTICE SUTHERLAND delivered the opinion of the Court.

The village of Euclid is an Ohio municipal corporation. It adjoins and practically is a suburb of the city of Cleveland. Its estimated population is between 5,000 and 10,000, and its area from 12 to 14 square miles, the greater part of which is farm lands or unimproved acreage. It lies, roughly, in the form of a parallelogram measuring approximately three and one half miles each way. East and west it is traversed by three principal highways: Euclid Avenue, through the southerly border, St. Clair Avenue, through the central portion, and Lake Shore boulevard, through the northerly border, in close proximity to the shore of Lake Erie. The Nickel Plate Railroad lies from 1,500 to 1,800 feet north of Euclid Avenue, and the Lake Shore Railroad 1,600 feet farther to the north. The three highways and the two railroads are substantially parallel.

Appellee is the owner of a tract of land containing 68 acres, situated in the westerly end of the village, abutting on Euclid Avenue to the south and the Nickel Plate Railroad to the north. Adjoining this tract, both on the east and on the west, there have been laid out restricted residential plats upon which residences have been erected.

On November 13, 1922, an ordinance was adopted by the village council, establishing a comprehensive zoning plan.

The entire area of the village is divided by the ordinance into six classes of use districts, denominated U-1 to U-6, inclusive; three classes of height districts, denominated H-1 to H-3, inclusive; and four classes of area districts, denominated A-1 to A-4, inclusive. The use districts are classified in respect of the buildings which may be erected within their respective limits, as follows: U-1 is restricted to single family dwellings, public parks, water towers and reservoirs, suburban and interurban electric railway passenger stations and rights of way, and farming, noncommercial greenhouse nurseries, and truck gardening; U-2 is extended to include two-family dwellings; U-3 is further extended to include apartment houses, hotels, churches, schools, public libraries, museums, private clubs, community center buildings, hospitals, sanitariums, public playgrounds, and recreation buildings, and a city hall and courthouse; U-4 is further extended to include banks, offices, studios, telephone exchanges, fire and police stations, restaurants, theaters and moving picture shows, retail stores and shops, sales offices, sample rooms, wholesale stores for hardware, drugs, and groceries, stations for gasoline and oil (not exceeding 1,000 gallons storage) and for ice delivery, skating rinks and dance halls, electric substations, job and newspaper printing, public garages for motor vehicles, stables and wagon sheds (not exceeding five horses, wagons or motor trucks), and distributing stations for central store and commercial enterprises; U-5 is further extended to include billboards and advertising signs (if permitted), warehouses, ice and ice cream manufacturing and cold storage plants, bottling works, milk bottling and central distribution stations, laundries, carpet cleaning, dry cleaning, and dyeing establishments, blacksmith, horseshoeing, wagon and motor vehicle repair shops, freight stations, street car barns, stables and wagon sheds (for more than five horses, wagons or motor trucks), and wholesale produce markets and salesrooms; U-6 is further extended to include plants for sewage disposal and for producing gas, garbage and refuse incineration, scrap iron, junk, scrap paper, and rag storage, aviation fields, cemeteries, crematories, penal and correctional institutions, insane and feeble-minded institutions, storage of oil and gasoline (not to exceed 25,000 gallons), and manufacturing and industrial operations of any kind other than, and any public utility not included in, a class U-1, U-2, U-3, U-4, or U-5 use. There is a seventh class of uses which is prohibited altogether.

Class U-1 is the only district in which buildings are restricted to those enumerated. In the other classes the uses are cumulative, that is to say, uses in class U-2 include those enumerated in the preceding class U-1; class U-3 includes uses enumerated in the preceding classes, U-2 and U-1; and so on. In addition to the enumerated uses, the ordinance provides for accessory uses; that is, for uses customarily incident to the principal use, such as private garages.

The height districts are classified as follows: In class H-1, buildings are limited to a height of 2 and 1/2 stories, or 35 feet; in class H-2, to 4 stories, or 50 feet; in class H-3, to 80 feet. To all of these, certain exceptions are made, as in the case of church spires, water tanks, etc.

The classification of area districts is: In A-1 districts, dwellings or apartment houses to accommodate more than one family must have at least 5,000 square feet for interior lots and at least 4,000 square feet for corner lots; in A-2 districts, the area must be at least 2,500 square feet for interior lots, and 2,000 square feet for corner lots; in A-3 districts, the limits are 1,250 and 1,000 square feet, respectively; in A-4 districts, the limits are 900 and 700 square feet, respectively. The ordinance contains, in great variety and detail, provisions in respect of width of lots, front, side, and rear yards, and other matters, including restrictions and regulations as to the use of billboards, signboards, and advertising signs.

Appellee's tract of land comes under U-2, U-3 and U-6. The first strip of 620 feet immediately north of Euclid Avenue falls in class U-2, the next 130 feet to the north, in U-3, and the remainder in U-6.

Annexed to the ordinance, and made a part of it, is a zone map, showing the location and limits of the various use, height, and area districts, from which it appears that the three classes overlap one another; that is to say, for example, both U-5 and U-6 use districts are in A-4 area districts, but the former is in H-2 and the latter in H-3 height districts.

The lands lying between the two railroads for the entire length of the village area and extending some distance on either side to the north and south, having an average width of about 1,600 feet, are left open, with slight exceptions, for industrial and all other uses. This includes the larger part of appellee's tract. Approximately one-sixth of the area of the entire village is included in U-5 and U-6 use districts. That part of the village lying south of Euclid Avenue is principally in U-1 districts. The lands lying north of Euclid Avenue and bordering on the long strip just described are included in U-1, U-2, U-3, and U-4 districts, principally in U-2.

The enforcement of the ordinance is intrusted to the inspector of buildings, under rules and regulations of the board of zoning appeals. Meetings of the board are public, and minutes of its proceedings are kept. It is authorized to adopt rules and regulations to carry into effect provisions of the ordinance. Decisions of the inspector of buildings may be appealed to the board by any person claiming to be adversely affected by any such decision. The board is given power in specific cases of practical difficulty or unnecessary hardship to interpret the ordinance in harmony with its general purpose and intent, so that the public health, safety and general welfare may be secure and substantial justice done. Penalties are prescribed for violations.

The ordinance is assailed on the grounds that it is in derogation of section 1 of the Fourteenth Amendment to the federal Constitution in that it deprives appellee of liberty and property without due process of law and denies it the equal protection of the law, and that it offends against certain provisions of the Constitution of the state of Ohio. The prayer of the bill is for an injunction restraining the enforcement of the ordinance and all attempts to impose or maintain as to appellee's property any of the restrictions, limitations or conditions. The court below held the ordinance to be unconstitutional and void, and enjoined its enforcement. The bill alleges that the tract of land in question is vacant and has been held for years for the purpose of selling and developing it for industrial uses, for which it is especially adapted, being immediately in the path of progressive industrial development; that for such uses it has a market value of about $10,000 per acre, but if the use be limited to residential purposes the market value is not in excess of $2,500 per acre; that the first 200 feet of the parcel back from Euclid Avenue, if unrestricted in respect of use, has a value of $150 per front foot, but if limited to residential uses, and ordinary mercantile business be excluded therefrom, its value is not in excess of $50 per front foot.

It is specifically averred that the ordinance attempts to restrict and control the lawful uses of appellee's land, so as to confiscate and destroy a great part of its value; that it is being enforced in accordance with its terms; that prospective buyers of land for industrial, commercial, and residential uses in the metropolitan district of Cleveland are deterred from buying any part of this land because of the existence of the ordinance and the necessity thereby entailed of conducting burdensome and expensive litigation in order to vindicate the right to use the land for lawful and legitimate purposes; that the ordinance constitutes a cloud upon the land, reduces and destroys its value, and has the effect of diverting the normal industrial, commercial, and residential development thereof to other and less favorable locations.

The record goes no farther than to show, as the lower court found, that the normal and reasonably to be expected use and development of that part of appellee's land adjoining Euclid Avenue is for general trade and commercial purposes, particularly retail stores and like establishments, and that the normal and reasonably to be expected use and development of the residue of the land is for industrial and trade purposes. Whatever injury is inflicted by the mere existence and threatened enforcement of the ordinance is due to restrictions in respect of these and similar uses, to which perhaps should be added, if not included in the foregoing, restrictions in respect of apartment houses.

A motion was made in the court below to dismiss the bill on the ground that, because complainant (appellee) had made no effort to obtain a building permit or apply to the zoning board of appeals for relief, as it might have done under the terms of the ordinance, the suit was premature. The motion was properly overruled. The effect of the allegations of the bill is that the ordinance of its own force operates greatly to reduce the value of appellee's lands and destroy their marketability for industrial, commercial and residential uses, and the attack is directed, not against any specific provision or provisions, but against the ordinance as an entirety. Assuming the premises, the existence and maintenance of the ordinance in effect constitutes a present invasion of appellee's property rights and a threat to continue it.

It is not necessary to set forth the provisions of the Ohio Constitution which are thought to be infringed. The question is the same under both Constitutions, namely, as stated by appellee: Is the ordinance invalid, in that it violates the constitutional protection "to the right of property in the appellee by attempted regulations under the guise of the police power, which are unreasonable and confiscatory"?

Building zone laws are of modern origin. They began in this country about 25 years ago. Until recent years, urban life was comparatively simple; but, with the great increase and concentration of population, problems have developed, and constantly are developing, which require, and will continue to require, additional restrictions in respect of the use and occupation of private lands in urban communities. Regulations, the wisdom, necessity, and validity of which, as applied to existing conditions, are so apparent that they are now uniformly sustained, a century ago, or even half a century ago, probably would have been rejected as arbitrary and oppressive. Such regulations are sustained, under the complex conditions of our day, for reasons analogous to those which justify traffic regulations, which, before the advent of automobiles and rapid transit street railways, would have been condemned as fatally arbitrary and unreasonable. And in this there is no inconsistency, for, while the meaning of constitutional guaranties never varies, the scope of their application must expand or contract to meet the new and different conditions which are constantly coming within the field of their operation. In a changing world it is impossible that it should be otherwise. But although a degree of elasticity is thus imparted, not to the *meaning*, but to the *application* of constitutional principles, statutes and ordinances, which, after giving due weight to the new conditions, are found clearly not to conform to the Constitution, of course, must fall.

The ordinance now under review, and all similar laws and regulations, must find their justification in some aspect of the police power, asserted for the public welfare. The line which in this field separates the legitimate from the illegitimate assumption of power is not capable of precise delimitation. It varies with circumstances and conditions. A regulatory zoning ordinance, which would be clearly valid as applied to the great cities, might be clearly invalid as applied to rural communities. In resolving doubts, the maxim "*sic utere tuo ut alienum non laedas*," which lies at the foundation of so much of the common law of nuisances, ordinarily will furnish a fairly helpful clew. And the law of nuisances, likewise, may be consulted, not for the purpose of controlling, but for the helpful aid of its analogies in the process of ascertaining the scope of the power. Thus the question whether the power exists to forbid the erection of a building of a particular kind or for a particular use, like the question whether a particular thing is a nuisance, is to be determined, not by an abstract consideration of the building or of the thing considered apart, but by considering it in connection with the circumstances and the locality. *Sturgis v. Bridgeman*, L.R. 11 Ch. 852, 865. A nuisance may be merely a right thing in the wrong place, like a pig in the parlor instead of the barnyard. If the validity of the legislative classification for zoning purposes be fairly debatable, the legislative judgment must be allowed to control.

There is no serious difference of opinion in respect of the validity of laws and regulations fixing the height of buildings within reasonable limits, the character of materials and methods of construction, and the adjoining area which must be left open, in order to minimize the danger of fire or collapse, the evils of overcrowding and the like, and excluding from residential sections offensive trades, industries and structures likely to create nuisances.

Here, however, the exclusion is in general terms of all industrial establishments, and it may thereby happen that not only offensive or dangerous industries will be excluded, but those which are neither offensive nor dangerous will share the same fate. But this is no more than happens in respect of many practice-forbidding laws which this court has upheld, although drawn in general terms so as to include individual cases that may turn out to be innocuous in themselves. The inclusion of a reasonable margin, to insure effective enforcement, will not put upon a law, otherwise valid, the stamp of invalidity. Such laws may also find their justification in the fact that, in some fields, the bad fades into the good by such insensible degrees that the two are not capable of being readily distinguished and separated in terms of legislation. In the light of these considerations, we are not prepared to say that the end in view was not sufficient to justify the general rule of the ordinance, although some industries of an innocent character might fall within the proscribed class. It cannot be said that the ordinance in this respect "passes the bounds of reason and assumes the character of a merely arbitrary fiat." Moreover, the restrictive provisions of the ordinance in this particular may be sustained upon the principles applicable to the broader exclusion from residential districts of all business and trade structures, presently to be discussed.

It is said that the village of Euclid is a mere suburb of the city of Cleveland; that the industrial development of that city has now reached and in some degree extended into the village, and in the obvious course of things will soon absorb the entire area for industrial enterprises; that the effect of the ordinance is to divert this natural development elsewhere, with the consequent loss of increased values to the owners of the lands within the village borders. But the village, though physically a suburb of Cleveland, is politically a separate municipality, with powers of its own and authority to govern itself as it sees fit, within the limits of the organic law of its creation and the state and federal Constitutions. Its governing authorities, presumably representing a majority of its inhabitants and voicing their will, have determined, not that industrial development shall cease at its boundaries, but that the course of such development shall proceed within definitely fixed lines. If it be a proper exercise of the police power to relegate industrial establishments to localities separated from residential sections, it is not easy to find a sufficient reason for denying the power because the effect of its exercise is to divert an industrial flow from the course which it would follow, to the injury of the residential public, if left alone, to another course where such injury will be obviated. It is not meant by this, however, to exclude the possibility of cases where the general public interest would so far outweigh the interest of the municipality that the municipality would not be allowed to stand in the way.

We find no difficulty in sustaining restrictions of the kind thus far reviewed. The serious question in the case arises over the provisions of the ordinance excluding from residential districts apartment houses, business houses, retail stores and shops, and other like establishments. This question involves the validity of what is really the crux of the more recent zoning legislation, namely, the creation and maintenance of residential districts, from which business and trade of every sort, including hotels and apartment houses, are excluded. Upon that question this court has not thus far spoken. The decisions of the state courts are numerous and conflicting; but those which broadly sustain the power greatly outnumber those which deny it altogether or narrowly limit it, and it is very apparent that there is a constantly increasing tendency in the direction of the broader view.

As evidence of the decided trend toward the broader view, it is significant that in some instances the state courts in later decisions have reversed their former decisions holding the other way.

The decisions . . . agree that the exclusion of buildings devoted to business, trade, etc., from residential districts, bears a rational relation to the health and safety of the community. Some of the grounds for this conclusion are promotion of the health and security from injury of children and others by separating dwelling houses from territory devoted to trade and industry; suppression and prevention of disorder; facilitating the extinguishment of fires, and the enforcement of street traffic regulations and other general welfare ordinances; aiding the health and safety of the community, by excluding from residential areas the confusion and danger of fire, contagion, and disorder, which in greater or less degree attach to the location of stores, shops, and factories. Another ground is that the construction and repair of streets may be rendered easier and less expensive, by confining the greater part of the heavy traffic to the streets where business is carried on.

The matter of zoning has received much attention at the hands of commissions and experts, and the results of their investigations have been set forth in comprehensive reports. These reports, which bear every evidence of painstaking consideration, concur in the view that the segregation of residential, business and industrial buildings will make it easier to provide fire apparatus suitable for the character and intensity of the development in each section; that it will increase the safety and security of home life, greatly tend to prevent street accidents, especially to children, by reducing the traffic and resulting confusion in residential sections, decrease noise and other conditions which produce or intensify nervous disorders, preserve a more favorable environment in which to rear children, etc. With particular reference to apartment houses, it is pointed out that the development of detached house sections is greatly retarded by the coming of apartment houses, which has sometimes resulted in destroying the entire section for private house purposes; that in such sections very often the apartment house is a mere parasite, constructed in order to take advantage of the open spaces and attractive surroundings created by the residential character of the district. Moreover, the coming of one apartment house is followed by others, interfering by their height and bulk with the free circulation of air and monopolizing the rays of the sun which otherwise would fall upon the smaller homes, and bringing, as their necessary accompaniments, the disturbing noises incident to increased traffic and business, and the occupation, by means of moving and parked automobiles, of larger portions of the streets, thus detracting from their safety and depriving children of the privilege of quiet and open spaces for play, enjoyed by those in more favored localities, until, finally, the residential character of the neighborhood and its desirability as a place of detached residences are utterly destroyed. Under these circumstances, apartment houses, which in a different environment would be not only entirely unobjectionable but highly desirable, come very near to being nuisances.

If these reasons, thus summarized, do not demonstrate the wisdom or sound policy in all respects of those restrictions which we have indicated as pertinent to the inquiry, at least, the reasons are sufficiently cogent to preclude us from saying, as it must be said before the ordinance can be declared unconstitutional, that such provisions are clearly arbitrary and unreasonable, having no substantial relation to the public health, safety, morals, or general welfare.

It is true that when, if ever, the provisions set forth in the ordinance in tedious and minute detail, come to be concretely applied to particular premises, including those of the appellee, or to particular conditions, or to be considered in connection with specific complaints, some of them, or even many of them, may be found to be clearly arbitrary and unreasonable. But where the equitable remedy of injunction is sought, as it is here, not upon the ground of a present infringement or denial of a specific right, or of a particular injury in process of actual execution, but upon the broad ground that the mere existence and threatened enforcement of the ordinance, by materially and adversely affecting values and curtailing the opportunities of the market, constitute a present and irreparable injury, the court will not scrutinize its provisions, sentence by sentence, to ascertain by a process of piecemeal dissection whether there may be, here and there, provisions of a minor character, or relating to matters of administration, or not shown to contribute to the injury complained of, which, if attacked separately, might not withstand the test of constitutionality. In respect of such provisions, of which specific complaint is not made, it cannot be said that the landowner has suffered or is threatened with an injury which entitles him to challenge their constitutionality. The gravamen of the complaint is that a portion of the land of the appellee cannot be sold for certain enumerated uses because of the general and broad restraints of the ordinance. What would be the effect of a restraint imposed by one or more or the innumerable provisions of the ordinance, considered apart, upon the value or marketability of the lands, is neither disclosed by the bill nor by the evidence, and we are afforded no basis, apart from mere speculation, upon which to rest a conclusion that it or they would have any appreciable effect upon those matters. Under these circumstances, therefore, it is enough for us to determine, as we do, that the ordinance in its general scope and dominant features, so far as its provisions are here involved, is a valid exercise of authority, leaving other provisions to be dealt with as cases arise directly involving them.

And this is in accordance with the traditional policy of this court. In the realm of constitutional law, especially, this court has perceived the embarrassment which is likely to result from an attempt to formulate rules or decide questions beyond the necessities of the immediate issue. It has preferred to follow the method of a gradual approach to the general by a systematically guarded application and extension of constitutional principles to particular cases as they arise, rather than by out of hand attempts to establish general rules to which future cases must be fitted. This process applies with peculiar force to the solution of questions arising under the due process clause of the Constitution as applied to the exercise of the flexible powers of police, with which we are here concerned.

Decree reversed.

[Dissent of MR. JUSTICE VAN DEVANTER, MR. JUSTICE MCREYNOLDS, and MR. JUSTICE BUTLER omitted.]

NOTES AND QUESTIONS

1. *The Development of "Euclidean" Zoning.* The movement for standard zoning clearly struck a receptive chord in America in the 1920s. By 1923, 208 municipalities with 22 million inhabitants representing 40% of the urban population of the United States were zoned. The finding by the U.S. Supreme Court that zoning was *prima facie* constitutional coupled with the enthusiastic reception of the Standard Zoning Enabling Act virtually guaranteed the success of so-called "Euclidean" zoning. Bettman, *Constitutionality of Zoning*, 37 HARV. L. REV. 834, 834–35 (1924).

2. *Prevention of Apartment Expansion.* Despite the rhetoric of the early proponents of zoning concerning the planning and health/safety basis of zoning (*see, e.g.*, BETTMAN, THE FACT BASIS OF ZONING, *in* COLLECTED PAPERS (1940)), it is difficult to read *Euclid* and other contemporary state court opinions without concluding that the primary purpose of zoning was to preserve residential neighborhoods from the incursion not only of commercial and industrial but also apartment uses. This would explain the special invective which the majority used against apartments, a use neither sought nor contemplated by the Ambler Realty Co. There is of course the language of the *Euclid* Court inveighing directly against such uses and their effect on light and air, increased traffic, and so forth. But for sheer property rights rhetoric, it is hard to beat the language of the California Supreme Court in *Miller v. Board of Public Works*, 234 P. 381 (Cal. 1925), which the Supreme Court cites in its opinion. While the court labors mightily to disclaim such bias ("We do not wish to unduly emphasize the single family residence as a means of perpetuating the home life of people." 234 P. at 387), it nevertheless says:

> In addition to all that has been said in support of the constitutionality of residential zoning as part of a comprehensive plan, we think it may be safely and sensibly said that justification for residential zoning may, in the last analysis, be rested upon the protection of the civic and social values of the American home. The establishment of such districts is for the general welfare because it tends to promote and perpetuate the American home. It is axiomatic that the welfare, and indeed the very existence, of a nation depends upon the character and caliber of its citizenry. The character and

> quality of manhood and womanhood are in a large measure the result of home environment. The home and its intrinsic influences are the very foundation of good citizenship and any factor contributing to the establishment of homes and the fostering of home life doubtless tends to the enhancement, not only of community life, but of the life of the nation as a whole.
>
> The establishment of single family residence districts offers inducements, not only to the wealthy, but to those of moderate means to own their own homes. With ownership comes stability, the welding together of family ties, and better attention to the rearing of children. With ownership comes increased interest in the promotion of public agencies, such as church and school, which have for their purpose a desired development of the moral and mental make-up of the citizenry of the country. With ownership of one's home comes recognition of the individual's responsibility for his share in the safeguarding of the community and increased pride in personal achievement which must come from personal participation in projects looking toward community betterment.

3. *Use Classifications*. In *Nectow v. Cambridge*, 277 U.S. 183 (1928), the United States Supreme Court struck down a municipal zoning ordinance *as applied* to a particular property owner. In that case, the zoning ordinance of the city of Cambridge, Massachusetts placed Nectow's property in a residential-use only category even though it was surrounded by business and industrial uses and had little if any value for residential purposes. In an opinion written by Justice Sutherland, the Court found that the general welfare of the community was not served by this restriction and that at least as applied to Nectow, it denied the landowner the use of his property without due process of law in violation of the Fourteenth Amendment.

Note the uses permitted on appellee's land in *Euclid* in each of the three use districts. How similar are these uses to those nearest adjacent? To other nearby uses? Under the *Nectow* decision, which of these, if any, could be construed to be unconstitutional classifications as applied?

4. *Facial vs. As-Applied Challenge*. Note that appellee attacks *Euclid*'s zoning ordinance in its "entirety." Might the result have been different if the attack had been merely upon the ordinance as it applied to appellee's property, as in *Nectow*?

5. *Overlay Zoning*. There is an odd structure to the *Euclid* zoning ordinance: it appears not to place all land use regulations relating to height, area, and so forth in the regulations pertaining to each use district, but to have different districts for such uses as height and area which are also drawn on the zoning map over the use zones. This "overlay" technique has recently become popular among planners for showing so-called natural site limitations such as steep slope, unsuitable soils, flood hazards, and so forth. *See, e.g.*, Art. 9, Land Use Ordinance for the City and County of Honolulu (2003) (creating eight such districts). The nature and legal structure of modern zoning ordinances are examined in much greater detail in Chapter II.

6. *Other Land Use Regimes*. The 20th century pattern of development in the United States focused on the expansion of urban areas on the periphery of

metropolitan areas (like Euclid, Ohio in the 1920s). Not all countries adopted this approach. In Europe, the focus was much more on a managed landscape and the protection of traditional housing patterns. *See* Light, *Different Ideas of the City: Origins of Metropolitan Land-Use Regimes in the United States, Germany, and Switzerland*, 24 YALE J. INT'L L. 577 (1999). Non-western systems are even farther from the United States approach. *See* Kremzner, *Managing Urban Land in China: The Emerging Legal Framework and Its Role in Development*, 7 PAC. RIM L. & POL'Y J. 611 (1998).

[2.] Regulatory Takings

In *Pennsylvania Coal Co. v. Mahon*, the Supreme Court ruled that a regulation that goes "too far" is a taking of property protected by the Fifth Amendment to the U.S. Constitution. However, after deciding that zoning as a regulatory technique survived Fourteenth Amendment challenge in *Village of Euclid v. Ambler Realty Co.* in 1926 (set out *supra* at [C][1]), and then striking down a particular application of a zoning ordinance in *Nectow v. Cambridge* in 1928, the Court rarely revisited the subject of takings and land use controls, leaving them to the state courts until the 1970s. When it did, land use regulations were almost always upheld. For the history of regulatory takings from the 1920s to the 1970s, see the relevant chapters of F. BOSSELMAN, D. CALLIES & J. BANTA, THE TAKING ISSUE: AN ANALYSIS OF THE CONSTITUTIONAL LIMITS OF LAND USE CONTROL (1973), and R. MELTZ, D. MERRIAM & R. FRANK, THE TAKINGS ISSUE (1999).

The Supreme Court reentered the fray on April Fool's Day, 1974, with its decision in *Village of Belle Terre v. Boraas*, 416 U.S. 1 (1974), which upheld a municipal ordinance that limited to two the number of non-related individuals who could occupy a "one-family" dwelling. More significantly, in 1978, it handed down its opinion in *Penn Central Transportation Co. v. New York*, a decision that 35 years later continues to be one of the two most significant regulatory takings decisions in its jurisprudence.

PENN CENTRAL TRANSPORTATION CO. v. CITY OF NEW YORK

United States Supreme Court
438 U.S. 104 (1978)

MR. JUSTICE BRENNAN delivered the opinion of the Court.

The question presented is whether a city may, as part of a comprehensive program to preserve historic landmarks and historic districts, place restrictions on the development of individual historic landmarks, in addition to those imposed by applicable zoning ordinances, without effecting a "taking" requiring the payment of "just compensation." Specifically, we must decide whether the application of New York City's Landmarks Preservation Law to the parcel of land occupied by Grand Central Terminal has "taken" its owners' property in violation of the Fifth and Fourteenth Amendments.

I

A

Over the past 50 years, all 50 States and over 500 municipalities have enacted laws to encourage or require the preservation of buildings and areas with historic or aesthetic importance.[10] These nationwide legislative efforts have been precipitated by two concerns. The first is recognition that, in recent years, large numbers of historic structures, landmarks, and areas have been destroyed[11] without adequate consideration of either the values represented therein or the possibility of preserving the destroyed properties for use in economically productive ways. The second is a widely shared belief that structures with special historic, cultural, or architectural significance enhance the quality of life for all. Not only do these buildings and their workmanship represent the lessons of the past and embody precious features of our heritage, they serve as examples of quality for today. "[H]istoric conservation is but one aspect of the much larger problem, basically an environmental one, of enhancing, or perhaps developing for the first time, the quality of life for people."

New York City, responding to similar concerns and acting pursuant to a New York State enabling Act,[12] adopted its Landmarks Preservation Law in 1965. The city acted from the conviction that "the standing of [New York City] as a world-wide tourist center and world capital of business, culture and government" would be threatened if legislation were not enacted to protect historic landmarks and neighborhoods from precipitate decisions to destroy or fundamentally alter their character. The city believed that comprehensive measures to safeguard desirable features of the existing urban fabric would benefit its citizens in a variety of ways: e.g., fostering "civic pride in the beauty and noble accomplishments of the past"; protecting and enhancing "the city's attractions to tourists and visitors"; "support-

---

[10] [1] *See* National Trust for Historic Preservation, A Guide to State Historic Preservation Programs (1976); National Trust for Historic Preservation, Directory of Landmark and Historic District Commissions (1976). In addition to these state and municipal legislative efforts, Congress has determined that "the historical and cultural foundations of the Nation should be preserved as a living part of our community life and development in order to give a sense of orientation to the American people," National Historic Preservation Act of 1966, 80 Stat. 915, 16 U.S.C. § .470(b) (1976 ed.), and has enacted a series of measures designed to encourage preservation of sites and structures of historic, architectural, or cultural significance. *See generally* Gray, *The Response of Federal Legislation to Historic Preservation*, 36 Law & Contemp. Prob. 314 (1971). 2[2] Over one-half of the buildings listed in the Historic American Buildings Survey, begun by the Federal Government in 1933, have been destroyed. *See* Costonis, *The Chicago Plan: Incentive Zoning and the Preservation of Urban Landmarks*, 85 Harv. L. Rev. 574, 574 n.1 (1972), *citing* Huxtable, *Bank's Building Plan Sets Off Debate on "Progress,"* N.Y. Times, Jan. 17, 1971, section 8, p. 1, col. 2.

[11] [2] Over one-half of the buildings listed in the Historic American Buildings Survey, begun by the Federal Government in 1933, have been destroyed. *See* Costonis, *The Chicago Plan: Incentive Zoning and the Preservation of Urban Landmarks*, 85 Harv. L. Rev. 574, 574 n.1 (1972), *citing* Huxtable, *Bank's Building Plan Sets Off Debate on "Progress,"* N.Y. Times, Jan. 17, 1971, section 8, p. 1, col. 2.

[12] [5] See N.Y. Gen. Mun. Law § .96-a (McKinney 1977). It declares that it is the public policy of the State of New York to preserve structures and areas with special historical or aesthetic interest or value and authorizes local governments to impose reasonable restrictions to perpetuate such structures and areas.

[ing] and stimul[ating] business and industry"; "strengthen[ing] the economy of the city"; and promoting "the use of historic districts, landmarks, interior landmarks and scenic landmarks for the education, pleasure and welfare of the people of the city."

The New York City law is typical of many urban landmark laws in that its primary method of achieving its goals is not by acquisitions of historic properties,[13] but rather by involving public entities in land-use decisions affecting these properties and providing services, standards, controls, and incentives that will encourage preservation by private owners and users. While the law does place special restrictions on landmark properties as a necessary feature to the attainment of its larger objectives, the major theme of the law is to ensure the owners of any such properties both a "reasonable return" on their investments and maximum latitude to use their parcels for purposes not inconsistent with the preservation goals.

The operation of the law can be briefly summarized. The primary responsibility for administering the law is vested in the Landmarks Preservation Commission (Commission), a broad based, 11-member agency[14] assisted by a technical staff. The Commission first performs the function, critical to any landmark preservation effort, of identifying properties and areas that have "a special character or special historical or aesthetic interest or value as part of the development, heritage or cultural characteristics of the city, state or nation." If the Commission determines, after giving all interested parties an opportunity to be heard, that a building or area satisfies the ordinance's criteria, it will designate a building to be a "landmark,"[15] situated on a particular "landmark site,"[16] or will designate an area to be a "historic district."[17] After the Commission makes a designation, New York City's Board of

[13] [6] The consensus is that widespread public ownership of historic properties in urban settings is neither feasible nor wise. Public ownership reduces the tax base, burdens the public budget with costs of acquisitions and maintenance, and results in the preservation of public buildings as museums and similar facilities, rather than as economically productive features of the urban scene. *See* Wilson & Winkler, *The Response of State Legislation to Historic Preservation*, 36 Law & Contemp. Prob. 329, 330–331, 339–340 (1971).

[14] [8] The ordinance creating the Commission requires that it include at least three architects, one historian qualified in the field, one city planner or landscape architect, one realtor, and at least one resident of each of the city's five boroughs. N.Y.C. Charter § .534 (1976). In addition to the ordinance's requirements concerning the composition of the Commission, there is, according to a former chairman, a "prudent tradition" that the Commission include one or two lawyers, preferably with experience in municipal government, and several laymen with no specialized qualifications other than concern for the good of the city.

[15] [9] " 'Landmark.' Any improvement, any part of which is thirty years old or older, which has a special character or special historical or aesthetic interest or value as part of the development, heritage or cultural characteristics of the city, state or nation and which has been designated as a landmark pursuant to the provisions of this chapter." § .207-1.0(n).

[16] [10] " 'Landmark site.' An improvement parcel or part thereof on which is situated a landmark and any abutting improvement parcel or part thereof used as and constituting part of the premises on which the landmark is situated, and which has been designated as a landmark site pursuant to the provisions of this chapter." § .207.-1.0(o).

[17] [11] " 'Historic district.' Any area which: (1) contains improvements which: (a) have a special character or special historical or aesthetic interest or value; and (b) represent one or more periods or styles of architecture typical of one or more eras in the history of the city; and (c) cause such area, by

Estimate, after considering the relationship of the designated property "to the master plan, the zoning resolution, projected public improvements and any plans for the renewal of the area involved," may modify or disapprove the designation, and the owner may seek judicial review of the final designation decision. Thus far, 31 historic districts and over 400 individual landmarks have been finally designated, and the process is a continuing one.

Final designation as a landmark results in restrictions upon the property owner's options concerning use of the landmark site. First, the law imposes a duty upon the owner to keep the exterior features of the building "in good repair" to assure that the law's objectives not be defeated by the landmark's falling into a state of irremediable disrepair. Second, the Commission must approve in advance any proposal to alter the exterior architectural features of the landmark or to construct any exterior improvement on the landmark site, thus ensuring that decisions concerning construction on the landmark site are made with due consideration of both the public interest in the maintenance of the structure and the landowner's interest in use of the property.

In the event an owner wishes to alter a landmark site, three separate procedures are available through which administrative approval may be obtained. First, the owner may apply to the Commission for a "certificate of no effect on protected architectural features": that is, for an order approving the improvement or alteration on the ground that it will not change or affect any architectural feature of the landmark and will be in harmony therewith. Denial of the certificate is subject to judicial review.

Second, the owner may apply to the Commission for a certificate of "appropriateness." Such certificates will be granted if the Commission concludes, focusing upon aesthetic, historical, and architectural values, that the proposed construction on the landmark site would not unduly hinder the protection, enhancement, perpetuation, and use of the landmark. Again, denial of the certificate is subject to judicial review. Moreover, the owner who is denied either a certificate of no exterior effect or a certificate of appropriateness may submit an alternative or modified plan for approval. The final procedure, seeking a certificate of appropriateness on the ground of "insufficient return," provides special mechanisms, which vary depending on whether or not the landmark enjoys a tax exemption,[18] to ensure that

---

reason of such factors, to constitute a distinct section of the city; and (2) has been designated as a historic district pursuant to the provisions of this chapter." § .207-1.0(h). The Act also provides for the designation of a "scenic landmark," *see* § .207-1.0(w), and an "interior landmark." *See* § .207-1.0(m).

[18] [13] If the owner of a non-tax-exempt parcel has been denied certificates of appropriateness for a proposed alteration and shows that he is not earning a reasonable return on the property in its present state, the Commission and other city agencies must assume the burden of developing a plan that will enable the landmark owner to earn a reasonable return on the landmark site. The plan may include, but need not be limited to, partial or complete tax exemption, remission of taxes, and authorizations for alterations, construction, or reconstruction appropriate for and not inconsistent with the purposes of the law. The owner is free to accept or reject a plan devised by the Commission and approved by the other city agencies. If he accepts the plan, he proceeds to operate the property pursuant to the plan. If he rejects the plan, the Commission may recommend that the city proceed by eminent domain to acquire a protective interest in the landmark, but if the city does not do so within a specified time period, the Commission must issue a notice allowing the property owner to proceed with the alteration or improvement as originally proposed in his application for a certificate of appropriateness.

designation does not cause economic hardship.

Although the designation of a landmark and landmark site restricts the owner's control over the parcel, designation also enhances the economic position of the landmark owner in one significant respect. Under New York City's zoning laws, owners of real property who have not developed their property to the full extent permitted by the applicable zoning laws are allowed to transfer development rights to contiguous parcels on the same city block. A 1968 ordinance gave the owners of landmark sites additional opportunities to transfer development rights to other parcels. Subject to a restriction that the floor area of the transferee lot may not be increased by more than 20% above its authorized level, the ordinance permitted transfers from a landmark parcel to property across the street or across a street intersection. The class of recipient lots was expanded to include lots "across a street and opposite to another lot or lots which except for the intervention of streets or street intersections f[or]m a series extending to the lot occupied by the landmark building[, provided that] all lots [are] in the same ownership." In addition, the 1969 amendment permits, in highly commercialized areas like midtown Manhattan, the transfer of all unused development rights to a single parcel. *Ibid.*

B

This case involves the application of New York City's Landmarks Preservation Law to Grand Central Terminal (Terminal). The Terminal, which is owned by the Penn Central Transportation Co. and its affiliates (Penn Central), is one of New York City's most famous buildings. Opened in 1913, it is regarded not only as providing an ingenious engineering solution to the problems presented by urban railroad stations, but also as a magnificent example of the French beaux-arts style.

The Terminal is located in midtown Manhattan. Its south facade faces 42d Street and that street's intersection with Park Avenue. At street level, the Terminal is bounded on the west by Vanderbilt Avenue, on the east by the Commodore Hotel, and on the north by the Pan-American Building. Although a 20-story office tower, to have been located above the Terminal, was part of the original design, the planned tower was never constructed.[19] The Terminal itself is an eight-story structure which Penn Central uses as a railroad station and in which it rents space

---

Tax-exempt structures are treated somewhat differently. They become eligible for special treatment only if four preconditions are satisfied: (1) the owner previously entered into an agreement to sell the parcel that was contingent upon the issuance of a certificate of approval; (2) the property, as it exists at the time of the request, is not capable of earning a reasonable return; (3) the structure is no longer suitable to its past or present purposes; and (4) the prospective buyer intends to alter the landmark structure. In the event the owner demonstrates that the property in its present state is not earning a reasonable return, the Commission must either find another buyer for it or allow the sale and construction to proceed.

But this is not the only remedy available for owners of tax-exempt landmarks. As the case at bar illustrates, if an owner files suit and establishes that he is incapable of earning a "reasonable return" on the site in its present state, he can be afforded judicial relief. Similarly, where a landmark owner who enjoys a tax exemption has demonstrated that the landmark structure, as restricted, is totally inadequate for the owner's "legitimate needs," the law has been held invalid as applied to that parcel.

[19] [15] The Terminal's present foundation includes columns, which were built into it for the express purpose of supporting the proposed 20-story tower.

not needed for railroad purposes to a variety of commercial interests. The Terminal is one of a number of properties owned by appellant Penn Central in this area of midtown Manhattan. The others include the Barclay, Biltmore, Commodore, Roosevelt, and Waldorf-Astoria Hotels, the Pan-American Building and other office buildings along Park Avenue, and the Yale Club. At least eight of these are eligible to be recipients of development rights afforded the Terminal by virtue of landmark designation.

On August 2, 1967, following a public hearing, the Commission designated the Terminal a "landmark" and designated the "city tax block" it occupies a "landmark site." The Board of Estimate confirmed this action on September 21, 1967. Although appellant Penn Central had opposed the designation before the Commission, it did not seek judicial review of the final designation decision.

On January 22, 1968, appellant Penn Central, to increase its income, entered into a renewable 50-year lease and sublease agreement with appellant UGP Properties, Inc. (UGP), a wholly owned subsidiary of Union General Properties, Ltd., a United Kingdom corporation. Under the terms of the agreement, UGP was to construct a multistory office building above the Terminal. UGP promised to pay Penn Central $1 million annually during construction and at least $3 million annually thereafter. The rentals would be offset in part by a loss of some $700,000 to $1 million in net rentals presently received from concessionaires displaced by the new building.

Appellants UGP and Penn Central then applied to the Commission for permission to construct an office building atop the Terminal. Two separate plans, both designed by architect Marcel Breuer and both apparently satisfying the terms of the applicable zoning ordinance, were submitted to the Commission for approval. The first, Breuer I, provided for the construction of a 55-story office building, to be cantilevered above the existing facade and to rest on the roof of the Terminal. The second, Breuer II Revised, called for tearing down a portion of the Terminal that included the 42d Street facade, stripping off some of the remaining features of the Terminal's facade, and constructing a 53-story office building. The Commission denied a certificate of no exterior effect on September 20, 1968. Appellants then applied for a certificate of "appropriateness" as to both proposals. After four days of hearings at which over 80 witnesses testified, the Commission denied this application as to both proposals.

The Commission's reasons for rejecting certificates respecting Breuer II Revised are summarized in the following statement: "To protect a Landmark, one does not tear it down. To perpetuate its architectural features, one does not strip them off." Record 2255. Breuer I, which would have preserved the existing vertical facades of the present structure, received more sympathetic consideration. The Commission first focused on the effect that the proposed tower would have on one desirable feature created by the present structure and its surroundings: the dramatic view of the Terminal from Park Avenue South. Although appellants had contended that the Pan-American Building had already destroyed the silhouette of the south facade and that one additional tower could do no further damage and might even provide a better background for the facade, the Commission disagreed, stating that it found the majestic approach from the south to be still unique in the city and that a 55-story tower atop the Terminal would be far more detrimental to its south facade than the Pan-American Building 375 feet away. Moreover, the Commission found that from closer vantage points the Pan Am Building and the other towers were largely cut off from view, which would not be the case of the mass on top of the Terminal planned under Breuer I. In conclusion, the Commission stated:

> [We have] no fixed rule against making additions to designated buildings, it all depends on how they are done. But to balance a 55-story office tower above a flamboyant Beaux-Arts facade seems nothing more than an aesthetic joke. Quite simply, the tower would overwhelm the Terminal by its sheer mass. The "addition" would be four times as high as the existing structure and would reduce the Landmark itself to the status of a curiosity.
>
> Landmarks cannot be divorced from their settings, particularly when the setting is a dramatic and integral part of the original concept. The Terminal, in its setting, is a great example of urban design. Such examples are not so plentiful in New York City that we can afford to lose any of the few we have. And we must preserve them in a meaningful way, with alterations and additions of such character, scale, materials and mass as will protect, enhance and perpetuate the original design rather than overwhelm it.

Appellants did not seek judicial review of the denial of either certificate. Because the Terminal site enjoyed a tax exemption, remained suitable for its present and future uses, and was not the subject of a contract of sale, there were no further administrative remedies available to appellants as to the Breuer I and Breuer II Revised plans. See n.13, *supra*. Further, appellants did not avail themselves of the opportunity to develop and submit other plans for the Commission's consideration and approval. Instead, appellants filed suit in New York Supreme Court, Trial Term, claiming, inter alia, that the application of the Landmarks Preservation Law had "taken" their property without just compensation in violation of the Fifth and Fourteenth Amendments and arbitrarily deprived them of their property without due process of law in violation of the Fourteenth Amendment. Appellants sought a declaratory judgment, injunctive relief barring the city from using the Landmarks Law to impede the construction of any structure that might otherwise lawfully be constructed on the Terminal site, and damages for the "temporary taking" that occurred between August 2, 1967, the designation date, and the date when the restrictions arising from the Landmarks Law would be lifted. The trial court granted the injunctive and declaratory relief, but severed the question of damages for a "temporary taking."

Appellees appealed, and the New York Supreme Court, Appellate Division, reversed. The Appellate Division held that the restrictions on the development of the Terminal site were necessary to promote the legitimate public purpose of protecting landmarks and therefore that appellants could sustain their constitutional claims only by proof that the regulation deprived them of all reasonable beneficial use of the property. The Appellate Division held that the evidence appellants introduced at trial, "Statements of Revenues and Costs," purporting to show a net operating loss for the years 1969 and 1971, which were prepared for the instant litigation, had not satisfied their burden.[20] First, the court rejected the claim that these statements showed that the Terminal was operating at a loss, for in the court's view, appellants had improperly attributed some railroad operating expenses and taxes to their real estate operations and compounded that error by failing to impute any rental value to the vast space in the Terminal devoted to railroad purposes. Further, the Appellate Division concluded that appellants had failed to establish either that they were unable to increase the Terminal's commercial income by transforming vacant or underutilized space to revenue-producing use, or that the unused development rights over the Terminal could not have been profitably transferred to one or more nearby sites. The Appellate Division concluded that all appellants had succeeded in showing was that they had been deprived of the property's most profitable use, and that this showing did not establish that appellants had been unconstitutionally deprived of their property.

The New York Court of Appeals affirmed. That court summarily rejected any claim that the Landmarks Law had "taken" property without "just compensation," indicating that there could be no "taking" since the law had not transferred control of the property to the city, but only restricted appellants' exploitation of it. In that circumstance, the Court of Appeals held that appellants' attack on the law could prevail only if the law deprived appellants of their property in violation of the Due Process Clause of the Fourteenth Amendment. Whether or not there was a denial of substantive due process turned on whether the restrictions deprived Penn Central of a "reasonable return" on the "privately created and privately managed ingredient" of the Terminal.[21] The Court of Appeals concluded that the Landmarks Law had not effected a denial of due process because: (1) the landmark regulation permitted the same use as had been made of the Terminal for more than half a century; (2) the appellants had failed to show that they could not earn a reasonable return on their investment in the Terminal itself; (3) even if the Terminal proper could never operate at a reasonable profit some of the income from Penn Central's extensive real estate holdings in the area, which include hotels and office buildings, must realistically be imputed to the Terminal; and (4) the development rights above the Terminal, which had been made transferable to numerous sites in the vicinity of the Terminal, one or two of which were suitable for the construction of office buildings, were valuable to appellants and provided "significant, perhaps 'fair,'

---

[20] [21] These statements appear to have reflected the costs of maintaining the exterior architectural features of the Terminal in "good repair" as required by the law. As would have been apparent in any case therefore, the existence of the duty to keep up the property was here and will presumably always be factored into the inquiry concerning the constitutionality of the landmark restrictions. The Appellate Division also rejected the claim that an agreement of Penn Central with the Metropolitan Transit Authority and the Connecticut Transit Authority provided a basis for invalidating the application of the Landmarks Law.

[21] [23] The Court of Appeals suggested that in calculating the value of the property upon which appellants were entitled to earn a reasonable return, the "publicly created" components of the value of the property, "i.e., those elements of its value attributable to the 'efforts of organized society' or to the 'social complex' in which the Terminal is located," had to be excluded. However, since the record upon which the Court of Appeals decided the case did not, as that court recognized, contain a basis for segregating the privately created from the publicly created elements of the value of the Terminal site and since the judgment of the Court of Appeals in any event rests upon bases that support our affirmance *see* [366 N.E.2d 1271, 1273 (N.Y. 1977)], we have no occasion to address the question whether it is permissible or feasible to separate out the "social increments" of the value of property.

compensation for the loss of rights above the terminal itself."

Observing that its affirmance was "[o]n the present record," and that its analysis had not been fully developed by counsel at any level of the New York judicial system, the Court of Appeals directed that counsel "should be entitled to present . . . any additional submissions which, in the light of [the court's] opinion, may usefully develop further the factors discussed." Appellants chose not to avail themselves of this opportunity and filed a notice of appeal in this Court. We noted probable jurisdiction. We affirm.

II

The issues presented by appellants are (1) whether the restrictions imposed by New York City's law upon appellants' exploitation of the Terminal site effect a "taking" of appellants' property for a public use within the meaning of the Fifth Amendment, which of course is made applicable to the States through the Fourteenth Amendment, and, (2), if so, whether the transferable development rights afforded appellants constitute "just compensation" within the meaning of the Fifth Amendment. We need only address the question whether a "taking" has occurred.[22]

Before considering appellants' specific contentions, it will be useful to review the factors that have shaped the jurisprudence of the Fifth Amendment injunction "nor shall private property be taken for public use, without just compensation." The question of what constitutes a "taking" for purposes of the Fifth Amendment has proved to be a problem of considerable difficulty. While this Court has recognized that the "Fifth Amendment's guarantee . . . [is] designed to bar Government from forcing some people alone to bear public burdens which, in all fairness and justice, should be borne by the public as a whole," this Court, quite simply, has been unable to develop any "set formula" for determining when "justice and fairness" require that economic injuries caused by public action be compensated by the government, rather than remain disproportionately concentrated on a few persons. Indeed, we have frequently observed that whether a particular restriction will be rendered invalid by the government's failure to pay for any losses proximately caused by it depends largely "upon the particular circumstances [in that] case."

In engaging in these essentially ad hoc, factual inquiries, the Court's decisions have identified several factors that have particular significance. The economic impact of the regulation on the claimant and, particularly, the extent to which the regulation has interfered with distinct investment-backed expectations are, of course, relevant considerations. So, too, is the character of the governmental action. A "taking" may more readily be found when the interference with property can be characterized as a physical invasion by government than when interference arises from some public program adjusting the benefits and burdens of economic life to promote the common good.

"Government hardly could go on if to some extent values incident to property

---

[22] [25] As is implicit in our opinion, we do not embrace the proposition that a "taking" can never occur unless government has transferred physical control over a portion of a parcel.

could not be diminished without paying for every such change in the general law," and this Court has accordingly recognized, in a wide variety of contexts, that government may execute laws or programs that adversely affect recognized economic values. Exercises of the taxing power are one obvious example. A second are the decisions in which this Court has dismissed "taking" challenges on the ground that, while the challenged government action caused economic harm, it did not interfere with interests that were sufficiently bound up with the reasonable expectations of the claimant to constitute "property" for Fifth Amendment purposes.

More importantly for the present case, in instances in which a state tribunal reasonably concluded that "the health, safety, morals, or general welfare" would be promoted by prohibiting particular contemplated uses of land, this Court has upheld land-use regulations that destroyed or adversely affected recognized real property interests.

Zoning laws generally do not affect existing uses of real property, but "taking" challenges have also been held to be without merit in a wide variety of situations when the challenged governmental actions prohibited a beneficial use to which individual parcels had previously been devoted and thus caused substantial individualized harm.

Pennsylvania Coal Co. v. Mahon, 260 U.S. 393 (1922), is the leading case for the proposition that a state statute that substantially furthers important public policies may so frustrate distinct investment-backed expectations as to amount to a "taking."

Finally, government actions that may be characterized as acquisitions of resources to permit or facilitate uniquely public functions have often been held to constitute "takings." *United States v. Causby*, 328 U.S. 256 (1946).

B

In contending that the New York City law has "taken" their property in violation of the Fifth and Fourteenth Amendments, appellants make a series of arguments, which, while tailored to the facts of this case, essentially urge that any substantial restriction imposed pursuant to a landmark law must be accompanied by just compensation if it is to be constitutional. Before considering these, we emphasize what is not in dispute. Because this Court has recognized, in a number of settings, that States and cities may enact land use restrictions or controls to enhance the quality of life by preserving the character and desirable aesthetic features of a city, appellants do not contest that New York City's objective of preserving structures and areas with special historic, architectural, or cultural significance is an entirely permissible governmental goal. They also do not dispute that the restrictions imposed on its parcel are appropriate means of securing the purposes of the New York City law. Finally, appellants do not challenge any of the specific factual premises of the decision below. They accept for present purposes both that the parcel of land occupied by Grand Central Terminal must, in its present state, be regarded as capable of earning a reasonable return, and that the transferable development rights afforded appellants by virtue of the Terminal's designation as a landmark are valuable, even if not as valuable as the rights to construct above the Terminal. In appellants' view none of these factors derogate from their claim that New York City's law has effected a "taking."

They first observe that the airspace above the Terminal is a valuable property interest, citing *United States v. Causby, supra*. They urge that the Landmarks Law has deprived them of any gainful use of their "air rights" above the Terminal and that, irrespective of the value of the remainder of their parcel, the city has "taken" their right to this superadjacent airspace, thus entitling them to "just compensation" measured by the fair market value of these air rights.

Apart from our own disagreement with appellants' characterization of the effect of the New York City law, the submission that appellants may establish a "taking" simply by showing that they have been denied the ability to exploit a property interest that they heretofore had believed was available for development is quite simply untenable. Were this the rule, this Court would have erred not only in upholding laws restricting the development of air rights, but also in approving those prohibiting both the subjacent and the lateral development of particular parcels.[23] "Taking" jurisprudence does not divide a single parcel into discrete segments and attempt to determine whether rights in a particular segment have been entirely abrogated. In deciding whether a particular governmental action has effected a taking, this Court focuses rather both on the character of the action and on the nature and extent of the interference with rights in the parcel as a whole, here, the city tax block designated as the "landmark site."

. . . Secondly, appellants, focusing on the character and impact of the New York City law, argue . . . that New York City's regulation of individual landmarks is fundamentally different from zoning or from historic-district legislation because the controls imposed by New York City's law apply only to individuals who own selected properties.

Stated baldly, appellants' position appears to be that the only means of ensuring that selected owners are not singled out to endure financial hardship for no reason is to hold that any restriction imposed on individual landmarks pursuant to the New York City scheme is a "taking" requiring the payment of "just compensation." Agreement with this argument would, of course, invalidate not just New York City's law, but all comparable landmark legislation in the Nation. We find no merit in it.

It is true, as appellants emphasize, that both historic-district legislation and zoning laws regulate all properties within given physical communities whereas landmark laws apply only to selected parcels. But, contrary to appellants' suggestions, landmark laws are not like discriminatory, or "reverse spot," zoning: that is, a land-use decision which arbitrarily singles out a particular parcel for different,

---

[23] [27] These cases dispose of any contention that might be based on *Pennsylvania Coal Co. v. Mahon*, 260 U.S. 393 (1922), that full use of air rights is so bound up with the investment-backed expectations of appellants that governmental deprivation of these rights invariably — i.e., irrespective of the impact of the restriction on the value of the parcel as a whole — constitutes a "taking." Similarly, *Welch*, *Goldblatt*, and *Gorieb* illustrate the fallacy of appellants' related contention that a "taking" must be found to have occurred whenever the land-use restriction may be characterized as imposing a "servitude" on the claimant's parcel. [Editor's note: The court's discussion of these earlier takings cases has been omitted from this edited version of the opinion.]

less favorable treatment than the neighboring ones. In contrast to discriminatory zoning, which is the antithesis of land-use control as part of some comprehensive plan, the New York City law embodies a comprehensive plan to preserve structures of historic or aesthetic interest wherever they might be found in the city, and as noted, over 400 landmarks and 31 historic districts have been designated pursuant to this plan.

Equally without merit is the related argument that the decision to designate a structure as a landmark "is inevitably arbitrary or at least subjective, because it is basically a matter of taste," thus unavoidably singling out individual landowners for disparate and unfair treatment. The argument has a particularly hollow ring in this case. For appellants not only did not seek judicial review of either the designation or of the denials of the certificates of appropriateness and of no exterior effect, but do not even now suggest that the Commission's decisions concerning the Terminal were in any sense arbitrary or unprincipled. But, in any event, a landmark owner has a right to judicial review of any Commission decision, and, quite simply, there is no basis whatsoever for a conclusion that courts will have any greater difficulty identifying arbitrary or discriminatory action in the context of landmark regulation than in the context of classic zoning or indeed in any other context.

Next, appellants observe that New York City's law differs from zoning laws and historic-district ordinances in that the Landmarks Law does not impose identical or similar restrictions on all structures located in particular physical communities. It follows, they argue, that New York City's law is inherently incapable of producing the fair and equitable distribution of benefits and burdens of governmental action which is characteristic of zoning laws and historic-district legislation and which they maintain is a constitutional requirement if "just compensation" is not to be afforded. It is, of course, true that the Landmarks Law has a more severe impact on some landowners than on others, but that in itself does not mean that the law effects a "taking." Legislation designed to promote the general welfare commonly burdens some more than others. The owners of the brickyard in *Hadacheck*, of the cedar trees in *Miller v. Schoene*, and of the gravel and sand mine in *Goldblatt v. Hempstead*, were uniquely burdened by the legislation sustained in those cases. Similarly, zoning laws often affect some property owners more severely than others but have not been held to be invalid on that account. For example, the property owner in *Euclid* who wished to use its property for industrial purposes was affected far more severely by the ordinance than its neighbors who wished to use their land for residences.

In any event, appellants' repeated suggestions that they are solely burdened and unbenefited is factually inaccurate. This contention overlooks the fact that the New York City law applies to vast numbers of structures in the city in addition to the Terminal, all the structures contained in the 31 historic districts and over 400 individual landmarks, many of which are close to the Terminal. Unless we are to reject the judgment of the New York City Council that the preservation of landmarks benefits all New York citizens and all structures, both economically and by improving the quality of life in the city as a whole, which we are unwilling to do, we cannot conclude that the owners of the Terminal have in no sense been benefited by the Landmarks Law. Doubtless appellants believe they are more burdened than benefited by the law, but that must have been true, too, of the property owners in

Miller, Hadacheck, Euclid, and *Goldblatt.*

Appellants' final broad-based attack would have us treat the law as an instance, like that in *United States v. Causby,* in which government, acting in an enterprise capacity, has appropriated part of their property for some strictly governmental purpose. Apart from the fact that *Causby* was a case of invasion of airspace that destroyed the use of the farm beneath and this New York City law has in nowise impaired the present use of the Terminal, the Landmarks Law neither exploits appellants' parcel for city purposes nor facilitates nor arises from any entrepreneurial operations of the city. The situation is not remotely like that in *Causby* where the airspace above the property was in the flight pattern for military aircraft. The Landmarks Law's effect is simply to prohibit appellants or anyone else from occupying portions of the airspace above the Terminal, while permitting appellants to use the remainder of the parcel in a gainful fashion. This is no more an appropriation of property by government for its own uses than is a zoning law prohibiting, for "aesthetic" reasons, two or more adult theaters within a specified area, or a safety regulation prohibiting excavations below a certain level.

C

Rejection of appellants' broad arguments is not, however, the end of our inquiry, for all we thus far have established is that the New York City law is not rendered invalid by its failure to provide "just compensation" whenever a landmark owner is restricted in the exploitation of property interests, such as air rights, to a greater extent than provided for under applicable zoning laws. We now must consider whether the interference with appellants' property is of such a magnitude that "there must be an exercise of eminent domain and compensation to sustain [it]." That inquiry may be narrowed to the question of the severity of the impact of the law on appellants' parcel, and its resolution in turn requires a careful assessment of the impact of the regulation on the Terminal site.

Unlike the governmental acts in *Goldblatt, Miller, Causby, Griggs,* and *Hadacheck,* the New York City law does not interfere in any way with the present uses of the Terminal. Its designation as a landmark not only permits but contemplates that appellants may continue to use the property precisely as it has been used for the past 65 years: as a railroad terminal containing office space and concessions. So the law does not interfere with what must be regarded as Penn Central's primary expectation concerning the use of the parcel. More importantly, on this record, we must regard the New York City law as permitting Penn Central not only to profit from the Terminal but also to obtain a "reasonable return" on its investment.

Appellants, moreover, exaggerate the effect of the law on their ability to make use of the air rights above the Terminal in two respects. First, it simply cannot be maintained, on this record, that appellants have been prohibited from occupying *any* portion of the airspace above the Terminal. While the Commission's actions in denying applications to construct an office building in excess of 50 stories above the Terminal may indicate that it will refuse to issue a certificate of appropriateness for any comparably sized structure, nothing the Commission has said or done suggests an intention to prohibit *any* construction above the Terminal. The Commission's report emphasized that whether any construction would be allowed depended upon whether the proposed addition "would harmonize in scale, material and character with [the Terminal]." Since appellants have not sought approval for the construction of a smaller structure, we do not know that appellants will be denied any use of any portion of the airspace above the Terminal.

Second, to the extent appellants have been denied the right to build above the Terminal, it is not literally accurate to say that they have been denied *all* use of even those pre-existing air rights. Their ability to use these rights has not been abrogated; they are made transferable to at least eight parcels in the vicinity of the Terminal, one or two of which have been found suitable for the construction of new office buildings. Although appellants and others have argued that New York City's transferable development-rights program is far from ideal, the New York courts here supportably found that, at least in the case of the Terminal, the rights afforded are valuable. While these rights may well not have constituted "just compensation" if a "taking" had occurred, the rights nevertheless undoubtedly mitigate whatever financial burdens the law has imposed on appellants and, for that reason, are to be taken into account in considering the impact of regulation.

On this record, we conclude that the application of New York City's Landmarks Law has not effected a "taking" of appellants' property. The restrictions imposed are substantially related to the promotion of the general welfare and not only permit reasonable beneficial use of the landmark site but also afford appellants opportunities further to enhance not only the Terminal site proper but also other properties.[24]

Affirmed.

[The dissenting opinion of Justice Rehnquist, joined by Chief Justice Burger and Justice Stevens, is omitted. Applying the test of the majority, the dissenters would have found that a taking occurred.]

NOTES AND QUESTIONS

1. *Partial vs. Complete Takings.* Notice that the argument here is not that the landmark designation deprives the building of all of its economical use, as in the *Lucas* case which follows. The Supreme Court analyzes the impact on the property owner as a partial taking. While the Court finds no taking in this case, it does tacitly acknowledge that there can be such a thing as a partial taking.

2. *The* Penn Central *Test.* The two-part test developed by the majority in *Penn Central* has played a central role in regulatory takings cases for the past quarter-century. What is that test?

What specific questions can be asked about justice and fairness in this context? Here is a partial list derived from modern takings cases: Was there unfair dealing? What representations did government make? Were those representations relied

---

[24] [36] We emphasize that our holding today is on the present record, which in turn is based on Penn Central's present ability to use the Terminal for its intended purposes and in a gainful fashion. The city conceded at oral argument that if appellants can demonstrate at some point in the future that circumstances have so changed that the Terminal ceases to be "economically viable," appellants may obtain relief.

upon in good faith? Was reliance reasonable? Did the landowner substantially change its position as a result of such reliance? How much time and money were invested? What led the investor to believe that the status quo would continue? Was government aware that the landowner was relying upon the status quo? From a public policy standpoint, can the government justify its regulation? Does the landowner have freedom to pursue other reasonable investment expectations? *See* G. Stein, *Takings in the 21st Century: Reasonable Investment-Backed Expectations After Palazzolo and Tahoe-Sierra*, 69 TENN. L. REV. 891 (2002). What is the status of other similarly situated properties? What development occurred prior to regulations on those properties? Would development of the investor's land as previously proposed be compatible with the rights of abutting property owners? Do government's prior planning efforts justify its regulations? Did government act for public or private purposes? Was there a change of conditions that triggered the need for new regulation? For a trenchant criticism of the first test, see J. David Breemer, *Playing The Expectations Game*, 38 URB. LAW. 81 (2006).

3. *Segmentation*. In *Penn Central*, the Supreme Court refuses to treat the air space as a separate unit of property. Of course, in measuring impact, the smaller the unit of property used, the greater the diminution. Is the approach in this case consistent with that of *Pennsylvania Coal v. Mahon*? In his dissent in *Mahon* recall that Justice Louis Brandeis faulted the majority for treating the mineral estate separate from the larger estate from which it was derived.

In *Keystone Bituminous Coal Ass'n v. DeBenedictis*, 480 U.S. 470 (1987), which involved a Pennsylvania anti-subsidence law strikingly similar to the one held invalid in *Pennsylvania Coal*, the Court rejected the argument that the coal that had to be left in place in a specific mine to prevent subsidence was the unit of property against which to measure the impact of the ordinance. Rather, the Court suggested that broader units, like the entire mining operations, or a specific mine, would be more reasonable units. Does this render *Pennsylvania Coal* obsolete?

4. "The Court's seemingly inconsistent approach to the segmentation of air and subterranean property rights in the above cases relates to one of the most persistent problems in takings jurisprudence — the "denominator" or "relevant parcel" issue. In many instances, the outcome of a takings claim depends on the unit of property that the court defines as relevant to the takings analysis, as discussed in greater detail later in this section."

5. *After* Penn Central. During the 1980s, the Supreme Court sidestepped the issue of what constitutes "too far" despite several opportunities to rule on the question. *See Agins v. City of Tiburon*, 447 U.S. 255 (1980); *Williamson County Regional Planning Comm'n v. Hamilton Bank*, 473 U.S. 172 (1985); *McDonald, Sommer & Frates v. Yolo County*, 477 U.S. 340 (1986) (mainly decided on the ground that the merits were not "ripe" for decision). The ripeness doctrine largely precludes courts from reaching the merits of regulatory taking cases; it has been much criticized. *See, e.g.*, T. ROBERTS, TAKING SIDES ON TAKINGS ISSUES (2002), Ch. X. Then, in 1992, it decided that a "total" taking by regulation was the functional equivalent of a physical taking by eminent domain.

LUCAS v. SOUTH CAROLINA COASTAL COUNCIL

United States Supreme Court
505 U.S. 1003 (1992)

JUSTICE SCALIA delivered the opinion of the Court.

In 1986, petitioner David H. Lucas paid $975,000 for two residential lots on the Isle of Palms in Charleston County, South Carolina, on which he intended to build single-family homes. In 1988, however, the South Carolina Legislature enacted the Beachfront Management Act, S.C. Code § 48-39-250 *et seq.* (Supp. 1990) (Act), which had the direct effect of barring petitioner from erecting any permanent habitable structures on his two parcels. *See* § 48-39-290(A). A state trial court found that this prohibition rendered Lucas's parcels "valueless." This case requires us to decide whether the Act's dramatic effect on the economic value of Lucas's lots accomplished a taking of private property under the Fifth and Fourteenth Amendments requiring the payment of "just compensation."

I

A

South Carolina's expressed interest in intensively managing development activities in the so-called "coastal zone" dates from 1977 when, in the aftermath of Congress's passage of the federal Coastal Zone Management Act of 1972, 86 Stat. 1280, as amended, 16 U.S.C. § 1451 *et seq.*, the legislature enacted a Coastal Zone Management Act of its own. *See* S.C. Code § 48-39-10 *et seq.* (1987). In its original form, the South Carolina Act required owners of coastal zone land that qualified as a "critical area" (defined in the legislation to include beaches and immediately adjacent sand dunes, § 48-39-10(J)) to obtain a permit from the newly created South Carolina Coastal Council (respondent here) prior to committing the land to a "use other than the use the critical area was devoted to on [September 28, 1977]." § 48-39-130(A).

In the late 1970s, Lucas and others began extensive residential development of the Isle of Palms, a barrier island situated eastward of the City of Charleston. Toward the close of the development cycle for one residential subdivision known as "Beachwood East," Lucas in 1986 purchased the two lots at issue in this litigation for his own account. No portion of the lots, which were located approximately 300 feet from the beach, qualified as a "critical area" under the 1977 Act; accordingly, at the time Lucas acquired these parcels, he was not legally obliged to obtain a permit from the Council in advance of any development activity. His intention with respect to the lots was to do what the owners of the immediately adjacent parcels had already done: erect single-family residences. He commissioned architectural drawings for this purpose.

The Beachfront Management Act brought Lucas's plans to an abrupt end. Under that 1988 legislation, the Council was directed to establish a "baseline" connecting the landward-most "point[s] of erosion . . . during the past forty years" in the region of the Isle of Palms that includes Lucas's lots. § 48-39-280(A)(2) (Supp. 1988). In an action not challenged here, the Council fixed this baseline landward of Lucas's parcels. That was significant, for under the Act construction of occupyable improvements[25] was flatly prohibited seaward of a line drawn 20 feet landward of, and parallel to, the baseline, § 48-39-290(A) (Supp. 1988). The Act provided no exceptions.

B

Lucas promptly filed suit in the South Carolina Court of Common Pleas, contending that the Beachfront Management Act's construction bar effected a taking of his property without just compensation. Lucas did not take issue with the validity of the Act as a lawful exercise of South Carolina's police power, but contended that the Act's complete extinguishment of his property's value entitled him to compensation regardless of whether the legislature had acted in furtherance of legitimate police power objectives. Following a bench trial, the court agreed. Among its factual determinations was the finding that "at the time Lucas purchased the two lots, both were zoned for single-family residential construction and . . . there were no restrictions imposed upon such use of the property by either the State of South Carolina, the County of Charleston, or the Town of the Isle of Palms." The trial court further found that the Beachfront Management Act decreed a permanent ban on construction insofar as Lucas's lots were concerned, and that this prohibition "deprive[d] Lucas of any reasonable economic use of the lots, . . . eliminated the unrestricted right of use, and render[ed] them valueless." The court thus concluded that Lucas's properties had been "taken" by operation of the Act, and it ordered respondent to pay "just compensation" in the amount of $1,232,387.50.

The Supreme Court of South Carolina reversed. It found dispositive what it described as Lucas's concession "that the Beachfront Management Act [was] properly and validly designed to preserve . . . South Carolina's beaches." Failing an attack on the validity of the statute as such, the court believed itself bound to accept the "uncontested . . . findings" of the South Carolina legislature that new construction in the coastal zone — such as petitioner intended — threatened this public resource. The Court ruled that when a regulation respecting the use of property is designed "to prevent serious public harm," no compensation is owing under the Takings Clause regardless of the regulation's effect on the property value.

III

A

Prior to Justice Holmes' exposition in *Pennsylvania Coal Co. v. Mahon* it was generally thought that the Takings Clause reached only a "direct appropriation" of

---

[25] [2] The Act did allow the construction of certain nonhabitable improvements, e.g., "wooden walkways no larger in width than six feet," and "small wooden decks no larger than one hundred forty-four square feet." §§ 48-39-290(A)(1) and (2) (Supp. 1988).

property, or the functional equivalent of a "practical ouster of [the owner's] possession." Justice Holmes recognized in *Mahon*, however, that if the protection against physical appropriations of private property was to be meaningfully enforced, the government's power to redefine the range of interests included in the ownership of property was necessarily constrained by constitutional limits. If, instead, the uses of private property were subject to unbridled, uncompensated qualification under the police power, "the natural tendency of human nature [would be] to extend the qualification more and more until at last private property disappear[ed]." These considerations gave birth in that case to the oft-cited maxim that, "while property may be regulated to a certain extent, if regulation goes too far it will be recognized as a taking." Nevertheless, our decision in *Mahon* offered little insight into when, and under what circumstances, a given regulation would be seen as going "too far" for purposes of the Fifth Amendment. In 70-odd years of succeeding "regulatory takings" jurisprudence, we have generally eschewed any "set formula" for determining how far is too far, preferring to "engag[e] in . . . essentially ad hoc, factual inquiries," *Penn Central Transportation Co. v. New York City*, 438 U.S. 104, 124 (1978). We have, however, described at least two discrete categories of regulatory action as compensable without case-specific inquiry into the public interest advanced in support of the restraint. The first encompasses regulations that compel the property owner to suffer a physical "invasion" of his property. In general (at least with regard to permanent invasions), no matter how minute the intrusion, and no matter how weighty the public purpose behind it, we have required compensation. For example, in *Loretto v. Teleprompter Manhattan CATV Corp.* we determined that New York's law requiring landlords to allow television cable companies to emplace cable facilities in their apartment buildings constituted a taking, even though the facilities occupied at most only 11/2 cubic feet of the landlords' property.

The second situation in which we have found categorical treatment appropriate is where regulation denies all economically beneficial or productive use of land. As we have said on numerous occasions, the Fifth Amendment is violated when land-use regulation "does not substantially advance legitimate state interests *or denies an owner economically viable use of his land.*" *Agins, supra*, 447 U.S. at 260 (citations omitted) (emphasis added).[26]

---

[26] [7] Regrettably, the rhetorical force of our "deprivation of all economically feasible use" rule is greater than its precision, since the rule does not make clear the "property interest" against which the loss of value is to be measured. When, for example, a regulation requires a developer to leave 90% of a rural tract in its natural state, it is unclear whether we would analyze the situation as one in which the owner has been deprived of all economically beneficial use of the burdened portion of the tract, or as one in which the owner has suffered a mere diminution in value of the tract as a whole. (For an extreme — and, we think, unsupportable — view of the relevant calculus, *see Penn Central Transportation Co. v. New York City*, 42 N.Y.2d 324, 333–334, 397 N.Y.S.2d 914, 366 N.E.2d 1271, 1276–1277 (1977), *aff'd*, 438 U.S. 104, 57 L. Ed. 2d 631 (1978), where the state court examined the diminution in a particular parcel's value produced by a municipal ordinance in light of total value of the takings claimant's other holdings in the vicinity.) Unsurprisingly, this uncertainty regarding the composition of the denominator in our "deprivation: fraction has produced inconsistent pronouncements by the Court. *Compare Pennsylvania Coal Co. v. Mahon*, 260 U.S. 393, 414 (1922) (law restricting subsurface extraction of coal held to effect a taking), *with Keystone Bituminous Coal Assn. v. DeBenedictis*, 480 U.S. 470, 497–502 (1987) (nearly identical law held not to effect a taking) . . . . The answer to this difficult question may lie in how the owner's reasonable expectations have been shaped by the State's law of property — *i.e.*, whether and to

We have never set forth the justification for this rule. Perhaps it is simply, as Justice Brennan suggested, that total deprivation of beneficial use is, from the landowner's point of view, the equivalent of a physical appropriation. *See San Diego Gas & Electric Co. v. San Diego*, 450 U.S. at 652 (Brennan, J., dissenting). "[F]or what is the land but the profits thereof[?]" 1 E. COKE, INSTITUTES ch. 1, § 1 (1st Am. ed. 1812). Surely, at least, in the extraordinary circumstance when *no* productive or economically beneficial use of land is permitted, it is less realistic to indulge our usual assumption that the legislature is simply "adjusting the benefits and burdens of economic life," . . . in a manner that secures an "average reciprocity of advantage" to everyone concerned. And the *functional* basis for permitting the government, by regulation, to affect property values without compensation — that "Government hardly could go on if to some extent values incident to property could not be diminished without paying for every such change in the general law," — does not apply to the relatively rare situations where the government has deprived a landowner of all economically beneficial uses.

On the other side of the balance, affirmatively supporting a compensation requirement, is the fact that regulations that leave the owner of land without economically beneficial or productive options for its use — typically, as here, by requiring land to be left substantially in its natural state — carry with them a heightened risk that private property is being pressed into some form of public service under the guise of mitigating serious public harm. *See, e.g., Annicelli v. South Kingstown*, 463 A.2d 133, 140–141 (R.I. 1983) (prohibition on construction adjacent to beach justified on twin grounds of safety and "conservation of open space"); *Morris County Land Improvement Co. v. Parsippany-Troy Hills Township*, 193 A.2d 232, 240 (N.J. 1963) (prohibition on filling marshlands imposed in order to preserve region as water detention basin and create wildlife refuge). As Justice Brennan explained: "From the government's point of view, the benefits flowing to the public from preservation of open space through regulation may be equally great as from creating a wildlife refuge through formal condemnation or increasing electricity production through a dam project that floods private property." *San Diego Gas & Electric Co., supra*, 450 U.S. at 652 (Brennan, J., dissenting). The many statutes on the books, both state and federal, that provide for the use of eminent domain to impose servitudes on private scenic lands preventing developmental uses, or to acquire such lands altogether, suggest the practical equivalence in this setting of negative regulation and appropriation. *See, e.g.*, 16 U.S.C. § 410ff-1(a) (authorizing acquisition of "lands, waters, or interests [within Channel Islands National Park] (including but not limited to scenic easements))"; § 460aa-2(a) (authorizing acquisition of "any lands, or lesser interests therein, including mineral interests and scenic easements" within Sawtooth National Recreation Area); §§ 3921–3923 (authorizing acquisition of wetlands); N.C. Gen. Stat. § 113A-38 (1990) (authorizing acquisition of, inter alia, "scenic easements" within the North Carolina natural and scenic rivers system); Tenn. Code Ann.

---

what degree the State's law has accorded legal recognition and protection to the particular interest in land with respect to which the takings claimant alleges a diminution in (or elimination of) value. In any event, we avoid this difficulty in the present case, since the "interest in land" that Lucas has pleaded (a fee simple interest) is an estate with a rich tradition of protection at common law, and since the South Carolina Court of Common Pleas found that the Beachfront Management Act left each of Lucas's beachfront lots without economic value.

§§ 11-15-101–11-15-108 (1987) (authorizing acquisition of "protective easements" and other rights in real property adjacent to State's historic, architectural, archaeological, or cultural resources).

We think, in short, that there are good reasons for our frequently expressed belief that when the owner of real property has been called upon to sacrifice *all* economically beneficial uses in the name of the common good, that is, to leave his property economically idle, he has suffered a taking.[27]

B

The trial court found Lucas's two beachfront lots to have been rendered valueless by respondent's enforcement of the coastal-zone construction ban. Under Lucas's theory of the case, which rested upon our "no economically viable use" statements, that finding entitled him to compensation. Lucas believed it unnecessary to take issue with either the purposes behind the Beachfront Management Act, or the means chosen by the South Carolina Legislature to effectuate those purposes. The South Carolina Supreme Court, however, thought otherwise. In its view, the Beachfront Management Act was no ordinary enactment, but involved an exercise of South Carolina's "police powers" to mitigate the harm to the public interest that petitioner's use of his land might occasion. By neglecting to dispute the findings enumerated in the Act[28] or otherwise to challenge the legislature's purposes, petitioner "concede[d] that the beach/dune area of South Carolina's shores is an

---

27 [8] Justice Stevens criticizes the "deprivation of all economically beneficial use" rule as "wholly arbitrary," in that "[the] landowner whose property is diminished in value 95% recovers nothing," while the landowner who suffers a complete elimination of value "recovers the land's full value." This analysis errs in its assumption that the landowner whose deprivation is one step short of complete is not entitled to compensation. Such an owner might not be able to claim the benefit of our categorical formulation, but, as we have acknowledged time and again, "[t]he economic impact of the regulation on the claimant and . . . the extent to which the regulation has interfered with distinct investment-backed expectations" are keenly relevant to takings analysis generally. *Penn Central Transportation Co. v. New York City*, 438 U.S. 104, 124 (1978). It is true that in at least some cases the landowner with 95% loss will get nothing, while the landowner with total loss will recover in full. But that occasional result is no more strange than the gross disparity between the landowner whose premises are taken for a highway (who recovers in full) and the landowner whose property is reduced to 5% of its former value by the highway (who recovers nothing). Takings law is full of these "all-or-nothing" situations. Justice Stevens similarly misinterprets our focus on "developmental" uses of property (the uses proscribed by the Beachfront Management Act) as betraying an "assumption that the only uses of property cognizable under the Constitution are *developmental* uses." We make no such assumption. Though our prior takings cases evince an abiding concern for the productive use of, and economic investment in, land, there are plainly a number of noneconomic interests in land whose impairment will invite exceedingly close scrutiny under the Takings Clause. *See, e.g.*, *Loretto v. Teleprompter Manhattan CATV Corp.*, 458 U.S. 419, 436 (1982) (interest in excluding strangers from one's land).

28 [10] The legislature's express findings include the following: . . .

(1) The beach/dune system . . . is extremely important to the people of this State and serves the following functions:

(a) protects life and property by serving as a storm barrier which dissipates wave energy and contributes to shoreline stability in an economical and effective manner;

(b) provides the basis for a tourism industry that generates approximately two-thirds of South Carolina's annual tourism industry revenue which constitutes a significant portion of the state's economy. The tourists who come to the South Carolina coast to enjoy the ocean and dry sand beach contribute significantly to state and local tax revenues;

extremely valuable public resource; that the erection of new construction, inter alia, contributes to the erosion and destruction of this public resource; and that discouraging new construction in close proximity to the beach/dune area is necessary to prevent a great public harm." In the court's view, these concessions brought petitioner's challenge within a long line of this Court's cases sustaining against Due Process and Takings Clause challenges the State's use of its "police powers" to enjoin a property owner from activities akin to public nuisances. *See Mugler v. Kansas*, 123 U.S. 623 (1887) (law prohibiting manufacture of alcoholic beverages); *Hadacheck v. Sebastian*, 239 U.S. 394 (1915) (law barring operation of brick mill in residential area); *Miller v. Schoene*, 276 U.S. 272 (1928) (order to destroy diseased cedar trees to prevent infection of nearby orchards); *Goldblatt v. Hempstead*, 369 U.S. 590 (1962) (law effectively preventing continued operation of quarry in residential area).

It is correct that many of our prior opinions have suggested that "harmful or noxious uses" of property may be proscribed by government regulation without the requirement of compensation. For a number of reasons, however, we think the South Carolina Supreme Court was too quick to conclude that that principle decides the present case. The "harmful or noxious uses" principle was the Court's early attempt to describe in theoretical terms why government may, consistent with the Takings Clause, affect property values by regulation without incurring an obligation to compensate — a reality we nowadays acknowledge explicitly with respect to the full scope of the State's police power. *See, e.g., Penn Central Transportation Co.*, 438 U.S. at 125 (where State "reasonably conclude[s] that 'the health, safety, morals, or general welfare' would be promoted by prohibiting particular contemplated uses of land," compensation need not accompany prohibition); *see also Nollan v. California Coastal Commission*, 483 U.S. at 834–835 ("Our cases have not elaborated on the standards for determining what constitutes a 'legitimate state interest[,]' [but] [t]hey have made clear . . . that a broad range of governmental purposes and regulations satisfy these requirements"). We made this very point in *Penn Central Transportation Co.*, where, in the course of sustaining New York City's landmarks preservation program against a takings challenge, we rejected the petitioner's

---

(c) provides habitat for numerous species of plants and animals, several of which are threatened or endangered. Waters adjacent to the beach/dune system also provide habitat for many other marine species;

(d) provides a natural health environment for the citizens of South Carolina to spend leisure time which serves their physical and mental well-being.

(2) Beach/dune system vegetation is unique and extremely important to the vitality and preservation of the system.

(3) Many miles of South Carolina's beaches have been identified as critically eroding.

(4) . . . [D]evelopment unwisely has been sited too close to the [beach/dune] system. This type of development has jeopardized the stability of the beach/dune system, accelerated erosion, and endangered adjacent property . . . .

(5) The use of armoring in the form of hard erosion control devices such as seawalls, bulkheads, and rip-rap to protect erosion-threatened structures adjacent to the beach has not proven effective . . . .

(8) It is in the state's best interest to protect and to promote increased public access to South Carolina's beaches for out-of-state tourists and South Carolina residents alike.

S.C. Code § 48-39-250 (Supp. 1991).

suggestion that *Mugler* and the cases following it were premised on, and thus limited by, some objective conception of "noxiousness."

> [T]he uses in issue in *Hadacheck, Miller*, and *Goldblatt* were perfectly lawful in themselves. They involved no "blameworthiness, . . . moral wrongdoing or conscious act of dangerous risk-taking which induce[d society] to shift the cost to a particular individual." Sax, *Takings and the Police Power*, 74 YALE L.J. 36, 50 (1964). These cases are better understood as resting not on any supposed "noxious" quality of the prohibited uses but rather on the ground that the restrictions were reasonably related to the implementation of a policy — not unlike historic preservation — expected to produce a widespread public benefit and applicable to all similarly situated property.

438 U.S. at 133–134, n.30. "Harmful or noxious use" analysis was, in other words, simply the progenitor of our more contemporary statements that "land-use regulation does not effect a taking if it 'substantially advance[s] legitimate state interests.' " *Nollan, supra*, 483 U.S. at 834 (quoting *Agins v. Tiburon*, 447 U.S. at 260) . . . .

The transition from our early focus on control of "noxious" uses to our contemporary understanding of the broad realm within which government may regulate without compensation was an easy one, since the distinction between "harm-preventing" and "benefit-conferring" regulation is often in the eye of the beholder. It is quite possible, for example, to describe in *either* fashion the ecological, economic, and aesthetic concerns that inspired the South Carolina legislature in the present case. One could say that imposing a servitude on Lucas's land is necessary in order to prevent his use of it from "harming" South Carolina's ecological resources; or, instead, in order to achieve the "benefits" of an ecological preserve.[29] *Compare, e.g., Claridge v. New Hampshire Wetlands Board*, 485 A.2d 287, 292 (N.H. 1984) (owner may, without compensation, be barred from filling wetlands because landfilling would deprive adjacent coastal habitats and marine fisheries of ecological support), *with, e.g., Bartlett v. Zoning Commission of Old*

---

[29] [11] In the present case, in fact, some of the "[South Carolina] legislature's 'findings' " to which the South Carolina Supreme Court purported to defer in characterizing the purpose of the Act as "harm-preventing," 404 S.E.2d 895, 900 (S.C. 1991), seem to us phrased in "benefit-conferring" language instead. For example, they describe the importance of a construction ban in enhancing "South Carolina's annual tourism industry revenue," S.C. Code § 48-39-250(1)(b) (Supp. 1991), in "provid[ing] habitat for numerous species of plants and animals, several of which are threatened or endangered," § 48-39-250(1)(c), and in "provid[ing] a natural healthy environment for the citizens of South Carolina to spend leisure time which serves their physical and mental well-being." § 48-39-250(1)(d). It would be pointless to make the outcome of this case hang upon this terminology, since the same interests could readily be described in "harm-preventing" fashion. Justice Blackmun, however, apparently insists that we must make the outcome hinge (exclusively) upon the South Carolina Legislature's other, "harm-preventing" characterizations, focusing on the declaration that "prohibitions on building in front of the setback line are necessary to protect people and property from storms, high tides, and beach erosion." He says "[n]othing in the record undermines [this] assessment," *ibid.*, apparently seeing no significance in the fact that the statute permits owners of *existing* structures to remain (and even to rebuild if their structures are not "destroyed beyond repair," S.C. Code Ann. § 48-39-290(B)), and in the fact that the 1990 amendment authorizes the Council to issue permits for new construction in violation of the uniform prohibition, *see* S.C. Code § 48-39-290(D)(1) (Supp. 1991).

Lyme, 282 A.2d 907, 910 (Conn. 1971) (owner barred from filling tidal marshland must be compensated, despite municipality's "laudable" goal of "preserv[ing] marshlands from encroachment or destruction"). Whether one or the other of the competing characterizations will come to one's lips in a particular case depends primarily upon one's evaluation of the worth of competing uses of real estate. *See* RESTATEMENT (SECOND) OF TORTS § 822, Comment g, p. 112 (1979) ("[p]ractically all human activities unless carried on in a wilderness interfere to some extent with others or involve some risk of interference"). A given restraint will be seen as mitigating "harm" to the adjacent parcels or securing a "benefit" for them, depending upon the observer's evaluation of the relative importance of the use that the restraint favors. *See* Sax, *Takings and the Police Power*, 74 YALE L. J. 36, 49 (1964) ("[T]he problem [in this area] is not one of noxiousness or harm-creating activity at all; rather it is a problem of inconsistency between perfectly innocent and independently desirable uses"). Whether Lucas's construction of single-family residences on his parcels should be described as bringing "harm" to South Carolina's adjacent ecological resources thus depends principally upon whether the describer believes that the State's interest in nurturing those resources is so important that *any* competing adjacent use must yield.[30]

When it is understood that "prevention of harmful use" was merely our early formulation of the police power justification necessary to sustain (without compensation) *any* regulatory diminution in value; and that the distinction between regulation that "prevents harmful use" and that which "confers benefits" is difficult, if not impossible, to discern on an objective, value-free basis; it becomes self-evident that noxious-use logic cannot serve as a touchstone to distinguish regulatory "takings" — which require compensation — from regulatory deprivations that do not require compensation. *A fortiori* the legislature's recitation of a noxious-use justification cannot be the basis for departing from our categorical rule that total regulatory takings must be compensated. If it were, departure would virtually always be allowed. The South Carolina Supreme Court's approach would essentially nullify *Mahon*'s affirmation of limits to the noncompensable exercise of the police power. Our cases provide no support for this: None of them that employed the logic of "harmful use" prevention to sustain a regulation involved an allegation that the regulation wholly eliminated the value of the claimant's land. *See Keystone Bituminous Coal Ass'n*, 480 U.S. at 513–514 (Rehnquist, C.J., dissenting).

Where the State seeks to sustain regulation that deprives land of all economically beneficial use, we think it may resist compensation only if the logically antecedent inquiry into the nature of the owner's estate shows that the proscribed use interests were not part of his title to begin with. This accords, we think, with our "takings" jurisprudence, which has traditionally been guided by the understandings of our citizens regarding the content of, and the State's power over, the "bundle of rights" that they acquire when they obtain title to property. It seems to us that the

---

[30] [12] In Justice Blackmun's view, even with respect to regulations that deprive an owner of all developmental or economically beneficial land uses, the test for required compensation is whether the legislature has recited a harm-preventing justification for its action. Since such a justification can be formulated in practically every case, this amounts to a test of whether the legislature has a stupid staff. We think the Takings Clause requires courts to do more than insist upon artful harm-preventing characterizations.

property owner necessarily expects the uses of his property to be restricted, from time to time, by various measures newly enacted by the State in legitimate exercise of its police powers; "[a]s long recognized, some values are enjoyed under an implied limitation and must yield to the police power." And in the case of personal property, by reason of the State's traditionally high degree of control over commercial dealings, he ought to be aware of the possibility that new regulation might even render his property economically worthless (at least if the property's only economically productive use is sale or manufacture for sale), *see Andrus v. Allard*, 444 U.S. 51, 66–67 (1979) (prohibition on sale of eagle feathers). In the case of land, however, we think the notion pressed by the Council that title is somehow held subject to the "implied limitation" that the State may subsequently eliminate all economically valuable use is inconsistent with the historical compact recorded in the Takings Clause that has become part of our constitutional culture.[31]

Where "permanent physical occupation" of land is concerned, we have refused to allow the government to decree it anew (without compensation), no matter how weighty the asserted "public interests" involved, *Loretto v. Teleprompter Manhattan CATV Corp.* — though we assuredly would permit the government to assert a permanent easement that was a pre-existing limitation upon the landowner's title. *Compare Scranton v. Wheeler*, 179 U.S. 141, 163 (1900) (interests of "riparian owner in the submerged lands . . . bordering on a public navigable water" held subject to Government's navigational servitude), *with Kaiser Aetna v. United States*, 444 U.S. at 178–180 (imposition of navigational servitude on marina created and rendered navigable at private expense held to constitute a taking). We believe similar treatment must be accorded confiscatory regulations, i.e., regulations that prohibit all economically beneficial use of land: Any limitation so severe cannot be newly legislated or decreed (without compensation), but must inhere in the title itself, in the restrictions that background principles of the State's law of property and nuisance already place upon land ownership. A law or decree with such an effect must, in other words, do no more than duplicate the result that could have been achieved in the courts — by adjacent landowners (or other uniquely affected persons) under the State's law of private nuisance, or by the State under its complementary power to abate nuisances that affect the public generally, or otherwise.

On this analysis, the owner of a lake bed, for example, would not be entitled to

---

[31] [15] After accusing us of "launch[ing] a missile to kill a mouse," Justice Blackmun expends a good deal of throw-weight of his own upon a noncombatant, arguing that our description of the "understanding" of land ownership that informs the Takings Clause is not supported by early American experience. That is largely true, but entirely irrelevant. The practices of the States *prior* to incorporation of the Takings and Just Compensation Clauses, *see Chicago, B. & Q. R. Co. v. Chicago*, 166 U.S. 226 (1897) — which, as Justice Blackmun acknowledges, occasionally included outright *physical appropriation* of land without compensation, were out of accord with any plausible interpretation of those provisions. Justice Blackmun is correct that early constitutional theorists did not believe the Takings Clause embraced regulations of property at all, but even he does not suggest (explicitly, at least) that we renounce the Court's contrary conclusion in *Mahon*. Since the text of the Clause can be read to encompass regulatory as well as physical deprivations (in contrast to the text originally proposed by Madison, *see* Speech Proposing Bill of Rights (June 8, 1789), *in* 12 J. Madison, The papers of James Madison 201 (C. Hobson, R. Rutland, W. Rachal, & J. Sisson ed. 1979) ("No person shall be . . . obliged to relinquish his property, where it may be necessary for public use, without a just compensation"), we decline to do so as well.

compensation when he is denied the requisite permit to engage in a landfilling operation that would have the effect of flooding others' land. Nor the corporate owner of a nuclear generating plant, when it is directed to remove all improvements from its land upon discovery that the plant sits astride an earthquake fault. Such regulatory action may well have the effect of eliminating the land's only economically productive use, but it does not proscribe a productive use that was previously permissible under relevant property and nuisance principles. The use of these properties for what are now expressly prohibited purposes was always unlawful, and (subject to other constitutional limitations) it was open to the State at any point to make the implication of those background principles of nuisance and property law explicit. *See* Michelman, *Property, Utility, and Fairness, Comments on the Ethical Foundations of "Just Compensation" Law*, 80 HARV. L. REV. 1165, 1239–1241 (1967). In light of our traditional resort to "existing rules or understandings that stem from an independent source such as state law" to define the range of interests that qualify for protection as "property" under the Fifth (and Fourteenth) Amendments, *Board of Regents of State Colleges v. Roth*, 408 U.S. 564, 577 (1972); . . . , this recognition that the Takings Clause does not require compensation when an owner is barred from putting land to a use that is proscribed by those "existing rules or understandings" is surely unexceptional. When, however, a regulation that declares "off-limits" all economically productive or beneficial uses of land goes beyond what the relevant background principles would dictate, compensation must be paid to sustain it.

The "total taking" inquiry we require today will ordinarily entail (as the application of state nuisance law ordinarily entails) analysis of, among other things, the degree of harm to public lands and resources, or adjacent private property, posed by the claimant's proposed activities, *see, e.g.*, RESTATEMENT (SECOND) OF TORTS §§ 826, 827, the social value of the claimant's activities and their suitability to the locality in question, *see, e.g.*, *id.*, §§ 828(a) and (b), 831, and the relative ease with which the alleged harm can be avoided through measures taken by the claimant and the government (or adjacent private landowners) alike, *see, e.g.*, *id.*, §§ 827(e), 828(c), 830. The fact that a particular use has long been engaged in by similarly situated owners ordinarily imports a lack of any common-law prohibition (though changed circumstances or new knowledge may make what was previously permissible no longer so, *see* RESTATEMENT (SECOND) OF TORTS, *supra*, § 827, comment g). So also does the fact that other landowners, similarly situated, are permitted to continue the use denied to the claimant.

It seems unlikely that common-law principles would have prevented the erection of any habitable or productive improvements on petitioner's land; they rarely support prohibition of the "essential use" of land, *Curtin v. Benson*, 222 U.S. 78, 86, 32 (1911). The question, however, is one of state law to be dealt with on remand. We emphasize that to win its case South Carolina must do more than proffer the legislature's declaration that the uses Lucas desires are inconsistent with the public interest, or the conclusory assertion that they violate a common-law maxim such as sic utere tuo ut alienum non laedas. As we have said, a "State, by *ipse dixit*, may not transform private property into public property without compensation." *Webb's Fabulous Pharmacies, Inc. v. Beckwith*, 449 U.S. 155, 164 (1980). Instead, as it would be required to do if it sought to restrain Lucas in a common-law action for public nuisance, South Carolina must identify background principles of nuisance and property law that prohibit the uses he now intends in the circumstances in which the property is presently found. Only on this showing can the State fairly claim that, in proscribing all such beneficial uses, the Beachfront Management Act is taking nothing.[32]

The judgment is reversed and the cause remanded for proceedings not inconsistent with this opinion. So ordered.

JUSTICE KENNEDY, concurring in the judgment.

The South Carolina Court of Common Pleas found that petitioner's real property has been rendered valueless by the State's regulation. The finding appears to presume that the property has no significant market value or resale potential. This is a curious finding, and I share the reservations of some of my colleagues about a finding that a beach front lot loses all value because of a development restriction.

The finding of no value must be considered under the Takings Clause by reference to the owner's reasonable, investment-backed expectations. The Takings Clause, while conferring substantial protection on property owners, does not eliminate the police power of the State to enact limitations on the use of their property. *Mugler v. Kansas*, 123 U.S. 623, 669 (1887). The rights conferred by the Takings Clause and the police power of the State may coexist without conflict. Property is bought and sold, investments are made, subject to the State's power to regulate. Where a taking is alleged from regulations which deprive the property of all value, the test must be whether the deprivation is contrary to reasonable, investment-backed expectations.

There is an inherent tendency towards circularity in this synthesis, of course; for if the owner's reasonable expectations are shaped by what courts allow as a proper exercise of governmental authority, property tends to become what courts say it is. Some circularity must be tolerated in these matters, however, as it is in other spheres. *E.g., Katz v. United States*, 389 U.S. 347, 88 S. Ct. 507, 19 L. Ed. 2d 576 (1967) (Fourth Amendment protections defined by reasonable expectations of privacy). The definition, moreover, is not circular in its entirety. The expectations protected by the Constitution are based on objective rules and customs that can be understood as reasonable by all parties involved.

In my view, reasonable expectations must be understood in light of the whole of our legal tradition. The common law of nuisance is too narrow a confine for the exercise of regulatory power in a complex and interdependent society. *Goldblatt v. Hempstead*, 369 U.S. 590, 593 (1962). The State should not be prevented from enacting new regulatory initiatives in response to changing conditions, and courts

---

[32] [18] Justice Blackmun decries our reliance on background nuisance principles at least in part because he believes those principles to be as manipulable as we find the "harm prevention"/"benefit conferral" dichotomy. There is no doubt some leeway in a court's interpretation of what existing state law permits — but not remotely as much, we think, as in a legislative crafting of the reasons for its confiscatory regulation. We stress that an affirmative decree eliminating all economically beneficial uses may be defended only if an *objectively reasonable application* of relevant precedents would exclude those beneficial uses in the circumstances in which the land is presently found.

must consider all reasonable expectations whatever their source. The Takings Clause does not require a static body of state property law; it protects private expectations to ensure private investment. I agree with the Court that nuisance prevention accords with the most common expectations of property owners who face regulation, but I do not believe this can be the sole source of state authority to impose severe restrictions. Coastal property may present such unique concerns for a fragile land system that the State can go further in regulating its development and use than the common law of nuisance might otherwise permit.

The Supreme Court of South Carolina erred, in my view, by reciting the general purposes for which the state regulations were enacted without a determination that they were in accord with the owner's reasonable expectations and therefore sufficient to support a severe restriction on specific parcels of property. The promotion of tourism, for instance, ought not to suffice to deprive specific property of all value without a corresponding duty to compensate. Furthermore, the means as well as the ends of regulation must accord with the owner's reasonable expectations. Here, the State did not act until after the property had been zoned for individual lot development and most other parcels had been improved, throwing the whole burden of the regulation on the remaining lots. This too must be measured in the balance. *See Pennsylvania Coal Co. v. Mahon*, 260 U.S. 393, 416 (1922).

With these observations, I concur in the judgment of the Court.

[The dissenting opinions of JUSTICES BLACKMUN and STEVENS have been omitted. JUSTICE SOUTER would have dismissed the writ of certiorari as having been improvidently granted.]

NOTES AND QUESTIONS

1. *Subsequent Developments in* Lucas. On remand, the South Carolina Supreme Court found that Lucas' proposed use of the land did not constitute a nuisance at common law and that he was entitled to compensation for the loss of his property from the time of the passage of the 1988 Act until the court's order. *Lucas v. South Carolina Coastal Council*, 424 S.E.2d 484 (S.C. 1992). The case was settled when the State of South Carolina agreed to purchase Lucas' two lots from him for $1.575 million ($850,000 for the lots, plus $725,000 for attorneys' fees and other expenses). The state then recouped some of its losses by selling the two lots to another developer. *See* Houck, *More Unfinished Stories: Lucas, Atlanta Coalition, and Palila/Sweet Home*, 75 U. COLO. L. REV. 331 (2004).

2. *A Categorical Taking.* The Court characterizes its rule in *Lucas* as "categorical," meaning that if there is no economically beneficial use left to the landowner, there is a taking requiring compensation. Does this reformulation leave room for inquiry into the owner's investment-backed expectations? Does it matter, in other words, if the owner purchases 10 acres of wetlands classified by the local government with jurisdiction as "preservation"? Note in this connection that Justice Scalia rejects the *Penn Central* test where, as in *Lucas*, the taking is "total" and not "partial," a test which Justice Kennedy would prefer to apply in total takings as well as partial ones. See his concurring opinion, above.

3. *Denial of All Economically Beneficial Use.* The test most consistently applied in *Lucas* is the taking of *all economically beneficial use.* Is this different from "all use"? How? At a minimum, the Court rejects counting so-called "salvage" uses, like camping or building a deck or pier, in deciding whether the taking is sufficiently "total" to fit the *Lucas* categorical rule. Notice that the court based its holding on the regulation's effect on the landowner's use of the land, rather than the value of the land.

4. *The Exceptions.* There are two exceptions to *Lucas*, according to the Court, which render the taking noncompensable: (1) nuisance and (2) background principles of state property law. What constitutes a nuisance? Although *Mugler v. Kansas*, 123 U.S. 623 (1887) was qualified by *Pennsylvania Coal v. Mahon*, it continues to stand for the so-called "nuisance exception." If a landowner uses his property in such a way as to pose a nuisance to the public, it may be confiscated or destroyed by the state without any obligation to compensation. Not all "nuisances" involve objectionable uses of property. In *Miller v. Schoene*, 276 U.S. 272 (1928), the Supreme Court upheld a Virginia law that required the removal of ornamental cedar trees affected with cedar rust. Although cedar rust posed no threat to the cedar trees themselves (or to humans or animals), the disease threatened nearby apple trees. (The apple growing business was an important part of the state's agricultural industry.) The Court's examples — earthquake faults and flood ways — are rather cataclysmic, but what else besides the obvious traditional examples would qualify? For two post-*Lucas* efforts to answer this question, see *M & J Coal v. United States*, 47 F.3d 1148 (Fed Cir. 1995), and *Darack v. Mazrimas*, 1996 Mass. Super. LEXIS 369 (July 1996). One consequence of *Lucas* is that the common law of nuisance becomes a constitutional category, since only common law nuisances — whatever they might be — can be abated completely without the state incurring an obligation to compensate. *See generally* Humbach, *Evolving Thresholds of Nuisance and the Takings Clause*, 18 Colum. J. Envtl. L. 1 (1993). See Chapter D for further elaboration of nuisance.

What is a background principle of state property law? There are only a handful of post-*Lucas* cases that attempt to define this exception — often in conjunction with nuisance. *See, e.g., United States v. 30.54 Acres of Land*, 90 F.3d 790 (3d Cir. 1996); *Stevens v. Cannon Beach*, 854 P.2d 449 (Or. 1993); *Esplanade Properties v. City of Seattle*, 307 F.3d 978 (9th Cir. 2002). In the above two cases find custom and public trust considerations, respectively, to be background principles of a state's law on property, which thus frees regulations enforcing them from the Lucas categorical takings doctrine. These holdings are not surprising, given the Lucas majority's language about a landowner having no property rights in something that was not part of his title to begin with. However, the *Lucas* majority also inveighed against newly-found "rights," particularly by legislatures, in an attempt to avoid regulatory takings.

Does *Thornton v. Hay* in Chapter 2 fall into this category? How could a landowner possibly have anticipated the expansive (and decidedly un-Blackstonian) customary rights in Oregon held by *all* the people on the entire coastline prior to the Oregon Supreme Court's decision? For one answer to this question, see the scathing dissent by Justice Scalia from the Court's failure to grant a petition for a writ of certiorari in the *Cannon Beach* case at 510 U.S. 1207 (1994) (another case involving these customary rights). What about public trust?

What about legislative acts? Are old and established statutes "background principles"? Obviously new statutes and ordinances are not, since such a statute was the subject of the *Lucas* case. For further discussion of all the categories of "background principles," see Callies & Breemer, *Selected Legal and Policy Trends in Takings Law: Background Principles, Custom and Public Trust Exceptions and the (Mis)Use of Investment Backed Expectations*, 36 VAL. U. L. REV. 339 (2002) and Callies, *Through a Glass Clearly: Predicting the Future in Land Use Takings Law*, 54 WASHBURN L.J. 43 (2014). See Chapter 2 for cases and further questions about custom and public trust.

5. *Does Notice Matter?* In *Palazzolo v. Rhode Island*, 533 U.S. 606 (2001) the Court held that notice of pre-existing limitations are irrelevant in a categorical or total taking case. However, such "notice" may well be an important factor in a Penn Central analysis. For further discussion, see Callies & Chipchase, Palazzolo v. Rhode Island*: Ripeness and "Notice" Rule Clarified and Statutory "Background Principles" Narrowed*, 33 URB. LAW. 907 (2001).

6. *The Denominator Issue*. One of the most vexing problems is the so-called "denominator" or "relevant parcel" issue raised in both *Penn Central* and *Lucas*. After *Lucas*, if a property owner can show that 10 of 100 acres has no economically beneficial use because of land use regulation, is this a total taking of the 10 acres, or a partial taking of the 100 acres? After Lucas, if a property owner can show that 10 of 100 acres lacks economically beneficial use because of land use regulation, is this a total taking of the 10 acres, or a partial taking of the 100 acres? The court's decision on this matter will drastically affect the landowner's changes of prevailing on a takings claim, as well as the compensation that he or she is entitled to thereafter. For cases that tackle this question, see *Loveladies Harbor Inc. v. United States*, 28 F.3d 1171 (Fed Cir. 1994); *Florida Rock Indus. v. United States*, 18 F.3d 1560 (Fed. Cir. 1994); *K & K Construction, Inc. v. Department of Nat. Resources*, 551 N.W.2d 413 (Mich. Ct. App. 1996), *review granted*, 562 N.W.2d 788 (Mich. 1997), *rev'd*, 575 N.W.2d 531 (1998); *Lost Tree Village Corp v. United States*, 707 F.3d 1286 (Fed. Cir. 2013). The U.S. Supreme Court specifically left this issue for another day in *Palazzolo v. Rhode Island*, 533 U.S. 606 (2001). For further discussion, see Merriam, *Rules for the Relevant Parcel*, 25 HAWAII L. REV. 353 (2003).

7. *How Did* Lucas *Affect* Penn Central? To what extent, if any, did the *Lucas* decision overrule or qualify part of the *Penn Central* decision? What are we to make of Justice Scalia's statement in his Footnote 7 that the "calculus" in *Penn Central* is unsupportable? Would the Supreme Court of 1992 have decided *Penn Central* differently? How, if at all, did *Lucas* change *Penn Central*'s investment-backed expectations factor? How does one measure these expectations in *Lucas*? What does one make of Justice Kennedy's concurrence on this point?

In 2002, the Court had the opportunity to clarify these and a number of other issues raised by *Lucas* in *Tahoe Regional Planning Agency v. Tahoe Regional Planning Agency*, 535 U.S. 302 (2002). Instead, it simply attempted an answer to the question: What if a temporary moratorium on development is imposed in order to allow the government to conduct environmental studies to determine what types of development should be allowed? Is that a per se taking of the value of the property during the time that the moratorium is imposed, or does a different test apply? In *Tahoe Regional Planning Agency*, the Court agreed with TRPA that the 3-factor test of *Penn Central* should apply, whereby courts consider "the regulation's economic effect on the landowner, the extent to which the regulation interferes with reasonable investment-backed expectations, and the character of the government action." For the rest, it ducked all but a controversy over whether "all economically beneficial use" means "all value." The majority read the per se test as requiring an "obliteration of value." If indeed the test is — contrary to the language in *Lucas* — value rather than use, is there anything left of the per se rule? After all, while the trial court in *Lucas* found the two lots to be "valueless," no one believed that. For discussions of the use v. value debate, see Douglas T. Kendall, *Defining the* Lucas *Box:* Palazzolo, Tahoe *and the Use/Value Debate*, Ch. 18 and James Burling, *Can the Existence of Value in Property Avert a Regulatory Taking When Economically Beneficial Use Has Been Destroyed?*, Ch. 19, *in* Taking Sides on Takings Issues Public and Private Perspectives (T. Roberts ed. 2002).

In *Lingle v. Chevron USA Inc.*, 544 U.S. 528 (2005), the U.S. Supreme Court abolished the "substantially advances a legitimate state interest" threshold standard for determining when a land use regulation becomes a taking under the Fifth Amendment to the U.S. Constitution. The opinion — which is unanimous — is more important for the Court's summary of present regulatory takings law, at least as applied to disputes involving the regulation of property. First, where the government requires an owner to "suffer a permanent physical invasion of her property — however minor — it must provide compensation." For this proposition, the Court cites its 1982 holding in *Loretto v. Teleprompter Manhattan CATV Corp.*, in which the Court struck down a state law requiring landlords to permit cable companies to install cable facilities on apartment buildings. Second, where government regulations completely deprive a landowner of "all economically beneficial use" of the land, government must pay compensation for a total regulatory taking except to the extent nuisance or the background principles of a state's law of property restrict the landowner's intended use. This is, of course, the rule established in *Lucas*. While a divided Court criticized that decision in *Tahoe-Sierra Preservation Council*, the Court's language in *Lingle* makes it clear that, rare as the deprivation of all economically beneficial use will be, the *Lucas* per se rule is alive, well and applicable when government regulation results in such total deprivation of use. For the rest, as the *Lucas* majority readily concurred, *Penn Central Transportation Company v. City of New York* sets out the criteria for the run-of-the-mill, partial taking by governmental regulation.

Finally, after reiterating that the right to exclude others is "perhaps the most fundamental of all property interests," the Court reviewed with approval its holdings in *Nollan v. California Coastal Commission* and *Dolan v. City of Tigard* (both principle cases set out in full later in this chapter), in which government required dedication of a public easement across part of the relevant parcels as a condition of obtaining a land development permit. These two cases establish that there must be a connection or nexus between a land development exaction and a proposed land use development, and the exaction must be proportional to the impact of the proposed development. *See* Dale Whitman, *Deconstructing Lingle: Implications for Takings Doctrine*, 40 J. Marshall L. Rev. 573 (2007).

8. *Regulatory Takings of Personal Property.* Although this chapter has dealt exclusively with the regulation of land, personal property can be the subject of a regulatory taking. *See generally Andrus v. Allard*, 444 U.S. 51 (1979), and *Horne v. Department of Agriculture*, 135 S. Ct. 2419 (2015). However, the sovereign is free to abate a noxious use of property or confiscate and destroy property used in the commission of a crime without having to pay compensation, a principle embraced by the United States Supreme Court in the landmark case of *Mugler v. Kansas*, 123 U.S. 623 (1887) (state constitutional amendment prohibited the manufacture and sale of alcoholic beverages). Furthermore, an absolute restraint on the ability to sell is not necessarily a taking. *Andrus, supra* (involving a provision in the Eagle Protection Act that prohibits commercial transactions involving parts of eagles legally killed before the statute was enacted). Although the case law is limited, it also appears that intellectual property can be the subject of a regulatory taking. *See Ruckelshaus v. Monsanto Co.*, 467 U.S. 986 (1984) (involving trade secrets) and *Horne v. Department of Agriculture*, 135 S. Ct. 2419 (2015).

9. The citation of U.S. property cases in judicial decisions outside the United States has been rare. However, this appears to be changing as countries throughout the world begin to wrestle with problems associated with increasingly restrictive land use conditions and government compulsory purchase of private property interests. Thus, for example, *Euclid*, *Pennsylvania Coal*, *Penn Central*, *Palazzolo*, *Nollan*, and *Dolan* have all been recently cited by, and cited to, Hong Kong's highest court. *See, e.g., Fine Tower Associates, Ltd. v. Town Planning Board* [2005] HKCU 504 (CFI), discussed with others, in Callies, *Takings: Physical and Regulatory*, 15 ASIA PACIFIC L. REV. 77 (2007).

10. *Regulatory Takings Outside the United States.* The "regulatory takings" problem is not a feature of land use regulation in many countries, but attitudes and standards appear to vary significantly from one country to another. *See* Rachelle Alterman, *Regulatory Takings Viewed Through Cross-National Comparative Lenses*, 5 WASH. U. GLOBAL STUD. L. REV. 469 (2006). For the contemporary situation in the western world, see the two volume symposium *Regulatory Takings in Land-Use Law: A Comparative Perspective on Compensation Rights*, published in Volume 5, Number 3 and Volume 6, Number 1, of the *Washington University Global Studies Law Review*. In addition to the Alterman article mentioned above and a *Conclusion* by Dan Mandelker, the symposium includes articles on regulatory takings in Canada, the United Kingdom, France, Greece, Poland, the Netherlands, Finland, Germany, Austria, and Israel. For a comparative discussion of foreign regulations of private land in Asia and Oceana, see TAKING LAND: COMPULSORY PURCHASE AND REGULATION IN ASIAN-PACIFIC COUNTRIES (Kotaka & Callies eds. 2002).

11. *A Note on Ripeness.* In order to get their claims into Federal Court in the first place, plaintiffs must meet the "ripeness" requirements articulated by the U.S Supreme Court in *Williamson County Regional Planning Comm'n v. Hamilton Bank of Johnson City*, 473 U.S. 172 (1985). The question of when a regulatory taking claim is "ripe" for review arises because unless a court can determine the extent of economic loss (whether partial or total), it cannot decide whether a regulatory taking has occurred. Additionally, particularly when the claimant sues under the U.S. Constitution's 5th Amendment, the issue of damages is critical since the amendment does not bar takings, but only takings without compensation.

The Williamson County ripeness doctrine test provides that a taking claim is not ripe until the landowner has satisfied the following two prongs: (1) obtained a "final decision" from the relevant state or county agencies on its application for development and (2) sought and failed to obtain compensation for the regulatory taking in state court. Ripeness has become a difficult hurdle for many litigants, especially based on its interaction with the judicial doctrine of issue preclusion. *See* Thomas E. Roberts, *Ripeness and Forum Selection in Fifth Amendment Takings Litigation*, 11. J. Land Use & Envtl. L. 37 (1995); Michael J. Berger, The "Ripeness Mess in Federal Land Use Cases, or How the Supreme Court Converted Federal Judges into Fruit Peddlers, Ch. 7, Inst. On Plan., Zoning and Eminent Domain (1991); J. David Breemer, *The Rebirth of Federal Takings Review? The Courts' "Prudential" Answer to Williamson County's Flawed State Litigation Ripeness Requirement*, 30 Touro L. Rev. 319, 340 (2014).

NOTES ON OTHER RELATED CONSTITUTIONAL CLAIMS

1. *The 14th Amendment and Equal Protection.* Challenges to government treatment of parties seeking development permission can often be framed in equal protection or substantive due process terms. Claims brought pursuant to the Equal Protection clause have a major advantage over substantive due process claims. No property interest need be shown. Also, judges who deny the existence of substantive due process outside the context of fundamental liberty interests (see Justice Scalia's comment, Note 1, *supra* following *Marks v. City of Chesapeake*, 883 F.2d 308 (4th Cir. 1989)), concede the existence of an equal protection claim. Nonetheless, equal protection claims that do not involve suspect classes or fundamental rights are subject to the highly deferential rational basis test. While this rule is not airtight, *see City of Cleburne v. Cleburne Living Center*, 473 U.S. 432 (1985), most land use cases fall into this category. *See e.g. Village of Belle Terre v. Boraas*, 416 U.S. 1 (1974).

2. *The 14th Amendment and Due Process.* Many constitutional land use claims are based on the Due Process clause of the Fourteenth Amendment rather than, or in addition to, the Fifth Amendment Takings Clause. While the takings claims discussed in the prior section are Fourteenth Amendment claims in that the Fifth Amendment is being applied to the states through the Fourteenth Amendment by incorporation, *Chicago, B. & Q. R. Co. v. City of Chicago*, 166 U.S. 226 (1897), in this section, we examine due process claims based directly and solely on the Fourteenth Amendment. Two due process claims exist: substantive and procedural. The essence of the former is protection against arbitrary state action; the essence of the latter is that a fair process (notice and hearing) accompany deprivations.

While substantive due process is most often expressed as imposing a requirement that a law promote a legitimate public end in a rational manner, the Court has said on occasion that substantive due process also means that laws ought not be unduly oppressive upon the affected class. *Lawton v. Steele*, 152 U.S. 133, 137 (1894); *Nollan v. California Coastal Commission*, 483 U.S. 825, 845 (1987) (dissenting opinion). In 1922 when the Court in *Pennsylvania Coal* said that otherwise valid regulations that went "too far" could only be sustained as Fifth Amendment takings, it became difficult to separate a takings claim from a substantive due process claim. Query: how do the tests of going "too far" and being "unduly onerous" differ? *Pennsylvania Coal*, in fact, was regarded as a substantive due process case by a few courts, but so long as the remedy for both was a declaration of invalidity, it mattered little how the claim was labeled. That changed when the Court held in the 1987 *First English* decision that the remedy for a regulatory taking was just compensation.

With the mandatory compensation remedy and the higher scrutiny used in some takings claims, there was a need to distinguish between the two claims. Yet, decades of case law, which discussed the two constitutional protections indiscriminately, left attorneys and judges understandably confused. For historical analyses of *Pennsylvania Coal* as a takings or due process case, see Robert Brauneis, *The Foundation of Our "Regulatory Takings" Jurisprudence: The Myth and Meaning of Justice Holmes's Opinion in* Pennsylvania Coal v. Mahon, 106 YALE L.J. 613, 679 (1996); James W. Ely, Jr., *The Fuller Court and Takings Jurisprudence*, 1996 J. SUP. CT. HIST., VOL. II at 120.

Regardless of the heritage of the *Lawton* "unduly oppressive" substantive due process claim that resembles, and in fact is sometimes labeled, a "due process takings," *see Warren v. City of Athens, Ohio*, 411 F.3d 697, 706 (6th Cir. 2005), cases suggest that the Fifth Amendment takings claim subsumes it. The Supreme Court has held in the context of the Fourth and Eighth Amendments that where there is an explicit textual source in the Constitution dealing with the governmental conduct in question, it must be the guide for analyzing liability, rather than Fourteenth Amendment substantive due process. *See City of Cuyahoga Falls v. Buckeye Community Hope Foundation*, concurrence of Justice Scalia, *infra* page 303. While courts show some confusion, several have held that this doctrine applies to eliminate a due process claim based on its allegedly unduly onerous nature or excessive impact. *See Banks v. City of Whitehall*, 344 F.3d 550 (6th Cir. 2003); *Madison v. Graham*, 316 F.3d 867 (9th Cir. 2002.). *See also* the discussion in *John v. City of Houston*, 214 F.3d 573, 583 (5th Cir. 2000). To avoid the *Williamson County* ripeness directive that takings claims be sued upon in state court, some landowners go directly to federal court trying to dress up their takings claim in due process language. Most courts recognize that careful analysis is necessary to ferret out these "masquerades." *See, e.g., Sandy Creek Investors, Ltd. v. City of Jonestown*, 325 F.3d 623 (5th Cir. 2003).

Unlike the obsolete substantive due process claim that a regulation is unduly oppressive, the arbitrary and capricious substantive due process claim does not assert that a regulation is "unduly oppressive," or goes "too far," but rather contends that the state either has no business regulating the conduct in question or that the state has chosen an irrational means to regulate. As one court observed, "[s]ome things a government cannot do at all, no matter the justification." *Gosnell v. City of Troy*, 59 F.3d 654, 657 (7th Cir. 1995). This claim does not duplicate the Fifth Amendment takings claim, and should not be subsumed. The *Lingle* Court, particularly Justice Kennedy's concurring opinion, makes this clear. Yet, old habits die hard and even the clear directive of *Lingle* hasn't been quickly absorbed by all. *See, e.g., Coates v. Hall*, 2007 U.S. Dist. LEXIS 26294 (W.D. Tex. Apr. 10, 2007) (arbitrary and capricious substantive due process claim subsumed into the Fifth Amendment takings cause of action.) Getting it right, *see Crown Point Develop-*

ment, Inc. v. City of Sun Valley, 506 F.3d 851, 855 (9th Cir. 2007) ("*Lingle* pulls the rug out from under our rationale for totally precluding substantive due process claims based on arbitrary or unreasonable conduct.").

Still, the arbitrary and capricious claim is often not well received. The lower federal courts, finding themselves inundated with land use claims based on allegedly arbitrary and capricious conduct, often belittle what they call "run of the mill, garden variety" zoning disputes. The Seventh Circuit dismissed one such suit declaiming it ought not "displace or postpone consideration of some *worthier object of federal judicial solicitude.*" *Coniston Corp. v. Village of Hoffman Estates*, 844 F.2d 461 (7th Cir. 1988). For a trenchant criticism of *Coniston*, see Richard Epstein, *Coniston Corp. v. Village of Hoffman Hills: How to Make Procedural Due Process Disappear*, 74 U. CHI. L. REV. 1689 (2007). Indeed, the Supreme Court has held that only "the most egregious conduct" that "shocks the conscience" is arbitrary in a Constitutional sense. *See County of Sacramento v. Lewis*, 523 U.S. 833, 834 (1998); *City of Cuyahoga Falls v. Buckeye Community Hope Foundation*, 538 U.S. 188 (2003). The Fourteenth Amendment also protects so called procedural due process. The decision making process in land use cases raise significant concerns with fairness, and courts have long held that decisions resulting in deprivation of poverty should at minimum follow a process that includes notice and a right to be heard. Procedural due process is most commonly implicated in the context of actions that are quasi-judicial in nature. As a general matter where an action is found to be adjudicative, the public body must: (1) allow all parties notice and an opportunity to be heard, so that they may adequately present and rebut evidence; (2) act impartially, without substantial pressure from outside interest; (3) keep a record of proceedings; and (4) make its decisions based on findings of fact and conclusions of law. One problem in this Constitutional field is the reluctance of some courts to hold that many decisions by city councils are legislative in name but quasi-judicial in fact. For an intriguing different approach to regulatory takings, see John Martinez, *A Cognitive Science Approach to Takings*, 49 U.S.F. L. Rev. 469 (2015).

3. *Section 1983 of the Civil Rights Act*. Section I of the Civil Rights Act of 1871, 42 U.S.C.A. § 1983, is the procedural vehicle for much constitutional land use litigation. Section 1983 provides:

> Every person who, under color of any statute, ordinance, regulation, custom, or usage, of any State or Territory of the District of Columbia, subjects, or causes to be subjected, any citizen of the United States or other person within the jurisdiction thereof to the deprivation of any rights, privileges, or immunities secured by the Constitution and laws, shall be liable to the party injured in an action at law, suit in equity, or other proper proceeding for redress.

The act creates no rights, but provides a vehicle which enables one to sue based on federal constitutional or statutory rights that are not self-executing. The Court's holdings that property rights as well as personal rights were protected by the statute, *Lynch v. Household Finance Corp.*, 405 U.S. 538 (1972), and that municipalities were "persons" covered by the act, *Monell v. Department of Social Services*, 436 U.S. 658 (1978), spurred use of § 1983 by land owners. *See generally* ROBERT H. FREILICH & RICHARD G. CARLISLE, SECTION 1983: SWORD & SHIELD (1983) and MARY MASSARON ROSS & EDWIN VOSS, SWORD AND SHIELD REVISITED: A PRACTICAL APPROACH TO SECTION 1983 (2d ed. 2006), in particular Ch. 7, *The Section 1983 Land Use Case.*

Wrongs actionable under other federal statutes may not also be actionable under § 1983. In *City of Rancho Palos Verdes v. Abrams*, 544 U.S. 113 (2005), the Court held that a § 1983 action was not available to enforce the rights created by the Telecommunications Act, 47 U.S.C. § 332(c)(7), since it sets out specific remedies.

The substantive issues in § 1983 land use litigation most often involve allegations that local government has deprived a particular landowner of one or more of the following federal rights: a taking of property without just compensation under the Fifth Amendment; a denial of procedural or substantive due process or equal protection under the Fourteenth Amendment; and/or a denial of freedom of speech or religion under the First Amendment.

While courts sometimes say that there is no direct cause of action under the constitution (except as against federal officials under *Bivens v. Six Unknown Named Agents of the Federal Bureau of Narcotics*, 403 U.S. 388 (1971), and that § 1983 is the sole remedy for federal constitutional violations by those acting under color of state law, *see, e.g.*, *Murphy v. Zoning Comm'n of Town of New Milford*, 223 F. Supp. 2d 377 (D. Conn. 2002), that is not true of a violation of the Takings Clause is it? After all, as the Court said in *First English*, the Fifth Amendment's Takings Clause is "self executing."

The Supreme Court has said that "the under-color-of-state-law requirement [of § 1983] does not add anything not already included within the state-action requirement of the Fourteenth Amendment . . . ." *Lugar v. Edmondson Oil Co.*, 457 U.S. 922, 935, n.18 (1982). For all practical purposes, § 1983 land use litigation almost always involves the actions of local governmental entities. Therefore, simply stated, the "state action" or "under color of state law" requirement of the Fourteenth Amendment and § 1983 are usually met, because the actions of a political subdivision of the state constitute state action. Problems, however, can arise in deciding which acts create liability of an individual official or of the government itself (or both). Note that States (in contrast to municipalities and counties) are not "persons" under § 1983. *Will v. Michigan Department of State Police*, 491 U.S. 58 (1989).

The paradigm for governmental liability was created in *Monell v. Department of Social Services*, 436 U.S. 658 (1978). The touchstone of a § 1983 action against a government body is an allegation that "official policy" was responsible for a deprivation of federal rights. In land use cases, the question of the liability of the municipality for decisions by lower municipal officials in zoning and subdivision related matters may be an issue. A municipality can be liable through the adoption of a zoning ordinance or through the acts of building inspectors, planning officials or the planning commission. *Video Intern. Production, Inc. v. Warner-Amex Cable Communications, Inc.*, 858 F.2d 1075 (5th Cir. 1988), *cert. denied*, 491 U.S. 906 (1989).

In *Pembaur v. City of Cincinnati*, 475 U.S. 469 (1986), the Court explained more precisely when an action by a government official on a single occasion may be enough to establish an unconstitutional municipal policy. Although unable to agree on a general standard, the *Pembaur* Court established four principles concerning municipal liability in § 1983 claims:

(1) a municipality is only liable under § 1983 for "acts which the municipality has officially sanctioned or ordered."

(2) only municipal officials who have "final policymaking authority" may subject the municipality to liability.

(3) whether an official has "final policymaking authority is a question of state law"; and,

(4) the challenged action must be in accordance with the policy adopted by the particular official for that official's designated area of the city's business.

Where a mayor vetoed a zoning ordinance in an attempt to bribe a developer, the municipality was not liable. Do you see why? *Manor Healthcare Corp. v. Lomelo*, 929 F.2d 633 (11th Cir. 1991). In *City of St. Louis v. Praprotnik*, 485 U.S. 112 (1988), the Court made it clear that the question of whether a government employee has the authority to establish official policy is a matter of law, and not one for the jury to decide.

The basis for individual liability was established by *Monroe v. Pape*, 365 U.S. 167 (1961). The *Monroe* Court found that public officials, sued in their individual capacities, could be liable because "[m]isuse of power, possessed by virtue of state law and made possible only because the wrongdoer is clothed with the authority of state law, is action taken under color of state law." *Monroe*, 365 U.S. at 184 (citing *United States v. Classic*, 313 U.S. 299, 326 (1941) (internal quotation marks omitted).

Unlike governments, individuals may be immune from suit.

4. *The First Amendment.* Land use controls frequently implicate First Amendment rights. The three principal activities touched by land use regulations sexually oriented businesses, billboards and other signs, and religious uses. In addition, when codes allow only "single family" use or exclude abortion clinics, First and Fourteenth Amendment (privacy) concerns arise. *See* discussion *infra*, on regulating nontraditional living arrangements. A fifth, increasingly raised claim alleges violation of the right to petition government when the government retaliates against property owners and developers who seek development permission.

The Supreme Court reentered the land use field in the mid-1970s after a nearly five decade hiatus. See introduction to this chapter. In doing so, the Court did not have difficulty sustaining zoning ordinances challenged under the First Amendment. Its initial foray came in *Young v. American Mini Theaters, Inc.*, 427 U.S. 50, 62 (1976), where the Court upheld a Detroit ordinance that regulated location of adult movie theaters. In that case the Court said that "[t]he mere fact that the commercial exploitation of material protected by the First Amendment is subject to zoning . . . is not a sufficient reason for invalidating these ordinances." *Id.* Rightly or wrongly, that statement led some to think that zoning controls were free from the constraint of the First Amendment. Thus, a state court, facing an ordinance that prohibited live entertainment in commercial zones, noted the above statement of *Young* and said that " 'First Amendment guarantees are not involved [since the case concerns] solely a zoning ordinance.' " *Schad v. Borough of Mount Ephraim*, 452 U.S. 61, 64 (1981), quoting the state trial court. On appeal in that case, the Supreme Court was obliged to make it clear that the zoning power "is not infinite and unchallengeable." The standard of review is dictated by the nature of the right affected rather than by the power being exercised, and "when a zoning law infringes upon a protected liberty, it must be narrowly drawn and must further a sufficiently substantial government interest." *Id.* at 68. Thus, when the action of a government entity is not carefully tailored and implicates fundamental rights of free speech, it may be invalidated. *See e.g. City of Ladue v. Gilleo*, 512 U.S. 43 (1994). In zoning's early years, the negative externalities of religious uses were negligible. Buildings devoted to religious use tended to be small, particularly when compared to today's "norms," and congregations served the neighborhoods in which they were located. Some courts viewed religious uses as presumptively or inherently beneficial to residential areas and lessened any burden of proof or shifted the burden on government to justify regulating them. Some still do. *See House of Fire Christian Church v. Zoning Bd. of Adjustment of City of Clifton*, 879 A.2d 1212, 1217 (N.J. Super. Ct. App. Div. 2005); *McGann v. Incorporated Village of Old Westbury*, 719 N.Y.S.2d 803 (2000).

Times have changed. Always a very religious society, the United States is, increasingly, religiously active and diverse. Activities conducted by many religious organizations are no longer limited to weekends and no longer limited to what many would think of as traditional religious services. They may operate day care centers or offer their buildings or grounds as homeless shelters. Multi-complex, multi-use religious organizations with thousands of members and daily activities that range beyond the "traditional" to include restaurants, coffee houses, bookstores, athletic fields, housing for elderly members, and radio and television broadcasting have spread across the country almost as fast as big box supercenters. *See* Sara C. Galvan, *Note, Beyond Worship: The Religious Land Use and Institutionalized Persons Act of 2000 and Religious Institutions' Auxiliary Uses*, 24 YALE L. & POL'Y REV. 207–208 (2006). These "mega-churches," as they are often called, often require substantial acreage and when a "supersized" project is announced by a religious organization or an existing religious use wants to expand, neighbors may voice concerns. While the objections of neighbors almost always relate to the anticipated impact on the community due to the size of buildings and multiplicity of activities that may occur, religious animus is not unknown. Religious orders that are new to a community may be viewed with skepticism. Ignorance or intolerance of those with different religious beliefs and "unusual" practices may well spark a zoning battle.

Economics also plays a role. Cities engaging in urban redevelopment or hoping for urban revitalization may prefer land uses that produce tax revenues and generate economic activity. A storefront, shoestring religious group that leases or buys a decrepit building in the urban center may preclude rehabilitation of the building and the entry of a taxpaying, new chic restaurant. *See* Lucinda Harper, *Storefront Churches: The Neighbors Upscale Stores Don't Love*, WALL ST. J., Mar. 15, 2000, at B1.

Some or all of these factors have led many communities to regulate religious uses more stringently than in the past. Often, this simply means treating religious uses on a par with other institutional uses since, as with much land development, they produce problems such as noise, traffic, parking, storm runoff, and erosion. At times, religious organizations may be treated unfavorably compared to other institutional uses. In either case, increasing regulation provokes an increase in First Amendment free exercise challenges, and it has led to congressional intervention into what traditionally has been a matter for local control.

Fearing litigation or believing religious uses should be treated more favorably than other like uses, some communities exempt religious uses from some or most controls. This favoritism may be challenged on establishment clause grounds. The dilemma then for regulators is to deal with the Catch 22: regulating religious uses may lead to free exercise claims but exempting religious uses from regulations others must follow may lead to establishment clause claims.

While it is fundamental that the free exercise clause absolutely protects religious beliefs, government can regulate religious conduct. However, the Court held in *Sherbert v. Verner*, 374 U.S. 398 (1963), that government regulation of conduct that substantially burdens the free exercise of religion cannot be sustained unless it furthers a compelling interest and uses the least restrictive means to advance this interest. In the *Sherbert* era, however, courts consistently found that land use regulations did not substantially burden the free exercise of religion and were thus not subject to the compelling interest test. *See Messiah Baptist Church v. County of Jefferson*, 859 F.2d 820 (10th Cir. 1988) (construction of a house of worship on particular tract of land not integrally related to the church's beliefs and church made no showing that alternative sites were unavailable); *Grosz v. City of Miami Beach*, 721 F.2d 729 (11th Cir. 1983) (valid to prevent rabbi from conducting organized religious services in his home to preserve the quiet of the neighborhood); and *Lakewood, Ohio Congregation of Jehovah's Witnesses v. City of Lakewood*, 699 F.2d 303 (6th Cir. 1983).

Religious exercise claims in the land use context became even in 1990 when the Court held that the strict scrutiny test of *Sherbert* does not apply to claims challenging neutral laws of general applicability. *Employment Division v. Smith*, 494 U.S. 872 (1990). The "right of free exercise does not relieve an individual of the obligation to comply with a 'valid and neutral law of general applicability on the ground that the law proscribes (or prescribes) conduct that his religion prescribes (or proscribes).' " *Id.* at 879.

The Court clarified the reach of *Smith* in *Church of Lukumi Babalu Aye, Inc. v. City of Hialeah*, 508 U.S. 520, 533–35 (1993), where it said that *Smith* did not grant government the power to target religious practices. In *City of Hialeah*, the Court found that a city violated the First Amendment when it applied its zoning, health, and animal cruelty ordinances prohibiting the ritual slaughter of animals to specifically target one church's religious conduct. Applying the compelling interest test, the Court found that the ordinances were not narrowly tailored to achieve the city's interests. Thus, under *City of Hialeah*, an ordinance that is neutral on its face will be subjected to strict scrutiny if shown to have been motivated by religious animus.

In *St. Bartholomew's Church v. City of New York*, 914 F.2d 348 (2d Cir. 1990), *cert. denied*, 499 U.S. 905 (1991), the court relied on *Employment Division v. Smith* to deny a free exercise claim by New York City's St. Bartholomew's Church involving the application of New York's historic landmark law. The church and its adjacent community building were designated historic landmarks in 1967. In 1983, the church wanted to raise revenue for a number of religious purposes and sought permission from the Landmarks Commission to replace its community house with a 59 story office tower. Its request was denied. In the litigation that followed, the court held that the church had to comply with the landmark law, which it found to be a facially neutral regulation of general applicability within the meaning of *Employment Division v. Smith.*

Dissatisfied with *Smith's* perceived narrowing of protection for religious uses, and decisions like *St. Bartholomew's*, Congress enacted the Religious Freedom Restoration Act of 1993 (RFRA), 42 U.S.C. § 2000bb *et seq.*, which purported to restore pre-*Smith* First Amendment law. When St. Peter's Catholic Church of Boerne, Texas proposed an addition to its 1923 mission style building, which could not accommodate the growing parish, the city denied its request. The building was a historic landmark, and the proposal would have replaced nearly 80% of it. Such an expansion, the city found, would impermissibly alter the exterior of the structure. The church claimed the denial violated RFRA. The Court, however, held RFRA an unconstitutional exercise of Congress' remedial powers under Section Five of the Fourteenth Amendment. *City of Boerne v. Flores*, 521 U.S. 507 (1997). *See generally* Alan C. Weinstein, CH. 4, PROTECTING FREE SPEECH AND EXPRESSION IN THE FIRST AMENDMENT AND LAND USE LAW (D. Mandelker & R. Rubin eds. 2001).

Attempting to overcome the Court's objections to RFRA, Congress enacted the Religious Land Use and Institutionalized Persons Act of 2000 (RLUIPA). 42 U.S.C. § 2000cc *et seq. See* Marci A. Hamilton, *Federalism and the Public Good: The True Story Behind the Religious Land Use and Institutionalized Persons Act*, 78 IND. L. J. 311 (2003). Land use litigation today relating to religious activities religious organizations generally raises First Amendment free exercise and RLUIPA claims and their neighbors raise establishment clause claims. For a recent case discussing RLUIPA claims *see World Outreach Conference Center v. City of Chicago and Trinity Evangelical Lutheran Church v. City of Peoria*, 591 F.3d 531 (7th Cir. 2009). *See generally* Smith and Donoho, *RLUIPA: Re-aligning Burdens of Proof, Clarifying Freedoms and Re-Defining Responsibilities*, 18 N.Y.U. J. OF LEGIS. & PUB. POL'Y 67 (2015).

[3.] Land Development Conditions

Not every constitutional controversy involving the application of the Takings Clause to land use restrictions involves statutes or ordinances. Administrative actions and decisions can raise similar questions. By justifying land development dedications and fees as police power regulations rather than "voluntary" costs of using the subdivision process, local governments invite judicial scrutiny under the Takings Clause of the Fifth Amendment to the U.S. Constitution. While early cases by and large upheld intrinsic dedications and fees, by the 1960s, charges of "impact fees" for the shared construction by several land developers of large and expensive public facilities (such as municipal waste water treatment plants and sanitary landfills) outside or extrinsic to the development upon which the fee was levied, led courts sympathetic to the rights of developers to scrutinize the connection between these fees and the need generated by the development for the particula question. Heyman & Gilhool, *The Constitutionality of Imposing Community Costs on New Suburban Residents Through Subdivision* 73 YALE L.J. 1119 (1964).

Nevertheless, it is generally agreed that the law applicable to ir exactions and in lieu fees, as well as to compulsory dedications, is the s that they all represent land development conditions levied at some point development process, such as subdivision approval, building permit, occupancy permit or utility connection. The major constitutional issue with respect to fees, dedications and exactions, is the relationship between such land development, and the land dedication or fee for the public facility, or other condition imposed or levied by government, as the following cases illustrate. For an extensive discussion of these issues, see R. FREILICH & M. SCHULTZ, MODEL SUBDIVISION REGULATIONS: PLANNING & LAW (1995); D. CALLIES, D. CURTIN & J. TAPPENDORF, *Land Development Conditions, in* BARGAINING FOR DEVELOPMENT: A HANDBOOK ON DEVELOPMENT AGREEMENTS, ANNEXATION AGREEMENTS, LAND DEVELOPMENT CONDITIONS, VESTED RIGHTS, AND THE PROVISION OF PUBLIC FACILITIES 5 (2003).

NOLLAN v. CALIFORNIA COASTAL COMMISSION

United States Supreme Court
483 U.S. 825 (1987)

JUSTICE SCALIA delivered the opinion of the Court.

James and Marilyn Nollan appeal from a decision of the California Court of Appeal ruling that the California Coastal Commission could condition its grant of permission to rebuild their house on their transfer to the public of an easement across their beachfront property. The California court rejected their claim that imposition of that condition violates the Takings Clause of the Fifth Amendment, as incorporated against the States by the Fourteenth Amendment. We noted probable jurisdiction.

The Nollans own a beachfront lot in Ventura County, California. A quarter-mile north of their property is Faria County Park, an oceanside public park with a public beach and recreation area. Another public beach area, known locally as "the Cove," lies 1,800 feet south of their lot. A concrete seawall approximately eight feet high separates the beach portion of the Nollans' property from the rest of the lot. The historic mean high tide line determines the lot's oceanside boundary.

The Nollans originally leased their property with an option to buy. The building on the lot was a small bungalow, totaling 504 square feet, which for a time they rented to summer vacationers. After years of rental use, however, the building had fallen into disrepair, and could no longer be rented out.

The Nollans' option to purchase was conditioned on their promise to demolish the bungalow and replace it. In order to do so, under Cal. Pub. Res. Code Ann. §§ 30106, 30212, and 30600 (West 1986), they were required to obtain a coastal development permit from the California Coastal Commission. On February 25, 1982, they submitted a permit application to the Commission in which they proposed to demolish the existing structure and replace it with a three-bedroom house in keeping with the rest of the neighborhood.

The Nollans were informed that their application had been placed on the administrative calendar, and that the Commission staff had recommended that the permit be granted subject to the condition that they allow the public an easement to pass across a portion of their property bounded by the mean high tide line on one side, and their seawall on the other side. This would make it easier for the public to get to Faria County Park and the Cove. The Nollans protested imposition of the condition, but the Commission overruled their objections and granted the permit subject to their recordation of a deed restriction granting the easement.

On June 3, 1982, the Nollans filed a petition for writ of administrative mandamus asking the Ventura County Superior Court to invalidate the access condition. They argued that the condition could not be imposed absent evidence that their proposed development would have a direct adverse impact on public access to the beach. The court agreed, and remanded the case to the Commission for a full evidentiary hearing on that issue.

On remand, the Commission held a public hearing, after which it made further factual findings and reaffirmed its imposition of the condition. It found that the new house would increase blockage of the view of the ocean, thus contributing to the development of "a 'wall' of residential structures" that would prevent the public "psychologically . . . from realizing a stretch of coastline exists nearby that they have every right to visit." The new house would also increase private use of the shorefront. These effects of construction of the house, along with other area development, would cumulatively "burden the public's ability to traverse to and along the shorefront." Therefore the Commission could properly require the Nollans to offset that burden by providing additional lateral access to the public beaches in the form of an easement across their property. The Commission also noted that it had similarly conditioned 43 out of 60 coastal development permits along the same tract of land, and that of the 17 not so conditioned, 14 had been approved when the Commission did not have administrative regulations in place allowing imposition of the condition, and the remaining 3 had not involved shorefront property.

The Nollans filed a supplemental petition for a writ of administrative mandamus with the Superior Court, in which they argued that imposition of the access condition violated the Takings Clause of the Fifth Amendment, as incorporated against the States by the Fourteenth Amendment. The Superior Court ruled in their favor on statutory grounds, finding, in part to avoid "issues of constitutionality," that the California Coastal Act of 1976, Cal. Pub. Res. Code Ann. § 30000 *et seq.* (West 1986), authorized the Commission to impose public access conditions on coastal development permits for the replacement of an existing single-family home with a new one only where the proposed development would have an adverse impact on public access to the sea. In the court's view, the administrative record did not provide an adequate factual basis for concluding that replacement of the bungalow with the house would create a direct or cumulative burden on public access to the sea. Accordingly, the Superior Court granted the writ of mandamus and directed that the permit condition be struck.

The Commission appealed to the California Court of Appeal. While that appeal was pending, the Nollans satisfied the condition on their option to purchase by tearing down the bungalow and building the new house, and bought the property. They did not notify the Commission that they were taking that action.

The Court of Appeal reversed the Superior Court. It disagreed with the Superior Court's interpretation of the Coastal Act, finding that it required that a coastal permit for the construction of a new house whose floor area, height or bulk was more than 10% larger than that of the house it was replacing be conditioned on a grant of access. It also ruled that the requirement did not violate the Constitution under the reasoning of an earlier case of the Court of Appeal, *Grupe v. California Coastal Commission*, 212 Cal. Rptr. 578 (Cal. App. 1985). In that case, the court had found that so long as a project contributed to the need for public access, even if the project standing alone had not created the need for access, and even if there was only an indirect relationship between the access exacted and the need to which the project contributed, imposition of an access condition on a development permit was sufficiently related to burdens created by the project to be constitutional. The Court of Appeal ruled that the record established that that was the situation with respect to the Nollans' house. It ruled that the Nollans' taking claim also failed because, although the condition diminished the value of the Nollans' lot, it did not deprive them of all reasonable use of their property. Since, in the Court of Appeal's view, there was no statutory or constitutional obstacle to imposition of the access condition, the Superior Court erred in granting the writ of mandamus. The Nollans appealed to this Court, raising only the constitutional question.

Had California simply required the Nollans to make an easement across their beachfront available to the public on a permanent basis in order to increase public access to the beach, rather than conditioning their permit to rebuild their house on their agreeing to do so, we have no doubt there would have been a taking. To say that the appropriation of a public easement across a landowner's premises does not constitute the taking of a property interest but rather (as Justice Brennan contends) "a mere restriction on its use," is to use words in a manner that deprives them of all their ordinary meaning. Indeed, one of the principal uses of the eminent domain power is to assure that the government be able to require conveyance of just such interests, so long as it pays for them. Perhaps because the point is so obvious, we have never been confronted with a controversy that required us to rule upon it, but our cases' analysis of the effect of other governmental action leads to the same conclusion. We have repeatedly held that, as to property reserved by its owner for private use, "the right to exclude [others is] 'one of the most essential sticks in the bundle of rights that are commonly characterized as property.' " *Loretto v. Teleprompter Manhattan CATV Corp.*, 458 U.S. 419, 433 (1982), quoting *Kaiser Aetna v. United States*, 444 U.S. 164, 176 (1979). In *Loretto* we observed that where governmental action results in "[a] permanent physical occupation" of the property, by the government itself or by others, "our cases uniformly have found a taking to the extent of the occupation, without regard to whether the action achieves an important public benefit or has only minimal economic impact on the owner." We think a "permanent physical occupation" has occurred, for purposes of that rule, where individuals are given a permanent and continuous right to pass to and fro, so that the real property may continuously be traversed, even though no particular individual is permitted to station himself permanently upon the premises.

Justice Brennan argues that while this might ordinarily be the case, the California Constitution's prohibition on any individual's "exclu[ding] the right of way to [any navigable] water whenever it is required for any public purpose," Art. X, § 4, produces a different result here. There are a number of difficulties with that argument. Most obviously, the right of way sought here is not naturally described as one to navigable water (from the street to the sea) but *along* it; it is at least highly questionable whether the text of the California Constitution has any *prima facie* application to the situation before us. Even if it does, however, several California cases suggest that Justice Brennan's interpretation of the effect of the clause is erroneous, and that to obtain easements of access across private property the State must proceed through its eminent domain power.[33]

Given, then, that requiring uncompensated conveyance of the easement outright would violate the Fourteenth Amendment, the question becomes whether requiring it to be conveyed as a condition for issuing a land-use permit alters the outcome. We have long recognized that land-use regulation does not effect a taking if it "substantially advance[s] legitimate state interests" and does not "den[y] an owner economically viable use of his land," *Agins v. Tiburon*, 447 U.S. 255, 260 (1980). *See also Penn Central Transportation Co. v. New York City*, 438 U.S. 104, 127 (1978) ("[A] use restriction may constitute a 'taking' if not reasonably necessary to the effectuation of a substantial government purpose"). Our cases have not elaborated on the standards for determining what constitutes a "legitimate state interest" or what type of connection between the regulation and the state interest satisfies the requirement that the former "substantially advance" the latter.[34] They have made

---

[33] [2] Justice Brennan also suggests that the Commission's public announcement of its intention to condition the rebuilding of houses on the transfer of easements of access caused the Nollans to have "no reasonable claim to any expectation of being able to exclude members of the public" from walking across their beach. He cites our opinion *in Ruckelshaus v. Monsanto Co.*, 467 U.S. 986 (1984), as support for the peculiar proposition that a unilateral claim of entitlement by the government can alter property rights. In *Monsanto*, however, we found merely that the Takings Clause was not violated by giving effect to the Government's announcement that application for *"the right to [the] valuable Government benefit," id.*, at 1007 (emphasis added), of obtaining registration of an insecticide would confer upon the Government a license to use and disclose the trade secrets contained in the application. *Id.*, at 1007–1008. But the right to build on one's own property — even though its exercise can be subjected to legitimate permitting requirements — cannot remotely be described as a "governmental benefit." And thus the announcement that the application for (or granting of) the permit will entail the yielding of a property interest cannot be regarded as establishing the voluntary "exchange," 467 U.S. at 1007, that we found to have occurred in *Monsanto*. Nor are the Nollans' rights altered because they acquired the land well after the Commission had begun to implement its policy. So long as the Commission could not have deprived the prior owners of the easement without compensating them, the prior owners must be understood to have transferred their full property rights in conveying the lot.

[34] Contrary to Justice Brennan's claim, our opinions do not establish that these standards are the same as those applied to due process or equal protection claims. To the contrary, our verbal formulations in the takings field have generally been quite different. We have required that the regulation "substantially advance" the "legitimate state interest" sought to be achieved, *Agins v. Tiburon*, 447 U.S. 255 (1980), not that "the State '*could rationally have decided*' that the measure adopted might achieve the State's objective." Justice Brennan relies principally on an equal protection case, *Minnesota v. Clover Leaf Creamery Co., supra*, and two substantive due process cases, *Williamson v. Lee Optical of Oklahoma, Inc.*, 348 U.S. 483, 487–488 (1955), and *Day-Brite Lighting, Inc. v. Missouri*, 342 U.S. 421, 423 (1952), in support of the standards he would adopt. But there is no reason to believe (and the

clear, however, that a broad range of governmental purposes and regulations satisfies these requirements. *See Agins v. Tiburon, supra*, 447 U.S. at 260–262, (scenic zoning); *Penn Central Transportation Co. v. New York City, supra* (landmark preservation); *Euclid v. Ambler Realty Co.*, 272 U.S. 365 (1926) (residential zoning); Laitos & Westfall, *Government Interference with Private Interests in Public Resources*, 11 Harv. Envtl. L. Rev. 1, 66 (1987). The Commission argues that among these permissible purposes are protecting the public's ability to see the beach, assisting the public in overcoming the "psychological barrier" to using the beach created by a developed shorefront, and preventing congestion on the public beaches. We assume, without deciding, that this is so — in which case the Commission unquestionably would be able to deny the Nollans their permit outright if their new house (alone, or by reason of the cumulative impact produced in conjunction with other construction)[35] would substantially impede these purposes, unless the denial would interfere so drastically with the Nollans' use of their property as to constitute a taking. *See Penn Central Transportation Co. v. New York City, supra.*

The Commission argues that a permit condition that serves the same legitimate police-power purpose as a refusal to issue the permit should not be found to be a taking if the refusal to issue the permit would not constitute a taking. We agree. Thus, if the Commission attached to the permit some condition that would have protected the public's ability to see the beach notwithstanding construction of the new house — for example, a height limitation, a width restriction, or a ban on fences — so long as the Commission could have exercised its police power (as we have assumed it could) to forbid construction of the house altogether, imposition of the condition would also be constitutional. Moreover (and here we come closer to the facts of the present case), the condition would be constitutional even if it consisted of the requirement that the Nollans provide a viewing spot on their property for passersby with whose sighting of the ocean their new house would interfere. Although such a requirement, constituting a permanent grant of continuous access to the property, would have to be considered a taking if it were not attached to a development permit, the Commission's assumed power to forbid construction of the house in order to protect the public's view of the beach must surely include the power to condition construction upon some concession by the owner, even a concession of property rights, that serves the same end. If a prohibition designed to accomplish that purpose would be a legitimate exercise of the police power rather

---

language of our cases gives some reason to disbelieve) that so long as the regulation of property is at issue the standards for takings challenges, due process challenges, and equal protection challenges are identical; any more than there is any reason to believe that so long as the regulation of speech is at issue the standards for due process challenges, equal protection challenges, and First Amendment challenges are identical. *Goldblatt v. Hempstead*, 369 U.S. 590 (1962), does appear to assume that the inquiries are the same, but that assumption is inconsistent with the formulations of our later cases.

35 [4] If the Nollans were being singled out to bear the burden of California's attempt to remedy these problems, although they had not contributed to it more than other coastal landowners, the State's action, even if otherwise valid, might violate either the incorporated Takings Clause or the Equal Protection Clause. One of the principal purposes of the Takings Clause is "to bar Government from forcing some people alone to bear public burdens which, in all fairness and justice, should be borne by the public as a whole." *Armstrong v. United States*, 364 U.S. 40, 49, (1960); *see also San Diego Gas & Electric Co. v. San Diego*, 450 U.S. 621, 656 (1981) (Brennan, J., dissenting); *Penn Central Transportation Co. v. New York City*, 438 U.S. 104, 123 (1978). But that is not the basis of the Nollans' challenge here.

than a taking, it would be strange to conclude that providing the owner an alternative to that prohibition which accomplishes the same purpose is not.

The evident constitutional propriety disappears, however, if the condition substituted for the prohibition utterly fails to further the end advanced as the justification for the prohibition. When that essential nexus is eliminated, the situation becomes the same as if California law forbade shouting fire in a crowded theater, but granted dispensations to those willing to contribute $100 to the state treasury. While a ban on shouting fire can be a core exercise of the State's police power to protect the public safety, and can thus meet even our stringent standards for regulation of speech, adding the unrelated condition alters the purpose to one which, while it may be legitimate, is inadequate to sustain the ban. Therefore, even though, in a sense, requiring a $100 tax contribution in order to shout fire is a lesser restriction on speech than an outright ban, it would not pass constitutional muster. Similarly here, the lack of nexus between the condition and the original purpose of the building restriction converts that purpose to something other than what it was. The purpose then becomes, quite simply, the obtaining of an easement to serve some valid governmental purpose, but without payment of compensation. Whatever may be the outer limits of "legitimate state interests" in the takings and land-use context, this is not one of them. In short, unless the permit condition serves the same governmental purpose as the development ban, the building restriction is not a valid regulation of land use but "an out-and-out plan of extortion." *J.E.D. Associates, Inc. v. Atkinson*, 432 A.2d 12, 14–15 (N.H. 1981).[36]

The Commission claims that it concedes as much, and that we may sustain the condition at issue here by finding that it is reasonably related to the public need or burden that the Nollans' new house creates or to which it contributes. We can accept, for purposes of discussion, the Commission's proposed test as to how close a "fit" between the condition and the burden is required, because we find that this case does not meet even the most untailored standards. The Commission's principal contention to the contrary essentially turns on a play on the word "access." The Nollans' new house, the Commission found, will interfere with "visual access" to the beach. That in turn (along with other shorefront development) will interfere with the desire of people who drive past the Nollans' house to use the beach, thus creating a "psychological barrier" to "access." The Nollans' new house will also, by a process not altogether clear from the Commission's opinion but presumably potent enough to more than offset the effects of the psychological barrier, increase the use of the public beaches, thus creating the need for more "access." These burdens on "access" would be alleviated by a requirement that the Nollans provide "lateral access" to the beach.

Rewriting the argument to eliminate the play on words makes clear that there is nothing to it. It is quite impossible to understand how a requirement that people

---

[36] [5] One would expect that a regime in which this kind of leveraging of the police power is allowed would produce stringent land-use regulation which the State then waives to accomplish other purposes, leading to lesser realization of the land-use goals purportedly sought to be served than would result from more lenient (but nontradeable) development restrictions. Thus, the importance of the purpose underlying the prohibition not only does not *justify* the imposition of unrelated conditions for eliminating the prohibition, but positively militates against the practice.

already on the public beaches be able to walk across the Nollans' property reduces any obstacles to viewing the beach created by the new house. It is also impossible to understand how it lowers any "psychological barrier" to using the public beaches, or how it helps to remedy any additional congestion on them caused by construction of the Nollans' new house. We therefore find that the Commission's imposition of the permit condition cannot be treated as an exercise of its land-use power for any of these purposes.[37] Our conclusion on this point is consistent with the approach taken by every other court that has considered the question, with the exception of the California state courts.

Justice Brennan argues that imposition of the access requirement is not irrational. In his version of the Commission's argument, the reason for the requirement is that in its absence, a person looking toward the beach from the road will see a street of residential structures including the Nollans' new home and conclude that there is no public beach nearby. If, however, that person sees people passing and repassing along the dry sand behind the Nollans' home, he will realize that there is a public beach somewhere in the vicinity. The Commission's action, however, was based on the opposite factual finding that the wall of houses completely blocked the view of the beach and that a person looking from the road would not be able to see it at all.

Even if the Commission had made the finding that Justice Brennan proposes, however, it is not certain that it would suffice. We do not share Justice Brennan's confidence that the Commission "should have little difficulty in the future in utilizing its expertise to demonstrate a specific connection between provisions for access and burdens on access," that will avoid the effect of today's decision. We view the Fifth Amendment's Property Clause to be more than a pleading requirement, and compliance with it to be more than an exercise in cleverness and imagination. As indicated earlier, our cases describe the condition for abridgement of property rights through the police power as a "*substantial* advanc[ing]" of a legitimate state interest. We are inclined to be particularly careful about the adjective where the actual conveyance of property is made a condition to the lifting of a land-use restriction, since in that context there is heightened risk that the purpose is [in] avoidance of the compensation requirement, rather than the stated police-power objective.

We are left, then, with the Commission's justification for the access requirement unrelated to land-use regulation: "Finally, the Commission notes that there are

---

[37] [6] As Justice Brennan notes, the Commission also argued that the construction of the new house would "increase private use immediately adjacent to public tidelands," which in turn might result in more disputes between the Nollans and the public as to the location of the boundary. That risk of boundary disputes, however, is inherent in the right to exclude others from one's property, and the construction here can no more justify mandatory dedication of a sort of "buffer zone" in order to avoid boundary disputes than can the construction of an addition to a single-family house near a public street. Moreover, a buffer zone has a boundary as well, and unless that zone is a "no-man's land" that is off limits for both neighbors (which is of course not the case here) its creation achieves nothing except to shift the location of the boundary dispute further on to the private owner's land. It is true that in the distinctive situation of the Nollans' property the seawall could be established as a clear demarcation of the public easement. But since not all of the lands to which this land-use condition applies have such a convenient reference point, the avoidance of boundary disputes is, even more obviously than the others, a made-up purpose of the regulation.

several existing provisions of pass and repass lateral access benefits already given by past Faria Beach Tract applicants as a result of prior coastal permit decisions. The access required as a condition of this permit is part of a comprehensive program to provide continuous public access along Faria Beach as the lots undergo development or redevelopment." That is simply an expression of the Commission's belief that the public interest will be served by a continuous strip of publicly accessible beach along the coast. The Commission may well be right that it is a good idea, but that does not establish that the Nollans (and other coastal residents) alone can be compelled to contribute to its realization. Rather, California is free to advance its "comprehensive program," if it wishes, by using its power of eminent domain for this "public purpose," *see* U.S. Const., Amend. 5; but if it wants an easement across the Nollans' property, it must pay for it.

Reversed.

JUSTICE BRENNAN, with whom JUSTICE MARSHALL joins, dissenting.

[Many of Justice Brennan's arguments are discussed in the majority opinion. However, the following comments on reciprocity of advantage are of particular interest.]

Examination of the economic impact of the Commission's action reinforces the conclusion that no taking has occurred. Allowing appellants to intensify development along the coast in exchange for ensuring public access to the ocean is a classic instance of government action that produces a "reciprocity of advantage." *Pennsylvania Coal*, 260 U.S. at 415. Appellants have been allowed to replace a one-story, 521-square-foot beach home with a two-story, 1,674-square-foot residence and an attached two-car garage, resulting in development covering 2,464 square feet of the lot. Such development obviously significantly increases the value of appellants' property; appellants make no contention that this increase is offset by any diminution in value resulting from the deed restriction, much less that the restriction made the property less valuable than it would have been without the new construction. Furthermore, appellants gain an additional benefit from the Commission's permit condition program. They are able to walk along the beach beyond the confines of their own property only because the Commission has required deed restrictions as a condition of approving other new beach developments. Thus, appellants benefit both as private landowners and as members of the public from the fact that new development permit requests are conditioned on preservation of public access.

NOTES AND QUESTIONS

1. *The Essential Nexus and Causal Connection.* The Court's "essential nexus" requirement establishes "a remoteness test where a court enquires into whether there exists a reasonable causal connection between the prevention of the perceived adverse impacts of the development project and the condition the government has imposed on the permit." Freilich & Morgan, *Municipal Strategies for Imposing Valid Development Exactions: Responding to* Nollan, 10 ZONING AND PLANNING L. REP., No. 11 at 170 (Dec. 1987). How the implications of the *Nollan* decision

radically affected the law is suggested in Been, *"Exit" As a Constraint on Land Use Exactions: Rethinking the Unconstitutional Conditions Doctrine*, 91 Colum. L. Rev. 473 (1991).

2. The *Nollan* decision was a bitterly divided 5-4 vote. However, in *Lingle v. Chevron, U.S.A.*, 544 U.S. 528 (2005), a unanimous Supreme Court reaffirmed the ruling that *Nollan* and *Dolan* state valid principles for constitutional takings review of land dedication and monetary conditions that are applied to subdivision review.

3. The *Nollan* opinion does not address the issue of when an exaction will be regarded as excessive or how the proportionality test is to be administered. For example, had the remoteness test been met in *Nollan*, there still would have been a question as to whether the required dedication was disproportionate. (The Court acknowledges the proportionality problem in Footnote 4 of its opinion, above.)The Court returned to the proportionality requirement seven years later in the following case

DOLAN v. CITY OF TIGARD

United States Supreme Court
512 U.S. 374 (1994)

Chief Justice Rehnquist delivered the opinion of the Court.

The State of Oregon enacted a comprehensive land use management program in 1973. The program required all Oregon cities and counties to adopt new comprehensive land use plans that were consistent with the statewide planning goals. The plans are implemented by land use regulations which are part of an integrated hierarchy of legally binding goals, plans, and regulations. Pursuant to the State's requirements, the city of Tigard, a community of some 30,000 residents on the southwest edge of Portland, developed a comprehensive plan and codified it in its Community Development Code (CDC). The CDC requires property owners in the area zoned Central Business District to comply with a 15% open space and landscaping requirement, which limits total site coverage, including all structures and paved parking, to 85% of the parcel. After the completion of a transportation study that identified congestion in the Central Business District as a particular problem, the city adopted a plan for a pedestrian/bicycle pathway intended to encourage alternatives to automobile transportation for short trips. The CDC requires that new development facilitate this plan by dedicating land for pedestrian pathways where provided for in the pedestrian/bicycle pathway plan.

The city also adopted a Master Drainage Plan (Drainage Plan). The Drainage Plan noted that flooding occurred in several areas along Fanno Creek, including areas near petitioner's property. The Drainage Plan also established that the increase in impervious surfaces associated with continued urbanization would exacerbate these flooding problems. To combat these risks, the Drainage Plan suggested a series of improvements to the Fanno Creek Basin, including channel excavation in the area next to petitioner's property. Other recommendations included ensuring that the floodplain remains free of structures and that it be preserved as greenways to minimize flood damage to structures. The Drainage Plan concluded that the cost of these improvements should be shared based on both direct and indirect benefits, with property owners along the waterways paying more due to the direct benefit that they would receive. The CDC and the Tigard Park Plan carry out these recommendations.

Petitioner Florence Dolan owns a plumbing and electric supply store located on Main Street in the Central Business District of the city. The store covers approximately 9,700 square feet on the eastern side of a 1.67 acre parcel, which includes a gravel parking lot. Fanno Creek flows through the southwestern corner of the lot and along its western boundary. The year round flow of the creek renders the area within the creek's 100 year floodplain virtually unusable for commercial development. The city's comprehensive plan includes the Fanno Creek floodplain as part of the city's greenway system.

Petitioner applied to the city for a permit to redevelop the site. Her proposed plans called for nearly doubling the size of the store to 17,600 square feet, and paving a 39 space parking lot. The existing store, located on the opposite side of the parcel, would be razed in sections as construction progressed on the new building. In the second phase of the project, petitioner proposed to build an additional structure on the northeast side of the site for complementary businesses, and to provide more parking. The proposed expansion and intensified use are consistent with the city's zoning scheme in the Central Business District.

The City Planning Commission granted petitioner's permit application subject to conditions imposed by the city's CDC. The Commission required that petitioner dedicate the portion of her property lying within the 100 year floodplain for improvement of a storm drainage system along Fanno Creek and that she dedicate an additional 15 foot strip of land adjacent to the floodplain as a pedestrian/bicycle pathway. The dedication required by that condition encompasses approximately 7,000 square feet, or roughly 10% of the property. In accordance with city practice, petitioner could rely on the dedicated property to meet the 15% open space and landscaping requirement mandated by the city's zoning scheme. The city would bear the cost of maintaining a landscaped buffer between the dedicated area and the new store.

II

The Takings Clause of the Fifth Amendment of the United States Constitution, made applicable to the States through the Fourteenth Amendment, provides: "[N]or shall private property be taken for public use, without just compensation." One of the principal purposes of the Takings Clause is "to bar Government from forcing some people alone to bear public burdens which, in all fairness and justice, should be borne by the public as a whole." *Armstrong v. United States*. Without question, had the city simply required petitioner to dedicate a strip of land along Fanno Creek for public use, rather than conditioning the grant of her permit to redevelop her property on such a dedication, a taking would have occurred. Such public access would deprive petitioner of the right to exclude others, "one of the most essential sticks in the bundle of rights that are commonly characterized as property." *Kaiser Aetna v. United States*.

On the other side of the ledger, the authority of state and local governments to engage in land use planning has been sustained against constitutional challenge as long ago as our decision in *Euclid v. Ambler Realty Co.* "Government hardly could go on if to some extent values incident to property could not be diminished without paying for every such change in the general law." *Pennsylvania Coal Co. v. Mahon.* A land use regulation does not effect a taking if it "substantially advance[s] legitimate state interests" and does not "deny an owner economically viable use of his land." *Agins v. Tiburon.*

The sort of land use regulations discussed in the cases just cited, however, differ in two relevant particulars from the present case. First, they involved essentially legislative determinations classifying entire areas of the city, whereas here the city made an adjudicative decision to condition petitioner's application for a building permit on an individual parcel. Second, the conditions imposed were not simply a limitation on the use petitioner might make of her own parcel, but a requirement that she deed portions of the property to the city. In *Nollan, supra,* we held that governmental authority to exact such a condition was circumscribed by the Fifth and Fourteenth Amendments. Under the well settled doctrine of "unconstitutional conditions," the government may not require a person to give up a constitutional right — here the right to receive just compensation when property is taken for a public use — in exchange for a discretionary benefit conferred by the government where the property sought has little or no relationship to the benefit.

Petitioner contends that the city has forced her to choose between the building permit and her right under the Fifth Amendment to just compensation for the public easements. Petitioner does not quarrel with the city's authority to exact some forms of dedication as a condition for the grant of a building permit, but challenges the showing made by the city to justify these exactions. She argues that the city has identified "no special benefits" conferred on her, and has not identified any "special quantifiable burdens" created by her new store that would justify the particular dedications required from her which are not required from the public at large.

III

In evaluating petitioner's claim, we must first determine whether the "essential nexus" exists between the "legitimate state interest" and the permit condition exacted by the city. If we find that a nexus exists, we must then decide the required degree of connection between the exactions and the projected impact of the proposed development. We were not required to reach this question in *Nollan,* because we concluded that the connection did not meet even the loosest standard. Here, however, we must decide this question.

A

[The Court summarizes *Nollan* and its holding.]

No such gimmicks are associated with the permit conditions imposed by the city in this case. Undoubtedly, the prevention of flooding along Fanno Creek and the reduction of traffic congestion in the Central Business District qualify as the type of legitimate public purposes we have upheld. It seems equally obvious that a nexus exists between preventing flooding along Fanno Creek and limiting development within the creek's 100 year floodplain. Petitioner proposes to double the size of her retail store and to pave her now gravel parking lot, thereby expanding the impervious surface on the property and increasing the amount of stormwater runoff into Fanno Creek.

The same may be said for the city's attempt to reduce traffic congestion by providing for alternative means of transportation. In theory, a pedestrian/bicycle pathway provides a useful alternative means of transportation for workers and shoppers: "Pedestrians and bicyclists occupying dedicated spaces for walking and/or bicycling . . . remove potential vehicles from streets, resulting in an overall improvement in total transportation system flow." Nelson, *Public Provision of Pedestrian and Bicycle Access Ways: Public Policy Rationale and the Nature of Private Benefits* 11, Center for Plan. Dev., Ga. Instit. of Tech., Working Paper Series (Jan. 1994).

B

The second part of our analysis requires us to determine whether the degree of the exactions demanded by the city's permit conditions bear the required relationship to the projected impact of petitioner's proposed development. Here the Oregon Supreme Court deferred to what it termed the "city's unchallenged factual findings" supporting the dedication conditions and found them to be reasonably related to the impact of the expansion of petitioner's business.

The city required that petitioner dedicate "to the city as Greenway all portions of the site that fall within the existing 100 year floodplain [of Fanno Creek] . . . and all property 15 feet above [the floodplain] boundary." In addition, the city demanded that the retail store be designed so as not to intrude into the greenway area. The city relies on the Commission's rather tentative findings that increased stormwater flow from petitioner's property "can only add to the public need to manage the [floodplain] for drainage purposes" to support its conclusion that the "requirement of dedication of the floodplain area on the site is related to the applicant's plan to intensify development on the site."

The question for us is whether these findings are constitutionally sufficient to justify the conditions imposed by the city on petitioner's building permit. Since state courts have been dealing with this question a good deal longer than we have, we turn to representative decisions made by them.

In some States, very generalized statements as to the necessary connection between the required dedication and the proposed development seem to suffice. We think this standard is too lax to adequately protect petitioner's right to just compensation if her property is taken for a public purpose.

Other state courts require a very exacting correspondence, described as the "specifi[c] and uniquely attributable" test. Under this standard, if the local government cannot demonstrate that its exaction is directly proportional to the specifically created need, the exaction becomes "a veiled exercise of the power of eminent domain and a confiscation of private property behind the defense of police regulations." We do not think the Federal Constitution requires such exacting scrutiny, given the nature of the interests involved.

A number of state courts have taken an intermediate position, requiring the municipality to show a "reasonable relationship" between the required dedication and the impact of the proposed development. Typical is the Supreme Court of Nebraska's opinion in *Simpson v. North Platte*, where that court stated:

The distinction, therefore, which must be made between an appropriate exercise of the police power and an improper exercise of eminent domain is whether the requirement has some reasonable relationship or nexus to the use to which the property is being made or is merely being used as an excuse for taking property simply because at that particular moment the landowner is asking the city for some license or permit."

Thus, the court held that a city may not require a property owner to dedicate private property for some future public use as a condition of obtaining a building permit when such future use is not "occasioned by the construction sought to be permitted.

We think the "reasonable relationship" test adopted by a majority of the state courts is closer to the federal constitutional norm than either of those previously discussed. But we do not adopt it as such, partly because the term "reasonable relationship" seems confusingly similar to the term "rational basis" which describes the minimal level of scrutiny under the Equal Protection Clause of the Fourteenth Amendment. We think a term such as "rough proportionality" best encapsulates what we hold to be the requirement of the Fifth Amendment. No precise mathematical calculation is required, but the city must make some sort of individualized determination that the required dedication is related both in nature and extent to the impact of the proposed development.[38]

Justice Stevens' dissent relies upon a law review article for the proposition that the city's conditional demands for part of petitioner's property are "a species of business regulation that heretofore warranted a strong presumption of constitutional validity." But simply denominating a governmental measure as a "business regulation" does not immunize it from constitutional challenge on the grounds that it violates a provision of the Bill of Rights. In *Marshall v. Barlow's, Inc.*, we held that a statute authorizing a warrantless search of business premises in order to detect OSHA violations violated the Fourth Amendment. And in *Central Hudson Gas & Electric Corp. v. Public Service Comm'n of N.Y.*, we held that an order of the New York Public Service Commission, designed to cut down the use of electricity because of a fuel shortage, violated the First Amendment insofar as it prohibited advertising by a utility company to promote the use of electricity. We see no reason why the Takings Clause of the Fifth Amendment, as much a part of the Bill of Rights as the First Amendment or Fourth Amendment, should be relegated to the

---

[38] [7] Justice Stevens' dissent takes us to task for placing the burden on the city to justify the required dedication. He is correct in arguing that in evaluating most generally applicable zoning regulations, the burden properly rests on the party challenging the regulation to prove that it constitutes an arbitrary regulation of property rights. Here, by contrast, the city made an adjudicative decision to condition petitioner's application for a building permit on an individual parcel. In this situation, the burden properly rests on the city.

status of a poor relation in these comparable circumstances. We turn now to analysis of whether the findings relied upon by the city here, first with respect to the floodplain easement, and second with respect to the pedestrian/bicycle path, satisfied these requirements.

It is axiomatic that increasing the amount of impervious surface will increase the quantity and rate of storm water flow from petitioner's property. Therefore, keeping the floodplain open and free from development would likely confine the pressures on Fanno Creek created by petitioner's development. In fact, because petitioner's property lies within the Central Business District, the Community Development Code already required that petitioner leave 15% of it as open space and the undeveloped floodplain would have nearly satisfied that requirement. But the city demanded more — it not only wanted petitioner not to build in the floodplain, but it also wanted petitioner's property along Fanno Creek for its Greenway system. The city has never said why a public greenway, as opposed to a private one, was required in the interest of flood control.

The difference to petitioner, of course, is the loss of her ability to exclude others. As we have noted, this right to exclude others is "one of the most essential sticks in the bundle of rights that are commonly characterized as property." *Kaiser Aetna.* It is difficult to see why recreational visitors trampling along petitioner's floodplain easement are sufficiently related to the city's legitimate interest in reducing flooding problems along Fanno Creek, and the city has not attempted to make any individualized determination to support this part of its request.

The city contends that recreational easement along the Greenway is only ancillary to the city's chief purpose in controlling flood hazards. It further asserts that unlike the residential property at issue in *Nollan*, petitioner's property is commercial in character and therefore, her right to exclude others is compromised. "The Constitution extends special safeguards to the privacy of the home[.]" The city maintains that "[t]here is nothing to suggest that preventing [petitioner] from prohibiting [the easements] will unreasonably impair the value of [her] property as a [retail store]."

Admittedly, petitioner wants to build a bigger store to attract members of the public to her property. She also wants, however, to be able to control the time and manner in which they enter. The recreational easement on the Greenway is different in character from the exercise of state protected rights of free expression and petition that we permitted in *PruneYard*. In *PruneYard*, we held that a major private shopping center that attracted more than 25,000 daily patrons had to provide access to persons exercising their state constitutional rights to distribute pamphlets and ask passersby to sign their petitions. We based our decision, in part, on the fact that the shopping center "may restrict expressive activity by adopting time, place, and manner regulations that will minimize any interference with its commercial functions." By contrast, the city wants to impose a permanent recreational easement upon petitioner's property that borders Fanno Creek. Petitioner would lose all rights to regulate the time in which the public entered onto the Greenway, regardless of any interference it might pose with her retail store. Her right to exclude would not be regulated, it would be eviscerated.

If petitioner's proposed development had somehow encroached on existing greenway space in the city, it would have been reasonable to require petitioner to provide some alternative greenway space for the public either on her property or elsewhere. But that is not the case here. We conclude that the findings upon which the city relies do not show the required reasonable relationship between the floodplain easement and the petitioner's proposed new building.

With respect to the pedestrian/bicycle pathway, we have no doubt that the city was correct in finding that the larger retail sales facility proposed by petitioner will increase traffic on the streets of the Central Business District. The city estimates that the proposed development would generate roughly 435 additional trips per day. Dedications for streets, sidewalks, and other public ways are generally reasonable exactions to avoid excessive congestion from a proposed property use. But on the record before us, the city has not met its burden of demonstrating that the additional number of vehicle and bicycle trips generated by the petitioner's development reasonably relate to the city's requirement for a dedication of the pedestrian/bicycle pathway easement. The city simply found that the creation of the pathway "could offset some of the traffic demand . . . and lessen the increase in traffic congestion."

No precise mathematical calculation is required, but the city must make some effort to quantify its findings in support of the dedication for the pedestrian/bicycle pathway beyond the conclusory statement that it could offset some of the traffic demand generated.

IV

Cities have long engaged in the commendable task of land use planning, made necessary by increasing urbanization particularly in metropolitan areas such as Portland. The city's goals of reducing flooding hazards and traffic congestion, and providing for public greenways, are laudable, but there are outer limits to how this may be done. "A strong public desire to improve the public condition [will not] warrant achieving the desire by a shorter cut than the constitutional way of paying for the change." *Pennsylvania Coal.*

The judgment of the Supreme Court of Oregon is reversed, and the case is remanded for further proceedings consistent with this opinion.

KOONTZ v. ST. JOHNS RIVER MGMT. DIST.

United States Supreme Court
133 S. Ct. 2586 (2013)

JUSTICE ALITO delivered the opinion of the Court.

Our decisions in *Nollan v. California Coastal Comm'n.*, 483 U. S. 825 (1987), and *Dolan v. City of Tigard*, 512 U.S. 374 (1994), provide important protection against the misuse of the power of land-use regulation. In those cases, we held that a unit of government may not condition the approval of a land-use permit of the owner's relinquishment of a portion of his property unless there is a "nexus" and "rough proportionality" between the government's demand and the effects of the proposed land use. In this case, the St. Johns Water Management District (District) believes that it circumvented Nollan and Dolan because of the way in which it structured its handling of a permit application submitted by Coy Koontz, Sr., whose estate is represented in this Court by Coy Koontz, Jr.[39] The District did not approve his application on the condition that he surrender an interest in his land. Instead, the District, after suggesting that he could obtain approval by signing over such an interest, denied his application because he refused to yield. The Florida Supreme Court blessed this maneuver and thus effectively interred those important decisions. Because we conclude that Nollan and Dolan cannot be evaded in this way, the Florida Supreme Court's decision must be reversed.

In 1972, petitioner purchased an undeveloped 14.9-acre tract of land on the south side of Florida State Road 50, a divided four-lane highway east of Orlando. The property is located less than 1,000 feet from that road's intersection with Florida State Road 408, a tolled expressway that is one of Orlando's major thoroughfares.

A drainage ditch runs along the property's western edge, and high-voltage power lines bisect it into northern and southern sections. The combined effect of the ditch, a 100-foot wide area kept clear for the power lines, the highways, and other construction on nearby parcels is to isolate the northern section of petitioner's property from any other undeveloped land. Although largely classified as wetlands by the State, the northern section drains well; the most significant standing water forms in ruts in an unpaved road used to access the power lines. The natural topography of the property's southern section is somewhat more diverse, with a small creek, forested uplands, and wetlands that sometimes have water as much as a foot deep. A wildlife survey found evidence of animals that often frequent developed areas: raccoons, rabbits, several species of bird, and a turtle. The record also indicates that the land may be a suitable habitat for opossums.

The same year that petitioner purchased his property, Florida enacted the Water Resources Act, which divided the State into five water management districts and authorized each district to regulate "construction that connects to, draws water from, drains water into, or is placed in or across the waters in the state." 1972 Fla. Laws cit. 72-299, pt. IV, § 1(5), pp. 1115, 1116 (codified as amended at Fla. Stat. § 373.403(5) (2010)). Under the Act, a landowner wishing to undertake such construction must obtain from the relevant district a Management and Storage of Surface Water (MSSW) permit, which may impose "such reasonable conditions" on the permit as are "necessary to assure" that construction will "not be harmful to the water resources of the district" 1972 Fla. Laws, § 4(1), at 1118 (codified as amended at Fla. Stat. § 373.413(1)).

In 1984, in an to protect the State's rapidly diminishing wetlands, the Florida Legislature passed the Warren S. Henderson Wetlands Protection Act, which made it illegal for anyone to "dredge or fill in, on, or over surface waters" without a Wetlands Resource Management (WRM) permit. 1984 Fla. Laws ch. 84-79, pt. VII, § 403.905(1), pp. 204–205. Under the Henderson Act, permit applicants are required to provide "reasonable assurance" that proposed construction on wetlands is "not contrary to the public interest," as defined by an enumerated list of criteria. See Fla.

---

[39] [1] For case of reference, this opinion refers to both men as "petitioner."

Stat. § 373.414(1). Consistent with the Henderson Act, the St. Johns River Water Management District, the district with jurisdiction over petitioner's, requires that permit applicants wishing to build on wetlands offset the resulting environmental damage by creating, enhancing, or preserving wetlands elsewhere.

Petitioner decided to develop the 3.7-acre northern section of his property, and in 1994 he applied to the District for MSSW and WRM permits. Under his proposal, petitioner would have raised the elevation of the northernmost section of his land to make it suitable for a building. graded the land from the southern edge of the building site down to the elevation of the high-voltage electrical lines, and installed a dry-bed pond for retaining and gradually releasing stormwater runoff from the building and its parking lot. To mitigate the environmental effects of his proposal, petitioner offered to foreclose any possible future development of the approximately 11-acre southern section of his land by deeding to the District a conservation easement on that portion of his property.

The District considered the 11-acre conservation easement to be inadequate, and it informed petitioner that it would approve construction only if he agreed to one of two concessions. First, the District proposed that petitioner reduce the size of his development to 1 acre and deed to the District a conservation easement on the remaining 13.9 acres. To reduce the development area, the District suggested that petitioner could eliminate the dry-bed pond from his proposal and instead install a more costly subsurface stormwater management system beneath the building site. The District also suggested that petitioner install retaining walls rather than gradually sloping the land from the building site down to the elevation of the rest of his property to the south.

In the alternative, the District told petitioner that he could proceed with the development as proposed, building on 3.7 acres and deeding a conservation easement to the government on the remainder of the property, if he also agreed to hire contractors to make improvements to District-owned land several miles away, Specifically, petitioner could pay to replace culverts on one parcel or fill in ditches on another. Either of those projects would have enhanced approximately 50 acres of District-owned wetlands. When the District asks permit applicants to fund offsite mitigation work, its policy is never to require any particular offsite project, and it did not do so here. Instead, the District said that it "would also favorably consider" alternatives to its suggested offsite mitigation projects if petitioner proposed something "equivalent." App. 75.

Believing the District's demands for mitigation to be excessive in light of the environmental effects that his building proposal would have caused, petitioner filed suit in state court. Among other claims, he argued that he was entitled to relief under Fla. Stat. § 373.617(2), which allows owners to recover "monetary damages" if a state agency's action is "an unreasonable exercise of the state's police power constituting a taking without just compensation."

We have said in a variety of contexts that "the government may not deny a benefit to a person because he exercises a constitutional right" *Regan v. Taxation With Representation of Wash.*,461 U.S. 540, 545 (1983). See also, *e.g. Rumsfeld v. Forum for Academic and Institutional Rights, Inc.*, 547 U.S. 47, 59–60 (2006); *Rutan v. Republican Party of Ill.*, 497 U.S. 62, 78 (1990). In *Perry v. Sindermann*, 408 U.S.

593 (1972), for example, we held that a public college would violate a professor's freedom of speech if it declined to renew his contract because he was an outspoken critic of the college's administration. And in *Memorial Hospital v. Maricopa County*, 415 U.S. 250 (1974), we concluded that a county impermissibly burdened the right to travel by extending healthcare benefits only to those indigent sick who had been residents of the county for at least one year. Those cases reflect an overarching principle, known as the unconstitutional conditions doctrine, that vindicates the Constitution's enumerated rights by preventing the government from coercing people into giving them up.

Nollan and *Dolan* "involve a special application" of this doctrine that protects the Fifth Amendment right to just compensation for property the government takes when owners apply for land-use permits, *Lingle v. Chevron U.S.A. Inc.*, 544 U.S. 528, 547 (2005); *Dolan*, 512 U.S. at 385 (invoking "the well-settled doctrine of 'unconstitutional conditions' "). Our decisions in those cases reflect two realities of the permitting process, The first is that land-use permit applicants are especially vulnerable to the type of coercion that the unconstitutional conditions doctrine prohibits because the government often has broad discretion to deny a permit that is worth far more than property it would like to take. By conditioning a building permit on the owner's deeding over a public right-of-way, for example, the government can pressure an owner into voluntarily giving up property for which the Fifth Amendment would otherwise require just compensation. See *id.*, at 384; *Nollan*, 483 U.S. So long as the building permit is more valuable than any just compensation the owner could hope to receive for the right-of-way, the owner is likely to accede to the government's demand, no matter how unreasonable. Extortionate demands of this sort frustrate the Fifth Amendment right to just compensation, and the unconstitutional conditions doctrine prohibits them. A second reality of the permitting process is that many proposed land uses threaten to impose costs on the public that dedications of property can offset. Where a building proposal would substantially increase traffic congestion, for example, officials might condition permit approval on the owner's agreement to deed over the land needed to widen a public road. Respondent argues that a similar rationale justifies the exaction at issue here: petitioner's proposed construction project, it submits, would destroy wetlands on his property, and in order to compensate for this loss, respondent demands that he enhance wetlands elsewhere. Insisting that landowners internalize the negative externalities of their conduct is a hallmark of responsible land-use policy, and we have long sustained such regulations against constitutional attack. See *Village of Euclid v. Ambler Realty Co.*, 272 U.S. 365 (1926).

Nollan and Dolan accommodate both realities by allowing the government to condition approval of a permit on the dedication of property to the public so long as there is a "nexus" and "rough proportionality" between the property that the government demands and the social costs of the applicant's proposal. *Dolan*, *supra*, at 391; *Nollan*, 483 U.S., at 837. Our precedents thus enable permitting authorities to insist that applicants bear the full costs of their proposals while still forbidding the government from engaging in "out-and-out . . . extortion" that would thwart the Fifth Amendment right to just compensation. *Ibid.* (internal quotation marks omitted). Under *Nollan* and *Dolan* the government may choose whether and how a permit applicant is required to mitigate the impacts of a proposed development, but it may not leverage its legitimate interest in mitigation to pursue governmental ends that lack an essential nexus and rough proportionality to those impacts.

The principles that undergird our decisions in *Nollan* and *Dolan* do not change depending on whether the government *approves* a permit on the condition that the applicant turn over property or *denies* a permit because the applicant refuses to do so. We have often concluded that denials of governmental benefits were impermissible under the unconstitutional conditions doctrine. See, *e.g.*, *Perry*, 408 U.S., at 597 (explaining that the government "*may not deny* a benefit to a person on a basis that infringes his constitutionally protected interests" (emphasis added); *Memorial Hospital*, 415 U.S. 250 (finding unconstitutional condition where government denied healthcare benefits). In so holding, we have recognized that regardless of whether the government ultimately succeeds in pressuring someone into forfeiting a constitutional right, the unconstitutional conditions doctrine forbids burdening the Constitution's enumerated rights by coercively withholding benefits from those who exercise them.

A contrary rule would be especially untenable in this case because it would enable the government to evade the limitations of *Nollan* and *Dolan* simply by phrasing its demands for property as conditions precedent to permit approval. Under the Florida Supreme Court's approach, a government order stating that a permit is "approved if "the owner turns over property would be subject to *Nollan* and *Dolan*, but an identical order that uses the words "denied until" would not. Our unconstitutional conditions cases have long refused to attach significance to the distinction between conditions precedent and conditions subsequent. See *Frost & Frost Trucking Co. v. Railroad Comm'n of Cal.*, 271 U.S. 583, 592–593 (1926) (invalidating " 'regulation that required the petitioner to give up a constitutional right "as a condition precedent to the enjoyment of a privilege"); *Southern Pacific Co. v. Denton*, 146 U.S. 202, 207 (1892) (invalidating statute "requiring the corporation. as a condition precedent to obtaining a permit to do business within the State, to surrender a right and privilege secured to it by the Constitution"). See also *Flower Mound*, 135 S.W.3d, at 639 ("The government cannot sidestep constitutional protections merely by rephrasing its decision from only 'if' to 'not unless' "). To do so here would effectively render *Nollan* and *Dolan* a dead letter.

The Florida Supreme Court puzzled over how the government's demand for property can violate the Takings Clause even though " 'no property of any kind was ever taken.' " 77 So. 3d, at 1225 (quoting 5 So. 3d, at 20 (Griffin. J. dissenting)); see also 77 So. 3d, at 1229–1230, but the unconstitutional conditions doctrine provides a ready answer. Extortionate demands for property in the land-use permitting context run afoul of the Takings Clause not because they take property but because they impermissibly burden the right not to have property taken without just compensation. As in other unconstitutional conditions cases in which someone refuses to cede a constitutional right in the face of coercive pressure, the impermissible denial of a governmental benefit is a constitutionally cognizable injury.

Nor does it make a difference, as respondent suggests, that the government might have been able to deny petitioner's application outright without giving him the option of securing a permit by agreeing to spend money to improve public lands. See *Penn Central Trans. Co. v. New York City*, 438 U.S. 104 (1978). Virtually all of our unconstitutional conditions cases involve a gratuitous governmental benefit of some kind. See, *e,g.*, *Regan*, 461 U.S. 540 (tax benefits); *Memorial Hospital*, 415 U. S. 250 (healthcare); *Perry*, 408 U.S. 593 (employment); *United States v. Butler*, 297 U. S. 1, 71 (1936) (crop payments); *Frost, supra* (business license). Yet we have repeatedly rejected the argument that if the government need not confer a benefit at all, it can withhold the benefit because someone refuses to give unconstitutional rights. *E.g.*, *United States v. American Library Assn, Inc.*, 539 U.S. 194, 210 (2003) ("[T]he government may not deny a benefit to a person on a basis that infringes his constitutionally protected . . . freedom of speech *even if he has no entitlement to that benefit*" (emphasis added and internal quotation marks omitted)); *Wieman v. Updegraff*, 344 U.S. 183, 191 (1952)(explaining in unconstitutional conditions case that to focus on "the facile generalization that there is no constitutionally protected right to public employment is to obscure the issue"). Even if respondent would have been entirely within its rights in denying the permit for some other reason, that greater authority does not imply a lesser power to condition permit approval on petitioner's forfeiture of his constitutional rights. See *Nollan*, 483 U.S. at 836–837 (explaining that "[t]he evident constitutional propriety" of prohibiting a land use "disappears . . . if the condition substituted for the prohibition utterly fails to further the end advanced as the justification for the prohibition"),

That is not to say, however, that there is *no* relevant difference between a consummated taking and the denial of a permit based on an unconstitutionally extortionate demand. Where the permit is denied and the condition is never imposed, nothing has been taken. While the unconstitutional conditions doctrine recognizes that this *burdens* a constitutional right, the Fifth Amendment mandates a particular *remedy* — just compensation — only for takings. In cases where there is an excessive demand but no taking, whether money damages are available is not a question of federal constitution law but of the cause of action — whether state or federal — on which the landowner relies. Because petitioner brought his claim pursuant to a state law cause of action, the Court has no occasion to discuss what remedies might be available for a *Nollan/Dolan* unconstitutional conditions violation either here or in other cases.

We turn to the Florida Supreme Court's alternative holding that petitioner's claim fails because respondent asked him to spend money rather than give up an easement on his land. A predicate for any unconstitutional conditions claim is that the government could not have constitutionally ordered the person asserting the claim to do what it attempted to pressure that person into doing. See *Rumsfeld*, 547 U.S., at 59–60. For that reason, we began our analysis in both *Nollan* and *Dolan* by observing that if the government had directly seized the easements it sought to obtain through the permitting process, it would have committed a *per se* taking. See *Dolan*, 512 U.S., at 384; *Nollan*, 483 U.S. at 831. The Florida Supreme Court held that petitioner's claim fails at this first step because the subject of the exaction at issue here was money rather than a more tangible interest in real property. 77 So. 3d, at 1230. Respondent and the dissent take the same position, citing the concurring and dissenting opinions in *Eastern Enterprises v. Apfel*, 524 U.S. 498 (1998), for the proposition that an obligation to spend money can never provide the basis for a takings claim. See *post*, at 5–8 (opinion of KAGAN, J.).

We note as an initial matter that if we accepted this argument it would be very easy for land-use permitting officials to evade the limitations of *Nollan* and *Dolan*. Because the government need only provide a permit applicant with one alternative that satisfies the nexus and rough proportionality standards, a permitting authority wishing to exact an easement could simply give the owner a choice of either surrendering an easement or making a payment equal to the easement's value. Such so-called "in lieu or fees" are utterly commonplace, Rosenberg, The Changing Culture of American Land Use Regulation: Paying for Growth with Impact Fees, 59 S.M.U. L. Rev. 177, 202–203 (2006), and they are functionally equivalent to other types of land use exactions. For that reason and those that follow, we reject respondent's argument and hold that so-called "monetary exactions" must satisfy the nexus and rough proportionality requirements of *Nollan* and *Dolan*.

Respondent and the dissent argue that if monetary exactions are made subject to scrutiny under *Nollan* and *Dolan*, then there will be no principled way of distinguishing impermissible land-use exactions from property taxes. See *post*, at 9–10. We think they exaggerate both the extent to which that problem is unique to the land-use permitting context and the practical difficulty of distinguishing between the power to tax and the power to take by eminent domain.

It is beyond dispute that "[t]axes and user fees . . . are not takings" *Brown*, supra, at 243, n. 2 (SCALIA, J., dissenting). We said much in *County of Mobile v. Kimball*, 102 U.S. 691, 703 (1881), and our cases have been clear on that point ever since. *United States v. Sperry Corp*, 493 U.S. 52, 62, n.9 (1989); see *A. Magnano Co. v. Hamilton*, 292 U.S. 40, 44 (1934); *Dane v. Jackson*, 256 U.S. 589, 599 (1921): *Henderson Bridge Co. v. Henderson City*, 173 U.S. 592, 614–615 (1899). This case therefore does not affect the ability of governments to impose property taxes, user fees, and similar laws and regulations that may impose financial burdens on property owners.

At the same time, we have repeatedly found takings where the government, by confiscating financial obligations, achieved a result that could have been obtained by imposing a tax. Most recently, in *Brown, supra* at 232, we were unanimous in concluding that a State Supreme Court's seizure of the interest on client funds held in escrow was a taking despite the unquestionable constitutional propriety of a tax that would have raised exactly the same revenue. Our holding in *Brown* followed from *Phillips v. Washington Legal Foundation*, 524 U.S. 156 (1998), and *Webb's Fabulous Pharmacies, Inc. v. Beckwith*, 449 U. S. 155 (1980), two earlier cases in which we treated confiscations of money as takings despite their functional similarity to a tax. Perhaps most closely analogous to the present case, we have repeatedly held that the government takes property when it seizes liens, and in so ruling we have never considered whether the government could have achieved an economically equivalent result through taxation. *Armstrong*, 364 U.S. 40; *Louisville Joint Stock Land Bank*, 295 U.S. 555.

Two facts emerge from those cases. The first is that the need to distinguish taxes from takings is not a creature of our holding today that monetary exactions are subject to scrutiny under *Nollan* and *Dolan*. Rather, the problem is inherent in this Court's long-settled view that property the government could constitutionally demand through its taxing power can also be taken by eminent domain.

Second, our cases show that teasing out the difference between taxes and takings is more difficult in theory than in practice. *Brown* is illustrative. Similar to respondent in this case, the respondents in *Brown* argued that extending the protection of the Takings Clause to a bank account would open a Pandora's Box of constitutional challenges to taxes. Brief for Respondents Washington Legal Foundation et al. 32 and Brief for Respondent Justices of the Washington Supreme Court 22, in *Brown v. Legal Foundation of Wash*, O. T. 2002, No. 01-1325. But also like respondent here, the *Brown* respondents never claimed that they were exercising their power to levy taxes when they took the petitioners' property. Any such argument would have been implausible under state law; in Washington, taxes are levied by the legislature, not the courts. See 538 U. S., at 242, n. 2 (SCALIA, J., dissenting).

The same dynamic is at work in this case because Florida law greatly circumscribes respondent's power to tax. See Fla. Stat. Ann. § 373.503 (authorizing respondent to impose ad valorem tax on properties within its jurisdiction); § 373.109 (authorizing respondent to charge permit application fees but providing that such fees "shall not exceed the cost . . . for processing, monitoring, and inspecting for compliance with the permit"). If respondent had argued that its demand for money was a tax, it would have effectively conceded that its denial of petitioner's permit was improper under Florida law. Far from making that concession, respondent has maintained throughout this litigation that it considered petitioner's money to be a substitute for his deeding to the public a conservation easement on a larger parcel of undeveloped land.[40]

This case does not require us to say more. We need not decide at precisely what point a land-use permitting charge denominated by the government as a "tax" becomes "so arbitrary . . . that it was not the exertion of taxation but a confiscation of property." *Brushaber v. Union Pacific* "the power of taxation should not be confused with the power of eminent domain," *Houck v. Little River Drainage Dist.*, 239 U.S. 254, 264 (1915), we have had little trouble distinguishing between the two.

Finally, we disagree with the dissent's forecast that our decision will work a revolution in land use law by depriving local governments of the ability to charge reasonable permitting fees. *Post*, at 8. Numerous courts — including courts in many of our Nation's most populous States — have confronted constitutional challenges to monetary exactions over the last two decades and applied the standard from *Nollan* and *Dolan* or something like it. See, *e.g.*, *Northern Ill. Home Builders Assn. v. County of Du Page*, 165 Ill. 2d. 25, 31–32, 649 N.E. 2d 384, 388–389 (1995); *Home Builders Assn. v. Beavercreek*, 89 Ohio St. 3d 121, 128, 729 N.E. 2d 349, 356 (2000); *Flower Mound*, 135 S.W.3d, at 640–641. Yet the "significant practical harm" the dissent predicts has not come to pass. *Post*, at 8. That is hardly surprising, for the

---

[40] [3] Citing cases in which state courts have treated similar governmental demands for money differently, the dissent predicts that courts will "struggle to draw a coherent boundary" between taxes and excessive demands for money that violate *Nollan* and *Dolan*. *Post*, at 9–10. But the cases the dissent cites illustrate how the frequent need to decide whether a particular demand for money qualifies as a tax under state law, and the resulting state statutes and judicial precedents on point, greatly reduce the practical difficulty of resolving the same issue in federal Constitutional cases like this one.

dissent is correct that state law normally provides an independent check on excessive land use permitting fees. *Post*, at 11.

The dissent criticizes the notion that the Federal Constitution places any meaningful limits on "whether one town is overcharging for sewage, or another is setting the price to sell liquor too high." *Post*, at 9. But only two pages later, it identifies three constraints on land use permitting fees that it says the Federal Constitution imposes and suggests that the additional protection of *Nollan* and *Dolan* are not needed. *Post*, at 11. In any event, the dissent's argument that land use permit applicants need no further protection when the government demands money is really an argument for overruling *Nollan* and *Dolan*. After all, the Due Process Clause protected the Nollans from an unfair allocation of public burdens, and they too could have argued that the government's demand for property amounted to a taking under the *Penn Central* framework. See *Nollan*, 483 U.S., at 838. We have repeatedly rejected the dissent's contention that other constitutional doctrines leave no room for the nexus and rough proportionality requirements of *Nollan* and *Dolan*. Mindful of the special vulnerability of land use permit applicants to extortionate demands for money, we do so again today.

We hold that the government's demand for property from a land use permit applicant must satisfy the requirements of *Nollan* and *Dolan* even when the government denies the permit and even when its demand is for money. The Court expresses no view on the merits of petitioner's claim that respondent's actions here failed to comply with the principles set forth in this opinion and those two cases. The Florida Supreme Court's judgment is reversed, and this case is remanded for further proceedings not inconsistent with this opinion.

It is so ordered.

NOTES AND QUESTIONS

1. At a minimum, *Nollan* and *Dolan* established a form of heightened scrutiny for regulations that constitute physical exactions. Thus, a traditional right of way dedication of a strip of land bordering a highway as a condition for a permit was invalidated in *Unlimited v. Kitsap County*, 750 P.2d 651 (Wash. Ct. App. 1988), where the court found a causal connection lacking. For other examples of courts trying to come to grips with the requirements of *Nollan* and *Dolan*, see *Sintra, Inc. v. City of Seattle*, 829 P.2d 765, 773 n.7 (Wash. 1992) (demolition fee for low income housing not subject to *Nollan* nexus because exaction was not physical); *Christopher Lake Dev. Co. v. St. Louis County*, 35 F.3d 1269 (8th Cir. 1994) (state mandated design specifications for disposal of storm water could be a taking of developer's property); *Walz v. Town of Smithtown*, 46 F.3d 162 (2d Cir. 1995) (plaintiff entitled to damages when town refused to issue an evacuation permit to which the plaintiff was entitled); *Burton v. Clark County*, 958 P.2d 343 (Wash. Ct. App. 1998) (county's decision to condition approval of plat plan on developer's willingness to construct a road for public use through his property constituted a taking of his property).

2. *Non-Physical Exactions.* Following *Koontz*, the heightened scrutiny requirement applies as well to non-physical exactions, like fees in lieu of land or impact fees where property owners or developers are required to make additional

payments as a prerequisite to development.

3. *Heightened Scrutiny and the Legislative v. Administrative Distinction.* What about "legislative" acts as opposed to administrative acts of agencies as in *Koontz, Nollan* and *Dolan*? While some courts agree with Justice Thomas that "a city can take property just as well as a planning commission," *Parking Assoc. v. City of Atlanta*, 515 U.S. 1116, 1117 (1995) (dissenting to denial of certiorari), many restrict application of intermediate scrutiny of the type applied in *Nollan* and *Dolan* to administrative decisions only. *See, e.g., Homebuilders Association of Metropolitan Portland v. Tualatin Hills Park and Recreation District*, 62 P.3d 404 (Or. Ct. App. 2003) (heightened scrutiny not applicable to legislative exaction). Some courts, however, have imposed *Nollan/Dolan* scrutiny on legislative decision. For a listing of such cases, *see* JUERGENSMEYER & ROBERTS, LAND USE PLANNING AND DEVELOPMENT REGULATION LAW § 10.5 (2012) and David L. Callies, *Through a Glass Clearly: Predicting the Future in Land Use Takings Law*, 54 WASHBURN L.J. 43 (2014), at 48–49.

4. *Exactions and Rezoning.* Exactions involving land dedication or facility construction as a condition of plan approval or rezoning are treated as immediately suspect both because they involve appropriation of property and because rezoning and plan approval do not generate a need for public facilities. When such exactions are imposed simply to conform to a community's general regulations, rather than to respond to specific project impacts on public facilities, they may fail to meet the *Dolan* proportionality test. But see the California Supreme Court's decision in *California Building Industry Association v. City of San Jose*, 351 P.3d 974 (Cal. 2015).

These types of exactions (which might seek to improve arterial streets or major park systems, for example) are hard to allocate to individual developments that yield incremental impacts because reasonably precise measurements of impacts are needed. In these cases, municipalities may use impact fees, which distribute costs for such improvements over many developments. Dedications can still be used as credits toward fee payments.

Furthermore, many states require land dedication or cash payments to mitigate adverse environmental impacts of development projects such as the one at issue in *Nollan* and *Dolan*. Under *Nollan*'s standards, these exactions logically come under greater scrutiny, although no doubt exists that their purposes are valid police-power objectives. The problem with imposing exactions for such purposes lies in the difficulty of quantifying adverse development impacts. Nevertheless, to satisfy the *Nollan* remoteness test, government agencies must document the relationship between development and the need for mitigating conditions, and incorporate the documentation into standards that govern the conditioning of development permits. *See* TAKINGS: LAND DEVELOPMENT CONDITIONS AND REGULATORY TAKINGS AFTER *NOLLAN* AND *LUCAS* 20–26 (Callies ed. 1996)

5. Two principal formulas have been used by communities to determine the amount of land that is required from the developer. The most common approach is to require a fixed percentage of the total amount of land in the subdivision — varying from three per cent to 15 per cent or more. The other approach is the "money in lieu of land" approach.

The fixed percentage approach has several disadvantages. It imposes the same burden on all development, irrespective of density or whether the subdivision contains multi-family or single-family units. In *Frank Ansuini, Inc. v. City of Cranston*, 264 A.2d 910 (R.I. 1970), the court upheld the constitutionality of dedication provisions but ruled that a seven per cent fixed percentage requirement, regardless of density, was fatally arbitrary.

The money in lieu of land approach is valuable when the subdivision is small and there is insufficient land to dedicate for parks or recreational facilities, where the land or topography is not well suited for park or recreational purposes, or where the comprehensive plan indicates a needed park or recreation site on land situated outside the boundaries of the subdivision. The "money in lieu of land" technique has met mixed reactions from the judiciary. Many jurisdictions have approved the approach: *Weingarten v. Town of Lewisboro*, 542 N.Y.S.2d 1012 (1989), *aff'd*, 559 N.Y.S.2d 807 (1990) (court upholds a $5000 per lot fee for park use); *City of College Station v. Turtle Rock Corp.*, 680 S.W.2d 802 (Tex. 1984) (an ordinance requiring park land dedication or money in lieu thereof as a condition of subdivision plat approval was not unconstitutionally arbitrary or unreasonable on its face). Other jurisdictions have found fault with the "money in lieu" approach: *Enchanting Homes, Inc. v. Rapanos*, 143 N.W.2d 618 (Mich. Ct. App. 1966) (no statutory authority to require money in lieu of land); *City of Montgomery v. Crossroads Land Co.*, 355 So. 2d 363 (Ala. 1978) (without specific legislative authorization, city had no power to require money in lieu of land for public parks; state enabling statute for "open spaces" insufficient).

6. *Subsequent Development of the Takings Standard.* In *Lingle v. Chevron USA, Inc.*, 544 U.S. 528 (2005), the Supreme Court had the opportunity to clarify the standards for regulatory takings. The case involved a challenge by Chevron (a major oil company) to a Hawaii statute that limited the rent that oil companies could charge dealers who leased service stations owned by the companies. The lower courts (the U.S. District Court for Hawaii and the Ninth Circuit) had found that the rent cap amounted to an uncompensated taking of private property in violation of the Fifth and Fourteenth Amendments because it did not substantially advance Hawaii's asserted interest in controlling retail gasoline prices, and, having reached that conclusion, entered summary judgment for Chevron. In so ruling, the two lower courts relied upon *Agins v. City of Tiburon*, 447 U.S. 255 (1980), in which the Supreme Court had stated that a regulation of private property effected a taking if it did not "substantially advance" a legitimate state interest. *Id.* at 260.

In a unanimous opinion written by Justice Sandra Day O'Connor, the Court repudiated the *Agins* language and the "substantially advances" formula for takings developed by the lower federal courts. After providing a lengthy summary of the Court's takings jurisprudence, O'Connor wrote:

> Today we correct course. We hold that the "substantially advances" formula is not a valid takings test, and indeed conclude that it has no proper place in our takings jurisprudence. In so doing, we reaffirm that a plaintiff seeking to challenge a government regulation as an uncompensated taking of private property may proceed under one of the other theories discussed above — by alleging a "physical" taking [Editor's note: as in *Loretta*], a

Lucas-type "total regulatory taking," a *Penn Central* taking, or a land-use exaction violating the standards set forth in *Nollan* and *Dolan*.

Because Chevron argued only a "substantially advances" theory in support of its takings claim, it was not entitled to summary judgment on that claim and the case was remanded to the trial court. Note that the majority in *Dolan* suggests that the first inquiry in determining the validity of an exaction should be the legitimacy of the governmental purpose. Of course, usually such an inquiry raises no barrier to imposition or collection because the use of fees is almost always for public facilities related to transportation, water, sewer, public recreation, and so forth. But what of the *Lingle* Court's abolition of *Agins*' first prong — "substantially advancing a legitimate state interest"? See for analysis of this issue D. Callies & C. Goodin, *The Status of Nollan v. California Coastal Commission and Dolan v. City of Tigard After Lingle v. Chevron U.S.A., Inc.*, 40 J. MARSHALL L. REV. 539 (2007).

Some observers have viewed *Lake Tahoe, Lingle*, and *San Remo Hotel v. City and County of San Francisco*, 545 U.S. 323 (2005), as reflecting a retreat on the part of the Supreme Court from the strongly pro-landowner perspective that produced decisions like *Kaiser Aetna, Loretto, Nollan, Lucas, and Dolan* from the late 1970s through the mid-1990s. Is this a fair reading of the these cases? Especially *Lingle*? (In *San Remo*, the Court, by a unanimous vote, ruled that the Full Faith and Credit statute, 28 U.S.C. § 1738, barred the plaintiffs from relitigating issues in their federal takings case that had been resolved against them in an earlier state court takings action.)

Requiring workforce/affordable housing is emerging as a special category of land development conditions, generally under the rubric of inclusionary zoning or linkage fees. According to one of this casebook's authors, "[Such] programs satisfy the nexus test only if the municipality can show that the downtown development contributes to the housing problem the linkage exaction is intended to remedy." MANDELKER, LAND USE LAW, at § 9.23, Note 2 (5th ed. 2003). But see *California Building Association v. City of San Jose*, 351 P.3d. 974 (Cal. 2015) which holds nexus and proportionality standards altogether inapplicable to housing exactions, despite the language in *Commercial Building v. City of Sacramento*, 941 F.2d. 872 (9th Cir. 1991), which the California Supreme Court failed to cite, despite its obvious relevance. *See* D. Callies, *Through a Glass Clearly: Predicting the Future in Land Use Takings Law*, 54 WASHBURN L.J. 43 (2014) at 55–60.

Part II

SHARED OWNERSHIP OF REAL AND PERSONAL PROPERTY

Chapter 4

ESTATES IN LAND AND FUTURE INTERESTS

[A.] THE ESTATE CONCEPT

Just as ownership may be divided between two or more individuals with simultaneous claims, it may be divided over time, with one owner entitled to the present use and another to its future use. Anglo-American law has regulated this form of joint ownership through the concept of the "estate" and corresponding future interests. Rooted in feudal land law, the estate concept recognizes that interests in land may be temporal and that ownership is more than just the right of present possession. The highest form of estate is the estate of *fee simple absolute* which means that the holder owns the property absolutely. The duration of his ownership is potentially infinite (fee); there are no restrictions on the inheritability of the property (simple); and no event will automatically divest the owner of his interest (absolute). When an owner possesses an estate in fee simple absolute, no future interests are held by anyone. It is, of course, possible for more than one individual to possess an estate in fee simple absolute in the same parcel of property. (This is typically the case with concurrent estates.)

Historically, the transfer of an estate in fee simple absolute required a writing which made use of the phrase "and his heirs," as in "to A and his heirs." In such a transaction, the heirs of A received nothing; the phrase (known as "words of limitation") simply indicated that an estate in fee simple was being transferred. At one time, the failure to use the wording "and his heirs" (or "and its assignees" if the transfer was to a corporation) meant that only a life estate was transferred, regardless of the intentions of the parties to the transfer. Today, there is no such requirement, and although the phrase is still widely used by real estate conveyancers, an estate in fee simple will be recognized if the evidence suggests that that was the intention of the parties to the transaction.

The owner of an estate in fee simple absolute may choose to alienate his entire estate to another owner; he may choose to alienate only a portion of it (in a temporal sense) and thus retain the possessory right to it at a future time; or he may transfer a portion of the estate to one party and the future interest in it to another. If he chooses either of the latter two, estates less than fee simple come into being. Present estates less than fee simple include the life estate and the estate for years (commonly referred to as a leasehold and available for any duration, including periods of less than one year). In addition, the estate of fee tail, which played an important role in pre-20th century English history, survives in a few American states in a truncated form.

There are also a number of "estates" that can be terminated by the holder of the future interest with little or no notice — the periodic tenancy, the tenancy at will, and the tenancy at sufferance. The periodic tenancy is an estate for a fixed period of time which continues for periods equal to the original one unless either the landlord or tenant gives notice of an intention to terminate the estate. The period may be of any length, although periodic tenancies of less than one week or more than one year are extremely rare. Under the traditional rule, notice of termination must be given prior to the beginning of the next period. Hence, in a week to week lease, one week's notice is required. In a month to month lease, one month's notice is necessary. The one exception is that a year to year tenancy can be terminated with six months' notice. In many jurisdictions, the notice period has been shortened by statute. A tenancy at will is an arrangement whereby either the landlord or the tenant can terminate the estate at any time. (If only one party has the right to terminate the estate, it is not a tenancy at will.) A tenancy at sufferance comes into being when an estate holder remains on the land after the expiration of his or her estate. The tenant at sufferance (also called a holdover tenant) can be evicted at any time. Under some circumstances, the landlord may renew the tenant's lease instead of evicting him. While those who hold property under these arrangements are not without legal rights, their ownership interest is so tenuous that it does not make a great deal of sense to characterize them as joint owners of the land with those who have the authority to terminate their possessory interest.

If O transfers Blackacre, which he owns in fee simple absolute, to A for five years or to B for the remainder of B's life, both the grantor and grantee retain an ownership interest in the tract. A or B have the present interest and with it the right of possession while O retains a future interest. The answer to the question: "Who owns Blackacre?" is that both do. O's interest in both of the above examples is known as a *reversion* in fee simple absolute. If O were to grant A an estate for life in Blackacre and then direct that after A's death Blackacre was to go to B and his heirs, A would still have a life estate, B would have a *remainder* (not a reversion) in fee simple absolute, and O would have nothing, since Blackacre would not revert back to him. The same characterization would apply if O had given A an estate for years. Reversions are retained by the original grantor while remainders are created for third parties by the original grantor. Remainders and reversions always take effect immediately upon the expiration of the preceding estate.

The life estate and the fee tail were known as freehold estates, while the estate for years, the periodic estate, the tenancy at will, and the tenancy at sufferance were designated non-freehold estates. (The freehold estates were also sometimes referred to as "particular" estates.) The conceptual difference lay in the fact that the holder of the freehold estate had "seisin," i.e., legal ownership, while the holder of a non-freehold estate had only possession. Consequently, the life estate and the fee tail were treated as real property interests while the leasehold was only a chattel, or personal property, interest. Under the traditional approach, if O transferred Blackacre to A for a term of one year (or 10 years, for that matter), O retained an estate in fee simple absolute (because there had been no transfer of seisin), subject to A's superior right to use the land. Conceptually, O and A both had present interests in Blackacre, and no future interest was created by the transfer. However, this distinction has never been an important part of American law, and today, the holder of the estate for years is usually treated as the present estate holder while O is said to hold a reversion. For an early discussion of the irrelevance of the freehold/non-freehold distinction in American law, see T. Walker, Introduction to American Law 266–69 (2d ed. 1846).

[B.] LIFE ESTATES

Life estates may be created either for the life of the grantee (as in O to A for the life of A) or for the life of a third party (O to A for the life of B). The latter is referred to as a life estate *pur autre vie* (for the life of another), and it will come to an end at B's death. When the language of the transaction is vague or ambiguous in regard to the measuring life for the estate, it will ordinarily be assumed that the estate is for the life of the grantee. Thus, O to A for life is presumed to be for the life of A (rather than O or some unnamed third party).

Because of the uncertainty in regard to their length, life estates are rarely used today, except in the context of transfers between members of the same family. The life estate can be used to provide for a surviving spouse or child while at the same time allowing the donor to designate a different individual as the ultimate owner of the property, as in O to O's wife for life, then to O's son A and his heirs (which creates a remainder in an estate in fee simple absolute for A.)

The holder of the life estate has the exclusive right of present possession and use of the property and can exclude all others, including the holder of the reversion or remainder. However, as the next case illustrates, the life tenant does not have the right to change the fundamental character or to diminish the economic value of the land subject to the life estate.

BROKAW v. FAIRCHILD

New York Supreme Court
237 N.Y.S. Supp. 6 (1929)

Hammer, J.

This is an action in which plaintiff [George Tuttle Brokaw] asks that it be declared and adjudged that the plaintiff, upon giving such security as the court may direct, has the right, and is authorized to remove the present structures and improvements on or affecting the real property No. 1 East Seventy-ninth street, or any part thereof, except the party wall, and to erect new structures and improvements thereon in accordance with certain proposed plans and specifications.

In the year 1886 the late Isaac V. Brokaw bought for $199,000 a plot of ground in the borough of Manhattan, city of New York, opposite Central Park, having a frontage of 102 feet 2 inches on the easterly side of Fifth avenue and a depth of 150 feet on the northerly side of Seventy-ninth street. Opposite there is an entrance to the park and Seventy-ninth street is a wide crosstown street running through the park. Upon the corner portion, a plot of ground 51 feet 2 inches on Fifth avenue and a depth of 110 feet on Seventy-ninth street, Mr. Brokaw erected in the year 1887, for his own occupancy, a residence known as No. 1 East Seventy-ninth street, at a cost of over $300,000. That residence and corner plot is the subject-matter of this action. The residence, a three story, mansard and basement granite front building, occupies the entire width of the lot. The mansard roof is of tile. On the first floor are two large drawing rooms on the Fifth avenue side and there are also a large hallway running through from south to north, a reception room, dining room and pantry. The dining room is paneled with carved wood. The hallway is in Italian marble and mosaic. There are murals and ceiling panels. There is a small elevator to the upper portion of the house. On the second floor are a large library, a large bedroom with bath on the Fifth avenue side and there are also four other bedrooms and baths. The third floor has bedrooms and baths. The fourth floor has servants' quarters, bath and storage rooms. The building has steam heat installed by the plaintiff, electric light and current, hardwood floors and all usual conveniences. It is an exceedingly fine house, in construction and general condition as fine as anything in New York. It is contended by plaintiff that the decorations are heavy, not of a type now required by similar residences, and did not appeal to the people to whom it was endeavored to rent the building.

It was offered to a great many people for rental at $25,000 with the statement that a lower figure might be considered and no offer of rental was obtained. Mr. Brokaw [the plaintiff] directed that the asking rental be $30,000 to start and finally reduced to $20,000. There is no demand for rental of private houses. There is a sporadic demand for purchase and sale on Fifth Avenue for use as private homes. Once in a while somebody will want a private house. The taxes are $16,881; upkeep for repairs, $750, and watchman, $300. The taxes for 1913 were $8,950.77.

Since 1913, the year of the death of Isaac V. Brokaw and the commencement of the life estate of plaintiff, there has been a change of circumstances and conditions in connection with Fifth avenue properties. Apartments were erected with great rapidity and the building of private residences has practically ceased. Forty-four apartments and only two private residences have been erected on Fifth avenue from Fifty-ninth street to One Hundred and Tenth street. There are to-day but eight of these fifty-one blocks devoted exclusively to private residences. Plaintiff's expert testified: "It is not possible to get an adequate return on the value of that land by any type of improvement other than an apartment house. The structure proposed in the plans of plaintiff is proper and suitable for the site and show 172 rooms which would rent for $1,000 per room. There is an excellent demand for such apartments . . . . There is no corner in the City of New York as fine for an apartment house as that particular corner."

The plaintiff testified also that his expenses in operating the residence which is unproductive would be at least $70,542 greater than if he resided in an apartment. He claims such difference constitutes a loss and contends that the erected apartment house would change this loss into an income or profit of $30,000. Plaintiff claims that under the facts and changed conditions shown the demolition of the building and erection of the proposed apartment is for the best interests of himself as life tenant, the inheritance, and the remaindermen. The defendants deny these contentions and assert certain affirmative defenses. (1) That the proposed demolition of the residence is waste, which against the objection of the adult defendant remaindermen plaintiff cannot be permitted to accomplish. (2) That Isaac V. Brokaw, before his death as well as by testamentary scheme by his will and codicil created and required the preservation, after his death, of a family center, embracing not only the premises in question but three other plots contiguous thereto or practically so, all of which are part of the original large parcel described above. The other parcels are: (a) No. 984 Fifth avenue, adjoining to the north, being twenty-five feet, six inches wide by one hundred and fifteen feet deep, devised to Howard Brokaw, a son, for life; (b) No. 985 Fifth avenue, adjoining to the north, being of the same dimensions, devised to Irving Brokaw, a son, for life; and (c) No. 7 East Seventy-ninth street, being a plot one hundred and two feet, two inches in depth by forty feet front and thirty-five feet in the rear, adjoining the corner plot to the east, given to the Farmers Loan and Trust Company in trust for the testator's daughter, Elvira Brokaw McNair, during the term of her life, with instructions to expend $250,000 under the direction of said daughter in the erection of a residence thereon. This trust also continues during the life of Elvira, daughter of Mrs. McNair. Residences palatial in character, each costing $344,536.26, had been erected by the testator during his life at 984 Fifth avenue and 985 Fifth avenue, and Howard and Irving Brokaw, respectively, have since resided therein with their families. As instructed by the will, another palatial residence was erected at 7 East Seventy-ninth street after the death of the testator at a cost of $250,000 for said daughter, Elvira Brokaw McNair, and she now occupies the same with her family.

Defendants claim that severance of the premises in question from the rest of the original plot would impair the plottage value of the other parcels and reduce the value of the buildings; the proposed plan of erecting such apartment on the premises is unsound because of the diminutive size of the lot in question in comparison with what is needed for a successful apartment and the increasing tendency to over-build. In addition, they assert a defense of res adjudicata, claiming that the questions raised here have already been passed upon and decided in the proceeding heretofore brought by the plaintiff for leave to mortgage the premises in question. (*Matter of Brokaw*, 219 App. Div. 337; *aff'd*, 245 N.Y. 614.)

Plaintiff's life estate, in my opinion, is not limited by the asserted testamentary scheme. The codicil reads:

> First. By the Fourth clause of my Last Will and Testament, dated and executed on the 20th day of April, 1907, upon the death or remarriage of my wife I gave and devised my residence, situated at the northeasterly corner of 79th Street and Fifth Avenue, in the City of New York, to my son, George Tuttle Brokaw, but directed that in the event he should not survive her then my executors should sell the said property and divide the proceeds of the sale among the surviving children and the issue of any deceased child of my said son, the issue of a deceased child to take by representation the parent's share.
>
> I now hereby modify that provision of my Will and after the death or remarriage of my wife I give and devise my said residence to my son George Tuttle Brokaw for and during the term of his natural life and after his death I give and devise the same to his children then living and to the issue, per stirpes, of any deceased child of him, their heirs and assigns forever. If my said son should not survive my wife or be living at her remarriage, then upon her death or remarriage I give and devise the said

> residence to his children then living and to the issue, per stirpes, of any deceased child of him, their heirs and assigns forever. In the event that no child nor any issue of any child or children of my son George Tuttle Brokaw shall be living at his death, or at the death or remarriage of my wife should he not survive her or be living at her remarriage, then upon his death or the death or remarriage of my wife, as the same may be, I give and devise my said residence in equal shares to my surviving children and the issue, per stirpes, of any deceased child of mine, their heirs and assigns forever.

In the 13th paragraph of testator's will, which devised 984 Fifth avenue to Howard Brokaw, and in the 14th paragraph, which devised 985 Fifth avenue to Irving Brokaw, each for life, there is contained a reciprocal restricting clause to the effect that "This property is devised, however, upon the express condition that so much of the land devised as has not been built upon shall forever remain open and unobstructed, in order that it may give access for light and air to this and the adjoining lot on the south (north), and that the airshaft occupying a portion of this lot, and which was provided for the common use and benefit of the buildings upon this lot and the lot adjoining it on the south (north), shall in no way be closed or obstructed. These restrictions of the use of the property hereby devised are intended as conditions subsequent, and immediately upon the violation of them or either of them the title of the devisees hereunder to said house and lot No. 985 (984) Fifth Avenue shall cease and determine and said property be and become a part of my residuary estate; either or both of these restrictions may be abrogated and canceled by the agreement of the owners in fee of the said two lots, or of my said sons Irving Brokaw and Howard Crosby Brokaw. In case such owners unite in an agreement to cancel such restrictions, or either of them, such agreement shall be evidenced by a writing executed in like manner as is required for the execution of a deed to be recorded under the laws of this State."

There is neither a similar nor any restriction in paragraph 15 in respect of premises No. 7 East Seventy-ninth street, the trust created for the testator's daughter, Elvira Brokaw McNair, during her life. There is no reference to a restriction or limitation upon No. 1 East Seventy-ninth street, either in the will or codicil. The testamentary scheme, therefore, which the defendants claim was contained in the will and codicil, clearly has no existence. The plaintiff received a plain, unconditional life estate. The plaintiff's estate in the premises involved is independent of the other life estates of the other defendants in their respective dwellings. (*Wiggin v. Wiggin*, 43 N. H. 561, and cases therein cited.)

Since the four life estates of the parties are separate and there is no testamentary scheme, it follows that the properties not being in a common ownership can have no plottage value, and such contention by defendants is entirely without merit. The claim of the unsoundness of the venture is also without merit. Indeed, defendants made little effort by proof to uphold such defense. If permissible it would be sound. [The court also rejected the defendants' argument that the issue in this case had been resolved by the earlier case of *Matter of Brokaw, supra.*]

Coming, therefore, to plaintiff's claimed right to demolish the present residence and to erect in its place the proposed apartment, I am of the opinion that such demolition would result in such an injury to the inheritance as under the authorities would constitute waste. The life estate given to plaintiff under the terms of the will and codicil is not merely in the corner plot of ground with improvements thereon, but, without question, in the residence of the testator. Four times in the devising clause the testator used the words "my residence." This emphasis makes misunderstanding impossible. The identical building which was erected and occupied by the testator in his lifetime and the plot of ground upon which it was built constitute that residence. By no stretch of the imagination could "my residence" be in existence at the end of the life tenancy were the present building demolished and any other structure, even the proposed thirteen-story apartment, erected on the site.

It has been generally recognized that any act of the life tenant which does permanent injury to the inheritance is waste. The law intends that the life tenant shall enjoy his estate in such a reasonable manner that the land shall pass to the reversioner or remainderman as nearly as practicable unimpaired in its nature, character and improvements. The general rule in this country is that the life tenant may do whatever is required for the general use and enjoyment of his estate as he received it. The use of the estate he received is contemplated and not the exercise of an act of dominion or ownership. What the life tenant may do in the future in the way of improving or adding value to the estate is not the test of what constitutes waste. The act of the tenant in changing the estate, and whether or not such act is lawful or unlawful, i.e., whether the estate is so changed as to be an injury to the inheritance, is the sole question involved. The tenant has no right to exercise an act of ownership. In the instant case the inheritance was the residence of the testator — "my residence" — consisting of the present building on a plot of ground fifty-one feet two inches on Fifth avenue by one hundred and ten feet on Seventy-ninth street. "My residence" — such is what the plaintiff under the testator's will has the use of for life. He is entitled to use the building and plot reasonably for his own convenience or profit. To demolish that building and erect upon the land another building, even one such as the contemplated thirteen-story apartment house, would be the exercise of an act of ownership and dominion. It would change the inheritance or thing, the use of which was given to the plaintiff as tenant for life, so that the inheritance or thing could not be delivered to the remaindermen or reversioners at the end of the life estate. The receipt by them at the end of the life estate of a thirteen-story $900,000 apartment house might be more beneficial to them. Financially, the objecting adults may be unwise in not consenting to the proposed change. They may be selfish and unmindful that in the normal course of time and events they probably will not receive the fee. With motives and purposes the court is not concerned. In *Matter of Brokaw* (245 N.Y. 614, App. Div.) their right to object to a proposed building loan and mortgage for the erection of the proposed apartment was established by decision. They have the same right of objection in this action. To tear down and demolish the present building, which cost at least $300,000 to erect and would cost at least as much to replace, under the facts in this case, is clearly and beyond question an act of waste.

The cases given by plaintiff are either cases where a prohibitory injunction against future waste has been sought and the parties have been refused the injunction and relegated to an action for damages for waste, or where, in condemnation proceedings or actions in equity, it appears that the equities between the parties are such that the technical waste committed has been ameliorated. The three cases upon which the plaintiff principally relies are *Melms v. Pabst Brewing Co.* (104 Wis. 7); *N.Y., O. & W. Ry. Co. v. Livingston* (238 N.Y. 300), and *Doherty v. Allman* (3 L.R. [App. Cas.] 709). These are readily distinguishable from the case at bar.

In *Melms v. Pabst Brewing Co.* (*supra*) there was a large expensive brick dwelling house built by one Melms in the year 1864. He also owned the adjoining real estate and a brewery upon part of the premises. He died in 1869. The brewery and dwelling were sold and conveyed to the Pabst Brewing Company. The Pabst Company used the brewery part of the premises. About the year 1890 the neighborhood about the dwelling house had so changed in character that it was situated on an isolated lot standing from twenty to thirty feet above the level of the street, the balance of the property having been graded down to fit it for business purposes. It was surrounded by business property, factories and railroad tracks with no other dwellings in the neighborhood. The Pabst Brewing Company, in good faith regarding itself as the owner, tore down the building and graded down the ground for business purposes.

Thereafter it was held, in the action of *Melms v. Pabst Brewing Co.* (93 Wis. 140), that the brewing company had only acquired a life estate in the homestead, although in another action between the same parties (93 Wis. 153) it was held that as to the other property the brewing company had acquired full title in fee. The action for waste in which the decision of 104 Wisconsin was delivered was brought and decided after the decisions in the other actions. We find it there said (at p. 9): "The action was tried before the Court without a jury, and the Court found, in addition to the facts above stated, that the removal of the building and the grading down of the earth was done by the defendant in 1891 and 1892, believing itself to be the owner in fee simple of the property, and that by the said acts the estate of the plaintiffs in the property was substantially increased, and that the plaintiffs have been in no way injured thereby." Again, it was stated (at p. 13): "There are no contract relations in the present case. The defendants are the grantees of a life estate, and their rights may continue for a number of years. The evidence shows that the property became valueless for the purpose of residence property as the result of the growth and development of a great city. Business and manufacturing interests advanced and surrounded the once elegant mansion, until it stood isolated and alone, standing upon just enough ground to support it and surrounded by factories and railroad tracks, absolutely undesirable as a residence and incapable of any use as business property. Here was a complete change of conditions, not produced by the tenant, but resulting from causes which none could control. Can it be reasonably or logically said that this entire change of condition is to be completely ignored, and the iron-clad rule applied that the tenant cannot make change in the uses of the property because he will destroy its identity? Must the tenant stand by and preserve the isolated dwelling house, so that he may at some future time turn it over to the reversioner equally useless?"

The facts in the above case are clearly not analogous to the facts here. Especially is this recognized from the fact that the plaintiff's dwelling house is far from being "isolated and alone, standing upon just enough ground to support it, surrounded by factories and railroad tracks, absolutely undesirable as a residence." It is located on the northeast corner of Fifth avenue and Seventy-ninth street. Across the avenue to the west is Central Park. To the south across Seventy-ninth street the block Seventy-eighth to Seventy-ninth streets is restricted to private dwellings. The residence itself is surrounded by the three other palatial Brokaw dwellings, forming a magnificent residential layout of the four plots. It may, of course, be that the situation will change in the future. The decision here is concerned only with the present.

N.Y., O. & W. Ry. Co. v. Livingston (*supra*) was a condemnation proceeding. The railroad company entered lawfully upon the land and under color of right improved it in good faith with buildings costing $49,000. A hostile right being asserted by the remaindermen, condemnation proceedings were instituted to acquire same. It was held that the railroad company, under the circumstances, could exclude the value of the improvements from the compensation due such remaindermen. *Doherty v. Allman* (*supra*) was an action for an injunction to restrain the converting of the building containing one old large store, which, the neighborhood having materially changed, had no practical use and yielded no income, into tenements which were useful, in demand, and profitable. The court refused the injunction, leaving the aggrieved party to an action for damages, stating, among other things, as follows: "the external walls of the building are to be retained, and those external walls, where one part of the building is of a lower height than the rest, are to be raised, so that the building may be of a uniform height; internal changes are to be made, internal party walls are to be introduced, the flooring is to be altered in its level and six dwelling-houses are to be made out of this which is now one long store." (P. 717.) "Suppose the change which is contemplated by the Respondent here is made in the internal arrangements of this which is now a store, will the injury be irremediable? Clearly not. Beyond all doubt as regards the immediate effect it would be beneficial and not injurious to the reversioner; he will have a much better security for his rent, and the property undoubtedly will be increased in value, and if, when the lease comes to an end, he should have that predilection which he now appears to have for a building of the character which we see represented in this photograph, it would be merely a question of money, and that not a very large sum of money, in order that the building might be brought back to the state in which it now is. Therefore there would be no injury which would be irremediable."

The facts, it is seen, in none of the cases cited are analogous to the case at bar. The law and procedure therein also contain no analogy. *Melms v. Pabst* was a law action for waste claimed to have been committed prior to the action. Upon the existing facts proved at the trial it was found as fact and in equity that the claimed waste was ameliorated and the plaintiff not damaged. *N.Y., O. & W. Ry. Co. v. Livingston*, a condemnation proceeding, simply involved the measure of damages under the facts and equities in the case, while *Doherty v. Allman*, in equity for injunction, decided only that under the equities an injunction would not be granted and an action at law was adequate.

From the foregoing I am of the opinion, and it will accordingly be adjudged and declared that, upon the present facts, circumstances and conditions as they exist and are shown in this case, regardless of the proposed security and the expressed purpose of erecting the proposed thirteen-story apartment, or any other structure, the plaintiff has no right and is not authorized to remove the present structures on or affecting the real estate in question.

NOTES AND QUESTIONS

1. Although the court which delivered the above opinion is designated the Supreme Court of New York, it is actually a trial court analogous to the circuit courts in most states. The highest court in New York is the Court of Appeals.

2. The doctrine of waste is one of the most important limitations on the rights of those who hold any estate less than fee simple. It is designed to protect future interest holders who, while not having the present right to use the land, have a substantial interest in it. Without such a principle, the holder of the present estate, whether it be a life estate or an estate for years, would have every incentive to exhaust the economic potential of the land during the term of his or her estate. If waste occurs, the holders of future interests may enjoin the conduct that constitutes waste, and they may recover damages. In many states, a successful action for waste entitles the plaintiff to double or treble damages. Why should there be an additional penalty?

There are two types of waste: affirmative and permissive. Affirmative, or voluntary, waste involves the destruction of buildings or structures on the land or the exploitation of natural resources. Permissive, or involuntary, waste occurs when the present estate holder allows the property to fall into disrepair or fails to make reasonable measures to protect the property from harm. A life tenant has at least a limited duty to make repairs on the property and to pay taxes, mortgage interest, and special assessments.

A number of doctrines help to limit the life tenant's liability for waste. When buildings are destroyed by fire, storm or other form of natural disaster not the doing of the tenant, the tenant is not guilty of waste. (Until the middle of the 19th century, this was not necessarily the case. See, e.g., N.Y. LAWS, 1860, p. 592, repealing the previous rule making the present estate holder liable for the cost of rebuilding structures "destroyed by fire, tempest, or other sudden and unexpected event.") Cutting down trees to convert unimproved land to farmland has long been held not to constitute waste, and the doctrine of estovers gave the life tenant the right to cut trees for purposes of repairing existing structures (including fences) and building necessary new ones. (A related doctrine, emblements, gave the representative of a deceased life tenant the right to enter the property to harvest annual crops planted by the life tenant.) Perhaps the most important modification is the doctrine of ameliorating (sometimes, just "meliorating") waste. Ameliorating waste is waste that actually increases the value of the land. Under certain circumstances, as the above case suggests, ameliorating waste on the part of the present estate holder is not actionable. Ameliorating waste is not actionable when there has been a dramatic change in conditions which make it impossible to carry out the grantor's intentions at the time the estate was created.

3. After losing at the trial court level, George Tuttle Brokaw appealed the decision to the New York intermediate appellate court which affirmed Judge Hammer's decision without opinion (although one judge dissented, accusing the

defendants of ulterior motives), *Brokaw v. Fairchild*, 231 A.D. 704 (N.Y. App. Div. 1930). An appeal to the New York Court of Appeals, the state's highest court, produced the same result, a per curiam affirmance without opinion, 177 N.E. 186 (N.Y. 1931). It was probably not coincidental that the events of this case took place during the depths of the Great Depression.

The *Brokaw* decision was ultimately overturned by an act of the New York legislature which provided that a life tenant or a tenant for years with an expectancy or unexpired term of more than five years could alter or replace a structure without incurring liability for waste if the following conditions were met:

1. The change would not reduce the market value of the future interests in the land.
2. The change or alteration was one that a prudent fee simple owner would likely make under the same circumstances.
3. The change would not violate any existing, legally binding agreement regulating the conduct of the present estate holder.
4. The owner of the present estate has given notice to all holders of future interests in the affected property.
5. The present estate holder has posted such security as the court has required to insure the completion of the proposed alteration.

N.Y. Laws 1937, c. 165.

Does the legislative action described above suggest that the court was wrong in concluding that this was not an appropriate situation for the application of the doctrine of ameliorative waste? Does Judge Hammer adequately distinguish the facts in this case from those of *Melms v. Pabst* which is discussed extensively in the opinion?

4. *The Creation of Life Estates*. Life estates can be created by operation of law (as in the case of dower and some spousal share statutes, discussed below) or by direct grant by deed. Often a grantor will wish to transfer property to a grantee, but subject to the life estate of another — as in a deed "to my son Bob subject to a life estate for my wife." However, such language in a deed has often been held to be inadequate to create a life estate. Under the common law rule, a grantor could not by reservation convey a life estate in real property to a party who is a stranger to the deed. *See Willard v. First Church of Christ Scientist, Pacifica*, 498 P.2d 987, 989 (Cal. 1972), for a discussion of the common law rule and cases applying it. (A "reservation" is "[a] clause in a deed or other instrument of conveyance by which the grantor creates, and reserves to himself, some right, interest, or profit in the estate granted, which had no previous existence as such, but is first called into being by the instrument reserving it; such as rent, or an easement." Black's Law Dictionary 1307 (6th ed. 1990).) Although the common law rule has been reaffirmed in New York as recently as 1987, *Estate of Thomson v. Wade*, 509 N.E.2d 309 (N.Y. 1987), in the past three decades, several courts have rejected the common law rule and allowed for the creation of a life estate by this method. For a recent case taking this position, see *Nelson v. Parker*, 687 N.E.2d 187 (Ind. 1997). *See also* W.W. Allen, Annotation, *Reservation or Exception in Deed in Favor of Stranger*, 88 A.L.R. 2d 1199, 1202 (1963 & Supp. 1993). For commentary on the effect of some life estates property

title and valuation, see Salzberg, *Zombie Life Estates, Ghost Value Transfer and Phantom Takings: Confusings of Title and Value in Property Law Legislation*, 22 QUINNIPIAC PROBATE L.J. 363 (2009).

5. *Premature Termination of Life Estates.* If the holder of the life estate and the reversioner or remaindermen agree, the life estate can be terminated and a fee simple absolute can be sold to a willing buyer. Where all the remaindermen cannot be ascertained or cannot consent (because of age or infirmity), courts will sometimes authorize the sale if other parties agree, and the court finds it to be within the best interests of all involved. Otherwise, courts have been traditionally unwilling to allow the life tenant to sell the property and place the sale proceeds in trust. There is, however, a modern movement to give life tenants greater authority to sell their land (with court approval) in situations where the original grantor was primarily concerned with the future economic well-being of the remaindermen rather than that a particular parcel of land be passed on to them.

[C.] REMAINDERS

The complexity of law of remainders supposedly prompted Oliver Cromwell to denounce English real property law as "a tortuous and ungodly jumble." Although many of the arcane features of the common law of remainders have been abolished or modified by statute, the area is still one of the most difficult in American law. The intricacies of the law of remainders, particularly as they relate to the disposition of personal property, are studied in much greater detail in courses on wills and trusts and estate planning.

[1.] Contingent Remainders

In *Brokaw v. Fairchild, supra*, you may have noticed that there was no guarantee that any of the defendants, the siblings and nieces and nephews of the plaintiff, would ever come into possession of the lot in question. According to the will of Issac Brokaw, the tract subject to George Brokaw's life estate was to go to the children of George Brokaw living at the time of George's death. Only if George were to die without surviving issue (children or other direct descendants) would the interests of his siblings and nephews and nieces vest in possession. (From other sources, we know that George Brokaw had one 4-year-old child at the time of this litigation.)

Because we have no way of knowing at the time of their creation if these remainders will ever become certain (or, in the vocabulary of future interests, "vested"), they are said to be contingent. Technically, even a vested remainder may not vest in possession,[1] so it is more accurate to say that remainders are contingent if there is an unsatisfied condition precedent, as there is in *Brokaw*, or if it is not yet possible to ascertain the identity of the remainderman. In *Brokaw*, the transaction that created the interests involved can be rendered as O to A for life, then to the surviving children of A and their heirs, otherwise to B, C, and D and

[1] In the transaction O to A for life, then to B for life, B has a *vested* remainder in a life estate even though B will never have the right of present possession if she predeceases A. See the discussion below.

their heirs. The remainders of B, C, and D are contingent, because there is an unsatisfied condition precedent, i.e., A must die without surviving children. That condition obviously cannot be satisfied until A actually dies. Even though A may have many children in his lifetime, there is no guarantee that any of them will survive him. The remainder interest in A's surviving children is doubly contingent. Do you see why?

A condition precedent is a condition expressly stated in the document creating the remainder which must be satisfied before the remainder interest can become possessory. However, the termination of the previous estate is not a condition precedent. Although it is true in one sense that a remainder cannot vest in possession unless the preceding estate ends, that requirement is not treated as a contingency. If it was, there could be no such thing as a vested remainder. In other words, the transaction O to A for life, then upon A's death, to B and his heirs does not contain a condition precedent, since the apparent "condition" is only the termination of A's preceding life estate.

Similarly, the holder of a contingent remainder is normally not required to survive the previous estate. For survivorship to be a condition precedent, it must be specifically so stated in the instrument creating the interest. For example, the transaction, O to A for life, then to B and her heirs, if B has graduated from law school, otherwise to C and her heirs, does not specifically require C to outlive A for C's interest to vest in possession. Consequently, the transaction creates alternate contingent remainders for both B and C (assuming that B has not graduated from law school; if he has, then C has nothing). C does not need to survive A or B for her interest to vest. Were she to predecease them, her remainder would then pass to her heir or devisee. If B died without ever graduating from law school, C's original remainder would then vest, even though C was no longer alive. Moreover, even if C had transferred her remainder to D during her lifetime and D was alive at the time of A's death, D would be entitled to Blackacre when A died. At one time, the common law prohibited the transfer of contingent future interests by deed or by will, but this restriction has long been abolished in most states. Consequently, contingent remainders may be sold or devised in the same manner as vested remainders.

A classic example of a remainder that is contingent because its holder cannot be ascertained is the transaction of O to A for life, then to A's heir. While we may assume that we can identify A's heir at any given time — today it is either his spouse or closest relative — we can actually only identify A's *heir apparent*, since it is possible that A will outlive anyone that we identify as his "heir." Consequently, we will only be able to identify A's heir after A's death. Similarly, if A has no children, the transaction O to A for life, then to the children of A, creates a contingent remainder in A's unborn children.

[2.] The Vesting of Remainders

A contingent remainder becomes vested when there are no remaining conditions precedent and when the holder of the remainder can be ascertained. It is not necessary that the holder of the remainder be eligible to take immediate possession for a contingent remainder to vest — as mentioned above, it may never vest in possession. For example, if O transfers Blackacre to A for life, then to B *for life*, if she has graduated from law school, B's remainder is initially contingent if she has not yet graduated from law school. The remainder becomes vested as soon as she graduates from law school, even if A is still alive. However, if B then dies before A, her vested remainder is divested without ever having become a present possessory right. Consequently, B's remainder is said to be *vested subject to divestment* during the period of time in which she has graduated from law school and A is still alive.

Unless there is a vested remainder in fee simple absolute, the original grantor retains a reversion. (Since all reversions are vested, there is no such thing as a contingent reversion.) In the transaction, O to A for life, then, if B has graduated from law school, to B *and her heirs*, B has a contingent remainder and O has a reversion. If B subsequently graduates from law school, her remainder becomes vested and O is divested of his reversion. In the transaction, O to A for life, then, if B has graduated from law school, to B *and her heirs*, otherwise to C and her heirs, B and C have alternate contingent remainders in fee simple absolute. Even though the right to Blackacre will pass to either B or C (or someone holding through them) after A's death, O nevertheless has a reversion until one or the other contingent remainders vests. Such reversions are said to be defeasible.

If a remainder is created for a class of individuals and some members of the class have met the condition precedent and others have not, then the remainders of those who have are said to be *vested subject to open*. For example, in the transaction O to A for life, then to the children of A, the living children of A all have vested remainders, but they are vested subject to open since it is possible that A will have more children. (Even if A is a 90 year old woman, she is presumed to be able to have more children, which with the institution of adoption is a legal possibility, even if not a biological one.) The unborn children of A are said to have contingent remainders (contingent on their subsequent birth).

If a vested remainder can be divested by a subsequent event, like death or dropping out of law school, the remainder is, as noted above, said to be *a vested remainder subject to divestment* or a *defeasibly vested remainder*. O to A for five years, then to B unless B gives up her U.S. citizenship would create a vested remainder in fee simple absolute subject to divestment for B, assuming that she is alive and a U.S. citizen at the time of the initial transaction.

[3.] The Destructibility of Contingent Remainders

Under the traditional rule of the destructibility of contingent remainders, all contingent remainders were required to vest at or before the termination of the preceding estate or else they were destroyed. Thus, in our example, if B had not graduated from law school upon A's death, her interest would have been destroyed, and her subsequent graduation from law school would have been irrelevant. Today, most (though not all) states have abolished the destructibility rule. In those jurisdictions, a contingent remainder that has not yet vested when the estate preceding it has come to an end will not be destroyed. Instead, it will remain a valid future interest and will vest in possession when the condition is satisfied. This will mean that the right of present possession will revert to the holder of the reversion, but that interest will be divested if the condition precedent is later fulfilled. Thus, if A dies and B has not yet finished law school, Blackacre reverts to O (or the current holder of O's reversion). However, if B subsequently graduates from law school, his future interest immediately divests O of the right of present possession. The effect of the abolition of the destructibility rule is to convert what was once a contingent remainder into an executory interest. (Executory interests are discussed below.)

It is also possible to destroy a contingent remainder through the principle of merger. If O, the fee simple owner of Blackacre, transferred a life estate to A, he divided his interest into a present estate and a vested future interest (a reversion). If the present estate and the reversion were transferred to a common owner, the component parts merged back into an estate in fee simple absolute. In the past, merger did not require the party reassembling the component parts to acquire title to contingent future interests like contingent remainders. Hence, if O transferred Blackacre to A for life, then to B if B has graduated from law school, B's contingent remainder could be destroyed by transferring A's life estate and O's reversion to the same party. Today, consistent with the abolition of the destructibility rule, most states no longer permit the destruction of a contingent remainder by this method.

ABO PETROLEUM CORP. v. AMSTUTZ

New Mexico Supreme Court
600 P.2d 278 (1979)

PAYNE, J.

This action was brought in the District Court of Eddy County by Abo Petroleum and others against the children of Beulah Turknett Jones and Ruby Turknett Jones to quiet title to certain property in Eddy County. Both sides moved for summary judgment. The district court granted Abo's motion, denied the children's motion, and entered a partial final judgment in favor of Abo. The children appealed, and we reverse the district court.

James and Amanda Turknett, the parents of Beulah and Ruby, owned in fee simple the disputed property in this case. In February 1908, by separate instruments entitled "conditional deeds," the parents conveyed life estates in two separate parcels, one each to Beulah and Ruby. Each deed provided that the property would remain the daughter's

> during her natural life, . . . and at her death to revert, vest in, and become the property absolute of her heir or heirs, meaning her children if she have any at her death, but if she die without an heir or heirs, then and in that event this said property and real estate shall vest in and become the property of the estate of . . . [her], to be distributed as provided by law at the time of her death.

At the time of the delivery of the deed, neither daughter was married, nor were any children born to either daughter for several years thereafter.

In 1911, the parents gave another deed to Beulah, which covered the same land conveyed in 1908. This deed purported to convey "absolute title to the grantee." In 1916, the parents executed yet another deed to Beulah, granting a portion of the property included in her two previous deeds. A second deed was also executed to Ruby, which provided that it was a "correction deed" for the 1908 deed. After all the deeds from the parents had been executed, Beulah had three children and Ruby had four children. These children are the appellants herein.

Subsequent to the execution of these deeds, Beulah and Ruby attempted to convey fee simple interests in the property to the predecessors of Abo. The children of Beulah and Ruby contend that the 1908 deeds gave their parents life estates in the property, and that Beulah and Ruby could only have conveyed life estates to the predecessors in interest of Abo. Abo argues that the 1911 and 1916 deeds vested Beulah and Ruby with fee simple title, and that such title was conveyed to Abo's predecessors in interest, thereby giving Abo fee simple title to the property.

We begin our inquiry by examining the nature of the estates James and Amanda Turknett conveyed in the 1908 deeds. First, the deeds gave each of the daughters property "during her natural life." As Abo apparently concedes, these words conveyed only a life estate.

Second, each deed provided that upon the daughter's death, the property would pass to her "heir or heirs," which was specifically defined as "her children if she have any at her death." Because it was impossible at the time of the original conveyance to determine whether the daughters would have children, or whether any of their children would survive them, the deeds created contingent remainders in the daughters' children, which could not vest until the death of the daughter holding the life estate. C. Moynihan, *Introduction to the Law of Real Property* 123 (1962).

Third, each deed provided that if the contingent remainder failed, the property would become part of the daughter's estate, and pass "as provided by law at the time of her death." The effect of this language would be to pass the property to the heirs of the daughter upon the failure of the first contingent remainder. Because one's heirs are not ascertainable until death (C. Moynihan, *supra* at 127), the grant over to the daughter's estate created a second, or alternative, contingent remainder.

The only issues that remain are whether the parents retained any interest, whether by their subsequent deeds to their daughters they conveyed any interest that remained, and whether those conveyances destroyed the contingent remainders in the children. The grantor-parents divested themselves of the life estate and contingent remainder interests in the property upon delivery of the first deed. Because both remainders are contingent, however, the parents retained a reversionary interest the property. C. Moynihan, *supra* at 124, n. 1.

Abo's position is that by the subsequent conveyances to the daughters, the parents' reversionary interest merged with the daughters' life estates, thus destroying the contingent remainders in the daughters' children and giving the daughters fee simple title to the property. This contention presents a question which this Court has not previously addressed — whether the doctrine of the destructibility of contingent remainders is applicable in New Mexico.

This doctrine, which originated in England in the Sixteenth Century, was based upon the feudal concept that seisin of land could never be in abeyance. From that principle, the rule developed that if the prior estate terminated before the occurrence of the contingency, the contingent remainder was destroyed for lack of a supporting freehold estate. The one instance in which this could happen occurred when the supporting life estate merged with the reversionary interest.

Although New Mexico has adopted the common law of England by statute, it has been repeatedly held that "if the common law is not 'applicable to our condition and circumstances' it is not to be given effect." *Flores v. Flores*, 506 P.2d 345, 347 (N.M. Ct. App. 1973), *cert. denied*, 506 P.2d 336 (1973). The doctrine of destructibility of contingent remainders has been almost universally regarded to be obsolete by legislatures, courts and legal writers. *See, e.g., Whitten v. Whitten*, 219 P.2d 228 (Okla. 1950), 1 L. Simes and A. Smith, *Law of Future Interests* § 209 (2d ed. 1956). It has been renounced by virtually all jurisdictions in the United States, either by statute or judicial decision, and was abandoned in the country of its origin over a century ago. Section 240 of the *Restatement of Property* (1936) takes the position that the doctrine is based in history, not reason. Comment (d) to § 240 states that "complexity, confusion, unpredictability and frustration of manifested intent" are the demonstrated consequences of adherence to the doctrine of destructibility. Furthermore, because operation of the doctrine can be avoided by the use of a trust to support the contingent remainder, the doctrine places a premium on the drafting skills of the lawyer. 49 Mich. L. Rev. 762, 764 (1951).

The only tenable argument in support of the doctrine is that it promotes the alienability of land. It does so, however, only arbitrarily, and oftentimes by defeating the intent of the grantor. Land often carries burdens with it, but courts do not arbitrarily cut off those burdens merely in order to make land more alienable. Because the doctrine of destructibility of contingent remainders is but a relic of the feudal past, which has no justification or support in modern society, we decline to apply it in New Mexico. As Justice Holmes put it:

> It is revolting to have no better reason for a rule of law than that so it was laid down in the time of Henry IV. It is still more revolting if the grounds upon which it was laid down have vanished long since, and the rule simply persists from blind imitation of the past.

Holmes, *The Path of the Law*, 10 Harv. L. Rev. 457 at 469 (1897).

We hold that the conveyances of the property to the daughters did not destroy the contingent remainders in the daughters' children. The daughters acquired no more interest in the property by virtue of the later deeds than they had been granted in the original deeds. Any conveyance by them could transfer only the interest they had originally acquired, even if it purported to convey a fee simple.

The summary judgment and partial final judgment entered in favor of Abo are reversed, and the cause is remanded for further proceedings consistent with this opinion.

NOTES AND QUESTIONS

1. This case reflects the modern tendency to preserve remainder interests and allow them to vest in possession. In addition to the widespread abolition of the destructibility rule, in ambiguous cases, American courts will generally apply a presumption that remainders are vested rather than contingent.

2. *The Rule in* Shelley's *Case*. In addition to having to concern themselves with the consequences of the merger rule and the destructibility doctrine, earlier generations of real estate conveyancers who sought to divide ownership between a life estate holder and remaindermen had to deal with the Rule in Shelley's Case. This rule, which predates the case that gave it its name — *Shelley's Case*, 1 Co. Rep. 93b, 76 Eng. Rep. 206 (K.B. 1581) — by more than 200 years, was famous as a trap for the unwary. It provided that if O conveyed or devised a life estate in land to A with a remainder in the heirs of A in fee simple, the remainder interest went to A, not A's heirs. Consequently, A's life estate and remainder then merged into a present estate in fee simple absolute, and A was able to transfer complete title if he chose to do so. The rule had its origins in English land law under which feudal incidents (essentially, a tax) attached to land that was inherited, but not to land that was "purchased." A could relieve his heirs from the obligation to pay future incidents by transferring Blackacre to O in fee simple and then having O transfer it back to him for life with a remainder to his heirs (which in accordance with primogeniture would be his eldest living male descendant at the time of his death). Thus when A died, A's heir would be entitled to Blackacre through the vesting of his remainder in possession, rather than through inheritance. The Rule in Shelley's Case was adopted to prevent such practices.

However, as was the case with many of the features of early modern real property law, the rule outlived the circumstances that had produced it. The rule applied to both legal and equitable interests, so long as both the life estate and the remainder were both legal or both equitable. (Equitable interests are those held in trust.) Because the law of feudal incidents had no applicability in the United States, the primary effect of the rule was to frustrate the efforts of grantors who attempted to tie up land in the same family for two generations, a practice that was otherwise permitted. The rule could be circumvented in most jurisdictions by avoiding the term "heir" or its equivalent and instead using the name of the heir apparent (as into A for life, remainder to B where B is A's heir apparent). Dissatisfaction with the rule led a number of courts to construe it extremely narrowly, and it was eventually abolished in most jurisdictions. Today, the rule survives only in Arkansas and Delaware and possibly in Colorado and Indiana. *See* W. STOEBUCK & D. WHITMAN, THE LAW of PROPERTY 115 (3d ed. 2000).

Because the abolition of the rule did not apply retroactively in many states, Rule in Shelley's Case cases still arise, and sometimes in jurisdictions where the rule has been long abolished. For example, the Chancery Division of the Superior Court of New Jersey was recently confronted with a case that turned on the application of the Rule in Shelley's Case, which was abolished in New Jersey in 1934. The case, *In the Matter of the Estate of Hendrickson*, 736 A.2d 540 (N.J. Super. Ct. Ch. Div. 1999), involved a provision in the will of Wycoff Hendrickson who died in 1928. Hendrickson's will, which was written in 1920, provided that his farm was to go to his son Earle for life and then to "such person or persons as shall be his sole heir or heirs." Earle took possession of the farm and maintained it until his death on May 31, 1997, 69 years after the death of his father. Although conceding that the Rule still applied in this case, the court concluded that the language used in the Wycoff Hendrickson will successfully avoided the Rule in Shelley's Case under the law as it existed in New Jersey in the 1920s. Thus, it ruled that the farm should pass to the heirs of Earle Hendrickson and not to his devisees (as would be the case if the Rule applied giving Earle a fee simple estate beginning in 1928).

3. *The Doctrine of Worthier Title.* Like the Rule in Shelley's Case, the Doctrine of Worthier Title prohibited devises of land to those who would otherwise inherit the property. Under this rule, if O's will provided that Blackacre was to go to A, and A was O's heir, A would take Blackacre by inheritance, as though the will had been silent on the disposition of Blackacre. As a practical matter, this aspect of the doctrine was of no particular consequence once the feudal incidents were abolished. The doctrine also provided that if O transferred a life estate, a fee tail (discussed in Section E, *infra*), or an estate for years, and created a remainder in his own heirs, the remainder was treated as a reversion in O. Hence, O to A for life, remainder to the heirs of O was treated as creating a reversion for O which would be inherited by O's heirs after O's death. However, if O outlived A, Blackacre returned to O in fee simple absolute, and O was free to alienate the property if he chose to do so. Today, the doctrine of worthier title is only a rule of construction; if the evidence shows that O intended to create a remainder which would vest in possession with his heirs upon the death of A, it will be so interpreted. The right of present possession will still revert back to O if O outlives A. Do you see why?

[4.] The Transfer of Remainders

Unless restrictions on alienation are imposed at the time of their creation, life estates and estates for years are freely transferable. The same is true for reversions and remainders. Hence, if O transfers Blackacre to A for A's life, A is free to transfer his estate to B. If B takes all of A's interest, he will have a life estate *pur autre vie*. A can create an estate for years or a life estate for the life of B, but in no case can the estate last longer than A's life. If A transfers Blackacre to B for 10 years and then dies shortly after the transaction, B's estate is terminated. Although the assignment of leases (estates for years) is quite common, there is only a limited market for existing life estates, given the uncertainty of the estate's duration. A could live for another 50 years or he could die tomorrow. A's life expectancy can be estimated from actuarial tables, but the element of risk remains for the purchaser.

While ordinary life estates cannot be passed along at death — for obvious reasons — life estates *pur autre vie* may be. Thus, if O transfers Blackacre to A for the life of B, and A dies before B, the estate would pass to A's heir or to whomever A designated if he had a valid will. This process could continue until the death of B, at which time the right of present possession would revert to O, or to whomever held O's interest. O's reversion could have been sold or passed to another party at the time of O's death. As the latter statement indicates, reversions and remainders may be transferred in much the same way. If O transfers Blackacre to A for life, O retains the reversion. If she transfers Whiteacre to A for life, remainder to B and her heirs, B has a remainder. Both interests can be freely transferred during A's life. Thus, if O or B transfers her interest to C, C will have the right of present possession in the respective parcels after the death of A.

The following case illustrates the complications and uncertainties that sometimes arise from the transfer of future interests.

RUTHERFORD v. KEITH

Kentucky Court of Appeals
444 S.W.2d 546 (1969)

EDWARD P. HILL, JUDGE.

This appeal concerns the construction of the will of Fount Cox, who died in 1910 a resident of Edmonson County. At stake is the title to a farm containing approximately one hundred acres. Fount Cox was survived by his wife Julia Cox. No children were born to this marriage. From the time of their marriage in 1899, Medie Woosley, a sister of Julia Cox, resided with Fount and Julia. She continued to live with Julia for some years after the death of Fount.

Also surviving Fount were two brothers, Sam W. Cox and J.M. Cox. The appellants, plaintiffs in the circuit court, are the children and grandchildren of Sam W. Cox and J.M. Cox. The apposite provisions of the Fount Cox will are quoted verbatim as follows:

> "I will to my said wife all my real estate for and during her natural life only after the deth of my said wife, should her Sister Miss Medie Woosley be living and unmarried. I will the whole of my real estate to her. In the event Miss Medie Woosely should die or marry before the deth of my said wife I will that at the deth of my Said Wife all of my real estate go to my two brothers J.M. Cox and S. W. Cox Share and Share alike and should either of my brother die before my Said Wife his child or children shall have what the father of said Child or children would have received had he been living at the time of my wife deth."

In 1916, Medie Woosley married a man by the name of Sambrook. The widow, Julia, married Andy F. Houchens in 1918. In the same year as her marriage to Houchens, Julia and her second husband conveyed the land involved to Sam W. Cox. Thereafter, and in the same year (1918), Sam W. Cox and his brother, J.M. Cox, executed a deed attempting to convey the farm to Mrs. O.H. Fishback. The appellees are the successors in title of Mrs. Fishback.

The husband of Medie died in 1928, and she never remarried. Both Sam W. Cox and J.M. Cox died in 1937. Julia Houchens died in 1954. In 1961, Medie Woosley Sambrook attempted to execute a deed to the farm to some of the defendants.

Appellants' action seeks to quiet their title to the farm in question and demands "rents, issues, and profits." Substantial improvements have been made on a two-acre tract, a part of the original farm. Appellees took the position in the trial court, and take the same position here, that the conveyance by Julia Houchens and her husband and the deed of Sam W. Cox and J.M. Cox conveyed good title to them.

The judgment appealed from held that the remarriage of Julia "terminated her life estate" and that the "remainder estate in the real estate of Fount Cox was thereby precipitated and the fee simple title in the said real estate thereupon vested in the remaindermen, J.M. and S.W. Cox." The title of appellees was quieted, and the complaint was dismissed. With this conclusion we cannot agree and reverse the judgment.

Unquestionably, Julia took a life estate in the farm. No mention is made in the will of a termination of her estate upon her remarriage. Her life estate did terminate in 1954 when she died. She could convey no greater interest in the property than that which she took under the will. Hence appellees and their predecessors have only the life estate of Julia. The fact that Sam W. Cox and J.M. Cox joined in the deed to Mrs. Fishback passed no title other than the life estate Julia conveyed to Sam, except Sam's and J.M.'s remainder interests under the will, which, however, were contingent on their surviving Julia, and thus never vested. *See Lepps v. Lee*, 17 S.W. 146 at 147, wherein this court said:

> But while a contingent interest may be conveyed or devised, * * * yet, if the grantor or devisor dies before it becomes effective, and no estate has ever vested in him, the grantee or devisee takes nothing. No right having ever vested in the devisor or grantor, nothing passes. It is merely a devise or grant that may become effective if the devise to him becomes so; and, this never having taken place in this case, it results that the appellant has no right to any part of the estate in contest. Judgment affirmed."

Under our construction of the will Julia was devised a life estate. Medie Woosley was given the first contingent remainder interest conditioned that she had not previously married and was still living at the time of Julia's death. Medie's marriage defeated her contingent remainder interest. It is apparent that Julia, Sam, J.M., and Medie considered Medie's marriage as a complete elimination or termination of Medie's contingent remainder interest in the property.

Sam and J.M. Cox were devised the second contingent remainder conditioned upon the death or marriage of Medie before the death of Julia and conditioned also upon their surviving Julia. No estate could vest in Sam and J.M. until the death of Julia, the life tenant. The will left the third contingent remainder to the children of Sam and J.M. in event the brothers predeceased Julia. The title to the remainder estate vested in these children in 1954, the date of the death of Julia. We have read and considered the authorities cited and relied on by appellees and find they contain sound law but are inapplicable to the facts of the present case. Most of these authorities hold that "the remainder vests in possession upon the elimination of the intervening estate." In the instant case, the first intervening estate, or contingent remainder, was eliminated by the marriage of Medie, and the second contingent remainder never vested in the two brothers because of their deaths before that of the widow. Therefore, the third remainder to the children and grandchildren of the two brothers vested in them on the death of the widow. The judgment is reversed for proceedings consistent herewith. All concur.

NOTES AND QUESTIONS

1. Note that there was nothing wrong with the two Cox brothers transferring their remainder interests to Mrs. Fishback. Those transfers were entirely valid. Why then did the right of ownership end up with the Cox children? Who was the owner of the right of present possession between 1918 and Julia's death in 1954?

2. *Transferability of Future Interests.* Vested future interests have always been freely alienable, and while there was a time when contingent future interests were viewed as inalienable, the modern rule is that all future interests can be transferred by will or by deed. As a general rule, attempted restraints on the alienation on future interests imposed by private parties are unenforceable. If O transferred Blackacre to A for life with a remainder in fee simple going to B, subject to the restriction that B could not transfer her future interest during A's lifetime, the limitation would be invalid and B would be free to transfer her remainder interest at any time during A's life. (The general subject of restraints on alienation is discussed in Chapter 8.)

[D.] THE ESTATE OF FEE TAIL

In early modern English property law the estate of fee tail was designed to ensure that land remained the property of a specific family, and it accomplished that purpose by requiring that the next owner of the land be the issue (the "heir of the body") of the current owner. Combined with the doctrine of primogeniture, which gave the oldest son the right to inherit all of the father's real property, the fee tail guaranteed that entailed estates would stay in the same family from one generation to the next. Land held subject to an estate in fee tail could not be alienated for more than the life of the present estate holder. If A took Blackacre from O in fee tail, the estate passed to A's direct descendant (either a child or a grandchild) upon A's death, regardless of what disposition A may have attempted to make of the property. For example, if A transferred his interest to B, B's right of possession expired upon the death of A.

An estate in fee tail was created through the use of the words "and the heirs of his body" in the instrument conveying title. This language was interpreted as words of limitation, not words of purchase, and as such, it created no immediate interest in the heirs of the body, i.e., the grantee's issue. Although a fee tail could theoretically go on forever — we are all the products of a line of descent going back to the beginning of time — in an era in which life spans were much shorter than they are today and infant mortality rates were high, it was assumed that any fee tail could end with the present generation. Consequently, the grantor retained a reversion in fee simple absolute which would vest in possession when the family line died out.

It was also possible to create specialized forms of fee tail, specifically fee tail male (to A and the male heirs of his body) and fee tail special (to A and the heirs of his body by his wife Agnes). The former was used to reclaim title to land if the grantee was survived only by daughters while the latter enabled the grantor to direct ownership down a particular biological line when the grantee had been married to more than one woman. Fee tails were subject to the Rule in Shelley's Case, but because the "heirs of the body" took no official future interest, they were not subject to the Rule against Perpetuities.

Whatever the merits of the fee tail, the desire to make land more freely alienable always made the estate unpopular with those who held entailed property. Between 1285 A.D. when the fee tail was created and 1925 when it was finally abolished in England, an extraordinary amount of effort was devoted to devising legal strategies that would work to convert fee tails into estates in fee simple absolute, a process known as disentailment or "knocking the tail." The most effective system was known as "common recovery." *See* A. W. B. SIMPSON, A HISTORY OF THE LAND LAW 130, et seq. (2nd ed. 1986).

The estate of fee tail was never popular in the United States and from a very early date, most states either abolished it or severely limited its application. Today, the fee tail exists in only four states (Maine, Massachusetts, Rhode Island, and Delaware) and in each of them an estate in tail can be disentailed at any time by the present estate holder. In a substantial majority of states, an effort to create a fee tail results in a fee simple estate. In about half of these states, the estate is automatically converted into an estate in fee simple absolute and the holder of the reversion or remainder takes nothing. In the other states, the future interests are preserved, but they can vest in possession if the original grantee dies without issue. For example, assume a transaction which provides, "O to A and the heirs of his body, but if A should die without issue, to B and her heirs." A goes into possession of Blackacre and then dies with no surviving lineal descendants (children, grandchildren, etc.). In the first group of states, A dies with an estate in fee simple absolute, and it passes through his will, or to his collateral heirs if he has no will. In the second group, B takes possession in fee simple absolute. If A is survived by issue, then the estate becomes one of fee simple absolute for all time.

In the rest of the states, the grantee takes a life estate, or its equivalent, and the issue of the grantee have a remainder in fee simple absolute. The effect of such statutes is to limit the duration of the fee tail to one generation. The following case illustrates the difficulties that can arise when parties nevertheless attempt to create estates in fee tail.

LONG v. LONG

Ohio Supreme Court
343 N.E.2d 100 (1976)

Plaintiff-appellees herein, Howard W. Long and Paul H. Olinger, the grandsons of Henry Long, commenced a declaratory judgment action in the Court of Common Pleas of Darke County, Probate Division, against the defendant-appellant herein, Bessie Long, the widow and beneficiary of Eugene Long, the deceased brother of appellee, Howard W. Long, to determine the ownership of certain real property.

The undisputed facts are as follows: On April 2, 1919, Henry Long conveyed three separate tracts of land in fee tail to each of his three children, Jesse Long, Edward W. Long and Emma Long Olinger. The latter two were survived by living children who took their respective tracts in fee simple, pursuant to R. C. 2131.08. Their parcels are not involved in the present controversy.

The granting clause in the deed from Henry Long to Jesse Long, which is similar to those conveying the other parcels to the other children, reads, in part: "to . . . Jesse S. Long, and the children of his body begotten, and their heirs and assigns forever . . . ." Henry Long died testate in August 1932. His will contained no general residuary clause, but provided in Item IV, as follows:

> At the decease of my wife I will and direct that my executor sell all my real estate, at public or private sale as deemed best at the time, and reduce all my personal estate into money, and from said funds then pay, — 1st to my then living grand-children the sum of Three Thousand Dollars ($3,000.00) to be divided equally among such grand-children and the residue to my three children, or their issue, if any be deceased with issue — if any of my children at the time of such division, be deceased, leaving no issue, no part of said funds shall pass to the estate of such deceased.

Edward Long died intestate in March 1946, survived by his wife, Emma, and sons, Howard and Eugene. Emma Long died testate on July 3, 1964, survived by Howard and Eugene. Her will contained a clause dividing her residuary estate equally between her sons. Eugene died testate in October 1966 without issue, and was survived by his wife, Bessie Long. His will made Bessie Long his sole beneficiary and specifically mentioned the real estate in controversy. Emma Long Olinger was predeceased by her husband and died intestate on October 19, 1954, survived by a son, Paul H. Olinger.

In 1945, Jesse Long executed a quitclaim deed conveying whatever interest he had in the property in question to Rosella Long, who died testate and made Marie Ethel Brown and her husband, John Brown, her sole beneficiaries. The Browns subsequently executed a quitclaim deed conveying whatever interest they had in the property to Howard W. Long and his wife, Esther Naomi Long. Jesse Long died intestate on March 4, 1974, without issue.

The appellant, Bessie Long, maintains that, "where a grantor deeds real estate to his son and to the children of his body begotten, their heirs and assigns forever, and such son dies without having sired a child, a possibility of reverter remains in the original grantor of such fee tail estate which is a descendible, devisable estate at the death of the original grantor of the estate tail." Appellant contends that, from the time Henry Long conveyed the fee tail estate to Jesse Long, there remained in him, as the grantor, a "possibility of reverter." Appellant argues that this "possibility of reverter" was a descendible, devisable interest and, therefore, passed at the grantor's death to his heirs existing at that time. Appellant contends that Item IV of Henry Long's will expressed an intention to convey the residue of his estate only to those surviving children who had issue and, therefore, Jesse Long's conveyance was ineffective. Appellant maintains that the possibility of reverter following Jesse Long's fee tail descended or was devised, one-half to Edward Long and one-half to Emma Long Olinger.

Appellant claims, through her deceased husband, Eugene Long, a one-fourth interest in the property from Edward's portion. Appellant also maintains that Howard W. Long received the other one-fourth interest from Edward's portion and that Paul Olinger, Emma Long Olinger's son, received, by descent, Emma's one-half interest in the possibility of reverter.

The Probate Court determined that a possibility of reverter is not an estate of inheritance and that, upon the happening of the contingency, the grantee's death without issue, the property passes to the next of kin and heirs at law of the grantor then living — in the present case the appellees, Howard Long and Paul Olinger. The Court of Appeals affirmed the judgment of the Probate Court, one judge dissenting.

J.J. P. Corrigan, Justice.

The unique issue in this case concerns the nature of the interest remaining in the grantor, Henry Long, after the creation by deed of a fee tail estate which was conveyed by the grantor to his son "Jesse S. Long, and the children of his body begotten, and their heirs and assigns forever." The parties agree that the estate created by the grantor was a fee tail.

Appellant maintains that the interest remaining in the grantor is a "possibility of reverter" which is a descendible, devisable estate at the death of the original grantor of the estate tail. Appellant contends that, upon the death of the first donee in tail without issue, the interest then passes to the heirs of the grantor living at his death, and to their descendants.

The appellees, too, maintain that the interest remaining in the grantor of a fee tail estate is a possibility of reverter. Appellees contend, however, that this possibility of reverter was not of sufficient quality to descend to an heir until the donee in tail dies without issue. At this point, appellees argue, the possibility ripens into a fee simple estate in the grantor and, where he has predeceased the donee in tail, the estate then passes by the law of intestate succession to his heirs living at the time of the ripening of the possibility.

Considerable confusion exists in the present case because of the term used to designate the nature of the grantor's future interest in the property conveyed. At early common law, prior to the enactment of the Statute of Westminster, 13 Edward I. Chapter 1, De Donis Conditionalibus, in 1285, the transfer of a fee restrained to some particular heirs exclusive of others, e.g., to the heirs of a man's body, created an estate designated a fee simple conditional. [Citations omitted.]

The future interest in the grantor of a conditional fee at common law was generally called a possibility of reversion or right of reverter. The usual practice at common law, however, was for the tenant in tail to alien the land conveyed and afterward repurchase, taking an absolute estate in the land which would descend to his heirs generally and prevent any reversion to the donor. To prevent this practice, the statute de donis was enacted, imposing a restraint upon the power of alienation by the tenant in tail. Prior to the enactment of the statute, a fee simple conditional became absolute upon the birth of issue. By operation of the statute the tenant now held an estate tail and the donor had a reversion of fee simple expectant on the failure of the issue in tail. The tenant could no longer alien, upon his having issue, but the feud (estate) was to remain to the issue according to the form of the gift, i.e., the issue of the donee in tail took per formam doni (by the form of the gift) or from the grantor rather than through any particular tenant in tail. The statute preserved the estate for the benefit of the issue of the grantee and the reversion for the benefit of the donor and his heirs by declaring that the intention of the donor manifestly expressed according to the form of the deed should be observed. The real source of the title was the donor, himself, who always retained a reversion expectant upon the failure of issue. It should be noted that the statute de donis did not create the estate tail but rather gave it perpetuity.

More importantly, for purposes of the present case, the statute de donis converted the donor's bare possibility of reversion or right of reverter into a reversion or fee simple expectant upon failure of issue. This distinction is important because a reversion in fee is a vested interest or estate and is descendible, alienable or assignable by deed or conveyance, and is also devisable. A reversion is the residue of an estate left in the grantor or other transferor, to commence in possession after the determination of some particular estate transferred by him. A reversion arises only by operation of law and is a vested right.

A reversion arises whenever a person having a vested estate transfers to another a lesser vested estate. Since the reversion is the undisposed of portion of a vested estate, it follows that all reversions are vested interests. A reversion is said to be vested because there is no condition precedent to the taking effect in possession other than the termination of the preceding estates. This does not mean, however, that every reversion is certain to take effect in possession and enjoyment. The distinguishing feature of the reversion is that it is not subject to a condition precedent to its taking effect in possession, and all other conditions defeating a reversion are regarded as conditions subsequent.

A reversion is historically distinguishable from a possibility of reverter in that a reversion arises when the estate transferred is of a lesser quantum than the transferor owns. A possibility of reverter arises when the estate conveyed is of the same quantum as the transferor owns.

The only remaining issue to consider is whether the Ohio enactment of 1811 (10 Ohio Laws 7), modifying fee tail estates, has had any effect on the reversionary interest in the grantor.[2] In Pollock v. Speidel, (17 Ohio St. 439), this court recognized the continued existence of estates tail in Ohio, subject to the statutory modification enacted in 1811, and now embodied in R. C. 2131.08, which converted estates tail into fees simple in the hands of the issue of the first donee in tail. Subsequent decisions, in Harkness v. Corning (1873), 24 Ohio St. 416; Broadstone v. Brown (1873), 24 Ohio St. 430; and Dungan v. Kline (1910), 81 Ohio St. 371, made it clear that the statutory enactment did not change the nature of the estate tail in the donee in tail from an inheritable estate to an estate for life merely but restricted the entailment to the immediate issue of such donee.

Ohio courts have also recognized the existence of a reversion in the grantor of an estate tail. [Citations omitted.] In accordance with the undisputed authority that the interest created in the grantor of a common-law fee tail estate is a vested reversion,

---

[2] [1] AN ACT to restrict the entailment of real estate. Sect. 1. Be it enacted by the General Assembly of the state of Ohio. That from and after the taking effect of this act, no estate in fee simple, fee tail, or any lesser estate in lands or tenements, lying within this state, shall be given or granted by deed or will to any person or persons, but such as are in being, or to the immediate issue or descendants of such as are in being at the time of making such deed or will, and that all estates given in tail shall be and remain an absolute estate in fee simple to the issue of the first donee in tail. This act to take effect and be in force from and after the first day of June next. . . . December 17, 1811.

and in view of the decisions to the effect that the Ohio enactment restricting fee tail estates does not alter the fundamental nature of the estate tail in the first donee in tail, we hold that such reversions are vested estates fully descendible, devisable and alienable inter vivos.

As a result, in the present case, the series of conveyances begun by Henry Long's deceased son, Jesse Long, were effective to convey his one-third reversionary interest in the property to appellee Howard W. Long, and Esther Naomi Long, one-sixth to each. As to Henry Long's son, Edward Long, who died intestate, his one-third reversionary interest in the property descended, one-half or a one-sixth share to his son, appellee Howard W. Long, and the other one-half interest or one-sixth share to his other son, Eugene Long. Eugene Long died testate in 1966, specifically devising his estate including the one-sixth share of the reversion to his wife, appellant Bessie Long. As to Henry Long's daughter, Emma Long Olinger, who died intestate, her one-third share of the reversion descended to her son, appellee Paul H. Olinger.

The present ownership of the realty in question rests, therefore, in the following undivided interests:

1. Esther Naomi Long, wife of Howard W. Long, one-sixth (from Jesse's portion)

2. Howard W. Long (Appellee), one-sixth (from Jesse's portion) and one-sixth (from Edward's portion). Howard Long's total interest is one-third.

3. Bessie Long (Appellant), one-sixth (from Edward's portion)

4. Paul H. Olinger, one-third (Emma Long Olinger's portion).

It should be noted that this distribution is consistent with that expressed in the minority opinion of the Court of Appeals for Darke County, written by Judge Sherer. It is not the precise distribution contended for by the appellant. The appellant urged that, although Henry Long's will contained no general residuary clause, Item IV thereof evidences a clear intention on the part of the testator that no part of the residue of his estate, including the reversion in the fee tail estate granted to Jesse Long, should pass to any of his children unless that child had issue. Appellant maintains, therefore, that Jesse Long did not qualify and no part of the reversion passed to him but passed, one-half to Emma Long Olinger and by descent to her son, appellee Paul H. Olinger, one-half to Edward Long, one-fourth descending to Howard W. Long and one-fourth descending to Eugene Long, devised by him to his surviving spouse, appellant Bessie Long. For reason of the foregoing, this contention has no merit. The Probate Court and Court of Appeals are correct in the holding that Item IV does not constitute a general residuary clause capable of transferring any of Henry Long's interest in the property in question. Oglesbee v. Miller (1924), 111 Ohio St. 426.

The judgment of the Court of Appeals is, therefore, reversed and judgment entered in accordance with this opinion. Judgment reversed.

NOTES AND QUESTIONS

1. The final resolution of this dispute differs from the results sought by both parties. Both plaintiffs and defendants (and their lawyers) had difficulty with the appropriate terminology, a feature that is not uncommon in cases involving estates in land and future interests. To understand the result in *Long v. Long*, one must focus on the whereabouts of Jesse Long's reversion as it moves from owner to owner during Jesse's life. Remember, Jesse's reversion is an undivided one-third interest in his father's original reversion that was created with Jesse's estate in fee tail and inherited by Jesse at his father's death.

2. *Fee Simple Conditional.* The estate of fee simple conditional, mentioned by the court in the above case, was an estate even older than fee tail. It resembled fee tail, except that it could be converted into a fee simple if the owner of the present estate transferred his or her interest to a third party after the birth of the owner's child or children. Although the estate of fee simple conditional was converted into fee tail by the statute *De Donis Conditionalibus* in 1285, the estate entered American law when a small number of states took the position that they had adopted the common law, but not the statute *De Donis*. Today, the fee simple conditional exists in South Carolina, and, at least in theory, in Iowa and Oregon.

3. *Fee Tail Followed by a Remainder Interest.* In theory, a fee tail estate could be followed by a vested remainder, as in O to A and the heirs of her body, then to B and his heirs. B's interest, however, is likely to be of value only if A dies without issue and without having terminated the fee tail. If A lives in a jurisdiction that automatically converts fee tail estates into estates in fee simple absolute, then B's interest will be completely worthless.

[E.] CONDITIONAL AND DETERMINABLE ESTATES

Many of the earliest efforts to impose restrictions on the use of land involved present estates that allowed the grantor to limit what the estate holder could do with the property. To accomplish this, English and American law recognized a number of qualified forms of the fee simple estate, known as the fee simple determinable, the fee simple subject to a condition subsequent, and the fee simple subject to an executory limitation. Each of these estates operated in accordance with the same general principle: the holder of the estate had all the rights of a fee simple owner so long as he or she did not violate a specific limitation or condition attached to the estate at the time of its creation. Consequently, the estate was of potentially infinite duration since it would never terminate if the limitation or condition were honored. However, if the limitation or condition was violated, either the estate ended automatically or the holder of the future interest had the power to terminate it. Either way, the offending owner effectively forfeited his ownership interest in the land.

The same devices could be used to transfer ownership of land upon the occurrence of an event that might or might not occur, as is a transfer from O to A and his heirs until such time as B reached age 21. If B died without reaching age 21, then O would hold title in fee simple absolute. However, once B reached age 21, A or his successor was automatically divested of title to Blackacre and B was now the owner in fee simple absolute.

The estate of *fee simple determinable* is an estate that *automatically* ends when some specified event occurs. The specified event is known as a "limitation" and may or may not be within the control of the estate holder. If the estate does terminate, the right of present possession reverts back to the grantor, or the current holder of the grantor's interest. The estate is created by the use of clear, unequivocal durational language, such as "To A for so long as the land is used for agricultural purposes for the next 20 years." Ordinarily, a document creating an estate in fee simple determinable will include the words "so long as," "until," or "while," all of which connote duration, or in the absence of such language, a specific statement that upon the happening of the event, the land will "revert" to the grantor. An estate of fee simple determinable can be transferred in any manner, but alienation does not alter its character.

The future interest retained by the grantor is known as the *possibility of reverter*. Although at common law, the possibility of reverter could not be transferred except by inheritance, in most states today, consistence with the principle of the free alienation of future interests, it may be transferred by any of the conventional means (i.e., by sale, by gift, or by devise).

The estate of *fee simple subject to a condition subsequent* differs from the fee simple determinable in that it does not automatically terminate upon breach of the stated restriction, called a "condition." Instead, the violation of the stated condition gives the grantor the option to terminate the estate if he or she chooses. A fee simple subject to a condition subsequent is created with language that attaches *words of condition* to the estate in fee simple and reserves the right or option to re-enter and re-take in the event of breach of the stated condition. Words of condition are usually signaled by the use of the conjunctive phrase, *but if*. For example, in the transaction "O to A, but if the land ceases to be used for agricultural purposes for the next 20 years, grantor reserves the right to re-enter and re-take," an estate of fee simple subject to a condition subsequent is created for A. Were A to cease to use the land for agricultural purposes within the stated period, the estate would not automatically end, as it would with a fee simple determinable, but it could be terminated if O chose to exercise his or her reserved right.

O's future interest in a fee simple subject to a condition subsequent is known as either a *right of entry* or the *power of termination*. As with the fee simple determinable, both the estate and the future interest can be transferred, although a minority of jurisdictions still prevent the transfer of the future interest by inter vivos conveyance. The Restatement Property Second §§ 161–62 endorses the minority position and states that powers of termination in land are not alienable unless certain very specific conditions are present.

The *fee simple subject to executory limitation* differs from the preceding estates in that it is accompanied by a future interest in a third party rather than the grantor. For example, "To A, his heirs, successor and assigns, so long as the premises are used as a church for the next 10 years, and if they cease to be so used, then to B and his heirs" creates an estate of fee simple subject to an executory limitation.

B's future interest is known as a *shifting executory interest*. (Executory interests are discussed in greater detail later in this chapter.) In regard to whether the forfeiture is automatic or elective, the fee simple subject to an executory limitation is like the fee simple determinable. The present estate is automatically forfeited in the event of breach of its accompanying condition, and the holder of the executory interest becomes the owner of the property. This is true, even if the language creating the estate contains terminology that would have created a fee simple subject to a condition subsequent had the future interest been retained by the grantor. Thus, an estate created by the transaction "O to A, but if the land ceases to be used for agricultural purposes for the next 20 years, B shall have the right to re-enter and re-take" will automatically terminate upon breach of the condition, even if B does nothing to assert his interest.

STORKE v. PENN MUTUAL LIFE INSURANCE CO.

Illinois Supreme Court
61 N.E.2d 552 (1945)

MR JUSTICE GUNN delivered the opinion of the court.

Appellants, as plaintiffs, prosecuted this action in the circuit court of Cook county as heirs-at-law of Jay E. Storke. Jay E. Storke and Bernard Timmerman, now both deceased, in 1889 subdivided approximately forty acres of land into lots. At that time the property was outside the limits of the city of Chicago. It is now located in the neighborhood of Halsted street between Seventy-fifth and Seventy-ninth streets. Part of the property involved was conveyed by deed containing the following covenant:

> And the party of the second part [the grantee in said deed], his heirs and assigns hereby covenant and agree that no saloon shall be kept and no intoxicating liquors be sold or permitted to be sold on said premises herein conveyed or in any building erected upon said premises; and that in case of breach in these covenants or any of them said premises shall immediately revert to the grantors, and the said party of the second part shall forfeit all right, title and interest in and to said premises.

It was agreed to be binding upon the heirs, executors, administrators and assigns of the respective parties. The balance of the premises involved had a covenant of substantially the same wording and with like effect. There was also one providing that the building erected upon the premises should cost at least $2,500, but no question is raised as to the value of the building upon the premises.

By mesne conveyances, appellee Penn Mutual Life Insurance Company, on November 19, 1934, acquired title to the premises involved herein by quitclaim deed, which did not contain the covenant prohibiting the use of saloons upon the premises. The premises have been occupied by Edward Walsh as tenant of Penn Mutual Life Insurance Company since 1934, and have been operated during all of that period as a saloon or tavern. The plaintiffs are the heirs-at-law of Jay E. Storke. The heirs of Bernard Timmerman are unknown. There are 491 lots in the sixteen blocks embraced in the subdivision, which are covered by the same restrictions as to the use of the premises.

The facts disclose this subdivision has become a built-up business section of the city of Chicago, and located in various parts of it are saloons or taverns, with at least sixteen saloons in the neighborhood of the property involved or in the adjoining blocks, and liquor has been almost continuously sold in this subdivision since 1933, the date of the repeal of the prohibition amendment. There have been numerous instances where the heirs-at-law of Timmerman or Storke have released and waived the restriction contained in the deed, from as far back as 1904 to as late as 1924.

In 1926, appellee Penn Mutual Life Insurance Company purchased a first mortgage on the premises herein involved for the sum of $42,500, and in November, 1934, it purchased the title to said property and released said mortgage lien and the personal liability of the mortgagor in reliance upon the abandonment of the possible right of reverter by the heirs of Jay E. Storke, and by their waiver of the restriction by acquiescing in the use of the said premises in said subdivision for saloon purposes and by releasing and relinquishing any possible right of reverter therein.

December 29, 1942, plaintiffs filed their complaint asking that the court establish title in the plaintiffs and the unknown heirs of Timmerman, and that defendant and appellee insurance company be decreed to have no right or title in the premises; that the interest of the plaintiffs and the heirs of Timmerman be ascertained; that partition be had of the premises; that the defendant Walsh be perpetually enjoined from maintaining a tavern, and that plaintiffs have further relief, etc. The case was tried upon a stipulation of facts, and anything not pointed out above, necessary to a decision of this case, will be referred to hereafter.

To reach a proper conclusion under the disclosed facts, it is necessary to determine the character of the condition, covenant, or reservation contained in the deed from the original grantors. Appellants say they do not deem it necessary to classify their supposed reversionary interests as either based upon a conditional limitation or as a condition subsequent, but assert that they rely upon the decision of *Pure Oil Co. v. Miller-McFarland Drilling Co., Inc.*, 34 N.E.2d 854 (Ill. 1941). Since the reversionary right in that case was held to arise from a deed containing a conditional limitation, we must infer that such is the basis of appellants' case. Appellee insurance company, however, contends the provisions in the deed upon which appellants seek to recover constitute conditions subsequent. Such different results follow from these different contentions that resolving the character of the restrictions contained in the deed will be determinative of the case.

The distinction between a conditional limitation and a condition subsequent is sometimes very refined, because of the language used under the different situations under which the question arises. Many distinctions are to be found in the books whether from the words used there is created a condition subsequent making the estate voidable, or words of limitation causing the estate to cease. The term "conditional limitation" in this State has been applied both where, upon the happening of certain events, the estate goes to third persons, and where a determinable or base fee is granted to the first taker followed by a possibility of reverter upon the happening of a contingency. (TIFFANY, 2d, sec. 90.) The term will be used herein in the latter sense.

The basic difference between estates upon conditional limitation and those upon condition subsequent is ascertained by the fact that, in the latter case, the entire estate has passed to another, but can be returned to the grantor upon the subsequent happening of a described event; while in the case of a conditional limitation, the estate passed to another contains within itself the ground for its return to the grantor. The accepted authorities of the common law are collected and aptly condensed with the following statement: "A condition determines an estate after breach, upon entry or claim by the grantor or his heirs, or the heirs of the devisor. A limitation marks the period which determines the estate, without any act on the part of him who has the next expectant interest. Upon the happening of the prescribed contingency, the estate first limited comes at once to an end, and the subsequent estate arises . . . . A conditional limitation is therefore of a mixed nature, partaking both of a condition and of a limitation; of a condition because it defeats the estate previously limited; and of a limitation, because, upon the happening of the contingency, the estate passes to the person having the next expectant interest, without entry or claim." *Proprietors of the Church in Brattle Square v. Grant*, 69 Mass. 142 (1855). To the same effect is *Smith v. Smith*, 23 Wis. 176 (1868).

Illustrations from our own decisions show these distinctions have been observed and followed. Thus, a conveyance to a grantee for so long as the property is used for church purposes may be forever, but if it ceased to be used for church purposes the condition upon which the grant is made ends (*Pure Oil Co. v. Miller-McFarland Drilling Co., Inc.*, 34 N.E.2d 854 (Ill. 1941); *North v. Graham*, 85 N.E. 267 (Ill. 1908)), or a grant upon condition that if said grantee herein shall die before the age of twenty-one years then the land shall revert to others (*Roberts v. Dazey*, 119 N.E. 910 (Ill. 1918)), or a deed to a grantee, and upon the death of grantee leaving no widow or children to another (*Cutler v. Garber*, 124 N.E. 441 (1919)), are all grants of estates upon conditional limitation. On the other hand, a deed for premises to be used as a church, and in case of failure of such use, grantee to pay a sum to the grantors (*Board of Education v. Trustees of Baptist Church*, 63 Ill. 204 (1872)), premises conveyed on condition to pay the debts of another (*Koch v. Streuter*, 83 N.E. 1072 (Ill. 1908)), or in consideration of support (*Phillips v. Gannon*, 92 N.E. 616 (Ill. 1910)), or a condition that grantee pay grantor's children $500 each (*Nowak v. Dombrowski*, 107 N.E. 807 (Ill. 1915)), or a conveyance to a village on condition that a town hall be erected, with a provision for reverter (*Village of Peoria Heights v. Keithley*, 132 N.E. 532 (Ill. 1921)), or a deed made subject to the payment of an annuity for the life of the grantor, with provision for reverter (*Powell v. Powell*, 167 N.E. 802 (Ill. 1929); *Plummer v. Worthington*, 152 N.E. 133 (Ill. 1926)), are all illustrations of conditions subsequent.

Courts prefer to construe provisions that terminate an estate as conditions subsequent rather than conditional limitations, and in doubtful cases will so construe them. (*Rooks Creek Evangelical Lutheran Church v. First Lutheran Church*, 290 Ill. 133 (Ill. 1919).) Conditions subsequent which destroy an estate are not favored and will not be enlarged. (*McElvain v. Dorris*, 131 N.E. 608 (Ill. 1921).) Such covenants are to be strictly construed. (*Dodd v. Rotterman*, 161 N.E. 756 (Ill. 1928).) If the parties intended the estate to vest and the grantee to perform acts, or refrain from certain acts after taking possession, it is a condition subsequent.

(*Hooper v. Haas*, 164 N.E. 23 (Ill. 1928).)

The foregoing cases clearly show the line of cleavage between an estate upon conditional limitation and a conveyance subject to a condition subsequent. If the deed contains language which purports to pass immediate title, but limits its duration by some event which may or may not happen, a conditional limitation is created, because there is always a possibility of reverter to the grantor. The estate fails upon the happening of the event by its own terms, because it comes within the condition which limits it, and it is self-operative.

On the other hand, a breach of a condition subsequent does not revest title in the original grantor or his heirs. Re-entry is necessary to revest title, and a court of equity will not aid a forfeiture where no right of re-entry is provided in the covenant. The deeds in question did not contain a right of re-entry. Under the authorities, the restrictions in the deed did not constitute a conditional limitation.

The action brought by the plaintiffs was partition. In order to maintain partition, it is requisite that the plaintiffs have title. (*Harris v. Ingleside Building Corp.*, 19 N.E.2d 585 (Ill. 1939).) Appellants rely upon the *Ingleside* case, which, among other things, held that an equitable title could, in the same proceeding, be converted into a legal title sufficient to support partition. Here, however, re-entry being necessary to effect the forfeiture, and there being no reservation of a right of re-entry, it was not within the power of equity to make the legal estate necessary to maintain a suit in partition. (*Newton v. Village of Glen Ellyn*, 27 N.E.2d 821 (Ill. 1940).) There being no title in the plaintiffs, and there having been no re-entry, or provision for re-entry, the case was properly dismissed, as lacking in the elements necessary to maintain a partition suit.

We have indicated above that there was not a conditional limitation which would terminate the estate of its own force, and that the plaintiffs have not established that they are entitled to a forfeiture under a condition subsequent. There is a finding by the court that the plaintiffs had actually a constructive knowledge of the sale of liquor, for a period of time, which would render it highly unjust and contrary to the doctrines of equity for them to divest the defendant of title purchased for a valuable consideration and in good faith.

The court also found that releases had been given to other owners in the subdivision by the plaintiffs, and by John W. Ellis, one of the plaintiffs' attorneys, which had created a change in the neighborhood from that contemplated in the original grant. If the provisions in the deed were construed as a restrictive covenant, they could not be enforced by the plaintiffs because the stipulation of facts and findings of the court show that the change in the circumstances and use of the property in the subdivision has been brought about by the acts of the grantors or their assigns. Under such circumstances, they cannot be enforced. (*Cuneo v. Chicago Title and Trust Co.*, 169 N.E. 760 (Ill. 1929); *Ewertsen v. Gerstenberg*, 57 N.E. 1051 (Ill. 1900); *Star Brewery Co. v. Primas*, 45 N.E. 145 (Ill. 1896).)

If the contention of appellants were correct, that the deed in question contained a conditional limitation, it would not aid them. In such case, as pointed out, no re-entry would be necessary and the estate would terminate immediately upon breach without action or re-entry. That being the case, the fourth paragraph of section 3 of the Limitations Act (Ill. Rev. Stat. 1943, chap. 83, par. 3), would apply. The statute provides that if a person claims an estate by reason of a forfeiture or breach of condition, his right shall be deemed to have accrued when the forfeiture occurred or the condition was broken. This section must be construed in connection with section 6 of the same act. The use of said premises as a saloon commenced before appellee obtained a deed therefor. The deed to appellee purporting to convey the entire estate constituted color of title in good faith, and taxes were paid for more than seven years. This would give appellee a good title, even if the position assumed by appellants was correct. Under either construction, the facts and the law bar the plaintiffs from recovery.

The deed to the original grantors cannot be construed as creating a conditional limitation. As a condition subsequent, appellants are not entitled to recover. Considered as a restrictive covenant, all rights of enforcement have been waived. And assuming appellants' contention that the estate was terminated by breach of condition, they are barred from recovery by the Statute of Limitations.

The decree denying the plaintiffs' right to recover, and confirming the title of the appellee, was correct, and is hereby affirmed.

NOTES AND QUESTIONS

1. As the *Storke* case illustrates, defeasible fees represent a risky form of land use control. Because they rely upon a draconian single sanction — divestment — courts have historically been hesitant to enforce them. On the theory that the law "abhors a forfeiture," courts usually construe limitations and conditions very narrowly and often will look for any reason to label the divesting interest invalid. (For example, in the above case, the Illinois court found the lack of a re-entry clause fatal to plaintiffs' claims.) Moreover, a desire on the seller's part to create a defeasible fee may have an adverse effect of the market for his land. Given a choice, buyers will prefer other parcels not subject to such a restraint, and even willing buyers will be unable to obtain mortgages, since lenders would be without protection if the limitation or condition were violated during the term of the mortgage.

2. *Rules of Construction.* As the court in *Storke* stated, when the language of the instrument creating a defeasible estate is unclear, it will be presumed that the grantor intended to create an estate subject to a condition subsequent rather than a determinable fee. This presumption also is a product of the prejudice against forfeitures. Some courts go even farther and hold that if the language is ambiguous, the court will presume that the party intended to agree to a mere covenant (a contractual agreement enforceable by money damages or equitable relief, but not forfeiture) rather than any type of defeasible estate. For such a case, see *Hagaman v. Board of Ed. of Woodbridge Twp.*, 285 A.2d 63 (N.J. Super. Ct. App. Div. 1971). In that case, a clause in a deed which conveyed land to the township "solely" for the purpose of building and maintaining a school was held to create a covenant which did not give the holders of the original grantor's interest any right to reclaim the land. In *MacDonald Properties, Inc. v. Bel-Air Country Club*, 72 Cal. App. 3d 693 (1977), the court acknowledged that the deed between the predecessors of the two parties used language sufficient to create a fee simple subject to a condition subsequent, but then stated, "But because conditions subsequent may result in forfeiture, they are disfavored at law and normally interpreted as covenants. (Civ. Code § 1442.) We so interpret the restrictions here." *Id.* at 699.

3. Not every court is as hostile to these types of restrictions as the court in *Storke*. In 1999, the Court of Appeals of New Mexico (the state's highest court) upheld language in a 1935 deed that prohibited the use of the property for immoral purposes or for the manufacture or sale of liquor. Were these restrictions to be violated, title was to revert to the grantor. The restrictions were challenged as an unlawful restraint on alienation. Without determining whether the deed in question created an estate in fee simple subject to a condition subsequent or a fee simple determinable, but acknowledging that it was one or the other, the court upheld the restriction as valid. *Prieskorn v. Maloof*, 991 P.2d 511 (N.M. Ct. App 1999).

4. *Defeasible Fees and Adverse Possession.* Had the court accepted the arguments of the plaintiffs in the above case that the original deeds created a determinable estate, the plaintiffs would still have lost because of an Illinois statute that required those who claim by right of forfeiture to assert their claims within seven years or lose them. Even without such a statute, the distinction between fee simple determinable and fee simple subject to a condition subsequent can have important consequences when the party who violated the limitation or condition stays in possession of the premises. If the estate was one of fee simple determinable, the previous estate holder's interest is hostile to that of the holder of the possibility of reverter from the moment the limitation is violated. Consequently, the clock immediately begins to run for purposes of adverse possession. In contrast, since the holder of the right of entry is not required to immediately enter and reclaim the property, the previous estate holder's presence is not adverse (and in a sense is permissory). Consequently, no adverse possession has begun. On the other hand, the holder of the right of entry who waits too long to reenter and claim the estate may find herself defeated by a claim of laches. As hostile as courts are to defeasible fees, they are even more hostile to holders of the accompanying future interests who fail to assert their rights in a reasonably timely fashion.

5. *Powers of Termination and the Doctrine of Laches.* What happens if O retains the right of re-entry upon the breach of a condition subsequent, but fails to exercise the right in a timely manner? Many courts have barred future interest holders from reclaiming title, if they have waited an unreasonably long time before attempting to reclaim the leasehold. For a relatively recent example of this, see *Martin v. City of Seattle*, 765 P.2d 257 (Wash. 1988).

6. *Defeasible Fees and Estates Less than Fee Simple.* Limitations and conditions subsequent are not restricted to estates in fee simple. Consequently, any estate can be subject to such restrictions, i.e., there could be a life estate determinable or, at least in theory, a fee tail subject to a condition subsequent (although English courts refused to recognize such an estate). It could be argued that most leaseholds are actually estates for years subject to a condition subsequent, since leases typically contain language that allow landlords to terminate the estate if the tenant engages in specified prohibited conduct.

7. *A Note on Terminology.* The terminology that has been used by American courts to describe defeasible fees and the future interests that accompany them has varied considerably from jurisdiction to jurisdiction, time period to time period, and even case to case. The estate of fee simple determinable is sometimes referred to as a "determinable fee," a "fee simple on a special limitation," a "base fee," a "qualified fee," and a "fee simple on a conditional limitation," while the estate of fee simple subject to a condition subsequent is also known as a "fee simple on a condition subsequent," a "conditional fee," and, as if to maximize confusion, a "base fee," a "qualified fee," and a "fee simple on a conditional limitation." The estate described above as the fee simple subject to an executory limitation is also known as a "fee simple with an executory limitation," "fee simple subject to a conditional limitation," and "fee simple determinable with an executory limitation" (if the restriction is a limitation rather than a condition subsequent).

Likewise, the possibility of reverter is sometimes referred to merely as a "reverter," as a "right of reverter," and as a "possibility of reversion." The interest usually called either a right of entry or the power of termination is also known as "the right to reenter" or "the right of reacquisition." Occasionally, executory interests are called "executory limitations," "conditional limitations" or, when they are created by will, "executory devises." Undoubtedly, other variations can be found.

8. *Defeasible Estates for Purposes Other than Land Use Control.* In addition to controlling the uses to which land could be put, these estates could also be used to influence the grantee's conduct or improve the chances that the land would end up where the grantor ultimately wishes it to be. The transactions "O to A, but if A marries B, then to C," and "O to A and his heirs, so long as A is survived by children of his own body," both make use of defeasible fees without imposing any restrictions on the use of the property. (These types of limitations were once quite common in wills.)

9. *The Place of Defeasible Estates in Modern Land Use Practice.* Although defeasible fees were somewhat popular in the late 19th and early 20th centuries as forms of land use control, they are seldom used today. Exceptions occur, however, when land is transferred by gift rather than sale. Obviously in such situations, the donee is unlikely to refuse the gift simply because of the restrictions attached. A frequently litigated issue arises when individuals donate land to public agencies or charitable institutions for a specific purpose (as for the maintenance of a school in the above-mentioned *Hagaman* case) and many years later the use is discontinued. For an examination of the role of the defeasible fee in the history of American land use planning, see Jost, *The Defeasible Fee and the Birth of the Modern Residential Subdivision*, 49 MO. L. REV. 695 (1984). For one view of the place of defeasible estates in modern land use law, see Korngold, *For Unifying Servitudes and Defeasible Fees: Property Law's Functional Equivalents*, 66 TEX. L. REV. 533 (1988). For a discussion of the role of future interests in modern law more generally, see Gallanis, *The Future of Future Interests*, 60 WASH. & LEE L. REV. 513 (2003).

10. *The Creation of New Estates.* Only legislatures have the authority to create new types of estates, and no such authority rests with private individuals. In *Johnson v. Whiton*, 34 N.E. 542 (Mass. 1893), the Massachusetts Supreme Judicial Court refuse to accept a grantor's effort to create a version of fee tail in which property was to descend down the grantee's male line, after an initial transfer to the grantor's granddaughter.

[F.] EXECUTORY INTERESTS

Executory interests are future interests created in a transferee which become possessory by *prematurely* terminating a preceding estate or vested future interest. Consequently, an executory interest is quite distinct from a remainder which becomes possessory only upon the natural termination of the preceding estate (as in the end of a life estate by death or the expiration of an estate for years). Consistent with this distinction, only an executory interest may follow a fee simple estate, since a fee simple estate never reaches an automatic termination point. An executory interest may, however, follow a lesser estate. In the transaction, "O to A for 10 years, but if the house is torn down during A's leasehold, to B for the remainder of the 10-year period," B receives an executory interest and O retains a reversion in fee simple absolute. (Do you understand why B's interest isn't a remainder?) As long as the house is still standing, A's estate will terminate as scheduled at the end of the 10-year period.

Executory interests can also divest other future interests. In "O to A for life, then to B, unless B marries C, in which case B's interest is to pass to D," B has a vested remainder which will vest in possession upon A's death. Thus, if B marries C while A is still living, his remainder is divested by D's interest even though A is still entitled to the present possession of Blackacre. Consequently, B is said to have a vested remainder subject to divestment, and D has an executory interest.

There are two types of executory interests: shifting and springing. *Shifting executory interests* are executory interests which divest an estate transferred to another by the grantor. Springing executory interests divest the grantor. All of the examples so far have involved shifting executory interests.

A *springing executory interest* comes into being only when the grantor creates a possessory interest to take effect in the future with no intervening estate other than what the grantor already holds. Thus, if O transfers Blackacre to A, a bachelor, subject to his marrying B, A takes no right of possession at the time of the transfer. Until he marries B, an event which may or may not occur, the estate remains with O. However, once A marries B, O's interest in Blackacre "springs" to A, who now owns the tract in an estate of fee simple absolute. Until the time of his marriage, A's interest is a springing executory interest (in an estate of fee simple absolute). O, meanwhile, has converted his estate in fee simple absolute into an estate in fee simple subject to an executory limitation. Do you see why?

Executory interests also play an important role in personal property, particularly in regard to assets held in trust.

[G.] THE RULE AGAINST PERPETUITIES

For more than 200 years law students have struggled to grasp the complexities of the Rule against Perpetuities. Although its traditional formulation is somewhat arcane, its central concept is not difficult to grasp: unvested future interests should either vest or fail to vest within a reasonable period of time. Otherwise, they have the potential to severely restrain the alienation of property which has long been viewed as an undesirable condition.

[1.] The Common Law Rule

A clever individual, wishing to insure that a particular piece land remain in his family forever, might attempt to accomplish his objective by creating a never ending sequence of life estates followed by remainders in life estates, as in O to A for life, remainder in a life estate to A's oldest surviving issue, then to A's oldest surviving issue for life, then to the oldest surviving issue of A's oldest surviving issue for life, and so on. However, this technique will not work because of the Rule against Perpetuities.

In its classic formulation by John Chipman Gray, the rule states: "No interest *is good unless it* must vest, if at all, not later than 21 years after some life in being at the creation of the interest." J. GRAY, THE RULE AGAINST PERPETUITIES 191 § 201 (4th ed. 1942). In the example above, the remainder interests are all contingent, because the identity of the surviving issue will not be known until the holder of the previous estate has died. Consequently, some of the remainders will not vest until some distant time.

The Rule worked to destroy any contingent future interest in a third party (whether a contingent remainder or an executory interest) that might not vest within 21 years of the death of some individual alive at the time of the creation of the interest. As traditionally applied, the actual time of vesting was irrelevant; all that mattered was whether or not the interest *must* vest (or fail) within the perpetuity period. We begin by examining the application of the Rule to contingent remainders. We will then turn to the subject of the Rule and executory interests.

The above example can be used to illustrate the rule's application. If we recharacterize our effort to insure continued family ownership as O to A for life, then to AA for life, then to AAA for life, then to AAAA for life, etc., the interests of AA, AAA, and AAAA are all contingent remainders for the reasons mentioned above. Assuming that A is alive at the time of the transaction (which he presumably is), AA's contingent remainder will definitely vest within the perpetuity period since it will automatically vest in possession upon the death of A, an event that must occur within a period defined by A's life plus 21 years. (In this case the 21 years is irrelevant.)

However, if the requirement was to A's oldest surviving issue who reaches age 22, AA's interest might not vest within the perpetuity period. AA could be born on the day of A's death, or if A is male, as late as nine months after his death. If this were the case, AA's interest would not vest until his 22nd birthday which would be more than 21 years after the period defined as A's life plus 21 years. In fact, there was no one alive on Earth at the time of AA's birth of whom it can be said with absolute certainty that person would be alive on AA's 22nd birthday. Thus AA's interest would be voided under the Rule against Perpetuities. Since AA's interest may not vest within the perpetuity period, then the same has to be true for all later contingent remainders in the sequence.

Note that in our example the remaindermen only have to be living at the time of the death of the preceding estate holder for their interest to vest. Therefore, AA's contingent remainder will definitely vest within the perpetuity period and thus is valid. We run into problems, however, with the contingent remainders of AAA and those of all the future interest holders who follow. Since AA may not have been alive at the time of the original transaction, AAA may not be born until many years after his or her interest was created, well beyond the life in being plus 21 years period.

For example, assume the original transaction occurred in 1850 when A was 10 years old. A dies at age 90 in 1930 and is survived by AA, who was not born until 1910. AA fathers AAA at age 60, and then dies at age 87 in 1997. AAA's remainder does not vest until 1997, 147 years after the transaction and almost certainly more than 21 years after the death of everyone alive in 1850. For purposes of the common law Rule against Perpetuities, the likelihood of this sequence of events was unimportant. All that mattered was that it might happen. Because it might vest outside of the perpetuity period, AAA's interest is void, even if it in fact vested within the period. Since AAA's interest is void, all subsequent remainders must be void as well, since they cannot vest any earlier than AAA's interest. Consequently, in our example, A would take a life estate, AA would have a contingent remainder in a life estate, and O would retain a reversion even though she intended to transfer away all of her ownership interest in Blackacre.

[2.] Remorseless Application (*Chenoweth v. Bullitt*)

The Rule against Perpetuities was legendary for the remorseless way in which it was applied. The case of *Chenoweth v. Bullitt*, 6 S.W.2d 1061 (Ky. Ct. App. 1928), is one such example. The will of William C. Bullitt devised a tract of land to his wife for the remainder of her life. Upon her death, the tract was to be divided equally between his children. His son Henry Bullitt's portion of the tract was to go to Henry and "his then wife during their natural lives, and to the survivor for life, and at the death of Henry and wife, his child or children, if any, or their lineal descendants." William was in fact survived by his wife.

The Kentucky Supreme Court read the clause in William's will pertaining to Henry Bullitt's interest as creating a life estate for William's widow, with a remainder in a life estate to Henry and his wife *at the time of his mother's death* for their joint lives, followed by a remainder in a life estate to the survivor, followed by a remainder in fee simple absolute to Henry's descendants. Having so characterized the transaction, the Court ruled that the interests created which followed the potential life estate of the surviving widow were voided by the Kentucky Rule against Perpetuities. Although both Henry and his wife, Mary Louisa Bullitt, were lives in being at the time of William Bullitt's death, the court noted that there was no guarantee that Henry's then current wife would be his wife on the date of his mother's death. Not only might Mary Louisa Bullitt die during the life of Mrs. William Bullitt and Henry remarry, it was also possible, though as the court acknowledged, not probable, that Henry might marry someone born after his father's death. In that situation, Henry and the new wife would become joint tenants in a life estate upon the death of Henry's mother and if the new wife survived Henry, she would have the land in a life estate for the remainder of her own life.

However, since the hypothetical new wife was not a life in being at the time of the creation of the interests (i.e., on the date of William Bullitt's death), it could not be said that the contingent remainder of the issue would necessarily vest within a life in being plus 21 years, 10 months (the period provided for by the Kentucky version of the Rule against Perpetuities). Consequently, the remainder interest created for Henry's descendants was void, meaning that a reversion was created in William's estate. This, in turn, meant that upon the death of Henry's widow the land would revert back to the holder of this reversion.[3] Of course, Henry Bullitt's widow turned out to be Mary Louisa Bullitt after all, but as the Kentucky court noted, "It is possibilities and not probabilities with which the rule deals."

NOTES AND QUESTIONS

1. *Class Gifts*. The Rule against Perpetuities often seemed particularly harsh when applied to class gifts. A class gift is a gift or transfer to a group of persons described in such a way as to form a distinct body of recipients. "A's children" and "the members of Harrison County High School Class of 1988" are examples of classes in this sense. If a class gift follows a life estate or an estate for years, the members of the class hold remainders. If there are no contingencies or the contingencies have been met, the remainders are vested.

Often, some members of the class have vested remainders subject to open, while others have contingent remainders. Suppose that O transfers Blackacre to A for life with a remainder to the children of A who reach age 25. Suppose also that A has three children, aged 31, 26, and 21. The remainders of the two oldest children are vested (subject to open); those of the youngest child and the unborn children who might be born are contingent. Only when there is no possibility of any other remainder vesting is the class said to be closed and the remainders said to be indefeasibly vested.

Under the traditional approach to the Rule against Perpetuities, if the future interest of any member of a class was void, then the interests of all members of the class were void. In our example, since it is possible that A may have another child after the transaction that created the interests, we cannot say with certainty that that child's interest will vest (which will not occur until its 25th birthday) within a life in being plus 21 years. Consequently, all of the interests fail; O retains a reversion; and after A's death, Blackacre will revert to the holder of O's reversion.

2. *Classic Perpetuities Problems*. The problem in *Chenoweth v. Bullitt* is known in perpetuities lore as the problem of the unborn widow. Other examples of the use

[3] In the actual case, the reversion was also subject to a power of appointment given to Henry which authorized him to designate the ultimate owner of the land from the ranks of William's lineal descendants if he (Henry) died without issue. This in fact happened, and much of the lengthy opinion in *Chenoweth v. Bullitt* deals with the legitimacy of the way in which Henry exercised the power of appointment. A power of appointment is "a power given by a deed or a will to a person to direct that an interest in property is to devolve on a person or persons, or on one or more of those within a designated and limited group of persons." D. WALKER, THE OXFORD COMPANION TO LAW 974 (1980).

of remote possibilities to strike down contingent interests include the fertile octogenarian problem and the problem of administrative contingency. The former is based on the assumption that no man or woman is ever too old to have an additional child. (With the possibility of legal adoption, this is literally true.) In the infamous case of *Jee v. Audley*, 1 Cox 324, 29 Eng. Rep. 1186 (Ch. 1787) — known as the "case that launched a thousand quips" — Edward Audley devised a sum of money to his niece Mary Hall for life, then to the issue of his niece, but when the last of her descendants died, "to be equally divided between the daughters then living of my kinsman John Jee and his wife Elizabeth Jee." At the time of Audley's death, Mary Hall was 40 years old and childless; John and Elizabeth Jee were both 70 years old; the Jees had four daughters; and legal adoption was not recognized by English law. Nevertheless, the court found that the interests of the daughters were void for remoteness, since it was legally, if not biologically, possible that the Jees might have another daughter who might be living at the time of the death of the last of the descendants of Mary Hall (of which there were none at the time). If this possibility occurred, then the interest of the afterborn daughter might vest outside the perpetuity period, and since the interests of the daughters constituted a class gift, the interests of the entire class failed.

The problem of the administrative contingency involves interests contingent upon the execution of routine procedures. In *Ryan v. Beshk*, 170 N.E. 699 (Ill. 1930), the testator's will provided, in part, "or in the event of the death of all or any of said persons mentioned I give and bequeath his or her part or share intended for him or her . . . to his or her executor or administrator to be applied by such as if the same had formed part of the estate of such person or legatee at his or her decease." The executors and administrators were to hold the property at issue only so long as it took to distribute to the heirs or devisees of the party named in the original will. However, the interests of those who were to take from the executors or administrators were determined to be void since they would only vest if the estates of the "said persons mentioned" in the will were probated — without probate, no executor or administrator could be appointed — and there was no absolute guarantee that the estates would be probated within 21 years of their death. It was possible, of course, that the estates would never be probated and, therefore, the subsequent interests would never vest. Consistent with the Rule against Perpetuities' focus on possibilities, it was no defense that the administrator or executor was in fact appointed within the perpetuity period.

DEISS v. DEISS

Illinois Court of Appeals
536 N.E.2d 120 (1989)

Presiding Justice McCullough delivered the opinion of the court.

Plaintiff Katie B. Deiss and her husband, Rudolph V. Deiss, established an irrevocable trust on January 29, 1969, with their son, Orville Deiss, as trustee. The corpus of this trust consists of a house in Mason City and farmland located in McLean, Logan, and Mason Counties in Illinois and farmland in Jewel County in Kansas. The trust provides that the trustee shall manage the real estate and pay the mortgages and other encumbrances on the property out of the income received from farming the property. Any net income is paid to Rudolph and Katie. The trustee is given the power to "lease and release" the real estate, including leasing the tract which the trustee then occupied to himself as well as leasing the remaining tracts to the other sons of the donors, Rudolph V. Deiss, Jr., Merle Deiss, and LeRoy Deiss. The trustee is also given the power to mortgage and remortgage the trust property.

At the first death of Rudolph and Katie, all of the income of the trust is paid to the survivor of them. Rudolph Deiss died on November 15, 1973. The trust continues until Katie's death and all of the mortgages on the trust property are paid in full. After both conditions are met, the corpus and accumulated income of the trust is divided as follows:

Orville Deiss farmland in Mason County

Rudolph V. Deiss, Jr. farmland in Logan County

Merle Deiss farmland in McLean County

LeRoy Deiss house in Mason City, Illinois, & farmland in Kansas

Each child of the donor receives a life estate in the property and the remainder passes to the children of each named child (grandchildren of the donors), or to his children (great-grandchildren of the donors), should a grandchild predecease his parent.

On July 1, 1987, the plaintiff filed a complaint for declaratory judgment, praying that the trust be declared void because it violates the rule against perpetuities and that the court declare that the defendants, the sons of the plaintiff as well as the present living grandchildren and great-grandchildren of the plaintiff, have no interest in the trust property. A guardian ad litem was appointed to represent the minor beneficiaries.

In the instant case, the remainder interest is described as follows: "[Upon] the death of the survivor [of the donors] this trust shall continue until mortgages on the real estate . . . has [sic] been paid in full and both [donors] are deceased. At the time that both of these conditions are met, the corpus and accumulated income of the trust shall be divided [with specific parcels going to each of the four sons for life] . . . with remainder [in such parcels] to his children, the children of any predeceased child to take the share their parent would have taken if living. . . . Should any of our children die leaving no child or children, or descendants of a child or children surviving, their share shall go, in equal shares, to their brothers or the children thereof per stirpes."

After hearing argument from the parties, the court found that the trust did not violate the rule against perpetuities and denied plaintiff's petition.

Plaintiff argued in the trial court that the remainder interests are contingent because two conditions must be met before the interests vest: the mortgages must be paid in full and the children must survive the death of the life tenant of the property. Plaintiff argued that the mortgage condition delayed vesting, and because it is possible that any of the children of the plaintiff, all lives in being at the creation of the interest, could die before the plaintiff and before the mortgages are paid, vesting may not occur within 21 years after their death. This violates the rule against perpetuities and, therefore, the trust is void.

The defendants, Merle, Sr.; Stacia; Merle, Jr.; Lynette; Steve; LeRoy; and Susan, argued in the trial court that the remainder interests were vested at the time the trust was created. These defendants urged that the payment of the mortgages affected the quantum or amount of the estate and not the time of its vesting. Because the remainder interests were vested, the defendants argued that the rule against perpetuities does not apply and therefore the trust is valid.

[S]everal of the defendants on appeal urge that the interests are vested remainders because there is no uncertainty as to who takes the property after the retirement of the mortgages and the deaths of the plaintiff, as surviving donor, and all the named life tenants.

Since the rule against perpetuities does not apply to vested interests, it must be determined whether the language in the document before us created a vested or contingent remainder. Initially, we note as did the Supreme Court in *Warren-Boynton State Bank v. Wallbaum* (1988), 528 N.E.2d 640, 643 (Ill.), that the law of future interests is confusing at best. We have thoroughly reviewed those cases relied upon by the parties and conclude that the language in the instrument in this case describes a vested remainder.

Plaintiff urges that the payment of the mortgages before the division of the trust property is a condition precedent which makes the remainder interest contingent and subject to the rule against perpetuities. Because the mortgages may never be paid in full, the remainder interests violate the rule and are void. Plaintiff next argues that the language used to describe the remainders in this case also makes them contingent and, therefore, subject to the rule against perpetuities. Specifically, plaintiff contends that the remainderman cannot be ascertained until the death of the life tenants — plaintiff's four sons.

Similar language to that used in the instant case has been found to be a vested interest, subject to divestment during the life of a life tenant where a remainderman predeceases a life tenant. [Citations omitted.] The language in the instant case does not require the survival of remainder beneficiary until the death of the donors' children as a condition precedent but contemplates that a child of any one of the four sons of the donors may die before his parent. We find the language used in the instant case describes a vested remainder.

The trial court held that the sons of the plaintiff will take an equitable life estate at the death of the plaintiff and their descendants will take equitable remainders with the trustee retaining legal title to accomplish the payment of the mortgages. We find that the instrument before us does not clearly and manifestly evidence an intent to postpone the vesting of the estates until the payment of the mortgages. What is postponed is full enjoyment of the property.

For the foregoing reasons, we agree with the trial court's findings and order that the trust is not violative of the rule against perpetuities. Therefore, the order of the trial court denying plaintiff's petition for declaratory judgment is affirmed.

NOTES AND QUESTIONS

1. Note that the court here is able to avoid applying the common law Rule against Perpetuities by interpreting the ambiguous language in such a way that the remainders at issue are vested, rather than contingent. Was it really necessary for the court to do this to prevent the interests of the children from being destroyed by the Rule?

2. *Deiss v. Deiss* differs from the previous cases in that instead of creating a legal life estate followed by a series of remainders, the Deisses transferred the land in question into a trust, thereby creating a number of simultaneous interests. The theory of the trust is one of divided ownership. The party establishing the trust (the settlor or grantor) transfers property, real or personal, to one party (the trustee) who holds it for the benefit of another (the beneficiary or cestui que trust). There may be both present and future beneficiaries. The trustee is said to hold "legal" title while the beneficiary has "equitable" title. Neither one can fairly be said to be the sole owner of the assets in the trust; as with the holder of the life estate and the reversioner, both own them. The death or resignation of the trustee will not terminate the trust; if no provision is made in the trust instrument (the document creating the trust), then a court will appoint a replacement trustee. The property, real or personal, that is the subject of the trust is known as the trust res.

There is no prohibition against multiple role-playing with a trust, so long as the entire legal and equitable interest is not held by one party. Thus T can establish a trust as the settlor and also name himself as trustee. He may also be either the present or future beneficiary, but not both.

3. Among the advantages of the land trust, as compared to the concurrent estate, is that a group of individuals (the beneficiaries) can derive the economic benefits of land ownership without having to worry about exercising control over the land itself, title to which remains with the trustee. It may also result in a saving of probate costs and guarantee a smoother transition of ownership between generations. Note that Katie and Rudolph Deiss reserved the right to income from the trust for the remainder of their lives, something that they would have had had they never placed it in trust. However, when they die, the beneficial ownership interest in the trust will pass to their children automatically upon the death of the last to survive (which turned out to be Katie). Until the land is free and clear of mortgage indebtedness, it remains with the trustee, and the land is distributed free and clear of the trust only after all mortgages are paid off. At no point is it necessary to initiate formal legal proceedings (i.e., probate) to effect the transfer from one generation to the next, as would be the case if the Deisses had used a will rather than a trust to deal with the issue of inter-generational transfer.

Other advantages of the land trust over the legal life estate include the ease with which the land can be sold if that course of action is deemed appropriate. If so authorized, the trustee can transfer a fee simple title to a third party and then replace the land in the trust res with the sale proceeds. This act can be taken without securing the approval of the beneficiaries (unless such approval is required by the trust instrument). While land subject to a life estate can be sold, to do so requires the unanimous assent of all those who hold present or future interests in the property, which is often difficult to obtain. The trustee will also be better able to borrow money on the land or secure a long-term tenant than would the holder of the life estate; the chances of waste occurring are reduced; and, since the trustee controls the property, disputes between the present and future interest holders can be resolved without going to court.

4. Why is Katie Deiss attacking the validity of a trust that she set up, ostensibly for her own benefit? One of the drawbacks of a trust is that unless the instrument creating the trust specifically reserves the right of revocation, the settlor cannot change his or her mind and revoke the trust. Do you understand why the interests of the future beneficiaries in the above case do not violate the Rule against Perpetuities? Do you understand Katie Deiss' argument that they do?

[3.] The Rule Against Perpetuities and Executory Interests

Since executory interests, possibilities of reverters, and rights of entry are inherently contingent future interests — there is no guarantee that they will ever vest in possession — it would seem logical that all would all be subject to the Rule against Perpetuities. However, in American law, first party future interests, whether vested or not, are not subject to the Rule. (The reasons for this are based on historical factors related to the concept of "tenure" and are of no present relevance.) The Rule against Perpetuities does apply to executory interests and, as a consequence, operates as a major limitation their use.

FLETCHER v. FERRILL
Arkansas Supreme Court
227 S.W.2d 448 (1950)

George Rose Smith, J.

This case involves the construction of a deed executed in 1923, by which J.W. Fletcher conveyed to a Masonic Lodge certain business property in the city of Batesville. In the deed Fletcher first reserved a life estate in himself. He then provided that when the property came into the possession of the Lodge it should be used exclusively for the benefit of a specified orphans home and school, "and when it ceases to be so used, or when said home and school shall be moved from Batesville, Arkansas, said property shall revert to the heirs of the said J.W. Fletcher." The parties concede that this deed created a determinable fee in the Lodge.

Fletcher died in 1930, leaving a will that named his widow, the principal appellant, as his residuary devisee. The Lodge took possession of the property upon Fletcher's death and used the rents for the benefit of the orphanage until 1948. In that year the orphanage ceased to exist, and the Lodge at once disclaimed any further interest in the property. The question now is whether the title then passed to the appellant as residuary devisee or to the forty-eight appellees, who are Fletcher's heirs under the statutes of descent and distribution. The chancellor decided in favor of the heirs, plaintiffs below.

The principal question is whether the language of the deed, "said property shall revert to the heirs of the said J.W. Fletcher," created (a) a possibility of reverter in

Fletcher himself or (b) an executory limitation to Fletcher's heirs, which would become a possessory interest upon termination of the determinable fee. We must first decide, however, whether a possibility of reverter is an interest that can be devised by will in Arkansas; for, if it is not, then the appellant's claim under the will obviously cannot be sustained. The early English cases held that a possibility of this kind cannot pass by will, but the opposite result has been reached in the great majority of American jurisdictions. REST., PROPERTY, § 164, Comment *c*, and § 165, Comments *a* and *f*. This holding is practically uniform in states having a statute like ours, which empowers the testator to devise real property "and all interest therein." Ark. Stats. (1947), § 60-102. Unquestionably the American rule carries out the grantor's intention more often than does the English rule. That is, if a landowner should convey property to a school, to be held as long as used for school purposes, he would undoubtedly assume that he still had an interest in the land and would be dismayed to learn that he could not leave that interest to any one he pleased — that it must inevitably go to his heirs at law, regardless of his own wishes. Yet that would be his unhappy position under the English doctrine. We have no hesitancy in following the American cases and holding that the broad language of our statute permits the testator to devise a possibility of reverter.

Returning to the principal question, we think the deed created a possibility of reverter in Fletcher rather than an executory interest in his heirs. This inquiry really narrows down to whether the word "heirs" is here a word of limitation or one of purchase. If it is a word of purchase, then the appellees took by virtue of the deed itself and not by inheritance from Fletcher. But if the word is one of limitation the title passed first to Fletcher's estate and thence to the appellant as residuary devisee.

In holding that the word is one of limitation rather than of purchase we stress the fact that Fletcher reserved a life estate in himself. In those circumstances there was no occasion for him to use the customary phrase — "the property shall revert to the grantor and his heirs" (in which the word is clearly one of limitation) — for it was unnecessary for him to provide for a possible reverter during his own lifetime. Thus there is a marked similarity between a reversion to the grantor's heirs in a deed that reserves a life estate and a reversion to the grantor and his heirs in a deed intended to transfer immediate possession.

Our holding in *Wilson v. Pharris*, 158 S.W.2d 274 (Ark. 1941), tends to support our present conclusion. There the grantor, after reserving a life estate in herself, conveyed to her daughter a life estate upon condition subsequent. The deed provided that upon the happening of the condition the property should revert "to the said grantor's heirs." We held that the grantor still owned the fee and could convey it during her life tenancy. This was of course a recognition that the right of re-entry was in the grantor at least during her lifetime.

Even if we should sustain the appellees' contention that in the case at bar the word "heirs" was used in the deed as a word of purchase, we should still have to decide the case in the appellant's favor. Under that construction the deed would vest a determinable fee in the Lodge, and upon termination of that estate the title would pass directly to the appellees, not by inheritance from Fletcher but by virtue of the executory limitation in the deed. The appellees would thus have had an executory interest in the property throughout the existence of the determinable fee. It is well settled, however, that such an executory interest is not a vested estate and therefore must vest within the period allowed by the rule against perpetuities. GRAY, THE RULE AGAINST PERPETUITIES, 4th ed., § 41; SIMES, FUTURE INTERESTS, § 768; REST., PROPERTY, § 44, Comment *o*, and § 229, Illustration 8. On the other hand, it is equally well settled that the retention by the grantor of a possibility of reverter does not offend the rule against perpetuities, even though the reverter may not take place for an indefinite period in the future. GRAY, § 41; SIMES, § 507; REST., § 372.

The leading case on this point is quite similar to the present case, if Fletcher's deed be construed as containing an executory limitation to his heirs. In *First Universalist Society of North Adams v. Boland*, 29 N.E. 524 (Mass. 1892), the deed provided that the grantee should hold the land as long as it should be devoted to the doctrines of the Christian religion, and when it was diverted from that use the title should vest in certain named persons. The court held that the limitation over was void for remoteness, and therefore a possibility of reverter remained in the grantor. We are not aware of any decision to the contrary. In the present case it is evident that the Lodge's determinable fee might have continued for a period far in excess of that allowed by the rule against perpetuities, and hence an executory limitation to Fletcher's heirs would necessarily be void. This leaves the possibility of reverter in the grantor, as an interest not conveyed by the deed. Thus it is clear that the appellant must prevail under either construction of this instrument.

The decree is reversed, and, as the title to real property is involved, the cause is remanded for the entry of a decree in accordance with this opinion.

[Two justices believed that the language of the deed did create an executory interest in the heirs, but they agreed with the majority that such interests were void under the Rule against Perpetuities, leaving Fletcher's estate with a possibility of reverter.]

NOTES AND QUESTIONS

1. *Fletcher's Heirs*. Under most contemporary inheritance statutes, surviving spouses are treated as heirs. However, traditionally, this was not the case. One's heirs were one's closest relatives by blood or adoption, and one's spouse was not likely to be a relative. At the time of this case, Arkansas law did not recognize a surviving spouse as an heir, hence the dispute between Mrs. Fletcher and her husband's many nephews and nieces.

2. *Words of Purchase and Words of Limitation*. The result in the above case turned on whether the court was to read the language pertaining to "heirs" as words of purchase or words of limitation. Words of purchase define who receives an interest; words of limitation define the estate they receive. For example, in "to A and his heirs," "and his heirs" are words of limitation: They define A's estate as one in fee simple absolute, but they create no interest for the heirs of A. Conversely in "to A for 10 years, then to the heirs of B," the "heirs of B" defines the owner of the remainder created by the transaction and not the size of their estate. (Presumably the heirs of B will take an estate in fee simple absolute, given the modern presumption in behalf of that estate.) The decision to interpret the words "said

property shall revert to the heirs of the said J.W. Fletcher" as words of limitation rather than words of purchase was apparently greatly influenced by Fletcher's reservation of a life estate for himself in the deed. Do you understand why?

In *McCrory Sch. Dist. v. Brogden*, 333 S.W.2d 246 (Ark. 1960), the same court interpreted the words "said property to revert to the heirs of the Patterson Estate if discontinued as School property" as works of purchase creating an executory interest in the heirs. The phrase appeared in a deed transferring a tract of land to a school district for the construction of a public school. Can these two constructions be reconciled?

3. The early English common law refused to recognize the creation of a third party interest analogous to the possibility of reverter and the right of entry. However, executory interests came to be recognized as a consequence of the Statute of Uses, enacted by Parliament in 1536.

4. *The Effect of an Invalid Executory Interest.* In *Fletcher*, had the court found that the deed created an executory interest in the heirs that was voided by the Rule against Perpetuities, the Masonic Lodge would not have taken title in fee simple absolute. Do you understand why? If the restriction is in the nature of a limitation — the type of restriction that would create a fee simple determinable were the future interest reserved by the grantor — the restriction survives even when the executory interest is destroyed. On the other hand, if the restriction is in the nature of a condition subsequent, it is destroyed along with the executory interest. The controlling premise is that if the grantor wanted the estate to terminate if the limitation was violated, it should terminate whether or not the executory interest was valid. However, such an intention will ordinarily not be implied, but must be expressed in the document creating the interest. Often the language used will dictate the resolution of this issue. For further discussion, see L. SIMES & A. SMITH, FUTURE INTERESTS 828 (2d ed. 1956). How important was it to this resolution of the above case that the Masonic Lodge expressed no further interest in the property?

5. For an example of a case where the court found both the condition and the executory interest to be invalid, see *Coleman House, Inc. v. Asbury Park*, 19 A.2d 889 (N.J. Ct. Ch. 1941). In 1876, a tract of land in Asbury Park, New Jersey, was transferred to one Sarah Coleman for a term of 999(!) years subject to the condition that she "erect a hotel" on an adjacent parcel (also conveyed by the grantor to Ms. Coleman) and that the leased parcel be used only as a "lawn for the hotel." Should she or her assigns fail to build the hotel, or should the operation of the hotel cease at any time, the parcel subject to the lease was to go to the city to use for "park and street" purposes. A hotel was constructed, and it was operated until torn down in 1934. No replacement hotel was built, and the city sought to obtain control of the leased premises. The court ruled that the executory interest created for the city was void since it could vest outside of the perpetuities period and that the condition did not survive the destruction of the executory interest. Consequently, the successor in interest to Coleman held the leased lot free of restriction. What will happen to this lot in the year 2875 A.D. when the lease expires?

6. *Perpetuities Saving Clauses.* Once it is known that executory interests are subject to the Rule against Perpetuities, the grantor who desires to create one has three options. He can abandon the restriction altogether; he can retain the future interest himself (since first party interests are not subject to the rule) and convey it to the third party at a later date; or he can impose a limit consistent with the rule as to the time during which the restriction is to be effective. The desire to accomplish the last of these often results in perpetuities saving clauses designed not only to square the interest created with the rule, but also to make sure that the restriction can be in effect for the maximum possible time.

For example, had Fletcher wished to create an executory interest for his heirs in the above case, he might have limited the restriction to a period of time defined as the lives of his heirs living at his death plus 21 years thereafter. Although it might prove difficult to determine precisely when this limitation would expire (if Fletcher had numerous heirs — as he apparently did — and they dispersed geographically), American courts are usually inclined to accept such clauses as satisfying the requirements of the Rule against Perpetuities. *See Norton v. Georgia R.R. Bank*, 322 S.E.2d 870 (Ga. 1984). The Restatement Second of Property § 1.3 endorses such an approach. However, if the measuring lives are defined too broadly — as in "for the life of the last to die of all those living on planet Earth at the time of this transaction" — or are corporations or long-lived animals, like Galapagos Island turtles — the restrictions are almost certain to be struck down. *See In re Moore*, [1901] 1 Ch. 936 (perpetuities period defined by the survivor of all those living at the death of the testator plus 21 years struck down as void for indefiniteness). Using all the children born in a particular hospital on a particular day has become a common feature of saving clauses, although the validity of such a clause remains suspect. Do you understand why?

7. *The Rule and Springing Executory Interests*. The conventional wisdom holds that all executory interests are contingent and therefore subject to the Rule against Perpetuities. However, in the transaction "O to A and his heirs in 25 years," is A's interest in any way contingent? Neither A nor O are required to survive for 25 years, and when the appropriate day arrives, the ownership interest in Blackacre will be transferred from the holder of O's interest (whomever that might be) to the holder of A's interest. Does it make sense to say that A's interest is voided by the Rule against Perpetuities? What result is accomplished by doing so? Isn't A's interest really a vested remainder following an estate for years reserved by O? Given the infrequency with which such transactions are made and the pace of perpetuities reform, there may never be a formal judicial answer to this question.

8. *Perpetuities and Option Contracts*. Although it has been argued that options to purchase land are executory interests, this argument has been regularly rejected. *Gearhart v. West Lumber Co.*, 90 S.E.2d 10 (Ga. 1955). However, options do share certain similarities with contingent future interests, and courts have applied the rule to them in numerous cases. Whereas the total number of reported cases involved executory interests as methods of land use control is actually quite small, options to purchase are a vital part of modern real estate practice. (For evidence of infrequent use of executory interests, see 45 A.L.R.2d 1154.) Suppose that O sells Blackacre to A but by contract reserves the right for himself, his heirs or assigns to repurchase it for $100,000 at any time. Because O's option is an interest in land, it is enforceable by specific performance. In effect, O and the future owners of his interest have the power to divest A of his interest in Blackacre at any time. Because

O has retained no possessory interest in the property, he is said to have an option in gross.

Ordinarily, courts will subject O's interest to the Rule against Perpetuities. *See Symphony Space, Inc. v. Pergola Properties, Inc.*, 669 N.E.2d 799 (N.Y. 1996). Since there is no requirement that it be exercised within the perpetuities period, and since it is not personal to O, O's option will be unenforceable. Consequently, if O demands that A sell the property to him, A is under no legal obligation to do so. Interestingly, in our example, O will not be able to claim that his first party future interest is in the nature of a possibility of reverter and thus exempt from the rule. For an example of such a case, see *Atchison v. City of Englewood*, 463 P.2d 297 (Colo. 1969). On the other hand, if the option to purchase is coupled with a lease, even one that runs longer than 21 years, courts routinely uphold the validity of the option, apparently seeing such options as in the nature of vested remainders and thus not subject to the rule.

9. *First Party Future Interests and Modern Reform.* Although possibilities of reverter and rights of entry are not subject to the Rule against Perpetuities, the rights of holders of such interests have been limited by statute in a number of states. The approach varies from jurisdiction to jurisdiction, but these statutes generally provide that if a contingent first party future interest has not vested in possession within a certain time period, usually 30 or 50 years, it is destroyed. These statutes usually apply to interests already in existence at the time of the statute's passage, a feature that initially touched off considerable debate, and litigation, as to their constitutionality (which was usually, although not always, upheld). *See, e.g., Cline v. Johnson County Bd. of Ed.*, 548 S.W.2d 507 (Ky. 1977). A few states, Kentucky and California in particular, have gone even farther and have abolished the estate of fee simple determinable.

10. *Defeasible Estates and Public Policy.* Regardless of the nature of the estate, limitations and conditions cannot be enforced if they illegal or contrary to public policy. If such a limitation is attached to an estate, the grantee takes the property in fee simple absolute. Among the most common forms of restrictions that violate public policy are excessive restraints on alienation. The limitation imposed by the transaction "O to A so long as A never attempts to sell Blackacre" would be unenforceable, leaving A with an estate in fee simple absolute.

11. As you by now may have gathered, the law of estates and future interests does not easily comport with modern notions of ownership transfer, and much of it is subject to statutory limitation if not abolition. Indeed, a committee draft of the American Law Institute Restatement of the Law Third relating to Donative Transfers suggests discontinuing the distinction between reversionary and non-reversionary interests altogether, "discontinuing the ancient distinctions among remainders, executory interests, reversions, possibilities of reverter and rights of entry," and abolishing the subcategories of defeasible interests (fee simple determinable, fee simple subject to an executory limitation, and fee simple subject to a condition subsequent) by subsuming those under the term fee simple defeasible and abolishing altogether the role of destructibility of contingent remainders, and the fee tale estate.

However, even if adopted by the ALI, for the definitive Restatement, it will not absolve at least one more generation of students from mastering these arcane interests in property since such adoption will have little effect on current controversies over estates and future interests.

[4.] Perpetuities Reform

For more than five decades, lawyers and law students have taken consolation in the holding of a California appellate court that a lawyer's error in the application of the Rule against Perpetuities was not evidence of professional negligence. According to that court, the rule is a "technicality-ridden nightmare" that is beyond the understanding of many attorneys of ordinary skill and diligence. *Lucas v. Hamm*, 364 P.2d 685 (Cal. 1961). Unfortunately, a number of courts, including at one in California, has since questioned the correctness of that case's holding. *See Millwright v. Romer*, 322 N.W.2d 30 (Iowa 1982); *Wright v. Williams*, 47 Cal. App. 3d 802 (1975).

However, over the past 50 years, dissatisfaction with the harshness of the traditional rule has led to calls for its modification. Initial efforts focused on interpretative rules, like the presumption in favor of vested interests apparently applied in *Deiss v. Deiss*, above. Another common approach was to permit courts to modify documents that inadvertently contained language that ran afoul of the Rule.

The most common modification has been the "Wait and See" approach which was first adopted in Pennsylvania in 1947. Although there is some variation from jurisdiction to jurisdiction as to the actual operation of the rule, all wait and see jurisdictions focus upon what actually happens, instead of what might happen. If a contingent interest vests within the perpetuity period, it is deemed to be valid, regardless of what *could* have happened (which was the test under the traditional rule). Interests that in fact vest beyond the period are still void.

The principal drawback of the wait and see rule is that it is sometimes necessary to wait for decades before knowing whether or not the interest will be valid (a fact that may seriously restrain the ability of the owner of the interest to alienate it). A second problem is the identification of a measuring life. Most wait and see jurisdictions limit measuring lives to those individuals whose lives somehow affect the interests created. The problems posed by the wait and see approach has been aggravated by the abolition of the doctrine of the destructibility of contingent remainders.

The measuring lives problem has been addressed by the Uniform Statutory Rule Against Perpetuities (USRAP), which has been adopted in slightly more than half of the states. The USRAP retains the common law Rule against Perpetuities, but imposes a 90-year waiting period before any interest may be destroyed. Because of the relative newness of this approach — the USRAP was only approved by the Commissioners on Uniform State Laws in 1986 — it is not entirely clear how this approach will operate when some interests begin to vest outside the perpetuities period sometime late in the 21st century.

A growing number of states have gone even farther and have abolished the rule altogether, although frequently limiting the abolition to personal property held in trust where the trustee retains the power to sell trust assets. Such statutes are motivated by a desire to attract so-called "dynasty" or "perpetual" trusts to the jurisdiction. As of 2016, 28 states plus the District of Columbia have laws permitting some form of perpetual trust, or at least trusts that could last for a minimum of 360 years. For a summary of the present state of the RAP on a state-by-state basis, see Foster, *Fifty-One Flowers: Current Perpetuities Law in the States*, 22 PROB. & PROP. 30 (July/Aug. 2008), and the American Bar Associations website, http://www.americanbar.org/content/dam/aba/events/real_property_trust_estate/joint_fall/2007/50_state_comparison_of_rule_against_perpetuities_laws.authcheckdam.pdf.

The common law Rule against Perpetuities was designed to limit the ability of property owners to control the identity of their successors in future generations. A life estate coupled with a remainder for life could guarantee that property would pass to the third generation, but any attempt to exercise control over ownership beyond that was doomed to fail. O could insure that title to his farm would pass to his grandchildren, but beyond that he had no ability to restrict the right of alienation. The abolition and modification of these rules now gives O greater authority to dictate how his property will be used and by whom it will be used for a longer period of time. Is this necessarily a positive development? For perspectives on the rise of the dynasty trust, see Dukeminier & Krier, *The Rise of the Perpetual Trust*, 50 UCLA L. REV. 1303 (2003); Sterk, *Jurisdictional Competition to Abolish the Rule Against Perpetuities: R.I.P. for the R.A.P.*, 24 CARDOZO L. REV. 2097 (2003).

In early 2011, the Rule Against Perpetuities is in its common law applied to all third-party contingent interests only in Alabama, Code of Ala. § 34-4-4, but the common law rule still applied to interests in land in a number of additional states.

Chapter 5

CONCURRENT ESTATES

American law has long permitted two or more ind rently. Concurrent owners have equal rights to posses property, and the general principle applies to persona most common form of concurrent ownership is ownership by husbands and concurrent owners are not required to have any mutual interests other than that in the property itself. Traditionally Anglo-American law has used the terminology of "estates" to describe different forms of concurrent ownership. However, in this context the estate terminology is used to describe the relationship of joint owners to each other and not the nature of the property ownership interest itself. Consequently, A and B can have a concurrent estate in Blackacre which they collectively hold in an estate of fee simple absolute.

[A.] JOINT TENANCIES AND TENANCIES IN COMMON

[1.] Basic Forms

GILES v. SHERIDAN
Nebraska Supreme Court
137 N.W.2d 828 (1965)

SPENSER, J.

This is an equitable action to determine and establish the interests of the parties in Lot 3, Randolph Terrace Third Addition to Lincoln, Lancaster County, Nebraska, on which a duplex is located, and for partition.

The plaintiff is Minnie Giles, who at the time of the acquisition of said property was 83 years of age. The initial defendants were John V. Sheridan and Helen M. Sheridan, husband and wife, who will hereafter be referred to as defendant and Helen. Helen was a niece of plaintiff. The petition was filed May 27, 1963. Helen died February 23, 1964, and was survived by defendant and their three children, Barbara Littlejohn, Sally Sheridan, and James Sheridan, the last two being minors.

The deed to the property in question is dated October 31, 1962, and describes as grantees Minnie Giles, a single person, and John V. Sheridan and Helen M. Sheridan, husband and wife, as joint tenants and not as tenants in common. Subsequent to the filing of the action, by a warranty deed dated November 9, 1963, plaintiff conveyed an undivided 1/20 of her interest in said property, subject to a life estate, to a nephew, Harley Giles. Trial was held July 21, 1964, and a decree was [illegible] March 5, 1965, confirming the shares of the parties and appointing a [illegible]e. Defendant has perfected an appeal to this court.

The petition of the plaintiff seeks to establish the interests of the parties on the basis of the contribution made to the purchase price of the property. Plaintiff attempted to prove that Helen came to her home in Hastings in 1961 to induce plaintiff to buy an apartment in Lincoln for joint occupancy and agreed to pay one-half of the costs thereof, and that pursuant to that agreement Helen found the duplex and the plaintiff signed an offer to purchase after looking it over with the Sheridans. This testimony was excluded as a transaction with a deceased, within the provisions of section 25-1202, R.R.S. 1943, the dead man's statute.

It is undisputed that the offer to purchase, dated August 25, 1962, which was signed only by the plaintiff, was prepared by the defendant. The purchase price was $33,325. Plaintiff deposited $1,000 with the offer, which was accepted, and agreed to assume a mortgage to the First Federal Savings and Loan Association of Lincoln in the approximate sum of $20,500, and to pay the balance on or before November 1, 1962. The sale was consummated October 31, 1962. Plaintiff paid $12,121.04 at that time to the grantors, and the deed described above was delivered. Plaintiff offered to prove the deed was executed in this manner because Helen demanded that she and her husband be included in the title, but the testimony was excluded. In this connection, it is of interest that on examination by his own attorney, defendant testified as follows: "Q. Mr. Sheridan, did you ever ask that your name be placed on this deed? A. My wife did. Q. Did you? A. I doubt if I did; I think it was my wife that did." The deed was drawn by a representative of the First Federal Savings and Loan Association of Lincoln, and the evidence is that the defendant told him how it was to be drawn.

The mortgage was paid December 28, 1962. On that date plaintiff gave a check to the First Federal Savings and Loan Association in the amount of $19,003.96, and Helen gave a check in the amount of $686.49. Plaintiff had previously paid $205.50 on the mortgage. On the same day, Helen issued a check to the county treasurer for taxes in the amount of $257.95.

It is defendant's contention that the Sheridans were to pay only $1,000 on the purchase price, and that the plaintiff was to pay the balance. It is his contention that the two items enumerated above constitute a part of the $1,000 they were to pay. There is no other testimony in this record to prove that the Sheridans actually paid $1,000 on the purchase price. Defendant's testimony is contradicted by plaintiff, who insists she always demanded one-half of the purchase price.

The trial court found as follows: "IT IS, THEREFORE ORDERED, CONSIDERED AND ADJUDGED, BY THE COURT, that said shares of each of the parties and their respective interests in said real estate are: 1. Minnie Giles, Plaintiff, Nineteen-twentieths (19/20) of a One-third (1/3) interest in said property, plus and in addition thereto the sum of $13,135.50 from her co-tenants and the survivor to reimburse said Minnie Giles for her payment of the mortgage on said premises, and said sum shall be and constitute a lien on said co-tenants (sic) share; and a life tenancy in the undivided one-sixtieth (1/60) interest of Harley Giles therein. 2. Harley Giles, an undivided one-sixtieth (1/60) interest therein, subject to the life estate of the plaintiff, Minnie Giles, who on November 9, 1963, was 85 years of age.

3. John V. Sheridan (his own interest and as surviving joint tenant of Helen M. Sheridan) two-thirds (2/3) interest in said property, subject to and charged with the payment and reimbursement of the said sum of $13,135.50 to Minnie Giles, advanced and contributed in payment and release of the mortgage lien thereon."

The plaintiff did not file a motion for a new trial or a cross-appeal on the finding of the interests of the parties in said property, so we limit our discussion of that phase except as it is necessary to an understanding of the other questions involved.

Plaintiff had the burden of the proof to establish that the estate described in the deed was other than it purported to be. If the plaintiff had not been prevented by the dead man's statute, the indication is that she would have attempted to prove a joint tenancy between the plaintiff and Helen, with each being required to make an equal contribution. This she could not do because of the statute. Reading the deed in the light of its expressed intent and in the absence of proof to indicate otherwise, we must conclude that the deed created a joint tenancy with the three grantees as joint tenants. As such they were seized of the entire estate for the purpose of tenure and survivorship, but only of an undivided interest for the purpose of conveyance. In *Hoover v. Haller*, 21 N.W.2d 450 (Neb.), we held: "Where a conveyance of property is made to two or more persons, and the instrument is silent as to the interest which each is to take, the rebuttable presumption is that their interests are equal."

When plaintiff on November 9, 1963, conveyed a portion of her interest to Harley Giles, she terminated the joint tenancy as to her, and converted her interest and that of her grantee to a tenancy in common. In *DeForge v. Patrick*, 162 Neb. 568, 76 N.W.2d 733, we said: "An estate in joint tenancy can be destroyed by an act of one joint tenant which is inconsistent with joint tenancy and such act has the effect of destroying the right of survivorship incidental to it. Any act of a joint tenant which destroys one or more of its necessarily coexistent unities operates as a severance of the joint tenancy and extinguishes the right of survivorship."

This, however, raises a question as to the nature of the interest of the other two joint tenants, Helen and defendant. If one of two joint tenants disposes of his interest by conveyance inter vivos, the other joint tenant and the grantee become tenants in common, while, if one of three or more joint tenants conveys his interest to a third person, the latter then becomes a tenant in common, instead of a joint tenant, with the others, though such others remain joint tenants as between themselves. [Citations omitted.]

With relation to the payment of the encumbrance on the property, a different question arises. The evidence is undisputed that plaintiff paid off the mortgage with a slight assist from Helen which defendant contends was to be applied on the $1,000 they were to pay on the purchase price. We note that the deed under which the defendant is claiming has the following provision: "subject to the unpaid balance of an existing mortgage to FIRST FEDERAL SAVINGS AND LOAN ASSOCIATION OF LINCOLN, which the grantees assume and agree to pay." The deed would indicate, therefore, that the mortgage is a joint obligation of all of the grantees and if defendant seeks to avoid the effect of this language he of course would have the burden to prove an agreement otherwise.

In *Carson v. Broady*, 77 N.W. 80 (Neb.), we said: "In the case of *Brown v. Homan*, 1 Neb. 448, it was held that the purchase by a tenant in common of an outstanding title to, or incumbrance on, the joint estate, would inure to the common benefit and entitle the purchaser to contribution. And this is believed to be the universal rule." In *Oliver v. Lansing*, 77 N.W. 802, we held: "As between themselves, co-tenants are liable for the payment of liens and incumbrances existing against the common estate, in proportion to their respective interest therein, each being surety for the others."

The deed which created the joint tenancy specifically provided that the grantees assumed and agreed to pay the mortgage. By its terms, therefore, the parties were equally liable for the discharge of the obligation. Defendant has not met his burden to prove that the mortgage was otherwise than the joint obligation of the parties. We hold that a joint tenant who pays off an encumbrance on the property, under such circumstances, does so for the common benefit of the joint tenants and is entitled to contribution. For the reasons given, we hold that the judgment of the trial court was correct and should be and is affirmed.

NOTES AND QUESTIONS

1. *Types of Concurrent Estates.* Joint tenancies and tenancies in common are the most common forms of concurrent estates. Both are forms of ownership in which the property is undivided, but a joint tenancy differs from a tenancy in common in two important respects. The former includes a right of survivorship while the latter does not. Moreover, all joint tenants have identical fractional interests in the property while the interests of tenants in common need not be identical (although they can be). For example, O can transfer a 1/2 interest in Blackacre to A, a 1/3 interest to B, and a 1/6 interest to C as tenants in common. She could not, however, affect such a division of ownership with a joint tenancy.

To create a valid joint tenancy, the traditional rule was that "four unities" must be satisfied. There must be unity of time, title, interest, and possession. To satisfy these requirements, prospective joint tenants must acquire interests for the same duration, from the same document, in the same amount, and with an equal right to use. If any of the unities are missing, the parties create a *tenancy in common* which requires only unity of possession. If any of the unities are destroyed, the joint tenancy is severed and becomes a tenancy in common. However, there is a modern trend toward a relaxation of the formal requirements for a valid joint tenancy and a greater focus on the intention of the parties. *See* Helmholz, *Realism and Formalism in the Severance of Joint Tenancies*, 77 NEB. L. REV. 1 (1998). California, Florida, Hawaii, Iowa, Maine, Massachusetts, Minnesota, and New Jersey have all relaxed the traditional requirements for a joint tenancy, and Alaska and Oregon has done away with the joint tenancy altogether.

2. *The Right of Survivorship.* The distinction between a joint tenancy and tenancy in common is often crucial to resolving questions of ownership, particularly after one of the original concurrent tenants dies. Note that the court in the above case finds that the deed in question created a joint tenancy between Minnie Giles, John V. Sheridan, and Helen M. Sheridan. Because a joint tenancy includes a right of survivorship, Giles and John Sheridan would have each owned an undivided one-half interest in the lot after the death of Helen, had Giles not previously severed the joint tenancy by her partial transfer to her nephew. Giles' severance of her share of the joint tenancy did not, however, affect the relationship of John and Helen who remained joint tenants in regard to their 2/3 interest. Consequently, when Helen died, her share went automatically to John, leaving no interest for her estate. (Had she and John been tenants in common, her interest would have passed according to the terms of her will, and if she had no will, by the inheritance laws of Nebraska.)

3. *The Creation of Joint Tenancies.* A joint tenancy can be created by deed, by will, or by joint adverse possession. It cannot, however, be created by inheritance. Those who take property when the owner dies intestate (without a will) take as tenants in common. Where the nature of the estate to be created is ambiguous, American law traditionally presumed that the grantor had intended a joint tenancy. However, in most states today a conveyance to two or more individuals who are not husband and wife is presumed to create a tenancy in common, unless there is evidence that the transferor intended to create a joint tenancy. (The situation with husbands and wives is discussed below.) Under the common law approach O, the sole owner of Blackacre, could not transfer Blackacre to himself and A as joint tenants. If he attempted to do so, a tenancy in common resulted. Today, in many states this result has been changed by statute so that a transfer from O to O & A as joint tenants will result in a joint tenancy.

4. *Terminating Joint Tenancies.* Any transfer by a joint tenant will ordinarily result in a severance of the joint tenancy. This is true whether the joint tenant transfers all or only a portion of his interest. A contract to convey a joint tenant's interest automatically severs the joint tenancy if the contract is specifically enforceable. On the other hand, a joint tenancy cannot be severed by a will, even if the will is validly executed. The will does not take effect until the death of the testator, and at that point the decedent's share has already passed to the other joint tenants.

Jurisdictions divide on the effect of certain types of transfers by joint tenants. In some states, a joint tenant can convert a joint tenancy into a tenancy in common by merely transferring the property to himself. In others, the common law rule that to be valid a transfer must be to another party is still followed. In such situations A can accomplish his purpose only by transferring his interest in Blackacre to X, a straw man, who then transfers the property back to A. Jurisdictions also divide on the effect of a joint tenant leasing her interest to a third party. The common law rule was that the lease severed the joint tenancy; the modern trend has been to hold that it does not. Those states which allow the joint tenancy to continue after the lease divide on the question of whether the estate of A's lessee survives A's death.

A similar split of opinion occurs in regard to mortgages. In states which follow the title theory of mortgage, a mortgage operates as a transfer of title from the mortgagor (who retains the right to redeem the mortgage) to the mortgagee. Consistent with this view, the joint tenancy is deemed to be severed. In the larger number of states which follow the lien theory of mortgages, the mortgagor takes only a security interest in the land; thus, the unities are not disturbed and the joint tenancy survives, at least until there is a court ordered foreclosure. *Knibb v. Security Ins. Co.*, 399 A.2d 1214 (R.I. 1979). As with the lease, states in this group divide over the question of whether the surviving joint tenant B takes A's share of Blackacre subject to or free of the mortgage.

In some circumstances, the joint tenancy is severed even when the four unities are preserved. If all joint tenants voluntarily agree to convert their ownership arrangement into a tenancy in common, their wishes will usually be honored without the necessity of formal transfer. Likewise, the divorce of husband and wife joint tenants will ordinarily produce a tenancy in common, and the murder of one joint tenant by another will sever the tenancy. See *State ex rel. Miller v. Sencindiver*, 275 S.E.2d 10 (W. Va. 1980), for a list of cases and statutes providing for this result. If A and B own Blackacre as joint tenants and the two die simultaneously in the same accident, what should be the result if they have different heirs, or different provisions in their wills?

[2.] Rights of Concurrent Tenants

McKNIGHT v. BASILIDES

Washington Supreme Court
143 P.2d 307 (1943)

SIMPSON, C.J.

This is an action for the partition of real estate and for an accounting of the income obtained by the defendant in possession. Judgment of default was entered against defendant Ruth Allison.

At the conclusion of the trial, the court made findings of fact and conclusions of law, and entered its decree of partition. The decree provided (1) that each of plaintiffs had an undivided one-sixth interest in two pieces of real estate, one at 5203 First avenue northwest, known as the "big house," and the other at 326 West Forty-first street, known as the "little house," both properties being situated in the city of Seattle; (2) that plaintiffs have judgment against Charles Basilides in the sum of $1,083.16 for their share of the rents and rental use of the property, and that the judgment was a lien upon the interest of Charles Basilides in the property; (3) that the house and lot at 5203 First avenue northwest be sold in the manner provided by law relative to partition and sale of real estate; (4) that the property at 326 West Forty-first street be not sold; (5) that plaintiffs be allowed an attorney's fee of five hundred dollars and that a like sum be allowed counsel for defendants. Both amounts were made a lien on the proceeds of the sale of the property at 5203 First avenue northwest. The decree further provided for the appointment of a referee to sell the First avenue property. Defendant Charles Basilides appealed.

In the year 1901 appellant married Alice King in the city of Chicago. At the time of her marriage to appellant, Mrs. King had two children by a former marriage, Alice, now Alice McKnight, and Fred W. King. Defendant Ruth Allison is the child of the appellant and his wife Alice. During the year 1907 the family moved to Seattle, where appellant engaged in business and acquired two pieces of real property, one known in the evidence as the "little house," located at 326 West Forty-first street, and the other, known as the "big house," located at 5203 First avenue northwest, both in the city of Seattle.

Alice Basilides died intestate November 20, 1929, and the estate has never been probated. Appellant has been in possession of both pieces of property since the death of his wife, and has paid all the taxes and assessments levied against the property. In addition, he made certain improvements upon the real estate. He rented the "little house" and occupied the "big house" as his home. During the time from the death of his wife, Alice, until a few days prior to the beginning of this action, appellant never made any claim to respondents that he was the sole owner of the property, nor did respondents make any claim to the property during the same period of time.

The assignments of error present three questions for consideration: (1) Did appellant obtain title to the real estate by adverse possession? (2) Should appellant be compelled to make an accounting of income from the property? (3) Were respondents entitled to a lien upon appellant's interest in the property for the amount found due after accounting? We will discuss the questions in the order set out above.

Appellant contends that the evidence shows him to have been in actual, uninterrupted, open, notorious, hostile, and exclusive possession of the property under claim of right since November 20, 1929, and for that reason he has acquired title by adverse possession.

The general rule relative to securing title to property owned in common by adverse possession is found in the following comprehensive statements:

> Since acts of ownership which, in case of a stranger, would be deemed adverse and per se a disseisin, are, in cases of tenancies in common, susceptible of explanation consistently with the real title, they are not necessarily inconsistent with the unity of possession existing under a cotenancy. For this reason, whether the acts of ownership will be such as to break and dissolve the unity of possession, constitute an adverse possession as against the cotenants, and amount to a disseisin, depends upon the intent with which they are done, and upon their notoriety and essential character. Accordingly, it is general rule that the entry of a cotenant on the common property, even if he takes the rents, cultivates the land, or cuts the wood and timber without accounting or paying for any share of it, will not ordinarily be considered as adverse to his cotenants and an ouster of them. Rather, such acts will be construed in support of the common title. Mere exclusive possession, accompanied by no act that can amount to an ouster of the other cotenant, or give notice to him that such possession is adverse, will not be held to amount to a disseisin of such cotenant. Mere intention, unannounced, is not sufficient to support a claim of adverse title. Although the exclusive taking of the profits by one tenant in common for a long period of time, with the knowledge of the other cotenant and without any claim of right by him, may raise a natural presumption of ouster upon which the jury may find the fact to exist, if it satisfied their minds, yet the law will not, from this fact, merely raise a presumption of such ouster.

1 Am. Jur., Adverse Possession, § 54. [Additional citations omitted.]

When we apply the rules just set out to the facts present in the case at bar, we hold that the evidence in this case was not sufficient to establish the claim that appellant made any adverse claim to the property, and that the facts indicate that his actions in living in the "big house" and collecting rents from the "little house" were not such outward acts as would amount to adverse possession.

The trial court compelled appellant to make an accounting. In so doing, appellant was given credit for repairs, improvements, taxes, and insurance in the amount of $4,753.46. He was then charged for the use of the properties between November 20, 1929, and May, 1943, in the total sum of $8,001. Respondents were given a judgment in the sum of $1,083.18 for their share of the rental use of the two properties, and the judgment was made a lien upon the interest that appellant owned in the properties. A portion of the income received consisted of rentals for the "little house," which was sold April 1, 1938, on a partial payment sales contract.

Since the date of the sale, appellant was charged a reasonable value for its use. The charge for the use of the "big house" was fixed at an amount which the court found from testimony to be the reasonable rental value thereof. The record discloses that the income was at all times sufficient to pay the taxes and other expenses. The improvements were of a minor nature and did not to any appreciable extent enhance the rental or sales value of the property. Appellant was responsible for and was properly held to an accounting of the rents he received from the "little house."

The charge for the occupancy of the "big house" and the reasonable rental value of the "little house" subsequent to its sale presents a more difficult problem.

The general rule is stated as follows in 62 C.J. 446, Tenancy in Common, § 64:

> While there is some authority in the United States to the contrary, based apparently upon the assumption that the Statute of Anne has become a part of the common law of the particular jurisdiction and upon an interpretation of that statute at variance with that adopted by the English courts, the generally accepted rule is that at common law one tenant in common who occupies all or more than his proportionate share of the common premises is not liable, because of such occupancy alone, to his cotenant or cotenants for rent or for use and occupation. He may become liable therefor, however, because of an express or implied agreement or if he stands in a fiduciary relationship to his cotenant, or where he has ousted his cotenant and, in some jurisdictions, liability is placed on him by virtue of express statute or because of the interpretation placed upon statutes similar in their terms to that of the Statute of Anne. Notwithstanding the rule may prevail in the particular jurisdiction that a cotenant may be charged for the use and occupancy of more than his proportionate share of the common premises, the circumstances of the particular case may require a denial of the application of the rule as inequitable, as where the occupancy has been with the acquiescence of the cotenants or the other cotenants have abandoned the occupancy of the property and declined to occupy it.

We are not disposed to follow the general rule laid down [above], for the reason that it is not an equitable one. There is no sound basis for the general rule of law.

No practical or reasonable argument can be advanced for allowing one in possession to reap a financial benefit by occupying property owned in common without paying for his personal use of that part of the property owned by his cotenants. The fairest method in cases in which the cotenant occupies and uses common property, instead of renting it out, is to charge him with its reasonable rental value. Of course there would be an exception to this holding in cases where the income resulted from improvements placed upon the property by the cotenant in possession. Appellant used the "big house" as a home for many years, and it was proper that he be charged with the reasonable rental value of that use and made to account to his cotenants for their share of that rental value. However, appellant should not be charged with the rental value of the "little house" after its sale, for the reason that he did not receive any rent, nor did he occupy or use it in any way.

Finally, it is argued that the court erred in impressing a lien upon the interest which appellant owned in the property. It is true that no lien exists in favor of one cotenant against the share owned by the others. However, the court may, in the exercise of its equitable powers and in order to do full justice to all parties concerned, impose a lien upon the interest in the property owned by the one who has benefitted by possession, and may provide for the payment of the judgment from the proceeds of the sale in a partition action. 14 Am. Jur. 107, Cotenancy, § 40.

The judgment will be modified by striking therefrom the charge for use of the "little house" subsequent to the time it was sold. In all other particulars, the judgment will be affirmed.

MALLERY, J. (dissenting).

"The generally accepted rule is that at common law one tenant in common who occupies all or more than his proportionate share of the common premises is not liable, because of such occupancy alone, to his cotenant or cotenants for rent or for use and occupation." 62 C.J. 446, Tenancy in Common, § 64.

This rule accords well with the rule that, in the absence of an ouster, the cotenant's possession is not adverse. In the face of the presumption of permission, the hostile character of the possession must fail. Therefore, the majority opinion rightly holds that appellant's claim to title by adverse possession cannot prevail. By the same token, since the adverse possession failed by reason of the permissive nature of his possession, he cannot be held liable for rent for the use of the "big house." His cotenants deliberately let him "carry the burden" during the depression years. They cannot now deny their permission without establishing his hostile possession. Of course, the rentals for the "little house" were received in trust for his cotenants.

Appellant has been charged in the accounting with his share of $8,001 of the rental value on the "big house" for the period beginning November 20, 1929, and ending May, 1943, which is over thirteen years. Rem. Rev. Stat., § 157 [P.C. § 8162], limits an action for the rents and profits or for the use and occupation of real estate to a period of six years. He should have been charged nothing. Even a stranger to the title could have been held for only six years. I dissent.

NOTES AND QUESTIONS

1. *Is the Decision in* McKnight *Correct?* States differ on the issue of the financial accountability of the occupying co-tenant. In most jurisdictions, a co-tenant must be ousted from the property before he or she can bring an action for the reasonable rental value of property that is occupied by a co-tenant in sole possession. (The share of the rent improperly held by the occupying co-tenant is known as the "mesne profits.") Which is the better rule? In a later case, *Fulton v. Fulton*, 357 P.2d 169 (Wash. 1960), the Washington Supreme Court adopted the majority rule.

2. The Statute of Anne, mentioned in *McKnight*, was adopted in England in 1704 and reversed the common law rule that a co-tenant in sole possession of land had no duty to account to his co-tenants for the income he received from his property. Most American states have either enacted their own version of the statute or else declared it to be part of the common law. In the United States, states differ as to whether the co-tenant in possession has to account for income derived from the use of the property (as from mining) or simply for rental income collected from third parties. Within a particular jurisdiction, the obligations of co-tenants are the same regardless of whether they are joint tenants or tenants in common. Absent an agreement, a co-tenant in possession is not entitled to contribution from non-possessory co-tenants for repairs or improvements, but in an accounting to his co-tenants, he will normally have the right to offset the costs of necessary repairs against income derived from the property. Any joint tenant or tenant in common has the right to bring an action for partition. The partition process is discussed below in Note 4.

3. *Concurrent Tenancies in Personal Property.* Joint tenancies and tenancies in common can be established in either real or personal property. Concurrent tenancies in bank accounts are quite common and are the source of numerous problems. Agency accounts (where one party is given the authority to write checks for the depositor) and survivorship accounts (which are will substitutes that entitle a designated individual to the balance of the account when the primary depositor dies, but to nothing prior to that time) are often incorrectly referred to as "joint accounts." If the account is a true joint account, there is not only a right of survivorship but each co-tenant can legally withdraw funds at any time.

However, while an individual joint tenant is entitled to withdraw the entire sum in the account, he or she may not be legally entitled to keep the entire balance. In fact, each joint tenant is entitled only to a proportionate share (1/2 if there are two joint tenants; 1/3 if there are three, etc.), and if he or she withdraws more than their share without the permission of the other joint tenants, the co-tenants may sue to recover the excess. The balance to which each joint tenant is entitled is known as the *moiety*. In *Estate of Kohn*, 168 N.W.2d 812 (Wis. 1969), a greedy second husband withdrew the balance from a joint bank account he held with his wife less than two days before his wife died of a lingering illness. The husband was forced to pay 50% of the balance into his wife's estate (which went to children from her first marriage) even though he would have been entitled to the entire sum as the surviving joint tenant had he merely waited until after his wife's death to make the withdrawal.

4. *Judicial Partition.* Both tenants in common and joint tenants [illegible] to terminate the concurrent ownership arrangement. This is don[illegible] proceeding in equity known as *partition.* A court hearing a partition [illegible] normally obligated to divide the property, even if other co-tenants object. [illegible] partition may be either in kind or by sale. In kind partition involves the phy[illegible] division of the land into separate tracts. If there are more than two co-tenants, o[illegible] of the tracts may be held by multiple owners as co-tenants if the parties so desire. If separate tracts are not equal in value, former co-tenants receiving the more valuable tracts will be required to make cash payments to the others to equalize the value. (Such payments are known as *owelty.*)

If there is no equitable way to physically divide the property (as in the case of a single family home or apartment building), the court will order a judicial sale with the proceeds to be divided among the co-tenants proportionate to their interest in the property. Joint tenants, of course, share equally in the proceeds.

5. *Heirs Property.* It is a general principle of the American law of inheritance that when multiple heirs take interests in a common parcel of property, real or personal, they take as tenants in common. Regardless of how the heirs themselves decide to use (or not use) the property, they remain tenants in common until such time as they transfer their interests to someone else or the property is portioned by judicial decree. As the following discussion illustrates, a wide variety of problems can arise in this situation, especially if the inherited shares are inherited by new tenants in common when one of the original tenants passes away. Retaining property as "heirs' property," i.e., taking no steps to alter the ownership structure is particularly common within in some cultural subgroups, especially African-Americans. The primary problem is that any one tenant in common, or even worse, the creditors of any one tenant in common can force a partition of the inherited property which can result in the property, often the family home, being sold to someone not at all related to the family.

To address this problem, the Uniform Laws Commission has prepared a Uniform Partition of Heirs Property Act (UPHPA) which establishes a series of simple due process protections designed to protect the heirs: notice, appraisal, right of first refusal, and if the other co-tenants choose not to exercise their right and a sale is required, a commercially reasonable sale supervised by the court to ensure all parties receive their fair share of the property. As of September 2015, the UPHPA has been adopted in Alabama, Arkansas, Georgia, Montana, Nevada, and Connecticut. It has also been introduced into the legislature of South Carolina and Hawaii.

6. *Other Forms of Concurrent Tenancy.* The common law recognized a *tenancy in coparcenary.* Under the English doctrine of primogeniture, the oldest surviving son inherited all real property. However, if there was no surviving son, then the land was held in equal, undivided shares by the surviving daughters who took as coparseners. Because the doctrine of primogeniture was never adopted in the United States, this particular form of concurrent estate was of no importance in the United States and it was abolished in England in 1925. Individuals who inherit simultaneous interests in real property today take as tenants in common.

Before the widespread adoption of the Uniform Partnership Act, many jurisdictions recognized a *tenancy in partnership.* This particular form of ownership was

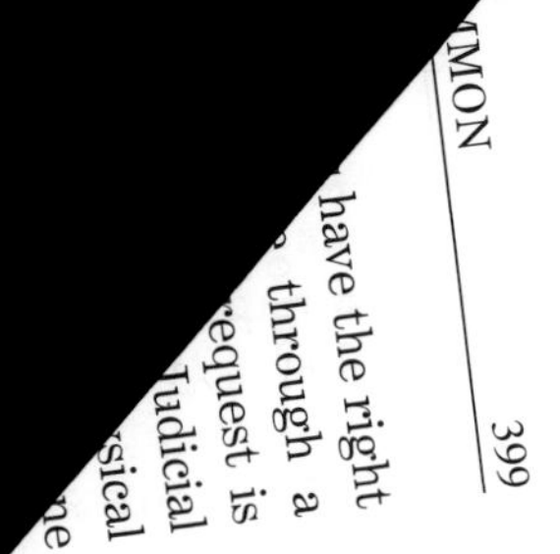

ı created by the rule that a partnership (unlike an d not own land in its own name. Under a tenancy in ners held property essentially as tenants in com- trust that required the survivor or assignee of an assets to the purposes of the partnership, rather ed a partnership to continue its operation without of survivorship for the partners. Thus, the profits o the successor of the original partner and were uccessor would be entitled to his or her (or its) successor had no authority to force a partition of

lopted by the American Law Institute, retained p" (§ 25), but it also allowed the partnership to ... name of the partnership (§ 8), a fact which reduced, but ... not entirely eliminate, the need for the concept of tenancy in partnership.

[3.] Concurrent Ownership in Condominiums

The concurrent estates imply a simultaneous right of possession of the entire tract for all co-tenants. In a condominium development, each individual residential or commercial unit is owned individually. In addition, the development also includes common areas which are typically held by the unit owners as tenants in common. However, this arrangement differs from the traditional tenancy in common in one important aspect: condominium owners are almost always prevented by statute from either forcing a partition of the common areas or from transferring their interest in the common areas separate from their interest in their primary unit.

The duties and obligations of the co-tenants are typically spelled out by a formal agreement entered into by each unit owner at the time of purchase and may include limitations on the rights of co-tenants to use all or some of the common areas. Control and upkeep of the common areas is typically delegated to a condominium association or a management firm. Unit owners also pay a fee collected at regular intervals which is used for the maintenance of common areas. The liability of unit owners for actions taken within the common areas has been the source of considerable litigation.

DUTCHER v. OWENS

Texas Supreme Court
647 S.W.2d 948 (1983)

C.L. Ray, Justice.

This is a case of first impression concerning the allocation of liability among condominium co-owners for tort claims arising out of the ownership, use and maintenance of "common elements." The defendant was found to be vicariously liable for the homeowners' association's negligence. The trial court ordered that the plaintiffs recover from the defendant an amount based upon the defendant's proportionate ownership in the condominium project. The court of appeals reversed in part the judgment of the trial court, holding "that each unit owner, as a tenant in common with all other unit owners in the common elements, is jointly and severally liable for damage claims arising in the common elements." 635 S.W.2d 208, 211. We reverse the judgment of the court of appeals and affirm the trial court's judgment.

J.A. Dutcher, a resident of San Diego, California, owned a condominium apartment in the Eastridge Terrace Condominiums, located in Dallas County, which he leased to Ted and Christine Owens. Ownership of the apartment includes a 1.572% pro rata undivided ownership in the common elements of the project. The Owenses suffered substantial property loss in a fire which began in an external light fixture in a common area.

The Owenses filed suit in Tarrant County against Dutcher, the Eastridge Terrace Condominium Association, Joe Hill Electric Company, IHS-8 Ltd. (the developer) and a class of co-owners of condominiums in Eastridge Terrace represented by the officers of the homeowners' association. All defendants with the exception of Dutcher obtained a change of venue to Dallas County. The case was tried before a jury, which found the following:

> (1) The fire was proximately caused by the lack of an insulating box behind the light fixture in the exterior wall air space;
>
> (2) The homeowners' association knew of this defect;
>
> (3) The homeowners' association alone was negligent in failing to install an insulating box with knowledge of the defect; and
>
> (4) The negligence of homeowners' association resulted in damage to the Owens' property in the amount of $69,150.00.

The trial court rendered judgment against Dutcher on the jury's verdict in the amount of $1,087.04. The award represents the amount of damages multiplied by Dutcher's 1.572% pro rata undivided ownership in the common elements of the Eastridge Terrace Condominium project.

By an agreed statement of facts filed with the court of appeals, the parties stipulated that the sole issue for determination on appeal was whether a condominium co-owner is jointly and severally liable or is liable only for a pro rata portion of the damages. In enacting the Texas Condominium Act (the Act), Tex. Rev. Civ. Stat. Ann. art. 1301a, the Texas Legislature intended to create "a new method of property ownership." A condominium is an estate in real property consisting of an undivided interest in a portion of a parcel of real property together with a separate fee simple interest in another portion of the same parcel. In essence, condominium ownership is the merger of two estates in land into one: the fee simple ownership of an apartment or unit in a condominium project and a tenancy in common with other co-owners in the common elements.

"General common elements" consist of, inter alia, the land upon which the building stands, the "foundations, bearing walls and columns, roofs, halls, lobbies, stairways, and entrances and exits or communication ways; . . . all other elements of the building desirable or rationally of common use or necessary to the existence, upkeep and safety of the condominium regime, and any other elements described in the declaration . . . ." Tex. Rev. Civ. Stat. Ann. art. 1301a, § 2 (l), subsections (1), (2) & (7). An individual apartment cannot be conveyed separately from the undivided interest in the common elements and vice versa. *Id.* § 9.

A condominium regime must be established according to the Act. The declaration must be filed with the county clerk, who must record the instrument in the Condominium Records. Once the declarant has complied with the provisions of the Act, each apartment in the project is treated as an interest in real property. Administration of the regime is established by the Act.

The condominium association or council is a legislatively created unincorporated association of co-owners having as their common purpose a convenient method of ownership of real property in a statutorily created method of ownership which combines both the concepts of separateness of tenure and commonality of ownership. The California Supreme Court has concluded that "the concept of separateness in the condominium project carries over to any management body or association formed to handle the common affairs of the project, and that both the condominium project and the condominium association must be considered separate legal entities from its unit owners and association members." *White v. Cox*, 95 Cal. Rptr. at 262.

Given the uniqueness of the type of ownership involved in condominiums, the onus of liability for injuries arising from the management of condominium projects should reflect the degree of control exercised by the defendants. We agree with the California court's conclusion that to rule that a condominium co-owner had any effective control over the operation of the common areas would be to sacrifice "reality to theoretical formalism," for in fact a co-owner has no more control over operations than he would have as a stockholder in a corporation which owned and operated the project. This does not limit the plaintiff's right of action. The efficiency found in a suit directed at the homeowners' association and its board of directors representing the various individual homeowners, as well as any co-owner causally or directly responsible for the injuries sustained, benefits both sides of the docket as well as the judicial system as a whole.

Such a result is not inconsistent with the legislative intent. While the Act creates a new form of real property ownership, it does not address the issue of the allocation of tort liability among co-owners. Nevertheless, we are guided in our decision by the other provisions in the Act which appear in pari materia, and which proportionately allocate various financial responsibilities. For example, the Act provides for pro rata contributions by co-owners toward expenses of administration and maintenance, insurance, taxes and assessments. Pro rata provisions also exist for the application of insurance proceeds. Tex. Rev. Civ. Stat. Ann. art. 1301a, §§ 15, 18, 19, & 20.

The theories of vicarious and joint and several liability are judicially created vehicles for enforcing remedies for wrongs committed. Justified on public policy grounds, they represent a deliberate allocation of risk. Texas follows the rule that statutes in derogation of the common law are not to be strictly construed. Tex. Rev. Civ. Stat. Ann. art. 10, § 8. Nevertheless, it is recognized that if a statute creates a liability unknown to the common law, or deprives a person of a common law right, the statute will be strictly construed in the sense that it will not be extended beyond its plain meaning or applied to cases not clearly within its purview. *Satterfield v.*

Satterfield, 448 S.W.2d 456, 459 (Tex. 1969). Since the Act is silent as to tort liability, we are dealing with rights and liabilities which are not creatures of statute but with the common law, which is our special domain. Hence, the rule we have reached is not a usurpation of the legislative prerogative. To the contrary, it is one reached in the public interest.

We hold, therefore, that because of the limited control afforded a unit owner by the statutory condominium regime, the creation of the regime effects a reallocation of tort liability. The liability of a condominium co-owner is limited to his pro rata interest in the regime as a whole, where such liability arises from those areas held in tenancy-in-common. The judgment of the court of appeals is reversed and the judgment of the trial court is affirmed.

NOTES AND QUESTIONS

1. Although it has existed in continental Europe since the time of the Roman Empire, the concept of the condominium was unknown in English and American law. Widely used in Europe and South America in the 19th and 20th centuries, it did not become an important part of American property law until the 1960s. 7 Powell on Real Property (Part III) c. 54.01 (Michael Wolf ed. 2005). Since that time its popularity has mushroomed. The Texas act at issue in the above case is typical of the condominium statutes enacted in every American state.

Although the term condominium is usually applied to apartment-like structures, the combination of individual unit ownership with joint ownership of common areas is used in many residential subdivisions as well. The legal authority of condominium boards and homeowner associations over individual unit owners is discussed in Chapter 8.

2. *Cooperatives.* Cooperative apartment buildings, on the other hand, are subject to a different type of ownership than the condominium. Typically, the cooperative is owned by a corporation whose shareholders are the residents of the building. The cooperative is thus run for the benefit of the owners who lease their units from the corporation, and thus is technically owned by a single legal entity, the corporation, and not the individuals who occupy or lease out the residential units.

3. *Time-Sharing.* Time-sharing arrangements present a third modern type of concurrent ownership in which multiple owners share common assets. Time-sharing divides property ownership (typically of a condominium) into a number of fixed periods of time (often weeks or months). Each purchaser then has the exclusive right to possession of the property during the period purchased. In most instances, the holder of the time unit is permitted to transfer his or interest to others.

There has been some disagreement as to the nature of the legal interests created by time-sharing arrangement. The Uniform Condominium Act (1977) defined a time-share in two different ways. It could be structured as a tenancy in common in which all the share owners were co-tenants whose right of occupancy was limited, by agreement, to the periods of time purchased from the developer. On the other hand, it could be set up as a sequence of short estates (one week, one month), each coupled with a remainder interest that entitled the owner to retake possession again after the expiration of intervening estates. (The estate and remainder concepts are discussed in Chapter 4.) On the other hand, the Uniform Real Estate Time-Sharing Act (1979) drew a distinction between those with recurring rights to use a particular unit (at least five discreet periods of use spread over at least five years) and those whose right to use was more short-lived. Under the latter act, those in the first category were viewed as owning an estate in the property while those in the second were said only to have a license to use the premises and not an ownership interest in the unit. (The concept of license is discussed in Chapter 7.)

4. *Party Walls.* In contrast to the interests discussed above, party walls are an ancient and somewhat modest form of concurrent ownership. A party wall is a common wall shared by two adjacent structures, normally constructed on the boundary line between the two parcels. The owners of the adjacent property may own the party wall as tenants in common, and each has a legal right to require the other to help maintain the wall. In other situations the wall may be owned entirely by one of the property owners subject to an easement held by the other. *C. & E. Partnership v. Donnelly*, 367 S.E.2d 490 (Va. 1988).

Party walls as a legal concept appears to be a more important matter in the United Kingdom than in the United States. The British parliament passed a Party Wall Act in 1996, and the Pyramis & Thisbe (named after the characters from Greek mythology who appear in the famous "wall" scene in Shakespeare's *A Midsummer's Night's Dream*) Society is an organization for professionals who specialize in party wall matters. *See* www.partywalls.org.uk; CHYNOWETH, THE PARTY WALL CASEBOOK (2003).

5. Uniform Common Interest Ownership Act § 3-111(a) (2008) rules out joint and several unit owner liability "for an injury or damage arising out of the condition or use of the common elements." Several states by statute have also limited unit owner liability to their proportionate share. Statutes may also require a unit owners association to carry insurance against risks on insurable common elements.

[B.] MARITAL PROPERTY

[1.] Tenancy by the Entirety

ROBINSON v. TROUSDALE COUNTY

Tennessee Supreme Court
516 S.W.2d 626 (1974)

HENRY, J.

This is an inverse condemnation suit involving the nature of the estate of tenancy by the entireties under Tennessee law and the common law disability of coverture. Petitioners, husband and wife, sued Trousdale County for damages for the taking of certain real estate owned by them as tenants by the entirety, for the purpose of widening a public road adjacent to their property, and for incidental damages. The answer of Trousdale County, among other defenses, asserts that petitioners are barred from seeking compensation and damages by virtue of a deed, executed by

property involved to Trousdale County, in fee

t Judge without the intervention of a jury. The
as estopped to claim any damage because of the
damages, and allowed the wife Five Hundred
damages for the value of the land taken. All
ls to the Court of Appeals. That court affirmed
all respects except as to the ownership and
representing the value of the land. The court
the Clerk of the trial court and invested by him
titioners; (2) that should the husband die first,
the wife; (3) that should the wife die first the
usdale County; and (4) in the event of a divorce,
reen the wife and Trousdale County.

ourt for certiorari. We granted the petition of
the disposition of the recovery. A proper
sarily involves a consideration of the nature of an estate by the entireties in Tennessee, the rights, benefits and privileges of the tenants, the right of a tenant to convey his or her interest, and the common law disability of coverture.

Our investigation leads us to the conclusion that the decisional law of Tennessee, not only is nebulous and confusing, but is in substantial conflict and out of harmony with justice, reason and logic. We, therefore, propose to clarify the law by a clear, comprehensive and definitive opinion.

We do not believe that the common law disability of coverture has any sanction in our jurisprudence or any relevance in our society. At best it is outmoded; at worst oppressive and degrading. The net result of [our earlier cases] may be summarized as follows:

a. A tenancy by the entirety confers upon the husband the right to possession, control, rents and profits from the estate.

b. The wife has no right to an accounting.

c. The common law disability of coverture is restored as to estates held by the husband and wife as tenants by the entirety.

d. The husband is the dominant tenant, the 1919 Amendment having restored his common law primacy.

To put the present law in proper perspective, let us assume that a husband and wife, having no other assets whatsoever, simultaneously inherit the sum of $250,000.00 each and that they pool their inheritances and purchase an apartment house, taking title as tenants by the entirety. The rental income starts coming in. The husband, the dominant tenant, appropriates all rental income and expends it in accordance with his desires, without the consent of the wife and over her protest. Short of resorting to the divorce courts, she has no legal remedy. One does not have to be a "Women's Libber" or even have an educated conscience, or anything beyond an elemental sense of justice to grasp the patent unfairness of such a situation. It is not only archaic; it is gross and unconscionable.

In *United States v. Yazell*, 382 U.S. 341 (1966), the Supreme Court of the United States refers to the disability of coverture as a "quaint doctrine" and a "peculiar institution . . . which is now, with some exceptions, relegated to history's legal museum."

The fact that Tennessee clings to the common law concept of coverture casts a shadow of doubt upon the intellectual consistency of our approach to the whole area of equality of the sexes, and points up the need for bringing this phase of our law into harmony with modern thinking.

We hold that the Married Women's Act (Ch. 26, Acts of 1913), fully and effectively eradicated the common law disability of coverture and that the amendatory act, Chapter 126, Acts of 1919, did not have the legal effect of restoring it. We abolish the last vestige of the common law disability of coverture in Tennessee.

We do not abolish the estate of tenancy by the entirety, but we strip it of the artificial and archaic rules and restrictions imposed at the common law, and we fully deterge it of its deprivations and detriments to women and fully emancipate them from its burdens.

From this date forward each tenant shall have a joint right to the use, control, incomes, rents, profits, usufructs and possession of property so held, and neither may sell, encumber, alienate or dispose of any portion thereof except his or her right of survivorship, without the consent of the other. Any unilateral attempt will be wholly and utterly void at the instance of the aggrieved tenant and any prospective purchaser, transferee, lessee, mortgagee and the like will act at his peril.

Lastly we reach the matter of the ownership of the fund now in the Registry of the Court. The husband conveyed his right of expectancy. The County has acquired the needed land for the public road. The result is that all parties in this case have received their just desserts except Mrs. Robinson. She gets the money.

HENRY, JUSTICE (concurring).

I wrote the main opinion to reflect the unanimous views of the Court. While I am in full accord with the conclusions we have reached on the common law disability of coverture and share with my colleagues a sense of pride in this progressive action, I am convinced that we should have based our decision to a substantial extent, on constitutional grounds. We can no longer countenance sex-based classifications.

I fully appreciate the traditional policy of the Courts to avoid constitutional questions where their resolution is not necessary to a decision. Sometimes issues of such overriding importance arise that the courts are under a duty to speak. This is such an issue.

I would hold that the application of the common law disability of coverture is violative of Section 1 of the Fourteenth Amendment to the Constitution of the United States in that married women are "citizens" of the United States and the application of this doctrine deprives them of their property without due process of law, and denies them the equal protection of the law. Moreover, said doctrine is an invidious and "suspect" classification based upon sex and marital status, and is predicated on no rational basis, and abridges their right to acquire, enjoy, lease, hold, own and benefit from their own property.

I would hold, for the same reasons, that the application of this doctrine is violative of Article 1, Section 8, of the Constitution of the State of Tennessee, in that it operates to deprive married women of their property and abridges their rights and privileges as citizens of the State, contrary to the law of the land. I am authorized to state that my brother Brock joins me in this concurring opinion.

NOTES AND QUESTIONS

1. Note that Justice Henry authors both the majority opinion and the concurrence in the above case. While not unprecedented, this is quite uncommon. Do you understand what prompted him to engage in this unconventional practice?

2. A tenancy by the entirety (sometimes called a tenancy by the entireties) can be created only between husband and wife. In most respects, it resembles a joint tenancy and includes a right of survivorship with the requirement of a valid marriage functioning as a fifth unity. However, because the tenancy by the entirety was originally rooted in the legal fiction that husband and wife were one person, it differed from the joint tenancy in that it could not be severed by the actions of one party. If either husband or wife attempts to transfer their interest, the attempted transfer fails. Similarly, neither party has the right to request a judicial partition. Furthermore, in most states where tenancy by the entirety exists, land so held is beyond the reach of creditors of either the husband or the wife (although obviously not beyond those of both), a feature that makes tenancy by the entirety particularly attractive. However, the United States Supreme Court has ruled that property held by tenants by the entirety is subject to a federal tax lien against one of the owners even if state law protects it against ordinary creditors. *United States v. Craft*, 535 U.S. 274 (2002).

A minority of states allow either spouse to transfer their own interest but not to defeat the right of survivorship. *Robinson v. Trousdale County* is an example of a case arising in such a jurisdiction.

If land is transferred to two unmarried persons as tenants in the entirety, courts differ as to the result. Some states recognize the resulting ownership as a joint tenancy, while others only a tenancy in common. A few states interpret the transaction as a tenancy in common in a life estate with a remainder interest in the co-tenant who survives the other. (Life estates and remainders are discussed in Chapter 4.) At common law, any transfer to a husband and wife was automatically treated as a tenancy by the entirety. (In fact, other forms of concurrent ownership were not permitted.) Today, approximately one-half of the states recognize tenancy by the entirety, although husbands and wives may hold as either joint tenants or tenants in common. In those jurisdictions, an ambiguous transfer to a husband and wife will result in a tenancy by the entirety.

3. *The Effect of Divorce.* A valid divorce terminates an estate of tenancy by the entirety. In most jurisdictions, former spouses hold the subject property as tenants in common, although in some they hold as joint tenants. Of course, a divorce settlement may result in only one, or neither, of the parties owning the property. If concurrent ownership survives the divorce proceedings, either party may initiate a partition suit.

4. *The Doctrine of Coverture.* Under the common law as it existed prior to the early 19th century, husbands and wives were treated as single entities at law with the legal personality of married women submerged in that of the husband. The status of the married woman was described as the disability of coverture. Under this doctrine, the husband had complete control over the wife's real property during the period of their marriage, and this control extended to property owned by the wife prior to the marriage as well as that acquired during it. In addition, all her personal property, including any income she might have, was under the control of her husband who could transfer his right if he so desired. In exchange, the husband was obligated to support the wife.

There were a limited number of exceptions to the general principle of the husband's absolute control. Equity would protect the wife's interest in property given to her specifically for her separate use, and a married woman who carried on a separate trade could, by agreement with her husband, retain the business and its profits for her own use, free from her husband's control. The disabilities associated with coverture were largely removed by statutes known as Married Women's Property Acts which date from the 1830s in the United States and from the 1850s in Great Britain. Vestiges of the doctrine of coverture nevertheless survived well into the 20th century.

5. *Dower and Curtesy.* Although a surviving wife took title to all land held with her husband as tenants by the entirety, under the common law husbands were under no obligation to hold real property as concurrent tenants with their wives. If a husband chose to acquire or hold land in his own name, the wife was said to hold a dower interest in the property. The dower interest, which was derived from the husband's obligation to support the wife even after the end of the marriage by death or divorce, was defined as a life estate in one-third in all lands of which the husband was "seised" during marriage and which were inheritable by issue (children or other direct descendants) born of the marriage. Lands that were "seised" by the husband were lands in which the husband held absolute title including the right to pass on the property after death (which would include all land held in fee simple including those that might be subject to a present estate for years). Not included were lands leased by the husband, lands in which he held a life interest, and lands in which he was a joint tenant. Dower did not extend to personal property nor to land in which the husband held only an equitable interest. (Equitable interests included land held in trust for his benefit.)

A life estate in one-third of all affected land entitled the widow to the right of possession of one-third of the property, or the income from it, for the remainder of her life. As long as the husband was alive, dower was inchoate. However, any property transferred by the husband during his marriage was subject to the wife's dower interest which could not be done away with other than by the consent of the wife. Consequently, to obtain an unrestricted ownership interest, a purchaser of land from a married man had to secure a waiver of the grantor's wife's dower interest. Otherwise the new purchaser took the land subject to the wife's inchoate dower interest which would have entitled her to a life estate in one-third of the property transferred, once her husband died. (Of course, if she predeceased her husband, the dower interest died with her.) The only other way to terminate the dower interest was by divorce, and even then it might survive if the wife had not been unfaithful.

The common law also recognized a counterpart to dower for men known as curtesy. Curtesy gave a surviving husband a life estate in his wife's lands (which he had controlled during the marriage), but only if children were born of the marriage. The children did not have to survive either parent; the only requirement was that they be born alive or "heard to cry within the four walls." In addition to the life estate in all of his wife's lands, curtesy also entitled the husband to any equitable interests that included a right of possession.

Common law curtesy has been abolished everywhere in the United States. Dower has also been abolished in most states, and, with one or two exceptions where it remains, it applies equally to men and women. A dower interest for women only is now believed to violate the constitutional guarantee of equal protection. *Boan v. Watson*, 316 S.E.2d 401 (S.C. 1984). Today, the principle way of protecting the interests of surviving spouses is the elective share which permits an inadequately provided for survivor to elect a statutorily prescribed share of the deceased spouse's estate (typically between 1/4 and 1/2).

[2.] Other Forms of Marital Property

HOAK v. HOAK

West Virginia Supreme Court of Appeals
370 S.E.2d 473 (1988)

BROTHERTON, JUSTICE.

This appeal from a divorce decree presents an issue of first impression in the courts of West Virginia: Is a professional degree earned during marriage "marital property" subject to equitable distribution? The circuit court in this case answered "no," and Rebecca Hoak, the working spouse, appeals. Based on our review of the record, the briefs, and the law of the many jurisdictions that have considered this issue, we conclude that a professional degree is not marital property. The Court adopts instead the concept of reimbursement alimony as a means of compensating the working spouse in this kind of "professional degree/divorce decree" case. We reverse the judgment of the lower court and remand the case for further proceedings, for reasons set out more fully below.

The appellant, Rebecca Hoak, and the appellee, Bruce Hoak, were married August 16, 1980. At that time, the appellee had completed his first year of medical school. The appellant had received a Bachelor of Science degree in horticulture, and was working for a landscape company. She changed jobs a year later, leaving her field of expertise in order to make more money. She intended to return to school for a degree in education or accounting after her husband completed his training. The appellee secured some odd jobs during medical school, but does not dispute that his wife provided the majority of the financial support and homemaker services for the household during the years 1980–1982.

The appellee graduated from medical school in the spring of 1983, and began a five-year surgical residency in Charleston, West Virginia, in July of that year. Thereafter, the appellee provided primary support for the couple, and the appellant worked only sporadically.

The parties separated in September, 1984, and on October 26, 1984, Bruce Hoak filed an action for divorce in the Circuit Court of Kanawha County. On December 14, 1984, the circuit court issued a temporary relief order requiring the appellee to pay $500 per month alimony to his wife and $400 per month child support for the couple's infant daughter. Depositions were taken in August and October, 1985, before Special Commissioner Alfred B. McCuskey. On November 15, 1985, the circuit court entered a second temporary relief order reducing monthly child support to $250. On March 12, 1986, the special commissioner filed his report, recommending that the appellee pay his wife $250 per month child support, and $150 per month rehabilitative alimony for two years or until the appellant was gainfully employed.

On August 29, 1986, the circuit court entered a final order dissolving the marriage. The court awarded the appellant $250 per month child support, plus the child's medical and dental expenses, and $500 per month rehabilitative alimony for two years. The court also ordered the appellee to pay attorney's fees in the amount of $1,875. [Note: The record showed that the couple had accumulated little marital property other than two cars and household items (and credit card debts). Neither party objected to the court's division of this property.]

Rebecca Hoak petitioned this Court for an appeal from the circuit court's order, alleging that the circuit court had erred by failing to hold that a license to practice medicine earned during marriage is marital property subject to equitable distribution under W. Va. Code §§ 48-2-1(e)(1) (1986) and 48-2-32 (1986). She also assigned as error the court's failure to award permanent alimony, and disputed its determination on the issue of attorney's fees, expert fees, and court costs. We granted the appeal and, after briefs and argument, address herein the questions presented.

I

Code § 48-2-32 governs the disposition of marital property upon divorce. It provides that such property shall be divided equally, unless the parties agree otherwise in a separation agreement, or unless the court alters the allocation based on its consideration of certain factors enumerated in the statute. Section 48-2-1(e) defines "marital property" as:

> (1) All property and earnings acquired by either spouse during a marriage, including every valuable right and interest, corporeal or incorporeal, tangible or intangible, real or personal, regardless of the form of ownership, whether legal or beneficial, whether individually held, held in trust by a third party, or whether held by the parties to the marriage in some form of co-ownership such as joint tenancy or tenancy in common, joint tenancy with the right of survivorship, or any other form of shared

ownership recognized in other jurisdictions without this state, . . . and

(2) The amount of any increase in value in the separate property of either of the parties to a marriage, which increase results from (A) an expenditure of funds which are marital property, including an expenditure of such funds which reduces indebtedness against separate property, extinguishes liens, or otherwise increases the net value of separate property, or (B) work performed by either or both of the parties during the marriage.

The appellant contends that her husband's medical degree is marital property subject to equitable distribution, because it falls within the broad statutory definition quoted above. The appellant argues that her ex-husband's medical degree is a valuable right or interest acquired during the marriage, and that she should share in the increased earning capacity achieved with the help of her financial and other contributions.

At this writing, the highest courts of almost half the states have considered this question, and only one, New York, has concluded that a professional degree is property. *See O'Brien v. O'Brien*, 489 N.E.2d 712 (N.Y. 1985). The rationale most often quoted for the majority view is that of the Supreme Court of Colorado:

> An educational degree, such as an M.B.A., is simply not encompassed even by the broad views of the concept of "property." It does not have an exchange value or any objective transferable value on an open market. It is personal to the holder. It terminates on death of the holder and is not inheritable. It cannot be assigned, sold, transferred, conveyed, or pledged. An advanced degree is a cumulative product of many years of previous education, combined with diligence and hard work. It may not be acquired by the mere expenditure of money. It is simply an intellectual achievement that may potentially assist in the future acquisition of property. In our view, it has none of the attributes of property in the usual sense of that term.

In re Marriage of Graham, 574 P.2d 75, 77 (Colo. 1978).

Other courts have added that a professional degree or license is too speculative to value, that characterizing spousal contributions as an investment in each other as human assets demeans the concept of marriage, that future earning capacity is a mere expectancy, and that a professional degree is personal to the holder and cannot, therefore, be apportioned. *See, e.g., Archer v. Archer*, 493 A.2d 1074, 1080 (Md. 1985); *Saint-Pierre v. Saint-Pierre*, 357 N.W.2d 250, 260 (S.D. 1984); *Mahoney v. Mahoney*, 453 A.2d 527, 532 (N.J. 1982).

Notwithstanding the overwhelming number of jurisdictions holding that a professional degree is not property, Rebecca Hoak urges us to adopt the minority view advanced most notably by the New York Court of Appeals, originally in the case of *O'Brien v. O'Brien*. In *O'Brien*, husband and wife were married when both held bachelor's degrees and were teaching at the same private school in New York State. The wife gave up her postgraduate training in order to support her husband through medical school, and moved with him to Mexico, where he attended medical school in Guadalajara. The husband filed for divorce two months after obtaining his medical degree. The court of appeals concluded that "marital property encompasses a license to practice medicine to the extent that the license is acquired during marriage." *Id.* at 746. The court noted that "marital property" is a statutory creature, which cannot be expected to fall within traditional property concepts. *Id.* It relied specifically on references in New York's equitable distribution statute to equitable claims or contributions "to the career or career potential" of the other party, and to difficulties in evaluating an interest in a "profession." *Id.* at 746–47. The court concluded that "an interest in a profession or professional career potential is marital property which may be represented by direct or indirect contributions of the non-titleholding spouse, including financial contributions and nonfinancial contributions made by caring for the home and family." *Id.* at 747. The court went on to say that the working spouse is entitled to an equitable portion of the present value of the professional spouse's enhanced earning capacity represented by the degree.

We have in prior cases construed our statutory definition broadly, concluding that "marital property" includes stock acquired by one party through a voluntary employee investment plan, *Raley v. Raley*, 338 S.E.2d 171 (W. Va. 1985), and nondisability retirement or pension benefits, *Butcher v. Butcher*, 357 S.E.2d 226 (W. Va. 1987); *Cross v. Cross*, 363 S.E.2d 449 (W. Va. 1987). These assets differ from the professional degree in issue in this case, however, because they have been earned during the marriage and have a definite, ascertainable value, even if that value cannot be realized until certain conditions are satisfied.

In contrast, the value of a professional degree is the value of the enhanced earning capacity of the degree-holder. Not only is that value speculative, but also it represents money or assets earned after dissolution of the marriage. As such, it falls outside our statutory definition of marital property as "all property and earnings acquired by either spouse *during a marriage*." W. Va. Code § 48-2-1(e)(1) (emphasis added). *Accord, Mahoney v. Mahoney*, 453 A.2d 527 (N.J. 1982).

Although, as appellant points out, courts often must place a value on human life and estimate the present value of future earning capacity in wrongful death or serious injury cases, such cases involve a third-party payor (usually an insurance company), and require speculation because the actual career will never take place. Here, even the best efforts of a trial judge would be disproved by actual events. A more accurate apportionment would result from awarding a percentage of the professional's actual earnings. Such methodology, however, runs afoul of the statute's reference to property "acquired during a marriage." W. Va. Code § 48-2-1(e)(1). The proper place for consideration of earning capacity is in an award of permanent alimony. *See* W. Va. Code § 48-2-16 (1986).

On the whole, a degree of any kind results primarily from the efforts of the student who earns it. Financial and emotional support are important, as are homemaker services, but they bear no logical relation to the value of the resulting degree. We therefore hold, in accordance with the majority view, that a professional degree or license earned during marriage is not marital property subject to equitable distribution.

II

Although we decline to follow New York in its holding on marital property, we agree that to allow a student spouse to leave a marriage with all the benefits of additional education and a professional license without compensating the spouse who bore many of the burdens incident to procuring the degree would be unfair. The supporting spouse in this case made financial contributions to her husband's education with the expectation that his degree would mean a higher standard of living for them both. She made personal financial sacrifices and consented to a lower standard of living than she would have enjoyed had her husband been employed. She postponed her own career plans and presumably overlooked many current needs for the prospect of future material benefits. The appellant's sacrifices would have been rewarded had the marriage endured. The divorce has left Rebecca Hoak at a substantial disadvantage when compared with her ex-husband.

Many courts have resolved this inequity by awarding "reimbursement alimony" to the working spouse. As the name indicates, reimbursement alimony is designed to repay or reimburse the supporting spouse for his or her financial contributions to the professional education of the student spouse. Unlike an award based on the value of a professional degree, reimbursement alimony is based on the actual amount of contributions, and does not require a judge to guess about future earnings, inflation, the relative values of the spouses' contributions, etc.

We note that reimbursement between former spouses as a general rule is neither desirable nor practical. Marriage is not a business arrangement, and this Court would be loathe to promote any more tallying of respective debits and credits than already occurs in the average household . . . . [H]owever, every joint undertaking has its bounds of fairness. Where a partner to marriage takes the benefits of his spouse's support in obtaining a professional degree or license with the understanding that future benefits will accrue and inure to both of them, and the marriage is then terminated without the supported spouse giving anything in return, an unfairness has occurred that calls for a remedy.

We therefore conclude that the trial judge in a divorce proceeding may in an appropriate case award reimbursement alimony to a working spouse who contributed financially to the professional education of a student spouse, where the contribution was made with the expectation of achieving a higher standard of living for the family unit, and the couple did not realize that expectation due to divorce.

Determining the amount of reimbursement alimony will be within the discretion of the trial court. Recognizing that the amount of reimbursement alimony depends on the facts in each case, we do not adopt a specific method for computing that amount. The trial court, if it concludes that reimbursement is merited, should try to make a fair and reasonable award based on whatever method it deems appropriate. In cases such as the one before us, both reimbursement and rehabilitative alimony may be appropriate.

We do not hold that every person who contributes to the education of a spouse is entitled to reimbursement alimony. As mentioned above, the supporting spouse in a marriage of many years should be compensated in the division of marital property. *See* W. Va. Code § 8-2-32(c)(3). Similarly, reimbursement alimony would be inappropriate where the professional degree was not sought with the expectation of achieving a higher standard of living for the family. When, for example, a homemaker of many years returns to school for a teaching certificate, or when a successful executive takes a sabbatical to pursue a doctorate in philosophy or literature, the supporting spouse should not ordinarily be reimbursed for contributions to the other's education.

NOTES AND QUESTIONS

1. *Is a Medical Degree Property?* In a footnote not reproduced above, Justice Brotherton raised a number of questions about the method one would use in evaluating a medical degree if it were deemed to be marital property. Brotherton wrote: "The writer cannot refrain from making a few observations on the difficulty of setting and apportioning the value of a professional degree. There is the obvious problem of guessing annual income correctly without enslaving the degree-holder to a lifestyle that he or she would not have chosen absent an obligation to pay half its value to a dependent spouse. Beyond that, should there be an offset for the discounted value of the homemaker and childbearing services that the professional spouse will never enjoy due to the divorce? Further, if we place a value on homemaker services in arriving at a fair ratio for distributing the value of the degree, should we also 'pay' the student for his or her contributions in the way of long hours in the lab and the library? And, to the same point, how much of a medical degree is attributable to the actual years spent in medical school, as opposed to undergraduate courses in biology and chemistry, or other life experiences that contribute to making a good doctor?" Is there an adequate response to the judge's questions?

2. *Defining Marital Property.* With no-fault divorce quite common in the United States and with the law of domestic relations becoming more emphatic that both spouses should share equitably in the assets of the marriage, the need to define "marital property" has become more and more pressing. Certain types of assets — pensions, disability payments, and personal injury awards — have posed particularly difficult problems akin to those in *Hoak v. Hoak*. Whether such assets constitute marital property often turns on whether they are viewed as compensation for past services or investments or as a replacement for future income. If they are the latter, then they are marital property; if the former, they are not. In regard to pensions, courts have become increasingly willing to acknowledge one spouse's property interest in the pension of the other. For a relatively recent case in which a badly divided court attempted to sort out such problems, see *Morrison v. Morrison*, 692 S.W.2d 601 (Ark. 1985).

3. *Business Goodwill.* In regard to intangible assets, courts have been more receptive to finding business goodwill to be a marital asset than they have professional degrees. For a summary of this development, see *Prahinski v. Prahinski*, 582 A.2d 784 (Md. 1990), a case in which the general principle was acknowledged, although the court determined that because of the special nature of the legal profession, a non-lawyer spouse could not claim an interest in her husband's law practice, even though she had worked with him as a legal secretary. (The court reasoned that she could not because lawyers are prohibited from taking

in non-lawyer partners in their practice.)

4. *Jobs as Property.* In 1986, the European Court of Human Rights ruled in *Van Marle and Others v. The Netherlands*, 8 Eur. H.R. Rep. 483 (1986), that Van Marle, an accountant, had a "property right" in the use of the title "accountant" that was protected by the European Convention for the Protection of Human Rights and Fundamental Freedoms. The Netherlands had adopted a new occupation licensing law that specified that only those with certain professional qualifications could use the title "accountant." Van Marle had worked as an accountant for several years but lacked the specified prerequisites. In *Board of Regents v. Roth*, 408 U.S. 564 (1972), the United States Supreme Court refused to recognize a property right per se in employment.

[3.] Community Property

The modern concept of community property is rooted in the idea of marriage as an economic partnership. In community property jurisdictions (Arizona, California, Idaho, Louisiana, Nevada, New Mexico, Texas, Washington, and Wisconsin), all earnings and property acquired with those earnings during a marriage are jointly owned by both spouses in undivided shares of equal value. Upon dissolution of the marriage by death or divorce, the surviving spouse is automatically entitled to a 50% share of community property. Community property does not include property owned by either spouse prior to marriage or separate property acquired by gift, devise, or inheritance during the marriage. Community property states divide over the question of whether income from separate property during the marriage is also community property.

Although the basic concept of community property is straightforward, the operation of a community property system can be quite complex. Couples who move back and forth between community property and common law jurisdictions pose particularly thorny problems. Issues also frequently arise relating to the right to manage the jointly owned property. In most community property states, gifts from one spouse to a third party can be set aside by the non-donor spouse if the object of the gift was jointly owned.

At one time, the situation in common law marital property states differed dramatically from that in community property jurisdictions. However, in recent years, common law jurisdictions have increasingly embraced community property concepts. The Uniform Marital Property Act incorporates so many features of community property that the difference almost disappears. The highly influential Uniform Probate Code has been amended to include many community property features, and in divorce cases, the American law of domestic relations now places greater emphasis on the equitable distribution of property than it does on maintenance and support of former spouses. While important differences remain, there is a clear trend toward ensuring that both spouses share equally in the economic acquisitions of the marriage, regardless of the income of the respective spouses.

[C.] TRIBAL PROPERTY

In *Johnson v. M'Intosh*, 21 U.S. (8 Wheat.) 543 (1823) (discussed in Chapter 1), Chief Justice John Marshall described the Native Americans of the United States as possessing a different conception of property than that held by European Americans. In invalidating land transfers between members of the Illinois and Piankeshaw tribes and non-Indian land speculators, Marshall ruled that title to Indian land was held by the United States government and the particular tribes, with the United States owning the fee interest and the tribes retaining a right of occupancy that could not be extinguished by private transfer. Tribal rights could be relinquished only to the federal government; hence Indian property rights were subject to a type of restraint on alienation which would ordinarily be unacceptable in the Anglo-American property system.

In 1887, the United States Congress enacted the Dawes Act (also known as the General Allotment Act) in an effort to convert tribally-owned land into individual parcels owned by individual Native Americans. Although the parcels transferred to individual Native American owners were subject to a 25 year restraint on alienation, the land was to be freely alienable after that. By 1934, when Congress repealed the Dawes Act, approximately 90 million acres of Indian land had been transferred to non-Indian owners. In order to stop such transfers, the Indian Reorganization Act restored or extended the restraints on alienation on lands still owned by Native Americans. The effect was to restrict ownership to what amounted to an endless series of life estates and remainders which could not be implemented. As the following case illustrates, this approach created a new set of problems.

BABBITT v. YOUPEE
United States Supreme Court
519 U.S. 234 (1997)

JUSTICE GINSBURG delivered the opinion of the Court.

In this case, we consider for a second time the constitutionality of an escheat-to-tribe provision of the Indian Land Consolidation Act (ILCA). 96 Stat. 2519, as amended, 25 U.S.C. § 220. Specifically, we address § 207 of the ILCA, as amended in 1984. Congress enacted the original provision in 1983 to ameliorate the extreme fractionation problem attending a century-old allotment policy that yielded multiple ownership of single parcels of Indian land. Amended § 207 provides that certain small interests in Indian lands will transfer — or "escheat" — to the tribe upon the death of the owner of the interest. In *Hodel v. Irving*, 481 U.S. 704 (1987), this Court held that the original version of § 207 of the ILCA effected a taking of private property without just compensation, in violation of the Fifth Amendment to the United States Constitution. We now hold that amended § 207 does not cure the constitutional deficiency this Court identified in the original version of § 207.

I

In the late Nineteenth Century, Congress initiated an Indian land program that authorized the division of communal Indian property. Pursuant to this allotment policy, some Indian land was parceled out to individual tribal members. Lands not allotted to individual Indians were opened to non-Indians for settlement. *See* Indian General Allotment Act of 1887, ch. 119, 24 Stat. 388. Allotted lands were held in trust by the United States or owned by the allottee subject to restrictions on alienation. On the death of the allottee, the land descended according to the laws of the State or Territory in which the land was located. In 1910, Congress also provided that allottees could devise their interests in allotted land. Act of June 25, 1910, ch. 431, § 2, 36 Stat. 856.

The allotment policy "quickly proved disastrous for the Indians." *Irving*, 481 U.S. at 707. The program produced a dramatic decline in the amount of land in Indian hands. F. Cohen, Handbook of Federal Indian Law 138 (1982). And as allottees passed their interests on to multiple heirs, ownership of allotments became increasingly fractionated, with some parcels held by dozens of owners. Lawson, Heirship: The Indian Amoeba, reprinted in Hearing on S. 2480 and S. 2663 before the Senate Select Committee on Indian Affairs, 98th Cong., 2d Sess., 77 (1984). A number of factors augmented the problem: Because Indians often died without wills, many interests passed to multiple heirs; Congress' allotment Acts subjected trust lands to alienation restrictions that impeded holders of small interests from transferring those interests; Indian lands were not subject to state real estate taxes, which ordinarily serve as a strong disincentive to retaining small fractional interests in land. The fractionation problem proliferated with each succeeding generation as multiple heirs took undivided interests in allotments.

The administrative difficulties and economic inefficiencies associated with multiple undivided ownership in allotted lands gained official attention as early as 1928. Governmental administration of these fractionated interests proved costly, and individual owners of small undivided interests could not make productive use of the land. Congress ended further allotment in 1934. *See* Indian Reorganization Act, ch. 576, 48 Stat. 984. But that action left the legacy in place. As most owners had more than one heir, interests in lands already allotted continued to splinter with each generation. In the 1960's, congressional studies revealed that approximately half of all allotted trust lands were held in fractionated ownership; for over a quarter of allotted trust lands, individual allotments were held by more than six owners to a parcel. In 1983, Congress adopted the ILCA in part to reduce fractionated ownership of allotted lands. Section 207 of the Act — the "escheat" provision — prohibited the descent or devise of small fractional interests in allotments. Instead of passing to heirs, such fractional interests would escheat to the tribe, thereby consolidating the ownership of Indian lands. Congress defined the targeted fractional interest as one that both constituted 2 percent or less of the total acreage in an allotted tract and had earned less than $100 in the preceding year. Section 207 made no provision for the payment of compensation to those who held such interests.

In *Hodel v. Irving*, this Court invalidated [§ 207] on the ground that it effected a taking of property without just compensation, in violation of the Fifth Amendment. The appellees in *Irving* were, or represented, heirs or devisees of members of the Oglala Sioux Tribe. But for [§ 207], the appellees would have received 41 fractional interests in allotments; under [§ 207], those interests would escheat to the tribe. This Court tested the legitimacy of [§ 207] by considering its economic impact, its effect on investment-backed expectations, and the essential character of the measure. Turning first to the economic impact of [§ 207], the Court in *Irving* observed that the provision's income-generation test might fail to capture the actual economic value of the land. The Court next indicated that [§ 207] likely did not interfere with investment-backed expectations. Key to the decision in *Irving*, however, was the "extraordinary" character of the Government regulation. As this Court noted, [§ 207] amounted to the "virtual abrogation of the right to pass on a certain type of property." Such a complete abrogation of the rights of descent and devise could not be upheld.

II

In 1984, while *Irving* was still pending in the Court of Appeals for the Eighth Circuit, Congress amended [§ 207]. [98 Stat. 3173]. Amended [§ 207] differs from the original escheat provision in three relevant respects. First, an interest is considered fractional if it both constitutes 2 percent or less of the total acreage of the parcel and "is incapable of earning $100 in any one of the five years [following the] decedent's death" — as opposed to one year before the decedent's death in the original [§ 207]. If the interest earned less than $100 in any one of five years prior to the decedent's death, "there shall be a rebuttable presumption that such interest is incapable of earning $100 in any one of the five years following the death of the decedent." Second, in lieu of a total ban on devise and descent of fractional interests, amended § 207 permits devise of an otherwise escheatable interest to "any other owner of an undivided fractional interest in such parcel or tract" of land. Finally, tribes are authorized to override the provisions of amended § 207 through the adoption of their own codes governing the disposition of fractional interests; these codes are subject to the approval of the Secretary of the Interior. In *Irving*, "we express[ed] no opinion on the constitutionality of § 207 as amended."

Under amended § 207, the interests in this case would escheat to tribal governments. The initiating plaintiffs, respondents here, are the children and potential heirs of William Youpee. An enrolled member of the Sioux and Assiniboine Tribes of the Fort Peck Reservation in Montana, William Youpee died testate in October 1990. His will devised to respondents, all of them enrolled tribal members, his several undivided interests in allotted trust lands on various reservations in Montana and North Dakota. These interests were valued together at $1,239. Each interest was devised to a single descendant. Youpee's will thus perpetuated existing fractionation, but it did not splinter ownership further by bequeathing any single fractional interest to multiple devisees.

In 1992, in a proceeding to determine the heirs to, and claims against, William Youpee's estate, an Administrative Law Judge in the Department of the Interior found that interests devised to each of the respondents fell within the compass of amended § 207 and should therefore escheat to the tribal governments of the Fort Peck, Standing Rock, and Devils Lake Sioux Reservations. Respondents, asserting the unconstitutionality of amended § 207, appealed the order to the Department of the Interior Board of Indian Appeals. The Board, stating that it did not have jurisdiction to consider respondents' constitutional claim, dismissed the appeal.

Respondents then filed suit in the United States District Court for the District of Montana, naming the Secretary of the Interior as defendant, and alleging that amended § 207 of the ILCA violates the Just Compensation Clause of the Fifth Amendment. The District Court agreed with respondents and granted their request for declaratory and injunctive relief. The Court of Appeals for the Ninth Circuit affirmed. On the petition of the United States, we granted *certiorari,* and now affirm.

III

In determining whether the 1984 amendments to § 207 render the provision constitutional, we are guided by *Irving.* The United States maintains that the amendments, though enacted three years prior to the *Irving* decision, effectively anticipated the concerns expressed in the Court's opinion. As already noted, amended § 207 differs from the original in three relevant respects: It looks back five years instead of one to determine the income produced from a small interest, and creates a rebuttable presumption that this income stream will continue; it permits devise of otherwise escheatable interests to persons who already own an interest in the same parcel; and it authorizes tribes to develop their own codes governing the disposition of fractional interests. These modifications, according to the United States, rescue amended § 207 from the fate of its predecessor. The Government maintains that the revisions moderate the economic impact of the provision and temper the character of the Government's regulation; the latter factor weighed most heavily against the constitutionality of the original version of § 207.

The narrow revisions Congress made to § 207, without benefit of our ruling in *Irving,* do not warrant a disposition different from the one this Court announced and explained in *Irving.* Amended § 207 permits a five-year window rather than a one-year window to assess the income-generating capacity of the interest . . . . [A]rgument that this change substantially mitigates the economic impact of § 207 "misses the point." Amended § 207 still trains on income generated from the land, not on the value of the parcel. The Court observed in *Irving* that "even if . . . the income generated by such parcels may be properly thought of as *de minimis,*" the value of the land may not fit that description. The parcels at issue in *Irving* were valued by the Bureau of Indian Affairs at $2,700 and $1,816, amounts we found "not trivial." *Ibid.* The value of the disputed parcels in this case is not of a different order. In short, the economic impact of amended § 207 might still be palpable.

Even if the economic impact of amended § 207 is not significantly less than the impact of the original provision, the United States correctly comprehends that *Irving* rested primarily on the "extraordinary" character of the governmental regulation. *Irving* stressed that the original § 207 "amount[ed] to virtually the abrogation of the right to pass on a certain type of property — the small undivided interest — to one's heirs." The *Irving* Court further noted that the original § 207 "effectively abolish[ed] both descent and devise [of fractional interests] even when the passing of the property to the heir might result in consolidation of property." As the United States construes *Irving,* Congress cured the fatal infirmity in § 207 when it revised the section to allow transmission of fractional interests to successors who already own an interest in the allotment.

Congress' creation of an ever-so-slight class of individuals equipped to receive fractional interests by devise does not suffice, under a fair reading of *Irving*, to rehabilitate the measure. Amended § 207 severely restricts the right of an individual to direct the descent of his property. Allowing a decedent to leave an interest only to a current owner in the same parcel shrinks drastically the universe of possible successors. And, as the Ninth Circuit observed, the "very limited group [of permissible devisees] is unlikely to contain any lineal descendants." Moreover, amended § 207 continues to restrict devise "even in circumstances when the governmental purpose sought to be advanced, consolidation of ownership of Indian lands, does not conflict with the further descent of the property." William Youpee's will, the United States acknowledges, bequeathed each fractional interest to one heir. Giving effect to Youpee's directive, therefore, would not further fractionate Indian land holdings.

The United States also contends that amended § 207 satisfies the Constitution's demand because it does not diminish the owner's right to use or enjoy property during his lifetime, and does not affect the right to transfer property at death through non-probate means. These arguments did not persuade us in *Irving* and they are no more persuasive today.

The third alteration made in amended § 207 also fails to bring the provision outside the reach of this Court's holding in *Irving*. Amended § 207 permits tribes to establish their own codes to govern the disposition of fractional interests; if approved by the Secretary of the Interior, these codes would govern in lieu of amended § 207. The United States does not rely on this new provision to defend the statute. Nor does it appear that the United States could do so at this time: Tribal codes governing disposition of escheatable interests have apparently not been developed. For the reasons stated, the judgment of the Court of Appeals for the Ninth Circuit is *Affirmed.*

JUSTICE STEVENS, dissenting.

Section 207 of the Indian Land Consolidation Act did not, in my view, effect an unconstitutional taking of William Youpee's right to make a testamentary disposition of his property . . . . [T]he Federal Government, like a State, has a valid interest in removing legal impediments to the productive development of real estate. For this reason, the Court has repeatedly "upheld the power of the State to condition the retention of a property right upon the performance of an act within a limited period of time." [Citation omitted.] I remain convinced that "Congress has ample power to require the owners of fractional interests in allotted lands to consolidate their holdings during their lifetimes or to face the risk that their interests will be deemed to be abandoned." The federal interest in minimizing the fractionated ownership of Indian lands — and thereby paving the way to the productive development of their property — is strong enough to justify the legislative remedy created by § 207, provided, of course, that affected owners have adequate notice of the requirements of the law and an adequate opportunity to adjust their affairs to protect against loss.

NOTES AND QUESTIONS

1. Note that the complaining parties in the above case are not objecting to the government-imposed restraint on alienation, but only to the escheat provision of the statute. In footnotes not reproduced above, Justice Ginsburg cited both *Penn Central* (under which *Hodel v. Irving* had been decided) and *Lucas*. Does it make sense to rely upon what are essentially land use cases to decide a question like the one posed in *Babbitt v. Youpee*?

2. *Tribal Property Rights.* A full discussion of Native-American property rights is far beyond the scope of this section. While many Native Americans own land outside of reservation borders, the 550 governmentally recognized Indian nations still own approximately 2% of the United States (or more than 52.5 million acres). Rules regulating the allocation and use of tribally owned land are the province of the tribes themselves (subject to federal law), and the reservations are not under the jurisdiction of the states in which they are located. Whether reservation land is held by the tribe collectively or by individual tribal members, the ownership interest is usually described as "trust status," implying a relationship with the land quite different than that traditionally associated with the Anglo-American fee simple owner.

3. *The Estate of Fee Tail.* The property rights afforded to Indian owners as a result of the Indian Reorganization Act of 1934 bear a certain resemblance to those associated with the old English estate of fee tail. The estate of fee tail was designed to ensure that land remain the property of a specific family, and it accomplished that purpose by requiring that the next owner of the land be the issue (the "heir of the body") of the current owner. Combined with the doctrine of primogeniture, which gave the oldest son the right to inherit all of the father's real property, the fee tail guaranteed that entailed estates would stay in the same family from one generation to the next. It also made it possible to avoid the fractionalization problem that prompted the statute at issue in *Babbitt v. Youpee*. The estate of fee tail, long abolished in the United States, is discussed in Chapter 4.

NOTES AND QUESTIONS

Chapter 6

LANDLORD AND TENANT LAW, HOUSING CODES, AND RENT CONTROL

This chapter examines property law concepts that affect the way in which individuals can find places to live. The first part of the chapter deals with the landlord-tenant relationship, one of the oldest legal relationships in Anglo-American law. The chapter then deals with public interventions that place limitations on that relationship, first considering local housing codes and then considering rent control legislation.

Today, about 34% of all Americans — about 40 million households — rent their dwellings. The collapse of the residential real estate market in the recent recession at the end of the previous decade led to an increase in the number of Americans who rent, rather than own, their residences. Leasing rather than ownership is also common for commercial and industrial uses of real property.

Widespread use of leasing as a form of property ownership requires consideration of the landlord and tenant relationship. Although it is conventional to say that the landlord and tenant share ownership of the property subject to the lease, the relationship is considerably more complicated than that. It is also customary to say that a revolution in the landlord-tenant relationship in the United States occurred in the second half of the 20th century. Certainly, the reality of modern landlord-tenant relationships shares little in common with traditional landlord-tenant law which was crafted in an agricultural era when leases typically dealt with open land. Real property concepts were imposed on the relationship of landlord and tenant, much to the advantage of the landlord and the disadvantage of the tenant.

The traditional, property-based law of landlord and tenant embodied the following principles:

(1) A tenancy is created by the landlord's conveyance of an interest in real property to the tenant.

(2) Conveyances will be construed according to express terms, conditions, and covenants. Few implied terms, conditions, or covenants, if any, are found in conveyances.

(3) The express covenants of both parties are generally independent of each other. A party is not excused from honoring its covenants or performing its duties because the other party has breached one or more of its material covenants.

(4) Absent an express covenant to the contrary, upon a party's breach, the non-breaching party has no obligation to minimize the loss incurred by the

non-breaching party. The non-breaching party is entitled to recover all its losses from the breaching party.

(5) Absent an express covenant to the contrary, the parties are under no obligation to act reasonably or to act in good faith while performing their respective duties and obligations. However, the parties will be liable to each other in tort for fraud, misrepresentation, and other similar wrongdoing.

(6) The tenant's interest is merely a purchase from the landlord for a prescribed period of time of the right to be in lawful, actual possession of the demised premises. If the tenant is wrongfully ousted from the demised premises, then the tenant's performance of covenants and obligations is not excused unless the ouster is caused by the wrongful conduct of the landlord or the landlord's agents. If the demised premises are totally useless to the tenant, then the tenant's performance of covenants and obligations is excused if the uselessness is caused by the wrongful conduct of the landlord or the landlord's agents.

Kelley, *Any Reports of the Death of the Property Law Paradigm for Leases Have Been Greatly Exaggerated*, 41 Wayne L. Rev. 1563, 1566–67 (1995).

However, courts eventually developed fictions to overcome the rigidities of this property-based landlord-tenant law and to mitigate some of the disadvantages imposed on tenants. But fictions are awkward, and it remained for courts and legislatures in the past five decades to recast the landlord-tenant relationship in modern doctrine more compatible with an urban society. While the conventional wisdom for some time has been that the traditional law was overturned in the 1960s and 1970s — *see* Rabin, *The Revolution in Residential Landlord-Tenant Law: Cases and Consequences*, 69 Cornell L. Rev. 517 (1984) — there is dissent from the view that the changes in those two decades were truly revolutionary. As Professor Maryanne Glendon of Harvard Law School noted about 30 years ago:

[W]hat has been called a revolution appears, in historical perspective, to have been no more or less than the culmination, in one area of the law, of certain long-standing trends that have transformed not only landlord-tenant law, but private law generally over the past century. Lease law was never pure property law. By the turn of the century, and up to the 1960s, it was an amalgam of real and personal property principles and of property and contract notions.

Glendon, *The Transformation of American Landlord-Tenant Law*, 23 B.C. L. Rev. 503, 504 (1982).

Professor Glendon also argues that statutes, more than case law, have been most instrumental in reshaping landlord and tenant doctrine. Most states have statutes on landlord and tenant obligations that have been substantially revised since the 1960s. Many have legislation based on the model Uniform Residential Landlord and Tenant Act (URLTA) proposed by the National Conference of Commissioners on Uniform State Laws. Throughout this chapter, the role of both courts and legislatures in shaping landlord-tenant law is explored. Remember, when you read the cases, that the parties can often, but not always, write terms into a lease that change the common law. For a discussion of the contemporary landlord-tenant landscape, see Schwemm, *Why Do Landlords Still Discriminate (and What Can Be Done About It)*, 40 J. MARSHALL L. REV. 455 (2007).

[A.] THE LANDLORD-TENANT RELATIONSHIP

[1.] Lease for Intended Use

ANDERSON DRIVE-IN THEATRE, INC. v. KIRKPATRICK

Indiana Court of Appeals
110 N.E.2d 506 (1953)

ROYSE, J.

Appellees brought this action against appellant for rent under the terms of a twenty-five year lease of real estate owned by appellees. The complaint was in the usual form. Appellant answered by a denial of the allegations of each rhetorical paragraph of the complaint. It also filed an amended second paragraph of answer and cross-complaint. Appellees' demurrer to that answer and cross-complaint was sustained. That ruling is the sole question presented by this appeal.

The lease which is the subject of this action provided the real estate was to be used for the construction and operation of a drive-in theatre and for any other lawful purpose not in competition with any business operated by a trailer camp situated immediately east of the leased property. The lease made no warranty as to the suitability of the land for the purpose which appellant intended to use it.

The material averments of the second amended paragraph of answer and cross-complaint may be summarized as follows: That appellees were farmers, and for a long time had been engaged in the cultivation of the land leased, and were possessed of full, accurate and complete knowledge of the future use of the land to be made by appellant; that appellees knew that appellant did not have knowledge of the nature and character of the land and depended upon representations of appellees that the said land was suitable for the purpose for which leased; that the land was either boggy or wet or muck ground; that it gave an outward appearance of being ordinary ground; but it would not carry or bear the weight of many tons of buildings and equipment necessary for appellant's purpose; that appellees knew that the surface of the land leased was soft and yielding, and that the weight of the necessary buildings and equipment for such outdoor theatre could not be borne by the land; that appellees, by the lease, warranted, either expressly or impliedly, that said land would be suitable for the purposes intended; that appellees, knowing the land was not fit and suitable for appellant's purposes, failed and neglected to give appellant the true facts as to the condition of said land, but purposely and knowingly either misrepresented the nature of said land or failed to reveal that the land was unsuitable for appellant's purposes; that after the lease was signed, appellant employed skilled and experienced persons to test the said land, and thereby learned that the land was entirely unfit for such purposes, and that appellees had concealed the fact that the land was unfit for appellant's purposes; that appellees knew that appellant did not know of the true character of the land, and that the only information appellant had about the character of the land was as described in the lease executed by both parties; that appellees knew that appellant would not execute the lease if the true facts as to the nature of the land were revealed to it.

The demurrer was on the grounds that the said answer and cross-complaint did not state facts sufficient to constitute an affirmative answer or cross-complaint against appellees.

In the memorandum to their demurrer appellees, in substance, asserted it is the law that because a lease designates the use to which the premises are to be put it does not imply that the premises are suitable or fit for the use intended; that in such matters the rule of caveat emptor applies; that nowhere in the written lease is there any warranty that the land was suitable for appellant's use; that any verbal representation made by appellees could not be claimed to vary the terms of the written agreement; that the cross-complaint avers after the execution of the lease appellant employed skilled and experienced persons to test the land to ascertain whether or not it would bear the weight of the buildings for its special use; that such allegation shows appellant was going to use the premises for a particular and special use with which it was familiar, but of which appellees had no knowledge, and it further shows appellant had the means and opportunity to have examined and tested the land prior to the execution of the lease.

Appellant contends its second paragraph of answer and cross-complaint alleges facts disclosing fraud which would vitiate the lease. In support of this contention it asserts its answer avers facts which show latent defects in the land which it was the duty of appellees to disclose to it.

In 51 C.J.S. (Landlord and Tenant), p. 964, § 304, it is stated:

> There is, as a general rule, no implied covenant on the part of the landlord that the demised premises are fit for the purposes for which they are rented or for the particular use for which they are intended by the tenant, as for the lessee's business, or that they comply with the requirements of public regulatory bodies, or that they shall continue fit for the purpose for which they were demised, and this is true, although the landlord knows the purpose for which the tenant intends to use the premises. In the absence of an express warranty or fraud, the rule of caveat emptor applies and the tenant is under a duty to investigate in order to determine the adaptability of the premises to the purposes for which they have been rented. It has been said, however, that an exception arises where there are concealed defects known to the landlord and not subject to disclosure by the tenant's examination, as where the landlord makes false representations concerning matters peculiarly within his own knowledge, and that the rule of caveat emptor does not apply as against the tenant where the landlord fraudulently represents the premises to be suitable for the tenant's use, although they contain latent defects rendering them unsuitable, which are unknown to the tenant. In this connection, however, it has been held that the landlord at the time of renting the premises need not exercise care to discover and inform the tenant of hidden defects.

In its brief appellant construes the foregoing to mean the landlord owes a duty to the tenant to disclose latent defects known to him and neither known to the tenant or reasonably discoverable by him.

The answer and cross-complaint herein do not allege appellees made any statements as to the nature of the land. They do not allege the defects were not reasonably discoverable. On the other hand it avers that after the execution of the lease it caused tests of the land to be made and thereby discovered its unsuitability. There are no averments that appellants did not have an opportunity to inspect the land or to make such tests before executing the lease.

A purchaser of property has no right to rely upon the representations of the vendor of the property as to its quality, where he has a reasonable opportunity of examining the property and judging for himself as to its qualities. *Shepard v. Goben* (Ind. 1895), 39 N.E. 506.

There is no implied warranty that leased premises are fit for the purposes for which they are let. When an action is based on fraudulent concealment, a duty to disclose the truth must be shown. The rule of caveat emptor applies in the relation of landlord and tenant unless material representations constituting fraud are specifically alleged, or there is a showing of a fiduciary relationship between the parties. *Swinton v. Whitinsville Sav. Bank* (Mass. 1942), 42 N.E.2d 808. In the last cited case the Supreme Judicial Court of Massachusetts stated the material allegations of the declaration in the following language:

> The declaration alleges that on or about September 12, 1938, the defendant sold the plaintiff a house in Newton to be occupied by the plaintiff and his family as a dwelling; that at the time of the sale the house "was infested with termites, an insect that is most dangerous and destructive to buildings"; that the defendant knew the house was so infested; that the plaintiff could not readily observe this condition upon inspection; that "knowing the internal destruction that these insects were creating in said house", the defendant falsely and fraudulently concealed from the plaintiff its true condition; that the plaintiff at the time of his purchase had no knowledge of the termites, exercised due care thereafter, and learned of them about August 30, 1940.

In affirming the action of the trial court in sustaining a demurrer, the court said:

> There is no allegation of any false statement or representation, or of the uttering of a half truth which may be tantamount to a falsehood. There is no intimation that the defendant by any means prevented the plaintiff from acquiring information as to the condition of the house. There is nothing to show any fiduciary relation between the parties, or that the plaintiff stood in a position of confidence toward or dependence upon the defendant. So far as appears the parties made a business deal at arm's length. The charge is concealment and nothing more; and it is concealment in the simple sense of mere failure to reveal, with nothing to show any peculiar duty to speak. The characterization of the concealment as false and fraudulent of course adds nothing in the absence of further allegations of fact.

If this defendant is liable on this declaration every seller is liable who fails to disclose any nonapparent defect known to him in the subject of the sale which materially reduces its value and which the buyer fails to discover. Similarly it would seem that every buyer would be liable who fails to disclose any nonapparent virtue known to him in the subject of the purchase which materially enhances its value and of which the seller is ignorant. The law has not yet, we believe, reached the point of imposing upon the frailties of human nature a standard so idealistic as this.

Based on the authorities referred to herein, we are of the opinion the trial court properly sustained the demurrer to the second amended answer and cross-complaint.

Judgment affirmed.

NOTES AND QUESTIONS

1. *Caveat Emptor.* The principal case, which states the accepted rule, illustrates the traditional set of concepts that apply to the landlord-tenant relationship. Notice the extent to which the court places its decision on property law (no implied covenant) as compared with tort law (no liability for fraudulent concealment). If the issue is really a question of risk distribution, why doesn't tort law apply? Do you agree with the way in which the court distributes the risk of loss? Courts have departed from the *caveat emptor* rule for defective conditions in vendor-purchaser cases, *Weintraub v. Krobatsch*, 317 A.2d 68 (N.J. 1974), and have found ways to hold landlords responsible for defective conditions in landlord-tenant cases. See the discussion of constructive eviction, *supra*.

2. *Commercial vs. Residential Leases.* This case also illustrates the difference between commercial and residential leases with respect to landlord and tenant responsibilities. There is no implied covenant in this commercial lease that the property be fit for its intended use. Likewise, there is no such implied covenant in a lease for a residence, but is the effect the same? The buyer of the house in *Swinton v. Whitinsville Sav. Bank* (cited in the above case) can have the bugs removed at minimal expense, but making the land fit for its intended purpose in the principal case is either impossible or prohibitively expensive. As the materials that follow will illustrate, American courts eventually took a more sympathetic view to the position of potential renters and home purchasers.

3. *Furnished House Exception.* Many jurisdictions that otherwise followed the rule of *caveat emptor* recognized an exception to the traditional "no guarantee" rule in the case of short term rentals of premises that were furnished. *Hacker v. Nitschke*, 39 N.E.2d 644 (Mass. 1942).

[2.] The Duty to Put the Tenant into Possession

ADRIAN v. RABINOWITZ

New Jersey Supreme Court
186 A. 29 (1935)

HEHER, J.

On April 30th, 1934, defendant, by an indenture, leased to plaintiff certain store premises in the main business district of the city of Paterson for the term of six months, commencing on June 15th next ensuing, at a stipulated monthly rent payable in advance; and the gravamen of this action is the breach of an obligation thereby imposed upon the lessor, as is said, to deliver to the lessee possession of the demised premises at the beginning of the term so prescribed. The state of demand is in two counts: The first seems to be grounded upon an asserted implied duty "to give and deliver possession" of the demised premises on the first day of the term; and the second, upon what plaintiff conceives to be an express covenant to put the lessee in possession on that day.

The lessee stipulated to devote the premises to the conduct of the shoe business; and he was given an option to renew the lease for an additional term of six months. Rent for the first month of the term was paid upon delivery of the lease[,] and the payment was acknowledged therein.

At the time of the execution of the contract, the premises were tenanted by another, who failed to respond to the landlord's notice to vacate on June 15th. The landlord deemed himself obliged to institute dispossess proceedings, which terminated in a judgment of removal. This judgment was executed on July 7th, 1934, and plaintiff took possession two days later.

The District Court judge, sitting without a jury, found for the plaintiff on the basic issue, and measured the damages at $500, "the loss sustained by plaintiff in the resale of the seasonable merchandise." He also ruled that plaintiff was not liable for rent for the portion of the term he was deprived of possession, and, making allowance for this, he awarded $25 to defendant on her set-off for rent due for the month beginning July 15th, 1934.

It is apparent that the tenant in possession when the lease was executed wrongfully held over after the termination of the tenancy; and the primary question, raised by motions to nonsuit and direct a verdict in defendant's favor, is whether, expressly or by implication, the contract imposed upon the lessor the duty of putting the lessee in actual and exclusive possession of the demised premises at the beginning of the term.

It seems to be the rule in this state that a covenant for quiet enjoyment, as one of the covenants of title, is not to be implied from the mere relation of landlord and tenant, even when that relation springs from a deed. But here the lessor expressly covenanted that the lessee, "on paying the said monthly rent, and performing the covenants aforesaid, shall and may peaceably and quietly have, hold and enjoy the said demised premises for the term aforesaid." And it has been held elsewhere that a covenant for quiet enjoyment, similarly phrased, imposed upon the lessor the obligation to deliver possession of the premises on the first day of the term. Yet a covenant for quiet enjoyment is generally interpreted to secure the lessee against the acts or hindrances of the lessor, and persons deriving their right or title through him, or from paramount title, and does not protect the lessee from interference by strangers with his possession.

It remains to consider whether the lessor, in the absence of an express undertaking to that effect, is under a duty to put the lessee in actual as well as legal possession of the demised premises at the commencement of the term. We are of the view that he is. There seems to be no dissent from the doctrine that the lessor impliedly covenants that the lessee shall have the legal right of possession at the beginning of the term. But there is a contrariety of view as to whether this implied obligation extends as well to actual possession, especially where, as here, the prior tenant wrongfully holds over.

In some of our American jurisdictions, the rule obtains that, while the lessee is entitled to have the legal right of possession, there is no implied covenant to protect the lessee against wrongful acts of strangers. The English rule is that, where the term is to commence in futuro, there is an implied undertaking by the lessor that the premises shall be open to the lessee's entry, legally and actually, when the time for possession under the lease arrives. This rule has the support of respectable American authority. And in an early case in this state, where the premises, while tenanted, were let for a term to begin on a fixed day in the future, and the lessor, in an action of covenant brought by the lessee for failure to deliver possession on the first day of the term, or any time thereafter, pleaded inability to deliver possession because of the wrongful holding over by the tenant, this court construed the stipulation for possession at the commencement of the term "as an express covenant to let the premises, and give possession" on the first day of the term, and held that the lessor, having failed in the performance of the duty thus undertaken, was liable to the action. *Kerr v. Whitaker*, 3 N.J.L. 247.

The English rule, so-called, is on principle much the better one. It has the virtue, ordinarily, of effectuating the common intention of the parties to give actual and exclusive possession of the premises to the lessee on the day fixed for the commencement of the term. This is what the lessee generally bargains for; and it is the thing the lessor undertakes to give. Such being the case, there is no warrant for placing upon the lessee, without express stipulation to that effect, the burden of ousting, at his own expense, the tenant wrongfully holding over, or the trespasser in possession of the premises without color of right at the commencement of the term; and thus to impose upon him who is not in possession of the evidence the burden of establishing the respective rights and duties of the lessor and the possessor of the lands inter se, as well as the consequences of the delay incident to the adjudication of the controversy, and the obligation to pay rent during that period. As was said by Baron Vaughan in *Coe v. Clay*, [5 Bing. 440, 130 Eng. Reprint 113] "He who lets agrees to give possession, and not merely to give a chance of a law suit." This doctrine is grounded in reason and logic. The underlying theory is that the parties contemplated, as an essential term of their undertaking, without which the lease would not have been made, that the lessor should, at the beginning of the term, have the premises open to the entry and exclusive possession of the lessee.

This is certainly the normal course of dealing, and, in the absence of stipulation to the contrary, is to be regarded as the parties' understanding of the lessor's covenant to deliver possession of the demised premises at the time prescribed for the commencement of the term.

There is an obvious distinction, which seems to have been overlooked in some of the cases rejecting the English doctrine, between a wrongful possession at the time fixed for the commencement of the term and the acts of trespassers who intrude after the lessee has been given the possession provided by the contract.

It is worthy of note that here the lessor, apparently conscious of a contractual obligation in the premises, initiated and prosecuted to a conclusion the proceedings requisite for dispossession of the hold-over tenant. She interpreted the contract as imposing the duty.

Therefore, the motions for a nonsuit and a direction of a verdict in defendant's favor on the ground that there was no evidence of a breach of her undertaking to deliver possession of the demised premises at the stipulated time were rightly denied.

NOTES AND QUESTIONS

1. *The Conflicting Rules on Delivery of Possession.* Both the American and English rules agree that the landlord must put the tenant in legal possession at the start of the term. This means the landlord must ensure that there is no third party with paramount title; must not attempt to create rights in a third party, e.g. leasing to a third party after already entering into the lease with the incoming tenant; and must not interfere in any other way with a tenant's attempt to take possession at the appointed time.

The issue is whether the landlord must ensure that the tenant can take actual possession at the start of the lease. The English rule applies unless this obligation has been expressly negated in the lease. This is the majority rule in the United States. If the tenant cannot take possession, the tenant may terminate the lease and has a cause of action against the landlord for damages, as in the principal case. The landlord in turn has a cause of action against the person wrongfully in possession. Another argument for the English rule is that the landlord is in a better position to prevent wrongdoers from coming on the premises, presumably because she has possession of the property prior to the beginning of the lease term. The landlord is only required to ensure actual possession on the first day of the term; subsequent interference is the tenant's problem.

Under the American rule, if someone has wrongful possession of the property, the tenant has a cause of action against them for damages and possession, but does not have a cause of action against the landlord, nor a basis for termination of the lease. Rationales for the American rule include 1) the tenant has an adequate legal remedy (for possession, damages or both) against the wrongful occupant, and 2) it is unreasonable to hold the landlord liable for a third party's independent wrong.

2. *The Correct Policy.* Which rule is preferable? How does the court in the principal case imply a covenant of quiet enjoyment in a transaction that is a

conveyance of property? Why is the intention of the parties critical? One commentator has suggested the English rule is supported by "principles involving the expectations of the parties and fundamental fairness." Weissenberger, *The Landlord's Duty to Deliver Possession: The Overlooked Reform*, 46 U. CIN. L. REV. 937, 942 (1977).

Are there any justifications for the American rule? In *Hannan v. Dusch*, 153 S.E. 824, 828 (Va. 1930), the court stated: "[The tenant's remedy is against] a former tenant who wrongfully holds over, because the landlord has not covenanted against the wrongful acts of another and should not be held responsible for such a tort unless he has expressly so contracted. This accords with the general rule as to other wrongdoers." Why is the allocation of tort liability a factor in a property case?

Noted legal historian Lawrence Friedman makes the following observation concerning the reasons behind the American rule.

> [T]he "American rule" was not quite so monstrous when applied to tracts of nonresidential land, and particularly under the conditions of cloudy titles and uncertainty, in nineteenth-century land law. To some courts, the rule seemed quite logical. A lease is a conveyance, and the lessee gets the right to possession when the lease goes into effect. Arguably, it is the lessee who then has the right to recover possession from a hold-over tenant, not the landlord. This assumes a kind of symmetrical relationship between the landlord and the tenant, and under the facts of the old cases, I suspect that was not so absurd.

Comments on Rabin, The Revolution in Residential Landlord-Tenant Law: Causes and Consequences, 69 CORNELL L. REV. 585, 587 (1984).

3. *Statutory Reform.* The Uniform Residential Landlord and Tenant Act (URLTA) § 301 states that "A landlord shall deliver physical possession of the dwelling unit to the tenant at the commencement of the term of the lease." If the landlord does not deliver possession, the tenant can terminate the lease before the landlord delivers possession, or demand damages and possession from the landlord. § 405.

For another example, see N.Y. Real Property Law § 223-a: "In the absence of an express provision to the contrary, there shall be implied in every lease of real property a condition that the lessor will deliver possession at the beginning of the term. In the event of breach of such implied condition the lessee shall have the right to rescind the lease and to recover the consideration paid. Such right shall not be deemed inconsistent with any right of action he may have to recover damages."

[3.] Sublease and Assignment

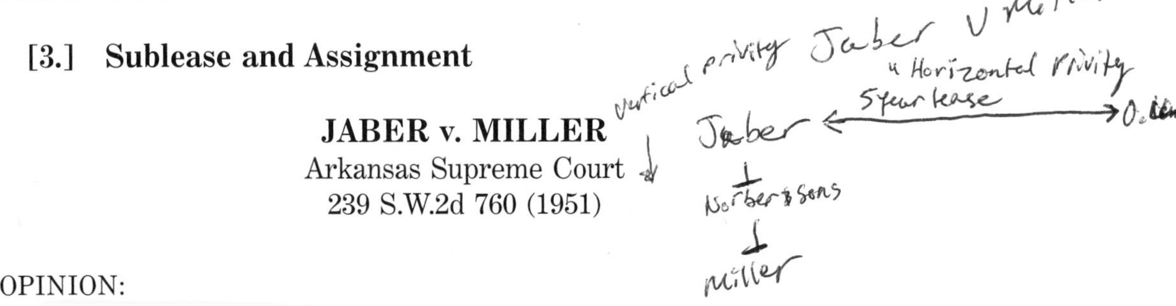

JABER v. MILLER

Arkansas Supreme Court
239 S.W.2d 760 (1951)

OPINION:

This is a suit to obtain cancellation of fourteen promissory notes, each in the sum of $175, held by the appellant, Jaber. The plaintiff's theory is that these notes represent monthly rent upon a certain business building in Fort Smith for the period beginning January 1, 1950, and ending March 1, 1951. The building was destroyed by fire on December 3, 1949, and the plaintiff contends that his obligation to pay rent then terminated. The defendant contends that the notes were given not for rent but as deferred payments for the assignment of a lease formerly held by Jaber. The chancellor, in an opinion reflecting a careful study of the matter, concluded that the notes were intended to be rental payments and therefore should be canceled.

In 1945 Jaber rented the building from its owner for a five-year term beginning March 1, 1946, and ending March 1, 1951. The lease reserved a monthly rent of $200 and provided that the lease would terminate if the premises were destroyed by fire. Jaber conducted a rug shop in the building until 1949, when he sold his stock of merchandise at public auction and transferred the lease to Norber & Son. Whether this instrument of transfer is an assignment or a sublease is the pivotal issue in this case.

In form the document is an assignment rather than a sublease. It is entitled "Contract and Assignment." After reciting the existence of the five-year lease the instrument provides that Jaber "hereby transfers and assigns" to Norber & Son "the aforesaid lease contract . . . for the remainder of the term of said lease." It also provides that "in consideration of the sale and assignment of said lease contract" Norber & Son have paid Jaber $700 in cash and have executed five promissory notes for $700 each, due serially at specified four month intervals. Norber & Son agree to pay to the owner of the property the stipulated rental of $200 a month, and Jaber reserves the right to retake possession if Norber & Son fail to pay the rent or the notes. The instrument contains no provision governing the rights of the parties in case the building is destroyed by fire.

Later on the plaintiff, Miller, obtained a transfer of the lease from Norber & Son. Miller, being unable to pay the $700 notes as they came due, arranged with Jaber to divide the payments into monthly installments of $175 each. He and the Norbers accordingly executed the notes now in controversy, which Jaber accepted in substitution for those of the original notes that were still unpaid. When the premises burned Miller contended that Jaber's transfer to Norber & Son had been a sublease rather than an assignment and that the notes therefore represented rent. Miller now argues that, under the rule that a sublease terminates when the primary lease terminates, his sublease ended when the fire had the effect of terminating the original lease.

In most jurisdictions the question of whether an instrument is an assignment or a sublease is determined by principles applicable to feudal tenures. In a line of cases beginning in the year 1371 the English courts worked out the rules for distinguishing between an assignment and a sublease. The doctrine established in England is quite simple: If the instrument purports to transfer the lessee's estate for the entire remainder of the term it is an assignment, regardless of its form or of the parties' intention. Conversely, if the instrument purports to transfer the lessee's estate for less than the entire term — even for a day less — it is a sublease, regardless of its form or of the parties' intention.

The arbitrary distinction drawn at common law is manifestly at variance with the usual conception of assignments and subleases. We think of an assignment as the outright transfer of all or part of an existing lease, the assignee stepping into the shoes of the assignor. A sublease, on the other hand, involves the creation of a new tenancy between the sublessor and the sublessee, so that the sublessor is both a tenant and a landlord. The common law distinction is logical only in the light of feudal property law.

In feudal times everyone except the king held land by tenure from someone higher in the hierarchy of feudal ownership. "The king himself holds land which is in every sense his own; no one else has any proprietary right in it; but if we leave out of account this royal demesne, then every acre of land is held of the king. The person whom we may call its owner, the person who has the right to use and abuse the land, to cultivate it or leave it uncultivated, to keep all others off it, holds the land of the king either immediately or mediately. In the simplest case he holds it immediately of the king; only the king and he have rights in it. But it well may happen that between him and the king there stand other persons; Z holds immediately of Y, who holds of X, who holds of V, who holds . . . of A, who holds of the king." POLLOCK & MAITLAND, HISTORY OF ENGLISH LAW (2d ed.), vol. I, p. 232. In feudal law each person owed duties, such as that of military service or the payment of rent, to his overlord. To enforce these duties the overlord had the remedy of distress, being the seizure of chattels found on the land.

It is evident that in feudal theory a person must himself have an estate in the land in order to maintain his place in the structure of ownership. Hence if a tenant transferred his entire term he parted with his interest in the property. The English courts therefore held that the transferee of the entire term held of the original lessor, that such a transferee was bound by the covenants in the original lease, and that he was entitled to enforce whatever duties that lease imposed upon the landlord. The intention of the parties had nothing to do with the matter; the sole question was whether the first lessee retained a reversion that enabled him to hold his place in the chain of ownership.

The injustice of these inflexible rules has often been pointed out. Suppose that A makes a lease to B for a certain rental. B then executes to C what both parties intend to be a sublease as that term is generally understood, but the sublease is for the entire term. If C in good faith pays his rent to B, as the contract requires, he does so at his peril. For the courts say that the contract is really an assignment, and therefore C's primary obligation is to A if the latter elects to accept C as his tenant. Consequently A can collect the rent from the subtenant even though the sublessor has already been paid. For a fuller discussion of this possibility of double liability on the part of the subtenant see Darling, *Is a Sublease for the Residue of a Lessee's Term in Effect an Assignment?*, 16 Am. L. Rev. 16, 21.

Not only may the common law rule operate with injustice to the subtenant; it can be equally harsh upon the sublessor. Again suppose that A makes a lease to B for a certain rental. B then makes to C what B considers a profitable sublease for twice the original rent. But B makes the mistake of attempting to sublet for the entire term instead of retaining a reversion of a day. The instrument is therefore an assignment, and if the original landlord acquires the subtenant's rights there is a merger which prevents B from being able to collect the increased rent. That was the situation in *Webb v. Russell*, 3 T.R. 393, 100 Eng. Reprint 639. The court felt compelled to recognize the merger, but in doing so Lord Kenyon said: "It seems to me, with all the inclination which we have to support the action (and we have hitherto delayed giving judgment in the hopes of being able to find some ground on which the plaintiff's demand might be sustained), that it cannot be supported. The defence which is made is made of a most unrighteous and unconscious nature; but unfortunately for the plaintiff the mode which she has taken to enforce her demand cannot be supported." Kent, in his Commentaries (14th ed.), p. 105, refers to this case as reaching an "inequitable result;" Williams and Eastwood, in their work on Real Property, p. 206, call it an "unpleasant result." Yet when the identical question arose in California the court felt bound to hold that the same distasteful merger had taken place. *Smiley v. Van Winkle*, 6 Calif. 605.

A decided majority of the American courts have adopted the English doctrine in its entirety. A minority of our courts have made timid but praiseworthy attempts to soften the harshness of the common law rule. In several jurisdictions the courts follow the intention of the parties in controversies between the sublessor and the sublessee, thus preserving the inequities of feudal times only when the original landlord is concerned.

In other jurisdictions the courts have gone as far as possible to find something that might be said to constitute a reversion in what the parties intended to be a sublease. In some States, notably Massachusetts, it has been held that if the sublessor reserves a right of re-entry for nonpayment of rent this is a sufficient reversionary estate to make the instrument a sublease. *Dunlap v. Bullard*, 131 Mass. 161. But even these decisions have been criticized on the ground that at common law a right of re-entry was a mere chose in action instead of a reversionary estate.

The appellee urges us to follow the Massachusetts rule and to hold that since Jaber reserved rights of reentry his transfer to Norber & Son was a sublease. We are not in sympathy with this view. It may be true that a right of re-entry for condition broken has now attained the status of an estate in Arkansas. Even so, the Massachusetts rule was adopted to carry out the intention of parties who thought they were making a sublease rather than an assignment. Here the instrument is in form an assignment, and it would be an obvious perversion of the rule to apply it as a means of defeating intention.

In this state of the law we do not feel compelled to adhere to an unjust rule which was logical only in the days of feudalism. The execution of leases is a very practical matter that occurs a hundred times a day without legal assistance. The layman appreciates the common sense distinction between a sublease and an assignment, but he would not even suspect the existence of the common law distinction. As Darling, *supra*, puts it: "Every one knows that a tenant may in turn let to others, and the latter thereby assumes no obligations to the owner of the property; but who would guess that this could only be done for a time falling short by something — a day or an hour is sufficient — of the whole term? And who, not familiar with the subject of feudal tenures, could give a reason why it is held to be so?" It was of such a situation that Holmes was thinking when he said: "It is revolting to have no better reason for a rule than that so it was laid down in the time of Henry IV. It is still more revolting if the grounds upon which it was laid down have vanished long since, and the rule simply persists from blind imitation of the past." *The Path of the Law*, 10 HARV. L. REV. 457, 469. The rule now in question was laid down some years before the reign of Henry IV.

The English distinction between an assignment and a sublease is not a rule of property in the sense that titles or property rights depend upon its continued existence. A lawyer trained in common law technicalities can prepare either instrument without fear that it will be construed to be the other. But for the less skilled lawyer or for the layman the common law rule is simply a trap that leads to hardship and injustice by refusing to permit the parties to accomplish the result they seek.

For these reasons we adopt as the rule in this State the principle that the intention of the parties is to govern in determining whether an instrument is an assignment or a sublease. If, for example, a tenant has leased an apartment for a year and is compelled to move to another city, we know of no reason why he should not be able to sublease it for a higher rent without needlessly retaining a reversion for the last day of the term. The duration of the primary term, as compared to the length of the sublease, may in some instances be a factor in arriving at the parties' intention, but we do not think it should be the sole consideration.

In the case at bar it cannot be doubted that the parties intended an assignment and not a sublease. The document is so entitled. All its language is that of an assignment rather than that of a sublease. The consideration is stated to be in payment for the lease and not in satisfaction of a tenant's debt to his landlord. The deferred payments are evidenced by promissory notes, which are not ordinarily given by one making a lease. From the appellee's point of view it is unfortunate that the assignment makes no provision for the contingency of a fire, but the appellant's position is certainly not without equity. Jaber sold his merchandise at public auction, and doubtless at reduced prices, in order to vacate the premises for his assignees. Whether he would have taken the same course had the contract provided for a cancellation of the deferred payments in case of a fire we have no way of knowing. A decision either way works a hardship on the losing party. In this situation we do not feel called upon to supply a provision in the assignment which might have been, but was not, demanded by the assignees.

NOTES AND QUESTIONS

1. *The Transfer of Interest Problem.* When tenants no longer need the premises they have leased, they can generally transfer the property to a third person. This secondary lease can take two forms, a sublease or an assignment. Whether the conveyance is in the form of a sublease or an assignment is a serious matter, because the two forms have very different legal consequences. This makes determining the form of a conveyance an important question for courts to answer.

The legal consequences of determining that a transfer is either a sublease or an assignment can be quite significant both to the transferee and to the landlord. Most important, an assignment creates "privity of estate" between the assignee and the landlord, whereas a sublease does not. This means a landlord has a legal cause of action against an assignee but not against a sublessee, because he has privity only with the assignee. (He remains in privity of contract with the assignor.) However, only those covenants that "run with the land," that is, those the original parties intended to exist between the landlord and any tenant of the property, are transferred to an assignee of the lease. Any covenants intended to be specific to the original tenant do not transfer to the assignee. A subtenant, by contrast, is insulated from the original lease between the landlord and the original tenant. She cannot enforce the covenants in the original lease, and the original landlord cannot enforce them against her. These rules do not apply if the subtenant specifically agrees to fulfill the tenant's duties to the landlord.

2. *Assignment or Sublease?* Courts have addressed the question of how to determine whether a transfer is a sublease or an assignment several different ways. The majority describes the "English doctrine," which has a relatively simple rule. If the tenant reserves some interest in the property, e.g. the last day of the term, it is a sublease. If the tenant conveys the entire interest to the subtenant, it is an assignment.

In its pure form, the "English doctrine" rule is pretty straightforward but, as often happens, some courts became concerned with the rigidity of rules based on feudal tenure. The principal case is an example. Courts have looked for ways to mitigate the uncompromising basis of a rule that requires the reservation of an estate to create a sublease. The principal way they have done this is to relax the definition of a "reservation of interest."

Courts have found tenants had reserved interests sufficient to create a sublease when 1) the tenant reserved a right of re-entry, 2) the transfer contained a covenant to surrender possession to the original tenant at the end of the sub-tenant's term, 3) the sub-tenant had to pay a different rent than in the original lease, and 4) the transfer was made on different terms or conditions from those contained in the main lease.

Faced with the alternative of only paying lip service to the reversion requirement in many cases, some courts chose to break new ground and decide the issue based solely on the intent of the parties, as in the principal case. In these cases, courts look at items in the written document such as whether it was titled "assignment" or "sublease," and whether the original tenant "assigns" or "subleases" the premises to the sub-tenant. If the written evidence of the parties' intent shows the parties intended a sublease, the court will find a sublease whether or not the original tenant reserved an interest. It is important to remember, however, that most jurisdictions still follow the feudal requirements of the English doctrine in determining whether a transfer is a sublease or an assignment.

3. *Policy Considerations.* The assignment vs. sublease problem is a good example of how early English legal principles have survived in landlord and tenant law. There are a number of competing considerations that influence how to deal with the problem, as the principal case indicates. Characterizing the transfer as a sublease, for example, makes it impossible for the landlord to evict, or collect rent from, the sublessee, although statutes have solved this problem in most jurisdictions. As usual, of course, relying on the intent of the parties rather than the reservation of an estate in land to decide these questions creates more uncertainty. Does the abandonment of feudal rigidity justify this risk?

For example, in *Lamont's Apparel, Inc. v. Si-Lloyd Assocs.*, 967 P.2d 905 (Or. App. 1998), the tenant sued claiming the landlord had improperly withheld consent to a sublease. The court held it did not have to reach this question because the tenant had proposed a "sublease" that was "different from the existing lease in a number of significant respects, including the use that the 'sublessees' could make of the property and the percentage rent that one would pay." *Id.* at 909. Korngold, *Whatever Happened to Landlord-Tenant Law?*, 77 NEB. L. REV. 703 (1998), points out that the intent rule is a market-based rule that reflects the expectations of the parties. When should market choices be overridden?

4. *Restricting the Right to Transfer.* At common law, now codified in many states, tenants have a presumptive right to transfer their interest to a third person. This means that unless a landlord specifically restricts a tenant's transfer rights, that tenant may sublease or assign the premises to anyone she chooses. Landlords may try to restrict transfer rights in a number of ways. Courts tend to disfavor restrictions on subleasing or assigning leases because restrictions lead to inefficient use of scarce housing and commercial resources.

Leases commonly contain a clause allowing a landlord to withhold her consent to a sublease or assignment. Again, the majority rule does not require the landlord to provide a reason for withholding consent under a clause of this type. For a recent case deciding to follow the minority rule and overruling an earlier majority rule case, see *Julian v. Christopher*, 575 A.2d 735 (Md. 1990). In addition to finding the majority rule violated the public policy against restraints on alienation, the court relied on "the public policy which implies a covenant of good faith and fair dealing in every contract." For discussion, see Wach, *Withholding Consent to Alienate: If Your Landlord Is in a Bad Mood, Can He Prevent You From Alienating Your Lease?*, 43 DUKE L.J. 671 (1993).

5. *The Landlord's Right to Withhold Consent to an Assignment or Sublease.* The withholding of consent problem illustrates the tensions between the rule that an owner of property may convey it freely to others and the accepted practice that parties to an agreement can restrict this freedom. A majority of courts still hold a landlord may withhold consent for any reason if the lease does not limit the right to withhold. This rule qualifies the tenant's presumptive right to transfer. A minority

holds that recognizing this right violates freedom of alienation: the land freely to others without restraint.

The majority rule can put a tenant in a difficult position. Assume a tena abandon a dwelling because of a job transfer. Even if he finds a creditw replacement and presents him to the landlord, under the majority rule, the landl need not accept the new tenant. On the other hand, it may be difficult for the landlord to refuse rent payments offered by the new tenant.

6. New York has adopted this statutory solution to the withholding of consent problem.

> 1. Unless a greater right to assign is conferred by the lease, a tenant renting a residence may not assign his lease without the written consent of the owner, which consent may be unconditionally withheld without cause provided that the owner shall release the tenant from the lease upon request of the tenant upon thirty days' notice if the owner unreasonably withholds consent which release shall be the sole remedy of the tenant. If the owner reasonably withholds consent, there shall be no assignment and the tenant shall not be released from the lease.

N.Y. Real Prop. Law § 226-b. The statute also provides that a tenant leasing a residence in a dwelling having four or more residential units "shall have the right to sublease his premises subject to the written consent of the landlord in advance of the subletting. Such consent shall not be unreasonably withheld." *Id.*, § 226-b(2)(a). A minority of states also have statutes providing that landlords must give good reasons for rejecting potential sub-tenants, such as a questionable financial situation or a use of the property that is inconsistent with that of other tenants.

Courts will strictly construe the wording in a clause restricting transfer. For example, if subleases are prohibited, courts will hold that assignments are not prohibited. Many courts have held that a landlord waives an objection to a transfer if she knows of the transfer and accepts rent from the transferee. See, for example, *Henrickson v. Freericks*, 620 P.2d 205 (Alaska 1980).

[B.] ABANDONMENT AND CONSTRUCTIVE EVICTION

A lease is entered into in the expectation that the tenant will pay rent and remain in the tenancy until it terminates. Problems arise, however, and the tenant may come to believe that she has to abandon the premises, either because she no longer wishes to continue the tenancy, or because she has found problems on the premises that she believes make it uninhabitable. The first section takes up the problems that occur when a tenant abandons. The second section considers the remedy of constructive eviction that is available when the tenant has cause to abandon.

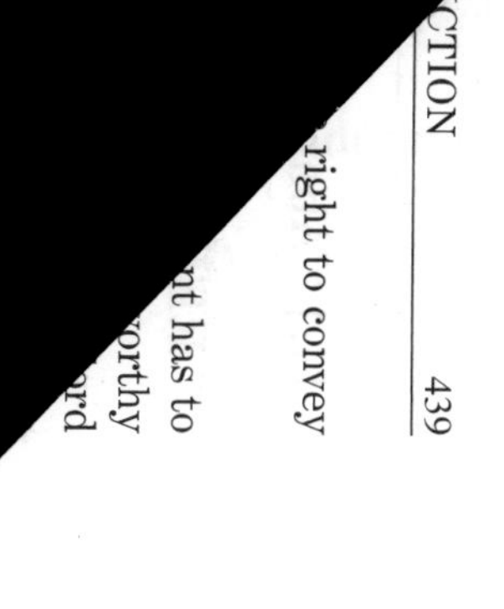

' OMAHA INSURANCE COMPANY

ah Supreme Court

76 P.2d 896 (1989)

appeals from a judgment in a nonjury trial finding Reid ("the Reids") for breach of a lease for office e trial court erred in rejecting its claim that the d Mutual and that it also erred in calculating the rm the judgment of liability for breach of the lease mination of damages.

In September of 1980, Mutual, as tenant, and the Reids, as landlord, entered a five-year lease agreement for office space at a monthly rate of $1,100. The lease term was to end in October of 1985. Mutual took possession of the premises, which it used to conduct an insurance sales business. Soon afterward, another tenant moved into adjoining space in the building. The other tenant, Intermountain Marketing ("Intermountain"), operated a door-to-door cookware sales business and used its office space to train its large sales force. Mutual made numerous complaints to the Reids that Intermountain's personnel were excessively noisy, occupied all of Mutual's parking spaces, and otherwise interfered with Mutual's business. Mutual felt that the Reids did not respond adequately to the frequent complaints and, in February of 1982, gave notice and vacated the premises. In April of 1982, the Reids filed suit, claiming that Mutual had breached the lease and was liable for the monthly rental for the three and a half years remaining on the five-year term. Mutual counterclaimed, contending that it had been constructively evicted by the Reids' failure to control the activities of Intermountain. While the litigation was proceeding, the Reids remodeled the premises at issue and leased them to Intermountain for the remainder of the five-year term at a rate comparable to what Mutual had been paying. However, in November of 1982, Intermountain vacated and declared bankruptcy; from that point through the date of trial, the premises were left vacant.

A bench trial was held in July of 1983. After hearing extensive evidence, the court found against Mutual on its counterclaim for constructive eviction, concluding that the noisy conditions were not sufficiently disruptive to amount to a constructive eviction. The court found that Mutual had breached the lease agreement and awarded the Reids damages under the terms of the agreement. These consisted of the total of the unpaid rents, including both those that had accrued through the date of trial and those that would accrue from the date of trial through the end of the lease term in 1985, less rents actually received from Intermountain during the time it occupied the Mutual premises, plus the costs of reletting and attorney fees . . . .

[The court upheld the finding on constructive eviction.]

Mutual next argues that even if the trial court properly rejected its constructive eviction claim and found it to have breached the lease, the Reids were entitled only to damages for nonpayment of rents measured by those rents that came due between the date of Mutual's last payment and the date of the reletting to Intermountain. Mutual contends that the trial court erred when it included in the measure of damages the unpaid rents that accrued after this reletting.

In support of this argument, Mutual relies upon the common law doctrine of "surrender and acceptance." Under that doctrine, when a tenant surrenders the premises to a landlord before a lease term expires and the landlord accepts that surrender, the tenant is no longer in privity of estate with the landlord and therefore has no obligation to pay any rents accruing after the date of the acceptance. [The court reviewed the evidence and concluded:]

At common law, a tenant raising the affirmative defense of surrender and acceptance has the burden of proving the landlord's intent to accept the surrender. Our previous cases have held that conduct such as the Reids' — reentering, remodeling, and reletting the premises — is relevant to, but not conclusive evidence of, an intent to accept the surrendered premises and terminate the lease.[1] We affirm the trial court's finding that the Reids' conduct was a reletting without termination.

Mutual next contends that even if it was liable for some rents accruing after the premises had been relet, the trial court erred in fixing the amount. This argument has several subparts, each of which attacks different parts of the damage award.

Mutual's second challenge relates to that portion of the award dealing with rents that were to accrue between the date of trial and the end of the original lease term. Mutual contends that the judgment entered fails to ensure that the Reids would mitigate their damages by reletting the premises.

We are thus faced with the question of whether Utah law imposes a duty upon landlords to mitigate their damages by reletting premises after a tenant has wrongfully vacated and defaulted on the covenant to pay rent. There is no controlling statute, and our research has revealed no case in which we have directly addressed the question. However, the concept of landlords mitigating their damages by reletting has been mentioned in several cases where the doctrine of

---

[1] [3] As we explain in the latter part of this opinion, lessors in the Reids' position have what effectively amounts to an obligation to mitigate damages by seeking to relet the premises. That duty to mitigate, which reflects general principles of contract law, was not expressly considered in our older cases in which reletting was viewed as relevant, although not conclusive, evidence of the acceptance of surrender. Our ruling today requires a reevaluation of those cases. Because we now hold that there is a duty to relet, it follows that it would be unfair and inappropriate to treat such reletting alone as sufficient evidence to show that the landlord intended to accept a surrender of the premises and free the tenant from all obligation for future rents. *See* Humbach, *The Common-Law Conception of Leasing: Mitigating Habitability, and Dependence of Covenants*, 60 Wash. U. L.Q. 1213, 1240–56 (1983).

[M]odern landlord-tenant relationships, while steeped in the tradition of ancient property law, have taken on substantive characteristics so similar to commercial transactions that certain of the legal principles developed in the law of contracts in the context of commercial transactions are now appropriately applied to leases, regardless of whether use is made of labels derived from the law of property conveyance or of contract. Our concern with substance rather than form is reflected in the law we apply in the present case with respect to the manner in which a lease may be terminated and to the requirement that a nonbreaching party must act reasonably to mitigate damages. Whether these rules are labeled as deriving from property law or contract law is of little concern.

surrender and acceptance was at issue.[2]

In looking to the law of other jurisdictions, we find a split of authority on the question. In states following what has been described as the traditional rule, landlords are not required to mitigate by reletting. *See* Restatement (Second) of Property § 12.1(3) (1977). A number of states have recently reconsidered the traditional view and, following what has been termed a trend rule, have imposed by statute or judicial decision some obligation to relet. These two competing rules reflect an evolution in the underlying doctrinal approach that has begun to have an impact on many issues of landlord-tenant law. As commentators have noted, the traditional rule imposing no duty to mitigate has its roots in ancient property law concepts under which leaseholds are considered estates in land. The trend rule reflects the more modern view that leases are essentially commercial transactions, contractual in nature.

A number of justifications have been advanced in support of the traditional rule. One is that forcing a landlord to mitigate is unfair when the conduct constituting mitigation might be viewed as evidence of an acceptance of a surrender, a result not actually in accordance with the landlord's intentions. Another justification is equitable in nature: it is unfair to allow the breaching tenant to force on the innocent landlord an affirmative duty to seek out new tenants and perhaps let the premises to tenants not entirely suitable in the landlord's subjective view. A final ground offered for retaining the traditional rule is simply that it is of long standing and in conformance with underlying property law notions.

The first of these justifications for the traditional rule can be easily obviated. As already noted, there is no reason to permit mitigating conduct to be used as indicia of an intent to accept a surrender. As for the second, there is some validity to the concern that the breaching party should not be able to force its landlord to seek other tenants on pain of losing bargained-for rents. However, we think this point is outweighed by the policy arguments in favor of the modern rule, and we think any unfairness to the landlord can largely be eliminated by careful application of a rule requiring reasonable mitigation efforts only.

As for the final justification offered for the traditional rule, it is true that that rule reflects ancient property law concepts; however, those concepts themselves are no longer consonant with most modern landlord-tenant relationships. First, the ancient law of leaseholds was developed in the context of leases of agricultural land. Those leases generally ran from growing season to growing season. If a tenant vacated after planting time had passed, it was unrealistic to expect the landlord to find a new tenant interested in leasing land that was essentially useless for the remainder of the term. *Cf.* Utah Code Ann. § 78-36-4 (1987) (statute allows agricultural land tenant to hold over for another year when landlord fails to object within 60 days to tenant's remaining in possession following lease term expiration). Therefore, a rule requiring mitigation by reletting would have been highly artificial in the practical context of most landlord-tenant relationships. But today, agricul-

---

[2] [8] The concept of mitigation of damages is grounded in traditional contract law principles and is also known as the doctrine of "avoidable consequences." Under this doctrine, a party injured by a contract breach may not recover damages that he or she, with reasonable effort, could have avoided.

tural leases constitute only a minor part of the modern leasing market. Growing seasons are irrelevant to the leasing of residential premises and commercial buildings.

Second, the traditional rule also stems from the ancient concept that a leasehold is a complete conveyance of a real property interest such that the tenant becomes, for a defined term of years, the owner of the property and the landlord simply has no present ownership interest in the property during the lease term. It would be logically inconsistent with this concept of a lease to impose upon the landlord, who has no interest in the property during the lease term, the obligation to relet the property for the remainder of that term. Today, leases are generally viewed as commercial transactions in which the landlord retains the estate but permits its use by another on specified conditions; leases are seldom seen as complete conveyances of the underlying property for a specified term. Our unlawful detainer statutes sub silentio recognize this changed view of a landlord's retained interest in the property when they authorize a landlord to evict a breaching tenant and reenter and relet the premises in very short order. *See* Utah Code Ann. §§ 78-36-8.5, -12, -12.6 (1987).

In sum, the principal justifications given to support the traditional rule are to a large extent anachronistic. In contrast, we find persuasive the reasons advanced in support of the trend rule requiring the landlord to take steps to mitigate its losses. For example, the economies of both the state and the nation benefit from a rule that encourages the reletting of premises, which returns them to productive use, rather than permitting a landlord to let them sit idle while it seeks rents from the breaching tenant.

In addition, the trend rule is more in keeping with the current policy disfavoring contractual penalties. Damages recoverable under a liquidated damages provision in a contract will generally be limited to an amount that represents a reasonable estimation, made at the time the contract was drafted, of what would be necessary to compensate the nonbreaching party for losses caused by the breach. This policy is based on the view that any liquidated damages provision not so limited results in the imposition of a penalty on the breaching party that is not permitted. Similarly, allowing a landlord to leave property idle when it could be profitably leased and force an absent tenant to pay rent for that idled property permits the landlord to recover more damages than it may reasonably require to be compensated for the tenant's breach. This is analogous to imposing a disfavored penalty upon the tenant.

Finally, the trend rule is more in line with the policy favoring mitigation that we have adopted in other areas of the law. For example, mitigation is generally required when damages are sought in tort cases, as well as in contract cases.

In light of these considerations, we conclude that a mitigation requirement is generally appropriate in the context of modern landlord-tenant transactions, and we join those courts now following the trend rule described above. We hold that a landlord who seeks to hold a breaching tenant liable for unpaid rents has an obligation to take commercially reasonable steps to mitigate its losses, which ordinarily means that the landlord must seek to relet the premises.

Certain aspects of our holding require some elaboration.

Another point warranting clarification is the affirmative nature of the mitigation obligation. Some courts imposing a mitigation requirement do not require landlords to show active efforts to relet; instead, the landlord can carry its proof-of-mitigation burden simply by showing that it was passively receptive to opportunities to relet the premises. We conclude that this minimal showing does not serve the policies that underlie the adoption of a mitigation requirement. We prefer to follow those courts that have required that the landlord take positive steps reasonably calculated to effect a reletting of the premises. Only by following such a course can we ensure that serious efforts are made to redeploy the rental property in a productive fashion by those who are best able to accomplish that end and who are also best able to prove that required mitigation efforts have been carried out.

A further word about the standard by which a landlord's efforts to mitigate are to be measured: the standard is one of objective commercial reasonableness. A landlord is obligated to take such steps as would be expected of a reasonable landlord letting out a similar property in the same market conditions. Obviously, the objective commercial reasonableness of mitigation efforts is a fact question that depends heavily on the particularities of the property and the relevant market at the pertinent point in time.

HOWE, ASSOCIATE CHIEF JUSTICE: (Concurring and Dissenting)

I concur in all of the majority opinion except in that part which holds that the trial court's determination that there had not been a constructive eviction of Mutual is supported by the evidence.

NOTES AND QUESTIONS

1. *Responsibilities When a Lease Is Breached.* The abandonment issue is yet another example of the shift in landlord-tenant law from property to contract. Is the court's adoption of an "avoidable consequences" or duty to mitigate rule justified? Flynn, *Duty to Mitigate Damages Upon a Tenant's Abandonment*, 24 REAL PROP. PROB. & TRUST J. 721 (1997), reviews additional reasons that favor the traditional majority view. She notes that the historic character of the leasehold as a conveyance means the tenant is the owner of the leased premises for the term, so her abandonment should not concern the landlord. In addition, under the traditional view of a lease, its covenants are independent of each other. Another argument is that the tenant should not be able to impose an obligation on the landlord because of her wrongdoing. Does the principal case adequately rebut these arguments?

Refusing to depart from the traditional view, one court reasoned that in "business transactions, particularly, the certainty of settled rules is often more important than whether the established rule is better than another or even whether it is the 'correct rule.' " *Holy Properties, Ltd. v. Kenneth Cole Prods., Inc.*, 661 N.E.2d 694, 696 (N.Y. 1995). Is this argument in favor of the non-mitigation rule persuasive? The RESTATEMENT (SECOND) OF PROPERTY follows the traditional view: "Abandonment of Property is an invitation to vandalism, and the law should not encourage such conduct by putting a duty of mitigation of damages on the landlord." RESTATEMENT (SECOND) OF PROPERTY 12.1(3) cmt. I (1977). See also Crump, *Should the Commercial Landlord Have a Duty to Mitigate Damages After the Tenant*

Abandons? A Legal and Economic Analysis, 49 WAKE FOREST L. REV. 187 (2014), arguing against the landlord's duty to mitigate in part because it encourages abandonment by tenants and discourages negotiation with the landlord over a negotiated solution.

A lease can contain a clause that states the obligation of the parties when a tenant abandons. *See Sylva Shops Ltd. P'ship v. Hibbard*, 623 S.E.2d 785 (N.C. Ct. App. 2006) (upholding commercial lease that expressly exempted landlord from mitigating damages upon a tenant's breach).

2. *"The Trend" and Statutory Reform on the Mitigation Issue.* As the principal case notes, the trend is to recognize a duty to mitigate. Though the duty to mitigate is often referred to as the minority rule, Flynn, *supra*, claims over half the states now recognize the duty, either in case law or by statute. For a comprehensive statute, see Wis. Stat. § 704.29(4), listing examples of acts on the part of the landlord that do not constitute an acceptance of a surrender of the premises. One such act is the landlord's entry, with or without notice, for the purpose of inspecting, preserving, repairing, remodeling and showing the premises. Compare the principal case, where the court held that conduct such as "reentering, remodeling, and reletting the premises is relevant to, but not conclusive evidence of, an intent to accept the surrendered premises and terminate the lease." Flynn, *supra*, states that avoiding acceptance of a tenant's surrender is not an issue in mitigation states because a landlord must take possession immediately after abandonment to mitigate losses by attempting to re-rent. The Uniform Residential Landlord and Tenant Act § 604 recognizes the duty to mitigate. Is there reason for distinguishing between residential and commercial leases when deciding whether a duty to mitigate should be recognized? *See Isbey v. Crews*, 284 S.E.2d 534 (N.C. Ct. App. 1981) (no distinction).

3. *Constructive Eviction.* The tenant claimed a constructive eviction in the principal case but lost on this issue. The next case considers when courts will hold that a tenant who abandons is excused from paying rent because there has been a constructive eviction by the landlord.

[2.] Constructive Eviction

PETROLEUM COLLECTIONS, INC. v. SWORDS

California Court of Appeal
48 Cal. App. 3d 841 (1975)

GARGANO, ASSOCIATE JUSTICE

Plaintiff is a collection agency, and it brought this action against the defendant in the court below to recover the sum of $6,043.24; the complaint alleged that the money was unpaid back rent due and owing by defendant to plaintiff's assignor, Texaco, Inc., hereinafter referred to as Texaco. Plaintiff appeals from the judgment entered in favor of the defendant.

The pertinent facts are undisputed.

On April 17, 1969, Texaco leased a parcel of land located on the northwest corner of the intersection of Adams Road and Freeway 99 near the City of Fowler to defendant, Edward Swords. The written lease was for a period of 10 years, called for a rental of $500 a month and embraced land, a service station and related buildings and facilities. It also embraced a large "modular" type sign which was located on top of the service station building and which could be seen approximately one-half mile down the freeway; the sign was equipped with individual letters five feet in height, illuminated from within by neon bulbs; the letters spelled out the word "Texaco."

On May 9, 1969, the Fresno County Building Inspector discovered that the modular type sign had been installed without a county building permit; also, he discovered that the sign had been fastened down improperly and constituted a fire hazard because it was too close to the vents to the gasoline storage tanks. The inspector ordered the hazardous condition rectified or the sign removed; the sign was taken down by the original builder at Texaco's request.

After taking down the sign, Texaco furnished defendant with an "antique," 30-year-old, dilapidated, enamel billboard which could not be seen from the freeway. Defendant then insisted that Texaco furnish him with a sign similar to the one which was on the service station when he leased the property; when Texaco failed to do so, defendant refused to pay any rent.

On March 13, 1970, Texaco and defendant cancelled the lease and defendant vacated the premises; however, approximately two months prior to cancellation, defendant subleased the premises to a third party; neither defendant nor the third party paid any rent to Texaco for any part of the 11-month period the premises were occupied.

At the conclusion of the court trial, the trial judge found, in essence, that when the leasing agreement in question was executed the parties contemplated that defendant would take advantage of the trade generated by the freeway and that the large sign on top of the service station was an integral part of the leased premises. The judge further found, in essence, that the sign was installed by Texaco, that the installation did not conform with county safety regulations, that the sign was a fire hazard, and that it was removed at Texaco's request even though the hazardous condition could have been rectified, readily, by the addition of elbow joints and extension pipe to the vents. The trial judge concluded that Texaco breached the lease's implied covenant of quiet enjoyment, that this implied covenant and defendant's covenant to pay rent were mutually dependent and that as a consequence defendant was not obligated to pay any rent to Texaco for the 11-month period he and his sublessee occupied the premises.

We turn to the nature and scope of the covenant of quiet enjoyment.

It has long been the rule that in the absence of language to the contrary, every lease contains an implied covenant of quiet enjoyment. Initially, the covenant related solely to the right of possession and only protected the lessee against any act of molestation committed by the landlord or anyone claiming under him, or by someone with paramount title, which directly affected the tenant's use and possession of the leased premises; the covenant was construed to protect the lessee against physical interference only. In recent years, the covenant of quiet enjoyment has been expanded, and in this state, for example, it insulates the tenant against any act or omission on the part of the landlord, or anyone claiming under him, which interferes with a tenant's right to use and enjoy the premises for the purposes contemplated by the tenancy. Under this view, the landlord's failure to fulfill an obligation to repair or to replace an essential structure or to provide a necessary service can result in a breach of the covenant if the failure substantially affects the tenant's beneficial enjoyment of the premises.

We consider next the question as to whether an implied covenant of quiet enjoyment and an express covenant to pay rent are mutually dependent; at common law, it was the traditional concept that covenants in leases were always independent.

The foundation for the tenant's obligation to pay rent is his right to use and possess the leased property for the purposes contemplated by the tenancy; rent is the compensation paid by the tenant in consideration for the use, possession and enjoyment of the premises. Consequently, when a tenant's possession of leased property has been interfered with, physically, by the landlord, or someone claiming under him, or by a person with paramount title, the tenant's covenant to pay rent is no longer supported by valid consideration and he is relieved of that obligation. The loss of possession, in short, goes to the very root of the consideration for the tenant's promise to pay rent, and after the eviction the obligation to do so ceases. It is in this sense that the implied covenant of quiet enjoyment and the covenant to pay rent are mutually dependent.

However, when the act of molestation merely affects the tenant's beneficial use of the premises, the tenant is not physically evicted and he has a choice in the matter. He can remain in possession and seek injunctive or other appropriate relief or he can surrender possession of the premises within a reasonable time thereafter. If the tenant elects to remain in possession, his obligation to pay rent continues unless the landlord has breached some other express or implied covenant which the covenant to pay rent is dependent upon. If, on the other hand, the tenant elects to surrender possession of the premises, a constructive eviction occurs at that time and, as in the case of an actual eviction, the tenant is relieved of his obligation to pay any rent which accrues thereafter. It is this doctrine, known as the doctrine of constructive eviction, "which expanded the traditional 'covenant of quiet enjoyment' from simply a guarantee of the tenant's possession of the premises [citations] to a protection of his beneficial enjoyment' of the premises." (*Green v. Superior Court*, [517 P.2d 1168, 1174 n.10 (Cal. 1974)].)

Stated in another manner, the covenant of quiet enjoyment is not broken until there has been an actual or constructive eviction; an actual eviction takes place when the tenant is physically dispossessed of the property; a constructive eviction occurs when the act of molestation merely affects the beneficial use of the property, causing the tenant to vacate the premises. If the tenant is evicted or if he surrenders possession of the premises within a reasonable time after the act of molestation has occurred, he is relieved of his obligation to pay rent accruing as of the date he surrendered; he also may sue for his damages or plead damages by way of offset in an action brought against him by the landlord to recover any unpaid rent that accrued prior to the surrender of the premises. If, in the case of an interference with the tenant's beneficial enjoyment of the premises, the tenant does not surrender the premises within a reasonable time after the date of the interference, he is deemed to have waived his right to abandon; what constitutes a reasonable period of time is a question of fact to be determined by the trier of fact after considering all of the circumstances.

In this case, there was sufficient evidence for the court to find that Texaco's failure to repair or replace the large modular sign, which was on top of the service station when the property was leased to defendant, substantially affected defendant's beneficial enjoyment of the property as contemplated by the parties; there was evidence to show that the parties knew that defendant would have to take advantage of the trade generated by the freeway in order to operate a service station successfully on the leased property at the monthly rental called for by the lease; there was also evidence to show that the sign was an integral part of the premises and that it was needed to attract drivers of vehicles traveling on the freeway. Nevertheless, we reverse the judgment. Defendant and his sublessee remained in possession of the service station for almost 11 months after the sign was removed by Texaco; albeit the trial judge found that during most of the period the parties continued to negotiate for a replacement sign, the judge made no finding as to whether defendant's conduct in staying in possession and in entering into a sublease with a third party was reasonable under the circumstances. Furthermore, even if we were to assume that defendant's conduct in remaining in possession during the 11-month period in question was reasonable under the circumstances, the covenant of quiet enjoyment did not relieve him of his obligation to pay rent during the period; the covenant was not breached until defendant vacated the premises on March 13, 1970. Defendant should have pled his damages by way of offset in the action brought against him for the stipulated rental by Texaco's assignee.

The judgment is reversed.

NOTES AND QUESTIONS

1. *The Origins of the Remedy.* As we have noted, at common law, a tenant's duty to pay rent was independent of the landlord's duty to fulfill his/her part of the lease covenants. Constructive eviction arose as a court-imposed limitation on this independent covenants doctrine, which many judges felt was unfair to tenants. Courts held that every lease included an implied covenant of quiet enjoyment, and that a landlord's acts materially and wrongfully depriving a tenant of the beneficial use and enjoyment of the property could act as a constructive eviction. Berger, *The New Residential Tenancy Law: Are Landlords Public Utilities?* 60 NEB. L. REV. 707 (1981).

The principal case traces the development of this doctrine, which is an extension (through a fiction) of the landlord's liability for a physical eviction. *Dyett v. Pendleton*, 8 Cow. 727 (N.Y. 1826) (prostitutes in dwelling held constructive eviction), was the first American case to adopt the constructive eviction defense and place it directly on the implied covenant of quiet enjoyment. Compare the way in which the court in *Reid* was able to find a duty to mitigate on abandonment with the way in which the courts have formulated the constructive eviction doctrine. Is constructive eviction a fiction?

2. *What is Necessary to Prove a Constructive Eviction?* Many law students can probably report examples of dwellings they rented that had conditions they did not appreciate. The question is how bad these conditions must be before a tenant can claim a constructive eviction defense. Since the defense is court-made, it is up to the courts to resolve this question.

The acts or omissions that give rise to claims of constructive eviction vary slightly from one jurisdiction to the next, but generally include problems with such "essential" services as heat, gas or electricity, running water, hot water, and waste disposal. Most courts use the requirements of the local housing maintenance code to establish the standards against which they judge landlords' actions. One court has held that renting an apartment without the legal right to do so can give rise to a constructive eviction. *Yochim v. McGrath*, 626 N.Y.S.2d 685 (City Ct. 1995).

Courts have also held that dangerous common areas and/or disturbing neighbors in multi-unit buildings can give rise to constructive eviction. In a case holding the presence of bugs was a constructive eviction, an Illinois court summarized the law on this point:

> A constructive eviction occurs where a landlord has done "something of a grave and permanent character with the intention of depriving the tenant of enjoyment of the premises." *Applegate v. Inland Real Estate Corp.*, 441 N.E.2d 379, 382 (Ill. App. 1982.) Because persons are presumed to intend the natural and probable consequences of their acts, constructive eviction does not require a finding that the landlord had the express intention to compel a tenant to leave the demised premises or to deprive him of their beneficial enjoyment. All that is necessary is that the landlord committed acts or omissions which rendered the leased premises useless to the tenant or deprived the tenant of the possession and enjoyment of the premises, in whole or part, making it necessary for the tenant to move. Whether there has been a constructive eviction is a question of fact, and the decision of the trier of fact will not be reversed unless it is against the manifest weight of the evidence.

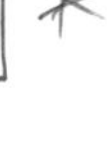

Home Rentals Corp. v. Curtis, 602 N.E.2d 859, 862, 863 (Ill. App. Ct. 1992).

What does this rule embrace? In the principal case, the court recognized economic interests as sufficient for a constructive eviction by holding the unavailability of an adequate sign sufficient. Isn't this just stretching the constructive eviction fiction to give the tenant a remedy for a breach of the lease?

Must there be some physical or other problem on the premises that is the basis for a constructive eviction claim? In *North Ridge Apartments v. Ruffin*, 514 S.E.2d 759 (Va. 1999), a tenant claimed a constructive eviction based on her fear of crime and because she did not feel safe on the premises. The court rejected the claim, noting a landlord has no duty to protect tenants against crime. Courts divide on this question, which is discussed *infra*. For a review of the constructive eviction doctrine, see Knight, *Constructive Eviction: An Illusive Tenant Remedy?*, 29 How. L.J. 13 (1986).

3. *The Move-Out Requirement.* The tenant lost in the principal case because he stayed in possession. Yet, how practicable would it have been for him to move out? In the *Home Rentals* case, *supra* Note 2, the college students left the bugs and moved out, but this may not be an option for poor tenants in tight urban housing markets.

Courts have experimented with ways to ameliorate the harsh move-out rule. In 1959, the Massachusetts Supreme Judicial Court utilized an "equitable constructive eviction" theory that allows a tenant to remain in possession and still receive equitable relief declaring a constructive eviction. *Charles E. Burt, Inc. v. Seven Grand Corp.*, 163 N.E.2d 4 (Mass. 1959). *But* see *Mac's Shell Serv., Inc. v. Shell Oil Products Co. LLC*, 559 U.S. 175, 184 n.6 (2010) (holding this is the minority view).The New York courts recognize a partial constructive eviction, but the tenant must physically vacate the affected portion of the premises. *See, e.g., Manhattan Mansions v. Moe's Pizza*, 149 Misc. 2d 43 (N.Y. Civ. Ct. 1990). This remedy is especially helpful to commercial tenants, who are not usually covered by the implied warranty of habitability. Even so, these reforms have not spread, and constructive eviction is a limited remedy for tenants in most states.

4. *The Uniform Residential Landlord Tenant Act (URLTA).* Many states have now codified the remedy of constructive eviction. URLTA imposes a duty on the landlord to maintain the premises in a habitable condition. This includes compliance with housing and other codes and essential facilities. § 302. Tenant remedies for noncompliance are provided in § 402. A tenant may withhold rent, recover damages, secure injunctive relief, make repairs and deduct the cost from the rent, or secure essential services or comparable substitute housing. Compare these statutory remedies with the remedies available without a statute.

5. *URLTA Revised.* A revised version of URLTA was adopted by the National Conference of Commissioners on Uniform State Laws in July 2015. The revised act is available at http://www.uniformlaws.org/shared/docs/residential%20landlord%20and%20tenant/RURLTA%202015_Final%20Act.pdf. Revisions deal with domestic violence, allowing the victim of domestic violence to terminate a lease, and security deposits. There were other changes throughout the Act, but the structure of the Act has been maintained. The earlier 1972 Act was adopted in at least 21 states. For a link to committee drafts and reports, go to http://www.uniformlaws.org/Committee.aspx?title=Residential%20Landlord%20and%20Tenant%20Act. For discussion of the act and proposed changes, see McDonough, *Then and Now: The Uniform Residential Landlord and Tenant Act and the Revised Residential Landlord and Tenant Act—Still Bold and Relevant?*, 35 U. ARK. LITTLE ROCK L. REV. 975 (2013).

[3.] Holdover Tenants

Types of Tenancies. The *estate for years* or *term for years* is the most common form of leasehold interest. An estate for years can be off any duration from, from one day (or less) to 999 years or more. The central features of the estate for years is the fact that it begins and ends on a specific date, and the termination of the tenant's possessory interest is automatic and requires no notice on the part of the landlord. The estate, however, may be terminated earlier on the happening of an event or condition (like the non-payment of rent). In a few states, like California, the duration of the term for years is limited—in California, to 99 years or 51 years, if the land is farmland. Cal. Civ. Code §§ 717, 718 (West 2007).

Not every leasehold contains an automatic expiration point. A *periodic tenancy* is a tenancy for a fixed duration that automatically renews if neither landlord nor tenant gives notice of a desire to terminate the arrangement. (The so-called "month-to-month lease" is a common example of the periodic tenancy.) Under the common law rules a periodic tenancy could only be terminated if notice was given at least one period length before the termination date. (In a month-to-month tenancy, notice must be given at least 30 days prior to the intended termination date.) For period of six-months or more, termination notice had to be given at least six months in advance. The traditional rule was that a periodic tenancy had to terminate on the final day of the rental period, which was normally the last day of a month.

In many states statutory modifications have reduced the notice requirement to 30 days, regardless of the date on which it is given. In Wisconsin, the notice requirement is 28 days, unless rent is payable on a basis less than monthly and then notice equal to the rent paying period is sufficient. Year-to-year agricultural tenancies by statute require notice of only 90 days. Notice must, however, be in writing. Wis. Stat. § 704.19(3)–(4)

Tenancies at will lack a fixed period of duration, but can be terminated at any point by either the landlord or the tenant. Ordinarily, the death of either party automatically terminates the tenancy at will, which is not a characteristic of the estate for years or the periodic tenancy. Although a tenancy at will can in theory be terminated at any point, in most states statutes require a period of notice. See the above-mentioned Wisconsin statute.

A *tenancy at sufferance* occurs when a tenant refuses to relinquish possession of the property when the lease expires. In this case, the lessee is said to be a "hold over" tenant. At common law, the landlord had two options when the hold over situation arose. He or she could evict the tenant and sue for damages, or else consent to the creation of a new lease. States now deal with the "hold over problem" in a variety of ways. Some states allow the landlord to collect double rent during the holdover period while others permit a limited holdover period. Many permit the expired term to be converted into a periodic tenancy. The following case illustrates some of the problems that can arise when a tenant stays beyond the expiration of the lease.

CRECHALE & POLLES v. SMITH

Mississippi Supreme Court
295 So. 2d 275 (1974)

RODGERS, PRESIDING JUSTICE, wrote the opinion. INZER, ROBERTSON, WALKER and BROOM, JJ., concur.

This action originated in the Chancery Court of the First Judicial District of Hinds County, Mississippi, pursuant to a bill for specific performance of a lease contract filed by Crechale and Polles, Inc., appellant herein. The court awarded the complainants one thousand seven hundred and fifty dollars ($1,750.00) in back rent payment, and seven hundred sixty dollars ($760.00) for damages to the leasehold premises, as well as costs incurred in the proceeding. From this judgment appellant files this appeal and appellees cross-appeal.

The testimony shows that on February 5, 1964, the appellant, Crechale and Polles, Inc., a Mississippi corporation, entered into a lease agreement with appellees, John D. Smith, Jr. and Mrs. Gloria Smith, with appellant as lessor and appellees as lessees. The lease was for a term of five (5) years commencing February 7, 1964, and expiring February 6, 1969, with rental in the amount of one thousand two hundred fifty dollars ($1,250.00) per month.

Smith was informed near the end of his lease that the new building which he planned to occupy would not be complete until a month or two after his present lease expired. With this in mind, he arranged a meeting with his landlord, Crechale, in late December, 1968, or early January, 1969, for the purpose of negotiating an extension of the lease on a month-to-month basis. The outcome of this meeting is one of the focal points of this appeal and the parties' stories sharply conflict. Crechale maintains that he told Smith that since he was trying to sell the property, he did not want to get involved in any month-to-month rental. Smith asserts that Crechale informed him that he was trying to sell the building, but that he could stay in it until it was sold or Smith's new building was ready. Smith's attorney drafted a thirty (30) day extension, but Crechale refused to sign it, saying, "Oh, go ahead. It's all right." Crechale denies that he was ever given the document to sign.

The following is a chronological explanation of the events which led to the subsequent litigation:

February 4, 1969 — Smith sent a letter to Crechale confirming their oral agreement to extend the lease on a monthly basis.

February 6, 1969 — Crechale wrote Smith denying the existence of any oral agreement concerning extension of the lease and requesting that Smith quit and vacate the premises upon expiration of the term at midnight, February 6, 1969. The letter also advised Smith that he was subject to payment of double rent for any holdover.

March 3, 1969 — Smith paid rent for the period of February to March. The check was accepted and cashed by Crechale.

April 6, 1969 — Smith paid rent for the period of March to April, but the check was not accepted by Crechale, because it was for "final payment."

April 7, 1969 — Smith sent a telegram to Crechale stating that he was tendering the premises for purposes of lessor's inventory. The telegram confirmed a telephone conversation earlier that day in which Crechale refused to inventory the building.

April 19, 1969 — Approximately three and one-half (3 1/2) months after the expiration of the lease, Crechale's attorney wrote Smith stating that since the lessee had held over beyond the normal term, the lessor was treating this as a renewal of the lease for a new term expiring February 6, 1974.

April 24, 1969 — Smith again tendered the check for the final month's occupancy and it was rejected by Crechale.

April 29, 1969 — Crechale's attorney wrote Smith again stating the lessor's intention to consider the lessees' holdover as a renewal of the terms of the lease.

There was no further communication between the parties until a letter dated May 15, 1970, from Crechale to Smith requesting that Smith pay the past-due rent or vacate the premises.

May 27, 1970 — Smith's attorney tendered the keys to the premises to Crechale.

Subsequently, this lawsuit was filed by Crechale to recover back rent and damages beyond ordinary wear and tear to the leasehold premises. From the chancellor's decision, appellant files the following assignments of error:

> (1) The lower court erred in holding that the appellees were not liable as holdover tenants for an additional term of one (1) year.
>
> (2) The lower court's award of damages to the appellant was so inadequate in its amount as to be contrary to the overwhelming evidence.

The cross-appellants, John D. Smith, Jr. and Mrs. Gloria Smith, assign the following as error:

> (1) That the chancellor erred in overruling cross-appellants' general demurrer to the original bill for specific performance.
>
> (2) That the lower court erred in assessing damages against the cross-appellants.

The appellant, Crechale and Polles, Inc., contends that the appellees became holdover tenants for a new term under the contract at the election of the landlord appellant, and that appellees owe appellant the rent due each month up to the filing of suit, less the rent paid; and, in addition thereto, it is entitled to specific performance of the holdover contract. This argument is based upon the general rule expressed in 3 Thompson on Real Property § 1024, at 65–66 (1959), wherein it is said:

> "As a general rule, a tenancy from year to year is created by the tenant's holding over after the expiration of a term for years and the continued payment of the yearly rent reserved. * * * By remaining in possession of leased premises after the expiration of his lease, a tenant gives the landlord the option of treating him as a trespasser or as a tenant for another year, . . ."

In support of this rule the appellant cites Tonkel, et al. v. Riteman, 141 So. 344 (Miss. 1932) wherein it is said:

> "It is firmly established that where, without a new contract, a tenant continues to occupy the property which he has held under an annual lease, he becomes liable as tenant for another year at the same rate and under the same terms. Love v. Law, 57 Miss. 596; Usher v. Moss, 50 Miss. 208. It is the duty of a tenant when his period of tenancy has expired to surrender the premises to his landlord or else to have procured a new contract, and, if he

fails to do either, the landlord may treat him as a trespasser or as a tenant under the previous terms, according to the option of the landlord." 141 So. at 344.

An examination of the testimony in this case has convinced us that the appellant is not entitled to specific performance so as to require the appellees to pay rent for a new term of the rental contract as a holdover tenant for the following reasons.

After receiving a letter from one of the appellees in which appellee Smith confirmed an alleged agreement to extend the lease on a month-to-month basis, Crechale immediately wrote Smith and denied that there was such an agreement, and demanded that Smith quit and vacate the premises at the end of the lease.

In addition to the rule expressed in 3 Thompson on Real Property § 1024, above cited, another rule is tersely expressed in American Law of Property § 3.33, at 237 (1952) as follows: "When a tenant continues in possession after the termination of his lease, the landlord has an election either to evict him, treat him as a trespasser it is said, or to hold him as a tenant."

The letter from the appellant dated February 6, 1969, was an effective election on the part of appellant to terminate the lease and to treat the appellees as trespassers.

After having elected not to accept the appellees as tenants, the appellant could not at a later date, after failing to pursue his remedy to evict the tenants, change the election so as to hold the appellees as tenants for a new term. . . .

Although the landlord, appellant, expressly refused to extend the lease on a month-to-month basis, nevertheless, the appellant accepted and cashed the rent check for the month of February. The normal effect of such action by the landlord is tantamount to extension of the lease for the period of time for which the check was accepted, unless, of course, the landlord had elected to treat the tenant as a holdover tenant.

The following excerpt from Annot., 45 A.L.R.2d 827, 831 (1956) points out this rule: "It is the rule that, absent evidence to show a contrary intent on the part of the landlord, a landlord who accepts rent from his holding-over tenant will be held to have consented to a renewal or extension of the leasing."

Although there is authority to the contrary [*see* Annot., 45 A.L.R.2d at 842] the overwhelming weight of authority has adopted the rule above expressed.

On April 6, 1969, the tenants mailed a check for rent for the month of March accompanied by a letter stating that the enclosed check represented the final payment of rent. The next day the tenants tendered the lease premises to the landlord and requested an inventory of certain personal property described in the lease. The landlord refused to accept the tender and rejected the check as a final payment. On April 19, 1969 [three and one-half (3 1/2) months after the expiration of the lease] the landlord attempted to change its position. It then notified the tenants that it had elected to treat them as holdover tenants so as to extend the lease for another term.

We are of the opinion that once a landlord elects to treat a tenant as a trespasser and refuses to extend the lease on a month-to-month basis, but fails to pursue his remedy of ejecting the tenant, and accepts monthly checks for rent due, he in effect agrees to an extension of the lease on a month-to-month basis. *See* Lally v. The New Voice, 128 Ill. App. 455 (1906); Stille v. Pellettieri, 173 Ill. App. 104 (1912).

There is authority to the contrary, but we believe this rule to be based on the best reasoned authority.

[The section of the opinion dealing with the adequacy of the trial court's award of damages is omitted.]

The cross-appellants, the Smiths, contend that the trial court erred in overruling their demurrer upon the ground that the landlord had an adequate remedy at law. They cite Roberts v. Spence, 209 So.2d 623, 626 (Miss. 1968) wherein this Court said: Ordinarily a court of equity will not attempt to enforce a contract by specific performance where the parties have an adequate remedy at law to recover damages growing out of the failure of a contracting party to carry out the terms of the contract."

The landlord does have a remedy at law to evict a tenant [Mississippi Code Annotated § 89-7-27 (1972)]; nevertheless, a landlord may also proceed in chancery to enforce specific performance of a renewed contract, and the mere fact that the chancellor held that specific performance would not be allowed does not retroactively deprive the chancery court of jurisdiction. This Court said in Roberts v. Spence, *supra*: "The application for specific performance is addressed to the sound discretion of the chancery court." [209 So.2d at 625]. The chancellor was correct in overruling the demurrer.

We cannot agree with the cross-appellants' contention that the chancellor was manifestly wrong in awarding the amount of damages for the items set out in the decree of the chancery court. We have carefully examined each item in the light of the briefs, and we find no reversible error in the ruling of the trial court.

We hold, therefore, that the decree of the trial court should be and is hereby affirmed.

NOTES AND QUESTIONS

1. *What Constitutes Holding Over?* How much of a presence on the property is necessary to constitute the failure to vacate the premises. In *Caserta v. Action for Bridgeport Community*, 377 A.2d 856 (Conn. Super. Ct. 1976), the court ruled that the failure to remove certain pieces of office equipment from the premises did not constitute holding over because the presence of the equipment did not interfere with the landlord's ability to make use of the premises. The question of whether the retention of keys by the former tenant constitutes holding over has been answered differently in different jurisdictions. *See Gooding Bay Realty Corporation v. Bristol Bay CVS*, 763 A.2d 650 (R. I. 2000), and cases cited therein. In the famous old case of *Herter v. Mullen*, 159 N.Y. 28 (1899), the highest court of New York ruled that tenants who were unable to remove their elderly mother from the premises because of her illness for 15 days were not subject to the penalties imposed on holdover tenants (in that case, the renewal of the lease for another year) because their

continued presence on the property was not voluntary but was at the command of their mother's physician.

2. *What Arrangements Are Not Estates of Any Sort?* Certain types of residential arrangements have been held to be in the nature of licenses rather than estates, although there has historically been a great deal of disagreement as to exactly which types of relationships fit into this category. Hotel guests are treated as licenses unless they actually live in the hotel, in which case they are more likely to be viewed as periodic tenants or holders of estates for years. The degree of control that the resident retains over the premises can be an important consideration in determining the nature of the arrangement. *Thomas v. Lenhart*, 444 A.2d 246 (Conn. 1982) (long term residents, or "lodgers," are protected by the state landlord tenant laws. Courts have split over the issue of whether employees who are required to live on the premises where they work are tenants or merely licensees. In *Chan v. Antepenko*, 203 Cal. App. 3d Supp. 21 (1988) (no) and *Bigelow v. Bullard*, 901 P.2d 630 (Nev. 1995) (yes), court reached opposite conclusions as to whether a building superintendent was a tenant. Similar problems arise with migrant farm workers who reside on the land on which they are working. *See De Bruyn Produce Co. v. Romero*, 508 N.W.2d 150 (Mich. Ct. App. 1993) (migrant farm workers who resided on the land on which they are working held not tenants within the meaning of Michigan's Landlord Tenant Relationship Act).

Similar problems have arisen in regard to college students residing in dormitories. In Kansas and New York, courts have ruled that they are tenants of the university, *Burch v. University of Kansas*, 756 P.2d 431 (Kan. 1988); *Green v. Dormitory Authority of the State of New York*, 173 A.D.2d 1 (N.Y. App. Div. 1991), while in Colorado and Illinois, courts have reached the conclusion that they are licensees in cases involving very similar facts, *Houle v. Adams State College*, 547 P.2d 926 (Colo. 1976); *Cook v. University Plaza*, 427 N.E.2d 405 (Ill. App. Ct. 1981).

[C.] CONTEMPORARY ISSUES IN LANDLORD-TENANT LAW

[1.] The Implied Warranty of Habitability

Doctrines like the constructive eviction doctrine modified traditional landlord-tenant law, including the doctrine of independent covenants, by introducing fictions. More recently, courts have moved aggressively to introduce new doctrines that add new legal dimensions to the landlord-tenant relationship. One of the most important of these doctrines is the implied warranty of habitability, which is considered next.

Some background on the landlord's responsibilities will provide perspective on this problem. At common law, the landlord was not liable in tort for injuries on the premises in the absence of fraud, concealment or an express assumption of liability in a lease. *See Bowles v. Mahoney*, 202 F.2d 320 (D.C. Cir. 1952). The court pointed out that the lessee assumed the risk of injury because the lease gave him possession and control of the premises.

The common law rule made sense in feudal England when leases generally were for agricultural land; any structures that might be on the land were secondary. Tenants could inspect the premises before signing the lease to discover any defects in the land. During the lease term, tenants were in a better position than the landlord to know what repairs might be needed to be made to the land. Tenant-farmers had an interest in maintaining the land in accordance with their particular agricultural needs. For a recent application of the common law rule in an urban setting, see *Gourdi v. Berkelo*, 930 P.2d 812 (N.M. 1996).

Courts became uncomfortable with this rule when the majority of landlord-tenant leases came to consist of renting a building or space in a building, and the land on which it sat became secondary. Tenants frequently were no longer able to discover defects by inspecting the premises. A dwelling could have structural problems even reasonably prudent tenants could not discover until they had lived in the dwelling for a time. Courts also came to believe landlords were in a better position to make the needed repairs, especially in the increasingly common cases of tenants renting apartments in multi-unit buildings. In some cases, courts found tenants actually were unable to make necessary repairs because they did not have access to all the required areas, such as common areas with plumbing and electrical facilities. Courts believed they should bring landlord-tenant law in line with the growing law of consumer protection and provide protection to lower-income tenants in urban housing markets where they often were at a disadvantage. The following case was the first to reject the common law doctrine and quickly became one of the most famous property law cases in American history.

JAVINS v. FIRST NATIONAL REALTY CORP.

United States Court of Appeals, District of Columbia Circuit
428 F.2d 1071 (1970)

J. Skelly Wright, Circuit Judge.

These cases present the question whether housing code violations which arise during the term of a lease have any effect upon the tenant's obligation to pay rent. The Landlord and Tenant Branch of the District of Columbia Court of General Sessions ruled proof of such violations inadmissible when proffered as a defense to an eviction action for nonpayment of rent. The District of Columbia Court of Appeals upheld this ruling.

Because of the importance of the question presented, we granted appellants' petitions for leave to appeal. We now reverse and hold that a warranty of habitability, measured by the standards set out in the Housing Regulations for the District of Columbia, is implied by operation of law into leases of urban dwelling units covered by those Regulations and that breach of this warranty gives rise to the usual remedies for breach of contract.

In our judgment the common law itself must recognize the landlord's obligation to keep his premises in a habitable condition. This conclusion is compelled by three separate considerations. First, we believe that the old rule was based on certain factual assumptions which are no longer true; on its own terms, it can no longer be justified. Second, we believe that the consumer protection cases discussed above require that the old rule be abandoned in order to bring residential landlord-tenant law into harmony with the principles on which those cases rest. Third, we think that the nature of today's urban housing market also dictates abandonment of the old rule.

The common law rule absolving the lessor of all obligation to repair originated in the early Middle Ages. Such a rule was perhaps well suited to an agrarian economy; the land was more important than whatever small living structure was included in the leasehold, and the tenant farmer was fully capable of making repairs himself. These historical facts were the basis on which the common law constructed its rule; they also provided the necessary prerequisites for its application.

Court decisions in the late 1800s began to recognize that the factual assumptions of the common law were no longer accurate in some cases. [The court discussed cases changing the common law rules by relieving the tenant of rent when a building is destroyed, and creating an exception to the no-repair rule for short term leases of furnished dwellings. It also mentioned the doctrines of quiet enjoyment and constructive eviction in a footnote.]

These as well as other similar cases demonstrate that some courts began some time ago to question the common law's assumptions that the land was the most important feature of a leasehold and that the tenant could feasibly make any necessary repairs himself. Where those assumptions no longer reflect contemporary housing patterns, the courts have created exceptions to the general rule that landlords have no duty to keep their premises in repair.

It is overdue for courts to admit that these assumptions are no longer true with regard to all urban housing. Today's urban tenants, the vast majority of whom live in multiple dwelling houses, are interested, not in the land, but solely in "a house suitable for occupation." Furthermore, today's city dweller usually has a single, specialized skill unrelated to maintenance work; he is unable to make repairs like the "jack-of-all-trades" farmer who was the common law's model of the lessee. Further, unlike his agrarian predecessor who often remained on one piece of land for his entire life, urban tenants today are more mobile than ever before. A tenant's tenure in a specific apartment will often not be sufficient to justify efforts at repairs. In addition, the increasing complexity of today's dwellings renders them much more difficult to repair than the structures of earlier times. In a multiple dwelling repair may require access to equipment and areas in the control of the landlord. Low and middle income tenants, even if they were interested in making repairs, would be unable to obtain any financing for major repairs since they have no long-term interest in the property.

Our approach to the common law of landlord and tenant ought to be aided by principles derived from the consumer protection cases . . . . In a lease contract, a tenant seeks to purchase from his landlord shelter for a specified period of time. The landlord sells housing as a commercial businessman and has much greater opportunity, incentive and capacity to inspect and maintain the condition of his building. Moreover, the tenant must rely upon the skill and bona fides of his landlord at least as much as a car buyer must rely upon the car manufacturer. In dealing with major problems, such as heating, plumbing, electrical or structural defects, the tenant's position corresponds precisely with "the ordinary consumer who cannot be expected to have the knowledge or capacity or even the opportunity to make adequate inspection of mechanical instrumentalities, like automobiles, and to decide for himself whether they are reasonably fit for the designed purpose." *Henningsen v. Bloomfield Motors, Inc.*, 161 A.2d 69, 78 (N.J. 1960).

Since a lease contract specifies a particular period of time during which the tenant has a right to use his apartment for shelter, he may legitimately expect that the apartment will be fit for habitation for the time period for which it is rented. We point out that in the present cases there is no allegation that appellants' apartments were in poor condition or in violation of the housing code at the commencement of the leases. Since the lessees continue to pay the same rent, they were entitled to expect that the landlord would continue to keep the premises in their beginning condition during the lease term. It is precisely such expectations that the law now recognizes as deserving of formal, legal protection.

Even beyond the rationale of traditional products liability law, the relationship of landlord and tenant suggests further compelling reasons for the law's protection of the tenants' legitimate expectations of quality. The inequality in bargaining power between landlord and tenant has been well documented. Tenants have very little leverage to enforce demands for better housing. Various impediments to competition in the rental housing market, such as racial and class discrimination and standardized form leases, mean that landlords place tenants in a take it or leave it situation. The increasingly severe shortage of adequate housing further increases the landlord's bargaining power and escalates the need for maintaining and improving the existing stock. Finally, the findings by various studies of the social impact of bad housing has led to the realization that poor housing is detrimental to the whole society, not merely to the unlucky ones who must suffer the daily indignity of living in a slum.

Thus we are led by our inspection of the relevant legal principles and precedents to the conclusion that the old common law rule imposing an obligation upon the lessee to repair during the lease term was really never intended to apply to residential urban leaseholds. Contract principles established in other areas of the law provide a more rational framework for the apportionment of landlord-tenant responsibilities; they strongly suggest that a warranty of habitability be implied into all contracts for urban dwellings.

The judgment of the District of Columbia Court of Appeals is reversed and the cases are remanded for further proceedings consistent with this opinion. So ordered.

NOTES AND QUESTIONS

1. *Social Activism. Javins* is the leading case establishing an implied warranty of habitability in residential leases. It was fortunate for the tenant's rights movement that the federal Court of Appeals for the District of Columbia had an opportunity to decide this case. The court, at that time, had a number of judges committed to social activism in judicial decision making. The late Skelly Wright, who wrote the *Javins* decision, was one.

Judge Wright and his colleagues on the bench may also have been influenced by events in the District of Columbia, where major slum clearance projects were under way and housing conditions were topical news. The court cited a recently-published report by a Presidential commission, led by an influential former Illinois Senator, that described slum housing conditions and proposed measures for their improvement. A number of state courts immediately adopted the rule in *Javins* and by the 1990's, most states had adopted it, either judicially or by legislation. For the current status of the implied warranty, see Lonegras, *Convergence in Contort: Landlord Liability for Defective Premises in Comparative Perspective*, 85 TUL. L. REV. 413 (2010).

2. *What the Implied Warranty Means. Javins* completed a modern trend that introduced new contract principles into certain areas of landlord-tenant law. This choice has several consequences. A tenant's obligation to pay rent is no longer independent of the landlord's duty to keep and maintain the premises in a habitable condition. As a result, in many jurisdictions with habitability warranties, tenants may either withhold rent until landlords repair defects or may deduct the cost of such repairs from their rent. The implied warranty of habitability also changed the common law rule that tenants had the duty to repair. Because tenants pay the same rent throughout their tenancy, the *Javins* court argued, landlords must keep units conforming to housing code standards throughout the tenancy. Merrill & Smith, *The Property/Contract Interface*, 101 COL. L. REV. 773 (2001), analyze these issues.

The *Javins* decision gave the municipal housing code the force of law governing civil landlord-tenant relationships. However, some courts do not limit a landlord's responsibility to housing code requirements. Do you agree with this shift in responsibility for standard-setting in the housing market? A review of the cases found that violations of the implied warranty fall into the following categories: "(1) "slum" conditions; (2) substandard structural conditions; (3) substandard physical conditions on the premises." Campbell, *Forty (Plus) Years After the Revolution: Observations on the Implied Warranty of Habitability*, 35 U. ARK. LITTLE ROCK L. REV. 793, 813 (2013)

Is the implied warranty recognized in *Javins* a sword as well as a shield? Could the tenant in that case successfully have sued the landlord in tort? What are the differences between the implied warranty recognized in *Javins* and the doctrine of constructive eviction? Under which doctrine is the tenant better off?

The *Javins* court imposed some consumer-protection limitations on the parties' freedom to contract. It held landlords cannot exclude the warranty by a provision in the lease or shift regulatory responsibilities to their tenants. The court and those following it reasoned that allowing a waiver would be contrary to the public policy of ensuring safe and sanitary housing. Most jurisdictions have adopted these limitations on waiver. Some states permit a full waiver. Miss. Code Ann. § 89-8-23(3). For an argument that the implied warranty should be extended to cover any violation of a tenant's reasonable expectations in a tenancy, see Smith, *Tenants in Search of Parity With Consumers: Creating a Reasonable Expectations Warranty*, 72 WASH. U. L.Q. 475 (1994).

3. *Commercial Leases.* The implied warranty of habitability initially applied only to residential leases. As its intent was to provide safe and sanitary housing for

families and individuals, it did not extend to commercial leases. This is still generally the rule, and several states have considered and rejected an extension to commercial leases. *See Seoane v. Drug Emporium, Inc.*, 457 S.E.2d 93 (Va. 1995); *Propst v. McNeill*, 932 S.W.2d 766 (Ark. 1996). For arguments for and against an implied warranty of habitability in commercial leases, see Vlatas, *An Economic Analysis of Implied Warranties of Fitness in Commercial Leases*, 94 COLUM. L. REV. 658 (1994).

The court partly based the adoption of the implied warranty in *Javins* on the tenants' unequal bargaining power and helplessness in the housing market. Do these policy reasons apply to commercial leases? In adopting an implied warranty of habitability for commercial leases, the Texas Supreme Court had this to say about the similarities between residential and commercial tenants:

> It cannot be assumed that a commercial tenant is more knowledgeable about the quality of the structure than a residential tenant. A businessman cannot be expected to possess the expertise necessary to adequately inspect and repair the premises, and many commercial tenants lack the financial resources to hire inspectors and repairmen to assure the suitability of the premises. Additionally, because commercial tenants often enter into short-term leases, the tenants have limited economic incentive to make any extensive repairs to their premises. Consequently, commercial tenants generally rely on their landlords' greater abilities to inspect and repair the premises.

Davidow v. Inwood North Prof'l Group-Phase I, 747 S.W.2d 373, 376 (Tex. 1988).

4. *Is the Implied Warranty an Effective and Desirable Reform?* There has been debate over whether the implied warranty of habitability is an effective and desirable reform since its adoption. One issue is whether the implied warranty raises rents, with the assumption that it harms lower-income tenants if it does. A recent study, Brower, *The "Backlash" of the Implied Warranty of Habitability: Theory vs. Analysis*, 60 DEPAUL L. REV. 849 (2011), conducted a statistical analysis over a substantial period of time that showed a statistically significant relationship between the implied warranty and rent increases. A waiver prohibition also led to increased rents. Left open is the question whether rent increases are balanced by benefits to tenants.

Another issue is whether the implied warranty has actually delivered as promised. Super, *The Rise and Fall of the Implied Warranty of Habitability*, 99 CAL. L. REV. 389 (2011), finds legal barriers to the implementation of the implied warranty. These include a waiver of the warranty that is allowed in some states, a requirement that tenants must show that their sole motive in rent withholding is to use repair issues, and availability of landlord protective orders that require tenants to deposit rent. Studies also show that tenants are not usually successful in court.

What arguments can you make for the implied warranty despite these studies? The student author of Note, *Law and Economics Meets Eviction Defense: The Interplay of Theory and Practice*, 13 YALE L. & POL'Y REV. 385 (1995), disagrees with conclusions in other studies that tenant representation by legal clinics unfairly delayed eviction proceedings of tenants without substantive defense who paid little or no rent during the period of delay. *See also* Singer, *Democratic Estates: Property*

Law in a Free and Democratic Society, 94 Cornell L. Rev. 1009, 1055 (2009).

5. *Codification.* Practically all states now have legislation enacting an implied warranty of habitability. Richards, *The Utah Fit Premises Act and the Implied Warranty of Habitability: A Study in Contrast*, 1991 Utah L. Rev. 55, 61 & n.47. Some have based their statutes on the Uniform Residential Landlord and Tenant Act (URLTA) § 302, which is discussed above in the section on constructive eviction. The 2015 revisions somewhat expand the provisions of the original 1972 act.

Landlords and tenants may agree that the tenant will undertake certain of the landlord's duties, but only under specified circumstances. These include a separate writing and consideration independent of the rental agreement. § 302(d). Tenant duties under URLTA are detailed in § 502. They include a duty to comply with housing and other codes, and to keep the premises in reasonably safe and sanitary condition. For discussion of the relationship between the implied warranty of habitability and landlord tort liability, see Green, *Paradoxes, Parallels and Fictions: The Case for Landlord Tort Liability Under the Revised Uniform Residential Landlord-Tenant Act*, 38 Hamline L. Rev. 407 (2015).

[2.] Landlord Responsibility for Crime

Landlord-tenant responsibility questions considered so far have all centered on problems related to the premises, such as maintenance, that are under the landlord's control. What about landlord responsibility for guaranteeing the safety of his tenants, a problem that may not be directly under her control? The next case raises, and addresses, this problem.

WALLS v. OXFORD MANAGEMENT COMPANY

New Hampshire Supreme Court
633 A.2d 103 (1993)

Horton, Justice

The United States District Court for the District of New Hampshire (Loughlin, J.) has certified to this court the following questions: (1) Does New Hampshire law impose a duty on landlords to provide security to protect tenants from the criminal attacks of third persons? (2) Does this State's law of implied warranty of habitability oblige landlords to provide security to protect tenants from the criminal attacks of third persons?

On December 13, 1988, the plaintiff, Deanna Walls, was sexually assaulted in her vehicle, which was parked on the premises of the Bay Ridge Apartment Complex in Nashua. The plaintiff lived with her mother, who leased an apartment at Bay Ridge. Gerard Buckley was arrested and subsequently convicted of sexually assaulting the plaintiff. Bay Ridge is owned by defendant Nashua-Oxford Bay Associates Limited Partnership (Nashua-Oxford), and managed by defendant Oxford Management Company, Inc. (Oxford). It consists of 412 apartments located in fourteen buildings. During the two years prior to the assault, the Bay Ridge complex had been the site of a number of crimes directed against property, including eleven automobile thefts, three attempted automobile thefts, and thirty-one incidents involving criminal mischief/theft. No sexual assaults or similar attacks against persons had been reported.

The plaintiff brought this action in federal court, charging that the defendants "had a duty to hire and contract with a competent management company, had a duty to provide reasonable security measures for the protection of residents of Bay Ridge, a duty to warn residents of its lack of security, as well as a duty to warn residents of the numerous criminal activities which had taken place on the premises of Bay Ridge and in the vicinity of Bay Ridge."

The plaintiff alleges that the defendants breached these duties, and that the breach was a proximate cause of the sexual assault. The record reflects that the questions were certified in advance of ruling on the defendants' motion to dismiss for failure to state a claim, and on the defendants' motion for summary judgment. The parties have agreed to certain facts and the record discloses other facts developed under the summary judgment procedure. The questions certified are general and not phrased in the context of these facts. Our answers, although general, are necessarily given in the context of these facts.

I. Landlord's Duty to Secure Tenants Against Criminal Attack

The issues raised by the first question place the court at the confluence of two seemingly contradictory principles of law. On one hand lies the accepted maxim that all persons, including landlords, have a duty to exercise reasonable care not to subject others to an unreasonable risk of harm. On the other hand, a competing rule holds that private persons have no general duty to protect others from the criminal acts of third persons.

Claims for negligence "rest primarily upon a violation of some duty owed by the offender to the injured party." [Case citations are omitted.] Absent a duty, there is no negligence. Whether a duty exists in a particular case is a question of law. Only after a court has determined that a defendant owed a plaintiff a duty, and identified the standard of care imposed by that duty, may a jury consider the separate question of whether the defendant breached that duty.

While of paramount importance to the analysis of a claim for negligence, duty "is an exceedingly artificial concept." In some cases, a party's actions give rise to a duty. A party who does not otherwise have a duty, but who voluntarily renders services for another, has been held to a duty of reasonable care in acting. In other cases, a duty to act exists based on a special relationship between two parties. In either case, the scope of the duty imposed is limited by what risks, if any, are reasonably foreseeable. As a general rule, "a defendant will not be held liable for negligence if he could not reasonably foresee that his conduct would result in an injury or if his conduct was reasonable in light of what he could anticipate." When charged with determining whether a duty exists in a particular case, we necessarily encounter the broader, more fundamental question of "whether the plaintiff's interests are entitled to legal protection against the defendant's conduct." The decision to impose liability ultimately rests on "a judicial determination that the social importance of protecting the plaintiff's interest outweighs the importance of immunizing the defendant from extended liability."

At one time, landlords enjoyed considerable immunity from "simple rules of reasonable conduct which govern other persons in their daily activities." A landlord owed no general duty to his tenants, and could be found liable for injuries caused by a defective or dangerous condition on leased property only if the injuries were "attributable to (1) a hidden danger in the premises of which the landlord but not the tenant [was] aware, (2) premises leased for public use, (3) premises retained under the landlord's control, such as common stairways, or (4) premises negligently repaired by the landlord." In *Sargent v. Ross*, 308 A.2d 528 (N.H. 1973), however, this court abolished landlord immunity, and held that a landlord has a duty to act as a reasonable person under all the circumstances. We acknowledged that "[c]onsiderations of human safety within an urban community dictate that the landowner's relative immunity, which is primarily supported by values of the agrarian past, be modified in favor of negligence principles of landowner liability." *Id.* at 533.

While we can state without reservation that landlords owe a general duty of reasonable care to their tenants, our efforts at resolving the first question presented are complicated by the competing common law rule that private citizens ordinarily have no duty to protect others from criminal attacks. This rule is grounded in the fundamental unfairness of holding private citizens responsible for the unanticipated criminal acts of third parties. "Under all ordinary and normal circumstances, in the absence of any reason to expect the contrary, the actor may reasonably proceed upon the assumption that others will obey the law . . . . Although [crimes] do occur . . . they are still so unlikely that the burden of taking continual precautions against them almost always exceeds the apparent risk." W. Page Keeton, et al., PROSSER AND KEETON ON THE LAW OF TORTS, § 33, at 201. In keeping with this rule, courts have largely refused to hold landlords to a general duty to protect tenants from criminal attack.

We agree that as a general principle, landlords have no duty to protect tenants from criminal attack. Without question, there is much to be gained from efforts at curtailing criminal activity. Yet, we will not place on landlords the burden of insuring their tenants against harm from criminal attacks.

Our inquiry is not concluded, however, as we must further consider whether exceptions to the general rule against holding individuals liable for the criminal attacks of others apply to the landlord-tenant relationship. A review of the law in this area suggests four such exceptions. The first arises when a special relationship, such as that of innkeeper-guest, or common carrier-passenger, exists between the parties. Courts have repeatedly held, however, that a landlord-tenant relationship is not a special relationship engendering a duty on the part of the landlord to protect tenants from criminal attack.

A second exception arises where "an especial temptation and opportunity for criminal misconduct *brought about by the defendant*, will call upon him to take precautions against it." Keeton, *supra* § 33, at 201 (emphasis added). This exception follows from the rule that a party who realizes or should realize that his conduct has created a condition which involves an unreasonable risk of harm to another has a duty to exercise reasonable care to prevent the risk from taking effect. Accordingly, in the majority of cases in which a landlord has been held liable for a criminal attack upon a tenant, a known physical defect on the premises foreseeably enhanced the risk of that attack. [The court cited cases where there was a defective deadbolt on an apartment door, a broken window latch, and inoperable lighting and a ladder left unattended near an unlocked window.]

A third exception is the existence of overriding foreseeability. Some courts have held landlords to a duty to protect tenants from criminal attacks that were clearly foreseeable, even if not causally related to physical defects on the premises. [The court cited cases where criminal activity was apparent in the neighborhood, where the apartment complex was plagued with a high incidence of serious crime, and where crimes had been perpetrated against tenants in a common area of the apartment complex.]

The fourth exception derives from the general tort principle that one who voluntarily assumes a duty thereafter has a duty to act with reasonable care. Thus, landlords who gratuitously or contractually provide security have been found liable for removing the security in the face of a foreseeable criminal threat. [Citing cases.] We hold that while landlords have no general duty to protect tenants from criminal attack, such a duty may arise when a landlord has created, or is responsible for, a known defective condition on a premises that foreseeably enhanced the risk of criminal attack. Moreover, a landlord who undertakes, either gratuitously or by contract, to provide security will thereafter have a duty to act with reasonable care. Where, however, a landlord has made no affirmative attempt to provide security, and is not responsible for a physical defect that enhances the risk of crime, we will not find such a duty. We reject liability based solely on the landlord-tenant relationship or on a doctrine of overriding foreseeability.

A finding that an approved exception applies is not dispositive of the landlord's liability for a tenant's injury. Where a landlord's duty is premised on a defective condition that has foreseeably enhanced the risk of criminal attack, the question whether the defect was a proximate or legal cause of the tenant's injury remains one of fact. Moreover, where a landlord has voluntarily assumed a duty to provide some degree of security, this duty is limited by the extent of the undertaking. For example, a landlord who provides lighting for the exterior of an apartment building might be held liable for failing to insure that the lighting functioned properly, but not for failing to provide additional security measures such as patrol services or protective fencing. The answer to the first certified question is no, subject to the pleading or proof, as appropriate, of facts supporting the approved exceptions.

II. Implied Warranty of Habitability

The second certified question concerns whether a landlord's implied warranty of habitability to provide a reasonably safe premises requires the landlord to secure tenants against criminal attack.

An agreement for the rental of an apartment unit contains an "implied warranty . . . that the apartment is habitable and fit for living," and that "there are no latent defects in facilities vital to the use of the premises for residential purposes." *Kline v. Burns*, 276 A.2d 248, 251–52 (N.H. 1971). A defect constituting a breach of this warranty "must be of a nature and kind which will render the premises unsafe, or unsanitary and thus unfit for living therein."

Until now, this court had not considered whether a landlord's failure to provide security against criminal attack renders a dwelling "unsafe" or "unfit for living" and thus in breach of the implied warranty of habitability. We therefore look for guidance in decisions from other jurisdictions. In *Williams v. William J. Davis, Inc.*, 275 A.2d 231, 231–32 (D.C. 1971), the District of Columbia Court of Appeals answered this question in the negative, holding that housing regulations referring to "clean, safe and sanitary conditions," and a "healthy and safe" premises, did not oblige a landlord to furnish protection against criminal attacks. According to the court, the terms "safe" and "safety" referred to structural defects, fire hazards, and unsanitary conditions, not to safety from criminal acts of third parties. *Id.* at 232. [The court also cited additional cases in accord from other states.]

We hold that the warranty of habitability implied in residential lease agreements protects tenants against structural defects, but does not require landlords to take affirmative measures to provide security against criminal attack. This holding in no way limits a tenant's recovery when a landlord has violated an express agreement to provide security measures, or has invited such an attack through a violation of an express housing code requirement. Our answer to the second certified question is no.

NOTES AND QUESTIONS

1. *Allocating Responsibility for Crime.* Holding landlords responsible for crimes committed on the premises is an extension of tort law. The principal case was willing to find distinctive features in the landlord-tenant relationship to make this extension. Not all courts agree. In *Bartley v. Sweetser*, 890 S.W.2d 250 (Ark. 1994), the court refused to find a special relationship between landlords and tenants. The court cited as policy reasons for its decision that the actions of third parties were a superseding cause, that the standard of care for landlords was vague, and that it was difficult to determine the foreseeability of criminal acts. The court was also concerned about the economic consequences of liability and was not willing to shift responsibility for crimes from government to landlords. It was willing to recognize exceptions only if the landlord contractually agreed to accept responsibility, or if a statute imposed this duty. Was the court correct in not extending the implied warranty of habitability to liability for crimes?

The principal case did not mention the possibility of liability for crimes committed in common areas. *Kline v. 1500 Massachusetts Ave. Apartment Corp.*, 439 F.2d 477 (D.C. Cir. 1970), is a leading case imposing liability on landlords in this situation. Though it conceded a landlord could not be the "insurer" of a tenant's safety, the court concluded:

> As between tenant and landlord, the landlord is the only one in the position to take the necessary acts of protection required. Not only as between landlord and tenant is the landlord best equipped to guard against the predictable risk of intruders, but even as between landlord and the police power of government, the landlord is in the best position to take the

> necessary protective measures. Municipal police cannot patrol the [common areas.]

Id. at 484.

The court also held there was an "implied" obligation in the contract between landlord and tenant on the landlord to provide protective measures within his reasonable capacity. Finally, the *Kline* case found a special relationship between landlords and tenants by analogizing it to the relationship between innkeepers and guests. *But see Sigmund v. Starwood Urban Retail VI, LLC*, 617 F.3d 512 (D.C. Cir. 2010), noting that in *Kline* the criminal acts were foreseeable because "the crimes of violence, robbery, and assault . . . had been occurring with mounting frequency on the premises," quoting *Kline*, at 480. Courts will deny liability if they do not find foreseeability. *Beato v. Cosmopolitan Associates, LLC*, 893 N.Y.S.2d 578 (App. Div. 2010).

2. *Voluntary Assumption of Duty.* Not all courts agree with the principal case that landlords must assume liability for criminal acts when they voluntarily provide security measures. As the Minnesota court pointed out in *Funchess v. Newman*, 632 N.W.2d 666 (Minn. 2001):

> We are not inclined to establish a rule that would discourage landlords from improving security. Transforming a landlord's gratuitous provision of security measures into a duty to maintain those measures and subjecting the landlord to liability for all harm occasioned by a failure to maintain that security would tend to discourage landlords from instituting security measures for fear of being held liable for the actions of a criminal.

Id. at 675.

The court rejected the deterrent effect of tort liability as counterproductive.

3. *Liability for the Acts of Other Tenants.* Does a landlord have a duty to police and screen tenants to keep his property free of persons likely to commit crimes? Courts may not find a special relationship, foreseeability or other basis for imposing this duty. *See, e.g., Conroy v. Solon Gershman, Inc.*, 767 S.W.2d 381 (Mo. App. 1989). However, the danger from criminal acts of tenants may be just as real as the danger from outsiders, and landlords may believe it is necessary to screen and reject potentially dangerous tenants if they believe that they, or members of their families, may commit criminal acts. What legal problems would rejection create?

4. *The Policy Issues.* Commentators are divided on the social benefits of placing greater responsibility on landlords in regard to crimes committed on the premises. Glesner, *Landlords as Cops: Tort, Nuisance & Forfeiture Standards Imposing Liability on Landlords for Crimes on the Premises*, 42 Case W. Res. L. Rev. 679 (1992), takes a negative view:

> Since the legal standards for landlord liability do nothing to address the causes of crime, increased landlord efforts to meet these legal standards primarily serve to relocate crime to other areas, failing to significantly decrease criminal activity overall. Compared to this minimal benefit, significant costs accompany the shift of criminal law enforcement duties to

> landlords. Besides the grave potential for violation of tenant rights, there is a danger of encouraging the "deputization" of the citizenry.

Id. at 775. What are the contrary arguments? Is the issue whether solutions to social problems should be loaded on to private relationships? Glesner discusses the use of statutory forfeiture and the law of public nuisance as other methods to control this problem.

5. *Lead and Lead Poisoning.* A million or more children suffer from lead poisoning in this country, a disease that can cause severe mental retardation or even death if not treated. Lead poisoning in children is usually caused by the ingestion of lead-contaminated dust or chips from lead-based paint still present in thousands of rental dwellings, even though the federal government prohibited the use of lead paint in 1978.

An action in negligence against the landlord is a common remedy for damage caused by lead contamination. As in cases where negligence actions are brought for damage resulting from crimes, a plaintiff must show a duty to act. Should there be a different presumption about this issue than in the crime cases? *Antwaun A. v. Heritage Mutual Ins. Co.*, 596 N.W.2d 456 (Wis. 1999), reversing summary judgment for the landlord in a suit brought for lead poisoning, held "a duty to test for lead paint arises whenever the landlord of a residential property constructed before 1978 either knows or in the use of ordinary care should know that there is peeling or chipping paint on the rental property." This is the minority view, but the court relied on the enactment of federal, state and local legislation, public service campaigns and media attention to reach a different conclusion. For discussion of cases rejecting public nuisance suits seeking damages from manufacturers for remediation costs see Pargola, *Childhood Lead Poisoning-Combating A Timeless Silent Killer*, 37 RUTGERS L. REV. 300 (2010).

For discussion of the complex federal, state and local regulation of lead paint, see Rechtschaffen, *The Lead Poisoning Challenge: An Approach for California and Other States*, 21 HARV. ENVTL. L. REV. 387 (1997). Federal legislation requires sellers and lessors to disclose lead-based paint or lead-based paint hazards before the sale or rental of a pre-1978 housing unit, but leaves the actual regulation of lead paint in private housing to the states. An EPA rule covers residential property renovations to remove lead-based paint, including child-occupied facilities. 40 C.F.R. Part 745. The rule requires workers to be certified and trained in the use of lead-safe work practices, and requires renovation, repair, and painting firms to be EPA-certified and follow work practice standards. For discussion go to http://www.epa.gov/lead/lead-renovation-repair-and-painting-program-rules State statutory intervention is limited. In evaluating legal approaches to this problem, consider that the cost of removing lead-based paint from a dwelling may average $20,000 a dwelling.

6. *Tenants and Consumer Protection Statutes.* As an alternative remedy, some jurisdictions permit tenants to sue their landlords under general consumer protection acts. While some courts have found that the landlord-tenant relationship was not that of business and consumer — *see Billings v. Wilson*, 493 N.E.2d 187 (Mass. 1986) — others have been more sympathetic. In *Romea v. Heiberger & Assocs.*, 163 F.3d 111 (2d Cir. 1998), Judge Calabresi of the Second Circuit Court of Appeals held that *Federal Debt Collections Practices Act*, a United States statute

applied in the landlord-tenant context. To date, there is no general consensus on this issue.

[D.] STATUTORY INTERVENTION IN THE LANDLORD TENANT RELATIONSHIP

[1.] The Modern Urban Housing Code

The *Javins* case relied on the mandatory maintenance provisions of the District of Columbia residential housing code as a basis for establishing an implied warranty of habitability in leases. Housing codes require the maintenance of housing in good condition, the provision of necessary facilities, and limit occupancy by requiring a minimum amount of space for each occupant of a dwelling. They apply to rental as well as owner-occupied housing.

The adoption of housing codes to require the maintenance of urban residential dwellings dates to the beginning of the 20th Century, when urban reformers in New York City campaigning for tenement reform successfully obtained the adoption of municipal ordinance requiring owners of multi-unit dwellings to maintain their properties in accordance with certain guidelines. Similar codes were adopted in other cities, but enforcement was always problematic as few cities devoted adequate resources to this aspect of municipal government. Small numbers of enforcement officials were usually overwhelmed by the magnitude of their responsibilities. Consequently, housing codes had fallen into disuse by the end of World War II. However, they were revived in the postwar era as part of a slum clearance and rehabilitation strategy adopted by the Federal Housing Agency and later the Department of Housing and Urban Development. Federal subsides provided financial incentives for slum clearance, and the federal government required the adoption of strict housing codes as a remedial measure to prevent the formation of new slums in areas that were deteriorating.

Housing codes contain lengthy and detailed regulations, but the following excerpt is an example of typical maintenance requirements in a housing code that provided the basis for the *Javins* opinion:

> General Requirements Relating to the Safe and Sanitary Maintenance of Parts of Dwelling and Dwelling Units
>
> 7.01. Every foundation, roof and exterior wall, door, skylight, and window shall be reasonably weather-tight, water-tight, and damp-free, and shall be kept in sound condition and good repair. Floors, interior walls, and ceilings shall be sound and in the good repair. All exterior wood surfaces, other than decay resistant woods, shall be protected from the elements and decay by paint or other protective covering or treatment. Toxic paint and materials will not be used where readily accessible to children. Walls shall be capable of affording privacy for the occupants. Every premises shall be graded, drained, free of standing water, and maintained in a clean, sanitary and safe condition.

This section is typical of generalized and qualitative maintenance provisions that appear in many codes. Note the extent to which this section requires a subjective and interpretive judgment by code inspection officials charged with determining housing code violations and, correspondingly, by courts asked to enforce the implied covenant of habitability. *See also* the International Property Maintenance Code (2012 Edition), available at http://publicecodes.cyberregs.com/icod/ipmc/2012/icod_ipmc_2012_3_par002.htm.

Housing codes depend on private, as well as public, enforcement. Most code enforcement agencies rely heavily on private reporting of code violations as the basis for their code enforcement programs. However, tenants in substandard housing run a risk of eviction if their landlord discovers that they reported code violations in his property. Because most of these tenants do not have a lease and are usually on a month-to-month tenancy, there is nothing to prevent their eviction under standard common law rules.

The following case introduced another new concept in landlord-tenant law by recognizing a defense of retaliatory eviction in cases of this type:

EDWARDS v. HABIB

United States Court of Appeals, District of Columbia Circuit
397 F.2d 687 (1968)

J. SKELLY WRIGHT, CIRCUIT JUDGE.

In March 1965 the appellant, Mrs. Yvonne Edwards, rented housing property from the appellee, Nathan Habib, on a month-to-month basis. Shortly thereafter she complained to the Department of Licenses and Inspections of sanitary code violations which her landlord had failed to remedy. In the course of the ensuing inspection, more than 40 such violations were discovered which the Department ordered the landlord to correct. Habib then gave Mrs. Edwards a 30-day statutory notice to vacate and obtained a default judgment for possession of the premises. Mrs. Edwards promptly moved to reopen this judgment, alleging excusable neglect for the default and also alleging as a defense that the notice to quit was given in retaliation for her complaints to the housing authorities. Judge Greene, sitting on motions in the Court of General Sessions, set aside the default judgment and, in a very thoughtful opinion, concluded that a retaliatory motive, if proved, would constitute a defense to the action for possession. At the trial itself, however, a different judge apparently deemed evidence of retaliatory motive irrelevant and directed a verdict for the landlord.

[Mrs. Edwards then appealed to the District of Columbia Court of Appeals, which affirmed. An appeal to the U.S. Court of Appeals then followed. After quoting provisions in the District of Columbia Code authorizing actions to evict tenants who unlawfully retained possession, Judge Skelly Wright found that protection against retaliatory eviction was necessary.]

These provisions [from the D.C. Code] are simply procedural. They neither say nor imply anything about whether evidence of retaliation or other improper motive should be unavailable as a defense to a possessory action brought under them. It is true that in making his affirmative case for possession the landlord need only show that his tenant has been given the 30-day statutory notice, and he need not assign any reason for evicting a tenant who does not occupy the premises under a lease. But while the landlord may evict for any legal reason or for no reason at all, he is not, we hold, free to evict in retaliation for his tenant's report of housing code violations to the authorities. As a matter of statutory construction and for reasons of public policy, such an eviction cannot be permitted.

The housing and sanitary codes, especially in light of Congress' explicit direction for their enactment, indicate a strong and pervasive congressional concern to secure for the city's slum dwellers decent, or at least safe and sanitary, places to live. Effective implementation and enforcement of the codes obviously depend in part on private initiative in the reporting of violations. Though there is no official procedure for the filing of such complaints, the bureaucratic structure of the Department of Licenses and Inspections establishes such a procedure, and for fiscal year 1966 nearly a third of the cases handled by the Department arose from private complaints. To permit retaliatory evictions, then, would clearly frustrate the effectiveness of the housing code as a means of upgrading the quality of housing in Washington.

As judges, "we cannot shut our eyes to matters of public notoriety and general cognizance. When we take our seats on the bench we are not struck with blindness, and forbidden to know as judges what we see as men." *Ho Ah Kow v. Nunan*, C.C.D. Cal., 12 Fed. Cas. 252, 255 (No. 6546) (1879). In trying to effect the will of Congress and as a court of equity we have the responsibility to consider the social context in which our decisions will have operational effect. In light of the appalling condition and shortage of housing in Washington, the expense of moving, the inequality of bargaining power between tenant and landlord, and the social and economic importance of assuring at least minimum standards in housing conditions, we do not hesitate to declare that retaliatory eviction cannot be tolerated. There can be no doubt that the slum dweller, even though his home be marred by housing code violations, will pause long before he complains of them if he fears eviction as a consequence. Hence an eviction under the circumstances of this case would not only punish appellant for making a complaint which she had a constitutional right to make, a result which we would not impute to the will of Congress simply on the basis of an essentially procedural enactment, but also would stand as a warning to others that they dare not be so bold, a result which, from the authorization of the housing code, we think Congress affirmatively sought to avoid.

The notion that the effectiveness of remedial legislation will be inhibited if those reporting violations of it can legally be intimidated is so fundamental that a presumption against the legality of such intimidation can be inferred as inherent in the legislation even if it is not expressed in the statute itself. Such an inference was recently drawn by the Supreme Court from the federal labor statutes to strike down under the supremacy clause a Florida statute denying unemployment insurance to workers discharged in retaliation for filing complaints of federally defined unfair labor practices. While we are not confronted with a possible conflict between federal policy and state law, we do have the task of reconciling and harmonizing two federal statutes so as to best effectuate the purposes of each. The proper balance can only be struck by interpreting 45 D.C. Code §§ 902 and 910 as inapplicable where the court's aid is invoked to effect an eviction in retaliation for reporting housing code violations.

This is not, of course, to say that even if the tenant can prove a retaliatory purpose she is entitled to remain in possession in perpetuity. If this illegal purpose is dissipated, the landlord can, in the absence of legislation or a binding contract, evict his tenants or raise their rents for economic or other legitimate reasons, or even for no reason at all. The question of permissible or impermissible purpose is one of fact for the court or jury, and while such a determination is not easy, it is not significantly different from problems with which the courts must deal in a host of other contexts, such as when they must decide whether the employer who discharges a worker has committed an unfair labor practice because he has done so on account of the employee's union activities. As Judge Greene said, "There is no reason why similar factual judgments cannot be made by courts and juries in the context of economic retaliation [against tenants by landlords] for providing information to the government."

Reversed and remanded.

[The concurring opinion by Judge McGowan and the dissenting opinion by Judge Danaher are omitted.]

NOTES AND QUESTIONS

1. *Retaliatory Eviction.* In *Habib*, the court relied on public policy and statutory intent to imply a defense of retaliatory eviction. The year before, in *Brown v. Southall Realty Co.*, 237 A.2d 834 (D.C. 1967), the court held that a lease on premises that violated the housing code was void and illegal. The defense of retaliatory eviction is now widely recognized. For a recent case, see *Building Monitoring Sys. v. Paxton*, 905 P.2d 1215 (Utah 1995). The court adopted and applied the definition of retaliatory eviction contained in Restatement (Second) of Property § 14.8 (1977). *Hosey v. Club Van Cortlandt*, 299 F. Supp. 501 (S.D.N.Y. 1969), held that the defense of retaliatory eviction was based on the Constitution.

Robinson v. Diamond Hous. Corp., 463 F.2d 853 (D.C. Cir. 1972), held the defense of retaliatory eviction is available even though the eviction is not for reporting a code violation, when the landlord attempted to evict a tenant who successfully set up housing code violations in a previous action for possession. That case also considered the landlord's argument, that the availability of the defense would give the tenant an indefinite tenancy. The court answered a landlord could always evict for a legitimate business justification. How much time must pass before a landlord can make this argument? *Imperial Colliery Co. v. Fout*, 373 S.E.2d 489 (W. Va. 1989), held the retaliatory eviction defense is not available for actions incidental to the tenancy (union activity in this case), but the true motive of the landlord may be difficult to determine. For a study showing that legal services attorneys represent poor and minority tenants with strong defenses to evictions, and that raising these defenses does not pose significant costs on landlords, see Gunn, *Eviction Defense for Poor Tenants: Costly Compassion or Justice Served?*, 13 Yale L. & Pol'y Rev. 385 (1995).

2. *Protecting the Tenancy.* In constructive eviction cases, the tenant must leave the premises to bring a case successfully, but the defense of retaliatory eviction is intended to protect the tenancy in cases where the tenant is not protected at common law. What if a tenant moves out of her property when threatened with eviction, or because a landlord has raised rents, and discovers later that she has a retaliatory eviction defense. Does she then have a cause of action against the landlord?

Murphy v. Smallridge, 468 S.E.2d 167 (W. Va. 1996), agreed with cases elsewhere and held yes. It held that denying the tenant a cause of action in this situation would lead to unfair treatment of analogous situations. If protecting the tenancy is the basis for the retaliatory eviction defense, is giving a cause of action to the tenant who moves out justified? *Twyman v. Johnson*, 655 A.2d 850 (D.C. 1995), held a tenant may be entitled to an award of damages through administrative relief, but that the D.C. statute did not create a private right of action for damages.

3. *A Statutory Solution.* About 30 states now have statutes that recognize the defense of retaliatory eviction. The Uniform Residential Landlord and Tenant Act, Article 9, deals with retaliatory eviction. Section 901 details retaliation that is protected, and includes complaints about code violations and housing discrimination. Section 902 authorizes tenant recovery of possession and rent. Section 903 enacts a rebuttable presumption of retaliation if a landlord engages in retaliation within six months after a tenant engages in protected activity.

Elk Creek Mgmt. Co. v. Gilbert, 303 P.3d 929, 940 (Or. 2013), held the statute prohibiting retaliatory eviction does not require an intent to injure the tenant, and a tenant need only prove that his "protected activity was a factor that made a difference in the landlord's decision." The court reviewed the adoption of a prohibition on retaliatory eviction in URLTA, and the different ways in which the states handled this statutory language.

4. *The Code Enforcement Alternative.* If a reliance on private complaints and enforcement of tenant rights is not enough to secure compliance with housing codes, what kind of public enforcement program will work best? Code enforcement is often reactive in response to complaints, and enforcement is discretionary. Ross, *Housing Code Enforcement and Urban Decline*, 6 J. Affordable Hous. 1 (1996). Cities may also take a triage approach, and enforce the code only in areas that have not fully declined, and where landlords have the resources to achieve compliance. For a case study of a successful attempt to implement a code enforcement program based explicitly on selective enforcement, see Kinning, *Selective Housing Code Enforcement and Low-Income Housing Policy: Minneapolis Case Study*, 21 Fordham Urb. L.J. 159 (1993). The author concludes that "[i]f there are no gentrification pressures and there exists a sufficient supply of affordable housing for low-income tenants, a selective code enforcement program can be administered without detriment to low-income tenants or neighborhoods." *Id.* at 197.

Is selective code enforcement unconstitutional if it has the effect of perpetuating bad housing in badly-deteriorated neighborhoods? *See 3004 Albany Crescent Tenants' Assoc. v. City of New York*, 1997 U.S. Dist. LEXIS 6138 (S.D.N.Y. May 5, 1997) (dismissing constitutional and statutory claims). For a thorough review of code enforcement, see J. SCHILLING & J. HARE, CODE ENFORCEMENT: A COMPREHENSIVE APPROACH (1994).

5. *Code Enforcement After the Housing Recession.* The housing recession, massive foreclosures, and the large residue of vacant dwellings have created serious enforcement problems. These include a fragmentation of enforcement functions and responsibilities, a large volume of violation, title defects that affect eligibility for special assistance, absentee ownership and speculation in distressed housing, large-scale resistance by the mortgage collection industry to lawful compliance, and financial incapability. Lind, *Collateral Matters: Housing Code Compliance in the Mortgage Crisis*, 32 N. ILL. U. L. REV. 445 (2012), discusses possible strategies for improving code enforcement after the mortgage crisis, including a shift in focus to target entire neighborhoods rather than individual homes.

Vacant property registration ordinances are one response to the crisis, and have been widely enacted. www.safeguardproperties.com/Resources/Vacant_Property_Registration.aspx is a web site that collects these ordinances from around the country. There are two basic models. "The classic model requires registration based on length of vacancy. The foreclosure model requires registration initiated at foreclosure." Davis, *A Comparative Analysis of State and Local Government Vacant Property Registration Statutes*, 44 URB. LAW. 399, 406 (2012). All models state the purpose and definition of vacant and abandoned properties, provide the specifics of the registration process, state the affirmative duties of potentially responsible parties, and have enforcement mechanisms. Martin, *Vacant Property Registration Ordinances*, 39 REAL EST. L.J. 6, 11 (2010). A growing trend is that some ordinances require a plan detailing how the unoccupied building will be secured, future plans for the property, or both. *Id. at* 24.

Anti-blight ordinances are another strategy. They include a definition of blighted premises, provide for notice and a hearing on probable violations, and a plan for abatement if a violation is found. The Westport, Connecticut ordinance is available at http://www.westportct.gov/modules/showdocument.aspx?documentid=5873.

6. *Retaliatory Eviction and Commercial Tenants.* As a general rule, the retaliatory eviction doctrine does not apply to commercial tenancies. Commercial tenants will normally have other remedies available in cases where a landlord fails to comply with property maintenance provisions in local buildings codes or in the lease itself. *Espenschied v. Mallick*, 633 A.2d 388 (D.C. 1993).

[2.] Rent Control

[a.] Rent Control in Theory and Practice

Rent control was in effect nationally during both World Wars, but it had virtually disappeared by the 1950s except in a few major urban centers like New York City. Inflationary trends in the 1970s and 1980s led to a renewed interest, and some cities are reconsidering rent control because of the rent inflation that is occurring since the recent housing recession displaced homeowners and increased the demand for rental housing. Rent controls exist today in California and some eastern seaboard states. However, an attack by property rights activists on rent controls has been effective in recent years. States such as Massachusetts have now prohibited rent controls altogether, and New York has modified its once extensive system.

Rent regulation rather than rent control is probably a better term to use for laws that limit tenant rents. Rents are not frozen, as due process requires that landlords earn a fair return. To meet this requirement, rent regulation ordinances usually allow for periodic increases, either a fixed statutory amount or a discretionary amount determined by a local agency that is based on increases in the cost of living index or in landlord costs. Some laws allow landlords to charge only a portion of the permitted increase, however. There may also be provisions for individual adjustments for landlords who require an exceptional rent increase because of extraordinary operating expenses or for other reasons. Adequate maintenance is required as a condition for a rent increase. *See Helmsley v. Borough of Ft. Lee*, 394 A.2d 65 (N.J. 1978) (ordinance limiting annual increases to 2.5% held confiscatory). Landlords are also allowed to recoup the cost of capital improvements, such as rehabilitation and repairs. For a description of some of the ordinances in the United States, see Baar, *Guidelines for Drafting Rent Control Laws: Lessons of a Decade*, 35 Rutgers L. Rev. 723, 756–841 (1983).

Rent control laws may provide for vacancy decontrol, which means that a housing unit is decontrolled once it becomes vacant. This option is subject to abuse because a landlord may trigger vacancy decontrol by moving into the unit and then re-renting at a higher rent once the previous tenant is evicted. There also are exemptions from controls, usually for new construction and for owners with only a few rental units.

Rent control may also contain additional protections for tenants. They may prohibit eviction except for just cause, and may regulate or restrict the demolition of rent-controlled units or their conversion to owner-occupied condominiums. This summary suggests that the economic impact of rent controls is to prevent excessive rent-charging, and that protections for tenants in the form of controls on evictions and other protections may be as important as restraints on rent levels.

Rent controls are either stringent or moderate, depending on how much they limit residential rents and landlord freedoms. A stringent law, for example, may not have a vacancy decontrol provision and may have very restrictive provisions for rent increases.

[b.] The Constitutionality of Rent Control: The Case of Mobile Homes

Although rent controls for apartment rentals may be diminishing, controls on rents for mobile homes in mobile home parks is still strong in states like California. "Mobile home" is actually the term used for a housing unit that is manufactured off-site and then shipped as a unit for site placement. "Manufactured housing" is now the acceptable term, but the case that follows uses the term "mobile home." Once sited, a mobile home is seldom moved. Mobile homes may be located on individual lots or placed, with others, in mobile home parks. Because mobile homes are more affordable than conventional housing, they are particularly attractive as a housing resource to the elderly and the relatively poor, and make up a substantial part of the housing stock in some municipalities and in rural areas. The preferred usage refers to them as manufactured housing.

Tenants own their mobile homes in mobile home parks, and pay a monthly rental for the mobile home "pad" to the park owner in addition to the mortgage payment on the home, if it is still being paid. Rent control determines the amount of rent a mobile home park owner can charge for a pad. Because zoning regulations usually limit the amount of land available for mobile home parks, the owners of parks would be able to charge a monopoly rent in the absence of controls.

Existing mobile home owners in parks benefit from this arrangement, but subsequent owners who purchase a mobile home from an existing owner will not benefit because they will probably have to purchase the mobile home at a premium. This is so because eviction from the park is severely restricted, and rent controls will diminish the monopoly rent the park owner would be able to charge in the absence of controls. These price and security of tenure advantages are what enable owners of mobile homes in parks to charge a premium price for their homes when they sell. *See* Rubinfeld, *Regulatory Takings: The Case of Mobile Home Rent Control*, 67 CHI.-KENT L. REV. 923 (1991).

This package of controls on mobile homes and mobile home occupancy makes substantial changes in the property rights of mobile home park owners and mobile home park occupants. The question is whether a taking has occurred because property rights normally belonging to the mobile home park owner have been extinguished. The Supreme Court considered these issues in a case arising out of the California mobile home rent control system.

YEE v. CITY OF ESCONDIDO

United States Supreme Court
503 U.S. 519 (1992)

JUSTICE O'CONNOR delivered the opinion of the Court.

The Takings Clause of the Fifth Amendment provides: "Nor shall private property be taken for public use, without just compensation." Most of our cases interpreting the Clause fall within two distinct classes. Where the government authorizes a physical occupation of property (or actually takes title), the Takings Clause generally requires compensation. *See, e.g., Loretto v. Teleprompter Manhattan CATV Corp.*, 458 U.S. 419 (1982). But where the government merely regulates the use of property, compensation is required only if considerations such as the purpose of the regulation or the extent to which it deprives the owner of the economic use of the property suggest that the regulation has unfairly singled out the property owner to bear a burden that should be borne by the public as a whole. The first category of cases requires courts to apply a clear rule; the second necessarily entails complex factual assessments of the purposes and economic effects of government actions.

Petitioners own mobile home parks in Escondido, California. They contend that a local rent control ordinance, when viewed against the backdrop of California's Mobile Home Residency Law, amounts to a physical occupation of their property entitling them to compensation under the first category of cases discussed above.

Issue: Is regulation of rent at trailer parks a physical taking?

I

The term "mobile home" is somewhat misleading. Mobile homes are largely immobile as a practical matter, because the cost of moving one is often a significant fraction of the value of the mobile home itself. They are generally placed permanently in parks; once in place, only about one in every hundred mobile homes is ever moved. Hirsch & Hirsch, *Legal-Economic Analysis of Rent Controls in a Mobile Home Context: Placement Values and Vacancy Decontrol*, 35 UCLA L. Rev. 399, 405 (1988). A mobile home owner typically rents a plot of land, called a "pad," from the owner of a mobile home park. The park owner provides private roads within the park, common facilities such as washing machines or a swimming pool, and often utilities. The mobile home owner often invests in site-specific improvements such as a driveway, steps, walkways, porches, or landscaping. When the mobile home owner wishes to move, the mobile home is usually sold in place, and the purchaser continues to rent the pad on which the mobile home is located.

In 1978, California enacted its Mobilehome Residency Law, Cal. Civ. Code Ann. § 798 (1982 and Supp. 1991). The Legislature found "that, because of the high cost of moving mobilehomes, the potential for damage resulting therefrom, the requirements relating to the installation of mobilehomes, and the cost of landscaping or lot preparation, it is necessary that the owners of mobilehomes occupied within mobilehome parks be provided with the unique protection from actual or constructive eviction afforded by the provisions of this chapter." § 798.55(a).

The Mobilehome Residency Law limits the bases upon which a park owner may terminate a mobile home owner's tenancy. These include the nonpayment of rent, the mobile home owner's violation of law or park rules, and the park owner's desire to change the use of his land. § 798.56. While a rental agreement is in effect, however, the park owner generally may not require the removal of a mobilehome when it is sold. § 798.73. The park owner may neither charge a transfer fee for the sale, § 798.72, nor disapprove of the purchaser, provided that the purchaser has the ability to pay the rent, § 798.74. The Mobilehome Residency Law contains a number of other detailed provisions, but none limit the rent the park owner may charge.

In the wake of the Mobilehome Residency Law, various communities in California adopted mobilehome rent control ordinances. *See* Hirsch & Hirsch, *supra*, at 408–411. The voters of Escondido did the same in 1988 by approving Proposition K, the rent control ordinance challenged here. The ordinance sets rents back to their 1986 levels, and prohibits rent increases without the approval of the City Council. Park owners may apply to the Council for rent increases at any time. The Council must approve any increases it determines to be "just, fair and reasonable," after considering the following nonexclusive list of factors: (1) changes in the Consumer Price Index; (2) the rent charged for comparable mobile home pads in Escondido; (3) the length of time since the last rent increase; (4) the cost of any capital improvements related to the pad or pads at issue; (5) changes in property taxes; (6) changes in any rent paid by the park owner for the land; (7) changes in utility charges; (8) changes in operating and maintenance expenses; (9) the need for repairs other than for ordinary wear and tear; (10) the amount and quality of services provided to the affected tenant; and (11) any lawful existing lease. Ordinance § 4(g).

Petitioners John and Irene Yee own the Friendly Hills and Sunset Terrace Mobile Home Parks, both of which are located in the city of Escondido. A few months after the adoption of Escondido's rent control ordinance, they filed suit in San Diego County Superior Court. According to the complaint, "the rent control law has had the effect of depriving the plaintiffs of all use and occupancy of [their] real property and granting to the tenants of mobilehomes presently in The Park, as well as the successors in interest of such tenants, the right to physically permanently occupy and use the real property of Plaintiff." The Yees requested damages of six million dollars, a declaration that the rent control ordinance is unconstitutional, and an injunction barring the ordinance's enforcement.

[The trial court sustained the city's demurrer and dismissed the complaint. The Court of Appeal affirmed.] The [latter] court concluded: "*Loretto* in no way suggests that the Escondido ordinance authorizes a permanent physical occupation of the landlord's property and therefore constitutes a per se taking." 224 Cal. App. 3d 1349, 1358 (1990). The California Supreme Court denied review.

We granted *certiorari*.

II

Petitioners do not claim that the ordinary rent control statutes regulating housing throughout the country violate the Takings Clause. *Cf. Pennell v. San Jose*, 485 U.S. 1 (1988); *Loretto*, *supra*, at 440. Instead, their argument is predicated on the unusual economic relationship between park owners and mobile home owners. Park owners may no longer set rents or decide who their tenants will be. As a result, according to petitioners, any reduction in the rent for a mobile home pad causes a corresponding increase in the value of a mobile home, because the mobilehome owner now owns, in addition to a mobile home, the right to occupy a pad at a rent below the value that would be set by the free market. *Cf.* Hirsch & Hirsch, 35 UCLA L. Rev., at 425. Because under the California Mobilehome Residency Law the park owner cannot evict a mobile home owner or easily convert the property to other uses, the argument goes, the mobile home owner is effectively a perpetual tenant of the park, and the increase in the mobile home's value thus represents the right to occupy a pad at below-market rent indefinitely. And because the Mobilehome Residency Law permits the mobile home owner to sell the mobile home in place, the mobile home owner can receive a premium from the purchaser corresponding to this increase in value. The amount of this premium is not limited by the Mobilehome Residency Law or the Escondido ordinance. As a result, petitioners conclude, the rent control ordinance has transferred a discrete interest in land — the right to occupy the land indefinitely at a sub-market rent — from the park owner to the mobile home owner. Petitioners contend that what has been transferred from park owner to mobile home owner is no less than a right of physical occupation of the park owner's land.

This argument, while perhaps within the scope of our regulatory taking cases, cannot be squared easily with our cases on physical takings. The government effects a physical taking only where it requires the landowner to submit to the physical occupation of his land. "This element of required acquiescence is at the heart of the concept of occupation." *FCC v. Florida Power Corp.*, 480 U.S. 245, 252 (1987). Thus whether the government floods a landowner's property, *Pumpelly v. Green Bay Co.*, 80 U.S. 166 (1872), or does no more than require the landowner to suffer the installation of a cable, *Loretto, supra*, the Takings Clause requires compensation if the government authorizes a compelled physical invasion of property.

But the Escondido rent control ordinance, even when considered in conjunction with the California Mobilehome Residency Law, authorizes no such thing. Petitioners voluntarily rented their land to mobile home owners. At least on the face of the regulatory scheme, neither the City nor the State compels petitioners, once they have rented their property to tenants, to continue doing so. To the contrary, the Mobilehome Residency Law provides that a park owner who wishes to change the use of his land may evict his tenants, albeit with six or twelve months' notice. Cal. Civ. Code Ann. § 798.56(g). Put bluntly, no government has required any physical invasion of petitioners' property. Petitioners' tenants were invited by petitioners, not forced upon them by the government. *See Florida Power, supra*, at 252–253. While the "right to exclude" is doubtless, as petitioners assert, "one of the most essential sticks in the bundle of rights that are commonly characterized as property," *Kaiser Aetna v. United States*, 444 U.S. 164, 176 (1979), we do not find that right to have been taken from petitioners on the mere face of the Escondido ordinance.

Petitioners suggest that the statutory procedure for changing the use of a mobile home park is in practice "a kind of gauntlet," in that they are not in fact free to change the use of their land. Because petitioners do not claim to have run that gauntlet, however, this case provides no occasion to consider how the procedure has been applied to petitioners' property, and we accordingly confine ourselves to the face of the statute. A different case would be presented were the statute, on its face or as applied, to compel a landowner over objection to rent his property or to refrain in perpetuity from terminating a tenancy.

On their face, the state and local laws at issue here merely regulate petitioners' use of their land by regulating the relationship between landlord and tenant. "This Court has consistently affirmed that States have broad power to regulate housing conditions in general and the landlord-tenant relationship in particular without paying compensation for all economic injuries that such regulation entails." *Loretto*, 458 U.S. at 440. *See also Florida Power, supra*, at 252 ("statutes regulating the economic relations of landlords and tenants are not per se takings"). When a landowner decides to rent his land to tenants, the government may place ceilings on the rents the landowner can charge, *see, e.g., Pennell, supra*, at 12, n.6, or require the landowner to accept tenants he does not like, *see, e.g., Heart of Atlanta Motel, Inc. v. United States*, 379 U.S. 241, 261 (1964), without automatically having to pay compensation. Such forms of regulation are analyzed by engaging in the "essentially ad hoc, factual inquiries" necessary to determine whether a regulatory taking has occurred. *Kaiser Aetna, supra*, at 175. In the words of Justice Holmes, "while property may be regulated to a certain extent, if regulation goes too far it will be recognized as a taking." *Pennsylvania Coal Co. v. Mahon*, 260 U.S. 393, 415 (1922).

Petitioners emphasize that the ordinance transfers wealth from park owners to incumbent mobile home owners. Other forms of land use regulation, however, can also be said to transfer wealth from the one who is regulated to another. Ordinary rent control often transfers wealth from landlords to tenants by reducing the landlords' income and the tenants' monthly payments, although it does not cause a one-time transfer of value as occurs with mobile homes. Traditional zoning regulations can transfer wealth from those whose activities are prohibited to their neighbors; when a property owner is barred from mining coal on his land, for example, the value of his property may decline but the value of his neighbor's property may rise. The mobile home owner's ability to sell the mobile home at a premium may make this wealth transfer more visible than in the ordinary case, *see* Epstein, *Rent Control and the Theory of Efficient Regulation*, 54 BROOK. L. REV. 741, 758–759 (1988), but the existence of the transfer in itself does not convert regulation into physical invasion.

Petitioners also rely heavily on their allegation that the ordinance benefits incumbent mobile home owners without benefiting future mobile home owners, who will be forced to purchase mobile homes at premiums. Mobile homes, like motor vehicles, ordinarily decline in value with age. But the effect of the rent control ordinance, coupled with the restrictions on the park owner's freedom to reject new tenants, is to increase significantly the value of the mobile home. This increased value normally benefits only the tenant in possession at the time the rent control is imposed. *See* Hirsch & Hirsch, 35 UCLA L. REV., at 430–31. Petitioners are correct in citing the existence of this premium as a difference between the alleged effect of the Escondido ordinance and that of an ordinary apartment rent control statute. Most apartment tenants do not sell anything to their successors (and are often prohibited from charging "key money"), so a typical rent control statute will transfer wealth from the landlord to the incumbent tenant and all future tenants. By contrast, petitioners contend that the Escondido ordinance transfers wealth only to the incumbent mobile home owner. This effect might have some bearing on whether the ordinance causes a regulatory taking, as it may shed some light on whether there is a sufficient nexus between the effect of the ordinance and the objectives it is supposed to advance. But it has nothing to do with whether the ordinance causes a physical taking. Whether the ordinance benefits only current mobile home owners or all mobile home owners, it does not require petitioners to submit to the physical occupation of their land.

The same may be said of petitioners' contention that the ordinance amounts to compelled physical occupation because it deprives petitioners of the ability to choose their incoming tenants.[3]

Again, this effect may be relevant to a regulatory taking argument, as it may be one factor a reviewing court would wish to consider in determining whether the ordinance unjustly imposes a burden on petitioners that should "be compensated by

[3] [1] Strictly speaking, the Escondido rent control ordinance only limits rents. Petitioners' inability to select their incoming tenants is a product of the State's Mobilehome Residency Law, the constitutionality of which has never been at issue in this case. (The State, moreover, has never been a party.) But we understand petitioners to be making a more subtle argument — that before the adoption of the ordinance they were able to influence a mobilehome owner's selection of a purchaser by threatening to increase the rent for prospective purchasers they disfavored. To the extent the rent control ordinance deprives petitioners of this type of influence, petitioners' argument is one we must consider.

the government, rather than remaining disproportionately concentrated on a few persons." *Penn Central Transp. Co. v. New York City*, 438 U.S. [104] at 124 [(1978)]. But it does not convert regulation into the unwanted physical occupation of land. Because they voluntarily open their property to occupation by others, petitioners cannot assert a per se right to compensation based on their inability to exclude particular individuals.

Petitioners' final line of argument rests on a footnote in *Loretto*, in which we rejected the contention that "the landlord could avoid the requirements of [the statute forcing her to permit cable to be permanently placed on her property] by ceasing to rent the building to tenants." We found this possibility insufficient to defeat a physical taking claim, because "a landlord's ability to rent his property may not be conditioned on his forfeiting the right to compensation for a physical occupation." *Loretto*, 458 U.S. at 439, n.17. Petitioners argue that if they have to leave the mobile home park business in order to avoid the strictures of the Escondido ordinance, their ability to rent their property has in fact been conditioned on such a forfeiture. This argument fails at its base, however, because there has simply been no compelled physical occupation giving rise to a right to compensation that petitioners could have forfeited. Had the city required such an occupation, of course, petitioners would have a right to compensation, and the city might then lack the power to condition petitioners' ability to run mobile home parks on their waiver of this right. But because the ordinance does not effect a physical taking in the first place, this footnote in *Loretto* does not help petitioners.

IV

We made this observation in *Loretto*:

> Our holding today is very narrow. We affirm the traditional rule that a permanent physical occupation of property is a taking. In such a case, the property owner entertains a historically rooted expectation of compensation, and the character of the invasion is qualitatively more intrusive than perhaps any other category of property regulation. We do not, however, question the equally substantial authority upholding a State's broad power to impose appropriate restrictions upon an owner's use of his property.

458 U.S. at 441.

Because the Escondido rent control ordinance does not compel a landowner to suffer the physical occupation of his property, it does not effect a per se taking under *Loretto*. The judgment of the Court of Appeal is accordingly Affirmed.

[Concurring opinions by Justices Blackmun and Souter are omitted.]

NOTES AND QUESTIONS

1. *The Constitutionality of Rent Control. Yee* indicates that restrictions on a landlord's rights in his property are not a physical taking of an interest in land per se. The court did not consider the regulatory taking problem. What about the argument that the combined effect of the two laws was to confer a windfall gain on existing tenants that properly belonged to the mobile home park owners? Isn't the transfer of this windfall gain a taking per se?

Would the Court's reasoning have been any different if it were considering a statute imposing an implied warranty of habitability? That requirement also transfers wealth from tenants to landlords, though in a different way. Could it be a regulatory taking?

The constitutionality of rent control was upheld by the United States Supreme Court as early as 1921. *Block v. Hirsh*, 256 U.S. 135 (1921). More than six decades later, it considered this issue again in *Pennell v. City of San Jose*, 485 U.S. 1 (1988). Plaintiffs facially challenged a provision in a rent control ordinance allowing a downward adjustment in rents if a local hearing officer found "hardship to a tenant." The Court held premature the claim that this provision violated the Takings Clause because it could reduce the "reasonable rent" to which a landlord was entitled under the ordinance. There was no evidence the tenant hardship clause had ever been applied, and an automatic reduction of rent under the clause was not required. The tenant hardship clause did not violate due process because it was a reasonable attempt to reduce the burden of housing costs on low-income tenants. The tenant hardship provision did not violate equal protection because it was rationally related to the legitimate objective of protecting tenants.

Guggenheim v. City of Goleta, 638 F.3d 1111 (9th Cir. 2010), rejected a facial takings claim that by locking in a rent below market rents, and allowing tenants to sell their mobile homes to buyers who will still enjoy the benefits of the controlled rent, the ordinance shifted much of the value of ownership from the landlord to the tenant. Although the Guggenheims might have paid a slight speculative premium over the value that legal stream of rent income would yield on the theory that rent control might end some day, that premium was no more than a speculative possibility that did not amount to a distinct investment-backed expectation.

To the extent the courts in some cases held a "taking" occurred because rent control did not advance a legitimate governmental interest, they are superseded at least as to federal law by the Supreme Court's recent decision in *Lingle v. Chevron USA*, discussed in Chapter 3, in the Notes following *Dolan*. *See* Note, *Rent Control and Rent Stabilization as Forms of Regulatory and Physical Takings*, B.C. ENVTL. L. REV. 361 (2007). Should mandatory affordable housing requirements be treated the same as rent control? The California Supreme Court recently so held in *California Building Industry Ass'n v. City of San Jose*, 351 P.3d 974 (Cal. 2015).

2. *Is Rent Control Good Social Policy?* There is a continuing and bitter controversy over the effects of rent controls on housing markets. A thorough review of studies published at the time of the *Pennell* case was cautiously mixed. A. DOWNS, RESIDENTIAL RENT CONTROLS: AN EVALUATION (1988). In his study, Downs found that only stringent rent controls reduce construction of multifamily housing; that stringent rent controls cause landlords to reduce service and maintenance expenditures, but that the evidence is ambivalent for moderate rent controls; that rent controls reduce tenant mobility and confer significant benefits on middle- and upper-income households; that rent controls cause a major transfer of resources from the owners of rental units to their tenants; and that rent controls tend to reduce the assessed values of rental housing. Downs concludes that "[r]ent controls harm low-income households in the long run by aggravating shortages of low-priced

rental units, thereby contributing to low vacancy rates and perhaps even homelessness among the very poorest households." *Id.* at 63.

For a review of even more negative studies from the 1980s and early 1990s, see Radford, *Why Rent Control is a Regulatory Taking*, 6 FORDHAM ENVTL. L.J. 755 (1995). These studies found:

> Rent control on both coasts of the United States has reduced the supply of affordable housing and imposed harsh costs on the poor, minorities, the elderly and other vulnerable population groups. The main beneficiaries appear to have been young, middle class professionals, who have a marked advantage in competing for the dwindling supply of rent controlled housing.

Id. at 769; *see also* Wagner, *Complexity, Governance and Constitutional Craftsmanship*, 61 AM. J. ECON. & SOC. 105 (2002) (arguing rent control too uncertain a measure to control market); Olsen, *Is Rent Control Good Social Policy?*, 67 CHI.-KENT L. REV. 931 (1991) (variance in annual benefits quite large among households with same characteristics; costs to landlords exceed benefits to tenants).

Advocates of rent control dispute these findings, claiming that studies with negative findings are flawed, and that changes in housing stock are due to market forces unrelated to rent control programs. *See, e.g.*, Gilderbloom, *Moderate Rent Control: Its Impact on the Quality and Quantity of the Housing Stock*, 17 URB. AFF. Q. 123 (1981); Olsen, *What Do Economists Know About the Effect of Rent Control on Housing Maintenance?*, 1 J. REAL EST. FIN. & ECON. 295 (1988). For a detailed examination of rent control, see RENT CONTROL: REGULATION AND THE URBAN HOUSING MARKET (W. Keating, M. Teitz & A. Skaburskis eds., 1998). For an argument of behalf of its continuing viability, see Block, *A Critique of the Legal and Philosophical Case for Rent Control*, 40 J. BUS ETHICS 75 (2002).

3. *What Happens When Rent Control Ends?* The termination of rent control in Massachusetts in 1994, where it had been in effect in Boston, and in Cambridge and Brookline in the Boston area, provides an insight into what may happen when rent control ends. Studies found that decontrolled rents increased by more than 50%, complaints of eviction rose by 33%, and in Cambridge, nearly 40% of tenants moved out after rent control ended. *The Morning After*, THE ECONOMIST, May 2, 1998, at 25. They also showed that investment in housing and repairs went up, that most people stayed put, and that the number of non-white tenants in formerly regulated units actually doubled. Cities in the area have also budgeted funds for affordable housing programs, while Boston secured federal rent subsidies for 400 units. *Id.* See Sims, *Out of Control: What We Can Learn from the End of Massachusetts Rent Control*, 61 J. URB. ECON. 129 (2007).

4. *Housing as a Fundamental Right.* In many countries, the right to housing is constitutionally protected. According to the Federal Constitutional Court of Germany, a tenant's interest in a rented apartment is a constitutionally protected property right. 89 BverfGE 1 [1993], and most European countries take a similar approach. *See* Ken, *One Nation's Dream, Another's Reality: Housing Justice in Sweden*, 22 BROOKLYN J. INT'L L. 63 (1996); SPRANKLING, COLETTA & MIROW, GLOBAL ISSUES IN PROPERTY LAW 59–68 (2006). Obviously, the United States has not adopted this approach. *See Lindsey v. Normet*, 405 U.S. 56 (1972) (rejecting fundamental

right argument); Berger, *Beyond Homelessness: An Entitlement to Housing*, 45 U. MIAMI L. REV. 315 (1991).

Chapter 7

SERVITUDES

To this point, the forms of shared ownership that have been examined have involved owners entitled to the right of possession, either at the present time or in the future. However, there are other forms of shared ownership in which some of the "owners" are never entitled to the right of possession. In these situations one party "owns" the subject property but holds it subject to the right of another to make use of it. While the parties are not joint owners in a technical sense, they do hold simultaneous real property interests in the same parcel. Neither can employ the property without taking into account the rights of the other, and thus are in a position of concurrent owners. Interests such as these are characterized as affirmative easements, profits, and licenses.

Easements and profits are traditionally described as servitudes which are nonpossessory interests created by agreements between private parties that entitle one party to use or restrict the use of the land of another. Licenses are not servitudes *per se*, but they perform a similar function. The other servitudes — the real covenant running with the land, the equitable servitude, and the negative easement — impose limitations or burdens on the use of land, but do not create a right to affirmatively use the affected property. As such they do not represent forms of concurrent ownership; rather, they resemble the restrictions on the ownership of land imposed by the sovereign through the exercise of the police and taxing powers. Consequently, these forms of servitudes are the subject Chapter 8: "The Transfer of Property Subject to Restriction."

[A.] EASEMENTS

[1.] Easements Appurtenant

If an easement is created for the use of the owner of an adjacent parcel of land, it is said to be an easement appurtenant. The tract of land burdened by the easement is said to be the servient tenement or estate while the parcel which benefits from the easement is known as the dominant tenement (or estate). For example, if A grants B a right of way across Blackacre so that B can more easily reach Greenacre which he owns, the easement holder, B, is deriving a benefit from Blackacre that is linked to B's physical use and enjoyment of Greenacre. In this situation, Greenacre is the dominant tenement and Blackacre, the servient tenement.

By contrast, an easement is in gross when it confers upon the easement holder some personal or pecuniary advantage that is not related to his use and enjoyment of his land. With an easement in gross, there is a servient tenement, but no dominant tenement, since the easement holder derives a gain that is independent of his or her ownership of land.

CUSHMAN VIRGINIA CORP. v. BARNES

Virginia Supreme Court
129 S.E.2d 633 (1963)

CARRICO, J., delivered the opinion of the court.

Cushman Virginia Corporation, hereinafter referred to as Cushman, filed a bill of complaint against Donald C. Barnes, hereinafter referred to as Barnes, praying that an adjudication be made that there was appurtenant to the land of Cushman a right of way over the land of Barnes. The bill also prayed that Barnes be enjoined from interfering with Cushman's use of the right of way. The trustees and beneficiaries under deeds of trust on the Cushman land were also made parties complainant, but their presence as such is not of concern on this appeal.

Barnes filed an answer to the bill denying that Cushman had any right of way over his property. The answer further alleged that if such a right of way had ever existed, it had been extinguished by "cessation of purpose" or abandonment. Barnes prayed for such relief "as may be appropriate."

The chancellor heard the evidence ore tenus, except for the deposition of one witness, and entered a final decree declaring that the right of way existed, but limiting its width and use to an extent that Cushman found objectionable. We granted Cushman an appeal. Barnes has assigned cross-error to the findings of the chancellor.

The evidence shows that the lands of Cushman and Barnes were originally parts of a large farm known as "Midway," containing approximately 955 acres, in Albemarle County. In 1895, "Midway" was divided among three heirs in a partition proceeding.

Lot 1, containing 410 3/4 acres which abutted on the public road, was conveyed to W.O. Durrette. The other two lots did not abut on the public road but lot 2, containing 255 acres, was conveyed to J. Frank Durrette, "together with the right of way by the present road through Lot No. 1 to the County road." Lot 3, containing 289 3/4 acres, "together with the right of way by the present road through Lots Nos. 2 and 1 to the County road," was conveyed to Mary M. Durrette (who later married G. Norris Watson), "her heirs and assigns."

The road thus established, and which is in controversy here, became known as the Durrette road. However, neither the plat of partition nor any of the deeds accomplishing the division showed the location or width of the "present road."

In 1930, Mary Durrette Watson acquired a portion of lot 2 of "Midway," containing 9.2 acres. This tract adjoined Mrs. Watson's lot 3 in the area near her home and was traversed by a portion of the Durrette road.

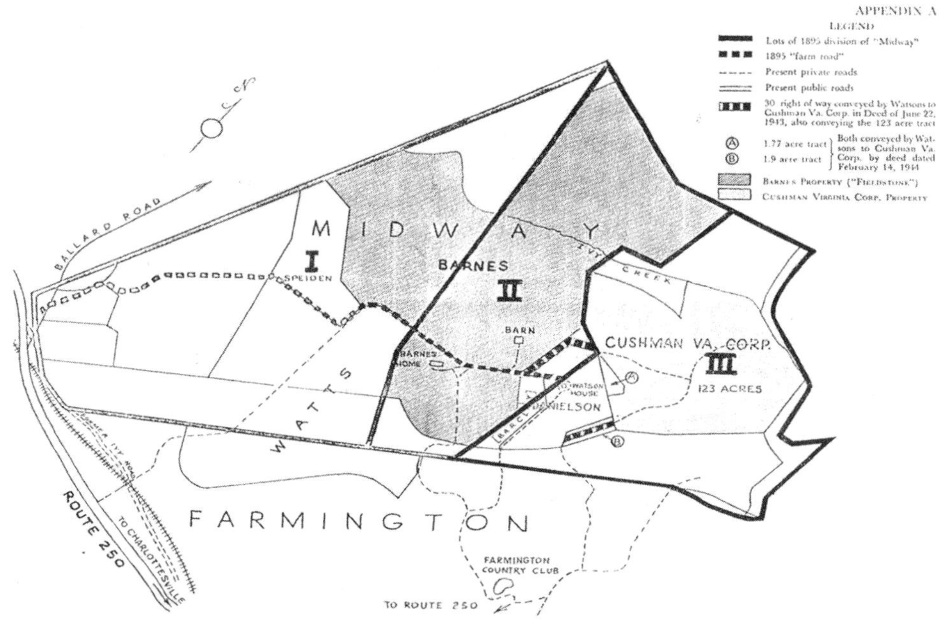

Cushman acquired its land, totaling 126.67 acres, all a part of lot 3 of "Midway," from Mrs. Watson and her husband by two deeds. The first deed, in 1943, conveyed 123 acres together with a right of way thirty feet wide, running from the 123 acre tract through the 9.2 acre portion of lot 2, "to the center of the Durrette Road," and also a right of way thirty feet wide, running from the 123 acre tract through the remaining portion of lot 3, "to the center of the branch in line of Farmington, Inc." The second deed, in 1944, conveyed tracts of 1.77 acres and 1.9 acres. No mention was made in the deeds of the right of way through lots 1 and 2 of "Midway" other than the reference to the termination of the thirty foot right of way in "the center of the Durrette Road."

Barnes acquired his land, totaling approximately 335 acres, made up of portions of lots 1, 2 and 3 of "Midway," by two deeds. The first deed, in 1947, conveyed 234.9 acres, being the major portion of lot 2 and traversed by the Durrette road, and 12.4 acres, being a portion of lot 3 but not so traversed. The second deed, in 1952, conveyed 88.4 acres, being a portion of lot 1 and traversed by the road. Each of these conveyances was made subject to the right of way established in the Durrette partition.

Barnes was also conveyed a right of way over the lands of Farmington, Inc., which he has used for access to his property. When he purchased his portion of lot 2 he found a sign marked "No Passin" on the right of way at the property line between lots 1 and 2.

In 1929, the Watsons had acquired a new right of way from their property through the lands of Farmington, Inc., and they ceased using the Durrette road as a means of access. A fence was erected across the road between the Watson land and that now owned by Barnes, although sliding bars were installed to permit the passage of members of the Farmington Hunt Club. A portion of the road on lot 2, near the Watson property, became overgrown with trees and brush.

However, occasional use was made of the old road on Barnes' land after 1929 by horseback riders, by a farmer hauling corn from the Cushman land and by one person who drove an automobile over it. And Mr. and Mrs. Watson, in 1942, conveyed a tract of 1.96 acres to George H. Barkley with, 'a right of way along the old right of way out to the old Ivy Road created' in the Durrette partition. In 1949, they conveyed to J. Deering Danielson a tract of 32.7 acres, together with a right of way over the old road.

The present controversy arose when Cushman advised Barnes of its intention to subdivide the 126.67 acre tract and to use the Durrette road in connection therewith.

At the hearing before the chancellor, there was no direct evidence of the width of the right of way or the scope of its use immediately after its establishment in 1895. There was testimony dating back to 1907 that the road served the three farms along its route to carry buggies, hay wagons, threshing machines, trucks and other farm equipment. One witness said that, "two people could pass most everywhere on that road except when you got out there on the mountain some places." However, there was other testimony that there was only, "a one track road, you could pass if you were to drive out in the field;" that the road, "in narrow places would give a buggy about six inches on each side;" that the road was 8 or 10 feet wide, and that there were gates across the road in seven or more different places, each being 10 to 12 feet wide.

Numerous photographs were introduced showing the condition of the road immediately prior to the hearing. They depict the remains of what had been a narrow, winding farm lane.

Cushman's assignments of error and Barnes' assignments of cross-error present several questions for our determination, the first of which is:

1. Did the chancellor err in finding that there was a right of way over Barnes' land appurtenant to the Cushman tract? This question arises from Barnes' contention that the deed of the 123 acre tract from Watson to Cushman in 1943 did not convey a right of way over the Durrette road. He also argues that since the 30 foot right of way granted to Cushman terminated in "the center of the Durrette Road," there was an expressed intention not to convey any rights beyond that point.

We think there is no merit in Barnes' contention in this respect. Code, § 55-50 provides as follows:

> Appurtenances, etc., included in deed of land. — Every deed conveying land shall, unless an exception be made therein, be construed to include all buildings, privileges and appurtenances of every kind belonging to the lands therein embraced.

The right of way over lots 1 and 2, established in the partition proceedings for the benefit of lot 3 of "Midway," was an appurtenance belonging to the latter lot, and to every portion thereof. When a portion of that lot was conveyed by the Watsons, it carried with it the use of the right of way, if accessible to it, unless an exception thereto was made in the deed. No such exception, as provided by Code, § 55-50, was contained in the deed to Cushman. To the contrary, by providing an easement from the tract conveyed to the Durrette road, the parties evidenced their clear intention that the owner of the tract should have the right to use the road. No other reasonable purpose can be conceived for providing the connecting easement.

In this connection, Barnes contends that the chancellor erred in excluding the testimony of G. Norris Watson that he and his wife did not intend to give Cushman the right to use the Durrette road when they made the conveyance of the 123 acre tract. This was not error. Since the intention of the parties was clearly expressed in the deed itself, parol evidence was not admissible to explain or to vary its terms.

The right of way over the Durrette road was, therefore, an appurtenance of the Cushman land. It passed with the land by operation of Code, § 55-50 and in furtherance of the expressed intention of the parties.

2. The next question is, did the court err in determining that the right of way, "does not exceed the width of the farm road existing in 1895, the traveled portion being limited to a single track, not exceeding 10 feet and the outside width, including cuts, fills, ditches, embankments, etc., at no point exceeding 15 feet?"

We think the chancellor did not err in this ruling. In *Stephen Putney Co. v. R.F. & R.R. Co.*, 81 S.E. 93 (Va. 1914), we said:

> Where an easement has been granted or reserved by deed, the ordinary rule which governs in the construction of other writings prevails, namely, that the rights of the parties must be ascertained from the words of the deed, and the extent of the easement cannot be determined from any other source. But where its language is ambiguous, the court in order to ascertain the intention of the parties looks to the language employed in the light of the circumstances surrounding the parties and the land at the time the deed was executed.

And in *Good v. Petticrew*, 183 S.E. 217 (Va. 1936), it was said, "Where the width of a right of way is not specified in the grant, then it is limited to the width as it existed at the time of the grant."

Applying these principles to the case before us, we find that the deeds creating the right of way did not specify its location, which is not in dispute here, or its width. It was, therefore, necessary to ascertain what the parties intended the width to be, by relating the words of the deed, "by the present road," to the circumstances surrounding the parties and their land. This is what the chancellor did and, as a result, found the right of way to be of the width set forth in his decree. The crucial question is, was there credible evidence to support his ruling?

It is true that there was no direct testimony of what width was actually established for the right of way in 1895. There was, nonetheless, ample evidence to show that the right of way existed then as it existed later — as a single lane farm road.

Cushman contends that since the deeds were silent as to the width of the right of way, it will be presumed that the parties intended that 30 feet would be its width. The basis for this presumption, Cushman says, is the fact that at the time the right of way was established all public roads in Virginia were 30 feet wide.

The Durrette road is not, nor has it ever been, a public road. Even Cushman does not now urge that it be so declared.

The testimony of the witnesses who had been familiar with the road since 1907; the technical evidence and expert testimony of the surveyor, Bailey; the photographic exhibits which displayed facts to which time has given testimony, and which cannot be refuted, all lead to but one conclusion — the Durrette heirs never intended, and did not establish, the right of way to be 30 feet wide. Instead, this evidence, all of which was credible, supports the chancellor's determination of its width.

3. The next question is, did the chancellor err in determining,

> that such right of way may not be used for the purpose of developing or serving the residential or commercial subdivision of the 126.67 acre tract and such right of way is accordingly limited to normal farm or residential use of not more than two single family dwellings together with any servant or tenant houses used solely for housing of the occupant employees of such dwellings located on any part of the 126.67 acre tract, regardless of the number of any future off conveyances or subdivisions of the 126.67 acre tract?

We are of opinion that the chancellor did err in this respect. His ruling unreasonably restricts Cushman's rights in the use of the right of way.

When a right of way is granted over land, the servient estate, for the benefit of other land, the dominant estate, and the instrument creating the easement does not limit the use to be made thereof, it may be used for any purpose to which the dominant estate may then, or in the future, reasonably be devoted. This rule is subject to the qualification that no use may be made of the right of way, different from that established at the time of its creation, which imposes an additional burden upon the servient estate.

And, as has been seen, the right to the use of the easement is an appurtenance of the dominant estate and of every portion thereof. When a portion of the dominant estate is conveyed away, without excepting the right of way, the owner of such portion has the right, in connection with the reasonable use of his land, to make use of the easement if his land is accessible thereto. The fact that the dominant estate is divided and a portion or portions conveyed away does not, in and of itself, mean that an additional burden is imposed upon the servient estate. The result may be that the degree of burden is increased, but that is not sufficient to deny use of the right of way to an owner of a portion so conveyed.

In the case before us, the deeds creating the right of way contained no terms of limitation upon its use. Mary Durrette Watson, the owner of lot 3 of "Midway," provided she devoted her land to a reasonable purpose which did not impose an additional burden upon lots 1 and 2, was entitled to make such use of the right of way as its narrow width permitted. That same right, subject to the same conditions, passed to Cushman as an appurtenance of the 126.67 acre tract acquired from Mrs. Watson. The final decree improperly limits Cushman's rights.

In so holding, we do not make any determination of the effect of local zoning or subdivision control ordinances upon the use of the right of way by Cushman. That question is not before us on this appeal.

4. The next question presented is, did the chancellor err in his finding that the right of way had not been extinguished by abandonment? This question arises from one of Barnes' cross assignments of error.

To support Barnes' theory that the right of way had been abandoned, there was testimony that after the Watsons had acquired the new right of way through Farmington in 1929, they abandoned the right of way over the Durrette road, erected a fence across it and never used it thereafter; that a "No Passin" sign was erected on the right of way between lots 1 and 2 when Barnes purchased his land, and that the right of way was permitted to become overgrown with trees and bushes.

To support Cushman's theory that the right of way had not been abandoned, there was testimony that occasional use had been made of the road since 1929, and that after the Watsons were supposed to have abandoned the right of way they made conveyances of portions of their land in which they granted the right to use the easement.

Thus, there was presented to the chancellor conflicting evidence upon this issue. He has determined to accept that version of the evidence which supports the theory of no abandonment. That version was credible and persuasive and he was justified in accepting it. Under these circumstances, we will not disturb his ruling. For the reasons given, the decree will be modified.

NOTES AND QUESTIONS

1. *The Scope of an Easement.* The Restatement of Property § 482 provides that "the extent of an easement created by a conveyance is fixed by the conveyance." In determining an express easement's scope, then, the language of the deed or instrument of conveyance controls. However, as *Cushman* reveals, if the court determines that the language is ambiguous, extrinsic evidence must be considered to ascertain the parties' intent. What sorts of considerations ought to be given weight? Restatement of Property § 483 suggests that an assessment should be made of the circumstances under which the conveyance was made, whether the grant was gratuitous, and the use made of the servient land before and after the conveyance. In *Barchenski v. Pion*, 402 N.E.2d 1095 (Mass. Ct. App. 1980), the court stated it would consider the purposes of easement, issues of public policy, and safety considerations to determine an easement's scope in the face of general language.

2. *Technological Change and the Scope of Easements.* As the *Cushman* case reveals, the passage of time and accompanying technological innovations (like automobiles) can raise difficult questions regarding the proper scope of an easement. As a general rule, owners of servient tenements must accept reasonable technological changes. As a Massachusetts court noted, "The progression from horse or ox teams to tractors and trucks is a normal development," and does not expand the scope of the easement. *Glenn v. Poole*, 423 N.E.2d 1030, 1033 (Mass. Ct. App. 1981). A California court reached a similar conclusion about the transition from electric street cars to diesel and gasoline-powered buses, *Faus v. City of Los*

Angeles, 431 P.2d 849 (Cal. 1967), and a Missouri court found that an easement for telephone and telegraph wires could be used for cable television lines. *Henley v. Continental Cablevision*, 692 S.W.2d 825 (Mo. Ct. App. 1985).

3. *Determining Reasonableness*. When the dominant tenement is expanded or altered, what factors ought to be relevant to a determination of reasonableness? Compare *Hayes v. Aquia Marina, Inc.*, 414 S.E.2d 820 (Va. 1992), in which the Virginia Supreme Court relied upon its *Cushman* decision to conclude that a dominant tenement owner's proposed expansion of a marina from 84 to 280 boat slips would not unreasonably burden the servient tenement, since the easement was created by general grant, without words limiting it to any particular use, with the same court's opinion in *Gordon v. Hoy*, 178 S.E.2d 495 (Va. 1971), which relied upon *Cushman* to conclude that an easement of right of way granted "as an inlet and outlet" prohibited the dominant tenement owner from installing underground water and gas pipes, since "no use may be made of the right of way, different from that established at the time of its creation, which imposes an additional burden upon the servient estate."

Suppose that the holder of an easement of right of way subdivides his dominant tenement into 100 tracts. Does each tract have the right of way across the servient tenement? *See Stiefel v. Lindemann*, 638 A.2d 642 (Conn. App. Ct. 1994), which held that when an easement is appurtenant and the dominant estate is subsequently divided into parcels, each parcel has right of use "as long as the easement is applicable to the new parcel, and provided the easement can be used by the parcels without additional burden to the servient estate." How could this not be an additional burden?

4. *Use of an Easement to Benefit Other Tracts*. What if Cushman had extended the easement to benefit lots that were not originally part of the Midway farm? *See Penn Bowling Recreation Ctr., Inc. v. Hot Shoppes, Inc.*, 179 F.2d 64 (D.C. Cir. 1949) (easement appurtenant may only serve the dominant tenement; easement holder enjoined from expanding right of way to benefit property adjacent to dominant tenement).

5. *Transfer of Easements Appurtenant*. Is the easement at issue in *Cushman* appurtenant, or could it be construed as an easement in gross? This distinction has significant consequences in respect to transferability. The easement appurtenant passes automatically with the dominant tenement and its burden passes with the servient estate. (The only exception is when the servient tenement is acquired by a bona fide purchaser with no actual or constructive notice of the easement. *See* Chapter 9.) By contrast, the easement in gross is presumed personal to its holder and is usually not transferable. (*See* Note 1 following the next case.)

Cushman reflects a judicial preference for easements appurtenant. Sometimes the distinction between the easement appurtenant and the easement in gross will blur, particularly when the easement holder owns land adjacent to the servient tenement that may or may not derive a benefit as a consequence of the easement. Also, parties to an agreement creating an easement are sometimes less than careful when drafting the terms of the grant. When the nature of the easement is unclear, how should a court construe the interest? How could the relevant language of the grant in *Cushman* have been drafted more carefully to ensure its categorization as such?

6. *Cooperation Among Interest Holders.* Since the owners of the dominant and servient tenement both share an interest in the same parcel of land, there is typically a need for cooperation and interaction between both interest holders (as there is with all holders of concurrent interests). Does the court's ruling in *Cushman* facilitate this end?

[2.] Easements in Gross

Examples of easements in gross include a utility company's entitlement to place a power line on privately owned land, the right to swim in another's lake, and the right to erect a billboard on another's private lot. In each of these examples, there is a servient tenement but no dominant tenement. Instead, there is an individual who reaps some personal or commercial benefit independent of the ownership of an adjacent tract of land.

MILLER v. LUTHERAN CONFERENCE & CAMP ASS'N
Pennsylvania Supreme Court
200 A. 646 (1938)

STERN, JUSTICE.

This litigation is concerned with interesting and somewhat novel legal questions regarding rights of boating, bathing and fishing in an artificial lake.

Frank C. Miller, his brother Rufus W. Miller, and others, who owned lands on Tunkhannock Creek in Tobyhanna Township, Monroe County, organized a corporation known as the Pocono Spring Water Ice Company, to which, in September 1895, they made a lease for a term of ninety-nine years of so much of their lands as would be covered by the backing up of the water as a result of the construction of a 14-foot dam which they proposed to erect across the creek. The company was to have "the exclusive use of the water and its privileges." It was chartered for the purpose of "erecting a dam . . . , for pleasure, boating, skating, fishing and the cutting, storing and selling of ice."[1] The dam was built, forming "Lake Naomi," somewhat more than a mile long and about one-third of a mile wide.

By deed dated March 20, 1899, the Pocono Spring Water Ice Company granted to "Frank C. Miller, his heirs and assigns forever, the exclusive right to fish and boat in all the waters of the said corporation at Naomi Pines, Pa." On February 17, 1900, Frank C. Miller (his wife Katherine D. Miller not joining), granted to Rufus W. Miller, his heirs and assigns forever, "all the one-fourth interest in and to the fishing, boating, and bathing rights and privileges at, in, upon and about Lake Naomi . . . ; which said rights and privileges were granted and conveyed to me by

---

[1] Editor's note: Before the advent of refrigerators, a number of lakes in the Poconos, including Lake Naomi, were created to produce ice for "ice boxes." The ice was stored in huge ice-houses and then, in the summer, would be shipped to major cities. *See* E. MILLER, WAYGOOD, CHANGING TIMES IN THE POCONOS (1972).

the Pocono Spring Water Ice Company by their indenture of the 20th day of March, A.D. 1899." On the same day Frank C. Miller and Rufus W. Miller executed an agreement of business partnership, the purpose of which was the erection and operation of boat and bath houses on Naomi Lake and the purchase and maintenance of boats for use on the lake, the houses and boats to be rented for hire and the net proceeds to be divided between the parties in proportion to their respective interests in the bathing, boating and fishing privileges, namely, three-fourths to Frank C. Miller and one-fourth to Rufus W. Miller, the capital to be contributed and the losses to be borne in the same proportion. In pursuance of this agreement the brothers erected and maintained boat and bath houses at different points on the lake, purchased and rented out boats, and conducted the business generally, from the spring of 1900 until the death of Rufus W. Miller on October 11, 1925, exercising their control and use of the privileges in an exclusive, uninterrupted and open manner and without challenge on the part of anyone.

Discord began with the death of Rufus W. Miller, which terminated the partnership. Thereafter Frank C. Miller, and the executors and heirs of Rufus W. Miller, went their respective ways, each granting licenses without reference to the other. Under date of July 13, 1929, the executors of the Rufus W. Miller estate granted a license for the year 1929 to defendant, Lutheran Conference and Camp Association, which was the owner of a tract of ground abutting on the lake for a distance of about 100 feet, purporting to grant to defendant, its members, guests and campers, permission to boat, bathe and fish in the lake, a certain percentage of the receipts therefrom to be paid to the estate. Thereupon Frank C. Miller and his wife, Katherine D. Miller, filed the present bill in equity, complaining that defendant was placing diving floats on the lake and "encouraging and instigating visitors and boarders" to bathe in the lake, and was threatening to hire out boats and canoes and in general to license its guests and others to boat, bathe and fish in the lake. The bill prayed for an injunction to prevent defendant from trespassing on the lands covered by the waters of the lake, from erecting or maintaining any structures or other encroachments thereon, and from granting any bathing licenses. The court issued the injunction.

It is the contention of plaintiffs that, while the privileges of boating and fishing were granted in the deed from the Pocono Spring Water Ice Company to Frank C. Miller, no bathing rights were conveyed by that instrument. In 1903 all the property of the company was sold by the sheriff under a writ of fi. fa. on a mortgage bond which the company had executed in 1898. As a result of that sale the Pocono Spring Water Ice Company was entirely extinguished, and the title to its rights and property came into the ownership of the Pocono Pines Ice Company, a corporation chartered for "the supply of ice to the public." In 1928 the title to the property of the Pocono Pines Ice Company became vested in Katherine D. Miller. Plaintiffs therefore maintain that the bathing rights, never having passed to Frank C. Miller, descended in ownership from the Pocono Spring Water Ice Company through the Pocono Pines Ice Company to plaintiff Katherine D. Miller, and that Frank C. Miller could not, and did not, give Rufus W. Miller any title to them. They further contend that even if such bathing rights ever did vest in Frank C. Miller, all of the boating, bathing and fishing privileges were easements in gross which were inalienable and indivisible, and when Frank C. Miller undertook to convey a one-fourth interest in them to Rufus W. Miller he not only failed to transfer a legal title to the rights but, in attempting to do so, extinguished the rights altogether as against Katherine D. Miller, who was the successor in title of the Pocono Spring Water Ice Company. It is defendant's contention, on the other hand, that the deed of 1899 from the Pocono Spring Water Ice Company to Frank C. Miller should be construed as transferring the bathing as well as the boating and fishing privileges, but that if Frank C. Miller did not obtain them by grant he and Rufus W. Miller acquired them by prescription, and that all of these rights were alienable and divisible even if they be considered as easements in gross, although they might more properly, perhaps, be regarded as licenses which became irrevocable because of the money spent upon their development by Frank C. Miller and Rufus W. Miller.

Coming to the merits of the controversy, it is initially to be observed that no boating, bathing or fishing rights can be, or are, claimed by defendant as a riparian owner. Ordinarily, title to land bordering on a navigable stream extends to low water mark subject to the rights of the public to navigation and fishery between high and low water, and in the case of land abutting on creeks and non-navigable rivers to the middle of the stream, but in the case of a non-navigable lake or pond where the land under the water is owned by others, no riparian rights attach to the property bordering on the water, and an attempt to exercise any such rights by invading the water is as much a trespass as if an unauthorized entry were made upon the dry land of another.

It is impossible to construe the deed of 1899 from the Pocono Spring Water Ice Company to Frank C. Miller as conveying to the latter any privileges of bathing. It is clear and unambiguous. It gives to Frank C. Miller the exclusive right to fish and boat. *Expressio unius est exclusio alterius.* No bathing rights are mentioned. This omission may have been the result of oversight or it may have been deliberate, but in either event the legal consequence is the same. It is to be noted that the mortgagee to whom the company mortgaged all its property in 1898 executed in 1902 a release of the fishing and boating rights to the company and to Frank C. Miller, thus validating the latter's title to these rights under the company's deed of 1899, but in this release also the bathing rights are omitted.

But, while Frank C. Miller acquired by grant merely boating and fishing privileges, the facts are amply sufficient to establish title to the bathing rights by prescription. True, these rights, not having been granted in connection with, or to be attached to, the ownership of any land, were not easements appurtenant but in gross. There is, however, no inexorable principle of law which forbids an adverse enjoyment of an easement in gross from ripening into a title thereto by prescription. Certainly the casual use of a lake during a few months each year for boating and fishing could not develop into a title to such privileges by prescription. But here the exercise of the bathing right was not carried on sporadically by Frank C. Miller and his assignee Rufus W. Miller for their personal enjoyment but systematically for commercial purposes in the pursuit of which they conducted an extensive and profitable business enterprise. The circumstances thus presented must be viewed from a realistic standpoint. Naomi Lake is situated in the Pocono Mountains district, has become a summer resort for campers and boarders, and, except for the ice it furnishes, its bathing and boating facilities are the factors which give it its prime importance and value. They were exploited from the time the lake was created, and are recited as among the purposes for which the Pocono Spring Water Ice Company was chartered. From the early part of 1900 down to at least the filing of the present bill in 1929, Frank C. Miller and Rufus W. Miller openly carried on their business of constructing and operating bath houses and licensing individuals and camp associations to use the lake for bathing. This was known to the stockholders of the Pocono Spring Water Ice Company and necessarily also to Katherine D. Miller, the wife of Frank C. Miller; no objection of any kind was made, and Frank C. Miller and Rufus W. Miller were encouraged to expend large sums of money in pursuance of the right of which they considered and asserted themselves to be the owners. Under such circumstances it would be highly unjust to hold that a title by prescription to the bathing rights did not vest in Frank C. Miller and Rufus W. Miller which is just as valid, as far as Katherine D. Miller is concerned, as that to the boating and fishing rights which Frank C. Miller obtained by express grant.

We are thus brought to a consideration of the next question, which is whether the boating, bathing and fishing privileges were assignable by Frank C. Miller to Rufus W. Miller. What is the nature of such rights? In England it has been said that easements in gross do not exist at all, although rights of that kind have been there recognized. In this country such privileges have sometimes been spoken of as licenses, or as contractual in their nature, rather than as easements in gross. These are differences of terminology rather than of substance. We may assume, therefore, that these privileges are easements in gross, and we see no reason to consider them otherwise. It has uniformly been held that a profit in gross — for example, a right of mining or fishing — may be made assignable. In regard to easements in gross generally, there has been much controversy in the courts and by textbook writers and law students as to whether they have the attribute of assignability. There are dicta in Pennsylvania that they are non-assignable. But there is forcible expression and even definite authority to the contrary. . . . There does not seem to be any reason why the law should prohibit the assignment of an easement in gross if the parties to its creation evidence their intention to make it assignable. Here . . . the rights of fishing and boating were conveyed to the grantee — in this case Frank C. Miller — "his heirs and assigns," thus showing that the grantor, the Pocono Spring Water Ice Company, intended to attach the attribute of assignability to the privileges granted. Moreover, as a practical matter, there is an obvious difference in this respect between easements for personal enjoyment and those designed for commercial exploitation; while there may be little justification for permitting assignments in the former case, there is every reason for upholding them in the latter.

The question of assignability of the easements in gross in the present case is not as important as that of their divisibility. It is argued by plaintiffs that even if held to be assignable such easements are not divisible, because this might involve an excessive user or "surcharge of the easement" subjecting the dominant tenement to a greater burden than originally contemplated. The law does not take that extreme position. It does require, however, that if there be a division, the easements must be used or exercised as an entirety. This rule had its earliest expression in *Mountjoy's Case*, which is reported in Co. Litt. 164b. 165a. It was there said, in regard to the grant of a right to dig for ore, that the grantee, Lord Mountjoy, "might assign his whole interest to one, two, or more; but then, if there be two or more, they could make no division of it, but work together with one stock." In *Caldwell v. Fulton*, 31 Pa. 475, 477, 478, and in *Funk v. Haldeman*, 53 Pa. 229, that case was followed, and it was held that the right of a grantee to mine coal or to prospect for oil might be assigned, but if to more than one they must hold, enjoy and convey the right as an entirety, and not divide it in severalty. There are cases in other jurisdictions which also approve the doctrine of *Mountjoy's Case*, and hold that a mining right in gross is essentially integral and not susceptible of apportionment; an assignment of it is valid, but it cannot be aliened in such a way that it may be utilized by grantor and grantee, or by several grantees, separately; there must be a joint user, nor can one of the tenants alone convey a share in the common right.

These authorities furnish an illuminating guide to the solution of the problem of divisibility of profits or easements in gross. They indicate that much depends upon the nature of the right and the terms of its creation, that "surcharge of the easement" is prevented if assignees exercise the right as "one stock," and that a proper method of enjoyment of the easement by two or more owners of it may usually be worked out in any given instance without insuperable difficulty.

In the present case it seems reasonably clear that in the conveyance of February 17, 1900, it was not the intention of Frank C. Miller to grant, and of Rufus W. Miller to receive, a separate right to subdivide and sub-license the boating, fishing and bathing privileges on and in Lake Naomi, but only that they should together use such rights for commercial purposes, Rufus W. Miller to be entitled to one-fourth and Frank C. Miller to three-fourths of the proceeds resulting from their combined exploitation of the privileges. They were to hold the rights, in the quaint phraseology of *Mountjoy's Case*, as "one stock." Nor do the technical rules that would be applicable to a tenancy in common of a corporeal hereditament apply to the control of these easements in gross. Defendant contends that, as a tenant in common of the privileges, Rufus W. Miller individually was entitled to their use, benefit and possession and to exercise rights of ownership in regard thereto, including the right to license third persons to use them, subject only to the limitation that he must not thereby interfere with the similar rights of his cotenant. But the very nature of these easements prevents their being so exercised, inasmuch as it is necessary, because of the legal limitations upon their divisibility, that they should be utilized in common and not by two owners severally, and, as stated, this was evidently the intention of the brothers.

Summarizing our conclusions, we are of opinion (1) that Frank C. Miller acquired title to the boating and fishing privileges by grant and he and Rufus W. Miller to the bathing rights by prescription; (2) that he made a valid assignment of a one-fourth interest in them to Rufus W. Miller; but (3) that they cannot be commercially used and licenses thereunder granted without the common consent and joinder of the present owners, who with regard to them must act as "one stock." It follows that the executors of the estate of Rufus W. Miller did not have the right, in and by themselves, to grant a license to defendant.

The decree is affirmed; costs to be paid by defendant.

NOTES AND QUESTIONS

1. *The Transferability of Easements in Gross.* The *Miller* court, mindful of the historical prohibition of the assignment of easements in gross, based its conclusion favoring transferability on the commercial nature of the entitlement. This distinction is still maintained. While noncommercial easements in gross, like recreational easements affording hunting, camping or fishing rights, are not assignable, commercial easements in gross are. *See* Restatement of Property § 489. Why shouldn't the intent of the original parties control? If the creators of an easement in gross clearly intend that the right be transferable, should it matter that the entitlement is for noncommercial purposes? *Compare Lindley v. Maggert*, 645 P.2d 430 (Mont. 1982) (allowing transfer of easement in gross for personal right of way on the basis of the parties' intent), *with LeMay v. Anderson*, 397 A.2d 984 (Me. 1979) (holding that easement in gross deemed personal to its holder was nonassignable, notwithstanding instrument's reservation of the easement in favor of "grantor and others").

At least one state legislature has abrogated the distinction, allowing all easements in gross to be assigned "if instruments that create such easements in real property so state." Ind. Code Ann. § 32-5-2-1 (Michie 1984). A less drastic approach is found in *Weber v. Dockray*, 64 A.2d 631 (N.J. Super. Ct. Ch. Div. 1949), where the New Jersey chancery court stated that the right to assign an easement in gross should depend on three factors: the intent of the parties, the burden on the servient tenement, and the relevant circumstances as they existed at the time of the grant.

2. *Public Commercial Easements in Gross.* When determining whether to permit the transfer of public commercial easements in gross, such as those held by governmental units and public utilities, courts have relied on the traditional commercial/noncommercial distinction as well as considerations of the benefit or gain conferred upon the larger community. See, for example, *Champaign Nat. Bank v. Illinois Power Co.*, 465 N.E.2d 1016 (Ill. App. Ct. 1984), where plaintiff's attempt to prohibit the transfer of an easement in gross conferring right of way to the defendant power company for construction of power lines was rejected. The court noted that "commercial easements in gross are alienable, especially when the easements are for utility purposes."

3. *The "One-Stock" Rule.* Notice that the *Miller* court found that the boating, fishing and bathing rights in Lake Naomi were assignable but not divisible. This limitation, which applies to profits as well, is known as the "one stock" rule. The rule has endured for more than 400 years as a way to avoid the "surcharge" or imposition of excessive, unreasonable use upon the servient estate. It has been criticized as vestigial and unworkable, and some have argued that commercial easements in gross should be freely divisible and separable, so long as the various interest holders do not exceed the extent and scope of the original burden. Kloek, *Assignability and Divisibility of Easements in Gross*, 22 Chi.-Kent L. Rev. 239, 255 (1944).

Today, most divisibility cases involve public commercial easements in gross for utilities or rights of way, where the parties do not or cannot act as "one stock," yet nonetheless confer significant public benefit. The traditional rule has yielded in some jurisdictions to an "original burden" standard. A number of courts have held divisibility to be permissible so long as the total burden does not exceed that contemplated in the original grant. *See, e.g.*, *Crowley v. New York Tel. Co.*, 363 N.Y.S.2d 292 (N.Y. Dist. Ct. 1975), where the court allowed the division of a telephone line easement to a cable company, mindful of the public benefit from access to cable television. Some courts have gone so far as to rule that divisibility will be upheld where the public interest in its favor outweighs the additional burden placed on the servient estate. In *Henley v. Continental Cablevision*, 692 S.W.2d 825 (Mo. Ct. App. 1985), and *Hoffman v. Capitol Cablevision Sys.*, 52 A.D.2d 313 (N.Y. App. Div. 1976), holders of easements in gross were permitted to divide their right to hang cables on utility poles and convey access to cable television companies. (Cable television did not exist when the easements were first created.) On the basis of this line of authority, can you imagine a scenario in which the parties could partition rights in Lake Naomi?

4. *The Role of Intent.* The determination of whether an easement is appurtenant or in gross is based on the parties' intent, as reflected in the language of the deed and relevant surrounding circumstances. Of the two, language is probably the most important. Failure to use words such as "heirs and assigns," "appurtenant" or "runs with the land" often creates a presumption that the easement is in gross. Similarly, courts have concluded that the enumeration of the dominant owner by name manifests the intent that the easement be in gross. For example, in *Stiefel v. Lindemann*, 638 A.2d 642 (Conn. App. Ct. 1994), a right-of-way was found to be in gross, since the reservation was for "grantors herein," with no mention of "heirs or assigns." Is this approach unduly formalistic? Since the determination of intent is considered a question of law, an appellate tribunal is unconstrained by the trial court's findings on the matter. Why should this be a matter of law and not fact?

[3.] The Creation of Affirmative Easements

Affirmative easements may be created expressly, by operation of law (both by necessity and by implication) and by prescription.

[a.] Express Easements

An easement that is created by a writing is an express easement. The writing itself is known as the deed of easement. (As real property interests, easements ordinarily require a writing that complies with the statute of frauds and the formal requirements of a deed.)

Express easements may be created by grant or by reservation. In the latter situation, the grantor of land explicitly reserves in a deed of transfer an easement in favor of him or herself. For example, A sells Blackacre to B, expressly reserving on A's behalf an easement of right of way across Blackacre. As with life estates (*see* Chapter 6), English and American courts traditionally prohibited the reservation of an easement in favor of a third party or stranger to the conveyance. *See Pitman v. Sweeney*, 661 P.2d 153 (Wash. Ct. App. 1983) (citing as majority rule refusal to enforce easement in favor of third party). However, as with life estates, the modern trend is to allow easements to be reserved on behalf of third persons. *See Willard v. First Church of Christ, Scientist, Pacifica*, 498 P.2d 987, 989–92 (Cal. 1972) (permitting seller's reservation of easement for parking on behalf of third party church); Restatement of Property § 472, Comment *b* (1944).

[b.] Easements by Operation of Law

HELLBERG v. COFFIN SHEEP CO.

Washington Supreme Court
404 P.2d 770 (1965)

Hill, Judge.

Hellberg leased some 3,000 acres from Coffin for a 10-year period, commencing January 1, 1958, and ending December 31, 1967; and, in addition, Coffin agreed to sell and Hellberg agreed to buy the property at the end of the lease period. This we will refer to as the Hellberg property. It is located in the southern part of Benton County in the Horseheaven Country, its southern boundary being the Columbia River. It is landlocked by the property of others (primarily, if not entirely, that of Coffin), except for a well defined road to which we will refer as the "old Coffin road" which connects the Hellberg land with Primary State Highway No. 8 (referred to herein as PSH 8). Its connection with PSH 8 is at the Coffin headquarters, and from that point it runs southeasterly (southerly about 2 miles and easterly 3 miles) traversing parts of five sections, all belonging to or controlled by Coffin, until it reaches the Hellberg property; it then continues south through that property to the Columbia River (roughly 3 miles).

The present litigation stems from Coffin padlocking a gate across the old Coffin road at its intersection with PSH 8. Hellberg brought this action to restrain any interference with the use of the old Coffin road and to have it declared a public road. Coffin contends there is another access road, but the evidence sustains the trial court's finding that there is no other practicable road which would give Hellberg access to PSH 8 or to any other practicable road out of the Horseheaven Country.

The trial court enjoined any interference with Hellberg's right to ingress and egress over the old Coffin road and upheld that right on several different legal theories.

The trial court found that the old Coffin road was a public highway because it had been used as such for 10 years, and because it had been worked and kept up at public expense for seven years. The trial court also found that Hellberg had an easement of necessity over that road and also an implied easement over it as an appurtenance to the lands leased to him by the defendants.

We are satisfied from the record that Hellberg is entitled to access to his property over the old Coffin road, either on the basis of a way of necessity or on the basis of an implied easement appurtenant to the land; hence, we see no necessity of discussing the other reasons given by the trial court for enjoining the interference with that access by Coffin. We entertain substantial doubt as to whether the use by the public of the old Coffin road was other than permissive. In the absence of some claim of interest on behalf of the public and because of the marked disinterestedness on the part of Benton County, we see no reason to impose any greater burden on the Coffin land than that necessary to give Hellberg the relief to which he is entitled.

Only the Hellbergs are seeking the right to use that road in the present litigation, and that can be secured for them on the trial court's holding that they had an easement of necessity, or that they had an implied easement appurtenant to the land, both of which are based on substantial evidence. Both easements arise by implication, but to avoid confusion we shall not refer to the easement of necessity as an implied easement.

An easement of necessity is an expression of a public policy that will not permit property to be landlocked and rendered useless. In furtherance of that public policy, we give the owner, or one entitled to the beneficial use of landlocked property, the right to condemn a private way of necessity for ingress and egress.

Condemnation, however, is not necessary where the private way of necessity is over the land of the grantor or lessor of the landlocked property.

The theory of the common law is that where land is sold (or leased) that has no outlet, the vendor (or lessor) by implication of law grants ingress and egress over the parcel to which he retains ownership, enabling the purchaser (or lessee) to have access to his property.

Under the findings of the trial court, Hellberg has no access from his leased land to any highway except over the land of Coffin, the lessor, by way of the old Coffin road. The right of the landlocked tenant to ingress and egress over his lessor's property cannot be gainsaid.

Concerning easement by implication as appurtenances to land, this court has said (*Bailey v. Hennessey*, 191 P. 863 (Wash. 1920)):

> Easements by implication arise where property has been held in a unified title, and during such time an open and notorious servitude has apparently been impressed upon one part of the estate in favor of another part, and such servitude, at the time that the unity of title has been dissolved by a division of the property or a severance of the title, has been in use and is reasonably necessary for the fair enjoyment of the portion benefited by such use. The rule then is that upon such severance there arises, by implication of law, a grant of the right to continue such use.

The essentials to the creation of an easement by implication are, as variously stated by this court, the following: (1) A former unity of title, during which time the right of permanent user was, by obvious and manifest use, impressed upon one part of the estate in favor of another part; (2) a separation by a grant of the dominant tenement; and (3) a reasonable necessity for the easement in order to secure and maintain the quiet enjoyment of the dominant estate.

And in *Adams v. Cullen*, 268 P.2d 451 (Wash. 1954), we said:

> An implied easement (either by grant or reservation) may arise (1) when there has been unity of title and subsequent separation; (2) when there has been an apparent and continuous quasi easement existing for the benefit of one part of the estate to the detriment of the other during the unity of title;

> and (3) when there is a certain degree of necessity (which we will discuss later) that the quasi easement exist after severance.
>
> Unity of title and subsequent separation is an absolute requirement. The second and third characteristics are aids to construction in determining the cardinal consideration — the presumed intention of the parties as disclosed by the extent and character of the user, the nature of the property, and the relation of the separated parts to each other.

We have here the former unity of title in Coffin, the separation by the lease of the 3,000 acres to Hellberg, and the quasi-easement of the old Coffin road over the Coffin land which furnishes the only practicable ingress and egress to the leased premises. Coffin, however, contends (if the implied easement applies to leases) that the evidence is insufficient to warrant a finding that this easement is reasonably necessary to the quiet enjoyment of the leased property.

The evidence fully substantiates the trial court's finding that there is no exit from land held by Hellberg and no road available other than the road in question (the old Coffin road) for convenient service to the areas leased by Coffin to Hellberg. The findings of the trial court leave no question as to the reasonable necessity for the use of the old Coffin road by Hellberg.

However, Coffin takes the position that there can be no implied easement because there has been no severance of title, and Hellberg is only a tenant. Hellberg is, at the moment, only a tenant and, by the same token, Coffin is his landlord. Rights and easements do pass to lessees by implication. The landlord-tenant relationship probably has produced more law relating to implied easements than any other.

It is pointed out in 3 TIFFANY, REAL PROPERTY § 788, at 274 (3d ed. 1939):

> An easement by implication based on a pre-existing quasi-easement, comes into being only in connection with a grant or transfer of title to an interest in land, but the creation of the easement does not depend upon the use of a particular form of instrument. . . . And it has been regarded as so passing upon a devise of land as well as of a conveyance, and upon a lease as well as upon a conveyance in fee simple.
>
> It is clear that the implication may be created by a lease. [Section] 475 reads:
>
> Creation of Easements by Implication — Form of conveyance.
>
> In order to create by implication an easement upon the conveyance
>
> (a) of an estate in land, the conveyance must satisfy the formal requisites established by local law for the creation of an *estate in land of the duration of that conveyed.* (Italics ours.)

In Comment *a*, on the above-quoted section, reference is made to § 9 (RESTATEMENT, PROPERTY (1936)), which defines "estate" as follows: "The word 'estate,' as it is used in this Restatement, means an interest in land which (a) is or may become possessory; and (b) is ownership measured in terms of duration."

The suggestion that Hellberg, as a tenant, has no right to an easement of necessity or an implied easement appurtenant to land is untenable. We have discussed the rights of these parties based on their present relationship as landlord and tenant. The easement of necessity could conceivably terminate before the termination of the lease upon the completion of another access road to the leased property, ending the necessity; but the old Coffin road is clearly appurtenant to the land during the period of the leasehold. Whether, when the lease terminates and the Hellbergs become the contract purchasers or owners of the leased property, the requisites will exist for either an easement of necessity or an implied easement appurtenant to land, we do not now determine. There is some authority that the situation at the time of the transfer of title may determine those issues.

The decree appealed from being too broad in its scope, the cause is remanded for the entry of a new decree. The decree appealed from is affirmed insofar as it requires the defendants not to interfere with the ingress and egress of the plaintiffs and their assignees or successors, at least so long as the landlord-tenant relationship continues; and insofar as it adjudges that the plaintiffs have, as lessees and tenants of the defendants, an easement of necessity, and an implied easement appurtenant to land over the old Coffin road.

NOTES AND QUESTIONS

1. *Easements by Implication Distinguished from Easements by Necessity.* Consider a situation where O owns Lots 1 and 2 and Lot 1 is hooked up to a sewage drain located on Lot 2. O then sells Lot 1 to A, with no mention of A's entitlement to continue using the drain located on O's remaining Lot 2. Should A be entitled to use the sewage drain? If the test is one of strict necessity, the answer is probably no. However, a court may nonetheless imply an easement by prior use if the previous use had been readily apparent to anyone viewing the premises and if the parties reasonably expected that its use would continue. A would receive the easement, but by implication rather than necessity.

Would the result be the same if the easement were for underground sewer pipes, drainpipes or utility lines? Could such a use be deemed apparent upon reasonable inspection? Some courts have said yes, applying a rather relaxed standard for "apparent." *See Romanchuk v. Plotkin*, 9 N.W.2d 421, 425 (Minn. 1943); *Van Sandt v. Royster*, 83 P.2d 698 (Kan. 1938). For that matter, if an easement is implied on the basis of prior use and the easement is hidden or obscured from view, should subsequent purchasers of the servient tenement who take without notice of the easement nonetheless be bound by it? *See* Eichengrun, *The Problem of Hidden Easements and the Subsequent Purchaser Without Notice*, 40 Okla. L. Rev. 3 (1987). If the same set of facts suggested both an easement by necessity and an easement by implication would it matter upon which theory the owner of the dominant tenement proceeded? Would the result differ?

2. *The Meaning of Necessity. The Hellberg* court construes the easement by necessity as "an expression of a public policy that will not permit property to be landlocked and rendered useless." Are there other justifications for the imposition of an easement on the facts of this case? Many states still require "strict necessity" for an easement by necessity, meaning that the proposed right of way must be the

only access. Under this standard, no easement will arise if there is any other way for the seemingly landlocked party to exit, no matter that those other paths are perilous or expensive or terribly impracticable. *See Othen v. Rosier*, 226 S.W.2d 622 (Tex. 1950).

Could an easement arise out of necessity for some purpose other than access out of a landlocked parcel? For example, could there be circumstances sufficient to permit a grantee to sustain a claim of necessity to lay power lines over his grantor's remaining land? There appears to be no authority for such a principle, and a number of cases involving claims of easements of necessity in regard to air and light uniformly reject that any such right can arise by necessity. It may be possible in many of the situations to argue for an easement by implication. *See generally* W. STOEBUCK & D. WHITMAN, THE LAW OF REAL PROPERTY 448 (3d ed. 2000). A number of states have repudiated the common law's insistence on "absolute necessity" and have instead imposed a standard of reasonableness under which an easement will be implied where alternative means of access do exist but are too inconvenient or too costly to utilize. *See* RESTATEMENT OF PROPERTY § 476 cmt. *g*.

On the other hand, a Wisconsin case decided just before the end of the previous century illustrates the limitations of arguments for easements by necessity or implication. Plaintiffs owned lake-front property that was bordered on the south by private land, on the north and east by a cliff and rocky terrain, and on the west by Green Bay (the bay, not the city). Although the plaintiffs could reach a public road on foot, their land could not be reached by motor vehicle. The plaintiffs submitted evidence that the cost of building a road over the cliff was at least $700,000; consequently, they requested that they be recognized as having an easement across the parcel of land to the south, even it had never been part of a common parcel with their lot. The Supreme Court of Wisconsin refused to recognize the existence of any such easement, stating that to do so would be "to sanction hidden easements." *Schwab v. Timmons*, 589 N.W.2d 1 (Wis. 1999).

3. *The Scope of an Easement by Necessity.* Since an easement by necessity arises in the absence of a creating document, it is necessary for the court to determine its scope. The general rule is that the scope of easement by necessity depends on reasonable needs, present and future, of the dominant estate as well as accommodation of full reasonable enjoyment of the servient estate. *See Soltis v. Miller*, 282 A.2d 369 (Pa. 1971).

4. *Policy Justifications.* Why is an easement by necessity implied? Is it to effectuate the parties' intent or are courts concerned primarily with the avoidance of wasteful consequences? Or is it a way of forcing neighbors to cooperate? On the latter, see Sterk, *Neighbors in American Land Law*, 87 COLUM. L. REV. 55 (1987). In *Bickel v. Hansen*, 819 P.2d 957 (Ariz. Ct. App. 1991), the court asserted that an easement by necessity results from the presumption that "whenever a party conveys property he conveys whatever is necessary for the beneficial use of that property and retains whatever is necessary for the beneficial use of the land he still possesses." Is this an adequate explanation?

5. *Easements Applied From Subdivision Plats.* Purchasers of lots in a subdivision are usually found to have acquired easements of access through the "common" areas (roads, streets, alleys, parks, open areas, etc.) of the subdivision.

This is particularly the case if the layout of the subdivision is platted, and the plat is available for inspection prior to purchase. The extent of these implied easements vary from jurisdiction to jurisdiction. Everywhere, the purchaser is entitled to access to the streets bordering his lot and to whatever streets are necessary for the purchaser to have access to public roads, even if the deed is completely silent on such issues. In jurisdictions which follow the "narrow" rule, this is the extent of the implied rights. *See Capitol Hill Methodist Church of Seattle v. Seattle*, 324 P.2d 1113 (Wash. 1958). In other jurisdictions, owners are held to have implicit access to all such areas that are reasonably beneficial to the use of his lot (the so-called "beneficial" or "full enjoyment" rule). *See Easter v. Mullins*, 289 S.E.2d 462 (W. Va. 1982). Finally, in other jurisdictions, the "broad" or "unity" rule prevails, and the owner has access to all common areas represented on the plat. *See Goss v. Johnson*, 243 N.W.2d 590 (Iowa 1976). The modern trend appears to be in the direction of the "broad" rule.

[c.] Easements by Prescription

MacDONALD PROPERTIES, INC. v. BEL-AIR COUNTRY CLUB

California Court of Appeals
72 Cal. App. 3d 693 (1977)

FLEMING, ACTING PRESIDING JUSTICE.

Plaintiffs appeal an adverse summary judgment in this action for declaratory relief and to quiet title to real property bordering defendant Bel-Air Country Club's golf course. The judgment (1) declared valid and binding on plaintiffs certain building restrictions in the deed by which Bel-Air conveyed the subject property in 1936 to Hilda Weber, plaintiffs' predecessor in interest, and (2) granted Bel-Air a prescriptive easement in the subject property.

The undisputed facts reveal the following: In 1936 Bel-Air owned a golf course, portions of which abutted Lot 35, Block 3, Tract 7656, in the County of Los Angeles. Hilda Weber owned the bulk of Lot 35, a wooded plateau of over seven acres jutting south from Bellagio Road almost 800 feet into Bel-Air's golf course. Weber had constructed a large mansion on Lot 35 but was dissatisfied with the entrance to her property from Bellagio Road. Her entry-way was steep, curving, and hazardous, and she wished to acquire a portion of the golf course to provide safer, more convenient access from Bellagio Road. In 1936 Bel-Air likewise had cause for dissatisfaction in that Weber's frontage on Bellagio Road separated the fifth green of its golf course from its sixth tee, thereby making surface movement between these two points difficult.

Accordingly, Weber and Bel-Air entered into an arrangement for their mutual satisfaction. Bel-Air undertook to convey to Weber the subject property of this action, approximately four-fifths of an acre of portions of Lots 33, 34, and 35 of Tract 7656, comprising a long strip of land bounded by Bellagio Road on the northeast and by Bel-Air's sixth fairway on the south west. Acquisition of the property would give Weber the entranceway she desired. However, the property served as rough for

Bel-Air's sixth fairway, and misdirected golf balls fell on it every day. To prevent interference with this use of the property for golfing purposes Bel-Air inserted certain building restrictions in its deed of conveyance to Weber. In her turn, Weber agreed to convey to Bel-Air a permanent easement and right of way for the construction, operation, and maintenance of a pedestrian tunnel under her portion of lot 35, a tunnel which would link the fifth green of Bel-Air's golf course with its sixth tee.

No money changed hands in the execution of this arrangement. Reciprocal conveyances were recorded on 28 August 1936, under which Weber granted the tunnel easement to Bel-Air, and Bel-Air deeded the subject property to Weber. Bel-Air's deed contained the building restrictions here in issue. In November 1950 plaintiff Hilton purchased the entire Weber property and mansion, including the subject property, and in March 1963 Hilton transferred a remainder interest in the property to plaintiff MacDonald Properties.

The trial court found that Bel-Air had acquired a prescriptive easement to use the subject property as rough in connection with its golf course. The relevant portions of the judgment are:

> a. Title to the following described easement and servitude is declared vested in defendant, to wit: An easement and servitude across and upon the entirety of the Subject Property to use the same as a "rough" area immediately adjacent to a fairway of Defendant's golf course, that is, an area where golf balls and other objects are frequently driven or cast in the ordinary pursuit of the game of golf, which area is regularly entered by Defendant, its officers, agents, employees, and members to retrieve such golf balls or other objects. A further incident to such easement and servitude is the right of Defendant, its officers, agents, employees, and members, to utilize the same without risk of injury or liability to persons or improvements upon the Subject Property, with consequent limitation of the use and improvement of the Subject Property to those uses which do not place persons or property in hazard from exercise of Defendant's rights to so utilize the Subject Property.
>
> b. The said easement and servitude is appurtenant to that real property owned by Defendant, adjoining the Subject Property. . . .
>
> c. The above defined title of Defendant to the said easement and servitude is forever quieted against any and all claims of Plaintiffs, or either of them, or any person claiming through or under them, or either of them; and each of Plaintiffs and all of such persons are enjoined from asserting any claim whatsoever adverse to Defendant in or to said easement and servitude or inconsistent therewith; and each of Plaintiffs and each of said persons is further enjoined from obstructing, impeding or interfering with Defendant's use and enjoyment of said easement and servitude.

A prescriptive easement in property may be acquired by open, notorious, continuous, adverse use, under claim of right, for a period of five years. (Code Civ. Proc., § 321.) The owner of the servient property must have actual knowledge of its use. Once knowledge of use is established, as was done here without contradiction, the key issue becomes one of permissive use under license as against adverse use under claim of right. The decisions on the burden of proving adverse use are widely divergent. *Clarke v. Clarke*, 66 P. 10 (Cal. 1901), puts the burden on the person asserting the easement to establish that his use was adverse under claim of right; whereas *Fleming v. Howard*, 87 P. 908 (Cal. 1906), holds that undisputed use of an easement for the prescriptive period raises a presumption of claim of right and puts the burden on the party resisting the easement to prove permissive use.

We think the better and more widely held rule is that continuous use of an easement over a long period of time without the landowner's interference is presumptive evidence of its existence. This rule, articulated in *Wallace v. Whitmore*, 117 P.2d 926 (Cal. App. 1941), was quoted as controlling in *Miller v. Johnston*, 270 Cal. App. 2d 289 (1969), as follows:

> It is true that title to an easement for the use of a private roadway must be established by clear and satisfactory evidence that it was used for more than the statutory period of five years openly, notoriously, visibly, continuously and without protest, opposition or denial of right to do so. But clear and satisfactory evidence of the use of the road in that manner creates a prima facie title to the easement by prescription. Such evidence raises a presumption that the road is used with an adverse claim of right to do so, and in the absence of evidence of mere permissive use of the road, it will be sufficient upon which to sustain a judgment quieting title to the easement therein.

At bench, the affidavits of both parties establish without contradiction that Bel-Air's use of the area as rough for its sixth hole continued for over forty years — from sometime prior to 1936 to the filing of suit in 1974 — and was well known to plaintiffs. Furthermore, in addition to the evidence of open and continuous use referred to in *Miller v. Johnston, supra*, we have at bench the crucial fact of the Weber deed with its building restrictions on the subject property designed to preserve Bel-Air's then existing use of its sixth hole. Extrinsic evidence established that such was the motivation for the restrictions, and no other plausible justification for them exists. The conduct of Bel-Air subsequent to the execution of the deed manifests the open and continuous use inferentially contemplated by the parties to the deed and effectuated through the creation of building restrictions. It is true that the deed does not in so many words grant an easement to Bel-Air to continue to use the property as rough for the sixth hole of its golf course. But the deed's existence, coupled with Weber's acquiescence in Bel-Air's use of the subject property as rough for many years (1936 to 1950), provides conclusive evidence that Bel-Air's use was adverse, under claim of right, and accepted as such by the owner of the subject property.

Plaintiffs did not acquire their interest in the subject property until later — 1950 for Hilton, 1963 for MacDonald. Accordingly, if open and continuous use of property for five years is presumed to be adverse and in the absence of other evidence establishes an easement, Bel-Air had already perfected its easement against plaintiffs' predecessor in title (Weber). Even if we disregard the historic record and assume that prescription did not begin until title to the servient property was acquired by its present owners, the evidence establishes that plaintiffs knew of the fall of golf balls on the subject property and their retrieval by defendant's players and agents (knowledge which plaintiffs concede) and failed to protest Bel-Air's continuous use of the subject property as rough, a failure that lasted 24 years in respect to Hilton and 11 years in respect to MacDonald. Nor did plaintiffs erect permissive use signs or take other steps to preserve their rights as they might have done (*see* Civ. Code, § 1008), a significant evidentiary fact in most jurisdictions. Clearly, it did not occur to plaintiffs to challenge Bel-Air's right to use the subject property until challenge acquired the appearance of profitability in the context of plaintiffs' desire to build.

Plaintiffs raise the specter that if Bel-Air prevails on the easement issue, all homeowners living near golf courses on whose property golf balls sometimes fall will find themselves subject to easements in favor of the golf course property if they permit players to retrieve golf balls. However, it is unlikely that many homes are so situated as to show the continuous usage without protest that occurred here (a minimum of "several balls per day frequently and regularly" driven onto the property and retrieved therefrom, amounting to "between three and five percent of the balls teed off from" a given location) or that the written record of the relationship between adjoining landowners will show as clearly as here what the intended use of the property had been. As discussed earlier, the Weber deed furnishes powerful evidence of the parties' actual intent that Bel-Air should continue to use the subject property as rough in the same fashion that it had when it owned the property in fee. Continuity of usage is really all the trial court granted Bel-Air by way of this unusual, but under the circumstances not incredible, prescriptive easement.

Plaintiffs argue that a grantor cannot acquire prescriptive rights against his grantee. We find no logical support for such a rule, and we find dictum to the contrary in the statement of the Supreme Court that a grantor can acquire title by adverse possession against his grantee. (*Allen v. Allen* (1911) 113 P. 160.) Bel-Air's grant of the fee interest in the subject property to Weber to give her better access to her property was not inconsistent with Bel-Air's continued use of the subject property adjacent to its sixth fairway as rough for misdirected golf balls.

Finally, no triable issue of fact existed on the subject of consent to the user, because, as stated, all affidavits indicated that plaintiffs knew of the use of the property and made no protest against it. The judgment is affirmed.

NOTES AND QUESTIONS

1. *Hostile or Adverse Use.* Was Bel-Air's use sufficiently hostile or adverse? Although the court cites Weber's "acquiescence" in Bel-Air's use of the property as part of the "rough" for the golf course as conclusive evidence that the use was adverse and under a claim of right, could it not be argued that the same pattern of facts could give rise to a presumption that the use was permissive from the very beginning? Given the Bel-Air court's interpretation of the appropriate legal standard, how could Weber have prevented the acquisition of the prescriptive easement?

2. *The Fairness Issue.* The traditional English law of prescription was rooted not in the principles of adverse possession, but in the fiction of the "lost grant." Long usage was presumed to be evidence of a previously granted right, the documentation for which was now lost. By the early 19th century, American courts had rejected the fiction of the lost grant, and instead developed the doctrine of prescription by analogy to adverse possession. What policy objectives are accomplished by such a legal principle? Why shouldn't the adverse user have to pay for the easement? Isn't his free usage of the servient tenement for the statutory period enough of a benefit? For a discussion of this and related issues, see Merrill, *Property Rules, Liability Rules, and Adverse Possession*, 79 NW. U. L. REV. 1122 (1984).

3. There are certain difficulties in juxtaposing traditional adverse possession doctrine upon the acquisition of an easement. For example, how is the "open and notorious" requirement satisfied when the easement is for an underground sewer pipe or utility line? *See Field-Escandon v. DeMann*, 204 Cal. App. 3d 228 (1988), in which the court ruled that a prescriptive easement could not be established unless the facts showed that there were visible signs of underground sewer. (The Indiana Supreme Court reached a similar conclusion in *Marengo Cave v. Ross*, discussed in Chapter 1.) How frequent does the adverse use have to be to be considered "continuous"?

4. *Public Prescriptive Easements.* Since acquisition of an easement by prescription is analogous to the acquisition of title by adverse possession, the tacking of successive adverse uses is permitted. Does that mean that the public's adverse uses can be added together to establish a prescriptive easement for the public at large? In view of the presumption favoring adversity, are landowners, particularly merchants or commercial owners, at risk that the public's use of their parking lots or private sidewalks could result in a public easement by prescription? What would landowners have to do to prevent this result? Should prescriptive users be required to give property owners actual notice that an adverse right is being claimed? Traditionally, American law frowned upon the idea of a public prescriptive easement. *See, e.g., State ex rel. Haman v. Fox*, 594 P.2d 1093 (Idaho 1979). In some states, however, prescriptive easements may be collectively acquired by large groups. *See Confederated Salish & Kootenai Tribes v. Vulles*, 437 F.2d 177 (9th Cir. 1971). In recent years, the concept of the public prescriptive easement has been more favorably received. *See Thornton v. Hay*, 462 P.2d 671 (Or. 1969) (which is discussed in Chapter 2; Finnell, *Public Access to Coastal Public Property: Judicial Theories and the Takings Issue*, 67 N.C. L. REV. 627 (1989).

[4.] Termination of Easements

PRESEAULT v. UNITED STATES

United States Court of Appeals, Federal Circuit
100 F.3d 1525 (1996)

Plager, Circuit Judge.

A. *Introduction and Summary*

In brief, the issue in this case is whether the conversion, under the authority of the Rails-to-Trails Act and by order of the Interstate Commerce Commission, of a long unused railroad right-of-way to a public recreational hiking and biking trail constituted a taking of the property of the owners of the underlying fee simple estate.

B. *Factual Background*

The Preseaults own a fee simple interest in a tract of land near the shore of Lake Champlain in Burlington, Vermont, on which they have a home. This tract of land is made up of several previously separate properties, the identities of which date back to before the turn of the century. The dispute centers on three parcels within this tract, areas over which the original railroad right-of-way ran. The areas are designated by the trial court as Parcels A, B, and C. Two of those parcels, A and B, derive from the old Barker Estate property. The third parcel, C, is part of what was the larger Manwell property.

The Rutland-Canadian Railroad Company, a corporation organized under the laws of Vermont, acquired in 1899 the rights-of-way at issue on Parcels A, B, and C, over which it laid its rails and operated its railroad. Over time the ownership interests of the Rutland-Canadian passed into the hands of several successor railroads with different names; except as it may be necessary to differentiate among them, they will be referred to collectively as the Railroad. Meanwhile, ownership of the properties over which the rights-of-way ran passed through the hands of successors in interest, eventually arriving in the hands of the Preseaults.

[Sections C and D of the Court's opinion, which deal with the constitutionality of the statute at issue, are omitted.]

E. *Abandonment*

The Preseaults contend that under Vermont law the original easements were abandoned, and thus extinguished, in 1975. If that is so, the State could not, over ten years later in 1986, have re-established the easement even for the narrow purposes provided in the original conveyances without payment of the just compensation required by the Constitution. *See, e.g., Loretto*, 458 U.S. at 441. It follows that if the State could not in 1986 use the parcels for railroad purposes without that use constituting a taking, then it surely could not claim the right to use the property for other purposes free of Constitutional requirements.

We have established that the effect of the turn-of-the-century transfers regarding Parcels A, B, and C was to create in the transferee Railroad an easement carrying the right to exclusive possession of the surface of the strips of land described in the conveyances for the limited purposes of railroad use, and to leave in the original owners of the property their fee simple estate, subject to the easement. An easement is not a possessory estate of freehold, but merely gives the easement holder a right to make use of the land over which the easement lies for the purposes for which it was granted. *See* 7 THOMPSON ON REAL PROPERTY § 60.02(c), (d) (David A. Thomas ed., 1994).

Typically the grant under which such rights-of-way are created does not specify a termination date. The usual way in which such an easement ends is by abandonment, which causes the easement to be extinguished by operation of law. *See generally* RESTATEMENT OF PROPERTY § 504. Upon an act of abandonment, the then owner of the fee estate, the "burdened" estate, is relieved of the burden of the easement. In most jurisdictions, including Vermont, this happens automatically when abandonment of the easement occurs. [Citations omitted.]

Vermont law recognizes the well-established proposition that easements, like other property interests, are not extinguished by simple non-use. As was said in *Nelson v. Bacon*, A.2d 140, 146 (Vt. 1943), "one who acquires title to an easement in this manner [by deed in that case] has the same right of property therein as an owner of the fee and it is not necessary that he should make use of his right in order to maintain his title." Thus in cases involving a passageway through an adjoining building (*Nelson*), or a shared driveway (*Sabins v. McAllister*, 76 A.2d 106 (Vt. 1950), overruled in part on other grounds by *Lague v. Royea*, 568 A.2d 357 (Vt. 1989)), the claimed easement was not extinguished merely because the owner had not made use of it regularly.

Something more is needed. The Vermont Supreme Court in *Nelson* summarized the rule in this way: "In order to establish an abandonment there must be in addition to nonuser, acts by the owner of the dominant tenement conclusively and unequivocally manifesting *either* a present intent to relinquish the easement or a purpose inconsistent with its future existence." *Nelson*, 32 A.2d at 146 (emphasis added); *see also Lague*, 568 A.2d at 359; *Barrett v. Kunz*, 604 A.2d 1278 (Vt. 1992).

The record here establishes that these easements, along with the other assets of the railroad, came into the hands of the State of Vermont in the 1960s. The State then leased them to an entity called the Vermont Railway, which operated trains over them. In 1970, the Vermont Railway ceased active transport operations on the line which included the right-of-way over the parcels at issue, and used the line only to store railroad cars. In 1975 the Railroad removed all of the railroad equipment, including switches and tracks, from the portion of the right-of-way running over the three parcels of land now owned by the Preseaults. *See* 24 Cl. Ct. at 822. In light of these facts, the trial court concluded that under Vermont law this amounted to an abandonment of the easements, and adjudged that the easements were extinguished as a matter of law in 1975.

In light of the facts before her and the arguments presented by the parties, the trial judge arrived at the conclusion that the facts meet the test of Vermont law, in that they manifest, conclusively and unequivocally, the requisite intent or purpose of the Railroad to abandon the easement in 1975.

We need not determine this issue for all time and for all cases. The question to be decided here is what was the intent or purpose of the Railroad in 1975, when, for all practical purposes, it ended railroad operations on this easement. It is enough, under the circumstances of this case and given the fullness of the factual record before the trial judge, as well as her carefully-considered analysis, that we here accord her traditional deference for factual determinations, and test her judgment against the usual standard of clear error. To do less would embroil this court in determining factual matters more intensively than customary for appellate courts, a position for which appellate courts are ill-equipped.

As noted, in 1970 the Vermont Railway ceased using the easement for active transport operations and used the tracks solely to store railroad cars, as the only freight customer serviced on that portion of the line had moved from the area. In 1975, Vermont Railway removed the rails and other track materials from the segment of line crossing the Preseaults' property. In the 1985 proceedings before the Interstate Commerce Commission (ICC), the State of Vermont and Vermont Railway filed a Verified Notice of Exemption (Corrected) dated December 16, 1985, in which they stated that no local traffic has moved over the line for at least two years and any overhead traffic on the line can be rerouted over other lines and that no formal complaint filed by a user of rail service on the line (or a State or local government entity acting on behalf of such user) regarding cessation of service over the line either is pending with the Commission or any U.S. District Court or had been decided in favor of the complainant within the two-year period.

The State sought approval from the ICC for a 30-year lease with the City of Burlington, indicating that the State fully recognized that railroad operations had ceased on the easement, and that none were contemplated in the foreseeable future. Although events occurring after 1975 cannot change the consequences of the facts then in place, these later declarations confirm the conclusion that the purpose of the Railroad's actions leading up to the track removal in 1975 was to abandon this stretch of rail line.

The Government and the State argue that there are facts inconsistent with that determination, but we are not persuaded that any of them significantly undercut the trial court's conclusion. For example, when the Vermont Railway removed its tracks in 1975, it did not remove the two bridges or any of the culverts on the line, all of which remained "substantially intact." That is not surprising. The Railroad was under no obligation to restore the former easement to its original condition. Tearing out existing structures would simply add to its costs, whereas the rails that were taken up could be used for repairs of defective rails elsewhere on the line. It is further argued that, since the rail line continues to operate to a point approximately one and one-third miles south of the Preseaults' property, it is possible to restore the line to full operation. The fact that restoration of the northern portion of the line would be technically feasible tells us little. The question is not what is technically possible to do in the future, but what was done in the past.

Almost immediately after the tracks were removed, members of the public began crossing over the easement. Perhaps illustrating the difficulty in getting government paperwork to catch up with reality, or perhaps indicating that revenue collectors do not give up easily, the State of Vermont and Vermont Railway, as they had done before the removal of the tracks, continued to collect fees under various license and crossing agreements from persons wishing to establish fixed crossings. In January 1976, the Preseaults executed a crossing agreement with the Vermont Railway which gave the Preseaults permission to cross the right-of-way. In March 1976, the Preseaults entered into a license agreement with the State and the Vermont Railway to locate a driveway and underground utility service across the railroad right-of-way. As late as 1991, 985 Associates [one of the plaintiffs in this action] (through Paul Preseault) paid a $10 license fee to "Vermont Railroad" (sic), presumably pursuant to one of the 1976 agreements. The Preseaults paid "under protest." Much of this activity suggests that, initially at least, the adjacent property owners decided it was cheaper to pay a nominal license fee to the State than to litigate the question of whether the State had the right to extract the fee. In view of all the contrary evidence of physical abandonment, we find this behavior by the State's revenue collectors unconvincing as persuasive evidence of a purpose or intent not to abandon the use of the right-of-way for actual railroad purposes.

One uncontrovertible piece of evidence in favor of abandonment is that, in the years following the shutting down of the line in 1970 and the 1975 removal of the tracks, no move has been made by the State or by the Railroad to reinstitute service over the line, or to undertake replacement of the removed tracks and other infrastructure necessary to return the line to service. The declarations in the 1985 lease between the State of Vermont, Vermont Railway, and the City of Burlington, which refer to the possible resumption of railroad operations at some undefined time in the future are of course self-serving and not indicative of the facts and circumstances in 1975.

We affirm the determination of the trial court that abandonment of the easements took place in 1975. [The court then concluded that the Rails-to-Trails Act, as applied in this case, effected an unconstitutional taking of the Preseault's property without just compensation.]

NOTES AND QUESTIONS

1. *Railroad Right-of-Ways.* Documents creating right-of-ways, many of which were executed in the 19th century, are often ambiguous as to whether the railroad (or the state) was acquiring title in fee simple to the area in which it would lay its tracks or merely an easement. (Title in fee simple determinable, discussed in Chapter 9, is a third possibility.) When the record is ambiguous, what should the court presume? A number of states have taken the position that the original transfer was in fee simple. *See State v. Hess*, 684 N.W.2d 414 (Minn. 2004). In 1981, New Hampshire enacted a statute that declared that all railroad right-of-ways held by the state were held in fee simple absolute. N.H. R.S.A. 228:60-a. Is a legislative declaration the proper way to resolve this issue? The U.S. Supreme Court weighed in on such easements in *Morris M. Brandt Revocable Trust v. U.S.*, 134 S. Ct. 1257 (2014), holding that once a railroad right-of-way conveyed by the Federal government was abandoned, the property reverted to the underlying landowner. For a highly critical analysis of the case and its financial repercussions, see Wright, *Doing a Double-Take: Rail-Trail Takings Litigation in the Post-Brandt Trust Era*, 39 Vt. L. Rev. 703 (2015)

2. *State Abandonment of Property.* Although the court in *Preseault* concluded that the state of Vermont could abandon the property interest in question, some state courts have held that states, unlike private owners, cannot abandon land or associated real property interests. The rationale is usually the same as that behind the widely held viewed that adverse users cannot adversely possess against the state. *Malnati v. State*, 803 A.2d 587 (N.H. 2002).

3. *Subsequent Developments in* Preseault. Since prevailing in the above case, J. Paul and Priscilla Preseault have continued to do battle with the United States government and the city government of Burlington, Vermont. Subsequent litigation has involved an effort to recover attorneys' fees and other expenses from the Rails-to-Trails dispute and a takings claim against the city based on the instillation of fiber optic cable along the existing telephone lines. *See In re Preseault*, 243 F.3d 558 (2d Cir. 2000); *Preseault v. United States*, 52 Fed. Cl. 667 (2002), *Preseault v. City of Burlington*, 2004 U.S. Dist. LEXIS 2713 (D. Vt. Feb. 5, 2004); *Preseault v. City of Burlington, Vt.*, 412 F.3d 96 (2d Cir. 2005); *Preseault v. City of Burlington*, 908 A.2d 419 (Vt. 2006); *Preseault v. City of Burlington, Vermont*, 464 F.3d 215 (2d Cir. 2006). The Preseaults, who operate a real estate firm known as 985 Associates have also been engaged in litigation with at least some of their tenants during the same period. *See 985 Associates, Ltd. v. Chiarello*, Vermont Supreme Court (2004), https://www.vermontjudiciary.org/UPEO2001-2005/eo03336.aspx

4. *Mechanisms for Terminating Easements.* Easements may be terminated in a number of ways:

By Their Own Terms. Express easements that are created for a defined period of time, or for the life of the holder, will expire at the conclusion of the designated period.

Unity of Title. An easement is extinguished when title to the easement and title to the servient tenement become vested in the same person. For example, A, the owner of Whiteacre, has a right of way across B's parcel, the servient tenement Greenacre. Later, A, the easement holder, purchases Greenacre. Now that merger of title has occurred, the easement is extinguished. If, subsequently, C purchases Whiteacre, she will not have an easement over Greenacre unless expressly granted. The original easement held by A will not automatically spring back to life.

Release. A written release complying with the statute of frauds and given by the holder of the easement to the owner of the servient tenement will succeed in terminating the easement.

Abandonment. An easement will be terminated on the basis of abandonment when the easement holder demonstrates, by physical action, an intention to never make use of the easement again. For example, A has a right of way across B's property. A now erects a structure on her parcel that precludes her from ever again reaching B's parcel. A's action signifies her intention to abandon the easement. By contrast, A's mere nonuse, or A's mere words indicating an intention to relinquish the easement, will not trigger termination by abandonment.

Estoppel. An easement may be extinguished if the servient owner materially acts in reasonable reliance on the easement holder's assurances that the easement will no longer be enforced. When this occurs, the easement holder, in equity, will be

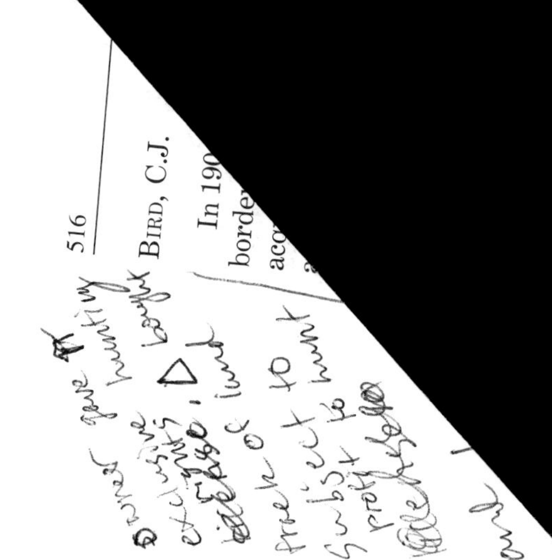

estopped from subsequently enforcing the easem easement of right of way across B's parcel. A tells I the right of way. A's mere words are insufficient to r by either abandonment (which requires affirmative holder) or release (which requires a writing). How reliance upon A's representation, B builds a swim had served the easement. In equity, A is now estopp

Prescription. By analogy to adverse possessi when the owner of the servient tenement interfer manner that is actual, adverse, open and notoriou statutory period, and, at least in some jurisdicti example, A has an easement of right of way acros fence on his servient tenement, precluding A from B may succeed in extinguishing the easement through prescription.

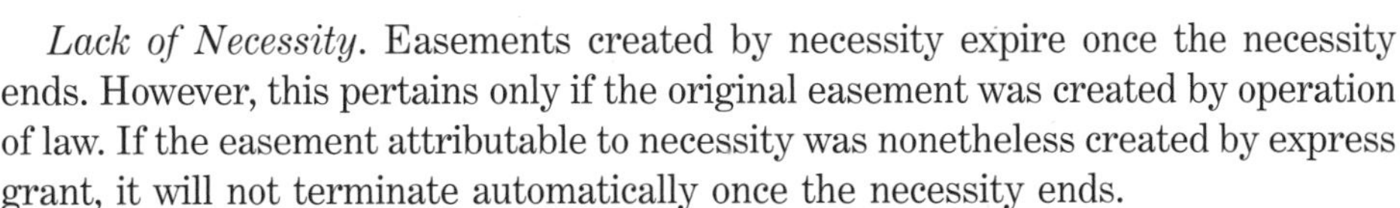

Lack of Necessity. Easements created by necessity expire once the necessity ends. However, this pertains only if the original easement was created by operation of law. If the easement attributable to necessity was nonetheless created by express grant, it will not terminate automatically once the necessity ends.

Condemnation of the Servient Estate. A governmental taking of the servient land by eminent domain serves to extinguish the easement. As a matter of constitutional law, the owner of the easement is entitled to "just compensation" from the government.

Misuse. If the owner of the easement exceeds his or her rights under the easement, the owner of the servient estate will entitled to injunctive relief to prevent continued misuse. However, if injunctive relief is ineffective, the easement may be deemed extinguished. (This outcome is not recognized in some jurisdictions, and easements rarely end this way. Normally injunctive relief will be adequate.)

[B.] PROFITS A PRENDRE

Profits a prendre (or just profits) resemble easements, but they include not just the right to enter the land of another but also the right to take or sever something from the land. Timber, mud, minerals, oil, gas, wild animals, and fish have all been subjects of profits.

ST. HELEN SHOOTING CLUB v. MOGLE

Michigan Supreme Court
207 N.W. 915 (1926)

Bill by the St. Helen Shooting Club against William H. Mogle and another to enjoin an infringement of an exclusive hunting privilege. From a decree dismissing the bill plaintiff appeals. Reversed, and decree entered for plaintiff.

…4 the St. Helen Development Company was the owner in fee of all the land …ring on Lake St. Helen, except certain rights which were subsequently …quired. In that year it conveyed the exclusive hunting rights to the plaintiff. An …dditional 12 acres of land bordering on the lake have been conveyed to the club. Upon this parcel a club house and cottages have been erected for the convenience of its members, and the club is being maintained and regulated by rules and enjoyed by the members thereof. The defendant Mogle purchased in fee a portion of the land bordering on the lake, subject to the exclusive hunting privileges theretofore granted to the plaintiff. He maintains a summer resort there. Defendant Winters is an employee of Mogle. The plaintiff filed this bill to restrain the defendant Mogle from infringing its hunting rights, it being claimed that defendant Mogle had not only himself infringed its exclusive hunting privilege, but had encouraged and enabled others to do so, by fitting up boats with blinds, and renting them to the public to enable it to enjoy the privileges which the plaintiff claims belong exclusively to the club.

The testimony and discussion took a wide range in the trial court. The chancellor concluded that such a lease or conveyance was void on the ground of public policy, and dismissed the bill. Plaintiff appeals.

After a somewhat extended consideration of the case, we are persuaded that there are but two important questions which need to be discussed and decided, namely:

(1) Whether the exclusive hunting privilege can be separated from the fee and conveyed by grant to another.

(2) Whether such a conveyance is against public policy, and, therefore, void.

1. It appears that the St. Helen Development Company, prior to the conveyance to plaintiff, was the owner in fee of all the land bordering upon the lake. If plaintiff were such owner we think it follows that it was the owner of the land under the lake. This court has decided that question so many times that we must regard that question as settled.

If the St. Helen Development Company was the owner of the shore and subaqueous lands, did it have the exclusive right of hunting on the shores and waters? We think this question is equally well settled by our authorities. There could be no other consistent conclusion. If it could not prevent trespasses on the shore in reaching the lake, its title to the land in fee simple would be of little value. But as we have said this court has, on several occasions, held the right of the owner to be exclusive in the hunting privileges. [Citations omitted.]

If the St. Helen Development Company was the owner of the shore and subaqueous lands and had an exclusive right of hunting thereon, may it separate this right from the fee of the land and convey it by grant to another? The right of hunting on premises is an incorporeal right, growing out of real estate, which, by the common law, was conveyed by grant, inasmuch as livery of seisin could not be made of it. This right has been termed by law writers a grant of a "profit a prendre." A "profit a prendre" is some right growing out of the soil. It is somewhat difficult to understand how, where one shoots a duck in the air while over the water, he is taking something from the soil, but, undoubtedly, the application of that term was made to this right so that it would become, in law, an incorporeal hereditament and thereby pass by grant and not become a mere license. But whatever inconsistencies appear, it is settled by all the authorities worth heeding that this right may be segregated from the fee of the land and conveyed in gross to one who has no interest and ownership in the fee, and when so conveyed in gross it is assignable and inheritable.

The rule laid down by 12 R.C.L. p. 689 is as follows:

> Though one person has no natural right to hunt on the premises of another, it is clear that a right to do so may be acquired by a grant from the owner. Or the owner can convey his premises and reserve to himself the hunting and fowling rights thereon. An owner of lands may convey exclusive hunting rights thereon to others so as to bar himself from hunting on his own premises. He may make a lease of the hunting privileges giving the lessee the exclusive right to kill game or water fowl on the premises, and at the same time reserve to himself the pasturage rights on the premises. The right to hunt on another's premises is not a mere license, but is an interest in the real estate in the nature of an incorporeal hereditament, and as such it is within the statute of frauds and requires a writing for its creation. Nor is the right of one person to hunt or fowl on premises owned and in the possession of another an easement, for, strictly speaking, an easement implies that the owner thereof shall take no profit from the soil. The right is more properly termed a profit a prendre. Unless the grant otherwise determines the rights of the parties, the owner of the hunting privileges may assign his rights to another, but he cannot give a pass or permit to another so as to allow the latter to exercise hunting privileges on the premises.

In the absence of anything to the contrary, in a grant of hunting or fowling privileges, the right to hunt and fowl is limited to the usual and reasonable methods generally used in the vicinity at the time of the execution of the grant, and the grantor is under no obligation to maintain a preserve for the pleasure and sport of the grantee, but the latter must exercise the right in the condition it may be at the time of the grant. Thus, if the owner of land conveys to others the right to hunt water fowl upon the waters thereof, he is not liable for depreciation in the value of such fowling rights from his acts in clearing and draining the land, provided he does so in good faith for the purpose of improving it.

The cases, both in United States and in England, have recognized the doctrine that a profit in gross may be created in fee without being appurtenant to a dominant estate. [Citations omitted.]

If this were a question of first impression in this court the writer would be in favor of holding that an exclusive hunting privilege could not be segregated from the fee of the land, except by a license revocable at the death of either party, or when the fee of the land was alienated. This rule would keep the exclusive right of hunting and the fee of the land together. We have, however, gone too far the other way to revert to such a holding without a legislative enactment. This holding, undoubtedly, deprives, to some extent, the man of modest means of the pleasure of hunting, which is regarded by some as great sport, but he will suffer no more in this respect than in other respects where he lacks the purchase price.

2. Is such a conveyance against public policy? It is not the policy of the law to unnecessarily restrict the right of persons to contract. When, however, the tendency of a contract, or a class of contracts, is manifestly injurious to the public interest, the court will avoid them. In determining what is public policy we must advert to the Constitution, statutes and judicial proceedings. 9 Cyc. p. 482, 13 C.J. p. 426.

In the present case the St. Helen Development Company was the owner in fee of these premises. As such owner it had the exclusive hunting privilege. It segregated therefrom the exclusive hunting rights and conveyed them to plaintiff, and the courts are nearly unanimous in saying that in so doing it simply exercised a legal right. We can see nothing in the act that has a tendency to be inimical to the public interest. While this holding somewhat restricts the hunting range of the average hunter, it simply gives to one the right to control and alienate what he owns. The State permits hunting companies to incorporate and exist under Act No. 171, Pub. Acts 1903 (2 Comp. Laws 1915, § 9054 *et seq.*). The State has also restricted the rights of such companies to hold more than 15,000 acres of land in one place for game preserves (Act No. 207, Pub. Acts 1923). It has not been brought to our attention that this court has in any way indicated that the tendency of such corporations was injurious to the public interest. This court had an opportunity in the case of *St. Helen Shooting Club v. Barber*, 150 Mich. 571, to disapprove of such contracts, but it did not do so. Our attention has not been called to any holding of any court elsewhere that such a contract is against public policy. We shall, therefore, have to disagree with the chancellor on this phase of the case.

The further question whether the contract or conveyance is a unilateral one is discussed. The appellee contends that the contract contained covenants for the St. Helen Shooting Club to perform, but that it was not signed by that company. We think it is pretty late in the day to raise that question after the lease has been accepted by plaintiff and the premises occupied and the consideration paid for upwards of 20 years. *Bakker v. Fellows*, 153 Mich. 428.

There is some discussion in appellee's brief of the question as to whether this contract is a deed or a lease. We think it is unimportant whether it is a deed or a lease. What we have said here would apply to either. 2 TIFFANY, REAL PROPERTY, § 381.

We conclude that the conveyance in question here is a valid one, and that it is not void on the ground of public policy. For these reasons the decree of the trial court must be reversed and one entered in accordance with this opinion. The plaintiff will recover its costs in both courts.

NOTES AND QUESTIONS

1. *Prior Litigation.* The St. Helen Shooting Club had appeared before the Michigan Supreme Court 18 years earlier in an attempt to vindicate its exclusive hunting privileges. *St. Helen Shooting Club v. Barber*, 114 N.W. 399 (Mich. 1908). As the opinion indicates, the concept of the exclusive hunting club was sufficiently popular in early 20th century Michigan to warrant special legislation.

2. *Incorporeal Hereditaments.* In the above case, the court identifies the interest created as an "incorporeal hereditament." This term refers to intangible, non-possessory legal interests that can be inherited. Easements, profits, and franchises are considered to be such interests. D. WALKER, THE OXFORD COMPANION TO LAW 607 (1980). The term is largely obsolete, due at least in part, as one group of commentators have noted, to the fact that "most persons find the phrase impossible to pronounce." R. CUNNINGHAM, W. STOEBUCK & D. WHITMAN, THE LAW OF REAL PROPERTY 436 (3d ed. 2000).

3. *Profits for Hunting, Fishing, and Drawing Water.* While it is clear that minerals, oil, sand, marble, gravel, and timber can be the subject of a profit, in the past, some courts have classified a right to come on to the land of another to hunt or fish or to draw water as an easement. *Butrick v. Tilton*, 29 N.E. 1088 (Mass. 1892) (hunting or fishing); *Thompson v. Finnerud*, 212 N.W. 497 (S.D. 1927) (hunting or fishing); *Diffendal v. Virginia Midland R.R. Co.*, 10 S.E. 536 (Va. 1890) (water). Do you understand why one might take this position? Reconsider the material in Chapter 1 on the ownership of wild animals and water. Most courts, however, have held that the right to hunt or fish is a profit, *see Hanson v. Fergus Falls Nat. Bank & Trust Co.*, 65 N.W.2d 857 (Minn. 1954), and that as to water, the question doesn't matter since the consequences are the same regardless of how the interest is classified. *Saratoga State Waters Corp. v. Pratt*, 125 N.E. 834 (N.Y. 1920).

Granting others the right to hunt on one's property, whether it be called an easement or a profit, may have consequences that the grantor did not anticipate. In *Figliuzzi v. Carcajou Shooting Club*, 516 N.W.2d 410 (Wis. 1994), the court held that the owner of the tract could not build condominiums on his land because to do so would interfere with a valid hunting easement.

4. *The Scope of Profits.* Profits share virtually all of the rules of easements, including those pertaining to classification, scope, creation, transferability and termination. Profits may be appurtenant or in gross, but unlike the case with easements, profits are presumed to be in gross since they usually are acquired to benefit the owner economically rather than in the use of his or her land. Rules pertaining to the transfer of profits in gross are usually more liberal than corresponding rules for easements in gross. Why should this be the case? Moreover, issues of scope produce additional problems with profits. For example, does a profit to cut firewood entitle the holder of the interest to cut down all the trees on a heavily wooded servient estate? Usually the scope of a profit is defined by a reasonableness standard.

5. *The Relationship of Easements and Estates.* Courts sometimes speak of profits and easements as though they were estates. In the above case, the parties used the term "lease" to describe their agreement, and the court and the sources cited generally accept this characterization. Given its modern meaning, a lease normally implies the creation of a present estate; therefore, it is probably not the correct term to use in such situation. In certain circumstances, the right granted by a profit or an easement so limits the use of the servient tenement that it seems tantamount to an estate. (For example, there is probably little difference between an easement for a railroad line and the lease of the land used for the track bed.) In

Miller v. City of New York, 203 N.E.2d 478 (N.Y. 1964), the court determined that a grant by the New York City Parks Commissioner to a private corporation of the right to construct and operate a golf-driving range with ancillary buildings for 20 years was an estate for years and not an easement.

In situations where it becomes necessary to determine if the document at issue created an estate or merely an easement or profit, courts will look to the totality of the circumstances and will not be bound by the language of the parties. *See Baseball Pub'g Co. v. Bruton*, 18 N.E.2d 362 (Mass. 1938), where an agreement labeled "lease," which permitted one party to place a sign on the exterior wall of another's building, was found to be an easement in gross, rather than an estate for years or a license.

6. *The One-Stock Rule and Profits.* The "one stock" rule discussed in *Miller v. Lutheran Conference & Camp Ass'n* in regard to easements in gross applies with equal force to profits. The traditional argument is that, given that profits can be assigned to multiple parties, without a rule like the "one stock" rule, the individual assignees would have an economic incentive to exhaust the resource as quickly as possible. Do you understand the rationale behind this explanation? Do you agree with it?

[C.] LICENSES

[1.] Licenses Distinguished from Easements and Profits

Most individuals who are lawfully on the premises of land owned by someone else are licensees — customers in stores, social guests, and spectators at public entertainments all possess this status. Unlike concurrent owners or the holders of easements or profits, none of these have an absolute right to be on the property.

In the terminology of legal philosopher Wesley Hohfeld, easements and profits are "rights" in land; that is, they are property interests which endure for a determinate period of time or "perpetually." By contrast, a license is a "privilege" — a revocable entitlement to enter the land of another for some narrow, delineated purpose. *See* Hohfeld, *Some Fundamental Legal Conceptions as Applied in Judicial Reasoning*, 23 Yale L.J. 16, 43–44 (1913). Although the distinction between a license and an easement or profit is easy to state, identifying a particular interest as one or the other is not always easy.

McCASTLE v. SCANLON

Michigan Supreme Court
59 N.W.2d 114 (1953)

Carr, J

The declaration filed by plaintiff in this cause alleged that on the 24th of May, 1951, the defendants were the owners of certain land in Muskegon county, and that a written agreement was executed by which they sold and conveyed to plaintiff all trees suitable for lumber, either standing or lying on the ground, on the premises in question, with permission to cut and haul the same within a period of one year. Plaintiff further claimed that he took possession of said timber and commenced to cut it, that defendants without justification repudiated the agreement, and that they refused to permit further operations thereunder. The pleading alleged, also, that plaintiff was engaged in the business of manufacturing and selling lumber, that he was purchasing the timber on defendant's property for use in his business, and that as a result of the defendants' refusal to allow him to proceed he sustained damages and loss of profits for which he sought recovery.

Defendants filed an answer denying material averments in the declaration and also filed a cross-declaration, defendant Evelyn Scanlon claiming the right to recover damages because of an alleged assault and battery on her person by plaintiff, and both defendants seeking the right to recover for timber that they claimed had been cut on their property after the revocation of permission to plaintiff to proceed under the agreement. A motion to strike defendants' cross-action, or counterclaims, was submitted. The trial judge concluded that such claims did not arise out of the contract that was the basis of plaintiff's alleged cause of action, that they were based on alleged tortious acts on the part of plaintiff after defendants had, as they claimed, terminated the agreement of May 24, 1951, and that, considered as pleas in recoupment, the assertion by defendants of rights to affirmative recoveries was not permissible. Such determination was correct, and the trial judge property refused to allow consideration of the counterclaims.

In appears from the pleadings and the proofs in the case that prior to the execution of the written agreement in controversy here the parties had, in August or September, 1950, entered into an oral arrangement under which plaintiff was granted permission to enter on the land of the defendant and to cut and remove timber. It is the claim of plaintiff that at that time he paid defendants the sum of $175, and that in the fall of 1950 he cut and removed approximately 3,500 feet of lumber. He did not continue with the operation during the winter, but in the late spring advised defendants that he wished to resume cutting. It was plaintiff's claim on the trial that after some conversation it was decided that the agreement between the parties should be put in writing, and that he should pay defendants as consideration the sum of $75. Thereupon, plaintiff prepared an instrument which was signed by the defendants and which read as follows:

> Dated this day of May 24th, 1951. Agreement by and between Carl Scanlon and wife, parties of the first part, and George McCastle, Jr., party of the second part. Parties of the first part agree to sell all trees suitable for lumber, either standing or lying on the ground, except some designated around buildings, on following description of land containing 35 acres, more or less, according to government survey, for the sum of 1 dollar and other valuable consideration, with permission to cut and haul same from said property for a period of 1 year from date. [Land description omitted.]

The principal question in the case involves the interpretation of the foregoing writing. It was plaintiff's theory on the trial in circuit court, as indicated by his amended declaration and by his testimony, that the agreement should be construed as a conveyance to him of the standing timber on defendants' property, subject to the exceptions indicated therein. Defendants contended that the agreement could not be construed as a grant or conveyance of the timber, and that in legal effect plaintiff had merely a license to enter on the property and to cut and remove trees so long as the license remained in effect. It was their claim that plaintiff had undertaken to convey to a third party rights that were personal to plaintiff under the agreement, and had in terms undertaken to sell to such party a part of the standing timber. Plaintiff's testimony on the trial disclosed that he had made such an agreement with one Morse, and had received by way of consideration the sum of $250. Thereafter Morse and others employed by him entered on the property for the purpose of cutting timber. Defendants forbade them to do so. Thereupon plaintiff undertook to resume cutting and was advised by defendants that he could not do so, and that his rights had been revoked. Such alleged revocation was pleaded by defendants in their answer, and the reason therefor indicated.

At the conclusion of plaintiff's testimony, defendants moved for a directed verdict in the ground that plaintiff had merely a license to cut and remove timber from their land, that no title to the standing timber had passed to him under the agreement, that the license was revocable, that plaintiff's arrangement with Morse constituted an attempted assignment of rights that were personal to plaintiff, and that defendants were justified in refusing to allow Morse to cut timber and likewise in refusing to permit plaintiff to resume operations. The motion was denied, and a subsequent motion made at the conclusion of plaintiff's proofs was also denied. Thereupon the case was submitted to the jury, the trial court specifically charging that plaintiff had the right to assign his interests under the contract to other persons, that his doing so was not a sufficient reason for the action of the defendants in refusing to permit plaintiff to continue under the agreement, that defendants were liable for damages unless plaintiff or others exercising his claimed rights cut trees that were not suitable for lumber, and that the measure of damages, if a verdict was returned in favor of plaintiff was the fair market value of the timber of which the plaintiff was deprived by the wrongful revocation of the agreement by the defendants at the time of such revocation in January, 1952. The jury returned a verdict in the sum of $1,000 and judgment was entered thereon. Defendants have appealed.

No claim is made that the oral agreement made in August or September, 1950, operated to pass title to the standing timber. Being an interest in land, such title could not have been conveyed other than by instrument in writing. CL 1948, § 566.106; *Wallace v. Kelly*, 148 Mich. 336. Plaintiff had merely a revocable license. *Marshall v. Heselschwerdt*, 304 Mich. 664. The payment by plaintiff to defendants of the sum of $175 does not change the situation in this respect.

May the written agreement of May 24, 1951, be construed as a conveyance of standing timber? It will be noted that the writing contains no words ordinarily found in a conveyance of an interest in real property. Neither was it executed with required formalities to permit it to be recorded. This Court has said in numerous decisions that a contract must be construed, if possible, to effectuate the intent of the parties. In the instant case such intent must be determined from the provisions of the written instrument. The Court may not construe the language used by the parties other than in its usual significance. It must be borne in mind, also, that the writing was prepared by plaintiff. The burden rests on him to sustain the theory under which his case was tried and submitted.

The situation in *Curran v. Gordon*, 169 Mich. 250, was very similar to that in the case at bar. There the owner of property gave to the plaintiff a writing setting forth that for a valuable consideration she did thereby sell to him all the timber on a certain described parcel of land. Subsequently the owner of the property died and title thereto passed to her sons who made a contract with defendant Gordon to cut and remove the timber. Plaintiff brought suit in equity for the purpose of obtaining injunctive relief. A demurrer to the bill of complaint was overruled by the trial court and defendants appealed. It was the claim of defendants in support of their motion that the writing created merely a license to cut timber. In determining that the demurrer should have been sustained, this Court said:

> The writing executed by the parties was a bill of sale of the timber with a license to enter upon the lands and remove it. The timber until it was severed was a part of the realty. The writing does not attempt to convey any interest in lands. Therefore no title to the timber would pass until it was severed from the realty. When severed, it became personal property and passed by the bill of sale. As was said in *Greeley v. Stilson*, 27 Mich. 153, it was the sale of a future chattel. Such a license may be revoked at any time before the timber is severed. If that were done in the present case, as it is claimed, it concluded the complainant's rights. But it is said the license was in writing, and could not be revoked. The writing would not prevent it. A license is not an interest in real estate, and therefore may as well rest in parol as in writing. The statute of frauds is not involved.

In *Wade v. Day*, 232 Mich. 458, the execution of a deed of real estate was accompanied by the giving of a bill of sale by the grantee to the grantor of standing timber on the property, the instrument reciting that said grantee "has bargained and sold, and by these presents does grant and convey" all of the timber on the land conveyed, with the privilege of entering on said lands from time to time to remove the same. It was further provided that should the grantee desire to clear up any part of the land he should give notice to such effect to his grantor, allowing "one winter's time" to do the work. It may be noted also that the writing which was apparently designated by the parties as a bill of sale ran not only to Day but to his "executors, administrators and assigns, forever." The Court held that in substance the transaction evidenced by the so-called bill of sale involved a reservation of the timber, and that in legal effect the writing was a conveyance of the timber rather than a mere license to remove it. Emphasis was placed on the "apt terms" employed by the parties to indicate their intention. Commenting on the situation, it was said:

> It will be found, upon an examination of cases of sales of standing timber, that the intention of the parties largely determines the question of whether there is a license, or a grant attaching to the realty. If the contract is made in contemplation of the timber being cut immediately, or the then condition of the timber is what is sold, and a reasonable time for the removal is agreed upon or implied under the circumstances, then the deal relates to personalty. But when the immediate severance of the timber from the land is not contemplated, and right to let it grow remains until the land is wanted for agricultural purposes and notice to remove is given, the conveyance deals with rights in realty.

The rule recognized by the Court in the language above quoted is applicable in the case at bar. The arrangement made between plaintiff and defendants did not contemplate that the standing timber should be allowed to remain for any extended period of time. The right of removal was limited to 1 year. It must be assumed that had the parties intended the conveyance of an interest in land appropriate terms to express such intention would have been used. The writing must be construed as granting a license to enter on the land and cut and remove timber.

Was the license personal to plaintiff? It will be noted that the agreement did not run to plaintiff and his assigns. There is nothing therein to indicate that the parties contemplated that plaintiff should have the right to transfer to another his interests under the agreement. As above pointed out, he did not become the owner of the standing timber, and it was beyond his power to sell it as such to Morse. This, however, is what he undertook to do. Obviously he was mistaken as to his rights.

In *Morrill v. Mackman*, 24 Mich. 279, it was held that the right to make exclusive use of land by flooding it, granted by a verbal agreement, created a lease from year to year. The difference between the facts in that case and those in the case at bar are clearly suggested by the following excerpt from the Court's opinion:

> A license is a permission to do some act or series of acts on the land of the licensor without having any permanent interest in it. It is founded on personal confidence, and therefore not assignable. It may be given in writing or by parol; it may be with or without consideration; but in either case it is subject to revocation, though constituting a protection to the party acting under it until the revocation takes place. Where nothing beyond a mere license is contemplated, and no interest in the land is proposed to be created, the statute of frauds has no application, and the observance of no formality is important.
>
> But there may also be a license where the understanding of the parties has in view a privilege of a less precarious nature. Where something beyond a mere temporary use of the land is promised; where the promise apparently is not founded on personal confidence, but has reference to the ownership and occupancy of other lands, and is made to facilitate the use of those lands in a particular manner and for an indefinite period, and where the right to revoke at any time would be inconsistent with the evident purpose of the permission; wherever, in short, the purpose has been to give an interest in the land, there may be a license but there will also be something more than a license, if the proper formalities for the conveyance of the proposed interest have been observed.
>
> What that interest shall be called in the law may depend upon the character of the possession, occupancy or use, the promisee is to have, the time it is to continue, and perhaps upon the mode in which the compensation, if any, is to be made therefor. It may be an easement or it may be a leasehold interest; or if the proper grant or demise has not been executed for the creation of either of these, the permission to make use of the land may still constitute a protection to the party relying upon it, until withdrawn.

In the case at bar the license granted by defendants to plaintiff must be regarded as personal in character. As above pointed out, the writing evidencing the agreement of the parties contains nothing indicating authority on plaintiff's part to assign to a third party the rights and privileges granted to him. The record discloses that there had been prior dealings between plaintiff and defendants, and it is a matter of inference that, based on their acquaintance with plaintiff and with his methods of operation, defendants were willing to grant the license to him but not to extend the privilege of entering on their property and cutting and removing timber to others to whom plaintiff might attempt to sell or assign. Under the circumstances defendants were within their rights in revoking the license and refusing to allow plaintiff or his assignee to cut additional timber. The motion for a directed verdict should have been granted.

The judgment of the trial court is reversed and the case remanded with directions to set aside the judgment in plaintiff's favor and to enter judgment for defendants. Appellants may have costs.

NOTES AND QUESTIONS

1. *Tickets as Licenses.* Tickets to sporting and theatrical events are usually treated as licenses, and thus are revocable. The latter feature may come as a surprise to the patron who has purchased a ticket. This issue reached the United States Supreme Court in 1913 in *Marrone v. Washington Jockey Club*, 227 U.S. 633 (1913), on appeal from the Court of Appeals for the District of Columbia. On consecutive days, Marrone was denied admission to the Bennings Race Track in the District of Columbia after buying a ticket of admission. Apparently he was denied entrance because the Washington Jockey Club believed that he had "doped" or drugged a horse entered in a race at this track a few days earlier. Marrone sued the Jockey Club for trespass to his person, arguing that it had no right to deny him admission to the grounds. He also accused the club of conspiring to defame him.

In a brief opinion for the court, Justice Oliver Wendell Homes wrote the following:

> But as no evidence of a conspiracy was introduced and as no more force was used than was necessary to prevent the plaintiff from entering upon the race track, the argument hardly went beyond an attempt to overthrow the rule commonly accepted in this country from the English cases, and adopted below, that such tickets do not create a right in rem. [Citations omitted.]
>
> We see no reason for declining to follow the commonly accepted rule. The fact that the purchase of the ticket made a contract is not enough. A contract binds the person of the maker but does not create an interest in the property that it may concern, unless it also operates as a conveyance. The ticket was not a conveyance of an interest in the race track, not only because it was not under seal but because by common understanding it did not purport to have that effect. There would be obvious inconveniences if it were construed otherwise. But if it did not create such an interest, that is

> to say, a right in rem valid against the landowner and third persons, the holder had no right to enforce specific performance by self-help.
>
> His only right was to sue upon the contract for the breach. It is true that if the contract were incidental to a right of property either in the land or in goods upon the land, there might be an irrevocable right of entry, but when the contract stands by itself it must be either a conveyance or a license subject to be revoked.

Is the right to sue on the contract an adequate remedy in such cases? What if Marrone was the "owner" of a stadium box in a modern (i.e., early 21st century) arena? Would he still be only a licensee?

2. *The Role of Language*. As with estates and easements, the determination of whether an interest is a license or an easement or profit does not turn entirely upon the language used by the parties. The nature of the interest created is more important than the language used to describe it. In *Beal v. Eastern Air Devices, Inc.*, 403 N.E.2d 438 (Mass. Ct. App. 1980), the parties' "License Agreement" was found to be misnamed, since the interest created by the agreement could not be revoked. However, in close cases, language can be dispositive.

3. *Licenses and the Statute of Frauds*. Because licenses are not viewed as real property interests, they fall outside the statute of frauds. Consequently, they may be created orally and can be enforced in the absence of a writing. If two parties attempt to create an easement through an oral contract, their efforts will usually be interpreted as creating a license, notwithstanding the parties' intentions or expectations to the contrary.

4. Suppose A agrees to pay B $5,000 for the right to erect a billboard on B's farm which is bordered on the west by an interstate highway. According to the terms of the agreement, A will have the exclusive right to maintain the billboard on B's property for one year. If the contract is in writing and signed, what interest has been created for A? A license? An easement? An estate for years for the land directly underneath the billboard? An estate for years for the land where the posts securing the billboard are sunk into the ground? Ordinarily, arrangements that allow one party to place items of personal property on the land of another are interpreted as licenses rather than easements. *See, e.g., Cooper v. Boise Church of Christ*, 524 P.2d 173 (Idaho 1974) (electric sign); *Linro Equip. Corp. v. Westage Tower Assocs.*, 233 A.D.2d 824 (N.Y. App. Div. 1996) (coin-operated washing machines and dryers in housing complex).

5. *Personal Property Licenses*. Licenses are also important legal instruments in the realm of personal property. This is particularly true in the world of intellectual property where the holder of the copyright or patent "licenses" the use of the property to others. The owners of the intellectual property, like the owners of land, have great leeway in determining the scope of the license. Normally, the rights and privileges created by the license are a matter of contract. For a well-known case dealing with the enforceability of "shrinkwrap licenses," the terms of which appear on or inside boxes containing computer software, see *ProCD, Inc. v. Zeidenberg*, 86 F.3d 1447 (7th Cir. 1996).

[2.] The Revocation of Licenses

The general rule is that licenses may be revoked at any time and are automatically revoked upon the death of the licensor or upon an attempt to transfer the interest. However, in some circumstances, licenses are not freely revocable. Estoppel principles may bar revocation, and the right to revoke cannot be exercised if the license is coupled with an interest. (Licenses coupled with an interest are discussed below.) The licensor will be estopped from revoking the license only when the licensee has invested substantial money and/or labor in reliance on the reasonable expectation that the license would not be revoked.

HOLBROOK v. TAYLOR

Kentucky Supreme Court
532 S.W.2d 763 (1976)

STERNBERG, JUSTICE.

This is an action to establish a right to the use of a roadway, which is 10 to 12 feet wide and about 250 feet long, over the unenclosed, hilly woodlands of another. The claimed right to the use of the roadway is twofold: by prescription and by estoppel. Both issues are heatedly contested. The evidence is in conflict as to the nature and type of use that had been made of the roadway. The lower court determined that a right to the use of the roadway by prescription had not been established, but that it had been established by estoppel. The landowners, feeling themselves aggrieved, appeal. We will consider the two issues separately.

In *Grinestaff v. Grinestaff*, 318 S.W.2d 881 (Ky. 1958), we said that an easement may be created by express written grant, by implication, by prescription, or by estoppel. It has long been the law of this commonwealth that "[an] easement, such as a right of way, is created when the owner of a tenement to which the right is claimed to be appurtenant, or those under whom he claims title, have openly, peaceably, continuously, and under a claim of right adverse to the owner of the soil, and with his knowledge and acquiescence, used a way over the lands of another for as much as 15 years." *Flener v. Lawrence*, 220 S.W. 1041 (Ky. 1920); *Rominger v. City Realty Company*, 324 S.W.2d 806 (Ky. 1959).

In 1942 appellants purchased the subject property. In 1944 they gave permission for a haul road to be cut for the purpose of moving coal from a newly opened mine. The roadway was so used until 1949, when the mine closed. During that time the appellants were paid a royalty for the use of the road. In 1957 appellants built a tenant house on their property and the roadway was used by them and their tenant. The tenant house burned in 1961 and was not replaced. In 1964 the appellees bought their three-acre building site, which adjoins appellants, and the following year built their residence thereon. At all times prior to 1965, the use of the haul road was by permission of appellants. There is no evidence of any probative value which would indicate that the use of the haul road during that period of time was either adverse, continuous, or uninterrupted. The trial court was fully justified, therefore, in finding that the right to the use of this easement was not established by prescription.

As to the issue on estoppel, we have long recognized that a right to the use of a roadway over the lands of another may be established by estoppel. In *Lashley Telephone Co. v. Durbin*, 228 S.W. 423 (Ky. 1921), we said:

> Though many courts hold that a licensee is conclusively presumed as a matter of law to know that a license is revocable at the pleasure of the licensor, and if he expend money in connection with his entry upon the land of the latter, he does so at his peril . . . , yet it is the established rule in this state that where a license is not a bare, naked right of entry, but includes the right to erect structures and acquire an interest in the land in the nature of an easement by the construction of improvements thereon, the licensor may not revoke the license and restore his premises to their former condition after the licensee has exercised the privilege given by the license and erected the improvements at considerable expense.

In *Gibbs v. Anderson*, 156 S.W.2d 876 (Ky. 1941), Gibbs claimed the right, by estoppel, to the use of a roadway over the lands of Anderson. The lower court denied the claim. We reversed. Anderson's immediate predecessor in title admitted that he had discussed the passway with Gibbs before it was constructed and had agreed that it might be built through his land. He stood by and saw Gibbs expend considerable money in this construction. We applied the rule announced in *Lashley Telephone Co. v. Durbin, supra*, and reversed with directions that a judgment be entered granting Gibbs the right to the use of the passway.

In *McCoy v. Hoffman*, 295 S.W.2d 560 (Ky. 1956), the facts are that Hoffman had acquired the verbal consent of the landowner to build a passway over the lands of the owner to the state highway. Subsequently, the owner of the servient estate sold the property to McCoy, who at the time of the purchase was fully aware of the existence of the roadway and the use to which it was being put. McCoy challenged Hoffman's right to use the road. The lower court found that a right had been gained by prescription. In this court's consideration of the case, we affirmed, not on the theory of prescriptive right but on the basis that the owner of the servient estate was estopped. After announcing the rule for establishing a right by prescription, we went on to say:

> On the other hand, the right of revocation of the license is subject to the qualification that where the licensee has exercised the privilege given him and erected improvements or made substantial expenditures on the faith or strength of the license, it becomes irrevocable and continues for so long a time as the nature of the license calls for. In effect, under this condition the license becomes in reality a grant through estoppel.

In *Akers v. Moore*, 309 S.W.2d 758 (Ky. 1958), this court again considered the right to the use of a passway by estoppel. Akers and others had used the Moore branch as a public way of ingress and egress from their property. They sued Moore and others who owned property along the branch seeking to have the court recognize their right to the use of the roadway and to order the removal of obstructions which had been placed in the roadway. The trial court found that Akers and others had acquired a prescriptive right to the use of the portion of the road lying on the left side of the creek bed, but had not acquired the right to the use of so much of the road as lay on the right side of the creek bed. Consequently, an appeal and a cross-appeal were filed. Considering the right to the use of the strip of land between the right side of the creek bed and the highway, this court found that the evidence portrayed it very rough and apparently never improved, that it ran alongside the house in which one of the protestors lived, and that by acquiescence or by express consent of at least one of the protestors the right side of the roadway was opened up so as to change the roadway from its close proximity to the Moore residence. The relocated portion of the highway had only been used as a passway for about six years before the suit was filed. The trial court found that this section of the road had not been established as a public way by estoppel. We reversed. In doing so, we stated:

> We consider the fact that the appellees, Artie Moore, et al., had stood by and acquiesced in (if in fact they had not affirmatively consented) the change being made and permitted the appellants to spend money in fixing it up to make it passable and use it for six years without objecting. Of course, the element of time was not sufficient for the acquisition of the right of way by adverse possession. But the law recognizes that one may acquire a license to use a passway or roadway where, with the knowledge of the licensor, he has in the exercise of the privilege spent money in improving the way or for other purposes connected with its use on the faith or strength of the license. Under such conditions the license becomes irrevocable and continues for so long a time as its nature calls for. This, in effect, becomes a grant through estoppel. It would be unconscionable to permit the owners of this strip of land of trivial value to revoke the license by obstructing and preventing its use.

In the present case the roadway had been used since 1944 by permission of the owners of the servient estate. The evidence is conflicting as to whether the use of the road subsequent to 1965 was by permission or by claim of right. Appellees contend that it had been used by them and others without the permission of appellants; on the other hand, it is contended by appellants that the use of the roadway at all times was by their permission. The evidence discloses that during the period of preparation for the construction of appellees' home and during the time the house was being built, appellees were permitted to use the roadway as ingress and egress for workmen, for hauling machinery and material to the building site, for construction of the dwelling, and for making improvements generally to the premises. Further, the evidence reflects that after construction of the residence, which cost $25,000, was completed, appellees continued to regularly use the roadway as they had been doing. Appellant J.S. Holbrook testified that in order for appellees to get up to their house he gave them permission to use and repair the roadway. They widened it, put in a culvert, and graveled part of it with "red dog," also known as cinders, at a cost of approximately $100. There is no other location over which a roadway could reasonably be built to provide an outlet for appellees.

No dispute had arisen between the parties at any time over the use of the roadway until the fall of 1970. Appellant J.S. Holbrook contends that he wanted to secure a writing from the appellees in order to relieve him from any responsibility for any damage that might happen to anyone on the subject road. On the other hand, Mrs. Holbrook testified that the writing was desired to avoid any claim which may be made by appellees of a right to the use of the roadway. Appellees testified that the writing was an effort to force them to purchase a small strip of land over which the roadway traversed, for the sum of $500. The dispute was not resolved and appellants erected a steel cable across the roadway to prevent its use and also constructed "no trespassing" signs. Shortly thereafter, the suit was filed to require the removal of the obstruction and to declare the right of appellees to the use of the roadway without interference.

The use of the roadway by appellees to get to their home from the public highway, the use of the roadway to take in heavy equipment and material and supplies for construction of the residence, the general improvement of the premises, the maintenance of the roadway, and the construction by appellees of a $25,000 residence, all with the actual consent of appellants or at least with their tacit approval, clearly demonstrates the rule laid down in *Lashley Telephone Co. v. Durbin, supra*, that the license to use the subject roadway may not be revoked.

The evidence justifies the finding of the lower court that the right to the use of the roadway had been established by estoppel. The judgment is affirmed.

NOTES AND QUESTIONS

1. *Length of Estoppel Period.* If the landowner is estopped from revoking a license, how long should the bar remain in effect? RESTATEMENT OF PROPERTY § 519(4) — licensee may continue the use "to the extent necessary to realize upon his expenditures" — implies that at some point the license becomes revocable again. A few courts, like the one above, have held that an irrevocable license is like an easement and can never be revoked. When equity intervenes to bar revocation, should the servient landowner be entitled to recover the value of the entitlement?

2. *Commercial Licenses.* For reasons similar to those cited in *Holbrook v. Taylor*, commercial licenses usually cannot be revoked at the whim of the party who granted the license. In most cases, the purchaser of the commercial license will have relied upon an expectation that the license would not be abruptly revoked, and the court will usually find that the licensor is estopped from revoking the license without reasonable notice. The licensee may also have an action for damages if the revocation was in violation of a contractual agreement between the two parties. Commercial licenses are also assignable, unless there is evidence that the license was personal to licensee or evidence that assignability would be inconsistent with the nature of the agreement that created the license.

3. *License Coupled with an Interest.* A license coupled with an interest is defined as "one which is incidental to the ownership of an interest in a chattel personal located on the land with respect to which the license exists." RESTATEMENT OF PROPERTY § 513. For example, if A, the owner and possessor of Whiteacre, sells B a car sitting on Whiteacre, B has a license coupled with an interest to go on Whiteacre to remove the vehicle. A license coupled with an interest is irrevocable for a reasonable period of time.

[D.] THE NATURE AND SCOPE OF NEGATIVE EASEMENTS

Although called easements, negative easements actually have less in common with affirmative easements than they do with defeasible estates, real covenants, and equitable servitudes, all of which are used to restrict the ways in which others can make use of their property. While an affirmative easement obviously restricts a property owner's ability to use his own property, those restrictions stem from the affirmative easement holder's right to use the servient tenement. Negative easements, however, give the holder no right to use the servient tenement but they do operate to restrict the way in which the owner of the affected property can make use of his land.

Unlike affirmative easements which can cover an almost unlimited array of usages, negative easements have been narrowly defined so as to apply in only limited circumstances. In fact, English and American courts have traditionally recognized only four types of negative easements: easements of light, air, subjacent or lateral support, and the flow of an artificial stream. Because the traditional negative easements provided the easement holder with no right to use the servient tenant but with the power to limit what the owner could do with his property, at one court recently referred to the negative easement as "a veto power." *Prospect Dev. Co. v. Bershader*, 515 S.E.2d 291, 299 (Va. 1999).

Moreover, courts have generally resisted the expansion of the types of negative easements. The following case represents a modest departure from that tradition.

PETERSEN v. FRIEDMAN

California Court of Appeals
162 Cal. App. 2d 245 (1958)

KAUFMAN, P.J.

The parties are owners of adjacent parcels of improved real estate situated on Franklin Street in San Francisco. Plaintiff's complaint sought to perpetually enjoin the defendants from violating an express easement of light, air and unobstructed view created in favor of plaintiff's property and to compel the defendants to remove certain television aerials and antennae. The trial court found all of the allegations of the complaint to be true, rendered judgment for the plaintiff, and issued both injunctions requested. Defendants appeal.

The nature and creation of the easement appurtenant to plaintiff's property is not in dispute. On November 6, 1942, Mary Petersen, now deceased, also known as Mrs. Chris Petersen, by a grant deed duly recorded conveyed a part of her property on Franklin Street to C. A. Petersen. The deed contained the followed reservation of an easement:

> Reserving, however, unto the first party, her successors and assigns, as and for an appurtenance to the real property hereinafter particularly described and designated as "Parcel A" and any part thereof, a perpetual easement of right to receive light, air and unobstructed view over that

> portion of the real property hereinabove described, to the extent that said light, air and view will be received and enjoyed by limiting any structure, fence, trees or shrubs upon said property hereinabove described or any part thereof, to a height not extending above a horizontal plane 28 feet above the level of the sidewalk of Franklin Street as the sidewalk level now exists at the junction of the southern and western boundary lines of the property hereinabove described. Any obstruction of such view above said horizontal plane except by a peaked gable roof extending the entire width of the front of the building referred to herein and extending 9 feet in an easterly direction from a point 1 foot 6 inches east of Franklin Street, the height of said peaked roof being 3 feet 2 inches together with spindles 3 feet in height on the peak of said roof, and except the necessary number of flues or vents constructed of galvanized iron and/or terra cotta not over 4 feet in height, shall be considered an unauthorized interference with such right or easement and shall be removed upon demand at the expense of second party, and his successors and assigns in the ownership of that real property described or any part thereof.

Thereafter, the defendants, by mesne conveyances from C.A. Petersen acquired all of the property conveyed by the deed of November 6, 1942, subject to the reservation. Plaintiff is the duly appointed and qualified executor of the estate of Mary Petersen, which is the owner of the dominant tenement.

Defendants' contentions on appeal are limited to the following: (1) that it could not have been the intent of the parties to preclude the erection of television aerials and antennae on the defendants' roof as the easement was created before such devices were known; (2) that the evidence does not support the judgment.

The language of the easement is clear and leaves no room for construction or determination of the intent of the parties, as contended by the defendant. Its purpose is to avoid any type of obstruction of the light, air and view without regard to the nature thereof. The reservation was not limited to the use then being made of the servient estate, but extended to all uses to which the servient estate might thereafter be devoted. Easements of light and air may be created in this state. Civ. Code, § 801; *Bryan v. Grosse*, 99 P. 499 (Cal.). Although we have not been able to find a California precedent on an easement of view, the weight of authority is that such an easement may be created by express grant. (*See* 142 A.L.R. 467 and cases collected therein.) It has been held in this state however, that interference with an easement of light, air or view by a structure in the street is ground for an injunction. *Williams v. Los Angeles R. Co.*, 89 P. 330 (Cal.).

As to defendant's second contention, the issue of whether or not the aerials and antennae obstructed plaintiff's view and otherwise interfered with the easement to the detriment of the plaintiff, were questions of fact for the lower court. The plaintiff offered evidence as to the size and nature of the obstructions and testified that because of the presence of the aerials and antennae, he received a lesser rental for the apartments on his property. The question of granting or refusing an injunction is addressed to the sound discretion of the lower court and its action will not be reversed on appeal unless there appears to be an abuse of discretion. *Williams v. Los Angeles R. Co., supra*. The record here supports the judgment.

Judgment affirmed.

NOTES AND QUESTIONS

1. *The Right to Light and Air.* Chapter 2 addressed the question of the right of one neighbor to interfere with another access to light and air as a matter of the law of nuisance. *See Whitesell v. Houlton* and *Prah v. Maretti, supra.* Presumably, a negative easement imposes more substantial limitations on the owner of the servient tenement than the general obligation to use one's land in a reasonable manner. A reasonableness requirement implies some sort of balancing test. Does the court appear to engage in any sort of balancing of interests in *Petersen*?

2. *Creation of Negative Easements.* Negative easements can only be created by an express writing. Unlike affirmative easements, they cannot arise by implication, necessity, or prescription. Arguments that a property owner could obtain a negative prescriptive easement of light against his neighbor were rejected by pre-Civil War American courts as inconsistent with the need for economic development. In doing so, they rejected the English common law doctrine of "ancient lights" which recognized a right to light and air based upon long and continuous enjoyment. *See Parker & Edgarton v. Foote*, 19 Wend. 309 (N.Y. Sup. Ct. 1838), perhaps the most significant of the American cases reflecting this view, where the court denounced the common law approach to light as "an anomaly in the law" and one which "cannot be applied in the growing villages and towns of this country, without working the most mischievous consequences." Does the experience of the second half of the 20th century suggest that a more liberal approach to negative easements might have enabled the American legal system to better deal with the complexities of urbanization?

3. Although American courts have been reluctant to expand the categories for negative easements, when they have, judges have typically been influenced by heightened environmental sensitivities, as the court appears to have been in *Petersen*. The use of solar collectors and windmills as alternative energy sources has prompted considerable discussion of the suitability of the negative easement doctrine to protect against interference with these technological devices. *See* Lyden, *An Integrated Approach to Solar Access*, 34 CASE W. RES. L. REV. 367 (1984). Many jurisdictions have by statute created a "solar skyspace easement" or "solar access easement." *See, e.g.*, Cal. Civ. Code § 801.5 (1982); Colo. Rev. Stat. §§ 38-32.5-100.3 to -103 (1982); N.Y. Real Prop. Law § 335-b (McKinney Supp. 1983). These entitle parties to *voluntarily* agree to a negative easement which would preclude the servient landowner from interfering with or causing detriment to the dominant tenement's access to solar energy.

Note, however, that such a *statute* would not necessarily have solved the homeowner's problem in *Prah v. Maretti, supra*, Chapter 2, since there was no such agreement in that case. Is the creation of a new type of negative easement (or at least a variation on an old type) the most efficient way to protect solar access or would zoning restrictions be more effective? Or is the recognition of a private nuisance action a preferable approach? *See* Gergacz & Houston, *Legal Aspects of Solar Energy: Limitations on the Zoning Alternative from a Legal and Economic Perspective*, 3 TEMP. ENVTL. L. & TECH. J. 5 (1984).

4. *Appurtenant or In Gross?* Negative easements created by private agreement are always appurtenant. As such they can only be enforced by the owner of the dominant tenement, i.e., the parcel which benefits from the restriction imposed by the easement. Unless specified in the creating instrument, a negative easement does not terminate when either the dominant or servient tenement is transferred.

5. *Conservation Easements.* The most significant new form of negative easement is the conservation easement, recognized over the last several decades as a way to preserve scenic areas and open space. A conservation easement is created when a landowner relinquishes the right to use a particular parcel of land in some specified way that would detract from, diminish, or extinguish its natural qualities. The easement holder, typically a public agency or a charitable organization, usually owns no dominant tenement but has the power to enforce the restriction against the servient landowner.

The Uniform Conservation Easement Act (UCEA) § 1 defines a conservation easement as "a nonpossessory interest of a holder in real property imposing limitations or affirmative obligations the purposes of which include retaining or protecting natural, scenic, or open-space values of real property, assuring its availability for agricultural, forest, recreational, or open-space use, protecting natural resources, maintaining or enhancing air or water quality, or preserving the historical, architectural, archaeological, or cultural aspects of real property." For a thorough analysis of the practical aspects of conservation easements, see Dietrich & Dietrich, *Conservation Easements: Tax and Real Estate Planning for Landowners and Advisors* (ABA Press 2011).

6. *Negative Easements in Gross.* The conservation easement is not without its problems. Since it can exist without a dominant tenement, it is technically a negative easement in gross which under traditional easement theory did not exist. States have dealt with this inconsistency in a number of ways, and not all have been sympathetic to the idea. A few have strained to treat conservation easements as easements appurtenant, thereby "running with the land," while still others avoid the term easement altogether, characterizing the new interest as a "conservation restriction" which is freely transferable. (The Uniform Act studiously avoids the phrase "easement in gross.")

Most states have simply recognized the anomalous nature of the conservation easement and have enacted statutes that render conservation easements enforceable, assignable, and perpetual in duration, even in the absence of a dominant tenement. Some states recognize a right to transfer conservation easements while others do not. States also differ in their approach to the enforcement of conservation easements.

See generally Federico Cheever & Nancy A. McLaughlin, *An Introduction to Conservation Easements in the United States: A Simple Concept and a Complicated Mosaic of Law*, 1 J. L. Prop. & Soc'y 107 (2015). The early history of the conservation easement is examined in Hegi, *The Easement in Gross Revisited: Transferability and Divisibility Since 1945*, 39 Vand. L. Rev. 109, 126–28 (1986). *See also* Colinvaux, *Conservation Easements: Design Flaws, Enforcement Challenges, and Reform*, 33 Utah. Envtl. L. Rev. 1 (2013); Jay, *When Perpetual Is Not Forever: The Challenge of Changing Conditions, Amendment, and Termination of Per-*

petual Conservation Easements, 36 HARV. ENVTL. L. REV. 1 (2012).

7. *How Conservation Easements Work.* By virtue of the broad discretion granted by enactments such as the Uniform Conservation Easement Act, landowners who are sympathetic to the idea of conservation can preclude any further development of their land even after their ownership ends. By granting a conservation easement that prevents future non-agricultural use of the land, for example, a present owner of land can severely limit what future owners may do. Were he to try to accomplish this end by means of a defeasible estate, he would be unlikely to succeed, either because the restraint would be deemed contrary to public policy or else, under modern statutes, his right to enforce the limitation would expire at some point in the not too distant future.

In contrast, the conservation easement is clearly enforceable and potentially infinite in duration. Moreover, even if the landowner isn't interested in conservation, the state's ability to condemn conservation easements through its power of eminent domain allows it to limit the land to a particular use at a fraction of what it would cost to condemn the entire parcel. This approach may, however, produce a political backlash if too widely used. For a discussion of these issues, see Korngold, *Privately Held Conservation Servitudes, A Policy Analysis in the Context of in Gross Real Covenants and Easements*, 63 TEX. L. REV. 433, 455–63 (1984).

Do conservation easement acts give too much power to those who support the idea of permanent classification? Should there be administrative commissions, akin to a zoning boards, to rule on the propriety of proposed conservation easements? Should conservation easements be subject to time limits?

[E.] RESTRICTIVE COVENANTS

At least two generations before the advent of systematic zoning, private landowners used the mechanisms of the restrictive covenant to create and enforce promises pertaining to the use of land, the maintenance of common facilities, and the race and religion of individuals to whom the land could be sold. *See* Jost, *The Defeasible Fee and the Birth of the Modern Residential Subdivision*, 49 MO. L. REV. 695 (1984). Even today, notwithstanding widespread governmental land use planning, restrictive covenants pervade all types of living arrangements from multi-unit urban buildings to the scattered housing of unzoned rural areas. Because of their flexibility and durability, as well as the relative ease with which they are created, restrictive covenants are often the most desirable form of land use restriction.

A note on terminology: Technically, a *restrictive covenant* imposes a restraint on another's land while an *affirmative covenant* imposes an obligation or duty upon the burdened landowner. Traditionally, restrictive covenants have also been divided, not by the type of interest they sought to enforce, but by the mechanism by which they were enforced; hence the traditional categories of equitable servitudes and real covenants running with the land.

[1.] Equitable Servitudes

Given the uncertainty of defeasible estates as an effective tool of land use control and the limited scope of the negative easement, it is not surprising that Americans turned to other land use control strategies in the 19thnineteenth century. Individuals who sought to limit the uses to which their neighbors could put their property and developers who wanted to offer a controlled environment turned to contract as a way of accomplishing their objectives. However, the contractual approach posed a very serious problem. While the current owner of the land could be bound by contract, what happened when the current owner sold the property to another owner?

To address this possibility, language was commonly inserted into the contract creating the restriction by which the party whose land was being burdened agreed that neither he, his heirs, or assigns would engage in the offending use. So long as original party to the contract (or covenant, as it was usually known) insisted on inserting a similar clause in his contract with the new buyer, the problem was at least partially addressed, although under 19thnineteenth century contract law, it was not clear that others not party to the specific contract could enforce the agreement.

The problem was solved at a surprisingly early date (the 1840s at the latest) by the willingness of American courts to enforce such agreements in equity against subsequent purchasers. So long as the restriction pertained to the land (and land use restrictions always did) and those who acquired the affected land had notice of the restriction and the fact that it was to bind subsequent owners, American courts were willing to enforce the terms of the original agreement, even between those who were not in privity of contract. In fact, from the mid-19thnineteenth century onward, American courts have usually dealt with covenants restricting the use of land as equitable servitudes and not as the older legal form, real covenants running with the land. W. Stoebuck, & D. Whitman, The Law of Property 472–73 (3d ed. 2000). (Real covenants running with the land are discussed in Subsection 2, below.)

[a.] Covenants in Equity

CHEATHAM v. TAYLOR
Virginia Supreme Court
138 S.E. 545 (1927)

Burks, J., delivered the opinion of the court.

This is an application for an appeal from a decree of the Circuit Court of the city of Lynchburg. We do not generally deliver opinions on such applications, but it is sometimes done in exceptional cases. We have been urged to do it in the instant case because of the supposed novelty of the main question involved.

In 1890 the Rivermont Company became the owner of a boundary of two thousand acres of land in the county of Campbell, abutting on the corporate limits of the city of Lynchburg. In order to connect with the business part of the city, the

Rivermont Company built an expensive viaduct across a deep ravine capable of carrying a double track street railway in the center and driveways and sidewalks on each side thereof. The Rivermont Company surveyed its property and laid it off in city blocks, lots, streets and alleys. It constructed an avenue called Rivermont Avenue, eighty feet wide, extending from the northern end of said viaduct through its property, a distance of three miles. All of this property is now within the city limits. It was expected to, and has since become, the principal residential part of the city. In order to make the lots on Rivermont avenue attractive for such purpose, the board of directors of the company, in April, 1891, passed a resolution declaring "that the building line of so much of Rivermont avenue as is beyond and northwest of Bedford avenue shall be twenty feet from the line of said avenue and no house or any part thereof shall be erected nearer to said street than said line, and all contracts of sale of lots on that part of said avenue and conveyances thereunder shall contain a covenant providing for such structure."

On July 4, 1891, and probably at other times, an advertisement was published in a daily paper in the city of Lynchburg, setting forth the advantages of the property of the Rivermont Company, in which, amongst other things, it was said: "The building restrictions, too, on this street, cannot fail to add to its other attractions. This consists in the fact that no house can be erected at a cost less than $1,500.00. From Bedford avenue west, and northwest, there is another restriction of a wholesome character which requires buildings to be set back twenty feet from the street line."

A plat of the property, showing the blocks, lots, streets and alleys, was recorded in the clerk's office of the county of Campbell, in which the property was then located, but this plat does not show the building line on Rivermont avenue hereinbefore referred to.

The appellant acquired title to two lots on the south side of Rivermont avenue, within the restricted area, and the appellees acquired title to three lots on the opposite side of Rivermont avenue, also within the restricted area. The Rivermont Company was the common source of title of all of the parties, and each of the deeds from the Rivermont Company contains the following clause:

> That the Rivermont Company in selling this lot sells with the distinct understanding and reservation that no house shall be built thereon now or at any other time the front line of which shall be nearer than 20 feet of the line of deed also contained the same said lot abuts, and further that no house shall be built thereon other than the stable, kitchen and other office on said premises which shall cost less than $1,500.00, . . . and the grantee accepts the foregoing reservations and restrictions as covenants running with the land.

The deed from the Rivermont Company to John A. Cassidy, the predecessor in title of the appellant, bears date November 29, 1892. The deed from Cassidy to appellant bears date March 30, 1908. The latter deed also contained the same restrictive covenants. In 1911, the appellant built a dwelling on one of the lots and a drug store on the other, both twenty feet from Rivermont avenue. In 1925, he added fifteen feet to the front of the drug store, thus bringing it to within five feet of the avenue.

In 1893 the Rivermont Company, after having sold not less than seventy per cent of its lots on Rivermont avenue, became insolvent, and, by deed bearing date June 2, 1893, conveyed all of its property, including the remaining lots on Rivermont avenue, to Wm. V. Wilson, Jr., in trust to secure its creditors. This deed did not contain the restrictive provisions above mentioned, and Wilson sold and conveyed the lots without such restrictions. The petition mentions but one lot on Rivermont avenue which was conveyed by the Rivermont Company without the restrictive provision.

When the appellees found that the appellant was about to make the addition to the drug store, they promptly notified him of their intention to apply for an injunction if he persisted in his purpose. He did persist, and this suit was brought to enjoin him from proceeding, and to require him to tear down and remove what he had constructed within twenty feet of Rivermont avenue. At the hearing on the merits, the trial court granted the injunction prayed for, and required appellant to tear down and remove what he had constructed within said twenty feet.

This is an application for an appeal from that decree, and the chief point insisted upon by counsel for the petitioner is that the covenant aforesaid is a personal covenant, which could, at any time, be waived or released by the Rivermont Company, and that the appellees cannot maintain this suit. His contention on this point is thus stated in the petition: "There is no privity of contract or obligation between the plaintiff and your petitioner. There is in existence no covenant or agreement whatever between the plaintiffs and the defendant. There is no mutual covenant between the plaintiffs and the grantors of this petition by virtue of which they may make any lawful demand on him, or interfere with his use of his own property." This position is elaborated in the petition by argument to show that in each of the deeds made by the Rivermont Company the covenant was a mere personal covenant between the grantor and grantee in that deed.

The petitioner insists that "privity of contract" is essential to the maintenance of the appellees' suit, when the weight of authority appears to be that no such privity is necessary. It is not a question of privity, but of intention. If when the covenant was entered into, it was the intention of the parties that the grantees were to be benefitted by the building restriction, they may maintain a suit in equity to protect and enforce the right conferred by the covenant.

It is not necessary, in order to sustain the equitable remedy, that there should be any privity of either estate or contract, if it clearly appears that the restriction was created for the plaintiffs, among others, or their grantor, and that the defendant had notice, actual or constructive, of the restriction. There is an equitable right in the plaintiffs, variously designated, which a court of equity will protect and enforce, although there may be no remedy, or an inadequate one, at law. Whether or not third persons, not parties to the instrument, are within its purview, is one of intention, and this intention may appear either from the instrument alone, or from the instrument with the aid of the surrounding facts and circumstances. If a person is within the benefits intended to be conferred, he has an equitable interest which a court of equity will protect.

Dean Harlan F. Stone, of Columbia Law School (now a justice of the United States Supreme Court), has a very thoughtful and able article on *The Equitable*

Rights and Liabilities of Strangers to a Contract, in 18 COLUM. L. REV. No. 4, pages 291–324, which will be hereinafter referred to. He discusses *Tulk v. Moxhay*, 2 Phillips 774, now to be referred to, and subsequent cases interpreting that case.

In *Tulk v. Moxhay, supra*, the owner of a piece of ground sold and conveyed a part of it, described as "Leicester Square Garden," to a purchaser in 1808, who, amongst other things, covenanted that no building should ever be erected upon it. "The piece of land so conveyed passed by diverse mesne conveyances into the hands of the defendant, whose purchase deed contained no similar covenants with his vendor; but he admitted that he had purchased with notice of the covenant in the deed of 1808." The purchaser asserted the right to build on it, if he thought fit, and the "plaintiff, who still remained the owner of several houses in the square, filed his bill for an injunction; and an injunction was granted by the Master of the Rolls." A motion to dissolve was made before Lord Chancellor Cottenham, which was refused. The Lord Chancellor said:

> That this court has jurisdiction to enforce a contract between the owner of land and his neighbor purchasing a part of it, that the latter shall either use or abstain from using the land purchased in a particular way, is what I never knew disputed. Here there is no question about the contract; the owner of certain houses in the square sells the land adjoining, with a covenant from the purchaser not to use it for any other purpose than as Square Garden. And it is now contended, not that the vendee could violate the contract, but that he might sell the piece of land, and that the purchaser from him may violate it without this court having the power to interfere. If that were so, it would be impossible for an owner of land to sell part of it without incurring the risk of rendering what he retains worthless. It is said that, the covenant being one which does not run with the land, this court cannot enforce it; but the question is, not whether the covenant runs with the land, but whether a party shall be permitted to use the land in a manner inconsistent with the contract entered into by his vendor, and with notice of which he purchased. Of course the price would be affected by the covenant, and nothing could be more inequitable than that the original purchaser should be able to sell the property the next day for a greater price, in consideration of the assignee being allowed to escape from the liability which he had himself undertaken.
>
> That the question does not depend upon whether the covenant runs with the land is evident from this, that if there was a mere agreement, and no covenant, this court would enforce it against a party purchasing with notice of it; for if an equity is attached to the property by the owner, no one purchasing with notice of that equity can stand in any different situation from the party from whom he purchased.

Here, then, Lord Cottenham puts the right of recovery upon "an equity attached to the land," and gives the right of recovery against any one "purchasing with notice of that equity."

In 8 AM. & ENG. ENCY. L. (2d ed.), page 140, it is said: "Courts of equity, however, irrespective of whether a privity of estate exists, or whether the covenants run with the land, upon equitable grounds enforce such covenants against purchasers with notice." In Northrup on the "Law of Real Property," page 377, it is said: "A purely equitable doctrine, of great importance in growing cities and entirely distinct from the common law doctrine of covenants running with the land, has arisen in modern times. It is often referred to, from the English case that is its foundation, as the doctrine of *Tulk v. Moxhay*. It is also called the doctrine of restrictive covenants in equity, and the rights and obligations established by it are known as equitable easements and equitable servitudes. The doctrine is, in brief, that when, on a transfer of land, there is a covenant or even an informal contract or understanding that certain restrictions in the use of the land conveyed shall be observed, the restrictions will be enforced by equity, at the suit of the party or parties intended to be benefitted thereby, against any subsequent owner of the land except a purchaser for value without notice of the agreement. The principal purposes of such agreements are to regulate the style and costs of buildings to be erected on a tract that is being sold in parcels for building lots, to restrict their location to certain distances from the street, and to prevent buildings in a locality from being put up or used for any other than residential purposes. Restrictive covenants are most commonly made in connection with such sales of building lots, but the principle of the doctrine of *Tulk v. Moxhay* is, of course, applicable to other kinds of restrictions on the use of land, and equitable easements are created for many miscellaneous purposes."

It was found from experience that the common law doctrine of easements and servitudes, and of covenants running with the land, were too narrow in their application, and left many substantial rights unprotected, and so courts of equity have intervened for the protection of such rights, making the intention of the parties the criterion of the existence of the right, and, when found to exist, enforcing it whether created by covenant or by simple contract. The equity enforced is the prevention of a third person from violating the equitable rights of another of which he has notice, actual or constructive.

In the establishment of the right, the intention of the parties is of great importance, but when once established no notice is necessary except of the existence of the right, and this notice may be actual or constructive.

From the authorities cited, and others along that line, it appears that equity will enforce restrictive covenants against takers with notice of the servient tenement; that privity is not necessary to entitle the injured party to sue; that the proper method to protect and enforce the covenant is by injunction; that the right to enjoin is not dependent upon the existence of a right of action at law; that the right of a third person to the protection of the covenant is an equitable right by whatever name called; and that the determination of the person who is entitled to sue is dependent on the intention of the parties to the covenant as disclosed by the language of the covenant, and the facts and circumstances surrounding its execution.

An injunction in this class of cases is addressed to the conscience of the court and will not be granted where it would be unfair and inequitable to do so, as where a residential section has become a business section and the enforcement of the covenant would be of little benefit to the covenantee, but cause serious pecuniary loss to the covenantor or his assigns, nor where it is contrary to public policy, as an undue restraint of trade. The contract to be enforceable must be reasonable.

The petitioner's view of the relation of the parties seems to be that it is purely contractual, that there must be a contract between the parties, or their privies, mutually assented to, by which certain rights are created and corresponding obligations are imposed. It is earnestly insisted by counsel for petitioner that the complainants could not maintain their suit because the petitioner and those under whom he claims had no notice of the rights now claimed by the complainants in their bill; that the resolution of the board of directors was not recorded, that the advertisement was not recorded, and that the recorded map did not show any building line restriction. It would have been better if the recorded map, with reference to which all of the lots were sold, had shown the building line, or if the deeds to the earlier grantees had contained a covenant by the grantor that like restrictions would be placed in all subsequent conveyances of lots within the restricted area, but these provisions were not essential prerequisites if the same result was otherwise accomplished. When the common grantor made the earlier conveyances there was an implied promise on its part, especially in view of the resolution of its board of directors and advertisement, that the entire property covered by the resolution should be subject to the restriction, and for a violation of this promise it could have been enjoined by a purchaser of one of the lots. An equity attached to the lots sold which the common grantor could neither violate nor alienate to a purchaser with notice. Such is the principle of *Tulk v. Moxhay, supra.*

The petitioner and those under whom he claims had constructive notice that a building plan was laid out by the recorded map for an annex to the city of property adjacent thereto, and that this property was laid off in blocks, lots, streets and alleys. He had constructive notice of every right, title or interest in the lot purchased by him which the common grantor had conveyed to any prior purchaser, including restrictions on its powers over the lot purchased by him. He had both actual and constructive notice of the equitable right of the complainants to have the building line maintained, and he covenanted that this building line should be maintained on the lot purchased by him. The right to build nearer than twenty feet to the avenue was, in effect, never conveyed to him. The layout of the recorded map showed one comprehensive plan, and a restricted building line would be of little advantage to one lot unless it was extended to practically all, and when the common grantor made the restriction in each conveyance, in pursuance of the resolution of its board of directors and its advertisement, it must have been intended for the benefit of all its grantees, antecedent and subsequent, as well as for itself. It had no right to violate its implied agreement with purchasers, whether antecedent or subsequent, that the entire property should be covered by the restriction, and the covenant must be taken to be with the common grantor for the benefit of all purchasers. The covenant being thus, in part at least, for the benefit of the complainants, they had the right to enforce it in their own names, even independent of the equitable right we have been discussing. Code, section 5143. We do not rely, however, solely on the statute, but also upon the equitable doctrine announced in *Tulk v. Moxhay, supra*, and the cases following it.

The petitioner violated the equitable rights of the complainants with full knowledge, actual and constructive, of the existence thereof.

In the instant case, no one can fairly doubt that it was the intention of the parties that the restrictive provisions in the deeds from the Rivermont Company were for the mutual benefit of the company and the several purchasers from it of lots on Rivermont avenue within the area designated. This intent on the part of the company was plainly manifested by the resolution of its board of directors and the newspaper advertisement hereinbefore quoted, and on the part of the purchasers it is hardly less plain from the stipulation that the "grantee accepts the foregoing reservations and restrictions as covenants running with the land." What else could this stipulation mean to the purchaser? Moreover, the purchasers acted on the covenant from 1892 till the institution of this suit, and built their houses with reference to the restricted line, and it would be extremely inequitable and unfair to them to allow the petitioner at this late date to violate its provisions.

This disposes of the main question presented by the petition. The deed made to Wm. V. Wilson, Jr., trustee, after the company became insolvent, was a practical necessity in insolvency proceedings, and did not show any purpose on the part of the Rivermont Company to change its policy and did not, if it could, affect the rights of prior purchasers. The decree of the trial court is plainly right, and the petition for an appeal is therefore refused.

NOTES AND QUESTIONS

1. *Elements of an Equitable Servitude.* For a covenant to be enforced as an equitable servitude against subsequent owners, the original parties to the covenant must have intended that the agreement to bind later owners and the later owners must have had notice of the restriction. Furthermore, the covenant must touch and concern the land. (That requirement is not discussed in the above case, presumably because the covenant at issue so obviously touches and concerns the land.) Since the action is in equity, the proper remedy is injunctive relief rather than money damages.

2. *Historical Origins of the Equitable Servitude.* The 1848 decision in *Tulk v. Moxhay*, discussed extensively in the above opinion, is usually cited as the origin of the equitable servitude (although that terminology is not used in that case). However, Lord Chancellor Cottenham, the author of the *Tulk* opinion, gave no impression that he considered the issue in the case to be a novel one. As he said,

> Here there is no question about the contract; the owner of certain houses in the square sells the land adjoining, with a covenant from the purchaser not to use it for any other purpose than as a square garden. And it is now contended, not that the vendee could violate that contract, but that he might sell the piece of land, and that the purchaser from him may violate it without this Court having any power to interfere. If that were so, it would be impossible for an owner of land to sell part of it without incurring the risk of rendering what he retains worthless. It is said that, the covenant being one which does not run with the land, this Court cannot enforce it: but the question is, not whether the covenant runs with the land, but whether a party shall be permitted to use the land in a manner inconsistent with the contract entered into by his vendor, and with notice of which he purchased.

In fact, there is considerable evidence that American courts were willing to enforce land use covenants against subsequent owners in equity well before the decision in *Tulk*. *See, e.g.*, *Hills v. Miller*, 3 Paige Ch. 254 (N.Y. Ch. 1832); *Barrow v. Richard*, 8 Paige Ch. 351 (N.Y. Ch. 1840). What is clear is that in the middle of the 19th century (if not earlier), American courts embraced the principle of the equitable servitude with great enthusiasm. *See Whitney v. Union Ry. Co.*, 77 Mass. 359 (1858); *Tallmadge v. East River Bank*, 26 N.Y. 105 (1862); *Clark v. Martin*, 49 Pa. 289 (1865); *Burbank v. Pillsbury*, 48 N.H. 475 (1869); *Hubbard v. Toledo*, 21 Ohio St. 379 (1871). As a member of the Virginia Supreme Court noted in 1886, quoting from Kerr on Injunctions, a widely-cited treatise first published in 1867:

> The jurisdiction of courts of equity over contracts and covenants is not confined to cases where an action at law can be maintained, but extends to cases where an action at law is not maintainable. It is in many cases a matter of much doubt whether a covenant with respect to the use and occupation of land runs with the land, so as to bind at law an assignee, although assigns be expressly named in the covenant; but covenants controlling the enjoyment of land, though not binding at law, will be enforced in equity, provided the person into whose hands the land passes has taken it with notice of the covenants.

Tardy v. Creasy, 81 Va. 553, 566 (1886) (Lewis, J.). (The requirements for maintaining an action at law on a covenant running with the land are discussed in Subsection [2] below.)

3. *Equitable Servitudes as Real Property Interests.* As you may have noticed, the court in *Cheatham v. Taylor* uses the terms equitable servitudes and equitable easements interchangeably. Many early equitable servitude cases involving restrictions on land use used the terminology of easement on the grounds that the interest created — the right to restrict another's use of his property — was analogous to a negative easement. Some courts even suggested that an equitable servitude was a form of easement. *See, e.g.*, *Trustees of Columbia College v. Lynch*, 70 N.Y. 440 (1877). The analogy to easements and the willingness of courts to enforce restrictive covenants in equity led courts to define the equitable servitude as a real property interest rather than a contractual right well before the end of the 19th century. Consistent with this view, the original party to the agreement is relieved of any further liability in equity once he or she disposes of their interest in the land, as is the case with other real property interests like easements and profits. (Under the theory of covenants running with the land, the contracting parties remain liable under the agreement, even after their interests are conveyed.)

4. *The Meaning of Notice.* As the court in *Cheatham v. Taylor* noted, the notice necessary to enforce a covenant as an equitable servitude may be actual or constructive. Constructive notice usually means record notice, i.e., that the agreement creating the restriction is recorded within the current owner's chain of title. There is some disagreement, however, as to what constitutes a chain of title for purposes of record notice.

The traditional view was that the chain of title included only those deeds in a direct line from the original private grantee from the sovereign to the current owner and did not include prior deeds from a previous grantor to other purchasers of lots in the same subdivision. Consequently, a failure to include restrictive covenants or at least a reference to them in a particular deed meant that the covenants were unenforceable against the current owner, even if such restrictions were included in all the other deeds in the subdivision. The rationale was that a buyer doing a title search would have no reason to examine other transfers made by the developer either before or after the issuance of the deed which he was searching. Many states still follow this approach. *See, e.g., Witter v. Taggart*, 577 N.E.2d 338 (N.Y. 1991). On the other hand, an equal number of states have held that such recordings are within the chain of title. *See Guillette v. Daly Dry Wall, Inc.*, 325 N.E.2d 572 (Mass. 1975). In 1995, California joined the ranks of the latter when the California Supreme Court held that purchasers had legal notice of all restrictions recorded for their subdivision prior to their purchase, whether or not they are included in the deed through which they held title. *Citizens for Covenant Compliance v. Anderson*, 906 P.2d 1314 (Cal. 1995). Dissenting Justice Kennard characterized the decision as one that "blasts a gaping hole through the structure of real property law."

5. *Inquiry Notice*. Some courts also recognize another form of constructive notice, known as inquiry notice. In the oft-cited *Sanborn v. McLean*, 206 N.W. 496 (Mich. 1925), the Supreme Court of Michigan found that because of the strictly uniform appearance of the area, the defendants could be held to notice of a covenant restricting the use of their land to a private dwelling even though the covenants were not in their chain of title, and they lacked actual knowledge of their existence. In *Sanborn*, the defendants sought to build a gasoline station on the back half of their lot in a residential section of Detroit. The record showed that of 91 lots fronting on defendants' street, 53 contained "residential use only" restrictions in their chains of title. Nevertheless, the Michigan Supreme Court found that the developer had intended that all the lots on the street be subject to the same restriction and that the restrictions were in effect when the McLeans purchased their lot in 1910 or 1911. Consequently, the court concluded that the McLeans should have realized that "the residences [on their street] were built and the lots occupied in strict accordance with a general plan" and were thus "put to inquiry." Had they inquired, they "would have found of record the reason for such general conformation"; therefore, the court reasoned, the McLeans could not plead the lack of notice as a defense to their neighbors' effort to enjoin the construction of their gasoline station.

What is the nature of the notice received by the defendants in *Cheatham v. Taylor*?

6. *General Plan or Common Scheme Doctrine*. The doctrine of general plan or common scheme was developed to address the situation in which restrictions that are generally applied to a development are omitted from the deeds of purchasers of individual lots. So long as it can be established that there was a consistent use of covenants to control development and that this common plan was in place at the time the defendant purchased the lot, the restriction in question will be enforced against a lot owner who lacks reference to it in his or her chain of title. The rationale for the common plan doctrine has varied from jurisdiction to jurisdiction, but it has usually involved notions of equitable estoppel (the defendant has received the benefit of the covenant in question) and inquiry notice. That a common plan could give rise to enforceable covenants was acknowledged by American courts before the

end of the 19th century. *Sharp v. Ropes*, 110 Mass. 381 (1872); *Clark v. McGee*, 42 N.E. 965 (Ill. 1896). For a case in which the presence of building restrictions in the deeds of 802 of 1621 lots in a common development was found insufficient to establish a "definite and uniform building scheme," see *Stevenson v. Spivey*, 110 S.E. 367 (Va. 1922).

Some jurisdictions do not recognize the general plan doctrine. Usually, this rejection is on the grounds that the statute of frauds prevents enforcement of a servitude as against a buyer whose lot is not expressly restricted in writing. Until recently, the most frequently cited case for this proposition was *Riley v. Bear Creek Planning Comm.*, 551 P.2d 1213 (Cal. 1976). In *Riley*, the Court relied upon the statute of frauds and the parol evidence rule to prevent the plaintiff homeowner association from demonstrating that the Rileys were aware of restrictive covenants that were inadvertently omitted from their deed and not recorded until after the sale. The impact of *Riley* in California may be restricted by the decision in *Citizens for Covenant Compliance v. Anderson*, discussed above.

[b.] The Power to Enforce

RODGERS v. REIMANN
Oregon Supreme Court
361 P.2d 101 (1961)

O'Connell, J.

This is a suit in equity to enforce a building restriction contained in a land sale contract under which defendants were purchasers of a lot in the city of Salem, Oregon. Defendants own the restricted lot, hereafter referred to as Lot 11, which abuts Kingwood Drive on the east. The lot owned by plaintiffs abuts Kingwood drive on the west, directly across the street from Lot 11. Plaintiffs purchased their lot from Dr. and Mrs. Lebold on January 31, 1957. We shall refer to plaintiffs' parcel as the Lebold lot. At the time plaintiffs purchased the Lebold lot, Mr. and Mrs. Willett owned the lot adjoining the Lebold lot on the north. At that time also, the Lebolds and the Willetts owned Lot 11. On December 15, 1959 the Lebolds and the Willetts joined together to convey Lot 11 under a land sale contract to the defendants. The contract contained the following covenant:

> That no dwelling house shall be constructed on said real premises the floor level of which shall be more than one foot higher than the street curb of Kingwood Drive adjacent to said real premises.

Soon after defendants entered into the contract for the purchase of Lot 11 they commenced construction of a dwelling house on the lot. Plaintiffs brought this suit to enjoin the construction of the dwelling house allegedly in violation of the covenant. The trial court entered a decree dismissing plaintiffs' complaint, from which decree plaintiffs appeal.

To be entitled to enforce the covenant plaintiffs must show that the building restrictions imposed upon Lot 11 were intended to benefit them as the owners of the Lebold lot and that defendants entered into the covenant with notice that the covenant was to have this effect. The plaintiffs have the burden of proof in establishing these facts and to carry that burden they must overcome the constructional preference against restrictions limiting the use of land. However, the intention to benefit a particular parcel of land through the imposition of the restrictions on the land conveyed need not be expressly recited in the contract or deed. *Hall v. Risley & Heikkila*, 213 P.2d 818 (Or. 1950). [Other citations, including *Cheatham v. Taylor*, are omitted.]

It is not reasonable to presume that building restrictions such as we are concerned with here are intended simply for the personal benefit of the vendors. Rather it is reasonable to presume that the covenant in the case at bar was intended to benefit at least the land which was retained by the Willetts at the time they joined with the Lebolds in conveying Lot 11.

It is somewhat more difficult to assume that such a covenant is intended to benefit a prior grantee of the vendor, or, as in this case, the prior grantee of one of the two co-grantors. Where the restrictions are a part of a general building plan the courts generally recognize that a prior purchaser from the covenantee can enforce the covenants subsequently entered into between his grantor and subsequent grantees. 2 AMERICAN LAW OF PROPERTY (1952), § 9.30; 5 RESTATEMENT, PROPERTY, SERVITUDES (1944), Intr. Note, Ch. 46, p. 3244, and § 541, Comment *f*. If the covenants touch and concern the land previously conveyed out of an area subdivided pursuant to a general building plan, it is ordinarily held that in the absence of evidence of a contrary intent it will be assumed that the parties intended to benefit such land.

However, where, as here, there is no general building plan, the inference that the covenant is intended to benefit land previously conveyed by the common grantor is ordinarily more difficult to draw. Some courts take the view that in the absence of a general building scheme a covenant cannot inure to the prior grantee even though the covenantor and covenantee intended to benefit the land previously conveyed. *Snow v. Van Dam*, 197 N.E. 224, 228 (Mass. 1935). But, as pointed out by the RESTATEMENT OF PROPERTY, the prevailing view is to the contrary: "It has, however, come to be the prevailing view that beneficiaries of a promise other than the promisee can enforce the promise (*see* RESTATEMENT OF CONTRACTS, Chapter 6) even though the promise is not part of a general plan. To the extent to which this is true, the fact that a promise respecting the use of land is not made pursuant to a general plan of land development is not a barrier to the enforcement of the promise by third parties who are beneficiaries of the promise." 5 RESTATEMENT, PROPERTY, SERVITUDES (1944), Intr. Note, Ch. 46, p. 3244. We adopt the prevailing view.

We find no difficulty in recognizing the principle that a prior grantee may sue upon a covenant subsequently made by his grantor, if all of the elements essential to the enforcement of the covenant are present. Some courts have regarded the prior grantee as a third party beneficiary of a contract entered into between his grantor and the covenantor. The Restatement adopts this view. 5 RESTATEMENT, PROPERTY, SERVITUDES (1944), § 541, Comments *c* and *f*. A second theory, recognized by some courts, recognizes the creation of an implied reciprocal servitude. This theory is explained in 2 AMERICAN LAW OF PROPERTY (1952), § 9.30, p. 426, as follows:

> [W]hen the prior purchaser acquires his land in expectation that he will be entitled to the benefit of subsequently created servitudes, there immediately arises an implied reciprocal servitude against the common grantor's remaining land. If so, then he is enforcing, not the express agreement made by the common grantor when he subsequently sells his remaining land, but this implied reciprocal servitude created by implication at the time of the conveyance to the prior purchaser.

We feel free to employ either of these theories, as the case may demand, in determining whether a prior grantee should be entitled to enforce a covenant inserted in a subsequent deed.

To establish a reciprocal servitude it is necessary to find that the prior grantee purchased his land in reliance upon his grantor's promise to impose restrictions upon the retained parcels when conveyed by the common grantor to subsequent purchasers. The evidence in the case at bar is not sufficient to establish such reliance by the plaintiffs. Dr. Lebold testified that he was not certain whether he discussed with plaintiffs the imposition of restrictions on Lot 11 before or after the conveyance to plaintiffs. Mr. Rodgers testified that he believed "quite strongly" that he discussed the matter with Dr. Lebold prior to purchasing his lot, but that he was not certain. This is not sufficient evidence to create a servitude upon Lot 11 in favor of the Lebold lot.

We are willing to recognize, as many courts do, that the Statute of Frauds is not an impediment in the creation of such a servitude. [Citations omitted.] But this relaxation of the requirement that the creation of interests in land must be in writing should be attended with the safeguard furnished by satisfactory evidence of a clear and unequivocal agreement between the prior grantee and his grantor, as well as a satisfactory showing that the subsequent grantee had notice of the agreement. In the present case Lebold and Rodgers did not clearly and unequivocally agree, as a part of their bargain in the sale of the Lebold lot, that Lebold would restrict Lot 11 for the benefit of the Lebold lot.

Will the evidence sustain the theory that a third party beneficiary contract was created? The scope of a third party beneficiary's rights and remedies in Oregon is not clearly defined. However, we shall not at this time attempt to reappraise our cases touching upon this part of the law. For purposes of this case it is enough to recognize that under accepted principles relating to the enforcement of restrictive covenants by third persons, plaintiffs do not make out a sufficient case to qualify as either creditor or donee beneficiaries. 5 RESTATEMENT, PROPERTY, SERVITUDES (1944), § 541, Comment *c*, p. 3248, states the following principle:

> In order to make a third person the beneficiary of a promise it must be shown that the promise was sufficiently comprehensive to include the benefit of the third person within its intended operation. In the case of promises respecting the use of land, it is often true that others besides the promisee would be equally benefitted by the performance of the promise. Such others are not entitled to enforce the performance of the promise merely because of that fact. It must be shown that benefit to them was one of the things bargained for between the promisee and the promisor.

In the case at bar it was not shown that the benefit to plaintiffs was one of the things bargained for between the promisee and the promisor. The requirement that benefit to plaintiffs' lot must be shown to be one of the things bargained for between the common grantor and the subsequent grantee may also be regarded as an application of the rule that a purchaser of land will not be bound by a restriction unless he has notice of it. The purchaser must not only have notice that there is a restriction imposed upon the land he is purchasing, but he must have notice of its scope, i.e. the extent to which others may enforce it. We recognize that such proof need not be direct and that it may rest upon "reasonable inferences from the circumstances under which the promise was made." 5 RESTATEMENT, PROPERTY, SERVITUDES (1944), § 541, Comment *e*. But the inferences are not strong enough in the present case. The evidence tending to prove that the bargain between defendants and their grantors had for one of its purposes the benefiting of plaintiffs' land was equivocal.

The evidence may be regarded as establishing that both the Lebolds and the Willetts intended the restriction on Lot 11 to benefit plaintiffs' lot. They purchased Lot 11 to protect their view. Dr. Lebold testified that they even contemplated building a dwelling house, of such size and location so as not to interfere with their view, on Lot 11 to assure themselves of an unobstructed view. Dr. Lebold further testified that the restriction was placed in the contract of sale with the intention of protecting the view from plaintiffs' lot, although he admitted that he did not directly participate in the drafting of the contract. Mr. Willett was in charge of closing the sale of Lot 11, but Dr. Lebold testified that "I felt that he [Willett] had the interest of both pieces of property in mind when we talked about selling that [Lot 11]." But, although the evidence is reasonably clear that at least the Lebolds intended the restrictions to benefit plaintiffs' lot, the evidence that defendants had either actual or constructive notice of this purpose was insufficient to meet plaintiffs' burden of proof.

Defendants could not have learned of the purpose of the restrictions from the Willetts or Lebolds because the sellers' negotiations for the sale of Lot 11 were handled exclusively by Mr. Hutchison, the real estate agent who showed Lot 11 to defendants. At no time prior to the purchase of Lot 11 did defendants discuss with the Lebolds or the Willetts the purpose of the restrictions. Mr. Hutchison testified that he informed the defendants that the Lebolds and Willetts would insist upon building restrictions as a condition to the sale of the lot. He also testified that he informed defendants of the purpose of the restrictions. But there was no evidence to show precisely what Mr. Hutchison understood this purpose to be, nor was it shown what he communicated to defendants. He simply testified that the sellers, i.e. the Lebolds and the Willetts, told him why the restriction would be imposed upon Lot 11 and that he communicated this purpose to Mr. Reimann. In order to conclude that Hutchison informed Reimann that the restrictions were to benefit plaintiffs' lot, we would have to infer that Hutchison was informed by the Lebolds (or by their representatives, the Willetts) that they wanted to benefit the lot they had previously conveyed to plaintiffs. We do not feel that we can supply this inference.

To be weighed against any inference which might be drawn that the parties intended the restriction to benefit the Lebold lot is the testimony of Mr. Reimann. He testified as follows:

[The court then presents excerpts from defendant's testimony to the effect that he was never told that the restrictions on the use of his land were for the benefit of the owner of the plaintiff's lot.]

Plaintiffs argue that the intention to benefit plaintiffs' lot can be inferred from the juxtaposition of plaintiffs' and defendants' lots. As we have already stated, the purpose of a restriction may be arrived at by drawing reasonable inferences from the circumstances under which the restriction was created. One of these circumstances is the location of the burdened property in relation to the land of the person claiming the benefit of the restriction. In the usual case the inference is drawn from the fact that the claimants' and defendants' land are a part of a general plan of development. And in some cases notice of restrictions has been imputed to the purchaser from the physical appearance of the neighboring land in the subdivision.

In the present case we would be willing to find that defendants had notice that the restrictions on Lot 11 were intended to benefit plaintiffs' lot if the circumstances strongly supported that inference. But as we read the record the inference is not strong. A dwelling house could be constructed on Lot 11 in such a way as to interfere with the view from the Willetts' lot. It is, therefore, possible and not unreasonable to construe the restriction to have been inserted in the contract of sale for the purpose of benefiting Willetts' lot only. And that, according to Mr. Reimann's testimony, was precisely his understanding of the purpose of the restriction. To accept plaintiffs' position we would have to disbelieve Reimann and, in addition, draw an inference from a highly equivocal circumstance. A burden on land, created by covenant, should rest upon a more substantial foundation of proof.

The decree of the trial court is affirmed. Neither party to recover costs.

NOTES AND QUESTIONS

1. Do you understand why Rodgers cannot simply claim that Reimann's lot was burdened for the benefit of his property? The court implies that had the lots been part of a larger tract developed according to a common scheme, the result might well have been different. Why should that matter?

2. When real covenants were enforced in equity rather than law, courts historically took a broader approach that allowed any individual for whose benefit the covenant had been adopted to enforce the covenant, regardless of whether or not there was a contractual relationship between the original beneficiary and the party seeking to enforce the covenant. As the court said in *Cheatham v. Taylor*, "the restrictions will be enforced by equity, at the suit of the *party or parties intended to be benefited thereby*, against any subsequent owner of the land except a purchaser for value without notice of the agreement." (Emphasis added.)

3. *Negative Reciprocal Servitudes.* When the first lot in a development was sold subject to a restrictive covenant, all the remaining lots received the benefit of the first agreement. However, when the second lot was sold subject to the same restriction, the benefit attached to the remaining unsold lots, but, at least in theory, not to the first lot which was already sold. To address the apparent unfairness of such a result, courts developed the concept of the negative reciprocal servitude which is discussed in the above case. (Perhaps the more precise term is reciprocal negative servitudes.) With the development of third-party beneficiary theory in the law of contract, courts have also embraced that basis for allowing third parties to enforce restrictive covenants when they are not in vertical privity with the original parties to the covenants. Not all states have embraced the approach as willingly as the Oregon Supreme Court. See, for example, *Jones v. Gaddy*, 380 S.E.2d 706 (Ga. 1989), in which the court refused to allow a prior purchaser in a subdivision to enforce a covenant against a later purchaser.

4. *Benefits in Gross.* Occasionally a covenant will be created which burdens a particular parcel of property, but fails to benefit anyone in their capacity as landowner. A covenant not to compete that restricts the usages a landowner may make of his land without attaching a benefit to any other parcel is such an agreement, as when A promises B that he will not open a law office on Blackacre which he is purchasing from B. B obtains the benefit of the covenant even if he owns no other land, hence the benefit is said to be in gross. Under the majority rule, neither the benefit nor the burden will be said to run with the land, and such a covenant cannot be enforced against A's successor C, even if A and B intended to bind subsequent owners of Blackacre and C purchases the tract with knowledge of the restriction. For a discussion of such covenants, see the court's opinion in *Pratte v. Balatsos*, 113 A.2d 492 (N.H. 1955).

5. *The Enforcement of Affirmative Covenants.* At one time, some American courts, following the English model, would not enforce affirmative covenants in equity. However, most of their American counterparts showed no such reluctance and thereby eliminated what might have been one of the principal distinctions between legal and equitable covenants. *See, e.g., Whittenton Mfg. Co. v. Staples*, 41 N.E. 441 (Mass. 1895); *Murphy v. Kerr*, 5 F.2d 908 (8th Cir. 1925); *Fitzstephens v. Watson*, 344 P.2d 221 (Or. 1959). Consequently, covenants to maintain fences and party walls, pay association dues, or drain swampland can be enforced as equitable servitudes, so long as the intent, notice, and touch and concern requirements are met. Ordinarily an equitable servitude will be enforced regardless of the obligation it imposes on the burdened property, unless it is deemed unenforceable for reasons of public policy. (*See* Chapter 8.)

[2.] Covenants Running With the Land

A real covenant is a promise to do or to refrain from doing something related to land. The real covenant "runs with the land" if it binds not just the current owner but future owners as well. Unlike the equitable servitude, the covenant running with the land is not a real property interest but a contractual limitation. The key to understanding the relationship of equitable servitudes and real covenants running with the land is to realize that a single covenant can be, and usually is, enforceable as either (or both). As noted above, most restrictive covenants have been, and are, enforced as equitable servitudes, since injunctive relief is usually the remedy of choice in such cases.

There are, nevertheless, a number of situations where a party may desire to enforce a covenant as a real covenant running with the land rather than as an equitable servitude. The most obvious situation is where the plaintiff desires money damages instead of, or in addition to, equitable relief. As long as the law/equity distinction is honored, money damages should not be available as a remedy for breach of an equitable servitude. A related situation occurs when the covenant is for some reason unenforceable in equity but nevertheless enforceable at law. In such situations, the only available remedy for the beneficiary of the covenant will be at law under a real covenant running with the land theory.

The other situation in which the running covenant analysis is preferable is when the successor owner of the burdened property had no notice of the restriction. While notice is a precondition for the enforcement of an equitable servitude, it is technically not a requirement for a valid covenant running with the land, although most modern recording acts make notice a de facto requirement.

The theory of the running covenant does play an important role in landlord-tenant law. Because assignees of estates for years may not be aware of the contents of their assignor's lease, it is not uncommon for them to take the present estate without knowing about valid covenants between the landlord and original tenant. Moreover, not all recording acts require that leases (particularly short-term ones) be recorded, so there is no guarantee of constructive notice to the assignee. The theory of running covenants, however, binds the assignee to covenants in the original lease that are intended to run with the land.

[a.] The Limits of Equity

MOSELEY v. BISHOP

Indiana Court of Appeals
470 N.E.2d 773 (1984)

Young, J

Edith Moseley brought suit against Merrill and Joanna Gates and sixteen others (hereinafter defendants) seeking damages for the defendants' failure to maintain a tile drain that served Moseley's farm and ran across the Gateses' land. This suit was based upon a contract made in 1896 by Henry Moseley, who then owned what is now the plaintiff's farm, and William Bohn, the defendants' predecessor in interest. The trial court ruled that this contract, which required Bohn to "permanently maintain" the drain at issue, did not run with the land and thus was not binding upon the defendants, Bohn's successors. The trial court also ruled that Moseley had not proved the defendants' failure to repair the drain caused the losses of which she complained. Moseley appeals, claiming the trial court's judgment was contrary to law. We reverse.

In 1896, Henry Moseley and William Bohn owned adjoining farms in Miami County, Indiana. Moseley's land was drained by an open ditch across Bohn's land. In August, 1896, they entered into a contract (hereinafter termed the Moseley-Bohn agreement), which read in part as follows:

> That Whereas; There exists an open public ditch known as the "Moseley Ditch" in the West half of the East half of Section 23 in Township 26 North, of Range 4 East, which real estate is owned by said Bohn, and Whereas; said Moseley is the owner of real estate lying immediately South of and

> adjoining said real estate and which has the ditch above referred to for the out-let for its drainage, and Whereas said Moseley and divers other persons have heretofore been assessed for the construction and repair of said Moseley Ditch, and said Bohn is desirous of straightening and placing drain tile the entire length of said ditch; Now Therefore, in consideration that said Moseley will consent to such straightening and tiling of said ditch, and in the further consideration of the sum of Forty Dollars to be paid by said Moseley when the tiling through that portion of said ditch which has been assigned to him for repairs shall have been completed, said William C. Bohn hereby agrees that he will place through the entire length of said ditch and permanently maintain drain tile of sufficient capacity to furnish adequate out-let for drainage from a twelve inch tile at the North line of said Moseley's land, being the south line of said Section 23. Backwater at said point to be conclusive evidence of lack of said capacity. In consideration of the foregoing premises, said Moseley hereby consents to the straightening and tiling of said ditch and agrees to pay to said Bohn the sum of $40.00 on the terms above stated.

This contract was duly recorded in the Miami County Recorder's Office.

In the course of time, Henry Moseley's farm came into the hands of Edith Moseley, the plaintiff. Bohn's farm has had several subsequent owners, most recently the Gateses — who farm the land — and the other defendants, most of whom own small residential tracts. Beginning in 1976, Moseley's son Harold noticed that her farm seemed to lack good drainage. This condition worsened each year to the point that, in 1981, there was standing water on Moseley's farm. In 1981 and again in 1982 Harold walked along the course of the drain at issue, which ran exclusively across the Gateses' land. On both occasions he observed eroded holes in the ground, some filled with water, indicating that the drain tile was broken or blocked. Harold requested Mr. Gates to fulfill his obligation under the Moseley-Bohn agreement and repair the drain tile. Gates refused to do so without Moseley's help, and he petitioned the Miami County Drainage Board to repair the drain and assess the cost equally against all the affected landowners. Moseley then brought this suit against the defendants, based on the Moseley-Bohn agreement, seeking damages for losses caused by flooding on her farm and asking that the defendants be made to pay any repair charges assessed against Moseley by the drainage board. After a bench trial the court entered judgment against Moseley, and this appeal ensued.

Moseley contends the trial court's ruling that the defendants had no contractual duty to repair the ditch was contrary to law. The central issue here is whether the Moseley-Bohn agreement runs with the land, so as to bind the defendants to "permanently maintain" the drain tile on their land. Generally, a covenant imposing an affirmative burden will run with the land if (1) the covenantors intend it to run, (2) the covenant touches and concerns the land, and (3) there is privity of estate between subsequent grantees of the original covenantor and covenantee. *Conduitt v. Ross*, 26 N.E. 198 (Ind. App. 1885); *Brendonwood Common v. Franklin*, 403 N.E.2d 1136 (Ind. App. 1980); J. CRIBBET, PRINCIPLES OF THE LAW OF PROPERTY 353 (2d ed. 1975). Because Moseley had the burden of establishing these elements, we may reverse the trial court's ruling against her only if the evidence is undisputed and shows that she is entitled to judgment as a matter of law.

The first element, the parties' intent that their covenant should run with the land, must be determined from the specific language used and from the situation of the parties when the covenant was made. *Thiebaud v. Union Furniture Co.*, 42 N.E. 741 (Ind. 1896); Cribbet, *supra*, at 354. Although a statement in the covenant that it is binding on the covenantor's heirs and assigns is strong evidence of intent that the covenant should run with the land, the omission of such language here, as the defendants concede, does not conclusively prove the covenant was not intended to run. *Geyer v. Lietzan*, 103 N.E.2d 199 (Ind. 1952).

In the contract at issue, Bohn agreed to "permanently maintain" a tile drain across his property. This language indicates an intention to bind not only Bohn but later grantees of the burdened property as well. Also relevant are the facts surrounding the covenant. Even before the agreement, Moseley's land was drained by an open ditch across Bohn's property. Thus, the installation of buried drain tile benefitted only Bohn, whose property gained additional usable surface area. Moseley, on the other hand, incurred an increased risk that his property might not be adequately drained, since it is more difficult to remove obstructions from a buried drain than from an open ditch. Under these circumstances, the importance of Bohn's promise to "permanently maintain" the drain is clear. Given the importance of this drain to Moseley's land, it is improbable that the parties intended their agreement to be purely personal and not binding on subsequent grantees of the land. Faced with similar agreements relating to ditches and drains, courts in other jurisdictions have generally found an intent that the covenant run with the land. *See* 20 Am. Jur. 2d Covenants, Conditions, and Restrictions § 42 (1965). We find as a matter of law that the facts surrounding the written agreement and the language used in it show an intent to create a covenant running with the land.

Having proved this intent, Moseley was also required to show the covenant touched and concerned the land with which it was to run. This requirement ensures that one purchasing land will be bound by his grantor's contract only where the contract has some logical connection to his use and enjoyment of the land. Thus, a successor to the covenantor's interest in property may be bound by the covenant if it is logically connected to that property interest. Conversely, a successor to the covenantee's property interest may enforce the covenant if it is logically connected to his property. *See* C. Clark, Real Covenants and Other Interests Which "Run With Land" 97 (1947). The covenant to maintain the tile drain at issue here is logically connected both to the Gateses' property — in which the drain is buried — and to the plaintiff's land, which is served by the drain. Because the drain runs exclusively across the Gateses' land, however, the agreement to maintain it has no logical connection to the land held by the other defendants, who own residential tracts in the old Bohn farm. Thus, the "touch and concern" requirement is met as to Moseley, the plaintiff, and the Gateses, but not as to the other defendants.

Finally, to establish a covenant running with the land, Moseley was required to prove she was in privity of estate with the defendants. Where, as here, neither of the original covenantors is a party to the suit, both "vertical privity" and "horizontal privity" must be proved. "Vertical privity" is established where the party seeking to enforce the covenant and the party against whom it is to be enforced are successors in title to the property of the covenantee and covenantor respectively. *See* CRIBBET, *supra*, at 354. Vertical privity clearly exists in this case.

The concept of "horizontal privity," however, is more difficult. "Horizontal privity" is generally established by evidence that the original parties to the covenant had some mutual or successive interest either in the land burdened by the covenant or the land benefitted by it. The requirement of horizontal privity may be met by proof that the covenantee has a leasehold and the covenantor has the reversion in the affected land. *E.g.*, *National Manufacturing & Engineering Co. v. Farmers Trust & Savings Bank*, 185 N.E. 146 (Ind. 1933). Similarly, the parties are in privity where one has an easement in land owned by the other, so long as the covenant concerns the easement. *E.g.*, *Conduitt v. Ross*, *supra*. Finally, privity of estate may be found between the original covenantors even where they did not hold simultaneous interests in the land if the covenant concerns land transferred by one party to the other. *E.g.*, *Brendonwood Common v. Franklin*, *supra*. Additionally, to establish privity, the plaintiff generally must prove the covenant was made in the context of a transfer of an interest in the affected land, whether by lease or by deed conveying the property or an easement therein. *Wheeler v. Schad*, 7 Nev. 204 (1871).[2]

We believe Moseley established the required privity of estate in this case. Where one landowner agrees to construct a drain across his property for the benefit of a neighbor's land, the agreement will generally create an easement appurtenant to

---

[2] [1] For several reasons, we make the foregoing statements of the law regarding horizontal privity with some trepidation. First, most of the legal scholars who have discussed real covenants argue that no privity of estate between the original covenantors should be required for their covenant to run with the land. CLARK, *supra*, 111-37; O.W. HOLMES, THE COMMON LAW 403, 404; Newman & Losey, *Covenants Running with the Land, and Equitable Servitudes; Two Concepts, or One?* 21 HASTINGS L.J. 1319 (1970); Stoebuck, *Running Covenants: An Analytical Primer*, 52 WASH. L. REV. 861 (1977). These writers point out that the requirement of horizontal privity, while frequently stated in dictum, is seldom used to bar the running of an otherwise valid real covenant. They also argue that this requirement is purely arbitrary, not vindicating any interest of the landowners involved or of society at large.

Second, the courts have made significant exceptions to the privity requirement. Thus, it has been held that a covenant need not be made as part of a transfer of an interest in land if "the promise is made in the adjustment of the mutual relationships arising out of the existence of an easement held by one of the parties to the promise in the land of the other." RESTATEMENT OF PROPERTY § 534(b) (1944); *see Morse v. Aldrich*, 36 Mass. 449 (Mass.1837). Further, it is unnecessary to prove privity of estate where the benefit of the covenant, rather than the burden, is to run with the land. *City of Reno v. Matley*, 378 P.2d 256 (Nev. 1963); RESTATEMENT OF PROPERTY § 548 (1944); 21 C.J.S. Covenants § 58 (1940 & Supp. 1984).

Finally, the horizontal privity requirement has been undermined by the courts' frequent resort to the doctrine of equitable servitudes. Under this doctrine, a landowner who has actual or constructive notice of a covenant concerning the land made by his predecessor in interest may be bound by the covenant even though the original covenantors were not in privity of estate. *Tulk v. Moxhay*, 2 Phillips 774 (1848); CRIBBET, *supra*, at 356; *see Howard D. Johnson Co. v. Parkside Development Corp.*, 348 N.E.2d 656 (Ind. Ct. App. 1976). Because virtually all promises giving rise to a real covenant also create an equitable servitude, this equitable doctrine has become a popular means of circumventing the technical requirements that govern real covenants — most notably the requirement of horizontal privity. *See, e.g., Neponsit Property Owners' Ass'n. v. Emigrant Industrial Savings Bank*, 15 N.E.2d 793 (N.Y. 1938); *Merrionette Manor Homes Improvement Ass'n. v. Heda*, 136 N.E.2d 556 (Ill. App. Ct. 1956); *see generally* Stoebuck, *supra*, 52 WASH. L. REV. at 919–21. For all these reasons, although we find the technical requirement of horizontal privity has been satisfied in this case, we doubt whether this requirement has much continuing vitality in Indiana.

the adjacent land. *Steinke v. Bentley*, 34 N.E. 97 (Ind. App. 1893); *see Hazlett v. Sinclair*, 76 Ind. 488 (1881) (agreement to maintain fence on one's land for neighbor's benefit creates easement in favor of that neighbor). Thus, we find that Bohn's agreement to construct a tile drain across his land for Moseley's benefit created an easement appurtenant to Moseley's land. Since Bohn's agreement to maintain the drain was contained in the same document, the covenant was clearly made in the context of a transfer to Moseley of an easement in Bohn's land. This satisfies the requirement of privity of estate between the original covenantors. We accordingly hold that the Moseley-Bohn agreement runs with the land now held by Moseley and the Gateses. Because the agreement does not affect the other defendants' property, however, the trial court correctly found it did not run with their land.

In their effort to avoid this contract, the Gateses point out that the ditch has been a public drain since 1883 — thirteen years before the contract was made. The Gateses argue that Bohn and Moseley could not, by their private agreement, deprive the county commissioners of jurisdiction over this public drain or bind other landowners served by it. This argument is correct, as far as it goes. *See Triplett v. Carlson*, 191 N.E. 82 (Ind. 1934) (private improvements by those served by a public drain do not deprive county commissioners of jurisdiction over it). We fail to see, however, how the agreement here interferes with the commissioners' jurisdiction or burdens other landowners served by the drain. Similarly, we believe Bohn was entitled to grant Moseley an easement across his land concurrent with the public drain and to impose upon himself contractual obligations beyond those imposed by the statutes governing public drains.

This private easement concurrent with the public drain across Bohn's land left both the county commissioners and Bohn's successors under a duty to maintain the drain tile on Bohn's land. If the county failed to maintain it, Moseley's successors could bind Bohn's successors to do so under the agreement. If, on the other hand, the county repaired the segment of the public drain crossing Bohn's land, Moseley could require Bohn to pay any repair charges assessed against Moseley. In either event, however, the contract would be enforceable between the parties absent some showing that enforcement of the contract would conflict with the county's overriding interest in maintaining the public drain. Because no such conflict has arisen in this case, we do not believe the Gateses can avoid liability on the contract based on the county commissioners' concurrent jurisdiction over the drain.

The Gateses further argue that they should not be bound by the contract at issue because its makers did not contemplate a duty to repair beyond the expiration of the original tile's normal useful life. An agreement in which the time of performance is not otherwise limited is presumed to continue for a reasonable time. *Grand Lodge Hall Ass'n v. Moore*, 70 N.E.2d 19 (Ind. 1945), *aff'd*, 330 U.S. 808 (1947). Nevertheless, absent some indication that the original covenantors intended to limit its duration, a real covenant generally survives as long as the estate with which it runs. In this case, Bohn agreed to "place through the entire length of said ditch and *permanently* maintain drain tile of sufficient capacity to furnish adequate outlet for drainage from a twelve inch tile . . . ." (Emphasis added). In light of this language and the fact that continuing maintenance of the drain is vital to keep the plaintiff's land tillable, it is improbable that the original covenantors intended Bohn to maintain the drain for no longer than twenty to forty years. Rather, we conclude that the original covenantors intended the duty to repair to extend beyond the useful life of the original tile.

The Gateses' final argument is that, even if they did breach a contractual duty to maintain the drain across their land, Moseley did not prove she was entitled to any damages as a result of that breach. In her complaint, Moseley claimed the defendants' failure to maintain the drain caused flooding in 1981 and 1982, resulting in reduced crops in those years. In its judgment, however, the trial court found Moseley had presented insufficient evidence to prove that her crop losses stemmed from the defendants' failure to maintain the drain as specified in the agreement. As noted above, we may reverse the trial court's negative judgment against Moseley only if the undisputed evidence conclusively shows she is entitled to judgment. The evidence of Moseley's losses does not meet this standard. The only evidence supporting Moseley's claim for damages was the testimony of her son — who farmed her land — that he was unable to plant crops on part of the land due to poor drainage. He testified that, if these wet areas had been dry enough to plant, they would have produced additional crops in 1981 worth $7,455 and in 1982 worth $720. Further, Moseley's son estimated the cost of reconditioning her flood-damaged soil at $1,530. There was other evidence, however, that the flooding on Moseley's farm, which caused these losses, was due to heavy rains in 1981 that flooded even well-drained property surrounding Moseley's farm. Thus, the trial court's ruling that Moseley was entitled to no damages was not contrary to law, and that part of the trial court's judgment must be affirmed.

Moseley's complaint also alleged, however, that the county drainage board had issued an assessment against her for a proposed reconstruction of the drain across the Gateses' land. Testimony at trial showed Moseley had not yet been required to pay the assessed amount, but might be required to pay after trial. When it entered judgment against Moseley, the trial court effectively denied this part of her claim against the defendants based on its finding that the Moseley-Bohn agreement did not run with the land. Because we find as a matter of law that the agreement ran with the Gateses' land, we conclude that the trial court erroneously precluded Moseley from holding the Gateses liable, should any assessments levied against her to repair the drain at issue.

The trial court's judgment denying Moseley damages for crop losses and rejecting her claim against the defendants other than the Gateses is affirmed; in all other respects, the trial court's judgment is reversed. Costs to the appellees.

NOTES AND QUESTIONS

1. *Moseley v. Bishop* nicely illustrates the binding consequences of a real covenant once it is determined to run with the land. Although the plaintiff Moseley failed to establish that the damages incurred in 1981 and 1982 were the result of defendant's failure to maintain the drain tile, the court in the above case otherwise upheld the validity of the covenant at issue. As a practical matter, this means that landowners in 1984 were still bound by an agreement made 88 years earlier by two individuals who were long dead by the time of this case.

2. *Additional Requirements.* In addition to the requirements for a covenant running with the land cited in the opinion above, real covenants must be created by a writing signed by the promisor. Like the negative easement, a real covenant cannot arise by implication, necessity or prescription. In most jurisdictions, the recording act (*see* Chapter 5) requires that covenants be recorded to be enforceable against subsequent owners. However, as the court above notes, the rules pertaining to covenants running with the land are in a state of considerable flux.

3. *Horizontal Privity.* As the court's lengthy footnote 1 indicates, the requirement that there be "horizontal privity" between the covenanting parties has been the source of much controversy. English law not only required that there be horizontal privity, but it limited it to situations where the covenanting parties were in a landlord-tenant relationship. (This was the situation in the celebrated *Spencer's Case*, 77 Eng. Rep. 72 (1583), which was the original source for much of the law of covenants.) As a consequence, the use of covenants running with the land as a form of land use control was highly restricted in England. In fact, the decision in *Tulk v. Moxhay* is often attributed to the difficulty English landowners had in establishing covenants at law that would run with the land.

Americans courts, almost without exception, were inclined to define horizontal privity more expansively and thus increase the number of covenants that could run with the land. Under the so-called Massachusetts rule, horizontal privity was found to exist when the covenanting parties shared a mutual interest in the affected land. In addition to a landlord-tenant relationship, this included situations where there was an easement or profit. The so-called "American rule" expanded the concept much farther by positing that horizontal privity existed if there was either a mutual interest or if the covenant at issue was created at the time the property was transferred from one owner to another. The American rule did require that the covenant be attached at the time of transfer, and covenants that were later agreed to by the parties could not apply back to the transaction, even if only a day or two had passed. *See Wheeler v. Schad*, 7 Nev. 204 (Nev. 1871) (covenant to repair dam agreed to six days after transfer of land adjacent to the dam lacked horizontal privity).

Under what might be called the "modern rule," embraced by a number of states and the Restatement (Third) of Property, Servitudes § 3.4, no horizontal privity is necessary to create a binding agreement. For an example of this approach, see *Orange & Rockland Utils. v. Philwold Estates*, 418 N.E.2d 1310, 1314 (N.Y. 1981) ("the party seeking to enforce the covenant need show only that he held property descendant from the promisee which benefited from the covenant and that the owner of the servient parcel acquired it with notice of the covenant").

The controversy over horizontal privity has had relatively little effect on the use of covenants to restrict the use of land, since, as mentioned above, such covenants can usually be enforced as equitable servitudes whether or not horizontal privity is present. Horizontal privity requirements have, however, made it more difficult to recover damages in breach of covenant cases. The scholarly literature has almost unanimously endorsed the abolition of the horizontal privity requirement. *See, e.g.*, C. Clark, Real Covenants and Other Interests Which "Run with the Land," 137–43, 206–62 (2d ed. 1947) (Judge Clark led the attack on horizontal privity in the

1930s and 40s); Walsh, *Covenants Running with the Land*, 21 N.Y.U. L. Q. REV. 28, 41–44 (1946); Newman & Losey, *Covenants Running with the Land and Equitable Servitudes: Two Concepts or One?*, 21 HASTINGS L.J. 1319, 1331 (1970); Browder, *Running Covenants and Public Policy*, 77 MICH. L. REV. 12, 16 (1979). In the last article, the author posits that recording statutes have rendered obsolete the horizontal privity requirement. Do you see why? Are there still reasons to retain a requirement of horizontal privity?

4. *Benefit and Burden.* Every real covenant creates a burden for one tract of land and a benefit for another. The horizontal privity rules are further complicated by the fact that many of the jurisdictions that recognize a horizontal privity requirement apply it only to the burden of a covenant and not its benefit. Thus, in these jurisdictions the benefit of a covenant will run with the land even if there is no horizontal privity. The logic behind this approach is quite simple. If adjacent property owners A and B enter into a contract which provides that A will not open a gas station on his land, and B subsequently sells his lot to C, the benefit runs to C. There is no unfairness in letting C enforce the agreement since A will be liable for damages only if he does what he agreed with B not to do. On the other hand, if A sells his property to D, and B or C is allowed to enforce the covenant against D, D's right to the land is limited by an agreement to which he was not part. Thus, the requirement that higher standards must be satisfied before the burden can run. Of course, even if the covenant is unenforceable as a covenant running with the land, it may still be enforceable as an equitable servitude if D had notice of the restriction.

5. *Vertical Privity.* In *Moseley*, the court stated that "vertical privity" is established "where the party seeking to enforce the covenant and the party against whom it is to be enforced are successors in title to the property of the covenantee and covenantor respectively." Traditionally, this meant that before the burden could run, the successor had to take the covenantor's entire estate (i.e., fee simple absolute, estate for years, etc.). If the previous owner retained any interest in the land (as in a reversion, possibility of reverter, etc.), the burden could not be enforced against the present possessor. The principal consequence of this requirement was that it was difficult to enforce covenants against the tenants of a covenanting party. More liberal jurisdictions allow the burden to run to a successor so long as he takes part of the predecessor estate. In regard to the benefit, the standards for vertical privity are typically more relaxed. Unlike the case with the burden, the successor has only to take part of the estate of his predecessor for the benefit to run.

6. Because covenants are said to follow with the estate and not with the land itself, it does not matter whether or not the successor takes the entire corpus of the affected land. Similarly, it is possible for the same estate to be both burdened and benefitted by the same covenant. This happens when A and B make mutual promises to restrict their land in an identical manner.

7. *The Enforcement of Covenants Running with the Land.* Ordinarily a running covenant is enforceable only by those who own land benefited by the covenant. However, it is now widely accepted that a homeowners association or condominium board may enforce such covenants on the theory that it is the agent of those who hold the benefitted estate. This principle was first acknowledged in

Neponsit Property Owners v. Emigrant Indus. Sav. Bank, 15 N.E.2d 793 (N.Y. 1938). Traditionally, courts were less restrictive in such matters when they were enforcing covenants as equitable servitudes. Is there any reason why the approach to enforcement should differ under the two theories?

[b.] Covenants that Touch and Concern the Land

In *Moseley*, there was little doubt that the covenant "touched and concerned the land." However, in other contexts, this is one of the most difficult determinations to make, given that covenants that do not touch and concern are unenforceable by subsequent owners, no matter what the intention of the covenanting parties may have been.

WHITINSVILLE PLAZA, INC. v. KOTSEAS

Massachusetts Supreme Judicial Court
390 N.E.2d 243 (1979)

Quirico, J.

These are civil actions commenced by Whitinsville Plaza, Inc. (Plaza), against Charles H. Kotseas and Paul Kotseas (Kotseas) and against Whitinsville CVS, Inc. (CVS). In its further amended complaint against Kotseas, Plaza alleged imminent violations of certain anticompetitive deed restrictions and requested declaratory, injunctive, and monetary relief under theories of breach of contract and unfair acts or practices within the meaning of G.L. c. 93A, § 2. Plaza's amended complaint against CVS likewise alleged imminent violations of the deed restrictions, and it requested declaratory, injunctive, and monetary relief on theories of breach of contract, unfair trade practices, and interference with contractual relations.

Plaza appealed from the dismissal of its actions, and we granted its application for direct appellate review in both cases. We hold that dismissal for failure to state a claim was erroneous as to some counts of each complaint.

In ruling on a motion to dismiss, "the allegations of the complaint [and annexed exhibits], as well as such inferences that may be drawn therefrom in the plaintiff's favor, are to be taken as true." *Nader v. Citron*, 372 Mass. 96, 98 (1977). In 1968, Kotseas conveyed certain land identified as "Parcel A" to four individuals as trustees of the "122 Trust" (Trust), a wholly owned subsidiary of Plaza. The deed set forth numerous, detailed, reciprocal restrictions and covenants designed to assure the harmonious development of a shopping center on Parcel A and on abutting land retained by Kotseas. In particular, Kotseas promised (a) not to use the retained land in competition with the discount store contemplated by the grantee and (b) to use the retained land only for enumerated business purposes. Among the permitted business uses of the land retained by Kotseas was a "drug store," defined in an appendix to the deed as a store selling prescribed types of merchandise. In addition, the deed recited that "[t]he foregoing restrictions shall be considered as covenants running with the land to which they are applicable and shall bind and inure to the benefit of the heirs and assigns of the respective parties to whom any part of the lands made subject to the above restrictions covenants and conditions shall at any time become or belong during the period hereinbefore set forth."

In 1975, the Trust conveyed Parcel A to Plaza and, thereafter, ceased operations. The deed to Plaza expressly made Plaza subject to, and gave it the benefit of, the restrictions and covenants in the 1968 deed from Kotseas to the Trust. At some later time, Kotseas leased a portion of its abutting land to CVS for use as a "discount department store and pharmacy." Plaza's complaints state that the lease to CVS, dated May 10, 1977, was expressly subject to the 1968 deed restrictions and that operation of the contemplated CVS store would violate those restrictions. Although the defendants controvert these allegations, we must, as we have said, accept them as true in ruling on the motion to dismiss.

As against Kotseas, Plaza sought (a) an injunction prohibiting the use of the retained land in violation of the restrictions and (b) damages suffered because of the alleged violations. In the alternative, Plaza prayed for a declaration that its own land was no longer subject to the anticompetitive restrictions. Plaza also requested the court to find that Kotseas had knowingly and wilfully violated G.L. c. 93A, § 2, and to award double or treble damages and counsel fees. As against CVS, Plaza requested similar relief and also requested damages on the theory that CVS had tortiously interfered with Plaza's contract by inducing Kotseas to violate its restrictions. The defendants filed motions to dismiss, stating as grounds that Plaza lacked standing to sue on the covenants and that the covenants were, in any event, unreasonable and in restraint of trade.

Real covenant analysis

Plaza has primarily sought to maintain its actions on the theory that the covenants contained in the 1968 deed run with the land. In our view, Plaza has alleged sufficient facts to be entitled to a hearing on its claims for legal and equitable relief on this theory. The covenants in question are evidenced by a writing signed by Kotseas, the covenantor. The language of the 1968 deed aptly expresses the intention of the original parties that the covenants run with the land. The deed also grants mutual easements sufficient to satisfy the requirement that Plaza and CVS be in privity of estate. Plaza's complaint alleges that CVS had actual knowledge of the restrictions and shows, in any event, that the restrictions were recorded with the deed.

One additional prerequisite for either legal or equitable relief is, however, arguably lacking in this case on the present state of our case law. It is essential that both the benefit and the burden of a real covenant "touch and concern" the affected parcels of land before it will be considered to run. *Orenberg v. Johnston*, 269 Mass. 312, 316 (1929). *Bronson v. Coffin*, 118 Mass. 156, 163 (1875). *Wheelock v. Thayer*, 16 Pick. 68, 70 (1835). This court has long held that a covenant not to compete contained in a deed, such as is involved in this case, does not "touch and concern" the land to be benefited and that, in consequence, such a covenant does not run with the land. *Shade v. M. O'Keefe, Inc.*, 260 Mass. 180, 183 (1927). *Norcross v. James*, 140 Mass. 188, 192 (1885). In *Shell Oil Co. v. Henry Ouellette & Sons*, 352 Mass. 725 (1967), we intimated that we might overrule *Norcross* and *Shade* in an appropriate case. *Id.* at 730–731 & n.8. We believe this is such a case.

It is essential to our task that we identify precisely the holding and rationale of the cases we propose to overrule. *Norcross* was an action seeking specific performance of a covenant not to quarry stone from a parcel of land. The covenant in question was contained in a deed by which one Kibbe conveyed a stone quarry to one Flynt, and it concerned adjoining land retained by Kibbe. The defendant James, a successor to Kibbe's interest, began operating a quarry on the restricted land. The plaintiff Norcross, a successor to Flynt's interest, sought an injunction to halt that operation. 140 Mass. at 188. In an opinion by Justice Holmes, this court denied relief. *Id.* at 192.

Justice Holmes analyzed the case before him in two steps. He first noted a distinction drawn in early English decisions between promises resembling warranties of title and those resembling grants of easements. Warranty-like covenants ran "with the estate" to grantees from the covenantee, but were enforceable only against the covenantor. Easement-like covenants, on the other hand, ran "with the land" in favor of and against subsequent owners. *Id.* at 188–190. *See also* O. W. Holmes, The Common Law 371–409 (1881) (developing historical analysis summarized later in *Norcross* opinion).

Having traced the development of the law of real covenants, Justice Holmes proceeded to determine whether the covenant could be encompassed within the easement-like class. He stated that a real covenant must "touch or concern" the land by conferring "direct physical advantage in the occupation of the dominant estate." 140 Mass. at 192. The covenant against operating a quarry did not do so because "[i]t does not make the use or occupation of [the dominant estate] more convenient. It does not in any way affect the use or occupation; it simply tends indirectly to increase its value, by excluding a competitor from the market for its products." *Id.* In addition, the covenant transgressed a supposed rule against attaching "new and unusual incidents" to land, for it attempted to create "an easement of monopoly, — an easement not to be competed with" not theretofore recognized. *Id.*

Two observations about *Norcross* are appropriate before we consider later developments. First of all, the benefit of the covenant surely touched and concerned the dominant estate within the ordinary sense and meaning of the phrase "touch and concern." Justice Holmes's analysis has been described as "overlook[ing] the purpose of all building restrictions, which is to enhance the market value of the promisee's land, whether for residential or for business purposes." 2 American Law of Property § 9.28, at 414 (Casner ed. 1952). It has been suggested that Justice Holmes's "real objection to [the covenant was] the policy against monopolies, and not any policy with reference to real covenants as such." C. Clark, Real Covenants and Other Interests Which "Run with Land" 84 n.26 (1929). *Cf. Norcross*, 140 Mass. at 193 (unnecessary to decide whether covenant would be invalid restraint of trade if enforcement attempted against Kibbe). If free-competition policies were indeed the basis for the *Norcross* decision, it would now seem preferable for us to deal with them explicitly rather than to condemn all anticompetitive covenants regardless of reasonableness.

Second, *Norcross* seems to turn on an assumption that there could be no other class of covenants, differing both from easements and from warranties, but which might nevertheless run with the land. Justice Holmes reasoned that neither the benefit nor the burden of the covenant could run because the benefit was personal to the original covenantee and was therefore inconsistent with the existence of any easement-like right appurtenant to the dominant land. Underlying such reasoning is the peculiar Massachusetts requirement of privity of estate, created by the existence of an easement between the parties to an action on a real covenant. CLARK, *supra* at 88. Cf. *Morse v. Aldrich, supra* at 452–454 (statement of Massachusetts privity rule); *Norcross*, 140 Mass. at 191 (citing Massachusetts privity cases). Yet, privity of estate in this sense had never been thought essential to an action in equity for specific performance of a covenant. *Beals v. Case*, 138 Mass. 138, 139–140 (1884). *Parker v. Nightingale*, 6 Allen 341, 344 (1863).

Notwithstanding the questions inherent in the *Norcross* decision, this court uncritically followed that case in *Shade v. M. O'Keefe, Inc.*, 260 Mass. 180 (1927). Like *Norcross, Shade* was a suit in equity by a successor to the promisee against a successor to the promisor seeking specific performance of an anticompetitive covenant. The covenant in question prohibited the operation of a grocery store on the defendant's land for ninety-nine years after 1902, the date of the original deed. The court reiterated that, for a covenant to be enforceable in equity, it must accompany or create "an easement or quasi easement" in the promisor's land for the benefit of the promisee's land. It thus followed the rule stated by Justice Holmes in *Norcross*. Without further analysis the court stated that the case before it was indistinguishable from *Norcross*, and it concluded that the action should be dismissed.

This court next confronted the question raised by *Norcross* in *Shell Oil Co. v. Henry Ouellette & Sons*, 352 Mass. 725 (1967), which was a suit in equity by a remote grantee of the promisee against the original promisor and a potential purchaser of part of the burdened land. We there considered a broad and sweeping covenant restraining all uses of the defendants' land that would compete with an existing use of the plaintiff's land. We wrote, "There is much to be said for the position advanced by one of the amici curiae that it is not 'unreasonable to approve covenants . . . which protect . . . [business] investments — very large in most instances — against competition close by,' where the protection will be very limited geographically and will not constitute, in the particular circumstances, an unreasonable restraint of trade. If we were without precedent, we might (in 1967 conditions) reach a conclusion different from that of our predecessors upon the facts which appeared in *Norcross v. James*, and in *Shade v. M. O'Keefe, Inc.*" We nonetheless held *Norcross* controlling and ordered that the complaint be dismissed. We did so primarily because of bare reliance on our earlier decisions, but we gave clear warning of our intention to reconsider *Norcross* "in the case of a reasonably limited covenant . . . hereafter made, which shows clearly the parties' intention that the burden and benefit of the covenant are to run to successors in title of the covenantor and the covenantee." *Id.* at 730–731 & 731 n.8.

Our most recent encounter with the *Norcross* rule was in *Gulf Oil Corp. v. Fall River Hous. Auth.*, 364 Mass. 492 (1974). In that case, the city of Fall River established a redevelopment plan for a certain area. The plan permitted an unlimited number of gasoline stations to be operated in a zone designated "A" and prohibited all but incidental or accessory use for gasoline sales in zone "B" if a gasoline station already existed in zone "A." The plaintiff obtained a parcel in zone

"A" by mesne conveyances from the defendant housing authority and was operating a gasoline station. Another defendant, the Mt. Hope Development Corporation (Mt. Hope), purchased a parcel in zone "B" from the authority, and it sought to operate a gasoline station as well. The deeds to Mt. Hope and to the plaintiff's predecessor both incorporated restrictions substantially equivalent to those set forth in the redevelopment plan.

In the *Gulf Oil* case, we ultimately held that the plaintiff might properly seek an injunction against the contemplated use by Mt. Hope. We did not, however, explicitly overrule *Norcross* to reach this result. Instead, we noted that application of the *Norcross* rule had been limited to cases where "the plain and practically exclusive reason for the covenant was to eliminate possible competition for the promisee." *Id.* at 499. Reasoning that the covenants in *Gulf Oil* were primarily designed to foster planned growth of the redevelopment area and not to grant an individual landowner a monopoly, we concluded that the "touch and concern" requirement was met.

Massachusetts has been practically alone in its position that covenants not to compete do not run with the land to which they relate. It has long been the opinion of text writers that our rule is anachronistic and in need of change. *See* 2 American Law of Property § 9.28, at 414 (Casner ed. 1952). The American Law Institute has suggested that an otherwise enforceable covenant not to compete should be held enforceable in the same manner as an equitable servitude. Restatement of Property § 539, Comment *k* (1944). Reasonable anticompetitive covenants are enforceable in the great majority of States where the issue has arisen. *See* Comment, *Covenants Not to Compete — Do They Pass?*, 4 Cal. W.L. Rev. 131, 133–134 (1968). Modern judicial analysis of cases like the one at bar appears to concentrate on the effects of particular covenants on competition and to avoid the esoteric convolutions of the law of real covenants. *See, e.g., Hall v. American Oil Co.*, 504 S.W.2d 313, 316 n.3 (Mo. App. 1973); *Quadro Stations, Inc. v. Gilley*, 7 N.C. App. 227, 231–235 (1970).

In addition to the doctrinal questions about the *Norcross* rule and the preference of most authorities for a more flexible approach, we may note the unfairness that would result from applying that rule to the facts of this case. In what appears to have been an arm's-length transaction, Kotseas agreed in 1968 not to use retained land in competition with the Trust. We may assume (a) that Kotseas received compensation for thus giving up part of his ownership rights by limiting the uses he could make of the retained land, and (b) that freedom from destructive, next-door competition was part of the inducement for the Trust's purchase and of the price paid by the Trust. Plaza, a closely associated business entity, succeeded to the Trust's interest in 1975. One of these entities established a business, presumably at great cost to itself and in reliance on the contractually obtained limitation of competition in its own narrow market area. Notwithstanding the promise not to do so, Kotseas proceeded to lease land to CVS for the purpose of carrying on the business that it knew would, at least in part, compete with Plaza and divert customers from Plaza's premises. Acting with full knowledge of the 1968 arrangement, CVS participated in this inequitable conduct by Kotseas. If we assume for the moment that the 1968 covenants are reasonable in their application to the present facts, we cannot condone the conduct of Kotseas and CVS. Yet, if *Norcross* remains the law, we are powerless to prevent Kotseas and CVS from indirectly destroying or diminishing the value of Plaza's investment in its business.

We think the time has come to acknowledge the infirmities and inequities of *Norcross*. Reasonable covenants against competition may be considered to run with the land when they serve a purpose of facilitating orderly and harmonious development for commercial use. To the extent they are inconsistent with this statement, *Norcross*, *Shade*, and *Ouellette* are hereby expressly overruled.

What we have said should not be construed as an invitation to legal draftsmen to insert unlimited, "boilerplate"-type covenants against competition in real estate documents. As we have said, an enforceable covenant will be one which is consistent with a reasonable over-all purpose to develop real estate for commercial use. In addition, the ordinary requirements for creation and enforcement of real covenants must be met. We have summarized many of these requirements earlier in this opinion. Others are found in G.L. c. 184, §§ 27, 30, which regulate enforcement of land-use restrictions generally. Within these limits, however, commercial developers may control the course of development by reasonable restrictive covenants free from resort to devious subterfuges in their attempts to avoid the doubts created by the *Norcross* rule and our efforts to apply or reconcile it in later cases.

To the extent they dismiss Plaza's claims for violation of real covenants or for interference with contractual relations, the judgments are erroneous and must be vacated. The cases are remanded to the Superior Court for further proceedings consistent with this opinion.

NOTES AND QUESTIONS

1. *Retroactive Application*. In a portion of its opinion not reproduced above, the Massachusetts court limited its ruling to those covenants not to compete executed on or after June 13, 1967, the date of the *Ouelletee* opinion discussed above. The court acknowledged that it would be unfair to penalize those who had relied upon the *Norcross* line of decisions. However, it asserted its belief that "parties who executed such covenants after *Ouellette* could not reasonably expect that the covenants would continue to be unenforceable under the rule of the *Shade* and *Norcross* decisions."

2. *Affirmative Obligations*. As with equitable servitudes, affirmative obligations (as opposed to restriction on use) can be enforced through real covenants running with the land if the obligation was sufficiently related to the land, or more precisely, to the owner's estate. As the above case indicates, at one time covenants not to compete posed difficult problems, as did covenants to insure and covenants to pay real estate taxes and assessments. The modern trend is to find that such covenants do in fact run with the land, although some courts continue to have problems with certain types of affirmative obligations. See, for example, *Chesapeake Ranch Club, Inc. v. C.R.C. United Members, Inc.*, 483 A.2d 1334 (Md. Ct. Spec. App. 1984), in which the court ruled that the burden of a covenant to pay membership dues for use of a recreational center did not touch and concern land, and therefore could not be enforced against successor owners.

3. *The Touch and Concern Requirement*. To run, both the burden and the benefit of a real covenant must touch and concern the land before they can transfer to subsequent owners. Typically, a burden is said to touch and concern if it affects the burdened party in his or her capacity as landowner. Thus a covenant which obligated A to sing at his neighbor B's daughter's wedding would not touch and concern the land since, while it may be a burden, it does not affect A in his capacity as landowner. Similarly, if the covenant imposes a limitation on what A can do with his land, it touches and concerns the land, but if the restriction is on A's conduct generally, it does not. The benefit of a covenant touches and concerns the land if it increases the covenantee's enjoyment of the land and the enjoyment comes directly from the ownership of the land. It is possible that the burden or the benefit of a particular promise, but not both, will touch and concern the land.

In the 20th century, the measure of touch and concern has moved away from the traditional focus on physical touching to one which focuses upon the economic impact of the benefit and burden. In spite of this more liberal approach, or perhaps because of it, there is some sentiment today for doing away with the touch and concern requirement. Critics from quite different ideological perspectives have argued that the touch and concern requirement frustrates the original parties' expectations and should be either abolished or significantly modified. *See* Epstein, *Notice and Freedom of Contract in the Law of Servitudes*, 55 S. Cal. L. Rev. 1353 (1982); Ellickson, *Alternatives to Zoning: Covenants, Nuisance Rules, and Fines as Land Use Controls*, 40 U. Chi. L. Rev. 681, 717 (1973). The Restatement (Third) of Property, Servitudes, § 3.2 (T.D. No. 2, 1991) "supersedes" the touch and concern requirement, insofar as "its vagueness, its obscurity, its intent-defeating character and its growing redundancy have become increasingly apparent." In its place, the Restatement imposes more specific tests, which "look to the legitimacy and importance of the purposes to be served by the servitude in the particular context, the fairness of the arrangement, its impact on alienability and marketability of the property, its impact on competition, and the degree to which it interferes with rights to personal autonomy and freedom from discrimination." *See also* Franzese, *Out of Touch: The Diminished Viability of the Touch and Concern Requirement in the Law of Servitudes*, 21 Seton Hall L. Rev. 235 (1991) (providing a detailed analysis of *Davidson v. Katz*, 579 A.2d 288 (N.J. 1990), which adopts a multi-factored test to determine whether the burden of a covenant not to compete runs with the land).

[3.] The Unification of Servitudes

While it has long been true that the vast majority of agreements that can be enforced as real covenants running with the land have also been enforceable as equitable servitudes, the overlap is even greater today, given the common recording act requirement that covenants be recorded to be enforced (grafting a notice requirement on to the covenant running with the land), the expansion of the third party beneficiary theory in contract, and the dramatic erosion of the horizontal privity requirement. Moreover, while most jurisdictions still honor the law/equity distinction in regard to remedies, there is some evidence that courts are willing to award money damages as well as injunctive relief in cases brought in equity. *Compare Runyon v. Paley*, 416 S.E.2d 177 (N.C. 1992) (acknowledging the distinction as still valid), *with Miller v. McCamish*, 479 P.2d 919 (Wash. 1971) (approving the award of damages in equity).

Because there now seem to be so few meaningful distinctions between negative easements, real covenants running with the land, and equitable servitudes, there has been considerable sentiment in recent years for unifying the three into a single legal interest. During the 1980s, legal scholars lined up on different sides on this question. Some advocates of unification went even further and argued for the consolidation of affirmative easements and profits as well. Reichman, *Toward a Unified Concept of Servitudes*, 55 S. CAL. L. REV. 1177 (1982); Epstein, *Notice and Freedom of Contract in the Law of Servitudes*, 55 S. CAL. L. REV. 1353 (1982). While there was general agreement that the law of servitudes was confusing and in need of clarification and simplification, many commentators were unconvinced that unification was the solution. French, *Servitudes Reform and the New Restatement of Property: Creation Doctrines and Structural Simplification*, 73 CORNELL L. REV. 928, 950–51 (1988); Berger, *Unification of the Law of Servitudes*, 55 S. CAL. L. REV. 1339 (1982).

The RESTATEMENT (THIRD) OF PROPERTY (SERVITUDES) embraces the call for a unification of servitudes. Section 1.4 dispenses with the terms "real covenant" and "equitable servitude," to wit, "The terms 'real covenant' and "equitable servitude" describe servitudes encompassed within the term 'covenant that runs with the land' and are not used in this Restatement except to describe the evolution of servitudes law." Section 1.3(3) states: "A 'restrictive covenant' is a negative covenant that limits permissible uses of land. A 'negative easement' is a restrictive covenant." In spite of everything, the traditional distinctions between servitudes hobble on into the 21st twenty-first century, and the old forms still have their defenders. *See* Tarlock, *Touch and Concern is Dead, Long Live the Doctrine*, 77 NEB. L. REV. 804 (1998); Stake, *Toward an Economic Understanding of Touch and Concern*, 1988 DUKE L.J. 925.

This casebook has attempted to sort out the confusion in the traditional law of servitudes by dividing the category between those servitudes that are essentially forms of concurrent ownership (affirmative easements, profits, and licenses) and those which function as mechanisms of land use restriction (negative easements, real covenants running with the land, and equitable servitudes). Would it make sense at this time to refer to the latter group simply as "negative easements"? Is the new RESTATEMENT's "covenants that run with the land" a better choice? What differences, if any, will accompany such changes in terminology?

Chapter 8

LIMITATIONS ON PRIVATE LAND USE CONTROLS

While the police power is available to regulate land usage and the behavior of those who occupy it, there are situations where like-minded individuals chose to adopt private rules and regulations designed to have the same force, although usually in a smaller geographic area — the subdivision, the condominium complex, the gated community. Such rules are a dominant fact in contemporary life in the United States.

In fact, most Americans today live in settings where they are subject to behavior-limiting rules based in contract and known as restrictive covenants. As a general rule such covenants enhance the value and attractiveness of the property they control and are, therefore, not particularly controversial. Individuals purchasing a home or an apartment may well take comfort in knowing that their neighbors will be legally obligated to use their property in accordance with certain guidelines. Even though local housing laws may not prohibit your neighbor from renting out his house to six male undergraduates, it can be comforting to know that such a rental is forbidden by the homeowners association by-laws that are in effect in your subdivision.

However, in recent years, it has become apparent that there are some situations in which current owners find the imposed restrictions unacceptably burdensome and inconsistent with their understanding of what they agreed to when they purchased their home or unit. This is particularly true in the case of condominiums and cooperatives and planned and gated communities where covenants are likely to be used not just to define the acceptable uses of the property but also to regulate the conduct of the residents in some detail. It is not uncommon for the original covenants to create an association which not only has the power to enforce existing rules but also the authority to make new rules. Disgruntled owners have increasingly turned to the judiciary to seek relief from restrictions that they view as unfair or inappropriate.

While lawfully executed covenants generally carry a presumption of validity, there are situations in which covenants are found to be unenforceable. The following materials explore the circumstances in which courts will and will not enforce covenants that on their face appear legally binding.

[A.] PUBLIC POLICY LIMITATIONS ON COVENANTS

It is hardly surprising that covenants that are prohibited by law or which require individuals to break the law are unenforceable. However, there are other covenants that are technically legal, but because of broad public policy concerns are deemed to be unenforceable.

[1.] Unlawful Restraints on Alienation

LAUDERBAUGH v. WILLIAMS

Pennsylvania Supreme Court
186 A.2d 39 (1962)

O'BRIAN, J.

These appeals are from decrees entered in an action to Quiet Title and an Equity Action to set aside a deed of conveyance of land. The cases involve the same questions and were tried together. In 1940, Mildred B. Lauderbaugh and her husband, Dayton S. Lauderbaugh, became the owners by purchase of land in Wayne and Monroe Counties which included a lake known as Watawga. The Lauderbaughs laid out some lots in a plan on the westerly shore and began the sale of lots in 1949. In June, 1951 the purchasers of the lots and the Lauderbaughs entered into an agreement whereby, as a condition precedent, future purchasers of land along the shore of the lake were required to be members of the Lake Watawga Association.

The Association was formed to control the development along the shore of the lake. Many attractive homes representing a substantial investment had been erected. After the formation of the Association and Agreement other lots were sold to those who became members of the Association and homes were built. Mrs. Lauderbaugh instituted an action to quiet title in March, 1958, her husband being deceased, to remove a cloud on her title by seeking to have the Agreement restricting the sale of property to members of the Association declared void. In February, 1960, Mrs. Lauderbaugh, together with Asher Seip, Jr., and Jacob Seip were named defendants in a complaint in Equity to set aside a deed of December 3, 1959, for land along the lake shore from Mrs. Lauderbaugh to Asher Seip, Jr.,— Jacob Seip being the partner of Asher Seip, Jr., grantee in the deed — as a violation of the Agreement of June 1951, and to enjoin Mrs. Lauderbaugh from conveying land along the lake shore except to persons approved for membership in the Lake Watawga Association.

The plaintiffs in the equity case were mostly the persons named as defendants in action to quiet title. The trial court entered a decree upholding the validity of the Agreement but restricted its application to the westerly shore of the lake and entered a decree setting aside the deed from Mrs. Lauderbaugh to Asher Seip, Jr., and enjoining her from conveying land on the western shore of the lake except in accordance with the Agreement of June, 1951, and in accordance with the rules, regulations and by-laws of the Lake Watawga Association. Both sides filed exceptions, which exceptions were dismissed, thereby giving rise to the instant appeals.

The Agreement of June, 1951 provides that: "The First Parties [the Lauderbaughs], for themselves, their heirs and assigns, agree that membership in the Lake Watawga Association shall be a condition precedent for future purchasers of land along the shore of Lake Watawga; that in the event such prospective purchasers qualify as members as aforesaid, the First Parties will, upon payment of purchase price, execute and deliver to them deeds."

The pertinent portions of the By-Laws of the Lake Watawga Association provide as follows:

> Article V — Membership
>
> Section 1. No person shall be eligible to membership in the Association who does not meet the requirements hereinafter specified. Such person shall be either the owner or a prospective owner of property along the shore of Lake Watawga, but such ownership or prospective ownership shall not in itself entitle such person or persons to become a member of this Association. This by-law can be amended only by a vote of three-fourths of the total membership of the Association.
>
> Section 4. Application for membership shall be made to the Secretary, and by him referred to the Board of Directors, who shall act upon the same at their earliest convenience. Notice of the application for membership shall be given to every member at least 10 days prior to the time when such application shall be acted upon. The Board of Directors shall carefully consider any objections made to applicants. An Investigation Committee composed of three members of the Board of Directors shall be appointed by the President of the Board, which Committee shall report its findings to the Board of Directors before the application is acted upon. If written objections are filed by one member of the Association, when the membership is less than ten, the applicant shall be rejected. If written objections are filed by three or more members, when the membership of the Association is more than ten, the applicant shall be rejected. If written objections are filed by less than three members, when the membership is more than ten, the applicant may be elected by a two-thirds vote of the Directors present when such application is considered.

Essentially the question is the legality of the Agreement restricting alienation of lake shore property to members of the Association only. This precise question has never before been decided by this court. However, while we do not have prior cases presenting similar factual conditions we are amply supplied with firmly established legal principles. Every restraint on alienation of real property is not necessarily void. True, such restraints are not favored in the law. Further, an absolute restraint is against public policy and, therefore, of no legal effect. However, a limited and reasonable restraint on the power of alienation may be valid. *See*, Restatement, Property, § 406.

Whether the Agreement of June, 1951 is construed to create a condition precedent, a covenant not to convey or anything else, it is clear that its effect, when read in conjunction with the requirements of membership in the Association, is to limit unreasonably the free alienation of land bordering Lake Watawga, since conveyances may be made only to members of the Association. Control over the membership of the Association lies not with the grantor, but with others, the consent of all but two of whom must be obtained in order for any prospective alienee to be eligible for membership.

We do not seek to impugn the motives of the members of the Association and, for the purposes of deciding the issues presented, assume that their motives are of the purest, their sole concerns being the orderly development of the area and, quite properly, the protection of their investments. Be that as it may however, the fact remains that no standards for admission to the Association are set out in its by-laws and it is possible that three members by whim, caprice or for any reason, good or bad, or for no reason, could deny membership to any prospective alienee, thereby depriving Mrs. Lauderbaugh of her right to alienate her land. It must be further noted that the restriction is not limited in time and purports to be a perpetual one, a fact which militates strongly against its enforcement.

The decree of the court below is reversed insofar as it declares the Agreement of June, 1951 to be valid and binding with respect to certain lots on the Westerly shore of Lake Watawga, and affirmed in all other particulars.

NOTES AND QUESTIONS

1. What is the nature of the legal action undertaken by the Williamses in the above case? Would the agreement at issue be enforceable but for the restraint on alienation? What would have happened if Mildred Lauderbaugh had died before the resolution of this matter? Note also that Mrs. Lauderbaugh initiated this litigation seeking to have declared invalid an agreement that she entered into voluntarily in 1951. Should she have the right to do this?

2. In English law, the prohibition against absolute restraints on alienation dates back to the Statute Quia Emptores (1290), which recognized the concept of free alienability by feudal tenants. Such restraints have long been viewed as undesirable because they render land unmarketable and discourage improvement of the land. The classic work on this subject is J. GRAY, RESTRAINTS ON ALIENATION (2d ed. 1895). Although technically not an unlawful restraint on alienation, the estate of fee tail posed obvious problems in this regard.

3. *Types of Restraints.* Restraints on alienation are divided into three types: forfeiture, disabling, and promissory restraints. A forfeiture restraint provides that the estate will be forfeited to an identified party if the grantee attempts to sell or transfer it. A disabling restraint simply prohibits the grantee from selling or transferring his interest, but contains no provision for forfeiture. Finally, a promissory restraint arises when a grantee promises on behalf of himself and his successors not to transfer his interest. Usually these distinctions are of little consequence, although in certain situations, forfeiture and promissory restraints have been upheld when disabling restraints are invalidated. The rationale is that the beneficiaries of forfeiture and promissory restraints can theoretically release the restriction, whereas there is no one who can terminate a disabling restraint.

4. *Reasonable Restraints.* Absolute restraints, whatever their nature, are *per se* void. As a general rule, partial restraints are also invalid. For example, a covenant which gave the developer the right to disapprove of any sale, lease, or mortgage of lots in the development unless a majority of the unit owners supported the proposed transaction in writing was struck down as an "unlawful restriction repugnant to the inherent nature and quality of a fee simple estate." *Kenney v. Morgan*, 325 A.2d 419 (Md. Ct. Spec. App. 1974).

Nevertheless, under certain circumstances, partial restraints will be upheld so long as they are reasonable and limited to a specific period of time. Rights of first refusal to repurchase, restraints on transfer for brief periods of time, sale approval rights for condominium boards, agreements on the part of co-tenants that they will not partition property during a specified period, forfeiture or promissory restraints on life estates, and restrictions on land use are all partial restraints on alienation that have been held to be reasonable. What should be the standard for reasonableness for a partial restraint on alienation? *See* Restatement (Second) of Property, Donative Transfers, Ch. 4 (1983); Bernhard, *The Minority Doctrine Concerning Direct Restraints on Alienation*, 57 Mich. L. Rev. 1173 (1959).

5. Would the following be a reasonable restraint on alienation? O devises the family home, which he owned in fee simple absolute, to his son, A, "provided that A shall permit his 70-year-old mother to reside there as long as she desires to do so. Any transfer of the home without his mother's consent during the time that she resides there shall be null and void."

6. In *Lauderbaugh v. Williams*, the justices state that they "assume that their [the members of the Lake Watawga Association] motives are of the purest, their sole concerns being the orderly development of the area and, quite properly, the protection of their investments." In reality, why do you think that the Association opposed the sale to the Seips?

[2.] Change of Circumstances

EL DI, INC. v. TOWN OF BETHANY BEACH
Delaware Supreme Court
477 A.2d 1066 (1984)

Upon appeal from the Court of Chancery.

Herrmann, Chief Justice (for the majority).

This is an appeal from a permanent injunction granted by the Court of Chancery upon the petition of the plaintiffs, The Town of Bethany Beach, et al., prohibiting the defendant, El Di, Inc. ("El Di") from selling alcoholic beverages at Holiday House, a restaurant in Bethany Beach owned and operated by El Di.

I

The pertinent facts are as follows: El Di purchased the Holiday House in 1969. In December 1981, El Di filed an application with the State Alcoholic Beverage Control Commission (the "Commission") for a license to sell alcoholic beverages at the Holiday House. On April 15, 1982, finding "public need and convenience," the Commission granted the Holiday House an on-premises license. The sale of alcoholic beverages at Holiday House began within 10 days of the Commission's approval. Plaintiffs subsequently filed suit to permanently enjoin the sale of alcoholic beverages under the license.

On appeal it is undisputed that the chain of title for the Holiday House lot included restrictive covenants prohibiting both the sale of alcoholic beverages on the property and nonresidential construction. The same restriction was placed on property in Bethany Beach as early as 1900 and 1901 when the area was first under development. As originally conceived, Bethany Beach was to be a quiet beach community. The site was selected at the end of the nineteenth-century by the Christian Missionary Society of Washington, D.C. In 1900, the Bethany Beach Improvement Company ("BBIC") was formed. The BBIC purchased lands, laid out a development and began selling lots. To insure the quiet character of the community, the BBIC placed restrictive covenants on many plots, prohibiting the sale of alcohol and restricting construction to residential cottages. Of the original 180 acre development, however, approximately 1/3 was unrestricted.

The Town of Bethany Beach was officially incorporated in 1909. The municipal limits consisted of 750 acres including the original BBIC land (hereafter the original or "old-Town"), but expanded far beyond the 180 acre BBIC development. The expanded acreage of the newly incorporated Town, combined with the unrestricted plots in the original Town, left only 15 percent of the new Town subject to the restrictive covenants.

Despite the restriction prohibiting commercial building ("no other than a dwelling or cottage shall be erected . . . "), commercial development began in the 1920s on property subject to the covenants. This development included numerous inns, restaurants, drug stores, a bank, motels, a town hall, shops selling various items including food, clothing, gifts and novelties and other commercial businesses. Of the 34 commercial buildings presently within the Town limits, 29 are located in the old-Town originally developed by BBIC. Today, Bethany Beach has a permanent population of some 330 residents. In the summer months the population increases to approximately 10,000 people within the corporate limits and to some 48,000 people within a 4 mile radius. In 1952, the Town enacted a zoning ordinance which established a central commercial district designated C-1 located in the old-Town section. Holiday House is located in this district.

Since El Di purchased Holiday House in 1969, patrons have been permitted to carry their own alcoholic beverages with them into the restaurant to consume with their meals. This "brown-bagging" practice occurred at Holiday House prior to El Di's ownership and at other restaurants in the Town. El Di applied for a license to sell liquor at Holiday House in response to the increased number of customers who were engaging in "brown-bagging" and in the belief that the license would permit restaurant management to control excessive use of alcohol and use by minors. Prior to the time El Di sought a license, alcoholic beverages had been and continue to be readily available for sale at nearby licensed establishments including: one restaurant mile outside the Town limits, 3 restaurants within a 4 mile radius of the Town, and a package store some 200–300 yards from the Holiday House.

The Trial Court granted a stay pending the outcome of this appeal.

II

In granting plaintiffs' motion for a permanent injunction, the Court of Chancery rejected defendant's argument that changed conditions in Bethany Beach rendered the restrictive covenants unreasonable and therefore unenforceable. Citing Restatement of Property, § 564; *Welshire, Inc. v. Harbison*, 91 A.2d 404 (Del. Supr. 1952); and *Cruciano v. Ceccarone*, 133 A.2d 911 (Del. Ch. 1957). The Chancery Court found that although the evidence showed a considerable growth since 1900 in both population and the number of buildings in Bethany Beach, "the basic nature of Bethany Beach as a quiet, family oriented resort has not changed." The Court also found that there had been development of commercial activity since 1900, but that this "activity is limited to a small area of Bethany Beach and consists mainly of activities for the convenience and patronage of the residents of Bethany Beach."

The Trial Court also rejected defendant's contention that plaintiffs' acquiescence and abandonment rendered the covenants unenforceable. In this connection, the Court concluded that the practice of "brown-bagging" was not a sale of alcoholic beverages and that, therefore, any failure to enforce the restriction as against the practice did not constitute abandonment or waiver of the restriction.

III

We find that the Trial Court erred in holding that the change of conditions was insufficient to negate the restrictive covenant.

A court will not enforce a restrictive covenant where a fundamental change has occurred in the intended character of the neighborhood that renders the benefits underlying imposition of the restrictions incapable of enjoyment. *Welshire v. Harbison*, 91 A.2d 404 (Del. Supr. 1952); *1.77 Acres of Land v. State*, 241 A.2d 513 (Del. Supr. 1968); *Williams v. Tsiarkezos*, 272 A.2d 722 (Del. Ch. 1970). Review of all the facts and circumstances convinces us that the change, since 1901, in the character of that area of the old-Town section now zoned C-1 is so substantial as to justify modification of the deed restriction. We need not determine a change in character of the entire restricted area in order to assess the continued applicability of the covenant to a portion thereof.

It is uncontradicted that one of the purposes underlying the covenant prohibiting the sale of intoxicating liquors was to maintain a quiet, residential atmosphere in the restricted area. Each of the additional covenants reinforces this objective, including the covenant restricting construction to residential dwellings. The covenants read as a whole evince an intention on the part of the grantor to maintain the residential, seaside character of the community.

But time has not left Bethany Beach the same community its grantors envisioned in 1901. The Town has changed from a church-affiliated residential community to a summer resort visited annually by thousands of tourists. Nowhere is the resultant change in character more evident than in the C-1 section of the old-Town. Plaintiffs argue that this is a relative change only and that there is sufficient evidence to support the Trial Court's findings that the residential character of the community has been maintained and that the covenants continue to benefit the other lot owners. We cannot agree.

In 1909, the 180 acre restricted old-Town section became part of a 750 acre incorporated municipality. Even prior to the Town's incorporation, the BBIC deeded out lots free of the restrictive covenants. After incorporation and partly due to the unrestricted lots deeded out by the BBIC, 85 percent of the land area within the Town was not subject to the restrictions. Significantly, nonresidential uses quickly appeared in the restricted area and today the old-Town section contains almost all of the commercial businesses within the entire Town. Moreover, these commercial uses have gone unchallenged for 82 years.

The change in conditions is also reflected in the Town's decision in 1952 to zone restricted property, including the lot on which the Holiday House is located, specifically for commercial use. Although a change in zoning is not dispositive as against a private covenant, it is additional evidence of changed community conditions.

Time has relaxed not only the strictly residential character of the area, but the pattern of alcohol use and consumption as well. The practice of "brown-bagging" has continued unchallenged for at least twenty years at commercial establishments located on restricted property in the Town. On appeal, plaintiffs rely on the Trial Court finding that the "brown-bagging" practice is irrelevant as evidence of waiver inasmuch as the practice does not involve the sale of intoxicating liquors prohibited by the covenant. We find the "brown-bagging" practice evidence of a significant change in conditions in the community since its inception at the turn of the century. Such consumption of alcohol in public places is now generally tolerated by owners of similarly restricted lots. The license issued to the Holiday House establishment permits the El Di management to better control the availability and consumption of intoxicating liquors on its premises. In view of both the ready availability of alcoholic beverages in the area surrounding the Holiday House and the long-tolerated and increasing use of "brown-bagging," enforcement of the restrictive covenant at this time would only serve to subvert the public interest in the control of the availability and consumption of alcoholic liquors.

Plaintiffs contend that the covenant prohibiting the sale of intoxicating liquors is separate from the other covenants. In the plaintiffs' view, the alcohol sale restriction serves a purpose distinct from the prohibition of nonresidential uses. Plaintiffs argue, therefore, that despite evidence of commercial uses, the alcohol sale restriction provides a substantial benefit to the other lot owners. We find the cases on which plaintiff relies distinguishable:

In *Jameson v. Brown*, 109 F.2d 830 (D.C. Cir. 1939), all of the lots were similarly restricted and there was no evidence of waiver or abandonment of the covenant prohibiting the sale of spirituous liquors. The court found evidence of one isolated violation — in contrast to the long-tolerated practice of "brown-bagging" in Bethany Beach. In *Brookside Community, Inc. v. Williams*, 290 A.2d 678, *aff'd*, 306 A.2d 711 (Del. Ch. 1972), the general rule in Delaware is stated as to the effect of a waiver of a separable covenant. The case is distinguishable because here we consider waiver in conjunction with our assessment of the change of conditions in the community. No such change was alleged or addressed in *Williams*. In Bethany Beach commercial uses have not simply crept in, but have been given official sanction through the 1952 Zoning Ordinance.

It is further argued that the commercial uses are restricted to a small area within the old-Town section. But significantly, the section in which Holiday House is located is entirely commercial. The business uses, the availability of alcohol in close proximity to this section, and the repeated use of "brown-bagging" in the C-1 district render the originally intended benefits of the covenants unattainable in what has become an area detached in character from the strictly residential surroundings to the west.

In view of the change in conditions in the C-1 district of Bethany Beach, we find it unreasonable and inequitable now to enforce the restrictive covenant. To permit unlimited "brown-bagging" but to prohibit licensed sales of alcoholic liquor, under the circumstances of this case, is inconsistent with any reasonable application of the restriction and contrary to public policy.

We emphasize that our judgment is confined to the area of the old-Town section zoned C-1. The restrictions in the neighboring residential area are unaffected by the conclusion we reach herein.

Reversed.

CHRISTIE, JUSTICE, with whom MOORE, JUSTICE, joins, dissenting.

I respectfully disagree with the majority. I think the evidence supports the conclusion of the Chancellor, as finder of fact, that the basic nature of the community of Bethany Beach has not changed in such a way as to invalidate those restrictions which have continued to protect this community through the years as it has grown. Although some of the restrictions have been ignored and a portion of the community is now used for limited commercial purposes, the evidence shows that Bethany Beach remains a quiet, family-oriented resort where no liquor is sold. I think the conditions of the community are still consistent with the enforcement of a restrictive covenant forbidding the sale of intoxicating beverages.

In my opinion, the toleration of the practice of "brown bagging" does not constitute the abandonment of a longstanding restriction against the sale of alcoholic beverages. The restriction against sales has, in fact, remained intact for more than eighty years and any violations thereof have been short-lived. The fact that alcoholic beverages may be purchased right outside the town is not inconsistent with my view that the quiet-town atmosphere in this small area has not broken down, and that it can and should be preserved. Those who choose to buy land subject to the restrictions should be required to continue to abide by the restrictions.

I think the only real beneficiaries of the failure of the courts to enforce the restrictions would be those who plan to benefit commercially. I also question the propriety of the issuance of a liquor license for the sale of liquor on property which is subject to a specific restrictive covenant against such sales.

I think that restrictive covenants play a vital part in the preservation of neighborhood schemes all over the State, and that a much more complete breakdown of the neighborhood scheme should be required before a court declares that a restriction has become unenforceable. I would affirm the Chancellor.

NOTES AND QUESTIONS

1. The court in *Bethany* states that a court "will not enforce a restrictive covenant where a fundamental change has occurred in the intended character of the neighborhood that renders the benefits underlying imposition of the restrictions incapable of enjoyment." On what basis does it conclude that the benefits of the covenant at issue can no longer be enjoyed? If no alcohol has been sold for 80 years and if the Town of Bethany is willing to sue to enforce the covenant, shouldn't that be evidence that the benefits continue? Why did both the trial court and the dissenting justices reach a different conclusion? Is the majority in fact applying a different standard than the one they assert in their opinion? Are they saying that if the degree of change is great enough, continued benefits are unimportant?

2. *Piecemeal Changes.* Change of circumstances arguments usually succeed only if the change is so pervasive that the entire area or subdivision's essential character has been altered. The party violating the covenant must demonstrate more than piecemeal or border lot change; a change in the character of the surrounding community is not sufficient. *See Western Land Co. v. Truskolaski*, 495 P.2d 624 (Nev. 1972), in which the Nevada Supreme Court concluded, "Even though nearby avenues may become heavily traveled thoroughfares, restrictive covenants are still enforceable if the single-family residential character of the neighborhood has not been thwarted." The court reasoned that as long as the restrictive covenant limiting land to residential uses remained of "real and substantial value to those homeowners living within the subdivision," increased commercialization and significant border lot change would be insufficient to extinguish the covenant. Similarly, in *River Heights Associates Ltd. v. Batten*, 591 S.E.2d 683 (Va. 2004), the Virginia Supreme Court upheld the enforcement of a 45 year old covenant that prohibited commercial development on the edges of a subdivision north of Charlottesville, even though the public road adjacent to the subdivision had been transformed over time from a "two-land country road" into "an eight- to ten-lane road that is highly developed commercially on both sides."

3. *Appropriate Remedy.* If a court refuses to enforce a restrictive covenant on the grounds of change of circumstances, is it saying that the covenant no longer exists or that it continues to exist, but is no longer enforceable? This distinction may be important when it comes to questions of remedy. If change in circumstances is an equitable defense (as it is usually said to be), is it an appropriate defense in a suit for damages? Apparently most courts have taken the position that it is, even though the original RESTATEMENT OF PROPERTY (1944) took a contrary position. (Comment *d* to § 564 stated that a court's refusal to grant an injunction enforcing a servitude on account of a change in conditions did not terminate the obligation and did not preclude an award of damages for its breach.) *See* Cross, *Interplay Between Property Law Change and Barriers to Property Law Reform*, 35 N.Y.U. L. REV. 1317 (1960).

A Massachusetts statute addresses this question by providing that the benefit of restrictive covenants can be enforced by damages only if certain conditions are present, including "changes in the character of the properties affected or their neighborhood . . . which reduce materially the need for the restriction or the likelihood of the restriction accomplishing its original purposes." Mass. Gen. Laws c.184 § 30. Would it make sense to borrow a principle from the law of affirmative easements and simply hold that once a covenant has served its purpose, it comes to an end? *See Union National Bank v. Nesmith*, 130 N.E. 251 (Mass. 1921). Which is the most desirable of the above approaches? For additional discussion of the damages remedy in this setting, see Robinson, *Explaining Contingent Rights: The Puzzle of "Obsolete" Covenants*, 91 COLUM. L. REV. 546 (1991); Note, *Termination of Servitudes: Expanding the Remedies for "Changed Conditions,"* 31 UCLA L. REV. 226 (1983).

4. *Criticism of the Change in Circumstances Doctrine.* In *Loeb v. Watkins*, 240 A.2d 513 (Pa. 1968), a divided Pennsylvania Supreme Court ruled that "Restrictive covenants are enforceable without the necessity of showing that the enforcement would work a substantial gain to the legal beneficiary of the covenant. The plaintiffs' right here to enforce the restrictive covenant is absolute, regardless of proof that they do or do not suffer damage as a result of the breach of the covenant." Writing for the majority, the legendary Justice Michael A. Musmanno denounced the idea that a restrictive covenant could expire because later owners disagreed with the original parties, understanding of its benefit:

> The learned Chancellor . . . erred further in his conclusion that equitable relief should be denied the plaintiffs because they did not show that upholding of the restriction would result in any substantial benefit to them. Who is to say that it will not result in damage to them if the antecedents in title believed a greater enjoyment would be theirs if the tract of land was restricted to 62 private dwellings? Who should say they did not have the right to limit the building operations to that extent? If a covenant running with land proclaims that a lake ornamenting the land must never be destroyed, no successor in title would have the right to argue that the lake is not pretty, the water muddy and no good for fishing, and, therefore, should be drained. Where a man's land is concerned, he may impose, in so far as the imposition does not violate any law or public policy, any restriction he pleases.

Other critics have accepted the legitimacy of the doctrine, but have called for more precise standards for its implementation. Professor Susan French has called for an expansion of the doctrine to deal effectively with obsolescence in servitudes. French has argued that relief from covenants should be provided "where an affirmative obligation has become unduly burdensome or where the economic arrangement implemented by the servitude obligation has become obsolete, wasteful, or unreasonable." French, *Toward a Modern Law of Servitudes: Reweaving the Ancient Strands*, 55 S. CAL. L. REV. 1261, 1313–17 (1982).

[3.] Abandonment and Selective Enforcement

MOUNTAIN PARK HOMEOWNERS ASS'N v. TYDINGS

Washington Supreme Court
883 P.2d 1383 (1994)

DOLLIVER, J.

Defendants Paddy L. Tydings and Richard Tydings seek reversal of a court of appeals decision that reversed and remanded a superior court's order of summary dismissal with prejudice. Defendants assign error to the Court of Appeals ruling that violations of other enumerated protective covenants in a subdivision were irrelevant to whether a covenant against antennas has been abandoned or not enforced uniformly by Plaintiff Mountain Park Homeowners Association. Defendants also claim that Plaintiff procedurally forfeited its right to challenge the trial court's original order. We affirm the decision of the Court of Appeals.

Defendants are resident homeowners in Mountain Park, a 244-unit planned community in Pierce County, Washington. Purchasers of property in the subdivision agree to be bound by the Declaration of Covenants, Conditions, and Restrictions for Mountain Park (CCR). Plaintiff Mountain Park Homeowners Association (Association) is a non-profit corporation established by the CCR whose membership consists of homeowners in the subdivision. The Association is empowered to enforce the CCR through the Architectural Control Committee (ACC).

The CCR enumerates certain protective covenants, including a prohibition on antennas: "No exposed or exterior radio or television transmission or receiving antennas shall be erected, placed, or maintained on any part of such premises except as approved by the ACC prior to installation or construction." CCR art. 9, § 17. In 1988, Defendants installed an exterior satellite receiving dish on their property. Acting on a complaint by another resident, Plaintiff notified Defendants by letter that they were in violation of the protective covenant against antennas and requested removal of the dish. Defendants refused to remove the dish and admit its continued presence on their property.

In October 1988, Plaintiff filed a complaint against Defendants seeking to enforce the covenant. At the same time, the Association brought a second suit to enforce the same antenna covenant against another homeowner's satellite dish; the trial court in that case granted summary judgment for the Association. In February 1989, the trial court in the present case denied Plaintiff's motion for summary judgment and ordered: "If all covenants and/or restrictions contained in the Mountain Park Declaration of Covenants, Conditions and Restrictions are not uniformly enforced this action found to be discriminatory will be dismissed."

Shortly thereafter, Plaintiff determined that 7 to 12 homeowners were in violation of various covenants, including stored disabled vehicles, campers, boats, building materials, and a traditional television antenna. Plaintiff notified these violators that continued non-compliance with the covenants would result in its seeking judicial enforcement. Nevertheless, in June 1989, the trial court denied Plaintiff's motion for reconsideration after deciding that the uniformity of enforcement remained in dispute. Meanwhile, Defendant Richard Tydings served as chairman of the ACC from 1989 to 1990.

In 1991, Defendants moved to dismiss the complaint by arguing that Plaintiff continued to fail to enforce the CCR against other violators. The trial court denied Defendants' motion to dismiss, deciding that a genuine issue of material fact regarding uniform enforcement persisted. Upon Defendants' motion for reconsideration, the court dismissed Plaintiff's complaint with prejudice. The court held the enforcement of the antenna covenant against Defendants was discriminatory as a matter of law "because Plaintiff has not uniformly enforced or attempted uniform enforcement of the [CCR] and has failed to take any action against the numerous violations of the [CCR] except for the proceedings against defendant herein." In addition, the court held the covenant was an unreasonable restraint on the use of property.

In December 1993, the Court of Appeals reversed the trial court's summary dismissal and remanded. *Mountain Park Homeowners Ass'n, Inc. v. Tydings*, 864 P.2d 392 (Wn. App. 1993). The court held as a matter of law that Plaintiff had not abandoned or selectively enforced the covenant against antennas and thus dismissal for Defendants was improper. The court also held the antenna covenant did not constitute an unreasonable restraint on the use of property. This court granted Defendants' petition for discretionary review solely on the issue of abandonment or selective enforcement.

[The court first dismissed the Tydings' claim that the plaintiff's assignment of error was procedurally insufficient.]

We turn next to the heart of Defendants' petition: the rejection by the Court of Appeals of their defense to enforcement. When reviewing an order for summary judgment, the appellate court engages in the same inquiry as the trial court. This court will affirm summary judgment if no genuine issue of any material fact exists and the moving party is entitled to judgment as a matter of law. All facts and reasonable inferences are considered in the light most favorable to the non-moving party, and all questions of law are reviewed de novo.

Property owners have a right in equity to enforce restrictive covenants. *See, e.g., Mains Farm Homeowners Ass'n v. Worthington*, 854 P.2d 1072 (Wash. 1993). A number of equitable defenses are available to preclude enforcement of a covenant: merger, release, unclean hands, acquiescence, abandonment, laches, estoppel, and changed neighborhood conditions. *St. Luke's Evangelical Lutheran Church v. Hales*, 534 P.2d 1379 (Wn. App. 1975). There is no question here that the antenna covenant applies to satellite dishes and that Defendants are in violation. Thus, Defendants can only avoid enforcement with facts supporting a viable defense.

The trial court accepted evidence of violations of other covenants to support a defense that the antenna covenant was abandoned or enforced selectively. The defense of abandonment requires evidence that prior violations by other residents have so eroded the general plan as to make enforcement useless and inequitable. *Mt. Baker Park Club, Inc. v. Colcock*, 275 P.2d 733 (Wash. 1954). "If a covenant which applies to an entire tract has been habitually and substantially violated so as to create an impression that it has been abandoned, equity will not enforce the covenant." *Sandy Point Imp. Co. v. Huber*, 613 P.2d 160 (Wn. App. 1980). Violations must be material to the overall purpose of the covenant, and minor violations are insufficient to find abandonment. *Reading v. Keller*, 406 P.2d 634 (Wash. 1965). This court has refused to find abandonment from evidence of a single violation. *Reading, supra.*

Washington courts have not directly addressed the relevance of a violation of one type of covenant to the enforcement of another. The covenants in prior cases were broad, generally prohibiting non-residential use and establishing setback or height restrictions. As a result, analysis has been limited to whether violations of the same covenant amount to abandonment. The case at hand is made unique by the nature of the CCR; instead of a single broad covenant, the CCR catalogs specific prohibitions in separate covenants.

The Court of Appeals repudiated the trial court's acceptance of a theory of abandonment based on violations of other covenants. The court held that a defense of abandonment or selective enforcement of the antenna covenant could only be supported by evidence of violations of that covenant. The court went on to note that Plaintiff had enforced the three violations of the antenna covenant in the record by court action or voluntary compliance. Because Defendants presented no evidence of failure to enforce the antenna covenant, as a matter of law their defense failed.

Defendants dispute the ruling of the Court of Appeals that violations of other covenants are irrelevant to a defense against enforcement of the antenna covenant. Defendants urge the court to adopt the analysis of other states apparently willing to consider violations of other independent covenants as relevant to abandonment. *See Swaggerty v. Petersen*, 572 P.2d 1309 (Or. 1977); *Condos v. Home Dev. Co.*, 267 P.2d 1069 (Ariz. 1954); *see also* 2 AMERICAN LAW OF PROPERTY § 9.38 (1952); *contra, Tompkins v. Buttrum Constr. Co.*, 659 P.2d 865 (Nev. 1983); *Dauphin Island Property Owners Ass'n, Inc. v. Kuppersmith*, 371 So. 2d 31, 34 (Ala. 1979).

Despite Defendants' contentions, the facts of the present case do not necessitate our reaching the legal issue of the viability of a defense based on violations of other independent covenants. Our review of the uncontroverted evidence in the record convinces us that the terms of the CCR itself bar a defense based on violations of other covenants. A court must construe restrictive covenants by discerning the intent of the parties as evidenced by clear and unambiguous language in the document. The court must consider the document in its entirety. Only in the case of ambiguity will the court look beyond the document to ascertain intent from surrounding circumstances.

The CCR contains an unequivocally unambiguous severability clause: "Invalidation of any one of these covenants or restrictions by judgment or court order shall not affect any other provisions which shall remain in full force and effect." CCR art. 14, § 4. Defendants do not deny their agreement to be bound by the provisions of the CCR, nor have they disputed the clarity, enforceability, or applicability of the severability clause to their circumstances. On its face, the severability clause indicates an intent to preclude the very defense accepted by the trial court. The CCR unambiguously mandates separate treatment of each covenant. As a result, we hold the terms of the CCR makes evidence of violations of other covenants irrelevant in the present case.

NOTES AND QUESTIONS

1. *CCRs.* Restrictive covenants imposed on a residential development are typically included in a governing document known as the declaration of covenants, conditions and restrictions (commonly abbreviated as CCRs or CC&Rs). This document is recorded before any units are sold and thus become part of the chain of title of all unit owners. Homeowners associations are typically created to enforce the CCRs. As the above case indicates, the CCR becomes the legislative code of the development.

2. Had there been no severability clause in the CCR, would the Tydings have prevailed? Is it fair to the homeowner to say that he or she cannot point to a pattern of violation and non-enforcement of other covenants as a defense?

3. *Other Equitable Defenses.* In addition to change of circumstances, abandonment and selective enforcement, the Washington Supreme Court also lists merger, release, unclean hands, acquiescence, laches, and estoppel as potential equitable defenses to preclude enforcement of a covenant. Other courts might add relative hardship to the list. There is considerable overlap among these categories, but all point to the fact that equity will not enforce a covenant if the violator has been led to believe that the covenant has been abandoned or if the party benefitted by the covenant has failed to assert his or her rights within a reasonable time.

Merger, which arguably is more a legal than an equitable defense, occurs when a common owner comes into possession of the burdened property and all the lots benefitted by the covenant. If he then resells some of the lots, the original covenants do not automatically come back to life. Under certain circumstances restrictive covenants have been held to be unenforceable in equity because they are too vague or too broadly worded. In such circumstances, money damages may be available. *See Amana Soc'y v. Colony Inn, Inc.*, 315 N.W.2d 101 (Iowa 1982).

4. *Termination of Covenants Generally.* In addition to being negated by changes in circumstances or abandoned, covenants may end if they expire by their own terms. A few states have even experimented with statutorily-defined expiration points. In addition, the beneficiaries of covenants may also voluntarily release their enforcement rights to the burdened party. If all those who are entitled to enforce the covenant release their rights, the covenant disappears.

5. *Eminent Domain.* If a parcel of land subject to restrictive covenants is condemned by the state through its exercise of eminent domain power, should the presence of the covenant be taken into account in computing the amount of just compensation owed? Should the owner of the property benefited by the covenant receive compensation as well, if the use undertaken by the state is inconsistent with the covenant? Courts have divided on this issue. *Compare Meagher v. Appalachian Elec. Power Co.*, 77 S.E.2d 461 (Va. 1953), *and Southern California Edison Co. v. Bourgerie*, 507 P.2d 964 (Cal. 1973) (owner of benefited property entitled to compensation), *with Ryan v. Town of Manalapan*, 414 So. 2d 193 (Fla. 1982) (benefit of covenant not a form of property for which compensation need be paid). The former is, however, clearly the majority view. Courts also differ on the question of whether the purchaser of land at a tax sale takes it free from the burden of covenants in effect at the time the government takes title for non-payment of taxes.

For a discussion of such cases, see *Easement, Servitude or Covenant as Affected by Sale for Taxes*, 7 A.L.R.5th 187 (1998). For a case that says that the tax sale does not eliminate the covenants, see *Lake Arrowhead Community Club, Inc. v. Looney*, 770 P.2d 1046 (Wash. 1989).

[4.] Covenants in Violation of Public Policy

CRANE NECK ASSOCIATION, INC. v. NEW YORK CITY/ LONG ISLAND COUNTY SERVICES GROUP

New York Court of Appeals
460 N.E.2d 1336 (1984)

Opinion of the Court (By Kaye, J.)

Beginning in 1945, as the Long Island estate of Eversley Childs was divided into residential parcels, each deed within the tract (called Crane Neck Farm) included an identical covenant restricting buildings to "single family dwellings." Respondent agencies, implementing a long-standing State policy to deinstitutionalize retarded persons and place them in community settings, in 1980 leased property within Crane Neck to house and care for eight severely retarded adults. Appellants, Crane Neck property owners, contending that this use violates the restrictive covenant, seek a judgment enforcing the covenant and enjoining continuation of the lease.

Special Term granted appellants partial summary judgment, concluding that the State facility was not a single-family dwelling and therefore violated the covenant, yet finding that there were fact issues as to whether the restrictions of the covenant had been waived by past violations and whether the character of the neighborhood had so changed as to render the covenant unenforceable in equity. The Appellate Division reversed and dismissed the complaint, determining that the facility could be considered a single-family dwelling consistent within the restrictive covenant, and that in any event the covenant could not be enforced to prevent the residence as a matter of public policy. On the latter ground, we affirm the order of the Appellate Division.

I

Pursuant to a lease effective September 1, 1980 between the owners of the subject property (respondents Jonathan Pool and Bernard Grofman) and respondent New York City/Long Island County Services Group (an agency of respondent New York State Department of Mental Retardation and Developmental Disabilities), eight profoundly retarded adults formerly in institutions came to reside in a six-bedroom home situated on two wooded acres at 3 Johns Hollow Road in the Hamlet of Crane Neck, Village of Old Field. These adults were in need of uninterrupted supervision.

According to the State's program, a nonresident professional staff of approximately 16 persons cares for the residents, trains them, and provides therapy where needed. While resident "houseparents" are in theory part of the program, it is not clear from the record that there have in fact been houseparents at 3 Johns Hollow Road. At least three supervisory persons are to be within the home around the clock.

In a family-type environment and under constant supervision, the disabled persons residing in Crane Neck are taught socialization as well as basic physical skills. Structured "day programming" lasting six or more hours a day is conducted in feeding, toilet training, personal grooming and health habits, dressing, housekeeping, and caring for property. After the initial period of intensive training, once sufficient independence is developed, the residents are enrolled in sheltered workshops in the area, such as the United Cerebral Palsy Center in Commack, the Industrial Home for the Blind in Melville, and the Suffolk Child Development Center in Smithtown, returning to 3 Johns Hollow Road each day. As they are able, also, they begin interacting with merchants and others in the neighborhood. The stays at 3 Johns Hollow are of indefinite duration, but it appears that residents upon reaching a certain degree of development are expected to leave and be replaced by others in need of care and training.

II

The question presented on this appeal is whether use of the leased premises at 3 Johns Hollow Road should be enjoined by equitable enforcement of the restrictive covenant in the lessors' deed. Any analysis of this issue of course must begin with language of the covenant.

Starting in 1945, and continuing for about 10 years, uniform deed restrictions were imposed on all parcels comprising the tract of Crane Neck. Each of these deeds, including the deed from which respondent lessors derived title, included the following:

> Subject to the following covenants and restrictions, which shall be construed as real covenants running with the land and shall be binding upon and enure to the benefit of the parties hereto, and their respective heirs, devisees, legal representatives, successors and assigns:
>
> (a) There shall not be constructed nor maintained upon the said premises any buildings other than single family dwellings and outbuildings. That no house or dwelling costing less than $3500 on the basis of 1944 material and labor costs shall be erected on the said premises, and that no building other than Cape Cod or Colonial design and architecture (and additional buildings shall conform in architecture to the main dwelling) shall be erected on said premises unless plans and specifications therefor have first been submitted to and approved in writing by the parties of the first part, or their duly authorized agent.

From a reading of the covenant and the undisputed evidence regarding the intent of the grantor, we conclude that the deed restriction was imposed to preserve Crane Neck as a neighborhood of single-family dwellings, not only architecturally but also functionally. We are therefore in agreement with both courts below that, to give the effect intended by its creator, the covenant must be read to apply not only to the physical construction of single-family dwellings within Crane Neck but also to their actual use.

We cannot agree, however, with the conclusion of the Appellate Division that the community residence at 3 Johns Hollow Road functions as a single-family dwelling. It fits neither a traditional concept of a single-family unit known in 1945 (*see What Constitutes a "Family" Within Meaning of Zoning Regulation or Restrictive Covenant*, Ann., 172 ALR 1172), by which its use must be measured (*Clark v. Devoe*, 124 NY 120, 123), nor even the expanded definitions of "family" of more recent origin (*see City of White Plains v. Ferraioli*, 34 NY2d 300, 306).

In support of their argument that the use is consonant with the covenant, respondent agencies point to the fact that the residence in theory functions as one housekeeping unit providing a homelike atmosphere for individuals who cannot remain in their natural families, meanwhile teaching them basic skills which will enable them to live independently. But these indicia of family life do not create a family.

We found in *City of White Plains v. Ferraioli* (34 NY2d 300, *supra*) that a group home consisting of a married couple, their two children and 10 foster children qualified as a family for purposes of a zoning ordinance, and in *Group House of Port Washington v. Board of Zoning & Appeals* (45 NY2d 266, 271), we concluded that a group home of seven children with two surrogate parents could not be distinguished from a natural family for that same purpose. Those decisions, which have in effect been codified in subdivision (f) of section 41.34 of the Mental Hygiene Law, are not controlling here. This case concerns the application of a private covenant, not a zoning ordinance. Furthermore, a much different factual situation is presented.

In this context, a home inhabited by eight unrelated adults each receiving uninterrupted professional supervision and care is not a single-family unit. The residents are twice outnumbered by a changing, nonresident staff of nurses, physical and recreational therapists, dieticians and others finding no equivalent in a biologically unitary family, or indeed in any expanded concept of the word "family." While neither the size of the resident group nor the nature of its daily activities would necessarily determine the issue (*see Incorporated Vil. of Freeport v. Association for Help of Retarded Children*, 94 Misc. 2d 1048, 1049, *aff'd*, 60 AD2d 644), the absence of regular houseparents and, most significantly, the presence of a large complement of nonresident professional attendants distinguish the residence at 3 Johns Hollow Road from a single-family unit.

The residence being operated by respondent agencies within Crane Neck, then, cannot be considered a single-family dwelling as contemplated by the deed restriction.

III

But even if use of the property violates the restrictive covenant, that covenant cannot be equitably enforced because to do so would contravene a long-standing public policy favoring the establishment of such residences for the mentally disabled.

Over the past three decades this State has developed a policy favoring the deinstitutionalization of mentally and developmentally disabled persons, and their placement in supervised residences housing small groups, called "community residences" (Mental Hygiene Law, § 1.03, subd. 28). The Mental Hygiene Law authorizes the Commissioner of Mental Retardation and Developmental Disabilities to operate these residences (Mental Hygiene Law, § 41.33), and provides for grants and reimbursements to others who offer such services (Mental Hygiene Law, §§ 41.36, 41.37, 41.38).

[The court then summarized the history of efforts in New York to move "toward community orientation in the provision of services to the mentally disabled."]

Even more directly pertinent to the present issues is the enactment of subdivision (f) of section 41.34 of the Mental Hygiene Law. Section 41.34 was added to the Mental Hygiene Law in 1978 to provide for a fair distribution of community residences and to bring municipalities into the process of site selection, thereby minimizing resistance and avoiding legal battles that had impeded the community residence program. The latter concern was a very real one as attempts to develop community residences and similar group homes in some areas had met with resistance in the form of injunctive actions based upon local ordinances limiting the use of property to single-family residences. In an effort to keep such legal challenges from frustrating the program, the Legislature provided as follows in the concluding subdivision of section 41.34 of the Mental Hygiene Law: "(f) A community residence established pursuant to this section and family care homes shall be deemed a family unit, for purposes of local laws and ordinances."

While the statute is limited to local laws and ordinances, this provision cannot be read without reference to the purpose that engendered it. A major purpose of section 41.34, and the very purpose for which subdivision (f) was enacted, was to eliminate the legal challenges that were impeding implementation of the State policy. (*See Zubli v. Community Mainstreaming Assn.*, 102 Misc. 2d 320, 327, *aff'd*, 74 A.D.2d 624, *mod on other grounds* 50 N.Y.2d 1024.)

Since the State's policy regarding placement of the mentally disabled as set forth in subdivision (f) would be frustrated by enforcement of the restrictive covenant, it cannot as a matter of public policy be enforced against the community residence at 3 Johns Hollow Road.

IV

Appellants urge that this court may not refuse to enjoin violation of the restrictive covenant on public policy grounds because it is a private contract which cannot be impaired by the State absent emergency circumstances not present here. (US Const., art I, § 10; *Home Bldg. & Loan Assn. v. Blaisdell*, 290 U.S. 398.) Appellants' argument, however, misconstrues the law.

Although the language of the contract clause is facially absolute, this court has long recognized that the State's interest in protecting the general good of the public through social welfare legislation is paramount to the interests of parties under private contracts, and the State may impair such contracts by subsequent legislation or regulation so long as it is reasonably necessary to further an important public purpose and the measures taken that impair the contract are reasonable and appropriate to effectuate that purpose. (*Matter of Subway-Surface Supervisors Assn. v. New York City Tr. Auth.*, 44 N.Y.2d 101, 109–112; *Matter of Farrell v. Drew*, 19 N.Y.2d 486, 493–494], *Matter of Department of Bldgs. v. Philco Realty Corp.*, 14 N.Y.2d 291, 297–298.)

While older cases such as *Blaisdell* [1934] (many of which concerned depression-era legislation prohibiting foreclosure of mortgages or other debts) may have suggested that some emergency requiring temporary State action should be present in order to allow impairment of contract rights, this is clearly no longer the law. "If the state regulation constitutes a substantial impairment, the State, in justification, must have a significant and legitimate public purpose behind the regulation * * * such as the remedying of a broad and general social or economic problem * * * Furthermore, since *Blaisdell*, the Court has indicated that the public purpose need not be addressed to an emergency or temporary situation." (*Energy Reserves Group v. Kansas Power & Light Co.*, 459 U.S. 400; *see, also, Allied Structural Steel Co. v. Spannaus*, 438 U.S. 234, 249, n 24.)

Here the State's interest in protecting the welfare of mentally and developmentally disabled individuals is clearly an important public purpose, and the means used to select the sites for community residences are reasonable and appropriate to effectuate the State's program of providing the most effective care in the least restrictive environment. In such circumstances, appellants' private contract rights may not override State policy.

V

Since public policy prohibits enforcement of the restrictive covenant against the "community residence" at 3 Johns Hollow Road, appellants' action seeking to enjoin such use was properly dismissed. Accordingly, the order of the Appellate Division should be affirmed, with costs.

NOTES AND QUESTIONS

1. *What Is Public Policy?* There appears to be no clear test as to what constitutes a "public policy" that will prevail over an otherwise legally enforceable covenant. Covenants that require the performance of an illegal or unconstitutional act are clearly unenforceable, as is a covenant which prohibits all uses of a particular parcel of land. However, the conduct at issue in the above case — limiting a neighborhood to single-family residences — was neither illegal nor unconstitutional. While at least one court has agreed with the New York Court of Appeals that a covenant that discriminates against group homes violates public policy — *see Westwood Homeowners Ass'n v. Tenhoff*, 745 P.2d 976 (Ariz. Ct. App. 1987) — numerous other courts have concluded that it does not and have allowed the enforcement of such covenants against the operators of group homes. *See Metzner v. Wojdyla*, 886 P.2d 154 (Wash. 1994); *Omega Corp. of Chesterfield v. Malloy*, 319 S.E.2d 728 (Va. 1984); *Hagemann v. Worth*, 782 P.2d 1072 (Wash. Ct. App. 1989); *Shaver v. Hunter*, 626 S.W.2d 574 (Tex. App. 1981).

For another example of a covenant held invalid on public policy grounds, see *Davidson Bros., Inc. v. D. Katz & Sons, Inc.*, 643 A.2d 642 (N.J. Super. Ct. App. Div. 1994), *on remand from same*, 559 A.2d 288 (Del. Ch. 1990) (covenant which prohibited the use of an inner city lot for a supermarket invalidated on public policy grounds.)

2. *The Restatement Approach.* The RESTATEMENT (THIRD) OF PROPERTY (SERVITUDES) (2000) takes an expansive approach to what constitutes public policy. Section 3.1 states that "Servitudes that are invalid because they violate public policy include, but are not limited to" a servitude (1) that is "arbitrary, spiteful, or capricious"; (2) that "unreasonably burdens a fundamental constitutional right"; (3) that imposes an "unreasonable restraint on alienation"; (4) that imposes "an unreasonable restraint on trade or competition"; or (5) that is "unconscionable."

In comment i to Section 3.1, the drafters of the RESTATEMENT describe "public policy concerns" in the following manner.

> Policies favoring privacy and liberty in choice of lifestyle, freedom of religion, freedom of speech and expression, access to the legal system, discouraging bad faith and unfair dealing, encouraging free competition, and socially productive uses of land have been implicated by servitudes. Other policies that become involved may include those protecting family relationships from coercive attempts to disrupt them, and protecting weaker groups in society from servitudes that exclude them from opportunities enjoyed by more fortunate groups to acquire desirable property for housing or access to necessary services.

Whether courts will follow the RESTATEMENT view of public policy limitations remains to be seen.

3. *Restrictions Favoring Single Family Homes.* Covenants restricting occupancy to single families are a standard feature of subdivision covenants. As a general rule they are enforceable. *See, e.g., Omega Corp. v. Malloy*, 319 S.E.2d 728 (Va. 1984). However, on some occasions, courts have avoided the public policy question by interpreting "single family" rather broadly. In *Hill v. Community of Damien of Molokai*, 911 P.2d 861 (N.M. 1996), the New Mexico Supreme Court concluded that a group home for four AIDS patients met the definition of "single-family." Other legal issues pertaining to the operation of group homes are explored in Chapter 10.

[5.] Unreasonable Covenants

NAHRSTEDT v. LAKESIDE VILLAGE CONDOMINIUM ASSOCIATION

California Supreme Court
878 P.2d 1275 (1994)

KENNARD, J.

A homeowner in a 530-unit condominium complex sued to prevent the homeowners association from enforcing a restriction against keeping cats, dogs, and other animals in the condominium development. The owner asserted that the restriction, which was contained in the project's declaration recorded by the condominium project's developer, was "unreasonable" as applied to her because she kept her three cats indoors and because her cats were "noiseless" and "created no nuisance." Agreeing with the premise underlying the owner's complaint, the Court of Appeal concluded that the homeowners association could enforce the restriction only upon proof that plaintiff's cats would be likely to interfere with the right of other homeowners "to the peaceful and quiet enjoyment of their property."

Those of us who have cats or dogs can attest to their wonderful companionship and affection. Not surprisingly, studies have confirmed this effect. But the issue before us is not whether in the abstract pets can have a beneficial effect on humans. Rather, the narrow issue here is whether a pet restriction that is contained in the recorded declaration of a condominium complex is enforceable against the challenge of a homeowner. As we shall explain, the Legislature, in Civil Code Section 1354, has required that courts enforce the covenants, conditions and restrictions contained in the recorded declaration of a common interest development "unless unreasonable."

Because a stable and predictable living environment is crucial to the success of condominiums and other common interest residential developments, and because recorded use restrictions are a primary means of ensuring this stability and predictability, the Legislature in Section 1354 has afforded such restrictions a presumption of validity and has required of challengers that they demonstrate the restriction's "unreasonableness" by the deferential standard applicable to equitable servitudes. Under this standard established by the Legislature, enforcement of a restriction does not depend upon the conduct of a particular condominium owner. Rather, the restriction must be uniformly enforced in the condominium development to which it was intended to apply unless the plaintiff owner can show that the burdens it imposes on affected properties so substantially outweigh the benefits of the restriction that it should not be enforced against any owner. Here, the Court of Appeal did not apply this standard in deciding that plaintiff had stated a claim for declaratory relief. Accordingly, we reverse the judgment of the Court of Appeal and remand for further proceedings consistent with the views expressed in this opinion.

Lakeside Village is a large condominium development in Culver City, Los Angeles County. It consists of 530 units spread throughout 12 separate 3-story buildings. The residents share common lobbies and hallways, in addition to laundry and trash facilities. The Lakeside Village project is subject to certain covenants, conditions and restrictions (hereafter CC & R's) that were included in the developer's declaration recorded with the Los Angeles County Recorder on April 17, 1978, at the inception of the development project. Ownership of a unit includes membership in the project's homeowners association, the Lakeside Village Condominium Association (hereafter Association), the body that enforces the project's CC & R's, including the pet restriction, which provides in relevant part: "No animals (which shall mean dogs and cats), livestock, reptiles or poultry shall be kept in any unit."

In January 1988, plaintiff Natore Nahrstedt purchased a Lakeside Village condominium and moved in with her three cats. When the Association learned of the cats' presence, it demanded their removal and assessed fines against Nahrstedt for each successive month that she remained in violation of the condominium project's pet restriction. Nahrstedt then brought this lawsuit against the Association, its officers, and two of its employees, asking the trial court to invalidate the assessments, to enjoin future assessments, to award damages for violation of her privacy when the Association "peered" into her condominium unit, to award damages for infliction of emotional distress, and to declare the pet restriction "unreasonable" as applied to indoor cats (such as hers) that are not allowed free run of the project's common areas. Nahrstedt also alleged she did not know of the pet restriction when she bought her condominium. The complaint incorporated by reference the grant deed, the declaration of CC & R's, and the condominium plan for the Lakeside Village condominium project.

The Association demurred to the complaint. In its supporting points and authorities, the Association argued that the pet restriction furthers the collective "health, happiness and peace of mind" of persons living in close proximity within the Lakeside Village condominium development, and therefore is reasonable as a matter of law. The trial court sustained the demurrer as to each cause of action and dismissed Nahrstedt's complaint. Nahrstedt appealed.

A divided Court of Appeal reversed the trial court's judgment of dismissal. In the majority's view, the complaint stated a claim for declaratory relief based on its allegations that Nahrstedt's three cats are kept inside her condominium unit and do not bother her neighbors. According to the majority, whether a condominium use restriction is "unreasonable," as that term is used in Section 1354, hinges on the facts of a particular homeowner's case. Thus, the majority reasoned, Nahrstedt would be entitled to declaratory relief if application of the pet restriction in her case would not be reasonable.

On the Association's petition, we granted review to decide when a condominium owner can prevent enforcement of a use restriction that the project's developer has included in the recorded declaration of CC & R's.

As mentioned earlier, under subdivision (a) of section 1354 the use restrictions for a common interest development that are set forth in the recorded declaration are "enforceable equitable servitudes, unless unreasonable." In other words, such restrictions should be enforced unless they are wholly arbitrary, violate a fundamental public policy, or impose a burden on the use of affected land that far outweighs any benefit.

When courts accord a presumption of validity to all such recorded use restrictions and measure them against deferential standards of equitable servitude law, it discourages lawsuits by owners of individual units seeking personal exemptions from the restrictions. This also promotes stability and predictability in two ways. It provides substantial assurance to prospective condominium purchasers that they may rely with confidence on the promises embodied in the project's recorded CC & R's. And it protects all owners in the planned development from unanticipated increases in association fees to fund the defense of legal challenges to recorded restrictions.

How courts enforce recorded use restrictions affects not only those who have made their homes in planned developments, but also the owners associations charged with the fiduciary obligation to enforce those restrictions. When courts treat recorded use restrictions as presumptively valid, and place on the challenger the burden of proving the restriction "unreasonable" under the deferential standards applicable to equitable servitudes, associations can proceed to enforce reasonable restrictive covenants without fear that their actions will embroil them in costly and prolonged legal proceedings. Of course, when an association determines that a unit owner has violated a use restriction, the association must do so in good faith, not in an arbitrary or capricious manner, and its enforcement procedures must be fair and applied uniformly.

There is an additional beneficiary of legal rules that are protective of recorded use restrictions: the judicial system. Fewer lawsuits challenging such restrictions will be brought, and those that are filed may be disposed of more expeditiously, if the rules courts use in evaluating such restrictions are clear, simple, and not subject to exceptions based on the peculiar circumstances or hardships of individual residents in condominiums and other shared-ownership developments.

Contrary to the dissent's accusations that the majority's decision "fray[s]" the "social fabric," we are of the view that our social fabric is best preserved if courts uphold and enforce solemn written instruments that embody the expectations of the parties rather than treat them as "worthless paper" as the dissent would. Our social fabric is founded on the stability of expectation and obligation that arises from the consistent enforcement of the terms of deeds, contracts, wills, statutes, and other writings. To allow one person to escape obligations under a written instrument upsets the expectations of all the other parties governed by that instrument (here, the owners of the other 529 units) that the instrument will be uniformly and predictably enforced.

The salutary effect of enforcing written instruments and the statutes that apply to them is particularly true in the case of the declaration of a common interest development. As we have discussed, common interest developments are a more intensive and efficient form of land use that greatly benefits society and expands opportunities for home ownership. In turn, however, a common interest development creates a community of property owners living in close proximity to each other, typically much closer than if each owned his or her separate plot of land. This proximity is feasible, and units in a common interest development are marketable, largely because the recorded declaration of CC & R's assures owners of a stable and predictable environment.

Under the holding we adopt today, the reasonableness or unreasonableness of a condominium use restriction that the Legislature has made subject to section 1354 is to be determined not by reference to facts that are specific to the objecting homeowner, but by reference to the common interest development as a whole. As we have explained, when, as here, a restriction is contained in the declaration of the common interest development and is recorded with the county recorder, the restriction is presumed to be reasonable and will be enforced uniformly against all residents of the common interest development unless the restriction is arbitrary, imposes burdens on the use of lands it affects that substantially outweigh the restriction's benefits to the development's residents, or violates a fundamental public policy.

We conclude, as a matter of law, that the recorded pet restriction of the Lakeside Village condominium development prohibiting cats or dogs but allowing some other pets is not arbitrary, but is rationally related to health, sanitation and noise concerns legitimately held by residents of a high-density condominium project such as Lakeside Village, which includes 530 units in 12 separate 3-story buildings.

We reverse the judgment of the Court of Appeal, and remand for further proceedings consistent with the views expressed in this opinion.

ARABIAN, JUSTICE, dissenting.

"There are two means of refuge from the misery of life: music and cats."

I respectfully dissent. While technical merit may commend the majority's analysis, its application to the facts presented reflects a narrow, indeed chary, view of the law that eschews the human spirit in favor of arbitrary efficiency. In my view, the resolution of this case well illustrates the conventional wisdom, and fundamental truth, of the Spanish proverb, "It is better to be a mouse in a cat's mouth than a man in a lawyer's hands."

I find the provision known as the "pet restriction" contained in the covenants, conditions, and restrictions (CC & R's) governing the Lakeside Village project patently arbitrary and unreasonable within the meaning of Civil Code Section 1354. Beyond dispute, human beings have long enjoyed an abiding and cherished association with their household animals. Given the substantial benefits derived from pet ownership, the undue burden on the use of property imposed on condominium owners who can maintain pets within the confines of their units without creating a nuisance or disturbing the quiet enjoyment of others substantially outweighs whatever meager utility the restriction may serve in the abstract. It certainly does not promote "health, happiness [or] peace of mind" commensurate with its tariff on the quality of life for those who value the companionship of animals. Worse, it contributes to the fraying of our social fabric.

From the statement of the facts through the conclusion, the majority's analysis gives scant acknowledgment to any of the foregoing considerations but simply takes refuge behind the "presumption of validity" now accorded all CC & R's irrespective of subject matter. They never objectively scrutinize defendants' blandishments of protecting "health and happiness" or realistically assess the substantial impact on affected unit owners and their use of their property. As this court has often recognized, "deference is not abdication." *People v. McDonald*, 690 P.2d 709 (Cal. 1984). Regardless of how limited an inquiry is permitted under applicable law, it must nevertheless be made.

Here, such inquiry should start with an evaluation of the interest that will suffer upon enforcement of the pet restriction. In determining the "burden on the use of land," due recognition must be given to the fact that this particular "use" transcends the impersonal and mundane matters typically regulated by condominium CC & R's, such as whether someone can place a doormat in the hallway or hang a towel on the patio rail or have food in the pool area, and reaches the very quality of life of hundreds of owners and residents. Nonetheless, the majority accept uncritically the proffered justification of preserving "health and happiness" and essentially consider only one criterion to determine enforceability: was the restriction recorded in the original declaration? If so, it is "presumptively valid," unless in violation of public policy. Given the application of the law to the facts alleged and by an inversion of relative interests, it is difficult to hypothesize any CC & R's that would not pass muster. Such sanctity has not been afforded any writing save the commandments delivered to Moses on Mount Sinai, and they were set in stone, not upon worthless paper.

Our true task in this turmoil is to strike a balance between the governing rights accorded a condominium association and the individual freedom of its members. To fulfill that function, a reviewing court must view with a skeptic's eye restrictions driven by fear, anxiety, or intolerance. In any community, we do not exist in vacuo. There are many annoyances which we tolerate because not to do so would be repressive and place the freedom of others at risk.

In contravention, the majority's failure to consider the real burden imposed by the pet restriction unfortunately belittles and trivializes the interest at stake here. Pet ownership substantially enhances the quality of life for those who desire it. When others are not only undisturbed by, but completely unaware of, the presence of pets being enjoyed by their neighbors, the balance of benefit and burden is rendered disproportionate and unreasonable, rebutting any presumption of validity. Their view, shorn of grace and guiding philosophy, is devoid of the humanity that must temper the interpretation and application of all laws, for in a civilized society that is the source of their authority. As judicial architects of the rules of life, we better serve when we construct halls of harmony rather than walls of wrath.

I would affirm the judgment of the Court of Appeal.

NOTES AND QUESTIONS

1. *Common Interest Communities.* One of the most significant developments in American housing patterns in the final quarter of the 20th century was the rise of the common interest community, often referred to as a "CIC." In 2007, more than 50 million Americans lived in such "communities."

As defined by the RESTATEMENT (THIRD) OF PROPERTY (SERVITUDES) § 6.2 (2000), common interest communities (CICs) are real estate developments or neighborhoods in which individual units are burdened by a servitude that requires either (1) payment for the maintenance of property held in common or (2) payments to an association which either maintains the common property or enforces other servitudes burdening the property. (To qualify as a CIC, unit owners must also be unable to avoid the obligations under the servitude by nonuse or withdrawal.) Such developments ordinarily include boards to which the rule-making authority is delegated. More commonly, the term is used to describe developments whose residents are subject to even more controls than the RESTATEMENT definition requires.

Common interest communities normally include planned unit developments (like so-called "gated communities"), condominiums, and cooperatives. Each owner occupies a distinct dwelling unit, and the entire community is governed by a private ownership association. Membership in the association is mandatory, and all members are obligated to comply with the restriction. All units are subject to comprehensive restrictions applicable only within the development, and common areas are owned by the unit owners as concurrent tenants or by the association. The association rules derive their authority from the law of restrictive covenants. For recent discussion of the common interest community generally, see Fennell, *Contracting Communities*, 2004 U. ILL. L. REV. 829; SPRANKLING, UNDERSTANDING PROPERTY LAW 595–606 (2d ed. 2007).

2. *The Reasonableness Test.* It is frequently stated that covenants must be "reasonable" to be valid. *Hidden Harbour Estates, Inc. v. Basso*, 393 So. 2d 637, 640 (Fla. Dist. Ct. App. 1981); *Ryan v. Baptiste*, 565 S.W.2d 196, 198 (Mo. Ct. App. 1978). However, as the above case illustrates, courts will not ordinarily invalidate a covenant on reasonableness grounds unless it appears to run afoul of some larger public policy concern, especially if the covenant was one that was included in the original declaration of covenants. This is true even if the state has, like California, a statute which specifically provides that unreasonable covenants cannot be enforced. Cal. Civ. Code § 1354. The standard rationale behind this "presumption of reasonableness" is that the property owners were aware of the restrictions (or should have been) at the time they purchased their unit, and if they believed that the restrictions were unreasonable, they should have purchased elsewhere. As a consequence, it is extremely difficult to challenge the reasonableness of a conduct or land use restriction in place when the initial sale of units begins.

The RESTATEMENT (THIRD) OF PROPERTY (SERVITUDES) appears to endorse this approach. Section 3.1 states: "A servitude created as provided in Chapter 2 [Creation of Servitudes] is valid unless it is illegal or unconstitutional or violates public policy." The section does not use the term "unreasonable" except in regard to covenants that restrain trade or the right to alienate. Section 3.7 does declare that an "unconscionable" servitude is invalid, but the examples of unconscionable covenants provided in the illustrations are limited to covenants that provide a continuing financial benefit to the developer. None of the illustrations deals with what could be referred to as "unreasonable" restrictions on the conduct or land use choices outside of the developer-benefit context.

3. *Rules Subsequently Adopted.* It is now quite common for developers to create homeowners or unit-owners associations with the authority to make rules for the benefit of the association at a later time. This is particularly true in the case of common interest communities. When an association has the power to adopt news

rules not spelled out in the original documents, rules that significantly affect the use of the property may not come into effect until after the property is purchased. While it is true that the purchaser has notice that the board had the power to make binding rules in the future, the individual buyer has no way of knowing what those rules will be.

As a principle of contract law, however, he or she is entitled to assume that the board will adopt only "reasonable" rules. As a consequence of the *post hoc* quality of such rules, courts appear more inclined to scrutinize the reasonableness of restrictions if they are not included in the original declaration but are later adopted pursuant to rule-making authority. In *Nahrstedt*, for example, the court acknowledged that a more rigorous standard of review would be appropriate if the rule in question had been adopted after the plaintiff had purchased her unit.

In *Ridgely Condominium Association v. Smyrnioudis*, 660 A.2d 942 (Md. Ct. Spec. App. 1995), a Maryland court was asked to consider the reasonableness of a rule adopted by the membership of a condominium association in Baltimore. The structure involved was a multi-story building whose units were limited to residential use except for seven units on the first floor which were used as professional offices. Concern over the presence of strangers in the building prompted the association membership to adopt a new rule prohibiting clients from entering the professional office via the lobby. (It was possible to enter the offices through little used external doors.) The court found that the owners of the first floor units had had no way of anticipating the adoption of such a rule and that the rule itself was "arbitrary or capricious" and bore "no relationship to the health, happiness, and enjoyment of life of the various unit owners." Consequently, the court refused to enforce the rule on the grounds that it was "unreasonable." In contrast, the Hawaii Court of Appeals recently upheld a subsequently adopted rule that allowed unit owners in a condominium development to expand their unit outward into common areas, even though many of the unit owners objected to this new policy. *Lee v. Puamana Community Ass'n*, 128 P.3d 874 (Haw. 2006).

Was the rule in *Ridgely* really "unreasonable"? Why isn't the concern about strangers entering the building through the lobby and then burglarizing residential units in the building a legitimate concern? Does it make sense to have one standard of reasonableness for rules included in the declaration of covenants and another for subsequently adopted rules?

4. *Rules that Apply to Some but Not All Unit Members*. A number of courts have been unwilling to enforce subsequently adopted rules that apply only to a minority of unit owners. Obviously, these ruling reflect a concern that a minority of unit owners ought not to be singled out for a special burden. *See Boyles v. Hausmann*, 517 N.W.2d 610 (Neb. 1994); *Walton v. Jaskiewicz*, 563 A.2d 382 (Md. 1989); *Ridge Park Home Owners v. Pena*, 544 P.2d 278 (N.M. 1975); *Montoya v. Barreras*, 473 P.2d 363 (N.M. 1970). On a related issue, the RESTATEMENT (THIRD) OF PROPERTY states that unanimous unit owner approval is required for any amendment to the covenants which "would prohibit or materially restrict the use of occupancy of, or behavior within, individually owned lots or units, or to change the basis for allocating voting rights or assessments among community members." RESTATEMENT (THIRD) OF PROPERTY: SERVITUDES § 6.10(3)(a)–(b).

5. *Theories of Consent.* As mentioned above, the enforcement of restrictions imposed on property by covenants is usually justified with the argument that residents freely made the choice to buy into a particular community and that the restrictions were a matter of public record at the time of purchase. Is this argument persuasive? The traditional answer was "yes," on the grounds that the decision to join such a community was purely voluntary. *See* Ellickson, *Cities and Homeowners Associations*, 130 U. Pa. L. Rev. 1519, 1523 (1982); Epstein, *Covenants and Constitutions*, 73 Cornell L. Rev. 906, 914–16 (1998).

However, in recent years, some critics have insisted that the "consent" in these situations is often less than voluntary. Prof. James Winokur has observed that "as more and more residential properties are bound by servitude regimes, and standard forms proliferate, the option to reject the model of servitude regimes prevailing in a given area becomes less realistic for substantial segments of the real estate market, particularly for those buyers who wish to enjoy either suburban or condominium living." Winokur, *The Mixed Blessings of Promissory Servitudes: Toward Optimizing Economic Utility, Individual Liberty and Personal Identity*, 1989 Wis. L. Rev. 1, 58. Proponents of the view that tight housing markets and the absence of less intensively regulated alternatives deprive would-be home or condominium purchasers of meaningful choices include: Alexander, *Freedom, Coercion and the Law of Servitudes*, 73 Cornell L. Rev. 883, 900–02 (1988); same, *Dilemmas of Group Autonomy: Residential Associations and Community*, 75 Cornell L. Rev. 1, 60 (1989); Brower, *Communities Within The Community: Consent, Constitutionalism and Other Failures of Legal Theory in Residential Associations*, 7 J. Land Use & Envtl. L. 203, 246–50 (1992); Frug, *Cities and Homeowners Associations: A Reply*, 130 U. Pa. L. Rev. 1589, 1589–90 (1982).

6. *Developer Rights.* Courts and legislatures do seem particularly concerned that developers not be able to manipulate the covenant enforcement process to make sweetheart deals for themselves or to retain too much authority over buyers. For examples of this attitude, see *Point E. Mgt. Corp. v. Point E. One Condominium Corp*, 282 So. 2d 628 (Fla. 1973) (dissenting opinion); *Kenney v. Morgan*, 325 A.2d 419 (Md. Ct. Spec. App. 1998 1974); *Davis v. Huey*, 620 S.W.2d 561 (Tex. 1981); *Wright v. Cypress Shores Dev. Co.*, 413 So. 2d 1115 (Ala. 1982); and Florida Condominium Act, Fla. Laws 1976, Ch. 76-222 § 3. In a similar spirit, to preclude developers from exerting protracted control over association governance, the Restatement (Third) of Property (Servitudes) § 6.19(2) (2000) provides that "the developer has a duty to transfer the common property to the association or its members and to turn over control of the association . . . [a]fter the time reasonably necessary to protect its interests in completing and marketing the project."

7. In an effort to create a perfect residential environment, common interest communities have frequently adopted quite specific rules, the enforcement of which sometimes produce results that border on the comic. Feighan, *Fight over Rights Gets Unneighborly, Lawsuits Grow as Homeowner Groups Enforce Rules*, Detroit News, Dec. 22, 2000, at A1. For example, in Atlanta, Georgia, a couple was fined $25 per day by its homeowners association because their lawn was green during the winter. An applicable servitude required that residents plant Bermuda sod in their front yards, which turns a telltale dormant brown during the winter. In Charlotte, North Carolina, a condominium owner was fined $75 per day because his dog

exceeded the prescribed weight limitations. The ultimate $11,000 in accrued fines forced him into bankruptcy. When a Houston, Texas resident, while undergoing treatment for a brain tumor, failed to pay $600 in dues, the association brought suit and, when he failed to pay on time, sold his $55,000 home at a forced sale for $17,000. (Fortunately for the ailing resident, the foreclosure was eventually voided.) For this and other seemingly absurd penalties imposed by homeowners associations, see Franzese, *Does it Take a Village? Privatization, Patterns of Restrictiveness and the Demise of Community*, 47 VILL. L. REV. 553, 574 (2002).

In spite of the legal difficulties facing those who attempt to overturn restrictions on "reasonableness" or public policy grounds, residents are becoming increasingly willing to take their homeowners associations to court. *See, e.g.*, Vanderpool, *But Isn't This My Yard? Revolt Against Neighborhood Rules*, CHRISTIAN SCI. MONITOR, Aug. 18, 1999 at 2; Trognitz, *Yes, It's My Castle*, A.B.A. J., June 2000 at 30. A 1995 survey of 600 homeowners associations revealed that more than 44% of the boards had been threatened with lawsuits during the previous year. Judd, *The Rise of the New Walled Cities*, *in* SPATIAL PRACTICES 158 (Liggett & Perry eds., 1995).

8. *Subsequent Developments in* Nahrstedt. Six years after the above decision, Natore Nahrstedt and Justice Arabian achieved a measure of vindication when the California legislature amended the state's civil code to require all "common interest developments" to permit their residents to keep at least one pet. For purposes of this provision, "pet" was defined to include "any domesticated bird, cat, dog, or aquatic animal kept within an aquarium." The statute took effect on January 1, 2001. Cal. Civ. Code § 1360.5.

[6.] Procedural Fairness

RISS v. ANGEL

Washington Supreme Court
934 P.2d 669 (1997)

MADSEN, J.

Members of the Mercia Heights homeowners association rejected Plaintiffs' building plans under a consent to construction clause in the subdivision's restrictive covenants. The trial court held that the association's rejection of the plans was unreasonable and arbitrary. The Court of Appeals affirmed and the homeowners sought review. We likewise affirm.

In 1992, Plaintiffs William and Carolyn Riss purchased lot 6 in Mercia Heights, a residential subdivision in Clyde Hill. The subdivision is subject to restrictive covenants recorded by the developer, which provide that new construction and remodeling must be approved by the Mercia Corporation, originally a nonprofit corporation consisting of the homeowners in the development. The corporation was administratively dissolved in 1985, and the subdivision is now governed by the homeowners as an unincorporated homeowners association which acts through an elected board of directors. The Mercia development includes many homes built in the 1950s which are one level or split-level ramblers. Many of the lots, which vary in shape, size, and slope, have distant views of Lake Washington, the Seattle skyline, and the Olympic Mountains.

The covenants, in existence since the 1950's, contain express restrictions on minimum square footage of residences, minimum setback requirements, and maximum roof heights, providing for homes with a minimum of 1,400 square feet and roof lines no higher than 20 feet above the highest point of finished grade on the lot. Paragraph 6 of the covenants provides that:

> As to improvements, construction and alterations in Mercia Heights . . . Mercia Corporation shall have the right to refuse to approve the design, finishing or painting of any construction or alteration which is not suitable or desirable in said addition for any reason, aesthetic or otherwise [considering] harmony with other dwellings . . . and any and all other factors which in their opinion shall affect the desirability or suitability of such proposed structure, improvement or alterations.

The covenants give the board of directors enforcement power and the authority to approve or disapprove construction or remodeling. The covenants provide that any lot owner may sue to enforce the covenants and the prevailing party is entitled to reasonable attorney fees and costs. In 1990, the covenants were amended to provide that a property owner aggrieved by a board decision may appeal to the Mercia homeowners, who will meet and decide by majority vote, with proxies allowed, whether to overturn the board's decision. Another amendment proposed in 1990 would have limited the height of new construction to the height of the existing dwelling on the lot unless written approval of a higher roof line was granted by the association. This amendment failed.

Plaintiffs wanted to remove the existing dwelling on lot 6 and construct a one-story home with a daylight basement. Plaintiffs submitted their plans to the homeowners' designee for covenant compliance and review. They were told that except in minor respects their plan satisfied the covenants. Plaintiffs knew the covenants required approval of the board and the homeowners.

Following November meetings where the board and homeowners discussed Plaintiffs' proposed plans, an open board meeting was held December 9, 1992, to consider Plaintiffs' plans. Prior to this meeting, the president of the homeowners association and his wife took photographs holding poles in front of various Mercia residences to show how high 23 feet was as referenced against existing dwellings. A montage of these photographs was presented at the meeting. The trial court found this photographic study lacked precision, failed to take into account either the height restriction of the covenants or the City of Clyde Hill's height restrictions (measured from the original topography), and were inaccurate and misleading as to the effect of Plaintiffs' proposed residence. Plaintiffs' plans called for a roof height within the maximum restrictive covenant height of 20 feet above the highest point of finished grade on a lot; the proposed residence would have a roof height 11 12 feet above the highest point of finished grade, some five feet higher than the existing structure. Also prior to the meeting, another Board member sent a letter to all other lot owners expressing concerns with Plaintiffs' plans and, the trial court found, inaccurately representing the height and square footage of the proposed residence.

Following the meeting, Plaintiffs were notified that the Board had rejected their plans. The Board's rejection was based upon the height of the structure, its bulk (width and depth), the design exterior finish, and proximity to neighboring houses. The letter notifying Plaintiffs of the rejection also explained that the Board was "not comfortable with giving specific guidelines at this time," and that "an arbitrary disapproval without any guidance would not be constructive." The Board said it would hire an architect to assist in describing guidelines that would allow Plaintiffs to design and construct a home on their property.

The architect the Board then consulted calculated the mass of the proposed home by adding square footage of the exterior surface walls when viewed in a plane, excluding the courtyard. This method was not communicated to Plaintiffs, and no comparison of their proposed home to other homes was made using this method. The architect recommended that a volume comparison be done, but none was made. On December 30, 1992, the Board president wrote to Plaintiffs, advising them of specific guidelines to aid in redesigning the house. The first required the roof line to remain at the same level as the existing structure to preserve views. The Board had never performed any view study or analysis, and Plaintiffs' evidence showed the proposed residence would not appreciably block views. The second guideline called for a 20 percent reduction in width and depth. Plaintiffs say this would result in a residence smaller than the existing residence. The sixth guideline concerned the width of the proposed residence; however, the proposed residence was 5 feet narrower than the existing residence. The remaining guidelines are not the subject of disagreement.

Testimony at trial also established that members of the homeowners association were concerned that lot 6 was special, or more visible to those entering the community.

Plaintiffs appealed the Board's decision to the homeowners. On January 2, 1993, the Board president wrote to the other Board members, urging them to assure a large turnout for the vote on Plaintiffs' appeal, or to vote by proxy, so that Plaintiffs would not be able to sway a small turnout. On January 8, 1993, the Board president wrote a letter to the owners advocating a vote against approval of Plaintiffs' plans at the January 18, 1993, meeting set to consider Plaintiffs' appeal. The homeowners voted against approval of Plaintiffs' plans. Defendants state that 24 of the 34 lot owners cast votes themselves or by proxy, and that the vote was 21-3 to reject Plaintiffs' proposal.

Plaintiffs brought this action against the homeowners individually, contending that the covenants were not enforceable, and, alternatively, that their plans complied with the covenants and the Board and association acted unreasonably in rejecting their plans.

The court ruled the covenants are binding, but it found the association acted unreasonably in rejecting Plaintiffs' plans. The court concluded that the covenants as written are reasonable, but do not permit the homeowners to impose restrictions more burdensome than those expressed in the covenants. Specifically, the court said that the homeowners could not restrict size, height, and proximity to neighbors beyond the minimum square footage and the maximum height restrictions, and the setback requirements set out in the covenants. The court concluded that paragraph

6's discretionary authority to reject proposals on the basis of design cannot be read as including authority to limit "bulk," i.e., size or scale. The court concluded the association does have wide discretion to control design aesthetics, which the court reasoned included authority to reject, for example, a geodome, A-frame, or Tudor castle. The court also rejected the homeowners' concerns that lot 6 is special, saying that if special restrictions on a specific lot were desired, the covenants must clearly say so.

The court also concluded that the association acted unreasonably because it rejected Plaintiffs' plans without comparing the width and depth of other homes in the neighborhood to Plaintiffs' proposed residence, failed to thoroughly investigate, and relied upon inaccurate information.

The court ruled in favor of the association, however, on its rejection of the proposed exterior. The court entered judgment declaring that Plaintiffs could build their proposed home, provided that they change the exterior finish to one reasonably specified by the association. Following trial on damages, which had been bifurcated from the liability issues, the court awarded Plaintiffs delay damages of $103,989.85, and attorney fees and costs of $102,250.31. The judgment was entered against the individual defendant homeowners jointly and severally.

The Court of Appeals affirmed. Appellants then petitioned for review, which this court granted.

Covenants providing for consent before construction or remodeling have been widely upheld, even where they vest broad discretion in a homeowners association or a committee or board through which it acts, so long as the authority to consent is exercised reasonably and in good faith. *E.g. Hannula v. Hacienda Homes, Inc.*, 211 P.2d 302 (Cal. 1949); *Rhue v. Cheyenne Homes, Inc.*, 449 P.2d 361 (Col. 1969). The Court of Appeals has similarly reasoned that consent to construction covenants must be reasonable and reasonably exercised to be valid.

Approval standards like "conformity and harmony of external design and general quality with the existing standards of the neighborhood" and "location of the building with respect to topography and finished ground elevations" have been upheld where covenants with such standards clearly established that discretion to approve had been granted. However, such a standard will not be enforced where it has been applied so inconsistently as to result in a wide variety of buildings. *See, e.g., Town & Country Estates, Ass'n v. Slater*, 740 P.2d 668, 669 (Mont. 1987) ("harmony of external design" too vague to be enforceable where development was a cacophony of styles).

We agree with the majority of courts that covenants providing for consent before construction or remodeling will be upheld so long as the authority to consent is exercised reasonably and in good faith. However, several courts have held that a consent to construction covenant cannot operate to place restrictions on a lot which are more burdensome than those imposed by the specific covenants. [Citations omitted.] We agree. If covenants include specific restrictions as to some aspect of design or construction, the document manifests the parties' intent that the specific restriction apply rather an inconsistent standard under a general consent to construction covenant.

In this case, the specific size, setback, and height requirements are in terms of minimums and maximums. The consent to construction covenant provides that the Board is to consider "harmony with other dwellings . . . the effect on outlook of adjoining or neighboring property and any and all other factors which in their opinion shall affect the desirability or suitability of such proposed structure, improvement or alterations." We construe these covenants to mean that the minimums must be satisfied, i.e., the Board has no discretion to permit anything smaller than a 1,400 square foot house or one having a height over 20 feet above the highest finished grade on the lot, but the Board does have discretion, for example, as to maximum size. This interpretation accords with the plain and ordinary language used, and rests on the premise that the specific covenants are not inconsistent with exercise of discretion as to size and height so long as the specific minimums and maximums are satisfied.

Moreover, we disagree with the trial court's conclusion that approval of "design" refers only to matters other than placement on the lot, size, and height in this set of covenants. "Design" commonly involves the whole of a structure, including size, configuration and height. Accordingly, the homeowners association had discretion to consider size, height, and proximity to neighbors in deciding whether to approve Plaintiffs' proposed residence.

The homeowners argue they acted in good faith and therefore cannot be held to have violated the covenants. The trial court did not enter findings or conclusions on the good or bad faith of the homeowners. Regardless of the good or bad faith of the homeowners, however, a decision under a consent to construction covenant must be reasonable. In examining whether rejection of a proposal is reasonable, courts have identified a number of factors which demonstrate unreasonable decisionmaking. Among other things, courts have found decisions unreasonable where there was no evidence in the record as to external design of any other structures in the subdivision aside from the applicant's residence and the record showed merely conclusory statements of the chairman of an architectural control committee that the proposed residence was not harmonious with surrounding structures. Also unreasonable was the failure to take neighbors' views into consideration as required, evidenced in part by an architectural control committee's failure to even view the site when deliberating on approval of an applicant's proposed addition. *Leonard v. Stoebling*, 728 P.2d 1358 (Nev. 1986). Further, unreasonable rejection of a building plan was found where there were two modern houses in a predominantly traditional subdivision, the applicant's nontraditionally styled home was not detrimental to the neighborhood, and the grantor would have approved the plans but for objections of neighbors whose houses were not depreciated in value by the building of the house. *Donaghue v. Prynnwood Corp.*, 255 N.E.2d 326, 329 (Mass. 1970).

In this case, the Board's decision reflected in the letter to Plaintiffs was in conclusory language about height, bulk, and proximity. An architect was consulted only after the decision was made. Three of the specific guidelines from the Board reflect unreasonable decisionmaking (reduction in roofline to preserve views where views were not appreciably affected by the proposed structure, reduction in size to less than the existing structure, and reduction in width to reflect the shapes of other homes where the proposed structure was fine but narrower than the existing structure).

Although view was allegedly a major concern, there is no evidence that the Board reasonably assessed the impact of Plaintiffs' proposed structure. Instead, the homeowners were presented with a misleading photo montage about the impact of Plaintiffs' plans. There is no evidence the Board visited the site, much less with an eye to neighbors' views or privacy. There is no evidence in the record that the Board made any objective comparisons with existing homes to compare size and height, though those were major reasons for rejecting the proposed plans. The trial court's finding that the Board president's photo montage was inaccurate and misleading is supported by the evidence. Its finding that another board member wrote a letter to homeowners inaccurately stating the height and size of the proposed structure is also supported by the evidence. While the height stated in this letter, a ridge height of 25 feet, was taken from structural plans, that height had nothing to do with the covenant restriction based upon measurement from the highest finished grade of the lot. These lobbying efforts by board members demonstrate less than a fair assessment of Plaintiffs' proposed structure.

Objections of neighbors should not be discouraged — that is often how restrictive covenants are enforced — but two of the board members inaccurately representing the impact of the structure is not part of a reasonable decisionmaking process. The trial court correctly concluded that the homeowners unreasonably and arbitrarily rejected Plaintiff's proposed building plans.

We hold that a homeowners association may not impose restrictions under a general consent to construction covenant which are more burdensome than provided for by specific objective restrictive covenants. Under the covenants at issue here, the homeowners had authority to consider size, height and proximity when considering approval of Plaintiffs' building plans under the general consent to construction covenant. However, the association's decision was unreasonable and arbitrary and in violation of the covenants because it was made without adequate investigation and was based upon inaccurate information. We affirm the trial court's determination that Plaintiffs may build their proposed home provided that a natural exterior finish reasonably approved by the association is used.

[The dissent of Justice Sanders is omitted.]

NOTES AND QUESTIONS

1. *Standards of Review.* In addition to having the power to enforce existing rules and adopt new ones, homeowners association boards are frequently given discretionary authority to approve proposals for new uses of property or to grant exceptions to the regulations imposed by the covenants. In such situations, what, if any, limits apply to the board's discretion?

In *Rhue v. Cheyenne Homes*, 449 P.2d 361 (Colo. 1969), an early case addressing this question, the Colorado Supreme Court ruled that to be valid, the decisions of the architectural review commission "must be reasonable and made in good faith and must not be arbitrary or capricious." For more than three decades, the "reasonableness" standard has been widely applied to the administrative processes of homeowners associations, condominium boards, and like entities.

While the standard articulated in *Rhue* has been widely adopted, there has been considerable disagreement as to what types of conduct are reasonable and to what extent courts should scrutinize the actions of private boards and commissions to determine whether or not they acted in a reasonable fashion. Although the Washington Supreme Court found that the architectural review committee and the homeowners association had acted unreasonably in the above case, a year earlier the Oregon Supreme Court held that an architectural review committee's decisions were nonreviewable in situations where the covenants gave it the broad discretion and the unlimited authority to make such decisions. *Valenti v. Hopkins*, 926 P.2d 813 (Or. 1996).

Which approach is preferable? On the one hand, judicial scrutiny of everyday decisions of a homeowners association often seems unduly intrusive and a waste of public resources. On the other, a policy of complete deference poses the risk of unchecked private oppression of one private group by another, or at least a pattern of arbitrary behavior. Moreover, when a court decides to examine the challenged behavior, how does it decide what is reasonable? In *Cohen v. Kite Hill Community Ass'n*, 142 Cal. App. 3d 642 (1983), the court defined reasonableness as "a fiduciary duty to act in good faith and to avoid arbitrary action." Is this the standard used in *Riss v. Angel*?

2. *Architectural Review*. What makes the decision of an architectural review commission unreasonable? The RESTATEMENT (THIRD) OF PROPERTY (SERVITUDES) § 6.13(1)(c) (2000) states that an association is required "to act reasonably in the exercise of its discretionary powers including rule-making, enforcement, and *design-control powers*" (emphasis added) but provides no specific guidance. If none of its members were architects, would its decision be unreasonable *per se*? (The case law suggests that the answer is no. *See Heath v. Uraga*, 24 P.3d 413 (Wash. Ct. App. 2001).) Is architectural review even a legitimate matter for an equitable servitude, or is it a matter too subjective to be enforced in equity? If a review commission's sole concern is that the introduction of an unconventional design will result in lower property values for existing units, is the denial of the unconventional design a reasonable or unreasonable decision? The legal aspects of these questions are addressed in Costonis, *Law and Aesthetics: A Critique and a Reformulation of the Dilemmas*, 80 MICH. L. REV. 355 (1982), and Karp, *The Evolving Meaning of Aesthetics in Land-Use Regulation*, 15 COLUM. J. ENVTL. L. 307 (1990).

3. *The Business Judgment Rule*. Some courts and commentators have argued that the "reasonableness" standard is too easy to satisfy. In its place, they have endorsed the use of the "business judgment rule," which imposes a higher standard of accountability on members of homeowners association boards and related entities. Under the business judgment rule, association board members have a duty to act in accord with the good faith exercise of business judgment, akin to the standard that is applied to corporate governance models. *See, e.g., Levandusky v. One Fifth Ave. Apartment Corp.*, 553 N.E.2d 1317 (N.Y. 1990); *Dockside Ass'n v. Detyens*, 362 S.E.2d 874 (S.C. 1987); *Lamden v. LaJolla Shores Clubdominium Homeowners Ass'n*, 980 P.2d 940 (Cal. 1999). The RESTATEMENT (THIRD) OF PROPERTY (SERVITUDES) § 6.13 (2000) adopts a somewhat expanded version of the "reasonableness" standard, but rejects the business judgment rule. *Id.* at cmt. b.

Critics of the contemporary regime have offered a variety of proposed alternatives. For an argument that courts should examine residential association regulations of all types through a two-step system: a "procedural, ultra vires analysis" followed by a "public policy review which candidly considers substantive values," see Brower, *Communities Within the Community: Consent, Constitutionalism, and Other Failures of Legal Theory in Residential Associations*, 7 J. LAND USE & ENVTL. L. 203 (1992). For an argument for the use of a governance system that emphasizes participatory structures and decentralized authority, see Drewes, *Note, Putting the "Community" Back in Common Interest Communities: A Proposal for Participation-Enhancing Procedural Review*, 101 COLUM. L. REV. 314 (2001). Could judicial review be avoided entirely by the inclusion of a clause in the governing articles obliging owners to submit to arbitration in lieu of recourse to the courts? Would this be a better system?

On the general issue of standards of review, see Franzese, *Common Interest Communities: Standards of Review and Review of Standards*, 3 WASH. U. J.L. & POL'Y 663 (2000).

4. The right to reasonable procedures is, of course, not limited to decisions of architectural review committees. In *Chateau Village N. Condominium v. Jordan*, 643 P.2d 791 (Colo. Ct. App. 1982), a Colorado appellate court overturned a lower court injunction permanently enjoining the appellant from keeping pets in her condominium unit. Although the condominium declaration gave the Association the authority to prohibit or limit the keeping of animals and its administrative rules and regulations forbade pets, the regulations also contained a provision that permitted exceptions to the general rule by the express permission in writing of the Board of Managers. When Ms. Jordan sought permission to keep two cats in her unit, her request was denied on the grounds that the board had a policy of allowing no new pets into the development. The appellate court found that by refusing to even consider her request, the Board had acted "arbitrarily and capriciously" and in excess of its authority and had failed to satisfy the "reasonable and good faith" requirement articulated by the Colorado Supreme Court in *Rhue v. Cheyenne Homes* 13 years earlier.

Although the case was clearly a victory for pet owners, most efforts to invoke *Chateau Village* on behalf of disgruntled condominium residents have been unsuccessful. For example, in *O'Buck v. Cottonwood Village Condominium Ass'n*, 750 P.2d 813 (Alaska 1988), a unit owner unsuccessfully cited the case of *Chateau Village* in an effort to have an association rule banning external television antennae overturned as arbitrary and capricious. In *Noble v. Murphy*, 612 N.E.2d 266 (Mass. Ct. App. 1993), a pet restriction was also upheld. For a recent discussion of the pet issue, in the context of the rights of the disabled, see Huss, *No Pets Allowed: Housing Issues and Companion Animals*, 11 ANIMAL L. 69 (2005).

5. Dissatisfaction with the actions of homeowners association boards have prompted the formation of a support group called "Homeowners Supporting Homeowners in Associations." The group has adopted a purple flamingo as its symbol of solidarity and protest against association overreaching. The organization's founder has a flamingo is his front yard, "just to bug" his homeowners association, and has sold at least 100 of the flamboyant steel birds to other disgruntled residents. The term "No HOA" (meaning, "No Homeowners Association") now appears in real estate ads because, in the words of one broker, "it is a real selling point." *See* Razzi Ru, *House Rules*, KIPLINGER'S PERS. FIN., Sept. 2000 at 88.

Increasing levels of discord have inspired some state legislatures to intervene in the name of consumer protection. In many states, legislation now governs issues such as association and member tort liability, association self-dealing, and the required disclosure of the association structure and powers. *See* Tarlock, *Residential Community Associations and Land Use Controls, in* RESIDENTIAL COMMUNITY ASSOCIATIONS: PRIVATE GOVERNMENTS IN THE INTERGOVERNMENTAL SYSTEM? 75–76 (U.S. Advisory Comm'n on Intergovernmental Relations, ed., 1989).

[B.] CONSTITUTIONAL LIMITATIONS

[1.] Racial Discrimination

SHELLEY v. KRAEMER

United States Supreme Court
334 U.S. 1 (1948)

MR. CHIEF JUSTICE VINSON delivered the opinion of the Court.

These cases present for our consideration questions relating to the validity of court enforcement of private agreements, generally described as restrictive covenants, which have as their purpose the exclusion of persons of designated race or color from the ownership or occupancy of real property. Basic constitutional issues of obvious importance have been raised.

The first of these cases comes to this Court on *certiorari* from the Supreme Court of Missouri. On February 16, 1911, thirty out of a total of thirty-nine owners of property fronting both sides of Labadie Avenue between Taylor Avenue and Cora Avenue in the city of St. Louis, signed an agreement, which was subsequently recorded, providing in part:

> . . . the said property is hereby restricted to the use and occupancy for the term of Fifty (50) years from this date, so that it shall be a condition all the time and whether recited and referred to as [sic] not in subsequent conveyances and shall attach to the land as a condition precedent to the sale of the same, that hereafter no part of said property or any portion thereof shall be, for said term of Fifty-years, occupied by any person not of the Caucasian race, it being intended hereby to restrict the use of said property for said period of time against the occupancy as owners or tenants of any portion of said property for resident or other purpose by people of the Negro or Mongolian Race.

The entire district described in the agreement included fifty-seven parcels of land. The thirty owners who signed the agreement held title to forty-seven parcels, including the particular parcel involved in this case. At the time the agreement was signed, five of the parcels in the district were owned by Negroes. One of those had been occupied by Negro families since 1882, nearly thirty years before the restrictive agreement was executed. The trial court found that owners of seven out of nine homes on the south side of Labadie Avenue, within the restricted district and "in the immediate vicinity" of the premises in question, had failed to sign the restrictive agreement in 1911. At the time this action was brought, four of the premises were occupied by Negroes, and had been so occupied for periods ranging from twenty-three to sixty-three years. A fifth parcel had been occupied by Negroes until a year before this suit was instituted.

On August 11, 1945, pursuant to a contract of sale, petitioners Shelley, who are Negroes, for valuable consideration received from one Fitzgerald a warranty deed to the parcel in question. The trial court found that petitioners had no actual knowledge of the restrictive agreement at the time of the purchase. On October 9, 1945, respondents, as owners of other property subject to the terms of the restrictive covenant, brought suit in the Circuit Court of the city of St. Louis praying that petitioners Shelley be restrained from taking possession of the property and that judgment be entered divesting title out of petitioners Shelley and revesting title in the immediate grantor or in such other person as the court should direct. The trial court denied the requested relief on the ground that the restrictive agreement, upon which respondents based their action, had never become final and complete because it was the intention of the parties to that agreement that it was not to become effective until signed by all property owners in the district, and signatures of all the owners had never been obtained.

The Supreme Court of Missouri sitting en banc reversed and directed the trial court to grant the relief for which respondents had prayed. That court held the agreement effective and concluded that enforcement of its provisions violated no rights guaranteed to petitioners by the Federal Constitution. *Kraemer v. Shelley*, 198 S.W.2d 679 (Mo. 1946). At the time the court rendered its decision, petitioners were occupying the property in question.

[The Court's discussion of the facts of the companion case, *McGhee v. Sipes*, 25 N.W.2d 638 (Mich. 1946), are omitted.]

Petitioners have placed primary reliance on their contentions, first raised in the state courts, that judicial enforcement of the restrictive agreements in these cases has violated rights guaranteed to petitioners by the Fourteenth Amendment of the Federal Constitution and Acts of Congress passed pursuant to that Amendment. Specifically, petitioners urge that they have been denied the equal protection of the laws, deprived of property without due process of law, and have been denied privileges and immunities of citizens of the United States. We pass to a consideration of those issues.

I.

Whether the equal protection clause of the Fourteenth Amendment inhibits judicial enforcement by state courts of restrictive covenants based on race or color is a question which this Court has not heretofore been called upon to consider. Only two cases have been decided by this Court which in any way have involved the enforcement of such agreements. The first of these was the case of *Corrigan v. Buckley*, 271 U.S. 323 (1926). There, suit was brought in the courts of the District of Columbia to enjoin a threatened violation of certain restrictive covenants relating to lands situated in the city of Washington. Relief was granted, and the case was brought here on appeal. It is apparent that that case, which had originated in the federal courts and involved the enforcement of covenants on land located in the District of Columbia, could present no issues under the Fourteenth Amendment; for that Amendment by its terms applies only to the States. Nor was the question of the validity of court enforcement of the restrictive covenants under the Fifth Amendment properly before the Court, as the opinion of this Court specifically recognizes. The only constitutional issue which the appellants had raised in the lower courts, and hence the only constitutional issue before this Court on appeal, was the validity of the covenant agreements as such. This Court concluded that since the inhibitions of the constitutional provisions invoked apply only to governmental action, as contrasted to action of private individuals, there was no showing that the covenants, which were simply agreements between private property owners, were invalid. Accordingly, the appeal was dismissed for want of a substantial question. Nothing in the opinion of this Court, therefore, may properly be regarded as an adjudication on the merits of the constitutional issues presented by these cases, which raise the question of the validity, not of the private agreements as such, but of the judicial enforcement of those agreements.

The second of the cases involving racial restrictive covenants was *Hansberry v. Lee*, 311 U.S. 32 (1940). In that case, petitioners, white property owners, were enjoined by the state courts from violating the terms of a restrictive agreement. This Court reversed the judgment of the state Supreme Court upon the ground that petitioners had been denied due process of law in being held estopped to challenge the validity of the agreement on the theory, accepted by the state court, that the earlier litigation, in which petitioners did not participate, was in the nature of a class suit. In arriving at its result, this Court did not reach the issues presented by the cases now under consideration.

It is well, at the outset, to scrutinize the terms of the restrictive agreements involved in these cases. In the Missouri case, the covenant declares that no part of the affected property shall be "occupied by any person not of the Caucasian race, it being intended hereby to restrict the use of said property . . . against the occupancy as owners or tenants of any portion of said property for resident or other purpose by people of the Negro or Mongolian Race." Not only does the restriction seek to proscribe use and occupancy of the affected properties by members of the excluded class, but as construed by the Missouri courts, the agreement requires that title of any person who uses his property in violation of the restriction shall be divested. [The Court then described the covenant in the Michigan case.]

It cannot be doubted that among the civil rights intended to be protected from discriminatory state action by the Fourteenth Amendment are the rights to acquire, enjoy, own and dispose of property. Equality in the enjoyment of property rights was regarded by the framers of that Amendment as an essential pre-condition to the realization of other basic civil rights and liberties which the Amendment was intended to guarantee. Thus, § 1978 of the Revised Statutes, derived from § 1 of the Civil Rights Act of 1866 which was enacted by Congress while the Fourteenth

Amendment was also under consideration, provides: "All citizens of the United States shall have the same right, in every State and Territory, as is enjoyed by white citizens thereof to inherit, purchase, lease, sell, hold, and convey real and personal property." This Court has given specific recognition to the same principle. *Buchanan v. Warley*, 245 U.S. 60 (1917).

It is likewise clear that restrictions on the right of occupancy of the sort sought to be created by the private agreements in these cases could not be squared with the requirements of the Fourteenth Amendment if imposed by state statute or local ordinance. We do not understand respondents to urge the contrary. In the case of *Buchanan v. Warley, supra*, a unanimous Court declared unconstitutional the provisions of a city ordinance which denied to colored persons the right to occupy houses in blocks in which the greater number of houses were occupied by white persons, and imposed similar restrictions on white persons with respect to blocks in which the greater number of houses were occupied by colored persons. During the course of the opinion in that case, this Court stated: "The Fourteenth Amendment and these statutes enacted in furtherance of its purpose operate to qualify and entitle a colored man to acquire property without state legislation discriminating against him solely because of color."

In *Harmon v. Tyler*, 273 U.S. 668 (1927), a unanimous court, on the authority of *Buchanan v. Warley, supra*, declared invalid an ordinance which forbade any Negro to establish a home on any property in a white community or any white person to establish a home in a Negro community, "except on the written consent of a majority of the persons of the opposite race inhabiting such community or portion of the City to be affected."

The precise question before this Court in both the *Buchanan* and *Harmon* cases involved the rights of white sellers to dispose of their properties free from restrictions as to potential purchasers based on considerations of race or color. But that such legislation is also offensive to the rights of those desiring to acquire and occupy property and barred on grounds of race or color is clear, not only from the language of the opinion in *Buchanan v. Warley, supra*, but from this Court's disposition of the case of *Richmond v. Deans*, 281 U.S. 704 (1930). There, a Negro, barred from the occupancy of certain property by the terms of an ordinance similar to that in the *Buchanan* case, sought injunctive relief in the federal courts to enjoin the enforcement of the ordinance on the grounds that its provisions violated the terms of the Fourteenth Amendment. Such relief was granted, and this Court affirmed, finding the citation of *Buchanan v. Warley, supra*, and *Harmon v. Tyler, supra*, sufficient to support its judgment.

But the present cases, unlike those just discussed, do not involve action by state legislatures or city councils. Here the particular patterns of discrimination and the areas in which the restrictions are to operate, are determined, in the first instance, by the terms of agreements among private individuals. Participation of the State consists in the enforcement of the restrictions so defined. The crucial issue with which we are here confronted is whether this distinction removes these cases from the operation of the prohibitory provisions of the Fourteenth Amendment.

We conclude, therefore, that the restrictive agreements standing alone cannot be regarded as violative of any rights guaranteed to petitioners by the Fourteenth

Amendment. So long as the purposes of those agreements are effectuated by voluntary adherence to their terms, it would appear clear that there has been no action by the State and the provisions of the Amendment have not been violated. *Cf. Corrigan v. Buckley, supra.*

But here there was more. These are cases in which the purposes of the agreements were secured only by judicial enforcement by state courts of the restrictive terms of the agreements. The respondents urge that judicial enforcement of private agreements does not amount to state action; or, in any event, the participation of the State is so attenuated in character as not to amount to state action within the meaning of the Fourteenth Amendment. Finally, it is suggested, even if the States in these cases may be deemed to have acted in the constitutional sense, their action did not deprive petitioners of rights guaranteed by the Fourteenth Amendment. We move to a consideration of these matters.

II.

That the action of state courts and judicial officers in their official capacities is to be regarded as action of the State within the meaning of the Fourteenth Amendment, is a proposition which has long been established by decisions of this Court. In the *Civil Rights Cases*, 109 U.S. 3, 11, 17 (1883), this Court pointed out that the Amendment makes void "State action of every kind" which is inconsistent with the guaranties therein contained, and extends to manifestations of "State authority in the shape of laws, customs, or judicial or executive proceedings." Language to like effect is employed no less than eighteen times during the course of that opinion.

One of the earliest applications of the prohibitions contained in the Fourteenth Amendment to action of state judicial officials occurred in cases in which Negroes had been excluded from jury service in criminal prosecutions by reason of their race or color. These cases demonstrate, also, the early recognition by this Court that state action in violation of the Amendment's provisions is equally repugnant to the constitutional commands whether directed by state statute or taken by a judicial official in the absence of statute. *Strauder v. West Virginia*, 100 U.S. 303 (1880).

The short of the matter is that from the time of the adoption of the Fourteenth Amendment until the present, it has been the consistent ruling of this Court that the action of the States to which the Amendment has reference includes action of state courts and state judicial officials. Although, in construing the terms of the Fourteenth Amendment, differences have from time to time been expressed as to whether particular types of state action may be said to offend the Amendment's prohibitory provisions, it has never been suggested that state court action is immunized from the operation of those provisions simply because the act is that of the judicial branch of the state government.

III.

Against this background of judicial construction, extending over a period of some three-quarters of a century, we are called upon to consider whether enforcement by state courts of the restrictive agreements in these cases may be deemed to be the acts of those States; and, if so, whether that action has denied these petitioners the equal protection of the laws which the Amendment was intended to insure.

We have no doubt that there has been state action in these cases in the full and complete sense of the phrase. The undisputed facts disclose that petitioners were willing purchasers of properties upon which they desired to establish homes. The owners of the properties were willing sellers; and contracts of sale were accordingly consummated. It is clear that but for the active intervention of the state courts, supported by the full panoply of state power, petitioners would have been free to occupy the properties in question without restraint.

These are not cases, as has been suggested, in which the States have merely abstained from action, leaving private individuals free to impose such discriminations as they see fit. Rather, these are cases in which the States have made available to such individuals the full coercive power of government to deny to petitioners, on the grounds of race or color, the enjoyment of property rights in premises which petitioners are willing and financially able to acquire and which the grantors are willing to sell. The difference between judicial enforcement and non-enforcement of the restrictive covenants is the difference to petitioners between being denied rights of property available to other members of the community and being accorded full enjoyment of those rights on an equal footing.

The enforcement of the restrictive agreements by the state courts in these cases was directed pursuant to the common-law policy of the States as formulated by those courts in earlier decisions. In the Missouri case, enforcement of the covenant was directed in the first instance by the highest court of the State after the trial court had determined the agreement to be invalid for want of the requisite number of signatures. The judicial action in each case bears the clear and unmistakable imprimatur of the State. We have noted that previous decisions of this Court have established the proposition that judicial action is not immunized from the operation of the Fourteenth Amendment simply because it is taken pursuant to the state's common-law policy. Nor is the Amendment ineffective simply because the particular pattern of discrimination, which the State has enforced, was defined initially by the terms of a private agreement. State action, as that phrase is understood for the purposes of the Fourteenth Amendment, refers to exertions of state power in all forms. And when the effect of that action is to deny rights subject to the protection of the Fourteenth Amendment, it is the obligation of this Court to enforce the constitutional commands.

We hold that in granting judicial enforcement of the restrictive agreements in these cases, the States have denied petitioners the equal protection of the laws and that, therefore, the action of the state courts cannot stand. We have noted that freedom from discrimination by the States in the enjoyment of property rights was among the basic objectives sought to be effectuated by the framers of the Fourteenth Amendment. That such discrimination has occurred in these cases is clear. Because of the race or color of these petitioners they have been denied rights of ownership or occupancy enjoyed as a matter of course by other citizens of different race or color. The Fourteenth Amendment declares "that all persons, whether colored or white, shall stand equal before the laws of the States, and, in regard to the colored race, for whose protection the amendment was primarily designed, that no discrimination shall be made against them by law because of their color." *Strauder v. West Virginia, supra* at 307. Nor may the discriminations imposed by the state courts in these cases be justified as proper exertions of state police power. *Cf. Buchanan v. Warley, supra.*

Respondents urge, however, that since the state courts stand ready to enforce restrictive covenants excluding white persons from the ownership or occupancy of property covered by such agreements, enforcement of covenants excluding colored persons may not be deemed a denial of equal protection of the laws to the colored persons who are thereby affected. This contention does not bear scrutiny. The parties have directed our attention to no case in which a court, state or federal, has been called upon to enforce a covenant excluding members of the white majority from ownership or occupancy of real property on grounds of race or color. But there are more fundamental considerations. The rights created by the first section of the Fourteenth Amendment are, by its terms, guaranteed to the individual. The rights established are personal rights. It is, therefore, no answer to these petitioners to say that the courts may also be induced to deny white persons rights of ownership and occupancy on grounds of race or color. Equal protection of the laws is not achieved through indiscriminate imposition of inequalities.

Nor do we find merit in the suggestion that property owners who are parties to these agreements are denied equal protection of the laws if denied access to the courts to enforce the terms of restrictive covenants and to assert property rights which the state courts have held to be created by such agreements. The Constitution confers upon no individual the right to demand action by the State which results in the denial of equal protection of the laws to other individuals. And it would appear beyond question that the power of the State to create and enforce property interests must be exercised within the boundaries defined by the Fourteenth Amendment. *Cf. Marsh v. Alabama*, 326 U.S. 501 (1946).

The task of determining whether the action of a State offends constitutional provisions is one which may not be undertaken lightly. Where, however, it is clear that the action of the State violates the terms of the fundamental charter, it is the obligation of this Court so to declare.

The historical context in which the Fourteenth Amendment became a part of the Constitution should not be forgotten. Whatever else the framers sought to achieve, it is clear that the matter of primary concern was the establishment of equality in the enjoyment of basic civil and political rights and the preservation of those rights from discriminatory action on the part of the States based on considerations of race or color. Upon full consideration, we have concluded that in these cases the States have acted to deny petitioners the equal protection of the laws guaranteed by the Fourteenth Amendment. Having so decided, we find it unnecessary to consider whether petitioners have also been deprived of property without due process of law or denied privileges and immunities of citizens of the United States.

For the reasons stated, the judgment of the Supreme Court of Missouri must be reversed. [The similar ruling of the Michigan Supreme Court was also reversed.]

NOTES AND QUESTIONS

1. Under what theory did the Missouri Supreme Court enforce the covenant at issue in this case? Notice that the covenant is to be in effect for only 50 years. Why was such a provision included?

2. *Racially Restrictive Covenants.* Covenants of the sort at issue in *Shelley v. Kraemer* were a staple of American land use restrictions from the end of the Civil War until the mid-1940s. It is entirely possible that they were the most common form of restrictive covenant, perhaps even more common that covenants limiting use to residential purposes. As *Shelley* indicates with cases from Missouri and Michigan, such covenants were not limited to the Deep South. Nor were the only targets of such covenants African-Americans. In a footnote, not included in the above version of the case, the Supreme Court reported that such covenants had been directed against "Indians, Jews, Chinese, Japanese, Mexicans, Hawaiians, Puerto Ricans, and Filipinos, among others."

3. *Subsequent Developments.* On May 3, 1948, the Supreme Court handed down its decisions in *Shelley v. Kraemer* and *Hurd v. Hodge*, 334 U.S. 24 (1948), the latter of which held that *federal court* enforcement of a racially restrictive covenant violated the Fifth Amendment. These two decisions were landmarks in the campaign for African-American civil rights, but they left many questions unanswered, particularly as to the scope of state action. Initially, some state courts interpreted its statements regarding state action quite narrowly. The Supreme Courts of both Missouri and Oklahoma subsequently found that while the Fourteenth Amendment prohibited judicial enforcement of a racially restrictive covenant, it did not prevent an award of money damages against the breaching party. *Weiss v. Leaon*, 225 S.W.2d 127 (Mo. 1949); *Correll v. Earley*, 237 P.2d 1017 (Okla. 1951). In *Barrows v. Jackson*, 346 U.S. 249 (1953), the Supreme Court rejected this reading of *Shelley* (although in *Barrows*, Chief Justice Vinson, the author of the *Shelley* decision agreed with the Missouri and Oklahoma state courts and dissented). However, like *Shelley, Barrows* held that the covenants were not illegal, but merely unenforceable.

It was not until *Jones v. Alfred H. Mayer Co.*, 392 U.S. 409 (1968) (reproduced in Chapter 5, Section F, above) that the Supreme Court extended the application of 42 U.S.C.A. § 1982 (part of the Civil Rights Act of 1866 discussed in *Shelley v. Kraemer*) to private discrimination in housing. That same year such practices were explicitly outlawed by the federal Fair Housing Act, enacted as Title VIII of the Civil Rights Act of 1968, 42 U.S.C.A. §§ 3601–3619 (1994). The Fair Housing Act renders unlawful the refusal to sell or rent a dwelling to any person because of race, color, sex, national origin, religion, handicap, or familial status. (Housing discrimination is examined in greater detail in the Chapter 10.)

4. *Racially Restrictive Limitations on Fee Simple Estates.* In 1955, the North Carolina Supreme Court ruled that a public park could revert to its original donor as the result of the violation of a racially restrictive limitation attached to a fee simple transfer without violating the rule set down in *Shelley v. Kraemer. Charlotte Park & Recreation Comm'n v. Barringer*, 88 S.E.2d 114 (N.C. 1955). Review of the decision was sought from the United States Supreme Court, but the Court declined to grant certiorari, *Leeper v. Charlotte Park & Recreation Comm'n*, 350 U.S. 983

(1956). Shortly thereafter, the city of Charlotte purchased the defendants' possibility of reverter, and the park was ultimately integrated. Whether or not the *Barringer* case was properly decided is still a matter of debate, but there is general agreement that had the defendant's reversionary interest been a right of entry rather than a possibility of reverter, the right could not have been enforced consistent with *Shelley v. Kraemer*. Do you understand why? On the issue of the proper resolution of *Barringer, see* Entin, *Defeasible Fees, State Action, and the Legacy of Massive Resistance*, 34 WM. & MARY L. REV. 769 (1993); J. NOWAK & R. ROTUNDA, CONSTITUTIONAL LAW 466 (4th ed. 1991).

5. *Racially Restrictive Covenants in Recorded Instruments*. The fact that racially restrictive covenants are unenforceable does not remove them from the chain of title. Even after the Civil Rights Act of 1968, it was apparently fairly common for racially restrictive covenants to be copied from old deeds into new ones even though such clauses were not only unenforceable but illegal. During the confirmation hearing for Chief Justice William Rehnquist in August of 1986, it was revealed that both Rehnquist and Sen. Joseph Biden (Del.), the ranking Democrat on the Senate Judiciary Committee and an opponent of the Rehnquist nomination, had owned homes that contained racially restrictive covenants in their chain of title. In the case of a Vermont summer home owned by Justice Rehnquist, the restriction was in Rehnquist's own deed. While the covenants were clearly unenforceable, and both men insisted that they had no intention of participating in a discriminatory scheme, the revelations were highly embarrassing. N.Y. TIMES, Aug. 1, 1986 at A8; Aug. 8, 1986 at A7. Do you understand why such covenants cannot simply be removed from the chain of title? Later that year, Chief Justice Rehnquist transferred his summer home to his lawyer who transferred it back to him with a new deed that made no reference to the controversial covenant which had prohibited sale or lease "to members of the Hebrew race." N.Y. TIMES, Nov. 16, 1986 at sec. 1, pt. 2, p. 50. What, if anything, was accomplished by this transaction?

6. *Extending* Shelley v. Kraemer *Beyond Issues of Race*. While the United States Supreme Court does not appear to have expanded its holding in *Shelley* beyond restrictive covenants with racial overtones, some state courts have extended the principle to covenants that discriminate against families with children, *Riley v. Stoves*, 526 P.2d 747 (Ariz. Ct. App. 1974); against individuals on the basis of age, *Franklin v. White Egret Condominium*, 358 So. 2d 1084 (Fla. Dist. Ct. App. 1977); and against those who wish to use property for public religious worship, *West Hill Baptist Church v. Abbate*, 261 N.E.2d 196 (Ohio C.P. 1969) (see below). The latter case raises important questions pertaining to the relationship of the First and Fourteenth Amendments to the enforcement of restrictive covenants that limit certain types of expression. If judicial enforcement of covenants which discriminate on the basis of race constitute state action, is the situation any different when courts are called upon to enforce covenants which restrict speech or religious expression and practice?

[2.] Restrictions on Religion

WEST HILL BAPTIST CHURCH v. ABBATE
Ohio Court of Common Pleas
261 N.E.2d 196 (1969)

CRAMER, J.

The plaintiff seeks a declaratory judgment declaring that certain restrictive covenants appearing in the chain of title of its real estate be declared invalid and unenforceable. United in interest with the plaintiff and seeking the same relief as does plaintiff, but seeking it by way of cross-petitions and joined as defendants here, are Adath Israel Anshe Sfard (hereinafter referred to as Anshe Sfard) and the Maronite Club of Akron, Ohio. These latter defendants are owners of land in the area involved, each seeking to erect houses of worship thereon.

There are two sets of covenants affecting the lands in question, one herein referred to as the Wright restrictions — recorded May 29, 1952 — and the other herein referred to as the Vaughn restrictions. The Wright restrictions covered a sizeable tract of land which has been subdivided into several areas. The Vaughn restrictions cover a smaller tract of land within the original Wright area. The land now owned by Anshe Sfard (also perhaps referred to herein as the Synagogue) is situated in an area covered by the Wright restrictions and partly by the Vaughn restrictions. The Maronite Club property is covered both by the Wright and Vaughn restrictions. This is also true as to the land of plaintiff.

The Wright restrictions seem to limit the use of land located therein to residential and agricultural and the Vaughn restrictions purport to limit the use of land located therein to agricultural and single family residential use. Both sets of restrictions contain provisions as to lot sizes, frontage, building setbacks and minimum structure size.

The pleadings and the evidence raise the issue as to whether the plaintiffs, The Maronite Club and Anshe Sfard, as property owners and religious organizations, have the right to construct and operate their respective churches and synagogue thereon notwithstanding the existence of two sets of restrictive covenants which prohibit the use of their property for other than single family residence purposes.

[The court then dismissed allegations that the covenants at issue were invalid because of a lack of uniformity and a lack of consistent enforcement.]

We come now to a consideration of the claim that the restrictions are, as they relate to houses of worship, violative of the Constitutions of the United States and of Ohio. Zoning is the exercise of police power regulating and controlling the uses of real property. Restrictive covenants, with which we are here dealing, and which, of course, purport to control the use of real property are in the nature of private zoning or zoning by contract.

Restrictive covenants do not supersede or in any way affect the requirements of a zoning ordinance. They may be less restrictive than the ordinance and, if so, the ordinance prevails and if the restrictive covenant is more restrictive than the ordinance the covenant prevails but, in either case, the ordinance is enforceable. The ordinance cannot abrogate or impair or enlarge the effect of a restrictive covenant and a valid covenant is not terminated or nullified by the enactment of a zoning ordinance nor is the validity of a restriction thereby affected (*see* 20 AMERICAN JURISPRUDENCE 2d 837 and 838).

It would follow, however, that if a zoning ordinance is, in its operation, unconstitutional, a restrictive covenant in the same area having the same effect would likewise be unconstitutional. In *Shelley v. Kraemer*, 334 U.S. 1, the court declared: "That the action of state courts and of judicial officers in their official capacities is to be regarded as action of the state, within the meaning of the 14th Amendment * * *" Therefore, if this court were to enforce (by declaratory judgment) the restrictive covenants here we would be engaging in state action.

In a majority of the states, churches cannot be wholly excluded from residential districts (through zoning legislation) because the courts have held that, under the circumstances, such exclusion amounts to unfair discrimination and, in any event, is contrary to the public welfare as a general rule, thus being an arbitrary and unauthorized exercise of the police power by the local authorities. *See* 81 HARVARD LAW REVIEW 338, and the citations referred to therein.

The courts have considered that the private enjoyment of surrounding property and maintenance of its economic value are not considered important enough to require exclusion of religious uses. It has also been held that a zoning ordinance which prohibits the use of certain residential land for church purposes does not bear any substantial relation to public health, safety, morals and general welfare and, therefore, is violative of constitutional rights. *See State, ex rel. Synod of Ohio of United Lutheran Church in America v. Joseph*, 139 Ohio St. 229. Also *Young Israel Organization of Cleveland v. Dworkin*, 105 Ohio App. 89. The annotation found in 74 A.L.R.2d 377 furnishes ample authority for the foregoing proposition.

Thus, it seems to us, that covenants such as those here in issue, which seek to limit an area to residential use only, thereby barring churches, would be unconstitutional as to houses of worship if they were in the form of zoning ordinances or resolutions rather than covenants.

Our question then is: Are such restrictive covenants which bar churches and synagogues from areas unconstitutional as to such institutions?

The concept of substantive due process, to have meaning, would require, in our opinion, a holding that if a zoning law which excludes churches is unconstitutional for that reason, a restrictive covenant accomplishing the same purpose likewise would be unconstitutional. Is such a restrictive covenant insulated against unconstitutionality because it is the result of a private agreement?

In *Kraemer, supra*, the United States Supreme Court held that judicial enforcement by a state court of a restrictive covenant excluding persons from purchasing real property because of their race or color was unconstitutional as state action within the prohibition of the 14th Amendment and thereby violated due process and equal protection of law. It would thus appear that the rationale of *Kraemer, supra*, applies with equal force here.

The right of freedom of religion safeguarded by the First Amendment to the Federal Constitution has been brought within the protection of the 14th Amendment to the Constitution of the United States. The fundamental concept of liberty embodied in the 14th Amendment embraces the liberties guaranteed by the First Amendment.

It is conceivable that to relegate houses of worship to areas other than those here in question thereby excluding them from residential districts not as fully populated would result in imposing a burden on the free right to worship and could conceivably result in prohibiting altogether the exercise of that right.

In the case of *Cantwell v. Connecticut*, 310 U.S. 296, it was stated that: "It cannot be left to the uncontrolled discretion of any public official as to when, where and under what conditions a religious organization may build a church or maintain a place of assembly." It has also been said that although the Supreme Court of the United States has been strict in its prohibition of prior restraint on the exercise of freedom of religion, it has been held that reasonable regulations of time and place for the exercise of such freedoms are valid.

Here, these restrictive covenants came as a result of the "uncontrolled discretion" of private individuals thus resulting in their unreasonable regulation of "time and place" for the exercise of religion by those coming into the area affected by the restrictions.

While it is true, of course, that when the effect of such a covenant upon the exercise of one's freedom of religion is small and the public interest to be protected is substantial such freedom is to give way to the public interest, that situation does not here exist. The private interests of the individuals, parties to the restrictive covenants, as distinguished from the public interest, were their chief and perhaps only concern. It is claimed the evidence shows that the excessive noise and increased traffic hazards engendered by the erection of three additional places of religious worship will occur, so that the public interest and welfare must be balanced against the freedom. We do not find that the evidence discloses that such results will take place to the extent claimed.

It is our conclusion that the enforcement of these covenants which would result in prohibiting the use by the plaintiff and the cross-petitioners of their property for the erection thereon of houses of worship, would constitute state action (through this court) violative of the free exercise of religion provision of the First Amendment of the Constitution of the United States and of comparable provisions of the Constitution of Ohio and against public policy, and that such action bears no reasonable relationship to the public health, safety, morals and general welfare.

We, therefore, declare that such restrictive covenants are not enforceable, so as to prevent the use of the properties of plaintiff and cross-petitioners to which they seek to put them, namely, the erection and maintenance of churches and a synagogue and all structures necessary to be used in connection therewith. Judgment for plaintiffs.

NOTES AND QUESTIONS

1. In a portion of the opinion not reproduced above, the court noted that the evidence showed that two churches had been constructed on lots subject to the covenants at issue in this case. While the court was not willing to find that these two "violations" were grounds for saying that the covenants had been abandoned, it did note that the presence of these two churches (which were not Baptist, Jewish, or Maronite) did give the "appearance of discrimination in favor of certain religious denominations." Would the result in this case have been different if those who had the benefit of the covenants had enforced them against all churches from 1952 onward?

2. *Restrictive Covenants and the Freedom of Religion.* On its face, the *Abbate* decision represents an extension of the principle of *Shelley v. Kraemer* to the area of religious liberty. Note, however, that the court here is only an Ohio trial court, and the defendants did not appeal. It appears that when this issue has been raised in other courts, no state has followed the lead of the court in *Abbate.* Instead, the standard response in cases of this sort has been to enforce covenants that effectively prohibit certain religious uses so long as the covenants at issue are not blatantly discriminatory against particular religions or so extreme as to be unreasonable under a contract analysis. Restrictions on religious meetings and the construction of houses of worship will normally be upheld and their enforcement will not be deemed state action. For example, both *Ginsberg v. Yeshiva*, 358 N.Y.S.2d 477, *aff'd mem.*, 325 N.E.2d 876 (N.Y. 1976), and *Ireland v. Bible Baptist Church*, 480 S.W.2d 467 (Tex. Ct. Civ. App. 1972), refuse to apply *Shelley* in cases enforcing residential use only covenants against parties who sought to use the property for religious purposes. For more evidence that *West Hill Baptist Church v. Abbate* is an atypical case, see *Church as Violation of Covenant Restricting Use of Property*, 13 A.L.R.2d 1239 (1950); *Note, Restrictive Covenants and Religious Uses: The Constitutional Interplay*, 29 Syracuse L. Rev. 993 (1978); Saxer, Shelley v. Kraemer's *Fiftieth Anniversary*, 47 Kan. L. Rev. 61 (1998).

[3.] Restrictions on Speech

COMMITTEE FOR A BETTER TWIN RIVERS v. TWIN RIVERS HOMEOWNERS' ASSOCIATION

New Jersey Supreme Court
929 A.2d 1060 (2007)

Wallace, Jr.

In this appeal, we determine whether the rules and regulations enacted by a homeowners association governing the posting of signs, the use of the community room, and access to its newsletter violated our state constitutional guarantees of free expression. The trial court held that the association's rules and regulations were not subject to the right of free speech embodied in our State Constitution. On appeal, the Appellate Division reversed. We granted certification and now reverse the judgment of the Appellate Division.

We start from the proposition that all citizens of this State, including the residents of Twin Rivers, possess the constitutional right to free speech and assembly. We acknowledge, however, that those rights are not absolute, as citizens may waive or otherwise curtail their rights. This case presents us with a hybrid setting to apply the standards set forth in *State v. Schmid*, 423 A.2d 615 (N.J. 1980), *appeal dismissed*, 455 U.S. 100 (1982) and *New Jersey Coalition Against War in the Middle East v. J.M.B. Realty Corp.*, 650 A.2d 757 (N.J. 1994), *cert. denied*, 516 U.S. 812 (1995). In applying the *Schmid/Coalition* multi-faceted standard, we conclude that the Association's policies, as set forth in its rules and regulations, do not violate our constitution.

I.

Twin Rivers is a planned unit development consisting of privately owned condominium duplexes, townhouses, single-family homes, apartments, and commercial buildings located in East Windsor, New Jersey. The community covers approximately one square mile and has a population of approximately 10,000 residents. The Twin Rivers Community Trust (Trust) is a private corporation that owns Twin Rivers's common property and facilities. The Trust was created by indenture on November 13, 1969, for the stated purpose of owning, managing, operating, and maintaining the residential common property of Twin Rivers. The administrator of the Trust certified that "Trust-owned property and facilities are for the exclusive use of Twin Rivers residents and their invited guests," and that the "general public is not invited" to use them.

The Twin Rivers Homeowners' Association (Association) is a private corporation that serves as trustee of the Trust. The Trust authorizes the Association to make rules and regulations for the conduct of its members while occupying the land owned or controlled by the Trust, to provide services to its members, and to maintain the common lands and facilities in Twin Rivers. The Association maintains the Trust's private residential roads, provides street lighting and snow removal, assigns parking spaces in its parking lots, and collects rubbish in portions of Twin Rivers. By acquiring property in Twin Rivers, the owner automatically becomes a member of the Association and subject to its Articles of Incorporation (Articles) and Bylaws.

The Articles authorize the Association to exercise all of the powers, rights, and privileges provided to corporations organized under the New Jersey Nonprofit Corporation Act, N.J.S.A. 15A:1-1 to -10. The Bylaws additionally authorize the Association to adopt, publish, and enforce rules governing the use of common areas and facilities. The Bylaws may be amended by a majority of a quorum of members present in person or by proxy at a regular or special meeting of the members.

The Association is governed by a Board of Directors (Board), whose members are elected by all eligible voting members of the Association. The Board is responsible for making and enforcing the rules, and for providing services to its members that are financed through mandatory assessments levied against residents pursuant to an annual budget adopted by the Board.

Prior to the commencement of this litigation, various residents of Twin Rivers formed a committee, known as the Committee for a Better Twin Rivers (Committee), for the purpose of affecting the manner in which Twin Rivers was governed. Eventually, the Committee and three individual residents of Twin Rivers (collectively, plaintiffs) filed a nine-count complaint against the Association and Scott Pohl, the president of the Association, seeking to invalidate various rules and regulations. Plaintiffs subsequently amended their complaint to include the Trust as a defendant. The thrust of the complaint was that the Association had effectively replaced the role of the municipality in the lives of its residents, and therefore, the Association's internal rules and regulations should be subject to the free speech and free association clauses of the New Jersey Constitution.

In count one of the complaint, plaintiffs sought to invalidate the Association's policy relating to the posting of signs. The Association's sign policy provided that residents may post a sign in any window of their residence and outside in the flower beds so long as the sign was no more than three feet from the residence. In essence, the policy limits signs to one per lawn and one per window. The policy also forbids the posting of signs on utility poles and natural features within the community. The stated purpose for the sign policy is to avoid the clutter of signs and to preserve the aesthetic value of the common areas, as well as to allow for lawn maintenance and leaf collection. Plaintiffs sought injunctive relief to permit the posting of political signs on the property of community residents "and on common elements under reasonable regulation," on the basis that the current policy was unconstitutional. [The plaintiffs also claimed that they were denied access to the Association's monthly newspaper which was used to defend the policies of the Association.]

The Association filed a motion for summary judgment, and plaintiffs filed a cross-motion for summary judgment. The material facts were not disputed. The trial court issued a comprehensive opinion, granting defendants' motion for summary judgment on the sign claims in count one and on the newspaper claims in count three.

Central to the trial court's decision was the determination that Twin Rivers was not a "quasi-municipality," and thus was not subject to the New Jersey Constitution's free speech and association clauses. The court noted that while the Association asserted considerable influence on the lives of Twin Rivers residents, that impact was a function of the contractual relationship that residents entered into when they elected to purchase property in Twin Rivers. The court applied the traditional test for evaluating the reasonableness of restrictive covenants and found that the covenant relating to the posting of signs was reasonable and enforceable.

Plaintiffs appealed. The Appellate Division reversed the trial court, holding that the Association was subject to state constitutional standards with respect to its internal rules and regulations. *Comm. for a Better Twin Rivers v. Twin Rivers Homeowners' Ass'n*, 890 A2d 947 (N.J. Super, App. Div. 2006). "[I]n balancing the interests of the parties," the panel found that "plaintiffs' rights to engage in expressive exercises . . . must take precedence over the [Association's] private property interests." The panel thus remanded counts one, two, and three for reconsideration in light of that determination. .The Association petitioned this Court for certification on whether the New Jersey Constitution applies to its internal rules and regulations. Plaintiffs cross-petitioned for certification on an issue unrelated to this appeal. We granted the Association's petition and denied plaintiffs' cross-petition. 897 A.2d 1062 (N.J. 2006).

II.

The Association argues that the test in *State v. Schmid, supra*, controls the disposition of this appeal, and contends that under that test, it was error to impose constitutional obligations on its private property. The Association urges this Court to follow the vast majority of other jurisdictions that have refused to impose constitutional obligations on the internal membership rules of private homeowners associations. In support of that view, the Association emphasizes that it does not invite public use of its property, and its members participate in the decision-making process of the Association. Additionally, its members are afforded extensive statutory protections, and the business judgment rule protects members from arbitrary decision-making. Further, the Association contends that the relationship with its members is a contractual one, set forth in reasonable and lawful restrictive covenants that appear in all property deeds.

In contrast, plaintiffs ask this Court to affirm the judgment of the Appellate Division to find that the New Jersey Constitution limits the manner in which the Association interacts with its members. They urge that political speech is entitled to heightened protection and that they should have the right to post political signs beyond the Association's restricted sign policy. Plaintiffs further contend that the excessive fees charged for the use of the community room are not reasonably related to the actual costs incurred by the Association. Finally, plaintiffs claim that the State Constitution requires that the Association publish plaintiffs' views on an equal basis with which the Association's views are published in its newspaper.

III.

Our constitution affirmatively grants to individuals the rights of speech and assembly. Every person may freely speak, write and publish his sentiments on all subjects, being responsible for the abuse of that right. No law shall be passed to restrain or abridge the liberty of speech or of the press. N.J. Const. art. I, ¶ 6. . . . The people have the right freely to assemble together, to consult for the common good, to make known their opinions to their representatives, and to petition for redress of grievances. N.J. Const. art. I, ¶ 18. This Court has long held that the rights of speech and assembly cannot be curtailed by the government. Moreover, under limited circumstances, we have determined that those constitutional rights may be enforced against private entities. *Schmid, supra*. In fact, our constitutional guarantee of free expression "is an affirmative right, broader than practically all others in the nation." *Green Party v. Hartz Mountain Indus., Inc.*, 752 A.2d 317 (N.J. 2000). Here, we must determine whether this case presents one of those limited circumstances where, in the setting of a private community, the Association's rules and regulations are limited by the constitutional rights of plaintiffs.

A.

Federal case law has evolved to require that there must be "state action" to enforce constitutional rights against private entities. *Marsh v. Alabama*, 326 U.S. 501 (1946), is recognized as the leading case in this area of law. In *Marsh*, a private company owned and controlled all aspects of the town. The company refused to allow solicitation and the distribution of religious literature. Marsh was arrested for trespassing while distributing religious literature on company-owned land that was otherwise open to the public. *Id.* The Court explained that "[t]he more an owner, for his advantage, opens up his property for use by the public in general, the more do his rights become circumscribed by the statutory and constitutional rights of those who use it." *Id.* at 506. The Court then balanced the constitutional rights of the property owners against the First Amendment rights of Marsh to find that "the latter occupy a preferred position." *Id.* at 509. The Court concluded that, in those limited circumstances, the property owner's action constituted "state action" and violated the First Amendment.

B.

Our jurisprudence has not been as confining. We briefly outline the development of our law expanding the application of free speech or similar constitutional rights against non-governmental entities.

In *State v. Shack*, 277 A.2d 369 (1971), this Court was asked to apply the principles of Marsh to a private farm operation. In *Shack*, two employees of federally funded organizations were arrested for trespassing when they entered private property to provide legal and medical assistance to migrant workers. The defendants challenged the constitutionality of the trespassing statute on several grounds. However, the Court declined to rule on the constitutional challenge, noting only that *Marsh* was inapplicable because the land in question was not open to the public. Applying our common law, this Court held that the defendants' conduct did not constitute trespass within the meaning of the statute under which they were prosecuted. Thus, the broader issue of whether the federal or State Constitution required access to the land remained unresolved.

Almost ten years passed before this Court decided the landmark *Schmid* case. In *Schmid*, Princeton University, a private, non-profit institution, prohibited persons not affiliated with the university from soliciting and distributing political literature on campus. The defendant, a non-student, was arrested and convicted for trespassing while distributing Labor Party materials on the Princeton campus. Princeton's regulations required off-campus organizations to obtain permission before distributing materials. The defendant claimed that his arrest was unconstitutional because distribution of political material was protected by both the First Amendment and Article I of the New Jersey Constitution. Princeton argued that as a private institution, it was not subject to the strictures of the federal or State Constitutions.

Analyzing Princeton's claim, the Court recognized that the constitutional equipoise between expressional rights and property rights must be similarly gauged on a scale measuring the nature and extent of the public's use of such property. Thus, even as against the exercise of important rights of speech, assembly, petition and the like, private property itself remains protected under due process standards from untoward interference with or confiscatory restrictions upon its reasonable use.

The Court crafted "the test to be applied to ascertain the parameters of the rights of speech and assembly upon privately owned property and the extent to which such property reasonably can be restricted to accommodate these rights." 423 A.2d 615. That test requires courts to consider (1) the nature, purposes, and primary use of such private property, generally, its "normal" use, (2) the extent and nature of the public's invitation to use that property, and (3) the purpose of the expressional activity undertaken upon such property in relation to both the private and public use of the property.

The Court explained that such a test would allow the court "to ascertain whether in a given case owners of private property may be required to permit, subject to suitable restrictions, the reasonable exercise by individuals of the constitutional freedoms of speech and assembly." *Id.* In assessing the reasonableness of any restrictions, the court shall consider "whether there exist convenient and feasible alternative means to individuals to engage in substantially the same expressional activity." *Id.* The Court applied the test to Princeton and found that the university had invited the public to use its facilities, the defendant's expressional activities were consonant with both the private and public uses of Princeton's campus, and Princeton's regulations contained no standards for governing the exercise of free speech. Therefore, the Court concluded that Princeton violated the defendant's constitutional rights of speech and assembly.

The Court expanded the *Schmid* test in *New Jersey Coalition Against War in the Middle East v. J.M.B. Realty Corp.*, 650 A.2d 757 (N.J. 1994), *cert. denied*, 516 U.S. 812 (1995). In *Coalition*, the plaintiffs sought judicial approval to permit their members to distribute leaflets in shopping centers to support opposition to any military action in the Middle East. The Court concluded that "each of the elements of the [*Schmid*] standard and their ultimate balance support the conclusion that leafleting is constitutionally required to be permitted." *Id.* Thus, the Court not only relied on the three-pronged test in *Schmid*, but also on the general balancing of expressional rights and private interests. Nevertheless, the Court recognized that regional shopping centers have broad powers to adopt reasonable conditions "concerning the time, place, and manner of such leafleting." *Id.* The Court limited its holding to "leafleting and associated speech in support of, or in opposition to, causes, candidates, and parties — political and societal free speech." *Id.* To avoid future questions, the Court addressed the "horribles" the defendants asserted would be the inevitable consequence of its decision. The Court emphasized that "[n]o highway strip mall, no football stadium, no theatre, no single high suburban store, no stand-alone use, and no small to medium shopping center sufficiently satisfies the standard of *Schmid* to warrant the constitutional extension of free speech to those premises, and we so hold." *Id.*

[The court's discussion of its application of the *Schmid/Coalition* rule in subsequent cases is omitted.]

IV.

We concluded in *Schmid, supra*, that the rights of free speech and assembly under our constitution are not only secure from interference by governmental or public bodies, but under certain circumstances from the interference by the owner of private property as well. Simply stated, we have not followed the approach of other jurisdictions to require some state action before the free speech and assembly clauses under our constitution may be invoked.

With those general principles as a backdrop, we turn now to apply the *Schmid/Coalition* test to the present matter. As noted, our constitution's free speech provision is "broader than practically all others in the nation." *Green Party, supra*, 752 A.2d 315. Consequently, we have not followed the approach of other jurisdictions to require some state action before the free speech and assembly clauses under our constitution may be invoked. Even in the absence of state action, we must determine whether the acts of a homeowners association violated its members' free speech and association rights in the setting of this private housing association.

This case presents an additional complication: it involves restrictions on conduct both on the private housing association's property and on the homeowners' properties. However, "[i]t is the extent of the restriction, and the circumstances of the restriction that are critical, not the identity of the party restricting free speech." *Coalition, supra*, 650 A.2d 757. We conclude that the three-pronged test in *Schmid* and the general balancing of expressional rights and private property interests in *Coalition* are the appropriate standards to decide this case.

As noted above, the *Schmid* test takes into account (1) the nature, purposes, and primary use of such private property, generally, its "normal" use, (2) the extent and nature of the public's invitation to use that property, and (3) the purpose of the expressional activity undertaken upon such property in relation to both the private and public use of the property. *Id.*

[Discussion of the three *Schmid* factors in this case is omitted.]

We find that plaintiffs' expressional activities are not unreasonably restricted. As the Association points out, the relationship between it and the homeowners is a contractual one, formalized in reasonable covenants that appear in all deeds. Moreover, unlike the university in *Schmid*, and the shopping center in *Coalition*, Twin Rivers is not a private forum that invites the public on its property to either facilitate academic discourse or to encourage public commerce. Rather, Twin Rivers is a private, residential community whose residents have contractually agreed to abide by the common rules and regulations of the Association. The mutual benefit and reciprocal nature of those rules and regulations, and their enforcement, is essential to the fundamental nature of the communal living arrangement that Twin Rivers residents enjoy. We further conclude that this factor does not weigh in favor of finding that the Association's rules and regulations violated plaintiffs' constitutional rights.

We are mindful that at least in regard to the signs on the property of the homeowners, it is the private homeowner's property and not that of the Association that is impacted. The private property owner not only is "protected under due process standards from untoward interference with or confiscatory restrictions upon its reasonable use," *Schmid, supra,* but also our constitution affirmatively grants the homeowner free speech and assembly rights that may be exercised on that property. Notably, the Association permits expressional activities to take place on plaintiffs' property but with some minor restrictions. Homeowners are permitted to place a single sign in each window and signs may be placed in the flower beds adjacent to the homes. Those limitations are clearly not an "untoward interference with" or a "confiscatory restriction" on the reasonable use by plaintiffs' on their property to implicate due process standards.

The outcome of the balancing of the expressional rights and the privacy interests is obvious. "We do not interfere lightly with private property rights." *Coalition, supra.* We find that the minor restrictions on plaintiffs' expressional activities are not unreasonable or oppressive, and the Association is not acting as a municipality. The Association's restrictions concerning the placement of the signs, the use of the community room, and access to its newspaper are reasonable "concerning the time, place, and manner of" such restrictions. Neither singularly nor in combination is the *Schmid/Coalition* test satisfied in favor of concluding that a constitutional right was infringed here. Consequently, we conclude that in balancing plaintiffs' expressional rights against the Association's private property interest, the Association's policies do not violate the free speech and right of assembly clauses of the New Jersey Constitution.

Additionally, plaintiffs have other means of expression beyond the Association's newspaper. Plaintiffs can walk through the neighborhood, ring the doorbells of their neighbors, and advance their views. As found by the trial court, plaintiffs can distribute their own newsletter to residents, and have done so. As members of the Association, plaintiffs can vote, run for office, and participate through the elective process in the decision-making of the Association. Thus, plaintiffs may seek to garner a majority to change the rules and regulations to reduce or eliminate the restrictions they now challenge.

V.

We recognize the concerns of plaintiffs that bear on the extent and exercise of their constitutional rights in this and other similar common interest communities. At a minimum, any restrictions on the exercise of those rights must be reasonable as to time, place, and manner. Our holding does not suggest, however, that residents of a homeowners association may never successfully seek constitutional redress against a governing association that unreasonably infringes their free speech rights.

Moreover, common interest residents have other protections. First, the business judgment rule protects common interest community residents from arbitrary decision-making. Pursuant to the business judgment rule, a homeowners association's rules and regulations will be invalidated (1) if they are not authorized by statute or by the bylaws or master deed, or (2) if the association's actions are "fraudulent, self-dealing or unconscionable."

Finally, residents are protected under traditional principles of property law — principles that specifically account for the rights afforded under our constitution's free speech and association clauses. Our courts have recognized that restrictive covenants on real property that violate public policy are void as unenforceable.

The judgment of the Appellate Division is reversed and we reinstate the judgment of the trial court.

NOTES AND QUESTIONS

1. *Restrictive Covenants and the Freedom of Speech.* The decision of the New Jersey Supreme Court in *Twin Rivers* was much anticipated when it was handed down in August, 2007. Because of the special protection provided to rights of expression by the New Jersey Constitution — as noted in the opinion, it is greater than that provided by the First Amendment to the United States Constitution — many observers anticipated that the court would rule in favor of the plaintiffs. Obviously, it did not. In upholding the enforceability of the restrictions, the New Jersey court fell in line with other courts that have visited this issue. *See Midlake on Big Boulder Lake Condominium Assoc. v. Cappuccio*, 673 A.2d 340 (Pa. Super. Ct. 1996).

2. Shelley v. Kraemer *and Restrictions on Speech.* Note that the court in *Twin Rivers* never mentions *Shelley v. Kraemer*. Early cases addressing the question of the validity of speech restrictions by covenant tended to view the question posed as one of whether or not *Shelley* applied. *See Midlake on Big Boulder Lake Condominium Assoc. v. Cappuccio, supra*, Note 1. However, the conclusion in such cases was that *Shelley* did not apply to restrictions of this sort.

Such an approach has been typical of courts facing efforts to extend the *Shelley* principle outside the realm of racial discrimination. While restrictive covenants are sometimes found to be unenforceable on the basis of public policy, most courts have been reluctant to extend the logic of *Shelley v. Kraemer* beyond those covenants that discriminate on the basis of race or some other immutable characteristic (*West Hill Baptist Church v. Abbate* notwithstanding). Why has this been the case? Does this reluctance suggest that *Shelley* was wrongly decided? Or, as Robert Bork suggested in his ill-fated 1987 Senate confirmation hearing for an appointment to the Supreme Court, rightly decided but for the wrong reason? (Bork argued that *Shelley* should have been decided on the basis of the 1866 Civil Rights Act.) Given that discrimination on the basis of race, religion, ethnic origin, or gender is currently outlawed by general civil rights laws, there would seem to be little need for *Shelley* in the one context in which it clearly does apply.

Is the enforcement of restrictions on speech (or religion) somehow less objectionable than the enforcement of racial discrimination? What if a challenged covenant had involved an absolute ban on political signs in a common interest community? In a traditional subdivision? What about a covenant that required residents of a subdivision to place signs in their yard encouraging people to vote for the representatives of one particular political party? Is it enough to say that the property owners voluntarily relinquished certain aspects of their right to speak when they purchased land subject to restrictions of this sort? When municipalities attempt to impose much less severe limitations, their efforts are usually declared unconstitutional. *See, e.g., Linmark Associates, Inc. v. Township of Willingboro*, 431

U.S. 85 (1977); *City of Ladue v. Gilleo*, 512 U.S. 43 (1994).

3. *The Restatement Approach.* The RESTATEMENT (THIRD) OF PROPERTY (SERVITUDES) § 3.1 appears to draw a distinction between reasonable and unreasonable restrictions on expression. Among the types of servitudes that are listed as unenforceable is the servitude which "unreasonably burdens a fundamental constitutional right." Among the illustrations of unenforceable covenants are those prohibiting the posting of signs on the property, at least to the extent that the covenant is applied to political signs or to flying the American flag. To date, there appear to be very few reported cases involving covenants imposing those sorts of restrictions, although the restrictions themselves are apparently widespread.

4. *Other Limitations on Expression.* In *Conrad v. Dunn*, 92 Cal. App. 3d 236 (1979), the defendant Dunn ignored a deed restriction in his subdivision and installed a citizen band (CB) radio antenna on the outside of his house. (The covenant forbade all outdoor antennae of any type.) When Dunn's next door neighbor sought a court order requiring him to remove the antenna, Dunn defended his conduct with the claim that the restriction violated his First Amendment right to free speech. The record showed that with an interior CB antenna, he could broadcast his signal only seven or eight blocks. With an exterior antenna, his range was 15 to 20 miles. When the trial judge ordered him to remove the antenna, Dunn appealed.

The Court of Appeals rejected Dunn's claim and awarded Conrad (the neighbor) attorney's fees. The Court found it was unnecessary to determine what standard applied — *Shelley v. Kraemer* was not even mentioned — since it found that a municipal ordinance imposing the same restrictions would be constitutional since it was a "reasonable, narrowly drawn restriction which concerns the time, place and manner of expression" and was "not a blanket prohibition on expression."

5. *Condominium and Homeowners Associations as State Actors.* Note that the cases in parts 1 and 2 of this section centered around claims that the *judicial* enforcement of covenants constituted a form of state action. An alternative approach, obviously present in *Twin Rivers*, is to characterize the association charged with enforcing the covenants as a "state actor." (The portion of the above opinion dealing with *Marsh v. Alabama* addresses this question.)

There has been considerable scholarly support for this position, particularly in the case of highly controlled developments. *See* Siegel, *The Constitution and Private Government: Toward the Recognition of Constitutional Rights in Private Residential Communities Fifty Years After* Marsh v. Alabama, 6 WM. & MARY BILL. RTS. J. 461 (1998); Askin, *Free Speech, Private Space and the Constitution*, 29 RUTGERS L.J. 947 (1998); Brower, *Communities Within the Community: Consent, Constitutionalism, and Other Failures of Legal Theory in Residential Associations, supra*; French, *The Constitution of a Private Residential Government Should Include a Bill of Rights*, 27 WAKE FOREST L. REV. 345 (1992); Weakland, *Condominium Associations: Living Under the Due Process Shadow*, 13 PEPP. L. REV. 297, 299 (1986).

In the second edition of this casebook, we wrote, "Regardless of scholarly opinion, there is little reason to believe that contemporary courts are inclined to characterize homeowners' associations as state actors." The decision in *Twin Rivers* would seem to confirm this judgment. In *Midlake, supra*, the court quickly rejected the claim that the Midlake development was like a company town or a municipality. After devoting only four sentences to the argument, the court announced, "We need not discuss this issue further." One searches in vain for cases which reach the opposite conclusion.

Moreover, given the United States Supreme Court's efforts to limit the state action doctrine in recent years, it seems highly unlikely that it will any time soon impose upon homeowners associations the same constraints applicable to state actors. In *Ball v. James*, 451 U.S. 355 (1981), for example, the Court held that a private water district was not subject to federal constitutional requirement of "one person, one vote" because it was not a state actor. The logic of that decision would seemingly apply to private planned communities as well, and there is little in the Court's jurisprudence of the past two decades to suggest that it has changed its mind on these matters. For a summary of these developments in the 1990s, see Madry, *State Action and the Due Process of Self-Help:* Flagg Bros. *Redux*, 62 U. PITT. L. REV. 1 (2000).

6. *Special Problems of Gated Communities.* Bear Creek Country Club is a gated residential development of 236 homes located near Woodinville, Washington and is approximately 17 miles east of Seattle. It has a community association that controls the development's private streets, private sewers, architectural restrictions and homeowners' fees. In place of local municipal rules, the association imposes and enforces restrictions including prohibitions of flag poles, visible clotheslines, satellite dishes, street-side parking, unsightly landscaping, and firearms. It does not operate a school or a library (factors cited in *Midlake*), but it does maintain Bear Paw Park for the recreational needs of its residents, and it contains a well-known private golf club to which 50% of residents belong. Egan, *Many Seek Security in Private Communities: The Serene Fortress*, N.Y. TIMES, Sept. 5, 1995, at 22. For more up to date information, see www.bearcreekcc.com (visited Feb. 2016).

Given this level of control, does it begin to make sense to think about communities like Bear Creek as the equivalent of a company town, at least for state action purposes? *See* Kennedy, *Residential Associations as State Actors: Regulating the Impact of Gated Communities on Nonmembers*, 105 YALE L.J. 761 (1995). Here again, it seems unlikely that any court will reach such a conclusion in the near future. In a gated community case decided almost a decade ago, the New Jersey Supreme Court — which in other cases in that era had been willing to impose "state-like" obligations on private owners — did not even address the possibility that the gated community association board was a state actor. *William G. Mulligan Foundation v. Brooks*, 711 A.2d 961 (N.J. 1998). For a discussion of the legal issues arising from gated communities generally, see E. BLAKELY & M. SNYDER, FORTRESS AMERICA: GATED COMMUNITIES IN THE UNITED STATES (1997); Callies, Franzese & Guth, *Gated Communities: Covenants and Concerns*, 34 URB. LAW 177 (2003).

7. *Whither Privatization?* The general process of privatization — the transfer of governmental services and functions to the private sector — is a significant factor in the public policy debates of the 21st century. The process seems certain to continue in regard to residential decisions, regardless of whether or not constitu-

tional standards are imposed on homeowners associations. What the ultimate consequences of this development will be is a matter of much debate. Privately regulated residential arrangements often offer more amenities than can be provided by local government, but critics argue that private communities reinforce undesirable exclusionary aims and erode important civic policies. On privatization and its consequences, see E. McKenzie, Privatopia: Homeowner Associations and the Rise of Residential Private Government (1994); Rosenberry, *Home Business, Llamas and Aluminum Siding: Trends in Covenant Enforcement*, 31 J. Marshall Rev. 443 (1998); Priest, *The Aims of Privatization*, 6 Yale L. & Pol'y Rev. 1 (1998); Franzese, *Does It Take a Village? Privatization, Patterns of Restrictiveness and the Demise of Community*, 47 Vill. L. Rev. 553 (2002).

Chapter 9

REAL ESTATE TRANSACTIONS

[A.] THE UNIQUENESS OF REAL ESTATE

The American legal system permits the transfer of most items of property with a minimum of formal requirements. For example, the owner of 100,000 shares of publicly traded common stock worth several million dollars can sell them simply by picking up the phone and calling a broker, but if the same individual tries to sell a small plot of land worth less than a thousand dollars, the transaction will ordinarily require a written contract of sale and a deed. Moreover, an interim period of several weeks, or even several months, will separate the signing of the contract and the transfer of the deed. In addition to the buyer and the seller, the transaction will ordinarily involve one or more real estate professionals, a lawyer for each side, a surveyor, a real estate title company, or an insurance provider. Even after the deal is "closed," the buyer cannot be sure that he has a valid legal title unless his deed is properly recorded in the public records in a timely fashion.

The reasons for this complexity are rooted in the historical significance of land ownership in the United States and in the belief that a stable system of land titles was a prerequisite for economic growth and social harmony.

[1.] The Statute of Frauds

TIMBERLAKE v. HEFLIN
West Virginia Supreme Court of Appeals
379 S.E.2d 149 (1989)

MILLER, J.

We consider in this case the enforceability of a parol contract for the transfer of certain joint property between husband and wife. The Berkeley County Circuit Court concluded that the contract was unenforceable due to the lack of a memorandum sufficient to comply with W. Va. Code, 36-1-3. We conclude that there was sufficient compliance.

I

Richard L. Timberlake and Sherry L. Timberlake were married on July 24, 1976. They purchased a two-bedroom home in Berkeley County on June 9, 1977. Their deed expressly provided that they were to hold the property as joint tenants with the right of survivorship. Mr. Timberlake asserts in this suit for specific performance that sometime prior to July, 1983, he and his wife (who has since remarried and is now named Ms. Heflin) contemplated a divorce. They entered into a parol contract for the division of their marital assets. Under that contract, Mr. Timberlake was to transfer his interest in a jointly owned automobile, motorcycle, and other personal property. Ms. Heflin, in turn, was to execute and deliver a deed for her interest in the marital home.

Mr. Timberlake's complaint states that on July 22, 1983, Ms. Heflin filed a suit for divorce in the Berkeley County Circuit Court. The divorce complaint was accompanied by a signed affidavit in which Ms. Heflin stated, under oath, that the averments set forth therein were true and accurate. One of these averments stated:

> Plaintiff [Ms. Heflin] says that [sic] she agrees to convey her interest to the Defendant in the jointly owned real estate, to wit: a two bedroom home located in Berkeley County, West Virginia, and known for postal purposes as P.O. Box 42, Hedgesville, West Virginia.

Mr. Timberlake's complaint also stated that upon being served with the divorce papers, he took no action in reliance on the parol agreement with his wife. On August 31, 1984, the circuit court entered a final order that divided some of the couple's joint assets, but made no disposition of the marital home.

The complaint further averred that so far as the contract dealt with real estate, it was not subject to W. Va. Code, 36-1-3, the statute of frauds, as "there [was] a writing, . . . duly verified and acknowledged, which operated as an exception to said statute." Mr. Timberlake requested entry of an order to direct the transfer of fee simple title in the marital home. Ronald Heflin was joined so as to require transfer of his dower interest. Mr. and Ms. Heflin filed a joint motion to dismiss the complaint because the statute of frauds barred enforcement of Mr. Timberlake's claim.

By order entered on October 24, 1986, the circuit court dismissed Mr. Timberlake's complaint. The court concluded that the averments in the divorce complaint, relied on by Mr. Timberlake, "[could] not be taken as fact and must be independently proved." For this reason, the suit remained subject to the statute of frauds and was barred. This appeal followed.

Mr. Timberlake died after his petition for appeal was accepted and Roxanne Timberlake, executor of his estate, was substituted as the appellant pursuant to Rule 26 of the Rules of Appellate Procedure. We shall, for purposes of clarity, refer to Mr. Timberlake as the appellant in the text of the opinion.

II

The prohibition in the statute of frauds against parol contracts for the sale of land, or the lease thereof for more than one year, is contained in W. Va. Code, 36-1-3, which provides: "No contract for the sale of land, or the lease thereof for more than one year, shall be enforceable unless the contract or some note or memorandum thereof be in writing and signed by the party to be charged thereby, or by his agent. But the consideration need not be set forth or expressed in the writing, and it may be proved by other evidence." This Code section is often referred to as the statute of frauds.

Mr. Timberlake's basic argument is that the divorce complaint filed by Ms. Heflin is a sufficient memorandum of their parol contract to meet the requirements of W. Va. Code, 36-1-3, and permit his suit for specific performance. Ms. Heflin says in response that the complaint contains bare assertions of fact and that it cannot, therefore, qualify as a memorandum. Thus, the initial issue is a rather limited one: Whether a judicial pleading can constitute a memorandum under the statute of frauds.

We note first that W. Va. Code, 36-1-3, does not itself specify a particular type of writing that is necessary to satisfy the memorandum requirement. Its wording suggests a degree of flexibility, as the language identifies several forms of writings: "the contract or some note or memorandum thereof." Certainly, our prior cases demonstrate that a memorandum under W. Va. Code, 36-1-3, need not take any particular form. E.g., *Connell v. Connell*, 46 S.E.2d 724 (W. Va. 1948) (deed of trust); *Tearney v. Marmiom*, 137 S.E. 543 (W. Va. 1927) (defective will); *Lawrence v. Potter*, 113 S.E. 266 (W. Va. 1922) (telegram).

We, along with other courts, have recognized that a pleading may, in appropriate circumstances, be sufficient to take a parol contract out of the statute of frauds. In a related line of cases, representative of the modern trend, courts have crafted a "judicial admission" exception to the statute of frauds. [Citations omitted.] These cases hold that any admission of a contract made in the course of judicial proceedings will render the statute of frauds inoperative. The "judicial admission" exception is read broadly to include even parol admissions in depositions or in open court. This result is said to be in harmony with the policy that underlies the statute of frauds: Its purpose is to prevent the fraudulent enforcement of unmade contracts, not the legitimate enforcement of contracts that were in fact made. 2 A. Corbin, Corbin on Contracts § 498 (1950 & 1984 Supp.). We also have settled law in this state that statements contained in pleadings may be judicial admissions and, therefore, conclusive of the facts so stated.

It would appear to us that, under the foregoing law, a pleading in a civil case may satisfy the requirement of a memorandum under W. Va. Code, 36-1-3.

III

It is important to recall that the statute of frauds, as applicable to contracts for the sale or lease of land, is a procedural bar to prevent enforcement of oral contracts unless the conditions expressed in W. Va. Code, 36-1-3, are met. Once they are met, then the terms of the oral contract can be proved. We summarized this principle in *Ross v. Midelburg*, 42 S.E.2d 185, 193 (W. Va. 1947): "The operation of the statute of frauds goes only to the remedy; it does not render the contract void. In *Drake* [*v. Livesay*], 341 S.E.2d 186, 188 (Va. 1986), the Virginia Supreme Court had this to say about its similar statute of frauds: "When the bar is removed, it is the oral contract which is subject to enforcement, not the memorandum. Because the memorandum serves only to remove a bar to the enforcement of the oral contract, the validity of the oral contract may be established by other evidence."

With these principles in mind, we proceed to review the sufficiency of the memorandum. W. Va. Code, 36-1-3, contains two express requirements. The memorandum must be (1) in writing, and (2) signed by the party against whom performance is demanded. These requirements are met in the case at hand. The complaint was typewritten and the affidavit accompanying it was signed by Ms. Heflin.

In addition to these express requirements, our cases require that the memorandum must contain a description of the involved land and must also contain the essential elements of the contract. *See Harper v. Pauley*, 81 S.E.2d 728 (W. Va. 1953); *Milton Bradley Co. v. Moore*, 112 S.E. 236 (W. Va. 1922).

We turn first to the property description. It need not be precise, but only reasonably certain, and the court can receive extrinsic evidence to complete the description. What is required is merely that the memorandum contain the "key" or "foundation" words from which the description may, by other evidence, be made complete and certain. We summarized these principles in *Harper v. Pauley, supra:*

> Every agreement required by the statute of frauds to be in writing must be certain in itself or capable of being made so by reference to something else, whereby the terms can be ascertained with reasonable certainty. And in contracts for the sale of lands the court may go outside of the writing for the purpose of identifying and ascertaining the land sold, where general words of description capable of being made certain are used in the writing.

We find the description of the property to be sufficient under *Harper*. The complaint refers to the couple's "jointly owned real estate," and provides a description of the home situated on that tract. Also provided is the town, county, and state, including the postal address of the home, from which a more complete metes and bounds description may readily be ascertained. Numerous jurisdictions have found a street or postal address to be a sufficient description under the statute of frauds. [Citations omitted.] In *Jones v. Hudson*, 236 S.E.2d 38 (W. Va. 1977), we held that a memorandum which identified certain farm property as "One hundred (100) acres, more or less, located on the waters of Big Run," was sufficient to withstand a motion to dismiss.

The question of what essential elements of a land contract must be placed in the memorandum is rather ambiguous. The statute expressly provides that "the consideration need not be set forth or expressed in the writing, and it may be proved by other evidence."

We have indicated in several cases that the memorandum must disclose an intent to sell. *E.g., Harper v. Pauley*, 81 S.E.2d at 735 (W. Va.); *see also Crookshanks v. Ransbarger*, 92 S.E. 78, 79 (W. Va. 1917). Here, there is no question of such an intention since the memorandum states that Ms. Heflin "agrees to convey her interest." Our cases often hold a memorandum sufficient when the party to be charged signs it, and the description is found to be adequate.

There also appear to be certain presumptions that are made by courts to establish the essential elements. One of these is that "where in a sale of land there is no time fixed for the payment of the consideration, courts will assume that the parties intended a cash transaction." *Donahue v. Rafferty*, 96 S.E. 935, 937 (W. Va. 1918).

Donahue illustrates another such presumption. Where there is some ambiguity in the memorandum "and the bill [for specific performance] sets forth in detail the terms . . . [,] when read together they set forth a contract sufficient upon demurrer to satisfy the statute of frauds." *Donahue v. Rafferty, supra.* In view of the foregoing authority, we find the memorandum to be adequate in this case.

[The remainder of the opinion deals with the effect of Mr. Timberlake's death during this litigation. The court concluded that Ms. Heflin was still legally obligated to fulfill the contract with Mr. Timberlake's representatives and that Ms. Heflin's right of survivorship as a joint tenant did not apply in this situation. The logic behind the court's reasoning is discussed in Subsection 3, below.]

For the foregoing reasons, we conclude that Mr. Timberlake's complaint was improperly dismissed. The judgment of the Circuit Court of Berkeley County is, therefore, reversed and the case is remanded for further proceedings not inconsistent with this opinion.

NOTES AND QUESTIONS

1. *The Concept of Fee Simple Absolute.* Mr. Timberlake requested the court to direct the transfer to him of "fee simple title" in the property in question. This phrase refers to the estate of *fee simple absolute* which signifies absolute ownership. An estate in fee simple absolute is one that has no termination point (as does a lease or an estate for life) and is free from any restriction, the violation of which could result in the forfeiture of the property. The concept of the estate is discussed more extensively in Chapter 4.

2. What policy objectives are advanced by forcing Ms. Heflin to relinquish her interest in the marital home in the above case? The plaintiff and defendant could easily have reduced their agreement to writing, but they failed to do so. Is the point of this case that all oral contracts should be enforced if it can be shown that the parties actually agreed to the transfer?

3. The original Statute of Frauds was enacted by the English parliament in 1677, 29 Car. II, c.3 (1677). Even before its enactment, English equity courts regularly refused to enforce oral contracts for the sale of land. The 1677 statute applied to "any contract for sale of lands, tenements or hereditaments or any interest in or concerning them" and it required either that the agreement be in writing or that there be "some memorandum or note" in writing evidencing the contract. A version of the statute has been enacted in every American state, and although its language varies slightly from jurisdiction to jurisdiction, American statutes typically require contracts for the sale of land to be in writing and signed by the party against whom the contract is enforced.

The required writing must identify the parties to the transaction, describe the land being transferred, and indicate the terms and conditions of the agreement. If there is no writing, or if the writing fails to contain the necessary information and signatures, the contract is unenforceable, even if it can be shown that both parties knowingly entered into the agreement.

4. *Exceptions to the Statute.* American courts have developed a number of doctrines that mitigate the potential harshness of the Statute of Frauds. Judicial admissions like the one in *Timberlake* are one example. Moreover, if the contract has been fully performed, then it is perfectly valid and neither party may rely upon the statute to subsequently back out of the agreement. Many courts interpret the concept of "necessary information" quite liberally and most will admit parol evidence to clarify ambiguous language. Courts also tend to be quite liberal in their interpretation of what constitutes a satisfactory writing (as the *Timberlake* case illustrates).

Perhaps the best-known exception is the doctrine of part performance. This equitable doctrine and the related doctrine of estoppel provide a basis in the enforcement of oral contracts for the sale of an interest in land over the objection of one of the parties. Ordinarily, if one or both parties to an oral contract for the sale of land make an "unequivocal" reference to the contract, the Statute of Frauds no longer bars its enforcement.

What constitutes "part performance" or an "unequivocal reference" varies from state to state, but ordinarily it requires action that makes sense only if it were undertaken pursuant to a contract. Examples include the buyer paying all or part of the purchase price or the buyer taking possession of the property and making improvements to it. Some states simply look for evidence that one party or the other has relied upon the oral contract to their serious detriment, making the refusal to enforce its terms unconscionable.

5. *Contract Revocation.* In most states, a written contract for the sale of land can be revoked by an oral agreement between the buyer and the seller. If one of the parties subsequently tries to enforce the agreement, he cannot plead the Statute of Frauds as a bar to proof that the contract for sale had been revoked. Does such a distinction make sense? In a minority of states, the revocation must be in writing to be valid. Obviously, any agreement to revoke a real estate sales contract *should* be in writing, regardless of the jurisdiction's rule in regard to the applicability of the Statute of Frauds.

6. *Gifts of Land.* Individuals are free to give land or other interests in real property to whomever they choose, at least so long as no fraud is involved. Since the Statute of Frauds applies to "transfers" rather than just to sales, gifts of land must be memorialized by writing. However, some jurisdictions will uphold a parol (i.e., oral) gift of land if the donee (recipient) takes possession of the land and makes substantial improvements. In such a case, the donee's actions are analogous to the buyer's part performance of an oral contract. *Hayes v. Hayes*, 148 N.W. 125 (Minn. 1914). This exception is justified on the grounds that it prevents injustice and in that sense, it is closely related to the doctrine of part performance.

To protect his or her interest, the donee of a gift of land must have something to record which ordinarily necessitates a deed. As the *Capozzella* case, below, illustrates, in transferring the deed, the requirements of a valid gift — donative intent, actual or constructive delivery — overlap with the delivery requirement necessary to give effect to a transfer by deed.

7. *Transfers at Death.* When individuals die intestate (i.e., without valid wills), land that they own ordinarily passes to their heirs which are either their surviving spouse or their closest relatives by blood or adoption. The Statute of Frauds has no effect on this type of transfer. If the transfer is by will, there is no Statute of Frauds issue, since all jurisdictions require wills that pass real property to be in writing. If the estate of the deceased is submitted to probate, the administrator or executor of the estate supervises the transfer of title to the new owner. When there is neither a will nor a probate proceeding, the heir sometimes has difficulty establishing ownership when he or she attempts to sell the property.

[2.] The Right of Specific Performance

In *Timberlake,* the plaintiff is not suing for damages resulting from his wife's alleged breach of contract but is asking the court (successfully, as it turns out) to order his ex-wife to transfer her half interest in the house to him. Although the general rule is that money damages are the appropriate remedy for injuries suffered as a result of another's breach of contract, contracts for the sale of land or other real property interests have been long held to be enforceable by specific performance. In this sense, purchasers and sellers of land are in a privileged position not shared by those who contract for the sale of personal property.

The rationale for this special remedy was rooted in the principle of contract law that damages were an inadequate remedy when the object of a sales contract was truly unique. For example, a contract for the sale of a highly valued and distinctive work of art may be enforced by specific performance because there is no way that the purchaser could ever acquire a substitute (and no way to realistically measure the damages suffered by the non-breaching party). Since every parcel of land is unique (or so it has been frequently stated), then damages were inadequate in every case of a breach of a real estate contract. Although this argument would logically seem to apply only in cases of seller's breach, courts have routinely applied specific performance both as a seller's and buyer's remedy.

However, as the case below illustrates, there has been some evidence in recent years of a movement to limit specific performance as a seller's remedy, particularly when the transactions at issue involve condominium sales and contracts to rent, rather than sell.

CENTEX HOMES CORP. v. BOAG

New Jersey Superior Court, Chancery Division
320 A.2d 194 (1974)

Gelman, J.S.C., Temporarily Assigned.

Plaintiff Centex Homes Corporation (Centex) is engaged in the development and construction of a luxury high-rise condominium project in the Boroughs of Cliffside Park and Fort Lee. The project when completed will consist of six 31-story buildings containing in excess of 3,600 condominium apartment units, together with recreational buildings and facilities, parking garages and other common elements associated with this form of residential development. As sponsor of the project Centex offers the condominium apartment units for sale to the public and has filed an offering plan covering such sales with the appropriate regulatory agencies of the States of New Jersey and New York.

On September 13, 1972 defendants Mr. and Mrs. Eugene Boag executed a contract for the purchase of apartment unit No. 2019 in the building under construction and known as "Winston Towers 200." The contract purchase price was $73,700, and prior to signing the contract defendants had given Centex a deposit in the amount of $525. At or shortly after signing the contract defendants delivered to Centex a check in the amount of $6,870 which, together with the deposit, represented approximately 10% of the total purchase of the apartment unit. Shortly thereafter Boag was notified by his employer that he was to be transferred to the Chicago, Illinois, area. Under date of September 27, 1972 he advised Centex that he "would be unable to complete the purchase" agreement and stopped payment on the $6,870 check. Centex deposited the check for collection approximately two weeks after receiving notice from defendant, but the check was not honored by defendants' bank. On August 8, 1973, Centex instituted this action in Chancery Division for specific performance of the purchase agreement or, in the alternative, for liquidated damages in the amount of $6,870. The matter is presently before this court on the motion of Centex for summary judgment.

Both parties acknowledge, and our research has confirmed, that no court in this State or in the United States has determined in any reported decision whether the equitable remedy of specific performance will lie for the enforcement of a contract for the sale of a condominium apartment. The closest decision on point is *Silverman v. Alcoa Plaza Associates*, 37 A.D. 2d 166 (App. Div. 1971), which involved a default by a contract-purchaser of shares of stock and a proprietary lease in a cooperative apartment building. The seller, who was also the sponsor of the project, retained the deposit and sold the stock and the lease to a third party for the same purchase price. The original purchaser thereafter brought suit to recover his deposit, and on appeal the court held that the sale of shares of stock in a cooperative apartment building, even though associated with a proprietary lease, was a sale of personalty and not of an interest in real estate. Hence, the seller was not entitled to retain the contract deposit as liquidated damages. [Under New York law, if the contract was deemed to be for the sale of realty, the seller could retain the deposit in lieu of damages.]

As distinguished from a cooperative plan of ownership such as involved in Silverman, under a condominium housing scheme each condominium apartment unit constitutes a separate parcel of real property which may be dealt with in the same manner as any real estate. Upon closing of title the apartment unit owner receives a recordable deed which confers upon him the same rights and subjects him to the same obligations as in the case of traditional forms of real estate ownership, the only difference being that the condominium owner receives in addition an undivided interest in the common elements associated with the building and assigned to each unit. *See* the Condominium Act, N.J.S.A. 46:8B-1 *et seq.*; 15 Am.Jur.2d, Condominiums and Cooperative Apartments, at 977 *et seq.*; Note, 77 HARV. L. REV. 777 (1964).

Centex urges that since the subject matter of the contract is the transfer of a fee interest in real estate, the remedy of specific performance is available to enforce the agreement under principles of equity which are well-settled in this state. *See Hopper v. Hopper*, 16 N.J. Eq. 147 (Ch. 1863); 5A Corbin on Contracts § 1143 (1964); 11 Williston on Contracts § 1418A (3d ed. 1968); 4 Pomeroy, Equity Jurisprudence (5th ed. 1941), § 1402; Restatement Contracts § 360.

The principle underlying the specific performance remedy is equity's jurisdiction to grant relief where the damage remedy at law is inadequate. The text writers generally agree that at the time this branch of equity jurisdiction was evolving in England, the presumed uniqueness of land as well as its importance to the social order of that era led to the conclusion that damages at law could never be adequate to compensate for the breach of a contract to transfer an interest in land. Hence specific performance became a fixed remedy in this class of transactions. *See* 11 Williston on Contracts (3d ed. 1968), § 1418A; 5A Corbin on Contracts § 1143 (1964). The judicial attitude has remained substantially unchanged and is expressed in Pomeroy as follows:

> [I]n applying this doctrine the courts of equity have established the further rule that in general the legal remedy of damages is inadequate in all agreements for the sale or letting of land, or of any estate therein; and therefore in such class of contracts the jurisdiction is always exercised, and a specific performance granted, unless prevented by other and independent equitable considerations which directly affect the remedial right of the complaining party . . .

1 Pomeroy, Equity Jurisprudence (5th ed. 1941), § 221(b).

While the inadequacy of the damage remedy suffices to explain the origin of the vendee's right to obtain specific performance in equity, it does not provide a rationale for the availability of the remedy at the instance of the vendor of real estate. Except upon a showing of unusual circumstances or a change in the vendor's position, such as where the vendee has entered into possession, the vendor's damages are usually measurable, his remedy at law is adequate and there is no jurisdictional basis for equitable relief. The early English precedents suggest that the availability of the remedy in a suit by a vendor was an outgrowth of the equitable concept of mutuality, i.e., that equity would not specifically enforce an agreement unless the remedy was available to both parties. See the discussion in *Stoutenburgh v. Tompkins*, 9 N.J. Eq. 332, 342–346 (Ch. 1853); 4 Pomeroy, Equity Jurisprudence (5th ed. 1941); § 1405; Annotation, 65 A.L.R. 7, 40 (1930); *Jones v. Newhall*, 115 Mass. 244 (Sup. Jud. Ct. 1874); Comment, 10 Vill. L. Rev. 557, 568–569 (1965).

So far as can be determined from our decisional law, the mutuality of remedy concept has been the prop which has supported equitable jurisdiction to grant specific performance in actions by vendors of real estate. The earliest reported decision in this State granting specific performance in favor of a vendor is *Rodman v. Zilley*, 1 N.J. Eq. 320 (Ch. 1831), in which the vendee (who was also the judgment creditor) was the highest bidder at an execution sale. In his opinion Chancellor Vroom did not address himself to the question whether the vendor had an adequate remedy at law. The first reported discussion of the question occurs in *Hopper v. Hopper*, 16 N.J. Eq. 147 (Ch. 1863), which was an action by a vendor to compel specific performance of a contract for the sale of land. In answer to the contention that equity lacked jurisdiction because the vendor had an adequate legal remedy, Chancellor Green said (at p. 148):

> It constitutes no objection to the relief prayed for, that the application is made by the vendor to enforce the payment of the purchase money, and not by the vendee to compel a delivery of the title. The vendor has not a complete remedy at law. Pecuniary damages for the breach of the contract is not what the complainant asks, or is entitled to receive at the hands of a court of equity.
>
> He asks to receive the price stipulated to be paid in lieu of the land. The doctrine is well established that the remedy is mutual, and that the vendor may maintain his bill in all cases where the purchaser could sue for a specific performance of the agreement.

No other rationale has been offered by our decisions subsequent to *Hopper*, and specific performance has been routinely granted to vendors without further discussion of the underlying jurisdictional issue. *E.g., Brown v. Norcross*, 59 N.J. Eq. 427 (Ch. 1900); *Moore v. Baker*, 62 N.J. Eq. 208 (Ch. 1901); *Van Riper v. Wickersham*, 77 N.J. Eq. 232 (Ch. 1910); *Gerba v. Mitruske*, 84 N.J. Eq. 79 (Ch. 1914); *Meyer v. Reed*, 91 N.J. Eq. 237 (Ch. 1920); *Morris v. Eisner*, 96 N.J. Eq. 538 (Ch. 1924); *Salter v. Beatty*, 101 N.J. Eq. 86 (Ch. 1927); *Mahaffey v. Sarshik*, 101 N.J. Eq. 297 (E. & A. 1927); *Harrington v. Heder*, 109 N.J. Eq. 528 (E. & A. 1931); *Hoffman v. Perkins*, 3 N.J. Super. 474 (Ch. Div. 1949).

Our present Supreme Court has squarely held, however, that mutuality of remedy is not an appropriate basis for granting or denying specific performance. *Fleischer v. James Drug Stores*, 1 N.J. 138 (1948); *see also*, RESTATEMENT, CONTRACTS § 372; 11 WILLISTON, CONTRACTS (3d ed. 1968), § 1433. The test is whether the obligations of the contract are mutual and not whether each is entitled to precisely the same remedy in the event of a breach. In *Fleischer* plaintiff sought specific performance against a cooperative buying and selling association although his membership contract was terminable by him on 60 days' notice. Justice Heher said:

> And the requisite mutuality is not wanting. The contention contra rests upon the premise that, although the corporation "can terminate the contract only in certain restricted and unusual circumstances, any 'member' may withdraw at any time by merely giving notice."
>
> Clearly, there is mutuality of obligation, for until his withdrawal complainant is under a continuing obligation of performance in the event of performance by the corporation. It is not essential that the remedy of specific performance be mutual. The modern view is that the rule of mutuality of remedy is satisfied if the decree of specific performance operates effectively against both parties and gives to each the benefit of a mutual obligation.

The fact that the remedy of specific enforcement is available to one party to a contract is not in itself a sufficient reason for making the remedy available to the other; but it may be decisive when the adequacy of damages is difficult to determine and there is no other reason for refusing specific enforcement. RESTATEMENT, CONTRACTS (1932), sections 372, 373. It is not necessary, to serve the ends of equal justice, that the parties shall have identical remedies in case of breach.

The disappearance of the mutuality of remedy doctrine from our law dictates the conclusion that specific performance relief should no longer be automatically available to a vendor of real estate, but should be confined to those special instances where a vendor will otherwise suffer an economic injury for which his damage remedy at law will not be adequate, or where other equitable considerations require that the relief be granted. *Cf. Dover Shopping Center, Inc. v. Cushman's Sons, Inc.*, 63 N.J. Super. 384, 394 (App. Div. 1960). As Chancellor Vroom noted in *King v. Morford*, 1 N.J. Eq. 274, 281–282 (Ch. Div. 1831), "whether a contract should be specifically enforced is always a matter resting in the sound discretion of the court and . . . considerable caution should be used in decreeing the specific performance of agreements, and . . . the court is bound to see that it really does the complete justice which it aims at, and which is the ground of its jurisdiction."

Here the subject matter of the real estate transaction — a condominium apartment unit — has no unique quality but is one of hundreds of virtually identical units being offered by a developer for sale to the public. The units are sold by means of sample, in this case model apartments, in much the same manner as items of personal property are sold in the market place. The sales prices for the units are fixed in accordance with schedule filed by Centex as part of its offering plan, and the only variance as between apartments having the same floor plan (of which six plans are available) is the floor level or the building location within the project. In actuality, the condominium apartment units, regardless of their realty label, share the same characteristics as personal property.

From the foregoing one must conclude that the damages sustained by a condominium sponsor resulting from the breach of the sales agreement are readily measurable and the damage remedy at law is wholly adequate. No compelling reasons have been shown by Centex for the granting of specific performance relief and its complaint is therefore dismissed as to the first count.

[The court also rejected Centex's claim that it was entitled to additional damages under the liquidated damages provision of the sale contract.]

NOTES AND QUESTIONS

1. Note that the court in the above case focuses upon the remedies of vendors. Would it make any difference if Centex was the breaching party? What if it offered the purchaser a different unit in the same development with an identical floor plan? Would the purchaser still be entitled to specific performance under the holding of this case? For a holding denying the remedy of specific performance for the landlord's breach of a rental contract, see *Van Wagner Advertising Corp. v. S & M Enter.*, 492 N.E.2d 756 (N.Y. 1986). Other cases in which courts have questioned the propriety of specific performance on the assumption that vendors are entitled to specific performance as a matter of course include *Wolf v. Anderson*, 334 N.W.2d 212 (N.D. 1983); *Perron v. Hale*, 701 P.2d 198 (Idaho 1985); and *Seabaugh v. Keele*, 775 S.W.2d 205 (Mo. Ct. App. 1989). The position taken in these decisions remains the minority position.

2. In California, damages are, by statute, *conclusively* presumed inadequate for purchasers of single-family dwellings who intend to occupy the premises. In vendor-breach cases involving other kinds of real property, damages are presumed to be inadequate, but the presumption can be rebutted. Cal. Civ. Code § 3387 (1984). This provision was adopted in 1984, apparently in response to a concern that courts were allowing the right of specific performance to erode.

3. *Other Remedies.* Of course, a party to a real property contract who is entitled to specific performance is not obligated to elect that remedy. In fact, there is usually a wide array of potential remedies available to the non-breaching party, including money damages, rescission, abatement of the sale price, restitution, or vendor's and vendee's liens.

4. *The Measure of Damages.* If the non-breaching party elects the damage remedy, what constitutes recoverable damages can vary from jurisdiction to jurisdiction. If the breach is by the purchaser, the seller is entitled to recover out of pocket expenses and loss of bargain damages. The latter are the difference between the agreed upon sale price and the market price of the property on the date that performance is due. Note that such damages will exist only when the sale price is greater than the market value. If the market value and the sale price are identical, then the seller has no loss of bargain damages because he can presumably sell the land to someone else at the same price. However, if the sale price is greater than the market price on the day the contract was completed, the seller is entitled to loss of bargain damages, even if the market price increases before the land is resold. On the other hand, it is often difficult to establish the actual market value of land on a particular day, and in some states a seller who later sells the land in question for a profit is barred from recovering loss of bargain damages regardless of the property's value on the original closing date.

If the breach is by the vendor, the rules are slightly more complicated. The buyer is entitled to out of pocket expenses and the return with interest of any sums deposited to secure the sale. However, the rule on loss of bargain damages varies. In the approximately one half of states which follow the so-called "English rule," loss of bargain damages are recoverable by a non-breaching buyer only if the seller wilfully refuses to convey or is guilty of fraud or deceit. In the other half of the states, the "American rule" prevails under which loss of bargain damages are recoverable irrespective of the nature of the reasons for the default. The classic case of a situation in which recovery is permitted under the American rule, but not under the English rule, is where the seller promised to deliver marketable title (i.e., title free from legal encumbrances — see Section B-2, below in this chapter), but through no fault of her own, is unaware of the existence of a cloud on her title that prevents her from fulfilling the contract.

5. *Liquidated Damages.* Contracts for the sale of land often state that the seller is entitled to keep the down payment (usually between 5% and 25% of the purchase price) if the purchaser proves unwilling or unable to complete the contract. If it can be shown that the parties intended this provision to be used to compensate the seller for his damages in lieu of other remedies, the seller's remedies will be limited to the down payment, so long as the amount deposited bears some reasonable relation to the amount of damages suffered by the seller. On

the other hand, if the provision can be shown not to have been in lieu of other remedies, then the seller can sue for the difference between his actual damages and the amount of the down payment. If the purpose of the liquidated damages clause can be shown to be primarily punitive or if the deposit is unreasonably large, the buyer may be able to sue for the return of part of the down payment.

[3.] Equitable Conversion

As mentioned earlier, in the typical real estate transaction the buyer and seller enter into a contract on one date and schedule the transfer of the deed on a future date. The presence of this "executory period" can give rise to difficult legal questions, particularly if the subject of the transaction is damaged during the interim period or if one of the parties to the agreement dies before closing. To address these problems, English judges developed the doctrine of equitable conversion in the early 19th century and most American jurisdictions followed suit. The complexity of the possible problems can be seen in the following case.

ROSS v. BUMSTEAD

Arizona Supreme Court
173 P.2d 765 (1946)

FARLEY, J.

On October 21, 1942, the parties entered into a contract whereby the plaintiff agreed to sell to defendant the premises known as the "Arizona Orchard," together with all the improvements thereon, all water and ditch rights, and all personal property on the said premises. The buyer agreed to pay for said property the sum of $75,000, payable $5,000 upon the execution of the agreement, $20,000 when title insurance policy, deed and mortgage were ready for delivery, and the balance in quarterly installments within six years. The contract recited that possession was to be given upon delivery of the title papers and deed, but when so given such possession should relate back to the date of the agreement, for the purpose of adjusting charges against the property and income from it. An inventory was to be taken of all personal property as of the date of the agreement, and one-half of the cost of packing materials and dates was to be added to the purchase price and paid by the buyer. The contract also provided that the vendor would be allowed a reasonable time, not to exceed ninety days, to meet any remedial requirement of the title insurance company, and all taxes, water assessment and insurance premiums were to be prorated as of the date of the agreement.

Following the execution of the agreement the defendant retained an auditor to conduct an inventory of the premises, and on October 29, 1942, eight days after the parties entered into the contract of sale, and while defendant was in Detroit, Michigan, the packing plant and warehouse, together with its contents, were destroyed by fire. The vendee thereupon requested the vendor to make an adjustment for the loss but the vendor refused to do so; whereupon defendant stopped payment on the $5,000 check he had given as a deposit and refused to complete the contract.

This action was then filed by the vendor to recover of the defaulting vendee the difference between the selling price as fixed by the contract made by the parties and the actual selling price to a third party. By way of defense defendant pleaded partial failure of consideration. From a judgment in favor of the plaintiff (vendor), defendant has appealed to this court.

Only two assignments of error were raised on appeal so that the issues are relatively simple of determination. Appellant contends that (1) the contract being a conditional one, and the condition not having been satisfied at the time of the destruction of the premises, the risk of loss falls upon the vendor; and (2) even if the contract is unconditional the risk of loss should fall upon the vendor.

In support of his first assignment of error appellant argues that the contract was conditional because the payment of $20,000 was not to be made until title insurance policy and deed were ready for delivery; possession was not to be given until delivery of title papers and deed; the seller was to give a warranty deed upon payment of $25,000 of the purchase price; and because certain taxes for the year 1942 had not been paid, as well as a mortgage held by the Valley National Bank. An examination of the record fails to sustain appellant's contention that the contract was a conditional one. The findings of the trial court disclose that plaintiff was ready, willing and able to convey good title, and that arrangements had been made to release the mortgage held by the bank. It further appears from the findings that plaintiff was ready and in a position to pay the unpaid taxes on the property, and the parties contemplated that such details would be taken care of by the plaintiff at the time of the execution of the contract.

A conditional contract has been defined as "an executory contract, the performance of which depends on a condition. It is not simply an executory contract, since the latter may be an absolute agreement to do, or not to do, something, but it is a contract whose very existence and performance depends on a contingency and condition." 17 C.J.S., Contracts, § 10, p. 329.

The contract did not depend upon any contingency, but at best its performance was suspended to a future time. As such a contract it is simply an executory contract containing unperformed but absolutely binding agreements.

Having determined that the contract is unconditional, our inquiry is directed solely to the rule of law to be applied to fix responsibility for the loss occasioned by the destruction of the packing shed during the interim between the signing of the contract and the time fixed for delivery of possession. This court, in the case of *Kresse v. Ryerson, supra*, undoubtedly committed itself to the so-called majority rule which holds that the risk of loss falls on the vendee; but in view of the fact that the rule as there announced was by way of obiter dictum, and the author of that opinion presided as trial judge in this action, we have re-examined the authorities and rationale of both majority and minority rules.

The early case of *Paine v. Meller*, 6 Ves. Jr. 349, 31 Eng. Reports 1088, first announced the majority rule, and it has been followed by a long line of cases both in England and America. 22 A.L.R. 575. The courts which have followed this rule have done so either upon the theory of an equitable conversion, whereby the vendor's interest in the property has been converted by the contract from realty into personalty and the vendor holds merely the bare legal title in trust for the vendee, who holds the equitable title; or upon the theory that the beneficial incidents of ownership are in the vendee.

The minority rule proceeds upon the theory that a contract for sale of realty contains an implied condition that since the vendee could not acquire all that he had bargained for by reason of the destruction of a portion of the premises, he should not be required to assume the loss. See cases cited in the Annot. 22 A.L.R. 575, at page 578, and also *Hawkes v. Kehoe*, 79 N.E. 766 (Mass); 41 A.L.R. 1272.

In this jurisdiction, both reason and authority require our reaffirmance of the majority rule as stated in *Kresse v. Ryerson, supra*. It is our view that the vendee under the contract had all the beneficial incidents of ownership, in that all income and charges were to be adjusted as of the date of the agreement. As was said by Lord Eldon in the case of *Paine v. Meller, supra*, "As to the mere effect of the accident itself, no solid objection can be founded upon that simply; for if the party by the contract has become in equity the owner of the premises, they are his to all intents and purposes. They are vendible as his, chargeable as his, capable of being incumbered as his; they may be devised as his; they may be assets and they would descend to his heir."

The authorities are numerous in holding that the rule placing the risk of loss on the vendee was the rule at common law. [Citations omitted.] Our statutes require the adoption of the common law as the rule of decision of the courts of this state, in so far as it is consistent with and adapted to the natural and physical conditions of this state and the necessities of the people thereof, and not repugnant to, or inconsistent with the Constitution of the United States, or the constitution and laws of this state, or established customs of the people of this state. Sec. 1-106, A.C.A. 1939. As a corollary of that premise it follows that the common-law rule, until changed by statute, is the rule this court must follow.

For the reasons stated the judgment of the lower court is in all respects affirmed.

NOTES AND QUESTIONS

1. *Criticism of the Doctrine of Equitable Conversion.* As the Arizona Court noted, the doctrine of equitable conversion is generally credited as originating in the decisions of the English Chancery Court early in the 19th century. *See Paine v. Muller*, 6 Ves. 349 (Ch. 1801); *Seaton v. Slade*, 7 Ves. Jun. 265 (Ch. 1802). Although the doctrine of equitable conversion has been adopted in at least 32 states, it has long been criticized. *See* Nock, Strait & Weaver, *Equitable Conversion in Washington: The Doctrine that Dares Not Speak Its Name*, 1 U.P.S. L. Rev. 121 (1977), for a list of jurisdictions in which the doctrine has been adopted.

As the above case illustrates, the traditional rationale for the doctrine was that the contract for sale should be treated as though the transaction had already been performed since equity would specifically enforce the contract. Although bare legal title remained in the possession of the vendor, the purchaser was viewed as having the more significant "equitable title." Academic criticism of the doctrine dates back at least to future United States Supreme Court Justice Harlan Fiske Stone's *Equitable Conversion by Contract*, 13 Colum. L. Rev. 369 (1913), and very few commentators have defended the doctrine in its traditional form. Moreover, it seems contrary to the expectations of the parties to the contract. As a practical matter, it most often means that the buyer, not the seller, is responsible for insuring the premises during the executory period, and this responsibility can be easily shifted by terms in the sale contract.

A number of jurisdictions have refused to follow the doctrine and others have modified it by statute, at least in regard to the risk of loss question. Shifting the risk of loss to the purchaser only if he or she takes possession in a fairly common modification. Both the Uniform Vendor and Purchaser Risk Act (1935) and the Uniform Land Transactions Act (1975) of the Commissioners on Uniform State Laws leave the risk with the seller until legal title is transferred to the buyer or the buyer takes possession, and excuse the buyer from the obligation to fulfill the contract if the property is materially damaged during the executory period.

Problems similar to those posed by damage to the premises arise when changes in zoning and building codes occur during the executory period and when eminent domain actions are initiated.

2. *The Death of a Party to the Contract During the Executory Period.* Since the execution of the real estate sales contract converts the seller's interest into one of personal property and the buyer's to one of real property before the exchange of land for money occurs, problems can occur if either party dies during the executory period and leaves a will that devises personal property to one individual and real property to another. For example, if T has a validly executed will that devises his real property to A and all of T's personal property to B, what happens if X and T enter into a valid contract of sale for Blackacre, but T dies before closing?

Under the theory of equitable conversion, T's interest in Blackacre was converted to personal property upon the execution of the contract even though he retains legal title to and possession of Blackacre. Consequently, Blackacre would go to B, the recipient of the personal property (who would be obligated to transfer it to X at the scheduled closing). What would be the result if X, not T, died before closing with a similar will? What would his devisee receive?

This distinction between real and personal property was of particular importance in England in the early 19th century when the doctrine of equitable conversion was created. At that time, real property descended to the eldest son while personal property was divided equally among the children. In the United States, this rule has at time produced unfair results, particularly when the will in question was made after the contract was executed and the parcel to be transferred, but not the decedent's personal property, was devised to a particular individual or institution. Some courts have awarded the purchase money of the land to the named devisee, not the recipient of the personal property, on the grounds that the testator must have intended such a result. For one such case, see *Father Flanagan's Boys Home v. Graybill*, 132 N.W.2d 304 (Neb. 1964).

3. *Equitable Conversion in* Timberlake v. Heflin. In *Timberlake*, Ms. Heflin argued that upon her ex-husband's death, his interest in the house automatically passed to her as a result of her status as joint tenant with right of survivorship. (Joint tenancies are examined in Chapter 5.) The court rejected this argument,

noting that "when the contract of sale was made, the doctrine of equitable conversion came into play." The court further noted: "The oral contract for the sale of land became enforceable when in July, 1983, Ms. Heflin acknowledged the contract in her divorce complaint. Mr. Timberlake, as the purchaser or vendee, acquired equitable title to Ms. Heflin's one-half interest in the property. Furthermore, on his death, his interest was not extinguished, but passed to his heirs at law." The court further concluded that it would be inequitable and improper to allow Ms. Heflin to exercise her survivorship rights to Mr. Timberlake's half interest in the property.

4. *Equitable Conversion and Option Contracts.* Even where the traditional rules as to equitable conversion apply, the acquisition of an option to purchase will not operate as a transfer of equitable title to the holder of the option. Equitable conversion occurs only when the option is exercised. Consequently, the seller of the option retains full legal title and his interest in the property remains a real property interest. If the seller dies before the option is exercised and his will directs his real property to one devisee and his personal property to another, the land subject to the option passes to the former. If the option is then exercised, that party is entitled to the full proceeds of the sale (and must complete the sale). Those were the facts in *Eddington v. Turner*, 38 A.2d 738 (Del. Ch. 1944).

Courts have also held that equitable conversion does not take place if the seller is unable to deliver marketable title, a concept explored in the next section of this chapter.

5. *The Installment Land Contract.* Throughout the 19th century and during much of the twentieth, land was often sold under an installment contract (also referred to as a contract for deed). In the modern land transaction, a buyer who cannot afford to pay the entire purchase price obtains a loan secured by a lien against the property to be purchased — this is called a purchase money mortgage — and pays the entire purchase price to the seller. However, the buyer under an installment land contract does not pay the full purchase price, but nevertheless takes possession of the land after the contract for sale is signed. He or she then makes a series of payments toward the outstanding balance according to a schedule set out in the contract. Only after the final payment is made, often years after the contract was executed, does legal title finally pass to the purchaser.

The prevalence of this type of financing in the 19th century helps explain the development of the doctrine of equitable conversion. In the context of the installment land contract, where the buyer takes equitable title and possession long before taking legal title, the doctrine's shifting liability for loss on to the holder of equitable title seems perfectly logical.

Under the typical installment land contract, the buyer's failure to make payments on schedule resulted in a forfeiture of equitable title back to the seller, and the buyer was left with no credit for payments already made. The perceived unfairness of this situation, particularly in times of economic depression, prompted many state legislatures to act to protect the interests of buyers under installment land contracts, usually by allowing the buyer to recover his or her "equity" in the contract. While the installment land contract has not entirely disappeared from the world of real estate transactions, it is clearly disfavored by courts and legislatures.

Note that the installment land contract is a different legal device than rent with option to purchase arrangements or forms of seller-financing in which the seller loans the purchase money to the buyer in exchange for a mortgage. In the former case, neither legal nor equitable title passes until the option to purchase is exercised; in the latter, legal title passes at closing as it does in situations involving third-party financing.

[B.] CONTRACTS FOR THE SALE OF LAND

[1.] The Sales Contract

To a great extent, the rules of real estate conveyancing are default rules that take effect when an issue arises — one that the contract for sale does not address. The parties to the transaction have a significant amount of leeway to change the rules governing the transaction so long as those changes are agreed upon and included in the sales contract.

Even so, few real estate sales contracts are drafted from scratch. Parties ordinarily begin with pre-printed form contracts and work from there. However, in the residential real estate context, the contract for sale is usually provided by a realtor and is signed by both parties without the assistance of attorneys (who are typically retained, if at all, only after the contract is signed). Consequently, the contents of a form contract drafted by neither of the parties is often controlling. Since the contract for sale is typically supplied by the real estate broker retained by the seller, should one expect the contract to favor the seller? The broker? At this point it might be useful to examine a residential real estate sales contract in use in your jurisdiction.

NOTES AND QUESTIONS

1. *The Role of the Real Estate Agent.* The responsibilities of the real estate agent to the buyer and seller have long been a source of controversy. The traditional rule was that the real estate broker and its employees were the agents of the seller and therefore owed a fiduciary duty to the seller. This was true even when the brokers or agents had no direct contact with the seller and when they were contacted by buyers to help locate a suitable piece of property. This position was justified by the fact that the seller, not the buyer, ordinarily paid the brokers the entire commission, even when it was shared with the agent assisting the buyer. In recent years, the latter relationship has been altered by statute in a number of jurisdictions. See, for example, Wis. Stat. §§ 452.133–139 (1995–1996), which states that an agent whose sole involvement with the transaction has involved assisting the buyer owes a primary fiduciary relationship to the buyer.

2. Residential real estate sales contracts often include a clause that allows either party to back out within a short period of time upon the advice of an attorney. Why is this clause included in a contract provided by a realtors' association? In whose interest does it operate?

3. *Fixtures.* The real estate sales contract is a contract for the sale of land and not the personal property located upon it. If personal property is to be exchanged as well as the land itself, that fact needs to be spelled out in the sales contract. However, certain items which were once personal property are treated as real property once they become affixed to the land. The most obvious fixture is a building. Although the components of the building are originally classified as personal property, they become a permanent part of the land once they are constructed. To become a fixture, an item must be intended to become a permanent part of the land; it must be actually annexed to the land or to something appurtenant to it (like a furnace in a house); and it must be specially adapted to the use of the land.

Sometimes the line between a fixture and a chattel is quite narrow. For example, wall to wall carpeting is usually treated as a fixture while a rug that covers the entire floor is not. Do you see the distinction? So-called mobile homes and other forms of pre-fabricated buildings pose recurring definitional problems. Questions pertaining to what is a fixture and what is not can and should be resolved in the purchase and sale agreement.

[2.] Marketable Title

In most contracts for the sale of land, the seller promises to deliver "marketable" or "merchantable" title. In fact, this requirement will normally be read into real estate contracts unless there is a provision in the contract to the contrary. Marketable title exists when the current owner's claim to a parcel of land is free, or virtually free, from the claims of others. Marketable title is not the same as fee simple title; a seller can own land in fee simple absolute but be unable to deliver marketable title because of the existence of easements, covenants, or liens which do not affect his ownership of the property but restrict the ways in which the property may be used.

A marketable title does not have to be a perfect title. So long as a prudent purchaser would accept the seller's title and so long as there is no reasonable probability that the buyer will be subjected to a lawsuit from another claiming an interest in the land, the title is said to be marketable. However, if the seller is unable to deliver marketable title at closing, the buyer has the right to withdraw from the contract.

TRI-STATE HOTEL CO. v. SPHINX INVESTMENT CO.

Kansas Supreme Court
510 P.2d 1223 (1973)

KAUL, JUSTICE.

This is an action to recover a deposit made under the terms of option purchase contracts entered into between the plaintiffs-appellants, other than the Fourth National Bank and Trust Company of Wichita, and the defendant-appellee.

The Fourth National Bank and Trust Company received the funds in question from the escrow agent, who was permitted to withdraw from the litigation with the consent of all parties. The Tri-State Hotel Company [and others] own interests in property known as the Broadview Hotel in Wichita and certain adjacent tracts and are the vendors in the option purchase contracts in question.

For convenience we shall refer to plaintiffs-appellants collectively as Tri-State and to defendant-appellee as Sphinx. The tracts of real estate involved in the option contracts, for purposes of identification, will be referred to as Tracts A, B, C and D. In negotiations leading up to the consummation of the option purchase contracts, plaintiffs-appellants were represented by Mr. R.C. McCormick, chairman of the board of directors of the Tri-State Hotel Company, Inc., which owned the Broadview Hotel. Negotiations for defendant-Sphinx were conducted primarily by Donald L. Herrick, treasurer and a member of the board of directors of Sphinx.

In December 1969 McCormick and Herrick reached an agreement in general terms for option purchase contracts of the properties involved. McCormick contacted John F. Eberhardt, a member of a Wichita law firm, and requested him to draw contracts on the basis of the general terms which had been agreed upon and which were summarized in a memo submitted to Eberhardt.

In his deposition, Eberhardt testified that he was requested to represent both parties in drafting the contracts; in processing all other paper work involved; in examination of titles; and was to act as escrow agent for the option deposits totaling $100,000.00 for the four tracts involved. Eberhardt further testified that he discussed the matter of his joint representation of the parties with both Herrick and McCormick and pointed out potential disadvantages to the parties and certain objections on his part in representing both parties to the contracts. Eberhardt testified that he told Herrick and McCormick that there was no way he could draw a contract and be perfectly fair to both sides; that there were things involved in any contract that could be drawn one way or the other. He also expressed concern about title defects which might appear in the abstracts. He told the parties that he knew of his own knowledge there was a "flock" of abstracts and that if title defects were encountered there would be problems, arising with respect to serious defects which a party would stand on or defects that could be waived. Eberhardt also testified that despite his expressed reservations about dual representation both McCormick and Herrick requested that he represent both parties.

Eberhardt proceeded to draft the contracts, discussing the details thereof from time to time with McCormick until the drafts were finalized. There were three separate contracts which were identical in terms except as to the different parties representing different ownerships in the various tracts and the diverse purchase prices for the particular property described. Each contract provided that it was contemporaneous with the other two contracts; that the obligations and terms of all three were interdependent; and that if any of the three contracts were canceled for nonmerchantability of title, the other two must also be canceled — that Sphinx must exercise its entitlement to cancel or its obligation to purchase, as the case might be, simultaneously with respect to all three contracts.

The portion of the contracts pertaining to delivery of abstracts disclosing marketable titles and providing for waiver of defects, which is relevant to this appeal, appears in Paragraph No. 3 of the contract which, in pertinent part, reads:

> As soon hereafter as is reasonably possible Tri-State shall deliver to attorney John F. Eberhardt of Foulston, Siefkin, Powers & Eberhardt, 600 Fourth National Bank Building, Wichita, Kansas, for purposes of title examination, abstracts of title to Tracts A, B and C certified to the approximate date of delivery by a bonded abstractor, which abstracts shall disclose good and marketable title in fee simple, free and clear of and from all liens and encumbrances except easements and restrictions of record, vested in Tri-State to all of Tract B, to an undivided one-half interest in Tract C, and to all of Tract A except the portion thereof in which an undivided 7/144ths fee interest is outstanding, and, with respect to said outstanding 7/144ths fee interest, said abstract shall show marketable title vested in Tri-State to a 99-year lease thereon requiring monthly rental payments of $15.07 and expiring in the year of 2019 A.D.
>
> Upon completion of the necessary title examination work said attorney's written title opinion shall be submitted to Tri-State and to Sphinx, and, in event said opinion reveals any merchantable defects in Tri-State's aforesaid title, Tri-State shall have a reasonable time thereafter within which to remedy all such defects at its own cost and expense. In event all such merchantable defects, if any, are not remedied by May 1, 1970, Sphinx shall have the right, at its discretion, to cancel this agreement, or, instead, to waive such defects and accept whatever title Tri-State is able to tender, which right shall be exercised by written notice to Tri-State on or before May 15, 1970, and failure to so notify Tri-State by that date shall constitute an irrevocable election by Sphinx to waive such defects and accept Tri-State's actual title. In event this agreement is canceled because of nonmerchantability of title to Tracts A, B, C, or D (as provided in following paragraph "4" hereof), Sphinx' initial $80,750.00 option payment hereunder shall forthwith be refunded to Sphinx, and the parties hereto shall be under no further obligation to each other hereunder. But if title to all of said tracts is merchantable or is rendered merchantable by May 1, 1970, or if on or before May 15, 1970, Sphinx waives all merchantable defects in the title to said tracts and no cancellation of this option contract is effected under paragraph "4" hereof, then and in such event Tri-State shall forthwith be entitled to unrestricted ownership of said $80,750.00 initial option payment. . . .

After the final drafts were completed the contracts were executed by McCormick and Herrick on December 23, 1969. On that day Eberhardt was in McCormick's office and after the signing of the contracts; McCormick, according to Eberhardt's testimony, "had a girl give me what he thought were all the rest of the abstracts." Mr. Eberhardt and two other members of his firm, whom he identified as Dick Harris and Phil Frick, commenced the examination of the abstracts.

It was soon discovered that a part of Tract A, upon which the Broadview is located, was not covered by any of the abstracts — as Eberhardt described the situation "we had abstracts that kept going to this place on all sides and we couldn't find anything that covered that particular tract." Efforts were made through the abstract company to locate the missing portion. Eberhardt had several more conversations with McCormick who was positive that he had complete abstracts of title. He told Eberhardt that he (McCormick) thought at one time they had already had a quiet title suit involving the same thing. Eberhardt testified that it took a month or two to locate all the abstracts on the property and finally it was necessary to have an abstract made. Ultimately, on April 16, 1970, a title opinion was rendered. The opinion was drafted in letter form by Mr. Eberhardt, addressed to Herrick and a copy sent to McCormick. The opinion revealed four merchantable title defects, three of which were said to be of no significance and could easily be cured before May 1, 1970, the cutoff date under the terms of the contract.

The fourth merchantable title defect which gives rise to this controversy was described by Eberhardt in this fashion:

> Although it is of no practical significance, the fourth merchantable title defect raises problems which cannot be remedied by May 1. As is explained in comment "(2)" of our title opinion covering Tract A, on June 30, 1925, The Arkansas Valley Improvement Company conveyed to The Siedhoff Hotel Company part of Holmes Addition (which is bounded by the Arkansas River on the west, by the south line of the NE/4 of Section 20-24S-1E on the north, by Waco Avenue on the east, and by Douglas Avenue on the south). However, in this deed the grantor excepted and retained a small wedge of land described by metes and bounds as set out in comment "(2)".
>
> When the Siedhoff Hotel Company reconveyed this part of Holmes Addition to The Tri-State Hotel Company, Inc. on July 31, 1964, the deed again excepted this same wedge of ground that is 10' 5" wide (north and south) at its east end, 2' 1" wide at its west end, 30' long on its southern side and 25' long on its northern side. From that time to this there has been no deed of any sort covering this diagonal strip of land, title to which is still vested in The Arkansas Valley Improvement Company, a Kansas corporation which is no longer in existence. So you can visualize this strip more readily I enclose a Zerox [sic] copy of a plat of Holmes Addition on which our troublesome wedge of land appears as a diagonal red mark immediately north of Lots 5 and 6. This strip is underneath the hotel improvements on Tract A. Beyond all shadow of doubt Tri-State has long since acquired indefeasible title to this strip by adverse possession, continued occupancy, and payment of real property taxes thereon. Nevertheless, since we can no longer obtain a quitclaim deed from the record title owner, our only remedy is to file quiet title proceedings. This, too, presents no problem whatever, except that it will require a minimum of 60 days to file suit, obtain service by publication, and secure judgment quieting Tri-State's title against The Arkansas Valley Improvement Company and its unknown successors, trustees, and assigns. By the same token, it is impossible to rectify this title defect by May 1, or even by May 15.
>
> Inasmuch as this defect cannot be removed by May 1, under paragraph "3" of the Sphinx-Tri-State base contract Sphinx has until May 15 to decide whether to cancel or retain its option. I would hope, though, that you can give me Sphinx' decision much sooner than May 15. Certainly I must know very quickly whether or not it will be necessary for Tri-State to prepay the last half of 1969 real property taxes and to prepay the two escrow contracts

> prior to May 1. Nor do I want to file quiet title proceedings until I know whether or not Sphinx will waive this one title defect, conditioned upon our promptly instituting and prosecuting quiet title action to final judgment at the sole cost of Tri-State. In this connection, having to represent both the seller and buyer puts me in an unhappy predicament. I must say, however, that I would strongly recommend that you waive this defect and accept Tri-State's title, conditioned upon Tri-State's authorizing us to conduct quiet title proceedings, even if I were representing Sphinx alone because the defect, although technically a "merchantable" one, is of no real consequence whatever and can easily be removed by a routine title suit.

The board of directors of Sphinx met on May 7, 1970, and considered the action which should be taken on Eberhardt's letter relating to the title defects. The action of Sphinx is reflected in the minutes of the board meeting and the deposition testimony of Herrick and Albert A. Kaine, Jr., vice-president and director. The discussion at the meeting centered around the problems Sphinx might encounter if it waived the defects in terms of being able to retain the financing commitment which Sphinx had previously arranged on the property. One of the directors, Glenn Jones, an attorney, warned of difficulties that might be encountered in various situations that were under negotiations by reason of not having merchantable title to the property.

Mr. Herrick testified that he had communicated with the correspondent for a mortgage lender on the property and was told that there would be a risk of having the mortgage lender back out completely or raise the interest rate, or require more personal signatures on the loan, or otherwise change existing commitments. The discussion culminated in a resolution adopted by the board of directors as follows:

> BE IT RESOLVED, that WHEREAS the Tri-State Hotel Company, Inc. through its attorney, John F. Eberhardt, had indicated it cannot deliver merchantable title by May 1, 1970, and WHEREAS under the Sphinx-Tri-State base contract, Sphinx Investment Co., Inc. has the option of waiving the defect or canceling the contract, Sphinx hereby elects not to waive the defect and authorizes its President to send notices of this fact by certified mail to all interested parties and to demand the return of its $100,000 option money plus interest from the escrow agent, John F. Eberhardt.

Thereafter, Sphinx sent notice of their election to terminate the contracts to the respective parties and made formal demand for the return of the option money paid in escrow to Eberhardt.

In the meantime, Eberhardt informed McCormick that he was going to hold the option deposit a few days and unless McCormick commenced litigation he was going to return the money to Sphinx. Thereafter this litigation was promptly instigated.

In their petition plaintiffs alleged that on or before May 1, 1970, they became unconditionally entitled to receive the option payments and that all conditions precedent to their rights to receive such payments had been performed or had occurred. Basically, plaintiffs contended that Sphinx had forfeited the deposit and that plaintiffs should be entitled to keep their property and have the option money as well.

Defendant answered setting out the title defect referred to and alleging that it had given written notice by certified mail that it was canceling its option contract with each of the plaintiffs inasmuch as Tri-State Hotel Company, Inc. did not have merchantable title to the property and that merchantable title could not be delivered on or before May 15, 1970. The case came on for trial to the court.

The evidence consisted of various exhibits, depositions and the testimony of several parties. The trial court held in favor of Sphinx and entered findings of fact and conclusions of law. It appears the trial court's conclusions were essentially based upon two premises. First, there was a merchantable defect giving Sphinx the discretionary right to cancel the contracts and, second, even if the title was merchantable Eberhardt's conclusion that Sphinx had the right to cancel was binding since he was acting as attorney and agent for plaintiffs. Specifically, the trial court concluded that the outstanding title in Arkansas Valley Improvement Company to the irregularly shaped strip of land lying beneath the hotel building constituted a marketable title defect and, even though Tri-State may have acquired title by adverse possession the title was not rendered marketable since a quiet title action would be required, thus Sphinx as purchaser would be exposed to the hazards of litigation. Specific findings and conclusions of the trial court will be considered and discussed in the course of this opinion.

The basic question on appeal is whether the outstanding fee title to an irregularly shaped strip of land approximately 6' 6" × 30' × 2" × 25", which now lies beneath an addition to the Broadview Hotel constructed in 1952, amounts to a merchantable defect which could not be cured within the time limit specified in the contract.

We deem it unnecessary for the purposes of our decision to trace in detail the devolution of title to the property in question. It will suffice to say that the tract causing the problem was described and expressly excepted from the property described in a warranty deed, dated June 30, 1925, from the Arkansas Valley Improvement Company to Seidhoff Hotel Company, Tri-State's predecessor in title. Arkansas Valley Improvement Company and its companion corporation, Arkansas Valley Interurban Railway Company, commenced assembling the properties in 1919 and 1920 for the purpose of developing a site for a hotel and railway depot. There were a number of lease assignments and exchanges of property between these two entities prior to the conveyance to Seidhoff. In 1935 there were several agreements simultaneously executed between the Arkansas Valley Improvement Company, the Arkansas Valley Interurban Railway Company and Seidhoff which dealt with easements for railroad purposes, none of which affected the fee title to the tract in question. Later, Seidhoff deeded all of the property owned by it to Tri-State and again the identical exception was expressly set out in the description of the property conveyed. Tri-State claims the easement conveyances between Arkansas Valley Improvement Company, Arkansas Valley Interurban Railway Company and Seidhoff should serve as a basis for an inference that it was intended that Seidhoff acquired the property in fee. It appears to be undisputed that fee title to the problem tract remains in the Arkansas Valley Improvement Company. Arkansas Valley Improvement Company was dissolved in 1943.

On appeal Tri-State attacks the trial court's judgment on a number of grounds. Its first contention gets to the meat of the issue in the case, whether the title defect, upon which Sphinx relied as a basis for cancellation of the contracts, amounted to a merchantable defect.

The contracts in this case are clear, specific and unambiguous. The language is neither doubtful nor obscure. They obligated the vendors to furnish abstracts disclosing good and merchantable title in fee simple. The terms "merchantable title" and "marketable title" are interchangeable when used in the context of a land contract, and they denote the same quality of title to be furnished. (*Darby v. Keeran*, 505 P.2d 710.)

Where a contract for the sale and purchase of land provides that the vendor shall furnish vendee or his representative an abstract disclosing a good and marketable title in fee simple, such as the contract here, the abstract must show on its face a marketable title in the vendor. (*Darby v. Keeran, supra*; *Hamilton v. Binger*, 176 P.2d 553 (Kan.); 55 Am.Jur., Vendor and Purchaser, § 297, p. 734.) A good or merchantable title within the meaning of a contract of sale, in the absence of provisions to the contrary, generally means a record title.

There can be no doubt regarding what constitutes a marketable or merchantable title in this jurisdiction. This court has been confronted with the question on many occasions, most recently in the case of *Darby v. Keeran, supra*, where we held: "A marketable title is one which is free from reasonable doubt and will not expose the party who holds it to the hazards of litigation."

Many of the cases in which the rule has been stated and approved are referred to in the *Darby* opinion and citations thereof will not be repeated at this early date. Guidelines for the application of the rule with respect to specific title defects have been set out in many of our decisions. For example in *Johnson Bros. Furniture Co. v. Rothfuss*, 349 P.2d 903 (Kan.), we held:

> To render the title to real estate unmarketable, the defect of which the purchaser complains must be of a substantial character and one from which he may suffer injury. Mere immaterial defects which do not diminish in quantity, quality or value the property contracted for, constitute no ground upon which the purchaser may reject the title. Facts must be known at the time which fairly raise a reasonable doubt as to the title; a mere possibility or conjecture that such a state of facts may be developed at some future time is not sufficient.

In the instant case, it is undisputed that Tri-State does not have title to the small irregular tract in question, the title to which remains in Arkansas Valley Improvement Company. In other words, title to the problem tract is outstanding. Tri-State says the defect could be cured or is extinguished by adverse possession; that it is not a defect of substantial character which might cause injury to the buyer; and thus cannot serve as a ground for cancellation by Sphinx. We cannot agree. In all probability, as Tri-State says, adverse possession could be established showing that the outstanding title in this case is barred. But the question is not whether adverse possession is or could be established by affidavits or a quiet title suit, it is whether, when delivered to Eberhardt, the abstracts disclosed a merchantable title which Sphinx must accept. The rule that where a contract calls for the delivery of abstracts disclosing merchantable title, a purchaser will not be compelled to accept a title based on adverse possession is in accord with decisions on the point in most other jurisdictions. [Citations omitted.]

Tri-State relies heavily upon the case of *Burton v. Mellor, supra*, in support of its argument that the defect here does not rise to the level of a merchantable defect. In that case, Burton, the vendor, brought the action to recover the agreed consideration for the sale of an oil and gas lease from the vendee, Mellor. Mellor defended on the alleged failure of Burton to furnish an abstract showing a merchantable title to the property. Mellor's objection to the title rested on a lease to a mining corporation executed by the then owner of the land about fifty-eight years prior to the sale in question. The previous lessee was a corporation which had forfeited its charter twenty-five years after the execution of the lease; had never complied with the terms of the lease or paid any rent thereunder; and had never attempted to assign or transfer any interest under the lease at any time. As in the instant case, there was no corporate entity available to receive a notice or to execute a quitclaim deed or release, but there the similarity between the two cases ends. In *Burton* the facts concerning the defunct corporation and its noncompliance with the terms of the lease were compiled in an affidavit of the secretary of the corporation and presented to Mellor and his counsel prior to the time Mellor refused to accept the title. In his affidavit the secretary averred that he was the sole surviving officer of the corporation; that at no time was there any prospecting for any mining products by the corporation on the lands covered by the lease; and that no payments provided for in the lease were ever made by the corporation. A lease which was subject to forfeiture and the terms of which had never been complied with cannot be equated with an outstanding fee such as in the case at bar. We view the *Burton* case as unpersuasive on the issue before us here.

In this action it was not the function of the trial court, nor of this court on appeal, to determine whether or not the title is or is not bad, but whether it is doubtful enough to cause it to be unmerchantable. Tri-State suggests the applicability of the principle that any conveyance of real estate passes all of the estate of the grantor therein unless the intent to pass a less estate should expressly appear or be necessarily implied in the terms of the grant (citing *Epperson v. Bennett*, 167 P.2d 606). The rule is sound and applicable when necessary in construing the effect of a written instrument, but it has no application where a deed contains an express, explicit and unequivocal exception such as in the instant case.

Tri-State contends that Eberhardt should have considered evidence discovered by it after the suit was filed. By the express terms of the contract, Tri-State was to deliver abstracts of title to Eberhardt; it was not incumbent upon him or Sphinx to furnish evidence of the title. However, according to Eberhardt's testimony, which is undisputed, he and other members of his firm searched diligently for abstracts and quiet title actions which McCormick insisted were in existence. It would fly in the face of the clear meaning of the contract to require Sphinx to base its decision whether to accept title, which it was required to do prior to May 15, on documents and title evidence not within the knowledge of either Tri-State or the examining attorneys at the time.

Despite the specific provisions pertaining to the dates, May 1 and May 15, Tri-State argues the contract should be construed so as to provide a reasonable time thereafter to cure defects. In his testimony Eberhardt explained that since the closing date of the option contract was July 1, 1970, dates in advance thereof had to be established for the clearing of title and the fixing of the time in which Sphinx had to cancel the contract or waive any defects which might appear. The significance of the dates May 1 and May 15 is emphasized in the language of Paragraph No. 3, first to provide that if defects are not remedied by May 1, then Sphinx has the right, at its discretion, to cancel by written notice before May 15, and failure therein would constitute an irrevocable election by Sphinx to waive any defects. The import of the dates was then restated in the alternative that "if title to all of said tracts is merchantable or is rendered merchantable by May 1, 1970, or if on or before May 15, 1970, Sphinx waives all merchantable defects in the title" then Tri-State would be entitled to unrestricted ownership of the initial option payment. The language used is explicit and the import and materiality of the dates, May 1 and May 15, are made clear. The provisions of the contract, in this regard, must be given the effect stated in the clear language employed. The law presumes that the parties understood their contract and that they had the intention which its terms import. It is not the function of courts to make contracts, but to enforce them as made, nor is it within the province of the court to reform an instrument by rejecting words of clear and definite meaning and substituting others therefor.

Tri-State further contends that Sphinx in continuing its efforts to market the property after receipt of Eberhardt's title opinion waived any defect mentioned therein and is estopped from claiming to the contrary. Viewing the evidence presented within the context of the express terms of the contract, we believe the trial court correctly disposed of Tri-State's claim of estoppel. When the title opinion was received, Herrick and Kaine did not know what the ultimate decision of the Sphinx board of directors might be. The evidence is that they continued to follow up and respond to contacts previously made. No new contacts were made and all activity ceased after the May 7th meeting of the Sphinx directors, which was the first meeting after receipt of the title opinion. There is no evidence that Tri-State was misled or that it changed its position in any way because of the continued activities of Herrick and Kaine. A party is not estopped by an act of his which does not mislead his adversary so as to cause him to act to his prejudice.

Finally, Tri-State argues the trial court erred in determining that Eberhardt's title opinion and notification to Sphinx of its right to cancel was binding on Tri-State since Eberhardt represented both parties and as such was the agent of Tri-State as well as Sphinx. On this point we are inclined to agree with the position taken by Tri-State. While it is true Eberhardt represented both parties, his duties and responsibilities were clearly defined in the contract, but they did not include that of arbiter. It is proper for the court, in determining marketability of a title, to take into consideration the fact a competent attorney has rendered an opinion the title is not marketable. But whether a title is in fact marketable presents a question of law for the court.

We rest our decision on the hypotheses that Tri-State failed to furnish abstracts disclosing a marketable title; that the defect was not remedied by May 1; and that Sphinx exercised its discretionary right to cancel prior to May 15, all as provided for in the explicit terms of the contract. The judgment is affirmed.

NOTES AND QUESTIONS

1. At the outset, lawyer John F. Eberhardt represented both parties to this transaction. While dual representation of both parties to a real estate contract is permitted in most jurisdictions, it is highly discouraged, and the lawyer must withdraw as soon as the interests of the parties become adverse. Should the real estate transaction be assumed to be an adversarial relationship? For a widely noted example of a lawyer who got into trouble attempting to represent both parties, see *In re Lanza*, 322 A.2d 445 (N.J. 1974).

2. Marketable title does not mean perfect title in the sense that there is no possibility that another party might have an interest in the property. It means, however, that the title being transferred is free of all reasonable risks of legal attack. Title may be unmarketable either because the seller cannot establish that he is the record owner of the property or because the property cannot be delivered to the buyer without legal encumbrances.

A defect in the chain of title means that the seller cannot trace a continuing line of ownership from his claim to the property back through all previous owners to the original transfer from the sovereign to the first private owner. This can be the result of the seller holding an invalid deed originating in fraud or forgery or it can be the result of an error in executing or recording what would have been an otherwise valid deed. Or, it may be, as in the case above, that the seller owns part, but not all, of the land he is purporting to transfer. Ordinarily, it is not necessary to trace title all the way back to the sovereign; in fact, breaks in the chain of title that date back more than 40 or 50 years are usually not seen as preventing the seller from delivering marketable title. Do you see why?

3. In rare cases, it may be possible that an owner who once had a valid chain of title to the land he seeks to convey can no longer deliver marketable title because of an adverse possession or an eminent domain taking, or because he has already knowingly or unknowingly transferred the property to someone else. Encumbrances which make title unmarketable include easements, restrictive covenants, mortgages, liens, and continuing zoning code violations. All represent legal interests in favor of other parties, and the presence of these interests could prevent the new owner from using the property as he saw fit. If such encumbrances exist and they are more than *de minimis*, the buyer may withdraw from the contract unless he has waived the right to do so. (In some jurisdictions, a purchaser must accept those encumbrances that are readily visible or known to him or her at the time the contract is signed.)

4. Of course, the existence of substantial encumbrances does not make the property literally unmarketable. While liens and mortgages can be paid off, and zoning code violations can be corrected, it may not be within the power of the owner to eliminate easements and covenants. Nevertheless, the property is not likely to be deprived of all value, and a prospective purchaser may still want the property, albeit at a lower price. Moreover, certain encumbrances, like utility easements and restrictive covenants designed to insure the residential character of a neighborhood, are actually quite desirable. Consequently, the right to object to specific encumbrances or even general types of encumbrances is frequently waived by the purchaser at the time the contract is executed.

5. *Marketable Title and Adverse Possession.* Jurisdictions differ on the issue of whether or not one who obtained title by adverse possession alone can deliver marketable title. As in the case above, some jurisdictions require more than just evidence that an adverse possession has been successfully completed — often a formal court action to quiet title is necessary. Others will find that clear and convincing evidence of an adverse possession will satisfy the requirements of marketable title unless the contract calls for "marketable title of record."

6. *Marketable Title and Zoning Restrictions.* The existence of zoning laws and building codes that affect the use of land do not affect marketable title, even if they severely restrict the uses to which the land may be put. The rationale is that such matters apply to the public generally and are matters of public record. In recent years, there has been a tendency to exempt subdivision-wide restrictive covenants from the marketable title requirements as well, even though the origin of these restrictions is private rather than public. *Seth v. Wilson*, 662 P.2d 745 (Or. Ct. App. 1983).

7. *Marketable Title vs. Insurable Title.* Sometimes real estate sale contracts call for "insurable title" rather than marketable title. This is ordinarily understood to mean that the seller is required only to provide title in sufficient quality to obtain an insurance policy from a title insurance company. This means that the presence of remote or insignificant encumbrances which technically prevent the seller from delivering marketable title but do not prevent the acquisition of title insurance cannot be used by the buyer to cancel the contract.

8. *Marketable Title Acts.* The inability to deliver marketable title can severely hamper the alienability of real property, even when there is very little chance of a third party asserting a valid claim against the parcel in question. Buyers are often understandably reluctant to purchase land which is subject to another's legal claim since it may be difficult for them to judge the seriousness of the impediment. To address this problem, many states have enacted legislation designed to make it easier for sellers to deliver marketable title.

Although the content of these acts varies considerably, they all seek to make land marketable by invalidating certain types of encumbrances, particularly those which are several decades old. By eliminating clouds on title, remedial acts of this nature allow buyers to purchase property free from risk. They also protect sellers by taking away from buyers, who change their mind during the time between the signing of the contract and closing, the right to back out of contracts.

The most conservative marketable title legislation — the so-called curative acts — merely validates deeds that were technically deficient but otherwise reflective of the intentions of the buyer and seller. Other acts limit the right to enforce specific types of legal encumbrances, usually older mortgages and certain types of future interests, specifically, possibilities of reverter and powers of termination (discussed in Chapter 9). "Marketable record title acts," which exist in approximately 20 states, go even farther and void most types of claims to land if they are not recorded or re-recorded in the official land records within a specific period of time following the "root of title." (The recording process is discussed in Section D of this chapter.)

While many of the third-party interests nullified by marketable title acts would be otherwise unenforceable because of the statute of limitations, the equitable doctrine of laches, adverse possession, legal abandonment, or other doctrines, there are situations in which they work to eliminate perfectly valid interests. That topic is discussed in Section D of this chapter.

[C.] THE DEED

[1.] Components of the Deed

The form and content of deeds varies from jurisdiction to jurisdiction, but all deeds must include the names of the grantor and grantee, words indicating an intention to transfer, a description of the land, the grantor's signature, and in some states, the signatures of two witnesses. As long as these requirements are satisfied, the deed will be valid, and American courts are usually liberal in their interpretation of these requirements. Deeds also typically include some reference to the consideration, warranties of titles, listing of existing encumbrances which the grantee accepts, and an acknowledgment clause. All of this can make the deed a lengthy document.

Description of Land. A deed must identify the boundaries of the property being conveyed. Ordinarily, a street address will not do this. Boundaries were traditionally defined by metes and bounds, i.e., a description of the perimeter of the property in relation to existing landmarks. In states that were subject to the government survey (all states north of the Ohio River or West of the Mississippi except Texas and including Florida, Alabama, and Mississippi) the description can be made in reference to the survey grid. In modern urban and suburban developments, deed descriptions are often in reference to a map or "plat" prepared by the developer and filed in the local land records after securing governmental approval. The plat itself contains a metes and bounds or government survey description of each lot in the development, but subsequent deeds make reference only to the lot number assigned to the particular parcel on the plat.

Types of Deeds. While both grantor and grantee may sign the deed, the Statute of Frauds requires only that it be signed by the party to be bound, i.e., the grantor. A deed signed by the grantor alone is called a deed poll. A deed signed by both parties is an indenture. At common law a deed had to be under seal, but this requirement has been largely abandoned (although it is retained in a few jurisdictions), and unsealed instruments are routinely referred to as deeds. Deeds are also classified by the degree of assurance offered by the grantor that the land transferred is free of encumbrances. Deeds that come with no guarantees are quitclaim deeds; those in which the grantor promises to come to the defense of the grantee if the title is challenged and to indemnify him if the challenge is successful are called warranty deeds. Deeds that warrant against title defects caused or created by the grantor personally are called *special warranty* deeds; those that warrant against all title defects, whatever their source, are *general warranty* deeds.

Spousal Interests. If the grantor owns the property in his or her own name, but is married, the spouse may have an interest in the property through dower, homestead, or community property laws. To relinquish these interests, the grantor's spouse must also sign the deed. For example, in *Timberlake v. Heflin*, above, Ms. Heflin's second husband, Hugh, was made a party to the action because of his dower interest. At the time of *Timberlake*, W. Va. Code § 43-1-1, provided:

> A surviving spouse shall be endowed of one third of all the real estate whereof the deceased spouse, or any other to his or her use, or in trust for him or her, was, at any time during the coverture, seised of or entitled to an estate of inheritance, either in possession, reversion, remainder, or otherwise, unless the right of such surviving spouse to such dower shall have been lawfully barred or relinquished.

The subject of marital property rights is discussed in Chapter 5.

The traditional deed is composed of the following parts: the premises, the habendum, the reddendum, warranties of title, signature, and acknowledgment. The premises identify the parties (or at least the grantor), describe the land being transferred, make some mention of the consideration, and include words of grant or transfer. The habendum is used for declarations of trust in those situations where the grantee is to hold the land for the benefit of someone else. If there is no intention to create a trust, as is usually the case, the habendum states that the grantee holds for his or her own use. In most cases the habendum clause is superfluous and is often omitted.

The reddendum is an exceptions and/or reservations clause and is used to retain or create an interest in the land for the grantor. An exception "excepts" some existing interest from the grant, such as where a grantor retains a small portion of an existing parcel. A reservation creates a new real property interest, like an easement of right of way, for the grantor. In most jurisdictions, a reservation cannot be made in favor of a third party. If one is desired, it must be handled through a two-step (two deed) process. For example, if A wishes to sell Blackacre to B subject to an easement of right of way for C (and no such easement currently exists), A must first deed the easement to C before conveying the parcel to B, or else secure from B a binding promise to convey the easement to C after she (B) receives the deed to Blackacre.

The warranties of title pledge the grantor to support the grantee if his title to the land is challenged. (Covenants of warranty are discussed in Subsection 3, below.) The signature and acknowledgment includes the grantor's signature and a notary's assertion that the signature is authentic. While no state requires deeds to be notarized to be valid, there are many advantages to doing so if the authenticity of the signature is ever put into question. Moreover, the recording acts of most states require that signatures be attested before the deed can be recorded.

While traditional deeds are still used in some places, the modern trend is toward a short form deed which dispenses with much of the archaic language of the granting clauses of deeds and the elaborate descriptions of the property conveyed. At this point it may be useful to examine a deed in use in your jurisdiction.

[2.] The Delivery Requirement

The writing requirement of the Statute of Frauds is ordinarily satisfied by a deed, the delivery of which legally marks the transfer of land. As the following case illustrates, it is the transfer of the deed, not its drafting or signing, that is the critical legal event.

CAPOZZELLA v. CAPOZZELLA

Virginia Supreme Court
196 S.E.2d 67 (1973)

POFF, JUSTICE.

This is an appeal from a final decree entered on December 20, 1971, granting the prayer of a bill of complaint filed by Harriet A. Capozzella against Lytton H. Gibson and Henry F. Capozzella for a mandatory injunction directing Gibson, as stakeholder, to deliver to the clerk for recordation a deed from Donald K. Graham and Rothwell J. Lillard, Trustees, to Henry F. Capozzella and Harriet A. Capozzella, his wife, as tenants by the entirety, conveying 51 acres of land with residence in Fairfax County. The deed was duly delivered and recorded, and we granted Henry F. Capozzella an appeal.

Pursuant to a separation agreement dated March 20, 1968, and for the purpose of waiving inchoate dower rights, Henry F. Capozzella and his first wife, Bette, executed a deed dated May 3, 1968 conveying the property to Capozzella's attorneys, Donald K. Graham and Rothwell J. Lillard, as trustees, with the understanding that upon payment of a sum of money to Bette the trustees would be empowered to convey title according to Capozzella's instructions. Payment was made in due course.

Harriet Capozzella testified that some time prior to their marriage, Henry F. Capozzella took her to the office of attorney Lytton Gibson and told Gibson, "I want to get my property out of the names of the trustees and put in this little girl's name, because if it weren't for her, I would be dead today." She explained that Capozzella was referring to help she had given him in obtaining employment as chief anesthetist at a large hospital. On June 19, 1970, four days after their marriage, the couple visited Gibson again, and Capozzella told the attorney that "[t]here is no reason not to take the trustees' names off, and have my wife's put on."

From Gibson's testimony concerning that meeting, it appears that Capozzella was eager to do whatever was necessary to prevent his first wife from attacking his will, and through their minor daughter, acquiring control over his property. Capozzella told Gibson that he trusted his new wife, and Gibson advised him that they should execute mutual wills and have the trustees convey the property to him and his new wife as tenants by the entirety with right of survivorship as at common law. Gibson explained the nature and effect of the tenancy "in detail."

By letter dated June 22, 1970, Gibson wrote to Lillard inquiring if the trustees were prepared to execute a deed. By letter dated June 25, 1970, Lillard advised Gibson in the affirmative, asked for written instructions from Capozzella and suggested a fee of $25.00 for each of the trustees.

On June 30, 1970, Gibson wrote to Capozzella telling him that the trustees had agreed to execute a deed, that the trustees' fees would be $25.00 each and that Capozzella should advise him the balance due on the trust note secured by the property in order that he could make appropriate provision in the deed he was preparing and properly calculate the recording fees.

Harriet testified that Capozzella telephoned her while she was in Massachusetts packing her effects to move to Virginia and asked her to call Gibson and give him the information requested in the letter, which, as Gibson confirmed, she did.

In late August 1970, she and her husband visited Gibson again and signed some document which she could not identify but which Gibson said he would send along with the deed to the trustees. Lillard testified that he never received written instruction signed by Capozzella but felt that Gibson had full authority to speak for him. Gibson testified that he estimated the costs of recordation of the deed would be about $1300.00 and "suggested that the parties just wait and see if the property was sold" and that Capozzella "agreed the deed was not to be recorded on account of the cost."

Dr. Alexander, Harriet's father, testified that at breakfast on the morning following the August meeting Capozzella told him and Mrs. Alexander "that they went and saw Mr. Gibson, and that he had the names of the trustees on the deed taken off, Lillard and Graham, and asked Mr. Gibson to have Harriet's name on the deed, and he was very happy to do that because that was the best gift he could give to her." Mrs. Alexander testified that Capozzella said, "Dr. Alexander, I want you to know that after we went in to see Mr. Gibson, and we signed the papers for the deed, I gave Harriet one-half of my property as a gift to her."

In a letter dated October 7, 1970 to Lillard, Gibson enclosed two $25.00 checks and a general warranty deed of tenancy by the entirety. At Lillard's request, Gibson re-drafted the deed to provide special warranty of title, dated it October 15, 1970 and sent it to Lillard.

By letter dated November 6, 1970 Gibson advised Capozzella that he had prepared the wills and received the executed deed from the trustees. He asked Capozzella to make an appointment to inspect the wills and "determine just what we want to do about recording the deed." Five days later the Capozzellas separated, the appointment was never made, and the wills were never signed. On account of the domestic dispute, Gibson retained the deed pending a court order. By letter dated December 11, 1970 Gibson submitted and Capozzella paid a bill of $350.00 for legal services rendered from April 13, 1970 to November 6, 1970 and "advanced costs" of $50.00.

Capozzella argues that the deed was void because he had given Gibson no instructions as to disposition of the deed and there was, therefore, no completed delivery of the deed; that the deed was void because Gibson, acting without his authority under seal, had no power to bind him to a deed under seal; and that the deed was void because the trustees, acting without his written authorization, violated their fiduciary duty in executing the deed.

For a deed to pass title, there must be delivery. For delivery to be operative, physical deposit with the named grantee is not essential. "The delivery may be actual, as by manual tradition to the grantee, or to another for his use, or it may be constructive. . . . . It may be proved by direct evidence or be inferred from circumstances." *Enright v. Bannister*, 77 S.E.2d 377, 379 (Va. 1953). *See also Schreckhise v. Wiseman*, 45 S.E. 745 (Va. 1903), approving the rule that delivery may be effective when a deed is deposited with a third person for transmittal to the grantee.

If delivery is made, recordation is not necessary to pass title. Even if the deed is lost or purposely destroyed by the grantor, delivery passes title. *Brewer v. Brewer*, 102 S.E.2d 303 (Va. 1958); *Garrett v. Andis*, 165 S.E. 657 (Va. 1932). And where the deed is made by one spouse to another in voluntary settlement of an antecedent promise, the formalities of delivery required of deeds of bargain and sale are not necessary.

What makes delivery operative is the grantor's intent. "There was a delivery if there was the intention to deliver which is effectuated by words or acts, and this is a question of fact to be gathered from all of the circumstances of the particular case." *Payne v. Payne*, 104 S.E. 712, 716 (Va. 1920).

Capozzella contends that he did not intend to deliver and delivery was incomplete because he had not given Gibson "specific instructions as to the disposition of the deed."

On the question of intent, the evidence is uncontradicted that Capozzella intended to remove title from the names of the trustees. If he intended the deed to be operative for one purpose, he must be taken to have intended it to be operative for all purposes apparent on its face.

Not once, until separated from his new wife, did he deny that he intended her to share ownership of his home. Prior to the marriage, he told Gibson that he wanted to put the property in her name. Only a few days after the marriage, he reaffirmed that purpose, and when Gibson advised how the deed should be drawn, his words and conduct justified Gibson in believing that he had full authority to pursue the course he recommended. A scant two weeks later, after receiving Gibson's letter telling him that the trustees were ready to execute the deed, Capozzella called his wife and asked her to supply the information necessary for Gibson to draft it, something he would not have done had he objected to its purpose.

When the couple returned to Gibson's office in August, Capozzella had another opportunity to protest what he knew Gibson was doing. Not only did he fail to challenge Gibson's authority, he accepted Gibson's further suggestion that he hold the deed and save recording costs until a decision had been reached about a possible sale. The following morning at breakfast, Capozzella told his wife's father that Gibson had made arrangements to effectuate the gift he was making her.

Even after receipt of Gibson's letter telling him that the executed deed was in his hands, Capozzella did not question Gibson's authority or repudiate what he had done. Rather, he paid Gibson for legal services rendered and reimbursed him for trustees' fees advanced.

When the deed, drafted and executed as Capozzella intended, was delivered to Gibson as Capozzella intended, there was an "intention to deliver . . . effectuated by words or acts" and therefore a "delivery" within the meaning of the rule in *Payne*. From the circumstances of this case, the chancellor decided the question of fact and found that delivery was complete. The evidence supports his finding. Upon delivery, title passed from the trustees to the Capozzellas. The fact that Henry F. Capozzella gave Gibson no instructions as to what he should do with the deed after delivery does not negate his intention to transfer title by such delivery.

We find no merit in Capozzella's argument that the trustees violated their fiduciary duty by acting without his written authority. Both trustees were Capozzella's attorneys in his first divorce case. Their authority to execute their deed was written into the deed Capozzella and his first wife made to them pursuant to the separation agreement. Both of these documents were signed by Capozzella. Neither required the trustees to await written instructions. Oral instructions, transmitted through Gibson by the sole beneficiary of the trust, were sufficient to justify the exercise of their fiduciary responsibility. Finding no error, we affirm the chancellor's decree.

HARRISON, J., dissents.

I dissent for the reason that appellee failed to carry the burden of proof which rested upon her "to show every fact and circumstance necessary to constitute a valid gift by clear and convincing evidence." *Rust v. Phillips*, 159 S.E.2d 628, 631 (Va. 1968). The record discloses neither intent nor delivery.

We are concerned here with property having an estimated value in excess of $1 million. The marriage between Dr. Henry F. Capozzella and Harriet A. Capozzella on June 15, 1970 was his second and her third. It lasted less than five months. Harriet claims that four days after their marriage Capozzella "because of his great love for her" made to her "a valid gift of the land" involved. She alleges that this gift was effectuated by the preparation of a deed, its execution by the trustees and its delivery to Lytton H. Gibson, who was, as she characterized him, the attorney for Capozzella.

Appellee supports her case by the testimony of her mother and father. Capozzella denies the gift and introduces the testimony of his two sisters. We must look to Gibson for an impartial version of the facts.

Capozzella did discuss with Gibson on June 19, 1970, in the presence of Harriet, the taking of title to the property in their joint names. However, it appears that he was then primarily concerned with the possibility that through his children, particularly his young daughter, his first wife might be able to exercise some control over his property. Gibson testified that at this time Capozzella "didn't know what to do" about his property; that he "wasn't given any instructions by Capozzella"; and that the suggestion that mutual wills be executed and the deed to the property taken in their joint names with right of survivorship "was done really the way I more or less dictated it." Gibson quoted the doctor as saying "well, I just don't know . . . you do the way you think it ought to be done."

Gibson testified repeatedly that the proposal to place the property in the joint names of Dr. and Mrs. Capozzella was his sole suggestion, and in the answer he filed as a defendant in the court below he stated: "The preparation of the deed in question by this defendant [Gibson] and the manner of taking title was done at the sole discretion of this defendant [Gibson]."

Following his conference with Capozzella on June 19, 1970 Gibson wrote to the trustees who were holding title to Capozzella's land and asked if they would convey the property to Capozzella. The trustees replied that they would execute a deed conveying the land as Capozzella instructed in writing. No such instructions in writing were ever given by Capozzella either to Gibson or to the trustees. While there were telephone calls and some correspondence between Gibson and the trustees, and Gibson prepared the deed, there was never a formal written request of the trustees by Gibson made on behalf of and as attorney and agent for Capozzella, directing and authorizing the trustees to convey title to Capozzella and Harriet.

It is significant that notwithstanding Capozzella is alleged to have made this gift on June 19, 1970 the deed from the trustees was not signed until October 19, 1970 (three weeks before the parties separated) and Gibson did not seek further instructions from Capozzella until his letter of November 6, 1970. Gibson's explanation of this June-to-October delay has a definite bearing on the intent of Capozzella to make the gift to his wife. Gibson said: "Very frankly I was dragging my feet. I wondered about this entire marriage, the marriage setup, etc." He said he was getting calls from New York and Boston, from Harriet, from her father and also from others. He "was wondering what the situation was" and "noticed some friction between the two of them." He said he "got kind of leery of this thing and I didn't know what to do."

We are not concerned here with the friction that developed between Dr. and Mrs. Capozzella which caused the dissolution of their union. Suffice it to say that by late-summer 1970 it existed, and Capozzella had abandoned any intent he ever entertained of taking title to his property jointly with Harriet. As the doctor's ardor waned, Harriet's interest in the property apparently increased. By December 11th Gibson realized that he was "in the middle." After the marriage fractured there was no reason for Capozzella to make a gift of the property to his wife or to deliver the deed, and he had no intention of doing so. Harriet was demanding that the deed be recorded or be delivered to her. Obviously Gibson could not comply with her request, for he was Capozzella's attorney, dealing with Capozzella's trustees and Capozzella's land. He realized that there could be no delivery or recordation of the deed unless and until such was directed by Capozzella and that such direction would not be forthcoming. Gibson then retired from the scene.

Even if we could assume an intent on Capozzella's part to make this purported gift to his wife, that intention must be accompanied by complete and unconditional delivery, actual or constructive. Here a deed had been signed by trustees and deposited with the donor's attorney. No delivery has ever been made to the alleged donee, her attorney or her agent. The donor, Capozzella, never surrendered control or dominion over the deed of his property.

Delivery need not be made to a donee personally; it may be made to a third person acting as agent for the donee. 38 Am.Jur.2d, Gifts, § 20. But "where the instrument relied upon to support a gift inter vivos is not delivered directly to the donee but is given to some third person . . . whether there was sufficient delivery of the instrument turns upon the decision whether the person taking delivery is to be regarded as the agent of the donor or of the donee." 48 A.L.R.2d 1419; *see* 9 M.J., Gifts, § 16.

Gibson was Capozzella's attorney and so regarded himself. He represented Capozzella in 1969 when the doctor divorced his first wife and settlement was effected with her. He was representing Capozzella when the doctor married Harriet. In her bill of complaint Harriet alleges that Gibson was Capozzella's attorney. The trial judge in his opinion referred to Gibson as Capozzella's attorney. Gibson so represented himself to the trustees, Graham and Lillard. All of Gibson's correspondence was to Capozzella, none to Harriet. It was Capozzella to whom he sent his bill for services. Harriet, when asked if Gibson billed her for services, responded: "He had no reason to. Everything I called him for was for the doctor, himself." She was then asked: ". . . and you never paid him?" She responded: "Well, I had no reason to." There is not a scintilla of evidence in the record that Gibson was the attorney or agent for any person other than Dr. Capozzella.

Aside from the questioned legality of the conveyance by the trustees, in which Capozzella did not unite and which was made without his written authorization, the only possible justification for the conveyance is that the trustees thought that they were conveying pursuant to the direction of Capozzella's attorney. Most certainly they would not have made the conveyance upon the representation of Harriet or her attorney, for she had no interest in or title to the property.

Since Gibson was the agent of Capozzella, execution of the deed and its delivery to Gibson are not sufficient "words or acts" which "effectuate" the donor's intent to deliver as required by *Payne v. Payne*, 104 S.E. 712 (Va. 1920), and it cannot be held, as the majority does, that "at that point, delivery was complete."

Viewing the evidence in the light most favorable to Harriet, we have here a case where a man expressed a desire to convey an interest in land to his wife but before the transaction could be consummated by delivery of the deed the parties separate, and he changes his mind. This was Capozzella's prerogative, for the trustees were his trustees; the property involved was his land; the attorney who requested execution of the deed and to whom the deed was delivered was his attorney. The deed was at all times under the control of Capozzella, and remains so to this date. The authorities universally hold that in order to constitute a valid gift, the deed must pass beyond the dominion and control of the donor and come within the power and control of the donee.

After his two consultations with Gibson in June and August, 1970 Capozzella obviously lost interest in making a gift of the land to Harriet. He therefore did not write or contact Gibson or pursue the matter further with his attorney. With his marriage disintegrating, and friction developing, Capozzella was not ready to "relinquish all dominion and control" over his property. He therefore declined to authorize delivery by his attorney. I would reverse.

NOTES AND QUESTIONS

1. It is obvious that Justices Richard Poff and Albertis Harrison reached quite different conclusions in regard to what the record showed in this case. Because this was an action in equity, rather than law, under Virginia procedure the case was tried by a court-appointed chancellor rather than a jury. Should this give the Virginia Supreme Court greater discretion in deciding what the facts actually are in this case? Is Justice Harrison's willingness to second guess the chancellor's conclusion that delivery occurred appropriate?

2. *What Constitutes Delivery?* As *Capozzella v. Capozzella* indicates, deeds do not transfer title to land unless they are delivered. The crucial component of delivery is not manual transfer, but the intent to deliver. Consequently, if A draws up a deed to Blackacre naming B as the grantee and then gives it to B with a stack of other papers to place in A's bank lock box, there has been no delivery. On the other hand, if A with the intent to deliver mails the deed to B at the wrong address and then dies before correcting his error, a valid delivery has probably occurred.

Delivery need not be to the grantee directly. Escrows are frequently used as intermediaries in real estate transactions. Once the grantor transfers the deed to the escrow without reserving the right to recall it, delivery has occurred. Whether or not Dr. Capozzella had reserved the right to recall the deed in his lawyer's possession was the critical issue in the above case.

3. The *Capozzella* case also illustrates the basic principles of the law of gifts. To effectuate a valid gift of real or personal property, there must be donative intent (on the part of the donor), delivery, and acceptance. Delivery and acceptance can be actual or constructive. Gifts *causa mortis* (i.e., those made in expectation of death) are subject to slightly different rules. The delivery requirements are relaxed, and the gift is returned if the donor survives. Gifts *causa mortis* are limited to items of personal property. Why should this be the case?

4. *A Note on Bailments.* With personal property, it is common for the owner to transfer possession of an object to another party without intending that the transfer be permanent or that any property rights be created in the transferee. When the owner of an appliance leaves it with a repairman, a bailment is created. The owner of the item is the *bailor*; the recipient who takes actual physical possession with the intention to possess is the *bailee*. A bailee is obligated to exercise reasonable care over the bailed goods and to redeliver them to the owner. Bailments are ordinarily consensual agreements, although under certain circumstances — as when lost property is found — an unintended possessor may be treated as a bailee. Such situations are known as constructive bailments.

A bailment differs from custody which occurs when an owner transfers literal possession to another without intending to relinquish control of the property. The classic example of custody occurs when the proprietor of a store allows a customer to take possession of, and examine, an item for sale.

5. *Deeds as Will Substitutes.* In the past, landowners have often mistakenly assumed that they could avoid the costs of probate by preparing completed deeds to their property for their chosen grantees, but retaining possession of the deeds until after their deaths. Under the traditional law of deeds (and wills) such deeds invariably fail for a lack of delivery. For a rare case where this approach apparently worked, albeit over a vigorous dissent, see *Estate of O'Brien v. Robinson*, 749 P.2d 154 (Wash. 1988).

Recognition of the desire to have a mechanism by which land can be transferred at death outside of the probate process has led several states to recognize a "transfer-on-death deed (also known as a TOD deed, or a beneficiary deed). TOD deeds must be recorded in local land records (see below) prior to the death of the grantor to be valid, but they can be revoked without penalty any time prior to death. If the TOD deed is not revoked, title passes to the grantee upon the death of the grantor. Such deeds have been authorized in Arizona, Arkansas, Colorado, Kansas, Minnesota, Missouri, Montana, Nevada, New Mexico, Ohio, Oklahoma, and Wisconsin. In July 2009, the National Conference of Commissioners on Uniform State Laws approved for adoption a Uniform Real Property Transfer on Death Act. As of February 2016, the Act had been adopted in 13 states and the District of Columbia.

6. *The Doctrine of Merger*. Once the buyer accepts the deed, the terms of the real estate sales contract are superseded by those of the deed, at least so far as they relate to the real property transferred. The contract is said to "merge" into the deed. This means that a provision (like the acceptance of a particular encumbrance) included in the contract but not in the deed cannot be enforced, even if the omission was inadvertent. In recent years, courts have become resistant to a strict application of the doctrine of merger, particularly when it appears to give one party an unfair advantage. It has been held not to apply in cases of fraud or mistake, and it does not apply to contractual provisions that refer to the physical condition of the property or agreed upon improvements. The effect of the doctrine can also be negated by a showing that the parties intended that the rule of merger not apply. The Uniform Land Transactions Act does away with the doctrine altogether except in cases in which the parties intend the deed to supersede all provisions in the contract for sale. For the general erosion of a strict merger principle, see *Reed v. Hassell*, 340 A.2d 157 (Del. Super. 1975); Dunham, *Merger by Deed — Was It Ever Automatic?*, 10 GA. L .REV. 419 (1976).

[3.] Covenants of Title

The fact that the contract for sale calls for marketable title does not guarantee that no impediments to sale will arise after the contract is executed. Certainly it is no defense to an action by a third party that both the seller and buyer thought that marketable title was being delivered. Moreover, because of the doctrine of merger, the buyer's recourse against the seller under the contract may be limited. To protect buyers, warranty deeds were developed. Under the warranty deed, the seller pledges to defend and indemnify the buyer if his title is challenged. Although there is some evidence that most deeds in early America lacked such guarantees, the warranty deed was clearly in wide use prior to the Civil War and a substantial body of law had developed around it. *See, e.g, Davis v. Smith*, 5 Ga. 274 (1848). The warranty is effected through the inclusion of covenants benefiting the purchaser in the deed itself.

There are six traditional title covenants which appear in warranty deeds: three are classified as present covenants, and three as future covenants. The present covenants are *seisin*, *right to convey*, and *against encumbrances*. The future covenants are *warranty*, *quiet enjoyment*, and *further assurances*. Ordinarily, a deed purporting to be a warranty deed will be interpreted to include all six of these covenants. The present covenants are breached, if at all, at the time the deed is accepted, and the Statute of Limitations begins to run at that time. On the other hand, the future covenants are breached only when the grantee is actually challenged by a third party with a superior legal interest to the property. (This is often referred to as an eviction, although loss of possession is not actually required.)

The covenant of *seisin* is a promise that the grantor owns the estate in land which the deed purports to convey. The covenant of *the right to convey* is a promise that the grantor has the right to transfer it. (Occasionally, one can be the owner without the right to convey; property owned by a minor is an example. Similarly, there are situations, as with a power of appointment, where the grantor may have the right to convey without seisin, i.e., the right of ownership). The covenant *against encumbrances* promises that there are no interests in third parties which would qualify, but not negate, the title being transferred (such as easements, profits, leases, restrictive covenants, mortgages, and other liens).

The future covenants of *warranty* and *quiet enjoyment* are essentially identical in their scope and coverage. They commit the grantor to come to the defense of the grantee if he suffers any loss to someone holding a superior claim to all or part of the land transferred or to someone holding an interest in the land. These covenants also obligate the grantor to come to the defense of the grantee if any legal attack is mounted against his title or possession, and they prevent the grantor from personally attacking the grantee's title. The covenant of *further assurances* is a promise that the grantor will execute any additional documents necessary to establish the grantee's title. Unlike the other deed covenants, which are enforceable only by damages, the covenant of further assurances can be enforced by specific performance. On the other hand, most necessary documents are completed at the time of closing, so this covenant rarely comes into play.

BROWN v. LOBER

Illinois Supreme Court
389 N.E.2d 1188 (1979)

MR. JUSTICE UNDERWOOD delivered the opinion of the court.

Plaintiffs instituted this action in the Montgomery County circuit court based on an alleged breach of the covenant of seisin in their warranty deed. The trial court held that although there had been a breach of the covenant of seisin, the suit was barred by the 10-year statute of limitations in section 16 of the Limitations Act (Ill. Rev. Stat. 1975, ch. 83, par. 17). Plaintiffs' post-trial motion, which was based on an alleged breach of the covenant of quiet enjoyment, was also denied. A divided Fifth District Appellate Court reversed and remanded. (63 Ill. App. 3d 727.) We allowed the defendant's petition for leave to appeal.

The parties submitted an agreed statement of facts which sets forth the relevant history of this controversy. Plaintiffs purchased 80 acres of Montgomery County real estate from William and Faith Bost and received a statutory warranty deed (Ill. Rev. Stat. 1957, ch. 30, par. 8), containing no exceptions, dated December 21, 1957. Subsequently, plaintiffs took possession of the land and recorded their deed.

On May 8, 1974, plaintiffs granted a coal option to Consolidated Coal Company (Consolidated) for the coal rights on the 80-acre tract for the sum of $6,000. Approximately two years later, however, plaintiffs "discovered" that they, in fact, owned only a one-third interest in the subsurface coal rights. It is a matter of public record that, in 1947, a prior grantor had reserved a two-thirds interest in the mineral rights on the property. Although plaintiffs had their abstract of title examined in 1958 and 1968 for loan purposes, they contend that until May 4, 1976, they believed that they were the sole owners of the surface and subsurface rights on the 80-acre tract. Upon discovering that a prior grantor had reserved a two-thirds interest in the coal rights, plaintiffs and Consolidated renegotiated their agreement to provide for payment of $2,000 in exchange for a one-third interest in the subsurface coal rights. On May 25, 1976, plaintiffs filed this action against the executor of the estate of Faith Bost, seeking damages in the amount of $4,000.

The deed which plaintiffs received from the Bosts was a general statutory form warranty deed meeting the requirements of section 9 of "An Act concerning conveyances" (Ill. Rev. Stat. 1957, ch. 30, par. 8). That section provides:

> Every deed in substance in the above form, when otherwise duly executed, shall be deemed and held a conveyance in fee simple, to the grantee, his heirs or assigns, with covenants on the part of the grantor, (1) that at the time of the making and delivery of such deed he was lawfully seized of an indefeasible estate in fee simple, in and to the premises therein described, and had good right and full power to convey the same; (2) that the same were then free from all encumbrances; and (3) that he warrants to the grantee, his heirs and assigns, the quiet and peaceable possession of such premises, and will defend the title thereto against all persons who may lawfully claim the same. And such covenants shall be obligatory upon any grantor, his heirs and personal representatives, as fully and with like effect as if written at length in such deed.

Ill. Rev. Stat. 1957, ch. 30, par. 8.

The effect of this provision is that certain covenants of title are implied in every statutory form warranty deed. Subsection 1 contains the covenant of seisin and the covenant of good right to convey. These covenants, which are considered synonymous assure the grantee that the grantor is, at the time of the conveyance, lawfully seized and has the power to convey an estate of the quality and quantity which he professes to convey. Subsection 2 represents the covenant against encumbrances. An incumbrance is any right to, or interest in, land which may subsist in a third party to the diminution of the value of the estate, but consistent with the passing of the fee by conveyance. Subsection 3 sets forth the covenant of quiet enjoyment, which is synonymous with the covenant of warranty in Illinois. By this covenant, "the grantor warrants to the grantee, his heirs and assigns, the possession of the premises and that he will defend the title granted by the terms of the deed against persons who may lawfully claim the same, and that such covenant shall be obligatory upon the grantor, his heirs, personal representatives and assigns." [Citations omitted.]

Plaintiffs' complaint is premised upon the fact that "William Roy Bost and Faith Bost covenanted that they were the owners in fee simple of the above described property at the time of the conveyance to the plaintiffs." While the complaint could be more explicit, it appears that plaintiffs were alleging a cause of action for breach of the covenant of seisin. This court has stated repeatedly that the covenant of seisin is a covenant in praesenti and, therefore, if broken at all, is broken at the time of delivery of the deed. *Tone v. Wilson* (1876), 81 Ill. 529; *Jones v. Warner* (1876), 81 Ill. 343.

Since the deed was delivered to the plaintiffs on December 21, 1957, any cause of action for breach of the covenant of seisin would have accrued on that date. The trial court held that this cause of action was barred by the statute of limitations. No question is raised as to the applicability of the 10-year statute of limitations. We conclude, therefore, that the cause of action for breach of the covenant of seisin was properly determined by the trial court to be barred by the statute of limitations since plaintiffs did not file their complaint until May 25, 1976, nearly 20 years after their alleged cause of action accrued.

In their post-trial motion, plaintiffs set forth as an additional theory of recovery an alleged breach of the covenant of quiet enjoyment. The trial court, without explanation, denied the motion. The appellate court reversed, holding that the cause of action on the covenant of quiet enjoyment was not barred by the statute of limitations. The appellate court theorized that plaintiffs' cause of action did not accrue until 1976, when plaintiffs discovered that they only had a one-third interest in the subsurface coal rights and renegotiated their contract with the coal company for one-third of the previous contract price. The primary issue before us, therefore, is when, if at all, the plaintiffs' cause of action for breach of the covenant of quiet enjoyment is deemed to have accrued.

This court has stated on numerous occasions that, in contrast to the covenant of seisin, the covenant of warranty or quiet enjoyment is prospective in nature and is breached only when there is an actual or constructive eviction of the covenantee by the paramount titleholder. *Biwer v. Martin* (1920), 294 Ill. 488; *Barry v. Guild* (1888), 126 Ill. 439; *Scott v. Kirkendall* (1878), 88 Ill. 465; *Bostwick v. Williams* (1864), 36 Ill. 65; *Moore v. Vail* (1855), 17 Ill. 185.

The cases are also replete with statements to the effect that the mere existence of paramount title in one other than the covenantee is not sufficient to constitute a breach of the covenant of warranty or quiet enjoyment: "[T]here must be a union of acts of disturbance and lawful title, to constitute a breach of the covenant for quiet enjoyment, or warranty." (*Barry v. Guild* (1888), 126 Ill. 439, 446.) "[T]here is a general concurrence that something more than the mere existence of a paramount title is necessary to constitute a breach of the covenant of warranty." (*Scott v. Kirkendall* (1878), 88 Ill. 465, 467.) "A mere want of title is no breach of this covenant. There must not only be a want of title, but there must be an ouster under a paramount title." *Moore v. Vail* (1855), 17 Ill. 185, 189.

The question is whether plaintiffs have alleged facts sufficient to constitute a constructive eviction. They argue that if a covenantee fails in his effort to sell an interest in land because he discovers that he does not own what his warranty deed purported to convey, he has suffered a constructive eviction and is thereby entitled to bring an action against his grantor for breach of the covenant of quiet enjoyment. We think that the decision of this court in *Scott v. Kirkendall* (1878), 88 Ill. 465, is controlling on this issue and compels us to reject plaintiffs' argument.

In *Scott*, an action was brought for breach of the covenant of warranty by a grantee who discovered that other parties had paramount title to the land in question. The land was vacant and unoccupied at all relevant times. This court, in rejecting the grantee's claim that there was a breach of the covenant of quiet enjoyment, quoted the earlier decision in *Moore v. Vail* (1855), 17 Ill. 185, 191:

> Until that time, (the taking possession by the owner of the paramount title,) he might peaceably have entered upon and enjoyed the premises, without resistance or molestation, which was all his grantors covenanted he should do. They did not guarantee to him a perfect title, but the possession and enjoyment of the premises.

88 Ill. 465, 468.

Relying on this language in *Moore*, the *Scott* court concluded:

> We do not see but what this fully decides the present case against the appellant. It holds that the mere existence of a paramount title does not constitute a breach of the covenant. That is all there is here. There has been no assertion of the adverse title. The land has always been vacant. Appellant could at any time have taken peaceable possession of it. He has in no way been prevented or hindered from the enjoyment of the possession by any one having a better right. It was but the possession and enjoyment of the premises which was assured to him, and there has been no disturbance or interference in that respect. True, there is a superior title in another, but appellant has never felt "its pressure upon him."

88 Ill. 465, 468–69.

Admittedly, *Scott* dealt with surface rights while the case before us concerns subsurface mineral rights. We are, nevertheless, convinced that the reasoning employed in *Scott* is applicable to the present case. While plaintiffs went into possession of the surface area, they cannot be said to have possessed the subsurface minerals. "Possession of the surface does not carry possession of the minerals . . . . To possess the mineral estate, one must undertake the actual removal thereof from the ground or do such other act as will apprise the community that such interest is in the exclusive use and enjoyment of the claiming party." *Failoni v. Chicago & North Western Ry. Co.* (1964), 30 Ill. 2d 258, 262.

Since no one has, as yet, undertaken to remove the coal or otherwise manifested a clear intent to exclusively "possess" the mineral estate, it must be concluded that the subsurface estate is "vacant." As in *Scott*, plaintiffs "could at any time have taken peaceable possession of it. [They have] in no way been prevented or hindered from the enjoyment of the possession by any one having a better right." (88 Ill. 465, 468.) Accordingly, until such time as one holding paramount title interferes with plaintiffs' right of possession (e.g., by beginning to mine the coal), there can be no constructive eviction and, therefore, no breach of the covenant of quiet enjoyment.

What plaintiffs are apparently attempting to do on this appeal is to extend the protection afforded by the covenant of quiet enjoyment. However, we decline to expand the historical scope of this covenant to provide a remedy where another of the covenants of title is so clearly applicable. As this court stated in *Scott v. Kirkendall* (1878), 88 Ill. 465, 469:

> To sustain the present action would be to confound all distinction between the covenant of warranty and that of seizin, or of right to convey. They are not equivalent covenants. An action will lie upon the latter, though there be no disturbance of possession. A defect of title will suffice. Not so with the covenant of warranty, or for quiet enjoyment, as has always been held by the prevailing authority.

The covenant of seisin, unquestionably, was breached when the Bosts delivered the deed to plaintiffs, and plaintiffs then had a cause of action. However, despite the fact that it was a matter of public record that there was a reservation of a two-thirds interest in the mineral rights in the earlier deed, plaintiffs failed to bring an action for breach of the covenant of seisin within the 10-year period following delivery of the deed. The likely explanation is that plaintiffs had not secured a title opinion at the time they purchased the property, and the subsequent examiners for the lenders were not concerned with the mineral rights. Plaintiffs' oversight, however, does not justify us in overruling earlier decisions in order to recognize an otherwise premature cause of action. The mere fact that plaintiffs' original contract with Consolidated had to be modified due to their discovery that paramount title to two-thirds of the subsurface minerals belonged to another is not sufficient to constitute the constructive eviction necessary to a breach of the covenant of quiet enjoyment.

Finally, although plaintiffs also have argued in this court that there was a breach of the covenant against encumbrances entitling them to recovery, we decline to address this issue which was argued for the first time on appeal. It is well settled that questions not raised in the trial court will not be considered by this court on appeal. *Kravis v. Smith Marine, Inc.* (1975), 60 Ill. 2d 141; *Ray v. City of Chicago* (1960), 19 Ill. 2d 593.

Accordingly, the judgment of the appellate court is reversed, and the judgment of the circuit court of Montgomery County is affirmed.

NOTES AND QUESTIONS

1. Most American states have recognized the right of surface owners to sever the mineral estates to their land and transfer them to others. As such, the mineral estate is another form of encumbrance and marketable title cannot be delivered if it is held by someone other than the surface owner. This feature of American property law greatly expedited the discovery and use of natural resources. However, as the above case illustrates, it has also produced numerous legal and political disputes. For perhaps the most famous property case involving mineral rights, see *Pennsylvania Coal v. Mahon*, discussed in Chapter 3.

2. The warranties at issue in this case are contained in a statutory warranty deed. Illinois, and many other states, have statutory provisions that define the warranties that are assumed to apply in deeds that fail to identify the type of deed or fail to include express warranties. Ordinarily, statutory deed warranties are implied from the parties' use of the term "grant" (or similar language) and are often called "grant deeds." Where such statutes exist, parties that wish to use only a quitclaim deed must state so explicitly in the deed itself or else the seller runs the risk of being bound by unintended warranties. In many jurisdictions, the statutory warranties are only those of a special warranty deed (i.e., they warrant only the acts of the grantor and not his predecessor). The Illinois statute, however, appears to imply a general warranty deed.

3. In *Lewicki v. Marszalkowski*, 455 A.2d 307 (R.I. 1983), the grantor was prevented from claiming by adverse possession a tract of land which she had conveyed with a covenant of warranty. Do you understand why? A related doctrine is that of estoppel by deed which provides that a grantor who purports to transfer by deed an interest in land that he does not own and subsequently acquires that interest, his after-acquired interest automatically passes to the original grantee. The grantor is estopped from asserting that he lacked title at the time of the original transfer, and he cannot elect to pay damages rather than transfer the property. Although the doctrine of estoppel by deed originally applied only to warranty deeds, it now applies to quitclaim deeds as well.

4. *Damages for the Breach of Deed Covenants.* Unlike the situation with the covenant of marketable title in a real estate sales contract, the only remedy available for the breach of a deed covenant is money damages. (The one exception is a breach of the covenant of future assurances which can require the covenantor to take affirmative steps.)

Whether or not the covenanting party will be liable under the deed for damages incurred by a future purchaser will depend upon whether the covenant breached is a present or future covenant. Because they are breached, if at all, at the time of transfer, grantors will normally be liable only to their original grantees under the present covenants. However, under the future covenants, grantors may be called upon to defend the title of remote grantees. This is because liability under these covenants arises only when there is an actual attack on title. Moreover, future covenants are understood to run with the land and therefore benefit not just the first but all subsequent purchasers. (The concept of running with the land is discussed in Chapter 9.)

While this obviously places the guarantor of a future covenant at risk for a long period of time, the potential liability is mediated by the rule that no matter which covenant is at issue, the covenantor is only liable for sums up to the amount that he or she received for the land. (This rule is apparently in force in every state except Connecticut, Massachusetts, Vermont, and Maine which allow recovery up to the value of the land at the time of eviction.) The party suing on the covenant may also be entitled to damages for lost interest and litigation expenses, including attorneys' fees, depending upon the jurisdiction.

5. If A receives Blackacre as a gift from B, and B conveys the parcel by a general warranty deed, may A recover from B if he is subsequently ousted by C who holds superior title to the land? If she can, what would be the measure of her recovery? This is an issue over which state courts have divided.

6. *Quitclaim Deeds.* A *quitclaim* deed transfers only the grantor's interest in the property conveyed (whatever that may be) and makes no representations as to the quality of the title transferred. An old property law joke has it that the Brooklyn Bridge is almost always sold by quitclaim deed. Quitclaim deeds are frequently used when the grantor's title to the land is in doubt, but the buyer wishes to purchase it anyway; when the transfer is by gift, or when the buyer wants to make sure that all collateral interests in a parcel of land are extinguished, as when the purchaser of land seeks quitclaim deeds from the seller's close relatives or business partners, just in case these parties might have interests in the property not known to the buyer.

Absent a statute imposing warranties, a deed that includes no warranties is presumed to be a quitclaim. Nevertheless, it is advisable to include the term "quitclaim" in a deed if it is the parties' intention that no guarantees are made as to the quality of title.

7. *Condition of the Premises.* The traditional deed warranties apply only to matters of title and have no effect on the physical condition of the premises. While the parties are free to negotiate a warranty of habitability or fitness as part of the contract for sale, the traditional rule is that no such warranty will be implied. This rule of caveat emptor is being slowly eroded by mandatory disclosure laws and by the widespread trend of reading an implied warranty of habitability into contracts for sale involving the builder of a new home. See Roberts, *Disclosure Duties in Real Estate Sales and Attempts to Reallocate the Risk*, 34 CONN. L. REV. 1 (2001). At least one court has held that sellers have a duty to disclose the fact that a house for sale was reputedly haunted by ghosts. *Stambovsky v. Ackley*, 572 N.Y.S.2d (N.Y. App. Div. 1991). In most states, sales of new, previously unoccupied homes are subject to an implied warranty of fitness or habitability. Normally the implied warranty extends only to significant defects and not to minor imperfections. *See Peterson v. Hubschman Constr. Co., Inc.*, 389 N.E.2d 1154 (Ill. App. Ct. 1979).

[4.] Title Insurance

Covenants of title have frequently proven to be an inadequate method of guaranteeing title. Not only are there problems inherent in the warranties themselves — the Statute of Limitations problem with present covenants, the "ouster" requirement for future covenants, the cap on the amount of damages that can be recovered, and the limited protection of the special warranty deed — but their value is also contingent on the seller's solvency and the ability of the buyer or successor owner to locate the seller once a problem arises. While deed covenants are still widely used and while curative and marketable title acts help correct many of the problems, title insurance has become the primary way by which purchasers of real estate protect themselves against clouds on title.

Title insurance is a guarantee, provided by an insurance company, that the title is of a certain quality. Ordinarily, this means a title free from encumbrances other than those specifically excepted in the title insurance policy. The policy is issued only after the insurance company, its agent, or an attorney has examined the chain of title to establish that the grantor does in fact have the right to convey the property and to identify all outstanding encumbrances. Basically, the title insurance policy guarantees that there are no defects other than those listed in the policy. If there are, the insurance company must indemnify the policy holder to cover any losses incurred. The insurer will also usually be liable for litigation costs arising out of challenges to the insured's ownership of the parcel. Unlike the future covenants of title, the title insurance policy normally protects only the grantee, his heirs, and devisees (and corporate successors if the grantee is a corporation), but not subsequent purchasers.

Title insurance typically requires a one-time premium and insures against any defects in the quality of title that may exist as of the date the policy is issued. While it indemnifies for all losses which result from attacks on the owner's title, it does not cover physical defects in the property or the consequences of zoning changes or other governmental actions. Policies protecting the interests of lenders are almost always purchased by the borrower (at the lender's insistence). Owner policies can be purchased by either the buyer or the seller, depending upon what the parties agree to in the contract or, more commonly, upon what the local custom is. In the eastern United States, owner policies are usually purchased by the buyer; in the western part of the country, it is customary for the seller to pay for the buyer's title insurance policy.

The title insurance market is highly concentrated. A government study found problems such as the extent of competition and the reasonableness of prices. Consumers find it difficult to comparison shop. Investigations have also found illegal activities, such as compensation to realtors and builders for consumer referrals. Effective federal and state regulation is a challenge. U.S. General Government Accountability Office, *Actions Needed to Improve Oversight of the Title Industry and Better Protect Consumers* (2007), *available at* http://www.gao.gov/products/GAO-07-401.

Title insurance policies usually reserve a right of subrogation for the insurer. The following case involves a situation where a title insurance company seeks to recover its losses by suing a seller under covenants of title.

FIDELITY NATIONAL TITLE INSURANCE CO. v. MILLER

California Court of Appeals
215 Cal. App. 3d 1163 (1989)

KREMER, P.J.

Plaintiff Fidelity National Title Insurance Company appeals summary judgment favoring defendant Clayton L. Miller on its complaint for breach of warranty and common counts. We reverse the summary judgment because the record discloses numerous triable factual issues.

In reviewing the propriety of summary judgment, we must accept the evidence and inferences most favorable to Fidelity. Applying that standard, the evidence shows: Miller owned Coronado property. In 1953 Miller encumbered the property with a restrictive covenant granting neighbor Whitby a "view easement." The

Whitby restrictive covenant was recorded. Years later Miller wanted to convey the property to his daughter and son-in-law, Jean and Raymond Gazzo (together Gazzo). Miller told Gazzo he had given Whitby a view easement. Apparently Miller was unsure whether Whitby had recorded her restrictive covenant. In 1986 Gazzo and Miller opened escrow. Fidelity issued a preliminary report not mentioning the Whitby encumbrance. Gazzo asked Fidelity whether the property was encumbered by a restriction not appearing on the preliminary report. Fidelity found nothing. Fidelity issued a title insurance policy to Gazzo not mentioning the Whitby encumbrance. Miller conveyed the property to Gazzo by unrestricted grant deed without excepting the Whitby restrictive covenant. After escrow closed, Gazzo discovered the Whitby encumbrance had been recorded. Gazzo made a claim against Fidelity under the title insurance policy. Fidelity paid Gazzo $125,000 under the title insurance policy for the diminution in the property's value resulting from the Whitby encumbrance. Gazzo executed a release and assignment of rights favoring Fidelity.

Fidelity sued Miller for breach of warranty and common counts. Fidelity's amended complaint alleged: Miller delivered to Gazzo a grant deed conveying a fee simple interest in the property. Under Civil Code section 1113, Miller impliedly covenanted the estate granted was free from any encumbrances made by Miller.[1] At the time Miller executed the deed, the property was subject to the Whitby restrictive covenant. As Gazzo's subrogee, Fidelity sought $125,000 from Miller for damages resulting from his breach of section 1113's implied covenant.

Miller sought summary judgment on Fidelity's complaint, asserting subrogee Fidelity had no right to recover against Miller because subrogor Gazzo knew the restrictive covenant might exist and thus was not entitled to recover from Miller for breach of section 1113's implied covenant. Miller characterized Fidelity's payment to Gazzo as voluntary. Miller also asserted Fidelity's recovery was barred because in executing the grant deed he relied on Fidelity's negligently prepared abstract of title. Supporting and opposing Miller's summary judgment motion, the parties presented portions of depositions by Miller, Gazzo, escrow agents and Fidelity's employee. [Miller also filed an answer to Fidelity's complaint and a cross-complaint of his own.]

After argument the court granted summary judgment. The court stated: "The basis for my ruling is that the rights of your carrier are no greater than the rights of their insured. And I don't think there's merit to the position that there is an implied covenant in this deed that there are no impediments to title when Miller came forth and told the escrow people that there was, in his opinion, a Whitby

---

[1] [1] Civil Code section 1113 provides: "From the use of the word 'grant' in any conveyance by which an estate of inheritance or fee simple is to be passed, the following covenants, and none other, on the part of the grantor for himself and his heirs to the grantee, his heirs, and assigns, are implied, unless restrained by express terms contained in such conveyance: [para.] 1. That previous to the time of the execution of such conveyance, the grantor has not conveyed the same estate, or any right, title, or interest therein, to any person other than the grantee; [para.] 2. That such estate is at the time of the execution of such conveyance free from encumbrances done, made, or suffered by the grantor, or any person claiming under him. [para.] 3. Such covenants may be sued upon in the same manner as if they had been expressly inserted in the conveyance."

covenant and it was necessary for them to check out the validity of it as part of the escrow transaction."

On this record the superior court should have denied Miller's motion for summary judgment. The record contains conflicting evidence requiring factual determinations bearing on the issues whether Miller breached section 1113's implied covenant against encumbrances by conveying the property to Gazzo by an unrestricted grant deed after encumbering the property with a restrictive covenant favoring Whitby, whether Gazzo could recover damages from Miller for any such breach, and whether Fidelity was entitled to subrogation from Miller. Also dependent upon resolution of disputed factual issues is the amount, if any, by which any recovery by Fidelity from Miller should be diminished if Miller prevails on any of his answer's affirmative defenses or his cross-complaint.

The superior court's ruling the grant deed did not contain an implied covenant was based on its conclusion Miller during escrow disclosed to Gazzo and Fidelity the potential existence of the Whitby encumbrance. However, the mere fact Gazzo and Fidelity may have known during escrow of the possibility a restrictive covenant might encumber the property does not necessarily preclude Fidelity from recovering in subrogation for Miller's breach of the implied covenant. For purposes of section 1113, a covenant running with the land restricting the use of property constitutes an encumbrance.

Section 1113 implies the covenants against prior conveyances and encumbrances ". . . from the use of the word 'grant' unless such covenants are restrained by express terms in the deed. Therefore, the grantor who does not want to imply the statutory warranties can specify that his grant is made without warranty of any kind or can specifically set forth in the deed the encumbrances to which the property is subject. The description of the encumbrances will negate any implication of warranty against those encumbrances." (3 Augustine & Zarrow, California Real Estate Law & Practice (1989) Deeds, § 80.21(6), p. 80-19.)

Miller contends the court could properly "construe the grant deed in light of all the circumstances surrounding the transaction" and conclude he and Gazzo impliedly agreed the grant deed would not contain an implied covenant against encumbrances. However, the construction of the grant deed propounded by Miller does not constitute the only reasonable construction that could be drawn from the evidence before the court. Thus, on the motion for summary judgment the court could not properly adopt such construction as a matter of law.

By its terms section 1113 implies a covenant against encumbrances in a grant deed "unless restrained by express terms contained in such conveyance." Miller presented no evidence compelling a finding as a matter of law that he and Gazzo expressly agreed to exclude from their contract section 1113's implied covenant against encumbrances. Indeed, in his points and authorities supporting his motion Miller admitted "none of the writings surrounding the transaction contain an exception from the conveyance of the Whitby Covenant." Further, Miller cites no authority suggesting the implied covenant can be deleted by implied agreement.

Assuming the statutorily implied covenant can be deleted by implied agreement, on this record the existence of such implied agreement would require resolution of triable factual issues. Indeed, the evidence before the court and reasonable inferences would support the contrary finding advanced by Fidelity that the grant deed did not exclude the statutorily implied covenant. On its face the grant deed appears to convey the property without limitation. The language of the grant deed itself constitutes evidence contradicting Miller's claim he and Gazzo impliedly agreed the grant deed would not contain section 1113's implied covenant against encumbrances.

At most Miller has suggested the meaning of the grant deed's language and the intentions of Gazzo and Miller are uncertain and thus may be explained by extrinsic evidence. Miller has not shown the grant deed is in any of its terms or provisions ambiguous or uncertain. For that reason alone, the court considering the motion for summary judgment could not properly adopt the interpretation of the grant deed advanced by Miller.

Further, on this record a fact finder could reasonably infer there was no agreement between Miller and Gazzo that the grant deed would not contain the statutorily implied covenant against encumbrances. Gazzo's surprise upon discovering the recorded Whitby covenant and his filing a claim against Fidelity suggest he had no such agreement with Miller. Also casting doubt on the existence of any such agreement is Miller's claim he executed the facially unrestricted grant deed because he in fact believed the property was unencumbered in justifiable reliance on Fidelity's representations.

Miller contends as a matter of law Fidelity should not be entitled to equitable subrogation because Miller disclosed to Gazzo and Fidelity the potential existence of the Whitby encumbrance. However, the ultimate determination whether Fidelity is entitled to equitable subrogation depends upon resolution of disputed factual issues.

The evidence would support findings the primary cause of any loss suffered by Gazzo was Miller's encumbering the property, Fidelity's issuance of the title insurance policy — though perhaps causing Gazzo to part with consideration — did not cause the encumbrance, Fidelity was contractually obligated to pay for any loss suffered by Gazzo as a result of the encumbrance, and Fidelity satisfied its primary contractual obligation to Gazzo by settling. Thus, the ultimate fact finder could reasonably determine any "sin" by Fidelity was "one of omission," while that of Miller was "one of commission and one which was the genesis of the problem." Further, a court might reasonably conclude Miller's retaining the entire consideration received from Gazzo would amount to unjust enrichment. Accordingly, the court might ultimately determine those considerations tilted the balance of the equities in favor of Fidelity's right to subrogation.

In an argument grounded on the allegations of his answer and cross-complaint, Miller contends Fidelity's recovery should be barred because he executed the grant deed to Gazzo in reliance on representations by Fidelity amounting essentially to an abstract of title. However, the evidence raises a triable factual issue about whether Fidelity issued only a preliminary report and a title insurance policy, not an abstract of title. The evidence also raises triable factual issues about whether Miller in fact justifiably relied on any representations by Fidelity regarding the state of the title.

Insurance Code sections 12340.10 and 12340.11 make "clear that no reliance may be placed on a preliminary report or a policy of title insurance to show the condition of title." A preliminary report is not an abstract of title. It only reflects the terms under which the insurer is willing to issue a policy of title insurance. The terms and conditions under which the policy of insurance may be issued may or may not reflect the true condition of record title.

Although Miller claims Fidelity effectively provided an abstract of title, Fidelity presented evidence it issued only a preliminary report and a title insurance policy. For purposes of Miller's summary judgment motion, we must accept Fidelity's evidence on that issue. Further, the record contains evidence to support findings Miller did not converse with any Fidelity employee and did not see the preliminary report or title insurance policy. The record also contains evidence to support a finding Miller executed the grant deed before Fidelity issued its preliminary report. Such evidence and reasonable inferences raise triable factual issues about Miller's asserted reliance on representations by Fidelity.

On this record resolution of the lawsuit cannot be determined as a matter of law. Triable factual issues abound. Miller is not entitled to summary judgment. The judgment is reversed.

HUFFMAN, J., dissenting.

The trial court granted summary judgment in favor of Miller on the basis Fidelity had no greater rights than Gazzo in whose place they stood on a theory of equitable subrogation. Since Gazzo was fully informed of the possible existence of the Whitby easement prior to the completion of the sale, the trial court correctly found no implied covenant of title on the basis of the grant deed.

The parties to the actual transaction diligently sought to determine if the Whitby easement had been perfected. They sought assistance from an escrow company and Fidelity to make that determination. Fidelity was negligent in its search. It failed to find a recorded easement which had been on the books for decades. It is patent from this record the parties, both Gazzo and Miller, relied on Fidelity's negligent representations and not any implied covenants in the grant deed.

The focus of the reliance is best understood when one realizes it was Gazzo, not Miller, who undertook to work with the escrow to investigate the Whitby easement. Miller had made full disclosure to Gazzo. In his testimony Gazzo described in detail his efforts through the escrow company to have Fidelity investigate the issue of title. Gazzo was advised, based on Fidelity's negligent representation: "Miller has fee title, except for this party wall thing [an unrelated matter]." He further pursued the issue with the escrow company and asked them to follow up on the easement specifically. Gazzo was advised that a Mr. Whitmoyer of Fidelity had specifically investigated the easement to Whitby and found it was nonexistent. In short, the person in whose shoes Fidelity seeks to stand made crystal clear he relied on Fidelity's representations, not on any "implied covenant" within a grant deed which Gazzo knew was prepared by the very escrow agent who was involved in the investigation of the Whitby easement. Clearly, Fidelity has no right to now seek to claim Gazzo's rights under such an "implied covenant."

The trial judge understood clearly what had transpired in this case and was absolutely correct in the grant of summary judgment. We should affirm his decision.

NOTES AND QUESTIONS

1. Note that the crux of Fidelity's claim against Miller is that he warranted (i.e., guaranteed) that the property he transferred to his daughter and son-in-law was free from legal encumbrances. The deed he delivered in fact said nothing about any such guarantee. Instead, the guarantee was imposed by statute (Cal. Civ. Code § 1113) which imposes such a warranty anytime the term "grant" is used in a conveyance. (See the discussion of statutory warranties in Note 2 following *Brown v. Lober, supra.*)

2. The court's principal holding in the above case — that the grantee's knowledge of an encumbrance is not a defense when the grantor has warranted that the property is free from encumbrances — has not been accepted by every court. For the contrary holding — that grantee's knowledge of encumbrance is a defense — see *Ludke v. Egan*, 274 N.W.2d 641 (Wis. 1979).

3. If there are no warranties imposed by statute, a deed alone does not constitute a guarantee that it conveys title of any particular quality. Deeds frequently contain lists of known encumbrances which the grantee has agreed to accept and which are, therefore, not subject to the deed covenants. It was the failure to do this in his deed to the Gazzos that led to Miller's problems.

4. The title insurance industry operates on the premise that it insures only against certain types of defects in title and not all challenges that might arise to the policyholder's title. Since the *PASH* litigation discussed in Chapter 2, all title policies in Hawaii contain a specific disclaimer with respect to traditional native Hawaiian rights over private land whether developed or undeveloped. This may prove to be an important issue in many states if the concept of Native American property rights is expanded along the lines of the Hawaii approach.

[5.] Transfers to the Sovereign: Implied Dedication

Ordinarily, when land is voluntarily transferred from a private owner to the sovereign, it is done so by deed. However, there are certain situations in which the transfer can be made without the issuance of a deed

ROGERS v. SAIN

Tennessee Court of Appeals
679 S.W.2d 450 (1984)

Opinion by FRANKS.

Defendants appeal from the circuit court judgment which states:

> The Oris Sain Road also known as Grundy County Road Number Seven (7) is a public road. The Plaintiffs, J.G. Rogers and Maurine Rogers, being

> abutting land owners to portions of said road are entitled to open and free ingress and egress to their property aforesaid over and across said Oris Sain Road.

The road in dispute was constructed by the late Oris Sain at the boundary between plaintiffs' and defendants' properties. The road has a graveled surface and extends six-tenths of a mile to the Sain homeplace. When Oris Sain died, defendants inherited his land and entered into negotiations with Rogers to purchase a tract of Rogers' land most easily accessible by the Oris Sain Road. Negotiations failed to result in a sale and plaintiffs leased the tract to a third party for farming purposes. Subsequently, defendants notified Rogers and the tenant that the road was closed to them. This action resulted, seeking a declaration that the road is a public road.

The trial judge filed an opinion finding facts which formed the basis for his conclusions. He stated:

> It appears by clear and convincing evidence that the road in question, hereafter referred to as the "Oris Sain Road," has been open, and unobstructed and a well-known road to the former home of Oris Sain, now deceased, for more than forty (40) years. This road lies wholly on the defendants' property, formerly Oris Sain property, and lies adjacent to plaintiffs' land for a long distance. The exact length of this contiguous relationship is not material to the question here in issue, but appears to be 62 poles in length and is the common boundary between the lands of plaintiffs and defendants. There was substantial proof of occasional use by plaintiffs of the subject road but not of such continued or uninterrupted use for so long as to constitute a private prescriptive easement. This road was used by the United States Post Office Department since 1960 as a public road for the delivery of mail. On more than one occasion, Oris Sain, now deceased, openly declared this road to be a public road.

The clear preponderance of the evidence indicated that Grundy County began some type of maintenance on this road in the 1930s and its activities increased thereafter especially during the 1960s. The defendants who were old enough to be aware of the activity of the Grundy County Highway Department have all frankly admitted that the County Highway Department did expend an undetermined amount of money on the maintenance of this road but stated that this was not an intention on their part to dedicate this land as a public road. They admitted sometimes requesting this service and received it because the county maintained many private roads in the county. The Court finds that the road had been substantially improved and maintained by the County Highway Department for more than twenty (20) years with the express request of defendants or their predecessors in title and to some extent for more than 40 years.

The Court further finds that the west fence maintained by Plaintiffs to be the common boundary between the real estate owned by the plaintiffs and the defendants and that some portion of this boundary line is adjacent to the road in question, sometimes known as the "Oris Sain Road." We agree with the trial court's assessment of the evidence and adopt the foregoing as our factual determinations.

Defendants' principal argument is the evidence does not establish an implied dedication of the road to public use. It has long been established that private land can be implicitly dedicated to use as a public road. *McCord v. Hays*, 302 S.W.2d 331 (1957); *Scott v. State*, 33 Tenn. 629 (1854). When an implied dedication is claimed, the focus of the inquiry is whether the landowner intended to dedicate the land to a public use. *McCord, supra; Johnson City v. Wolfe*, 52 S.W. 991 (1899); *Nicely v. Nicely*, 232 S.W.2d 421 (1949). The proof on the issue of intent to dedicate must be unequivocal, *Cole v. Dych*, 535 S.W.2d 315 (Tenn. 1976), but intent may be inferred from surrounding facts and circumstances, *Cole, supra*, including the overt acts of the owner. *Wolfe, supra.*

The significance of the conduct of the landowner is assessed in *Wolfe*, where the court said:

> The public, as well as individuals, have a right to rely on the conduct of the owner as indicative of his intent. If the acts are such as would fairly and reasonably lead an ordinarily prudent man to infer an intent to dedicate [the court will find that the road has been so dedicated].

Wolfe, 103 Tenn. at 282, quoting from ELLIOTT ON ROADS AND STREETS, at 92.

Among the factors which indicate an intent to dedicate are: the landowner opens a road to public travel; *Wolfe, supra; Burkitt v. Battle*, 59 S.W. 429 (Tenn. Ch. App. 1900); acquiescence in the use of the road as a public road, *Nicely* and *Burkitt, supra*; and the fact the public has used the road for an extended period of time, *McCord, supra; Scott, supra.* While dedication is not dependent on duration of the use, extended use is a circumstance tending to show an intent to dedicate. *Cole, supra.* Finally, an intent to dedicate is inferable when the roadway is repaired and maintained by the public. *Burkitt, supra*, citing *Sharp v. Mynatt*, 69 Tenn. 375 (1878).

The foregoing authorities support the trial judge's conclusion, derived from the facts, that the road was dedicated by implication as a public road. We affirm the judgment of the trial court and remand at appellants' cost.

NOTES AND QUESTIONS

1. *Eminent Domain vs. Dedication.* Although an eminent domain action and a dedication both result in the transfer of land from a private owner to the public (or the sovereign), the underlying premise is different. With a dedication, the private owner voluntarily transfers title to the public. While many dedications are made by written deeds, no deed is required, as the above case illustrates. The element of involuntariness arises when the private owner denies that any dedication occurred. This problem normally arises when the original dedication was oral or by implication.

2. *Elements of an Implied Dedication.* Many jurisdictions recognize that a dedication may be made without any statement, written or spoken. While an intent to dedicate is still required (at least in theory), an implied dedication is established by a showing that the private owner has invited or permitted the public to use the land in question for a long period of time. Either complete title to the land or an easement of use may be conveyed by implied dedication. If the court concludes that the private owner intended to implicitly dedicate the land to the public, a subsequent attempt to exclude the public from the property, even by the original owner, will be ineffective.

Transfer of title by implied dedication differs from adverse possession or prescription in that it is based on a theory of voluntary transfer rather than a loss of rights through a failure to protest adverse use. In fact, the two are often difficult to distinguish since both rely on proof of long and continuous use by parties other than the original owner. At least one court has concluded that there is no meaningful distinction between implied dedication and prescription. *Nature Conservancy v. Machipongo Club, Inc.*, 419 F. Supp. 390 (E.D. Va. 1976).

3. One of the most controversial implied dedication cases is *Gion v. City of Santa Cruz*, 465 P.2d 50 (Cal. 1970), in which the California Supreme Court found that the owners of a private beach had dedicated an easement of use to the public. The court reached this conclusion on the ground that the public had made use of the beach for many years. The fact that the private owners denied any intention to dedicate an easement to the public and had made half-hearted efforts to prevent public use over the years were found not to be controlling. The court reasoned that a dedication was implied from the public use for the prescriptive period (which in California was only five years) and from the owners' inadequate efforts to bar others from the property.

Although the *Gion* decision was hailed in some quarters, it was also the subject of intense criticism. At least two courts outside of California have explicitly rejected the decision, *Department of Nat. Resources v. Mayor & Council of Ocean City*, 332 A.2d 630 (Md. 1975); *Automotive Prods. Corp. v. Provo City Corp.*, 502 P.2d 568 (Utah 1972). Moreover, in the aftermath of the case, California enacted legislation which limited dedications arising out of public use to cases in which the private owner made an express written offer of dedication. Cal. Civ. Code § 1009. Was the legislative response an overreaction?

[D.] SECURITY OF TITLE

[1.] The Recording System

Once a deed has been delivered, the buyer ordinarily takes it to a county office where it is recorded into the public land records. The recording of deeds has been a feature of American land transactions since the seventeenth 17th century. In a society in which land was freely alienable and in which individual parcels of property frequently changed ownership, the value of a system of land registration in which prospective purchasers could determine whether prospective sellers actually held title to property was quickly appreciated. No such system existed in England, a fact that created numerous problems even though land transfers were far less frequent there than in the United States. (For example, the "English rule" that a buyer could not recover loss of bargain damages from a seller who had promised marketable title in good faith but could not deliver it was a product of the difficulty of determining the quality of title to land.)

In a typical American recording system, a county government office maintains a library of deeds and other written instruments relating to land transactions. Individuals who have acquired new interests in real property may bring the appropriate documents to be "recorded." Individuals are not required to record their deeds, and the failure to record has no effect on the validity of the document between the buyer and seller. However, a purchaser of an interest in real estate who fails to record may find that his interest is legally inferior to that of a subsequently acquired interest held by a third party.

Any document directly or indirectly affecting title to land may be recorded (including liens of all types and divorce and probate decrees), although in many jurisdictions documents must first be acknowledged or notarized. The officials who operate the recording system do not attempt to judge the validity of the documents presented to them, but merely record them once the requisite fees are paid. The records are open to the public.

Equally important, the governmental office also maintains an index to these documents which, in a densely populated area, would otherwise be unsearchable. Documents submitted for recording are typically recorded in chronological sequence. Access to desired records is made possible through the indexes. The most common form of index is one which provides a brief description of each land transaction and lists it alphabetically by the name of both grantor and grantee. A prospective purchaser of property can locate the seller's previous deed by looking up the seller's name in the grantee index. Having found the previous seller's name, his deed can be located in the same manner. If the buyer is concerned that the seller may have already sold the property or an interest in it to another purchaser, she can go to the grantor index to see if any such transactions have been recorded. A title search involves tracking all previous owners of a parcel of property for a substantial period — usually forty to sixty years — through the use of the grantee index. Each of the previous owners is then looked up in the grantor index to make sure that other interests in the land in question have not been created. The indexes will also indicate the location in the records of every deed in the chain of title. Ordinarily all of these deeds will be examined to make sure that the deeds themselves were properly executed and did not create any additional interests in other parties.

In some urban areas, tract indexes are used. Entries in a tract index are made by block and lot number, rather than by the name of the grantor or grantee. The great advantage of a tract index is that all transactions relating to a particular parcel of property appear on a single page. However, tract indexes do not work very well with land that is subdivided or consolidated with other parcels. Nevertheless, a title search with a tract index is often a relatively simple process.

An alternate form of recording is deed registration, or the Torrens System (named after its inventor, Sir Richard Torrens). Under this system, deeds are replaced by title certificates which are conclusive as to ownership. The name on the certificate of title is the owner of the property, and when land changes hands, the grantee must present the previous owner's certificate of title to the appropriate governmental agency which issues a new title. The originals of the title certificates are held by the state and are accessible through a tract index. All interests in the land held by third parties are either noted on the face of the certificate or else are invalid. (Reference to restrictions or covenants filed elsewhere is usually held to be insufficient.) Although the Torrens System has generated periodic bursts of interest since its introduction in Australia in the 1850s, enthusiasm for it has waned noticeably in the United States. In one form or another, it is available in approximately ten states, although in no state is it the dominant system of recording.

[2.] Recording Acts

To encourage purchasers of interests in land to record their deeds, American Recording Acts have long included provisions that reward timely recording and, perhaps more importantly, raise the possibility of serious, adverse consequences for those who fail to do so. Under the common law rule, the superiority of one claim to another was ordinarily a temporal matter. If A sold Blackacre to B, and then one day later sold it again to C, B would always prevail against C (short of C establishing title by adverse possession), because B's claim was first in time. Similarly if A executed a mortgage to B and then a second mortgage to C (which, unlike the first example, is perfectly legal), B would have first priority to any proceeds from the sale if it became necessary for her to foreclose against A. Under a recording act, B, who acquired her interest first in time in both examples might not be able to recover at all if she failed to properly record her interests in a timely fashion.

There are three major types of recording acts: race, notice, and race-notice. Under a "race" statute, priority among competing grantees of the same parcel of land is determined solely by the order in which the grantees recorded. If A sold Blackacre to B on Monday and to C on Tuesday, and C recorded on Wednesday, and B on Thursday, C would have the superior claim to Blackacre, even if he was aware of B's prior purchase. Although the earliest recording acts were "race" statutes, their potentially inequitable consequences have made them unpopular and only a handful of states still have recording statutes of this type.

Under a notice statute, a subsequent bona fide purchaser prevails over an earlier grantee who has failed to record so long as the later purchaser has no actual or constructive notice of the prior transaction at the time of his purchase. Actual notice means that the purchaser is aware of the previous transaction at the time he or she acquires the real property interest. Subsequent notice is irrelevant. Constructive notice usually means notice through the land records. Any prospective purchaser is held to have notice of properly recorded legal instruments, whether or not he knows in fact of their existence. Approximately half of the states have notice statutes.

Under race-notice recording acts, subsequent grantees who purchase without notice are protected against prior purchasers who have failed to record, so long as they record prior to the previous grantee. (Notice statutes impose no such requirement.) Race-notice statutes also exist in approximately half the states.

LEASING ENTERPRISES, INC. v. LIVINGSTON

South Carolina Court of Appeals
363 S.E.2d 410 (1987)

CURETON, JUDGE.

This case involves the effort by a judgment creditor to attack a conveyance of real property between a debtor and a family member. The Master-in-Equity set aside the conveyance. The family member, Margaret Schlee, appeals. We affirm.

Leasing Enterprises Inc. (Leasing) is a California corporation. In 1980, Leasing entered into a Lease Purchase Agreement with Joe E. Livingston for a forklift. Livingston failed to comply with the agreement and Leasing obtained a default judgment against him in California in November of 1981. The record is not clear concerning the disposition of the forklift but the judgment was not satisfied.

Leasing filed this action in Oconee County in May of 1984. In its complaint, Leasing sought to domesticate its foreign judgment. It also alleged Livingston had represented to Leasing through financial documents in 1980 that he owned a one-half undivided interest in approximately thirty-seven (37) acres in Oconee County. This land was allegedly jointly owned by Livingston and Margaret Schlee, his mother. In 1980, real estate records in Oconee County would have reflected this situation. On April 21, 1983, a purported quitclaim deed from Livingston to Schlee was recorded in Oconee County. This deed conveyed all of Livingston's interest in the property to Schlee for the stated consideration of love and affection. The deed was executed in California. It bears the date of October 21, 1977. It is prepared on what appears to be a standard California form. The sole witness on the deed is Earl Schlee. The October, 1977, date is reflected in the notary certification where a California notary attests to the signature of Livingston. There is no certification of the witness's signature. Leasing recorded its domesticated judgment against Livingston in December of 1984.

There is no challenge to the validity of the judgment against Livingston or the domestication of the California judgment. Livingston did not appear in this case although he was served and subsequently found to be in default. The controversy concerns the deed from Livingston to Schlee. Leasing claims the deed constitutes a fraudulent conveyance and also alleges the deed was not validly recorded under the South Carolina recording statute. The relevant chronology is: (1) the quitclaim deed relating to South Carolina property executed in California in October 1977; (2) the financial arrangement between Leasing and Livingston in 1980; (3) the California judgment against Livingston in 1981; (4) the recording of the quitclaim deed from Livingston to Schlee in Oconee County in 1983; and (5) the domestication of the California judgment and its recording in Oconee County in 1984.

The case was referred to the Master-in-Equity for entry of a final judgment with direct appeal to the South Carolina Supreme Court. The Master found for Leasing. He directed the Clerk of Court to cancel the deed from Livingston to Schlee in order to allow Leasing's judgment to attach to Livingston's one-half interest in the property. The Master's decision was based upon a number of grounds but we find it necessary to address only certain issues in affirming the decision of the Master.

Although not directly discussed by the parties or the Master, it is clear South Carolina law governs the validity of the conveyance between Livingston and Schlee. The deed was executed in California but it concerns real property located in South Carolina. The law of the situs would be applied to determine whether a conveyance transfers an interest in land and the nature of the interest transferred. RESTATEMENT (SECOND) OF CONFLICTS Section 223(1) (1971).

Section 27-7-10, Code of Laws of South Carolina, 1976, sets forth a form of conveyance of fee simple. The section provides the form shall be valid to transfer a fee simple interest from one person to another "if it shall be executed in the presence of and be subscribed by two or more credible witnesses."

In 1840, the Court of Errors of South Carolina was asked to determine if a deed with one subscribing witness was valid in this state. The Court held the form adopted by the Legislature was intended to operate "as a deed for the conveyance of freehold, [and to do so] it must have two subscribing witnesses." *Craig v. Pinson*, 25 S.C.L. (Chev.) 272 (1840). The requirement of two witnesses was recognized in subsequent decisions. *Jones v. Crawford*, 26 S.C.L. (1 McMul.) 373 (1841); *Little v. White*, 7 S.E. 72 (S.C. 1888) ("There can be no doubt that two subscribing witnesses are necessary to the validity of a deed designed to convey real estate."); *Hunt v. Smith*, 202 S.C. 129, 24 S.E.2d 164 (1943).

Schlee argues the absence of two witnesses does not destroy the validity of a deed to transfer title. In making this argument she relies upon *Farmer's Bank & Trust Co. v. Fudge*, 100 S.E. 628 (S.C. 1919) and *Smith v. Hawkins*, 175 S.E.2d 824 (S.C. 1970). Both of these cases indicate a deed or mortgage without competent or sufficient witnesses is good as between the parties. However, this case deals with the effect of the purported transfer upon a third party in the position of Leasing (i.e., a subsequent creditor of the grantor). Accordingly, we must consider the recording of the deed because recording is the method by which a third party without actual notice is alerted to the possible transfer of interests in real property.

Section 30-7-10, Code of Laws of South Carolina, 1976, is the recording statute. If this deed was acceptable for recording, Leasing's judgment would not have priority over Schlee under the current recording statute unless Leasing shows the deed is a fraudulent conveyance.

In 1958 the recording statute was amended to require a subsequent lien creditor without notice to file the instrument evidencing his lien in order to claim under the statute. Further, the statute was amended to declare priority would be determined by the time of filing for record. This amendment by the Legislature was apparently designed to obviate the result in the case of *South Carolina National Bank v. Guest*, 102 S.E.2d 215 (S.C. 1958). *See, Atlas Supply Co. v. Davis*, 256 S.E.2d 859 (S.C. 1979). In the *Guest* case an individual obtained two loans from two different banks on the same day. He executed chattel mortgages on the same vehicle to secure the loans. He represented to the second bank that the vehicle was free of any liens. Both banks recorded their mortgages the next day and the first bank to loan money was the first to record. The question arose as to the priority of the mortgages. The South Carolina Supreme Court interpreted the then existing recording act to give priority to the second bank even though it recorded its mortgage forty-five minutes after the first bank. The Court pointed out that even though the first bank had executed and recorded its mortgage first in point of time the mortgage was not of record when the second bank had loaned money and its mortgage was executed. The Court classified the South Carolina recording act as being of the "notice" type which will invalidate an instrument as against a subsequent instrument acquired in good faith before the first instrument is recorded. Prior to the 1958 amendment to the statute the "subsequent purchaser" without notice was protected under the recording act regardless of when or whether he recorded his own conveyance. *Guest*, 102 S.E.2d at 217 (S.C.). Our reading of the current statute indicates the recording act is a race-notice act which will provide protection to the subsequent purchaser or creditor provided he records first. Therefore, even though Leasing had no actual or constructive notice of the deed between Livingston and Schlee when the Lease Purchase agreement was made and was a subsequent creditor of Livingston, it has no protection under the recording statute unless either the deed from Livingston to Schlee was not valid for recording thereby causing Schlee to lose her filing priority or Leasing can demonstrate a fraudulent conveyance.

The comment of the Supreme Court in *Young v. Young* concerning a mortgage is instructive on this controversy.

> An instrument purporting to be a mortgage but imperfectly executed by the omission of a seal, or in some other manner, so as to be defective in form is wholly nugatory at law as a valid mortgage or as giving any interest in or claim upon the parcel of land described. Equity, however, not saying that the instrument is a true legal mortgage, declares that it is an efficient agreement to give a mortgage, and as such creates an equitable lien upon the land, valid for all purposes, and as against all parties, *except a purchaser of the land for a valuable consideration and without notice.*

Young v. Young, 3 S.E. 202, 205 (S.C. 1887) (emphasis added).

Because of its facial defect in containing the signature of only one witness the deed was not entitled to be recorded in Oconee County. The South Carolina Supreme Court has indicated the right to record a deed is conditioned upon the fact of having been witnessed by two witnesses. *Arthur v. Hollowell*, 98 S.E. 202 (S.C. 1919). "Certain irregularities unquestionably must be regarded as material ones disqualifying an instrument for record. Thus, the record of a deed or mortgage having only one witness . . . does not constitute notice of the existence of such deed or mortgage." Means, *The Recording of Land Titles in South Carolina*, 10 S.C.L.Q. 346, 407 (1958). *See, Harper v. Barsh*, 31 S.C. Eq. (10 Rich.) 149 (1858) (mortgage attested by only one witness is incomplete in execution and is not entitled to be recorded).

Schlee argues the acknowledgment of the signature of Livingston by a notary public in California makes the deed proper in form for purposes of recording in South Carolina. Whether the acknowledgment complies with the "Uniform Recognition of Acknowledgments Act" in Section 26-3-10 *et seq.*, Code of Laws of South Carolina, 1976, has nothing to do with the statutory requirement of two subscribing witnesses to the deed. We concur with the analysis expressed by the Office of the South Carolina Attorney General in Opinion No. 3373, 1972 Op. Atty. Gen. 225. "The Acts [Section 26-3-20 *et seq.* and Section 30-5-30] do recognize and permit the recording of a deed or other instrument *properly subscribed by the required number of witnesses* (emphasis added) if execution is provided by affidavit of a subscribing witness under terms of the Uniform Recognition of Acknowledgment Act . . . or an acknowledgment of the person executing the instrument under the conditions prescribed therein." 1972 Op. Atty. Gen. at 226.

The deed from Livingston to Schlee was not effective to convey title with respect to a party in the position of Leasing and was not entitled to be recorded so as to obtain record priority. Accordingly, the judgment of the Master-in-Equity is Affirmed.

NOTES AND QUESTIONS

1. In this case, the creditor prevails because the deed in question was not validly executed under South Carolina law. However, had the deed been signed by two witnesses, Leasing would not have been able to enforce its lien against the property even though the deed was recorded two years after Leasing obtained its judgment against Livingston in California. Do you understand why?

2. Recording acts usually apply to all real property interests, not just the transfer of land. Under many statutes, easements and profits, restrictive covenants, long-term leases, mortgages and other liens must be recorded to be fully effective. Note also that to fully protect the purchaser, an interest should be recorded immediately. In the 19th century, recording acts often provided for a grace period in which the new owner could record without risk of being displaced by a subsequent purchaser. The last such provision, a Delaware statute which gave purchasers fifteen days to record their deeds, was repealed in 1968.

3. The language of recording acts often seems highly arcane, especially upon a first reading. Consider, for example, the following three statutes:

> Every (i) such contract in writing, (ii) deed conveying any such estate or term, (iii) deed of gift, or deed of trust, or mortgage conveying real estate or goods and chattels, and (iv) such bill of sale, or contract for the sale of goods and chattels, when the possession is allowed to remain with the grantor, shall be void as to all purchasers of valuable consideration without notice not parties thereto and lien creditors, until and except from the time it is duly admitted to record in the county or city wherein the property embraced in such contract, deed or bill of sale may be.

Va. Code Ann. § 55-96(A)(1).

> No (i) conveyance of land, or (ii) contract to convey, or (iii) option to convey, or (iv) lease of land for more than three years shall be valid to pass any property interest as against lien creditors or purchasers of a valuable consideration from the donor, bargainor or lessor but from the time of registration thereof in the county where the land lies.

N.C. Gen. Stat. § 47-18 (1997).

> Every conveyance (except patents issued by the United States or this state, or by the proper officers of either) which is not recorded as provided by law shall be void as against any subsequent purchaser in good faith and for

> valuable consideration of the same real estate or any portion thereof whose conveyance shall first be duly recorded.

Wis. Stat. § 706.08 (1995–1996).

The first of these is a notice statute; the second, a race statute; and the third, a race-notice statute. Do you understand why? For a relatively recent breakdown of types of recording statutes by state, see Sweat, *Race, Race-Notice and Notice Statutes: The American Recording System*, PROB. & PROP. (May–June 1989).

4. Ordinarily, recording acts only protect bona fide purchasers, that is, those who pay valuable consideration for the interest transferred. The practical effect of this distinction is that subsequent heirs, devisees, and donees are not protected by these statutes. However, transfers from such parties to bona fide purchasers will usually be protected. For example: A sells Blackacre to B, but B fails to record. A then deeds Blackacre to C as a gift and C records. B will still prevail over C, even though he hasn't recorded because C is not a purchaser for value. However, if C sells the property to D, who has no notice of the earlier transaction between A and B, D will prevail over B, so long as B had still not recorded at the time of the C-D transfer. For a once well-known case involving a version of this problem, see *Earle v. Fiske*, 103 Mass. 491 (1870). For similar reasons, recording acts only apply to voluntary transfers, not involuntary ones. Consequently, a validly recorded deed will not defeat a claim of adverse possession, implied easement, or dower right.

5. *What Constitutes Constructive Notice?* While constructive notice ordinarily means record notice, in some jurisdictions a purchaser is required to make additional inquiries. In a minority of states, a buyer who takes by quitclaim deed must inquire into the existence of prior, unrecorded conveyances. This requirement is justified on the grounds that the quitclaim deed is an inherently suspicious device. In a majority of jurisdictions, a purchaser is obligated to inspect the premises and is held to know whatever a reasonable inspection of the property would reveal. For example, if O sells Blackacre to A who takes possession but fails to record his deed, B, a subsequent purchaser of Blackacre from O, will be held to have notice of the first transaction if an inspection of the premises would have alerted a prospective buyer to the possibility of a prior sale, i.e., A's presence on the premises. The fact that B made no such inspection is no defense.

6. *The Shelter Rule.* Suppose O sells Blackacre to A, who fails to record, and then to B, who purchases it for value and without notice of the prior sale to A. B then records. Under any recording statute, B will prevail over A. What happens, however, if B then sells to C, who had notice of the original O to A transaction? To further complicate the situation, A now records. Should C prevail over A?

Under the so-called "shelter rule," C prevails. The rule is justified on the grounds that were the rule otherwise, B, who is entirely blameless, would be penalized. Do you see why? What should be the result if B sells to O instead of C?

7. What if O agrees to sell Blackacre to A and then, before the scheduled closing date, sells it to B, who records? Should A be able to recover Blackacre from B? What, after all, could A have done to protect his interest? According to an Iowa appellate court, A's equitable interest during the executory period was unaffected by the subsequent transfer. *In re Estate of Clark*, 447 N.W.2d 549 (Iowa Ct. App. 1989).

Is such a result fair to B? Ordinarily, contracts for the sale of land are not recorded. Should they be?

8. Recording acts not only affect the right of ownership and possession, but also affect the priority of mortgages and other liens. Consider the following situation in a jurisdiction with a notice recording act. O owes A $7,000. To secure the obligation, O gives A mortgage for that amount. A does not record. O then gives B, who has actual knowledge of A's mortgage, a second mortgage for $5,000. B records. Finally, O gives C, who has no knowledge of A's mortgage, a $3,000 mortgage. [Notice that unlike the situation involving multiple sales of the same property, there is nothing inherently dishonest about these transactions.] O defaults on all three mortgages without having repaid any of the loans. Blackacre is sold for $10,000. To whom, and in what amounts, should the proceeds be distributed?

In *Day v. Munson*, 14 Ohio St. 488 (1863), which involved similar facts, the court gave C the amount available above B's claim, and then gave A first claim to what remained with any remainder going to B. In the above example, C would get $3,000; A, $7,000; and B would get nothing. Is this the proper result?

9. In most instances, submitting an instrument for recording means that it will be entered into the local records in a timely fashion. However, there are occasions where deeds are indexed under the wrong name or where official records are destroyed. In such cases, should future purchasers be deemed to have constructive notice even though they could not locate these records if they tried? Courts have divided on this question. *Compare United States v. Lomas Mortgage, USA, Inc.*, 742 F. Supp. 936 (W.D. Va. 1990) (as long as deed is entered into the deed books, proper indexing is not necessary for constructive notice), *with Hochstein v. Romero*, 268 Cal. Rptr. 202 (Cal. App. 1990) (misindexed interests are unrecorded). There may be a slight trend toward the latter position. The argument for favoring the second purchaser is that while both parties are essentially innocent of wrongdoing, the first purchaser could have prevented the problem by checking to see if his deed was properly indexed.

[3.] Marketable Title Acts

In addition to removing clouds on title, marketable title acts may also eliminate what might otherwise be a valid claim to ownership had it been asserted earlier. The process is illustrated in the following case.

MARSHALL v. HOLLYWOOD, INC.
Florida Supreme Court
236 So. 2d 114 (1970)

CARLTON, JUSTICE.

We now review an application of the Marketable Record Titles to Real Property Act, Chapter 712, Florida Statutes. The District Court of Appeal, Fourth District, has certified that its decision in this cause, reported at 224 So. 2d 743, is one which passes upon a question of great public interest. The District Court held, in effect, that the Act confers marketability to a chain of title arising out of a forged or a wild deed, so long as the strict requirements of the Act are met. We affirm this decision.

The complex facts involved in this case have been presented extensively and with clarity in the opinion of the District Court. We will only briefly summarize these facts. In 1912 Mathew Marshall and Carl Weidling owned a large tract of land in South Florida. In 1913 they organized and incorporated the Atlantic Beach Company ["Company"]. They transferred their property interests in the large tract to the Company, and in return they received two-thirds and one-third, respectively, of the Company's total authorized and issued stock, in direct proportion to their initial ownership interests in the tract. Marshall and Weidling were the sole officers of the Company and they alone participated in its stock.

Mr. Marshall died in December 1923, leaving Louise Marshall as his widow and sole surviving heir. Mrs. Marshall was totally unaware of her husband's interests in the Company, and within a month after his passing, she left the State without ever returning. After her departure, a man named Frank M. Terry, apparently aided and abetted by certain associates, set into motion a clever scheme calculated to defraud the Marshall estate of all interests in the Company and its property. Although there is some question as to exactly who played what part in this scheme, for purposes of this opinion we shall ascribe all responsibility to Mr. Terry.

Within a few days after Mrs. Marshall's departure, Terry forged her name to an Application for Letters of Administration concerning Mathew Marshall's estate. Letters were subsequently issued by the County Judge, Dade County, to Mrs. Marshall and Terry received them. About this same time, Terry wrote up certain "Minutes of Dissolution of Atlantic Beach Company" and he also prepared a deed conveying all of the Company's property to himself and others residing out of the State, who were alleged in the spurious Minutes to be the remaining stockholders of the Company. Thereafter, these Minutes were purportedly acknowledged, and the deed conveying all of the Company's property was executed by those who were alleged to be the stockholders.

Next, Terry prepared a petition seeking an Order dissolving the Company which was then filed in Circuit Court, Broward County, along with the Minutes of Dissolution. The Court granted the petition since it appeared in order, and a decree dissolving the Company was entered in February 1924. The day before this petition was filed, Terry and the other grantees under the deed from the Company joined in executing a deed conveying the tract to Hollywood Realty Company, a Florida corporation. This deed was recorded in April 1924. In August 1924 Hollywood Realty in turn executed a deed conveying this same property to Homeseekers Realty Company, which was recorded August 22, 1924.

All of the foregoing transactions are alleged by petitioner to have been part of a scheme to defraud the Mathew Marshall estate. The record is silent as to why Carl Weidling, initially owner of a one-third undivided interest in the tract, and subsequently holder of one-third of the Atlantic Beach Company stock, never raised any objections or questions. Mr. Weidling died in 1963; his interests are not represented in this suit. Mrs. Marshall died in 1945 without ever having learned of her husband's interests in the Company. The Company itself was never legally dissolved until September 14, 1936, when it was dissolved by proclamation of the Governor on account of failure to pay capital stock tax.

Homeseekers Realty Company disposed of approximately one-third of the initial Atlantic Beach Company tract through sales before it lost its control over the remainder by forced sheriff's sale in 1929. In that year, the Highway Construction Company of Ohio, Inc., obtained a judgment against Homeseekers and caused the sale at which Highway purchased the remaining unsold two-thirds of the initial tract. A sheriff's deed evidencing the judgment sale was recorded December 30, 1930. Highway Construction Company then conveyed its interests in the tract to respondent Hollywood, Inc., and this deed was recorded on February 21, 1931.

Respondent Hollywood, Inc., still retains title to the two-thirds of the original Atlantic Beach tract which was conveyed to it as a result of the forced sheriff's sale. The other respondents are those numerous persons, or their successors, who derived title to parcels on the one-third portion of the original tract from Homeseekers Realty prior to the 1929 judgment sale.

It was not until November 1966, that petitioner, a brother of Mathew Marshall, uncovered Terry's actions. Petitioner obtained appointment as Administrator of the Marshall estate, and subsequently, in his capacity as Administrator, he filed his initial complaint on July 13, 1967. An amended complaint was filed on April 5, 1968. The amended complaint sought a decree establishing the equitable interest of petitioner in the tract initially belonging to the Atlantic Beach Company, confirmation of the ownership of Atlantic Beach stock by petitioner, and also the appointment of a trustee for the Company who could convey legal title to the interest in the original tract to the heirs of Marshall.

Upon respondents' motion, the amended complaint was dismissed by final judgment with prejudice. The order of dismissal stated that petitioner's amended complaint failed to state a cause of action because the estate's claims were barred by operation of the [Florida] Marketable Record Title Act. The dismissal was appealed to the District Court. The issue framed on appeal was whether or not the Act applied to the claim of title asserted in petitioner's amended complaint in a manner which would extinguish the claim.

The arguments raised by the litigants before the District Court were similar to the arguments presented here. Petitioner asserted that dismissal by the Circuit Court was an error because: (1) the Legislature did not intend that such claims be barred by the Act; (2) the Act preserves case law which is inconsistent with dismissal; (3) the language of the Act does not support dismissal; (4) though the Act calls for a liberal construction, such construction cannot supersede restraints imposed by the Act itself.

Respondents contended that dismissal was proper because: (1) it comports with the Legislative intent behind the Act; (2) the Act goes beyond previous statute of limitations, curative acts, and recording acts, and, therefore, case law arising out of these prior enactments is not necessarily pertinent; (3) the language of the Act requires dismissal; (4) petitioner does not qualify under any of the exceptions provided for by the Act; (5) the Act would be totally deprived of meaning if dismissal were not granted.

The Florida Bar has been active in this case, both here and in the District Court, as amicus curiae because the Act was submitted to the Legislature by the Bar's Real

Property, Probate and Trust Law Section, and this case represents its first reported construction. The Bar's position is that petitioner's interpretation of the Act and its effect is clearly erroneous. The Bar also presented arguments here and below regarding the constitutionality of the Act. However, we join with the District Court in declining to consider such arguments because the constitutionality of the Act was not framed as an issue in petitioner's amended complaint, which is the only complaint now before us. For purposes of disposing with this litigation, we will act on the assumption that the Act is constitutional.

The most persuasive argument of petitioner is that the Marketable Record Title Act preserves case law which is inconsistent with dismissal of petitioner's amended complaint. F.S. § 712.07, F.S.A. states:

> Nothing contained in this Act shall be construed to extend the period for the bringing of an action or for the doing of any other act required under any statute of limitations or to affect the operation of any statute governing the effect of the recording or the failure to record any instrument affecting land. This law shall not vitiate any curative act.

Petitioner asserts that by preserving the operation of statutes of limitations, and curative and recording acts, the Legislature intended that the Act must be construed in a manner consistent with these previous enactments and all case law interpreting them. In cases dealing with wild or forged deeds under these various acts, it has consistently been held, according to petitioner, that such deeds are void and of no effect even though they may have been recorded. As examples, petitioner cites *Reed v. Fain*, 145 So. 2d 858 (Fla. 1961, *rev'd on rehearing*, 1962); *Poladian v. Johnson*, 85 So. 2d 140 (Fla. 1955); and *Wright v. Blocker*, 198 So. 88 (1940). Therefore petitioner suggests that the Act cannot bar a complaint which demonstrates that the chain of title involved in a cause initiated out of a forgery or a wild deed, even though the forgery or the wild deed came into being more than thirty years before marketability was being determined.

The answer to this argument is simply that the Act in question goes beyond previous enactments and is in a category of its own. We quote with approval the following commentary. Boyer & Shapo, *Florida's Marketable Title Act: Prospects and Problems*, 18 U. Miami L. Rev. 103, 104:

> The Marketable Title concept is simple, although it has fathered many variations in draftsmanship. The idea is to extinguish all claims of a given age (thirty years in the Florida Statute) which conflict with a record chain of title which is at least that old. The act performs this task by combining several features, which generally, are singly labeled as "statutes of limitations," "curative acts," and "recording acts."
>
> The new act is in fact all of these: It declares a marketable title on a recorded chain of title which is more than thirty years old, and it nullifies all interests which are older than the root of title. This nullification is subject to a group of exceptions — including interests which have been filed for record in a prescribed manner.
>
> The act is also more: It goes beyond the conventional statute of limitations because it runs against persons under disability. It is broader

> than the kind of legislation generally described as a curative act, because it actually invalidates interests instead of simply "curing" formal defects. It also differs from a recording act by requiring a re-recording of outstanding interests in order to preserve them.

Also, CATSMAN, THE MARKETABLE RECORD TITLE ACT AND UNIFORM TITLE STANDARDS, III FLORIDA REAL PROPERTY PRACTICE (1965), § 6.2:

> The chief purpose of the act is to extinguish stale claims and ancient defects against the title to real property, and, accordingly, limit the period of search. The act is different from a statute of limitations. In a statute of limitations a claim of a vested, present interest is cut off because of the claimant's failure to sue. If suit is not filed, the claim is lost. By the Marketable Record Title Act, any claim or interest, vested or contingent, present or future, is cut off unless the claimant preserves his claim by filing a notice within a 30-year period. If a notice is not filed, the claim is lost. The act also goes beyond a curative act. Curative legislation only corrects certain minor or technical defects through the passage of time, whereas under the Marketable Record Title Act, most defects or clouds on title beyond the period of 30 years are removed and the purchaser is made secure in his transaction.

In view of the special nature of this Act and its special purpose, the assertion that its construction and application must be bound by precedents relating to less comprehensive acts does not make good sense and cannot make good law. The clear Legislative intention behind the Act, as expressed in F.S. § 712.10, F.S.A., was to simplify and facilitate land title transactions by allowing persons to rely on a record title as described by F.S. § 712.02, F.S.A., subject only to such limitations as appear in F.S. § 712.03, F.S.A. To accept petitioner's arguments would be to disembowel the Act through a case dealing with a factual situation of a nature precisely contemplated and remedied by the Act itself. This we cannot do.

In summary, although the Atlantic Beach Company/Terry deed initiating the chain of title involved here was forged, this deed formed but one link in the chain coming before the effective roots of title in this case as defined by the Act, i.e., transactions with either The Highway Construction Company or the Homeseekers Realty Company as grantors. Claims arising out of transactions, whether based upon forgeries or not, predating the effective roots of title are extinguished by operation of the Act unless claimants can come in under any of the specified exceptions to the Act. In this case, petitioner fails to qualify under any of the exceptions to the Act, and, therefore, petitioner's claims are barred.

The certified question involved in this cause was, in effect, whether the Marketable Record Titles to Real Property Act, Ch. 712, F.S. confers marketability to a chain of title arising out of a forged or wild deed, so long as the strict requirements of the Act are met. This question is answered in the affirmative.

The decision of the appellate court here reviewed having properly affirmed the decree of the lower court, the writ heretofore issued in this cause should be and it is hereby discharged.

NOTES AND QUESTIONS

1. Does the increased alienability of land justify a result like the one in this case? Isn't it likely that Hollywood, Inc. and the other landowners whose claim to the Marshall property traces back to the wild deed could establish title by adverse possession? Do they need an additional remedy?

Although adverse possession has cleared more title defects than any other legal device, those who hold title by adverse possession often have trouble selling their property to a buyer who insists upon marketable title. (Remember the problem in *Tri-State Hotel Co. v. Sphinx Inv. Co.*, above.) While some states will allow an adverse possessor to establish marketable title by written documents or other evidence admissible in court, owners without a valid deed are ordinarily required to go through a formal legal proceeding to quiet title before they can establish marketable title. A successful action to quiet title concludes with the court issuing what is in effect a new deed from the sovereign to the adverse possessor. Some jurisdictions distinguish between mere marketable title and marketable title "of record." If the contract for sale specifies the latter, then an action to quiet title is necessary.

2. Short of suing to reclaim possession of the land itself, what could Marshall's estate have done to prevent the result in the above case? As the court notes, quoting a commentator on the Florida act, interests are "cut off unless the claimant preserves his claim by filing a notice within a 30-year period." In other words, had Marshall's estate or his heir or devisee rerecorded a deed to the property any time within in the 30-year period preceding their 1967 complaint, they would have prevailed. Does this mean that all property owners in Florida should refile their deeds every thirty years to protect themselves against those who may claim through a forged deed?

3. *Constitutional Issues.* Although the Florida Supreme Court did not feel it was appropriate to address the question of the constitutionality of the Florida Marketable Title Act, such acts are frequently subject to constitutional challenges on the grounds that they constitute the taking of property without due process of law. Such challenges rarely succeed. For an example of a successful attack, see *Chicago & N.W. Transp. Co. v. Pedersen*, 259 N.W.2d 316 (Wis. 1977) (involving an act extinguishing unexercised claims to mineral rights). However, a nearly identical statute was upheld in *Short v. Texaco*, 406 N.E.2d 625 (Ind. 1980). The latter decision was upheld by the United States Supreme Court in *Texaco, Inc. v. Short*, 454 U.S. 516 (1982).

4. *Root of Title.* The root of title is technically the transfer from the sovereign to the first private owner. However, under most modern marketable title acts, the root of title is the first transaction in the chain of title that predates the marketable title period. For example, in a state with a 40-year marketable title period, a title search done in 2008 would stop once the searcher located a deed in the grantor index that predated 1968. Interests created in earlier deeds would be invalid because they would predate the "root of title." For a more detailed explanation of the operation of the modern marketable title statutes, see W. STOEBUCK & D. WHITMAN, THE LAW OF PROPERTY 898–905 (3d ed. 2000).

[E.] FRAUDULENT TRANSFERS

[1.] Forged Deeds

As we saw in *Marshall v. Hollywood*, a forged or wild deed can gain priority over a legitimate deed through the operation of a marketable title act. However, such a result can occur only if the true owner fails to enforce his or her right over a long period of time. If the true owner objects in a more timely fashion, nothing will validate a chain of title that originates in a forgery, even if the ultimate owner is a bona fide purchaser for value who acquired the property without notice of the fraud. Recording a deed is usually said to give rise to a rebuttable presumption that the deed is valid, but proof of forgery will always overcome that presumption. However, when the deed involves something other than forgery, the situation may be more complicated.

[2.] Deeds Fraudulently Acquired

HAUCK v. CRAWFORD

South Dakota Supreme Court
62 N.W.2d 92 (1953)

RUDOLPH, JUDGE.

Although in form an action to quiet title, the real purpose of this action is to cancel and set aside a certain mineral deed admittedly signed by plaintiff and certain other deeds transferring the mineral rights by the grantee named in the original deed. No one has questioned the form of the action. The trial court entered judgment canceling the deeds and defendants have appealed.

Cancellation was asked because of alleged fraud, and it was upon this basis that the trial court entered its judgment. The defendants contend, first, that there was no fraud and second, that the mineral rights were transferred to a bona fide purchaser for value and are not, therefore, subject to cancellation even though obtained by fraud in the first instance.

The facts most favorable in support of the judgment of the trial court are as follows: Plaintiff is a farmer owning and operating a farm located partly in South Dakota and partly in North Dakota. He lives on that part of the farm located in South Dakota in McPherson County. Plaintiff is 44 years old, has an 8th grade education, married and has a family. His farm consists of two sections of land which he purchased at three different times.

On May 23, 1951, while plaintiff was at a neighbor's place, three men approached him and discussed leasing plaintiff's land for oil and gas. A Mr. Crawford was the principal spokesman. Plaintiff testified that after some discussion Crawford offered 25 cents an acre for a lease. Plaintiff agreed, and one of the men apparently prepared the necessary papers on a typewriter while sitting in the back seat of the car. When the papers were prepared they were clamped to a board or pad and presented to plaintiff while in the car for signing. Printed forms were used which contained much fine print. The man who prepared the papers indicated where plaintiff should sign, and after signing in one place, partially turned the signed sheet and asked plaintiff to sign again, stating that this second sheet was a part of the lease, which plaintiff believed. Plaintiff testified that no mention was ever made of a mineral deed and to this extent is corroborated by Crawford who in response to the question, "Did you ever describe to Mr. Hauck one of the instruments as a mineral deed?," answered, "No, sir." Separate instruments were required for the land in each state. Plaintiff never received a copy of any of the instruments he signed.

It now appears that somehow plaintiff had signed a mineral deed conveying one half the minerals in his land to D.W. Crawford. This deed was filed for record June 1, 1951, but on May 29, 1951, Crawford, the grantee, conveyed such mineral rights to the defendants White and Duncan at Gainsville, Texas. The trial court made no finding relating to the knowledge of White and Duncan concerning the conditions under which [Crawford] obtained the deed, but decided the case on the basis that they were in fact bona fide purchasers for value. This statement of the facts is sufficient for our present purpose.

We are concerned with a type of fraud which the trial court, texts and decided cases refer to as "fraud in the factum" or "fraud in the execution" as distinguished from "fraud in the inducement." This type of fraud relates to misrepresentation of the contents of a document by which one is induced to sign a paper thinking that it is other than it really is. It was this type of fraud with which this court was dealing in the case of *Federal Land Bank v. Houck*, 4 N.W.2d 213, 218 (S.D. 1942). In this cited case we held that, as between the original parties, when a person is fraudulently induced to sign a paper believing that it is something other than it really is "the contractual knot was never tied" and such paper or instrument is not only voidable but actually void. In that case it was further held in conformity with prior holdings that "neither reason nor policy justifies the reception of a showing of negligence on the part of him who is overreached, as a countervailent or neutralizer of fraud." In other words, the perpetrator of the fraud cannot avoid his acts by a showing that the person upon whom the fraud was committed was negligent.

The *Houck* case, we are convinced, settles the issue of fraud. Accepting as a verity testimony of the plaintiff the misrepresentation and trickery of Crawford was complete. Crawford not only misrepresented the effect of the papers plaintiff signed, but by "manipulation of the papers" as found by the trial court tricked plaintiff into signing the deed thinking it was the lease. Under the rule of the *Houck* case plaintiff's negligence, if any, does not neutralize this fraud. As stated in the *Houck* case there was "no intention to do the act or say the words which manifest a volition to assent." It must therefore be held that as between *Hauck*, the grantor, and Crawford, the grantee, the deed was void.

The deed being void as distinguished from voidable it had no effect whatsoever, conveyed nothing to Crawford, and he in turn had nothing to convey to White and Duncan. As stated by Judge McCoy in the case of *Highrock v. Gavin*, 179 N.W. 12, 23 (S.D. 1920), "The grantee under this void deed was as powerless to transmit title as would be the thief of stolen property. Said deed had no more force or effect than a forged deed, and, in principle, was legally analogous to a forged deed. The recording statutes furnish no protection to those who claim as innocent purchasers under a forged or otherwise void deed, where the true owner has been guilty of no negligence or acts sufficient to create an estoppel. DELVIN ON DEEDS (3d ed.) § 726; 8 R.C.L. 1029; *Vesey v. Solberg*, 132 N.W. 254 (S.D. 1911); *Pry v. Pry*, 109 Ill. 466 (1884)."

Throughout these proceedings appellant has contended that plaintiff is an intelligent farmer, operating a large farm, and that if he failed to detect the fact that he signed a deed such failure was due to his negligence and therefore he should not be permitted to prevail in these proceedings. We have pointed out above that plaintiff's negligence will not neutralize the fraud, or give validity to the deed, but we are convinced that this holding is not decisive as against a purchaser for value without notice. As indicated in the *Highrock-Gavin* case, *supra*, even though the deed is void if plaintiff were negligent or committed acts sufficient to create an estoppel he should bear the brunt of such negligence, rather than a bona fide purchaser.

"An 'estoppel' arises when, by his conduct or acts, a party intentionally or through culpable neglect induces another to believe certain facts to exist, and such other party rightfully relies and acts on such belief so that he will be prejudiced if the former is permitted to deny the existence of such facts." *Lambert v. Bradley*, 42 N.W.2d 606, 607 (S.D. 1950). As applied to civil actions the words "culpable negligence" mean the same as actionable negligence. *State v. Studebaker*, 66 S.W.2d 877, 881 (Mo. 1933). The action being in form an action to quiet title there was no opportunity for appellants to plead an estoppel. There being no opportunity to plead it, the defense is not waived. *Smith v. Cleaver*, 126 N.W. 589 (S.D.1910); 31 C.J.S., Estoppel, § 153, p. 445.

As we view this case, therefore, we must revert to the issue of whether plaintiff was negligent when he affixed his signature to this deed not knowing that it was a deed he signed. On this issue the trial court made no specific determination. Whether plaintiff was negligent under all the facts and circumstances presented by this record we believe to be a question of fact which should be determined by the trial court. The question is, did plaintiff act as a person of reasonable and ordinary care, endowed with plaintiff's capacity and intelligence, would usually act under like circumstances?

We are not inclined to accept the trial court's holding that the manner in which plaintiff's signature was obtained constituted a forgery. As disclosed by the notes in 14 A.L.R. 316 and 56 A.L.R. 582, such holding is a minority view, and seems to us unsound. We believe the rule we have announced in *Federal Land Bank v. Houck*, *supra*, and in this opinion will better sustain the ends of justice. Our holding, we believe, recognizes actualities. The signature was the real signature of the plaintiff. True, plaintiff was induced to sign by a false representation, but to hold a signature thus obtained a forgery seems artificial and out of harmony with the actual facts.

The judgment appealed from is reversed.

NOTES AND QUESTIONS

1. *Bona Fide Purchasers.* So long as the land in question is held by the grantee, a fraudulent deed is void, or at least voidable. However, as the court in the above case indicates, once the land is conveyed to a bona fide purchaser without notice of the fraud, the bona fide purchaser will prevail if the defrauded party was sufficiently negligent to share part of the blame. In such a situation, the grantor will not be able to reclaim the land, but will still have a cause of action against the grantee (if it can be found).

2. In *Houston v. Mentelos*, 318 So. 2d 427 (Fla. Dist. Ct. App. 1975), Marie Houston orally agreed to lease her home in Miami to Thomas Mentelos, a man she believed to be a representative of Paramount Studios in Hollywood, California. (Ms. Houston's home had earlier been used for the filming of the movie "Tony Rome," starring Frank Sinatra.) When she was presented with what she was told was the lease, she signed, apparently without reading, a "Sale of Property Agreement" and a "Warranty Deed" transferring ownership of her home to Mentelos. The deed was subsequently recorded.

Mentelos then used the property to acquire a mortgage from a Henry Gordon. When Houston learned of this transaction, she filed suit to quit title. The trial court found that the transaction was void, but held that Gordon was a bona fide mortgagee for value and as such held a valid lien against Ms. Houston's home. The appellate court found that the deed had been void from the beginning and that no mortgage ever attached. One concurring judge questioned the correctness of his colleagues' reasoning that the deed was void rather than merely voidable. He nevertheless voted to deny the mortgagee any interest in the property on the grounds that Ms. Houston's continued presence on the property should have put the mortgagee on notice as to the fraudulent nature of the transfer.

3. *The Role of Consideration.* In fraud cases, a critical fact is often whether there is a bona fide purchaser who has acquired an interest in the real property in question for "valuable consideration" without notice of unrecorded prior transactions. (Such individuals stand in contrast to donees, heirs, devisees, and those who are allowed to purchase land for far less than the market price.) Valuable consideration does not have to be as much as the market value of the land, but it must be more than nominal payment — neither a peppercorn nor one dollar are sufficient.

Since the effect of a finding of valuable consideration will often be the divestment of a prior purchaser of his right to land, to justify such a remedy the payment must be enough to convince the court that the buyer was not just a donee in disguise. "Love and affection" does not constitute valuable consideration, nor does a mortgage given to secure a pre-existing debt. On the other hand, a promise to care for someone in their old age or a transfer in exchange for the release of a pre-existing debt ordinarily will be deemed sufficient.

4. *Estoppel by Deed.* If the seller conveys land that he or she does not own by warranty deed to an unknowing buyer and subsequently acquires the land, title automatically passes to the original buyer. Whether or not the seller intended to defraud the buyer is irrelevant. The same principle, known as estoppel by deed,

applies to lesser property interests as well, including mortgages. *See Ayer v. Philadelphia & Boston Face Brick Co.*, 34 N.E. 177 (Mass. 1893).

[F.] LIENS AND MORTGAGES

Purchasers of real property frequently borrow money from a lender as part of the purchase and sale process. To protect their interest, lenders normally insist of taking a formal legal interest in the land or other property transferred. This is ordinarily referred to as a mortgage. Officially, a mortgage is "the conveyance of an interest in real property as security for performance of an obligation." Restatement (Third) of Property: Mortgages § 1.1 (1997). Mortgages are normally coupled with promissory notes which represent an obligation on the part of the borrower/mortgagor to repay a particular sum to the lender/mortgagee pursuant to the terms of the note. When the mortgagor fails to comply with the terms of the note, the mortgagee's interest is protected by the security interest. The property subject to the mortgage may be sold or transferred to the mortgagee, depending on the law of the relevant jurisdiction. This process is known as foreclosure.

[1.] Strict Foreclosure

Ordinarily, a foreclosure requires the intervention of the judicial system and in most states, the lost property does not immediately pass directly to the creditor who initiated the foreclosure. Instead, the property is sold at auction, and if the sale results in an amount greater than the debt, the mortgagor (the debtor) gets to keep the surplus. However, in a very small number of states, including Vermont, the mortgagee (the creditor) has the right to take title to the property directly, even if it is worth more than the amount owed. This procedure is called strict foreclosure, and it permits the mortgagee to take the property in cancellation of the debt. In this event, the mortgagor gives up any right to a surplus of value upon a sale, and the mortgagee gives up any right to pursue a deficiency in the event that the property value is less than the existing debt.

DIEFFENBACH v. ATTORNEY GENERAL OF VERMONT

United States Court of Appeal, Second Circuit
604 F.2d 187 (1979)

Oakes, Circuit Judge.

Appellant *pro se* challenges on equal protection and due process grounds the so-called "strict foreclosure" laws of the state of Vermont under which on foreclosure of a real estate mortgage the mortgagee owns the mortgaged property absolutely and need not apply the proceeds of any sale in satisfaction of the mortgage debt. Appellant also seeks to challenge on constitutional grounds a Vermont statute, 12 Vt. Stat. Ann. § 4601, which provides that a defendant (but not a plaintiff) in a foreclosure action needs leave of court to appeal. And he also claims a violation of his right to due process by the failure of a deputy clerk of the Vermont Supreme Court to give him adequate notice of a hearing on the mortgagee's motion to dismiss his appeal from the state foreclosure decree for failure to secure from the lower court the needed permission to appeal. The United States District Court for the District of Vermont, James S. Holden, Chief Judge, granted the defendants' motion for summary judgment. We affirm.

I. *The Facts*

Appellant purchased certain real estate in Shoreham, Vermont, on February 25, 1974, financing the property with a first mortgage issued by the First National Bank of Orwell, Inc. (the Bank), in the amount of $10,000. The mortgage did not contain a clause providing for a power of sale; indeed, a statute permitting foreclosure by judicial sale in the case of mortgage deeds containing such clauses did not become effective until July 1, 1974. Appellant became delinquent in the payments due sometime before December, 1975, and the Bank commenced foreclosure proceedings on January 20, 1976, by filing an action in the Addison Superior Court, together with a motion for summary judgment and a motion to shorten the statutory time of redemption of six months. On February 18, 1976, appellant filed his answer and opposition to the Bank's motions. The Superior Court on April 13, 1976, found no material facts in issue concerning appellant's execution of the mortgage note and his default of payments, granted the Bank summary judgment on its motion for foreclosure, but set down for hearing the amount owing for principal, interest, taxes, insurance, attorney's fees and legal costs, under the terms of the mortgage deed, following Vt. R. Civ. P. 80.1(e). On June 18, 1976, the Superior Court held a hearing on the accounting pursuant to the judgment of foreclosure and found that appellant was indebted to the Bank in the total sum of $11,252, covering principal, interest, taxes, insurance premium, and reasonable attorney's fees, plus interest at the rate of $2.04 per day from the date of the decree to the date of payment. The court gave appellant six months from the date of the decree during which to redeem.

The Addison Superior Court on March 2, 1977, issued a writ of possession to the Bank, and appellant was subsequently evicted from the premises by act of the sheriff.[2] Appellant then filed on April 21, 1977, a motion to stay judgment with the Vermont Supreme Court. This motion was set for hearing on April 29, 1977, and the Bank filed a motion to dismiss the appeal on April 27, 1977. The clerk of the Supreme Court mailed notice of the Bank's motion to appellant on April 27, together with notice that the second motion would also be heard on April 29. Appellant appeared before the Supreme Court on April 29, 1977, and the court proceeded to deny his motion to stay and grant the Bank's motion to dismiss for lack of jurisdiction, presumably because appellant had not complied with the Superior Court's conditions for leave to file the second appeal, i.e., filing a bond.

In October, 1977, the Bank sold the property to a third person for $20,000. The Bank was entitled to sell because the period for redemption had expired on

---

[2] [5] This was in accordance with 12 Vt. Stat. Ann. § 4528 which provides:

> If a decree is made foreclosing the right of redemption, the time of redemption shall be six months from the date of the decree unless a shorter time be ordered. If the premises are not redeemed agreeably to the decree, the clerk of the court may issue a writ of possession. Such writ shall have the same force and effect and be executed in the same manner as similar writs issued after judgment by a court of law in ejectment proceedings

December 8, 1976, and the Bank had been installed in possession of the premises by virtue of the writ issued on March 2, 1977, so that it could deliver both legal title and possession to a purchaser.[3] Under Vermont law, once the period for redemption has expired following a decree of foreclosure and the mortgagee has lawfully acquired full legal title, it need not repay the mortgagor any excess sum recovered from a subsequent sale of the property over the amount owing on the mortgage.[4]

Appellant filed suit in the United States District Court for the District of Vermont on March 17, 1978, against the Vermont Attorney General, the deputy clerk of the Supreme Court, the Addison County sheriff, the Bank, and a Bank officer, Robert D. Young.

II. *Jurisdiction*

[Omitted.]

III. *Strict Foreclosure*

Appellant's attack on Vermont's strict foreclosure statute is substantive, not procedural. In effect, the laws permit a mortgagee to receive any surplusage remaining after the proceeds from the mortgaged land have been applied in payment of the mortgagee's debt and costs as found in the foreclosure decree. This form of strict foreclosure has been a part of Vermont law from Vermont's earliest days and until 1973 no statute has permitted foreclosure by judicial sale. *See* H. Harmon, Vermont Court Procedure § 173, at 221 (1912). Yet interestingly, the state Attorney General appears to concede that strict foreclosure permits the inequitable enrichment of the mortgagee; indeed, the Attorney General reasons that insofar as the mortgagee still has a cause of action under the note to sue the borrower/mortgagor if the property is worth less than the debt, there "would seem to be a clear violation of equal protection rights" because the borrower has no right to seek a refund of overage that the mortgagee receives on the sale. And here in fact the mortgagee did ultimately receive an amount several thousand dollars in excess of the mortgage debt.

---

[3] [8] Legal title could be delivered because the law treated the legal estate in mortgaged premises as absolutely vested in the mortgagee upon the mortgagor's default in compliance with the condition of the mortgage; until a foreclosure decree, however, the mortgagor was the equitable owner of the fee, with legal title vested in the mortgagee only for the protection of his security interest. By early statute foreclosure in Vermont was by suit in equity, whereby the sum due was ascertained, execution might be stayed, and a time for payment limited after which the "equity of redemption" would expire. As Harmon, the leading Vermont commentator, pointed out:

> The Vermont method (of foreclosure) is favorable to the debtor, giving him considerable time in which to pay, with only a moderate addition of costs. While it does not always bring the money promptly to the creditor, he can sell the land at public auction if he desires (or, we would add, at private sale), after the equity of redemption has been foreclosed.

Id.

[4] [9] It should be pointed out that a mortgagee who takes possession under a foreclosure decree that has become absolute cannot sue on the debt unless he has established in the foreclosure proceedings that the property is worth less than the debt. Ordinarily the mortgagee can recover any established deficiency only in a later action at law on the debt.

However, absent any suggestion that the foreclosure laws operate to burden a suspect group or fundamental interest, the appropriate standard for analyzing the foreclosure laws under the Equal Protection Clause is whether they are rationally related to a conceivable legitimate state interest. *City of New Orleans v. Dukes*. In an economic matter such as this, we owe an extraordinary deference to state objectives, almost the equivalent of a strong presumption of constitutionality, and we must uphold any classification based "upon a state of facts that reasonably can be conceived to constitute a distinction, or difference in state policy." *Allied Stores v. Bowers*. The substantive due process test similarly, is whether the laws are rationally related to a legitimate state interest, though the focus of substantive due process analysis is not whether the State has treated similarly situated classes differently but whether its interest in burdening a single class outweighs the due process interests of that class.

Applying these tests, we hold the Vermont mortgage foreclosure laws constitutional. In the first place strict foreclosure has a long history in the state. At the time of the American Revolution strict foreclosure was the only method of foreclosure recognized by the English chancellors. In the early days a mortgage would be foreclosed by a bill in equity drawn with all the circumlocution of the English practice so vividly described in Dickens' Bleak House.

Historical basis does not, of course, alone establish rational relationship, but it does indicate that the people of the state of Vermont have managed fairly well to conduct their commercial affairs despite the allegations of unfairness that can be directed against "strict foreclosure." Property is bought and sold, and mortgages are given and generally paid, if sometimes foreclosed. It has always been open to the courts, as matters of equity, to extend a time for redemption in the event that a property seemed to be more valuable than the debt which it secured, or to enlarge or reopen the right of redemption if the mortgagee accepts payment outside the terms of the redemption order. Creditors and debtors have worked out numerous accommodations, sometimes without the aid of the courts, sometimes by virtue of court mandate, with little or no apparent dissatisfaction and certainly no challenge on this basis over the years.

But what is that rational relationship? One possible purpose of strict foreclosure is to make it easier for banks or other creditors to lend by giving them a speculative interest in the property, for the bank realizes that it may retain the excess if the property's value happens to exceed the debt. Another purpose might be to compensate the bank for its administrative expense, its employees' time, and its general overhead for any effort involved in a foreclosure suit and subsequent resale. A third possibility is that, in an implicit quid pro quo, the legislature has granted the banks this speculative interest in return for requiring the banks to lend mortgage money at lower interest rates, and to permit prepayment without penalty. Of course, although the favorable interest rates and the nonpenalty provision benefit those who are able to obtain loans, these provisions may also operate as a brake on the volume of mortgage lending in Vermont; but strict foreclosure may mitigate somewhat that braking effect and thus may itself indirectly benefit the class of potential mortgagors.

Moreover, perhaps an even more important element of the implicit quid pro quo is that strict foreclosure, as interpreted in Vermont, imposes on banks a substantial delay before they may recover some value for uncollectible debts. To the typical six-month period for redemption one must add two periods of time from default in payments to the entry of the initial foreclosure decree and from the final decree to the execution of the writ of possession. These may be lengthy, especially in counties whose courts have widely spaced semi-annual terms and long periods of recess or whose courts have crowded dockets. These delays certainly diminish the profitability of mortgage lending in Vermont and may in the minds of the legislature help justify an occasional "windfall" benefit to the banks. In the instant case, for example, at least fourteen months elapsed from the time after default that the Bank notified appellant it intended to foreclosure until it actually obtained possession.

Thus, with respect to the distinction between the bank's right to a deficiency and the mortgagor's right to recover a surfeit, the laws do not operate unfairly, in either the equal protection[5] or substantive due process sense. But one might object that the laws create a different kind of unfairness in their differential treatment of mortgagors because they burden only those mortgagors whose property happens to have a value in excess of the outstanding debt. The bank's administrative expenses and losses from uncollectible debts should, one might argue, be collected not from these unfortunate mortgagors, but from the class of mortgagors (or potential mortgagors) generally, in the form of higher interest payments or lesser availability of loans.[6] But this objection is unpersuasive. The legislature may reasonably have concluded that strict foreclosure laws equitably distribute the commercial costs of mortgages because every mortgagor, when he executes a mortgage, is equally subject to the risk that his property's value will exceed the portion of his debt that he is unable to pay. The State's failure to "insure" against the unequal actual incidence of this risk by permitting banks to absorb the risk in their interest rates does not amount to a violation of equal protection.

Moreover, to a significant degree mortgagors in the situation of appellant who are burdened by the strict foreclosure laws have in a very real sense brought the misfortune upon themselves because nothing in the law and so far as we can see nothing in fact prevents them from selling the property while the foreclosure is pending; if the property really has an excess value it can be realized by the mortgagor on such a sale. To be sure, conceivably the pendency of a foreclosure proceeding might in some cases operate so as to depress the market for the mortgaged real estate though it is a little difficult to see just how or why unless the mortgagee is the only available lending institution in the particular area. But in this day of several state-wide lending institutions, with easy telephonic communications and ready transportation available, it is difficult to see save in the remotest circumstances how this could be the case. At least one can readily view the legislature as taking the position that to protect those few mortgagors who might

---

[5] [21] Indeed, the strict foreclosure laws' award of a deficiency to the mortgagee but not to the mortgagor fits awkwardly within the usual framework of equal protection analysis, for it is not obvious in what respect the bank and the borrower are "similarly situated." The existence of commercial incentives appropriate only to lending institutions reveals that the banks' "situation" differs from their borrowers' and justifies different treatment

[6] [22] Presumably if strict foreclosure were abolished, either one of these two consequences would occur or banks would enjoy lower profits.

be thus adversely affected would not be more desirable than, say, to make mortgage money more readily available through the strict foreclosure "incentive."

And that is the nub of it. In the ordinary situation a mortgagor will have six months from the entry of a decree (which itself may occur some considerable time after default in payments) within which he can sell his property, and there is nothing that a bank can do to forestall any such sale. Vermont land generally is a marketable, now a highly marketable, commodity. Numerous banks, state and national, as well as savings and loan associations are available for borrowing purposes. Moreover, appellant also had the options of attempting to refinance his loan or of seeking an extension of the redemption period. In light of these several alternatives, the legislature may well suppose that it will only be the extraordinarily recalcitrant debtor who will be injured by strict foreclosure.

NOTES AND QUESTIONS

1. *State Mortgage Law and Lien Enforcement*. State mortgage law determines the means of enforcement in each jurisdiction. Whether a state is a "title state" or a "lien state" will be the determining factor. For example, in a "title state," a mortgage temporarily conveys title to the property to the mortgagee (lender) while the mortgagor (borrower) generally remains in possession. In comparison, in a "lien state," the title to the property does not pass to the mortgagee, but instead creates an enforceable lien (or security interest) in favor of the mortgagee. Today most states subscribe to the lien theory, although the title theory is still in place in Alabama, Arkansas, Connecticut, Maine, Massachusetts, Mississippi, Rhode Island, Tennessee, and Vermont. SINGER, PROPERTY 556–557 (3d ed. 2010).

2. *Methods of Foreclosure*. Although once common, strict foreclosure today exists only in Vermont and Connecticut. However, the doctrine appears to be entrenched in those two jurisdictions. Statutes remain on the books in both states, Vt. Stat. Ann. Tit. 12 § 4528; Conn. Gen. Stat. Ann. §§ 49-15 & 49-24, and appellate courts in both states have upheld the practice in the not too distant past. *Stowe Center, Inc., v. Burlington Savings Bank*, 451 A.2d 1114 (Vt. 1982); *Farmers & Mechanics Bank v. Arbucci*, 589 A.2d 14 (Conn. App. Ct. 1991).

Judicial mortgage foreclosure is the most commonly used tool for mortgagees to minimize their losses upon default by the mortgagor. This procedure is available in every state and is the only permitted form of foreclosure in about 50 % of jurisdictions. Under judicial foreclosure, the land subject to the lien is sold, usually at public auction, and the mortgagees is paid off, if the sale produces sufficient funds. If there is a surplus it is returned to the mortgagor. If the proceeds of the sale are not enough to pay off the remaining debt, the mortgagee may, depending on the state, have the right to proceed personally against the debtor.

In some states, a deed of trust is used to secure the creditors' interest in a mortgage. If O borrows money from A and pledges Blackacre as security, he transfers legal title to T who holds the plot for O's benefit. Day-to-day control of the property, however, usually remains with O. However, should O fail to comply with the terms of the loan agreement, T has the power to sell Blackacre and transfer to A any unpaid sums stemming from the loan. Any surplus would be paid to O. The deed of trust allows parties to conduct foreclosure proceedings without having to initiate a formal court proceeding.

3. *Rights of Redemption.* In most states, homeowners who lose their property as a result of foreclosure (strict or otherwise) have opportunities to reacquire their land if they can arrange to pay off the underlying debt. The borrower's *equity of redemption* entitles him or her to pay off the debt any time prior to foreclosure, even if the due date for the debt has past. In many states, there is also a *statutory right of redemption* that allows the mortgagor to buy back the property for the amount of the highest bid at the foreclosure sale. This right extends for a specified period of time after foreclosure, usually one year.

4. *Installment Land Contracts.* The installment land contract, discussed above in Sec. A-3, are an alternative to mortgage financing. While they are treated as the equivalent of mortgages in some states, in others they do not qualify for all of the legal protections provided for mortgagors. NELSON & WHITMAN, REAL ESTATE FINANCE LAW 70–85 (4th ed. 2001).

[2.] Mortgage Priorities

COUNTRYWIDE HOME LOANS, INC. v. FIRST NAT'L BANK OF STEAMBOAT SPRINGS

Wyoming Supreme Court
144 P.3d 1224 (2006)

KITE, JUSTICE.

In this mortgage foreclosure action, the district court declined to apply the doctrine of equitable subrogation and instead strictly applied Wyoming's "first in time is first in right" recording statute. The result was an order granting summary judgment in favor of First National Bank of Steamboat Springs, N.A. (First National Bank), holding its mortgage had priority over all other recorded liens and allowing it to proceed with foreclosure. In their appeal from the order, Countrywide Home Loans, Inc., (Countrywide) and America's Wholesale Lender (AWL) ask this Court to reverse the district court and adopt the doctrine of equitable subrogation so as to place Countrywide in the primary lien position formerly occupied by AWL.

Elmer Lee Ketcham, Jr. and Anita Ketcham owned real property located in Carbon County, Wyoming. On November 12, 1997, they obtained a loan of $100,000 from AWL, which they secured by executing a mortgage on the Carbon County property. The AWL mortgage was recorded in the Carbon County clerk's office on November 13, 1997. AWL assigned the mortgage to the Bank of New York and the assignment was recorded in the clerk's office on May 26, 1998.

On June 4, 2002, the Ketchams pledged the Carbon County property as collateral for a business loan made by First National Bank to Blue Gate West, a Colorado corporation in which the Ketchams were principles. This mortgage was recorded in the Carbon County clerk's office on July 22, 2002.

On April 2, 2003, the Ketchams executed a third mortgage on the property in favor of Countrywide and MES in exchange for a loan of $97,500. The purpose of this loan was to pay off the 1997 AWL mortgage. Countrywide obtained a title insurance commitment, which listed the 1997 AWL mortgage and the 2002 First National Bank mortgage as prior liens on the property. The 2003 Countrywide mortgage was recorded in the Carbon County clerk's office on April 15, 2003. The Ketchams used the funds borrowed from Countrywide to pay off the 1997 AWL mortgage, making the final payment in August of 2004.

Meanwhile, in June of 2003, the Ketchams failed to make their monthly payment to First National Bank on the 2002 mortgage. Under the terms of the loan agreement, the failure to make the payment constituted a default entitling First National Bank to foreclose on the property. First National Bank filed a complaint for foreclosure naming the Ketchams, Countrywide, the Bank of New York, MES and AWL as defendants and claiming the First National Bank lien was the first and senior lien on the Carbon County property.

[Portions of the opinion dealing with the timeliness of the response of the Bank of New York and MES are omitted.]

In the meantime, First National Bank filed a motion for summary judgment requesting the district court to declare as a matter of law that its lien on the Ketchams' Carbon County property was superior to the interests of all others; the Ketchams were in default; and First National Bank was entitled to foreclose. Countrywide and AWL also moved for summary judgment. They asked the district court to apply the doctrine of equitable subrogation and hold as a matter of law that the 2003 Countrywide mortgage was subrogated to the 1997 AWL mortgage, making the Countrywide mortgage superior in priority to all encumbrances recorded after 1997.

The district court issued a decision letter in which it declined to apply the doctrine of equitable subrogation. Instead, the court applied Wyo. Stat. Ann. § 34-1-121 to hold that First National Bank's 2002 mortgage had priority over all other encumbrances on the Ketchams' property, including the 2003 Countrywide mortgage. The district court denied Countrywide's summary judgment motion and granted summary judgment in favor of First National Bank.

Countrywide and AWL ask this Court to reverse the district court's ruling, adopt the doctrine of equitable subrogation and apply it in the instant case so that Countrywide's 2003 lien would be subrogated to the priority position of the 1997 AWL lien. They urge this Court to adopt the doctrine as set out in Restatement (Third) of Property (Mortgages) § 7.6 (1997):

> (a) One who fully performs an obligation of another, secured by a mortgage, becomes by subrogation the owner of the obligation and the mortgage to the extent necessary to prevent unjust enrichment. Even though the performance would otherwise discharge the obligation and the mortgage, they are preserved and the mortgage retains its priority in the hands of the subrogee.
>
> (b) By way of illustration, subrogation is appropriate to prevent unjust enrichment if the person seeking subrogation performs the obligation:

(1) in order to protect his or her interest;

(2) under a legal duty to do so;

(3) on account of misrepresentation, mistake, duress, undue influence, deceit, or other similar imposition; or

(4) upon a request from the obligor or the obligor's successor to do so, if the person performing was promised repayment and reasonably expected to receive a security interest in the real estate with the priority of the mortgage being discharged, and if subrogation will not materially prejudice the holders of intervening interests in the real estate.

In declining to apply the Restatement, the district court relied on § 34-1-121, which provides in relevant part as follows:

> (a) Each and every deed, mortgage, instrument or conveyance touching any interest in lands, made and recorded, according to the provisions of this chapter, shall be notice to and take precedence of any subsequent purchaser or purchasers from the time of the delivery of any instrument at the office of the register of deeds (county clerk), for record.

Reading this provision strictly to mean that lien priority is determined by the date of recording, the district court held First National Bank's 2002 mortgage had priority over Countrywide's subsequent 2003 mortgage. In reaching this result, the district court concluded application of the Restatement was not appropriate:

> where a lender has actual and constructive notice of a junior mortgagee and could have taken any one of a number of steps to protect its interests.[Countrywide] could have asked for a subordination agreement or an assignment of the AWL mortgage; it did neither of these things and now seeks to rely upon the concept that it "expected" to step into AWL's priority without anything more. The argument goes that, in recognizing the doctrine of equitable subrogation, [First National Bank] is not prejudiced and "loses nothing" because it remains second in priority (before it was behind AWL; now it would be behind [Countrywide]). But, this Court believes equity requires looking at things from a different perspective: [Countrywide] entered into the third mortgage on the property with knowledge of [First National Bank's] prior loan to Ketcham. Why should [Countrywide] get the benefit (and be unjustly enriched) by leaping over [First National Bank] to assume AWL's priority status. [Countrywide] has done nothing to deserve this advantage.

Countrywide argues the district court's approach does not account for the equities of this case and ignores the purpose equitable "subrogation serves in the modern mortgage re-financing context." Countrywide contends the modern trend among courts is to apply equitable subrogation as set forth in the Restatement. Countrywide asserts the district court's approach is contrary to the purpose served by applying the doctrine because: 1) the Ketchams, Countrywide and AWL reasonably expected Countrywide would have first priority; 2) Countrywide would not have agreed to re-finance the 1997 AWL mortgage if it had known it would not have first priority; 3) First National Bank's position would not change if subrogation were allowed; 4) First National Bank should not be moved forward in priority simply because Countrywide knew of the 2002 mortgage when it paid off the AWL mortgage; 5) First National Bank accepted the risks inherent in accepting a second priority lien when it demanded additional collateral from the Ketchams; and 6) giving the 2002 mortgage priority results in an inappropriate windfall to First National Bank. Before addressing these assertions, we consider § 34-1-121 and our precedent on the doctrine of equitable subrogation.

By statute and case decision, Wyoming is a filing date priority jurisdiction. Section 34-1-121; That is, as the Wyoming legislature expressly provided in § 34-1-121, a mortgage properly recorded in the county clerk's office provides notice to subsequent purchasers and takes precedence over later conveyances. As stated in *Crozier v. Malone*, 366 P.2d at 127, a subsequent purchaser (or mortgagee) has constructive notice of any burden upon title from the date of recordation.

Countrywide asks this Court to recognize an equitable exception to Wyoming's "first in time" statutory provision. Specifically, Countrywide asks us to recognize the doctrine of equitable subrogation as set forth in the Restatement and apply it in this case so Countrywide, by extending a loan to the Ketchams in 2003 to pay off their 1997 mortgage with AWL, is subrogated to AWL's primary lien position. In other words, by executing the 2003 mortgage which allowed the Ketchams to pay off the 1997 mortgage, Countrywide seeks to stand in the shoes of AWL and be given priority over all post-1997 encumbrances.

This Court has not previously considered the Restatement version of equitable subrogation. However, in addressing the concept of subrogation, this Court long ago stated:

> The right of subrogation may arise and sometimes must arise from contract. This is conventional subrogation. The right is sometimes given in the absence of contract, is then a creation of the court of equity, and is given when otherwise there would be a manifest failure of justice. This is legal subrogation. It is a mode which equity adopts to compel the ultimate payment of a debt by one who in justice, equity, and good conscience ought to pay it, though it is not exercised in favor of a mere intermeddler. This principle, adopted from the Roman law and at first sparingly exercised, has come to be one of the great principles of equity of our jurisprudence, and courts incline to extend it rather than restrict it. One instance in which legal subrogation is applied is in connection with the protection of a lien, and the rule is universal that one who has an interest in property by lien or otherwise, in making payment of prior liens, including taxes, is not a mere volunteer, and that he will be entitled, upon payment of a superior lien in order to protect his own lien, to be subrogated to the rights of the superior lienholder.

Wyoming Bldg. & Loan Ass'n v. Mills Constr. Co., 38 Wyo. 515, 269 P. 45, 48–49 (1928) (citations omitted).

[The Court then discusses other Wyoming decisions dealing with the doctrine of equitable subrogation.] Thus, we have recognized equitable subrogation in Wyoming as a creation of courts of equity to prevent manifest injustice. We have specifically applied it to compel payment of a debt by one who in justice, equity, and good conscience ought to pay it and to allow one who pays a superior lien in order to protect his own lien to be subrogated to the rights of the superior lien holder. We have recognized the appropriateness of the doctrine where one pays the debt of another under a reasonable belief that such payment is necessary for his own protection. We have not, however, applied the doctrine of equitable subrogation as set forth in the Restatement to allow a refinancing mortgagee to step into the shoes of a prior mortgagee for purposes of obtaining lien priority.

Having considered our statute and the cases from other states in which courts have applied equitable subrogation in the context of mortgage re-financing, we decline to adopt the Restatement. Unlike the trend in other courts, we are not persuaded any manifest injustice results from applying the express language of § 34-1-121 and adhering to the clear legislative intent that lien priority in Wyoming is to be determined by the date of recording. Here, the AWL mortgage was recorded in 1997, the First National Bank mortgage was recorded in 2002 and Countrywide's mortgage was recorded in 2003. Countrywide knew of the existence of First National Bank's lien before it extended the loan to the Ketchams.

Thus, Countrywide knew First National Bank had a prior recorded lien on the property when it executed the 2003 mortgage. Countrywide was charged with knowing Wyoming is a "first in time" jurisdiction. *United Pacific Insurance Co. v. Wyoming Excise Tax Division, Dept. of Revenue and Taxation*, 713 P.2d 217, 226 (Wyo. 1986). We are charged with the duty of giving effect to the statutes our legislature has enacted. Where the language of a statute is plain and unambiguous and conveys a clear and definite meaning, the court has no right to look for and impose another meaning, but has the duty to give full force and effect to the legislative product. *Thomson v. Wyoming In-Stream Flow Comm.*, 651 P.2d 778 (Wyo. 1982). Contrary to Countrywide's assertion, it had no reason to expect under Wyoming law that its 2003 mortgage would be given priority over First National Bank's 2002 mortgage. Although Countrywide makes the policy argument that equitable subrogation will make refinancing more readily available to the public and thereby, serves the public interest, those arguments are properly directed to the legislature.

In addition, the primary purpose of our recording statute is to secure certainty of title. *Condos v. Trapp*, 717 P.2d 827, 832 (Wyo. 1986). This countervailing public policy interest in clarity and certainty in matters of land title arguably outweighs the interests of private lending institutions which can be protected by simple due diligence.

As this Court stated in *Wyoming Bldg. & Loan Ass'n*, 269 P. at 48, equitable subrogation is "a creation of the court of equity, and is given when otherwise there would be a manifest failure of justice." "It is a mode which equity adopts to compel the ultimate payment of a debt by one who in justice, equity and good conscience ought to pay it, though it is not exercised in favor of a mere intermeddler." *Id.* These factors, which may compel application of the doctrine of equitable subrogation in other contexts, simply are not present in the case of a mortgagee who agrees to refinance a prior mortgage. In this context, the mortgagee does not pay the debt (or extend the loan) because "in justice, equity and good conscience he ought to pay it." Nor in the context of mortgage re-financing does the mortgagee pay the debt because he must do so in order to protect his own interest. To the contrary, the mortgagee who refinances a prior mortgage more closely resembles a volunteer or intermeddler in whose favor courts have not been inclined to apply equitable subrogation. In our view equitable subrogation simply has no application where a financial institution extends a loan for the purpose of enabling a mortgagor to pay off an existing mortgage, knowing that a subordinate lien exists on the real estate. Other mechanisms are available for a re-financing lender to obtain first priority without invoking equity to achieve that result. Affirmed.

NOTES AND QUESTIONS

1. *Priority of Mortgages.* There is nothing inappropriate about using a single piece of property to secure multiple mortgages, so long as the value of the land exceeds the combined amount of the mortgages. In cases of foreclosure, the mortgage or lien with the highest priority is paid first; then the one with the second highest priority; and so on. As the court in the opinion above indicates, priority is normally determined by the recording act and the general rules used to establish priority of title.

Mortgages do not take priority over other liens on the property. However, an exception exists for what are called "purchase money mortgages." Purchase money mortgages are created when the buyer of land pays all or part of the purchase price with a note made out to the seller that is secured by the land being purchased. Even if the buyer is subject to a judgment lien at the time he purchases the property — and the judgment lien would normally automatically attach to the property — the seller's interest in the purchase money mortgage takes priority over the judgment lien (which still attaches, but not with first priority).

2. *Equitable Subrogation.* Courts differ on the question of whether the doctrine of equitable subrogation ought to apply in cases like the one above. A year later, the Washington Supreme Court reached the opposite conclusion in a case involving very similar facts. *Bank of America v. Prestance Corp.*, 160 P.3d 17 (Wash. 2007). The RESTATEMENT OF MORTGAGES § 7.6 (1997) takes the position that the Washington approach is the better one. The rationale is that the holder of the second mortgage should be aware that the first mortgage may be refinanced and thus is in no different position when refinancing occurs. The Restatement approach does appear to have the effect of making it less expensive for homeowners to obtain refinancing. Do you see why? The ability (or inability) to refinance home mortgages was, of course, an integral part of the recent subprime mortgage crisis that was already underway when the above case was decided.

Chapter 10

HOUSING DISCRIMINATION

Discrimination in housing is a serious social problem in our society. Integration indices developed over the years continue to show that many major cities are seriously segregated, and studies by the U.S. Department of Housing and Urban Development (HUD) show that discrimination in the sale and rental of housing is still a serious problem. This chapter examines the federal Fair Housing Act, Title VIII of the Civil Rights Act of 1968, and how it applies to discrimination in the housing market.

[A.] FEDERAL FAIR HOUSING LEGISLATION

Congress adopted the Fair Housing Act with little debate or legislative history as a response to the assassination of Martin Luther King in 1968. Congressional action on fair housing had not been expected. Many states and municipalities had fair housing laws in effect for some time, and President Kennedy issued a limited Executive Order on discrimination in housing in 1962, but opposition to a more aggressive federal role in housing discrimination had stalled congressional action. For an account indicating the Act was the product of a political deal between President Johnson and Republican Senator Everett Dirksen, see Jonathan Zasloff, *The Secret History of the Fair Housing Act*, 53 Harv. J. Legis. ___ (forthcoming 2016). Title VIII is not the only federal legislation that applies to discrimination in housing. The Civil Rights Act of 1866, 42 U.S.C. § 1982, provides:

> All citizens of the United States shall have the same right, in every State and Territory, as is enjoyed by white citizens thereof to inherit, purchase, lease, sell, hold, and convey real and personal property.

The Supreme Court upheld the constitutionality of this law under the Thirteenth Amendment in *Jones v. Alfred H. Mayer Co.*, 392 U.S. 409 (1968), and pointed out the differences between that law and the more comprehensive Title VIII that Congress had just passed:

> At the outset, it is important to make clear precisely what this case does not involve. Whatever else it may be, 42 U.S.C. § 1982 is not a comprehensive open housing law. In sharp contrast to the Fair Housing Title (Title VIII) of the Civil Rights Act of 1968, the statute in this case deals only with racial discrimination and does not address itself to discrimination on grounds of religion or national origin. It does not deal specifically with discrimination in the provision of services or facilities in connection with the sale or rental of a dwelling. It does not prohibit advertising or other representations that indicate discriminatory preferences. It does not refer explicitly to discrimination in financing arrangements or in the provision of brokerage services.

empower a federal administrative agency to assist aggrieved akes no provision for intervention by the Attorney General. In ough it can be enforced by injunction, it contains no provision horizing a federal court to order the payment of damages.

ing Act can be enforced through litigation, and litigants who bring s face a number of issues that decide whether their case will be cal issue is how to prove a violation of the Act has occurred. A hown either by proof of disparate treatment or disparate effect. Proof of disparate treatment requires some proof of intent. Proof of disparate impact can be shown by proof of disparate impact on a protected group. The availability of proof through disparate impact varies from the standard of proof required under the equal protection clause of the federal constitution, where proof of discriminatory intent is required. *Washington v. Davis* , 426 U.S. 229 (1976).

In the following case, the Supreme Court held that proof of disparate impact is acceptable, and outlined the basis for proving a violation of the Act:

TEXAS DEPARTMENT OF HOUSING AND COMMUNITY AFFAIRS v. THE INCLUSIVE COMMUNITIES PROJECT, INC.

United States Supreme Court
135 S. Ct. 2507 (2015)

Justice Kennedy delivered the opinion of the Court.

The underlying dispute in this case concerns where housing for low-income persons should be constructed in Dallas, Texas — that is, whether the housing should be built in the inner city or in the suburbs. This dispute comes to the Court on a disparate-impact theory of liability. In contrast to a disparate-treatment case, where a "plaintiff must establish that the defendant had a discriminatory intent or motive," a plaintiff bringing a disparate-impact claim challenges practices that have a "disproportionately adverse effect on minorities" and are otherwise unjustified by a legitimate rationale. *Ricci v. DeStefano*, 557 U.S. 557 (2009) (internal quotation marks omitted). The question presented for the Court's determination is whether disparate-impact claims are cognizable under the Fair Housing Act (or FHA), 82 Stat. 81, as amended, 42 U.S.C. § 3601 *et seq.*

I.

A.

Before turning to the question presented, it is necessary to discuss a different federal statute that gives rise to this dispute. The Federal Government provides low-income housing tax credits that are distributed to developers through designated state agencies. 26 U.S.C. § 42. Congress has directed States to develop plans identifying selection criteria for distributing the credits. § 42(m)(1). Those plans must include certain criteria, such as public housing waiting lists, § 42(m)(1)(C), as well as certain preferences, including that low-income housing units "contribut[e] to a concerted community revitalization plan" and be built in census tracts populated predominantly by low-income residents. §§ 42(m)(1)(B)(ii)(III), 42(d)(5)(ii)(I). Federal law thus favors the distribution of these tax credits for the development of housing units in low-income areas.

In the State of Texas these federal credits are distributed by the Texas Department of Housing and Community Affairs (Department). Under Texas law, a developer's application for the tax credits is scored under a point system that gives priority to statutory criteria, such as the financial feasibility of the development project and the income level of tenants. Tex. Govt. Code Ann. §§ 2306.6710(a)–(b) (West 2008). The Texas Attorney General has interpreted state law to permit the consideration of additional criteria, such as whether the housing units will be built in a neighborhood with good schools. Those criteria cannot be awarded more points than statutorily mandated criteria. Tex. Op. Atty. Gen. No. GA–0208, pp. 2–6 (2004), 2004 WL 1434796, *4–*6.

The Inclusive Communities Project, Inc. (ICP), is a Texas-based nonprofit corporation that assists low-income families in obtaining affordable housing. In 2008, the ICP brought this suit against the Department and its officers in the United States District Court for the Northern District of Texas. As relevant here, it brought a disparate-impact claim under §§ 804(a) and 805(a) of the FHA. The ICP alleged the Department has caused continued segregated housing patterns by its disproportionate allocation of the tax credits, granting too many credits for housing in predominantly black inner-city areas and too few in predominantly white suburban neighborhoods. The ICP contended that the Department must modify its selection criteria in order to encourage the construction of low-income housing in suburban communities.

The District Court concluded that the ICP had established a prima facie case of disparate impact. It relied on two pieces of statistical evidence. First, it found "from 1999–2008, [the Department] approved tax credits for 49.7% of proposed non-elderly units in 0% to 9.9% Caucasian areas, but only approved 37.4% of proposed non-elderly units in 90% to 100% Caucasian areas." 749 F. Supp. 2d 486, 499 (N.D. Tex. 2010) (footnote omitted). Second, it found "92.29% of [low-income housing tax credit] units in the city of Dallas were located in census tracts with less than 50% Caucasian residents." *Ibid.* . . . [The Department appealed.]

While the Department's appeal was pending, the Secretary of Housing and Urban Development (HUD) issued a regulation interpreting the FHA to encompass disparate-impact liability. See Implementation of the Fair Housing Act's Discriminatory Effects Standard, 78 Fed. Reg. 11460 (2013). The regulation also established a burden-shifting framework for adjudicating disparate-impact claims. Under the regulation, a plaintiff first must make a prima facie showing of disparate impact. That is, the plaintiff "has the burden of proving that a challenged practice caused or predictably will cause a discriminatory effect." 24 CFR § 100.500(c)(1) (2014). If a statistical discrepancy is caused by factors other than the defendant's policy, a plaintiff cannot establish a prima facie case, and there is no liability. After a plaintiff does establish a prima facie showing of disparate impact, the burden shifts to the defendant to "prov[e] that the challenged practice is necessary to achieve one or more substantial, legitimate, nondiscriminatory interests." § 100.500(c)(2). HUD has clarified that this step of the analysis "is analogous to the Title VII requirement that an employer's interest in an employment practice with a disparate impact be job related." 78 Fed. Reg. 11470. Once a defendant has satisfied its burden at step two, a plaintiff may "prevail upon proving that the substantial, legitimate, nondiscriminatory interests supporting the challenged practice could be served by another practice that has a less discriminatory effect." § 100.500(c)(3). . . . [The court of appeals reversed and remanded, and the Supreme Court granted certiorari. The Court, comparing the Fair Housing Act with similar statutes, held it allowed proof of disparate impact. It then explained how the disparate impact test should be applied:]

Recognition of disparate-impact claims is consistent with the FHA's central purpose. The FHA, like [similar statutes], was enacted to eradicate discriminatory practices within a sector of our Nation's economy. See 42 U.S.C. § 3601 ("It is the policy of the United States to provide, within constitutional limitations, for fair housing throughout the United States"); H.R. Rep., at 15 (explaining the FHA "provides a clear national policy against discrimination in housing").

These unlawful practices include zoning laws and other housing restrictions that function unfairly to exclude minorities from certain neighborhoods without any sufficient justification. Suits targeting such practices reside at the heartland of disparate-impact liability. See, *e.g.*, [*Town of Huntington, N.Y. v. Huntington Branch, N.A.A.C.P.*, 488 U.S. 15, at 16–18 (1988)], (invalidating zoning law preventing construction of multifamily rental units); [*United States v. City of Black Jack, Missouri*, 508 F.2d 1179, 1182–88 (8th Cir. 1974)] (invalidating ordinance prohibiting construction of new multifamily dwellings); *Greater New Orleans Fair Housing Action Center v. St. Bernard Parish*, 641 F. Supp. 2d 563, 569, 577–578 (E.D. La. 2009) (invalidating post-Hurricane Katrina ordinance restricting the rental of housing units to only " 'blood relative[s]' " in an area of the city that was 88.3% white and 7.6% black). The availability of disparate-impact liability, furthermore, has allowed private developers to vindicate the FHA's objectives and to protect their property rights by stopping municipalities from enforcing arbitrary and, in practice, discriminatory ordinances barring the construction of certain types of housing units. See, *e.g.*, *Huntington*, *supra*, at 18. Recognition of disparate-impact liability under the FHA also plays a role in uncovering discriminatory intent: It permits plaintiffs to counteract unconscious prejudices and disguised animus that escape easy classification as disparate treatment. In this way disparate-impact liability may prevent segregated housing patterns that might otherwise result from covert and illicit stereotyping.

But disparate-impact liability has always been properly limited in key respects that avoid the serious constitutional questions that might arise under the FHA, for instance, if such liability were imposed based solely on a showing of a statistical disparity. Disparate-impact liability mandates the "removal of artificial, arbitrary, and unnecessary barriers," not the displacement of valid governmental policies. The FHA is not an instrument to force housing authorities to reorder their priorities. Rather, the FHA aims to ensure that those priorities can be achieved without arbitrarily creating discriminatory effects or perpetuating segregation.

Unlike the heartland of disparate-impact suits targeting artificial barriers to housing, the underlying dispute in this case involves a novel theory of liability. See Seicshnaydre, Is Disparate Impact Having Any Impact? An Appellate Analysis of Forty Years of Disparate Impact Claims Under the Fair Housing Act, 63 Am. U. L. Rev. 357, 360–363 (2013) (noting the rarity of this type of claim). This case, on remand, may be seen simply as an attempt to second-guess which of two reasonable approaches a housing authority should follow in the sound exercise of its discretion in allocating tax credits for low-income housing.

An important and appropriate means of ensuring that disparate-impact liability is properly limited is to give housing authorities and private developers leeway to state and explain the valid interest served by their policies. This step of the analysis is analogous to the business necessity standard under Title VII [the employment discrimination act] and provides a defense against disparate-impact liability. See 78 Fed. Reg. 11470 (explaining that HUD did not use the phrase "business necessity" because that "phrase may not be easily understood to cover the full scope of practices covered by the Fair Housing Act, which applies to individuals, businesses, nonprofit organizations, and public entities"). As the Court explained in *Ricci*, an entity "could be liable for disparate-impact discrimination only if the [challenged practices] were not job related and consistent with business necessity." 557 U.S., at 587. Just as an employer may maintain a workplace requirement that causes a disparate impact if that requirement is a "reasonable measure[ment] of job performance," [citing *Griggs v. Duke Power Co.*, 401 U.S. 424, 436 (1971)] so too must housing authorities and private developers be allowed to maintain a policy if they can prove it is necessary to achieve a valid interest. To be sure, the Title VII [the employment discrimination act] framework may not transfer exactly to the fair-housing context, but the comparison suffices for present purposes.

It would be paradoxical to construe the FHA to impose onerous costs on actors who encourage revitalizing dilapidated housing in our Nation's cities merely because some other priority might seem preferable. Entrepreneurs must be given latitude to consider market factors. Zoning officials, moreover, must often make decisions based on a mix of factors, both objective (such as cost and traffic patterns) and, at least to some extent, subjective (such as preserving historic architecture). These factors contribute to a community's quality of life and are legitimate concerns for housing authorities. The FHA does not decree a particular vision of urban development; and it does not put housing authorities and private developers in a double bind of liability, subject to suit whether they choose to rejuvenate a city core or to promote new low-income housing in suburban communities. As HUD itself recognized in its recent rulemaking, disparate-impact liability "does not mandate that affordable housing be located in neighborhoods with any particular characteristic." 78 Fed. Reg. 11476.

In a similar vein, a disparate-impact claim that relies on a statistical disparity must fail if the plaintiff cannot point to a defendant's policy or policies causing that disparity. A robust causality requirement ensures that "[r]acial imbalance . . . does not, without more, establish a prima facie case of disparate impact" and thus protects defendants from being held liable for racial disparities they did not create. *Wards Cove Packing Co. v. Atonio*, 490 U.S. 642, 653 (1989), superseded by statute on other grounds, 42 U.S.C. § 2000e-2(k). Without adequate safeguards at the prima facie stage, disparate-impact liability might cause race to be used and considered in a pervasive way and "would almost inexorably lead" governmental or private entities to use "numerical quotas," and serious constitutional questions then could arise. 490 U.S., at 653.

The litigation at issue here provides an example. From the standpoint of determining advantage or disadvantage to racial minorities, it seems difficult to say as a general matter that a decision to build low-income housing in a blighted inner-city neighborhood instead of a suburb is discriminatory, or vice versa. If those sorts of judgments are subject to challenge without adequate safeguards, then there is a danger that potential defendants may adopt racial quotas — a circumstance that itself raises serious constitutional concerns.

Courts must therefore examine with care whether a plaintiff has made out a prima facie case of disparate impact and prompt resolution of these cases is important. A plaintiff who fails to allege facts at the pleading stage or produce statistical evidence demonstrating a causal connection cannot make out a prima facie case of disparate impact. For instance, a plaintiff challenging the decision of a private developer to construct a new building in one location rather than another will not easily be able to show this is a policy causing a disparate impact because such a one-time decision may not be a policy at all. It may also be difficult to establish causation because of the multiple factors that go into investment decisions about where to construct or renovate housing units. And as Judge Jones observed below, if the ICP cannot show a causal connection between the Department's policy and a disparate impact — for instance, because federal law substantially limits the Department's discretion — that should result in dismissal of this case. 747 F.3d, at 283–284 (specially concurring opinion).

The FHA imposes a command with respect to disparate-impact liability. Here, that command goes to a state entity. In other cases, the command will go to a private person or entity. Governmental or private policies are not contrary to the disparate-impact requirement unless they are "artificial, arbitrary, and unnecessary barriers." *Griggs*, 401 U.S., at 431. Difficult questions might arise if disparate-impact liability under the FHA caused race to be used and considered in a pervasive and explicit manner to justify governmental or private actions that, in fact, tend to perpetuate race-based considerations rather than move beyond them. Courts should avoid interpreting disparate-impact liability to be so expansive as to inject racial considerations into every housing decision.

The limitations on disparate-impact liability discussed here are also necessary to protect potential defendants against abusive disparate-impact claims. If the specter of disparate-impact litigation causes private developers to no longer construct or renovate housing units for low-income individuals, then the FHA would have undermined its own purpose as well as the free-market system. And as to governmental entities, they must not be prevented from achieving legitimate objectives, such as ensuring compliance with health and safety codes. The Department's *amici*, in addition to the well-stated principal dissenting opinion in this case, (opinion of Alito, J.), call attention to the decision by the Court of Appeals for the Eighth Circuit in *Gallagher v. Magner*, 619 F.3d 823 (2010). Although the Court is reluctant to approve or disapprove a case that is not pending, it should be noted that

Magner was decided without the cautionary standards announced in this opinion and, in all events, the case was settled by the parties before an ultimate determination of disparate-impact liability.

Were standards for proceeding with disparate-impact suits not to incorporate at least the safeguards discussed here, then disparate-impact liability might displace valid governmental and private priorities, rather than solely "remov[ing] . . . artificial, arbitrary, and unnecessary barriers." *Griggs*, 401 U.S., at 431. And that, in turn, would set our Nation back in its quest to reduce the salience of race in our social and economic system.

It must be noted further that, even when courts do find liability under a disparate-impact theory, their remedial orders must be consistent with the Constitution. Remedial orders in disparate-impact cases should concentrate on the elimination of the offending practice that "arbitrar[ily] . . . operate[s] invidiously to discriminate on the basis of rac[e]." *Ibid.* If additional measures are adopted, courts should strive to design them to eliminate racial disparities through race-neutral means. See *Richmond v. J.A. Croson Co.*, 488 U.S. 469, 510 (1989) (plurality opinion) ("[T]he city has at its disposal a whole array of race-neutral devices to increase the accessibility of city contracting opportunities to small entrepreneurs of all races"). Remedial orders that impose racial targets or quotas might raise more difficult constitutional questions.

While the automatic or pervasive injection of race into public and private transactions covered by the FHA has special dangers, it is also true that race may be considered in certain circumstances and in a proper fashion. Cf. *Parents Involved in Community Schools v. Seattle School Dist. No. 1*, 551 U.S. 701 (2007) (Kennedy, J., concurring in part and concurring in judgment) ("School boards may pursue the goal of bringing together students of diverse backgrounds and races through other means, including strategic site selection of new schools; [and] drawing attendance zones with general recognition of the demographics of neighborhoods"). Just as this Court has not "question[ed] an employer's affirmative efforts to ensure that all groups have a fair opportunity to apply for promotions and to participate in the [promotion] process," *Ricci*, 557 U.S., at 585, it likewise does not impugn housing authorities' race-neutral efforts to encourage revitalization of communities that have long suffered the harsh consequences of segregated housing patterns. When setting their larger goals, local housing authorities may choose to foster diversity and combat racial isolation with race-neutral tools, and mere awareness of race in attempting to solve the problems facing inner cities does not doom that endeavor at the outset.

The Court holds that disparate-impact claims are cognizable under the Fair Housing Act upon considering its results-oriented language, the Court's interpretation of similar language in [similar statutes], Congress' ratification of disparate-impact claims in 1988 against the backdrop of the unanimous view of nine Courts of Appeals, and the statutory purpose. . . .

Much progress remains to be made in our Nation's continuing struggle against racial isolation. In striving to achieve our "historic commitment to creating an integrated society," *Parents Involved, supra*, at 797 (Kennedy, J., concurring in part and concurring in judgment), we must remain wary of policies that reduce homeowners to nothing more than their race. But since the passage of the Fair Housing Act in 1968 and against the backdrop of disparate-impact liability in nearly every jurisdiction, many cities have become more diverse. The FHA must play an important part in avoiding the Kerner Commission's grim prophecy that "[o]ur Nation is moving toward two societies, one black, one white — separate and unequal." Kerner Commission Report 1. The Court acknowledges the Fair Housing Act's continuing role in moving the Nation toward a more integrated society.

The judgment of the Court of Appeals for the Fifth Circuit is affirmed, and the case is remanded for further proceedings consistent with this opinion.

It is so ordered.

[Dissent of JUSTICE THOMAS omitted.]

[Dissent of JUSTICE ALITO, with whom THE CHIEF JUSTICE, JUSTICE SCALIA, and JUSTICE THOMAS join, omitted.]

NOTES AND QUESTIONS

1. *Understanding the Kennedy Opinion.* All of the circuits held proof of disparate impact acceptable, but the Supreme Court had not passed on the question until this case. The Court accepted jurisdiction in two earlier cases. One was dismissed by the city that appealed, and the other settled.

Kennedy does not indicate how disparate impact should be proved statistically. Courts disagree on this point. The next reproduced case provides one answer. His citation of the HUD regulation suggests he approves it, but the regulation does not discuss this problem either.

Kennedy also made some changes in the disparate impact rule. The requirement, that the burden shifts to the plaintiff to prove a nondiscriminatory alternative once government shows its action is nondiscriminatory, was only adopted by some circuits. It converts the case into a requirement to prove nondiscrimination rather than a defense of discrimination. What is also new in the Kennedy opinion are the limitations he places on disparate impact proof. The most important are his holdings that defendants can assert valid policy interests, and that plaintiffs must prove causation. These limitations are not present in circuit court cases applying the disparate impact test. His comment that the disparate impact test may raise constitutional questions is puzzling. He is apparently referring to the possibility that defendants may use racial quotas defensively.

2. *The Government Discrimination Case.* Justice Kennedy refers to the *Texas* case as a rare case of government discrimination. In another case of government discrimination, *Gallagher v. Magner*, 619 F.3d 823 (8th Cir. 2010), wrongly described factually by Justice Alito in his dissenting opinion, the city adopted a housing code enforcement campaign targeted at minority rental housing. The court found a violation. The court held there was a shortage of rental housing in the city; that minorities, especially African-Americans, made up a disproportionate portion of lower-income households; that the city's aggressive housing code enforcement policy increased costs for owners of rental property; and that this increase in housing costs resulted in less affordable housing in the city. "These premises, together, reasonably demonstrate that the City's aggressive enforcement of the Housing Code resulted in a disproportionate adverse effect on racial minorities, particularly African-Americans." *Id.* at 834. This approach to statistical analysis differs from most because it does include a comparison of majority and minority groups. The Supreme Court granted certiorari, but the city withdrew the case because it feared an adverse decision on the disparate impact issue. Kennedy did not comment on the decision in his opinion.

The dissent cited *Reinhart v. Lincoln County*, 482 F.3d 1225 (10th Cir. 2007), where the county changed its land use regulations to prohibit a development of residential housing. The court held "[i]t is not enough for the Reinharts to show that (1) a regulation would increase housing costs and (2) members of a protected group tend to be less wealthy than others." *Id.* at 1230. It contrasted cases where the court had compared the impact of a restriction on majority and minority groups.

Cases like the *Texas* case can remedy an instance of individual discrimination. Cases like *Magner* get at more systemic discriminatory practices, rules and laws that deny housing to groups protected under the Act because they have a discriminatory impact on the housing market. Other examples of discriminatory practices that have market effects are considered in the cases that follow.

[B.] FACIALLY NEUTRAL DISCRIMINATION

[1.] Rental Housing

The typical case of discrimination in a failure to rent housing is discrimination based on race or color or any of the other factors listed under the federal law. These cases present a clear violation of federal law if discrimination can be proved. Other types of discrimination do not fit the legislative categories but arguably should fall within them. Discrimination based on source of income is one important example. It can occur in the federally subsidized Section 8 Housing Choice Voucher Program, 42 U.S.C. § 1437f, named for the section of the federal housing law that authorizes it, which subsidizes 2,447,016 units with 5,322,160 people. Here is how the program works:

> The Section 8 Housing Choice Voucher Program provides eligible low-income individuals with vouchers equal to 30% of their adjusted income. Tenants may apply the vouchers toward rent for a privately owned dwelling advertised at or below a locally established Fair Market Rent (FMR). The legislation authorizes the federal Department of Housing and Urban Development (HUD) to enter into annual contribution contracts with local public housing authorities, which subsidize the remainder of tenants' rent. Landlords who choose to accept a Section 8 tenant are obligated to maintain units rented by Section 8 tenants in compliance with HUD's Housing and Quality Standards (HQS).

Note, *Section 8, Source of Income Discrimination, and Federal Preemption: Setting the Record Straight*, 32 Cardozo L. Rev. 1407, 1410 (2010). There were 2,318,706 units in the program in 2011. It is 70% minority.

No federal requirement mandates participation in the program; landlord participation is voluntary. The author of the Note points out that "[h]ousing reform advocates argue that source of income discrimination acts as a proxy for discrimination based on race, gender, or other family characteristics, as many Section 8 tenants exhibit those protected traits." *Id.* at 1417. Landlords have what they think are legitimate reasons for discriminating against Section 8 tenants, such as tenant reputation, administrative difficulties and delays in the program. *See* Note, *Housing Discrimination and Source of Income: A Tenant's Losing Battle*, 32 IND. L. REV. 457, 460–461 (1999). As a result, as many as 40% of Section 8 voucher holders are unable to find housing in some jurisdictions. This problem may be aggravated, as the demand for Section 8 vouchers has increased, and there are long waiting lists. Baurlein, *Crowds Chase Scarce Housing Vouchers*, WALL STREET JOURNAL, vol. 256, no. 38, at A3, Aug. 14, 2010.

The following is a case of income source discrimination brought under the Fair Housing Act that can be a proxy for racial discrimination.

BRONSON v. CRESTWOOD LAKE SECTION 1 HOLDING CORP.

United States District Court, New York Southern District
724 F. Supp. 148 (1989)

MARY JOHNSON LOWE, UNITED STATES DISTRICT JUDGE.

Before this Court is plaintiffs' motion for a preliminary injunction. For the reasons stated below, the motion is granted.

Background

This proposed class action involves a challenge under Title VIII of the Civil Rights Act of 1968 (also known as the Fair Housing Act) to the rental policies of Crestwood Lake ("Crestwood"), an apartment complex located in the city of Yonkers, New York. Specifically, plaintiffs allege that Crestwood's rental policies — variously consisting of its refusal to consider the applications of any person who receives Section 8 federal housing assistance or whose income is not at least three times the rent of the apartment for which that person is applying — disproportionately and adversely impact upon black and Hispanic ("minority") applicants for tenancies in comparison to white applicants. Plaintiffs additionally allege that these policies were intentionally crafted to exclude minorities from apartments at Crestwood.

Plaintiff Ruth Bronson currently resides with her child and grandchild in the Southwest portion of Yonkers, New York. A recipient of public assistance, Bronson also holds a Section 8 housing assistance voucher issued by the Yonkers Housing Authority. Plaintiff Lisa Carter also resides, with her three children, in the Southwest portion of Yonkers. She, too, is a recipient of public assistance and holds a Section 8 housing assistance voucher. In addition to these subsidies, Carter receives $693.00 per month in child support. Both Carter and Bronson are black.

The Southwest section of Yonkers in which plaintiffs currently reside has been the subject of extensive litigation elsewhere in this District. Most notable for its extreme concentration of the city's minority population — 80.7% of Yonkers' minorities reside there — it is also the site for virtually all of the city's government subsidized housing projects. According to plaintiffs' affidavits, this community is also riddled with drug users and dealers, many of whom actively engage in their trade directly across the street from Carter's apartment complex. Dealers' solicitations are not infrequent; Bronson's twelve year old grandchild is himself regularly recruited, though unsuccessfully, for drug-related tasks. Not all of the neighborhood's children, many of them truants, have succeeded, as he has, in their resistance to the drug culture. The Southwest section of Yonkers also abounds with other forms of criminal activity. The apartment building in which the Bronsons live is "not secure, so that strangers often enter the building and roam the halls." Fearing a break-in or assault, the Bronson family often sleeps poorly at night. Carter, too, fears for the safety and welfare of herself, her children and her home.

It is against this backdrop and in the hope of relocating to another area of Yonkers, that plaintiffs Bronson and Carter looked to Crestwood Lake Apartments, a housing development with over one thousand units located on the east side of the city. Crestwood is owned by defendant Crestwood Lake Section 1 Holding Corporation ("Crestwood Corporation").

To that end, Ruth Bronson went to defendants' rental office at Crestwood on June 23, 1989 in search of a two bedroom apartment for herself and her child and grandchild. While there, she spoke with rental agent Margaret Naughton ("Naughton") who informed Bronson that rent for such an apartment is $875 per month. Bronson indicated to Naughton that she could meet this rent entirely through the shelter component of her public assistance grant and her Section 8 housing voucher. Naughton thereupon asserted that Bronson "probably would not pass the credit check because [she did] not have earned income." Bronson's initial contact with Crestwood apparently concluded at this juncture.

Later that day, Bronson related these events to two attorneys employed by Westchester Legal Services, Inc. — John Hand and Jerrold Levy — both of whom accompanied Bronson back to the rental office to question the rental manager about Bronson's application. While there, Levy and Hand spoke with Michael D. Aiello, the Property Manager for defendant Jonathan Woodner Company, who initially stated that Bronson could not pass the credit check because she did not have earned income. When informed by one of the attorneys that such a requirement would constitute unlawful race discrimination because it would have a disparate impact on minority persons, Aiello stated that the management would allow Bronson to apply for a tenancy and that, if Bronson passed the credit check, her name would be placed on a waiting list for an apartment.

Bronson returned to Crestwood on June 26 to fill out an application for a credit check and was told by Naughton that the results would be returned within two days. When ten days had passed, Bronson called Naughton to determine the status of her application and was informed that the credit check had not, in fact, been returned to the office.[1] Naughton went on to inform Bronson that, at any rate, she had just spoken with her manager and was told that Crestwood was "not accepting Section 8." Bronson's application was subsequently rejected.

Carter's application process followed a considerably less tortuous course. When she appeared at defendants' rental office on July 18, 1989 to apply for either a two or three bedroom apartment, she was informed by Naughton that the rent for such apartments began at $850 and $1000 per month, respectively. Like Bronson before her, Carter indicated that she could afford either of these rents through her public assistance grant, Section 8 voucher, and a reasonable portion of her monthly child support payments. Carter thereafter proceeded to fill out an initial application, but was told that a credit check would be executed only after an apartment became available. According to the Complaint, Naughton further questioned Carter about the sources of her income and attempted to discourage her from applying to Crestwood. Since this initial interview, Carter's application has been placed on a waiting list. However, because defendants consider her "ability to pay [to be] in serious doubt," Carter is unlikely to be offered an apartment at Crestwood.

A "settlement" conference between the parties apparently took place on July 24, 1989. It was at this meeting that Charles Macellaro, counsel for Crestwood Lake Corporation, represented to Westchester Legal Services that further attempts to secure plaintiffs' tenancies at Crestwood would generate considerable political controversy and community opposition. Macellaro further stated that attempts should not be made to increase the racial "mix" at Crestwood because it would induce white residents to leave. When asked about Crestwood's policy on accepting Section 8 vouchers, Macellaro disavowed Naughton's earlier representation that Crestwood would not accept the vouchers and, instead, articulated, apparently for the first time, Crestwood's policy of accepting only those applicants who have an annual income at least equal to three times the annual rent (hereinafter "the triple income test"). . . .

[In an earlier "Part I" hearing, plaintiffs obtained an order temporarily enjoining defendants from entering into a lease for the occupancy of two currently available two bedroom apartments which, plaintiffs claim, would have been made available to them but for the enforcement of defendants' allegedly discriminatory application policies.] It should be noted that during the course of the hearing before Judge Wood, counsel for Crestwood disavowed Naughton's earlier representation that Crestwood did not accept Section 8 applicants. Indeed, he stated on the record that Crestwood currently has eight tenants who receive such subsidies.[2]

In their Complaint, plaintiffs allege that defendants' refusal to rent to Section 8 voucher holders or to applicants who do not meet the triple income test (i.e. effectively all Section 8 voucher holders), has a substantially disproportionate and adverse impact upon minority persons and is therefore violative of plaintiffs' rights under the Fair Housing Laws, 42 U.S.C. § 3601 *et seq.*, as well as under state law.

---

[1] [4] It should be noted that, in her affidavit to this Court, Naughton now admits that the credit report had, in fact, been returned to her on the date of this conversation.

[2] [6] Counsel has also stated that Crestwood actually has four tenants currently receiving Section 8 subsidies, all of whom are white.

Plaintiffs also claim that the aforementioned policies constitute an attempt to restrict the minority composition at Crestwood and, as such, have a racially discriminatory purpose. For the purpose of the instant motion for a preliminary injunction, however, plaintiffs are asserting only their disparate impact claim. . . . [After a hearing, the court granted the plaintiffs' request for a preliminary injunction, and ordered that the two apartments subject to the temporary restraining order remain vacant until the issuance of an opinion in this proceeding.]

DISCUSSION

Irreparable Harm

[The court found that plaintiffs had shown irreparable harm. Even if plaintiffs could find another apartment, a move to Crestwood should they succeed in this case would be disruptive.]

Likelihood of Success on the Merits

One of the principal functions of Title VIII is to promote "open, integrated residential housing patterns." *Otero v. New York Housing Authority*, 484 F.2d 1122, 1134 (2d Cir. 1973). To that end, and pursuant to its powers under the Thirteenth Amendment, Congress has made it unlawful "to refuse to sell or rent after the making of a bona fide offer or to refuse to negotiate for the sale or rental of, or otherwise make unavailable or deny, a dwelling to any person because of race, color, religion, sex, or national origin." 42 U.S.C. § 3604. "Housing practices unlawful under Title VIII include not only those motivated by a racially discriminatory purpose, but also those that disproportionately affect minorities." *United States v. Starrett City Associates*, 840 F.2d 1096, 1100 (2d Cir. 1988). Under this basis for liability, known as the disparate impact theory, "a prima facie case is established by showing that the challenged practice of the defendant 'actually or predictably results in racial discrimination; in other words that it has a discriminatory effect.' " *Huntington Branch, NAACP v. Town of Huntington*, 844 F.2d 926, 934 (2d Cir. 1988) (quoting from *United States v. City of Black Jack*, 508 F.2d 1179, 1184–85 (8th Cir. 1974), *cert. denied*, 422 U.S. 1042 (1975)). Accordingly, plaintiffs under Title VIII need not show that the policies complained of were fashioned with discriminatory intent. This Circuit's rejection of an intent requirement under the Fair Housing Act rests principally upon the long recognized parallel between Title VIII and Title VII jurisprudence and upon the fact that, under the latter statute, discriminatory effect alone is sufficient to establish a violation. *See, e.g., Griggs v. Duke Power Co.*, 401 U.S. 424, 429–36 (1971). Once plaintiffs have succeeded in making a prima facie showing of discriminatory effect, the burden shifts to the defendants to present bona fide and legitimate justifications for their policies.

Using alternative statistical approaches, plaintiffs have demonstrated that the challenged application policies utilized by the defendants do indeed have a substantial disparate impact on minority persons. Under all of these statistical approaches, plaintiffs have used as the general applicant pool all Yonkers renters who, after payment of taxes and rent required for residence at Crestwood, would have income equal to or greater than the New York State-determined standard of need. According to 1980 Census figures, that pool consists of 16,883 households, of which 2,820 (16.70%) are minority households, and of which 14,063 (83.30%) are non-minority households. Application of Crestwood's policy of rejecting holders of Section 8 vouchers, alone, would have the effect of disqualifying from tenancies 6.06% of the minority households in the applicant pool, but only 0.25% of non-minority households in the pool. Stated another way, the odds of being excluded from Crestwood on the basis of the Section 8 policy is over 25 times greater for minority persons than for non-minorities. These figures are hardly surprising given the fact that, while only 16.7% of the total applicant pool represents minority households, 82.6% of the Section 8 voucher holders within that pool are minorities.

While the application of Crestwood's triple income test does not result in equally dramatic figures, it too has a substantially disparate impact upon otherwise qualified minority households. Of the roughly 14,063 non-minority households within the applicant pool, 3,945 or 28% qualify for tenancies at Crestwood under the triple income test. By contrast, only 14% of the minority households otherwise capable of affording defendants' apartments qualify under the test. Consequently, non-minorities qualify at a rate of more than twice that for minorities. Using these same statistical figures, an odds analysis demonstrates that the odds of being excluded by the triple income test are 2.5 times greater for minority persons than non-minority persons. . . . [The court accepted the use of 1980 census data as accurately reflecting the present racial composition of renters in Yonkers.]

Besides challenging the accuracy of plaintiffs chosen methodology, defendants also argue that a wholly different statistical approach should be utilized. Defendants would have this Court concentrate on the actual distribution of minority persons currently residing at Crestwood vis-'A-vis the distribution of minority persons in the overall population of Yonkers. Yet, this is precisely the kind of statistical approach the Supreme Court has emphatically rejected under analogous Title VII disparate-impact cases. *See Connecticut v. Teal*, 457 U.S. 440 (1982); *Wards Cove Packing Co., Inc. v. Atonio*, 490 U.S. 642 (1989). Thus, even if a "bottom-line" racial balance in the actual tenancies at Crestwood exists, as defendants assert they do, plaintiffs would still have a case under Title VIII "if they could prove that some particular [application] practice has a disparate impact on minorities." *Id.* This Court is satisfied that plaintiffs' statistical formulations meet that prima facie burden. Accordingly, I now turn to the second prong of the disparate-impact analysis.

Under this second prong, the burden is upon the defendant to show that the challenged practices serve legitimate and genuine business goals. In support of its application policies, defendants assert that the Section 8 voucher prohibition and the triple-income requirement are necessary to insure the payment of rent and adequate protection in the case of a default. Specifically, defendants advance the following justifications of their policies: 1) there is no guarantee from any government agency that either Bronson or Carter will set aside the necessary amount of their public assistance grants to meet the balance of their monthly rental payments after the Section 8 assistance is advanced; and 2) the form of lease which the Section 8 Housing Voucher Contract would require Crestwood to enter into contains provisions not within its standard lease and which it finds objectionable. For example, should the tenant vacate the premises during the term of the tenancy, under the standard lease, but not the Section 8 lease, Crestwood would be able to collect the full amount of rent for the remainder of the term. Moreover, under the Crestwood lease, the tenant must waive his right to a trial by jury in any ensuing court proceedings between the parties. This waiver is not included in the Section 8 lease.

In setting forth these justifications, defendants quite correctly argue that nothing under Title VIII forbids a landlord from seeking "assurance that prospective tenants will be able to meet their rental responsibilities." *Boyd v. Lefrak Organization*, 509 F.2d 1110, 1114 (2d Cir.), *reh'g denied*, 517 F.2d 918 (2d Cir.), *cert. denied*, 423 U.S. 896 (1975). The application policies at issue in this litigation, defendants urge, are designed to do nothing more than advance this legitimate and genuine business goal of maximizing the probability of collecting rent.

However, under the limited circumstances of the instant motion, these justifications must be rejected as insubstantial. First, other than general conclusory assertions and broad references to an apartment management manual, defendants have not offered any evidence to show that the challenged policies are reasonably necessary to insure payment of rent or that Crestwood has, in past experience, encountered losses or defaults as a result of accepting Section 8 tenants or tenants who fail to meet the triple income test.

Second, defendants have in the past participated in the Section 8 certificate program which is very similar to the Section 8 voucher program that they now allege is so objectionable. Crestwood currently has four tenants receiving Section 8 subsidies, under the certificate program.[3] As a result, defendants' willingness to accept Section 8 certificate subsidies casts doubt on their claim that their refusal to accept Section 8 voucher applicants stems from their reluctance to depart from their standard lease agreement.[4] . . . [In addition, both plaintiffs have agreed to make payment arrangements that would alleviate any risk of nonpayment.]

Finally, I note that one factor that may affect my determination here is evidence of discriminatory intent on the part of the defendants. As this Circuit has explained, while "intent is not a requirement of the plaintiff's prima facie case, there can be little doubt that if evidence of such intent is presented, that evidence would weigh heavily on the plaintiff's side of the ultimate balance." *Huntington*, 844 F.2d at 936. Indicia of such intent include, inter alia, "the specific sequence of events leading up to the challenged decision." *Village of Arlington Heights v. Metropolitan Housing Development Corp.*, 429 U.S. 252, 267 (1977); *see also Robinson* [*v. 12 Lofts Realty*

---

[3] [9] These tenants were not receiving Section 8 subsidies at the time they applied for apartments. Rather, after they came into occupancy, they applied for Section 8 certificates and were awarded them. All of these four tenants are white.

[4] [12] The record does not indicate whether the lease agreements between Crestwood and its Section 8 certificate tenants contain jury waiver provisions. In any event, the waiver of jury trial in this instance is of minimal importance, because Bronson and Carter have effectively guaranteed their rental payments. Since Bronson and Carter cannot default on these guarantees, there should never be a non-payment proceeding and, therefore, no jury trial. Moreover, should they abandon the apartments, no eviction proceedings will be required and the apartments will promptly be relet.

Co.], 610 F.2d at 1038 (2d Cir. 1979). Without passing on the merits of plaintiffs' discriminatory intent claim — a claim which for the present purposes of the instant motion, plaintiffs have relinquished — I note that defendant's inconsistent articulation and application of its tenant selection policies cast the sincerity of those policies in a somewhat questionable light. Throughout the course of their application process, for example, plaintiffs were never made aware of Crestwood's triple income test. It was not until well after she had submitted her credit check application, moreover, that Bronson was informed of Crestwood's Section 8 policy. Carter, on the other hand, was never told that such a policy existed. Indeed, defendant's post hoc objections to the Section 8 lease were, themselves, never articulated until after the Temporary Restraining Order hearing, although Crestwood was certainly given an opportunity to present such objections before the Part I judge. Moreover, despite these very objections, it does in fact appear that Crestwood currently rents apartment units to four Section 8 recipients. It is not insignificant that all four of these tenants are white. Perhaps most perplexing of all, is the inconsistent treatment conferred upon the plaintiffs' applications. Both Bronson and Carter occupy identical positions with respect to defendant's Section 8 and triple income policies, yet while Bronson's application has been flatly rejected, Carter remains on the waiting list for tenancy. These inconsistencies only serve to undermine the sincerity with which defendants advance their "business necessity" policies.

RELIEF

[The court considered the prayers for relief by both parties and concluded:]

As an initial matter, this Court must stress that it seeks to avoid creating a situation whereby in every instance that defendants make a tenant selection, this Court would have to review claims challenging the basis of that decision. Moreover, defendants' ability throughout the limited course of these proceedings to offer an ever-changing array of justifications for their refusal to accept plaintiffs' applications only further highlights the difficulty this Court foresees were it to grant relief which merely required defendants to give a non-discriminatory reason for choosing other applicants. These concerns reveal the primary flaws of defendants' suggested remedy.

On the other hand, this Court is not unmindful of the unfairness inherent in forcing Crestwood to accept an applicant who though able to afford the rent at Crestwood presents some other genuine risk. Crestwood does have a right to exercise its own judgement in choosing its applicants so long as it relies on legitimate, objective criteria in so doing. . . . [The court ordered the defendants to evaluate plaintiff's applications without regard to whether they are employed, to whether they have income in excess of three times the rent, and to whether their tenancies require entry into standard Section 8 leases. The court also ordered defendants to offer plaintiffs the two apartments held open pursuant to the temporary restraining order unless the defendants could demonstrate "legitimate, objective grounds" for denying plaintiffs' applications. The court refused to stay the operation of this injunction pending an appeal of the order.]

NOTES AND QUESTIONS

1. *Income Source Discrimination.* This type of discrimination is not explicitly covered by the Fair Housing Act, but the judge in *Bronson* was able to find that the refusal to rent to a Section 8 tenant was actionable racial discrimination. Notice the court's concerns in *Bronson*, however, about infringing too far on a landlord's privilege to choose tenants who will be financially responsible. How did the court balance this concern against the landlord's duty to offer rental property in a nondiscriminatory manner? Would the landlord's business reasons be acceptable under the holding in the Texas case? *See Woods v. Real Renters, Ltd.*, 2007 U.S. Dist. LEXIS 19631 (S.D.N.Y. 2007) (upholding poor credit as reason for rejecting minority tenant). For a study of the impact of Section 8 vouchers, see Varady & Walker, NEIGHBORHOOD CHOICES: SECTION 8 HOUSING VOUCHERS AND RESIDENTIAL MOBILITY (2007).

A landlord may also decide to withdraw from the program rather than face challenges to tenant denials. The Sixth Circuit held that withdrawal could be a Title VIII violation if it has a disproportionate impact on minorities, though it cites cases holding a withdrawal can never be a violation. *Graoch Assocs. #33, L.P. v. Louisville/Jefferson County Metro Human Rels. Comm'n*, 508 F.3d 366 (6th Cir. 2007). However, the Second Circuit held that withdrawal is permissible because the program is voluntary. *Salute v. Stratford Greens Garden Apartments*, 136 F.3d 293 (2d Cir. 1998). *See* Note, *Using Disparate Impact Analysis Fair Housing Act Claims: Landlord Withdrawal from the Section 8 Voucher Program*, 78 FORDHAM L. REV. 1971 (2010). Congress repealed a provision in the act that prevented a landlord who participated in the program from refusing to rent to a tenant who was eligible for assistance under the voucher program. Keep in mind that the Supreme Court has modified the disparate impact test as stated and applied in the *Bronson* case.

A number of state and local governments have laws prohibiting income source discrimination. *See* POVERTY & RACE RESEARCH ACTION COUNCIL, KEEPING THE PROMISE: PRESERVING AND ENHANCING HOUSING MOBILITY IN THE SECTION 8 HOUSING VOUCHER PROGRAM, APP. B (2009), http://prrac.org/pdf/source-of-income.pdf. For discussion of these laws see Note, *Bringing Real Choice to the Housing Choice Voucher Program: Addressing Housing Discrimination Under the Federal Fair Housing Act*, 98 GEO. L.J. 769, 777–779 (2010), arguing that some of these laws do not provide adequate protection. *See Austin Apartment Ass'n v. City of Austin* , 89 F. Supp. 3d 886 (W.D. Tex. 2015) (upholding a city source of income ordinance).

2. *Preventing Discrimination in Rentals.* Cases claiming discrimination in rentals fall into two categories: cases in which the plaintiff claims he or she has been unfairly treated, and cases in which the plaintiff claims a rental practice of a landlord is discriminatory. *Bronson* falls in the second category. Cases challenging discriminatory practices are called discriminatory impact cases, and cases challenging discriminatory refusals to rent are called discriminatory treatment cases.

3. *Proving the Disparate Impact Case.* The statute does not specify what kind of proof is required in a disparate impact case. For a review of the different rules in the circuits *see* Casenote, 78 U. CIN. L. REV. 371 (2009). Note how the statistical proof was made in *Bronson*. The court rejected a suggestion that it consider the distribution of minorities in the project as compared with the distribution of

minorities in the Yonkers population. The court applied a proportionality test. It considered the proportionate impact of the rule on minorities. It did not compare the absolute number of minorities affected with the absolute number of non-minorities affected. This approach is borrowed from the Title VII cases, but it is not always followed. *See Summerchase Limited Partnership I v. City of Gonzales* , 970 F. Supp. 522 (M.D. La. 1997) (applying absolute numbers approach and holding rejection of development not discriminatory). Does an absolute numbers approach ever make sense in a housing discrimination case? Justice Kennedy did not discuss the statistical proof problem in the *Texas* case, and the *Magner* case did not use a comparison approach.

4. *The Disparate Treatment Case.* In *Bronson*, the project owner did not want to accept the plaintiffs as tenants because they violated his rules for tenant selection. But what if a minority tenant meets all the formal selection criteria, yet a project owner rejects her for other reasons? For example, the project owner may claim that references from previous landlords are bad. This is a disparate treatment case, which can also occur in the sale of housing.

The leading case on disparate treatment is *Robinson v. 12 Lofts Realty Co.*, 610 F.2d 1032 (2d Cir. 1979), in which the plaintiff claimed discrimination in a refusal to sell him a cooperative apartment in New York City. The court first adopted a prima facie case rule from *Smith v. Anchor Bldg. Corp.*, 536 F.2d 231 (8th Cir. Mo. 1976), where the court held a prima facie case is proved when a black rental applicant meets the landlord's objective requirements, and the rental "would likely have been consummated" if the applicant had been white.

Robinson then applied a disparate treatment test adopted for employment discrimination cases by *McDonnell Douglas Corp. v. Green*, 411 U.S. 792 (1973). As adapted for housing discrimination cases, that test requires a showing (1) that the applicant is black, (2) that he applied for and was qualified to rent or purchase the housing, (3) that he was rejected, and (4) that the housing opportunity remained available.

Cases like this often present a mixed motive problem, because the landlord often claims he had a nondiscriminatory reason for rejecting the applicant. Prior to 1989, most courts took the position that a rejection was discriminatory despite the presence of a valid reason for rejecting an applicant. However, in 1989 the Supreme Court held in a Title VII employment discrimination case that an employer may avoid liability, despite proof of racial motivation, by showing she would have made the same decision for nondiscriminatory reasons. *Price Waterhouse v. Hopkins*, 490 U.S. 228 (1989). This rule, though modified by Congress for employment discrimination cases, may make housing discrimination cases harder to prove. The *Price Waterhouse* rule places considerable discretion with the trial court. As attorney for a plaintiff claiming discrimination, what can you do help ensure a favorable finding?

5. *Remedies. Bronson* also indicates the importance of effective remedial relief in housing discrimination cases. Preliminary injunctions of this type are standard in private discrimination cases. Justice Kennedy called for caution in granting relief in the *Texas* case.

The subsequent history of the *Bronson* litigation indicates why remedial relief in housing discrimination cases can be problematic. In a later proceeding in this case, *Glover v. Crestwood Lake Section 1 Holding Corps.*, 746 F. Supp. 301 (S.D.N.Y. 1990), the original plaintiffs withdrew because the defendants' actions over the course of the litigation convinced them they no longer wanted an apartment in the project. The court then granted class certification and partial summary judgment to the plaintiffs on some counts. It held the defendant's refusal to rent to Section 8 tenants violated the antidiscrimination provision of the federal housing act, and that defendant's refusal to rent to a single parent with children constituted discrimination based on familial status, which the statute prohibits. Questions concerning discrimination based on marital status, familial status and age were to be resolved at trial.

Yonkers was also the site of a major lawsuit brought to challenge racial discrimination in schools and public housing. *United States v. Yonkers Bd. of Ed.*, 624 F. Supp. 1276 (S.D.N.Y, 1985), *aff'd* , 837 F.2d 1181 (2d Cir. 1987).

[2.] Affirmative Marketing and Steering

Racial discrimination in housing does not occur only because of the discriminatory acts of individual owner. Practices in the real estate industry also contribute. One such practice, known as "steering," perpetuates housing discrimination in the housing market. The Supreme Court defined steering as a practice that occurs when:

> real estate brokers and agents preserve and encourage patterns of racial segregation in available housing by steering members of racial and ethnic groups to buildings occupied primarily by members of such racial and ethnic groups and away from buildings and neighborhoods inhabited by members of other races or groups.

Havens Realty Corp. v. Coleman, 455 U.S. 363, 366 n1 (1982).

Another, benign form of steering occurs when communities engage in affirmative marketing programs that attempt to maintain integration by maintaining racial balance. The next case considers whether this practice violates the Fair Housing Act.

SOUTH-SUBURBAN HOUSING CENTER v. GREATER SOUTH SUBURBAN BOARD OF REALTORS

United States Court of Appeals, Seventh Circuit
935 F.2d 868 (1991)

These consolidated appeals deal with a variety of constitutional and Fair Housing Act challenges to real estate marketing activities and municipal ordinances affecting the real estate market in a number of the southern suburbs of Chicago, Illinois. [Park Forest is one of these municipalities.] The court disposed of these issues following a bench trial consisting of approximately eight weeks of testimony presented intermittently between March 23, 1987, and September 1, 1987.

I. *Facts*

The municipal defendants are located in an area bordered on the north by the City of Chicago, on the west approximately by Harlem Avenue or Interstate 57, on the south roughly by Will County and on the east by the Indiana State line. The district court found that these formerly all-white suburbs have become integrated, but now face the threat of resegregation as a result of

> a complex mix of market forces. These market forces include racial prejudice: some whites and some blacks prefer to live in segregated communities; the belief that high concentrations of blacks result in a drop in home values; the expectation that an integrated community will eventually become segregated; and housing search practices that are reinforced by certain real estate practices.

South-Suburban Housing Center v. Greater South Suburban Board of Realtors, 713 F. Supp. 1068, 1074 (N.D. Ill. 1988). In order to stem the tide of these market forces and promote integrated housing patterns, the plaintiff, [South-Suburban Housing Center, now referred to as] SSHC, "attempted to influence the housing market by encouraging the sales and marketing of real estate in what it terms to be 'non-traditional' ways, i.e., encouraging whites to move to black or integrated areas and blacks to move to white or integrated areas." *Id.* at 1075. A controversy between South-Suburban Housing Center and the Realtors over the propriety of SSHC making special efforts to market houses in black neighborhoods to white home buyers spawned the initial complaint in this litigation.

The plaintiff, SSHC, is an Illinois, non-profit corporation whose "purposes are to 'promote and encourage multiracial communities in the South Suburbs' of Chicago and 'promote open housing to all people regardless of race.' " *Id.* at 1073. SSHC engages in a program of "affirmative marketing" of real estate, which "consists of race conscious efforts to promote integration or prevent segregation through special marketing of real estate to attract persons of particular racial classifications who are not likely to either be aware of the availability or express an interest in the real estate without such special efforts." *Id.* at 1075.

The defendants/counterplaintiffs are two realtor trade associations, the Greater South Suburban Board of Realtors (GSSBR) and the National Association of Realtors (NAR). The GSSBR is an Illinois, non-profit corporation which is an organization of licensed real estate brokers and salesmen operating in the south suburbs of Chicago. One of GSSBR's activities is the operation of a multiple listing service (MLS) in the south suburbs. The district court described the MLS as follows:

> [the] multiple listing service ("MLS") [is] a facility by which a MLS member broker makes a blanket unilateral offer of subagency to all other MLS participants with respect to a home listed with that broker. The MLS computer data base contains information about homes listed for sale with its members. MLS members and their home-seeking prospects can review this data via computer terminals or by reviewing printed compilations distributed to members on a bi-weekly basis.

Id. at 1077. The NAR is also an Illinois non-profit corporation and an organization of licensed real estate brokers that "provides policy guidance and materials and services of various sorts to its local affiliates, including the GSSBR." *Id.* at 1073.

A. Affirmative Marketing

This action originated as a result of the Realtors' reaction to South-Suburban Housing Center's attempts to promote a racial balance in the Village of Park Forest through making special efforts to interest white home buyers in property there. The current racial imbalance came about during the 1970s when many black families moved into an area in the northeast corner of the Village of Park Forest, Illinois known as the Eastgate subdivision. At the time of the 1980 census, the census block including the homes at issue here had become more than fifty-six percent black, more than double the black population of any other census block in the Eastgate subdivision. As a result of the area's reputation as "a black block," few white families were interested in buying property. The area became less attractive to home buyers as VA and FHA mortgage foreclosures led to abandoned homes and neighborhood blight. In response to the problem of abandoned homes in the Eastgate subdivision, in 1982 the Village of Park Forest instituted a program of purchasing vacant or abandoned homes for rehabilitation and resale, including vacant homes at numbers 9, 15 and 26 Apache Street. SSHC submitted a proposal, which included affirmative marketing, to Park Forest for the acquisition, rehabilitation and resale of these three homes.

After the Park Forest Board of Trustees accepted the proposal and sold the homes to the South-Suburban Housing Center, the SSHC agreed to list the homes for sale with Century 21-Host Realty through one of its salesmen, William H. Motluck. The parties utilized a standard real estate contract form with the exception of provisions that Century 21-Host Realty was "to implement the affirmative marketing plan attached as appendix." In addition to securing a buyer, Century 21-Host Realty's receipt of a commission was conditioned upon its "performance of the attached affirmative marketing plan."

The affirmative marketing plan (AMP) directed that the realtor "use its best efforts to attract minority and majority groups persons" to the particular Apache Street home, and stated that the SSHC and the Realtor "agree that white home seekers are not likely without special outreach efforts to be attracted to the Apache St. home." The AMP also provided that the Realtor would use "the following special outreach activities to attract white home seekers to the Apache Street home:

> A. Placement of advertisements in newspapers with a predominantly white circulation;
>
> B. Distribution of information to selected rental developments; and
>
> C. Distribution of information to selected employers.

The Plan also provided that "Realtor shall not take any action which prohibits, restricts, narrows or limits the housing choice of any client on the basis of race." Century 21 was further required to maintain "a list of all persons, by race, who are shown the Apache Street home."

. . . .

[GSSBR removed the Apache Street homes from the MLS and filed a complaint against Motluck with the Professional Standards Committee of the Illinois Realtors Association. It believed the AMP marketing program could be considered racial steering, and that Motluck violated an article in the code of ethics that prohibited realtors from providing services in a discriminatory manner. The committee, after holding a hearing, found there was insufficient evidence of a violation because Motluck was merely conducting his business in an ordinary manner. The district court held these actions by GSSBR did not violate the Fair Housing Act.]

C. The Realtors' Fair Housing Act Claims

The trial court determined that SSHC and Park Forest did not violate the Fair Housing Act in their implementation of the Apache Street Plan.

1. 42 U.S.C. § 3604(a)

We turn to the Realtors' claim that SSHC and Park Forest violated 42 U.S.C. § 3604(a), which prohibits the "refus[al] to sell or rent . . . or otherwise make unavailable or deny, a dwelling to any person because of race, color, religion, sex, or national origin." The Fair Housing Act is concerned with both the furtherance of equal housing opportunity and the elimination of segregated housing. As we observed in *Southend Neighborhood Improvement Association v. County of St. Clair*, 743 F.2d 1207, 1209–10 (7th Cir. 1984):

> The Fair Housing Act prohibits both direct discrimination and practices with significant discriminatory effects. For example, although Section 3604(a) applies principally to the sale or rental of dwellings, courts have construed the phrase "otherwise make unavailable or deny" in subsection (a) to encompass mortgage "redlining," insurance redlining, racial steering, exclusionary zoning decisions, and other actions by individuals or governmental units which directly affect the availability of housing to minorities. Of course, *the alleged illegal actions must lead to discriminatory effects on the availability of housing. The Act is concerned with ending racially segregated housing. Section 3604(a) applies to the availability of housing.* That section thus is violated by discriminatory actions, or certain actions with discriminatory effects, that affect the availability of housing.

(Emphasis added) (footnote and citations omitted). The Realtors argue that the affirmative marketing plan furthers the goal of "ending racially segregated housing" at the expense of limiting the "availability of housing" for black people. They assert that this alleged subordination of equal housing opportunity to the goal of integration is invalid, just as the courts held in *United States v. Starrett City Associates*, 840 F.2d 1096 (2d Cir.), *cert. denied*, 488 U.S. 946 (1988), and *United States v. Charlottesville Redevelopment and Housing Authority*, 718 F. Supp. 461 (W.D. Va. 1989). In *Starrett City*, owners of a government subsidized housing development sought to maintain an ethnic distribution of tenants in their project consisting of sixty-four percent white persons, twenty-two percent black persons and eight percent Hispanic persons through a "tenanting procedure" that filled apartment vacancies with "applicants of a race or national origin similar to that of the departing tenant." 840 F.2d at 1098. In *Charlottesville*, a "tenant selection policy . . . gave preferential treatment to white applicants for public housing," based upon an intent to "achieve a 50/50 mix of black and white residents in . . . public housing." 718 F. Supp. at 462. The courts determined that each of these "quota" programs violated the Fair Housing Act. In *Charlottesville*, the court recognized that the Fair Housing Act's twin purposes of eliminating discrimination in housing and furthering integration in housing are both important, but may occasionally be incompatible:

> The legislative history of the Fair Housing Act suggests to this court that the prime focus or the "quickening" force behind that legislation is prohibition of discrimination in the provision of housing, but also that integration was seen by the creators of that legislation as a prominent goal and a value of great worth. From the perspective of over two decades, it is perhaps excusable to find the unexamined assumption in the Act's legislative history that the principles of nondiscrimination and integration will always necessarily go hand in hand. With our later perspective, that assumption may be unfounded, but it does not detract from the observation that this legislation was created with both legal (and moral) principles in mind, although primary weight is given to the prohibition of discrimination. However, cases such as *Trafficante* [*v. Metropolitan Life Ins. Co.*, 409 U.S. 205 (1972)] illustrate that the legal principle of integration and concern for the achievement of that goal cannot be considered mere surplusage.

718 F. Supp. at 467. The court determined that Charlottesville's "quota" program presented a conflict between the Act's purposes of nondiscrimination and integration, and held that:

> In the present conflict between these two legal principles, nondiscrimination and integration, the obligation of [the Charlottesville Redevelopment and Housing Authority (CRHA)] to avoid discrimination must "trump" CRHA's obligation to promote integration, as regards the promotion of integration through the specific policy mechanism and controversy before this court. It is not that this court ascribes to integration a status inferior to nondiscrimination in the pantheon of legal values. It is, rather, that the duty to avoid discrimination must circumscribe the specific particular ways in which a party under the duty to integrate can seek to fulfill that second duty.

718 F. Supp. at 468. Similarly, the Second Circuit in *Starrett City* held that while integration maintenance with its concern over

> the "white flight" phenomenon may be a factor "take[n] into account in the integration equation," *Parent Ass'n of Andrew Jackson High School v. Ambach*, 598 F.2d 705, 720 (2d Cir. 1979), it cannot serve to justify attempts to maintain integration at Starrett City through inflexible racial quotas that are neither temporary in nature nor used to remedy past racial discrimination or imbalance within the complex.

Starrett City, 840 F.2d at 1102. Thus, *Starrett City* and *Charlottesville* both mandate the conclusion that an interest in racial integration alone is insufficient to justify a racial quota system which favors whites and thereby lessens housing opportunities for minorities.

In contrast to the subordination of the goal of equal housing opportunity to the goal of integration presented by the facts in *Starrett City* and *Charlottesville*, the Realtors' challenge to the Apache Street affirmative marketing plan presents the question of whether a real estate organization may engage in limited race conscious marketing which does not exclude minorities from housing opportunities. Thus, we are not dealing with conflicting goals, for the affirmative marketing plan furthers the goal of integration while providing equal opportunities to all.

Essentially, the Realtors' contention is that the AMP constitutes invalid "steering" of blacks from Park Forest in that it "deterred blacks from buying on Apache Street and in Park Forest generally by directing essential information about housing availability away from blacks and towards whites, and by stigmatizing black residents and home seekers." This Court has not previously addressed the question of whether an attempt to interest white homeowners in property located in an area of predominant interest to black home buyers constitutes "steering" violative of the Fair Housing Act. However, we recently addressed the analysis applicable to an allegation of more traditional, non-benign "steering" in *Village of Bellwood v. Dwivedi*, 895 F.2d 1521, 1529–30 (7th Cir. 1990). [In that case the court held that the mental element required in steering cases is proof of disparate treatment, which "means treating a person differently because of his race; it implies consciousness of race, and a purpose to use race as a decision-making tool." Proof of discriminatory motive is critical.]

In analyzing the question of whether directing information to predominantly white audiences concerning the Apache Street homes violates the Fair Housing Act, we must recognize that these homes likely would have been primarily of interest to black home buyers. But SSHC's affirmative marketing plan in no way deters black home buyers from pursuing their interest in the Apache Street homes; it merely creates additional competition in the housing market. If the AMP resulted in realtors "refusing to show properties because of the race of the customer, or misleading the customer about the availability of properties because of his race, or cajoling or coercing the customer because of his race to buy this property or that or look in this community rather than that," *id.* at 1530, we would agree that racial steering may possibly have been involved. In the absence of concrete evidence of this nature, however, we see nothing wrong with SSHC attempting to attract white persons to housing opportunities they might not ordinarily know about and thus choose to pursue.

The district court explicitly found that:

> The SSHC's stated purpose in entering into and implementing the Apache Street listings was to add some "white traffic to the properties in addition to the black traffic," not to decrease or restrict the black traffic. The relevant evidence supports a finding that that was in fact the SSHC's purpose.

South-Suburban Housing Center, 713 F. Supp. at 1085. With respect to the ultimate factual finding of whether the Realtors had proven intentional dis trial court found:

> Since counterplaintiffs offered no evidence respecting any p sought to purchase or rent homes and who were denied that r SSHC, or that the SSHC denied or made housing available to a any way restricted or limited anyone's housing choice, the cour that the counterplaintiffs have failed to prove an "intent" case Fair Housing Act.

Id. at 1088. The record contains neither cases of particular adversely affected black home buyers nor statistical evidence that would lead us to conclude that the trial court's finding of an absence of intentional discrimination was clearly erroneous.

In addition to furthering the Fair Housing Act's goal of integration, we are of the opinion that the AMP also advances the purpose of the Act through making housing equally available to all by stimulating interest among a broader range of buyers. Furthermore, this marketing may simply be a wise business move in that it stimulates interest in housing among new and/or potential customers. We disagree with the Realtors' argument that increased competition among black and white home buyers for the same homes constitutes a violation of the Fair Housing Act. Instead, this is precisely the type of robust multi-racial market activity which the Fair Housing Act intends to stimulate. Because the Apache Street affirmative marketing plan merely provided additional information to white home buyers concerning properties they might not ordinarily know about nor consider, and involved no lessening of efforts to attract black home buyers to these same properties, we conclude that the plan was not in violation of 42 U.S.C. § 3604(a).

NOTES AND QUESTIONS

1. *Integrating the Housing Market and Steering.* Integration in the housing market requires affirmative action as well as action against specific acts of discrimination. Yet, as the *South-Suburban* case shows, the line between affirmative action which does not violate the housing act and affirmative action that does is difficult to draw.

One question in the *South-Suburban* case was whether the affirmative marketing plan constituted steering. This plan was an example of benign steering rather than non-benign steering. Although not explicitly covered by the Fair Housing Act, the courts have held that non-benign steering violates the Act as a refusal to make housing available in a nondiscriminatory manner. Non-benign steering is usually defined as a practice through which real estate brokers direct potential buyers away from homes or neighborhoods because their race or other protected status, such as religion. In the typical case, black homebuyers are steered away from all-white neighborhoods. Steering is a discriminatory practice that has not declined. A report by the National Fair Housing Alliance found that steering occurred 87% of the time in transactions studied for the report. 2008 Fair Housing Trends Report, at 29, *available at* www.nationalfairhousing.org. One disturbing trend is the use of school quality as a proxy for steering. *See* Zimmerman, *Opening the Door to Race-Based Real Estate Marketing:* South-Suburban Housing Center v. Greater South Suburban Board of Realtors, 41 DePaul L. Rev. 1271 (1992).

2. *The Steering Dilemma.* Proof of non-benign steering presents a dilemma. The difficulty is to distinguish between non-benign steering and consumer preference, as illustrated by the *Bellwood* case discussed in the principal opinion, an influential steering case. Testing evidence in that case showed that a realty company generally sent black homeseekers to integrated areas and white homeseekers to majority white areas. The court held that agents could steer on the basis of race in response to consumer preference, even though no evidence showed the testers requested housing based on race. The court noted that the plaintiffs could not provide an explanation for the discrimination, there were real customers of the real estate company who testified they were not steered, and black suburban migration would be harmed if agents were deterred from providing housing in integrated communities. Evidence of disparate impact was not acceptable because real estate agents, unlike government, cannot control the racial composition of communities.

The court then held that plaintiffs can make a disparate treatment claim in steering cases. "They can therefore use evidence that blacks were shown primarily houses in black areas and whites primarily houses in white areas to place on the defendants the burden of giving a noninvidious reason for the difference in treatment." *Id.* at 1531. There has been little development of the case law since *Bellwood*. Letters from the U.S. Department of Housing and Urban Development subsequent to the case agreed that meeting consumer housing preferences based on race is acceptable.

The judicial response to ambiguous situations is difficult. A preference for areas with good schools and low crime or even diversity could allow an agent to guide buyers to neighborhoods where segregated patterns are perpetuated. *See* Note, *The Forty-Year "First Step": The Fair Housing Act as an Incomplete Tool for Suburban Integration,"* 107 Colum. L. Rev. 1617, 1642 (2007).

3. *Quotas.* The affirmative marketing program upheld in *South-Suburban* carried an implicit quota, because the assumption behind the program was that an "ideal" integrated neighborhood should have an appropriate mixture of whites and minorities. However, the quota level was not specified, unlike in *Starrett City*, where the court struck down an explicit quota as a violation of the Fair Housing Act. Are you satisfied with the way in which *South-Suburban* distinguished these two cases? Do you believe that quotas are valid or a violation of the Act?

In *Starrett City*, the court had this to say about the validity of quotas:

> Starrett's allocation of public housing facilities on the basis of racial quotas, by denying an applicant access to a unit otherwise available solely because of race, produces a "discriminatory effect . . . [that] could hardly be clearer," *Burney v. Housing Auth.*, 551 F. Supp. 746, 770 (W.D. Pa. 1982).

Id. at 1100. Why wasn't this true in *South-Suburban*? Why didn't that court also apply an effects test?

Racial quotas have a stormy and uneven history in the courts, and the law is too complex to summarize here and is still developing. It is worth noting that the court in *Starrett* analogized to cases on race-conscious quotas in employment, but held they did not apply because there was no prior history of discrimination in the *Starrett City* complex, as required by these cases. Rather, it was initiated as an integrated project. Is this a proper distinction? Daye, *Whither Fair Housing: Meditations on Wrong Paradigms, Ambivalent Answers and a Legislative Proposal*, 3 WASH. U. J.L. & POL'Y 241 (2000), discusses the quota problem and ambiguities in national policy on how integration in housing should be accomplished.

4. *Blockbusting.* Blockbusting is a practice in which real estate agents attempt to scare homeowners in white neighborhoods into selling to other groups, particularly to African-Americans. The Fair Housing Act's section on blockbusting states it is unlawful

> For profit, to induce or attempt to induce any person to sell or rent any dwelling by representations regarding the entry or prospective entry into the neighborhood of a person or persons of a particular race, color, religion, sex, handicap, familial status, or national origin.

42 U.S.C. § 3604(e).

Some states have outlawed blockbusting. *See, e.g.*, Ohio Rev. Code Ann. § 4112.02(H)(10); Cal. Gov't Code § 12955(h).

In the typical blockbusting situation, a real estate agent will attempt to obtain listings from residents in a neighborhood by convincing them that the area is "tipping" or turning into a minority neighborhood. This type of scare tactic may lead homeowners to list their property when they previously had no intention of doing so. It may lead eventually to sales to blacks or other minority group members at depressed prices as the scare of turnover spreads. The neighborhood then tips and changes to a minority-occupied neighborhood.

One court provided a commonly-accepted definition of the offense:

> Section 3604(e), therefore, is aimed at both overt "blockbusting" and other uninvited solicitations in racially transitional neighborhoods where it can be established (1) that the solicitations are made for profit, (2) that the solicitations are intended to induce the sale of a dwelling, and (3) that the solicitations would convey to a reasonable man, under the circumstances, the idea that members of a particular race are, or may be, entering the neighborhood.

Zuch v. Hussey, 394 F. Supp. 1028, 1049 (E.D. Mich. 1975). *Compare Heights Community Congress v. Hilltop Realty*, 774 F.2d 135 (6th Cir. 1986) (no violation when neighborhood transitional but not in grip of panic).

Blockbusting no longer seems to be serious problem. *New York State Ass'n of Realtors, Inc. v. Shaffer*, 27 F.3d 834 (2d Cir. 1994), struck down an anti-blockbusting regulation because it violated the Free Speech Clause. The court noted the state had not produced "any direct evidence of systematic blockbusting in the last 10 years." For an argument that the harms of blockbusting were overstated, that they hampered neighborhood integration, and that laws against blockbusting were racist-motivated, see Mehlhorn, *A Requiem for Blockbusting: Law, Economics, and Race-Based Real Estate Speculation*, 67 FORDHAM L. REV. 1145 (1998). What is it about blockbusting that might support the racist charge?

5. *Housing Segregation Today*. Black/white segregation has declined steadily, though it remains high in many metropolitan areas. U.S. Dep't of Housing & Urban Development, HOUSING DISCRIMINATION AGAINST RACIAL AND ETHNIC MINORITIES 2012, at 12. *See* J. Logan & B. Stults, THE PERSISTENCE OF SEGREGATION IN THE METROPOLIS: NEW FINDINGS FROM THE 2010 CENSUS 1–2 (2011).The most blatant forms of discrimination have declined, but the HUD study reported that more subtle forms of discrimination still exist. For example, "minority homeseekers are told about and shown fewer homes and apartments than whites." *Id.* at 1.

For discussion of new strategies, see Dillman, *New Strategies for Old Problems: The Fair Housing Act at 40*, 57 CLEV. ST. L. REV. 197 (2009) (suggesting more activism by housing activists). King, *Affirmatively Further: Reviving the Fair Housing Act's Integrationist Purpose*, 88 N.Y.U. L. REV. 2182 (2013) (discussing "affirmatively further fair housing" provision); Powell, *Reflections on the Past, Looking to the Future: The Fair Housing Act at 40*, 41 IND. L. REV. 605 (2008) (attack segregation in the suburbs, ensure integration in the federal low income housing tax program, and attack predatory lending). On the increase in suburban segregation see Fischer, *Shifting Geographies: Examining the Role of Suburbanization in Blacks' Declining Segregation*, 43 URBAN AFF. REV. 475, 490–91 (2008).

[3.] Group Homes

Congress amended the Fair Housing Act in 1988 to apply to discrimination against the handicapped. The amendments cover state and local restrictions, such as zoning, that limit or restrict the operation of group homes for the handicapped. The following case considers the validity of such a restriction under the Act:

LARKIN v. STATE OF MICHIGAN DEPARTMENT OF SOCIAL SERVICES

United States Court of Appeals, Sixth Circuit
89 F.3d 285 (1996)

ALDRICH, DISTRICT JUDGE. [Sitting by designation]

Defendant-Appellant State of Michigan Department of Social Services appeals from an order of the district court granting summary judgment in favor of plaintiff-appellee Geraldine Larkin and intervenor-appellee Michigan Protection and Advocacy Services. The district court held that the spacing and notice requirements of the Michigan Adult Foster Care Licensing Act are preempted by the federal Fair Housing Act and violate the equal protection clause of the fourteenth amendment to the United States Constitution. Because we agree that the Fair Housing Act preempts the spacing and notice requirements of the Michigan Adult Foster Care Licensing Act, we affirm without reaching the equal protection issue.

I.

Geraldine Larkin sought a license to operate an adult foster care (AFC) facility which would provide care for up to four handicapped adults in Westland, Michigan. The Michigan Adult Foster Care Licensing Act (MAFCLA), M.C.L. §§ 400.701 *et seq.*, governs the issuance of such licenses. It prevents the issuance of a temporary license if the proposed AFC facility would "substantially contribute to an excessive concentration" of community residential facilities within a municipality. M.C.L. § 400.716(1). Moreover, it requires compliance with section 3b of the state's zoning enabling act, codified as M.C.L. § 125.583b. M.C.L. § 400.716(3). Section 3b of the zoning act provides in part:

> At least 45 days before licensing a residential facility [which provides resident services or care for six or fewer persons under 24-hour supervision], the state licensing agency shall notify the council . . . or the designated agency of the city or village where the proposed facility is to be located to review the number of existing or proposed similar state licensed residential facilities whose property lines are within a 1,500-foot radius of the property lines of the proposed facility. The council of a city or village or an agency of the city or village to which the authority is delegated, when a proposed facility is to be located within the city or village, shall give appropriate notification . . . to those residents whose property lines are within a 1,500-foot radius of the property lines of the proposed facility. A state licensing agency shall not license a proposed residential facility if another state licensed residential facility exists within the 1,500-foot radius of the proposed location, unless permitted by local zoning ordinances or if the issuance of the license would substantially contribute to an excessive concentration of state licensed residential facilities within the city or village.

M.C.L. § 125.583b(4). MAFCLA also requires notice to the municipality in which the proposed AFC facility will be located. M.C.L. § 400.732(1).

Michigan Department of Social Services (MDSS) notified Westland of Larkin's application in accordance with MAFCLA. Westland determined that there was an existing AFC facility within 1,500 feet of the proposed facility and so notified MDSS. It also notified MDSS that it was not waiving the spacing requirement, so that MDSS could not issue a license to Larkin. When MDSS informed Larkin of Westland's action, Larkin withdrew her application.

Larkin filed suit in the United States District Court for the Eastern District of Michigan, alleging that Michigan's statutory scheme violates the Fair Housing Act (FHA) as amended by the Fair Housing Amendments Act (FHAA). Larkin also alleged that MAFCLA violates the equal protection clause of the fourteenth amendment to the constitution. In addition, Larkin named Westland as a defendant, alleging that it had violated the FHAA by not waiving the 1500-foot requirement. Michigan Protective and Advocacy Services (MPAS) moved to intervene as of right on the ground that it had a federal mandate to protect the rights of the handicapped. The district court granted that motion.[5]

The parties agreed that there were no disputed issues of material fact and filed cross-motions for summary judgment. After oral argument, the district court ruled that the 1500-foot spacing requirement and the notice requirements of M.C.L. § 125.583b(4), as incorporated into MAFCLA by M.C.L. § 400.716(3), were preempted by the FHAA because they were in conflict with it. The court also ruled that these statutes violated the equal protection clause of the fourteenth amendment. Accordingly, the court enjoined the defendants from enforcing §§ 125.583b(4) & 400.716(3).[6] MDSS appeals this decision.

[The court also held that Westland did not violate the FHAA because it lacked the authority to waive the 1500-foot requirement under Michigan law. Plaintiffs did not appeal this ruling. The court also clarified its ruling to hold that M.C.L. § 400.732(1), which requires MDSS to notify the municipality of the proposed facility, also violated the FHAA and the equal protection clause, and enjoined its enforcement. The defendants also appealed this order. As the appeal was from a summary judgment, and as there were no disputes about material facts, the only question was whether plaintiffs were entitled to judgment based on the agreed upon facts.]

III.

Congress passed the Federal Fair Housing Act (FHA) as Title VIII of the Civil Rights Act of 1968 to prohibit housing discrimination on the basis of, inter alia, race, gender, and national origin. In 1988, Congress passed the Fair Housing Amendments Act (FHAA), which expanded the coverage of the FHA to include people with disabilities. The FHA, as amended by the FHAA, makes it unlawful to:

> discriminate in the sale or rental, *or to otherwise make unavailable or deny*, a dwelling to any buyer or renter because of a handicap of —
>
> . . .
>
> (B) a person residing in or intending to reside in that dwelling after it is so sold, rented, or made available.

42 U.S.C. § 3604(f)(1) (emphasis added). It is well-settled that the FHAA applies to the regulation of group homes. Moreover, Congress explicitly intended for the FHAA to apply to zoning ordinances and other laws which would restrict the placement of group homes. *See* H. Rep. No. 711, 100th Cong., 2d Sess. 24, reprinted in 1988 U.S.C.C.A.N. 2173, 2185.

A. Preemption

[The court held the FHAA preempts state laws with which it conflicts.]

---

[5] [1] For ease of reference, Larkin and MPAS will be referred to collectively as "plaintiffs."

[6] [2] Although the district court referred to the excessive concentration provisions in M.C.L. §§ 125.583b(4) & 400.716(1), it did not hold that they violated the FHAA or the equal protection clause, and it did not enjoin the enforcement of M.C.L. § 400.716(1).

B. Discrimination

This brings us to the crux of the case: whether the statutes at issue discriminate against the disabled in violation of the FHAA. The district court held that two different aspects of MAFCLA violate the FHAA: (1) the 1500-foot spacing requirement of M.C.L. § 125.583b(4); and (2) the notice requirements of M.C.L. §§ 125.583b(4) & 400.732(1).

[The court noted that courts apply either a discriminatory treatment or discriminatory impact test to violations of the Fair Housing Act.] Some courts have identified a third type of case where a challenged practice discriminates against the handicapped on its face. However, facially discriminatory actions are just a type of intentional discrimination or disparate treatment, and should be treated as such.

Here, the challenged portions of MAFCLA are facially discriminatory. The spacing requirement prohibits MDSS from licensing any new AFC facility if it is within 1500 feet of an existing AFC facility. M.C.L. § 125.583b(4). The notice requirements require MDSS to notify the municipality of the proposed facility, and the local authorities to then notify all residents within 1500 feet of the proposed facility. M.C.L. §§ 125.583b(4) & 400.732(1). By their very terms, these statutes apply only to AFC facilities which will house the disabled, and not to other living arrangements. As we have previously noted, statutes that single out for regulation group homes for the handicapped are facially discriminatory.

MDSS argues that the statutes at issue cannot have a discriminatory intent because they are motivated by a benign desire to help the disabled. This is incorrect as a matter of law. The Supreme Court has held in the employment context that "the absence of a malevolent motive does not convert a facially discriminatory policy into a neutral policy with a discriminatory effect." [*International Union, United Auto. Aerospace & Agricultural Implement Workers v.*] *Johnson Controls*, 499 U.S. [187] at 199 [(1991)]. Following *Johnson Controls*, all of the courts which have considered this issue under the FHAA have concluded the defendant's benign motive does not prevent the statute from being discriminatory on its face. MDSS relies on *Familystyle of St. Paul, Inc. v. City of St. Paul*, 728 F. Supp. 1396 (D. Minn. 1990), *aff'd*, 923 F.2d 91 (8th Cir. 1991), for the proposition that proof of a discriminatory motive is required for a finding of discriminatory intent. However, both decisions in *Familystyle* preceded the Supreme Court's opinion in *Johnson Controls*. Thus, they have been implicitly overruled by *Johnson Controls* in this regard.

Because the statutes at issue are facially discriminatory, the burden shifts to the defendant to justify the challenged statutes. However, it is not clear how much of a burden shifts. MDSS urges us to follow the Eighth Circuit and rule that discriminatory statutes are subject to a rational basis scrutiny, i.e., they will be upheld if they are rationally related to a legitimate government objective. *See Oxford House-C v. City of St. Louis*, 77 F.3d 249, 252 (8th Cir. 1996). Plaintiffs urge us to reject the rational basis test and adopt the standard announced by the Tenth Circuit, which requires the defendant to show that the discriminatory statutes either (1) are justified by individualized safety concerns; or (2) really benefit, rather than discriminate against, the handicapped, and are not based on unsupported stereotypes. *Bangerter* [*v. Orem City Corp.*], 46 F.3d [1491] at 1503–04 [10th Cir. 1989].

Although we have never explicitly decided the issue, we have held that in order for special safety restrictions on homes for the handicapped to pass muster under the FHAA, the safety requirements must be tailored to the particular needs of the disabled who will reside in the house. *Marbrunak,* [*Inc. v. City of Stow*, 974 F.2d [43,] at 47 [(6th Cir. 1992)]. We rejected the ordinances at issue in that case because they required

> nearly every safety requirement that one might think of as desirable to protect persons handicapped by any disability — mental or physical; and all the requirements applied to all housing for developmentally disabled persons, regardless of the type of mental condition that causes their disabilities or of the ways in which the disabilities manifest themselves.

Id. Therefore, in order for facially discriminatory statutes to survive a challenge under the FHAA, the defendant must demonstrate that they are "warranted by the unique and specific needs and abilities of those handicapped persons" to whom the regulations apply. *Id.*

MDSS has not met that burden. MDSS claims that the 1500-foot spacing requirement integrates the disabled into the community and prevents "clustering" and "ghettoization." In addition, it argues that the spacing requirement also serves the goal of deinstitutionalization by preventing a cluster of AFC facilities from recreating an institutional environment in the community.

As an initial matter, integration is not a sufficient justification for maintaining permanent quotas under the FHA or the FHAA, especially where, as here, the burden of the quota falls on the disadvantaged minority. [Citing, inter alia, *Starrett City.*] The FHAA protects the right of individuals to live in the residence of their choice in the community. If the state were allowed to impose quotas on the number of minorities who could move into a neighborhood in the name of integration, this right would be vitiated.

MDSS argues that the state is not imposing a quota because it is not limiting the number of disabled who can live in a neighborhood, it is merely limiting the number of AFC facilities within that neighborhood. However, as we have previously noted, disabled individuals who wish to live in a community often have no choice but to live in an AFC facility. Alternatively, if the disabled truly have the right to live anywhere they choose, then the limitations on AFC facilities do not prevent clustering and ghettoization in any meaningful way. Thus, MDSS's own argument suggests that integration is not the true reason for the spacing requirements.

Moreover, MDSS has not shown how the special needs of the disabled warrant intervention to ensure that they are integrated. MDSS has produced no evidence that AFC facilities will cluster absent the spacing statute. In fact, this statute was not enforced from 1990 to 1993, and MDSS has offered no evidence that AFC facilities tended to cluster during that period.

Instead, MDSS simply assumes that the disabled must be integrated, and does not recognize that the disabled may choose to live near other disabled individuals. The result might be different if some municipalities were forcing the disabled to segregate, or cluster, in a few small areas. However, Michigan already prohibits such behavior:

> In order to implement the policy of this state that persons in need of community residential care shall not be excluded by zoning from the benefits of a normal residential surroundings, a state licensed residential facility providing supervision or care, or both, to 6 or less persons shall be considered a residential use of property for purposes of zoning and a permitted use in all residential zones, including those zoned for single family dwellings, *and shall not be subject to a special use or conditional use permit or procedure different from those required for other dwellings of similar density in the same zone.*

M.C.L. § 125.583b(2) (emphasis added). The only clustering or segregation that will occur, then, is as the result of the free choice of the disabled. In other words, the state's policy of forced integration is not protecting the disabled from any forced segregation; rather, the state is forcing them to integrate based on the paternalistic idea that it knows best where the disabled should choose to live.

In contrast, deinstitutionalization is a legitimate goal for the state to pursue. However, MDSS does not explain how a rule prohibiting two AFC facilities from being within 1500 feet of each other fosters deinstitutionalization in any real way. Two AFC facilities 500 feet apart would violate the statute without remotely threatening to recreate an institutional setting in the community. In fact, the spacing requirement may actually inhibit the goal of deinstitutionalization by limiting the number of AFC facilities which can be operated within any given community.

MDSS relies again on *Familystyle*, where both the district court and the Eighth Circuit found that the goal of deinstitutionalization justified facially discriminatory spacing requirements. However, *Familystyle* is distinguishable from the present case. In *Familystyle*, the plaintiff already housed 119 disabled individuals within a few city blocks. The courts were concerned that the plaintiffs were simply recreating an institutionalized setting in the community, rather than deinstitutionalizing the disabled.

Here, however, Larkin seeks only to house four disabled individuals in a home which happens to be less than 1500 feet from another AFC facility. The proposed AFC facility, and many more like it that are prohibited by the spacing requirement, do not threaten Michigan's professed goal of deinstitutionalization. Because it sweeps in the vast majority of AFC facilities which do not seek to recreate an institutional setting, the spacing requirement is too broad, and is not tailored to the specific needs of the handicapped.[7]

In summary, MDSS's justifications do not pass muster under the standard announced in *Marbrunak*. Therefore, the 1500-foot spacing requirement violates the FHAA and is preempted by it . . . . [The court also invalidated the notice provision, for which MDSS has offered the same justifications.]

By this holding, we in no way mean to intimate that the FHA, as amended by the FHAA, prohibits reasonable regulation and licensing procedures for AFC facilities.

---

[7] [4] We express no opinion on whether a more narrowly tailored law prohibiting such a concentration would pass muster under the FHAA.

As was stated in *Marbrunak*, "the FHAA does not prohibit the city from imposing *any* special safety standards for the protection of developmentally disabled persons." *Marbrunak*, 974 F.2d at 47 (emphasis in original). Rather, it merely prohibits those which are not "demonstrated to be warranted by the unique and specific needs and abilities of those handicapped persons." *Id.*

V.

For the foregoing reasons, the judgment of the district court is affirmed.

NOTES AND QUESTIONS

1. *Applying the Fair Housing Act to Zoning.* The 1988 amendments to the Fair Housing Act prohibit a number of disability-specific practices in the sale or rental of housing. These prohibitions do not explicitly include zoning, but they prohibit acts that "otherwise make unavailable or deny" a dwelling because of a handicap. Similar language appears in other parts of the Act, and the courts have applied it to prohibit discriminatory zoning.

The House Judiciary Committee Report quoted in the *Larkin* decision had the following to say about discriminatory zoning practices:

> The Committee intends that the prohibition against discrimination against those with handicaps apply to zoning decisions and practices. The Act is intended to prohibit the application of special requirements through land-use regulations, . . . and conditional or special permits that have the effect of limiting the ability of such individuals to live in the residence of their choice in the community.

Does this language have any bearing on the problem in the *Larkin* case? The Fair Housing Act thus adds a new dimension to the zoning problems discussed in Chapters 3 and 11 when the disabled are affected. Do you agree with this approach to the disability problem, or is it a one-dimensional solution to difficult issues that ignores the complexities of zoning for the disabled? It is estimated there are about one million persons with disabilities in group homes. They have gotten smaller in recent years, and may have only three or four residents. There is no accurate count on person with mental illness in group homes.

2. *Standards for Violation and Burden of Proof.* Notice that the *Larkin* decision held that the statute raised a discriminatory treatment problem. Why do you suppose the court declined to apply the discriminatory effect standard, which is easier to satisfy? The court also made it more difficult to show a justification for the state statute by rejecting the rational basis standard of judicial review. It held the state statutes must be "warranted by the unique and specific needs and abilities of those handicapped persons" to which they apply. Do you believe this ruling is justified by the policy of the Act? Why didn't the court apply this standard in the *South-Suburban* case? The courts divide on who has the burden of proof in these cases. *See Lapid Laurel, L.L.C. v. Zoning Bd. of Adjustment*, 284 F.3d 442 (3d Cir. 2002) (different for different issues).

3. *Zoning and Spacing Requirements.* Zoning ordinances can include barriers to group homes. They may not qualify as a single "family" in a single family zoning district, and occupancy limits may disqualify group homes over a certain size. There is some statutory protection. More than half of the states allow group homes as a permitted use in residential districts. Some prohibit discriminatory treatment of group homes. Most courts exempt group homes with state licenses from zoning restrictions.

Most courts also invalidate spacing requirements like those in the *Larkin* case, which impose an implicit quota on the number of group homes in a community. In a related case, one court held invalid a local law that allowed a county to object to a group home because there was no need for it, or because it would result in a concentration of group homes that substantially altered the nature and character of an area. *Human Res. Research & Mgmt Group v. County of Suffolk*, 687 F. Supp. 2d 237 (E.D.N.Y. 2010). For discussion, see Mandelker, *Housing Quotas for People with Disabilities: Legislating Exclusion*, 43 Urb. Law. 915 (2011).

Enforcement efforts by the Department of Justice to implement a Supreme Court decision on the right of persons with disabilities to integration have included settlements that require quota requirements. *See* Golik, *Is Integration for Persons with Disabilities Resulting in Contradictory Barriers to Housing?*, 16 Fla. Coastal L. Rev. 205 (2015). Spacing requirements are an implicit quota.

4. *Conditional Uses and Variances.* Many zoning ordinances require approval as a conditional use or variance for group homes. These are discretionary approvals that have the effect of allowing a use not permitted by the zoning ordinance, and municipalities can use these requirements to deny approval of a group home. *Regional Economic Community Action Program, Inc. (RECAP) v. City of Middleton*, 294 F.3d 35 (2d. Cir. 2002), illustrates how discretionary decision-making can raise questions under the Act. The city denied special use permits for a half-way house for recovering alcoholics, and the district court granted summary judgment in the city's favor. On the evidence presented, the court found that a jury could find that the city's reasons for denying the permits were pretextual, and that it was motivated wholly or in part by animus towards the class. On the disparate impact claim, however, it upheld the grant of summary judgment because the plaintiffs only challenged the denial of their own permits and made no effort to show that the facially neutral special permit requirement, which applied to a variety of uses in the zones in question, had a disproportionate impact on plaintiffs as opposed to other groups. *See also Valley Housing LP v. City of Derby*, 802 F. Supp. 2d 359 (D. Conn. 2011) (city's proffered reasons for preventing development of supportive housing for disabled was pretext for discrimination).

An even more basic objection is that a conditional use requirement for group homes violates a statutory provision that requires a "reasonable accommodation" in rules, policies and practices when such accommodations are necessary in order to afford handicapped persons an opportunity to use and enjoy a dwelling. 42 U.S.C. § 3604(f)(3)(B) (which applies only to discrimination against the handicapped).

In *United States v. Village of Palatine*, 37 F.3d 1230 (7th Cir. 1994), the government argued a conditional use requirement violated this provision because it placed an unacceptable burden on disabled persons and owners of group homes who were required to go through the conditional use review process. The court disagreed and held that any burdens that residents of a group home might suffer from going through the conditional use process did not outweigh the municipality's interest in requiring this process for all applicants for conditional use approval. Public input, it held, is an important element in municipal decision making. Not all courts agree. For an argument that the negative effects of participation in variance and conditional use proceedings require an exemption as a special accommodation, see Note, *The "Usual Incidents of Citizenship": Rethinking When People With Disabilities Must Participate in Public Variance Proceedings*, 109 COLUM. L. REV. 2044 (2009).

A NOTE ON THE CONSTITUTIONAL ALTERNATIVE

The Fair Housing Act is especially critical as a basis for challenges to discriminatory housing practices because constitutional litigation is not likely to be successful. Heightened judicial review is available under the Equal Protection Clause if a fundamental constitutional right is implicated or if a suspect class, such as race, is affected. However, *James v. Valtierra*, 402 U.S. 137 (1971), upheld a constitutional California provision that required a referendum on public housing, and eliminated arguments based on fundamental rights by holding there is no fundamental constitutional right to housing. *Village of Arlington Heights v. Metropolitan Hous. Dev. Corp.*, 429 U.S. 252 (1977), substantially limited equal protection claims against zoning that are based on race as a suspect class. A developer applied for a multi-family rezoning on a vacant tract surrounded by single-family residential development so it could build a federally-subsidized multi-family housing project. A "buffer policy" that had been in the comprehensive plan for some time, and that was applied in a reasonably consistent manner, allowed multi-family zoning only on sites placed between single-family residential and other more intensive development. The village relied on this policy to deny the rezoning, and also claimed the denial was necessary to protect the adjacent single-family area from the adverse effects of multi-family development.

The Supreme Court upheld the village's decision. It applied a case it had recently decided, *Washington v. Davis*, 426 U.S. 229 (1976), to hold that a violation of the Equal Protection Clause requires proof of a racially discriminatory intent as a motivating factor, although proof of "disproportionate impact" could be relevant as evidence of intent. The Court emphasized the village had relied on "zoning factors" that were "not novel criteria in the Village's rezoning decision," and that neighboring property owners had relied on the maintenance of single-family zoning on the developer's site.

Though *Arlington Heights* was a zoning case, its restrictive application of the Equal Protection Clause makes it clear that proof of racial discrimination in housing is difficult under the Constitution. Most of the lower federal court cases since *Arlington Heights* have not found a discriminatory intent sufficient to prove a violation of the Constitution. *See, e.g., Kawaoka v. City of Arroyo Grande*, 17 F.3d 1227 (9th Cir. 1994). *But see Dews v. Town of Sunnyvale*, 109 F. Supp. 2d 526, 570–73 (N.D. Tex. 2000), *decree modified*, 2001 U.S. Dist. LEXIS 13086 (N.D. Tex. Aug. 24, 2001), where the court used the *Arlington Heights* factors to conclude that plaintiffs had established intentional racial discrimination. *Pacific Shores Properties, LLC v. City of Newport Beach*, 730 F.3d 1142 (9th Cir. 2013), applied these factors under the Fair Housing Act to refuse dismissal of an intentional violation claim when the city adopted restrictive zoning to reduce the number of group home in the city.

Chapter 11

ZONING AS A FORM OF LAND USE CONTROL

Chapter 3 discussed the basis for exercising control over land use in the United States. This chapter continues this review by examining the elements of zoning and subdivision control, still the forms of land use control which affect most Americans. It also examines more specialized land use controls, such as aesthetically motivated regulations and historic preservation. Through zoning, land use controls came into their own in the United States. In this respect, the first quarter of the 20th Century was a critical period. New York claimed the first comprehensive zoning ordinance in 1916, though more rudimentary forms appeared in both Boston and Los Angeles at least 10 years earlier. *See* Bettman, *Constitutionality of Zoning*, 37 HARV. L. REV. 834 (1924); Garner & Callies, *Planning Law in England and Wales and in the United States*, 1 Anglo-Am. L. Rev. 292, 304–305 (1972). Like the Euclid ordinance which was modeled upon it, the New York law, called the New York Building Zone Resolution, divided New York City into use districts, area districts and height districts. It was challenged and upheld by the New York Court of Appeals in *Lincoln Trust Co. v. Williams Building Corp.*, 128 N.E. 209 (N.Y. 1920). *See* TOLL, ZONED AMERICAN, Ch. 6 (1969); D. Callies, *Village of Euclid v. Ambler Realty Co.*, Ch. 12 *in* G. Korngold & A. Morris (eds.) PROPERTY STORIES 2d Ed. (2009); M. WOLF, THE ZONING OF AMERICA (2008). The drafting of a standard zoning act and its dissemination by the United States Department of Commerce greatly facilitated the spread of the zoning movement across the United States. The "Standard State Zoning Enabling Act Under Which Municipalities May Adopt Zoning Regulations" was the product of an advisory commission appointed by Herbert Hoover, then Secretary of Commerce, and was part of the Hoover Commerce Department's efforts to disseminate information throughout the country on methods to improve agriculture, forestry, mining and fisheries. The first version "published" in 1922 was mimeographed, and revised in 1923. The first printed version followed in 1924 and quickly sold over 55,000 copies. BASSETT, ZONING, 1940, at 28–29; ROHAN, 8 ZONING AND LAND USE CONTROLS § 53.01(1), Standard State Zoning Enabling Act, Note 14 (1926). For further reading, see BABCOCK & WEAVER, CITY ZONING: THE ONCE AND FUTURE FRONTIER (1979); and MERRIAM, THE COMPLETE GUIDE TO ZONING (2004). For a summary of current, specialized zoning issues, see ZONING FROM A TO Z (Salkin, ed. 2001).

.] THE ZONE

PIERRO v. BAXENDALE

New Jersey Supreme Court
118 A.2d 401 (1955)

JACOBS, J.

In 1939 Palisades Park adopted a zoning ordinance which divided the borough into residential, business and industrial districts. District AA was generally restricted to one- and two-family dwellings and District A to one- and two-family dwellings and apartment houses. Hotels and motels were not expressly permitted in Districts AA and A although "boarding and rooming houses" (and other limited uses not pertinent here) were expressly permitted. The ordinance defined a boarding house as "any dwelling in which more than six persons not related to the owner or occupant by blood or marriage are lodged and boarded for compensation;" it defined a rooming house as "any dwelling where furnished rooms are rented to more than six persons for compensation, provided however, the lodging of relatives, by blood or marriage, of the owner or occupant of such dwelling shall not come within these terms."

The plaintiffs are the owners of land located within residential District A. On May 19, 1954 they applied to the building inspector of the borough for a permit to erect a 27-unit motel on their land but the application was denied; no administrative appeal from the denial was taken by the plaintiffs nor did they ever seek a variance under N.J.S.A. 40:55-39. On May 25, 1954 the borough adopted a supplemental zoning ordinance which expressly prohibited the construction within Palisades Park of "motels, motor courts, motor lodges, motor hotels, tourist camps, tourist courts, and structures of a similar character intended for a similar use." On May 28, 1954 the plaintiffs filed a complaint in the Law Division seeking a judgment directing the issuance of a permit to them in accordance with their application to the building inspector and setting aside the supplemental ordinance.

[T]he parties in open court entered into a short stipulation on which the judgment ultimately entered must rest. The stipulation set forth that the Borough of Palisades Park is approximately a mile square and is located about a mile and a half south(west) of the George Washington Bridge; it is a residential community composed principally of one-family homes and "is zoned percentage[-]wise as follows: 80 percent for residential purposes, 9 percent for business purposes, 3 percent for light industry, and 8 percent for heavy industry, which area lies solely west of the Northern Railroad tracks;" there are no motels in Palisades Park but there are motels in the Borough of Fort Lee (which lies immediately to the north(east) thereof) and in other nearby communities; the plaintiffs' property is located on Temple Terrace in a residential area "and on the same block, or immediately adjacent to the property, there is a two-family house with considerable shrub area immediately adjacent to it," and "on the opposite side of Temple Terrace there is a large ranch type house presently being built;" "both sides of (nearby) Sunset Place have been built up with one-family residences, many of them within the last 4 or 5 years;" and "another large ranch type home is being built on East

Edsal Boulevard near the property in question." In answer to an interrogatory submitted by the plaintiffs, the Borough of Palisades Park stated that it had issued 19 tavern licenses and 12 licenses for the sale of alcoholic beverages for off-premises consumption; apparently all of these establishments are in the business district.

After considering the arguments and briefs of counsel the trial judge expressed the view that "a motel is a rooming house" and that there is no "fair and reasonable discrimination between a motel as a rooming house and some other type of rooming house;" he therefore concluded that the supplementary ordinance was invalid and that the plaintiffs were entitled to a building permit for the erection of a motel on their property in residential District A, provided its manner of construction was in conformity with the borough's building requirements . . . .

The plaintiffs do not attack the validity of the 1939 ordinance which placed their property in a residential zone. And in the absence of an affirmative showing of unreasonableness they admittedly could not attack the right of the borough to exclude all private business operations, including boarding and rooming houses, hotels, motels and tourist camps, from the residential zones within the borough. They do, however, deny the borough's right to permit boarding and rooming houses in residential zones and at the same time exclude motels therefrom; as we view the terms of the 1939 ordinance the borough contemplated the exclusion of hotels, motels and similar businesses from the residential zones without, nevertheless, curbing the right of dwelling house owners or occupants to use their premises for boarding and rooming house purposes. If this classification by the borough has no reasonable basis then it must fall as the plaintiffs contend; if, on the other hand, it has reasonable basis then it may be permitted to stand and serve to exclude the operation of a motel in a residential zone as proposed by the plaintiffs.

[L]egislative bodies may make such classifications as they deem necessary and as long as their classifications are based upon reasonable grounds "so as not to be arbitrary or capricious" they will not be upset by the courts.

[W]e recently upheld a zoning ordinance which permitted public and parochial elementary and high schools, but prohibited colleges and other schools of higher learning, in residential areas. In the course of his opinion, Justice Burling set forth grounds for differentiating schools for the education of community children from institutions of higher learning and quoted approvingly from the *Euclid* case where Justice Sutherland pointedly remarked that "if the validity of the legislative classification for zoning purposes be fairly debatable, the legislative judgment must be allowed to control." . . .

[T]he business of selling used cars may properly be "distinguished from the selling of new cars," and holding that the classification by the borough was not "unreasonable, arbitrary or capricious," Justice Heher similarly remarked that the classification between new and used car businesses was not "vicious on its face."

See also 28 Am. Jur. 543 (1940) where the editors have the following to say under the caption "Inns and Hotels Distinguished from Boarding, Lodging and Rooming Houses":

> While there is a certain similarity between inns and hotels on the one hand, and boarding, lodging, and rooming houses on the other, the two classes of

houses differ from each other by definition in certain fundamental characteristics. The principal distinction is that in the case of houses of the latter class; the proprietor deals with his customers individually with respect to terms and accommodations and exercises the right to reject any or all applicants at his pleasure, while in the case of inns and hotels the proprietor deals with the public generally on the basis of an implied contract and may not arbitrarily refuse to receive as a guest one who is entitled to be so received, as has been pointed out in prior sections. A boardinghouse has also been said to differ from an inn or hotel both in being less public in character and in arranging with its patrons to provide for them during some more or less definite period.

Motels have some but by no means all of the aspects of hotels. It is true that motels and hotels both furnish overnight lodging to transient guests but they differ generally in their structural design and location, in the services they render and the uses to which they are put, and in the extent of control or supervision readily available to their operators. However, passing the differences between motels and hotels, it seems clear to us that motels may without difficulty be differentiated from boarding and rooming houses. Motels are business institutions which cater to members of the general public and by and large are obliged to serve them indiscriminately. As such business institutions they possess, in substantial degree, the attributes which have led to the exclusion of businesses generally from residential zones. On the other hand, boarding and rooming houses may select guests with care and are admittedly "less public in character." They are located in buildings which have the outward appearances of private dwelling houses and their commercial features and incidents are insignificant when compared to those of motels.

The officials of Palisades Park viewed boarding and rooming houses as being consistent with residential areas and motels as being inconsistent therewith; it seems clear to us that their views may not be said to be wholly without reasonable basis and that the lower court's conclusion to the contrary was erroneous. It must always be remembered that the duty of selecting particular uses which are congruous in residential zones was vested by the Legislature in the municipal officials rather than in the courts. Once the selections were made and duly embodied in the comprehensive zoning ordinance of 1939 they became presumptively valid and they are not to be nullified except upon an affirmative showing that the action taken by the municipal officials was unreasonable, arbitrary or capricious. No such showing was made in the instant matter and, consequently, the plaintiffs were not legally entitled to the building permit which they requested for the construction of a motel in a residential zone.

The judgment entered in the lower court not only directed the issuance of the building permit but also set aside the supplemental ordinance enacted on May 25, 1954. In support of this action the plaintiffs have advanced the far-reaching contention that no municipality in the State has power to exclude motels from all zoning districts within its territorial limits and that the supplemental ordinance must, therefore, be deemed void on its face. They cite cases where the courts disapproved municipal zoning ordinances which sought to exclude particular types of residences such as three-family houses and particular types of businesses such as gasoline stations. However, . . . this court sustained a zoning ordinance which excluded heavy industry from all districts in the borough, an ordinance which prohibited the construction of very small houses (containing less than 768 square feet for a one-story dwelling) anywhere in the township was sustained by this court, a zoning restriction which excluded apartment houses from substantially the entire borough, a five-acre zoning requirement and rested our holding on the primary ground that there was "ample justification for the ordinance in preserving the character of the community, maintaining the value of property therein and devoting the land throughout the township for its most appropriate use."

The environmental characteristics of many of our beautiful residential communities are such that the establishment and operation of motels therein would be highly incongruous and would seriously impair existing property values. We know of no sound reason why such communities may not, as part of their comprehensive zoning, reasonably exclude such enterprises. On the other hand, there are many communities which are so constituted and located that they could not properly advance any sound objections to motels within their borders; although such communities may not entirely exclude them, they may reasonably confine them to compatible districts. In the instant matter the parties have not given us any oral testimony with respect to the characteristics of Palisades Park and its surrounding territory, nor have they suggested that we take judicial notice thereof. They have told us in their short stipulation that the borough is mostly residential with part of its territory zoned for business and industrial purposes, but we know little or nothing about the nature of its residences or the nature of its businesses and industries or the need for additional motel facilities in the general area. The burden of the attack by the plaintiffs has not been directed against the supplemental ordinance in its particular application to the evidence before the lower court; instead their contention has consistently been that the supplemental ordinance is void on its face and should therefore be stricken without more, and that they are entitled to construct and operate their proposed motel within an area which has long been zoned for residential purposes. This contention has been rejected by us in both of its aspects. And, in any event, we do not feel free to say on the inadequate record before us and at the behest of objectors whose property is in a residential zone, that the borough's general restriction against motels is wholly invalid in the light of its own and surrounding characteristics.

Reversed.

HEHER, J. (dissenting).

By the supplement to the zoning ordinance adopted May 25, 1954, "motels, motor courts, motor lodges, motor hotels, tourist camps, tourist courts, and structures of a similar character intended for a similar use, by whatever name the same may be called, whether one or more stories in height," are forbidden within the borough.

The preamble to this local legislative act recites that the mayor and council deemed such uses "contrary to the best interests of the people of the Borough." Conceding that motels "as such are admittedly not immoral *per se*," it is said in argument that it is the "expressed conviction" of the mayor and council that "such structures offer great temptation to the conduct of immoral actions" and the design of the supplement was to "remove such temptation," and to avoid the "potential evils" attending on occasion the operation of such facilities, unfavorable publicity and police action, and "For such valid and legitimate purposes as motels may serve the traveling public, accommodations may be had in the neighboring municipalities of Fort Lee, or in other communities nearby," thus acknowledging a legitimate public need that must be denied because lax operation of such facilities gives rise to police problems of supervision, a "burden" to be borne by the neighboring communities.

But this community-wide interdiction evinces, I would suggest, a basic misconception of the philosophy of zoning and the constitutional and statutory zoning process. The supplement is *ultra vires* the local municipal corporation.

The essence of zoning, we have so often said, is territorial division according to the character of the lands and structures and their peculiar suitability for particular uses, and uniformity of use within the division. Due process demands that the exercise of the power shall not be unreasonable, arbitrary or capricious, and the means selected for the fulfillment of the policy shall bear a real and substantial relation to that end. There must be a rational relation between the regulation and the service of the common welfare in an area within the reach of the police power. Restraints upon property cannot be exorbitant or unduly discriminatory. A police regulation that goes beyond the public need is not effective to curtail the rights of person or of private property made the subject of constitutional guaranties. Arbitrary or unreasonable restraints may not be put upon the exercise of the basic right of private property.

Thus, the genius of the constitutional and statutory zoning process is the regulation of land and buildings by districts according to the nature and extent of their use; and the particular regulation is not in that category. The fields of regulation authorized in state enabling acts are usually height, area, and use of buildings, use of land, and density of population. It is fundamental that zoning is not based on the doctrine of common-law nuisance. Zoning regulations and common-law nuisances involve different legal principles.

And it is generally recognized that in the nature of the business and the accommodations furnished, there is no substantial difference between motels or bungalow courts and hotels or multiple dwellings. Zoning ordinances permitting the operation of hotels or multiple dwellings in certain areas have been held to apply with equal force to the maintenance of motels or bungalow courts.

Here, my brethren say: "[A]s we view the terms of the 1939 ordinance the Borough contemplated the exclusion of hotels, motels and similar businesses from the residential zones without, nevertheless, curbing the right of dwelling house owners or occupants to use their premises for boarding and rooming house purposes;" and "If this classification by the Borough has no reasonable basis then it must fall as the plaintiffs contend."

But in District A, as shown *supra*, "multiple family dwellings," "group houses" and "garden-type apartments" are permissible uses, and "boarding and rooming houses," as well.

It cannot be that motels are beyond effective regulation. They are now in general use throughout the country, providing in many areas reasonably priced, comfortable living facilities on a par with hotel service, in keeping with the highest standards of conduct, in many cases serving a distinct public need. The fact that there are occasional operational faults and lapses does not justify the complete suppression of the use as a public nuisance, or otherwise a peremptory requirement in the essential public interest; there is no showing here that such is the case. If and when the need arises, the police power may be exerted to supply the remedy. . . .

[H]ere we have, by the supplement to the ordinance, not a regulation, but rather a prohibition of the motel use throughout the community, in a residence zone by express provision open to multiple-family dwellings, group houses, garden-type apartments, and boarding and rooming houses, and in the business and industrial zones as well; and so, I submit, the rule of the supplement is utterly unreasonable, arbitrary and discriminatory, at odds with the constitutional and statutory zoning policy and violative of the basic standards of due process and equal protection. See Professor Haar's penetrating analysis of the principles determinative of the issue of discrimination, *In Accordance with a Comprehensive Plan*, 68 HARV. L. REV. 1154 (1955). Even motels of more than one story are banned. There is in all this no distinction of substance reasonably related to any of the constitutional and statutory considerations to be served by zoning; the classification is illusive and unreal.

I would affirm the judgment.

NOTES AND QUESTIONS

1. *Included vs. Excluded Uses*. One of the thorniest problems in the drafting of use district regulations is illustrated in the *Pierro* case: how to differentiate between included and excluded uses. In *Pierro*, the court struggles with types of guest accommodations, which may have different land use characteristics. In other contexts, courts have struggled with different types of halfway houses. *See* Merriam, *Ozzie and Harriet Don't Live Here Anymore: Time to Redefine Family*, ZONING PRACTICE 2 (Feb. 2007); Comment, *Is the Group Home "Like a Pig in the Parlor"?*, 62 NEB. L. REV. 742 (1983); Boyd, *Zoning for Retarded Citizens*, 25 VILL. L. REV. 273 (1980); Hopperton, *A State Legislative Strategy for Ending Exclusionary Zoning of Community Homes*, 19 URB. L. ANN. 47 (1980).

2. *Reliance Upon Other Jurisdictions*. The *Pierro* court cites extensively to the experiences in other jurisdictions. Among the cases cited (although omitted from the edited version above) are *State ex rel. Howard v. Village of Roseville*, 70 N.W.2d 404 (Minn. 1955) (sustaining an ordinance which prohibited trailer parks in residential zones), and *Menger v. Pass*, 80 A.2d 702 (Pa. 1951) (where the court refused on nuisance grounds to exclude a motel or tourist court from an "unrestricted" and "unzoned" residential area). In *Menger*, the trial judge found:

> The purpose of the tourist court is to rent rooms by the night to transients. There will be a parking place for approximately 25 cars. Nearly that number are likely to be there almost every night of the year. Some guests will come in the late afternoon, leave again for dinner and come back. Some will arrive in the early evening, but some undoubtedly will arrive later. The

> lights to attract them will be on until 11:30. If there are vacancies in the court, motorists will be received later. Some of those who stop are bound to leave early in the morning, some later. Car doors will bang, not only to permit passengers to leave and enter the vehicle, but also to remove the luggage, and often again for the forgotten package. Trunks too will bang. And a certain amount of loud talk during the unloading, the "don't forget" variety of calls from the cabin door to the parked car, is inevitable.

80 A.2d at 703.

In *Von Der Heide v. Zoning Bd. of Appeals*, 204 Misc. 746 (N.Y. Sup. Ct. 1953), while denying a permit to erect a motel in a business district, the court dealt extensively with the definition of a motel as compared with an inn or hotel:

> The court has come to the conclusion that the petitioner's motel is not an "inn" within the ordinary meaning of such word. True, the word "motel" is a coined and modern word derived from, and an abbreviation of the words "motorists" hotel, i.e., "motel" (WEBSTER'S NEW COLLEGIATE DICTIONARY, 1949; FUNK & WAGNALL'S NEW STANDARD DICTIONARY, 1951), and the word "inn" in present day use is synonymous with the word "hotel." But a motel is commonly understood to be an establishment essentially different from an inn or hotel in design, purpose and use. From early times, an inn or hotel was "a house of entertainment for travelers," or "a house where a traveler is furnished, as a regular matter of business, with food and lodging while on his journey." An inn or hotel more elaborately defined, may be considered as an establishment where guests, transient or otherwise, are lodged for a consideration and where they may receive for a consideration, meals, maid or room-service, telephone or desk service and all other necessities, conveniences and facilities to completely take care of all their ordinary and proper wants, day and night, for a stay of one day, several days or a long period. On the other hand, a motel, as one generally understands the term, and as typified by the building sought to be erected by this petitioner, merely furnishes the transient guest with sleeping quarters and bath and toilet facilities, with linen service and a place to park his car.

123 N.Y.S.2d at 729. How persuasive do you find these distinctions today?

3. *Appearance and Aesthetic Concerns*. Note the emphasis of the *Pierro* majority on the welfare clause, neighborhood appearance and aesthetic concerns, as well as the almost cavalier treatment of the potentially exclusionary and discriminatory effects of their decision. Contrast this with the dissent's seemingly sensible suggestion that if there is behavior in motels that is offensive, there are less onerous means of dealing with them than exclusion.

Both federal and state courts dealt extensively with these issues beginning in the 1960s. In *Village of Belle Terre v. Boraas*, 416 U.S. 1 (1974), the United States Supreme Court upheld a municipal ordinance which restricted land use in the less than one square-mile sized community to one-family dwellings and excluded lodging houses, boarding houses, fraternity houses, and other forms of multiple-dweller houses. The effect of *Belle Terre* has been to make exclusion an easy, and usually preferred, way of dealing with less popular uses. Fifteen states have followed *Belle*

Terre, but some have rejected it. A leading case rejecting it is *State v. Baker*, 405 A.2d 368 (N.J. 1979).

4. *The Court's Analysis.* Note the test that the court indicates must be met before it can interfere with a decision below. Is the court correct that this is the standard established by *Village of Euclid v. Amber Realty*?

5. *Application to an Industrial Zone.* How would you expect this court to decide a challenge on behalf of a small strip of commercial development to an industrial zone which forbids residential and commercial use? See *Katobimar Realty Co. v. Webster*, 118 A.2d 824 (N.J. 1955), and its stinging dissent by Justice Brennan.

6. What about "fiscal" zoning — zoning to economically protect the viability of downtown commercial uses? *See Hernandez v. City of Hanford*, 159 P.3d 33 (Cal. 2007).

7. *Further Examples of Use Districts.* The principal case by no means exhausts the issues raised by various kinds of uses and use districts. Others include: cemeteries (*Cedar Park Cemetery v. Hayes*, 334 A.2d 386 (N.J. Super. Ct. 1975)); condominium conversions (*McHenry State Bank v. City of McHenry*, 446 N.E.2d 521 (Ill. App. Ct. 1983)); funeral homes (*Johnson v. Board of Adjustment*, 239 N.W.2d 873 (Iowa 1976)); mobile homes and house trailers (*Anderson v. Washington Dep't of Ecology*, 664 P.2d 1278 (Wash. Ct. App. 1983)); radio and TV towers (*Rode v. Village of Northbrook*, 462 N.E.2d 843 (Ill. App. Ct. 1984); *Hopengarten v. Board of Appeals of Lincoln*, 459 N.E.2d 1271 (Mass. Ct. App. 1984)). *See also City of Monterey v. Carrnshimba*, 215 Cal. App. 4th 1068 (2013) (medical marijuana dispensary was public nuisance per se under city planning ordinance).

[B.] AMENDMENTS

Amending the zoning ordinance is the most extreme method for a landowner to obtain permission for a presently non-permitted land use. In theory at least, a zoning amendment follows a legislative determination that the amendment reflects the general welfare of the community. However, not every amendment reflects an actual public purpose. What is the public purpose served by the amendments in the following case? Note the concern of the courts (and the local legislative body) with the nature of the proposed development on "rezoned" land. If the amendment is a general legislative act, entitling the property so zoned to a range of uses "of right" in the new zone, is the specific use proposed by the landowner any of their business?

BARTRAM v. ZONING COMMISSION OF CITY OF BRIDGEPORT

Connecticut Supreme Court of Errors
68 A.2d 308 (1949)

MALTBIE, CHIEF JUSTICE.

This is an appeal by the defendants from a judgment sustaining an appeal from a decision of the zoning commission of the city of Bridgeport taken in accordance with the provisions of § 845 of the General Statutes. The commission changed the classification of a Sylvan Avenue lot, with a frontage of 125 feet and a depth of 133 feet, from a residence zone to a business No. 3 zone.

With some corrections to which the defendants are entitled, the controlling facts found by the court are these: Zoning regulations became effective in Bridgeport on June 1, 1926. They provided for three classes of residence zones, two classes of business zones, and two classes of industrial zones. In 1937 the regulations were amended to establish business zones No. 3 and special regulations were adopted as to them. These regulations, as further amended, contain provisions as to the type of construction of buildings and require open yards about them, a setback of thirty feet from the street and parking facilities for cars on private property; the sale of liquors was originally restricted but this provision was amended to forbid sales of liquor under any permit for a tavern, restaurant or all-liquor package store. The territory surrounding the lot in question is contiguous to the northern boundary of the city and quite a distance from its shopping and business center. Previous to 1936, both sides of Sylvan Avenue to a depth of 100 feet had for a considerable distance been in a business No. 1 zone, but in that year the classification was changed to residence A; and since that date, as before, a considerable territory in the neighborhood of the premises in question has been in residential zones. When zoning was originally adopted, the area was sparsely built up and contained much farm land. Beginning before 1936, people desiring to get away from the noise and congestion of the center of the city began to build homes there; at present it is quite generally built up with residences, at least 40 per cent of which have been constructed since 1936. Most of the houses in the immediate vicinity of the premises in question are comparatively new; they are neat, one-family homes, with well-kept lawns and attractive plantings; and they give every indication that a self-respecting community of people of moderate means have moved to this outlying section of the city. In the vicinity of the premises in question there exist as nonconforming uses four stores, three selling groceries or meat and one a liquor package store. One of the former is a small store in a building almost opposite the premises in question, the second floor of which is occupied as a residence. There is no drugstore in the vicinity. There is also, near the premises in question, a small church. Sylvan Avenue is a street sixty feet wide and it is a principal traffic artery to and from the section surrounding it.

The application for the change of zone was made by the defendant Rome. He presented to the commission at the hearing before it plans for a building he proposes to erect, which in all respects would comply with the regulations for a business No. 3 zone, which would contain provision for five places of business "a drug, a hardware and a grocery store, a bakeshop and a beauty parlor" and which would provide for the parking of cars in the rear of the building, and between it and the street line. Aside from Rome, no one appeared to support his application, but ten residents and property owners in the neighborhood opposed it. They gave various reasons for the position they took, among them these: They desired to have the residential character of the section preserved from business development; in many instances they had purchased or developed their properties in reliance upon the residence zoning of the area and in the expectation that this zoning status would remain unchanged; they were fearful that the business zoning of any portion of the area would be destructive of the peace and quiet they desired to have preserved; they believed that the business zoning of any part of it, however small and wherever located, would have a tendency to break down the residence zoning of the area by making further business zoning in it more likely; and there was no present need for further and more adequate shopping facilities in the neighborhood. A remonstrance against granting the application signed by more than seventy residents in the neighborhood was also filed with the commission; but only some forty-six different addresses of the signers appear on it; in a number of instances the signers were husband and wife or two or more residing in the same house; and many of them lived at a considerable distance from the premises in question. Within a radius no longer than the distance to the addresses given by some of the signers are more than 200 residences.

The commission gave the following reasons for its decision: 1. The location is on Sylvan Avenue, a sixty-foot street, and there is no shopping center within a mile of it. To the north of this tract there is a very large development but only small nonconforming grocery stores to serve the people. 2. There is practically only one house, adjacent to this tract on the north, which will be directly affected by this change of zone. 3. Business No. 3 regulations, with their thirty-foot setback and liquor restrictions, were designed to meet conditions like this and help alleviate the great congestion in the centralized shopping districts. The court also found that a member of the commission testified that it was its policy to encourage decentralization of business in order to relieve traffic congestion and that, as part of that policy, it was considered desirable to permit neighborhood stores in outlying districts; and nowhere in the record is there any suggestion that this testimony is not true.

The trial court concluded that the change was an instance of "spot zoning." A limitation upon the powers of zoning authorities which has been in effect ever since zoning statutes were made applicable generally to municipalities in the state is that the regulations they adopt must be made "in accordance with a comprehensive plan." Public Acts, 1925, c. 242, § 3, Rev. 1949, § 837. "A 'comprehensive plan' means 'a general plan to control and direct the use and development of property in a municipality or a large part of it by dividing it into districts according to the present and potential use of the properties.' " Action by a zoning authority which gives to a single lot or a small area privileges which are not extended to other land in the vicinity is in general against sound public policy and obnoxious to the law. It can be justified only when it is done in furtherance of a general plan properly adopted for and designed to serve the best interests of the community as a whole.

The vice of spot zoning lies in the fact that it singles out for special treatment a lot or a small area in a way that does not further such a plan. Where, however, in pursuance of it, a zoning commission takes such action, its decision can be assailed only on the ground that it abused the discretion vested in it by law. To permit business in a small area within a residence zone may fall within the scope of such a plan, and to do so, unless it amounts to unreasonable or arbitrary action, is not unlawful. The zoning regulations of Bridgeport were adopted under the provisions of the General Statutes which gave the commission power to divide the municipality into districts and in each district to regulate the construction and use of buildings and land, and to change the regulations from time to time. The commission might be guilty of spot zoning either in the original regulations it made or in later amendments, but, if in one or the other it decides, on facts affording a sufficient basis and in the exercise of a proper discretion, that it would serve the best interests of the community as a whole to permit a use of a single lot or small area in a different way than was allowed in surrounding territory, it would not be guilty of spot zoning in any sense obnoxious to the law. That was the situation in this case, and we cannot sustain the conclusion of the trial court that the action of the commission was improper as an instance of spot zoning.

The trial court also concluded that the change in zoning was in violation of the declared objects of the zoning regulations of Bridgeport, as stated in their first section. That section states among the purposes to be served by them the promotion of the health, safety, morals and general welfare of the community and the lessening of congestion in streets. The reasons which led the commission to take the action it did, as we have stated them above, fall well within the scope of these purposes. The fact that the change was advocated only by Rome at the hearing and was opposed by numerous property owners and residents in the neighborhood did not, as the trial court concluded, deprive the commission of power to make it. It does not appear that there was anything like unanimous opposition to the change by property owners in the surrounding territory; but, even if there had been, it was the duty of the commission to look beyond the effect of the change upon them to the general welfare of the city. The reasons given before the commission by those who opposed the change were quite largely based on fear that other like changes might be made rather than upon the effect of the particular one in question. The property of no one was taken by the commission's decision; nor is there any finding or, indeed, evidence that property values would be affected . . . . Property owners in the neighborhood had no right to a continuation of the existing situation which could be effective against a decision by the commission reached legally and properly. The state, through the authority it vests in zoning authorities, "may regulate any business or the use of any property in the interest of the public health, safety, or welfare, provided this be done reasonably. To that extent the public interest is supreme and the private interest must yield." The commission could not properly be held, upon the record in this case, to have acted in violation of law in making the change it did.

How best the purposes of zoning can be accomplished in any municipality is primarily in the discretion of its zoning authority; that discretion is a broad one; and unless it transcends the limitations set by law its decisions are subject to review in the courts only to the extent of determining whether or not it has acted in abuse of that discretion. A court is without authority to substitute its own judgment for that vested by the statutes in a zoning authority. In view of the facts present in this case, the trial court could not properly find that the policy which determined the decision of the commission would so clearly fail to serve the proper purposes of zoning in the city that the court might set aside that decision; nor do the facts show that it was unreasonable to apply that policy in the situation before us. This is illustrated by the fact that, had this lot been placed in a business No. 3 zone as an incident to the adoption of an original plan for zoning the city as a whole, that action could not on this record be held an unreasonable exercise by the commission of its powers.

There is error, the judgment is set aside and the case is remanded with direction to enter judgment dismissing the appeal.

DICKENSON, JUDGE (dissenting).

This, as the trial court held, seems to be a clear instance of spot zoning. The trial court has found no comprehensive plan to permit single lots or small areas to be used for business purposes in residential zones. The only evidence of such a plan is the testimony of a member that it was the "policy" of the commission to encourage decentralization of business in order to relieve traffic congestion and permit stores in outlying residential areas. So radical a departure from the general purpose of zoning to separate business from residential districts should not be left to the whims of a zoning board. It should come within "a comprehensive plan for zoning the town."

NOTES AND QUESTIONS

1. *Classic Map Amendment.* The *Bartram* case represents a classic map amendment situation, in which a particular piece of property is "rezoned" to another land use classification. There is, however, one distinction. Who does the rezoning for Bridgeport? Who usually rezones property from one classification to another? What role does the rezoning agency in *Bartram* usually play? *See* §§ 4–6 of the Standard Zoning Enabling Act (SZEA).

2. *New Standard?* Note the standard which the *Bartram* court imposes on the trial court. Is it consistent with the tests laid down in previous cases? What about the standard of review of the appellate court? While courts are inclined to defer to local boards, it is not unusual for them to overturn rezoning decisions when they think the city or county has gone awry. In *Greater Yellowstone Coalition, Inc. v. Board of Commissioners of Gallatin County*, 25 P.3d 168 (Mont. 2001), the commissioners rezoned a 323 acre tract from one single family home unit per 10 acres (a total of 32 homes) to a planned unit development classification that could have allowed 969 single family homes. The land was adjacent to Yellowstone National Park and the county's plan provided that the area's natural resources should be protected allowing a minimal amount of development. The trial court found the rezoning to be invalid spot zoning, and the state supreme court upheld that finding. *Greater Yellowstone Coalition, Inc. v. Board of County Commissioners of Gallatin County*, 25 P.3d. 168 (Mont. 2001) has been distinguished by *North 93 Neighbors, Inc., v. Board of County Commissioners of Flathead County*, 137 P.3d. 557 (Mont. 2006). Whereas in *Greater Yellowstone*, the court held that zoning amendment was invalid spot zoning, the *North 93* court held that the zoning amendment was not spot zoning. *Greater Yellowstone* is still good law, however. *See also Board of Commissioners v. Parker*, 88 S.W.3d 916 (Tenn. Ct. App. 2002), where the court found the commission's decision not to rezone to be arbitrary where similar land had been recently been rezoned.

3. *Vested Rights.* One of the most troublesome areas of current zoning law is the question of vested rights: at what point may a landowner rely on an existing zone classification or zoning code to commence or proceed with a development which later changes render illegal? As we will see, the basis for such vested rights is

usually found in the law pertaining to nonconformities. Who is claiming vested rights here? To what? What are the merits of this claim? *See* Kupchak et. al., *Arrow of Time: Vested Rights, Zoning Estoppel and Development Agreements in Hawai'i*, 27 HAWAII L. REV. 17 (2004).

4. *Evidentiary Testimony*. Note the plans presented by Rome for his proposed development. Reread the introductory paragraph to Section A, subsection 2. Note also the relative weight and interpretation given to the testimony and evidence presented to the rezoning agency. Where was it presented? How? In what manner did the rezoning agency decide the application? Did they give any reasons? Did they have to? Why?

If Rome were to open otherwise allowable business uses that did not serve community as well as those he described to the commission, could the city enjoin him? See *Cherokee County v. Martin*, 559 S.E.2d 138 (Ga. Ct. App. 2002), where the county authorized a planned unit development on the understanding that it would contain assisted living facilities for the elderly. After the county rezoned the land to multi-family uses, the developer found there was no market for assisted living facilities but that there was a market for apartments. Unhappy with this turn of events, the county sought to enjoin the developer. Since both uses were multi-family uses, the court refused. How might the county have prevented this from happening?

5. *Timing of Placement on the Official Zoning Map*. Not all land use districts found in the text of a zoning ordinance are initially drawn on the official zoning map. Some are purposely held back to "float" until an "appropriate" development for which such zoning was formulated comes along. Thereafter, once "mapped," the zone no longer floats. The method of creating it probably does not thereafter materially differ from any other rezoning or map amendment; however, when first "mapped," it is obviously not placed contiguous to any other like-zoned parcel. Then, particularly if the parcel is small and the abutting districts significantly inconsistent, the ancient cry of "spot zoning" is raised. (*See* Note 6, below).

The rationale for the coming to rest of the floating zone is often critical. If the use thus permitted is articulated in the comprehensive plan in a fashion which justifies its placement in that vicinity on the zoning map, so much the better. A Maryland Court so held in *Floyd v. County Council*, 461 A.2d 76 (Md. 1983). The same is often true for a newly discovered community need, such as for low- or moderate-income housing. *See, e.g., Lee v. District of Columbia, Zoning Comm'n*, 411 A.2d 635 (D.C. 1980); *see also* Reno, *Non-Euclidean Zoning: The Law of the Floating Zone*, 23 MD. L. REV. 105 (1963).

6. *Spot Zoning*. The principal charge of the neighbors appears to be that the reclassification will amount to spot zoning. If one were to sketch the zones alone and superimpose the proposed scheme upon them, wouldn't it look like an isolated "spot"? Why does the court hold that it is not? Note the dissent's radically different characterization of the Commission's decision. Given the court's characterization of the area affected, what factors should determine what uses are or are not appropriate, or at least worth considering in deciding the appropriateness of a map amendment? See *Plains Grains Limited Partnership v. Board of County Commissioners of Cascade County*, 238 P.3d 332 (Mont. 2010), for a discussion of zoning amendments that may amount to spot zoning.

7. Assume a community decides that it wants to encourage light industrial development or multi-family housing. Rather than rezone land for those uses, the legislative body may create a light industrial zone or a multi-family zone. It will then await application by a landowner to have a particular parcel rezoned to that unmapped, or floating, classification. It is thus a two-step process, with the second step constituting the actual rezoning. The neighbors who then wind up with the industrial use or multi-family project next door may not be too happy with where the floating zone landed. For some courts such an approach is "the antithesis of zoning . . . [since actual land use] await[s] solicitation by individual landowners." *Eves v. Zoning Bd. of Adjustment of Lower Gwynedd Twp.*, 164 A.2d 7, 11 (Pa. 1960) (invalidating rezoning of a 103-acre tract from single family to light industrial for a sewage treatment plant). For others the approach is "the first step in a reasoned plan of rezoning, . . . [which ought not be condemned] merely because the board employed two steps to accomplish what may be, and usually is, done in one." *Rodgers v. Village of Tarrytown*, 96 N.E.2d 731, 735–36 (N.Y. 1951) (upholding the rezoning of a 10 acre tract from single family to multi-family housing for garden apartments). *Eves v. Zoning Bd. of Adjustment of Lower Gwynedd Twp.*, 164 A.2d 7 (Pa. 1960) has been declined to extend by *Newtown Square East, L.P. v. Township of Newtown*, 101 A.3d 37 (Pa. 2014); *Rodgers v. Village of Tarrytown*, 96 N.E.2d 731 (N.Y. 1951) has been distinguished by *Carnat Realty, Inc. v. Town of Islip*, 34 A.D.2d 780 (N.Y. App. Div. 1970).

Why would a legislative body employ such a scheme? Is the use of a floating zone scheme an abdication of the legislative responsibility to zone, as charged in the *Eves* case? Does it invite rezoning petitions? Is that wise? Could Bridgeport have used a floating zone scheme to accommodate its decentralization policy?

[C.] SPECIAL OR CONDITIONAL USES

In many local (and some state) land use schemes, it is possible to obtain a change of use without obtaining an amendment by means of a special or conditional use permit, or special exception. According to some courts and authorities, this avoids the problem of spot zoning, though if indeed the problem is the use proposed (and it usually is), this seems to exalt form over substance. Nevertheless, permitting a use which is not listed under the permitted use category of the subject property's zoning does provide the local authority with more flexibility, at least in theory, than it has when faced with a simple map or text amendment request. Why?

Consider, first, what kinds of special requirements or conditions ought to be placed upon the special permit requests made in the following case and notes that follow so that they "fit into" the districts in which they are proposed; second, how the text of a zoning ordinance could be amended so that such uses could be permitted "of right"; and third, how one would go about amending the text of a zoning ordinance to deal with a use not permitted by name in the district in which a client owns property he or she wishes to so use. *See* FREILICH & QUINN, THE EFFECTIVENESS OF FLEXIBLE AND CONDITIONAL ZONING TECHNIQUES — WHAT THEY CAN AND CANNOT DO FOR CITIES, INST. ON PLANNING, ZONING AND EMINENT DOMAIN 167 (1979); Shapiro, *The Case for Conditional Zoning*, 41 TEMP. L. REV. 267 (1968).

GORHAM v. TOWN OF CAPE ELIZABETH

Maine Supreme Judicial Court
625 A.2d 898 (1993)

CLIFFORD, JUSTICE.

Coleman Gorham owns a single family residence on Bowery Beach Road in Cape Elizabeth. The property is in a Residence — A zoning district. R-A zone permitted uses include single family dwellings, agricultural uses, and schools. Multi-unit dwellings are permitted as a conditional use upon a showing of compliance with conditions set out in the Cape Elizabeth zoning ordinance. In August 1989, Gorham filed with the Cape Elizabeth Zoning Board of Appeals an application for a conditional use permit in order to convert his single family home to a multi-unit dwelling. Gorham sought approval for an apartment within his home; there were to be no changes to the exterior of the building or to the parking facilities. The Board held three public hearings, and considered several letters, three reports from real estate appraisers and the oral comments of a number of residents before it unanimously denied Gorham's application. The Board, in denying the application, determined that the use of Gorham's home as a multi-family unit would "adversely affect the value of adjacent properties" under Section 19-4-7(b)(4) of the zoning ordinance.

Gorham brought a three-count complaint in the Superior Court (Cumberland County) naming as defendants the Town of Cape Elizabeth and its code enforcement officer. In Count I, Gorham alleges that decision was not supported by substantial evidence in the record and was arbitrary and unreasonable. In Count II, Gorham seeks a declaratory judgment that Section 19-4-7(b) of the zoning ordinance is unconstitutional because it bears no substantial relationship to the public health, safety, and general welfare, and it impermissibly delegates legislative authority to the Board. In Count III, Gorham alleges, *inter alia*, that his constitutional right to due process was violated because of the Board's bias and predisposition against multi-family dwellings. The Superior Court rejected Gorham's appeal, entering a judgment for the Town on Count I (*Brennan, J.*), and granting a summary judgment to the Town on Counts II and III (*Lipez, J.*). Gorham then appealed to this court. We find no error and affirm the judgment.

CONSTITUTIONAL CHALLENGES

A. Substantial Relationship to Health, Safety, and General Welfare and Delegation of Legislative Power

Under Section 19-4-7(b) of the Cape Elizabeth zoning ordinance, one of the criteria that has to be satisfied before a conditional use application is approved is that "[t]he proposed use will not adversely affect the value of adjacent properties." Gorham, under the due process clause, challenges the constitutionality of the ordinance's "adverse affect" criterion in two respects. First, he contends that the criterion does not bear a substantial relationship to the public health, safety, or welfare. *See Warren v. Municipal Officers of Town of Gorham*, 431 A.2d 624, 627

(Me. 1981). Gorham also contends that Section 19-4-7(b)(4) constitutes an improper delegation of legislative authority. We are unpersuaded by either contention.

The constitutionality of a zoning ordinance is presumed. Gorham, in attacking the ordinance, has the burden of proof of demonstrating its unconstitutionality. *Warren*, 431 A.2d at 627–28. Contrary to Gorham's first contention, the maintenance of property values is a legitimate interest served by zoning restrictions. *Id. at 628; Barnard v. Zoning Bd. of Appeals of Town of Yarmouth*, 313 A.2d 741, 745 (Me. 1974). Therefore, the Cape Elizabeth zoning ordinance meets the due process requirement that it bear a reasonable relationship to the public health, safety, morals, or general welfare. *Warren*, 431 A.2d at 627.

Gorham also contends that the "adverse affect" criterion set out in Section 19-4-7(b)(4) constitutes a constitutionally impermissible delegation to the Board of discretionary authority not sufficiently limited by legislative standards, *see Stucki v. Plavin*, 291 A.2d 508, 510 (Me. 1972), and argues that the criterion is too subjective and not measurable, leading to favoritism and discrimination. *See Wakelin v. Town of Yarmouth*, 523 A.2d 575, 577 (Me. 1987).

Because conditional uses are those uses that the legislature has determined to be ordinarily acceptable in a particular zone, in order to withstand attack as an impermissible legislative delegation of authority, ordinances that establish criteria for acceptance of a conditional use must specify sufficient reasons why such a use may be denied. *Bass v. Town of Wilton*, 512 A.2d 309, 310 (Me. 1986). A conditional use standard must be sufficiently specific "to guide both an applicant in presenting his case . . . and the Board in examining the proposed use . . . . " *Wakelin*, 523 A.2d at 577.

In this case, the Town has determined that in order for multi-family use of property to be allowed in an R-A zone, the Board must determine, among other criteria, that such use "will not adversely affect the value of adjacent properties."[1] Although we have not previously decided whether such a criterion is sufficiently

---

[1] [3] Section 19-4-7(b) of the Cape Elizabeth Zoning Ordinance provides: (b) *Conditional Use Applications*. The Board shall consider requests for the issuance of permits for any of the conditional uses of land or buildings permitted in the various districts, upon submission to the Building Inspector of an application and the materials listed in Section 19-2-9(b)(2), (A) through (F), (I) and (K). The Board shall, after review of required materials, authorize issuance of a conditional use permit, upon a showing that: [Amended 7/29/87]

1. Any conditions prescribed for such conditional use will be satisfied.
2. The proposed use will not create hazardous traffic conditions when added to existing and foreseeable traffic in its vicinity.
3. The proposed use will not create unsanitary conditions by reason of sewage disposal, emissions to the air, or other aspects of its design or operation.
4. The proposed use will not adversely affect the value of adjacent properties.
5. The proposed site plan and layout are compatible with adjacent property uses and with the Comprehensive Plan.
6. The design and external appearance of any proposed building will constitute an attractive and compatible addition to its neighborhood, although it need not have a similar design, appearance or architecture.

Upon such showing to the satisfaction of the Board, it shall authorize the issuance of permits for such conditional use, but may impose such conditions upon such use as it deems necessary in order to assure that the foregoing objectives shall be attained.

specific to survive constitutional scrutiny, *see Cope v. Town of Brunswick*, 464 A.2d 223, 225 n. 3 (Me. 1983), we conclude that Section 19-4-7(b)(4) gives sufficient guidance to a conditional use applicant, such as Gorham, as to what facts must be presented "to gain the Board's approval" and to the Board itself in examining the proposed use. *Wakelin*, 523 A.2d at 577. Gorham and the parties opposing his application presented a substantial amount of evidence directed to the precise issue addressed in Section 19-4-7(b)(4), namely, whether the proposed multi-family use of Gorham's property would adversely affect values of surrounding property.

In *Bass*, the constitutionality of the conditional use criterion "devalue adjacent property" was raised by the parties but, because the case was decided on other grounds, was not addressed by the court. We agree with the Superior Court, however, that the reasoning of Justice Scolnik in his dissent in *Bass*, urging that such a standard was sufficiently specific to be constitutional, is persuasive when applied to the instant case.

> The plain meaning of the term "devalue" is sufficient to guide the Board in its application of [that section of the zoning ordinance] to a requested conditional use permit. The term "devalue," in this zoning context, obviously means to cause the reduction or loss in the value of adjacent property. By the employment of this objective standard, the Board does not assume for itself an unfettered discretion to grant or deny the permit. As this case illustrates, evidence may be presented by expert appraisers as well as the owners of the adjacent land. Such evidence provides a sufficient basis for an evaluation of whether the proposed project would cause a reduction in the value of the adjacent properties. If so, [the section] requires that the permit be denied. In short, the standard of whether adjacent property is devalued is a sufficient guide for the Board to employ in its decision-making process, and it enables those to whom the law is to be applied reasonably to determine their rights thereunder.

Bass, 512 A.2d at 312 (*Scolnik, J.*, dissenting) (citations omitted). *See* R.M. Anderson, *American Law of Zoning* 3d § 21.14 at 689 (1986) ("[A] board of zoning appeals may deny a special permit where the record discloses that the proposed use will depreciate surrounding property").

Contrary to Gorham's contention that his application must be approved unless there is present some characteristic of his property, such as changes to the building's exterior, apart from its use as a multi-family dwelling, that adversely affects neighboring properties, the ordinance plainly states that a single family dwelling can be converted to multi-family use in an R-A zone only if such "use will not adversely affect the value of adjacent property." The wording of the ordinance does not require that the conversion be allowed *unless* the property has unique characteristics that impact property values.

Gorham also argues, relying on our decision in *Cope*, that the ordinance is based on a presumption that the conditional uses allowed will not adversely affect the value of adjacent property and that the burden should have been on those opposing Gorham's application to demonstrate such an adverse effect. We disagree. In *Cope* we concluded that whether an exceptional use under the ordinance would "generally comply with the health, safety and welfare of" the area is a legislative question that could not be delegated to the board of appeals. Although uses that are classified as exceptions or conditional uses may result from a legislative determination that such uses will not *ordinarily* be "detrimental or injurious to the neighborhood," *Cope* does not prohibit a zoning ordinance from requiring compliance with specific and measurable criteria, including the criterion that the conditional use of the property will not adversely affect the values of adjacent properties.

Although an ordinance *could* be written to allow the conditional use absent a showing that the use will adversely effect the values of adjacent properties, in effect placing on the opponents of the conditional use the burden to demonstrate that certain conditions have *not* been met, under *this* ordinance the burden to show compliance with all conditions is on the applicant. Moreover, this case did not turn on a failure to meet the burden of proof. The Board's finding was not that it was not persuaded that there was no adverse affect on property values. Rather, the Board made an affirmative finding that the use by Gorham of his home as a multi-family unit would actually adversely affect the values of adjacent property.

The Board heard the evidence and made a factual conclusion in accordance with the ordinance that Gorham's use of his property as a multi-family dwelling would adversely impact the property value of an adjacent property. Accordingly, pursuant to Section 19-4-7(b)(4) of the zoning ordinance, the Board denied his application. Because the maintenance of property values is a legitimate interest served by zoning restrictions, and because Section 19-4-7(b)(4) specifically required the Board to determine the effect of the conditional use on property values, a specific and discernible standard that the evidence addressed, Gorham's constitutional challenge must fail.

Gorham also contends that he was denied due process because of the Board's bias, prejudice, and predisposition against multi-unit dwellings. It is true that an applicant before an administrative board is entitled under the due process clause of the United States and Maine constitutions to a fair and unbiased hearing. *See Mutton Hill Estates, Inc. v. Town of Oakland*, 468 A.2d 989 (Me. 1983). In *Mutton Hill Estates* we upheld, on due process grounds, the Superior Court's setting aside of a planning board denial of an application for approval of a subdivision. In that case, the board had invited admittedly biased opponents of the subdivision to participate in an *ex parte* session when the board made its findings of fact to support a denial of the application. *Mutton Hill Estates*, 468 A.2d at 992.

In this case, to support his claim of a due process violation, Gorham relies on statements he alleges were made to him by the code enforcement officer, that the Board does not want two-family houses in Cape Elizabeth, and that "you don't stand a prayer [on your application]." In addition, Gorham relies on statements made by various members of the Board at the public hearing on his application and during the Board's deliberations. The statements of the code enforcement officer, who is not a member of the Board, do not demonstrate denial of due process to Gorham. The statements of the Board members themselves, contrary to Gorham's contention, do not reflect an unlawful bias or predisposition. Rather, the entire record indicates that Board members listened attentively, questioned witnesses, both for and against the petition, and discussed the evidence with a view toward making a sincere effort to fairly decide the issue before them.

Prior to rendering its decision denying the application, the Board held three hearings (the matter was tabled at the first two), received and considered a number of documents submitted by both Gorham and opponents to his application, including reports from appraisers on the effect of the multi-family use of Gorham's residence on the property values of adjoining properties, and heard comments from a number of residents. At the close of the hearing, the Board openly deliberated before concluding that Gorham's application should be denied. The evidence is inadequate to support Gorham's contention that he was denied due process because of bias and predisposition. * * *

SUFFICIENCY OF THE EVIDENCE

Gorham also contends that the Board's decision is not supported by substantial evidence in the record, that the findings of the Board are inadequate, and that the decision is based on the personal opinions of residents and on Board members' own personal opinions. We disagree.* * *

In this case, the Board had before it conflicting evidence as to the effect that the conversion of Gorham's single family residence to two family use would have on the adjacent properties. There was evidence, in the form of the opinions of two expert appraisal witnesses, that there would be no adverse impact. That evidence would have supported a conclusion by the Board that the multi-family use of Gorham's property would not adversely affect the property values in the area. There was contrary evidence, however, from an expert appraiser, from a real estate broker, and from owners of neighboring properties, that the conversion would have an adverse impact on the value of the adjacent properties. This constitutes substantial evidence to support the ultimate conclusion of the Board that the use of the property by Gorham as a multi-family unit would adversely affect the value of adjacent properties. See *Hrouda*, 568 A.2d at 826. To vacate the Board's decision for insufficient evidence, we would have to conclude that the Board was compelled to find that there would be no adverse impact on property values. *See Total Quality, Inc. v. Town of Scarborough*, 588 A.2d 283, 284 (Me. 1991). This we are unable to do.

Moreover, the Board's denial of Gorham's application was based on the clearly stated finding that Gorham's use of his property as a multi-family residence would adversely affect the value of adjacent properties. The finding was made after a lengthy hearing and discussion of the evidence by the Board members. No request for further findings was made. *See Pearson v. Town of Kennebunk*, 590 A.2d 535, 537 n. 1 (Me. 1991). Contrary to Gorham's contention, the findings of the Board are adequate, and are based on substantial evidence in the record. We cannot conclude that they constitute unsubstantiated opinion. * * *

ROBERTS, JUSTICE, with whom RUDMAN, J., joins, dissenting.

I respectfully dissent. For the purpose of this dissent, I accept the Court's determination that the standard set out in section 19.4.7(b)(4) of the ordinance, i.e., "will not adversely affect the value of adjacent properties," provides adequate guidance to a conditional use applicant and to the Zoning Board of Appeals. I also agree with the Court's interpretation on page 7 of the slip opinion of our decision in

Cope v. Town of Brunswick, 464 A.2d 223 (Me. 1983). On the record before us, however, I conclude that the Board's rejection of Gorham's conditional use application was arbitrary and capricious.

The Town of Cape Elizabeth has determined, through its legislative process, that multi-family dwellings are consistent with the zoning scheme, provided there is a showing that the multi-family unit will not adversely affect the value of adjacent properties. In the words of the Court's opinion, that is "a legislative determination that such [a use] will not *ordinarily* be 'detrimental or injurious to the neighborhood.' "

Gorham presented uncontested evidence that his proposal would not change the external appearance of his home and contested evidence by two appraisers that there would be no adverse affect on the value of adjacent properties. The evidence of a third appraiser and of neighbors, who predicted an adverse affect on the adjacent properties, did not explain what there was about Gorham's particular proposal that made it harmful to the value of adjacent properties. Rather, all the opponents' comments were addressed to the more general idea that multi-family units adversely affect the value of single family homes.

Because the Town of Cape Elizabeth has already made a legislative determination that multi-family units will not ordinarily affect the value of surrounding properties, it was inimical for the Board to accept evidence contrary to that determination. In fact, the Board's adoption of the theory that multi-family units devalue surrounding property effectively precludes approval of any plan proposing a multi-family unit, clearly contravening the legislative intent. We have previously said that allowing a zoning board to decide whether a particular use complies with a legislative dictate is

> improper if the Board is permitted to decide that same legislative question anew, without specific guidelines which permit the Board to determine what *unique* or *distinctive* characteristics of, a particular [proposed use] will render it detrimental or injurious to the neighborhood.

Cope, 464 A.2d at 227 (emphasis added).

The Board, therefore, could have properly rejected Gorham's proposal only in reliance on evidence that his specific proposed use, because of its particular characteristics, would adversely affect the value of adjacent properties. Without any such evidence, the Board's decision was arbitrary, capricious, and contrary to the terms of the ordinance.

NOTES AND QUESTIONS

1. *Gorham* represents a classic special use problem: how specific the standards for dealing with permit requests must be to guard against unbridled discretion while preserving flexibility. Consider the degree of discretion delegated to the board. Would it be better to tell the board to grant a permit only if it finds "that the general welfare would be promoted"?

2. Was the legislative will followed in *Gorham*? Are you satisfied with the way the majority handled the dissent's concern? Compare *Gorham* with *City of Chicago*

Heights v. Living Word Outreach Full Gospel Church and Ministries, Inc., 749 N.E.2d 916 (Ill. 2001). A church acquired a building located in a business district in which churches were listed as a special use. The church was required to satisfy the city, among other things, that its use would not be injurious to other property in the immediate vicinity nor be unreasonably detrimental to the public interest. The city denied the permit because it determined that religious use of the land would frustrate the city's plan to develop the area as a strong commercial corridor. The state supreme court reversed, finding that the city's rationale for denying the permit was the equivalent of a declaration that churches were per se incompatible uses in the district, and thus contrary to the ordinance recognizing churches as permissible special uses. The court ordered the city to issue the permit.

3. Traditionally special use permit applications are heard by an administrative board or hearing officer. In many cities, however, the legislative body retains the power to issue permits for certain uses, typically those that have community-wide impact. Some courts interpret the Standard Zoning Enabling Act (the board "may" grant special use permits) to vest the power to issue special use permits exclusively in the Board of Adjustment. *See Holland v. City Council of Decorah*, 662 N.W.2d 681 (Iowa 2003). If the legislative body issues a special permit, is its action legislative or quasi-judicial? *See* JUERGENSMEYER & ROBERTS, LAND USE PLANNING AND DEVELOPMENT REGULATION LAW § 5. 25 (2nd ed.2007). Is there a meaningful difference between a legislatively granted special permit and the mapping of a floating zone discussed in the prior section? With a special permit, the underlying zone is not changed. On the face of it, at least, the permit decision cannot be spot zoning. But, does that exalt form over substance?

4. The landowner in *Gorham* attacks the standards for obtaining a conditional use permit as "too subjective" and not sufficiently specific to guide the board. He lost on this issue. What if he had won?

5. If the landowner in *Gorham* had obtained the permit, would the neighbors have had standing to challenge the permit's issuance? *See* § 7, SZEA. What if the neighbor's property is used for rental purposes, and the newly granted permit would constitute competition? *See Nernberg v. City of Pittsburgh*, 620 A.2d 692 (Pa.Cmwlth.1993) (standing to challenge special permit for apartment use denied to apartment owner in vicinity).

6. In addition to legislative criteria, the board typically can add "appropriate conditions and safeguards" to a permit. SZEA, § 7. Assume you are a neighbor of the special use proposed in *Gorham*. What conditions would you suggest? What if the proposed use is a group home for the mentally retarded? What conditions should attach?

7. Does the multi-family use involved in *Gorham* follow the rationale for special permits set out in the headnote to this section? Why do you suppose the legislative body in Cape Elizabeth added multi-family use to its special use category? A community bent on excluding or limiting multi-family use may allow it only as a special use. Such a limitation, however, might violate exclusionary zoning rules in some states.

8. Special uses often involve uses that are unpopular in residential districts: residential care facilities and halfway houses. By relegating these to conditional or special use status, the authorities can control their location in residential districts. The discretionary nature of such permits makes it difficult to attack the refusal of local authorities to grant such permits in the event of successful local opposition to a particular facility at a particular location. The Fair Housing Act, however, may limit such municipal denials.

[D.] VARIANCE

Among the troublesome issues confronting early zoning ordinance draftsmen was the problem of how to avoid the potential hardships caused to individual property owners by the immediate and literal application of the zoning ordinance to a particular piece of property. The new ordinance could cause what was formerly a legal use of land to be illegal. This problem was addressed through the recognition of "nonconformities" (which are discussed in the following section) and through the availability of the variance (sometimes also called a variation or a special exception). Variances may alter the use to which property may be put (e.g., commercial use in a residential zone), or grant area or bulk concessions (e.g., modify setback lines or height requirements). In the case that follows, note which type of variance is sought. The Standard Zoning Enabling Act, which has served as a model for zoning enabling acts in many jurisdictions, provides for a local zoning board of appeals primarily for the purpose of granting such variances after a hearing, but some jurisdictions converted such boards into hearing agencies only. Note who then granted the variance. While arguably hedged in by a host of administrative restrictions, the variance is one of the most important and commonly used techniques for changing the land use regulations which apply to particular parcels. Shapiro, *The Zoning Variance Power*, 29 MD. L. REV. 1 (1969); Dukeminier & Stapleton, *The Zoning Board of Adjustment: A Case Study in Misrule*, 50 KY. L.J. 273 (1962).

TOPANGA ASS'N FOR A SCENIC COMMUNITY v. COUNTY OF LOS ANGELES

California Supreme Court
522 P.2d 12 (Cal. 1954)

TOBRINER, JUSTICE.

The parties in this action dispute the future of approximately 28 acres in Topanga Canyon located in the Santa Monica Mountains region of Los Angeles County. A county ordinance zones the property for light agriculture and single family residences; it also prescribes a one-acre minimum lot size. Upon recommendation of its zoning board and despite the opposition of appellant-petitioner, an incorporated nonprofit organization composed of taxpayers and owners of real property in the canyon, the Los Angeles County Regional Planning Commission granted to the Topanga Canyon Investment Company a variance to establish a 93-space mobile home park on this acreage. Petitioner appealed without success to the county board of supervisors, thereby exhausting its administrative remedies.

1. *An administrative grant of a variance must be accompanied by administrative findings. A court reviewing that grant must determine whether substantial evidence supports the findings and whether the findings support the conclusion that all applicable legislative requirements for a variance have been satisfied.*

A comprehensive zoning plan could affect owners of some parcels unfairly if no means were provided to permit flexibility. Accordingly, in an effort to achieve substantial parity and perhaps also in order to insulate zoning schemes from constitutional attack, our Legislature laid a foundation for the granting of variances. Enacted in 1965, section 65906 of the Government Code establishes criteria for these grants; it provides: "Variances from the terms of the zoning ordinance shall be granted only when, because of special circumstances applicable to the property, including size, shape, topography, location or surroundings, the strict application of the zoning ordinance deprives such property of privileges enjoyed by other property in the vicinity and under identical zoning classification." Any variance granted shall be subject to such conditions as will assure that the adjustment thereby authorized shall not constitute a grant of special privileges inconsistent with the limitations upon other properties in the vicinity and zone in which such property is situated.[2]

Applicable to all zoning jurisdictions except chartered cities, section 65906 may be supplemented by harmonious local legislation. We note that Los Angeles County has enacted an ordinance which, if harmonious with section 65906, would govern the Topanga Canyon property here under consideration. Los Angeles County's Zoning Ordinance No. 1494, section 522, provides: "An exception [variance] may . . . be granted where there are practical difficulties or unnecessary hardships in the way of carrying out the strict letter of the ordinance, and in the granting of such exception the spirit of the ordinance will be observed, public safety secured, and substantial justice done."

Both state and local laws thus were designed to establish requirements which had to be satisfied before the Topanga Canyon Investment Company should have been granted its variance. Although the cases have held that substantial evidence must support the award of a variance in order to insure that such legislative requirements have been satisfied, they have failed to clarify whether the administrative agency must always set forth findings and have not illuminated the proper relationship between the evidence, findings, and ultimate agency action.

[W]e hold that regardless of whether the local ordinance commands that the variance board set forth findings, that body must render findings sufficient both to enable the parties to determine whether and on what basis they should seek review and, in the event of review, to apprise a reviewing court of the basis for the board's action. We hold further that a reviewing court, before sustaining the grant of a

---

[2] [5] A third paragraph added to section 65906 declares: "A variance shall not be granted for a parcel of property which authorizes a use or activity which is not otherwise expressly authorized by the zone regulation governing the parcel of property." This paragraph serves to preclude "use" variances, but apparently does not prohibit so-called "bulk" variances, those which prescribe setbacks, building heights, and the like. The paragraph became effective on November 23, 1970, 19 days after the Los Angeles County Regional Planning Commission granted the variance here at issue. Petitioner does not contend that the paragraph is applicable to the present case.

variance, must scrutinize the record and determine whether substantial evidence supports the administrative agency's findings and whether these findings support the agency's decision. In making these determinations, the reviewing court must resolve reasonable doubts in favor of the administrative findings and decision.

We . . . conclude that implicit in section 1094.5 is a requirement that the agency which renders the challenged decision must set forth findings to bridge the analytic gap between the raw evidence and ultimate decision or order. If the Legislature had desired otherwise, it could have declared as a possible basis for issuing mandamus the absence of substantial evidence to support the administrative agency's action. By focusing, instead, upon the relationships between evidence and findings and between findings and ultimate action, the Legislature sought to direct the reviewing court's attention to the analytic route the administrative agency traveled from evidence to action. In so doing, we believe that the Legislature must have contemplated that the agency would reveal this route.

Among other functions, a findings requirement serves to conduce the administrative body to draw legally relevant subconclusions supportive of its ultimate decision; the intended effect is to facilitate orderly analysis and minimize the likelihood that the agency will randomly leap from evidence to conclusions.

In addition, findings enable the reviewing court to trace and examine the agency's mode of analysis.

Absent such roadsigns, a reviewing court would be forced into unguided and resource-consuming explorations; it would have to grope through the record to determine whether some combination of credible evidentiary items which supported some line of factual and legal conclusions supported the ultimate order or decision of the agency. Moreover, properly constituted findings[3] enable the parties to the agency proceeding to determine whether and on what basis they should seek review.

They also serve a public relations function by helping to persuade the parties that administrative decision-making is careful, reasoned, and equitable.

By setting forth a reasonable requirement for findings and clarifying the standard of judicial review, we believe we promote the achievement of the intended scheme of land use control. Vigorous and meaningful judicial review facilitates, among other factors, the intended division of decision-making labor. Whereas the adoption of zoning regulations is a legislative function, the granting of variances is a quasi-judicial, administrative one. If the judiciary were to review grants of variances superficially, administrative boards could subvert this intended decision-making structure. They could "[amend] . . . the zoning code in the guise of a variance" and render meaningless, applicable state and local legislation prescribing variance requirements.

---

[3] [16] Although a variance board's findings "need not be stated with the formality required in judicial proceedings," they nevertheless must expose the board's mode of analysis to an extent sufficient to serve the purposes stated herein. We do not approve of the language in *Kappadahl v. Alcan Pacific Co.*, 35 Cal. Rptr. 354 (Cal. App. 1963), and *Ames v. City of Pasadena*, 334 P.2d 653 (Cal. App. 1959) which endorses the practice of setting forth findings solely in the language of the applicable legislation.

Moreover, courts must meaningfully review grants of variances in order to protect the interests of those who hold rights in property nearby the parcel for which a variance is sought. A zoning scheme, after all, is similar in some respects to a contract; each party foregoes rights to use its land as it wishes in return for the assurance that the use of neighboring property will be similarly restricted, the rationale being that such mutual restriction can enhance total community welfare. If the interest of these parties in preventing unjustified variance awards for neighboring land is not sufficiently protected, the consequence will be subversion of the critical reciprocity upon which zoning regulation rests.

Abdication by the judiciary of its responsibility to examine variance board decision-making when called upon to do so could very well lead to such subversion. Significantly, many zoning boards employ adjudicatory procedures that may be characterized as casual. The availability of careful judicial review may help conduce these boards to insure that all parties have an opportunity fully to present their evidence and arguments. Further, although we emphasize that we have no reason to believe that such a circumstance exists in the case at bar, the membership of some zoning boards may be inadequately insulated from the interests whose advocates most frequently seek variances. Vigorous judicial review thus can serve to mitigate the effects of insufficiently independent decision-making.

2. *The planning commission's summary of "factual data," its apparent "findings," does not include facts sufficient to satisfy the variance requirements of Government Code.*

The variance can be sustained only if all applicable legislative requirements have been satisfied. Since we conclude that the requirements of section 65906 have not been met, the question whether the variance conforms with the criteria set forth in Los Angeles County Zoning Ordinance No. 1494, section 522 becomes immaterial.[4]

We summarize the principal factual data contained in the Los Angeles County Regional Planning Commission's report, which data the commission apparently relied on to award the variance. The acreage upon which the original real party in interest sought to establish a mobile home park consists of 28 acres; it is a hilly and in places steep parcel of land. At the time the variance was granted, the property contained one single-family residence. Except for a contiguous area immediately to the southeast which included an old and flood-damaged subdivision and a few commercial structures, the surrounding properties were devoted exclusively to scattered single-family residences.

The proposed mobile home park would leave 30 percent of the acreage in its natural state. An additional 25 percent would be landscaped and terraced to blend in with the natural surroundings. Save in places where a wall would be incompatible with the terrain, the plan contemplated enclosure of the park with a wall; it further called for rechanneling a portion of Topanga Canyon Creek and anticipated that the

---

[4] [18] We focus on the statewide requirements because they are of more general application. If we were to decide that the criteria of section 65906 had been satisfied, we would then be called upon to determine whether the requirements set forth in the county ordinance are consistent with those in section 65906 and, if so, whether these local criteria also had been satisfied.

developers would be required to dedicate an 80-foot-wide strip of the property for a proposed realignment of Topanga Creek Boulevard.

The development apparently would partially satisfy a growing demand for new, low cost housing in the area. Additionally, the project might serve to attract further investment to the region and could provide a much needed fire break. Several data indicate that construction on the property of single-family residences in conformance with the zoning classification would generate significantly smaller profits than would development of the mobile home park. Single-family structures apparently would necessitate costly grading, and the proposed highway realignment would require a fill 78 feet high, thereby rendering the property unattractive for conventional residential development. Moreover, the acreage is said not to be considered attractive to parties interested in single-family residences due, in the words of the report's summary of the testimony, to "the nature of the inhabitants" in the vicinity and also because of local flood problems.

These data, we conclude, do not constitute a sufficient showing to satisfy the section 65906 variance requirements. That section permits variances "*only* when, because of *special* circumstances applicable to the property, . . . the strict application of the zoning ordinance deprives such property of privileges enjoyed by other property in the vicinity and under identical zoning classification." (Emphasis added.) This language emphasizes *disparities* between properties, not treatment of the subject property's characteristics in the abstract. It also contemplates that at best, only a small fraction of any one zone can qualify for a variance.

The data contained in the planning commission's report focus almost exclusively on the qualities of the property for which the variance was sought. In the absence of comparative information about surrounding properties, these data lack legal significance. Thus knowledge that the property has rugged features tells us nothing about whether the original real party in interest faced difficulties different from those confronted on neighboring land.[5] Its assurances that it would landscape and terrace parts of the property and leave others in their natural state are all well and good, but they bear not at all on the critical issue whether a variance was necessary to bring the original real party in interest into substantial parity with other parties holding property interests in the zone.

The claim that the development would probably serve various community needs may be highly desirable, but it too does not bear on the issue at hand. Likewise, without more, the data suggesting that development of the property in conformance with the general zoning classification could require substantial expenditures are not relevant to the issue whether the variance was properly granted. Even assuming for the sake of argument that if confined to the subject parcel and no more than a few others in the zone, such a burden could support a variance under section 65906, for all we know from the record, conforming development of other property in the area would entail a similar burden. Were that the case, a frontal attack on the present ordinance or a legislative proceeding to determine whether the area should be

[5] [21] Indeed, the General Plan for Topanga Canyon suggests that the subject property is not uniquely surfaced; it states that the entire area is characterized by "mountainous terrain, steep slopes and deep canyons interspersed with limited areas of relatively flat or rolling land."

rezoned might be proper, but a variance would not.

Although they dispute that section 65906 requires a showing that the characteristics of the subject property are exceptional, the current real parties in interest would nevertheless have us speculate that the property is unlike neighboring parcels. They point out that the plot has rugged terrain and three stream beds and that the Topanga Creek Boulevard realignment would bisect the property. Speculation about neighboring land, however, will not support the award of a variance. The party seeking the variance must shoulder the burden of demonstrating before the zoning agency that the subject property satisfies the requirements therefor. Thus neither an administrative agency nor a reviewing court may assume without evidentiary basis that the character of neighboring property is different from that of the land for which the variance is sought.

Moreover, the grant of a variance for non-conforming development of a 28-acre parcel in the instant case is suspect. Although we do not categorically preclude a tract of that size from eligibility for a variance, we note that in the absence of unusual circumstances, so large a parcel may not be sufficiently unrepresentative of the realty in a zone to merit special treatment. By granting variances for tracts of this size, a variance board begins radically to alter the nature of the entire zone. Such change is a proper subject for legislation, not piecemeal administrative adjudication. Since there has been no affirmative showing that the subject property differs substantially and in relevant aspects from other parcels in the zone, we conclude that the variance granted amounts to the kind of "special privilege" explicitly prohibited by Government Code section 65906.

We submit, in summary, that this case illumines two important legal principles. First, by requiring that administrative findings must support a variance, we emphasize the need for orderly legal process and the desirability of forcing administrative agencies to express their grounds for decision so that reviewing courts can intelligently examine the validity of administrative action. Second, by abrogating an unsupported exception to a zoning plan, we conduce orderly and planned utilization of the environment.

We reverse.

NOTES AND QUESTIONS

1. *Adequacy of the Record.* Note the court's concern for an adequate record in *Topanga*. Why is it so critical here? Does the distinction the court draws between legislative and administrative actions offer a clue?

2. *Options Other than a Variance.* The *Topanga* court appears to favor the proposed development on the subject property, yet it denies the variance. Why? If you represented the property owner, what form of zoning change would you seek?

3. *What Constitutes Hardship?* How much of a land use change ought to be permitted by means of a variance, and what constitutes hardship? As the *Topanga* court notes, the hardship is also supposed to be unique to the property and not affecting nearby property. What is before the court is essentially a use variance rather than a bulk variance. Can a hardship of a land use nature justify a use

variance? If so, what kind? In *Kensington South Neighborhood Advisory Council v. Zoning Bd. of Adjustment*, 471 A.2d 1317 (Pa. 1984), a variance to sell wholesale fresh produce where only retail distribution was permitted was deemed improperly granted. The petitioner unsuccessfully argued that the permit should be granted because the distinction between retail and wholesale produce operations was minimal. Since the owner failed to demonstrate that compliance with the zoning code would result in unnecessary hardship, the use variance could not be granted.

On the other hand, the Illinois court in *Kleidon v. City of Hickory Hills*, 458 N.E.2d 931 (Ill. App. Ct. 1983), upheld a variance allowing parking for a restaurant to be located in a residential district. The restaurant was located in a commercial district. The court held that a parking problem existed in the street and in the adjoining parcel which was the site of the restaurant, which satisfied the "practical difficulties or particular hardships" standard that had to be met. In discussing what constitutes hardship, one may be able to include a brief discussion regarding the applicability of personal hardships. From the Land Use textbook (Note 6, p. 195): "It is well established that variances are not to be granted for personal hardships, but rather for hardships generated by the land. Thus, parents who wanted a variance form setbacks to build a deck in their backyard for their child to play failed to meet the unnecessary hardship standard. *See* Larsen v. Zoning Bd. Of Adj. of Pittsburgh, 672 A.2d 286, 290 (Pa. 1996). The rule, however, may need to bend when the Fair Housing Act or the Americans with Disabilities Act is invoked. *See* JUERGENSMEYER AND ROBERTS, LAND USE PLANNING AND DEVELOPMENT REGULATION LAW § 5. 17B (3rd ed. 2012). Size also matters. See *Surfrider Foundation v. Zoning Board of Appeals*, 358 P.3d 664 (2015), where the Hawaii Supreme Court overturned charter mandated hardship findings at administrative zoning appeals board and circuit court levels in holding a variance of several stories for a new hotel legal.

4. *Variance Granted to Extent Needed.* An applicant is entitled only to that degree of variance that will relieve him of his particular hardship. Thus, if a homeowner can show that his side yard requirements leave only eight feet in which to construct a garage and he needs nine, a variance granting an encroachment of one foot would presumably not be harmful to the public, assuming the side yard requirements are ample. Should the standard size car in the neighborhood enter into the decision on his application? What about the community standard for sheltering cars? In parts of the country, carports are the rule rather than the exception, often open on all sides but the rear. If such a shelter was inadvertently constructed so that two side support posts and the concrete "apron" infringe upon a four-foot side yard requirement by, say, four inches, but the roof overhangs into the side yard by two feet, should a variance be granted to make the carport "legal"? What if the aforementioned carport were a brick garage? What would be the status of a "third bedroom" constructed on top of the garage, with the same perimeter dimensions, constructed for new-born twins into a family of four? For a licensed daycare center as a condition of the license, assuming such a center is a permitted home occupation in the district? For criticism of area variances generally, *see* C. Durkin, *The Exclusionary Effect of "Mansionization": Area Variances Undermine Efforts to Achieve Housing Affordability*, 55 CATH. L. REV. 439 (2006).

5. *After-the-Fact Variances.* What about variances to cure alleged hardships "after the fact"? In *Board of Adjustment, Corpus Christi v. McBride*, 676 S.W.2d

705 (Tex. App. 1984), a landowner who had spent $75,000 on construction of a home that was 80% complete was told to stop construction work for failure to obtain a variance from a 25-foot setback requirement. The court noted that compliance with the setback restrictions would adversely affect the structural integrity of the house, would cost at least $4,200, would render the house unsightly, and would serve no useful function. The court ordered the variance granted in view of unrefuted findings showing hardship and evidence that the variance would not adversely affect the public interest. The landowner in *McBride* might be described as lucky, since self-created hardships normally are not grounds for a variance. *See Korean Buddhist Dae Won Sa Temple of Hawaii v. Sullivan*, 953 P.2d 1315 (Haw. 1998), where a Buddhist Temple was constructed nine feet higher than the building permit allowed. Upon discovery of the violation, the Temple sought a variance to maintain the illegal structure. The request was denied and the roof was lowered.

6. By express or implied authority, conditions can be attached to variances. They must relate to the land and be reasonable. Conditions on fencing and lighting are common. What about limiting the number of employees allowed to work on site? What about limiting employees to persons who are related to the owner? New Jersey courts have approved variances issued on the condition that if the neighbors offer to buy the property at its fair market value, the variance will not issue. Why? Does this make sense? *Davis Enterprises v. Karpf*, 523 A.2d 137 (N.J. 1987).

[E.] NONCONFORMITIES

The rapid spread of comprehensive zoning to most urban areas of the United States after the *Euclid* case resulted in many existing structures and uses no longer permitted in the new use districts. As the case which follows illustrates, most state zoning enabling acts provided expressly for such "nonconformities." Local governments were uniformly prohibited from eliminating most nonconforming uses and buildings at once. Obviously, the same potential for creating nonconformities exists upon a rezoning or map amendment, or in changing the list of permitted or special uses in an existing district. To qualify for nonconformity status, a use or structure must have been legally commenced or used *ab initio*.

CITY OF LOS ANGELES v. GAGE

California Court of Appeals
127 Cal. App. 2d 442 (1954)

VALLEE, JUSTICE.

In 1930 Gage acquired adjoining lots 220 and 221 located on Cochran Avenue in Los Angeles. He constructed a two-family residential building on lot 221 and rented the upper half solely for residential purposes. He established a wholesale and retail plumbing supply business on the property. He used a room in the lower half of the residential building on lot 221 as the office for the conduct of the business, and the rest of the lower half for residential purposes for himself and his family; he used a garage on lot 221 for the storage of plumbing supplies and materials; and he constructed and used racks, bins, and stalls for the storage of such supplies and materials on lot 220. Later Gage incorporated defendant company. The realty and the assets of the plumbing business were transferred to the company. The case is presented as though the property had been owned continuously from 1930 to date by the same defendant. The use of lots 220 and 221 begun in 1930, has been substantially the same at all times since.

In 1930 the two lots and other property facing on Cochran Avenue in their vicinity were classified in "C" zone by the zoning ordinance then in effect. Under this classification the use to which Gage put the property was permitted. Shortly after Gage acquired lots 220 and 221, they were classified in "C-3" zone and the use to which he put the property was expressly permitted. In 1936 the city council of the city passed Ordinance 77,000 which contained a comprehensive zoning plan for the city. Ordinance 77,000 re-enacted the prior ordinances with respect to the use of lots 220 and 221. In 1941 the city council passed Ordinance 85,015 by the terms of which the use of a residential building for the conduct of an office in connection with the plumbing supply business was permitted. Ordinance 85,015 prohibited the open storage of materials in zone "C-3" but permitted such uses as had been established to continue as nonconforming uses. The use to which lots 220 and 221 was put by defendants was a nonconforming use that might be continued. In 1946 the city council passed Ordinance 90,500. This ordinance reclassified lots 220 and 221 and other property fronting on Cochran Avenue in their vicinity from zone "C-3" to zone "R-4" (Multiple dwelling zone). Use of lots 220 and 221 for the conduct of a plumbing business was not permitted in zone "R-4." At the time Ordinance 90,500 was passed, and at all times since, the Los Angeles Municipal Code (§ 12.23 B & C) provided: "(a) The nonconforming use of a conforming building or structure may be continued, except that in the 'R' Zones any nonconforming commercial or industrial use of a residential building or residential accessory building shall be discontinued within five (5) years from June 1, 1946, or five (5) years from the date the use becomes nonconforming, whichever date is later . . . .

> "(a) The nonconforming use of land shall be discontinued within five (5) years from June 1, 1946, or within five (5) years from the date the use became nonconforming, in each of the following cases: (1) where no buildings are employed in connection with such use; (2) where the only buildings employed are accessory or incidental to such use; (3) where such use is maintained in connection with a conforming building."

Prior to the passage of Ordinance 90,500, about 50% of the city had been zoned. It was the first ordinance which "attempted to zone the entire corporate limits of the city." Prior to its passage, several thousand exceptions and variances, were granted from restrictive provisions of prior ordinances, some of which permitted commercial use of property zoned for residential use, "and in some cases permitted the use of land for particular purposes like or similar to use of subject property which otherwise would have been prohibited." Under Ordinance 90,500, the uses permitted by these exceptions and variances that did not carry a time limit may be continued indefinitely.

The business conducted by Gage on the property has produced a gross revenue varying between $125,000 and $350,000 a year. If he is required to abandon the use of the property for his business, he will be put to the following expenses: "(1) The value of a suitable site for the conduct of its business would be about $10,000; which would be offset by the value of $7,500 of the lot now used. (2) The cost incident to removing of supplies to another location and construction of the necessary racks, sheds, bins and stalls which would be about $2,500. (3) The cost necessary to expend to advertise a new location. (4) The risk of a gain or a loss of business while moving, and the cost necessary to reestablish the business at a new location, the amount of which is uncertain."

The noise and disturbance caused by the loading and unloading of supplies, trucking, and the going and coming of workmen in connection with the operation of a plumbing business with an open storage yard is greater than the noise and disturbance that is normal in a district used solely for residential purposes.

The court found: the business conducted by Gage has a substantial value; he could not, either prior to June 1, 1951, or at any time thereafter or in the future, remove the business without substantial loss or expense; the value of Gage's property has not been increased or stabilized by the passage of Ordinance 90,500, nor will observance or enforcement of the ordinance increase the value of the property; the use of the property for the purpose that it has been used continuously since 1930 will not adversely and detrimentally effect [sic] the use or value of other property in the neighborhood thereof; the use to which the property has been put by Gage has not been unsanitary, unsightly, noisy, or otherwise incompatible with the legal uses of adjoining property; Gage has not, nor will he in the future, operate to disturb the peace and quiet of the residents of the neighborhood as long as the property is operated substantially as it was operated at the date of the filing of the complaint; the use to which the property has been put does not interfere with the lawful and reasonable use of the streets and alleys in the vicinity by the residents in the neighborhood or others entitled thereto.

The court concluded: Gage became vested with the right to use the property for the purpose that it was used; insofar as the Los Angeles Municipal Code purports to require the abandonment of the use of the building on lot 221 as an office for the plumbing and plumbing supply business or the use of lot 220 for the open storage of plumbing supplies in the manner that it has been and is being used by Gage, it is void and of no legal effect; Ordinance 90,500 is void insofar as it affects Gage's use of the property in that it deprives him of a vested right to use the property for the purpose it has been used continuously since 1930 and deprives him of property without due process of law. Judgment was that plaintiff take nothing. Plaintiff appeals.

Plaintiff contends that the mandatory discontinuance of a nonconforming use after a fixed period is a reasonable exercise of the police power, and that on the agreed facts the Los Angeles ordinance is a valid exercise of such power as applied to Gage's property. Gage does not question the validity of the ordinance as a whole, but he contends it may not be constitutionally applied to require the removal of his existing business. He asserts that under *Jones v. City of Los Angeles*, [295 P. 14] the decision of the trial court was correct.

A nonconforming use is a lawful use existing on the effective date of the zoning restriction and continuing since that time in nonconformance to the ordinance. A provision permitting the continuance of a nonconforming use is ordinarily included in zoning ordinances because of the hardship and doubtful constitutionality of compelling the immediate discontinuance of nonconforming uses. It is generally held that a zoning ordinance may not operate to immediately suppress or remove from a particular district an otherwise lawful business or use already established therein.

No case seems to have been decided in this state squarely involving the precise question presented in the case at bar. Until recently zoning ordinances have made no provision for any systematic and comprehensive elimination of the nonconforming use. The expectation seems to have been that existing nonconforming uses would be of little consequence and that they would eventually disappear. The contrary appears to be the case. It is said that the fundamental problem facing zoning is the inability to eliminate the nonconforming use. The general purpose of present-day zoning ordinances is to eventually end all nonconforming uses. There is a growing tendency to guard against the indefinite continuance of nonconforming uses by providing for their liquidation within a prescribed period. It is said, "The only positive method of getting rid of non-conforming uses yet devised is to amortize a non-conforming building. That is, to determine the normal useful remaining life of the building and prohibit the owner from maintaining it after the expiration of that time." Crolly & Norton, *Termination of Nonconforming Uses*, 62 Zoning Bull. 1, Regional Plan Ass'n, June 1952.

Amortization of nonconforming uses has been expressly authorized by recent amendments to zoning enabling laws in a number of states. Ordinances providing for amortization of nonconforming uses have been passed in a number of large cities. The length of time given the owner to eliminate his nonconforming use or building varies with the city and with the type of structure.

Jones v. City of Los Angeles, relied on by Gage, held unconstitutional, as applied to existing establishments, an ordinance making it unlawful to erect, operate, or maintain, in certain residential areas, a sanitarium for the treatment of persons suffering from mental or nervous diseases. The *Jones* case was distinguished in the recent case of *Livingston Rock, etc., Co. v. County of Los Angeles*. In the *Livingston* case an ordinance of the County of Los Angeles allowed certain existing nonconforming uses to continue for 20 years unless such exception should be revoked as provided in the ordinance. One ground of revocation specified was if the use was so exercised "as to be detrimental to the public health or safety, or so as to be a nuisance." Distinguishing the *Jones* case the court said,

> "Moreover, the ordinance under consideration in the *Jones* case differed materially from the one here involved. There the ordinance, cast in the form of a penal statute rather than in the form of a comprehensive zoning law, prohibited the maintenance of sanitariums of a certain type in designated districts. By its terms the ordinance, unlike the ordinary zoning laws, purported to have both a retroactive as well as a prospective effect, thereby automatically prohibiting the continued maintenance of several established sanitariums representing large investments. In other words, no provision was made for any automatic exception for existing nonconforming uses. In the present case, the zoning ordinance does provide for automatic exceptions of reasonable duration for existing nonconforming uses, subject,

however, to earlier revocation of the automatic exception if the use for which approval was granted is so exercised 'as to be detrimental to the public health or safety, or so as to be a nuisance' (§ 649, *supra*); and the power to determine, upon notice, the question of whether the property was being so used was vested in the Regional Planning Commission."

Assuming, as suggested by Gage, that the foregoing was dictum, we think it a correct statement of the distinction between the *Jones* case and the case at bar. There are other differences between *Jones* and the present case. There the regulation was of one type of commercial use. Here the regulation is of all commercial uses. There the ordinance affected a substantial investment in land and special buildings designed and built for the use to which they were being put. Here the ordinance affects only the use of land and the nonconforming use of a conforming building. The building has been, and may continue to be, used for the purpose for which it was designed and built. There the property could not have been used immediately for other purposes. Here the property can be used immediately for the uses for which it is zoned. In the *Jones* case the court said: "We do not mean to hold that those engaged in the zoning of cities must always be faced with the impossibility of eradicating the nonconforming uses. Our conclusion is that where, as here, a retroactive ordinance causes *substantial* injury and the prohibited business is not a nuisance, the ordinance is to that extent an unreasonable and unjustifiable exercise of police power." (Italics added.)

The theory in zoning is that each district is an appropriate area for the location of the uses which the zone plan permits in that area, and that the existence or entrance of other uses will tend to impair the development and stability of the area for the appropriate uses. The public welfare must be considered from the standpoint of the objective of zoning and of all the property within any particular use district. It was not and is not contemplated that preexisting nonconforming uses are to be perpetual. The presence of any nonconforming use endangers the benefits to be derived from a comprehensive zoning plan. Having the undoubted power to establish residential districts, the legislative body has the power to make such classification really effective by adopting such reasonable regulations as would be conducive to the welfare, health, and safety of those desiring to live in such district and enjoy the benefits thereof. There would be no object in creating a residential district unless there were to be secured to those dwelling therein the advantages which are ordinarily considered the benefits of such residence. It would seem to be the logical and reasonable method of approach to place a time limit upon the continuance of existing nonconforming uses, commensurate with the investment involved and based on the nature of the use; and in cases of nonconforming structures, on their character, age, and other relevant factors.

Exercise of the police power frequently impairs rights in property because the exercise of those rights is detrimental to the public interest. Every zoning ordinance effects some impairment of vested rights either by restricting prospective uses or by prohibiting the continuation of existing uses, because it affects property already owned by individuals at the time of its enactment. In essence there is no distinction between requiring the discontinuance of a nonconforming use within a reasonable period and provisions which deny the right to add to or extend buildings devoted to an existing nonconforming use, which deny the right to resume a nonconforming use after a period of nonuse, which deny the right to extend or enlarge an existing nonconforming use, which deny the right to substitute new buildings for those devoted to an existing nonconforming use, all of which have been held to be valid exercises of the police power.

The distinction between an ordinance restricting future uses and one requiring the termination of present uses within a reasonable period of time is merely one of degree, and constitutionality depends on the relative importance to be given to the public gain and to the private loss. Zoning as it affects every piece of property is to some extent retroactive in that it applies to property already owned at the time of the effective date of the ordinance. The elimination of existing uses within a reasonable time does not amount to a taking of property nor does it necessarily restrict the use of property so that it cannot be used for any reasonable purpose. Use of a reasonable amortization scheme provides an equitable means of reconciliation of the conflicting interests in satisfaction of due process requirements. As a method of eliminating existing nonconforming uses it allows the owner of the nonconforming use, by affording an opportunity to make new plans, at least partially to offset any loss he might suffer. The loss he suffers, if any is spread out over a period of years, and he enjoys a monopolistic position by virtue of the zoning ordinance as long as he remains. If the amortization period is reasonable the loss to the owner may be small when compared with the benefit to the public. Nonconforming uses will eventually be eliminated. A legislative body may well conclude that the beneficial effect on the community of the eventual elimination of all nonconforming uses by a reasonable amortization plan more than offsets individual losses.

The ordinance in question provides, according to a graduated periodic schedule, for the gradual and ultimate elimination of all commercial and industrial uses in residential zones. These provisions require the discontinuance of nonconforming uses of land within a five-year period, and the discontinuance of nonconforming commercial and industrial uses of residential buildings in the "R" zones within the same five-year period. These provisions are the only ones pertinent to the decision in this case. However, it may be noted that other provisions of the ordinance require the discontinuance of nonconforming billboards and, in residential zones, the discontinuance of nonconforming buildings and of nonconforming uses of nonconforming buildings, within specified periods running from 20 to 40 years according to the type of building construction.

We have no doubt that Ordinance 90,500, in compelling the discontinuance of the use of defendants' property for a wholesale and retail plumbing and plumbing supply business, and for the open storage of plumbing supplies within five years after its passage, is a valid exercise of the police power. Lots 220 and 221 are several blocks from a business center and it appears that they are not within any reasonable or logical extension of such a center. The ordinance does not prevent the operation of defendants' business; it merely restricts its location. Discontinuance of the nonconforming use requires only that Gage move his plumbing business to property that is zoned for it. Such property can be found within a half mile of Gage's property. The cost of moving is $5,000, or less than 1% of Gage's minimum gross business for five years, or less than half of 1% of the mean of his gross business for five years. He has had eight years within which to move. The property is usable for residential purpose. Since 1930 lot 221 has been used for residential purposes. All of the land within 500 feet of Gage's property is now improved and used for such purposes. Lot 220, now unimproved, can be improved for the same purposes.

We think it apparent that none of the agreed facts and none of the ultimate facts found by the court justify the conclusion that Ordinance 90,500, as applied to Gage's property, is clearly arbitrary or unreasonable, or has no substantial relation to the public's health, safety, morals, or general welfare, or that it is an unconstitutional impairment of his property rights.

It is enough for us to determine and we determine only that Ordinance 90,500 of the city of Los Angeles, insofar as it required the discontinuance of Gage's wholesale and retail plumbing business on lots 220 and 221 within five years from the date of its passage, is a constitutional exercise of the police power.

NOTES AND QUESTIONS

1. *Termination of Dangerous Uses.* To the requirement that a nonconforming use be "legal," that is, established legally, the California Supreme Court in the *Jones v. City of Los Angeles* case discussed in *Gage*, added that it be "not dangerous" as well. What remedy does that court seem to suggest for terminating dangerous uses? What, therefore, would be useful to show in the operation of a nonconformity if it were challenged in a jurisdiction which strictly interprets statutory language forbidding zoning ordinances to have a retroactive effect? The *Gage* court is not so strict. See *Lachapelle v. Town of Goffstown*, 225 A.2d 624 (N.H. 1967), for a case where the nuisance characteristics of a junkyard seem to sway the court in the direction suggested by the *Jones* court.

2. *Cost of Relocation.* In upholding a delayed termination of *Gage*'s plumbing business, the court is clearly swayed by the economic (and monopolistic) success of the use and the relatively low costs of relocating it. But does it pick and choose its facts too randomly? Note that it all but characterizes the business as nuisance-like, despite evidence that the business is apparently conducted quietly and without demonstrable adverse land use consequences for the neighboring properties, except for the lowering of property values. Nevertheless, the *Gage* court stops considerably short of advocating the immediate termination of such uses as *Gage*'s, holding only that five years were enough. What is a "reasonable duration" for a nonconformity? Should a use be treated differently from a structure for purposes of determining a proper termination period? If so, why? What special problems can you foresee in terminating a structure? What about other uses, like the sanitariums in *Jones*? Should a use be treated differently from a structure for purposes of determining a proper termination period? If so, why? What special problems can you foresee in terminating a structure? *See City of La Mesa v. Tweed and Gambrell Planing Mill*, 146 Cal. App. 2d 762 (1956) (five years insufficient for building with remaining economic life of 20 years).

3. *Period of Amortization.* What considerations go into deciding the reasonableness of the amortization period? One is the justification for regulating the use. A billboard that is a menace to traffic safety can be immediately removed, but signs targeted due to their unattractive qualities provide a less compelling reason for immediate termination. *Modjeska Sign Studios, Inc. v. Berle*, 373 N.E.2d 255 (N.Y.

1977). A second is the investment. "[A]s the financial investment increases in dimension, the length of the amortization period should correspondingly increase. While an owner need not be given that period of time necessary to recoup his investment entirely the amortization period should not be so short as to result in a substantial loss of his investment." *Id.* at 262. Investment factors to consider may include initial capital investment, investment realization to date, life expectancy, and the existence, and binding nature, of lease obligations. What would be a reasonable amortization period for a two-story duplex in a single-family, single-story residence zone? *See generally* Cobb, *Amortizing Nonconforming Uses*, LAND USE L. & ZONING DIG., vol. 37 no. 3 at 3 (1985).

Most courts have upheld the amortization concept, *LaChapelle v. Town of Goffstown, supra*, Note 1 (amortization of one year valid as to junkyards); *National Advertising Co. v. City of Raleigh*, 947 F.2d 1158, 1164, n.6 (4th Cir. 1991) (citing cases), and limit their review to the reasonableness of specific clauses in as applied challenges. *See North Carolina v. Joyner*, 211 S.E.2d 320 (N.C. 1975). A few courts invalidate amortization provisions on their face. *See Pennsylvania Northwestern Distribs., Inc. v. Zoning Hearing Bd.*, 584 A.2d 1372 (Pa. 1991), where the court found an amortization clause to be a facial taking under state constitution. The case involved a 90 day amortization period for adult book stores. Ohio and Indiana agree with Pennsylvania. *See Ailes v. Decatur County Area Planning Comm'n*, 448 N.E.2d 1057 (Ind. 1983); *Sun Oil Co. v. City of Upper Arlington*, 379 N.E.2d 266 (Ohio App. 1977).

4. *Amortization of Billboards*. From enormous billboards to small flashing temporary ones, signs are the targets of many amortization ordinances. How much time do signs get? *See Art Neon Co. v. City & County of Denver*, 488 F.2d 118, 122–23 (10th Cir. 1973) (amortization period of five years valid for non-conforming signs; a mere 30 days valid for flashing, blinking, fluctuating, animated, or portable signs). Federal law inhibits the use of amortization on certain federally funded highways by threatening withdrawal of federal money. In *Adams Outdoor Advertising, L.P. v. Board of Zoning Appeals*, Board of Zoning Appeals (Va. 2007), the city prohibited the erection of billboards, and the court held the replacement of a static face with an electronic message board was an "enlargement" and "structural alteration" of a nonconforming use not permitted by the zoning ordinance. The message board added 3000 to 3500 pounds to the sign and increased its depth.

5. *Repairs on Nonconforming Uses*. Most ordinances provide that nonconforming structures may not be repaired or enlarged so as to extend their "lives." What does that mean? Can a nonconforming residence thus permissibly violate fire and housing codes? Indeed, can such repairs be legally made if their effect would be to prolong the life of the structure? Ordinances may allow conversion to another use, but not if it is deemed more harmful. In Pennsylvania, the "natural expansion" of a nonconforming use is constitutionally protected. *See Sweeney v. Zoning Hearing Bd.*, 626 A.2d 1147 (Pa. 1993).

Most ordinances also provide that nonconforming structures which are partially destroyed by fire, usually 50% or more, may not be reconstructed except according to the then-existing zoning regulations. What are the rights of homeowners who have had houses destroyed by fire or flood on lots which now have but a fraction of the minimum area now required for a single-family house in that zone?

Finally, a nonconforming use that has been discontinued cannot be recommenced. What constitutes an intent to abandon? *See Hartley v. City of Colorado Springs*, 764 P.2d 1216 (Colo. 1988) (no showing of intent required). *See also* Strauss & Giese, *Elimination of Nonconformities: The Case for Voluntary Discontinuance*, 25 URB. LAW. 159 (1993).

6. *Administrative Problems with Termination of Nonconformities*. There are a host of administrative problems involved in terminating nonconformities according to useful life, value and other standards over time. Someone must first find, then keep track of each nonconformity, as well as make some determination of value, useful life, and so forth. Equitable, if not legal, notions of due process also would seem to require some sort of notice to the nonconforming user both concerning an official determination of nonconformity and the applicable "amortization" period.

A NOTE ON VESTED RIGHTS AND DEVELOPMENT AGREEMENTS

Vested Rights

Despite the sustained effort of regulators to do away with nonconformities (see the preceding section), they persist, nonconforming status affords a property owner significant protection. However, as zoning controls change over time, and often in response to a specific development proposal, it is critical to know whether, and if so when, developments in the permitting process or projects partially constructed are subject to new regulations.

One of the most vexing problems in comprehensively amending a zoning ordinance is the public notice it provides the private landowner contemplating development. Public discussion proposing a zoning classification from a use permitting reasonably intensive development (multiple family residential or commercial, for example) to something like single-family or agricultural classifications, or the reduction of permitted uses in existing zone classifications, is likely to result in a "race" by the landowner to commence the still-permitted, more intense development — or to change position sufficiently to acquire vested rights to proceed in the face of any subsequently enacted amendment making such development illegal. This is particularly true if the amendment process is prolonged by multiple hearings and/or required comprehensive plan changes in advance of the zoning amendment. It is for these reasons that many local governments attempt to preserve the status quo pending such amendments by means of moratoria and other interim land use controls in order to prevent the comprehensive amendments from being rendered ineffective through the grandfathering in of a host of new nonconformities.

Specific development proposals often trigger rezoning petitions. Once neighbors learn that a big box superstore is planned next door or a nearby parcel of open land is about to be developed into a residential subdivision and that existing zoning permits such uses, they may well petition the city to downzone the land. Then, the race is on.

The point at which a developer-landowner has proceeded sufficiently far enough with a project so that the right to proceed is "vested" is a land management problem of vast proportions. For an analysis of the theories upon which courts have rested decisions for and against vested rights generally, together with a discussion of the range of governmental actions held to vest landowner rights, *see* David L. Callies, Daniel J. Curtin, Jr., & Julie A. Tappendorf, Bargaining for Development: A Handbook on Development Agreements, Annexation Agreements, Land Development Conditions, Vested Rights, and the Provision of Public Services (2003). Charles L. Siemon, Wendy U. Larsen & Douglas R. Porter, Vested Rights: Balancing Public and Private Development Expectations (1982); Kupchak et. al., *Arrow of Time: Vested Rights, Zoning Estoppel and Development Agreements in Hawai'i*, 27 Hawaii L. Rev. 17 (2004).

Development Agreements

Decisions vesting development rights late in the process, like the *Avco* case from California and the *Nukolii* case from Hawaii, together with the need for more public facilities than could be legally exacted from the development community through impact fees and exactions, led developers and government to seek common ground upon which both needs (vested rights and additional public facilities) could be negotiated. What resulted was the development agreement. *See* David L. Callies, Daniel J. Curtin, Jr., & Julie A. Tappendorf, Bargaining for Development: A Handbook on Development Agreements, Annexation Agreements, Land Development Conditions, Vested Rights, and the Provision of Public Services (2003). The development agreement is provided for by statute in at least 14 states,[6] and is particularly prolific in rapidly developing, multi-permit jurisdictions like California. *See* Daniel J. Curtin & Scott A. Edelstein, *Development Agreement Practice in California and Other States*, 22 Stetson L. Rev. 761 (1993). Nearly every court ruling on the validity of development agreements has upheld them. *See, e.g., Santa Margarita Area Resident Together v. San Luis Obispo County Bd. of Supervisors*, 84 Cal. App. 4th 221 (2000).

[F.] SPECIALIZED CONTROLS

[1.] Aesthetics and Historic Preservation

The use of the police power through zoning to regulate for aesthetic concerns raises some difficult philosophical and legal problems. It is one thing to agree that the popular target of municipal regulation, the billboard, is so generally offensive, and its small number of supporters so uniformly economically interested, that its regulation on aesthetic grounds is a reasonable exercise of the police power. However, one can usually concoct other rationales for regulating billboards — indeed for most signs. The same can be said for junkyards, but what about housing design or color? What is acceptable and what is not? Who is to decide? If the answer is experts, which ones? Architects? Planners? Art historians? What

[6] Arizona, California, Colorado, Florida, Hawaii, Idaho, Louisiana, Maine, Maryland, Nevada, New Jersey, Oregon, Virginia, and Washington.

standards should govern the prohibition of certain usages on aesthetic grounds? Are there special places which, for economic reasons, have a particular interest in remaining "attractive"? *See* J. COSTONIS, ICONS & ALIENS: LAW, AESTHETICS, AND ENVIRONMENTAL CHANGE (1989); Costonis, *Law and Aesthetics: A Critique and a Reformulation of the Dilemmas*, 80 MICH. L. REV. 355 (1982). A recent review of judicial views on aesthetic regulation finds that all states today allow the use of aesthetic concerns in some fashion, and that almost half the states accept aesthetics alone as a basis for regulation. The remaining states accept the use of aesthetics with other factors. Some of these have held that the use of aesthetic concerns alone is not appropriate, but a number appear to be moving away from that position. Pearlman, et al, *Beyond the Eye of the Beholder Once Again: A New Review of Aesthetic Regulation*, 38 URB. LAW. 1119 (2006).

Review *Penn Central Transportation Co. v. New York* in Ch. B. In that case, how does New York City proceed in the designation of historic property? What criteria does it use? How much of a burden should the owner of a historic property have to bear without compensation? For an overview of historic preservation law in the United States, *see* Callies, *Historic Preservation Law in the United States*, 32 ELR 10348 (2002), and [more recent summary needed here].

REID v. ARCHITECTURAL BOARD OF REVIEW OF CITY OF CLEVELAND HEIGHTS

Ohio Court of Appeals
192 N.E.2d 74 (Ohio Ct. App. 1963)

KOVACHY, PRESIDING JUDGE

Donna S. Reid, plaintiff appellant, hereinafter designated applicant, applied to the Building Commissioner of the City of Cleveland Heights for a permit to build a residence on a lot owned by her and her husband on North Park Boulevard in Cleveland Heights. As required by ordinance, the plans and specifications were referred to the Architectural Board of Review, which Board, after due consideration, made the following order:

> This plan is for a single-story building and is submitted for a site in a multi-story residential neighborhood. The Board disapproves this project for the reason that it does not maintain the high character of community development in that it does not conform to the character of the houses in the area.

Upon appeal to the Court of Common Pleas, that court rendered a judgment in favor of the Board, holding (1) that the Codified Ordinances were constitutional enactments under the police power of the City; (2) that the Board had the power and authority to render the decision appealed from; (3) that the Board did not abuse its discretion; and (4) that due process was accorded applicant.

The Board is composed of three architects registered and authorized to practice architecture under Ohio laws with ten years of general practice as such.

Section 137.05 of the Codified Ordinances of the City of Cleveland Heights, titled

"Purpose" reads as follows:

> The purposes of the Architectural Board of Review are to protect property on which buildings are constructed or altered, to maintain the high character of community development, and to protect real estate within this City from impairment or destruction of value, by regulating according to proper architectural principles the design, use of materials, finished grade lines and orientation of all new buildings, hereafter erected, and the moving, alteration, improvement, repair, adding to or razing in whole or in part of all existing buildings, and said Board shall exercise its powers and perform its duties for the accomplishment of said purposes only.

This ordinance is intended to:

1. protect property,
2. maintain high character of community development,
3. protect real estate from impairment or destruction of value, and the Board's powers are restricted "for the accomplishment of said purposes only."

These objectives are sought to be accomplished by regulating:

1. design,
2. use of material,
3. finished grade lines,
4. orientation (new buildings).

The City of Cleveland Heights is a suburb of the City of Cleveland and was organized to provide suitable and comfortable home surroundings for residents employed in Cleveland and its environs. It has no industry or railroads within its confines and is a well-regulated and carefully groomed community, primarily residential in character. An ordinance designed to protect values and to maintain "a high character of community development" is in the public interest and contributes to the general welfare. Moreover, the employment of highly trained personages such as architects for the purpose of applying their knowledge and experience in helping to maintain the high standards of the community is laudable and salutary and serves the public good.

We determine and hold that Ordinance 137.05 is a constitutional exercise of the police power by the City Council and is, therefore, valid. *State ex rel. Saveland Park Holding Corp. v. Wieland.*

Section 137.05, as outlined above, sets out criteria and standards for the Board to follow in passing upon an application for the building of a new home which are definite as to the objective to be attained, to protect property, to maintain high character of community development, to protect real estate from impairment and destruction of value; specific as to matters to be considered and regulated, design, use of material, finished grade lines, orientation; instructive as to the method by which the matters specified are to be adjudged, "proper architectural principles" and informative as to the bounds within which it is to exercise these powers, "for the accomplishment of said purposes only."

When borne in mind that the members of the Board are highly trained experts in the field of architecture, the instruction that they resolve these questions on "proper architectural principles" is profoundly reasonable since such expression has reference to the basic knowledge on which their profession is founded.

It is our view, therefore, that Section 137.05 contains all the criteria and standards reasonably necessary for the Board to carry on the duties conferred upon it.

We have read the bill of exceptions filed in this case carefully. It discloses that North Park Boulevard is in a district zoned for Class 1A residences not to exceed thirty-five feet in height or two and one-half stories, whichever is lesser, and which are required to cover not less than fifteen thousand square feet of lot space. This district extends through a park area with buildings on the north side and trees, ravines, and bushes hundreds of feet wide on its south side. The buildings on this Boulevard are, in the main, dignified, stately and conventional structures, two and one-half stories high.

The house designed for the applicant, as described by applicant, is a flat-roofed complex of twenty modules, each of which is ten feet high, twelve feet square and arranged in a loosely formed "U" which winds its way through a grove of trees. About sixty per cent of the wall area of the house is glass and opens on an enclosed garden; the rest of the walls are of cement panels. A garage of the same modular construction stands off from the house, and these two structures, with their associated garden walls, trellises and courts, form a series of interior and exterior spaces, all under a canopy of trees and baffled from the street by a garden wall.

A wall ten feet high is part of the front structure of the house and garage and extends all around the garden area. It has no windows. Since the wall is of the same height as the structure of the house, no part of the house can be seen from the street. From all appearances, it is just a high wall with no indication of what is behind it. Not only does the house fail to conform in any manner with the other buildings but presents no identification that it is a structure for people to live in.

The Board, as well as the architect for the applicant, concede that this structure would be a very interesting home placed in a different environment. It is obvious that placed on North Parks Boulevard, it would not only be out of keeping with and a radical departure from the structures now standing but would be most detrimental to the further development of the area since there are two vacant lots immediately to the west and a third vacant lot on the street bordering the westernmost lot.

Esthetics was a consideration that played a part in the ruling of the Board, but there were many other factors that influenced its decision. The structure designed is a single-story home in a multi-story neighborhood; it does not conform to general character of other houses; it would affect adjacent homes and three vacant lots; it is of such a radical concept that any design not conforming to the general character of the neighborhood would have to be thereafter approved; when viewed from the street, it could indicate a commercial building; it does not conform to standards of the neighborhood; it does not preserve high character of neighborhood; it does not preserve property values; it would be detrimental to neighborhood on the lot where proposed and it would be detrimental to the future development of the neighborhood.

16 C.J.S. Constitutional Law § 195, Esthetic Conditions, p. 939, states:

> The concept of the public welfare is broad and inclusive. The values it represents are spiritual as well as physical, esthetic as well as monetary. It is within the power of the legislature to determine that the community should be beautiful as well as healthy, spacious as well as clean, well-balanced as well as carefully patrolled. Nevertheless, it is held that esthetic conditions alone are insufficient to support the invocation of the police power, although if a regulation finds a reasonable justification in serving a generally recognized ground for the exercise of that power, the fact that esthetic considerations play a part in its adoption does not affect its validity.

It is our determination and we hold that the record in this case discloses ample evidence to support the judgment of the trial court that the Board did not abuse its discretion in its decision in this matter.

CORRIGAN, JUDGE (dissenting).

That the Board's determination was based entirely on [an aesthetic] consideration is, to this member of the court, conclusively established by the record before us. Take for example these questions and answers in connection with the interrogation of the witness, Russell Ralph Peck, a registered architect, who is a member of the Board of Architectural Review, at the trial in the Common Pleas Court. It should be remembered that it was stipulated by counsel for both parties that, if the other two members of the Board of Architectural Review would have testified, their testimony would be the same as the testimony of Mr. Peck. It is to be remembered also that both of these other members are likewise registered architects.

Q: Now the Board never took the position that this house would hurt property values along North Park Boulevard, did it?

A: Our issue was the fact that it was a single story house in a multi-story neighborhood.

Q: In other words, you were concerned.

A: . . . *and it did not conform to the aesthetics of the neighborhood.* (Emphasis added)

Q: Your objection was grounded upon the appearance of this house and not upon any market value depreciation possibility?

A: There is no question that the house would be in a class cost-wise with those in the neighborhood.

Q: The application for the permit was denied solely on the ground that the house did not conform to the character of the other houses along North Park Boulevard; is that correct?

A: Yes.

Q: And the application wasn't denied because of any purported or existing violation of technical requirements of the building code?

A: Oh, no.

Q: At the meeting of January 2nd and February 6th, was there any evidence before the Board that this house, if built, would threaten, endanger or impair the public health or public safety?

A: No.

Q: Any evidence before the Board that if that house were built it would adversely affect the public welfare, Mr. Peck?

A: It might affect public opinion.

Q: Might affect public opinion?

A: Yes, but not welfare.

Q: But not welfare?

A: Yes.

Q: How are the other houses affected, sir?

A: By the fact that this house did not conform to the multi-story designs of the houses in the neighborhood.

Q: In other words, you can't tell us what practical effect this house would have on the other houses or any other house in that neighborhood?

A: From a value standpoint, it probably would be as valuable dollar-wise.

Q: I take it from what you say that the Board's essential concern was with the appearance of this house from the outside?

A: Exactly.

Q: The Board wasn't concerned with the architectural treatment of the interior?

A: No.

Q: Its sole consideration was the exterior appearance; is that right?

A: Yes, sir. . . .

A: We don't like the appearance of that house in this neighborhood.

Therefore, the question presented under this assignment of error is: does the Board have the right to prohibit a citizen from building a house that does not conform to the other houses in the neighborhood, as Mr. Peck testified, *supra*, or in other words, on aesthetic considerations alone, where the design and plans of such house meet the zoning and building code requirements and will not threaten, endanger or impair the public health, safety or welfare, and will not impair property values in the neighborhood?

This member of the court is of the opinion that the answer is an emphatic negative in the light of the law that is applicable to the situation.

First, to take up the decision of the Board: what answers do the evidence provide as to "the character of the houses in the area," as stated in the Board's decision. North Park Boulevard is an important motor vehicle thoroughfare running generally east and west. On the south side of the boulevard, there is a park area. There are no sidewalks on either side of the boulevard in the block, at least, where appellant's site is located. The homes along North Park Boulevard show examples of Tudor, flat-roofed contemporary or modern, Spanish, Colonial, and other types. Some are two and one-half or three storied homes. The plaintiff's lot abuts to the north on the south end of lots on Colchester Road. This latter street on both sides presents a prosaic succession of two family homes, some of brick construction, some of wood, and some of a combination of both, all of two and one-half stories in height. Two lots west of the plaintiff's property and clearly within view from her lot are the modest frame single homes of two stories on both sides of Woodmere Drive. So here in one small area in Cleveland Heights we find a mélange of architectural styles and of obviously varying lot sizes and price values. Then the question occurs as to what is the "character of the houses in the area." A fair definition would appear to consider "character" as the sum of qualities or features by which the area is distinguished from others or a sum of traits conferring distinctiveness. But, is there any distinctiveness to this area? It seems to reflect the result observable in any American suburb of the age of Cleveland Heights with localities of residences constituted of a mixture of architectural designs and of varying price values, most of which were obviously constructed at least from twenty five to forty years ago. This is not the new suburbia, the packaged villages that are becoming the barracks of the new generation.

The residence proposed to be constructed on her lot by appellant does have character, in the opinion of this member of the court, judging from the description of the plans given by the architect and the model of the proposed construction introduced as an exhibit. It does have attributes conferring distinctiveness. It is one story with a flat roof. But there are other one story modern homes on North Park Boulevard with flat roofs. The plans include a wall to be built at the setback line, 106 feet from North Park Boulevard, approximately seven feet high with walls describing irregular courses on the easterly and westerly sides and a wall on the north line. If appellant does not wish to be bothered with a view of the "round the clock" vehicular traffic swishing past on North Park Boulevard to and from the marts of trade, she should be permitted this peace. If she wishes to screen out the view of the neighboring mixture of architectural styles and enjoy her trees and garden and other beauties of nature and whatever decoration she introduces within her walls and her home, these should be permitted to her. She feels that the plan submitted calls for a residence of beauty and utility and so does her architect.

It should be borne in mind that there is an important principle of eclecticism in architecture which implies freedom on the part of the architect or client or both to choose among the styles of the past and present that which seems to them most appropriate.

Should the appellant be required to sacrifice her choice of architectural plan for her property under the official municipal juggernaut of conformity in this case?

Should her aesthetic sensibilities in connection with her selection of design for her proposed home be stifled because of the apparent belief in this community of the group as a source of creativity? Is she to sublimate herself in this group and suffer the frustration of individual creative aspirations? Is her artistic spirit to be imprisoned by the apparent beneficence of community life in Cleveland Heights? This member of the court thinks not under the record in this case and the pertinent legal principles applicable thereto.

NOTES AND QUESTIONS

1. *Legitimate Exercise of Police Power.* A longstanding issue is whether aesthetic considerations constitute a legitimate basis for the exercise of the police power. Early courts rejected the idea, but the clear trend has been toward acceptance of the proposition. Most courts today take the position that aesthetic considerations alone justify an exercise of the police power. Among the minority of states which are unwilling to say that such concerns alone are enough, most recognize aesthetic factors as a valid auxiliary consideration. *See* 3 ZONING AND LAND USE CONTROLS §§ 16.03–05 (Rohan ed. 1992). Some scholars trace the use of the police power "purely" for aesthetic purposes to dictum in the famous United States Supreme Court decision, *Berman v. Parker*, 348 U.S. 26 (1954). This language is quoted, though not identified, by the *Reid* majority in the penultimate paragraph of the opinion. *Berman*, an eminent domain case, is discussed in Ch. 4.

Where does the *Reid* case stand on the question of whether aesthetic concerns alone can justify a police power regulation? The court lists numerous "other factors" that warrant examination. If not aesthetic considerations, what are they?

What do courts and legal commentators mean by "aesthetics"? Dean Costonis suggests that the aesthetics of the law not be treated as the aesthetics of the museum. It is, he says, not taste or beauty that legal aesthetics deals or ought to deal with, but stability and protection for that which we have come to expect. J. COSTONIS, ICONS & ALIENS: LAW, AESTHETICS, AND ENVIRONMENTAL CHANGE (1989). Does this thesis conform to the concerns of the *Reid* court? (Note that the court itself never uses the word "aesthetics" as a noun, but only "aesthetic" as an adjective.)

2. *The* Reid *Ordinance.* Observe the basic thrust of the ordinance in this case. As in the designation and regulation of historic buildings and sites, the constitutionality of architectural preservation schemes often depends upon the process used to evaluate the merits of the proposed structure and the finality of the decision. Should one be satisfied with the fact that "highly trained personages such as architects," as the *Reid* court puts it, are entrusted with the decision of whether the applicant gets to build the kind of house she wants? Does the ordinance adequately guide their decision-making and limit their discretion? For some courts, standards directing a board to determine whether a proposed house is "inappropriate" or "incompatible" with surrounding property are unconstitutionally vague. *See Waterfront Estates Dev., Inc. v. City of Palos Hills*, 597 N.E.2d 641, 649 (Ill. App. Ct. 1992); *Anderson v. City of Issaquah*, 851 P.2d 744 (Wash. Ct. App. 1993). Would it be better to have a standard that "no permit shall issue if the proposed structure will be so incompatible so as to cause substantial depreciation in the value of surrounding property"? *See State ex rel. Saveland Park Holding Corp. v. Wieland*,

69 N.W.2d 217 (Wis. 1955); *see also Anderson v. City of Issaquah*, 851 P.2d 74 (Wash. Ct. App. 1993) (ordinance, which required that buildings be "harmonious," "interesting," and "compatible," and where one commissioner denied approval in part because the suggested "Tahoe blue may be too dark," found unconstitutionally vague); *Rolling Pines Ltd. Partnership v. City of Little Rock*, 40 S.W.3d 828 (Ark. Ct. App. 2001) (compatibility standard not unconstitutionally vague to determine whether to allow manufactured homes in "residential" subdivision).

3. *First Amendment Implications*. One of the earliest state court cases raising First Amendment rights against an ordinance that is clearly aesthetically-based is *New York v. Stover*, 191 N.E.2d 272 (N.Y. 1963). There, property owners protesting increased taxes hung clotheslines full of rags in their front yard in violation of a local ordinance prohibiting clotheslines in front or side yards. Despite evidence that the ordinance was clearly directed at the protesters, the New York Court of Appeals held that the ordinance did not unconstitutionally burden the right of free speech, especially as it was directed to the protection of property values, even though it was clearly aesthetically motivated. The decision prompted a strong dissent on the ground that aesthetic judgments are so much a matter of personal taste that regulation for such purposes ought to be sharply curtailed lest individual preferences and tastes be gradually eliminated by local governments seeking "to placate the wishes of other property owners who constitute a larger segment of the electorate." 191 N.E.2d at 278. *See generally* Williams, *Subjectivity, Expression, and Privacy: Problems of Aesthetic Regulation*, 62 MINN. L. REV. 1 (1977); Poole, *Architectural Appearance Review Regulations and the First Amendment: The Good, the Bad, and the Consensus Ugly*, 19 URB. LAW. 287 (1987); Pak, Note, *Free Exercise, Free Expression, and Landmark Preservation*, 91 COLUM. L. REV. 1813 (1991); Regan, Note, *You Can't Build That Here: The Constitutionality of Aesthetic Zoning and Architectural Review*, 58 FORDHAM L. REV. 1013 (1990). Does the dissenting justice's discomfort suggest that First Amendment rights are implicated here? Does architecture constitute protected speech? *See First Covenant Church of Seattle v. City of Seattle*, 840 P.2d 174 (Wash. 1992), where the court says that, according to United States Supreme Court authority, conduct constitutes speech within the meaning of the First Amendment when there is " 'an intent to convey a particularized message' and a great 'likelihood . . . that the message would be understood by those who view it.' " *Id.* at 182. Pursuant to that test, the Washington court found that a church building itself was speech. Does this make sense?

In 1993, Congress passed the Religious Freedom Restoration Act, which, inter alia, expressly forbade control of religious uses by local governments. In *City of Boerne v. Flores*, 521 U.S. 507 (1997), the Supreme Court struck it down on grounds that it went beyond the powers of the federal government. Congress responded with the Religious Land Use and Institutionalized Persons Act of 2000, which specifically mentions zoning in its list of forbidden controls. It also prohibits governments from adopting "a land use regulation in a manner that imposes a substantial burden on the religious exercise of a person, including a religious assembly or institution" unless the regulation is linked to "a compelling governmental interest." 42 U.S.C. §§ 2000cc to 2000cc-5. Literally dozens of cases interpreting RLUIPA have been filed and decided in the ensuing half-dozen years. One must conclude that core religious activity is protected, but ancillary activities — like coffee shops and counseling t, even if all were allegedly related to the subject religion. *See* owley and Kenneth Pearlman, Six Flags Over Jesus: RLUIPA, d Zoning, 21 TUL. ENVTL. L.J. 203 (2008); Shelly Ross Saxer, *Faith us Accessory Use and Land Use Regulation*, 2008 Utah L. Rev. aimo and Lucero (eds), RLUIPA READER: RELIGIOUS LAND USES, OURTS (2009).

ISION AND PLANNING

land development through the subdivision process is a relatively modern regulatory device. The subdivision ordinance developed from so-called "plat acts" which required that no parcels be divided and sold without the filing of a "plat," a drawing of the parcel showing the division or divisions into which it had been carved. The plat acts help facilitate real estate conveyancing by producing a more useful property description which could be recorded in deeds and real estate sale contracts in the official land records. (The mechanics of conveyancing and recording are the subject of Chapter 5.)

Until late into the 19th century, land was usually described by its "metes and bounds." Beginning at a relatively immovable landmark, like an oak tree, a boulder, an iron stake, or a stone boundary marker, a series of measurements consisting of angles, feet, degrees, and directions would give the boundary of a lot, ultimately ending or "closing" the perimeter description at the "point of beginning." The metes and bounds description was not only cumbersome — some descriptions running for pages — but also fraught with legal peril. A mistake in the description, often resulting in a measurement that did not close or return to the point of beginning, created a defect in title that often voided the transfer. D. MANDELKER, LAND USE LAW (6th edition 2012). However, by taking the same parcel, giving it a name, dividing it or "subdividing" it into two or more parts, numbering or lettering the parts or lots, and recording the whole drawing or plat, it was possible thereafter to provide a complete legal description by referring to the individual lots on the plat rather than the cumbersome metes and bounds.

As a land development tool, early subdivisions were often an unmitigated disaster. In particular, larger subdivisions with many lots often were badly planned both internally and externally in relation to adjacent parcels. Streets were often not only poorly laid out within the subdivision but also failed to connect with streets outside the development. Major streets in one subdivision could, and did, lead directly into minor streets in another, and some streets ended abruptly at the property line. These and other design and public facility shortcomings led to state subdivision enabling legislation permitting local communities to adopt subdivision regulations (usually ordinances) to deal with these problems.

At first, local subdivision ordinances dealt primarily with an increasing volume of so-called design standards: width and composition of streets and sidewalks, road perimeter linkage, uniformity of building set backs, and the like. Street and road standards often incorporated by reference an official map showing where the community had decided to place its streets. From the design and location of public facilities needed to serve new subdivisions, it was an easy (if not necessarily logical) step to require their construction as a condition of subdivision approval. Thus, many state enabling acts directed local subdivision codes to require the building and dedication (donation to the community) of streets, sewers, water mains, sidewalks, and other public facilities. The subdivision was well on its way to becoming a development code by the 1950s. LAND USE LAW, *supra*, at Ch. 4-B.

A logical step from regulating the design of public facilities and their dedication was the mandatory reservation of open space and public building sites on subdivision plats and later their dedication to the public as well. The first of these, the reserving of sites for public uses and consequent prohibition (even for a short time) of an owner's developing such sites, was both common and practical. Increased residential construction creates the need for schools, police and fire stations, and parks. A number of state enabling acts directed that such sites be left undeveloped by private owners only for a specified length of time, usually a year, by which time the local government either had to purchase the site or let the owner develop it. Even this limited requirement met with owner resistance, sometimes resulting in litigation.

The process of subdivision approval is much the same everywhere. Usually, a preliminary plat is first submitted to the local plan commission for review. Streets, sidewalks, lots, and public facilities are sketched on such plats, and conditions and dedication requirements are either written directly on it, or if more lengthy, attached to it. After review by appropriate officials (usually building department staff), it is either approved, approved with modifications, or rejected. A more detailed final plat is then submitted, similarly viewed, and, if accepted, sent to the city or county council for formal approval, execution, and recording. The restrictions and conditions so recorded thus become burdens that "run with the land"; that is, they become binding on later purchasers of the lots. *See generally* R. FREILICH & S. MARK WHITE, 21ST CENTURY LAND DEVELOPMENT CODE (2008).

YOUNGBLOOD v. BOARD OF SUPERVISORS OF SAN DIEGO COUNTY

California Supreme Court
586 P.2d 556 (1978)

TOBRINER, JUSTICE.

These consolidated cases involve the Rancho Del Dios subdivision in West-Central San Diego County. On December 10, 1974, the Board of Supervisors of San Diego County approved a tentative subdivision map providing for one-acre lots, a land use permitted by the then zoning and general plan. On December 31, however, the county amended its general plan to limit density for Rancho Del Dios to one dwelling unit for each two acres; thus when the county approved the final subdivision map on October 25, 1975, the subdivision did not conform to the existing general plan.

Plaintiffs, neighbors of the subdivision, filed two mandamus actions against the board of supervisors; both suits contend that the board acted illegally in approving the tentative and final maps and that it was under a mandatory duty to rezone the subdivision to conform to the new general plan.

While the appeal was pending before this court, the board of supervisors amended the zoning for Rancho Del Dios to conform to the general plan, thus mooting the principal issue of this appeal. The only remaining issue relates to the board's approval of the tentative and final subdivision maps. With respect to those issues, we hold that the board did not act unlawfully in approving the tentative map; once the developer complied with the conditions attached to that approval and submitted a final map corresponding to the tentative map, the board performed a ministerial duty in approving the final map. We therefore affirm the judgment of the superior court.

1. *Summary of issues and proceedings.*

On June 26, 1974, real party in interest Santa Fe Company filed an application for a tentative subdivision map for Rancho Del Dios. The map divides the 217-acre parcel into 131 lots, many of which would be only 1 acre or slightly larger in size. Because the developer proposed to retain a 40-acre parcel and several smaller parcels in an undeveloped state, the density of the subdivision would approximate .6 dwelling units per acre.

On October 11, 1974, the San Diego County Planning Commission (Planning Commission) approved the proposed tentative map, expressly finding that it conformed to the existing zoning and general plan. The Planning Commission recommended, however, that a number of conditions be imposed upon approval of a final subdivision map. Although one such condition was that the developer apply for a zoning change from A-4(1) to E-1 (one-acre residential), a zone the commission believed more suitable for a residential subdivision, the Planning Commission refused to require the zoning change as a condition to approval of a final map. On December 10, the board of supervisors approved the tentative map subject to the conditions proposed by the Planning Commission.

2. *The board of supervisors did not abuse its discretion in approving the tentative subdivision map for Rancho Del Dios.*

Plaintiffs assert that the board abused its discretion when it approved the tentative subdivision map.[7] They first argue that the tentative map was not approved until April 1975, after the enactment of the new San Dieguito Community Plan, and that such approval was ineffective because the tentative map conflicted with the new general plan. The record shows, however, that the board approved the tentative map on December 10, 1974, subject to certain conditions, among which was the condition that Santa Fe Company apply for E-1(B) zoning; on April 24, 1975, the board determined that Santa Fe had fulfilled this condition.

The Subdivision Map Act contemplates that the local agency, when it approves a tentative map, will normally attach conditions to that approval, such as the completion of planned subdivision improvements, and will approve the final map

[7] [2] Approval of a tentative subdivision map is a quasi judicial act subject to judicial review for abuse of discretion under Code of Civil Procedure section 1094.5. (*See Woodland Hills Residents Ass'n, Inc. v. City Council* (1975) 118 Cal. Rptr. 856 (Cal. App.).)

only after certifying that the subdivider has complied with those specified conditions. (*See generally* LONGTIN, CAL. LAND USE REGULATIONS (1977) ch. 10.) This statutory structure compels the conclusion that the approval of a tentative map subject to conditions is nonetheless an approval for the purpose of determining that map's consistency with the existing general plan. Since the board conditionally approved the tentative subdivision map on December 10, 1974, the features of that map must be measured against the general plan in effect on that date.

3. *The board of supervisors properly approved the final subdivision map for Rancho Del Dios.*

On October 25, 1975, when the board of supervisors approved the final subdivision map for Rancho Del Dios, the new San Dieguito Community Plan called for two-acre homesites in the area of the subdivision. Plaintiffs contend that the final subdivision map providing for lots of less than two acres conflicted with the general plan then in effect, and thus that the board's approval of that map violated Business and Professions Code sections 11526 and 11549.5.[8] The county and the developer in response maintain that under Business and Professions Code sections 11549.6 and 11611 the county *was required* to approve a final map which conformed to a properly approved tentative map if the subdivider had complied with all conditions attached to the approval of the tentative map. We shall explain why we agree with the county's construction of the governing statutes.

The requirement that subdivision maps conform to a general plan was added by the enactment of Assembly Bill No. 1301 in 1971. When first passed by the Assembly, the bill contained two provisions requiring final maps to conform to a general plan. Section 11526, subdivision (c) stated that "No city or county shall approve a tentative or final subdivision map unless the governing body shall find that the proposed subdivision . . . is consistent with *applicable* general or specific plans of the city or county." (Emphasis added.) Section 11549.5 then specifically listed all grounds which require the governing body to "deny approval of a final or tentative subdivision map;" the first ground listed, in subdivision (a), is "That the proposed map is not consistent with *applicable* general and specific plans." (Emphasis added.) Since no statute specified which general plan is "applicable" when the governing body takes up the question of approval of a final map, sections 11526 and 11549.5 could have been construed either to require a final map to conform to the general plan in effect when that map came before the governing body for approval, as plaintiffs contend, or to require it only to conform to the general plan in effect when the tentative map was approved.

The purpose of section 11549.6, as we perceive it, was to confirm that the date when the tentative map comes before the governing body for approval is the crucial date when that body should decide whether to permit the proposed subdivision. Once the tentative map is approved, the developer often must expend substantial sums to comply with the conditions attached to that approval. These expenditures

---

[8] [4] The board's decision approving the final subdivision map is a ministerial act reviewable by ordinary mandamus pursuant to Code of Civil Procedure section 1085. (*See Great Western Sav. & Loan Ass'n v. City of Los Angeles* (1973) 107 Cal. Rptr. 359 (Cal. App.).)

will result in the construction of improvements consistent with the proposed subdivision, but often inconsistent with alternative uses of the land. Consequently it is only fair to the developer and to the public interest to require the governing body to render its discretionary decision whether and upon what conditions to approve the proposed subdivision when it acts on the tentative map. Approval of the final map thus becomes a ministerial act once the appropriate officials certify that it is in substantial compliance with the previously approved tentative map. (*Great Western Sav. & Loan Ass'n v. City of Los Angeles*, *supra*, 107 Cal. Rptr. 359; LONGTIN, CAL. LAND USE REGULATIONS, *op. cit. supra*, at p. 600.)

Plaintiffs do not contend that the final map for Rancho Del Dios does not substantially comply with the tentative map or that Santa Fe Company failed to fulfill the conditions attached to approval of the tentative map. Having held, as we stated earlier, that the board of supervisors properly approved the tentative map, we conclude that the board acted properly in approving the final map.

NOTES AND QUESTIONS

1. Note the court's characterization of the tentative map approval as quasi-judicial, and the subsequent approval of the final map as ministerial. What is the difference, and why does it matter here? If additional land development conditions were added by the board at the final map approval stage, would the court still characterize the decision as ministerial?

2. This case raises a classic vested rights question: at what point does a landowner have the right to proceed with a development rendered illegal under new land use regulations? Usually the courts require a measure of good faith on the part of the landowner, as well as a substantially changed position in the form of expenditures in reliance on preexisting regulations and/or approvals. While good faith may not be an issue in the principal case, what about the changed position? If, as the court seems to indicate, the landowner has vested rights to proceed, what precisely does the landowner have a right to do or expect from the county? Would the result be the same if the county had changed the zoning to agriculture? If the state's coastal commission had placed the land in a coastal zone and required a coastal zone permit? See, for extended discussion, D. CALLIES, D. CURTIN & J. TAPPENDORF, BARGAINING FOR DEVELOPMENT: A HANDBOOK ON DEVELOPMENT AGREEMENTS, ANNEXATION AGREEMENTS, LAND DEVELOPMENT CONDITIONS, VESTED RIGHTS, AND THE PROVISION OF PUBLIC FACILITIES (2003).

COMMERCIAL BUILDERS OF NORTHERN CALIFORNIA v. SACRAMENTO

United States Court of Appeals, Ninth Circuit

941 F.2d 872 (1991)

SCHROEDER, CIRCUIT JUDGE

In 1987, the City and County of Sacramento commissioned a consulting firm, Keyser-Marston Associates, to study the need for low-income housing, the effect of nonresidential development on the demand for such housing, and the appropriateness of exacting fees in conjunction with such development to pay for such housing. Keyser-Marston submitted its report, estimating the percentage of new workers in the developments that would qualify as low-income workers and would require housing. As instructed, it also calculated fees for development based on a yearly subsidy of $12,000 per qualified household that would be connected to the development. This figure represented the difference between $42,000, the minimum cost of building a two-bedroom apartment, and $30,000, the maximum rental income expected from a low-income household. Also as instructed, however, in the interest of erring on the side of conservatism in exacting the fees, it reduced its final calculations by about one-half.

Based upon this study, the City of Sacramento enacted the Housing Trust Fund Ordinance on March 7, 1989. The Ordinance lists several city-wide findings, including the finding that nonresidential development is "a major factor in attracting new employees to the region" and that the influx of new employees "creates a need for additional housing in the City." Pursuant to these findings, the Ordinance imposes a fee in connection with the issuance of permits for nonresidential development of the type that will generate jobs. The fees, calculated using the Keyser-Marston formula, are to be paid into a fund to assist in the financing of low-income housing. The city projects that the fund will raise about $ 3.6 million annually, nine percent of the projected annual cost of $42 million for the needed housing. Additional money will come from other sources, such as debt funding and general revenues.

Commercial Builders does not argue that the city lacks a legitimate interest in expanding low-income housing. Rather, it contends that this Ordinance constitutes an impermissible means to advance that interest, because it places a burden of paying for low-income housing on nonresidential development without a sufficient showing that nonresidential development contributes to the need for low-income housing in proportion to that burden. We affirm because we find the Ordinance sufficiently related to the legitimate purpose it seeks to achieve.

We have held that a condition placed upon the granting of a permit to develop land may constitute an impermissible taking, but we have done so only where the condition lacked any rational relationship to the project for which the permit was sought. In *Parks v. Watson*, 716 F.2d 646 (9th Cir. 1983), we held that where a developer seeking vacation of platted streets offered to pay for such vacation, a city could not insist that the developer dedicate its geothermal wells to the city as a precondition for such vacation. The dedication requirement, we held, "had no rational relationship to any purpose related to the vacation of the platted streets." 716 F.2d at 653. The condition therefore violated the *fifth amendment.*

We noted in *Parks* that the analysis we applied was based upon a consensus among the states that had considered the constitutionality of subdivision exaction regulations. 716 F.2d at 653. Prior to *Nollan*, other federal courts similarly upheld ordinances placing restrictions or conditions upon development where the ordinances were reasonably related to legitimate public purposes . . . . Under this analysis, the Ordinance here at issue cannot be said to work an unconstitutional taking. It was enacted after a careful study revealed the amount of low-income housing that would likely become necessary as a direct result of the influx of workers that would be associated with the new nonresidential development. It assesses only a small portion of a conservative estimate of the cost of such additional housing. The burden assessed against the developers thus bears a rational relationship to a public cost closely associated with such development.

The appellants contend that, even if the Ordinance would pass constitutional muster under these principles, it must be struck down because the Supreme Court has now articulated a more stringent standard under which courts must analyze the imposition of conditions upon development. The appellants point out that in *Nollan v. California Coastal Comm'n*, 483 U.S. 825, 107 S. Ct. 3141, 97 L. Ed. 2d 677 (1987), the Court held that such conditions must not only be ones that the government might "rationally have decided" to employ for a given legitimate public purpose; they must also substantially advance such a purpose. *See* 483 U.S. at 834 & n.4. They argue that under the standard articulated in *Nollan*, an ordinance that imposes an exaction on developers can be upheld only if it can be shown that the development in question is directly responsible for the social ill that the exaction is designed to alleviate.

As a threshold matter, we are not persuaded that *Nollan* materially changes the level of scrutiny we must apply to this Ordinance. The *Nollan* Court specifically stated that it did not have to decide "how close a 'fit' between the condition and the burden is required," because it found that the regulation in question "d[id] not meet even the most untailored standards." 483 U.S. at 838. It also noted that its holding was "consistent with the approach taken by every other court that has considered the question," citing *Parks* as the lead case in its string cite. *Id.* at 839. Other circuits that have considered the constitutionality of ordinances that placed burdens on land use after *Nollan*. None have interpreted that case as changing the level of scrutiny to be applied to regulations that do not constitute a physical encroachment on land. . . .

We therefore agree with the City that *Nollan* does not stand for the proposition that an exaction ordinance will be upheld only where it can be shown that the development is directly responsible for the social ill in question. Rather, *Nollan* holds that where there is no evidence of a nexus between the development and the problem that the exaction seeks to address, the exaction cannot be upheld. Where, as here, the Ordinance was implemented only after a detailed study revealed a substantial connection between development and the problem to be addressed, the Ordinance does not suffer from the infirmities that the Supreme Court disapproved in *Nollan*. We find that the nexus between the fee provision here at issue, designed to further the city's legitimate interest in housing, and the burdens caused by commercial development is sufficient to pass constitutional muster. . . .

NOTES AND QUESTIONS

1. Note the detailed study which preceded the workforce housing exaction imposed by the City of Sacramento. How much of the 9th Circuit's opinion is dependent upon this demonstration of need?

2. California courts of appeal have twice considered mandatory housing exactions, both on residential projects, since the *Commercial Builders* case, with different results. *In Home Builders Ass'n of Northern California v. C* 535 U.S. 954 (2001), the court upheld a 10% mandatory affordable housi but in the context of significant density bonuses and other benefits pr developer, and 700 pages of explanatory documentation from the *Building Industry Ass'n of Central California v. City of Patterson,* 4th 886 (2009), another court of appeals struck down a substantial in- housing fee imposed on a residential development accompanied justification study. Observing that the study appeared to be based on the City's need alone, the court said: "No connection is shown, by the Fee Justification Study or by anything else in the record, between the 642-unit figure and the need for affordable housing generated by the new market rate development." *Id.* at 74. Then in June of 2015 the California Supreme Court overruled the Patterson case on the surprising ground that, despite the City of Sacramento decision, which it failed to cite altogether, the law of exactions and land development conditions was entirely inapplicable to workforce/affordable housing set-asides. *California Building Industry Ass'n v. City of San Jose*, 351 P.3d 974 (Cal. 2015). According to the court, such set-asides are the same as standard zoning requirements. The court's failure to understand basic zoning and land use is breathtaking and the case is currently the subject of a petition for certiorari to the U.S. Supreme Court. Both cases should be read in the context of a California statute requiring density bonuses for any developer seeking them in return for providing affordable housing, which bonuses become mandatory at the 5% affordable housing requirement (if any) level. A 2004 survey of California local governments which impose such requirements, report density bonuses in exchange for affordable housing in 91% of the 98 (out of 107) local governments responding to the survey. *See* California Coalition for Rural Housing and the Non-Profit Housing Association of Northern California, *Inclusionary Housing in California: 30 years of Innovation* (2003). For further commentary and analysis, *see* D. Callies, *Mandatory Set-Asides as Land Development Conditions for Affordable/Workforce Housing*, 42 The Urban Lawyer 307 (2010).

Chapter 12

ENVIRONMENTAL PROTECTIONS

Although the line between environmental and land use controls is hardly bright (as the United States Supreme Court's many opinions in *California Coastal Commission v. Grallite Rock Co.*, 480 U.S. 572 (1987), case amply demonstrate), some land use regulations are more clearly designed to improve environmental conditions than others. Indeed, many of the cases in this section often find their way into environmental law texts as often as in land use and property texts. Nevertheless, it is difficult to appreciate the full spectrum which the law of property embraces without at least some introduction to the protection of coastal areas, land use implications of the Clean Air, Clean Water, and Endangered Species statutes, and public land law. The cases which follow are designed to provide this introduction. They are neither the most recent nor, for the most part, the most famous. They are, however, among the most fundamental.

[A.] COASTAL ZONE

Coastal zone management has been the subject of state and local regulation through much of the last three decades in the United States. This is not particularly surprising, since fully three-quarters of our population lives in the coastal zone. However, it was not until the mid-1970s that a national program of coastal zone management commenced under the federal Coastal Zone Management Act ("CZMA"). Designed largely to encourage states in coastal areas to plan, manage, and regulate the use of land therein, the CZMA provides funds for the creation and implementation of state coastal zone management plans, on the condition that they follow various coastal land regulatory and management guidelines.

The federal Coastal Zone Management Act of 1972 was passed during the heady days of national land use and environmental activism in response to competing development and preservation demands on the nation's coastal areas. Congress found that population growth and development in coastal areas resulted in the destruction of marine resources, wildlife, open space, and other important ecological, cultural, historic, and aesthetic values. In response, Congress created a management and regulatory framework and appropriated money for the development and implementation of state-run coastal zone management programs. The framework is imposed if, but only if, a state chooses to accept the money and — except for Alaska — all of the 35 eligible coastal states and territories have so chosen. The program consists of three parts: a management plan/program, implementation regulations, and consistency regulations.

The CZMA requires a state's coastal zone management program to include nine planning elements, the most important plan themes of which are a definition of the boundaries of that part of a coastal zone that is subject to the program, objectives and policies for coastal area protection, a statement of permissible land and water uses, and the identification of special management areas.

The program's coastal boundaries are defined as coastal waters and adjacent shorelands that are strongly influenced by each other. While it is not particularly difficult to find the seaward boundary, the trick is to identify the vaguely defined inland boundary. The zone extends seaward to the outer limit of the U.S. territorial sea, but the inland boundary of the zone is based on the extent of area necessary to control shorelands, the use of which has a direct and significant impact on coastal waters. According to federal regulations, areas that might be included are areas of particular concern — salt marshes and wetlands, beaches, state — determined floodplains, islands and watersheds. However vague the regulations, a state must define its inland boundary with sufficient precision so that "interested parties" can determine whether their activities are controlled by the management program. CZMA regulations also set out criteria for determining permissible uses subject to the management program.

TOPLISS v. PLANNING COMMISSION

Hawaii Intermediate Court of Appeals
842 P.2d 648 (1993)

HEEN, JUDGE.

On April 30, 1990, Petitioner-Appellant Larry T. Topliss, dba Pacific Land Company (Petitioner), filed a petition (Permit Petition) with Appellee Planning Commission of the County of Hawaii (Commission) for a Special Management Area (SMA) permit (SMAP) pursuant to the Coastal Zone Management Act (CZMA), Hawaii Revised Statutes (HRS) chapter 205A (1985 and Supp. 1991), to develop two multi-story office buildings on his property (property) in Kailua-Kona.

The property lies on the northern comer of the intersection of Kuakini Highway and Seaview Circle. Kuakini Highway has an 80-foot right-of-way with a 24-foot pavement, while Seaview Circle has a 6O-foot right-of-way with a 20-foot pavement. The Permit Petition acknowledges that the property "lies on a vital intersection and is adjacent to a high-traffic highway." The Permit Petition also describes the intersection as "a high-traffic intersection."

The property consists of two adjacent lots within the 143-lot Kona Sea View Lots Subdivision, most of which are in single family residential use.[1] [The Court then summarized the applicable land use regulations and plans and concluded the property was appropriately classified for the proposed development.]

The property has an area of approximately one-half acre and is nearly 400 feet above sea level and about 3600 feet from the shoreline. The property is rather severely sloped away from Kuakini Highway with a grade of approximately 20%. The difference in elevation between the property's mauka and makai boundaries is approximately 40 feel. The roof line of the proposed building abutting Kuakini

[1] [1] The two lots have areas of 15,001 and 7,502 square feet.

Highway would extend approximately six feet above the elevation of the property's boundary. Between the property and the coastline lies most of the Kona Sea View Lots Subdivision, a "non-transgressable thicket," hotels and apartments along Alii Drive, and Alii Drive itself, which is the paved county roadway closest to and paralleling the coastline. Two circuitous vehicular routes measuring 2.7 miles in the southerly direction and 1.5 miles in the northerly direction are the only accesses to the coastline.

The property came within the purview of the CZMA in 1980 when the Commission designated all of the area makai of Kuakini Highway from Kailua southward to Keauhou as a SMA. At that time, the Commission cited "anticipated development pressures" in the area, the steep topography, soil composition, the Hawaii County General Plan designation of "the entire Kuakini right of way . . . as an important scenic resource," and the need to "better coordinate the overall development of the area" as the grounds for its action.

The Commission denied the Permit Petition and Petitioner appealed to the third circuit court. By stipulation of the parties, the matter was remanded to the Commission for the entry of findings of fact (FOF) and conclusions of law (COL). Meanwhile, on September 4, 1990, Petitioner filed a petition with the Commission to amend the boundaries (Boundary Petition) of the SMA to exclude his property.

The Boundary Petition was heard by the Commission on January 31, 1991. At the same hearing, the Commission denied Petitioner's request to reconsider the denial of the Permit Petition. On February 21, 1991, the Commission entered separate FOF, COL, and Orders denying both Petitions. Petitioner appealed both orders to the third circuit court and on September 5, 1991, that court entered an order affirming the Commission. The matter is here on Petitioner's appeal from the circuit court's order.

I

Although Petitioner does not challenge the validity of the CZMA, the thrust of his attack is that when the Commission denied his Petitions it violated the CZMA's clear objectives and purposes.[2] We disagree with respect to the Boundary Petition, but agree with respect to the Permit Petition.

The dispositive question is construction of the CZMA. Our duty in construing statutes is to ascertain and give effect to the legislature's intention and to implement that intention to the fullest degree. *State v. Briones*, 784 P.2d 860 (Haw. 1989). Petitioner argues that the CZMA is simply a zoning statute which must, as a general rule, be strictly construed against further derogation of common-law property rights. The rule cited by Petitioner is inapplicable here, however, since the language of the CZMA is clear and unambiguous and the legislature's intent is beyond peradventure. *See Maui County v. Puamana Management Corp.*, 631 P.2d 1215 (Haw. App. 1981).

The CZMA is "a comprehensive State regulatory scheme to protect the

---

[2] [3] We reject Petitioner's arguments that the Commission's refusal to remove the property from the CZMA was "spot zoning" and amounted to a "taking."

environment and resources of our shoreline areas." *Mahuiki v. Planning Comm'n*, 654 P.2d 874, 881 (Haw. 1982).

The CZMA imposes special controls on the development of real property along the shoreline areas in order "to preserve, protect, and where possible, to restore the natural resources of the coastal zone of Hawaii." HRS § 20SA-21. *Sandy Beach Defense Fund v. City Council*, 773 P.2d 250, 254 (Haw. 1989)

When it enacted the CZMA. the Hawaii legislature specifically found that "special controls on developments within an area along the shoreline are necessary to avoid permanent losses of valuable resources and the foreclosure of management options, and to ensure that adequate access, by dedication or other means, to public owned or used beaches, recreation areas, and natural reserves is provided." HRS § 205A-21 (1985). The legislature therefore declared it to be "The state policy to preserve, protect, and where possible, to restore the natural resources of the coastal zone of Hawaii." *Id.* In order to carry out the CZMA's policies and objectives, the legislature authorized the counties to establish SMAs. HRS § 205A- 23 (1985). Development within a SMA is controlled by a permit system administered by the counties pursuant to HRS § 205A-28 (1985).

II.

The Boundary Petition

A.

Petitioner argues that the Commission exceeded its lawful authority when it established Kuakini Highway as the mauka [towards the mountains, inland, away from the beach] boundary of the SMA. He contends that the CZMA authorizes the Commission to include within the SMA lands that have a "direct and significant impact" on the coastal waters protected by the CZMA.[3] He asserts that in this case the property has "no potential for direct or substantial impact upon either the coastal water or the coastal resources to be protected" and should not be included within the SMA.[4] The argument is without merit.

---

[3] [4] Petitioner claims that the following findings or fact do not support the Commission's conclusion that the property should not be removed from the SMA:

> 63. Upon mandatory review and update or the SMA maps. the [Planning] Department recommended that the SMA in the North Kana district should include the area along Alii Drive, bounded by Kailua. Keauhou and Kuakini Highway. The rationale for this expansion focused on the rapid growth experienced in the area and a need to ensure that development evaluates the physical constraints as well as the scenic viewplanes from Kuakini Highway, which has been identified as an important scenic resource in the General Plan.
>
> 68. It is important that the boundary line be retained at Kuakini Highway since viewplanes have been identified as an area or critical concern.
>
> 71. If the development or Property is round to have no significant adverse impacts on viewplanes or open space, this does not mean that the Property can be removed from the SMA.

[4] [5] Any contraction of an SMA boundary is subject to review by State authorities for compliance

Among the CZMA's stated objectives and policies are the protection, preservation, restoration and improvement of the "quality of coastal scenic and open space resources[,]" HRS § 205A-2(b)(3) and (c)(3)(C) (1985), and the "designing and locating" of new "developments to minimize the alteration of . . . existing public views to and along the shoreline[.]" HRS § 205A-2(c)(3)(B) (1985).[5]

In order to protect and preserve the coastal zone's scenic and open space resources, the CZMA requires the Commission to "minimize, where reasonable . . . [a]ny development which would substantially interfere with or detract from the line of sight toward the sea from the state highway nearest the coast[.]" HRS § 205A-26(3)(D) (1985).

The intent of the CZMA is clearly to authorize inclusion in the SMA of lands that have a significant impact on the scenic resources in the area and whose development would alter the public views to and along the shoreline. Protection of the coastal areas and waters from adverse environmental or ecological impact is only one of the CZMA's objectives. Another clear objective is protection against interference with or alteration of coastal scenic resources. Where a property or development has the potential for such interference, then it may be included within a SMA even though it is not in close proximity to the coastline.

Petitioner's arguments that (1) the Commission's "rapid growth" finding"[6] is "factually incorrect" because the area surrounding the property "had already become substantially developed as early as 1977[,]" and (2) the property "is one of the very last parcels in the neighborhood which is yet to be developed[,]" is without merit.

First, the finding is merely a reiteration of the original finding made in 1980 when the SMA boundary was established at Kuakini Highway. There is nothing in the record to support Petitioner's argument that the area was already substantially developed at the time the finding was made. Moreover, whether the growth in the area was rapid or slow is really of no import. The aim of the CZMA is to control growth of whatever rapidity. See *Sandy Beach Defense Fund.*

Second, the fact that the property is among the last to be developed in the neighborhood does not vitiate the finding. The objective of controlling growth relates to the entire SMA not just the neighborhood in which the property is located.

Since control of growth in the SMA is an objective of the CZMA, it cannot be said, as Petitioner argues, that control of rapid growth is the Commission's attempt to use general planning and zoning objectives to justify imposition of the special controls of the CZMA.

---

with the objectives and policies of the CZMA. HRS § 205A-23 (1985).

[5] [6] In a report of the United States Senate Commerce Committee on the Coastal Zone Management Act of 1972, S. Rep. No. 92·753. 92 Cong., 2d Sess. 3, *reprinted* in U.S. Code Congo & Admin. News 4776 (1972), the committee suggested that a State coastal zone management program should include "both visual and physical" access "to the coastline and coastal areas[.]" *Id.* at 4786. Hawaii's coastal management program arises from the federal enactment, and the above sections of the CZMA clearly are meant to be in accord with the Commerce Committee's suggestion.

[6] [7] See note 4, *supra.*

B.

Petitioner acknowledges that the CZMA expresses the legislature's concern for "views along the shoreline." However, he contends that the "scenic viewplanes" cited by the Commission in FOF No. 63 is purely a creation of the Commission and is not among the "state interests" advanced by the CZMA.[7] Consequently, the continued inclusion of the property in the SMA unconstitutionally deprived him of his property. The argument is without merit.

First, Petitioner misstates the language of the CZMA. HRS § 20SA-2(c)(3)(B) clearly establishes the protection of views to and along the shoreline as among the legislature's policies regarding scenic and open space resources.[8]

Second, as stated above, HRS § 205A-26(3)(D) requires the Commission to minimize a development's interference with the line of sight from Kuakini Highway toward the sea.

In our view, the term scenic viewplanes employed in FOF No. 63 relating to the Boundary Petition is merely a paraphrase of the statutory terms "views to and along the shoreline" or "line of sight toward the sea," and clearly comports with the intent of the statute.

C.

Petitioner also argues that since the shoreline itself, as defined in the CZMA,[9] cannot be seen from the property, the continued inclusion of the property in the SMA goes beyond the legislature's authorization to protect "views *to and along* the shoreline" and "shoreline open space and scenic resources." We disagree.

HRS § 205A-26(3)(D) clearly mandates the Commission to protect and preserve more than just the view of the shoreline. As noted above, the statute, by its very language, is intended to protect the view toward the sea even though the "shoreline" cannot be seen either because of intervening development or natural growth.

Petitioner also contends that even if "protecting panoramic coastal views" is within the legislative mandate, it is not a reasonable basis for imposing SMA

---

7 [8] See note 4, *supra.*

8 [9] HRS§ 205A-2(c) (3)(B)(1985) reads as follows:

> Coastal Zone Management Program; objectives and policies
>
> (c) Policies.
>
> (3) Scenic and open space resources;
>
> (B) Insure that new developments are compatible with their visual environment by designing and locating such developments to minimize the alteration of natural landforms and *existing public views to and along the shoreline*[.]

(Emphasis added.)

9 [10] HRS §205A-1 (Supp. 1991) defines shoreline as:

> the upper reaches of the wash of the waves, other than storm and seismic waves, at high tide during the season of the year in which the highest wash of the waves, other than storm and seismic waves, at high tide during the season of the year in which the highest wash of the waves occurs, usually evidenced by the edge of vegetation growth, or the upper limit of debris left by the wash of the waves.

regulations, since Hawaii County may impose height and setback limitations under its zoning powers. However, the fact that the County can impose the same restrictions through the exercise of one power does not make the proper exercise of another specifically authorized power unreasonable.

D.

Petitioner asserts that since there is no significant view of either the ocean or the shoreline from the portion of Kuakini Highway that abuts the property, the inclusion of the property in the SMA did not advance the State's interest in preserving the viewplane from the highway. We disagree.

Admittedly, Petitioner's evidence indicates that the view from the portion of Kuakini Highway abutting the property is limited. However, that does not affect the Commission's finding as to the significance of the total viewplane from the highway. If, in fact, Petitioner's development would not have a significant, adverse impact on the total viewplane, the Commission could consider that as favoring the development or could impose conditions on the development to minimize the impact. However, that would not necessarily support removal of the property from the SMA.

E.

Petitioner argues that "[t]he original enactment of Hawaii's CZMA in 1975 . . . defined the SMA to exclude 'portions of [lands in] which there are numerous residential commercial or other structures of a substantial nature in existence as of the effective date of [CZMA]," and there is no indication that that exclusion should not be continued. The argument misstates the statute.

The original enactment excluded from SMAs only such built up areas that may be located on lands "which abut any *inland* waterway or body of water wholly or partially improved with walls[.]" Act 176, 1975 Haw. Sess. Laws § 1 (emphasis added). That is not the situation here and there is nothing to indicate the legislature intended to continue that exclusion or to expand it.

III

The Permit Petition

In denying the Permit Petition, the Commission made the following FOF:

> 62. Rule 9-IO(H)(5) says that one factor which should be considered in constituting a "significant adverse effect" is when the proposed use, activity or operation "involves substantial secondary impacts . . . such as effect on public facilities."
>
> 69. Based upon the evidence adduced, including that submitted with the Petition, the testimony of the public and the Petitioner, and the information contained in the [Planning] Department's Background Report, the Commission concluded that the Petitioner's proposed development would have

cumulative and significant adverse effects and impact on the public roadway facilities and system in the area of said development, to wit:

(A) Increased traffic congestion;

(B) Decreased pedestrian safety, especially with a school bus stop in the vicinity;

(C) Potential increase in vehicular accidents at the intersection of Kuakini Highway and Sea View Circle.

Petitioner challenges the quoted FOF as not being based on substantial evidence. We disagree. The record contains substantial evidence showing that the development will impact on the roads in the vicinity of the Kuakini Highway-Sea View Circle intersection. Nevertheless, after a thorough review of the record, we have a definite and firm conviction that a mistake has been made.

Pursuant to HRS § 205A-26(2) (1985), development cannot be approved within a SMA unless findings are made that the development (A) will not have any substantial adverse environmental or ecological effect except, however, where the substantial adverse effect is practicably minimized and "clearly outweighed by public health, safety, or compelling public interests;" (B) is consistent with the objectives, policies, and SMA guidelines of the CZMA; and (C) is consistent with the county general plan and zoning. In our view, where a proposed development meets those statutory requisites, the Commission's denial of a SMAP would be in excess of its authority.

The purpose of the CZMA is to control development within a SMA through the device of the SMAP, not to totally prevent or prohibit such activity. It follows that, where an administrative record indicates that a proposed development within a SMA would not contravene the statute's policies, objectives, and purposes, the Commission would exceed its authority by denying a SMAP that may have been requested for that project. The question, here, is whether the Commission's findings satisfied its duty and authority under the statute.

Here, the Commission in other FOF found that the development would have no significant impact on archaeological or historical sites, "floral" and "faunal" resources of the coastal area, or on the coastal waters.[10] The Commission made no finding regarding any impact on the viewplanes and open space.

The only reason given by the Commission for denying the permit, as noted in FOF 62 and 69, is that the development would have cumulative and significant

---

[10] [12] The Commission made the following pertinent findings of fact:

46. The project site has been previously altered and is unlikely to contain any surface archaeological sites of significance.

47. The Department of Land and Natural Resources commented, "It is our understanding that the lots in this subdivision were graded some time ago, making it unlikely that significant historic sites are present. The project should have 'no effect' on such sites.'

49. Because the land has been altered, it is not likely to be a habitat for any rare or endangered species of flora or fauna.

50. The project site is located approximately 3,600 feet from the shoreline.

adverse effects on the roadway system at the intersection in question. However, at oral argument in this court, the Commission's counsel conceded that the traffic generated by the development in this case would have very little, if any, impact on the coastal zone's environment or ecology.

Under the circumstances of this case, absent a finding that the impact on the public facilities would result in a substantial adverse environmental or ecological effect, or render the development inconsistent with the objectives, policies, and guidelines of the CZMA, the Commission's finding that the development would have significant adverse effects and impact on the existing highway system in the area of the development does not provide a sufficient basis for denying the Permit Petition. In other words, if traffic from a development within a SMA is not shown to have a substantial adverse effect on the coastal environment, such impact as the traffic may otherwise have on the existing roadway system in the area of the development cannot be the basis for denying a SMAP application.

Additionally, even if the development in this case is shown to have a substantial adverse effect in accordance with the statute, the Commission was required under HRS § 205A-26(2)(A) to determine whether that effect could be practicably minimized and, when minimized, whether the effect is clearly outweighed by public health, safety, or compelling public interests. *See Mahuiki*, 654 P.2d at 881 no. 10. That was not done in this case. Here, Petitioner represented to the Commission that he would be willing to design the development so as to minimize the traffic impact as much as possible. It does not appear from the record that the Commission considered Petitioner's offer as we think it was required to do under the statute.

On remand, the Commission should reconsider the Permit Petition and determine whether the traffic generated by the development will or *will not* have a substantial adverse environmental or ecological effect on the coastal zone. If the Commission finds that the traffic *will not* have such a substantial adverse effect, then the Commission should approve the Permit Petition without conditions relating to the traffic.

If the Commission finds that the traffic *will* have such a substantial effect, but that the effect can be practicably minimized and, as minimized, the effect is clearly outweighed by public health, safety, or compelling public interests, the Commission should approve the Permit Petition. In order to achieve the minimization, the Commission may impose reasonable conditions on the development. If, of course, the development cannot be made to conform to HRS § 205A-26(2)(A), then the Commission should deny the Permit Petition.

This opinion is not meant to prevent the Commission from imposing other reasonable conditions affecting mailers within the purview of the CZMA, such as the viewplanes to the ocean, where such may be deemed necessary to comply with the intent of the CZMA.

Conclusion

We affirm the Commission's denial of the Boundary Petition. We vacate the denial of the Permit Petition and remand the mailer to the Commission for further proceedings consistent with this opinion,

NOTES AND QUESTIONS

1. *The Definition of the Coastal Zone*. Defining the landward part of the coastal zone for purposes of CZMA can be difficult, especially for regulatory purposes, since the federal government looks to the states, to which it gives the money for program development and implementation, for enforcement. What if the statutory definition would result in CZM regulations covering the entire developable area of the state? This is what happened in Hawaii, which then developed two coastal zones: the all-inclusive one for "administrative" purposes, and a second, usually only a few hundred yards wide (defined county-by county), for regulatory purposes. *See* D. Callies, Regulating Paradise: Land Use Controls In Hawaii, Ch. 7 (2d ed. 2010).

2. *The Purpose of the CZMA*. The Coastal Zone Management Act appears to be directed at preserving critical coastal natural resources and values. Assuming it is possible to obtain a permit from an appropriate local agency under an approved coastal zone management program, what would you expect restrictions on development to look like? What kind of bulk and height standards would you expect to be imposed? Consider these questions in light of the materials in this Chapter on flood hazard protection and the dilemma of the landowner subject both to coastal zone protection and flood hazard prevention regulations enforced at the local level. *See* Davidson, *Coastal Zone Management and Planning in California: Strategies for Balancing Conservation and Development*; Winters, *Environmentally Sensitive Land Use Regulation in California*, 10 San Diego L. Rev. 693 (1973).

3. *Coastal Zone Management and the Climate Change*. Today, coastal zone issues cannot be addressed without considering the effects of climate change on coastal areas and developments. *See, e.g.*, M. Burkett and Denzin, et al., *Land Use Law: Zoning in the 21st Century*, pp. 30 *et seq.*

[B.] WETLANDS

SOLID WASTE AGENCY OF NORTHERN COOK COUNTY v. UNITED STATES ARMY CORPS OF ENGINEERS

United States Supreme Court
531 U.S. 159 (2001)

Chief Justice Rehnquist delivered the opinion of the Court.

Section 404(a) of the Clean Water Act (CWA or Act), 86 Stat. 884, as amended, 33 U.S.C. 1344(a), regulates the discharge of dredged or fill material into "navigable waters." The United States Army Corps of Engineers (Corps) has interpreted § 404(a) to confer federal authority over an abandoned sand and gravel pit in northern Illinois which provides habitat for migratory birds. We are asked to decide whether the provisions of § 404(a) may be fairly extended to these waters, and, if so, whether Congress could exercise such authority consistent with the Commerce Clause, U.S. Const., Art. I, § 8, c1.3. We answer the first question in the negative and therefore do not reach the second.

Petitioner, the Solid Waste Agency of Northern Cook County (SWANCC), is a consortium of 23 suburban Chicago cities and villages that united in an effort to locate and develop a disposal site for baled nonhazardous solid waste. The Chicago Gravel Company informed the municipalities of the availability of a 533 acre parcel, bestriding the Illinois counties Cook and Kane, which had been the site of a sand and gravel pit mining operation for three decades up until about 1960. Long since abandoned, the old mining site eventually gave way to a successional stage forest, with its remnant excavation trenches evolving into a scattering of permanent and seasonal ponds of varying size (from under one-tenth of an acre to several acres) and depth (from several inches to several feet).

The municipalities decided to purchase the site for disposal of their baled nonhazardous solid waste. By law. SW ANCC was required to file for various permits from Cook County and the State of Illinois before it could begin operation of its balefill project. In addition, because the operation called for the filling of some of the permanent and seasonal ponds, SWANCC contacted federal respondents (hereinafter respondents), including the Corps, to determine if a federal landfill permit was required under § 404(a) of the CWA, 33 U.S.C. 1344(a).

Section 404(a) grants the Corps authority to issue permits "for the discharge of dredged or fill material into the navigable waters at specified disposal sites." The term "navigable waters" is defined under the Act as "the waters of the United States. including the territorial seas." 1362(7). The Corps has issued regulations defining the term "waters of the United States" to include

> "waters such as intrastate lakes. Rivers, streams (including intermittent streams), mudflats, sandflats, wetlands, sloughs, prairie potholes, wet meadows, playa lakes. or natural ponds, the use, degradation or destruction of which could affect interstate or foreign commerce . . . ." 33 CFR 328.3(a)(3) (1999).

In 1986, in an attempt to "clarify" the reach of its jurisdiction, the Corps stated that 404(a) extends to intrastate waters:

> "a. Which are or would be used as habitat by birds protected by Migratory Bird Treaties; or
>
> "b. Which are or would be used as habitat by other migratory birds which cross state lines; or
>
> "c. Which are or would be used as habitat for endangered species; or
>
> "d. Used to irrigate crops sold in interstate commerce." 51 Fed. Reg. 41217.

This last promulgation has been dubbed the "Migratory Bird Rule."[11]

The Corps initially concluded that it had no jurisdiction over the site because it contained no "wetlands," or areas which support "vegetation typically adapted for life in saturated soil conditions," 33 CFR 328.3(b) (1999). However, after the Illinois Nature Preserves Commission informed the Corps that a number of migratory bird species had been observed at the site, the Corps reconsidered and ultimately

[11] [1] The Corps issued the "Migratory Bird Rule" without following the notice and comment procedures outlines in the Administrative Procedure Act, 5 U.S.C. § 553.

asserted jurisdiction over the balefill site pursuant to subpart (b) of the "Migratory Bird Rule." The Corps found that approximately 121 bird species had been observed at the site, including several known to depend upon aquatic environments for a significant portion of their life requirements. Thus, on November 16, 1987, the Corps formally "determined that the seasonally ponded, abandoned gravel mining depressions located on the project site, while not wetlands, did qualify as 'waters of the United States'. . . based upon the following criteria: (1) the proposed site had been abandoned as a gravel mining operation; (2) the water areas and spoil piles had developed a natural character; and (3) the water areas are used as habitat by migratory bird [sic] which cross state lines."

During the application process, SWANCC made several proposals to mitigate the likely displacement of the migratory birds and to preserve a great blue heron rookery located on the site. Its balefill project ultimately received the necessary local and state approval. By 1993. SWANCC had received a special use planned development permit from the Cook County Board of Appeals, a landfill development permit from the Illinois Environmental Protection Agency, and approval from the Illinois Department of Conservation.

Despite SWANCC's securing the required water quality certification from the Illinois Environmental Protection Agency. the Corps refused to issue a 404(a) permit. The Corps found that '1be Corps issued the "Migratory Bird Rule" without following the notice and comment procedures outlined in the Administrative Procedure Act, 5 U.S.C. § 553.

SWANCC had not established that its proposal was the "least environmentally damaging, most practicable alternative" for disposal of nonhazardous solid waste; that SWANCC's failure to set aside sufficient funds to remediate leaks posed an "unacceptable risk to the public's drinking water supply"; and that the impact of the project upon area — sensitive species was "unmitigatable since a landfill surface cannot be redeveloped into a forested habitat."

Petitioner filed suit under the Administrative Procedure Act, 5 U.S.C. § 701 et seq., in the Northern District of Illinois challenging both the Corps' jurisdiction over the site and the merits of its denial of the§ 404(a) permit. The District Court granted summary judgment to respondents on the jurisdictional issue, and petitioner abandoned its challenge to the Corps' permit decision. On appeal to the Court of Appeals for the Seventh Circuit, petitioner renewed its attack on respondents' use of the "Migratory Bird Rule" to assert jurisdiction over the site. Petitioner argued that respondents had exceeded their statutory authority in interpreting the CWA to cover nonnavigable, isolated, intrastate waters based upon the presence of migratory birds and, in the alternative, that Congress lacked the power under the Commerce Clause to grant such regulatory jurisdiction.

The Court of Appeals began its analysis with the constitutional question, holding that Congress has the authority to regulate such waters based upon "the cumulative impact doctrine, under which a single activity that itself has no discernible effect on interstate commerce may still be regulated if the aggregate effect of that class of activity has a substantial impact on interstate commerce." 191 F.3d 845, 850 (C.A.7 1999). The aggregate effect of the "destruction of the natural habitat of migratory birds" on interstate commerce, the court held, was substantial because each year millions of Americans cross state lines and spend over a billion dollars to hunt and observe migratory birds.[12] The Court of Appeals then turned to the regulatory question. The court held that the CW A reaches as many waters as the Commerce Clause allows and, given its earlier Commerce Clause ruling, it therefore followed that respondents' "Migratory Bird Rule" was a reasonable interpretation of the Act.

We granted certiorari, 529 U.S. 1129, 120 S. Ct. 2003, 146 L. Ed. 2d 954 (2000), and now reverse.

Congress passed the CWA for the stated purpose of "restor[ing] and maintain-[ing] the chemical, physical, and biological integrity of the Nation's waters." 33 U.S.C. § 1251(a). In so doing, Congress chose to "recognize, preserve, and protect the primary responsibilities and rights of States to prevent, reduce, and eliminate pollution, to plan the development and use (including restoration, preservation, and enhancement) of land and water resources, and to consult with the Administrator in the exercise of his authority under this chapter." 1251(b). Relevant here, 404(a) authorizes respondents to regulate the discharge of fill material into "navigable waters," 33 U.S.C. § 1344(a), which the statute defines as "the waters of the United States, including the territorial seas," 1362(7). Respondents have interpreted these words to cover the abandoned gravel pit at issue here because it is used as habitat for migratory birds. We conclude that the "Migratory Bird Rule" is not fairly supported by the CWA.

This is not the first time we have been called upon to evaluate the meaning of 404(a). In United States v. Riverside Bayview Homes, Inc., 474 U.S. 121, 106 S. Ct. 455, 88 L. Ed. 2d 419 (1985), we held that the Corps had 404(a) jurisdiction over wetlands that actually abutted on a navigable waterway. In so doing, we noted that the term "navigable" is of "limited import" and that Congress evidenced its intent to "regulate at least some waters that would not be deemed 'navigable' under the classical understanding of that term." But our holding was based in large measure upon Congress' unequivocal acquiescence to, and approval of, the Corps' regulations interpreting the CWA to cover wetlands adjacent to navigable waters. We found that Congress' concern for the protection of water quality and aquatic ecosystems indicated its intent to regulate wetlands "inseparably bound up with the 'waters' of the United States."

It was the significant nexus between the wetlands and "navigable waters" that informed our reading of the CWA in Riverside Bayview Homes. Indeed, we did not "express any opinion" on the "question of the authority of the Corps to regulate discharges of fill material into wetlands that are not adjacent to bodies of open water . . . ." In order to rule for respondents here, we would have to hold that the jurisdiction of the Corps extends to ponds that are not adjacent to open water. But we conclude that the text of the statute will not allow this.

Indeed, the Corps' original interpretation of the CWA, promulgated two years

---

[12] [2] Relying upon its earlier decision in *Hoffman Homes, Inc. v. EPA*, 999 F.2d 256 (C.A.7 1993), and a report from the United States Census Bureau, the Court of Appeals found that in 1996 approximately 3.1 million Americans spent $1.3 billion to hunt migratory birds (with 11 percent crossing state lines to do so) as another 17.7 million Americans observed migratory birds (with 9.5 million traveling for the purpose of observing shorebirds). See 191 F.3d, at 850.

after its enactment, is inconsistent with that which it espouses here. Its 1974 regulations defined 404(a)'s "navigable waters" to mean "those waters of the United States which are subject to the ebb and flow of the tide, and/or are presently, or have been in the past, or may be in the future susceptible for use for purposes of interstate or foreign commerce." 33 CFR § 209.120(d)(1). The Corps emphasized that "[i]t is the water body's capability of use by the public for purposes of transportation or commerce which is the determinative factor." , 209.260(e)(I). Respondents put forward no persuasive evidence that the Corps mistook Congress' intent in 1974.[13]

Respondents next contend that whatever its original aim in 1972, Congress charted a new course five years later when it approved the more expansive definition of "navigable waters" found in the Corps' 1977 regulations. In July 1977, the Corps formally adopted 33 CFR 323.2(a)(5) (1978), which defined "waters of the United States" to include "isolated wetlands and lakes, intermittent streams, prairie potholes, and other waters that are not part of a tributary system to interstate waters or to navigable waters of the United States, the degradation or destruction of which could affect interstate commerce." Respondents argue that Congress was aware of this more expansive interpretation during its 1977 amendments to the CWA. Specifically, respondents point to a failed House bill, H.R. 3199, that would have defined "navigable waters" as "all waters which are presently used, or are susceptible to use in their natural condition or by reasonable improvement as a means to transport interstate or foreign commerce." 123 Congo Rec. 10420, 10434 (1977). They also point to the passage in 404(g)(1) that authorizes a State to apply to the Environmental Protection Agency for permission "to administer its own individual and general permit program for the discharge of dredged or fill material into the navigable waters (other than those waters which are presently used, or are susceptible to use in their natural condition or by reasonable improvement as a means to transport interstate or foreign commerce . . . , including wetlands adjacent thereto) within its jurisdiction . . . ." 33 U.S.C. 1344(g)(1). The failure to pass legislation that would have overturned the Corps' 1977 regulations and the extension of jurisdiction in 404(g) to waters "other than" traditional "navigable waters," respondents submit, indicate that Congress recognized and accepted a broad definition of "navigable waters" that includes nonnavigable, isolated, intrastate waters.

Although we have recognized congressional acquiescence to administrative interpretations of a statute in some situations, we have done so with extreme care. "[F]ailed legislative proposals are 'a particularly dangerous ground on which to rest an interpretation of a prior statute.' " Central Bank of Denver, N.A. v. First Interstate Bank of Denver, N.A., 511 U.S. 164, 187, 114 S. Ct. 1439, 128 L. Ed. 2d 119 (1994) (quoting Pension Benefit Guaranty Corporation v. LTV Corp., 496 U.S.

---

13 [3] Respondents refer us to portions of the legislative history that they believe indicate Congress' intent to expand the definition of "navigable waters." Although the Conference Report includes the statement that the conferees "intend that the term 'navigable waters' be given the broadest possible constitutional interpretation," S. Conf. Rep. No. 92B1236, p. 144 (1972), U.S. Code Cong. & Admin News 1972 pp. 3668, 3822, neither this, nor anything else in the legislative history to which respondents point, signifies that Congress intended to exert anything more than its commerce power over navigation. Indeed, respondents admit that the legislative history is somewhat ambiguous.

633, 650, 110 S. Ct. 2668, 110 L. Ed. 2d 579 (1990)). A bill can be proposed for any number of reasons, and it can be rejected for just as many others. The relationship between the actions and inactions of the 95th Congress and the intent of the 92d Congress in passing 404(a) is also considerably attenuated. Because "subsequent history is less illuminating than the contemporaneous evidence," Hagen v. Utah, 510 U.S. 399, 420, 114 S. Ct. 958, 127 L. Ed. 2d 252 (1994), respondents face a difficult task in overcoming the plain text and import of 404(a).

We conclude that respondents have failed to make the necessary showing that the failure of the 1977 House bill demonstrates Congress' acquiescence to the Corps' regulations or the "Migratory Bird Rule," which, of course, did not first appear until 1986. Although respondents cite some legislative history showing Congress' recognition of the Corps' assertion of jurisdiction over "isolated waters,"[14] as we explained in Riverside Bayview Homes, "[i]n both Chambers, debate on the proposals to narrow the definition of navigable waters centered largely on the issue of wetlands preservation." Beyond Congress' desire to regulate wetlands adjacent to "navigable waters," respondents point us to no persuasive evidence that the House bill was proposed in response to the Corps' claim of jurisdiction over nonnavigable, isolated, intrastate waters or that its failure indicated congressional acquiescence to such jurisdiction.

Section 404(g) is equally unenlightening. In Riverside Bayview Homes we recognized that Congress intended the phrase "navigable waters" to include "at least some waters that would not be deemed 'navigable' under the classical understanding of that term." But 404(g) gives no intimation of what those waters might be; it simply refers to them as "other . . . waters." Respondents conjecture that "other . . . waters" must incorporate the Corps' 1977 regulations, but it is also plausible, as petitioner contends, that Congress simply wanted to include all waters adjacent to "navigable waters," such as nonnavigable tributaries and streams. The exact meaning of 404(g) is not before us and we express no opinion on it, but for present purposes it is sufficient to say, as we did in Riverside Bayview Homes, that "" 404(g)(1) does not conclusively determine the construction to be placed on the use of the term 'waters' elsewhere in the Act (particularly in 502(7), which contains the relevant definition of 'navigable waters') . . . .[15]

We thus decline respondents' invitation to take what they see as the next ineluctable step after Riverside Bayview Homes: holding that isolated ponds, some only seasonal, wholly located within two Illinois counties, fall under 404(a)'s definition of "navigable waters" because they serve as habitat for migratory birds. As counsel for respondents conceded at oral argument, such a ruling would assume

---

[14] [6] Respondents cite, for example, the Senate Report on S.1952, which referred to the Corps' "isolated waters' regulation. See No 95B370, p. 75 (1977), U.S. Code Cong. & Admin. News 1977 pp. 4326, 4400. However, the same report reiterated that "[t]he committee amendment does not redefine navigable waters."

[15] [7] Respondents also make a passing reference to Congress' decision in 1977 to exempt certain types of discharges from 404(a), including, for example, "discharge of dredged or fill material . . . for the purposes of construction or maintenance on a farm or stock ponds or irrigation ditches, or the maintenance of drainage ditches." 67, 91 Stat. 1600, 33 U.S.C. § 1344(f)(C). As § 404(a) only regulates dredged or fill material that is discharged "into navigable waters," Congress' decision to exempt certain types of these discharges does not affect, much less address, the definition of "navigable waters."

that "the use of the word navigable in the statute . . . does not have any independent significance." We cannot agree that Congress' separate definitional use of the phrase "waters of the United States" constitutes a basis for reading the term "navigable waters" out of the statute. We said in Riverside Bayview Homes that the word "navigable" in the statute was of "limited import" 474 U.S., at 133, 106 S. Ct. 455, and went on to hold that 404(a) extended to nonnavigable wetlands adjacent to open waters. But it is one thing to give a word limited effect and quite another to give it no effect whatever. The term "navigable" has at least the import of showing us what Congress had in mind as its authority for enacting the CWA: its traditional jurisdiction over waters that were or had been navigable in fact or which could reasonably be so made.

Respondents relying upon all of the arguments addressed above contend that, at the very least, it must be said that Congress did not address the precise question of 404(a)'s scope with regard to nonnavigable, isolated, intrastate waters, and that, therefore, we should give deference to the "Migratory Bird Rule." See, e.g., Chevron U.S.A., Inc. v. Natural Resources Defense Council, Inc., 467 U.S. 837, 104 S. Ct. 2778, 81 L. Ed. 2d 694 (1984). We find 404(a) to be clear, but even were we to agree with respondents, we would not extend Chevron deference here.

Where an administrative interpretation of a statute invokes the outer limits of Congress' power, we expect a clear indication that Congress intended that result. See Edward J. DeBartolo Corp. v. Florida Gulf Coast Building & Constr. Trades Council, 485 U.S. 568, 575, 108 S. Ct. 1392, 99 L. Ed. 2d 645 (1988). This requirement stems from our prudential desire not to needlessly reach constitutional issues and our assumption that Congress does not casually authorize administrative agencies to interpret a statute to push the limit of congressional authority. See *ibid.* This concern is heightened where the administrative interpretation alters the federal-state framework by permitting federal encroachment upon a traditional state power. See United States v. Bass, 404 U.S. 336, 349, 92 S. Ct. 515, 30 L. Ed. 2d 488 (1971)("[U]nless Congress conveys its purpose clearly, it will not be deemed to have significantly changed the federal-state balance"). Thus, "where an otherwise acceptable construction of a statute would raise serious constitutional problems, the Court will construe the statute to avoid such problems unless such construction is plainly contrary to the intent of Congress." DeBartolo, supra, at 575, 108 S. Ct. 1392.

Twice in the past six years we have reaffirmed the proposition that the grant of authority to Congress under the Commerce Clause, though broad, is not unlimited. See United States v. Morrison, 529 U.S. 598, 120 S. Ct. 1740, 146 L. Ed. 2d 658 (2000); United States v. Lopez, 514 U.S. 549, 115 S. Ct. 1624, 131 L. Ed. 2d 626 (1995). Respondents argue that the "Migratory Bird Rule" falls within Congress' power to regulate intrastate activities that "substantially affect" interstate commerce. They note that the protection of migratory birds is a "national interest of very nearly the first magnitude," Missouri v. Holland, 252 U.S. 416, 435, 40 S. Ct. 382, 64 L. Ed. 641 (1920), and that, as the Court of Appeals found, millions of people spend over a billion dollars annually on recreational pursuits relating to migratory birds. These arguments raise significant constitutional questions. For example, we would have to evaluate the precise object or activity that, in the aggregate, substantially affects interstate commerce. This is not clear, for although the Corps has claimed jurisdiction over petitioner's land because it contains water areas used as habitat by migratory birds, respondents now, post litem motam, focus upon the fact that the regulated activity is petitioner's municipal landfill, which is "plainly of a commercial nature." But this is a far cry, indeed, from the "navigable waters" and "waters of the United States" to which the statute by its terms extends.

These are significant constitutional questions raised by respondents' application of their regulations, and yet we find nothing approaching a clear statement from Congress that it intended 404(a) to reach an abandoned sand and gravel pit such as we have here. Permitting respondents to claim federal jurisdiction over ponds and mudflats falling within the "Migratory Bird Rule" would result in a significant impingement of the States' traditional and primary power over land and water use. See, e.g., Hess v. Port Authority TransHudson Corporation, 513 U.S. 30, 44, 115 S. Ct. 394, 130 L. Ed. 2d 245 (1994) ([R]egulation of land use [is] a function traditionally performed by local governments"). Rather than expressing a desire to readjust the federal-state balance in this manner, Congress chose to "recognize, preserve, and protect the primary responsibilities and rights of States . . . to plan the development and use . . . of land and water resources . . . . 33 U.S.C. § 1251 (b). We thus read the statute as written to avoid the significant constitutional and federalism questions raised by respondents' interpretation, and therefore reject the request for administrative deference.

We hold that 33 CFR 328.3(a)(3) (1999), as clarified and applied to petitioner's balefill site pursuant to the "Migratory Bird Rule," 51 Fed. Reg. 41217 (1986), exceeds the authority granted to respondents under § 404(a) of the CWA. The judgment of the Court of Appeals for the Seventh Circuit is therefore

REVERSED.

JUSTICE STEVENS, with whom JUSTICE SOUTER, JUSTICE GINSBURG, and JUSTICE BREYER join, dissenting.

In 1969, the Cuyahoga River in Cleveland, Ohio, coated with a slick of industrial waste, caught fire. Congress responded to that dramatic event, and to others like it, by enacting the Federal Water Pollution Control Act (FWPCA) Amendments of 1972, 86 Stat. 817, as amended, 33 U .S.C. § 1251 et seq., commonly known as the Clean Water Act (Clean Water Act, CWA, or Act). The Act proclaimed the ambitious goal of ending water pollution by 1985. § 1251(a). The Court's past interpretations of the CWA have been fully consistent with that goal. Although Congress' vision of zero pollution remains unfulfilled, its pursuit has unquestionably retarded the destruction of the aquatic environment. Our Nation's waters no longer burn. Today, however, the Court takes an unfortunate step that needlessly weakens our principal safeguard against toxic water.

It is fair to characterize the Clean Water Act as "watershed" legislation. The statute endorsed fundamental changes in both the purpose and the scope of federal regulation of the Nation's waters. In 13 of the Rivers and Harbors Appropriation Act of 1899 (RHA), 30 Stat. 1152, as amended, 33 U.S.C. 407, Congress had assigned to the Army Corps of Engineers (Corps) the mission of regulating discharges into certain waters in order to protect their use as highways for the transportation of interstate and foreign commerce; the scope of the Corps' jurisdiction under the RHA accordingly extended only to waters that were "navigable." In the CWA, however, Congress broadened the Corps' mission to include the purpose of protecting the quality of our Nation's waters for esthetic, health, recreational, and environmental uses. The scope of its jurisdiction was therefore redefined to encompass all of "the waters of the United States, including the territorial seas." 1362(7). That definition requires neither actual nor potential navigability.

The Court has previously held that the Corps' broadened jurisdiction under the CWA properly included an 80 acre parcel of low-lying marshy land that was not itself navigable, directly adjacent to navigable water, or even hydrologically connected to navigable water, but which was part of a larger area, characterized by poor drainage, that ultimately abutted a navigable creek. United States v. Riverside Bayview Homes, Inc., 474 U.S. 121, 106 S. Ct. 455, 88 L. Ed. 2d 419 (1985). Our broad finding in Riverside Bayview that the 1977 Congress had acquiesced in the Corps' understanding of its jurisdiction applies equally to the 410 acre parcel at issue here. Moreover, once Congress crossed the legal watershed that separates navigable streams of commerce from marshes and inland lakes, there is no principled reason for limiting the statute's protection to those waters or wetlands that happen to lie near a navigable stream.

In its decision today, the Court draws a new jurisdictional line, one that invalidates the 1986 migratory bird regulation as well as the Corps' assertion of jurisdiction over all waters except for actually navigable waters, their tributaries, and wetlands adjacent to each. Its holding rests on two equally untenable premises: (1) that when Congress passed the 1972 CWA, it did not intend "to exert anything more than its commerce power over navigation," and (2) that in 1972 Congress drew the boundary defining the Corps' jurisdiction at the odd line on which the Court today settles.

As I shall explain, the text of the 1972 amendments affords no support for the Court's holding, and amendments Congress adopted in 1977 do support the Corps' present interpretation of its mission as extending to so-called "isolated" waters. Indeed, simple common sense cuts against the particular definition of the Corps' jurisdiction favored by the majority.

[Discussion of the statutory issue omitted.]

III

Although it might have appeared problematic on a "linguistic" level for the Corps to classify "lands· as "waters" in Riverside Bayview, we squarely held that the agency's construction of the statute that it was charged with enforcing was entitled to deference under Chevron U.S.A., Inc. v. Natural Resources Defense Council, Inc., 467 U.S. 837, 104 S. Ct. 2778, 81 L. Ed. 2d 694 (1984). Today, however, the majority refuses to extend such deference to the same agency's construction of the same statute. This refusal is unfaithful to both Riverside Bayview and Chevron. For it is the majority's reading, not the agency's, that does violence to the scheme Congress chose to put into place.

Contrary to the Court's suggestion, the Corps' interpretation of the statute does not "encroac[h]" upon "traditional state power" over land use. "Land use planning in essence chooses particular uses for the land; environmental regulation, at its core, does not mandate particular uses of the land but requires only that, however the land is used, damage to the environment is kept within prescribed limits." California Coastal Comm'n v. Granite Rock Co., 480 U.S. 572, 587, 107 S. Ct. 1419, 94 L. Ed. 2d 577 (1987). The CWA is not a land-use code; it is a paradigm of environmental regulation. Such regulation is an accepted exercise of federal power. Hodel v. Virginia Surface Mining & Reclamation Assn., Inc., 452 U.S. 264, 282, 101 S. Ct. 2352, 69 L. Ed. 2d 1 (1981).

It is particularly ironic for the Court to raise the specter of federalism while construing a statute that makes explicit efforts to foster local control over water regulation. Faced with calls to cut back on federal jurisdiction over water pollution, Congress rejected attempts to narrow the scope of that jurisdiction and, by incorporating 404(g), opted instead for a scheme that encouraged States to supplant federal control with their own regulatory programs. S. Rep. No. 95B370, at p. 75, U.S. Code Congo & Admin. News at p. 4400, reprinted in 4 Leg. Hist. of CWA 708 ("The committee amendment does not redefine navigable waters. Instead, the committee amendment intends to assure continued protection of all the Nation's waters, but allows States to assume the primary responsibility for protecting those lakes, rivers, streams, swamps, marshes, and other portions of the navigable waters outside the [C]orps program in the so-called phase I waters" (emphasis added). Because Illinois could have taken advantage of the opportunities offered to it through 404(g), the federalism concerns to which the majority adverts are misplaced. The Corps' interpretation of the statute as extending beyond navigable waters, tributaries of navigable waters, and wetlands adjacent to each is manifestly reasonable and therefore entitled to deference.

IV

Because I am convinced that the Court's miserly construction of the statute is incorrect, I shall comment briefly on petitioner's argument that Congress is without power to prohibit it from filling any part of the 31 acres of ponds on its property in Cook County, Illinois. The Corps' exercise of its 404 permitting power over "isolated" waters that serve as habitat for migratory birds falls well within the boundaries set by this Court's Commerce Clause jurisprudence.

In United States v. Lopez, 514 U.S. 549, 558–559, 115 S. Ct. 1624, 131 L. Ed. 2d 626 (1995), this Court identified "three broad categories of activity that Congress may regulate under its commerce power": (1) channels of interstate commerce; (2) instrumentalities of interstate commerce, or persons and things in interstate commerce; and (3) activities that "substantially affect" interstate commerce. The migratory bird rule at issue here is properly analyzed under the third category. In order to constitute a proper exercise of Congress' power over intrastate activities that "substantially affect" interstate commerce, it is not necessary that each individual instance of the activity substantially affect commerce; it is enough that, taken in the aggregate, the class of activities in question has such an effect. Perez v. United States, 402 U.S. 146, 91 S. Ct. 1357, 28 L. Ed. 2d 686 (1971) (noting that it is the "class" of regulated activities, not the individual instance, that is to be considered in the "affects" commerce analysis); see also Hodel, 452 U.S., at 277, 101 S. Ct. 2352; Wickard v. Filburn, 317 U.S. 111, 127–128, 63 S. Ct. 82, 87 L. Ed. 122 (1942).

The activity being regulated in this case (and by the Corps 404 regulations in general) is the discharge of fill material into water. The Corps did not assert jurisdiction over petitioner's land simply because the waters were "used as habitat by migratory birds." It asserted jurisdiction because petitioner planned to discharge fill into waters "used as habitat by migratory birds." Had petitioner intended to engage in some other activity besides discharging fill (i.e., had there been no activity to regulate), or, conversely, had the waters not been habitat for migratory birds (i.e., had there been no basis for federal jurisdiction), the Corps would never have become involved in petitioner's use of its land. There can be no doubt that, unlike the class of activities Congress was attempting to regulate in United States v. Morrison, 529 U.S. 598, 613, 120 S. Ct. 1740, 146 L. Ed. 2d 658 (2000) ("[g]ender-motivated crimes"), and Lopez, 514 U.S., at 561 (possession of guns near school property), the discharge of fill material into the Nation's waters is almost always undertaken for economic reasons. See V. Albrecht & B. Goode, Wetland Regulation in the Real World, Exh. 3 (Feb. 1994) (demonstrating that the overwhelming majority of acreage for which 404 permits are sought is intended for commercial, industrial, or other economic use).

Moreover, no one disputes that the discharge of fill into "isolated" waters that serve as migratory bird habitat will, in the aggregate, adversely affect migratory bird populations. See, e.g., 1 Secretary of the Interior, Report to Congress, The Impact of Federal Programs on Wetlands: The Lower Mississippi Alluvial Plain and the Prairie Pothole Region 79B80 (Oct. 1988) (noting that "isolated," phase 3 waters "are among the most important and also [the] most threatened ecosystems in the United States" because "[t]hey are prime nesting grounds for many species of North American waterfowl . . . " and provide"[u]p to 50 percent of the [U.S.] production of migratory waterfowl"). Nor does petitioner dispute that the particular waters it seeks to fill are home to many important species of migratory birds, including the second-largest breeding colony of Great Blue Herons in northeastern Illinois, and several species of waterfowl protected by international treaty and Illinois endangered species laws.

In addition to the intrinsic value of migratory birds, see Missouri v. Holland, 252 U.S. 416, 435, 40 S. Ct. 382, 64 L. Ed. 641 (1920) (noting the importance of migratory birds as "protectors of our forests and our crops" and as "a food supply"), it is undisputed that literally millions of people regularly participate in bird watching and hunting and that those activities generate a host of commercial activities of great value. The causal connection between the filling of wetlands and the decline of commercial activities associated with migratory birds is not "attenuated," Morrison, 529 U.S., at 612, 120 S. Ct. 1740; it is direct and concrete. Cf. Gibbs v. Babbitt, 214 F.3d 483, 492–493 (C.A. 4 2000) ("The relationship between red wolf takings and interstate commerce is quite direct with no red wolves, there will be no red wolf related tourism . . . .").

Finally, the migratory bird rule does not blur the "distinction between what is truly national and what is truly local." Morrison, 529 U.S., at 617–618, 120 S. Ct.

1740. Justice Holmes cogently observed in Missouri v. Holland that the protection of migratory birds is a textbook example of a national problem. 252 U.S., at 435, 40 S. Ct. 382, 64 L. Ed. 641 ("It is not sufficient to rely upon the States [to protect migratory birds]. The reliance is vain . . . "). The destruction of aquatic migratory bird habitat, like so many other environmental problems, is an action in which the benefits (e.g., a new landfill) are disproportionately local, while many of the costs (e.g., fewer migratory birds) are widely dispersed and often borne by citizens living in other States. In such situations, described by economists as involving "externalities," federal regulation is both appropriate and necessary. Revesz, Rehabilitating Interstate Competition: Rethinking the "Race-to-the-Bottom" Rationale for Federal Environmental Regulation, 67 N.Y.U. L. Rev. 1210, 1222 (1992) ("The presence of interstate externalities is a powerful reason for intervention at the federal level"); cf. Hodel, 452 U.S., at 281–282, 101 S. Ct. 2352 (deferring to Congress' finding that nationwide standards were "essential" in order to avoid "destructive interstate competition" that might undermine environmental standards). Identifying the Corps' jurisdiction by reference to waters that serve as habitat for birds that migrate over state lines also satisfies this Court's expressed desire for some "jurisdictional element" that limits federal activity to its proper scope.

The power to regulate commerce among the several States necessarily and properly includes the power to preserve the natural resources that generate such commerce. Cf. Sporhase v. Nebraska ex rel. Douglas, 458 U.S. 941, 953, 102 S. Ct. 3456, 73 L. Ed. 2d 1254 (1982) (holding water to be an "article of commerce"). Migratory birds, and the waters on which they rely, are such resources. Moreover, the protection of migratory birds is a well-established federal responsibility. As Justice Holmes noted in Missouri v. Holland, the federal interest in protecting these birds is of "the first magnitude." 252 U.S., at 435, 40 S. Ct. 382. Because of their transitory nature, they "can be protected only by national action."

Whether it is necessary or appropriate to refuse to allow petitioner to fill those ponds is a question on which we have no voice. Whether the Federal Government has the power to require such permission, however, is a question that is easily answered. If, as it does, the Commerce Clause empowers Congress to regulate particular "activities causing air or water pollution, or other environmental hazards that may have effects in more than one State," Hodel, 452 U.S., at 282, 101 S. Ct. 2352, it also empowers Congress to control individual actions that, in the aggregate, would have the same effect. Perez, 402 U.S., at 154, 91 S. Ct. 1357; Wickard, 317 U.S., at 127–128, 63 S. Ct. 82. There is no merit in petitioner's constitutional argument. Because I would affirm the judgment of the Court of Appeals, I respectfully dissent.

NOTES AND QUESTIONS

1. The majority's charge that there "are significant constitutional questions raised by" the Corps' application of its regulation to isolated waters is particularly ominous after the groundbreaking commerce clause cases of *Lopez* and *Morrison* described by the dissent. Is the regulation of wetlands a local land use issue or a national environmental issue? Does it make sense to distinguish between regulations by using the labels "land use" and "environmental" ? See the discussion of this issue infra, in *Granite Rock.* For recent decisions testing the validity of the Endangered Species Act under the commerce clause, see the Notes, *infra.* Are the commerce clause connections of endangered plants and wildlife similar to wetlands?

2. Does *SWANCC* limit the Corps' jurisdiction under the CWA to navigable waters and waters adjacent to hem? Certainly, a non-navigable tributary of a navigable stream is covered. But, what about a man-made ditch? Is that a tributary? Yes, according to *United States v. Deaton,* 332 F.3d 698 (4th Cir. 2003) (wetlands adjacent to a 32 mile ditch that passed through several nonnavigable streams before reaching Chesapeake Bay within Corps' jurisdiction).

The Court refers to "the significant nexus between the wetlands and 'navigable waters' that informed"[its] reading of the CW A in *Riverside Bayview Homes.* Is this nexus, or hydrological connection, met by an intermittent surface flow of water that is sufficient to carry pollution to a navigable waterway? *See North Carolina Shellfish Growers Assn. v. Holly Ridge Associates, LLC,* 278 F. Supp. 2d 654 (E.D.N.C. 2003) (yes).

Lower courts have differed on the impact of SWANCC. In addition to the Fourth Circuit in *Deaton,* at least three other circuits have given SWANCC a narrow reading, allowing the Corps to exercise jurisdiction where there is an indirect hydrologic connection: the Sixth, *United States v. Rapanos,* 339 F.3d 447 (6th Cir. 2(03)), Seventh, *United States v. Krilich,* 303 F.3d 784 (7th Cir. 2(02)), and Ninth, *Headwaters. Inc. v. Talent Irrigation Dist.,* 243 F.3d 526 (9th Cir. 2001). The Fifth Circuit has disagreed, finding SWANCC requires a navigable waterway or adjacency to navigable waterway. *Rice v. Harken Exploration Co.,* 250 F.3d 264 (5th Cir. 2001). *See* Lawrence Liebesman, *Judicial. Administrative and Congressional Responses to SWANCC.* 33 ENVT. L. REP. 10899 (2003). In the face of continued Corps intransigence over the limits of its jurisdiction as suggested in *SWANCC,* the U.S. Supreme Court attempted to tighten the definition of wetlands subject to Corps regulation in *Rapanos.* However, the Court was unable to concur on much beyond the need for a "nexus" between a wetland and a waterway, leaving the entire field so fact-specific that anything beyond *SWANCC's* holding remains speculative.

3. *SWANCCs* invalidation of the migratory bird rule is limited to the Court's reading of the statute. There have been several attempts to amend the statute (as well as EPA attempts to amend the relevant regulations) but so far, to no avail.

4. Regulating wetlands based on the discharge language of 404 results in less than comprehensive protection. The language does not cover the draining of a wetland a major loophole. *See Save Our Community v. United States Envtl. Protection Agency,* 971 F.2d 1155, 1158. n.5 (5th Cir. 1992). The Corps of Engineers adopted a rule in 1993 that partially closed this loophole by defining a discharge as "any addition of dredged material . . . including any redeposit of dredged material" into a wetland. C.F.R. I 323.2 (d)(I). The rule covered so-called incidental "fallback," the inevitable redeposit of some material that occurs with any dredging. This so-call *Tulloch* rule (named after a settlement in *North Carolina Wildlife Federation v. Tulloch,* Civ. No. C90-713-CIV-5-BO (E.D.N.C. 1992), was held invalid in *National Mining Association v. U. S. Army Corps of Engineers,* 145 F.3d 1399 (D.C. Cir. 1998). *See* Joseph J. Kalo. *"Now Open for Development?": The Present State of Regulation of Activities in North Carolina Wetlands,* 79 N.C. L. REV. 1667 (2001).

After the National Mining decision, the Corps issued a new rule that gave the decision a narrow reading. The new regulations replaced "any redeposit of dredged material" with "redeposit of dredged material other than incidental fallback." Then, in a footnote, the Corps stated that "incidental fallback results in the return of dredged material to virtually the spot from which it came." 33 C.F.R. I 323.2(d)(2). *See Greenfield Mills, Inc. v. O'Bannon*, 189 F. Supp. 2d 893 (N.D. Ind. 2002). applying the new regulation. *See also* J. Juergensmeyer & T. Roberts, Land Use Planning and Development Regulation Law 11, 11 (2003).

5. In 2006, the U.S. Supreme Court decided *Rapanos v. United States*, 547 U.S. 715 (2006). Widely expected to take the next step following SWANCC and unequivocally hold that the Corps's § 405 permit process unconstitutionally extended wetland protection "too far," instead the Court announced only a four justice plurality for that position. Instead, thanks largely to a concurring opinion, Justice Kennedy, the Court formulated a "nexus" rule which is so fact sensitive as to be nearly meaningless, as Chief Justice Roberts taciturnly observed in his own brief concurring opinion.

[C.] PUBLIC LANDS

Much of the land that was eventually to become the vast majority of federal land called "the public domain" was acquired through fortuitous purchases. Alaska, Florida, the Louisiana Purchase, and the Mexican Purchase, totaling 54% of the land area of the United States, come most readily 10 mind. The land was for the most part acquired during a decidedly expansionist period in U.S. history (between 1803 and 1867). The major thrust of legislation and other programs governing its use was to put as much public land as possible rapidly and expeditiously into private hands. The wholesale "giveaways" (usually in the form of below market-price sales) that characterized early United States land policy did not abate until the first part of the 20th century, which saw the setting up of a national park system, followed by national forests, reserves, and a host of other federal land classifications designed to hold and conserve, rather than dispose of, public land. (For more discussion, see the notes following *Plume v. Seward & Thompson* in Chapter 1.) Today, federally-owned land constitutes roughly one-third of the nation. One-half are in Alaska. Huge percentages of western states are also publicly owned: Nevada, 85%; Idaho and Utah, 65%; Wyoming and Oregon, 50%; California, 45%; Colorado, 35%; Montana, 30%. In the east, the percentages are smaller, but still constitute significant amounts of acreage: Virginia, 10% (25 million acres); Georgia, 6%; Florida, 12%; Michigan, 10% (36 million acres); New Hampshire, 13%; Tennessee, 6%; West Virginia, 7%. All of this is owned in fee simple. The government also owns subsurface mineral rights in some 60 million acres. In addition, the federal government controls the outer continental shelf, which is the area from three to two-hundred miles off- shore. 43 U.S.C. § 1331 to 1356. This enormous area, controlled by the Department of the Interior, is of great commercial importance for its oil, gas, and fisheries resources. *See* "Congress Spars over proposed 'ocean zoning,' " Miami Herald, Oct. 04, 2011.

KLEPPE v. NEW MEXICO

United States Supreme Court
426 U.S. 529 (1976)

ICE MARSHALL delivered the opinion of the Court.

At issue in this case is whether Congress exceeded its powers under the Constitution in enacting the Wild Free-roaming Horses and Burros Act.

I

The Wild Free-roaming Horses and Burros Act, was enacted in 1971 to protect "all unbranded and unclaimed horses and burros on public lands of the United States," from "capture, branding, harassment, or death." The Act provides that all such horses and burros on the public lands administered by the Secretary of the Interior through the Bureau of Land Management (BLM) or by the Secretary of Agriculture through the Forest Service are committed to the jurisdiction of the respective Secretaries, who are "directed to protect and manage [the animals) as components of the public lands . . . in a manner that is designed to achieve and maintain a thriving natural ecological balance on the public lands." If protected horses or burros "stray from public lands onto privately owned land, the owners of such land may inform the nearest Federal marshal or agent of the Secretary, who shall arrange to have the animals removed."

Section 6, authorizes the Secretaries to promulgate regulations, and to enter into cooperative agreements with other landowners and with state and local governmental agencies in furtherance of the Act's purposes. On August 7, 1973, the Secretaries executed such an agreement with the New Mexico Livestock Board, the agency charged with enforcing the New Mexico Estray Law. The agreement acknowledged the authority of the Secretaries to manage and protect the wild free-roaming horses and burros on the public lands of the United States within the State and established a procedure for evaluating the claims of private parties to ownership of such animals.

The Livestock Board terminated the agreement three months later. Asserting that the Federal Government lacked power to control wild horses and burros on the public lands of the United States unless the animals were moving in interstate commerce or damaging the public lands and that neither of these bases of regulation was available here, the Board notified the Secretaries of its intent

> to exercise all regulatory, impoundment and sale powers which it derives from the New Mexico Estray Law, over all estray horses, mules or asses found running at large upon public or private lands within New Mexico . . . . This includes the right to go upon Federal or State lands to take possession of said horses or burros, should the Livestock Board so desire.

The differences between the Livestock Board and the Secretaries came to a head in February 1974. On February 1, 1974, a New Mexico rancher, Kelley Stephenson, was informed by the BLM that several unbranded burros had been seen near Taylor Well, where Stephenson watered his cattle. Taylor Well is on federal property, and

Stephenson had access to it and some 8,000 surrounding acres only through a grazing permit issued pursuant to § 3 of the Taylor Grazing Act. After the BLM made it clear to Stephenson that it would not remove the burros and after he personally inspected the Taylor Well area, Stephenson complained to the Livestock Board that the burros were interfering with his livestock operation by molesting his cattle and eating their feed.

Thereupon the Board rounded up and removed 19 unbranded and unclaimed burros pursuant to the New Mexico Estray Law. Each burro was seized on the public lands of the United States and, as the director of the Board conceded, each burro fit the definition of a wild free-roaming burro under § 2(b) of the Act. On February 18, 1974, the Livestock Board, pursuant to its usual practice, sold the burros at a public auction. After the sale, the BLM asserted jurisdiction under the Act and demanded that the Board recover the animals and return them to the public lands. . . .

II

The Property Clause of the Constitution provides that "Congress shall have Power to dispose of and make all needful Rules and Regulations respecting the Territory or other Property belonging to the United States." U.S. Const., Art. IV, § 3, cl. 2. In passing the Wild Free-roaming Horses and Burros Act, Congress deemed the regulated animals "an integral part of the natural system of the public lands" of the United States, and found that their management was necessary "for achievement of an ecological balance on the public lands." According to Congress, these animals, if preserved in their native habitats, "contribute to the diversity of life forms within the Nation and enrich the lives of the American people." . . .

For these reasons, Congress determined to preserve and protect the wild free-roaming horses and burros on the public lands of the United States. The question under the Property Clause is whether this determination can be sustained as a "needful" regulation "respecting" the public lands. In answering this question, we must remain mindful that, while courts must eventually pass upon them, determinations under the Property Clause are entrusted primarily to the judgment of Congress.

Appellees argue that the Act cannot be supported by the Property Clause. They contend that the Clause grants Congress essentially two kinds of power: (1) the power to dispose of and make incidental rules regarding the use of federal property; and (2) the power to protect federal property. According to appellees, the first power is not broad enough to support legislation protecting wild animals that live on federal property; and the second power is not implicated since the Act is designed to protect the animals, which are not themselves federal property, and not the public lands. As an initial matter, it is far from clear that the Act was not passed in part to protect the public lands of the United States[16] or that Congress cannot assert a property interest in the regulated horses and burros superior to that of the

[16] [7] Congress expressly ordered that the animals were to be managed and protected in order "to achieve and maintain a thriving natural ecological balance on the public lands." § 3(a), 16 U.S.C. §1333(a)(1970 ed., Supp. IV).

State. But we need not consider whether the Act can be upheld on either of these grounds, for we reject appellees' narrow reading of the Property Clause.

Appellees ground their argument on a number of cases that, upon analysis, provide no support for their position. Like the District Court, appellees cite Hunt v. United States, for the proposition that the Property Clause gives Congress only the limited power to regulate wild animals in order to protect the public lands from damage. But Hunt, which upheld the Government's right to kill deer that were damaging foliage in the national forests, only holds that damage to the land is a sufficient basis for regulation; it contains no suggestion that it is a necessary one.

Next, appellees refer to Kansas v. Colorado, referenced passage in that case states that the Property Clause "clearly . . . does not grant to Congress any legislative control over the states, and must, so far as they are concerned, be limited to authority over the property belonging to the United States within their limits." But this does no more than articulate the obvious: The Property Clause is a grant of power only over federal property. It gives no indication of the kind of "authority" the Clause gives Congress over its property.

Camfield v. United States, is of even less help to appellees. Appellees rely upon the following language from Camfield:

> While we do not undertake to say that congress has the unlimited power to legislate against nuisances within a state which it would have within a territory, we do not think the admission of a territory as a state deprives it of the power of legislating for the protection of the public lands, though it may thereby involve the exercise of what is ordinarily known as the "police power," so long as such power is directed solely to its own protection.

Appellees mistakenly read this language to limit Congress' power to regulate activity on the public lands; in fact, the quoted passage refers to the scope of congressional power to regulate conduct on private land that affects the public lands. And Camfield holds that the Property Clause is broad enough to permit federal regulation of fences built on private land adjoining public land when the regulation is for the protection of the federal property. Camfield contains no suggestion of any limitation on Congress' power over conduct on its own property; its sole message is that the power granted by the Property Clause is broad enough to reach beyond territorial limits.

Lastly, appellees point to dicta in two cases to the effect that, unless the State has agreed to the exercise of federal jurisdiction, Congress' rights in its land are "only the rights of an ordinary proprietor . . . ." Fort Leavenworth R. Co. v. Lowe. See also Paul v. United States. In neither case was the power of Congress under the Property Clause at issue or considered and, as we shall see, these dicta fail to account for the raft of cases in which the Clause has been given a broader construction.

In brief, beyond the Fort Leavenworth and Paul dicta, appellees have presented no support for their position that the Clause grants Congress only the power to dispose of, to make incidental rules regarding the use of, and to protect federal property. This failure is hardly surprising, for the Clause, in broad terms, gives Congress the power to determine what are "needful" rules "respecting" the public lands. And while the furthest reaches of the power granted by the Property Clause have not yet been definitively resolved, we have repeatedly observed that "[t]he power over the public land thus entrusted to Congress is without limitations." United States v. San Francisco.

The decided cases have supported this expansive reading. It is the Property Clause, for instance, that provides the basis for governing the Territories of the United States. And even over public land within the States, "[t]he general government doubtless has a power over its own property analogous to the police power of the several states, and the extent to which it may go in the exercise of such power is measured by the exigencies of the particular case." Camfield v. United States. We have noted, for example, that the Property Clause gives Congress the power over the public lands "to control their occupancy and use, to protect them from trespass and injury, and to prescribe the conditions upon which others may obtain rights in them . . . ." And we have approved legislation respecting the public lands "[i]f it be found to be necessary, for the protection of the public or of intending settlers [on the public lands]." Camfield v. United States. In short, Congress exercises the powers both of a proprietor and of a legislature over the public domain. Although the Property Clause does not authorize "an exercise of a general control over public policy in a State," it does permit "an exercise of the complete power which Congress has over particular public property entrusted to it." In our view, the "complete power" that Congress has over public lands necessarily includes the power to regulate and protect the wildlife living there.

III

Appellees argue that if we approve the Wild Free-roaming Horses and Burros Act as a valid exercise of Congress' power under the Property Clause, then we have sanctioned an impermissible intrusion on the sovereignty, legislative authority, and police power of the State and have wrongly infringed upon the State's traditional trustee powers over wild animals. The argument appears to be that Congress could obtain exclusive legislative jurisdiction over the public lands in the State only by state consent, and that in the absence of such consent Congress lacks the power to act contrary to state law. This argument is without merit.

Appellees' claim confuses Congress' derivative legislative powers, which are not involved in this case, with its powers under the Property Clause. Congress may acquire derivative legislative power from a State pursuant to Art. I, § 8, cl. 17, of the Constitution by consensual acquisition of land, or by nonconsensual acquisition followed by the State's subsequent cession of legislative authority over the land.[17] In

---

[17] [11] Article I, §8, cl. 17 of the Constitution provides that Congress shall have the power:

> To exercise exclusive Legislation in all Cases whatsoever, over such District (not exceeding ten Miles square) as may, by Cession of Particular States, and the Acceptance of Congress, become the Seat of the Government of the United States, and to exercise like Authority over all Places purchased by the Consent of the Legislature of the State in which the Same shall be, for the Erection of Forts, Magazines, Arsenals, dock-Yards, and other needful Buildings . . . .

The Clause has been broadly construed, and the acquisition by consent or cession of exclusive or partial jurisdiction over properties for any legitimate governmental purpose beyond those itemized is

either case, the legislative jurisdiction acquired may range from exclusive federal jurisdiction with no residual state police power, to concurrent, or partial, federal legislative jurisdiction, which may allow the State to exercise certain authority.

But while Congress can acquire exclusive or partial jurisdiction over lands within a State by the State's consent or cession, the presence or absence of such jurisdiction has nothing to do with Congress' power under the Property Clause. Absent consent or cession a State undoubtedly retains jurisdiction over federal lands within its territory, but Congress equally surely retains the power to enact legislation respecting those lands pursuant to the Property Clause. And when Congress so acts, the federal legislation necessarily overrides conflicting state laws under the Supremacy Clause. U.S. Const., Art. VI, cl. 2. As we said in Camfield v. United States, in response to a somewhat different claim: "A different rule would place the public domain of the United States completely at the mercy of state legislation."

Thus, appellees' assertion that "[a]bsent state consent by complete cession of jurisdiction of lands to the United States, exclusive jurisdiction does not accrue to the federal landowner with regard to federal lands within the borders of the state," is completely beside the point; and appellees' fear that the Secretary's position is that "the Property Clause totally exempts federal lands within state borders from state legislative powers, state police powers, and all rights and powers of local sovereignty and jurisdiction of the states," is totally unfounded. The Federal Government does not assert exclusive jurisdiction over the public lands in New Mexico, and the State is free to enforce its criminal and civil laws on those lands. But where those state laws conflict with the Wild Free-roaming Horses and Burros Act, or with other legislation passed pursuant to the Property Clause, the law is clear: The state laws must recede.

Again, none of the cases relied upon by appellees are to the contrary. Surplus Trading Co. v. Cook, merely states the rule outlined above that, "without more," federal ownership of lands within a State does not withdraw those lands from the jurisdiction of the State. Likewise, Wilson v. Cook, holds only that, in the absence of consent or cession, the Federal Government did not acquire exclusive jurisdiction over certain federal forest reserve lands in Arkansas and the State retained legislative jurisdiction over those lands. No question was raised regarding Congress' power to regulate the forest reserves under the Property Clause. And in Colorado v. Toll, the Court found that Congress had not purported to assume jurisdiction over highways within the Rocky Mountain National Park, not that it lacked the power to do so under the Property Clause.[18] In short, these cases do not support appellees' claim that upholding the Act would sanction an impermissible

---

permissible. Collins v. Yosemite Park Co., 304 U.S. 518, 528–530, 58 1009, 1013–14, 82. 1502 (1938).

[18] [12] Referring to the Act creating the National Park, the Court said:

> There is no attempt to give exclusive jurisdiction to the United States, but on the contrary the rights of the State over the roads are left unaffected in terms. Apart from those terms the state denies the power of Congress to curtail its jurisdiction or rights without an act of cession from it and an acceptance by the national government. The statute establishing the park would not be construed to attempt such a result. As the [park superintendent] is undertaking to assert exclusive control and to establish a monopoly in a matter as to which, if the allegations of the bill are maintained, the State has not surrendered its legislative power, a cause of action

intrusion upon state sovereignty. The Act does not establish exclusive federal jurisdiction over the public lands in New Mexico; it merely overrides the New Mexico Estray Law insofar as it attempts to regulate federally protected animals. And that is but the necessary consequence of valid legislation under the Property Clause.

Appellees' contention that the Act violates traditional state power over wild animals stands on no different footing. Unquestionably the States have broad trustee and police powers over wild animals within their jurisdictions. But, as Geer v. Connecticut cautions, those powers exist only "in so far as [their] exercise may be not incompatible with, or restrained by, the rights conveyed to the federal government by the constitution." "No doubt it is true that as between a State and its inhabitants the State may regulate the killing and sale of [wildlife], but it does not follow that its authority is exclusive of paramount powers." Thus, the Privileges and Immunities Clause, U.S. Const., Art. IV, § 2, cl. I, precludes a State from imposing prohibitory licensing fees on nonresidents shrimping in its waters; the Treaty Clause, U.S. Const., Art. II, § 2, permits Congress to enter into and enforce a treaty to protect migratory birds despite state objections; and the Property Clause gives Congress the power to thin overpopulated herds of deer on federal lands contrary to state law. We hold today that the Property Clause also gives Congress the power to protect wildlife on the public lands, state law notwithstanding.

IV

In this case, the New Mexico Livestock Board entered upon the public lands of the United States and removed wild burros. These actions were contrary to the provisions of the Wild Free-roaming Horses and Burros Act. We find that, as applied to this case, the Act is a constitutional exercise of congressional power under the Property Clause. We need not, and do not, decide whether the Property Clause would sustain the Act in all of its conceivable applications.

Appellees are concerned that the Act's extension of protection to wild free-roaming horses and burros that stray from public land onto private land, will be read to provide federal jurisdiction over every wild horse or burro that at any time sets foot upon federal land. While it is clear that regulations under the Property Clause may have some effect on private lands not otherwise under federal control, Camfield v. United States, we do not think it appropriate in this declaratory judgment proceeding to determine the extent, if any, to which the Property Clause empowers Congress to protect animals on private lands or the extent to which such regulation is attempted by the Act. We have often declined to decide important

---

is disclosed if we do not look beyond the bill, and it was wrongly dismissed. 268 U.S., at 231, 45, at 506 (citations omitted).

While Colorado thus asserted that, absent cession, the Federal Government lacked power to regulate the highways within the park, and the Court held that the State was entitled to attempt to prove that it had not surrendered legislative jurisdiction to the United States, as most the case stands for the proposition that where Congress does not purport to override state power over public lands under the Property Clause and where there has been no cession, a federal official lacks power to regulate contrary to state law.

questions regarding "the scope and constitutionality of legislation in advance of its immediate adverse effect in the context of a concrete case", the absence of "an adequate and full-bodied record." We follow that course in this case and leave open the question of the permissible reach of the Act over private lands under the Property Clause.

NOTES AND QUESTIONS

1. *Federal vs. Local Jurisdiction.* What would happen if the Secretary of the Interior were to lease, say, 40 acres in an abandoned military base to a private developer for 99 years for the construction of high-rise condominium and apartment buildings, in an area zoned by the local government in whose jurisdiction the land would otherwise fall, for open space, or zoned for low-density residential use?

2. *The Extent of Federal Jurisdiction.* The extent of the type of peripheral land use regulation designed to protect federal land but exercised over private land is becoming an issue around national forests and other public lands. How far does such control physically extend? What about acid rain or mist from nearby, but nonadjacent, chemical works which defoliates national forests or parklands? What kind of police power is this? How does it differ from that exercised by the states? *See* Sax, *Helpless Giants: The National Policy and the Regulation of Private Lands*, 75 MICH. L. REV. 239 (1976).

3. *Preemption.* Should Congress expressly preempt state regulation? Is the burden of going through two systems for permits too great? If Congress does preempt, how can the state's interest be protected?

4. *The Sale of Federal Lands and the Accompanying Controversies.* Disposal of much of federal land, especially military land, takes place under the Federal Property and Administrative Services Act of 1949, 40 U.S.C. § 472 *et seq.* ("FPASA"). Indeed, it was under this Act that the Administration attempted to sell off perhaps the most controversial part of the "national estate," the 72-acre Fort DeRussy on Waikiki Beach in Honolulu, Hawaii. Part of 715 acres designated for disposal under the aforementioned Asset Management Program by the Property Review Board was a parcel containing 17 of the Fort's 72 acres which were to be sold for real estate development purposes. Among the issues was whether the land should have been offered first to the City at a discount for a public park (which was more or less its current use). *See* Comment, *The Sale of Fort DeRussy: An Analyses of the Reagan Administration's Federal Land Sales Program*, 7 U. HAW. L. REV. 105 (1985); *Government Land Bank v. General Servo Admin.*, 671 F.2d 663 (1st Cir. 1982), for possible answers. For a policy analysis of the issues raised by federal land disposal in a historical context, *see* RETHINKING THE FEDERAL LANDS, (Brubaker ed., 1984); M. CLAWSON, THE FEDERAL LANDS REVISITED (1983).

5. Not all federal land is either condemned by the federal government or part of the public domain. In Hawaii, for example, thousands of valuable acres are held in a variety of defeasible fee by the federal government, and must be returned to the State — less improvement costs, if any — when the Administrator of the General Services Administration and the federal agency user declare it to be "surplus." Ceded Lands Act, 77 U.S. Statutes at Large, 472 (1963). Can the state force such a declaration of surplus if it can show the land is not being used? For federal purposes? *See Hawaii v. Gordon*, 373 U.S. 57 (1963). *See Comment, Hawai'i's Ceded Lands*, 3 U. Haw. L. Rev. 101 (1981); Callies, Regulating Paradise: Land Use Controls In Hawaii, Ch. 12 "Public Lands" (2010).

[D.] CLEAN AIR, CLEAN WATER

[1.] Clean Water Act

It is difficult to make effective use of land without discharging something into a waterway. Therefore, the repeated attempts by Congress to see that the United States — and in particular its states and local governments — does what is possible to clean up the nation's waterways has had significant consequences for real property. The Federal Water Pollution Control Act, as amended by the Clean Water Act of 1977 (the "Clean Water Act"), is the complex legislation that was passed to implement the Congressional intent.

The Clean Water Act contains several parts that have a particularly strong bearing on the use of land: Section 208 wastewater planning, pollution discharge (point and nonpoint source), U.S. Army Corps of Engineers' dredge and fill permit programs, and wastewater treatment plant construction. Drinking water preservation (the "injection" issue) is the subject of separate legislation, closely related to the Clean Water Act. With clean air, coastal zone, flood hazard, and other programs, the federal government drastically affects land use control, long considered to be the domain of state and local government.

The Clean Water Act has as its principal purpose the cleaning and maintenance of the nation's waters. It attacks the problem broadly by means of so-called "structural" and "nonstructural" techniques. The structural techniques pertain to the financing and construction of wastewater treatment plants and ancillary facilities. Nonstructural techniques pertain primarily to regulatory mechanisms, such as planning and land use controls. The purpose of both is to eliminate the discharge of pollutants into the nation's waterways. Initially, most federal money went into the former category, even though there was little, if any, early planning or consideration of the growth-generating potential of large municipal wastewater treatment plants. It became increasingly apparent that all the hardware the federal government could afford for the treatment of pollutants discharged into individual waterway segments was not going to significantly improve the nation's waterways without plans required by other sections of the Clean Water Act. The shift in emphasis, together with the increased role of the Corps of Engineers in granting or not granting permits to dredge and fill navigable waterways, appears to represent current EPA policy.

Inherent in the federal programs, both structural and nonstructural, is the emphasis on their implementation by state and local governments. While it is the federal government that provides most of the money for municipal wastewater treatment facilities, it is the local government unit — city, county, village, special district — that constructs, operates, and maintains the facility and attempts to implement the various rules and regulations concerning connections, pretreatment of effluent, and the like, which come with the money. It is also a regional unit of state or local government that is to do the planning — especially the wastewater management planning upon which much regulatory implementation depends. To state and local governments also falls the job of monitoring, regulating, and enforcing compliance.

HOMESTAKE MINING CO. v. UNITED STATES ENVIRONMENTAL PROTECTION AGENCY

United States District Court, South Dakota District
477 F. Supp. 1279 (1979)

Memorandum Opinion

BOGUE, DISTRICT JUDGE.

This case is before the Court on cross-motions for summary judgment. It concerns defendant South Dakota's adoption and Defendant Environmental Protection Agency's (EPA) approval of water quality standards under the Federal Water Pollution Control Act (FWPCA). These standards were incorporated in a National Pollution Discharge Elimination System (NPDES) permit issued to Plaintiff Homestake Mining Company.

The FWPCA

The cornerstone of the FWPCA is § 301(a), which prohibits "the discharge of any pollutant by any person" unless certain sections of the Act are complied with. An existing pollutant source, such as plaintiff, can continue to discharge waste pursuant to a NPDES permit. A permit is issued upon application and an opportunity for public hearing. It sets limits on the amount of pollutants that can be discharged from anyone source.

The Act provides for two types of restrictions on the discharge of pollutants. First, there are federal technology-based effluent limitations which are established in two stages. The first stage is to be met by July I, 1977, and is to be based upon "the best practicable technology currently available" (BPT). The second stage is to be met by July I, 1984, and is to be based on "the best available technology economically achievable" (BAT).

The second type of restriction on the discharge of pollutants is provided for in §§ 301(b)(1)(c) and 510, 33 U.S.C. §§ 1311(b)(1)(c) and 1370. In this case, plaintiff argues that these restrictions have been improperly implemented by the defendant.

Facts

Plaintiff contends that EPA's approval of South Dakota's water quality standards, which are somewhat stricter than those mandated by the FWPCA, was arbitrary, capricious and contrary to law. In 1974, South Dakota revised its water quality standards and designated Whitewood Creek for use as a cold water permanent fishery and for recreation in and on the water. This designation affected plaintiff in that plaintiff discharges waste into Gold Run Creek which is a tributary of Whitewood Creek. On October 28, 1977, South Dakota again revised its water quality standards as required by § 303(c) of the FWPCA. These revisions did not change the designation of Whitewood Creek as a cold water permanent fishery.

Under § 402(a) of the FWPCA, EPA issued draft NPDES permits to plaintiff in 1975 and 1976. These permits contained effluent limitations based on BPT and the more stringent state water quality standards. Plaintiff was given a chance for a hearing on the terms of its permit, but eventually declined this opportunity and accepted the permit on September 17, 1976.

Plaintiff is now asking this Court to declare EPA's approval of South Dakota's more stringent water quality standards to be violative of the FWPCA. Such a declaration by this Court would free plaintiff from the requirements of its NPDES permit. I n its prayer for relief plaintiff asks this Court to enjoin the application to it of both South Dakota's water quality standards and the Cheyenne River Basin Plan.

In support of its claim, plaintiff argues three main points: (1) That EPA's approval of South Dakota's water quality standards was arbitrary, capricious, an abuse of discretion and not in accordance with the FWPCA; (2) That §§ 302 and 303 of the FWPCA have been improperly interpreted, implemented and applied by the defendants; (3) That EPA's approval of the Cheyenne River Basin plan was arbitrary, capricious and not in accordance with the law. Each of these three issues will be addressed separately.

Approval of the Cheyenne River Basin Plan

Plaintiff next challenges EPA's approval of the § 303(e), Cheyenne River Basin Plan. A large part of western South Dakota, including Whitewood Creek, is included in the Cheyenne River Basin. The Plan establishes South Dakota's strategy for correcting water pollution and thereby improving and maintaining water quality in the Cheyenne River Basin. It specifies the process of planning and managing pollution abatement operations to achieve South Dakota's standards for pollutant discharges to, and water quality in the Basin's, lakes, rivers and tributaries.

This plan was implemented pursuant to § 303(e) of the FWPCA.

Section 303(e) provides for the establishment, by the states, of a continuing planning process. Section 303(e)(3)(c) reads as follows:

> The Administrator shall approve any continuing planning process submitted to him under this section which will result in plans for all navigable waters within such State, which include, but are not limited to, the following: . . .
>
> (c) total maximum daily load for pollutants in accordance with subsection (d) of this section.

The method of establishing the daily load is set out in § 303(d)(I). That section provides:

> A) Each State shall identify those waters within its boundaries for which the effluent limitations required by section 1311(b)(I)(A) and section 1311 (b)(I)(B) of this title are not stringent enough to implement any water quality standard applicable to such waters. The State shall establish a priority ranking for such waters, taking into account the severity of the pollution and he uses to be made of such waters. . . .
>
> (C) Each State shall establish for the waters identified in paragraph (I)(A) of this subsection, and in accordance with the priority ranking, the total maximum daily load, for those pollutants which the Administrator identifies under section 1314(a)(2) of this title as suitable for such calculation. Such load shall be established at a level necessary to implement the applicable water quality standards with seasonal variations and a margin of safety which takes into account any lack of knowledge concerning the relationship between effluent limitations and water quality.

Section 304(a)(2)(0) of the FWPCA, requires EPA to identify pollutants which are suitable for maximum daily load calculations by October 18, 1973. Prior to the adoption of South Dakota's water quality standards defendants failed to comply with these sections of the Act in that maximum daily loads for pollutants were not established.

These procedures were meant to assist EPA and the states in implementing the requirements of the Act. Plaintiff contends that these procedures are mandatory requirements of the FWPCA. Furthermore, plaintiff argues that the failure to comply with these procedures should invalidate the entire Cheyenne River Basin Plan.

Although South Dakota did not establish total maximum daily loads as required by § 303(d), this was not required of the state until 180 days after EPA's identification of pollutants. Section 304(d)(2), 33 U.S.C. § 1314(d)(2). Because EPA had not identified the pollutants at the time of the Basin Plan's adoption, South Dakota cannot be said to have failed to comply with this portion of the FWPCA. The question then becomes whether EPA's failure to identify pollutants suitable for maximum daily load calculations pursuant to § 304(a)(2)(D) is of such magnitude as to invalidate the Cheyenne River Basin Plan and in turn, to invalidate plaintiffs NPOES permit.

It appears to this Court that EPA's failure to identify pollutants does not invalidate the Basin Plan. First of all, plaintiffs attack on the entire Basin Plan is clearly an attempt to avoid having to comply with the terms of its NPOES permit. Section 509(b)(I)(F) provides that a challenge to an NPDES permit can be made within 90 days of the permit's issuance in the applicable Circuit Court of Appeals. This, plaintiff did not do. Furthermore, plaintiff withdrew its request for an adjudicatory hearing regarding its permit under 40 CFR § 125.36(b). Since plaintiff neglected its other opportunities to challenge its NPOES permit, the Court is unwilling to invalidate the entire Cheyenne River Basin Plan because of plaintiffs dissatisfaction with its permit.

Furthermore, it appears that § 402(a)(1) of the FWPCA allows the issuance of a permit prior to the taking of all implementing actions. This statute provides in part as follows:

> [T]he Administrator may, after opportunity for public hearing, issue a permit for the discharge of any pollutant, .. , prior to the taking of necessary implementing actions relating to all such requirements, such conditions as the Administrator determines are necessary to carry out the provisions of this chapter.

It appears to this Court that Congress anticipated that some of the Act's requirements would not, or could not, be complied with prior to the issuance of permits. Therefore, § 402 was included in the Act to insure that the permit issuance program was not stymied because another part of the Act had not been strictly complied with.

The FWPCA is a complex statute. EPA clearly has more experience working with it than do most other public or private entities. In implementing and interpreting such a complex statute, EPA's interpretation must be given a great deal of weight. In approving South Dakota's Cheyenne River Basin Plan, EPA substantially complied with the Act's requirements. Furthermore, plaintiffs right to challenge the effluent limitation and its NPDES permit was preserved. Therefore, this Court sees no reason to declare the Basin Plan invalid or to find EPA's approval of it to be arbitrary and capricious.

NOTES AND QUESTIONS

1. *Ground Water.* The EPA also has responsibilities for keeping increasingly endangered ground water supplies unpolluted. This is essential, as there is twice as much usable groundwater in North America as there is water in the major lakes, and its use is increasing at twice the rate of total freshwater use. U.S. Water Resources Council, Second National Assessment of the Nation's Water Resources, Part II, 38, 39, and 51 (1958). Indeed, some cities like Honolulu and San Antonio get most of their fresh water from underground water sources. The EPA has limited authority to regulate certain discharges into such sources under the Clean Water Act, *United States Steel Corp. v. Train*, 556 F.2d 822 (7th Cir. 1977). *But see United States v. GAF Corp.*, 389 F. Supp. 1379 (S.D. Tex. 1975); *Exxon Corp. v. Train*, 554 F.2d 1310 (5th Cir. 1977). However, its principal authority comes from the Safe Drinking Water Act, 42 U.S.C. § 300f *et seq.*, which establishes a national regulatory program for injection of pollutants into certain underground water sources.

The thrust of the Act is to prevent the pollution of underground drinking water sources by requiring states to establish a permit program for underground injection wells which may endanger such water supplies. In addition, section 300h-3(e) — the so-called Gonzales Amendment to the Act, also protects those underground water formations known as aquifers — which are also the sole or principal source of drinking water for an area by forbidding any federally assisted project which might contaminate such an aquifer through its recharge zone "so as to create a significant hazard for public health." As the use and development of land generates considerable waste, the effects on local development controls can be considerable. Consider that approximately 200 "deep" and 40,000 "shallow" injection wells for the disposal of commercial and industrial waste are in operation across the country, and that an estimated 17 million septic tanks and cesspools discharge 800 billion gallons of wastewater into the ground each year. EPA, Report to Congress, Waste Disposal Practices and Their Effects on Ground Water 362, 508 (1977).

2. *Pollution Sources.* Note the similarity in approach in the Clean Air Act and the Clean Water Act, especially comparing effluent and emission standards. As with the Clean Air Act, the Clean Water Act requires different standards for new and existing sources of pollution. As industrial and commercial dischargers turned increasingly to the largely federally-funded, publicly-owned treatment works to dispose of highly-polluted wastewater, the EPA issued guidelines requiring the pretreatment of such wastewater to avoid undue burdening of the treatment works. Consider the effect of such regulations on private decisions to locate a new facility.

3. *NPDES.* It is illegal to discharge pollutants into a waterway without a permit from a state agency under the National Pollution Discharge Elimination System (NPDES). Intensive use of land is impossible without some provision for sewage and other waste disposal (usually in waterways); how this program is administered critically affects that use. The NPDES permit requirement extends to both private and public-facility discharges — including publicly owned treatment works (POTWs). The permits are issued by an approved state agency only upon condition that such discharge will meet the effluent and other standards set by the administrator of the EPA. For the EPA administrator to approve a state permitting program, the state agency must have the power to revoke a permit violating its terms. The state program must also insure that any permit for a POTW will include conditions that guarantee compliance with pretreatment standards for private-source hookups (industrial/commercial facilities connected to the POTW). These standards require the treatment of sewage for the removal of some pollutants before the sewage reaches a POTW, in order to avoid overburdening the plant. The cost of this pretreatment is a factor in the locating of private industry in an area. The effect on growth is in many areas predictably substantial, as treatment works, new or expanded, with substantial treatment excess capacity to accommodate future needs attracted development to the areas they served.

4. *Plans and Permits.* While the structural solutions have been vastly better funded, emphasis in the late 1970s moved to what was intended to precede the construction of wastewater treatment facilities: the areawide waste treatment management or "208" plans (so named because they are required in section 208 of the Clean Water Act) and 404 permits. The Section 208 plans were originally intended to be the basis for the water cleanup effort. The purpose of the plans was to abate water pollution through the management of water quality and the regulation of land use in metropolitan regions. Such plans are required for any area identified as having substantial water quality control problems as a result of urban-industrial concentrations or other factors. A representative organization capable of developing effective area — wide waste treatment management plans for that area is then designated to prepare such a plan within one year. Unfortunately, many of the regional bodies so designated — like Council of Governments (COGS) and regional councils — had just planning powers and no more. The next step — implementation — has been lacking in many areas. Land use controls, as you now know, rest principally with local governments and not with the states and regional agencies. Sanctions — which amount to loss of POTW construction grant funding and no NPDES permits for point sources which conflict with the plan — have not proven particularly effective. *See* Goldfarb, *Water Quality Management Planning: The Fate of 208*, 8 U. Tol. L. Rev. 105 (1976); Comment, *Sewers, Clean Water and Planned Growth*, 86 Yale L.J. 733 (1977). They may not be entirely toothless, however. In *Smoke Rise, Inc. v. Washington Suburban San. Comm'n*, 400 F. Supp. 1369 (D. Md. 1975), a 208 plan proved remarkably effective as a basis for upholding a rather long moratorium on sewer hookups. What effect do you suppose this had on residential construction in the area?

The purpose of Section 404 of the Clean Water Act is to prohibit discharge of dredged or fill materials into navigable — including coastal — waters of the United States without a permit from the U.S. Army Corps of Engineers. Until the late I 960s, the Corps granted or refused such permits based primarily on the likely effect on navigation of such materials. Thereafter, the Corps, in response to a growing national concern for environmental values and related federal legislation, commenced implementation of a so-called "public interest" permit review process to consider the effect of proposed dredge and fill upon fish and wildlife, conservation, pollution, aesthetics, ecology, and the general public interest. Then, in the mid-1970s, the Corps listed additional factors to be considered — economics, historic values, flood damages prevention, land use classification, recreation. and water supply/water quality — together with a policy to protect wetlands from unnecessary destruction. The result is the slow conversion of a relatively simple permitting process directed at preserving navigation into a full-fledged land use — environmental review of proposed projects in coastal and coastal wetland areas. The *SWANCC* case, *supra*, reflects implementation of the Corps' section 404 mandate.

[2.] Clean Air

Government, and in particular the federal government, got into the air pollution control business in 1970 with amendments to the Air Quality Act of 1967. In many ways, the Clean Air Act is the toughest of federal laws affecting the use of land and the one that has had a substantial effect. This is so at least in part because it deals directly with the use of land. State and local governments, the actual administrators of the federally mandated clean air program, have no choice about whether or not to participate. The Clean Air Act requires state and local governments to implement clean air measures in substantial part through land use controls.

Basically, the Clean Air Act provides for geographically uniform federal quality standards for ambient air (the air around us) to be established with respect to certain key pollutants by the administrator of the Environmental Protection Agency (EPA). The standards are to be enforced by the states through a state implementation plan (SIP), which the EPA administrator may approve only if it meets the federal standards. If not, the administrator may draw up and issue a SIP for a recalcitrant state. The act also provides for the promulgation of emission standards (for air at a point of discharge into the atmosphere) for new stationary sources of pollution (factories, power plants, and the like), for certain hazardous air pollutants, and for pollutants from motor vehicles. Various lawsuits and amendments to the Clean Air Act have added requirements for the prevention of significant deterioration of air quality in clean air regions, the designation of air quality maintenance areas, and the need for preconstruction reviews of new major stationary sources of pollution. Finally, the amendments suggest that a state divide all its air quality maintenance regions into three zones, which, other things being equal, regulate the number of new pollution sources — and, hence, the use of land — in each.

CITIZENS AGAINST REFINERY'S EFFECTS, INC. v. UNITED STATES ENVIRONMENTAL PROTECTION AGENCY

United States Court of Appeals, Fourth Circuit
643 F.2d 183 (1981)

K.K. Hall, Circuit Judge.

Citizens Against the Refinery's Effects (CARE) appeals from a final ruling by the Administrator of the Environmental Protection Agency (EPA) approving the Virginia State Implementation Plan (SIP) for reducing hydrocarbon pollutants. The plan requires the Virginia Highway Department to decrease usage of a certain type of asphalt, thereby reducing hydrocarbon pollution by more than enough to offset expected pollution from the Hampton Roads Energy Company's (HREC) proposed refinery. We affirm the action of the administrator in approving the state plan.

The Act

The Clean Air Act establishes National Ambient Air Quality Standards (NAAQS) for five major air pollutants.[19] The EPA has divided each state into Air Quality Control Regions (AQCR)[20] and monitors each region to assure that the national standard for each pollutant is met. Where the standard has not been attained for a certain pollutant, the state must develop a State Implementation Plan designed to bring the area into attainment within a certain period. In addition, no new source of that pollutant may be constructed until the standard is attained.

The Clean Air Act created a no-growth environment in areas where the clean air requirements had not been attained. EPA recognized the need to develop a program that encouraged attainment of clean air standards without discouraging economic growth. Thus the agency proposed an Interpretive Ruling in 1976 which allowed the states to develop an "offset program" within the State Implementation Plans. The offset program, later codified by Congress in 1977 Amendments to the Clean Air Act, permits the states to develop plans which allow construction of new pollution sources where accompanied by a corresponding reduction in an existing pollution source. In effect, a new emitting facility can be built if an existing pollution source

---

[19] [1] The five major pollutants for which standards have been developed are sulfur dioxides, carbon monoxide, nitrogen dioxide, particulates, and photochemical oxidants. 40 CFR § 50 (1976)

[20] [2] There are 247 AQCRs in the nation. Virginia has seven AQCRs

decreases its emissions or ceases operations as long as a positive net air quality benefit occurs.

If the proposed factory will emit carbon monoxide, sulfur dioxide, or particulates, the EPA requires that the offsetting pollution source be within the immediate vicinity of the new plant. The other two pollutants, hydrocarbons and nitrogen oxide, are less "site-specific," and thus the ruling permits the offsetting source to locate anywhere within a broad vicinity of the new source.

The offset program has two other important requirements: first, a base time period must be determined in which to calculate how much reduction is needed in existing pollutants to offset the new source. This base period is defined as the first year of the SIP, or where the state has not yet developed a SIP, as the year in which a construction permit application is filed. Second, the offset program requires that the new source adopt the Lowest Achievable Emissions Rate (LAER) using the most modem technology available in the industry.

The Refinery

HREC proposes to build a petroleum refinery and offloading facility in Portsmouth, Virginia. Portsmouth has been unable to reduce air pollution enough to attain the national standard for one pollutant, photochemical oxidants, which is created when hydrocarbons are released into the atmosphere and react with other substances. Since a refinery is a major source of hydrocarbons, the Clean Air Act prevents construction of the HREC plant until the area attains the national standard.

In 1975, HREC applied to the Virginia State Air Pollution Control Board (VSAPCB) for a refinery construction permit. The permit was issued by the VSAPCB on October 8, 1975, extended and reissued on October 5, 1977 after a full public hearing, modified on August 8, 1978, and extended again on September 27, 1979. The VSAPCB, in an effort to help HREC meet the clean air requirements, proposed to use the offset ruling to comply with the Clean Air Act.

On November 28, 1977, the VSAPCB submitted a State Implementation Plan to EPA which included the HREC permit. The Virginia Board proposed to offset the new HREC hydrocarbon pollution by reducing the amount of cutback asphalt used for road paving operations in three highway districts by the Virginia Department of Highways. By switching from "cutback" to "emulsified" asphalt, the state can reduce hydrocarbon pollutants by the amount necessary to offset the pollutants from the proposed refinery. The standard of review here is whether the agency action was arbitrary, capricious, an abuse of discretion, or otherwise not in accordance with law.

The Geographic Area

CARE contends that the state plan should not have been approved by EPA since the three highway-district area where cutback usage will be reduced to offset refinery emissions was artificially developed by the state. The ruling permits a broad area (usually within one AQCR) to be used as the offset basis.

The ruling does not specify how to determine the area, nor provide a standard procedure for defining the geographic area. 41 Fed. Reg. 55529 (1976). Here the Virginia Board originally proposed to use four highway districts comprising one-half the state as the offset area. When this was found to be much more than necessary to offset pollution expected from the refinery, the state changed it to one highway district plus nine additional counties. Later the proposed plan was again revised to include a geographic area of three highway districts.

The agency action in approving the use of three highway districts was neither arbitrary, capricious, nor outside the statute. First, Congress intended that the states and the EPA be given flexibility in designing and implementing SIPs. Such flexibility allows the states to make reasoned choices as to which areas may be used to offset new pollution and how the plan is to be implemented. Second, the offset program was initiated to encourage economic growth in the state. Thus a state plan designed to reduce highway department pollution in order to attract another industry is a reasonable contribution to economic growth without a corresponding increase in pollution. Third, to be sensibly administered the offset plan had to be divided into districts which could be monitored by the highway department. Use of any areas other than highway districts would be unwieldy and difficult to administer. Fourth, the scientific understanding of ozone pollution is not advanced to the point where exact air transport may be predicted. Designation of the broad area in which hydrocarbons may be transported is well within the discretion and expertise of the agency.

The Base Year

Asphalt consumption varies greatly from year to year, depending upon weather and road conditions. Yet EPA must accurately determine the volume of hydrocarbon emissions from cutback asphalt. Only then can the agency determine whether the reduction in cutback usage will result in an offset great enough to account for the new refinery pollution. To calculate consumption of a material where it constantly varies, a base year must be selected. In this case, EPA's interpretive Ruling establishes the base year as the year in which the permit application is made. EPA decided that 1977 was an acceptable base year. CARE argues that EPA illegally chose 1977 instead of 1975.

Considering all of the circumstance, including the unusually high asphalt consumption in 1977, the selection by EPA of that as the base year was within the discretion of the agency. Since the EPA interpretive Ruling allowing the offset was not issued until 1976, 1977 was the first year after the offset ruling and the logical base year in which to calculate the offset. Also, the permit issued by the VSAPCB was reissued in 1977 with extensive additions and revisions after a full hearing. Under these circumstances, 1977 appears to be a logical choice of a base year.

The Legally Binding Plan

For several years, Virginia has pursued a policy of shifting from cutback asphalt to the less expensive emulsified asphalt in road-paving operations. The policy was initiated in an effort to save money, and was totally unrelated to a State implementation Plan. Because of this policy, CARE argues that hydrocarbon emissions were decreasing independent of this SIP and therefore are not a proper offset against the refinery. They argue that there is not, in effect, an actual reduction in pollution.

The Virginia voluntary plan is not enforceable and therefore is not in compliance with the 1976 Interpretive Ruling which requires that the offset program be enforceable. The EPA, in approving the state plan, obtained a letter from the Deputy Attorney General of Virginia in which he stated that the requisites had been satisfied for establishing and enforcing the plan with the Department of Highways. Without such authority, no decrease in asphalt — produced pollution is guaranteed. In contrast to the voluntary plan, the offset plan guarantees a reduction in pollution resulting from road-paving operations.

The Lower Achievable Emissions Rate

Finally, CARE argues that the Offset Plan does not provide adequate Lowest Achievable Emission Rates (LAER) as required by the 1976 interpretive Ruling because the plan contains only a 90% vapor recovery requirement, places an excessive 176.5 ton limitation on hydrocarbon emissions, and does not require specific removal techniques at the terminal. EPA takes the position that the best technique available for marine terminals provides only a 90% recovery and that the 176.5 ton limit may be reduced by the agency after the final product mix at the terminal is determined.

Since the record shows no evidence of arbitrary or capricious action in approving the HREC emissions equipment, the agency determination of these technical matters must be upheld.

NOTES AND QUESTIONS

1. *Air Quality Zoning.* The Portsmouth refinery was a highly controversial project that required a number of other federal permits in addition to air quality clearance. Since the refinery was in an area where the air quality standards had not been attained, the state had to use the emission offset policy to justify air quality compliance. This led to an exercise in air quality zoning. The three highway districts used in the offset decision spanned most of the eastern, mainly rural, third of the state and cut across four Air Quality Control Regions (ACQR). In effect, the state was zoned so that air pollution could be "averaged" in a way that would make the refinery acceptable. Was this decision justified?

2. *Restricting Offsets.* The interpretive ruling at issue in the *Citizens* case favored keeping emission offsets at least within the same AQCR as the proposed source and hydrocarbon offsets in particular within 85 miles of urban areas, where they are abundant. In 1977 Congress codified the emission offset policy as follows:

> The owner or operator of a new or modified major stationary source may comply with any offset requirement in effect under this part for increased emissions of any air pollutant only by obtaining emission reductions of such air pollutant from the same source or other sources in the same nonattain-

> ment area, except that the State may allow the owner or operator of a source to obtain such emission reductions in another nonattainment area if (A) the other area has an equal or higher nonattainment classification than the area in which the source is located and (B) emissions from such other area contribute to a violation of the national ambient air quality standard in the nonattainment area in which the source is located. Such emission reductions shall be, by the time a new or modified source commences operation, in effect and enforceable and shall assure that the total tonnage of increased emissions of the air pollutant from the new or modified source shall be offset by an equal or greater reduction, as applicable, in the actual emissions of such air pollutant from the same or other sources in the area

42 U.S.C. § 7503(c)(1).

Would the offset allowed in the *Citizens* case qualify under this statute? Note that states had begun the switch to water-based paving asphalt at the time this offset was approved and was eventually approved by EPA as an emission control strategy. Virginia had been slow to make the change. How did this affect the outcome in the case? Was it correct to allow the state to use water-based asphalt as an emission offset when it was cheaper, a better energy conservation strategy, readily available, and about to be approved by the EPA?

3. *Regional Impacts*. What was the regional impact of the refinery's approval? One commentator noted:

> The economic benefit dimension of the offset policy indicates the importance of limiting the offset area to the vicinity of the source. The offset policy was intended to create an economic incentive to reduce air pollution. The Portsmouth area may reap an economic benefit from the refinery, but distant rural regions in the offset area will not. They will contribute their emission reductions to the refinery offset. without receiving an economic benefit comparable to that enjoyed by the Portsmouth area. An industry that wanted to locate in a remote region of the refinery offset area might be forced, or might find it cheaper, to locate elsewhere because offset credits have been exhausted.

Rudykoff, *Recent Development, Citizens Against the Refinery's Effects, Inc. (CARE) v. United States Environmental Protection Agency (EPA)*, 643 F.2d 183 (4th Cir., 1981), 12 Envtl. L. 811, 819 (1982). For an argument that fragmented statutes prevented a comprehensive review of the project, see Liroff, *Oil vs. Oysters — Lessons for Environmental Regulation of Industrial Siting from the Hampton Roads Refinery Controversy*, 11 B.C. Envtl. Aff. L. Rev. 70S, 714 (1984).

[E.] ENDANGERED SPECIES PROTECTION AND PROPERTY RIGHTS

Congress enacted the Endangered Species Act (ESA) to:

> provide a means whereby the ecosystems upon which endangered species and threatened species depend may be conserved, to provide a program for the conservation of such endangered species and threatened species, and to

> take such steps as may be appropriate to achieve the purposes of the treaties and conventions set forth [in the act].

16 U.S.C. § 1531(b).

In crafting the act, Congress demonstrated an awareness that wildlife not only has "esthetic" value but "ecological, educational, historical, recreational, and scientific value" as well. Passage of the Endangered Species Act was an affirmation of our Nation's commitment to and understanding of the need for species preservation and protection.

Largely in response to criticism from business interests, Congress amended the ESA several times to strike a better balance between species protection and development. One of the more controversial issues under the ESA is whether the modification of habitat on private lands constitutes a "taking" of an endangered or threatened species. Section 9 of the ESA explicitly prohibits the "taking" of any endangered species of animal or plant. The term "take" is defined as meaning: "to harass, harm, pursue, hunt, shoot, wound, kill, trap, capture, or collect or to attempt to engage in any such conduct."

DEFENDERS OF WILDLIFE v. BERNAL

United Stated Court of Appeals, Ninth Circuit
204 F.3d 920 (2000)

Chief Justice Hug delivered the opinion of the Court.

Defenders of Wildlife and the Southwest Center for Biological Diversity (collectively "Defenders") appeal the district court's order lifting a temporary restraining order and denying their motion for a permanent injunction to halt the construction of a new school on property which Defenders contend contains potential habitat for the cactus ferruginous pygmy owl (pygmy-owl), listed as endangered under the Endangered Species Act (ESA), 16 U.S.C. §§ 1531–1543. At issue in this case is whether the construction of a critically-needed new high school by the Amphitheater School District (the School District) in northwest Tucson will result in the "take" of the endangered pygmy-owl in violation of section 9 of the ESA, 16 U.S.C. § 1538(1)(B).

After a three-day bench trial the district court found that the proposed construction would not result in the take of a pygmy-owl and denied the permanent injunction. In this appeal Defenders assert that the district court (1) erroneously concluded that plaintiffs failed to meet their burden of proof, (2) should have required the School District to apply for an incidental take permit, (3) inappropriately excluded expert testimony and (4) incorrectly denied Defender's Motion for a New Trial. We have jurisdiction over final judgments of the district court pursuant to 28 U.S.C. § 1291, and we affirm.

I. *Factual and Procedural Background*

In 1994, the School District paid $1.78 million to purchase a 73 acre site in northwest Tucson, upon which a new high school would be built. The high school complex is intended to accommodate 2,100 students and is composed of several buildings, athletic fields and parking areas for students, faculty and visitors. In December 1994, after the purchase of the school site, the United States Fish and Wildlife Service (FWS) formally published a proposed rule to list the pygmy-owl as an endangered species under the ESA. On March 10, 1997, after the required procedures and commentary period, the FWS listed the pygmy-owl as an endangered species under the ESA.

The pygmy-owl is a small reddish brown owl known for its relatively long tail and monotonous call which is heard primarily at dawn and dusk. The pygmy-owl nests in a cavity of a large tree or large columnar cactus. Its diverse diet includes birds, lizards, insects, and small mammals and frogs. The pygmy-owl occurs from lowland central Arizona south through portions of western Mexico and from southern Texas south through other portions of Mexico on down through portions of Central America.[21] The FWS indicates that there are a total 54,400 acres of suitable pygmy-owl habitat in northwest Tucson, which includes the 73 acre school site. The school site falls within the area designated by the FWS as critical habitat for the pygmy owl. *See* 64 Fed. Red. 37,419 (1999).[22]

Within the 73 acre parcel acquired by the School District in 1994, there are three "arroyos," defined as "dry washes" or "ephemeral desert waterways." The U.S. Army Corps of Engineers designated the arroyos as "jurisdictional waters" pursuant to the Clean Water Act, 33 U.S.C. § 1251 *et seq.* The original design of the School District complex called for some construction within the "jurisdictional waters," thereby requiring the School District to obtain a permit under the Clean

---

[21] [1] The cactus ferruginous pygmy-owl is one of four subspecies of the ferruginous pygmy-owl. It is the cactus ferruginous pygmy-owl that we are concerned with in this case, and the term "pygmy-owl" as used in this opinion refers to that subspecies.

[22] [2] Critical habitat is defined as "i) the specific areas within the geographical area occupied by the species, at the time it is listed in accordance with [the Act], on which are found those physical or biological features (I) essential to the conservation of the species and (II) which may require special management considerations or protection; and (ii) specific areas outside the geographical area occupied by the species at the time it is listed in accordance with the provisions [the Act], upon a determination by the Secretary that such areas are essential for the conservation of the species." 16 U.S.C. § 1532(5)(A).

At the time the FWS issued its regulation determining that the pygmy owl is an endangered species on March 10, 1997, it did not designate the critical habitat for the species as provided for in 16 U.S.C. § 1533(a)(3)(A). During the pendency of this appeal, in response to a lawsuit instituted on October 1997, the FWS issued a regulation on July 12, 1999, 64 Fed. Reg. 37419–37440, that designated the critical habitat of the pygmy-owl. We requested supplemental briefs from the parties discussing what effect, if any, this identification of critical habitat by the FWS on this case. The regulation designated 731,712 acres, including the 54,000 acres north of Tucson and the 90-acre school site that had been discussed in the trial. It does not affect the result in this case brought under Section 9 of the ESA involving private land because the district court found that there was no "taking" of the endangered species (the pygmy-owl). There is legal significance under section 7 of the ESA, which pertains to federal agency actions and federally authorized or funded projects. The regulation itself makes this clear:

> The designation of critical habitat has no effect on non-Federal actions taken on private land even if the private land is within the mapped boundary of designated critical habitat. Critical habitat has possible effects on activities by private landowners only if the activity involves Federal funding, a Federal permit, or

64 Fed. Reg. 37428 (1999). Critical habitat designation is only applicable to Federal lands and to private lands if a Federal nexus exists. 64 Fed. Reg. 37444(1999).

Water Act. Because a federal permit was at issue, the FWS informed the Corps that "formal consultation" pursuant to section 7 of the ESA was required to assess the impact of the proposed project on the pygmy-owl[23] was initiated, but before completion of the process the School District withdrew its application for the permit because it had redesigned the project so that construction would not affect the jurisdictional waterways. As a result of the redesigned project, no development is planned for the 30 acres containing the arroyos in the western portion of the property. The School District has acquired or will acquire 17 acres to the east of the initially acquired property for utilization in the redesigned school project. Thus, the entire school site is 90 acres, including the 30 acres containing the arroyos. The 30 acre parcel will remain undeveloped and fenced off. For ease in identification in this opinion, the entire 90 acre parcel will be referred to as the "school site." The 60 acres upon which the school complex is designed to be built will be referred to as the "60 acre parcel" The undeveloped 30 acre parcel, which contains the arroyos, will be referred to as the "30 acre parcel."

In March 1998, the School District began plant salvaging operations as a precursor to beginning construction. Defenders immediately filed suit seeking a temporary restraining order and a preliminary injunction against the School District to prevent any action on the school site. Defenders alleged that the proposed construction violated Section 9 of the ESA because it was likely to harm or harass a pygmy-owl, which Defenders assert inhabit or use the site. Section 9 of the ESA applies to private parties, whereas Section 7 of the ESA, which had earlier been resolved, applies only to actions carried out, funded, or authorized by a federal agency. The district court entered a temporary restraining order. The court later consolidated the hearing on Defenders' request for a preliminary injunction with the trial on the merits. Following a three-day trial, the district court issued its final order, denying the request for a permanent injunction, and lifting the temporary restraining order. We granted Defenders' motion for an injunction pending appeal.

II. *Statutory Framework*

Section 9 of the ESA makes it unlawful to "take" a species listed as endangered or threatened. *See* 16 U.S.C. § I 538(a)(1)(B). "The term 'take' means to harass, harm, pursue, hunt, shoot, wound, kill, trap, capture or collect, or to attempt to engage in any such conduct." 16 U.S.C. § 1532(19). The take alleged is that the proposed construction will harass or harm the pygmy-owl. The Department of the Interior has promulgated a regulation further defining harm and harass as follows:

> Harm in the definition of "take" in the Act means an act which actually kills or injures wildlife. Such act may include significant habitat modification or

---

[23] [3] The pertinent part [of] Section 7 provides:

> Each federal agency shall, in consultation with and with the assistance of the Secretary, insure that any action authorized, funded, or carried out by such agency is not likely to jeopardize the continued existence of any endangered species or threatened species or result in the destruction or adverse modification of habitat of such species with is determined by the Secretary . . . to be critical . . .

16 U.S.C. § 1536(a)(2).

> degradation where it actually kills or injures wildlife by significantly impairing essential behavioral patterns, including breeding, feeding or sheltering. Harass in the definition of "take" in the Act means an intentional or negligent act or omission which creates the likelihood of injury to wildlife by annoying it to such an extent as to significantly disrupt normal behavioral patterns which include, but are not limited to, breeding. feeding or sheltering.

50 C.F.R. § 17.3.

Harming a species may be indirect, in that the harm may be caused by habitat modification, but habitat modification does not constitute harm unless it "actually kills or injures wildlife." The Department of Interior's definition of harm was upheld against a facial challenge to its validity in the case of *Babbitt v. Sweet Home Chapter of Communities for a Great Oregon*, 515 U.S. 687 (1995). In upholding the definition of "harm" as encompassing habitat modification, the Supreme Court emphasized that "every term in the regulation's definition of 'harm' is subservient to the phrase 'an act which actually kills or injures wildlife.' " *Id.* at 700 n. 13.

Three months prior to the *Sweet Home* decision we held in *Forest Conservation Council v. Rosboro Lumber Co.*, 50 F.3d 781, 783 (9th Cir. 1995), that habitat modification that is reasonably certain to injure an endangered species by impairing their essential behavioral patterns satisfied the actual injury requirement and was sufficient to justify a permanent injunction. In a subsequent action, it was contended that *Sweet Home* had overruled *Rosboro* and that an actual violation of the ESA was required before an injunction could issue. However, in *Marbled Murrelet v. Babbit*, 83 F.3d 1060, 1066 (9th Cir. 1996), we held that the Supreme Court's decision in *Sweet Home* does not overrule *Rosboro* and that a reasonably certain threat of imminent harm to a protected species is sufficient for issuance of an injunction under section 9 of the ESA.

III. *Harm and Harassment Claims*

In order to prevail in this action Defenders had to prove that the School District's actions would result in an unlawful "take" of a pygmy-owl. An injunction would be appropriate relief. *See Marbled Murrelet*, 83 F.3d at 1064. Defenders had the burden of proving by a preponderance of the evidence that the proposed construction would harm a pygmy-owl by killing or injuring it, or would more likely than not harass a pygmy-owl by annoying it to such an extent as to disrupt its normal behavioral patterns. *See Rosboro*, 50 F.3d at 784. The district court's final order was a thorough, detailed and carefully reasoned discussion and analysis of the testimony of the expert witnesses and other evidence produced at the trial. The judge framed his discussion and analysis as follows:

> In this case, there are primarily two material factual Questions: 1) Does a pygmy-owl use or occupy any part of the school site? 2) Will the construction and operation of the site result in as 9 "take" through the "harm" or "harassment" of a pygmy-owl? The Court has concluded that the evidence supports a finding that an owl or owls use a portion of the site which the Defendants do not intend to develop. Accordingly, the Court's inquiry has

> further devolved into two remaining questions: 1) whether clearing the unused portion of the property could "take" the owl, in spite of what the FWS has concluded in the Final Rule,[24] and 2) what proof is offered that the construction and operation of the school will harm or harass the owl.

The district judge first discussed his factual findings as to the territory that was occupied or used by the pygmy-owls. He found from the expert testimony and other evidence produced that the pygmy-owls used territory to the north of the boundary and the west of the boundary of the school site and that no pygmy-owl had been detected anywhere within the school site itself. However, he found that there was a reasonable inference that one or more pygmy-owls used the area of the arroyos between the north boundary and west boundary of the school site. These arroyos are within the 30 acre parcel that will remain undeveloped. He also found that there was insufficient evidence to prove that a pygmy-owl used any portion of the 60 acre parcel upon which the school complex is to be built.

The judge explained at some length what evidence he relied on to support his findings. The judge stated that the opinion of scientific experts, the evidence of the habits of the pygmy-owl, and the recent aural detection of the bird, supports a logical inference that the bird or birds currently use the areas where they have been detected near the north and west boundaries of the site, and the area between those two points within the arroyo. He noted that because habitat within this arroyo area is suitable for pygmy-owls, provides cover and prey for birds, provides a natural corridor for the owl to travel from the north boundary to the west boundary where it has been frequently sighted, an inference can be drawn that the owl uses this area. The judge then contrasted the 30 acre parcel, which he refers to as "the Area," with the rest of the school site:

> Contrarily, there have been no sightings of the owl beyond the clusters of detections near the north and west boundaries of the property and extensive surveys of the entire property have failed to produce one single detection of a pygmy-owl. A search of 361 cavities of saguaro cacti on the site, in which pygmy owls prefer to nest, produced no pygmy-owls. There is therefore little factual basis to conclude that the owl uses the rest of the school site, outside of the Area.
>
> Because owls display site fidelity and have been seen near the Area but never detected on the school site outside of the Area, in spite of concentrated efforts to find them there, a logical inference can be made that the owl is not using the remainder of the site. Finally, the heaviest concentrations of sightings confirmed by the [Arizona Game and Fish Department] near the site are in Residential areas west of the school site where there is low impact housing (one house on a 3–5 acre plot with minimal disturbance to native vegetation). This supports the inference that the "core" of the owl's activity may not be in the Area but may be west of the school site, and that the 30 acre Area may be the outer fringe of the territory the bird uses.

---

[24] [4] The FWS said in its Final Rule that the clearing of unoccupied habitat would not be a § 9 take, whereas the "clearing or significant modification of occupied habitat" could potentially harm, harass, or otherwise take the pygmy owl. 62 Fed. Reg. 10746 (1997).

The district court next discussed the basis for his finding that harm to the pygmy owl was not proven. He observed that while the inference that an owl uses the 30 acre parcel is based on solid factual premises and well-founded expert opinion, the allegation that the construction of the high school will harm the owl lacks this support and is weakened by seemingly inconsistent facts. The judge noted that although he gives weight to the opinions of the experts, he cannot blindly rely on their opinions and must consider how the conclusions were reached and whether they are relevant and reliable, citing *Daubert v. Merrell Dow Pharmaceuticals, Inc.*, 509 U.S. 579 (1993). One of Defenders' experts had testified that a school would increase the amount of human activity on the school site and that although pygmy-owls can tolerate some level of human activity, he suspected that level would be enough to render or cause a pygmy-owl not to occupy the area. The judge noted that in contradiction to the expert's suspicions that the owl would be harmed by human activity associated with the high school, there was evidence that pygmy-owls can tolerate a fairly high degree of human presence. The Arizona Game and Fish Department had reported that "pygmy-owls are not intimidated by the presence of people or can acclimate to low density urbanization and associated activities." In 1995–96, a K-8 school was constructed and has been operating a short distance north of the proposed school site. One neighbor testified that she had chased an owl shouting at it and waving a broom, but the owl had returned to the residence. At one residence, an owl family was found in a grapefruit tree close to the house and was inspected at close range for weeks on end by the resident and his guests.

The judge stated that the facts do not support a finding that the owl will be harassed. He noted that there was evidence that the owl can tolerate and even benefit from human activity, and that Defenders have only offered speculation that the activity associated with the school would harass the owl. He observed that the experts made little or no attempt to support their opinions with recorded observations of pygmy owls in similar circumstances or to draw analogies from other similar birds. The judge found that this failure to support opinion with fact seriously degraded the value of the expert opinions. He stated "the limited data about the owls which was presented did not show with clarity that breeding, feeding, and sheltering would be adversely impacted by the construction or operation of the school." The judge summarized his findings as follows:

> The contradictory facts presented by Plaintiffs and assumptions about what will harm the bird do not support a conclusion that the owl will actually be injured or will likely be harassed. Finally, the FWS has concluded that clearing of unoccupied habitat will not "take" an owl and the Court has concluded that construction of the school, as planned, will not involve clearing of occupied habitat.

We review a district court's finding of fact under the clearly erroneous standard. *See* Fed. R. Civ. P. 52(a); *Russian River Watershed Protection Comm. v. Santa Rosa*, 142 F.3d 1136, 1140 (9th Cir. 1998). The well supported factual findings of the district judge are not clearly erroneous, and we affirm the conclusion of the district court that the construction of the school complex will not "take" a pygmy-owl.

IV. *Failure to Apply for an Incidental Take Permit*

Defenders contend that the district court should have required the School District to apply for an Incidental Take Permit (ITP). The district court concluded that the permitting provisions found in Section 10 of the ESA are not mandatory. We review a district court's conclusion on a question of law de novo. *See Russian River*, 142 F.3d at 1141.

If a proposed action constitutes a take under Section 9 of the ESA, a party may apply for an ITP under Section 10. 16 U.S.C. § 1539(a)(1)(B). If the FWS grants the ITP, the party can proceed with the proposed activity despite the taking of an endangered species. The School District declined to apply for an ITP because its position was that the proposed construction would not result in the take of an endangered pygmy-owl. Defenders argue that the district court erred by failing to require the School District to seek an ITP based on the expert scientific testimony presented.

We have established that pursuing an ITP is not mandatory and a party can choose whether to proceed with the permitting process. *See Rosboro*, 50 F.3d at 783. However, if a party chooses not to secure a permit and the proposed activity, in fact, takes a listed species, the ESA authorizes civil and criminal penalties. *See* 16 U.S.C. § 1540. Thus a party may proceed without a permit, but it risks civil and criminal penalties if a "take" occurs. The district court did not err in concluding that the School District was not required to seek an ITP.

Conclusion

Based on the foregoing, the judgment of the district court is AFFIRMED.

B. FLETCHER, CIRCUIT JUDGE, concurring:

I concur in the opinion but make these observations to clarify the limited precedential value of our opinion – the principal reason for our declining to publish in the first instance. Future cases that involve action or contemplated action in pygmy owl habitat in Arizona will be informed by the critical habitat designation and accompanying explanation in the new Final Rule. At the time this case was tried and argued to us on appeal no final designation on critical habitat had been made. We concluded that the critical habitat designation had no legal significance in this action brought under Section 9, which involves private land. We concluded that the critical habitat designation did not alter the outcome in this case because, in the end, this case turned on the sufficiency of plaintiffs' evidence, not on the inclusion or exclusion of the school site from critical habitat. As explained in the FWS regulation, "[c]ritical habitat has possible effects on activities by private landowners only if the activity involves Federal funding, a Federal permit, or other Federal action." 64 Fed. Reg. 37428 (1999). Here, the district court made a factual determination that, based on plaintiffs' evidence, the pygmy owl did not occupy the school construction site. We concluded that that factual decision was not clearly erroneous. In light of the earlier FWS rule stating that the clearing of unoccupied habitat does not result in a "take," the district court concluded that plaintiffs offered insufficient evidence to demonstrate a take. We do not hold that the designation of critical habitat will never have any bearing on actions on private lands within designated critical habitat, and thus, our decision has limited value for any other case involving either the pygmy owl or private lands that lie within the mapped boundary of designated critical habitat. *See Palila v. Hawai'i Dep't of Land & Natural Resources*, 639 F.2d 495 (9th Cir. 1981).

NOTES AND QUESTIONS

1. The protection of habitat for endangered species drastically affects the use which owners can make of land. Habitat protection plans, negotiated among landowners, government agencies and environmental groups, were designed to protect endangered species while leaving some economically beneficial use of land. If such effects are unsuccessful, does the Act result in a taking of private property without compensation?

2. Once a species is listed as endangered, controversy over the effects of critical habitat designation under § 1532 of the ESA is the predictable consequence of such designations. Technically directed at federal activities only, such designations are easily used as a basis for restricting private land use for fear of "taking" a species by harming its habitat. Moreover, state and local laws may require special protections for species preservation, which habitat designation arguably triggers. Given proposed designations of thousands of acres of land in states like California and Hawaii for the protection of red tree frogs and subterranean-dwelling cave spiders, the economic analysis which the Fish and Wildlife Service is obligated to undertake during the habitat designation process is coming under increasing scrutiny. The ESA requires the consideration of economic impact before the designation of a critical habitat. ESA § 4(b)(2), 16 U.S.C. § 1533 (b)(2). Courts differ over the proper methodology used to carry out this mandate. Use of the so-called "base-line" approach, comparing the current state of affairs (the base-line) with how things would look after designation of critical habitat, has been upheld on the 9th Circuit. *Home Builders Ass'n v. United States Fish & Wildlife Serv.*, 616 F.3d 983 (9th Cir. 2010), *cert. denied*, 131 S. Ct. 1475 (2011). The Tenth Circuit has held that the FWS must use a "co-extensive" approach, which "would take into account all of the economics of the [critical habitat designation], regardless of whether those impacts are caused co-extensively by any other agency action (such as listing) and even if those impacts would remain in the absence of the [designation]." *New Mexico Cattle Growers Ass'n v. United States Fish & Wildlife Serv.*, 248 F.3d 1277 (10th Cir. 2001). Compare, *e.g., New Mexico Callie Growers Ass'n v. U.S. Fish and Wildlife Service*, 248 F.3d 1277 (10th Cir. 2001), *with Arizona Callie Growers Ass'n v. Salazar*, 606 F.3d 1160 (9th Cir. 2010).

3. The decision in *Bernal* was originally delivered as an unpublished opinion, but the court was persuaded to publish it to provide guidelines as to what constitutes a "take" and what constitutes "harm." In her concurring opinion, Judge Fletcher attempts to limit the effect of the decision. How persuasive do you find her arguments? How would you advise a landowner whose property is subject of a hearing to designate it as a critical habitat?

TABLE OF CASES

[References are to pages.]

A

B

[References are to pages.]

C

[References are to pages.]

[References are to pages.]

D

E

[References are to pages.]

[References are to pages.]

H

[References are to pages.]

I

J

[References are to pages.]

K

L

[References are to pages.]

M

[References are to pages.]

N

[References are to pages.]

O

P

[References are to pages.]

Q

R

[References are to pages.]

S

[References are to pages.]

T

[References are to pages.]

U

V

W

[References are to pages.]

Y

Z

INDEX

[References are to sections.]

[References are to sections.]